AF718453

New Works in Accounting History

Richard P. Brief, *Series Editor*

Leonard N. Stern School of Business
New York University

A Garland Series

Commerce, Accounts & Finance

Volumes IV-V, January 1902-May 1903

Introduction by
Paul J. Miranti, Jr.

Garland Publishing, Inc.
New York and London 1993

Introduction copyright © 1993 by Paul J. Miranti, Jr.
All rights reserved.

Library of Congress Cataloging-in-Publication Data

Commerce, Accounts & Finance. Published from January 1901 to May 1903.
This reprint has been classified by the Library of Congress as a serial.

ISBN 0-8153-1214-8 (pt. 2)
ISSN 1068-2929

Printed on acid-free, 250-year-life paper.
Manufactured in the United States of America.

Design by Marisel Tavarez

CONTENTS

Volume IV

Nos. 1-12, January-December 1902

THE NEW YORK PUBLIC LIBRARY. 292235

COMMERCE ACCOUNTS & FINANCE

Volume 4 New York January 1902 Number 1

CONTENTS

Published Monthly by the Commerce Accounts & Finance Company Twenty-five Pine Street New York

McKinley National Memorial Association

The McKinley National Memorial Association having been incorporated according to law, met in Cleveland. Ohio. October 10th, 1901, for the purpose of effecting an organization by the election of officers and adoption of regulations for its government. The President of the United States, at the request of Mrs. McKinley and members of the family, named the following Board of Trustees:

Cornelius N. Bliss, New York,
Thomas Dolan, Philadelphia,
W. Murray Crane, Boston,
Alexander H. Revell, Chicago,
Charles W. Fairbanks, Indianapolis,
Henry M. Duffield, Detroit,
George B. Cortelyou, Washington,
Ell Torrance, Minneapolis,
William A. Lynch, Canton,
John G. Milburn, Buffalo,
William McConway, Pittsburgh,
David R. Francis, St. Louis,
Robert J. Lowry, Atlanta,
Henry C. Payne, Milwaukee,
Henry T. Scott, San Francisco,
Franklin Murphy, Newark,
E. S. Hammond, Memphis,
E. W. Bloomingdale, New York,
William R. Day, Canton,
Marcus A. Hanna, Cleveland,
Myron T. Herrick, Cleveland.

The Trustees having qualified, proceeded to the election of officers as follows:

President, William R. Day, Canton, Ohio.
Vice-President, Marcus A. Hanna, Cleveland, Ohio.
Treasurer, Myron T. Herrick, Cleveland, Ohio.
Secretary, Ryerson Ritchie, Cleveland, Ohio.

The purposes of the Association, as defined in its certificate of incorporation, are the erection and maintenance at Canton, Ohio, of a suitable memorial to the late President, and raising the necessary funds for said purposes; and after fully providing therefor, the surplus of such funds, if any, to be devoted to such memorial as may be provided for the late President at the National Capitol. The memorial will be erected at Canton, that city having been his home throughout his public life and selected by him as his final resting place.

The memorial is to be, in the highest sense, the sincere expression of all the people of the country of their love for President McKinley and of their admiration for the qualities expressed so eminently in his life and deeds.

It is the purpose to have the offerings of the people voluntary, with a full opportunity to all to contribute.

The co-operation of the Governors and officers of the States and municipalities of the United States, and all religious, educational, labor, civic, patriotic, fraternal, benevolent, and other organizations is invited.

All public officials, organized bodies, and the press are requested to take immediate steps to secure, at the earliest possible time, a full response to this appeal. The Association looks to the press of the country to lend its efficient aid to the collection and forwarding of subscriptions.

The Association will prepare and distribute to all donors to the fund a souvenir certificate which will be worthy of preservation, as evidence of the holder's participation in the work. The name and postoffice address of each contributor should be forwarded to the Treasurer of the Association, with the fund remitted, for preservation in the permanent archives of the Association.

It is hoped that the response of the people will be so liberal that a memorial may be erected which will fittingly honor the memory of our martyred President, and emphasize their loyalty to our institutions, and their abhorrence of that spirit of lawlessness which inspired the assault upon his life.

THE NEW YORK STATE ORGANIZATION.

Auxiliary to the above-mentioned National Association, it was decided to form a State Association in the State of New York, and at a meeting held at the Chamber of Commerce of the State of New York, 32 Nassau Street, New York City, October 23d, a State organization was effected, with the following officers:

President, Governor B. B. Odell, Jr.
Chairman Executive Committee, Cornelius N. Bliss.
Treasurer, James G. Cannon.
Secretary, F. B. Thurber.

It is proposed that the Executive Committee shall be representative of the various industries and interests of the State.

Offices have been taken at 100 Broadway, New York City, and subscriptions, large or small, are solicited from the people of this State. Moneys may be deposited in banks and other financial institutions throughout the State or with Postmasters, who are requested to receive and transmit them to the office of the McKinley Memorial Association, 100 Broadway, New York, payable to the order of James G. Cannon, Treasurer, together with the name, amount, and address of each donor. Respectfully yours.

CORNELIUS N. BLISS, *Chairman Executive Committee.*

NEW YORK UNIVERSITY
School of Commerce, Accounts and Finance

A college course in Higher Accountancy arranged in accordance with the requirements of the Certified Public Accountants' Act of the State of New York and fitting students for the Regents' Examination for the C. P. A. degree. The course in Accountancy is rounded out by instruction in finance, commerce and commercial law leading to the University Degree of Bachelor of Commercial Science.

NEW YORK UNIVERSITY
Washington Square NEW YORK CITY

Business Law

By
Thomas Raeburn White, B.L., LL.B.
Lecturer on Law in the University of Pennsylvania.

A compact, comprehensive work, presenting in plain understandable English the elementary principles of law relating to common business transactions. Size, 5x7½ inches; 367 pages. Bound in Cloth. Back title gilt.

PRICE, $1.50.
Sent prepaid on receipt of price.

Commerce, Accounts & Finance
25 Pine Street,
New York, N.Y.

THE NEW YORK PUBLIC LIBRARY
ASTOR, LENOX AND TILDEN FOUNDATIONS
1903

Accounting for Cotton Mills—I.*

By GEORGE YOUNG

The conversion of the fiber or lint of the cotton plant into its various products, commonly known as cotton manufacturing, is one of the world's great industries. It follows naturally then, that the subject of accounting for cotton mills is one fraught with great interest, and great importance. Indeed, in an industry of such magnitude, in which the units of production are so many and the profit margins so narrow that a very slight fluctuation in cost or selling price may represent the difference between a deficit and a dividend, the importance of proper accounting can hardly be overestimated.

Just so in the erection of a system of accounting for any business, the specific needs of that particular business must be studied; even the characteristics—I had almost said the peculiarities—of the men in control must be considered, and so in each case the result may be a superstructure like to no other, excepting as all buildings have points in common; but we must have for our foundation those bed-rock principles which never change.

In respect of the broad results to be attained accounting for cotton mills does not differ one iota from accounting for any other business. To quote again from Mr. Kittredge, the books should reveal "The thing which the manager wants to know, at the time he wants to know it, in the form best adapted to his needs."

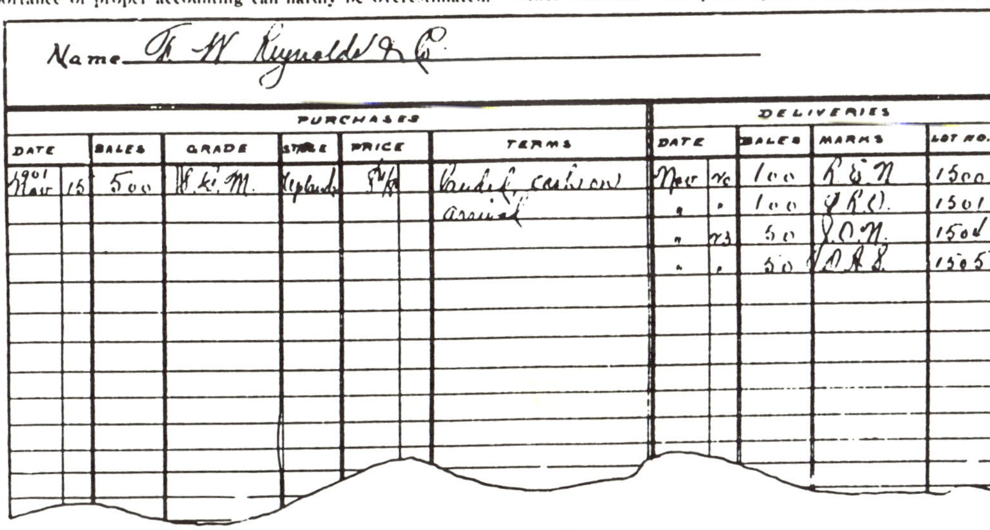

Name F. W. Reynolds & Co.

PURCHASES							DELIVERIES				
DATE		BALES	GRADE	STAPLE	PRICE	TERMS	DATE		BALES	MARKS	LOT NO.
1901 Nov	15	500		Upland		arrival	Nov	16	100		1500
							"	"	100		1501
							"	23	50		1504
							"	"	50		1505

FIG. 1. PURCHASE RECORD.

Good bookkeeping is well enough, but good bookkeeping, although important, is not sufficient. It is not enough that the accounts reflect accurately the relations to the business of its customers and its creditors, not enough that the books be kept in a way to enable the bookkeeper to construct from them at long intervals a balance sheet; the need, the demand, is for something better than this, and to meet this imperative need many men trained in the work and familiar with the needs are giving their best endeavors.

Much has been accomplished in recent years in the direction of better accounting for the textile industries, but it has not all been done, and there is still plenty of room, not only at the top, but also in the broader, if more populous levels farther down—room for men with minds peculiarly constituted and specially trained for the work, and ample opportunity for the exercise of all their best talents and equipment.

If I may be allowed to paraphrase a saying of your learned professor of the theory of accounts, "The principles of accounting are eternal and unchangeable, but the applications of these principles are new every morning and fresh every evening;" and it is these applications or adaptations with which the accountant has to do.

ENGINEERING AN IMPORTANT FEATURE.

A most important feature of accounting today is engineering, if you please, the careful, intelligent study of the needs of each specific case, and the erection therefor of a system which shall accomplish the desired results, and at the same time be economical in its operation. You have noticed that all railroad stations are not alike, but in their construction the topography of the city, the volume and character of the traffic and a hundred other things seen only by the architect specially trained in that work are considered.

There are three principal things which the cotton mill man wishes to know about his business, not the average cotton mill man, but every cotton mill man; he wants to know the cost of his output, the profits or losses on his transactions, and the actual financial condition of his business;

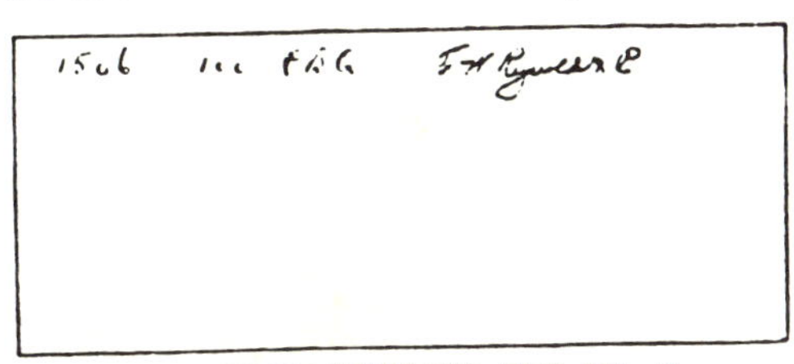

FIG. 2. FILING ENVELOPE. SIZE, 4¾ x 11.

briefly, he wants costs, results and condition; and all of these things the books should show.

I lay special emphasis on the statement that these things should be shown by the books.

THE SUBJECT OF COSTS.

No other branch of our subject has received so much attention as costs; but in very few instances is the cost system a part of the accounting scheme—it is usually a thing apart and distinct from the bookkeeping of the institution, related to it only as the costs may be proven from the books, perhaps at the close of the fiscal year.

This is wrong. The cost system should be an integral part of the accounting system, and only by making it such can accurate and satisfactory results be obtained.

What more natural place to look for costs than in the

*A series of addresses before the Junior Class in Accounting, School of Commerce, Accounts and Finance, New York University, by George Young, manager Textile Division, Account, Audit and Assurance Co., Ltd., New York and Boston.

books of account, in which is recorded every expenditure? And what more logical cost system than the segregation, classification and distribution of these expenditures in a way to give us the desired result?

Our books should show labor costs, divided into producing and non-producing labor, and sub-divided by departments to any extent which may be desirable or expedient. Our books should show the cost of mill supplies, repairs, coal, taxes, insurance, depreciation and all those sundry costs commonly known as general expenses in as fine detail as the managers of the business may wish, and all these must be distributed equitably over product in a way to work no injustice to any portion of the output nor to any period of the fiscal year, be it long or short, a thing which though not commonly practiced is easily accomplished.

The costing of output should be concurrent with our accounting, a vital part of it. The final result of our cost accounts should be the actual cost of each kind of goods. If we wish to know the cost of a given roving, or warp, or filling, our books should give this information.

All the expenditures should be recorded in a way to make analysis of costs and expenses for a year or any other fiscal period an easy matter. The final costs should be actual—not estimated on the basis of last year's summary of general manufacturing costs, nor subject to the explanation that they are too high because taxes or insurance or some other annual, semi-annual or quarterly charge has been paid in this period.

PROFIT AND LOSS STATEMENT.

Our profit and loss showings or statements of **expenses and** revenues should be made for short periods of uniform length, say every four weeks. The revenues should be particularized in a way to show the results in each department of the business—what mills, what classes of goods, what departments of the business are most profitable; and the expense accounts should record in detail those expenditures which are no part of the cost of the goods, but are expenses of administration and marketing.

THE BALANCE SHEET.

Our balance sheet should be a true statement of the condition of our business; not merely a basis of loss and gain calculation, but a statement which may be presented to a bank

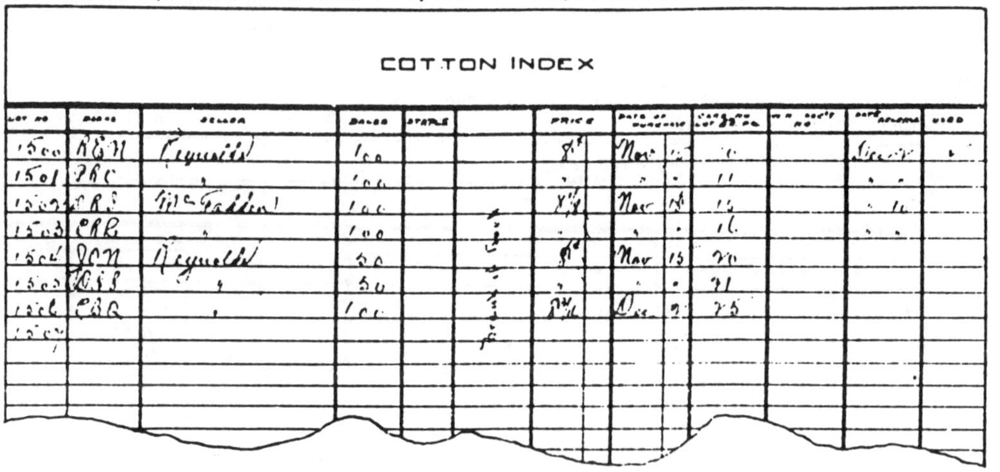

FIG. 3. COTTON INDEX.

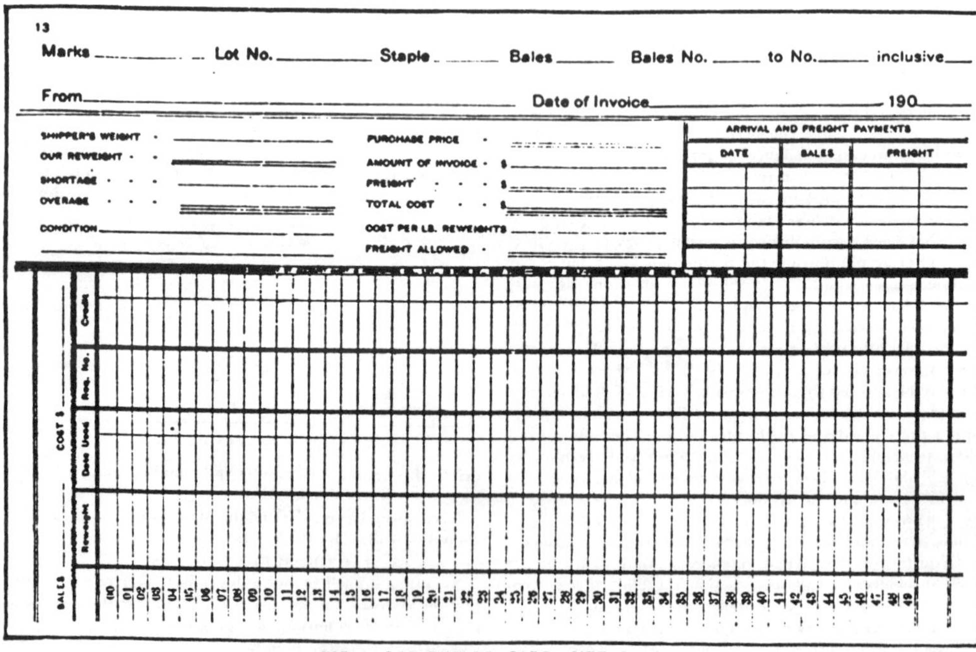

FIG. 4. LOT RECORD CARD. SIZE, 5 x 8.

or trust company as an actual schedule of our assets and liabilities. It should be, not a thing constructed from our books at intervals, but an essential, a vital part of our bookkeeping, the most important part of all, the one thing above all others which we shall keep going.

These things are not only possible but entirely practicable; not as easy perhaps as plodding along in the old ruts worn deep by long years of grinding, but let us not be content

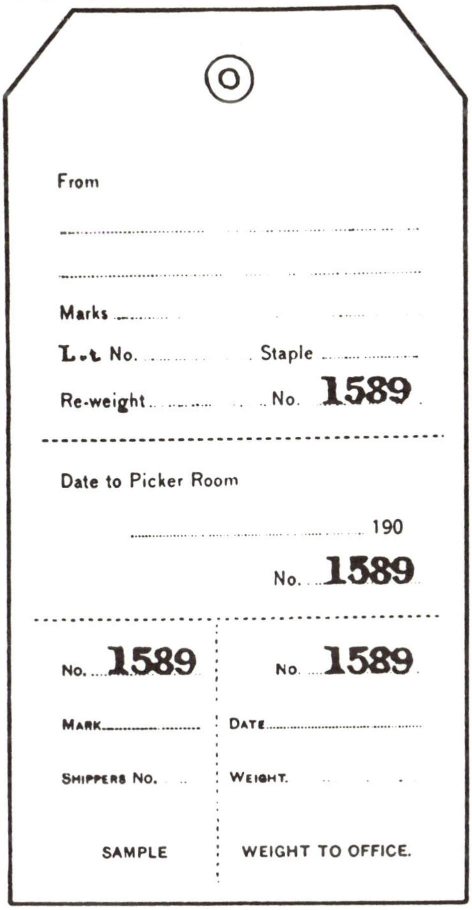

FIG. 5. COTTON TAG.

with unthinking plodding. "Set your affections on things above"—"Hitch your wagon to a star."

RECORDS.

One of the difficulties encountered in a cotton mill office is that of getting satisfactory results from our cotton records and accounts; and we must have cotton records which are reliable or we are handicapped at the outset.

Our records should be kept in a way to show us, first, that the cotton bought is actually shipped to us—that is a simple matter—second, that the cotton shipped to us is actually received by us—that is not so simple; and third, they should show the number of bales of each grade and character on hand and due to arrive at any time; and the cotton account in our ledger should show at all times the cost value of the cotton owned by us; in other words, should represent the cotton inventory.

First, then, we want a Purchase Record. Fig. 1 shows a form for this purpose.

We will assign a page, or as many pages as may be needed to each cotton firm with whom we are dealing. We will enter each purchase on the left-hand side of the page and will reserve against the record of purchase as many lines as we estimate will be needed for the record of deliveries, by checking them as shown in the illustration. Cotton is usually delivered in lots of 50 or 100 bales, and if on a purchase of 500 bales we reserve ten lines we will be safe. We will enter the invoices which we receive against a given purchase on the right-hand side of the page, opposite the record of the purchase, on the lines reserved for that purpose. The difference between the number of bales purchased as recorded on the left of the page, and the number of bales invoiced as recorded on the right of the page will be the number of bales due us on the purchase.

LOT NUMBER.

We have in the illustration a column headed "Lot No." The serial numbering of lots affords a convenient means of tracing and checking, and of identifying and assembling the papers relating to the lots; but it may be made to cover a much wider scope by making the numbers not only to represent the serial numbers of the lots, but also to operate as a cipher to indicate the grade, character, and, if we choose, the ownership of the lots.

Suppose our mill is using several grades and say three general characters, for example, 1 1-16 to 1 1-8, which, for convenience, we will call weaving cotton; uplands of high grade which we will call hosiery cotton, and 1 3-16 and above, which we will designate as peeler cotton. We will indicate the grades by hundreds and the characters by thousands

Thus, let 00 stand for Low Middling.
100 for Strict Low Midling.
200 for Middling.
300 for Strict Middling.
400 for Good Middling.
500 for Strict Good Middling.
600 for Middling Fair.

Let 000 stand for Weaving Cotton.
1,000 for Hosiery Cotton.
2,000 for Peeler Cotton.

By using these figures in combination we will have in our lot numbers a key to the grade and character of each lot of cotton. Thus, the first lot of Strict Good Middling hosiery would be numbered 1,500, the second lot, 1,501, and so on to 1,599. All the papers, including invoice, bale tags, freight vouchers, classing sheets, etc., will bear this lot number, and everybody concerned in the handling of the cotton will know at a glance that a lot bearing any number from 1,500 to 1,599 inclusive is Strict Good Middling hosiery cotton, because 1,000 means hosiery, and 500 means Strict Good Middling.

For filing our cotton papers we will use a heavy manila envelope of large size, say 4 3-4 by 11, on the upper margin of which we will write the lot number, number of bales, marks and name of shipper, as in Fig. 2.

We will stand these envelopes on edge in a drawer, in numerical order, and in them we will file all the papers of the respective lots as they come to hand. The original invoice will be kept in the envelope until it is wanted for entry, when it goes into our invoice file for posting to the ledger, and becomes part of our invoice file or book. It may then be replaced in the envelope, either by a copy, or by a memorandum slip giving the number of the invoice in the invoice file.

Suppose we have the books of two corporations in one office. We may indicate ownership by using numbers up to say 5,999 for corporation A and 6,000 and upwards for corporation B. Lot No. 1,300 would then be Strict Middling weaving cotton of corporation A; No. 7,300 would indicate cotton of the same grade and character belonging to B.

Or, suppose some of our cotton is carried by the sellers, covered by our warehouse receipts. In that case we must safeguard the cotton against use before the warehouse receipt is surrendered to us and cancelled; and we will be aided in this by having our lot numbers indicate those lots which have been receipted for and can only be used after they have been released; so we will let 3,000 stand for weaving, 4,000 for hosiery and 5,000 for peeler cotton covered by receipts. Under this scheme 4,400 would indicate Good Middling hosiery cotton contracted for by A but covered by warehouse receipts, and so on.

This lot number scheme is a most useful one, and it may be developed and extended as circumstances may indicate.

COTTON INDEX.

We must now have a cotton index, which should be a small book, convenient to handle, ruled as in Fig. 3.

Besides furnishing an index to our files and books this will give us a condensed description and history of every lot of cotton handled by us, as we shall see later on. We will divide the leaves of this book into two sections. The first half we will index through alphabetically, from A to Z. The other half we will index numerically by hundreds, according to our lot number scheme.

If we were using several of the thousand series, we would not have room on the margin of our book to index throughout by hundreds, and we would then index on the outside by thousands, and sub-index inside by hundreds.

We must have a lot record, that is, a record of the particulars as per invoice, the arrival in detail, and the consumption by the mill of each lot. We may use a card for this purpose, or we may use a book, as may seem best in the premises. The form illustrated in Fig. 4 is printed on a 5x8 card, which is a standard size. There are two of these cards

We turn next to the record of bale numbers assigned, and find that the highest number used thus far is 499, so we assign to this lot bale numbers 500 to 599 and give a memorandum of the fact to the office boy, who takes out 100 tags bearing these numbers (See Fig. 5), and putting on them the details of the lot, either with a pen or by some simple printing device such as the Multigraph, he gives them to the warehouse man, or to the man in charge of the unloading.

We record the details of the lot in our lot book, or on our lot card, whichever we are using, and we are now ready for the cotton to arrive.

All this doubtless looks like rather a complex proposition; but, as a matter of fact, it is perfectly simple, and very little time is required to make the entries which have been described.

NUMBERED TAGS.

As the cotton of this lot arrives, one of the numbered tags will be attached to each bale. When it is weighed, the reweight will be noted on the body of the tag and also on the

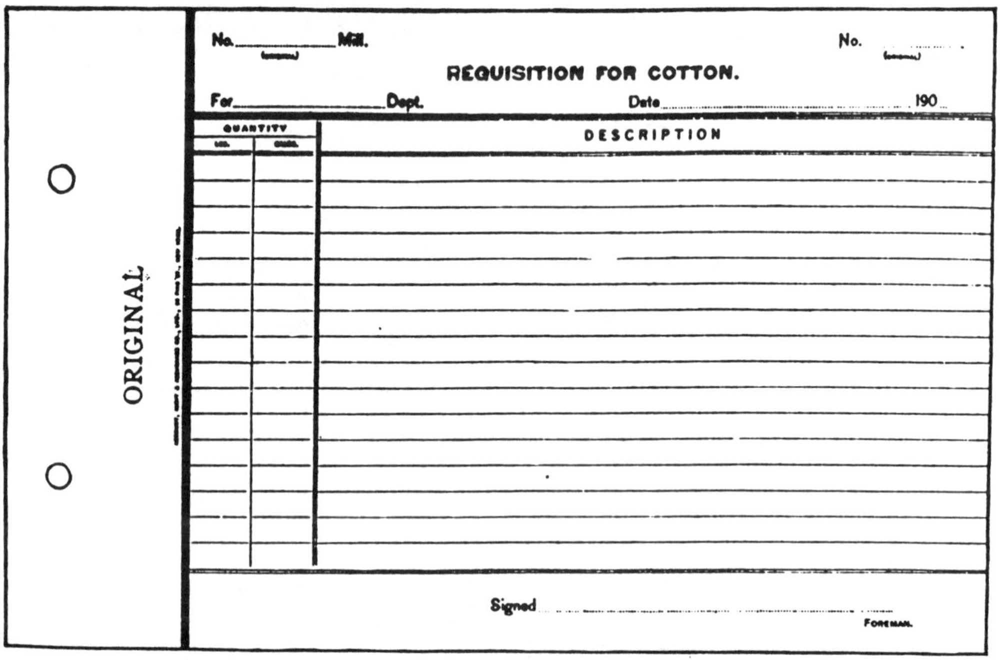
ORIGINAL

No.______ Mill. No.______

REQUISITION FOR COTTON.

For______ Dept. Date______190__

QUANTITY		DESCRIPTION

Signed______
FOREMAN.

FIG. 6. REQUISITION FOR COTTON. SIZE, 5 1-2 x 8 1-2.

in a set, one with marginal numbers 00 to 49, and the other 50 to 99. The scheme of writing a master number at the head of the column and reading this master number and the printed marginal numbers in conjunction to avoid the necessity of writing each number is pretty generally understood and need not be explained in this connection.

RECORD OF INVOICE.

We are ready now to record an invoice. We get an invoice of 100 bales C B Q from F. W. Reynolds & Co. First, we compare it with our purchase record to see that the price, terms, etc., are correct. Since it is Strict Good Middling grade and hosiery character, it will go in the 1,500 series. We open our index in the numerical division at the 1,500 page, and find that the last lot entered there was No. 1,505, so this will be lot 1,506. We record the marks, number of bales, name of seller, price and date of purchase, and here our record stops for the present. We write the lot number across the face of the invoice with a blue pencil, and then opening the alphabetical section of our index at the C page we record the same particulars there. This will enable us to locate the lot in our records either by the bale marks or by the lot num-

We now credit the invoice to the purchase in the purchase record.

lower right-hand coupon. Both the lower coupons will then be removed; the re-weight coupon will be sent to the office as a report of the re-weight, and the sample coupon will be rolled in the sample, which will go to the man in charge of the classing.

The re-weight will be noted in the office in the lot record opposite the proper number, and if we wish to give the seller a memorandum of the re-weights, we can have our cards padded with thin sheets above them, and by using carbon paper can make the seller's memorandum and our own record at one writing.

The bales are now identified in all our records by numbers, and we have a means of accounting for each individual bale, which is quite as important as tracing each package of our mill product.

Cotton is one of our valuable assets, and we will lay down the rule that it is not to be taken for use on the help-yourself plan, but is to be taken from the warehouse only on a requisition (See Fig. 6), which will serve as a receipt to the warehouse man; and delivery to the mill is to be recorded bale by bale on a delivery report, as per Fig. 7, which shall bear the same number as the corresponding requisition, and shall be made in duplicate by the carbon process, the original to go to the office and the duplicate to be filed in the warehouse for record.

All of these blanks should be of standard sizes for filing in post binders or filing cabinets of standard makes.

It will be well to establish the rule that cotton is to be used only as it is released by an order from the office. This rule will be necesary if we are issuing warehouse receipts, but whether we are or not, it will be a great convenience, enabling the office to know what lots the mill is working on, and preventing the promiscuous breaking of lots.

DELIVERY REPORT.

From our delivery report, Fig. 7, we will post to the lot record, and as we record the consumption of each bale we will note on the delivery report the cost of the bale, or where a number of bales of a lot are used at one time, their total cost, which may be at the actual cost on the re-weight, or the average cost per bale of the lot.

A summary of these delivery reports for a given period will give us the total cost of the cotton used, and will post to

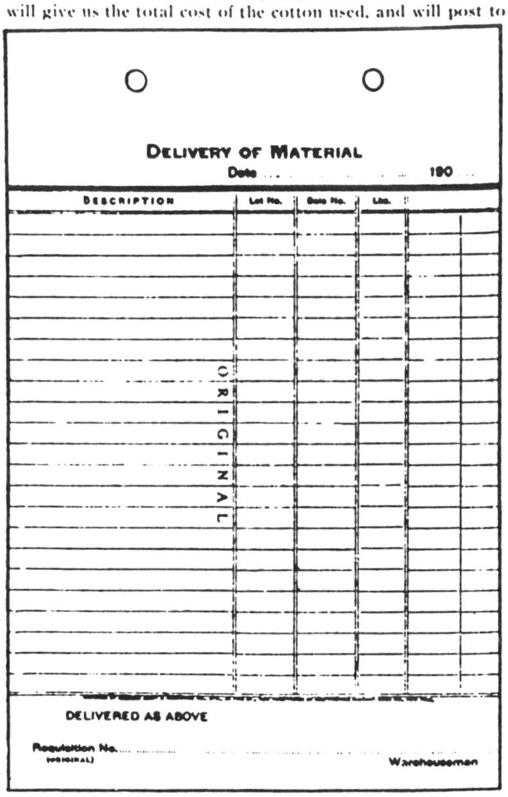
DELIVERY OF MATERIAL
Date 190
DESCRIPTION | Lot No. | Bale No. | Lbs.
ORIGINAL
DELIVERED AS ABOVE
Requisition No.
(ORIGINAL)
Warehouseman

FIG. 7. DELIVERY REPORT. SIZE, 8 1-2 x 5 1-2

the credit of the cotton account and the debit of the manufacuring account of the mill.

Now, if we debit our cotton account with the cost of all cotton bought, and credit that account with the cost of all cotton used as evidenced by our delivery reports the balance in the cotton account will represent the cost value of the cotton on hand, in other words, we shall have in our ledger a going inventory of cotton at cost, which we can prove by our detail lot accounts.

Ordinarily, our inventory, whether of raw material, stock in process, or finished product, should be at cost, should represent the amount of money which we have invested in it, without regard to market conditions.

Occasion might arise in which deviation from this rule would be expedient. For example, in the event of a big slump in the cotton market, the management might decide to write off the depreciation as a loss; but it is neither good business nor good accounting to change inventory to meet every fluctuation in market, to deceive ourselves into the belief that we have made or lost money trading with ourselves.

If our company is operating two or more mills, it is unnecessary under this plan to run a separate cotton account and a separate cotton inventory for each mill. The mills will be charged only with the cotton taken into their opening rooms for use.

COTTON OF DIFFERENT GRADES AND CHARACTERS.

Let us see now what we can learn from our records with reference to our standing on cotton of different grades and characters. Suppose our treasurer wishes to know how we stand on Strict Good Middling hosiery cotton. We turn first to our purchase record, Fig. 1, and find that there are 200 bales due us on purchases of Nov. 15, and 600 on other purchases, making a total of 800 bales due to be shipped. We next open our index at the 1,500 page, that is, the page on which all lots bearing any numbers from 1,500 to 1,599 are recorded, and we find that the first lot recorded there has all been used as indicated by the check mark in the "Used" column, put there when the last bale of the lot was taken to the mill as recorded on the Delivery Report, so we pass that lot. The next three lots have been released for use, but they have not all been used, so we note the numbers of the record cards, 11, 15 and 16, and by reference to the cards we find that there are still unused 10 bales of P R O, 40 bales of D R I, and 35 bales of C R L, making 85 bales released for use, but not yet taken into the mill. J O N and D A S have not yet been released, and we find by reference to our record cards that these lots are all in, so we put down 100 bales as available for immediate use. The lot of C B Q has just been shipped, so we put this down as in transit.

REPORT TO THE TREASURER.

We now turn to the 4,500 page of our index, on which are recorded the Strict Good Middling hosiery lots which may be covered by warehouse receipts, and by the same process we find there 500 bales covered by receipts, and 260 bales in broken lots, that is, released but not all used.

Our report to the treasurer will be as follows:—

Strict Good Middling Hosiery Cotton, December 21.

		Bales.
Due on purchases.		800
Covered by warehouse receipts.		500
In transit.		100
Released, unused.	345	
Available for immediate release.	100	445
Total.		1,845

The making of this report has occupied only a very few minutes, and we may present it to the treasurer with some assurance that it is correct. The element of estimate is entirely eliminated, and we are not dependent on reports from the warehouseman as to the quantity on hand; the whole thing is a matter of record in the office.

We are in position to prove our work step by step. The arrival of the cotton is evidenced by the re-weight coupons, and also by car reports and the warehouse records. The requisition, of which we get a copy, advises us that a certain number of bales of a certain grade and character are to be taken from the warehouse for use, and the delivery report shows what bales are actually taken, and this report is checked by the tag coupons "To Picker Room." It would be a rare combination of circumstances whereby requisition, delivery report and tag coupon all failed of reaching the office.

We have in our ledger an account which represents the actual asset of cotton on hand, and this we can prove by the balances from the individual lot records.

If we will keep accounts in the same way with work in process, finished product and other items of inventory, we shall have all of our inventory in our books, and since every set of books is supposed to contain all of the liabilities of the business and all of the assets, with the exception of inventory, by carrying a going inventory in our books we are enabled to complete the balance sheet and also to render a profit and loss statement as often as may seem best in the premises.

Systematic Bookkeeping for Retailers

IMPORTANT MOVE BY THE NATIONAL ASSOCIATION OF CREDIT MEN

Prize Competition for a Simple System of Bookkeeping for Retail Stores

The subject of a simple system of bookkeeping for retail stores, giving a comprehensive statement of condition as a basis for credit, has been under consideration for several years by the National Association of Credit Men. Several schemes have been submitted and investigated, but, up to the present time, nothing has appeared combining the essentials of simplicity, economy and clearness.

The growing importance of the matter elicited considerable discussion at the annual convention of the Association, at Cleveland, in June last, and the following resolutions were adopted:—

> **RESOLVED, That the Committee on Credit Department Methods be instructed to formulate a simple plan of bookkeeping for the use of the owners of retail stores, including a simple form of monthly statement showing in a comprehensive manner an analysis of resources and liabilities, purchases and collections, sales and the various expense accounts in detail, so that comparisons may be readily made month by month and year by year.**
>
> **RESOLVED, further, that the members of the Association be requested to distribute copies of this plan among their customers and secure its adoption through that means.**

To bring out, if possible, a system of bookkeeping which will answer the requirements of the situation the Board of Directors has arranged a competition in which a prize of $50 is offered for the best system submitted, and a prize of $25 for the second best system.

The competition has been placed in charge of a committee consisting of Mr. F. H. Meadow, of the Staver Carriage Co., Chicago, chairman; Mr. A. O. Kittredge, president of the Account, Audit & Assurance Company, Ltd., of New York, and Mr. Wm. A. Prendergast, national secretary of the Association. The conditions under which the competition is to be conducted are as follows:—

1. Plans submitted under this contest must be sealed and mailed to Mr. W. A. Prendergast, secretary of the National Association of Credit Men, 20 Nassau street, New York city, and bear a postmark not later than March 15, 1902.
2. The theory of each plan must be fully explained in typewriting, and must be accompanied by all necessary blanks and forms, with a sufficient number of entries thereon to exemplify the system. Explanatory matter must be typewritten on letter paper about eight inches wide and eleven inches long, such typewriting to be on one side of the paper only.
3. It is expressly stipulated that the National Association of Credit Men shall have the right to use all or any part of any plan submitted in this competition.
4. The decisions of the committee of award are to be final, that is without argument or appeal.

Contestants will be allowed the broadest latitude consistent with the requirements of the resolutions adopted by the National Association of Credit Men, upon which the competition is based. All essential particulars are presented above, and in justice to all competitors, no letters of inquiry will be answered other than to refer to what precedes.

IMPROVEMENTS IN BOOKKEEPING.

Several well-known credit men have recently prepared and read papers on various bookkeeping subjects showing the necessity of the methods for which the National Association is working. At a recent meeting of the Detroit Credit Men's Association, Mr. C. A. Simon, of the Acme White Lead & Color Works, explained the methods employed in that concern. Mr. Simon devoted his remarks largely to an explanation of the advantages of the loose-leaf system. "The Safeguard System previously in use," said Mr. Simon, "had the great disadvantage of necessitating the carrying forward or re-writing the balances every month, whether the account had been increased in amount or not; also it was necessary to tear off the perforated extension sheets every six months or so, and carry the balance over on the other side of the page. These disadvantages have been done away with entirely by the loose leaf system and other advantages gained with its aid, which were never possible of execution in connection with the safe guard or the old systems, only at great expenditure of time and labor. The loose leaf system is economical in not only money but time and labor as well. There is a saving of at least 50 per cent in the cost of the ledgers and ledger leaves at the end of the second year, as it is only necessary to invest in one set of current and transfer ledgers, instead of purchasing a new set of ledgers every two years or so. The ledgers need not be larger than 9x12 inches, therefore there is no necessity for heavy binding. While the ledger leaves are utilized to the very last line, therefore no waste of paper or space is made. You also have the advantage, at any time you wish it to change the printed matter or form of your ledger leaves, which is out of the question with the old style.

"One of the most satisfactory results from an economical standpoint, which we have derived, is the fact that during the four (4) years we have had our present ledgers, we have only had them repaired at nominal expense but once, whereas were we using the old system it would have cost us the price of an entire set of books ere this, and we would now be looking after our third set with which to start the fifth year. As a time saver the loose leaf system has yet to meet its competitor. One of the nightmares of a bookkeeper's existence is the trial balance to be drawn off the first of each month, which is usually accompanied with a question mark as to its correctness. This injustice to the individual behind the pen should not be and to a great extent this feeling will not exist if the employer will keep up to date and install the modern loose leaf system. In taking off the trial balance the bookkeeper encounters none but the live or current accounts. There is no fingering of the silent accounts, and also less chance for error. This system has enabled us to take off a trial balance by the second or third of each month, and seldom later. In our business we endeavor to render statements to our customers the 1st or 2d of each month, but not later than the 2d. We do this every month, and have done so for the last four (4) years."

TIME SAVING METHODS.

Mr. Thos. C. Kincella, in discussing bookkeeping methods of the present day, said that modern bookkeeping differs materially from the old school. The practice of journalizing all transactions and spending hours of valuable time re-writing from original entries have been abolished. The chief aim now is to avoid all unnecessary work, and to arrive at results with the utmost dispatch, consistent with accuracy.

"Advanced double-entry bookkeeping," continued Mr. Kincella, "consists first, in posting direct from the books of original entry to the ledgers, and, secondly, in so classifying business transactions by the use of special books and extra columns as to require but a single posting for each of the transactions, and as far as posible only a single monthly posting for the aggregate of each class of transactions appertaining to other than personal accounts.

"When a system is thus organized it requires but little extra labor over the simplest system of single entry, and is at the same time the most advanced system of double entry.

"By keeping a sales book and posting directly therefrom to the ledger, we reduce that portion of our bookkeeping to single entry, because we simply post the amount of sales recorded therein to the debit of the respective personal account, and at the same time post no credit whatever. All such amounts are, however, extended into the outer columns in the sales book, and the footings there are carried forward from page to page until the end of the month, when the aggregate of all the amounts, which were entered during the month posted to the debit of each customer's account, is posted direct from this book to the credit of merchandise account. The same result is acquired in the cash book, day book and credit book, by using extra columns for non-personal accounts.

"Reducing labor lessens the liability to commit errors, enhances the value of the bookkeeper's services.

"More work is accomplished, and a saving is made to his principals, of salaries for assistants. Moreover, the satisfaction is had of knowing that no part of the time has been wasted upon unnecessary work. The more books a transaction passes through before it reaches the ledger the more labor. The fewer it passes through the more it is diminished. To accomplish the work with as little writing as possible, posting should be direct, from the book of original entry to the ledger.

"The bookkeeper that is wise in his day and generation should employ his spare moments in calculating the gain of time, which would accrue through the eliminating of work where losses are occasioned, and in the pursuit of methods whereby gains are made.

"Thus assisting in placing bookkeeping upon a still higher plane of excellence than that upon which it now stands, for it is only through such attention that the science can be advanced. Experience teaches the alert accountant how to economize work, and he soon learns to dispose of all unnecessary labor. Old habits sometimes cling to one for years, but they generally yield to reason, and new ideas assert themselves."

WHY AND HOW.

Mr W. D. Gridley discussed the why and how of bookkeeping. "In the practical application of the art or science of bookkeeping," said he, "there is one great why and an infinite quantity and quality of hows. Every individual, firm, corporation, municipality and state, aims at the one idea, and strike it with varying degrees of success. In so far as they keep the definition mentioned clearly in mind, and make their systems conform, do they get the best results from their bookkeeping departments.

"When old Nicholas Vedder wanted to know how much poor old Rip Van Winkle was in for, he swung the shutter and there was the score fully exposed to view. How many firms can tell the amount they have in stock without taking their whole force and working from one to six weeks before they make up their minds. In my opinion, you have not reduced our bookkeeping problem to its final solution until you have got to the point where you can turn to your merchandise of stock account and tell what you have on hand without being obliged to see and sort and calculate the articles themselves. As it is now ninety-nine out of every hundred merchants go from one year to the next without knowing to a certainty whether they are running ahead of the game or behind, and when they make or lose they do not know, as a rule, which department is ahead and which is behind.

"Why not have your books so arranged that you can tell by turning to an account what goods you have in stock of any particular department, what the profit and loss is in that department, etc.?

"This, it seems to me, is the mark above all others that the accounting branch of any establishment should aim at. Your books are not fulfilling their duty unless they are made to tell you exactly what you want to know and when you want to know it.

"This, then, is the end sought, but how to accomplish it.

"The great stumbling block is the merchandise account. We charge merchandise with purchases, we credit it with sales, we charge it with returned goods and credit with returned purchases, and in the end, what does it tell you? Not what you have in stock, nor your gross profits, unless your stock is always kept at a fixed value, which I think is very unusual. It is my belief that the merchandise account is not performing its full duty until it tells you by inspection the amount of merchandise in stock. If you have separated your business into different departments, then the merchandise account of each department should be the indicator of the amount on hand in that department, and instead of waiting from year's end to year's end to know whether you are making or losing you can tell every month, fortnight or week, as you will.

"The reform in the treatment of the merchandise account will lead naturally to the opening of a revenue account, into which channel turn every account representing a source of revenue.

"It is true in many cases that the interest and discount accounts are run together, so that it neither tells you what you are allowing for discounts, getting for discounts, or receiving for interest. This account should also be classified, so that the revenue and expense will be shown separately.

"Regarding the treatment of the account covering the loss occasioned by bad debts, a matter that must appeal very strongly to all you gentlemen, I would urgently recommend that a fixed percentage arrived at by taking the average loss of say five years last passed be charged to P & L each month, and set aside in a reserve account, and losses, as they occur, charged against it. This will be an object lesson to the management, as regards the results of your efforts as credit men, that cannot be overlooked.

"This same principle applied to all accounts coming under the expense head will be found of great benefit in contrasting expense accounts with revenue accounts of each month, and different months."

THE NATIONAL DEBT OF ENGLAND

Every great nation, like every small church, has a debt. England's debt is a good-sized one, which of couse is what the debt of such a great nation should be, and it also is of ancient beginnings.

The English national debt, in its present form, has a contiuous history of over 200 years. Its beginning can be traced to a breach of faith of Charles II. Before that event, English monarchs were undoubtedly familiar with the practice of borrowing, but they only borrowed for short terms, generally a few months, or perhaps a year, and they always paid back. The history of these earlier borrowings is so full of interest that it may be worth while to dwell for a few moments upon the subject. In essence, these borrowings by the earlier kings of England were only anticipations of current revenue: the very form in which the loan was contracted is incidental evidence of that fact. From the time of the Norman conquest, it was the practice of the exchequer to acknowledge the receipt of revenue by means of a wooden tally. A tally (French, taille) is a stick cleft down the middle and cut across the cleavage with a series of notches. One-half or side of the cleft stick is handed over to the payer of the money, and the other is retained by the receiver. The system forms a perfect check on receipts, for, in case of dispute, all that is needed is to bring the two halves of the stick together and see that the notches coincide. The present writer saw such tallies in daily use a few years ago in a baker's shop in the capital of Normandy. As evidence of their recent use by unlettered people in England, it may be mentioned that in Kentish hop gardens, the man who keeps the books and checks the earnings of each picker is still called the "tally man." The official use of tallies in the English exchequer continued down to 1824. Ten years later a caretaker in the buildings where these now useless bits of wood were stored, was instructed to get rid of them by burning them in ordinary fire-grates. He heaped on too many at once, and the Houses of Parliament were burned to the ground.

THE LEADING FORTUNE TELLER

"That's funny," she said, puzzling over the city directory. "I'm sure that's the name Mr. Kidder gave me, but I can't find it."

"What is it?" asked her friend.

"Why, we were talking about fortune tellers, and he said the best and surest one in town was named Bradstreet, but I can't find her at all."—Catholic Standard and Times.

What an Accountant Should Know

By EDWARD P. MOXEY

Synopsis of an Address Delivered Before the Students of the School of Commerce, Accounts and Finance of the University of New York.

In speaking upon what an accountant should know, I will not attempt to state all that he should know, for were I to try to do so, I would find that, when I was through speaking, there would be many subjects omitted that should have been included, and no doubt some would be important ones. I will therefore confine my remarks to those which all will concede are necessary for the accountant to be versed in.

WHAT AN ACCOUNTANT IS.

Before giving any of the subjects that an accountant should know, let us first consider what an accountant is. Webster tells us that "an accountant is a person who is skilled in, or who keeps accounts; an officer in a public office who has charge of the accounts." The Century Dictionary describes him as "One who is skilled in or who keeps accounts; one who makes the keeping or examination of accounts his profession; an officer in a public office who has charge of the accounts."

In business affairs we hear repeatedly used the words, clerk, bookkeeper, auditor, accountant. Many persons are prone to confuse the work of one with that of another; while it is true that they all deal with figures, there is as much difference in the character of the work performed by one compared with that done by another, as there is between the light of an electric light and that of a candle. The accountant is the electric light of the world where figures are involved, while the clerk for the time being must content himself to be the candle.

The accountant should possess the qualifications of the clerk, bookkeeper and auditor, for unless he is master of the work that should be performed by them, he lacks the underlying knowledge absolutely necessary to be possessed by him as the stepping-stone to his proficiency. Without the training of the auditor, he would be a mere bookkeeper, and lacking the knowledge of the methods of bookkeeping, which the bookkeeper should possess, he would be nothing more than a clerk.

THE CLERK AND HIS DUTIES.

The clerk, what is he and what are his duties? In the counting house, banking offices or other places in the business world, the tireless driver of the pen is always to be found. Webster describes him as "o ie who is employed to keep records and accounts; a scribe; a penman." The Century Dictionary classes him as "one who is employed in an office, public or private, or in a shop or warehouse, to keep records or accounts."

The clerk in nearly all business concerns is a mere scribe, transcribing into books whatever is given him to copy therein, knowing little or nothing, and in some cases caring less, of the relevancy of the entries he makes, recording the transactions made; working more like an automatic machine. The little knowledge of bookkeeping he possesses has been acquired, not so much in performing his own work, as from assisting the bookkeeper in his. The work of a clerk is the A B C of bookkeeping, and his position a stepping-stone to that of a bookkeeper.

THE BOOKKEEPER.

According to Webster's definition, a bookkeeper is "one who keeps accounts; one who has charge of keeping the books and accounts in an office; " while bookkeeping is defined as "the art of keeping accounts; the art of recording mercantile transactions in a regular and systematic manner, so that a man may know thr true state of his business and property by an inspection of his books." The Century Dictionary gives the vocation of a bookkeeper as that of "one who keeps accounts; one whose occupation is to make a formal balance record of pecuniary transactions in account books." Bookkeeping is defined as "the art of keeping accounts in such a manner as to give a permanent record ot business transactions from which the true state or history of one's pecuniary affairs or mercantile dealings may at any time be ascertained."

I very much doubt if in any vocation there exists so many persons with such various degrees of proficiency as are to be found in that of a bookkeeper. All grades, from the one who is master of his calling to the thoroughly incompetent one, are to be found.

A mistaken idea prevails that any one who is able to perform the duties of a clerk, no matter how limited his knowledge of bookkeeping may be, is capable of keeping a set of books, and I am sorry to say that this idea is entertained by a large number of business men; and it very often requires the sustaining of a financial loss, caused by stupid bookkeeping, to convince them of their error.

The thoroughly competent bookkeeper is as much of a necessity to the successful conuducting of a business as is any part of the working force thereof. His work is in many respects as important as that performed by the one who handles the finances of the concern. He is the source of information upon which the directing head relies for all data as to the business done by the concern and the financial status thereof. In order to be fully qualified for this position, he should possess a thorough knowledge of double-entry bookkeeping, and of the business, the transactions of which he records upon the books.

THE AUDITOR AND HIS WORK.

The next step in advancement is the auditor. This individual is best described as a person appointed and authorized to examine an account or accounts, compare the charges with the vouchers, examine parties and witnesses, allow or reject charges, and state the result. It is usual with courts to refer accounts involved in litigation to auditors for adjustment, and their report, if received, is the basis of the judgment. Sometimes an auditor is a standing officer of political or corporate bodies. State Municipal Auditors are persons appointed or elected to examine the public accounts as they approve, or at such intervals as may be designated.

From this it will be seen that, varied as the different offices of the auditor are, he must possess the same fundamental requirements in whatever line of auditing he may be engaged upon, whether municipal, corporate or otherwise.

He should possess all the qualifications of a competent bookkeeper, which of necessity must include those of the clerk, and be able to discern the correctness of all entries upon the books or accounts which he is auditing after he has examined the same.

In conducting an examination the auditor should be capable of verifying all disbursements with the vouchers or other evidences of payment, and be able to tell whether expenditures made for conducting the business, enlarging the plant, etc., etc., have been charged to the proper accounts. In other words, that the books correspond with the facts.

THE ACCOUNTANT.

The work of the accountant covers the broadest field imaginable; it is of such a diversified character that it is impossible for him to acquire any knowledge of business transactions and the methods of conducting various businesses that will not be indispensable to enable him to perform his duties in a proper manner. The accountant should possess all the requisites that go to make the competent clerk, bookkeeper and auditor, and, in addition to these qualifications, should have a thorough business training, possessing at least a general knowledge of how the principal businesses are conducted and the relation of one business to another.

A noted English accountant, in commenting along these lines in 1886, said: "No accountant can successfully carry on his practice in all the above-mentioned branches unless he is a person of considerable knowledge, skill and experience, for he must be not only acquainted with bookkeeping, which is to him as the alphabet only, but, to put it very briefly, he must have some general knowledge of various trades and their customs. He ought also to have some knowledge of the practice of the Stock Exchange, and so on. No unprejudiced person could deny the advantages of such a knowledge as is here advocated; the only question being whether a standard is not being set so high as to be virtually unattainable, and, consequently, impracticable. The reply to this is that, in accountancy, as elsewhere, it is only he who aims at absolute perfection who can expect to attain even to a decent mediocrity. A complete knowledge of everything is not readily attained in three score years and ten, and is not to be expected as the results of five years' study under articles, but the author never yet heard it seriously suggested that the standard set for the final examination of the Institute indicated the limit of desirable or useful knowledge. Only let the accountant make the most of his opportunities and he will find that liquidation and bankruptcies, as well as audits, will afford him many—and he will be surprised at the amount of knowledge he can acquire, even in a short time, and perhaps, even more astonished at the vast amount of service such knowledge will be to him in his profession."

Many persons confound the accountant with the auditor. The work of each is as separate and distinct as that of the surgeon and the physician. The accountant is the surgeon in the business world, where books, figures and accounts are concerned. His work is analytical in its character, while that of the auditor is purely inspective.

DIFFERENCE BETWEEN ACCOUNTING AND AUDITING.

I cannot better illustrate the distinction between the scopes of the work of the accountant and that of the auditor than to state a case in point.

A corporation which owned a large blast furnace, was the producer of pig iron. It had an extensive plant and employed a large number of men. The volume of its business was great and the profit derived therefrom naturally varied yearly with the fluctuations of the iron trade, some years being large and others small, but even under the most depressed conditions of trade, it always succeeded in making a profit. Its plant was well located for the receipt of the coal, coke, ores and materials used in its furnace, and for the shipment of its product.

The stock of the corporation was owned by a few individuals who gave a banking house an option to purchase the same at a stated price. During the period covered by the option there arose an enormous demand for iron, which caused it to advance rapidly in the market.

The bankers, in order to determine whether or not they would avail themselves of the option held and become they owners of the furnace, decided to have the books of the company examined by an accountant, so as to be fully informed upon all matters appertaining to the business of the company which could in any manner affect the value of the shares of the stock thereof.

The accountant made an examination of the books, covering a period of many years, and prepared statements showing the number of tons of pig iron produced each year and the cost of the same, the tons of pig iron sold yearly and the amount realized therefrom; the yearly profits made in the business, which showed gratifying results, and also a statement of the assets and liabilities, as shown by the books.

Had the accountant been only an auditor he no doubt would have ceased his work with the preparation of the statements I have outlined, and flattered himself with the idea that he had made a complete investigation and that from the data given a close valuation of the shares of the stock of the corporation could be made, based upon earnings, assets and liabilities.

The accountant was more than an auditor, he brought to play his analytical powers and the knowledge he had acquired as to how the business of producing pig iron was conducted, and very soon ascertained that the company was in a far better condition financially than was shown by the prepared statements taken from its books.

The accountant knew that it was the custom for iron producers to contract in advance for the coal, coke, ores and materials for the use of the plant, and that generally the contract was made yearly for an amount deemed necessary to produce the estimated yearly product of the furnace, and that it was also the custom to sell pig iron for future delivery and before the same had been puroduced.

The accountant ascertained that the company, whose affairs he was examining, had made contracts for both purchases of raw materials and for sales of pig iron to be produced. An examination of these contracts, the only record of which was kept in a memorandum book, revealed the fact, that of the iron ores contracted for, deducting the amount that would necessarily be used to produce the pig iron sold, there would be many tons of the same on hand when the contract for delivery to the furnace had been completed, and that the difference between the cost of the ores and what they could then be sold for was many thousands of dollars, which cut quite a figure in the value of the stock of the corporation. It is needless to say that the option to purchase the stock was exercised by the bankers, and that they made a handsome profit upon the transaction.

ORGANIZING OF ACCOUNTING SYSTEMS.

An important branch of the accountant's work is the designing and organizing of systems of keeping accounts. Many a business man has been financially ruined by not having his books and accounts kept in such a form as to give at a glance all information that is absolutely necessary for the prudent and profitable conducting of the business in which he is engaged. This is particularly true of a manufacturer, for the very foundation upon which he conducts his business is the knowledge of the cost price of the goods he manufactures. A system of keeping accounts must therefore be used that will give this information in an accurate and readily accessible form.

It devolves upon the accountant to construct the system which must meet the requirements, not only of the business itself but also of the volume of the business. A system that would be an eminent success where a large business was transacted would be a flat failure in a small concern; and that which would be perfection in one character of business would be worthless in another. What accountant could therefore devise a good system for any business without having considerable knowledge of that business? Absolutely none.

It must be admitted that the knowledge of many businesses can be acquired only after long years of experience; nevertheless, a fundamental knowledge of the most important ones is absolutely necessary before the professed accountant can emerge from the sphere of the auditor.

AN EXAMPLE OF THE NEED OF ACCOUNTANCY.

A partner of a manufacturing concern doing an extensive business was thunderstruck upon receiving from the bookkeeper at the close of their fiscal year, a statement of the business for the year, which showed a good sized loss instead of a large profit, as had confidently been expected.

The concern had made a profit upon the business of the preceding year, and during the last year it had increased its business over 25 per cent, and had sold the goods it manufactured at the same prices before obtained; the partners therefore counted upon an increase in the profits for that year, over the preceding one, of at least 25 per cent, and when the statement of their bookkeeper was submitted, showing a considerable loss, they concluded that the same must be the result of a defalcation, and that the approximate amount thereof was the estimated profits plus the loss shown by the statement. An accountant was engaged to discover the supposed defalcation. He made a thorough audit and found everything correct, as far as receipts and payments of money were concerned; every dollar that had been received had been properly entered upon the books, and there were no entries of payments where the money was not actually and properly disbursed. He therefore did not discover the defalcation that the partners were convinced existed.

The accountant, in analyzing the books and accounts, soon discovered that a grievous error had been made in the calculations of the cost of the goods manufactured. The quality of the goods manufactured had been improved at a considerable cost; the removal of the factory to a site adjacent to their salesroom and warehouse had made a large increase in the rates of insurance upon the latter building and its contents; goods had been sold upon six months' credit, and in many cases, even longer time of payment was given, instead of being sold upon four months' time as had been the custom; large amounts of money had been borrowed at high rates of interest to provide capital to carry on the increased business. All of these things with other expenses were lost sight of in the calculations made of the cost price of the goods manufactured.

Had the several items which went to make up the cost of each description of goods manufactured been classed in proper accounts, this error in the calculation of cost could not have been made. This clearly exemplifies the difference between the work of the bookkeeper and that of the accountant.

On more illustration will suffice for the purpose of showing the absolute necessity of the accountant having a knowledge of many businesses and business transactions.

THE CARTER CASE.

For illustration I will take the Oberlin M. Carter case. In speaking of this I will only give those parts which have become public property through testimony offered in court, which therefore is not now confidential information. Captain Oberlin M. Carter, of the Engineer Corps of the U. S. Government, had charge of the construction work in the river and harbor improvements near Savannah, Ga., and Fernandina, Fla. After some time he was transferred to another district, and another engineer officer placed in charge, who discovered that the quality of the work done by the contractors was far below that called for by the contract. Further investigation revealed the fact that the Government had been victimized out of an enormous sum of money. Captain Carter was courtmartialed, found guilty and sentenced to Leavenworth penitentiary, where he is now imprisoned for his crime.

Before President McKinley confirmed the finding of the courtmartial and the sentence thereof, the financial phase of the transactions of the contractors with the Government, also those of Captain Carter, were investigated by an expert accountant called in for that purpose, and it was after the attorney-general had received the expert's report that the sentence was confirmed.

The payments made to the contractors were all by checks on the U. S. Sub-Treasury, at New York, or on the Government Depository, at Savannah, Ga. These checks, which aggregated about $3,100,000, were about the only tangible pieces of evidence in the possession of the Government and its accountants. A number of these checks aggregating a very large amount of money were paid in currency by the paying teller of the U. S. Ass't. Treasurer, at New York, while others were deposited in various banks and trust companies in New York and other cities, to the credit of one or more of the contractors.

After the contractors had obtained the money upon the Government checks, either by having them cashed at the Sub-Treasury or depositing them in banks, they made a monthly division with Captain Carter, the payments to Captain Carter always being made in currency. Some of the Government checks received by the contractors were deposited to their or their representatives' credit in several banks at Savannah, Ga., the total of these was about $800,000, which was the amount paid by the contractors for the work done under the contract and for which the Government paid them about $3,100,000. The remainder of the Government checks received by the contractors, aggregating about $2,300,000, represented the profits made on the contract, of which Captain Carter received one-third, or over $700,000.

As I have said, the payments to Captain Carter were made in currency, and on the same day that many of them were made, large amounts of currency were deposited in a trust company in New York, to the credit of Captain Carter, or to that of his father-in-law, or paid to bond brokers for stocks and bonds purchased by Carter. In many cases the total amount thus used on a particular date was exactly one-third of the amount of the Government checks deposited by the contractors in New York city on the same day.

A large portion of the over $700,000 received by Captain Carter was invested in gilt edge railroad stocks and bonds. The numbers of the bonds purchased from various bond brokers—which were all coupon bonds and payable to bearer—were obtained, and at various dates the coupons were deposited by Captain Carter in a trust company, to the credit of his account, about the time that the coupons became due and payable.

Several years after these investments were made by Captain Carter, some of the identical bonds were traced to some of his relatives and friends, principally through their collecting the coupons. Within the last few weeks securities and money in their possession belonging to Captain Carter, aggregating over $400,000, have been attached by the Government, and are now in the custody of the court pending proof of their ownership.

None except those who have had experience in this particular line of accounting can estimate the amount of tact and labor it involves to trace money, when different accounts in many banks and trust companies in various cities have been used in the endeavor to conceal the transactions, and how apparently hopeless the task seems when the same is currency.

This is only the beginning of the end of this celebrated case. It is one of those few cases in which the Government, after having been defrauded of a large amount of money, has recovered any large portion of it, and where any of the perpetrators of the swindle were convicted of the criminal charges made.

COLLEGE COURSE OF ACCOUNTING.

Having, as I think, shown some of the important qualifications that the accountant should possess, in order to qualify him for his very high calling, it would be presumption on my part to dogmatize as to how these are to be acquired in a college course. As I have already said, some of the knowledge that an accountant should possess can only come through years of experience, and this of course, cannot be acquired in a college course of a few years; nevertheless a thorough knowledge of bookkeeping in all of its branches, as well as a general knowledge of the more important businesses of the country is absolutely necessary before any one is entitled to the appellation of an accountant. This knowledge can be acquired in a college course.

If I were asked what I considered should be included in a college course of accounting, I would suggest the following outline, for Commercial Geography, Industry and Business Practice:—

FIRST.—COMMERCIAL GEOGRAPHY.

a The situation of the United States in relation to the other continents with reference to our foreign trade.

b The situation, topography, soil, climate, agricultural and forest resources and mineral resources, considered in relation to the location of the industries of the United States.

SECOND.—INDUSTRY: A STUDY OF THE METHODS AND PROCESSES IN THE FOLLOWING INDUSTRIES:

a The cereals and flour manufacture.

b Iron and coal mining, and the iron and steel industry.

c Live stock and the packing industry.

d Cotton, wool, silk and flax growing and the textile industry.

e The lumber industry.

f The industry of transportation, including the principles of railway location and construction. Relation of railways to canals and other waterways. Principles determining the choice of railway routes. The technical side of railroading.

THIRD.—BUSINESS PRACTICE.

a A study of the business methods of production and distribution. Methods of getting control of natural resources. United States land laws and mining laws. Methods of optioning property. Terms of sale. Mining royalties, etc.

b Methods of transportation. Principles of railway rates. Terms of payment. Descriptions of operations of shipments.

c Organization of wholesale markets. Produce Exchanges and produce speculation. Methods of dealing in wheat, cotton, petroleum, coffee and pig iron. Contrast of foreign and domestic methods.

d Principles determining the location of manufacturing industries. Methods of erecting plant, collecting labor force, purchasing machinery. Organization of purchasing and inspection departments. Operation of plant. Relations of responsibility. Methods of promotion and selection of foremen and overseers. Methods of wage payment. Relation between employers and employees. Business aspects of Trades Unions. Management of labor difficulties. Rights of employers and employees. Restrictions upon employers in the matter of protection of laborers from accident. Methods of cost keeping and keeping depreciation account. Methods of sale.

Distribution of the products. Relations between manufacturer and wholesaler. Manufacturers' agent. Organization of wholesale house. Relations between wholesale house and traveling salesmen. Relations between wholesaler and retailer. Principles of granting credit to retailer. Advantages to retailer of discounting. Management of retail stores. Management of stock. Principles of giving credit to customers. Management of clerks. Principles of advertising.

This outline does not include the studies in banking, finance, political economy, business law and other subjects which are of equal importance, an analysis of which I will not enter into.

Let me say to the student that whatever work he does in college, with the purpose of qualifying himself for this important and exacting vocation, must be done thoroughly and conscientiously and with the thought that all such knowledge acquired is but the foundation stone upon which his future success as an accountant depends.

To those of you who are members of the School of Commerce, Accounts and Finance of the University of New York, let me say that you are to be congratulated in having such an able corps of instructors, who have made a life-long study of those things which are fundamentally necessary for the preparation of an accountant. In the future, and no doubt soon, these instructors, by their efforts, will turn out able men who will take their places among the ranks of the greatest accountants of the age. It is these instructors who are best qualified to determine as to what subjects are to be included in the college course of an accountant's training and the best methods to pursue in teaching the same.

Let me close with a quotation from a noted English accountant: "Lastly but not least, may be placed those desirable qualifications of the auditor which are not acquired by careful study, but, rather by living. Tact, caution, firmness, good temper, courage, integrity, discretion, industry, judgment, patience, clear headedness and reliability. In short, all those qualities that go to make a good man contribute to the making of a good auditor, while that judicious and liberal education which is involved in the single word 'culture' is most essential for all who would excel. Accountancy is a profession calling for a width and variety of knowledge to which no man has yet set the limit: the foremost accountants are not ashamed to say that, like Epaminondas, they learn something in addition every day; let us, therefore, see no shame in following their example."

SECRETARY GAGE

Secretary of the Treasury Lyman J. Gage, whose contemplated retirement from the Cabinet is announced, is one of America's typical self-made men. He has been in the banking business all his life, beginning as an office boy in the Central Bank, of Oneida, N. Y. He has been three times elected president of the American Bankers' Association and was president of the board of directors of the World's Columbian Exposition in 1893. President McKinley appointed him Secretary of the Treasury in 1897, and he has served since then to the eminent satisfaction of financiers and bankers all through the country. Secretary Gage is much interested in the work of the American Institute of Bank Clerks and has made one address before one of its chapters, that in Denver. He is a thorough believer in the practical education of the bank clerk and his remarks on the need of competent men in financial positions and the princely salaries to be paid such men, if they can be found, have been widely quoted. The accompanying fine portrait of Secretary Gage at his desk in the Treasury Department is reproduced here by the courtesy of the New York Commercial Advertiser.

SECRETARY GAGE AT HIS DESK IN THE TREASURY DEPARTMENT.

NEW ISSUE OF AN OLD ALMANAC

"The Old Farmers' Almanac for 1902 has appeared, and the perusal of it will give pleasure to many old eyes," says the New York Sun. "Founded in 1793, it has been published annually ever since; and it will be published, we presume, when 2000 has gone to join 1900. The founder was Robert Baily Thomas, of Boylston, Mass., who edited it for more than fifty years. The prefaces used to be, and we believe are still, signed with his name in script. Folks used to believe as firmly that Robert B. Thomas was alive as in Santa Claus or any other authentic and venerable character. There was a quotation from some poet at the head of the page devoted to each month. We would give most of contemporary literature for the sound advice that was in the righthand column, if it was the righthand column of each page. There you learned the time for hanging gates, for sodding the house, for picking over the potatoes, for all the operations of the year. The meteorological predictions have never been equalled in accuracy and unpretentiousness. Was the month February? 'About this time look out for snow,' would be spread over the whole calendar for that month. You were not told to look out for thunder in December or frost in July. Robert B. Thomas may not have been brilliant, but he was safe. He built one of the too few monuments of real popular literature in the United States."

The Negotiable Instruments Law*

By THOMAS B. PATON

Restrictive Indorsements — Responsibility — Qualified and Conditional Indorsements — Payable to Cashiers.

NOTE.—As enacted in New York, the Negotiable Instrument law is divided into nineteen articles as follows:—

1. GENERAL PROVISIONS (Sections 1—17)
2. NEGOTIABLE INSTRUMENTS: Form and Interpretation (20—42)
3. Consideration (50—55)
4. Negotiation (60—80)
5. Rights of holder (90—98)
6. Liabilities of parties (110—119)
7. Presentment for payment (130—148)
8. Notice of Dishonor (160—189)
9. Discharge (200—206)
10. BILLS OF EXCHANGE (210—215)
11. Acceptance (220—230)
12. Presentment for acceptance (240—248)
13. Protest (260—268)
14. Acceptance for honor (280—290)
15. Payment for honor (300—306)
16. Bills in a set (310—315)
17. PROMISSORY NOTES AND CHECKS (320—325)
18. Notes given for patent rights (330—332)
19. Law repealed: When takes effect (340—341)

The provisions of the law naturally fall under four general classifications.

a. General Provisions.
b. Negotiable Instruments in General.
c. Bills of Exchange.
d. Promissory Notes and Checks.

The text of the law is the same in all the states (with some slight exceptions which will be noted), but the numbering of the sections, and in some states of the articles, is not uniform. There is, however, the same continuity of articles and text, except that in some instances, "General Provisions" follow, instead of precede, the remainder of the act. By following this course of study with reference to the New York act, as above outlined, the reader in each state can apply the same to the law of his own state.

We pass from the forms of special and blank indorsement, by which the title to negotiable instruments is freely and unrestrictedly transferred to those other forms of indorsement known as restrictive, qualified, or conditional, which, as their respective designations imply, impose some restriction, qualification or condition upon the transfer.

RESTRICTIVE INDORSEMENT.

Sec. 66. When Indorsement Restrictive.—An indorsement is restrictive which either:—

1. Prohibits the further negotiation of the instrument; or
2. Constitutes the indorsee the agent of the indorser; or
3. Vests the title in the indorsee in trust for or to the use of some other person.

But the mere absence of words implying power to negotiate does not make the indorsement restrictive.

Restrictive indorsements have their uses in the commercial world. For good and satisfactory reasons, the payee or indorsee owning a negotiable instrument may, for example, desire that its ownership pass to another without the power being possessed by that other of further negotiating the instrument. He will, thereupon, make a restrictive indorsement designed to "(1) prohibit the further negotiation of the instrument." If he indorses it "Pay to John Smith only," the use of the word "only," will make the indorsement restrictive, and prohibit John Smith from further negotiating it. If, however, he merely indorses "Pay to John Smith," without adding "or order," the indorsement will not so operate, but will confer upon John Smith the title and unrestricted power of negotiation, for the act provides that "the mere absence of words implying power to negotiate does not make an indorsement restrictive."

Again, the payee or indorsee owning a negotiable instrument may desire to retain his title thereto, but to transfer the instrument to another merely for purposes of receiving payment thereof, and accounting to him therefor. In such event he will use a form of restrictive indorsement designed to "(2) constitute the indorsee the agent of the indorser." A common form of indorsement of this character is "Pay to A, or order, for collection."

It has often happened that A, the collecting agent of the indorsing owner, has failed while holding the paper or its proceeds, before paying the same over to the indorser, and the courts have frequently been called upon to decide conflicting questions of ownership of such paper and its proceeds, between the indorsing owner, on the one hand, and the bankrupt estate of the indorsee, or some one claiming such proceeds as due from such bankrupt estate, on the other.

QUESTIONS OF RESPONSIBILITY.

Growing out of restrictive indorsements in this form—i. e., constituting the indorsee agent of the indorser—have also arisen many legal questions of responsibility of A, the restrictive indorsee, as an indorser warranting the genuineness of prior indorsements and correctness of amount, to those to whom he has sub-indorsed the instrument for collection, or to those from whom he has received payment. These questions have had peculiar importance to those engaged in the banking business, for bankers, upon whom negotiable instruments are drawn for payment, are in the habit of honoring them upon the responsibility of the immediate presentors, it being impracticable for a drawee bank to investigate the history and genuineness of the signatures of indorsers, prior to the last indorsee who presents the instrument for payment, or to determine the financial responsibility of prior parties with reference to making good to them the amount paid, in case it turns out that some prior indorsement has been forged, or the amount for which the instrument was originally drawn, enlarged.

As the courts have decided in several cases that a restrictive indorsee, being a mere agent and not owner, is not responsible for genuineness, and cannot be compelled to refund a payment received of a raised check or draft, or one bearing a forged indorsement, after he has paid the amount to his principal, indorsements "for collection," and all other forms of restrictive indorsements whereunder the indorsee is a mere agent of the indorser, have come into disfavor in the banking world, and their use has been largely curtailed by resolutions adopted by clearing-house associations excluding restrictively indorsed paper from the clearings, and by the refusal of bankers to handle instruments having this character of indorsement.

A third variety of restrictive indorsement is one which "vests the title in the indorsee in trust for or to the use of some other person." The legal title to property is often held by one person, in trust for some other person, in whom resides the beneficial ownership, and the right to have the property managed and applied according to the terms of the trust upon which it is held. Checks, drafts or other negotiable instruments indorsed payable to "A in trust for B" or to "A, for the use of B" or to "A, for account of B," exemplify a form of restrictive indorsement whereunder the legal title to the money passes to A; but the indorsement is restrictive to the extent of showing that the instrument cannot be negotiated by A for his own benefit, or passed away for his own personal debt.

EFFECT OF RESTRICTIVE INDORSEMENT.

We now come to consider the effect of a restrictive indorsement and the rights of the restrictive indorsee:—

Sec. 67. Effect of Restrictive Indorsement: rights of indorsee.—A restrictive indorsement confers upon the indorsee the right:—

1. To receive payment of the instrument;
2. To bring any action thereon that the indorser could bring;
3. To transfer his rights as such indorsee, where the form of the indorsement authorizes him to do so.

But all subsequent indorsees acquire only the title of the first indorsee under the restrictive indorsement.

This section very clearly shows the right of the restrictive indorsee to receive payment of the instrument, and if payment is refused, to bring an action on the paper in his own name to enforce payment through the courts. Before the enactment of the Negotiable Instruments Law the courts in several states differed as to this last-named proposition, some

*Republished from the Banking Law Journal, by permission. Copyright, 1899, 1900 and 1901, by T. B. Paton, all rights secured. To be revised and published in book form by the author.

holding that an indorsee "for collection" could bring suit on the instrument, but others denying the right and power of the restrictive indorsee so to do.

This section further empowers the indorsee to transfer his rights as such indorsee "where the form of the indorsement authorizes him so to do," but of course he cannot transfer, nor can a subsequent indorsee acquire from him, any further title or rights than possessed by the first restrictive indorsee.

Having seen that under one form of restrictive indorsement the indorsee acquires title, but shorn of the power of further negotiation; that under another form, he merely acquires possession for purposes of collection as agent of the indorser, but not the title, which remains in the indorser; and that under a third form, the indorsee acquires title, but in trust for another, so that he cannot negotiate the instrument as his own, we come now to that form of indorsement known as "qualified."

Sec. 68. Qualified Indorsement.—A qualified indorsement constitutes the indorser a mere assignor of the title to the instrument. It may be made by adding to the indorser's signature the words "without recourse" or any words of similar import. Such an indorsement does not impair the negotiable character of the instrument.

Ordinarily, as we have seen, when the owner of a negotiable instrument transfers it to another, he does so by a special or blank indorsement, which not only passes full title to the indorsee, but also carries certain warranties that the instrument is genuine, his title good, etc., and certain engagements on his part that on due presentment the instrument will be accepted or paid, or both, as the case may be, and that if it be dishonored, and the necessary proceedings on dishonor be duly taken, he will pay the amount thereof to the holder or to any subsequent indorser who may be compelled to pay it. But sometimes the owner desires to transfer title to the instrument free from the contingent liability or engagement last specified, namely, that if dishonored on due presentment and notice, he will make it good. To accomplish this object he has recourse to the "qualified" indorsement. This is usually made by the use of the words "without recourse" in connection with the indorsement; or other words of similar import, will answer the same purpose. By this form of indorsement, title to the instrument is transferred and its negotiable character is not impaired. If the instrument is not genuine and in all respects what it purports to be, if the indorser has not had a good title to it, if prior parties have not had capacity to contract, or if the indorser, at the time of negotiation, has had knowledge of any fact which would impair the validity of the instrument or render it valueless,—in any such event, the qualified indorser is liable, but if there is nothing against him in these respects, he cannot be held, as can an indorser by special or blank indorsement, because the instrument is not paid at maturity.

CONDITIONAL INDORSEMENT.

We now approach the subject of conditional indorsement.

Sec. 69. Conditional Indorsement. Where an indorsement is conditional, a party required to pay the instrument may disregard the condition, and make payment to the indorsee or his transferee, whether the condition has been fulfilled or not. But any person to whom an instrument so indorsed is negotiated, will hold the same, or the proceeds thereof, subject to the rights of the person indorsing conditionally.

Every indorsement, special or in blank, is conditional to the extent that the indorser binds himself to pay only in the event of due presentment, notice of dishonor, etc. But such indorsements are not regarded as conditional, or other than absolute, for this reason. A conditional indorsement is one by which the indorser annexes some other condition to his indorsement. For example, A owning a negotiable instrument may indorse it "Pay to B or order if before maturity B pays a promissory note (specified) held by C against me;" or, taking an example from an actual case, a bill of exchange was drawn by F upon K to order of R, indorsed by R.

"Pay the within sum to Messrs. C & R, or order, upon my name appearing in the Gazette, as ensign in any regiment of the line, between the 1st and 64th, if within two months from this date. R."—
and accepted by K after such indorsement. This bill was afterwards negotiated by the indorsees to others and finally was discounted by the Bank of England, to whom, at maturity, it was paid by the acceptors. As the condition upon which the indorsement by the payee, R, was made had never been fulfilled, he brought an action against the acceptors to recover the amount of the bill. The court held that the acceptors were bound by the condition, and if it was not performed, the property in the bill reverted to the payee, who was entitled to the amount against the acceptors. (Robertson vs. Kensington, 4 Taunt. 30).

At common law, therefore, we see that where a bill was indorsed conditionally, the acceptor paid the bill at his peril, if the condition was not fulfilled. But this common law rule has been altered by the first paragraph of section 69 of the Negotiable Instruments Law which, as is seen, provides that where the indorsement is conditional, the payor may "disregard the condition and make payment to the indorsee or his transferee, whether the condition has been fulfilled or not." The reason given is that any other rule is too hard on an acceptor. If he dishonors the bill, he may be liable to damages, and yet it may be impossible for him to find out if the condition has been fulfilled.

But the act goes on to provide that "any person to whom an instrument so indorsed is negotiated, will hold the same, or the proceeds thereof, subject to the rights of the person indorsing conditionally." Thus, we see, that if the condition has not been performed, while the payor is allowed to make payment, the one who receives payment holds the proceeds, not absolutely, but subject to the rights of the person indorsing conditionally.

It seems a peculiar thing to permit a negotiable instrument, which has been indorsed conditionally, to remain in the category of negotiable instruments, so as to be transferable as a negotiable instrument subject to the condition. One of the requisites of negotiability, as set forth in section 20, is that the instrument "must contain an unconditional promise or order to pay a sum certain in money." Yet, after the instrument, in negotiable form, is once put forth, it would seem that any indorser may make its payment uncertain and conditional by affixing some condition to his indorsement, and the Negotiable Instruments Act, instead of providing, that such an indorsement destroys its further negotiability, provides that the instrument shall be certainly payable, condition or no condition, but that the last indorsee who collects it, is not absolutely entitled to the money, but holds the proceeds "subject to the rights of the person indorsing conditionally." After an instrument is so indorsed, it is certainly unfit for further circulation as a negotiable instrument, being shorn of that certainty of payment to—or rather, right to retain the proceeds by any subsequent taker, which must be present in order to enable him, when acquiring it, to correctly gauge its value.

PAYABLE TO BEARER.

The next section treats of indorsements of instruments payable to bearer.

Sec. 70. Indorsement of Instrument Payable to Bearer.—Where an instrument, payable to bearer, is indorsed specially, it may nevertheless be further negotiated by delivery; but the person indorsing specially is liable as indorser to only such holders as make title through his indorsement.

We discussed this section in connection with the subject of special and blank indorsements.

We are still on the subject of negotiation of the instrument by delivery or by indorsement, and approach the case where a negotiable instrument, instead of having a single payee, is made payable to the order of two or more persons. This is provided for by

PAYABLE TO TWO OR MORE PERSONS.

Sec. 71. Indorsement where payable to two or more persons.—Where an instrument is payable to the order of two or more payees or indorsees who are not partners, all must indorse, unless the one indorsing has authority to indorse for the others.

This is the rule of the law merchant. If a note, for example, is drawn payable to order of John Smith and Peter Jones, the indorsement by either, alone, will be insufficient to transfer title to the instrument, unless the one indorsing has authority to indorse for the other. No commercial purchaser should acquire the instrument upon the single indorsement, without first being satisfied of the existence of such authority, for if he had to take it into court for enforcement, the single indorsement alone would be insufficient to prove his title, and he would have to prove authority by the non-indorsing payee to the indorsing payee, to indorse for him. The following case arose in Michigan and was passed upon by the federal court. (Dwight vs. Pease, 3 McLean, 94.) A promissory note was executed as follows:—

"Detroit, January 1, 1837. Two years after date, I promise to pay to the order of Walter Chester, and Pease Chester & Co., one thousand five hundred dollars, for value received, at the Farmers' & Mechanics' Bank of Michigan, with interest. (Signed) John Chester."

This note was indorsed:—

"Pease, Chester & Co.,
"D. E. Jones."

The note came into the hands of one Dwight, who after demand of payment of the maker, and notice of dishonor to the indorsers, brought suit against Pease, Chester & Co. as indorsers of the note. As the note had never been indorsed by Walter Chester, one of the payees, Dwight was held to have no right of recovery. The court said:—

"Walter Chester, one of the promisees in the note, seems not to have indorsed it, and this is fatal to the right of the plaintiff. The interest of the promisees is joint in the note, and not being in partnership, they must each transfer the note.

"Only one-half of the note was transferred by the indorsement of Pease, Chester & Co., and this does not give a right to their, or any subsequent, assignee to sue on the note. Recourse against the maker cannot thus be divided and suits multiplied. The plaintiff seeks by this action to recover the full amount of the note against the defendants, as indorsers. But as he holds but one-half of the note under the assignment, the indorsement, at most, can only be evidence of that amount. The declaration is defective in not averring that Walter Chester, one of the payees, did indorse the note."

If a note is payable to a partnership, then indorsement by a single partner is sufficient, but the indorsement must be in the name of the partnership, not in the individual name of the indorsing partner.

PAYABLE TO CASHIER OR CORPORATION OFFICERS.

The next section treats of instruments drawn payable to cashiers of banks, or to fiscal officers of banks or corporations.

Sec. 72. Effect of instrument drawn or indorsed to a person as cashier. Where an instrument is drawn or indorsed to a person as "cashier" or other fiscal officer of a bank or corporation, it is deemed prima facie to be payable to the bank or corporation of which he is such officer; and may be negotiated by either the indorsement of the bank or corporation, or the indorsement of the officer.

The practice is very common, in transmitting paper to banks for collection, to make the indorsement to "John Jones, Cashier," instead of to the "Bank of Smithville," of which such John Jones is the cashier. In making remittances to banks, also, drafts are likewise commonly made payable to the cashier as such. Several cases have come before the courts wherein objection has been made to the title of the bank to such paper, on the ground that it was not in reality payable to the bank, but to the cashier individually. In all such cases, exception has been made to the general rule that the affixing of a representative capacity, merely describes the person of the payee, and it has been held that the paper is payable to the bank of which the named payee is cashier. Section 72 embodies this rule as part of the Negotiable Instruments Law, but extends it so that it becomes applicable, not alone to paper drawn to cashiers of banks, but to all paper made payable to "fiscal" officers of banks or corporations. "Treasurers" are undoubtedly fiscal officers, but it may require some judicial construction in particular cases to define just what officers of a corporation would or would not be comprehended within the meaning of the term "fiscal."

MISSPELLED NAME.

Sec. 73. Indorsement where name is misspelled, etc.—Where the name of a payee or indorsee is wrongly designated or misspelled, he may indorse the instrument as therein described, adding, if he think fit, his proper signature.

This section greatly promotes convenience in the transfer of negotiable paper. Very numerous are the cases where a party in executing or indorsing an instrument, mistakes the correct spelling, or even the correct name, of the proposed payee or indorsee, and merely inserts what he thinks is right, but what, in reality, is more or less erroneous. Under this section, the intended payee or indorsee, is authorized to indorse in the name by which he is described, and then, if he chooses, he may add his proper signature. The necessity, in thousands of cases, of refusing payment because of "incorrect indorsement," or of requiring "guaranties" of correctness and sufficiency of signature before payment, is obviated where this rule is followed by payees or indorsees in the indorsement of paper wherein they have been wrongly designated, or their names misspelled.

Further, as illustrative of the benefits of this section, the case of Bolles vs. Stearns, decided nearly half a century ago, 11 Cushing (Mass.) 320, may be cited. A man named Joseph P. Reed, made a loan to a man named Bolles, for which the latter gave Reed his promissory note. But in drawing the note, Bolles mistakenly made it payable to "John P. Reed or order." There was a John P. Reed living in the same town, but the note was in fact given to, and intended for, Joseph P. Reed. Joseph P. Reed indorsed the note in his own name to one Stearns. Stearns owed Bolles money, and Bolles sued Stearns therefor. Stearns sought to set off the note given by Bolles to Reed and indorsed by Reed to him. But the court refused to allow him to do it. Following is its reasoning:—

"The note given by the plaintiff, payable to John P. Reed, or order, and indorsed to the defendant by Joseph P. Reed, cannot be allowed to the defendant by way of set-off. That note, though given for money lent to the plaintiff by Joseph P. Reed, was made payable, not to him, but to John P. Reed, a person in esse. Now it is certain that the legal interest in that note was not transferred to the defendant by Joseph P. Reed's indorsing his name on it. He was not the payee, nor the legal representative of the payee; and a transfer by indorsement can be made in the first instance only by the payee, or by some one claiming in his right, as his executor, administrator, or assignee in bankruptcy or insolvency. If there had been no such person as John P. Reed, perhaps the note might have been regarded as payable to bearer, and might have been passed to the defendant by delivery, as if it had in terms been made payable to bearer. Of this, however, we give no opinion. But as the note was made payable, not to a fictitious person, but to a person in being, the indorsement of a third person transferred no legal title to it."

This reasoning is to the effect that a note made payable to John P. Reed, an existing person, but delivered to and intended to be made payable to, Joseph P. Reed, cannot be lawfully transferred by the latter's indorsement, as it would be the indorsement of a third person, not the payee in the note. We are inclined to think, to the contrary, that Joseph P. Reed's indorsement was the indorsement of the intended and real payee, and a title-conveying indorsement, and that if the existing John P. Reed had indorsed his name to this note, it would have been a forgery. But, however this may be, the Negotiable Instruments Law now provides a remedy for such a case of wrong designation of a payee, under which his indorsee would derive protection. If such a case should now arise, wherein a note, intended for Joseph P. Reed was erroneously drawn payable to John P. Reed, all that Joseph would have to do, would be to sign the name of John P. Reed, and then, if he chose, add his correct name, Joseph P. Reed; then if he transferred it to a Mr. Stearns, who owed Mr. Bolles, the maker, a sum of money, which the latter sought to collect from him through the Massachusetts courts, the decision of the Supreme Court of that commonwealth would be different from that rendered in 11 Cushing, namely, that Bolles' note to John P. Reed, intended for and indorsed by Joseph P. Reed in the manner provided in the Negotiable Instruments Law, and transferred to Stearns, was a good subject of set-off in the suit of Bolles vs. Stearns.

REPRESENTATIVE CAPACITY.

We come to the next section, which treats of indorsement in a representative capacity.

Sec. 74. Indorsement in representative capacity.—Where any person is under obligation to indorse in a representative capacity, he may indorse in such terms as to negative personal liability.

A man may die, and be succeeded by an executor or administrator. He may fail, and be succeeded by an assignee in bankruptcy or insolvency. It may become part of the duty of such a representative to indorse negotiable paper of his predecessor. An ordinary indorsement, in addition to its title conveying power, carries with it certain liabilities. The rule has been laid down in many cases that "an administrator or executor can only bind himself by his contracts; he cannot bind the assets of the deceased. Therefore, if he make, indorse, or accept negotiable paper, he will be held personally liable, even if he adds to his own name, the name of his office; signing a note, for example, 'A as executor of B,' for this will be deemed only a part of his description, or will be rejected as surplusage."

In view of the above, the object of section 74 is plain. It confers authority upon any person who is obliged to indorse in a representative capacity, to indorse in such terms as to negative personal liability. This authority, it will be observed, seems to be confined to an indorsement. It does not, in terms, cover the case of the making or acceptance of a negotiable instrument by an executor, administrator or other person acting in a representative capacity.

SCHOOL OF COMMERCE, ACCOUNTS & FINANCE

Diary of the Month's Work

Senior Class

RECORD FOR WEEK ENDING DECEMBER 6, 1901.

MONDAY.
8-9 Lecture on Life Insurance by Mr. C. S. Jones.
9-10 Lecture on Trust Accounts by Mr. Jos. Hardcastle.

TUESDAY.
8-10 Lecture on Money by Prof. Jos. F. Johnson.

WEDNESDAY.
8-9 Lecture by Dr. Edward T. Devine, Gen. Sec. of Charity Organization Soc., on "Standard of Living Among the Poor."
9-10 Lecture on History, Theory and Geography of Commerce by Dr. Webster.

THURSDAY.
8-10 Lecture on Accounting by Mr. Conant, C. P. A.

FRIDAY.
8-10 Mr. Walsh lectured on Commercial Law.

RECORD FOR WEEK ENDING DECEMBER 13, 1901.

MONDAY.
8-9 Lecture on Life Insurance by Mr. C. S. Jones.
9-10 Lecture on Trust Accounts by Mr. Jos. Hardcastle.

TUESDAY.
8-10 Lecture on Money by Prof. Jos. F. Johnson.

WEDNESDAY.
8-9 Dr. John Quincy Adams, of Philadelphia, lectured on "Art and Labor Reform."
9-10 Lecture on History, Theory and Geography of Commerce by Dr. Webster.

THURSDAY.
8-10 Lecture on Accounting by Mr. Conant, C. P. A.

FRIDAY.
8-10 Mr. Walsh lectured on Commercial Law.

RECORD FOR WEEK ENDING DECEMBER 20, 1901.

MONDAY.
8-9 Lecture on Life Insurance by Mr. C. S. Jones.
9-10 Lecture on Trust Accounts by Mr. Jos. Hardcastle.

TUESDAY.
8-10 Lecture on Money by Prof. Jos. F. Johnson.

WEDNESDAY.
8-9 Lecture by Mr. Edw. P. Moxey on "What an Accountant Should Know."
9-10 Lecture on History, Theory and Geography of Commerce by Dr. Webster.

THURSDAY.
8-10 Lecture on Accounting by Mr. Conant, C. P. A.

FRIDAY.
8-10 Mr. Walsh lectured on Commercial Law.

RECORD FOR WEEK ENDING DECEMBER 27, 1901.

MONDAY.
8-9 Lecture on Life Insurance by Mr. C. S. Jones.
9-10 Lecture on Trust Accounts by Mr. Jos. Hardcastle.
Christmas Recess Tuesday.

Junior Class

RECORD FOR WEEK ENDING DECEMBER 6, 1901.

MONDAY.
8-10 Prof. Jos. F. Johnson on Political Economy.

TUESDAY.
8-10 Lecture on Cotton Mill Accounting by Mr. Geo. Young.

WEDNESDAY.
8-9 Lecture by Dr. Edward T. Devine, Gen. Sec. of Charity Organization Soc., on "Standard of Living Among the Poor."
9-10 Lecture by Mr. Eaton on Transportation.

THURSDAY.
8-10 Lecture by Mr. Bacon on Law of Contracts.

FRIDAY.
8-10 Lecture by Mr. George Young on Cotton Mill Accounting.

RECORD FOR WEEK ENDING DECEMBER 13, 1901.

MONDAY.
8-10 Prof. Jos. F. Johnson on Political Economy.

TUESDAY.
8-10 Lecture on Cotton Mill Accounting by Mr. Geo. Young.

WEDNESDAY.
8-9 Lecture on "Art and Labor Reform" by Dr. John Quincy Adams, of Philadelphia, Pa.
9-10 Lecture by Mr. Eaton on Transportation.

THURSDAY.
8-10 Lecture by Mr. Bacon on Law of Contracts.

FRIDAY.
8-10 Lecture on Cotton Mill Accounting by Mr. Geo. Young.

RECORD FOR WEEK ENDING DECEMBER 20, 1901.

MONDAY.
8-10 Prof. Jos. F. Johnson on Political Economy.

TUESDAY.
8-10 Mr. Vedder lectured on Practical Accounting.

WEDNESDAY.
8-9 Lecture by Mr. Edw. P. Moxey on "What an Accountant Should Know."
9-10 Lecture by Mr. Eaton on Transportation.

THURSDAY.
8-10 Lecture by Mr. Bacon on Law of Contracts.

FRIDAY.
8-9 Lecture by Mr. Geo. Young on Purchase Record and Invoice System.
9-10 Lecture by Mr. Vedder on Sales Systems.

RECORD FOR WEEK ENDING DECEMBER 27, 1901.

MONDAY.
8-10 Prof. Jos. F. Johnson on Political Economy.
Christmas Recess Began Tuesday.

COMMERCIAL EDUCATION

The following graceful allusion to the usefulness of the School of Commerce, Accounts and Finance is from a recent issue of the New York Commercial:—

"The Commercial notes with satisfaction the splendid and public-spirited effort of New York University to train men for the higher duties of commercial life, in establishing, on a broad basis of advanced instruction in Political Economy, Accounting and Commercial Law, a School of Commerce, Accounts and Finance. The objects of this school cannot be better set forth than by quoting the following extract from one of its announcements:—

"'In the more general higher commercial education, the plan of the school is elastic. The courses of study now offered furnish a thorough training in the principles and practice of banking, in commercial law, in the foreign exchanges, in stock brokerage, in transportation, and in foreign commerce, and must prove of positive and practical value to any young man who wishes to prepare himself for usefulness in the office of a bank or kindred financial institution, or in the employ of a railroad corporation. The plan of study is broad enough in scope, it is believed, to meet the wants of those who are to be administrators of affairs, to whom a working knowledge of accountancy, commercial law, and economics is of the first importance. The courses in law are intended to furnish so much of the law relating to commercial subjects as is essential to the education of a properly trained accountant and man of affairs.'

"New York University is to be congratulated for being one of the first in the United States to recognize the present general movement in behalf of the higher commercial education. We hope that the day is not far distant when every university throughout the land will have, as one of its component parts, this twentieth century necessity."

COMMERCE ACCOUNTS & FINANCE

A Monthly Magazine of Higher Business Education and Practical Administration. Acknowledged Authority in the Profession of Commerce and Consistent Advocate of Methods Up to Date and Above the Table.

GEORGE E. ALLEN, Editor.

Published Monthly by the Commerce, Accounts & Finance Company, 25 Pine Street, New York. Subscription One Dollar a Year. Postage prepaid by the Publishers. In the absence of specific orders to stop at the end of the subscription term the paper will be continued and a bill sent. Entered at the New York Postoffice as Second Class mail matter.

* * *

The old year has gone. Welcome the new! The year just passed was one of unparalleled business prosperity—for this nation at least—of wonderful strides in invention and discovery, of unprecedented combinations of capital in corporations and upon the community-of-interest basis, of terrible crimes against society, as witness the assassination of the President; of sharp financial crises, as witness the Northern Pacific corner of last May; and of wonderful forbearance and self-possesion, as witness the behavior of the business public in the trying days succeeding the President's death. The new year is ushered in with wireless telegraphy on the one hand and aerial navigation on the other—two most promising propositions, both of which remain to be commercialized and made useful in a business way. During the year 1901 much was done to improve the conditions under which business is transacted. The banks in various ways have been brought into closer relationship with each other, and acting together are now in position to fend off the disastrous results of a panic, as never before. The conference of various representative labor leaders with conspicuous managers of capital near the close of the year, and which resulted in the selection of a board of arbitration, in the composition of which there are included some of the best minds of the period, representing the three elements in interest—labor, capital and the general public—promises a freedom from wage disputes and strikes for other reasons which we have never before known.

*

The old year is gone. Its lessons are before us. Its results are accomplished facts. The present is in our grasp—but what of the future? All the financial and business reviews which the turn of the year has called forth dwell at considerable length upon the satisfactory condition of business at present and the probability of a continuation of those conditions for some time to come. And yet we seem to hear at times the ominous mutterings of a storm that is gathering somewhere, be it east or west or north or south, none of us has yet taken time to observe. Like children at play on a summer afternoon, we propose to run to shelter whenever the raindrops begin to fall. Speculation has been hard hit in copper and in street railway and telephone building. Certain of the great staple industries in the matter of production seem to have reached a point where consumption has been overtaken and passed by production. Perhaps the storm is only a sun-shower or will pass around, never showing more than a little cloud along the horizon. Surely we would not be alarmists, and yet our philosophy says night always succeeds the day, and there has never been a period of financial distress in the history of this nation that was not preceded by "good" times. Or to put it otherwise, the present is the only period of "good" times that has not been followed by a season of stringency and business distress.

*

In peace prepare for war, is a bit of ancient wisdom. It may be variously paraphrased. In summer prepare for winter. In sunshine prepare for storm. In time of financial prosperity prepare for the period of stringency that may not unreasonably be expected sooner or later. In what does such preparation consist? What do sailors do before the breaking of a storm? They make everything snug and tight. They securely fasten in place whatever might be blown away, and last but not least, they stand ready to shorten sail at the word of command. There is many a business enterprise that at present is apparently prosperous because of the profit showing that its statements make, that would be a much safer investment if things were snugged up, and arrangements made to shorten sail on call, even if in part the sails were not taken in before the storm actually breaks. Does the manager of the business know the cost of his goods? Are the profits on goods sold constantly contrasted with the expenses of conducting the business? Are credits being carefully scanned, and are collections kept close up? In purchases, are discounts being carefully taken? In short, is the business completely in hand so that in the event of necessity the manager can handle it as requirements may be, just as the master of a ship would handle his vessel in a storm while getting every possible help out of the crew? The next financial storm may be several years away. We hope it may be very slow in coming, if come at all it must, but we risk nothing in the reader's interest in advising him to get into a condition of preparedness at the earliest possible date. That business which is best ready to withstand a storm will in almost all cases make the most money during seasons of prosperity weather. Therefore we argue that the prudent man, foreseeing the danger and preparing for it, has everything to make and nothing to lose.

* * *

Large space in the daily papers has been devoted to the announcement of the Commercial High School, New York, the cornerstone of which was laid a few days since. Not only have the daily papers of the metropolis considered this event of sufficient interest to warrant the attention given it, but the journals of neighboring cities—Boston, Philadelphia, Buffalo and Chicago—have likewise noticed the matter. If the man from Mars were among us, he would be justified, from the newspaper accounts alone, in reaching the conclusion that what has been done is of very great importance to the community, and that the inauguration of the school is something of great moment to the business world. For ourselves, we think his conclusions, whether based upon newspaper report or upon a more careful investigation of the subject, would be fully justified. At the same time, the proposition as stated in the daily press will bear investigation. Is the community, as a fact, so greatly interested in this undertaking? Does it promise such wonderful results as to warrant the high hopes that are entertained for it?

*

All that has so far been done clusters around that time-honored custom of laying a cornerstone. Speeches have been made, promises have been recited, and all future has been drawn upon in support of the general undertaking. Primarily, there is a building, and the pages of our contemporaries, the editorial columns of which have bristled with the articles referred to, have also contained elevations and plans of the school. Left to himself, the average citizen reaches the conclusion that New York is to be graced with one more architectural feature. Beyond that, for the present at least, he has nothing very definite to gaze upon. But, as a fact, what has a building to do with a school? Of course, a school, like any other institution, must be housed, but the housing has little to do with the school beyond contributing somewhat to its dignity and standing.

*

Andrew Carnegie, of library fame, in making the proposition of an endowment of ten million dollars for a university in Washington, was very careful to eliminate from his plans the buildings which the average citizen would suppose would consume more or less of the amount named. For this care in doing something different from what is ordinarily done in founding a university, Mr. Carnegie was warmly praised by many of the foremost journals in the country. It was pointed out that his millions were not to be spent for mere stones and mortar, but instead, that they were to be used in what was, for lack of better terms, likened to the maintenance of post-graduate courses, wherein all existing government buildings, whether postoffices, libraries, museums, the halls of congress or the executive departments of the government should be the school houses, class rooms, or study places of those making use of the opportunities and advantages of the new university. In marked contrast to that is what is being done by the City of New York in starting a commercial high school, the first feature of which is the erection of a large building.

*

Upon further inquiry concerning this building and having in mind the school which it is to house, one is naturally interested in the appointments of the building. There are school houses and school houses in New York, as well as educational buildings of still greater dignity, but this is declared to be a school of commerce, or rather, a commercial high school. It is announced that it is to be unlike other schools. Let us see what the building offers in this regard. We learn from the particulars given to the public that the frontage on Sixty-fifth street is one hundred and fifty feet, and Sixty-sixth street, one hundred feet, and that the total depth of the building is two hundred feet. The structure is to contain five stories with a basement. The basement, which, the veracious reporter says, "is not to be the least important part of the building," will cover the entire plot, and among its appointments will have an overhead running track, a gymnasium and a natatorium, with a "plunge bath forty-two feet long and twenty-one feet wide." It will also be fitted with shower baths, etc. Now we submit in all seriousness the following question: What parts of commercial education are served by a gymnasium and a swimming pool? It occurs to us to suggest that while it is expedient for the young business man of the future to be athletic and to maintain his body in the best sanitary condition, still there are other places than high schools built at the expense of the taxpayer to which he should go for a bath, when he needs a bath,—assuming for the moment that his home is not provided with this very necessary adjunct to health. What part has a running track, and also what part has a gymnasium in commercial education? There are athletic clubs almost beyond number. Why, then, compete with an existing institution in this regard when trying to supply something which the business community needs, because that something does not at present exist?

*

Turning to another part of the newspaper description of the building we are interested in discovering what the school is to be. The statement is made that "high schools are in existence now, but a high school devoted to the scientific and systematic study of commercial affairs will be somewhat of a novelty." Perhaps the business public would think it still more of a novelty if the reporter had said right there that a high school was to be called into existence to be devoted to the combined object of securing to the young man a scientific and systematic study of commercial affairs, and at the same time skill not only as a swimmer, but also as a practical gymnast. But, to continue our investigation of what the school is to be. We are told that it has been in contemplation for a number of years and that Miles M. O'Brien, president of the Board of Education, has been its chief sponsor. Quoting from remarks that this gentleman has made we gain the following: "The probable expansion of American trade will call for a class of young Americans capable not only of understanding international commercial problems, but of carrying out the practical propositions which the growing trade of the country will present. The object of the school is to educate students primarily on questions of international commerce. It will fit them for consular positions abroad, instruct them in general commercial affairs, acquaint them with the laws of supply and demand, make them familiar with the possibilities of the trade relations of the United States, and particularly with the great fields which the new American possessions open up."

*

It is asserted that the course of instruction has not yet been arranged, but still is in an advanced stage of preparation. It is declared that the school is designed to be an institution on a higher plane than what is generally denominated business or commercial schools. It will be recalled that these latter institutions do not ordinarily contain swimming pools and gymnasiums. This is certainly one difference to be noted at the outset. But, continuing: "The school is intended to provide a scientific study of commerce in all its relations, so as to enable its graduates to enter upon the duties of a commercial life fully equipped to understand the requirements of the same. While it will give a good foundation to theory, it will at the same time pay close attention to the equipment of the student for practical work." Still further on we read: "In view of the fact that the objects of the school and the scope of the work are to be different from those found in any other school of its kind in this country, the selection of a suitable head for the institution has necessitated a great deal of consideration from those who have the matter in charge. Whether the head of the school will be called 'principal' of 'president' has not yet been determined upon. The general idea of the new school is to fit its graduates for higher positions than mere clerkships, and to give them such a breadth of view in all matters relating to commerce as will practically insure their after success."

*

Here is at once a declaration and a confession. A stream cannot rise above its fountain head. A school cannot expect its pupils to be essentially superior to the instructors employed. The head of this school has not yet been selected, and in all probability the instructors occupying subordinate positions are likewise yet unnamed. So we reach this conclusion, that public money is being spent for a building containing swimming baths and gymnasium, with general assembly room and class rooms to a considerable number, but there is yet to be worked out and announced all that is practical in the school. The scheme of education, the instructors, the courses of study are all yet in the future. It would seem to us, from our humble point of view, that those who have the matter in charge have left the weightier matters until the last. What is a cage without a bird to put in it? What is an educational building without a school to be housed therein? Evidently the building is assured, but the school may or may not materialize.

*

Those who have given thought to the matter of a commercial high school seem to have caught on to the idea that expansion is a good watchword, and therefore they talk about the increasing needs of the United States for consular service of a high grade, etc. The little that is said about the courses that are to be pursued emphasizes this. Quoting again: "The study of languages best adapted to the increasing commercial demands of the United States will be an important feature in the curriculum of the high school of commerce. The Spanish language will receive particular attention because of not only the possible growth of trade with the South American Republics, but on account of the relations between the United States and Cuba, Porto Rico and the Philippine Islands. The German language will also be taught in the new school with a view to applying it to commercial purposes." Were we disposed to be captious we could point out that there are already in existence well organized, ably-conducted schools where the student can get most satisfactory instruction in Spanish, German and various other modern languages. If languages are the only matters to be developed in this new school, then there were no need of this magnificent building, which is about to be erected.

*

Let us turn from the preliminary announcements to what has been offered by those who were called upon to address the assembly that witnessed the laying of the corner-stone.

Mr. Andrew Carnegie delivered the leading address, although that honor had first been reserved for ex-mayor Abram S. Hewitt. Mr. Hewitt was, however, detained by sickness. Mr. Carnegie, eminently practical though he is, seemed to get no further along in a translation of the scheme of the school than that which had been offered him by the reporters who had previously interviewed those who have been thinking about this scheme. He said: "This school is the pioneer high school of commerce in New York, or in the country, and it owes its creation to the fact that the United States has become the leading commercial nation in the export of its products, even Britain being now second. . . . For the most of the other avocations of life, schools designed to give the student the best suitable start have for generations been established, but schools to instruct the youth desirous of entering upon a business career are of recent origin even in the older countries of Europe. With us they are as yet unknown, if we except a few private schools, charging fees, which give instruction only in the rudiments of commercial knowledge."

*

Far be it from us to intimate that we are in any respect opposed to the undertaking referred to. Quite the contrary. We believe in schools and we believe in schools of higher business, but we regret that the establishment of a school, where a school is really needed, is reduced to the mere matter of erecting a building and providing it with gymnasium equipments. It is too much like what our Methodist brethren are sometimes charged with doing. For lack of any other religious service for the moment they take up a collection. Our school commissioners build a bathhouse. The business community will begin to find an interest in this school whenever the school is organized, whether it has a building or not. They will scan the faculty, they will correctly measure the president or principal, whichever he may be called, and they will be very apt in this work to apply the yardstick of severe practical common sense.

*

The Board of Education in launching a school of this kind gets beyond that which is ready at hand in the way of teachers and lessons. It will have to originate, invent, adapt. Its teachers, including the principal or president, will have to be recruited not from college professors nor from among the graduates of universities, but instead from among the hard-handed practical men of business. Reference is made in several articles that we have seen relating to this school to the failure of the so-called commercial schools, or, rather, the shortcomings of these institutes, which therefore leave something for this school to do. One of the worst things that can be said at the expense of the so-called commercial schools is that they have never had the courage to go out into the field of practical business and bring into their faculty men of actual experience. Have these schools taught accounting? So they say. But what has it been based upon? Not upon accounting in practice but the interpretation of accounting in a book which some teacher has written. Have they taught something of banking? So they say. But what they have taught has not been practical banking, but banking seen through the dim spectacles of a professor.

*

There is ample room for a commercial high school. There is a crying need for what this institution ought to do, but what it accomplishes will depend upon its teachers. They must be men of practical experience in that which they teach, not mere theorists, not mere book men. There will be difficulty in securing men of this kind. To be able to teach the twelve of fifteen hundred pupils, which this school is intended to have, those subjects which legitimately fall to the scope of the school will require a talent which, if exercised commercially, would bring the individual an income of fifty thousand dollars a year. Does the school expect to pay so high a salary? Salaries among teachers are low, and we venture to say that sooner or later this school will be searching for teachers at salaries of about 10 per cent of what they are worth in the commercial world, if their talents were to be devoted to business instead of to teaching.

SCHOOLS OF COMMERCE

The High School of Commerce, which has just been founded as a part of the public school system of New York is greeted as the first of its kind—a free public high school of commerce—in America. We must not, however, regard it as the first in the world. The New York Tribune says that there are many state schools of commerce, as also of industry, in other lands, while the fundamental idea of the institutions is an old one, having existed in this country for many years and in others for generations. Probably the first real school of commerce was the "Aula do Commercio," founded in Lisbon in 1759. Ten years later the first in Germany was founded by J. G. Busch, and was conducted by him until his death, in 1799. The first in France was organized in Paris in 1820, and it was acquired by the Paris Chamber of Commerce in 1868, and has since that date been known as the High School of Commerce. Switzerland followed the example of Zurich in 1827, Belgium in 1837, and Austria in 1856. In the United States so-called business colleges had their rise about 1840, while in late years—as in New York University in 1899—schools of commerce, finance and accounts have been organized as legitimate university departments.

All these, however, were private or corporate undertakings. Only in recent years have commercial schools been organized under state auspices. We remember the noteworthy showing made by German commercial schools at the Centennial Exhibition of 1876, at Philadelphia, which gave a vast impetus to similar work throughout the world. Yet the schools represented there were all private, or at most municipal, institutions. As late as ten years ago only one school of commerce was maintained by the German Imperial Government, and only twenty-three were maintained by municipalities in that country, against eleven by chambers of commerce, twenty by mercantile guilds and 110 by private corporations and individuals. The Government granted subsidies, however, to fifty-four of them. In France there are numerous commercial schools, both elementary and high, under state control or subsidy. Since about a dozen years ago practically all the commercial high schools of France have become state institutions, or at least have received state recognition, so that their students are partially exempted from the military conscription and are made eligible to consular and diplomatic appointments. Switzerland has between fifty and sixty state subsidized schools of commerce, chiefly dating from or since 1891. Belgium has a veritable commercial university in the Institute of Commerce at Antwerp, the three years' students of which have since 1897 been eligible to consular appointments; and the Government is now introducing commercial education into the common public schools. Austria's system of commercial schools was reorganized under state direction in 1888. Sweden has only private schools of commerce. Norway has some municipal ones, Denmark has private ones aided with small state subsidies; Holland has one partly subsidized by the state and one maintained by the municipality of Amsterdam. Italy has one subsidized by the state, and Japan has one fine state school of commerce at Tokio.

In the United States, as we have said, private "business colleges" are numerous, more than five hundred of them being officially reported. These range from mere schools of penmanship and bookkeeping up to such fine degree granting institutions as those of the New York University, the University of Pennsylvania and other leading universities in various parts of the land. There has in recent years, largely to afford preparation for these university schools, been a considerable development and extension of commercial instruction in the public schools. And now the radical "new departure" —for this country—is made in New York of establishing as a part of the public school system a high school of commerce. We have hitherto dwelt upon some phases of its significance. It is in all respects an interesting experiment.

NEW YORK
PUBLIC LIBRARY.
TILDEN FOUNDATIONS

Along the Highways and Byways of Business

By VANNANT

When the editor of COMMERCE, ACCOUNTS & FINANCE, the other day, invited me to become a contributor to the columns of his journal, saying that various subscribers had suggested that a revival of "Round-About-Notes," which years since has been published in Office and Business over my name, would please them, I was both surprised and gratified. I was surprised that the editor of this latter-day business exponent should have found me out, and I was gratified that any one should have remembered my screeds of seven to twelve years ago with so much of appreciation as to desire more of the same kind. In reply to the editor's most courteous communication I said that it would be impossible for me now to do the same as I had done in the past for several reasons. First, because in the interval I have formed the reprehensible but confirmed habit of growing old. Of a fact, I see things differently from what I used to. Perhaps it is because my eyes are getting dim, and perhaps also it is because time has tempered in other respects my mental and physical powers. Second, things in the business world have changed in the interval during which my pen has been resting in the rack over my dried up ink-well, more than I have changed. Numerous improvements have been introduced in almost every direction. Distinct progress has been made all along the line, and struggle though I have, I am afraid I have not kept up with the stream. I am not so nearly abreast of the on-rushing tide, perhaps, now as I fondly imagined myself to be in the days when my remarks and criticisms were found to be acceptable to the readers of the old papers above mentioned. And last, but not least, many of those who were both suggestion and inspiration to me in by-gone days, and from whose conversation I derived many of the thoughts my manuscript recorded are no longer to be found in their accustomed places. Some have already passed over the line; their accounts have been footed and balanced for the last time, and their successors are much younger men, with whom I have not got acquainted. Still others are quietly waiting—waiting the summons of the great auditor, which must come before long; meanwhile their wonted tasks are being discharged by younger men also. It sometimes seems to me that only Old "Vannant" is left. So I said to the editor that while I was willing to do anything I could to entertain and instruct the readers of his up-to-date periodical, about all I could bring forward of the old was my name. I could not attempt to sing the old songs, and I very much doubted if they were sung that they would please the majority of the present generation of readers. He urged that observations of the business world at present, from my itinerant point of view, would be as valuable to the reader now as were the notes penned in the past. So I capitulated as best I could, and said that with a new title and the privilege at the outset of a personal explanation (which I have taken all this space to make), I would try to realize his expectations. If I please those subscribers who are responsible for suggesting my return to the habit of writing out my observations, and also enough more to cause the editor to feel that he has made a profitable investment in thus arranging with me, all will be well. On the other hand, if a considerable number of readers write to the editor, complaining that my contributions are like myself, somewhat old and overworked, and therefore should give place to the thoughts of a younger and healthier brain, I presume I shall be forthwith and unconditionally dropped from the pay roll. But such dropping is something that a man who is getting old in the business ranks learns to expect. He ought to get used to it because of the frequency of its occurrence, but as a fact he never does. Hope rises eternal in the breast, and each time he hopes it will not turn out the usual way. However, the editor did not invite me to become lugubrious nor yet to occupy space with personal lamentations.

* * *

One of the great changes that have occurred in the past few years in the conduct of business is the appreciation of the work of the public accountant. Whereas a short time since the average business concern knew him not, and felt no need of his services, now he is in request in all directions. Another change, or perhaps I should call it development, which the recent past has witnessed, is the effort that is being made to educate public accountants in a way to raise the dignity and usefulness of the profession. However we may be disposed to make up the account of the last few years, the fact that the School of Commerce, Accounts and Finance, of the New York University, has been established and has done most excellent work, is not to be overlooked. From how small a seed do some great and useful plants grow! Years ago, then working in its prime, was the Institute of Accounts, composed of lofty aspirations and a high ambition to be serviceable to the business public. It was never a large body in point of membership, but was able always to count in its ranks a number of progressive and far-seeing men. Within the Institute of Accounts was drafted the bill that has since became the Accountants' Law of the State of New York, and which was so happily conceived as to merit and receive the support of the various accountants' societies then existing. With the law on the statute book, what was more natural than that the public accountants who received certificates under it should form a society? So the New York State Society of Public Accountants was established. In the progress of events, this body appointed a committee to consider the question of education—particularly of the young men in accountants' offices, and from the ranks of whom the public accountants of the near future must be recruited. Out of the work of this committee on education grew the school of Commerce, Accounts and Finance. Referring again to the parent organization, the Institute of Accounts, it is at present represented in the school in a marked degree. From among its members were chosen the dean of the school and several of the professors, while one of the prominent lecturers the present term, Joseph Hardcastle, although not a member of the Institute of late, was for many years very prominent in its counsels. So the little seed that was planted when the Institute of Accounts was formed, has not grown in vain. Just how large and spreading will be its influence in the future I do not attempt to guess. Suffice it for the present to measure it by the work that is now in progress.

* * *

Speaking of Mr. Hardcastle,—I wonder what it was, an attempt at a joke or the irony of fate, that caused a certain journal, a few weeks since, to publish one of his most earnest and labored mathematical articles, the subject being, "Depreciation," under the head of "Profitable Publicity?" Perhaps after all it was only superior enterprise upon the part of the editor, if indeed the paper referred to has an editor. It is becoming much the fashion for business enterprises, large corporations in particular, to make public their statements. The U. S. Steel Corporation is an example in point. Now depreciation is a fact with which every business statement must deal in one way or another. Possibly, therefore, the promulgation to the world of the principle of depreciation in accounts, as Mr. Hardcastle sees it, appeared to the editor, or the office cat, whichever was in charge, to be an example of "profitable publicity," and so it was dubbed.

* * *

So far I have not seen in print a report of Prof. Joseph French Johnson's lecture before the New York Society of Certified Public Accountants, delivered a few weeks since at the Waldorf-Astoria, on the "Relation of Economics to Higher Accounting," although I noticed that stenographers were present. Perhaps it will yet greet a larger audience through the press than was present on the occasion named. For fear that the one bright and particular rhetorical and scientific gem that adorned the address, and which those who listened to it took away with them, to repeat on various and sundry occasions, may be expurgated or edited out of existence, I am going to refer to it here. Besides the professor's definition affords me the chance to supplement it by another which he may see the chance to make good use of on some other occasion. To appreciate the definition it should be borne in mind that the address the month before had been by one of the members of the society, on "The Balance Sheet." The word to be defined was "lie." The speaker said: "There are only three kinds of lies: lies, d—n lies, and balance sheets." He did not make any application of this chunk of erudite investigation. Neither shall I make any application of the following: In school a pupil was asked to define a lie, and promptly answered: "An abomination in the eyes of the Lord, but a very present help in the time of trouble."

* * *

The credit men of the country through their local organizations, and in co-operation with the national association, have in a measure exhausted their subject, in-so-far as the literature and mechanics of credits are concerned. All the members of the organization who are able to speak or write upon credits have put themselves on record. The subject of credits has been exploited from almost every point of view, and it would be a smart man indeed who could take up his pen at the present time and write freely on the subject, without repeating so much of what has preceded as to cause a suspicion of rank plagiarism. The morals of credits have been exhaustively presented. The duty of rendering statements has been forced home upon every retailer. The profits of discounting have been dangled before his eyes by wholesalers and manufacturers in the hope thereby to make the country merchant prompter in remitting. Model credit departments have been worked out and set up that the employees of the sellers might be more efficient in managing credits. The duty of the country dealer to keep abundantly insured had been so carefully urged that some have thought there might possibly be a rake-off by way of commission to the wholesalers. And even the law has been invoked. In every state where they could command the necessary following the credit men have more or less moulded legislation to help the seller by guarding his claims, and making the way of the dishonest debtor not only hard but actually dangerous. What more could the credit men do? And yet the human nature of the country merchant and the average retailer remains much the same. He is in business to make money. He desires to be honest, but he must make money. He clearly perceives the animus of the many things that have ostensibly been done in his interest, and does not fail to tell the credit man from time to time, when opportunity presents, how much he feels his obligations for the service. But then he straightaway forgets to send in that signed statement that is due, and yields it up only on urgent demand. He neglects his insurance because it is not his nature to keep everything right up to date. He stops discounting his purchases because he has neglected his own collections. And the credit man naturally becomes desperate over the obduracy of his pet pupils, and reflects that after all, if it was not for the stern arm of the law to which he can resort if he must, business in general would be a very hard road to travel.

* * *

But as I gather in my walks about town a new idea has occurred to some of the leading minds among the credit men. They are going to try their pet pupils with a new remedy for all the ills that business is heir to. The retailer is in business to make money. He could make more money than at present if he was only an abler business man. If he was an abler business man and made more money, he would be a better customer. Then let us make him an abler business man, with more profit to sweeten his temper and a larger bank account against which to draw in paying our bills. Accounting is the vital element of business. It is the glass through which alone the business man, be he large or small, can see what he is doing. If we give the retailer good accounting, and encourage him to regard his business analytically, he will soon see where he is making money, and therefore what parts of his business should be driven the hardest, and where he is losing money and what parts therefore should be cut off. We will appeal to his own interests, giving him the lion's share of the advantage. And so they—the credit men—have set out to find the best system of retail accounts. When they have found it they will send it out to the country merchants, very much as the agricultural department of the government distributes new varieties of seed among the farmers. It is certainly an experiment worth trying, and I shall watch the result with interest.

THE WEIGHT OF UNITED STATES COINS

These are the weights of the American coins now in circulation:—

Gold Coins—The twenty-dollar gold piece, or double eagle, weighs 516 grains; the ten-dollar gold piece, or eagle, weighs 258 grains; the five-dollar gold piece, or half-eagle, weighs 129 grains; the three-dollar gold piece (authorized February 21, 1853, and discontinued September 26, 1890), weighed 77.4 grains; the two-dollar-and-a-half gold piece, or quarter eagle, weighs 64.5 grains, and the one-dollar gold piece (authorized March 3, 1849, and discontinued September 26, 1890), weighed 25.8 grains.

Silver Coins—The silver dollar weighed originally 416 grains, and then it was reduced to its present weight of 412.5 grains. The trade dollar (authorized February 12, 1873, and discontinued February 19, 1887) weighed 420 grains. The silver half-dollar weighs 192.9 grains; the "Columbian" silver half-dollar weighs 192.9 grains; the common silver quarter-dollar weighs 96.45 grains; the silver twenty-cent piece (authorized March 3, 1875, and discontinued May 2, 1878) weighed 77.16 grains; the silver dime weighs 38.58 grains; the silver half-dime (authorized April 2, 1792, and discontinued February 12, 1873) weighed first 20.8 grains, then changed to 20.625 grains, and finally to 19.2 grains; and the silver three-cent piece (authorized March 3, 1851, and discontinued February 12, 1873) weighed first 12 5-8 grains and then 11.52 grains.

Nickel Coins—The five-cent nickel piece (75 per cent copper and 25 per cent nickel) weighs 77.16 grains; the three-cent nickel piece (authorized March 3, 1865, and discontinued September 26, 1900) weighed 30 grains (75 per cent copper and 25 per cent nickel); the one-cent nickel piece (authorized February 21, 1857, and discontinued April 22, 1864) weighed 72 grains (88 per cent copper and 12 per cent nickel).

Bronze or Copper Coins—The old-fashioned copper cent (authorized April 2, 1792) weighed first 264 grains; it was then changed to 208 grains, then to 168 grains, and its coinage was discontinued February 21, 1857. The copper (or bronze) two-cent piece (authorized April 22, 1864, and discontinued February 12, 1873) weighed 96 grains (95 per cent copper and 5 per cent tin and zinc); the present copper cent was authorized April 22, 1864, and weighs 48 grains, of which 95 per cent is copper and 5 per cent tin and zinc; and the copper half-cent (authorized April 2, 1792, and discontinued February 21, 1857) weighed originally 132 grains; then it was changed, first to 104 grains and finally to 84 grains.

A QUESTION OF METHOD

Mortimer. "There ought to be some way to prevent bank defalcations."

Newton. "Yes; but whether it would be the proper thing to lock up the cashier before he has a chance to embezzle, or to lock up the directors so they can't avoid seeing all that is going on.

WHAT EACH OF US IS WORTH

The human body of average weight contains three pounds thirteen ounces of calcium. Calcium, at present market rates, is worth $300 an ounce, so that the amount of it contained in one human body has a money value of $18,300. Few of our fellow citizens realize that they are worth so much intrinsically.—American Analyst.

American "Trusts," as an Englishman Sees Them*

By ARCH. B. CLARK, M. A.

A British* View of American "Trusts" in Their Economic Aspect, by the Lecturer on Political Economy in St. Mungo's College, Glasgow, Scotland

The last three years have witnessed a rapid development in the formation of, and a consequent marked revival of interest in, those great industrial combinations most generally known by their American title as "Trusts." The situation, in fact, has been reminiscent of the years immediately preceding 1890. For the trust fever has now its recognized place in the credit cycle. It is in the years of "boom" which precede a crisis that the formation of "trusts," like the promotion of companies generally, goes on most merrily. It is quite true that in the original sense of the term—the sense in which it was used when these great industrial monopolies or market dominations first attracted attention—the trust has never been known here, and has ceased to exist in America itself.

In its original form the trust was the union of a number of joint-stock companies by means of a majority of the shareholders handing over their stock with its voting powers to a board of trustees who undertook to manage the combined undertakings, and who issued to each of the original shareholders a certificate for the amount of his shares deposited, which certificate entitled him to a proportionate interest in all the property and earnings of the trust. This was the form in which the most famous of all the American combinations—Mr. Rockefeller's Standard Oil Trust—existed for ten years (1882-1892). In 1888, however, the American public awoke to the existence of trusts and their dangers. On common law principles the surrender by the shareholders of their powers into the hands of trustees was held to be ultra vires, and under pressure of the law courts and of public opinion the great trusts were one after another formally and ostentatiously dissolved. But though the legal form was altered, the thing itself—the industrial combination—in most cases remained unchanged, or was merely further consolidated. Either the different competing businesses actually amalgamated to form one great corporation, as in the case of the Sugar Trust, or the moving spirits in the management of one great business obtained through the purchase of shares in rival concerns a preponderating voice in their management, and thus secured a monopoly, or at all events such a market domination as to enable them to control prices. This is now the position of the Standard Oil Trust.

TRUSTS IN ENGLAND.

In this country, within the last few years, several large combinations have been formed, such as J. & P. Coats, Limited, the Calico Printers' Association, the English Sewing Cotton Company, the Yorkshire Wool Combers' Association, the United Alkali Company, Sir W. G. Armstrong, Limited, and others. But, for reasons to be dealt with subsequently, the economic environment is not so well adapted for fostering monopoly as that of America, and, with a few exceptions, such as the Coats Company, the British "combines" have made but a poor return to their shareholders.

The great American trusts claim that, owing to various economies resulting from their organization, they can produce more cheaply than independent competing establishments, and are thus really in the interest of the consumer. Their so-called advantages, however, are, as we shall see, in many cases assets of very doubtful value. The confidence of the trust leaders in their reality, moreover, can scarcely be said to be attested by that dread of "interlopers," the interminable struggle with whom is quite as marked a feature of the history of the trusts as it was of the medieval British foreign trade companies. No sooner has one or other of the trusts secured something approaching to a market domination, and thus placed itself in a position in which it may reasonably expect to enjoy the sweets of monopoly at the expense of the consumer, than in tantalizing fashion the cup is dashed from its lips, and its position threatened by the appearance of independent rivals, which testify with remarkable persistence to the enduring vitality of the spirit of competition. These, in turn, are bought up by the trusts at figures which belie the confidence professed by the latter in their boasted advantages. And, with every step in the process of absorption, after a certain point, the financial position of the mammoth monopolist becomes less and less secure.

THE TRUSTS AND PUBLIC WELFARE.

Let us now consider how the interest of the consuming public is affected by the operation of the trusts. The aim of a monopolist company, in the intelligent pursuit of the immediate interests of its shareholders, naturally is to fix the price at such a level that the amount sold will yield the greatest possible net revenue. The monopolist would clearly gain nothing from his monopoly if he placed on the market an amount so great that the price obtained would just cover the monopoly expenses of production, including ordinary profits. According to Adam Smith, indeed, "The price of monopoly is upon every occasion the highest which can be got. The natural price, or the price of free competition, on the contrary, is the lowest which can be taken, not upon every occasion indeed, but for any considerable time together. The one is upon every occasion the highest which can be squeezed out of buyers, or which it is supposed they will consent to give; the other is the lowest which the sellers can commonly afford to take, and at the same time continue their business."

Now, if "price of monopoly" be interpreted as the aggregate net return to the monopolist, there is no doubt that to maximize this is the goal of his efforts. And it is equally certain that competition tends to make the return such as will yield merely the ordinary rate of profits. But it is clear that, in the above statement, Adam Smith is referring to the price per unit of the commodity, and that he considers the amount produced under a monopoly will be less, and the price necessarily higher than the competitive price. This, however, is by no means certain. Owing to the economies resulting from production on a large scale, and the avoidance of the waste involved in free competition, it is at least theoretically possible, if we assume for the time being equal ability and enterprise on the part of the management, that the monopoly expenses of production for a given amount may be less than the competitive expenses. In this case—especially if the commodity is one for which a small fall in price causes a great increase in demand—it may well be that the amount produced will be greater, and the price less, under monopoly than under free competition.

In practice, however, the monopolist, it appears, tends to prefer the certain simplicity of a high price with small sales, to the prospective gain from large sales at a low price. This is the natural tendency of trusts when they happen to secure a monopoly, save in so far as it may be thought expedient to maintain a large scale of production for a time in order to obtain interest on the machinery and other fixed capital invested in the different businesses at the time of amalgamation. That trusts possessed of anything approaching a monopoly, or able to dominate the market, do tend to raise the price to the consumer, or at all events to check the fall which would naturally take place under free competition, is a truth which finds abundant illustration in the history of American trusts, as, for example, in the case of the great Sugar Trust. The evidence on this head is judiciously summed up by Professor Jenks: "The facts, then, in the United States, seem to lead to the conclusion regarding trusts and combines, so far as their effect on prices is concerned, that while they have it in their power to make profits at somewhat lower prices than would be possible under free competition, they nevertheless do probably check slightly the normal decrease in prices that comes with in-

*Lecture delivered before the students at St. Mungo's College, and printed in the Accountants' Magazine.

creasing facilities for manufacturing. At any rate, they hold prices so that they can make much better profits than under free competition. Competition, however, and the checked demand that would come with too high prices, generally in the long run prevent the prices from being much higher than under free competition. Trusts cannot be entirely arbitrary in fixing prices. This seems to be the universal testimony."

HISTORY OF THE GROWTH OF TRUSTS.

The movement towards industrial monopoly in America has a history extending over at least thirty years. It may be said to have begun with the Standard Oil Company, and to have reached its greatest development so far in the present year with the formation of the gigantic United States Steel Corporation. But the causes of the movement and its economic significance are still matters of dispute. According to some, it is the natural outcome of the modern system of production on a large scale. In many industries the advantages in production and in marketing which result from production on a large scale lead, it is said, to a continual increase in the size of the business unit, and often to an actual decrease in the number of competing businesses. But this, it is held, brings no relief. It simply intensifies the struggle for supremacy, and the economies resulting from large-scale production are dissipated in that "cut-throat" competition which aggravates market fluctuations and renders depressions more severe and prolonged, till the survivors are glad to come to terms. But the rule which it is to the interest of the whole industry to observe, it is often the immediate interest of the individual manufacturer to infringe Thus, for example, it is said that in the Birmingham bedstead trade twelve articles were invoiced and thirteen sent, or an 18s. article invoiced and a 20s. one sent. To avert such secret infringements of the agreement the bonds of union are gradually drawn tighter. Thus combination presents itself as a haven of refuge against the evil results of competition.

This view has the support of the deservedly high authority of Professor Ashley: "The trusts are, in the main, simply an attempt to lessen, and, if it may be, avert altogether the disastrous and harassing effects of cut-throat competition, after a completer experience of what that competition means than any country has ever been through before. Their formation has, in most cases, followed upon a period of over-production and consequent depression. For the nerves of the American business man have at last revolted and demanded some decently comfortable measure of stability. This, I am convinced, is the underlying cause of the movement towards combination, of which the 'trusts' are but the culminating examples."

But, in the first place, it may be objected that industrial depression is not, as is commonly assumed, the only or even the chief cause of the formation of trusts. They may follow upon a period of depression, but the fact already noted that for the most part they have actually come into existence in years of prosperity, when hope once more gilds the industrial horizon and the speculative spirit is abroad—this alone is surely more suggestive of the guileless simplicity of the company promoter and of a sensitive finger on the pulse of the Stock Exchange.

Again, though the evils incident to a competitive regime cannot be denied, it will not do to quietly ignore its virtues and assume that through these monopolistic combinations lies the road to industrial salvation. As a matter of fact, the belief that the trend of industrial evolution is towards monopoly, and through that to a socialist regime, is unsupported by history. On the contrary, the gradual displacement of privilege and monopoly by competition has been one of the most striking features in the history of Western civilization for at least a thousand years. The spirit of monopoly, like the poor, we have always with us. But though in the United States and Germany, aided by tariff laws, its operations have lately been on an imposing scale, the experience is as yet too limited to show that it is actually displacing competition, and that it will prevail in a country such as this there is nothing whatever to show.

ARGUMENTS OF THE TRUST ADVOCATES.

The advocates of the trusts argue that they are bound to prevail by reason of their numerous advantages in production and marketing as compared with independent producers. But, on investigation, it appears that the great bulk of these economies are equally accessible to large independent establishments. Take, for example, the claim that they can afford to employ experts whose business it is to devise improved methods of production, and that they can secure abler management through the opportunity they afford for specialization of skill. Both these claims may equally well be made on behalf of any large independent business. Other economies, again, which are undoubtedly peculiar to these large monopolistic combinations are frequently greatly overrated. Thus, for example, one of the advantages commonly claimed for trusts is the saving in freights which such an organization can effect, especially in the case of bulky articles, by supplying its customers from its nearest establishment. This looks like a substantial gain, till we reflect with Professor Jenks that, in the case of bulky products, each of the incorporated establishments would naturally, when independent, produce chiefly for the supply of its own locality, while in the case of light articles the saving in freight charges can never be great. In the case of advertising, in all its forms, the wastefulness of the competitive system is obvious, and it might reasonably be thought that here, if anywhere, a combination possessing a monopoly of supply has an undoubted advantage—that it can sit still and pocket the saving, since consumers must come to it or want. This, however, though true of the necessaries of life, does not hold good of most commodities, the demand for which is largely dependent on their being continually brought to the notice of the public. Hence it appears that the possible saving to the monopolist, even under this head, is easily capable of over-valuation.

But if the economies claimed for the trusts are in most cases of doubtful value, there is no doubt of the reality of the difficulties under which they work. The advantages accruing from production on a large scale in manufactures—such as economy in respect of materials, machinery, and skill, and facilities for buying and selling—are generally admitted. But, after a business has attained a magnitude sufficient to secure adequate specialization in production and marketing facilities, there is nothing to gain from further consolidation, while every accretion brings with it a serious increase in the difficulties of management and control. The burden tends to become too great for even a master-mind. Hence the inevitable tendency of these huge businesses is towards routine management. There is delegation of duties with ineffective supervision. When the combination becomes so great as to secure a practical monopoly, there falls to be added the further drawback of the absence of that stimulus to exertion and enterprise which energetic competition alone can supply. The able and enterprising management that distinguishes many of the existing trusts in their efforts to secure a monopoly affords no evidence that, monopoly once secured, a similar spirit of enterprise would prevail.

INDUSTRIAL LEADERS MADE GREAT BY THE COMPETITIVE SYSTEM.

In this connection it should not be forgotten that the great industrial leaders of America, the men whose organizing genius has startled the world, the men who have made the trusts, are the men whom competition has made. A regime of monopoly, with its system of patronage and its bureaucratic methods, may produce an admirable race of trained officials, but it is scarcely the field to which we should look for a continuous supply of that ability, enterprise, and self-reliance which in the long-run are essential to success in the struggle for international trade. This consideration is worthy of emphasis in view of the prevailing apprehension in this country that the growth of these gigantic American trusts is a serious menace to British industrial supremacy. That there will be temporary disturbance and displacements of trade seems probable, but that these mushroom monopolies will ultimately prevail over free enterprise is contrary to all experience. For, as already pointed out, monopoly is not a new thing. Its form may have changed, but its essence and its weakness are enduring. The danger to British industry from American competition lies not so much in the existence of the trusts as in the greater energy and enterprise of American business men, and their clearer insight into the nature and operation of economic forces. In this country we train the engineer, the mechanic, the bookkeeper, but we do not train the business manager—the man on whose action depends the fruitfulness or the reverse of the labor of hundreds, or it may be thousands, of men. The recent relatively rapid industrial progress of America and Germany should be carefully pondered, in the light of the comparative neglect of the economic study in this country.

UNSTABLE POSITION OF THE MONOPOLIST.

But to resume. Even in America, if we leave out of account the so-called "natural monopolies," such as railroads, telegraphs, telephones, water-works, etc., all which when in private hands are regulated by the state, the position of the great monopolist trusts in the manufacturing industries is seen to be in most cases thoroughly unstable. It rests, as M. de Rousiers remarks, sometimes on the system by which the railways are permitted to charge preferential rates, as in the notorious case of the Standard Oil Trust; while in other cases, such as the Sugar Trust, the high protective tariff is its basis. Indeed the system of high protection is responsible for the trusts in another sense. For in the United States at present, just as in England at the beginning of last century, high protection aggravates the fluctuations in trade which the trusts in turn as ostensibly created to cure. Thus state interference to create monopoly leads to the development of further monopolies, and the abuses of these again call for further state interference. The removal of the protective tariff and the enforcement of uniform charges by the railway companies would do much to weaken the hold of the trusts in all industries save those which—like the monopoly of anthracite coal—depend on the control of limited supplies of raw material, or, as in the case of grain, of facilities for storage and transport. In these and similar cases it is the obvious duty of the state to regulate the monopoly in the interest of the public. But before the state is called upon, as Professor Ashley suggests, to "assume the duty of in some way controlling prices" of monopolized articles in general, it would surely be wise to abolish the existing restrictions and privileges, and to allow competition to do its perfect work. If this were done it is probable that the industrial combinations in the states would prove no more inimical to the public interest than they are here, where, with few exceptions, their shareholders alone have been the sufferers. And it is well that this is so, for that "fairly efficient administrative service," to which Professor Ashley would entrust the wholesale regulation of prices, is still, it is to be feared, a vision for which we shall have to dip into the future a little further than human eye can see.

WHY THE SENIOR PARTNER LOST

In some manner, says a Philadelphia exchange, the cheeky man gained admittance to the senior partner's private office.

"Don't want any books, brooms or soap," said the senior partner.

"Sir!" exclaimed the cheeky man, "I would inform you that I am no peddler."

"Then who are you?"

"A sporting gentleman, sir."

"What business can you have with me?"

"I wish to make a bet."

"Look here! I am no—"

"Of course you are no gambler. This is a gentleman's bet. I bet you, sir, that I can hold up my thumb and after I lower it you will leave the room."

The senior partner threw down his pen.

Up went the cheeky man's thumb.

"Wait!" called the senior partner, "this is so easy that I would like to make it ten dollars."

"Make it twenty dollars if you like."

"All right, it is twenty dollars."

The cheeky man raised and lowered his thumb.

"You don't see me leaving the room," said the senior partner.

"No," admitted the cheeky man.

The senior partner labored with his pen for thirty minutes.

"I'm still here."

"So I see."

Fifteen minutes passed.

"You'd just as well pass over the twenty dollars."

"It is early yet."

"Look here!" said the senior partner suddenly, "when is the time up?"

"There is no time limit, sir. If you remain in this room the money is yours; when you leave I win. This evening, tomorrow, next week; it makes no difference to me."

Then the senior partner gave in.

"Take the money!" he roared; "but if it wasn't for catching the Oak Park train I would stick you out and win."

THE SHIPPING OF MONEY

The recent mysterious disappearance of a trunk containing jewelry valued at $13,000, between Providence and this city, caused an inquiry to be made of one of the large express companies as to the methods employed for the protection of large sums of money while in transit between two cities, says the Boston Transcript. An official, who did not care to have his name used, was willing to explain some of the ways in which his company protected the property entrusted to it for shipment.

"For instance," he said, "suppose certain banks in one city want a large sum of money sent to them from some city hundreds of miles away. In the first place, we use as much secrecy as possible, never allowing our messengers to know until the last minute that a large amount of cash is to be entrusted to their care. The entire amount is not sent on one train, as there are just as 'bad men' in the East as in the West, and were it to become known that on a certain date, and by some particular train, $100,000 was to be shipped out of Boston, there are plenty of desperate men who would not hesitate to wreck a train here in New England as quickly as in the West. So we send the money by different routes and divide it into several packages.

"Of course each messenger is armed, and oftentimes another man rides in the car, ostensibly as a passenger, through the courtesy of the company, but in reality another guard for the money, also 'armed to the teeth,' and unknown as a company employee to the regular messenger. When the money arrives at its destination, other men, also unknown to the messenger, are there awaiting the train, and the messenger is followed and watched very closely until the money is actually delivered to the bank to which it is consigned, and a receipt is taken for it.

"While, of course, a messenger occasionally 'goes wrong' and runs away with a large amount of money, this seldom happens. Most of the men seem to take a pride in their hazardous line of work, and, considering the enormous sums of money and valuable packages which are constantly being shipped by express, few go astray."

THE DULL BOY

Who is the "dull boy?" asks an exchange. To the Greek professor, he is the boy who cannot learn Greek. To the whole literary or classical faculty, he is the poor fool whose brains will only absorb facts of physics and chemistry. To the witty man, he is that awful creature who sits solemn over the latest joke or epigram. To the serious man he is the laughing jackass who persists in treating life as a comedy.

In brief, the "dull boy" is the square peg whom somebody is trying to fit into a round hole.

Correspondence

The Get-Rich-Quick Scheme

From Teduis Baldus, New York.

Is there a nigger in the wood-pile? Sure! The game is not very different from what some long-whiskered country folks know as a "gold brick." We smart city folks think we know it all—well, perhaps, but for instance. There sits Mr. Cityman perusing his penny paper—his eye lights on the page containing all varieties of "get-rich-quick," "what-is-the-use-of-working" advertisements. Ha, says Mr. C., that is the ticket. Good as finding a wad of Standard Oil stock. The article goes on to tell of miraculous inducements—how to invest one dollar and live in comfort for the remainder of life on the income. Musingly he wonders why the benevolent editor has so little faith in his own advertisements as not to sell out his whole blamed printing outfit to take advantage of such a "cinch" and corner the market without letting the public into the deal. Must be worked on a sort of "fresh-air-fund" basis of charity on the theory than there is enough for all. Blessed be the man who invented editors.

Well, thinks he to himself (as he fingers a bill or two that is left over after a pay-day-night's argument with wifey), this is not like a bald-headed man investing in hair restorer—this is a sure thing and hair restorer aren't—so here goes.

Accordingly, he issues a buying order for say three links of the endless chain variety for one dollar. Now he isn't greedy—doesn't want all the money, so he gives his friend Yap the opportunity to buy one of his links so that he may open negotiations with the main foundry for obtaining privilege of doing further business in the link line. Yap promises to pull together with Mr. C., but when the final welding of links is over and the strain is put on the chain, Mr. C. finds to his sorrow that Mr. Y. was troubled with that tired feeling, financially, of course, and as the chain bursts Mr. C. lands in a heap in the bottomless pit of experience with a dull thud and a lamb-like countenance.

Such bait, however, is rarely palatable a second time. So he places that dollar to credit of experience account and lives happily ever after.

A Hartford Man's Views

From C. D. K., Hartford Conn.

I was very much interested in an article entitled "Get-Rich-Quick Scheme," which appeared in a recent issue of your paper, wherein the American Street Car Company, of Brooklyn, was interested. I enclose for the editor's attention an article on the same subject which recently appeared in one of the daily papers of this city, and as you have invited letters on this matter I send this forward thinking it may be of some interest.

Note—What our correspondent encloses is a clipping from a Hartford, Conn., daily paper, wherein is described the plans of the Aetna Street Car Transportation Company. The details of the scheme are practically identical with those which already have been presented to the reader. The stub or coupon which the buyer receives reads as follows:

"When introductions are all disposed of, return these stubs to us. Upon receipt of introduction we give you tickets as follows. For one, eight tickets; two, sixteen tickets; three, a book of twenty-five tickets, each good for one ride on any street car line in the United States."

The article commenting on this says:

"The volunteer agent who has thus been induced to peddle tickets has obtained the idea from a hasty glance at the wording of the contract that if he sells his three tickets and returns the stubs, and if the purchasers of his tickets turn them in, he will receive twenty-five car tickets, and as he has received 75 cents from his friends he has expended but twenty-five cents. He is pleased. He can sell his tickets for $1.25 and be a dollar richer than when he started in."

Continuing the comments the article says:

"That is all very well for him to think, but that is not what the contract says. It reads that if he sends back the stub and his three purchasers also return the coupons, and if each one then buys a new book, each paying 75 cents, then he will get the car tickets, but if they don't buy the books he does not get the car tickets and he is out 25 cents. His friends also lose 25 cents each.

In explanation of how it really works the article enclosed by this correspondent presents the following:

"A pays 25 cents for his first ticket or 'letter of introduction,' and the opportunity to invest more money. He then pays 75 cents more and becomes the agent of the concern to help along the scheme. But suppose he chooses to keep on investing his own money, what happens?

"In that case A sends back his three tickets and three stubs and $2.25 more for three more 'books,' each containing three 'introductions,' making his total investment $3.25. He then receives twenty-five car tickets, worth $1.25, which, deducted from $3.25, leaves $2 in the hands of the Aetna Street Car Transportation Company."

"On the next turn A sends back nine tickets and nine stubs, with $6.75, for which he receives nine books, containing twenty-seven tickets, and he receives seventy-five car tickets, worth $2.25, leaving a profit in the hands of the company of $4.50.

"Finding that he is doing a flourishing business A comes up once more with his 27 tickets and planks down $20.25. He then receives 81 tickets in 27 'books,' and he also receives 225 car tickets worth $11.52, leaving $9 this time in the hands of the Aetna Transportation Company. The total profits of the concern thus far are $2; plus $4.50, plus $9—$15.50 in all.

"The result is exactly the same to the concern if these 'tickets' are distributed among 40 individuals and handed in by them, instead of all being owned by one purchaser.

"It is simply a case of geometrical progression in paying something for nothing, and the scheme is devised to induce people to aid in pushing it along. If the scheme prospers the community not only buys car tickets at cost of the Aetna Transportation Company, but for every 325 car tickets purchased through the company it pays $17.25, a premium of $15.50, or not quite 10 cents each. The Aetna Transportation Company makes a profit of $15.50 on a total business of $32.75."

Loose Leaf Ledgers

From W. G. D., Pittsburg, Pa.

Referring to loose-leaf ledgers, I desire to inquire if it is not advisable where over six hundred accounts are required to use two ledgers? What are the real advantages of loose-leaf ledgers over old-fashioned bound volumes?

Answer.—We were in a bank in this city wherein loose-leaf ledgers are employed for certain classes of accounts the very day that this letter came to hand. In fact, it was the morning before the letter reached us, so that the information that we picked up at that time was in no respect connected with this question. Nevertheless, it is apropos. We asked the question of the cashier in charge whether or not he liked loose-leaf ledgers. He said, "Yes and No." The principal objection to them was that they were so bulky; that where there was a considerable number of accounts there had to be two or more volumes employed. Accordingly, when a depositor presented his smiling face at the window and asked concerning his account, it might be in the ledger on which the ledger clerk was working at the moment, or in view of the usual way in which Fate manages affairs, it might be in the ledger out of use for the moment; therefore it would necessitate closing one book and opening another.

Theoretically, where as many as six hundred accounts are required more than one volume should be used, but whether the advantages or having the accounts in two volumes, which are numerous, will overcome the objection which this cashier raises is something that we leave to our practical readers for determination. There are among those who read this item many who are in position to contribute in this regard and we should like to hear from them.

Referring now to our correspondent's inquiry concerning the advantages of loose-leaf ledgers over the old style bound volume, we submit the following. It would seem that the genius of the present day is a loose sheet of paper (never mind the size or the character of the paper for the moment), on which something is written in the nature of a record and which afterwards, with items of its class, goes into a binder or holder; in other words, the binding follows after the paper has been used instead of preceding it. Loose-leaf ledgers are merely one of a large number of interpretations of this principle. The card index, the ordinary letter file and various other devices that might be mentioned are other exemplifications of it.

Loose-leaf systems are not nearly so much in use in banks as they are in mercantile and manufacturing institutions. It is safe to say that there are comparatively few mercantile institutions and still fewer manufacturing institutions today that could keep up with the procession, in the accounting sense, if they did not employ more or less of loose-leaf principles. With order sheets coming along from salesmen in shape to be instantly bound for permanent preservation whenever the orders have been filed, with invoices being made out in duplicate so that the carbon copy forms the sales book, and with various other applications of the same idea, a plurality of clerks can be employed in a given department where otherwise only one or two could find space.

A short time since we were in the office of a very well known mercantile concern, which, much to its disadvantage as we see the case, adheres to the bound-book idea, and found no less than six men waiting for a sight at the pages of a given book. The book in question was a copy of orders. No two men wanted to look at the same order. They were obliged to wait until each in his turn had gotten the information he wanted. The cost to the establishment was considerable, while the wear and tear upon the nerves and tempers of the clerks was also to be considered. With the bound book broken up into small units so that the pages which were to be inspected by these different clerks could be used away from the binding, sorted up by one of them so as to give each one what he required, there would have been a great saving in time as well as temper.

These general remarks answer in part the question which our correspondent has asked with reference to the advantages of loose-leaf ledgers. All that applies to the card index system now in almost universal use, and all that applies to modern schemes of filing letters, likewise applies in this case.

In this question, as in others, points are raised which hundreds of our readers are able to answer from their own practical experience, and therefore we should be glad to have communications upon it. What advantages do ledger clerks perceive in the handling of loose-leaf ledgers? What disadvantages do they encounter?

We have not given special attention in what precedes to one advantage that must appear to every thinking person, and that is the possibility of holding the book, ledger or other volume, whatever it may be, to live matter. All the dead and out-of-date matter is at once removed from the file, leaving in the binder only that which is required for current use.

THE LONDON TIMES "AMERICANIZED"

All England is trembling, for the American invader is invading. American manufactured goods, American canned beef, American wheat, American machinery, American plays and American actors are pouring in upon the helpless Briton, and, worse than all, they are, by their very excellence, convincing the said helpless one that he is slow, very, very slow. As the Chicago Tribune puts it:—

"There's a panic on the Strand, there's grave apprehension in Piccadilly, there is a fear and trembling in Hyde Park, in Kensington and Chelsea, and anxious forebodings and white faces all the way from the bank to the farthermost limits of Dun Cow Road. All London is under arms waiting the bugle call to summon them to the breastworks."

You see, Mr. Morgan has been in England and has returned with his pockets full of steamship lines and other little souvenirs. Mr. Chas. T. Yerkes has also been in London, and he has "Americanized" the street railroads of that great city. American shoes are walking the British product out of the market. American office furniture long ago displaced the clumsy and old-fashioned desks and chairs that the Englishman built from the patterns left by his grandfather.

The Times.

No. 17,895 JULY 20th, 1910. Five Cents.

CONTENTS.

TOWN TOPICS.

WHAT WE THINK.

Opening of a SARDINE TIN in Hyde Park, By Congressman J. P. MORGAN.

Rank and Fashion and Talent Crowd In to Assist At the Ceremony.

Britisher Arrested for WANTING TO KNOW What it is all about.

SEETHING CROWDS WATCHED THE CEREMONY

Full Page Illustration of the Sardine Tin.

MORGAN TALKS To a "Times" Man.

WEPT IN A COFFEE CUP.

Stall-Keeper Jones Specially Snapped.

In the Awful Conflagration COFFEE STALL KEEPER Loses All.

DREADFUL HOLOCAUST OF BACON.

EGGS Surrounded by Flames and many Burnt.

Plucky Rescue of Eighteen Sandwiches by Police Captain Murphy.

TEA-URN EXPLODES WITH HEART-RENDING SHRIEK.

"Times" Reporter first on the Scene.

The Big Store—A City in Itself.

MACLURE'S DEPARTMENT STORE.

A Great Line of Silk Waists.

THEY COST $1. $1. $1.

AND THEY ARE WORTH $1. $1. $1.

FINE THINGS—LOW PRICES.

$100 will buy. $160

If you want anything else it's here.

MACLURE'S DEPARTMENT STORE.

PAGE OF THE "AMERICANIZED" LONDON TIMES.—LONDON WEEKLY KING.

So there is woe in England, real woe and a lot of make-believe woe. Johnny Bull is inclined to take the American invasion as something of a grimly practical joke, and it is probable that the good feeling between the United States and Great Britain has not been so much in evidence since before the day when Miss Columbia shook the dust of Mother Brittannia's kitchen from her shoes and tripped daintily off to set up business on her own hook. Some clever chap recently printed in the London Weekly *King* a page supposed to be clipped from the London Times of July 20, 1910. It is a prophecy of a sort calculated to make the staid old "Thunderer" sit up and gasp with indignation. Incidently it is a pretty good burlesque on a certain kind of American newspaper. We reproduce this page herewith.

Current Business Cartoons

We reproduce two cartoons from Punch in this issue. The first very cleverly portrays what the situation may become if

Col. Jonathan J. Bull; or What John B. May Come to.—Punch.

the Boer leaders continue to keep out of the way of General Kitchener and the British forces. The Boer war is materially affecting British commerce and trade, and, in fact, there is a great deal of opposition in England toward the further continuance of the war, although it is not at all probable that hostilities will cease until the Boers are subjugated. In the

"You Can't Tie Up at This Dock."—Phila. North American.

cartoon the only remaining Boer is on crutches, and Kitchener has become an old man with his beard below his waist, but they do not seem to have reached an understanding, even in 1950.

In the second English cartoon, Bernard Partridge, one of Punch's best cartoonists, has pictured what John Bull may become if American ideas continue to dominate in Great Britain. John Bull has become "Colonel Jonathan Bull."

Time 1950.—The Aged Rip-Van-Kitchener (aside to his venerable Tommies)—"Aha! The only survivor 'coming in' at last!"
The Last of the Boers—"Wait a moment! What terms? Complete independence or I go out again on commando."—Punch.

and his waistcoat with the British cross, is spangled with the stars of the United States; in like manner his trousers are

A Message for Each of Them.—Minn. Journal.

striped with red and white. The British lion is now an eagle with a lion's head and tail, and behind the figures are American "skyscrapers," telegraph wires and smoke.

Lamb Stew.—N. Y. Tribune.

The cartoons for the early part of the month of December

dealt principally with the President's Message and the convening of Congress. President Roosevelt's Message was generally well liked, and there were no open words of complaint. The message was a long one, and treated the subjects of importance before the nation carefully and with much common sense. Among the subjects about which the President expressed an opinion were the Trusts, the Exclusion of Chinese Laborers, Reciprocity, the Indian Question and the Isthmian Canal. In the cartoon from the Minneapolis Journal each of these various subjects is personified by a typical character, who is listening to the message as it comes from the phonograph. The Canal and Reciprocity appear to be pleased,—the others do not look happy.

"The Cyclone's Coming!"—N. Y. World.

In the President's Message he especially advocated more strict enforcement of the Chinese Exclusion Act. The Chinese, he thinks, are not the best class of people coming to our shores, particularly as they do not come here to become citizens, but merely to make money with the intention of returning to China as soon as they have laid by a few dollars. In the cartoon from the Philadelphia North American the situation is typified in clever fashion, the drawing being much better than in the majority of cartoons.

Likely to Catch the Whole Group.—Minn. Journal.

The New York World evidently thinks that Congress has its eye principally upon Uncle Sam's dollars, and is anxious to disburse them as quickly as possible. At any rate, that is what one might gather from the cartoon in which President Roosevelt is shown helping Uncle Sam to get the sack containing the $130,000,000 surplus into the cyclone cellar before Congress arrives.

New Picture of Uncle Sam; Drawn by a European Artist.—Chicago. Record-Herald.

The Amalgamated Copper Stock has had a bad tumble in the past month, and Wall Street has fattened once more on the lambs. In the cartoon from the New York Tribune, Wall Street is a cook, tasting with delight the lamb stew which he is preparing.

Waiting for the Minister.—Cleveland Plain Dealer.

Although arrangements are not yet perfected for the purchase of the Danish West Indies, it is practically settled that these islands will become the property of the United States. By right of situation and by common sense principles of trade, all of the West Indian group should belong to this country. It may be that all will eventually so belong. The cartoon of the Minneapolis Journal shows them as birds attracted to the trap by the bait of the American dollar. When the hat falls it seems likely to cover a goodly number.

The horrible looking creature on the screen, in the car-

292235

toon from the Chicago Record-Herald, with hands like a spider, reaching for everything in sight, is the German conception of the United States. They are having a terrible time in Germany over the invasion of American manufactured products, and German legislators are advocating all sorts of prohibitory measures to keep us out of the German markets. McCutcheon, the artist, shows the German lecturer holding up the horrible creature Uncle Sam as an awful warning to all Europe.

Uncle Sam's Lamp Beats Aladdin's.—Boston Herald.

The artist of the Cleveland Plain Dealer has some very clever ideas. We reproduce one of them. The Atlantic and Pacific oceans sit side by side on the Isthmus of Panama and are waiting for the Rev. Uncle Sam to join them in the ties of "canal-lock." It is a good idea, well drawn.

The dividends and interest on the stocks and bonds of our great investment companies amount each year to an enormous sum, and they have amounted to more in the last year than ever before. Williams, of the Boston Herald, shows Uncle Sam rubbing the lamp of progress, which summons the genii with the sack of riches. Uncle Sam's lamp, compared with Alladin's, makes the latter look like a candle beside an arc light.

Another One so Soon?—Des Moines (Ia.) Leader.

New combinations of capital are being formed every month. The artist of the Des Moines (Ia.) Leader pictures Mr. Morgan holding the new baby, "Northern Securities Company," in his lap, while the little boy, "Steel Trust," who, by the way, is not so very little either, is playing about. The nurse, New Jersey, is bringing in another newcomer into the room, labelled, "Southern Securities Company." Mr. Morgan looks surprised, but rather happy.

The new treaty with England has been ratified and the United States will dig the Isthmian canal. It is now merely a question of route. The cartoon from the Chicago Journal shows Uncle Sam with a shovel in his hand and determination written on his countenance, just as he was shown, by the way, in an original cartoon which appeared in Commerce, Accounts and Finance one year ago, except that, in the latter the old gentleman was shown as actually digging.

I Will!—Chicago Journal.

A WAIL FROM THE BRITON

Oh, here's a wail from the London Mail, that voices Briton's anguish! We "Yanks" invade her marts of trade, and England's products languish. We come with nails and jam in pails, with desks and beef and bonnets, with soup and soap and rails and rope and peaches, plays and sonnets. In short, we win, and, with chagrin, this pill the Briton swallows; so wipe your eyes and sympathize and read the plaint that follows:—

We have got to this: The average Englishman rises in the morning from his New England folding bed, shaves himself with Yankee soap and a Yankee safety razor, pulls on his Boston boots over his socks from North Carolina, fastens his Connecticut braces, slips his Waltham or Waterbury watch in his pocket and sits down to breakfast. There he congratulates his wife on the way her Illinois straight-front corset sets off her Massachusetts blouse, and he tackles his breakfast, where he eats bread made from prairie flour (possibly doctored at the special establishment on the lakes), tinned oysters from the Pacific coast, and a slice of Kansas City bacon, while his wife plays with a slice of Chicago ox tongue. The children are given a dish of "Puritan" oats. At the same time he reads his morning paper printed by American machines and possibly on American paper.

He rushes out, catches the electric tram (New York) to Shepherd's Bush, where he gets in a Yankee elevator to take him onto the American-fitted railway to the city. In his office, of course, everything is American. At lunch time he hastily swallows some cold roast beef that comes from a cow in Iowa, and flavors it with the latest New England pickles, followed by a few Florida tinned peaches.

To follow his course all day would be wearisome. But when evening comes he seeks relaxation at the latest American musical comedy, and finishes up with a couple of "little liver pills" "made in America."

SINGLE TICKET

Farmer Cloverleaf (to railway ticket agent)—I want a ticket to Buffalo.

Ticket Agent (briskly)—Single?

Farmer Cloverleaf—No, married; but wife can't leave home at this time of year, we're too busy.

C. W. HASKINS, C. P. A. E. W. SELLS, C. P. A.

HASKINS & SELLS

Certified Public Accountants

CABLE ADDRESS, "HASKSELLS." THIRTY BROAD STREET, NEW YORK

Accounts of Municipalities, Corporations, Firms and Individuals Inspected and Audited; Methods of Accounting Originated and Adapted to Conditions; Books of Accounts Opened, Regulated and Closed; Irregularities Discovered; Financial Situations Examined.

Experts under the Joint Commission of the Fifty-third Congress to Revise the Accounting System of the UNITED STATES GOVERNMENT.

Michigan University
Course in
Higher Commercial Education

It is the aim of this course to give special training in the construction and organization of modern industry and commerce. While placing special stress upon what is technical or professional in a course preparatory to a business career, ample provision is made for instruction in history, language, science and other lines of study which contribute to a general education. This course is designed to provide an education equal in scope and mental discipline to any which the University offers.

Michigan University, Ann Arbor, Mich.

About a Pay Roll which proves itself, corrects all mistakes in figuring, divides up Pay Roll into several amounts needed to pay each person.

But let us send you a sample leaf, with circular, which tells the whole story.

BARLOW BROS., Grand Rapids, Mich.

It's Good for You

To use our Typewriter Ribbons and Carbons, because they write better and last longer than the ordinary kind; they do not smut, blur nor fill the type, but they make fine copies.

No. 1 Ribbons, 75c. ea., $7.00 doz.
No. 1 Carbon, $3.00 pr. bx., 40c. doz.
Silkarbon, $4.00 pr. bx., 50c. doz.

We pay express or mail charges.

IMPERIAL MANUFACTURING CO.
289-297 Washington St., Newark, N. J.

W. G. Mowat
Public Accountant
831 Ellicott Sq., Buffalo, N. Y.

PRENTISS CLOCKS

for offices, stores and homes. They run two months on one winding and are excellent timekeepers.

Also Frying-pan, Program and Electric Clocks. Send for Catalogue No. 940.

THE PRENTISS CLOCK IMPROVEMENT CO.
Dept. 84, 49 Dey St., New York City

A **Systematist** is one who makes or reduces systems.—*Webster.*

My forte is the scientific systematic care and arrangement of advertising details. I also expertly devise and apply automatic methods and devices for the *recording* and *despatching* of business.

It might surprise some were they to become acquainted with the list of leading representative concerns in mechanical and electrical circles for whom I am working along lines as above—and of the satisfaction expressed. Any inquiry will receive careful consideration.

RAY D. LILLIBRIDGE, Systematist,
90 Broad Street, New York City. Tel. 11 Cortlandt.

STATIONERY

For business use. Embossed in color from Steel Dies—Nothing else. Capacity, 50,000 sheets daily. Samples and quotations gladly furnished.

THE AMERICAN EMBOSSING CO.
73 Lock St., Buffalo, N. Y

Ralph H. Brown
Public Accountant and Auditor,
318 Temple Court, Atlanta, Ga.

Leon Brummer, C. P. A.
Public Accountant and Auditor,
7 Pine Street, New York, N. Y.

Textile Accounting

HOW THE BALANCE SHEET SYSTEM SOLVES THE PROBLEM OF MANUFACTURING COSTS

THE BALANCE SHEET SYSTEM OF ACCOUNTING, as applied to the textile industry, gives to the management at all times the exact information required for intelligent business administration.

In cotton manufacturing, for example, THE BALANCE SHEET SYSTEM gives a perpetual or going inventory of the ootton on hand, subdivided in detail to any required degree.

THE BALANCE SHEET SYSTEM also gives a going inventory in similar fashion of all other materials and supplies.

In like manner THE BALANCE SHEET SYSTEM gives a going inventory of stock in process of manufacture and of finished product on hand. Such inventory may be in gross or in as much detail as desired.

THE BALANCE SHEET SYSTEM provides for a going balance sheet and a going profit and loss statement, constantly showing results in every department of the business.

THE BALANCE SHEET SYSTEM provides an accurate record of cost of product, including an equitable distribution of general manufacturing costs as they accrue.

Incidental to the installation of THE BALANCE SHEET SYSTEM the manufacturer is provided with up-to-date office methods and mechanisms—in fact, with the best of everything in modern accounting.

A TYPICAL COTTON MILL.

BALANCE SHEET.

Assets.

- CASH.
- IMPREST CASH.
- BANK.
- NOTES RECEIVABLE.*
- Accounts Receivable.
  - CUSTOMERS.*
  - SUNDRY DEBTORS.*
- COTTON AND OTHER MATERIALS.*
- ACCRUING MANUFACTURING COSTS.*
  - Heat, Light and Power.
  - Superintendence and Foremanship.
  - Clerical Labor.
  - Repairs of Plant.
  - Depreciation of Plant.
  - Taxes.
  - Insurance.
  - Accidents.
  - Incidentals.
- MANUFACTURING.
  - Mill No. 1.
    - Roving.
      - Materials.
      - Labor.
      - Mfg. Costs.
    - Yarn.
      - Same as above.
    - Cloth.
      - Same as above.
  - Mill No. 2.
    - Same as above.
  - Dye Works.
    - Materials.
    - Labor.
    - Manufacturing Costs.
  - Bleachery.
    - Same as above.
  - Machine Shop.
    - Same as above.
  - Carpenter Shop.
    - Same as above.
  - Paint Shop.
    - Same as above.
- FINISHED PRODUCT.*
- MANUFACTURING PLANT.*
  - Land and Buildings.
  - Power Plant.
  - Machinery and Fixtures.
  - Tools and Furniture.
- TENEMENT PROPERTY.*
- HORSES AND WAGONS.*
- STOCKS AND BONDS.*
- ITEMS IN SUSPENSE.*
  - Taxes.
  - Insurance.
  - Experimental Work.
  - Construction Accounts.

Liabilities.

- NOTES PAYABLE.*
- Accounts Payable.
  - PURCHASE CREDITORS.*
  - SUNDRY CREDITORS.*
- ACCRUED LABOR.
- RESERVES.*
  - Taxes.
  - Repairs of Manufacturing Plant.
  - Depreciation of Manufacturing Plant.
  - Repairs of Tenement Property.
  - Depreciation of Tenement Property.
  - Depreciation of Product.
  - Bad Debts and Collection Charges.
  - Interest.
  - Accidents.
- FOUR-WEEK LOSS AND GAIN.
- GENERAL LOSS AND GAIN.
- IMPAIRMENT AND SURPLUS.
- CAPITAL STOCK.

PROFIT AND LOSS STATEMENT.

Expenses.

- ADMINISTRATIVE.*
  - Fees Directors' Meetings.
  - Interest on Borrowed Money.
  - Incidentals.
- COMMERCIAL.*
  - Traveling.
  - Freights Outward.
  - Advertising.
  - Salaries.
  - Bad Debts and Collection Charges.
  - Depreciation of Finished Product.
  - Interest.
  - Commissions.
  - Teaming.
  - Warehousing.
  - Incidentals.
- MISCELLANEOUS.*
  - Taxes on Tenement Property.
  - Insurance of Tenement Property.
  - Repairs of Tenement Property.
  - Depreciation of Tenement Property.
  - etc., etc.

Revenues.

- SALES OF MATERIALS AND SUPPLIES.
- SALES OF ROVING.
- SALES OF YARN.
- SALES OF FINISHED PRODUCT.
- REVENUE FROM DYE WORKS.
- REVENUE FROM BLEACHERY.
- REVENUE FROM MACHINE SHOP.
- REVENUE FROM CARPENTER SHOP.
- REVENUE FROM PAINT SHOP.
- REVENUE FROM TEAMING.
- REVENUE FROM WAREHOUSING.
- SALES OF SCRAP, WASTE AND REFUSE.
- RENTS OF TENEMENTS.
- INCOME FROM STOCKS AND BONDS.
- DISCOUNTS ON PURCHASES.

COTTON MILL ACCOUNTING.

Chart and analysis of classification accompanying paper read before the New England Cotton Manufacturers Association, at the semi-annual meeting, Boston, April 24-25, 1901, by A.O. Kittredge, C.P.A., Professor of Theory of Accounts, School of Commerce, Accounts and Finance, New York University, and president of the Account, Audit & Assurance Company, Limited, 25 Pine Street, New York.

Copyright, 1901, by Account, Audit & Assurance Co., Ltd., New York.

The cost-account features of THE BALANCE SHEET SYSTEM OF ACCOUNTING are the cheapest to install and maintain, and the most efficient and satisfactory to use.

Installations of THE BALANCE SHEET SYSTEM OF ACCOUNTS are made on the specification plan exclusively. The foundation in every case is a chart of the accounts. See typical illustration above. Everything is in writing. There are no oral instructions. No changes in existing routine are made until time and opportunity are given to study THE BALANCE SHEET SYSTEM and make sure that all details are going to be satisfactory.

Lump prices for installations are quoted after a survey has been made determining what is necessary. Correspondence solicited.

A copy of the paper read by A. O. Kittredge, C. P. A., before the New England Cotton Manufacturers' Association, from which the chart shown above is taken, will be sent on application. Address:—

Account, Audit & Assurance Co., Limited

25 Pine Street, New York — 502 Exchange Building, Boston

PUBLIC LIBRARY

COMMERCE ACCOUNTS & FINANCE

Volume 4 New York February 1902 Number 2

CONTENTS

Published Monthly by the Commerce Accounts & Finance Company Twenty-five Pine Street New York

KNICKERBOCKER TRUST CO.

234 FIFTH AVENUE, CORNER 27TH STREET,
BRANCH OFFICES:
66 BROADWAY, AND 125TH STREET AND LENOX AVE.,
NEW YORK CITY.

CAPITAL AND UNDIVIDED PROFITS, $2,508,399.11.

LEGAL DEPOSITORY FOR STATE, CITY, AND COURT FUNDS.

Interest allowed on Time Deposits. Deposits also received subject to Demand Checks, which pass through the Clearing House as do those upon any city bank.

Authorized to act as Executor or Administrator of Estates, and as Guardian, Receiver, Registrar, Transfer and Financial Agent for States, Cities, Towns, Railroads, and other corporations, and to accept any other Trusts in conformity with the laws of any State or of the United States.

LETTERS OF CREDIT FURNISHED.
BUSINESS AND PERSONAL ACCOUNTS SOLICITED.

CHAS. T. BARNEY, - - - - - - - - President.
JOSEPH T. BROWN, - - - - - - 2d Vice-President.
JULIAN M. GERARD, - - - Asst. Sec. and Asst. Treas.
FRED'K K. ELDRIDGE, - - - - 1st Vice-President.
FRED'K GORE KING, - - - Secretary and Treasurer.
WM. B. RANDALL, - - - - - - - Trust Officer.

BOARD OF DIRECTORS:

JOSEPH S. AUERBACH,
HARRY B. HOLLINS,
JACOB HAYS,
CHARLES T. BARNEY,
A. FOSTER HIGGINS,
ANDREW H. SANDS,
JAMES H. BRESLIN,
I. TOWNSEND BURDEN,
HON. E. V. LOEW,
HENRY F. DIMOCK,
CHARLES F. WATSON,
FREDERICK G. BOURNE,
C. LAWRENCE PERKINS,
CHARLES R. FLINT,
AMZI L. BARBER,
CHARLES T. COOK,
JOHN MAGEE,
HENRY A. MORGAN,
HENRY C. BERLIN,
CHARLES W. GOULD,
FRED'K L. ELDRIDGE,
HENRY W. DE FOREST,
ALFRED B. MACLAY
HARRY W. McVICKAR.

HALL'S Fireproof and Burglar Proof SAFES

Sold since 1840. Never fail to protect contents.

KNOWN EVERYWHERE

393 BROADWAY, N.Y.

Telephones: 3133-3136-307 Franklin.

Accounting for Cotton Mills—II.*

By GEORGE YOUNG

If, as we are told, "the object of all bookkeeping is to produce a perfect balance sheet," then the construction of the balance sheet is a matter demanding very careful treatment at the hands of the accountant, and the arrangement of records and the classification of entries in a way to make the production of a proper balance sheet at frequent intervals a feature of the regular routine work is worthy of the most careful consideration, not only of the accountant, but of the business man as well.

THE BALANCE SHEET.

In its final analysis the balance sheet is a statement of the assets and liabilities of the business.

Some definitions mention the "difference between the two sides of the balance sheet," or the "excess of assets over liabilities," as being the net capital; but why a difference between assets and liabilities? There can be no difference between the totals of the two sides of a balance sheet; it must balance, or else it is not what it purports to be.

All of the capital of a business belongs to the owners of the business, is a liability to them; therefore a statement of liabilities will include all items of capital, both of original investment and accumulated earnings.

The balance sheet is complete only as it is corrected in the light of the profit and loss statement, but it is not a profit and loss statement in itself. The functions of the two things are quite different, and therefore they are to be treated as two separate and distinct propositions.

It is customary, in presenting to the managers of the business a balance sheet which has been corrected to the extent of the profits accrued during a given fiscal period, to show such profits in one item, separate from the earnings which may have accumulated prior to the period under review, and this is perfectly proper, but profit and loss, undivided profits, surplus, call it what you will, it is all an increment of capital belonging to the owners of the business, and is therefore a liability to be shown in the balance sheet.

A perfect balance sheet is one in which all of the assets and all of the liabilities are stated accurately, classified correctly and listed in proper form and order.

Behind it must be records in detail of every transaction of the business, and these records should be systematized in a way to make the postings to controlling or balance sheet accounts a matter of totals only, without the necessity of rewriting.

This result is readily accomplished by the use of modern accounting methods and machinery. The most important of these, including, among others, the cash received record, the check register, the imprest cash method, the ACX invoice system, the bill and sales sheet system and the balance sheet ledger have been fully discussed before this class by other lecturers, and therefore need not be explained in this connection.

Every well-kept set of books is supposed to contain, immediately after the balance sheet has been completed by the process known as closing the books, all of the assets and all of the liabilities of the business, a supposition which is not usually borne out by the facts; but for present purposes we will presume that the books do reflect the true condition of the business.

Under ordinary bookkeeping this state of affairs will cease to exist as soon as there are sales to record, and yet to continue balance sheet conditions in the books it is only necessary to preserve the proper relationship between cost values and selling prices, and to establish and maintain the proper classification of entries on balance sheet principles.

A GOING BALANCE SHEET.

To put it another way: Since the books reflect all the liabilities, and all the assets, with the one exception of inventory, it is only necessary to supply the missing asset to complete the circle, and with a going inventory in our books it is only a step to a going profit and loss statement and a going balance sheet. The analysis of profit and loss and of expenses becomes then a mere matter of detail.

We have in our books an account with Cash. We do not inventory our cash to ascertain how much we have; the balance in the account is the asset of cash, and we count the money only to prove the accuracy of the book balance. How do we keep this account in a way to show at all times the asset of cash in hand? Simply by debiting it with all receipts and crediting it with all disbursements; the balance is bound to be the remaining asset. By extending the application of this principle to accounts to represent all of the assets of the business we shall get in each the same result, namely, a balance representing the net asset, and the only necessity for physical inventory will be for proof purposes.

To illustrate: If we will open an account called Customers, debiting it with all of our charges against all of our customers and crediting it with all of our credits to all of our customers, including cash received from them, discounts and other allowances made to them, etc., the balance in the account will be the total amount due us from all of our customers. This asset, called Customers' Accounts Receivable, must agree with the total of the balances in the customers' ledger. The arrangement of records in a way to make the accomplishment of this result simple and economical is a mere matter of office mechanics.

We have seen how this result may be accomplished with the asset of cotton. The same rule will apply to supplies and to any other material. If we will debit an account called Materials and Supplies with the cost of all the materials and supplies purchased, and will credit that account at cost prices with all materials and supplies used or withdrawn, the balance in the account will represent the asset of materials and supplies on hand.

It would be folly to attempt to keep such an account without making some provision for the discovery and correction of discrepancies which we know must creep in. By providing detail record accounts of supplies according to kinds and arranging for regular systematic comparison of balances with stock, the detection and adjustment of differences may be made a matter of regular routine, and the Materials and Supplies account may be kept down to an actual representation of the asset of supplies on hand.

Incidentally the use of such a scheme furnishes advantages quite distinct from those pertaining to the accounting. For example, the information which it may be made to convey to the purchasing agent; and you as accountants, in designing and installing a system in any business, are bound to consider the needs and the interests, not merely of the accounting department, but of the business as a whole.

Let us take another step forward. If you will debit an account called Manufacturing, with all raw materials put into process of manufacture and with all labor and general manufacturing costs as they accrue, and will credit that account with the manufactured product at the cost of manufacture, as the finished goods come out, the resulting balance will represent the cost of work in process. In other words, it will be a mill inventory at cost. Here, again, we must provide means of proving and checking our work as we proceed, which, you will remember, was emphasized as an important feature of the cost methods which we have discussed together. Whatever application or adaptation of the proof-by-balance cost system may be made—and this is a matter which must be decided in the light of the conditions and the needs existing in each individual case—whether the up-set rate plan, the factory order plan pure and simple or a combination of the two, the items of cost entering into the manufacturing account must be segregated in a way to enable those who have in charge the administration of the system to

* An address before the Junior Class in Accounting School of Commerce, Accounts and Finance, New York University, by George Young, manager Textile Division of the Account, Audit and Assurance Co., Ltd., New York and Boston.

keep this account well in hand, to safeguard it against the danger of inflation, and provision must also be made for frequent proof of balances. To this end the manufacturing account may be subdivided into subordinate accounts to any extent which may be desirable or expedient in the premises.

Never lose sight of the fact that your cost accounts constitute a feature of your accounting system, not merely related to the books of account, but a vital part of the general bookkeeping scheme.

With costs established, the handling of the Mill Product account becomes easy, a simple matter of debiting it with goods manufactured and crediting it with goods sold, always at cost.

FORM OF BALANCE SHEET.

The balance sheet of a typical cotton manufacturing corporation constructed on the principles would look something like this:—

ASSETS.				
Cash ....$	500			
Banks	30,000			
Imprest Cash	1,000	31,500		
Notes Receivable*.....		42,000		
Ac's Re. Customers*	110,000			
Ac's Re. Sun'y Debt's*	90,000	200,000		
Cotton*	150,000			
Materials & Supplies*..	25,000			
Manufacturing*	100,000			
Finished Product*	250,000	525,000		
Stocks and Bonds		60,000	858,500	
Manfacturing Plant*..		1,200,000		
Finishing Plant*		350,000		
Tenement Property*.		225,000		
Horses and Wagons.		2,500	1,777,500	
Items in Suspense* ...			8,500	
LIABILITIES.				
Notes Payable*		490,000		
Act's Pay. Pur. Cred.*	60,000			
Act's Pay. Sun. Cred.*	90,000	150,000		
Accrued Labor.......		15,000		655,000
Reserves*		260,000		
Four-W'k Loss & Gain.	15,000			
General Loss & Gain..	114,000			
Impairment & Surplus.	300,000	429,500		689,500
Capital Stock Preferred		300,000		
Capital Stock Common		1,000,000		1,300,000
			$2,644,500	$2,644,500

Following a well-established rule, the quick assets are stated first and are listed in the order of their availability. The amounts are extended short, and the total of quick assets is carried into the asset column in one item, and the plant values or items representing fixed assets are treated in the same manner. Accounts receivable from Customers and those due from Sundry Debtors are separated, because it is fair to presume that the balances due from Customers will be maturing in regular course, while Sundry Debtors may represent long time accounts or those which have no definite maturity dates. The total amount due from these two classes of debtors appears in the quick assets group in one item.

Under liabilities the same reasons suggest the separation of Purchase Creditors and Sundry Creditors, and the extension of the total of current liabilities in one item.

ANALYSIS OF ACCOUNTS.

Those items or accounts which require analysis are indicated by asterisks. Notes Receivable account is analyzed in the note book; Customers and Sundry Debtors in the Accounts Receivable ledger or ledgers; Cotton in the individual lot accounts, and other accounts in other subordinate ledgers. The term ledger does not necessarily mean a bound volume; it may refer to such a book or it may be applied to any one of half a dozen different groups or classes of accounts in the same volume.

ACCRUING MANUFACTURING COSTS.

The Accruing Manufacturing Costs account may be given as an example of subdivision into subsidiary accounts. This account belongs in the assets division of the ledger, although ordinarily it will show no balance at the close of a fiscal period, and therefore would not appear in the balance sheet. It may be subdivided for statistical and analytical purposes something like this:—

Accruing Manufacturing Costs:
- Superintendence
- Clerical Labor
- Non-Producing Labor
- Heat, Light and Power
- Repairs of Plant
- Taxes
- Insurance
- Depreciation of Plant
- Accidents
- Incidentals

The spreading of these general manufacturing costs over product period by period will be in total from the controlling amount. The subordinate accounts will finish the analysis, and at the end of a given period will show total expenditures for each item in the group.

The question may be raised, "Why should Accruing Manufacturing Costs be treated as an asset?" The answer is, "Because it is an asset."

The cost of the cotton which we buy for manufacturing purposes represents money invested; it is an asset; we pay for labor to convert that cotton into manufactured product; the cost of the material is increased to the extent of the labor cost expended upon it. The investment in labor is an asset; we pay for superintendence, repairs, taxes, insurance and other costs necessary to manufacturing; we are still investing money for the purpose of converting our raw material into something more valuable, and the money thus invested is still an asset, whether it has been spread over product or appears temporarily in an account by itself.

Among the items which do not ordinarily appear in books are Suspense, Reserves and Accrued Labor.

ACCRUED LABOR.

The last-named account is designed to show the liability of wages earned by employees, but not yet paid. In some cases a special account is opened to show this liability at the time of closing the books, a plan which might answer well enough with long fiscal periods, but we are discussing new plans for a going balance sheet, and we need the liability of unpaid wages stated in our books all the time.

ITEMS IN SUSPENSE.

The controlling account entitled Items in Suspense is designed to carry advance payments of costs and expenses. To illustrate: Insurance is invariably paid in advance, and is usually charged in full to costs or expenses at the close of the fiscal period. Unless the fiscal period is a full year (and what modern manufacturer is willing to wait a year to know the results of his business?) this makes an unequal distribution of the cost of insurance, and also an incorrect balance sheet, since unearned insurance premiums constitute an asset, not only in the sense of being chargeable to future periods for value to be received during those periods, but also in the sense of being collectible in the event of cancellation; and having such an asset, it should be carried in the books, and should be stated in the balance sheet. Again, interest paid in advance should not be charged off at the time of payment, but should be spread equitably over the period during which the use of the money is obtained, the unprorated balance being carried meantime as an asset, in suspense.

RESERVES.

The liability account of Reserves should include those items of costs and expenses which have accrued, but are not yet due for payment, such as taxes, interest payable at maturity, etc.

By the proper use of Suspense and Reserve accounts all general manufacturing costs, and all expenses of administration and marketing may be pro-rated equitably over any number of fiscal periods without reference to the payment dates.

The treatment of plant account and depreciation is an interesting subject and one which has been much discussed. We will take it up briefly even at the risk of covering ground already well trodden.

PLANT ACCOUNT AND DUPLICATION.

One of the methods in vogue is that of charging the plant account with all expenditures for machinery and betterments, and crediting it at the close of each fiscal period with a certain percentage for depreciation. Another is that of carrying all new machinery and adjustments in a betterments account until the close of the fiscal period and then charging the whole amount to profit and loss on the theory that the betterments only keep the plant good. Still another plan is that of writing off from the asset of plant at the close of the year whatever amount, in the judgment of the management, the business can afford.

Under none of these plans, after they have been in operation for any considerable time, will the plant account reflect the true value of the plant. It is beyond analysis; no one can tell how near it is to actual values without an appraisal of the property.

A better plan is to carry in the books all machinery and other items of plant at cost, so long as they are in service, debiting all new machinery and other additions, and crediting at cost all machinery sold or rendered useless by wear or invention and therefore withdrawn from use, creating in the meantime a reserve against which to charge losses by depreciation when the same become apparent through alterations.

Classify and subdivide your subordinate plant accounts to any extent which may be desirable, as, for example:—

Manufacturing Plant:
- Mill Site
- Buildings
- Power Plant
- Machinery and Fixtures
- Tools and Furniture.

and have records, classified after the same plan, giving in detail the cost of each item of plant, to enable you to give at any time the details which make up the one item in your balance sheet called Plant, a thing which might prove very valuable in a case of serious loss by fire.

To illustrate the plan: Suppose our Machinery and Fixtures account stands at $200,000, which represents the cost (or, in the case of an old plant, the appraised value) of the items of plant belonging in this account, and suppose we run for ten years without making any changes in plant, reserving for depreciation of machinery meantime at the rate of 7 per cent per annum on the cost. At the end of the ten years Machinery and Fixtures will still be represented in the asset account of Plant at $200,000, and we shall have a reserve for depreciation of machinery and fixtures of $140,000. Suppose, now, that we purchase fifty new cards at a cost of $800 each, and throw out forty old ones which are carried on our books at $750 each. We will charge machinery and fixtures with the cost of the fifty new cards, $40,000, and will credit it with the cost of the forty old cards thrown out, $30,000.

For purposes of illustration we will say that the old cards are worthless. When we credit plant account with their cost, $30,000, we must debit that amount somewhere; we will change it to Reserves for Depreciation. The transaction does not affect surplus nor any other profit account at all; we have simply reduced the asset account of plant by the cost of some machinery which is no longer a part of plant, and have reduced by the same amount the liability account of Reserves for Depreciation, which was created for this very purpose.

With a classified plant account at cost we shall have a good guide for insurance purposes.

In case of a disastrous fire we would have a right to expect a settlement by the insurance companies on the basis, not of the market value of the property destroyed, but of the cost of replacement; and in this same plant account, backed up by detail records, we shall have an excellent basis of adjustment.

And now, gentlemen, in all your work, whether for the textile industries or for other lines of manufacture or of trade, let me urge you to stand for good accounting, for accounting which is true in principle and right in practice; for complete and accurate records; for correct classification; for profit and loss statements which show actual results, and for balance sheets which reflect true conditions, always remembering that the accountant should be able to show "the thing which the manager wants to know, at the time he wants to know it, and in the form best adapted to his needs."

THE HONESTY OF THE AVERAGE MAN

When a sneak-thief attempts to walk off with our overcoat, or if a stranger borrows our best umbrella, we say man has no honesty; but we do not really mean this, for instances of the average person's honesty are brought to our attention every day. In New York city, and in other cities, there are restaurants where one may step up to the counter, help himself to such articles of food as he wishes, and after finishing his meal pay the cashier what he pleases; that is to say, there are no checks and no apparent means of ascertaining whether the amount stated by the customer is the full value of the food that he has eaten. Here is an opportunity of cheating that would seem to be just what the cheat and swindler are looking for, but the restaurant pays and has enlarged its business premises several times. It could not pay if it were not for the honesty of its patrons. A writer in the Chicago Inter Ocean claims that the average person is scrupulously honest. He says:—

"This may be denied by the skeptics who question the existence of any good traits in humanity, but it is nevertheless a statement founded not upon mere sentimental belief, but upon exact knowledge. There is proof of it in the experience of people who have to do with the 'lost and found' columns of the newspapers and the bureaus established by the railway companies, the traction companies, the theaters, the hotels and the great stores for the reception and restitution of lost articles. Not everything that is lost finds its way back to the loser, but in these bureaus there is constantly more property awaiting owners than there are claimants for it.

"Because now and then somebody loses something which is never found the impression is created, perhaps, in that person's mind that the average human being is dishonest, but the fact remains that only an insignificant fraction of the money or articles lost in public conveyances and public places is unrecovered by the losers.

"Recognition of the fact that the people, generally speaking, are not only honest, but scrupulously so, has given rise within the last twenty-five years to the establishment of a retail credit system that now spreads into every line of trade. The people as a whole are trusted as they never have been trusted before in all the world's history. Successful merchants in the credit line no longer regard it in the light of a risk to deliver valuable property to a man upon the receipt of a small payment.

"Costly books are sent by express on the receipt of a nominal sum. Furniture, pianos, clothing, watches, diamonds, everything that one can name almost, are now sold on 'instalments,' and in the great majority of cases absolutely without other security than the purchaser's bare promise to pay.

"The pessimist will find no satisfaction in the contemplation of these facts, but, as they are presented only to encourage the optimist, that does not make any difference."

THE PRACTICAL VALUE

"Do you really think it paid to give Josh all this education?" asked Farmer Corntassel.

"Course I do," answered the fond mother. "It's wuth money to know better 'n to say 'crops are bad' instid o' 'crops is bad.'"

"Well, if you say so, I reckon it's all right. But I can't say as I see how it kin make any difference in the crops."—Washington Star.

The Relation of Economics to Higher Accounting*

By JOSEPH FRENCH JOHNSON, Ph.D.

Mr. Chairman and Gentlemen of the Society: I regret to say that I must begin with the usual stereotyped formula of an apology, for I have not had time to prepare carefully an address for you, as I had hoped to do. I must talk to you informally about my subject, economics and its relation to higher accounting.

I have always had, as most men seem to have, a rather hazy idea of what is called the science of accounting, and of the exact difference between the work of the accountant and the work of the bookkeeper. There is a difference, however, and in my remarks I shall endeavor to make clear the distinction as well as the relation of each to political economy.

Economics is a science concerned with a certain set of phenomena. Just as the science of chemistry endeavors to classify the phenomena in the elements of matter, and lay down the laws which regulate them, so the science of economics studies the phenomena of the production and consumption of all things that are exchangeable; that is, of things that have value, things which we ordinarily call wealth. Economics is not concerned with what ought to be or with what ought not to be, but with what is. The political economist, as such, is concerned solely with what takes place and with understanding and explaining the facts of the business world. When he undertakes to suggest improvements in the methods of production or distribution, he is outside the sphere of science and is over in the field of art; he is applying the principles which he has learned from the science of political economy. So the economist who advocates a high protective tariff, or free trade, or the free coinage of silver, or a bank note system based on assets, the banks being allowed to issue as many notes as they can keep in circulation, is, in such advocacy not a pure scientist; he is in the realm of useful or applied arts. Most of the great debates and disputes which have arisen in the field of political economy have been with respect to these practical applications of principles, and have not concerned the truth of the principles themselves.

MISTAKES OF THE EARLY ENGLISH ECONOMISTS.

The early English economists in developing their science made the mistake of assuming that the facts of the business world were so complex and intricate that they could not be classified. To them it did not seem necessary to go into the markets, into the fields, into the mines, and into the forest, and there watch the processes of production and exchange, in order that, through a study of the facts, they might arrive at the laws governing wages, prices, rent, the rate of interest, and the rate of profits. They founded their science largely on assumptions. They assumed that man was an economic animal; that is, that all men were governed by the desire to get rich; and that every man would necessarily sell in the dearest and buy in the cheapest market. They thus developed what is known as a deductive science of political economy. You are doubtless all familiar with the names of the celebrated English economists, Adam Smith, David Ricardo and John Stuart Mill. Those were the most celebrated, and all of them lived a little too much in their studies, and so developed a science of political economy which applied to no country and to no people that had ever been in existence.

I call your attention to this characteristic of the so-called "Classical School" of English political economy, because it seems to me possibly to contain an important lesson for the modern accountant. I will refer to this later.

What should the economist do? He should get as close to the facts which he wishes to explain as possible. Can an accountant theorize to advantage with regard to a statement, of defalcation, or about the profits of a concern, unless he examines, not merely the books, but the whole property, and looks accurately and critically into all the details of the business? Of course he cannot. If he should try it, he would grope in the dark. Yet that is something like the work which has been too often attempted in the past by the economists. Now, however, they are endeavoring to get away from the old method and to adopt what is known as the inductive method, and in the pursuit of their investigations they are coming into very close relation, it seems to me, with the work which you gentlemen are doing. It is now recognized that the economist who wishes to explain the phenomena of the business world, must be very familiar with those phenomena and with their significance.

SOURCE OF WEALTH.

The earth is the original source of all wealth. The physiocrats of France, who made the products of the earth the most important wealth, were not far from the truth. The raw materials of all our wealth come from the earth. Here, therefore, is where the economist must begin his investigations. He must trace the extraction of the raw materials from the earth, know just how those raw materials are produced, know the cotton industry, the coal industry, and the iron and steel industry; know where iron and steel are found and under what conditions, in what climate and in what soil cotton grows, what wages are paid, why the wages are low or high, and so on. The economist must get facts like these. He must go into the business world and watch, not hypothetical dummies, but the actual producers and exchangers of wealth. And that, I am glad to say, is what economists are now trying to do.

You probably are familiar with the large number of books, monographs and articles which have been published in the last fifteen or twenty years, giving information of the kind that I have just described. Our universities, instead of asking young men to write disquisitions on the theory of value or the iron law of wages, are sending them out into the world and making them learn exactly how things are made and under what conditions, what wages the employees receive, how the goods are sold, how the raw materials are obtained, how they are transported, and the cost of transportation from the mine or farm to the factory, the relations between the manufacturer and the wholesaler, the relations between the wholesaler and the retailer, and the means of payment. That is the kind of work which the political economist of the present day is trying to do.

POLITICAL ECONOMY NOT AN EXACT SCIENCE.

I would have you notice that political economy is not an exact science. It is essentially inexact, for it is founded upon something that is always fluctuating, always shifting. It does not rest on bed rock like mathematics, or physics, or chemisty, which rest on nature's laws, but has its basis on your nature and my nature, your wants and my wants, and these are constantly undergoing change. Hence the economist who makes a positive prediction based on the events of today, which are all due to your wants and tastes of today, is liable to go astray. He can only say that the tendency is that such and such things will happen, other things remaining unchanged. The economist must always hedge when he predicts. Nevertheless, while economics must always be an inexact science, the pursuit of it is neither profitless nor inconclusive. Its greatest need today is facts. The economist wants accurate information in all the fields of production, industry and commerce. The statistical bureaus of the United States and of various states are putting forth a good deal of useful material, yet the facts within the reach of the economist are still very inadequate. They furnish only the most slender foundation for inductions.

ACCOUNTANT AND ECONOMIST.

Where does the accountant appear in all of this work which I have described as being within the field of the economist? Before we look for him, I want to run over

* An address delivered before the New York State Society of Certified Public Accountants, December 12, 1901.

rapidly the outline of a proposed course of study for the New York University School of Commerce, Accounts and Finance, in which it is proposed to bind economics and accounting closely together.

Outline of Announcement in Economic and Commercial Geography, Industry and Business Practice

I. COMMERCIAL GEOGRAPHY.

A. The situation of the United States in relation to the other continents—soil, climate, topography, mineral resources, with reference to the composition of our foreign trade.

B. The situation, topography, soil, climate, agricultural and forest resources, and mineral resources, considered in relation to the location of the industries of the United States.

II. INDUSTRY.

A. Study of the methods and processes in use in the following industries:—

a. The cereals and flour manufacture.
b. Iron and coal mining and the iron and steel industry.
c. Live stock and the packing industry.
d. Cotton, wool, silk and flax growing, and the textile industry.
e. The lumber industry.
f. The industry of transportation.

Principles of railway location and construction. Relations of railways to canals and other water ways. Principles determining the choice of railway routes. The technical side of railroading.

III. BUSINESS PRACTICE. A study of the business methods of production and distribution.

A. Methods of getting control of natural resources. United States land laws and mining laws. Methods of optioning property. Terms of sale, mining royalties, etc.

B. Methods of transportation. Principles of railway rates. Terms of payment. Description of operations, etc.

C. Principles determining the location of manufacturing industries. Methods of erecting plant, collecting labor force, purchasing machinery; organization of purchasing and inspection departments; operation of plant. Methods of promotion and selection of foremen and overseers. Methods of wage payment. Relations between employer and employee. Business aspects of trades unions. Management of labor difficulties. Rights of employer and employee. Restriction upon employers in the matter of protection of laborers from accident. Methods of cost keeping and of keeping a depreciation account. Methods of sale.

D. Organization of wholesale markets. Produce exchanges and produce speculation. Methods of dealing in wheat, cotton, petroleum, coffee and pig iron. Contrast of foreign and domestic methods.

E. Distribution of the products. Relations between manufacturers and wholesalers; dating ahead; manufacturers' agent.

That outline will give you an idea of the kind of preliminary work that must be done by the economist. It is the purpose of such a course of study to make the student familiar with the development of wealth from its rough birthplace in mother earth on through the myriad transformations wrought by the toil of hands and machinery, together with the part played by the railroad, the ship, the tradesman, the produce exchange, and the stock exchange. To the economist the world is a vast and complicated machine for the production and distribution of wealth, and it is his business to study that machine until he understands the function of each part and can explain the laws governing every movement.

THE BOOKKEEPER AND THE ACCOUNTANT.

But where is the accountant in all this work? Well, I think I have discovered a person who looks like an accountant. All through these processes of production and distribution and exchange, this person is everywhere hard at work. He is called a bookkeeper. In my opinion, he is not an accountant, but a servant of the accountant. The bookkeeper is a routine worker. He keeps the record of all the work that is done, and he keeps it in the way that he has been taught. His work is valuable, but he is not *per se* a thinker. I know just enough about bookkeeping to see how it is possible for books to be kept so as to give an intelligent record of the world's great industrial processes and its commercial transactions, without a single bookkeeper fully understanding the significance of the particular piece of work which he is doing. His work bears an important relation to economics, but he does not need to understand economics any more than the elevator boy out here needs to understand the laws of hydraulics or of steam engines. He has simple motions to go through, and the elevator rises or descends. But without the bookkeeper all this mighty sweep of industrial forces would be without significance, as meaningless as the blowing of the north wind. The bookkeeper furnishes the economist with the data from which he steps to the thing in which he is particularly interested, namely, profits. Profit is the incentive to all of our work. What profits are to the capitalist wages are to the laboring man, and the rewards of each are calculated from the data furnished by the bookkeeper.

But isn't the accountant also present in that work? Yes, he certainly is. I think he was there before the bookkeeper was there. I think the accountant had something to do with industry, with commerce and with political economy, for that matter, long before the bookkeeper—the record keeper—existed. He antedates the bookkeeper, just as Edison antedates the electric light, just as Franklin antedates the lightning rod. The accountant is not a refined bookkeeper, not an especially intelligent bookkeeper; he is not a bookkeeper raised to the nth power. He is not a bookkeeper multiple. He is a bookkeeper plus something—plus the wisdom of economics, plus a knowledge of law, plus an understanding of business, plus initiative, plus an uncommon measure of common sense. The perfect accountant understands every movement and the significance of every process in the world of industry, and is able to make an intelligent synthesis of all the records of each bookkeeper. In fact, he provides the system according to which the bookkeeper must work. Thus I conceive accounting to be much older than bookkeeping; not a development from bookkeeping, but rather the father or inventor of bookkeeping. The first bookkeeper must have been an accountant.

CREDIT.

What is now the significance of the accountant's work? Having invented bookkeeping and set him at his important task, is the accountant's work done? Before I can answer that question to my satisfaction, I must examine a certain great organization or machine which has contributed a vast amount to the production and distribution of wealth. This machine is the most important one which business men use. If any cog slips in it we have a catastrophe that brings suffering and loss to all the people. It is a machine which must always be looked after, night and day; it must always be in order; it must always be well oiled. It is the machine known as credit. Credit instruments have been used a good many thousand years, for the explorer's shovel in Babylon has upturned records of promissory notes and of sales on account; but the credit system as we know it today is barely a century old. At the present time the greatest part of the world's wealth is created and exchanged every year by the aid of credit machinery. Destroy that machinery and production and trade will come to a standstill.

Credit, if we define it concretely, is merely a promise to pay money. It is founded on confidence in the prosperity of the community in which it is given, and on the taker's confidence in the giver's ability to pay and in his willingness to pay. It is sometimes called a substitute for money, but it is more than that; it does more than take the place of money. It adds more to the productivity of industry than any mere substitute for money could do. I should say that it is rather a device or machine to increase the efficiency of money, and to make money capable of doing manifold more work than it could do alone; a device, we may say, like the lever, which increases the efficiency of gravity. You know that if we have a light weight on the long arm of a lever and a heavy weight at the end of the short arm, they will balance. Just so one dollar in the cash reserve of a bank can be made to do the work of ten dollars on the outside. The dollar, of course, must be in the bank. It is impossible to develop a credit system without any money at all behind it, but having the money, then by the aid of banks and clearing houses, which are part of our credit machinery, men are able to do a great deal more business than they could do if credit were not used.

Credit does the work of business with much more convenience and much more rapidity than it could be done with money. Credit, as compared with money, is like lightning compared with the old stage coach. A man can complete a transaction for a million dollars by a stroke of the pen, and since one credit instrument is generally cancelled and offset by another, many payments can be made without the exchange of any money whatever. Inasmuch as credit is the most convenient and the swiftest medium of exchange which the world knows, it is the one which all men prefer to use, and so it has come about that in the civilized world of today exchanges are reeled off, as it were, upon credit machines in astounding and ever-increasing totals.

One of the first steps in the progress of the human race was doubtless coincident with the invention or evolution of money. It is an interesting study to trace the development of the use of money as peoples and nations have increased in intelligence and in industrial efficiency. But the greatest advance in material civilization has been made since credit appeared. The remarkable increase in the world's wealth that has been made in the last hundred years has been *pari passu* with a marvelous development of the world's credit machinery, and at the present time all our prosperity is dependent upon the condition of that machinery. If it gets out of order we have panic, idle labor and general distress. It is, furthermore, the most sensitive piece of machinery in use. Through its agency economic forces, good and bad, are flashed around the world, so that short crops in the Argentine Republic, over-production in Brazil, over-speculation in Germany, or destruction of capital in South Africa by war, all tending to injure the delicate machinery of credit, are bound to react upon and injure the United States, even though we have committed no economic sins.

RELATION OF CREDIT TO ACCOUNTING.

What has all this got to do with accounting? It is my opinion that we have found a point of close contact between the accountant and the science of political economy. Of all the phenomena which economists are seeking to explain, credit is one of the most important, and credit is merely a matter of accounting. With imperfect accounting you will have an imperfect credit machine. With imperfect accounting, the production of wealth will decrease, and bankruptcy and poverty will increase. The accountant, it seems to me, is the inventor, the creator of the credit machine. Not only did he invent it, but he is the man who has the care of it, who protects it from violence. He must see that every part is doing the work which it is intended to do. The bookkeeper, to be sure, is also there doing what he has been told to do. I have a great respect for the bookkeeper, and I am inclined to think that there are many bookkeepers who deserve, on account of their intelligence and their knowledge of the processes of which they are a part, to be classed as accountants, and not as mere routine workers. Nevertheless, bookkeeping seems to me to be only a trade, involving a lot of routine work and a minimum use of the brain; while accounting I would put among the professions, where the maximum is done by the brain and the minimum by the fingers, the body and the muscles.

It is the accountant, and not the bookkeeper, who is responsible for this modern credit system. The responsibility is great. If the accountant is to perform the full service which his profession has charged him with, he must understand the industrial and commercial processes which the machine that he has invented is helping to carry on. In short, I think I would make him both an economist and a lawyer. He must know a good deal about business, or he cannot help the man who comes to him for advice with a story about a defalcation or tangled books or losses where there should be profits; he should know the nature of the business, the chances for loss, how the goods are sold, and the laws which govern the sales. It seems to me that the accountant, if he is to carry his profession to its logical goal, must be a very highly educated man; he must know both the law and political economy; just as the lawyer and the political economist should know accounting. The economist goes out in search of the truth and sometimes he comes home with only a bookkeeper's statement. Now, you know there are three kinds of lies; white lies—lies, and balance sheets. The economist like many other people, is often baffled by balance sheets, for example, by such balance sheets as the railroads used to publish in their annual reports. The accountant has a lot of work cut out for him. He must, for one thing, convince the managers of great railroads and industrial corporations that it is worth while to keep their accounts in such fashion that he who runs, having sense, may read and understand; and he must be ready to provide them promptly with the proper system of accounts. The accountant must recognize the full significance of the distinction between himself and the bookkeeper. His work, it seems to me, can be compared to the work of the United States mint, which takes a piece of raw gold and coins it into money available for use; or to the work of the bank, which takes your and my raw, unavailable credit, and coins it into a credit everywhere acceptable in the shape of a draft; for in like manner the accountant must take a lot of raw, heterogeneous facts and coin them into intelligible propositions.

FUNDAMENTAL PRINCIPLES OF ACCOUNTING.

I would like, for the sake of the discussion that I hope will follow, to suggest one or two principles which are fundamental in accounting, and which seem to bear a close relationship to certain economic propositions. One is that familiar law that debits must equal credits. That is analagous to an established proposition in economics, to wit, that the marginal utility of a good which is sold must equal the marginal utility of the money price which it fetches. Marginal utility is a term that economists have adopted to express a thought which perhaps can be more simply expressed. The marginal or final utility of a good is the utility of the last bit of the good that is in the supply sold, and it fixes the price. In the case of wheat, for instance, if it is offered at 90 cents a bushel, and only part of it can be sold at that figure, the holders must and will lower their price to a figure that will bring into the market buyers enough to take up the whole stock.

The accountant's treatment of money has suggested to me the thought that the first accountant must have been a political economist. Money, of course, is nothing but a go-between. Men are producing goods in order that they may exchange them for other goods. Money is simply a medium, and that is exactly the way the accountants treat it. You make money a person. You treat it as a sort of messenger, the Mercury of business, to whom goods are entrusted and from whom goods must be received in equal amounts, money itself being only the common carrier. The economist in his theory of money has reached the same conclusion, but he would appear to have reached it a little later than the accountant.

DETRIMENTAL INFLUENCE OF THE ENGLISH CLASSICAL SCHOOL.

I have no doubt that many other parallels can be found between accountancy and political economy, but I will not continue the subject, for I want to discuss something else. In the beginning of my talk I intimated that our political economy in its development had been hampered somewhat by the influence of the English Classical School. I am wondering if accountancy in America, since it must have been very largely modeled after English methods, has not suffered very much in the same way. I would not be understood as condemning either English economists or English accountants. The former were certainly the greatest that the world has yet produced. No country has given birth to any economist whose name deserves so high a place in our esteem as the names of Adam Smith, David Ricardo and John Stuart Mill. Yet these great thinkers were under the influence of their narrow environment; they were primarily interested in the economic phenomena of England alone. Their theories were all constructed to explain English conditions. During their lifetime England, from a modern point of view, was practically an isolated economic unit. The people were dependent for their support upon the products of one season, one soil and one climate. Goods were not pouring into England from all parts of the world, for that was before the day of the railroad, the telegraph, the cable and the steamship.

As a result of these conditions, the economists developed a peculiar theory with regard to capital, namely, that the amount of capital, or wealth, in a country determined absolutely the amount of possible industry. By capital they meant especially food stuffs and raw materials, of which England possessed only a definite amount at the beginning of each year. The English economists made the wages of labor dependent on the amount of foodstuff that had been stored up in the country, and so the rate of wages varied with the number of workingmen among whom it was to be divided. Increase the number of workingmen, that is the denominator, and you would lower the rate of wages. Increase the amount of capital, that is the numerator, and you would increase the rate of wages. This so-called wage fund theory has been abandoned by modern economists, for it certainly does not apply to modern conditions. There is no fixed capital fund in any country, and no limited amount of food upon which the population must subsist. No country is now dependent upon the products of a single season, but has tributary to it all the soils and climates of the earth.

IMPROVED METHODS NEEDED.

It seems to me quite possible that English accountancy, like English economics, may have failed to keep up with the rapid development of recent years, and that, perhaps, American methods of accounting, if modeled too closely after the English, may not be doing for industry all that they should. The custom, for example, of closing books only once a year, it strikes me, is antiquated. The 31st of December is a day of no more consequence in business than any other day. The business of the United States is no longer limited by the products of the season or by the products of a single country. The flow of goods into our factories and markets is perpetual, for they come from all countries, and find a sale in all markets. I am unable to indicate the improvements in our accounting methods demanded by these new conditions, but it seems to me certain that the old methods must have been outgrown. The entrepreneur cannot now be contented, I am sure, with a yearly balance sheet or yearly statement of profits. I should say that he ought to know where he stands every day, for not otherwise can he steer his enterprise wisely, keep clear of breakers, take due advantage of the shifting winds in the markets, and be always in trim for a financial gale.

Wonderful improvements have been made in recent years in the organization of industry. You are all familiar with the results, the vast aggregations of capital in great corporations and so-called trusts, the gigantic combination of railroads. Accountancy must keep pace with these movements. I do not know that it has failed to do so, but I merely call attention to the necessity for progress. The systems of accounting in vogue in England fifty years ago cannot be applicable here. Even that in vogue in this country twenty-five years ago will not suffice to meet the requirements of modern conditions. So I find here urgent need for the work of the scientific accountant. It will keep him side by side constantly with the economist, who is also trying to keep in touch with the marvelous development of industry.

I will close with a story which I heard in Austria last spring. I asked an officer of the government his opinion of the financial condition of Russia. He shrugged his shoulders. That was an answer I often got over there. I remarked that Russia seemed to be very prosperous, Minister De Witte having made out in his report that the financial condition of the empire was first class. "Yes," he said, "yes, yes, but—I will tell you a story. There was a man once who was very well off, and who had a son whom he wanted to give a good education, so that he might continue the father's business. He sent this son to a commercial school to learn bookkeeping. Finally the young fellow came home and the father said: 'Now, my boy, I have never kept any very strict accounts of my affairs. I wish you would go around and get all the information you can and tell me just exactly what my condition is.' So the young fellow started out and inquired into his father's business affairs on all sides, and after some weeks he came to his father with a good many pages of figures, and said: 'Well, father, I have got through.' 'What is the result?' The son said: 'Father, I find that you are bankrupt.' And it may be that if you send a fellow through all the figures about Russia, you will find that Russia is bankrupt."

The story points still another moral, for it appears that the father was disgusted with the reply and said: "Boy, you go back and learn some more; you go back and learn how to figure me out of bankruptcy." It is my opinion that the father was talking to a bookkeeper and wanted to make his son an accountant.

The Balance Sheet System of Accounting–V.

By GEORGE E. ALLEN

From E. K., Milwaukee, Wis.

Your articles on "The Balance Sheet System of Accounting," publised in COMMERCE, ACCOUNTS & FINANCE, are of such general interest and the arguments are so clear and conclusive that I am thereby induced to respectfully request you to favor its readers with some remarks on "Present Worth." In my sixteen years of experience as an accountant I find that the majority of business men and bookkeepers think that if they know their present worth today, and in a year from now ascertain their then present worth, the difference between the two will represent their profit or loss. I say profit or loss because they immagine that the business has earned or lost such difference, but they forget that a large part of their assets has not been converted into money or collectable accounts and that the gain or loss represented by the increase or decrease in value of the unsold assets may never be realized. Present worth seems to be more important to them than profit or loss on the goods actually sold and delivered. They do not seem able or willing to understand that in order to find the profit or loss on the business done, it is necessary to know the cost of the commodities sold and that therefore the inventory must be figured, at cost, instead of at present market value, or what it would cost to replace them. I trust that I have conveyed my idea to you and thank you in advance for anything you may be pleased to favor us (your readers) with.

Answer.—Present worth, to which our esteemed correspondent refers, is a very indefinite term. Judging from the foregoing communication, present worth would seem to be looked upon as the estimated value of any business at the last of a series of inventories made annually or at other infrequent intervals. Present worth, according to a proper dictionary definition, would mean such a business condition as is shown by a going balance sheet, wherein all proper allowances and provisions are made through adequate suspense and reserve accounts.

What our correspondent says, however, in regard to business men who estimate or inventory their assets at market values one year and go through a similar process the year following, imagining that, wherever a comparison shows an advance in values, they have thereby made money, is very much to the point. To compare goods or other assets on hand with the market value of the same is a harmless sort of speculation, which must afford a certain amount of excitement to one who indulges in it. To people who crave excitement such mental financiering, or, to use a slang expression, "making money in your mind," is much more commendable than to secure excitement by means of gambling or strong drink.

As a business proposition, however, there is no such thing as making money without selling something which has been acquired at a less price. It is a regretable fact, as our correspondent says, that many people do not seem able or willing to understand that in order to find the profit or loss on business done it is necessary to know the cost of the commodities sold, and that therefore any inventory must be figured at cost, instead of at market value or what it would cost to replace them. Any system of accounting must inevitably fall down which does not maintain a distinct and actual record of costs and another record of the expense of doing business. To keep mixing up current market quotations with the actual cost of merchandise is scarcely less illogical than to confuse cost prices with selling prices. In either case the result is a hopeless jumble, followed by the necessity of taking a new inventory as if no record at all had been kept.

Charging interest to certain departments or certain quantities of goods on hand and crediting the same to other accounts is another exercise of imagination more or less current. How anybody can make money doing business with himself is something that the writer has not yet been able to comprehend. Speculation between the different departments of any business as a mental exercise should not be too severely criticised, but as a serious business proposition it is scarcely creditable to the participants, yet this very thing is done by some business concerns that ought to know better.

The application of scientific accounting principles to any business can have but one logical result. There must be a division of all property into assets and liabilities. The additions to such assets and liabilities, and the subtractions therefrom, must at short intervals be incorporated into the primary statement of what is owned and what is owed. There may be endless subdivision of accounts, but everything is susceptible to this simplest of all classification.

From R. O. W., Toronto, Canada.

In a recent number of COMMERCE, ACCOUNTS & FINANCE, I noticed an article on the subject of the Balance Sheet System of Accounting, in which the author states that the sales account is credited with sales and debited with the goods returned and the cost of the goods that are sold. In following such a system, I presume you have some method of finding the volume of business carried on without analyzing this account, and would be pleased to know what the method is.

I might say that the system used by enterprising Canadian Accountants is to open a sales account and credit it with the goods sold, and debit it with the sales returned, the difference showing the volume of business, and in order to keep account of the profit or goods sold, an account is opened. "Cost-of-goods-sold account," which is debited with the cost price of the items appearing in the sales account, and an adjustment account is created and credited with the corresponding entries, the difference, of course, between the cost account, and the sales account, representing the profit. I would be pleased to know the method you use for determining the volume of business.

The Sales Account in the "Balance Sheet System of Accounting," while primarily a revenue account, and used for the purpose of ascertaining the profits on sales, and corresponding to the adjustment account referred to in our correspondent's letter as used by Canadian accountants, still it furnishes readily statistical records of the gross amount of sales and the amount of goods returned.

Along the Highways and Byways of Business

By VANNANT

The term "higher accounting," which one occasionally encounters nowadays not only when talking with the teachers in commercial schools, but also among business men, is peculiar, to say the least, whenever we come to look at it. I was talking with a business man of wide experience a short time since, when our conversation turned upon the use of peculiar terms in business, and this was one that was cited as an illustration. Among other things he said: "Some time since I determined to investigate the meaning of 'higher accounting,' and in an effort to exploit the real significance of the term I asked questions of several people. The first man I met was determined to be facetious, for he said, 'I suppose that higher accounting refers altogether to the price we business men are called upon to pay for the services of expert auditors and accountants, for, according to my observation, it is getting higher and higher all the time.' Leaving him I met another man, who likewise attempted to be funny, but his play upon words was altogether in a different direction. He said that higher accounting was that which was 'hired,' and that accordingly it meant so-called expert accounting or anything that had to be brought into the office from the outside."

* * *

After this much conversation I determined to investigate on my own account and find what I could by way of comfort in any direction whatsoever. I discovered there was such a thing, for example, as higher mathematics, and I commenced asking what comparison there could be between higher mathematics and higher accounting. Again, when I got among the theologians I found there was such a thing as higher criticism, referring to discussion along theological lines, and I asked myself the question, "What can there be by way of comparison between higher criticism and higher accounting?" The further I went in this latter direction the further I was off, for there seemed to be very few who accept the so-called higher criticism in a real whole-souled, old-fashioned way, and many there were that led me to think that higher criticism was something scarcely to be defined. It appeared to be one of those things for which there was no other good name, and in order to emphasize it and make it appear as something before the people, writers and speakers upon the subject lugged in the term of "higher" criticism.

* * *

It is to be noted in this connection that when we say higher criticism, we don't say what it is higher than. In turn, when we say higher mathematics, it does not appear to be determined just where we commenced measuring to obtain the relative height. The term higher is comparative. If there is higher mathematics, then there must be low or lower mathematics; if there is higher criticism, then there must be ordinary criticism, and, accordingly, if there is higher accounting, then there must be accounting that is not high. Now it seems to me that all this is ridiculous, and that there is no reason why the teachers in the schools and the authors of text books on bookkeeping should make use of such terms as higher accounting. Genial Bob Burdette, in one of his lectures, to which I was an interested listener years ago, advised young men to distinguish themselves from others in the community by some peculiarity. He said: "For example, you might be honest; not tolerably honest, but honest. Think of a tolerably good egg." What Burdette meant is, that a man is either honest or dishonest. There is no middle ground. By the same token either there is accounting or there is not accounting. Accounting is the whole thing. Like truth, which is its foundation, there is nothing with which it can be compared. Such a term, then, as higher accounting is an insult to every right thinking man.

* * *

The carlessness with which terms may be used, even by those who do, or, at least, should know better, was very strikingly illustrated by something that occurred some time since in the office of a well-known publisher. The gentleman in question was a compositor in his younger days. He had also "read proof," and therefore should have known the meaning of terms. He did not ordinarily read proof in the later days, after prosperity had overtaken him, but on a certain occasion he was personally looking after a circular that was to be issued. The type in which one of the paragraphs was set did not suit him. It was too large. He wanted it much smaller. So he wrote in the margin, "Set in smallest possible type." The foreman-compositor, recognizing the source of this most explicit direction, believed it meant what it said, and therefore he obeyed literally. He brought into requisition the resources of the nearest type foundry, and in due season returned the proof with the paragraph referred to set in type of microscopic dimensions. It was practically unreadable with the naked eye. With this went the apology that there was still a smaller size, sometimes made, but the foundry did not have it in stock at present. The publisher was aghast, and at first thought a joke had been attempted, but every one concerned kept a straight face and pointed to his plainly written instructions. He declared afterwards that the lesson was worth all it cost, including the bill for the new type purchased.

* * *

Is not "higher" accounting of the same nature as the growing rye about which the farmer offered to bet. He declared no one could reach to the top of his growing rye with his hands stretched as far as possible above his head. This apparently made the grain seven or eight feet high. On reaching the field, however, the rye was found to be just sprouting through the top crust of the soil. Of course no one could reach the top of it with his hands in the ridiculous position indicated. Is it not possible that what is called "higher" accounting is that which is just sprouting through the crust of the gray matter in the heads of those who employ the term? And that they use it simply to impress their hearers, whom they take to be geese, if not fools outright? It certainly will not measure up by any reasonable standard, any more than would the farmer's rye. Give it time and favorable weather and perhaps it will grow—but not any higher than the ordinary variety.

* * *

Speaking seriously, there is undoubtedly higher bookkeeping, but not higher accounting. Accounting and bookkeeping are as unlike as a fluid,—water, for example,—and a quart measure. Sometimes the circumstances of the case make a measure of the size named all that is necessary. On other occasions gallons and barrels are requisite. In extreme cases lakes and oceans become the only possible units of measurement, and yet all the time we are dealing with water. Accounting is the same for large and small enterprises, for mercantile and manufacturing ventures, for transportation and mining, for insurance and the affairs of the commonwealth and the nation. Accounting principles are unvarying, inflexible and eternal. Bookkeeping, on the other hand, is as plastic as clay and as elastic as rubber. It may be measured in the light of the requirements of the peanut stand and corner grocery, or according to the necessities of the transcontinental railway and the United States Steel Corporation. Let us give up all thought of "higher" accounting as we would the idea of "higher" honesty. Let us seek to know accounting as we would to know truth. On the other hand, let us cherish bookkeeping, higher bookkeeping and highest bookkeeping, so that we may be in position to choose discriminatingly, from time to time, as our requirements may be.

WHAT TO DO WITH $500

This is the day of big things; big piles of money among others. In the days of our grandpas, five hundred was a lot of currency, and a great deal could be done with it. The New York Commercial says:—

"While reading daily about the millions of capital in the great corporations of the country, and Mr. Rockefeller's income of $16,000,000 from Standard Oil stock, one cannot refrain from smiling at the recollection of good old times when the young man who had learned his trade started out for himself with a capital of $500. In those days reputation counted as capital, and if the young man possessed the nerve and ability, his own employers sometimes trusted him with goods on six months' time. One of the largest wholesale drug houses in Maine was started in this way, but it was many years ago. What can the young man of today do for himself with $500? He finds store rents in a city are from $500 to $5,000 at least, and in New York he might be required to pay down his $500 to secure a lease. In other words, it would be the first month's rent. Hopeless, then, to start here. In the West, however, he can find opportunities in trade, or in fruit culture, or sheep raising, and his $500 will put him on his feet and give him the independence which he craves, but which he cannot hope to gain in the East."

WOODEN BOOKKEEPING

We have read of the bookkeeping of the ancient Babylonians, who were said to have scratched their accounts upon clay and baked the clay in an oven, thus making a permanent record.

This method of accounting seems fitting and appropriate for a period of some thousands of years before Christ, but one hardly expects to meet with a system of accounts fully as elemental in these twentieth century times, but, according to the New York Herald, there is in Switzerland a body of peasantry who keep their accounts upon wooden tablets like those shown in the accompanying cut.

Very peculiar and little known to the outside world is the village of Vesperterminen, situated on a high plateau

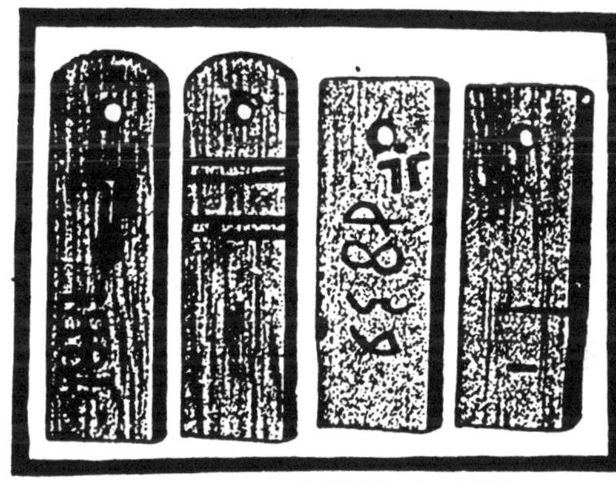

BOOKKEEPING ON WOODEN TABLETS.

which overhangs the Visp-Zermatt Mountain Railway, in Canton Wallis, Switzerland. One of the most striking peculiarities of these villagers is their method of keeping accounts, which are never written on paper, but always carved on wooden tablets. Another specialty of the place is the communal system of irrigation, which is of great and unknown antiquity.

The illustration shows the front and back of two tablets relating to irrigation. On the face are initials and private marks, which indicate the possessor of the water right, while the marks on the back show how much water he is entitled to. A groove cut entirely across the tablet denotes the right to turn on the water four hours daily for three weeks. A groove half way across authorizes two hours, a circle twenty minutes and a semi-circle ten minutes' daily use during the same period.

The water comes from glaciers, and, like that of the Nile, contains a fructifying alluvium. It fertilizes not only pasture and meadow, but vineyards, probably the most elevated in Europe—four thousand feet above sea level—from which a strong, sweet wine is obtained.

But these little tablets, which are about three inches long, are used for records of all sorts and strung on cords. There are bake tablets, which mark the order in which families may use the village oven, for each family bakes only twice a year.

Tithes, rents, interest and many other things are recorded on certain tablets, or "tesslen," as they are called. Some of them are kept by their respective owners, others are filed away in the communal archives. The legends, superstitions, manners and customs of this isolated community are very singular and interesting. The place has just been "discovered" by a Zurich professor, who has described it in the annual of the Swiss Alpine Club.

ORIGINAL DEFINITIONS

Here are some examples in which the child has been asked to define the meanings of words with such results as: "Alias, a good man in the Bible; Ammonia, the food of the gods; Emolument, a headstone to a grave; Eucharist, one who plays euchre; Ipecac, a man who likes a good dinner."

The Isthmian Canal

The ratification of the new canal treaty by the Senate practically settles the question of the Isthmian Canal. That is to say, it insures the digging of this waterway by the United States and its operation under the auspices of this country. The immense importance of the work is appreciated by every one. Its completion will simply mean this: that a vessel bound from New York to the western coast of the United States, or to any point in the Pacific Ocean or the Far East north of Hong Kong, will be enabled to make the passage in a much shorter time than is now possible, and avoid all the dangers of the South American coast, Cape Horn in particular. Vessels from New York bound for ports south of Hong Kong will still find the quicker passage via the Suez Canal or around the Cape of Good Hope.

FIRST REPORT OF THE GOVERNMENT COMMISSION.

A month ago it seemed that the question of the route of the canal was practically settled in favor of the Nicaragua route, in preference to that through Panama, the commission appointed by the government to inquire into the merits of the two routes having then decided that the Nicaragua was the better. The commission in its first report estimated the cost of the Nicaragua Canal at $189,864,062. It, at that time, estimated also that the cost of the construction of the Panama Canal would be about $144,233,358, but that it would cost $109,141,000 to obtain the Panama concession. A newspaper writer, discussing this report at the time of its appearance, said:—

The report says the Panama route is feasible as a sea level canal, while the Nicaragua route must be by locks, but Lake Nicaragua will furnish an inexhaustible supply of water for the canal. The Nicaragua route has no natural harbors at either end, but satisfactory harbors may be constructed. Harbors already exist at each end of the Panama route, but considerable work must be done at the entrance of the harbor on the Atlantic side.

With adequate force and plant the commission estimate that the Nicaragua Canal can be completed in six years, exclusive of two years for preparation. Ten years is estimated to complete the Panama Canal.

The total length of the Nicaragua route is 183.66 miles, and the Panama route 49.09 miles. The estimated cost of operating and maintaining the Nicaragua Canal annually is $1,350,000 greater than that of the Panama Canal. The estimated time for a deep draught vessel to pass through the Panama Canal is twelve hours, and through the Nicaragua Canal thirty-three hours. The Nicaragua route, the report says, is most advantageous for commerce save that originating on the west coast of South America. Hygienic conditions also favor Nicaragua.

The commission says the United States should acquire control of a strip of territory ten miles wide from sea to sea through which to build the canal. The consent of Nicaragua and Costa Rica must be obtained to construct the canal, but the report says this can easily be secured. The report concludes as follows: "This commission is of the opinion that the most practicable and feasible route for an Isthmian canal, to be under the control, management and ownership of the United States is that known as the Nicaragua route."

But this first report of the commission was based on the fact that France refused to sell the plant, right of way, construction machinery, etc., belonging to the Panama Canal except at a very high figure. Since that time, however, her price has dropped to $40,000,000, instead of $109,000,000, as previously quoted. In view of this reduced price the commission reconsidered the matter and at once decided that the Panama route was the more feasible and should be adopted by the United States. The situation is somewhat complicated, as the House of Representatives, prior to the receipt of the second report of the canal commission, passed a bill for the construction of the canal through Nicaragua. The Senate is now wrestling with the problem, and the debate on the question of route seems likely to be somewhat protracted.

THE TWO ROUTES COMPARED.

A recent writer on the subject has very ably compared the relative advantages of the Nicaragua and Panama route. He says, in part:—

The value of an isthmian canal depends upon the difference between the tolls charged by the canal and the expense it saves in shortened voyages and transfers of freight. To be a public benefit its tolls must be less than the cost of transferring freight to the Panama Railroad, hauling it across the forty-seven miles of that line and reloading it on the other side. The canal will be compelled also to compete with the Tehauntepec Railroad, 190 miles in length, on a route very much shorter between points in the northern hemisphere than by way of either canal. For these reasons to be a success the interoceanic canal must not only be a first-class canal, operated at low rates, but must be located on the most favorable route.

While both the Panama and Nicaragua routes involve engineering feats of great magnitude, they are both entirely feasible. Both have ample and certain water supplies and can control their surplus waters with certainty and safety. Both can be constructed in about ten years, and can be maintained in a high state of efficiency. In all these respects the routes are about equal.

No construction work has been done in Nicaragua, while in Panama about $60,000,000 worth of work has been done, but the partly constructed canal with its concessions belongs to a French company which is prohibited from transferring it to any government. It might, however, relinquish its rights for a sufficient consideration, thus leaving the Columbian Government free to negotiate a new concession with the United States. The Isthmian Canal Commission in its preliminary report, estimates that a canal of 35 feet depth, 150 feet bottom width and duplicate locks of large dimensions, would cost $58,000,000 more at Nicaragua than the completion of the Panama Canal on a similar basis. We will assume that this figure represents the present value of the Panama Canal, and that the works could be purchased

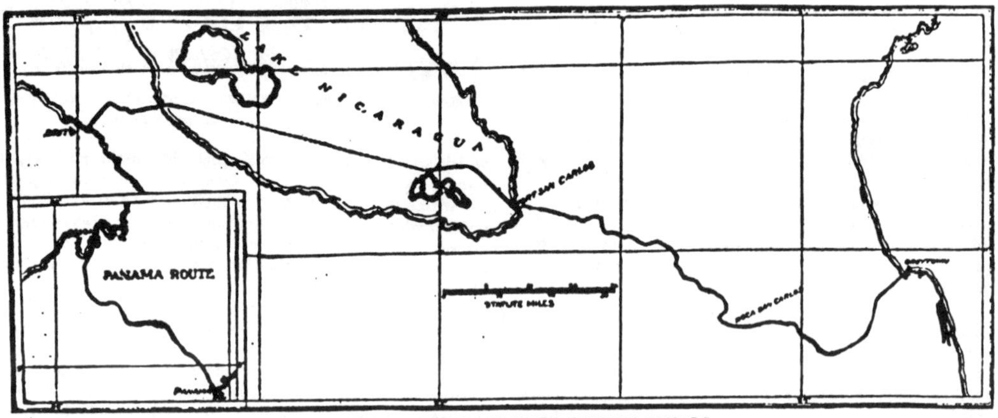

MAP SHOWING ROUTES OF THE ISTHMIAN CANALS.

and a satisfactory concession could be obtained from Colombia for that amount, making the completed canal cost the same as the Nicaragua. It then remains to compare the canals as to cost of operation and maintenance, and relative utility. In making this comparison we will adopt the plans

Miss Panama—"I assure you, sir, this model canal only wants a little careful attention, and it will work beautifully!"

Uncle Sam—"Ah, but this firm reckons to make me a brand new one for less money!"—Punch.

recommended by the Isthmian Canal Commission, and accept, as far as they go, the official estimates and figures.

To arrive at the cost of maintaining and operating the canal, we have recourse to comparison with other canals already constructed and in operation. The following table

Uncle Sam—"Take your choice."—Cleveland Plain Dealer.

shows the traffic and expenses for recent years of the principal canals of the world, according to their official reports:

TRAFFIC AND COST OF OPERATION OF SHIP CANALS.

Year.	Traffic in tons.	Annual cost.	Cost per ton-mile.
Manchester—35.5 Miles.			
1898	$2.595.585	$861,976	$.0093
1899	2,778,108	927,140	.0094
1900	3,060,516	1,004,333	.0092
Mean cost per ton-mile			$.0093
Suez—80 miles.			
1898	9,238,603	1,592,834	.0022
1899	9,895,630	1,661,042	.0021
1900	9,738,152	1,742,717	.0022
Mean cost per ton-mile			$.0022
Keil—61.6 miles.			
1898	3,117,840	492,080	.0026
1899	3,488,767	540,128	.0025
Mean cost per ton-mile			$.0025

King Edward—"Build the canal! Why certainly; you may do anything you please."—Philadelphia North American.

Year.	Traffic in tons.	Annual cost.	Cost per ton-mile.
Sault Ste. Marie—1.6 miles.			
1897	17,619,933	78,104	.0028
1898	18,622,754	58,890	.0020
1899	21,958,347	90,307	.0026
1900	22,315,834	79,293	.0022
Mean cost per ton-mile			$.0024
Average of all four			$.0041

These figures show a wide divergence in traffic cost, which may be explained in part by examination of the following table comparing the canals in length, alignment, locks, traffic, etc.:

COMPARISON OF SHIP CANALS.

	Suez.	Manchester.	Keil.	Panama.	Nicaragua.	Sault Ste. Marie
Length, miles	88	35.5	61.6	47	187	1.6
In natural lakes	8	0	4	0	49	0
Bottom width, feet	122	120	72	150	150	108
Depth, feet	28	26	29.5	35	35	21
Cost, million dollars	115	76	37	200	200	7.85
Number of locks	0	5	2	5	9	1
Maximum lift, feet	0	16.5	16	43	37	18
Radius sharpest curve, in feet	5900	1980	3280	6234	4000	*—
Percentage, straight	..	56	63	57	..	100
Traffic began	1870	1894	1895	..	..	1855
Traffic, 1890 in 1000 tons	9985	2778	3489	..	..	21,958

*Infinite.

The questions of curvature and number of locks have, of course, much to do with the traffic cost. The writer from whom we have quoted goes on, in the course of an elaborate argument, to prove that the Panama Canal, generally speaking, would be cheaper to operate than that through Nicaragua. He quotes figures to show that if tolls were made to just cover expenses, their sum would be thirty-six cents per ton lower by the Panama than by the Nicaragua route:—

The total length of the Nicaragua route is 187 miles, of which forty-nine are deep water in the lake, where vessels can travel at full speed, and are not properly part of the canal, leaving 138 miles of river and canal proper. Eighteen miles of the river require no improvement other than the construction of the dam, and will require little attention for maintenance, but will require lighting, attendance of tugs, telegraph service, etc., and will be included in cost of operation and maintenance, while the lake will be excluded, though it will also require some lights, and telegraph wires must go around it.

The length of the Panama Canal is about forty-seven

Panama Promoter—"Hold on, Uncle Sam, here's a cheaper one—already broken."—Chicago Record-Herald.

miles, of which ten are in Lake Bohio, which is really the Chagres River impounded by the Bohio dam, but being of the same nature as the eighteen miles of San Juan River on the Nicaragua route, it will, like that, be charged for operation and maintenance.

No trade between Europe and the Orient can use with profit the Isthmian Canal. Trade of this kind will still continue to use the Suez route. There are, however, eight typical routes of traffic that will use the Isthmian Canal.

The following table shows the relative distances saved for these eight classes of traffic, allowing for delay in transit, as above indicated:

COMPARISON OF DISTANCES SAVED BY NICARAGUA AND PANAMA CANALS.

To San Francisco

From	Via Nicaragua. Miles.	Via Panama. Miles.	Saved Via Nicaragua. Miles.
New York	5,040	5,340	300
Liverpool	7,770	8,080	310
New Orleans	4,240	4,740	500

How happy could I be with either,
Were t'other dear charmer away!"—N. Y. Tribune.

To Yokohoma via Honolulu

	Miles.	Miles.	Saved Via Nicaragua. Miles.
New York	10,870	11,050	180
New Orleans	10,070	10,450	380

To Guayaquil, Ecuador

	Miles.	Miles.	Saved Via Panama. Miles.
New York	3,367	2,904	463
Liverpool	6,097	5,643	454
New Orleans	2,564	2,303	261

It will be observed that Nicaragua holds the advantage in five of the eight classes, estimated at about two-thirds of the

"Well, now, this offer is worth considering."—Philadelphia Inquirer.

traffic, while Panama holds the advantage in three, estimated at about one-third of the total. The largest advantage in favor of Nicaragua is on voyages typified by that from New Orleans to San Francisco, in which its saving is 500 miles.

Uncle Sam—"Well, I can't adopt both."—Washington Evening Star.

If we allow one-half mill per ton-mile for moving ships over the ocean, which is the annual estimate, we find that such vessels could use Panama in preference to Nicaragua, by reason of the cheaper rate of tolls. In all other seven classes of routes the conditions are still more favorable for Panama than this.

To sum up, sailing vessels to and from the north, or, say, five per cent. of the total traffic, would prefer Nicaragua;

steam vessels from Gulf ports to the west coast of North America, or, perhaps, twenty-five per cent. of the total, would prefer Panama, but might use either route with nearly equal advantage; while all the rest, or seventy per cent., would much prefer Panama, and the traffic to and from the west coast of South America in steam vessels, or about thirty per cent., would, by the way of Panama, save an average of nearly 400 miles in distance and thirty-six cents per ton—always assuming that these are to be based on expenses.

A glance at the map which accompanies this article will show the reader that the Panama route is very much shorter and that the Nicaragua route has the natural advantages of a river and lake. The people of the United States are much interested in the proposed canal, and the question of route is being discussed pretty thoroughly in the newspapers. The subject has furnished cartoonists with much material for clever sketches, and we reproduce a few of these. These cartoons need no explanation. They were published at various dates, and as they picture the various changes and phases of the subject they make a rather good history in themselves. One of the cartoons is from Punch, and gives an idea of how our British cousins view the canal question.

SCHOOL OF COMMERCE, ACCOUNTS & FINANCE

Diary of the Month's Work

Senior Class

RECORD FOR WEEK ENDING JANUARY 10, 1902.

MONDAY.
- 8-9 Lecture on Life Insurance Law, by Mr. Stevens.
- 9-10 Lecture on Surrogate Accounting, by Mr. Jos. Hardcastle.

TUESDAY.
- 8-10 Lecture on Banking, by Prof. Jos. F. Johnson.

WEDNESDAY.
- 9-10 Lecture on the History, Theory and Geography of Commerce, by Dr. Webster.

THURSDAY.
- 8-10 Lecture on Accounting, by Mr. Conant.

FRIDAY.
- 8-10 Lecture on Corporation Law, by Mr. Walsh.

RECORD FOR WEEK ENDING JANUARY 17, 1902.

MONDAY.
- 8-9 Lecture on Life Insurance Law, by Mr. Stevens.
- 9-10 Lecture on Surrogate Accounting, by Mr. Jos. Hardcastle.

TUESDAY.
- 8-10 Lecture on Banking, by Prof. Jos. F. Johnson.

WEDNESDAY.
- 8-9 Lecture on Evolution of Bank Credits, by Hon. Milton E. Ailes, Asst. Sec'y U. S. Treasury.
- 9-10 Lecture on the History, Theory and Geography of Commerce, by Dr. Webster.

THURSDAY.
- 8-10 Lecture on Accounting, by Mr. Conant.

FRIDAY.
- 8-10 Lecture on Corporation Law, by Mr. Walsh.

RECORD FOR WEEK ENDING JANUARY 24, 1902.

MONDAY.
- 8-9 Lecture on Life Insurance Law, by Mr. Stevens.
- 9-10 Lecture on Surrogate Accounting, by Mr. Jos. Hardcastle.

TUESDAY.
- 8-10 Lecture on Banking, by Prof. Jos. F. Johnson.

WEDNESDAY.
- 9-10 Lecture on the History, Theory and Geography of Commerce, by Dr. Webster.

THURSDAY.
- 8-10 A Talk on the Qualifications of a Railroad Auditor and Accountant, by Mr. Whitehead, Chief Auditor of the Atchison, Topeka and Santa Fe R. R.

FRIDAY.
- 8-10 Lecture on Corporation Law, by Mr. Walsh.

RECORD FOR WEEK ENDING JANUARY 31, 1902.

MONDAY.
- 8-9 Lecture on Fire Insurance Law, by Mr. Stevens.
- 9-10 Lecture on Surrogate Accounting, by Mr. Jos. Hardcastle.

TUESDAY.
- 8-10 Lecture on Banking, by Prof. Jos. F. Johnson.

WEDNESDAY.
- 8-9 Lecture on the Eight-Hour Day in the United States, by Dr. F. W. Speirs, of Philadelphia.
- 9-10 Lecture on Real Estate Values, by R. M. Hurd, Asst. Sec. of the U. S. Mortgage and Trust Co., New York.

THURSDAY.
- 8-10 Lecture on Accounting, by Mr. Conant.

FRIDAY.
- 8-9 Lecture on Corporation Law, by Mr. Walsh.
- 9-10 Examination on Corporation Law.

Junior Class

RECORD FOR WEEK ENDING JANUARY 10, 1902.

MONDAY.
- 8-10 Lecture on Money and Credit, by Prof. Jos. F. Johnson.

TUESDAY.
- 8-10 Lecture on the Theory of Accounting, by Prof. Kittredge.

WEDNESDAY.
- 9-10 Lecture on Transportation and Domestic Commerce, by Mr. Eaton.

THURSDAY.
- 8-10 Lecture on the Law of Contracts, by Mr. Bacon.

FRIDAY.
- 8-10 Lecture on the Theory of Accounting, by Prof. Kittredge.

RECORD FOR WEEK ENDING JANUARY 17, 1902.

MONDAY.
- 8-10 Lecture on Money and Credit, by Prof. Jos. F. Johnson.

TUESDAY.
- 8-10 Lecture on Instalment Accounts, by Mr. H. W. Courter.

WEDNESDAY.
- 8-9 Lecture on "The Evolution of Bank Credits," by Hon. Milton E. Miles, Asst. Sec'y U. S. Treasury.
- 9-10 Lecture on Transportation and Domestic Commerce, by Mr. Eaton.

THURSDAY.
- 8-10 Lecture on the Law of Contracts, by Mr. Bacon.

FRIDAY.
- 8-10 Lecture on Instalment Accounts, by Mr. H. W. Courter.

RECORD FOR WEEK ENDING JANUARY 24, 1902.

MONDAY.
- 8-10 Lecture on Money and Credit, by Prof. Jos. F. Johnson.

TUESDAY.
- 8-10 Lecture on Loose Leaf System, by Mr. F. E. Webner.

WEDNESDAY.
- 9-10 Lecture on Transportation, by Mr. Eaton.

THURSDAY.
- 8-10 Lecture on the Law of Contracts, by Mr. Bacon.

FRIDAY.
- 8-10 Lecture on Card Index System, by Mr. F. E. Webner.

RECORD FOR WEEK ENDING JANUARY 31, 1902.

MONDAY.
- 8-10 Lecture on Money and Credit, by Prof. Jos. F. Johnson.

TUESDAY.
- 8-10 Lecture and Review on First Term's Work on Accounting, by Mr. H. M. C. Vedder.

WEDNESDAY.
- 8-9 Lecture on the Eight-Hour Day in the United States, by Dr. F. W. Speirs, of Philadelphia.
- 9-10 Lecture on Real Estate Values, by Mr. R. M. Hurd, of the United States Mortgage and Trust Co.

THURSDAY.
- 8-10 Lecture on the Law of Contracts, by Mr. Bacon.

FRIDAY.
- 8-10 Lecture on the Balance Sheet, by Mr. Young.

REFUSED TO FIGURE

Apropos of the rising generation: A youngster in one of the lower primary grades recently had a small rabbit given to him. His mother found him the next day on his knees with the rabbit held before him in both hands, and alternately shaking it, and exclaiming: "Three times four." "Twice five." "Four times six." Shocked at this seemingly cruel action on the part of her usually gentle boy, she said: "Why, Harry, why on earth are you shaking that rabbit so? You'll kill it." "Well," replied Master Harry, "papa said this morning that rabbits multiply rapidly, but I can't make this one say a thing."

HIS PRESENTIMENT

"Raynor," said Shine, as he pocketed the money he had borrowed and gave his note for the amount, "you may think I am superstitious, but when I signed my name to that I. O. U. I had a vivid presentiment of coming trouble."

"Don't let that bother you, old boy," replied Raynor.

"I won't if you say so," rejoined the other, with alacrity. "The presentiment was that I'd have to pay you some day."

COMMERCE ACCOUNTS & FINANCE

A Monthly Magazine of Higher Business Education and Practical Administration. Acknowledged Authority in the Profession of Commerce and Consistent Advocate of Methods Up to Date and Above the Table.

GEORGE E. ALLEN, Editor.

Published Monthly by the Commerce, Accounts & Finance Company, 25 Pine Street, New York. Subscription One Dollar a Year. Postage prepaid by the Publishers. In the absence of specific orders to stop at the end of the subscription term the paper will be continued and a bill sent. Entered at the New York Postoffice as Second Class mail matter.

* * *

A "community of interests" is a phrase particularly pertinent to the changing conditions extant and clearly apparent to the thinking mind in this the opening of the twentieth century. The very foundation of the Republic are laid down and understood to be a community of interests. Each individual is recognized as a unit. Men in communities form towns and cities. They in turn form themselves into broader and more expansive communities embraced in the State interests. The national government discriminates on all matter pertaining to the greatest number of individual units.

*

These broad conditions hold true in every phase of political, industrial or social existence. The railroads, the great arteries through which the life blood of commercial or mental activity are carried to every part of the anatomy of the country, are pulsing more and more rapidly with the vital principles of the force of the nation. The business man must today recognize the force of this magnificent community of interests. Not alone must he understand that the interest of his own town are to be considered, but he must face clearly and understandingly the community of interest which is rapidly affecting the whole world. The development of transportation facilities, the telegraph, telephone, railroad and steamship service make the Orient and the Occident more neighbors than were New York and Boston a lifetime ago.

*

These unmeasured and unmeasurable conditions must and are affecting the promotion of business propositions. Today a man entering the business field faces competition not alone of his own town; but the competition of—in many lines of trade—the state and the country, and, in some cases, the world. This competition must be recognized. An understanding of the *why* that enables America to compete in building bridges in Africa or constructing railroads in standing of the why that enables America to compete in Siberia is found in the general discussion of every topic of interest, to the unit of community of units through the almost all powerful and certainly all pervading newspaper. In short the advertising medium. The dessemination of knowledge on every subject through the medium of Printers' Ink puts in touch and brings together the community of interest of the subject in hand however abstruse the matter may be. The entire field of human thought is voiced by the press. A subject perhaps of incidental interest to the world at large is, "briefed," in the news the world over, and thoroughly discussed and elucidated in the medium of the particular class of the community it represents.

*

Starting with the production of any article advertising becomes at once imperative. The statement by word of mouth advertises its advantage. Letter and circular tell the story to their recipients and the newspaper and magazine are eligible to carry the tale to all. From the multiplicity of mediums the business man must be able to descriminate publications which will be read by the persons who want or may need their goods. Taking COMMERCE, ACCOUNTS & FINANCE as an example, upon investigation its circulation is found to reach the man dictating the management of the office and interested in the simplification of business methods. This means the credit man, manager and superintendent. It means the very large industrial and financial enterprise where the bulk of business necessitates the economy of time in the production of the facts required, costs of production, maintenance, etc. This medium would then be particularly valuable in presenting announcement of any articles or financial propositions which would be of interest to this particular community of interest.

Printers' ink publicity under the various postal classifications commands the attention which largely insures success.

* * *

Chancellor McCracken, of New York University, recently contributed to the New York Herald a short article entitled "A Glance at a Year of Wonderful Educational Achievements." Dr. McCracken began by asserting that the initial year of the twentieth century had set a standard for educational achievement, which, if maintained through the hundred years, will see the whole world educated by 2000 A. D. He then went on to recite what, to him, seemed the greatest educational achievements of the various nations during the year 1901. Italy, France, Germany, Great Britain and Russia were spoken of in turn and their educational improvements named. Our own country was named last of all, and the following is what Prof. McCracken said of educational improvements in America:—

*

"In America, the events of 1901 are the immense gifts to higher education, beginning with Mrs. Stafford's transfer of $30,000,000 as the greatest, and next to that Mr. Carnegie's gifts to Pittsburg for technical education, and his proffer for educational work at the national capital, which is not, at this writing, accepted. After these come several million-dollar funds secured by various universities. University care for pedagogy has shown marked advance this year, especially in the Chicago, New York and Columbia Universities. Medical research has been greatly promoted by Mr. John D. Rockefeller's gift, to be administered by a board of seven trustees, each of whom is a professor in one of five universities, namely, Harvard, Columbia, New York, Pennsylvania and Johns Hopkins. A great gift for medical work has been received by Harvard from Mr. Pierpont Morgan. The bicentennial of Yale has marked a notable advance in that venerable university. The opening of the Hall of Fame by New York University is exerting a marked educational influence. Secondary schools are given this year important help by the College Entrance Examinations Board, which prescribes uniform entrance examinations for the universities and colleges in New England and Middle States and Maryland. A pedagogic crusade to the Philippines is proclaimed by the United States. Of nearly a thousand teachers, which the plan calls for, between one and two hundred have already gone. They will find vast obstacles, especially in the former managers of education there, who are mostly Jesuits, as well as in the ignorance and savagery of many Filipinos. Encouraging advance marks the work this year in Puerto Rico under an American superintendent."

*

The reader will note that only once is technical education mentioned, this once being in reference to Mr. Carnegie's gift to Pittsburg. Commercial education, in the strict sense of the word, is not mentioned at all, and yet the movement in behalf of technical education in this country has been greater than ever before. At least four universities of note have added schools of commerce or departments of commerce to their curriculums, and these schools or departments have competent faculties and goodly numbers of students. A great high school of commerce has been planned for New

York City. In Chancellor McCracken's own university, the School of Commerce, Accounts and Finance has made a marked stride forward, and the attendance is considerably greater than in 1900. New commercial schools and manual training schools have been built all over the country, and commercial and technical education has been systematized as never before, but the chancellor did not deem these facts of sufficient moment to be even mentioned. The reader will notice, however, that the Hall of Fame was referred to quite prominently. It was also mentioned in a part of the article not here quoted.

*

The Hall of Fame may or may not be a good thing. There are people who think it is a good thing, and there are others who deem it of somewhat questionable value. Dr. McCracken, it is needless to say, is not one of the latter class. We will not comment on the Hall of Fame idea further than to say that to attempt to choose by popular vote from the noted names of history those which should be recorded upon the tablets in such a hall is a decidedly difficult, not to say delicate, task. We will not speak of the practical value of such a hall, for it is not a question of practical value, but of sentimental and patriotic value.

*

But it is of the practical value of commercial and technical education that we wish to speak. There can be no question that a great majority of the youths of this country, and, for that matter, of other countries, will, after finishing their schooling, enter upon commercial careers. Surely the education which fits these prospective merchants and manufacturers and financiers for their life work is of real practical value, and of patriotic value also. It is of more practical value than the so-called "classical education," with its months of Greek and Latin and other ornamental flourishes. But Dr. McCracken, looking, we fear, through the spectacles of the pedant, does not deem the great improvements in and the systematization of commercial education which the year 1901 brought forth worth more than a line or two in an article of over a thousand words.

*

Commercial education, it is needless for us to assert, has come to stay, writers of Dr. McCracken's class to the contrary notwithstanding. It is more than an infant: it is a healthy youngster, and is growing very, very rapidly. We will venture to say that ten years from now no writer on the subject of educational advancement will dare to omit the subject of commercial and business education.

* * *

Foreigners are just beginning to realize the immense size and resources of the United States of America. It is doubtful if the citizens of this country realize this size and importance as thoroughly as do outsiders. It is only when we stop to consider what our great extent of territory and our 76,000,000 of population mean that we begin to understand how thoroughly independent our country has become. We need depend upon no other land for our bread stuffs, our clothing and most of our luxuries.

*

At this period when our merchants are struggling for foreign trade and are gaining it, when our manufactured products are selling in the "uttermost parts of the earth" and when we are acknowledged as the kings of commerce, it is well to consider this fact of our absolute independence. A writer in the Saturday Evening Post figures that our tremendous export trade amounts to only $20 for each one of our population. This writer goes on to say that a very little improvement in the consuming and purchasing power of our people will reduce that amount to insignificance. Let us consider what this means. Our boot and shoe manufacturers are sending their finely made productions all through Europe. This, of course, means a large amount of profit to them, but suppose each one of our citizens should agree to buy one more pair of shoes a year, or one extra pair and that at a minimum price—say, $3. That would mean an increase in the boot and shoe business of $228,000,000 a year. With that increase we could laugh at the German or Russian shoemakers should they prohibit the importation of American shoes. The same thing would apply to any line of industry. Only a very little more money spent by each of us would bring the industry upon which it was spent up to an astonishing amount. Our population is growing. If it grows at the rate in which it has grown in the past fifty years we shall, fifty years hence, have a population which will be astounding in its immensity. Our climate ranges from the semi-tropical to the arctic and almost every product of the globe may be raised somewhere within our borders. We are a great country and that's a fact, and the eagle does not need to scream in order to proclaim it to the world.

* * *

The interest in athletics continues to grow in this country. This tendency has called forth and is calling forth continually, frightened wails from scholars and pedagogues of a certain class, who see in it the decline of mentality and the pushing forward of the brutal part of man. They, the pedagogues and scholars before mentioned, point to ancient Rome and its gladatorial combats and say, "This is what we are coming to." But we think there is no cause for alarm, rather that there is cause for congratulation in the growth of the interest in athletic sports. This is a busy country. Almost everyone works and works hard. A healthy relaxation from the grind of business is afforded by our football games and college contests and our baseball leagues. They give us something else to think about and chase the musty office cobwebs out of our minds for a while.

*

The clerk who takes part in a football game on Saturday afternoon feels the better for it afterwards, provided, of course, that he doesn't lose an ear or meet with some accident of this kind. He does, or should, come back to his work on Monday morning with a clearer brain and a better feeling in his muscles. He does not need to carry his athletic ideas into business hours, and he doesn't need to think athletics when he should be thinking interest and discount. Our non-athletic friends, the pedagogues, seem to think that because a man kicks a football between the goal posts on Saturday that he will be tempted to kick the ledger over the chandelier on Monday, but he isn't so tempted, at least he isn't if he is good for anything. There is a time for outdoor sports and for indoor work and both are necessary. As the old jingle used to tell us, "There's a time for work and a time for play."

A PUZZLER

Last week one of the big banks, under the management of shrewd financiers and expert accountants, had to give up a puzzle that a young girl solved in a second, says the Pittsburg Dispatch. Through the mail came a typewritten letter that presented some strange hieroglyphics, puzzling to all, from the letter clerk up to the president.

In part the letter said: "I will require 4&("&."

"What does it mean?" asked one of the other, as the letter passed from hand to hand, and no one could tell.

"Show it to your typewriter," said the president to the cashier. He did so and she smiled.

"That's plain enough," she said. "It means $7,927."

"How do you make that out?"

"Easily enough," was the answer. "The writer simply blundered, neglected the shift key of his machine when he should have used it and used it when he should not. By not pressing it when he wanted to make the dollar mark he made a four, and by holding it while he thought he was making the four figures he made the characters above them on their keys."

She was right.

An Interesting Voucher Check

From G. J. R., Kansas City, Kan.

In a recent issue of your valuable paper the editor suggested to those who handle checks that they send in drawings of documents of this kind that, in their estimation, would not be objectionable to bank clerks. What I enclose is a rough outline of a voucher check that, in my opinion, would be entirely satisfactory to bank clerks, and I may say further that it also has the approval of the issuing parties, and the form submitted is not the same as the one now in use by the Armour Packing Company, of Kansas City, but has the same printing, same space for bills, for notation, for receipt, etc., as the one at present employed. The advantage of the plan upon which the sketch is made is that all the bank clerks handling this check can see all that they need to see on the face and back, the same as in the case of the ordinary check, without having to open it up and read the inside.

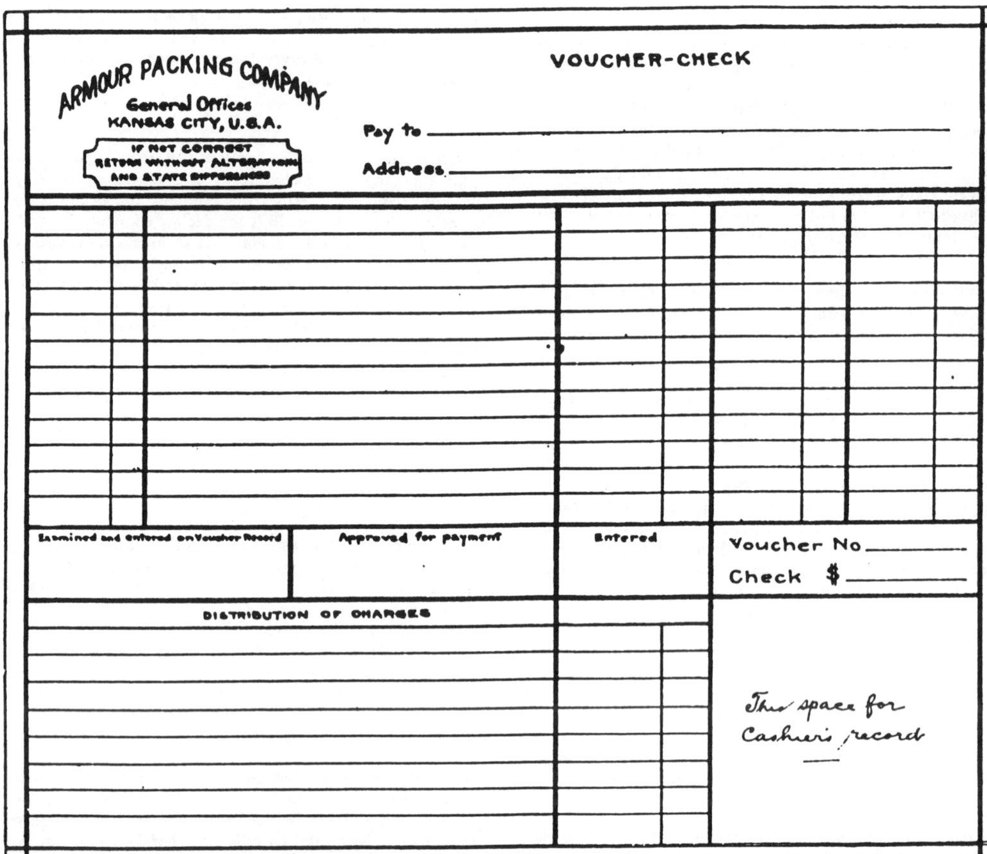

ARMOUR PACKING COMPANY
General Offices
KANSAS CITY, U.S.A.
IF NOT CORRECT RETURN WITHOUT ALTERATION AND STATE DIFFERENCES

VOUCHER-CHECK

Pay to ______

Address ______

Examined and entered on Voucher Record	Approved for payment	Entered	Voucher No ______ Check $ ______

DISTRIBUTION OF CHARGES

This space for Cashier's record

FIG. 1. FACE OF VOUCHER CHECK USED BY THE ARMOUR PACKING CO.

I hope what I have submitted may be of advantage to some who are afflicted the same as we are in this bank, and that those who issue voucher checks will take the bank clerk into consideration when giving their next orders to the printers.

Note.—We have much pleasure in reproducing by photo process what was enclosed by this correspondent and present the same for the reader's attention in this connection. The form, it will be seen, is similar in some respects to others that have been presented in these columns. The sheet of paper on which the check is printed when folded one way gives on one face the usual check items and affords space on the other for necessary indorsements. The inside of the form affords space for the analysis of the account and the signatures of the subordinates in the office in which it is prepared, together with description of charges. In that it is a folded piece of paper it does not meet in all respects the objections which have been formulated by some of our correspondents who have discussed voucher checks in the past. Perhaps at this stage of the voucher check investigation it will be considered entirely proper for us to offer a few words concerning the use of voucher checks and the principles underlying their design. A voucher check of late years has come to be a very important part of what is sometimes described as the "voucher system of account keeping." Voucher checks are legion in number when considered with respect to their design, but for the most part are included in the following general description. A piece of paper nearly square, on one side of which are spaces for ordinary check particulars with other spaces for signatures of subordinatees and the final signature of the disbursing officer and also space for the receipt of the voucher by the signature of the payee. On the other side is space for a statement of the account paid and the particulars of distribution according to the accounting system employed by the establishment issuing the checks. Originally the voucher was one thing and the check the other. Some bright man combined the two, thus putting upon bank clerks the labor and responsibility of which various correspondents have complained.

The question may fairly be asked, why should voucher checks be employed? Or, to put it otherwise, what is the use of the voucher system? Without fear of contradiction it may be asserted broadly that the voucher system is one of the best methods that has ever been devised for keeping check on the disbursements of the treasurer's department, in other words, of making up the treasurer's accounts. On the other hand, it is the poorest imaginable system from various other points of view. Upon the old plan where invoices received from the seller were fastened to and made a part of the voucher, the filing of the vouchers put those invoices away in a manner to make them practically inaccessible for any other purpose except only to check up the cash account. They were out of reach of the superintendent, of the foreman of the department, of the purchasing agent, and of everyone else, save only the treasurer, who might want to know sets of the business until they have been paid for or have been credited to the seller's account. It is best therefore, from every consideration, to pass upon invoices and make adjustments and distributions at the time the goods are received, instead of waiting until they are paid for. The best and most progressive business managers pay accounts instead of paying bills. The appearance of the voucher check in use with provision for distribution of charges, etc., is a confession that the accounting system, of which it is a part, is somewhat behind the times, or that the business facts of the concern are not correctly stated in the ordinary course of business.

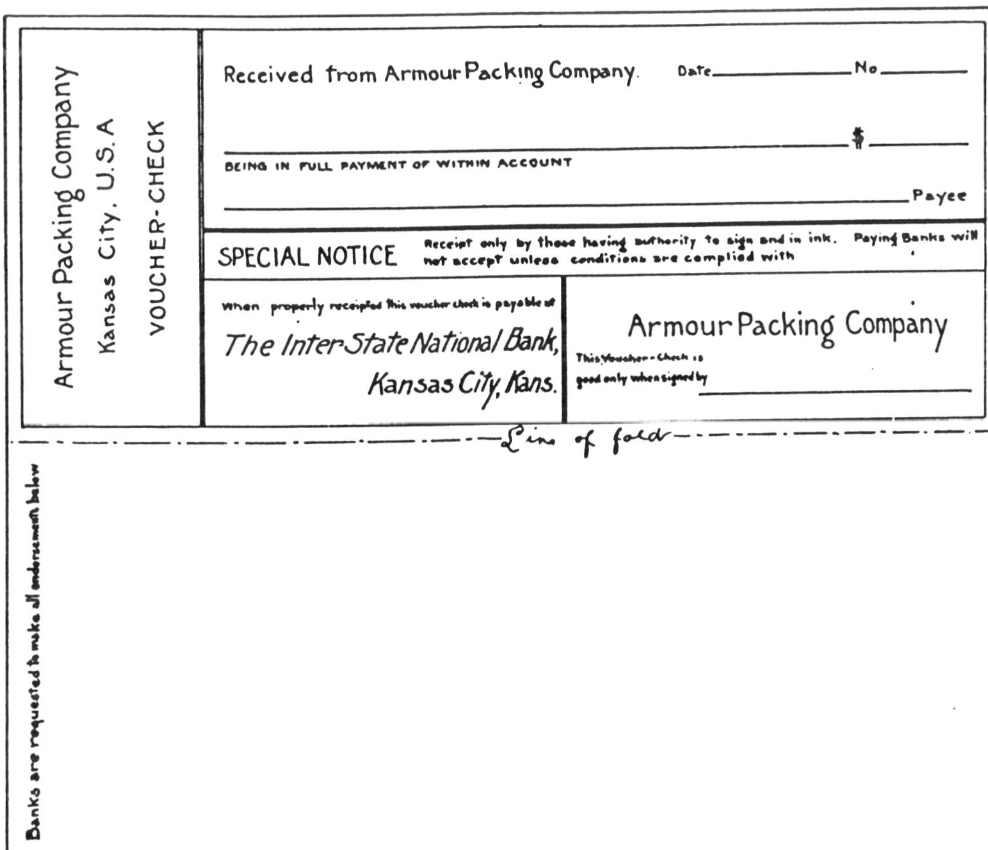

FIG. 2. BACK OF VOUCHER CHECK USED BY THE ARMOUR PACKING CO.

something about the items of the transaction. This objection is in part removed by the use of the modern voucher check, but at the same time this late article has brought us to question the extra work that it gives bankers and bank clerks. Why should manufacturers or jobbers, as the case may be, put upon their respective banks the labor and responsibility which the use of the ordinary voucher check requires? We think that the banks have good cause for complaint and objection to the system.

Continuing the question from the standpoint of mere accounting it has been proven in hundreds of cases that better results are secured by ledgerizing accounts at the time invoices are received, and afterwards paying accounts instead of paying bills. It is a mistaken business policy that does not recognize the presence of materials or merchandise in the possession of the business until the bill is paid, particularly when the payment of the bill may be delayed in various clerical processes, or may be voluntarily held up by the treasurer in view of the condition of his finances. Materials and merchandise purchased are very generally required for use instantly upon receipt. Ostensibly they become assets of the business. In fact they do not become as-

THE NAMES OF THE MONTHS

The titles of the months are modernized forms of those in use among the Romans, namely: January, in honor of Janus, a deity who presided over the beginning of everything. February, from the Latin word febru, to purify, because the purification of women took place in this month; March, from Mars, the god of war; April, from aperio, to open, this being the month in which the buds shoot forth; May, after Maia, the mother of Mercury, to whom sacrifices were offered on the first day of this month; June, from Juno, the queen goddess; July, the name given to this month by Marc Antony, in honor of Julius Caesar, who was born in it; August, named by Augustus Caesar after himself, because in this month he celebrated three distinct triumphs, reduced Egypt to subjection and put an end to the civil wars; while September, October, November and December literally express the seventh, eighth, ninth and tenth months of the old Roman calendar, counted from March, which commenced the year, previous to the addition of January and February by Numa in the year 713 B. C.

The Negotiable Instruments Law*

By THOMAS B. PATON

Place of Indorsement—Continuation of Negotiable Chapters—Transfer without Indorsement—Reissue.

NOTE.—As enacted in New York, the Negotiable Instrument law is divided into nineteen articles as follows:—

1. GENERAL PROVISIONS (Sections 1—17)
2. NEGOTIABLE INSTRUMENTS: Form and Interpretation (20—42)
3. Consideration (50—56)
4. Negotiation (60—80)
5. Rights of holder (90—98)
6. Liabilities of parties (110—119)
7. Presentment for payment (130—148)
8. Notice of Dishonor (160—189)
9. Discharge (200—206)
10. BILLS OF EXCHANGE (210—215)
11. Acceptance (220—230)
12. Presentment for acceptance (240—248)
13. Protest (260—268)
14. Acceptance for honor (280—290)
15. Payment for honor (300—306)
16. Bills in a set (310—316)
17. PROMISSORY NOTES AND CHECKS (320—325)
18. Notes given for patent rights (330—332)
19. Law repealed: When takes effect (340—341)

The provisions of the law naturally fall under four general classifications.

a. General Provisions.
b. Negotiable Instruments in General.
c. Bills of Exchange.
d. Promissory Notes and Checks.

The text of the law is the same in all the states (with some slight exceptions which will be noted), but the numbering of the sections, and in some states of the articles, is not uniform. There is, however, the same continuity of articles and text, except that in some instances, "General Provisions" follow, instead of precede, the remainder of the act. By following this course of study with reference to the New York act, as above outlined, the reader in each state can apply the same to the law of his own state.

The following section provides the presumption as to time of indorsement:—

Section 75. Time of indorsement; presumption. Except where an indorsement bears date after the maturity of the instrument, every negotiation is deemed prima facie to have been effected before the instrument was overdue.

The general practise in indorsing negotiable paper is to make the indorsement undated, although occasionally the date is added. In order to constitute one a holder in due course of a negotiable instrument he must have acquired the instrument before it became overdue. Section 75 provides that, prima facie, every indorsement, except where it bears date after the maturity of the instrument, is deemed to have been made before the instrument was overdue. This section is, therefore, important in providing the presumption of negotiation before maturity in case of the large class of unplace of indorsement:—

PLACE OF INDORSEMENT.

The following section provides the presumption as to the place of indorsement:

Section 76. Place of indorsement; presumption. Except where the contrary appears, every indorsement is presumed prima facie to have been made at the place where the instrument is dated.

A negotiable note may be dated and made in one state and indorsed in another. The law of the state where the indorsement is made governs the contract of indorsement, and if this is different, as it sometimes is, from the law of the state where the note is executed, upon the point of the indorser's liability, the place where the indorsement is made is a matter of importance. Section 76 provides that, presumptively, the place of indorsement is the place where the instrument is dated. If the indorsement has been made elsewhere, this must be proved.

CONTINUATION OF NEGOTIABLE CHARACTER.

We now approach section 77, which provides for the continuation of the negotiable character of the instrument.

Section 77. Continuation of Negotiable Character. An instrument negotiable in its origin continues to be negotiable until it has been restrictively indorsed or discharged by payment or otherwise.

Until, therefore, the negotiable character of an instrument is destroyed by a restrictive indorsement, or the instrument is discharged by payment or otherwise, it continues to be negotiable, even after maturity. But, in reading this section, an important distinction must be borne in mind between the rights of the holder who acquires it before and one who acquires it after maturity. Before maturity a negotiable instrument is transferable free from equities; after maturity, while the instrument may be transferred and indorsed in the same manner as before maturity, it is subject to equities. The rule of the common law, which the above section perpetuates, is well expressed by a New Jersey court in the case of Cumberland Bank vs. Hamm, 18 N. J. Law, 230, as follows:—

"Bills and notes remain negotiable, at common law, after maturity. They must be treated, after maturity, as negotiable instruments, subject only to such equities and defenses or to such objections to them or impeachment of them as they are exposed to in the hands of the last indorser."

The New York Court of Appeals, in Leavitt vs. Putnam, 3 N. Y. 494, also say on the same subject:—

"A bill or note does not lose its negotiable character by being dishonored. If originally negotiable, it may still pass from hand to hand ad infinitum until paid by the drawer. Moreover, the indorser after maturity writes in the same form, and is bound only upon the same condition of demand upon the drawer and notice of non-payment as any other indorser. Thus the paper preserves its mercantile existence and retains the main attributes of a proper bill or note, and circulates as such in the mercantile community."

But this court, and all courts, recognize the vital distinction that before maturity a negotiable instrument is transferable free from equities, while after maturity it is subject to equities; and if we regard the term "negotiable" as defining that peculiar characteristic or attribute of an instrument known as "freedom from equities," an instrument does not in this sense retain its negotiable character after maturity. There is, however, a continuation of the negotiable character as defined in the act if the instrument is not discharged at maturity, except that the holder acquiring a negotiable instrument after maturity holds it subject to equities. This exception is provided for in later sections of the act under the title, "Rights of the holder." To constitute a "holder in due course" who is entitled to enforce the instrument "free from any defect of title of prior parties, and free from defenses available to prior parties among themslves" (Sec. 96) he must have taken the instrument "before it was overdue" (Sec. 91). "In the hands of any holder other than a holder in due course, a negotiable instrument is subject to the same defenses as if it were non-negotiable." (Sec. 97).

Although we see that legally a negotiable instrument continues to be negotiable after maturity, with the single exception that it is subject to equities, this single exception is, after all, the main destroyer of the vitality of the instrument for all commercial uses. The chief value of a negotiable instrument is its utility as a medium of circulation from hand to hand, payable at its full face, free from hidden defects, and this value only continues with it so long as it remains unmatured. If it is dishonored at maturity, its utility as an instrument of commerce ceases; the mere shell is left, but the vital part has gone.

In connection with the transfer of a negotiable instrument after maturity, it is important, also, to remember the new character it possesses with reference to the time of its payment. The period at which the instrument was made payable by its original terms has passed; it now becomes an instrument payable on demand. This is provided for by Sec. 26 of the act which we have already considered: "Where an instrument is issued, accepted or indorsed when overdue, it is, as regards the person so issuing, accepting or indorsing it, payable on demand."

Republished from the Banking Law Journal by permission. Copyright, 1899, 1900 and 1901, by T. B. Paton, all rights secured. To be revised and published in book form by the author.

STRIKING OUT INDORSEMENT.

The next section relates to striking out indorsements upon a negotiable instrument.

Sec. 78. Striking out Indorsement. The holder may at any time strike out any indorsement which is not necessary to his title. The indorser whose indorsement is struck out, and all indorsers subsequent to him, are thereby relieved from liability on the instrument.

Reading this section, the student will naturally inquire when and under what circumstances is it advantageous for a holder to strike out any indorsements not necessary to his title? What object is to be gained by so doing, and thus relieving the indorser whose name is stricken out and all indorsers subsequent to him from liability on the instrument? The answer is that this right is generally availed of when a holder brings the instrument into court for enforcement against some prior indorser and desires to obviate tracing his title through certain indorsees previous to himself and subsequent to the indorser whom he is suing. If the indorser sought to be held on the paper has indorsed in blank, none of the subsequent indorsements are necessary to the holder's title, and he can strike them all out and claim title direct from the indorser in blank.

TRANSFER WITHOUT INDORSEMENT.

Sec. 79. Transfer Without Indorsement; Effect of. Where the holder of an instrument payable to his order transfers it for value without indorsing it, the transfer vests in the transferee such title as the transferer had therein, and the transferee acquires, in addition, the right to have the indorsement of the transferer. But for the purpose of determining whether the transferee is a holder in due course the negotiation takes effect as of the time when the indorsement is actually made.

Negotiable instruments payable to bearer are transferable by delivery, but, as we have seen, the mode of transferring a negotiable instrument payable to a named payee or his order is by indorsement by the payee or indorsee in one of the forms which have already been considered. But it sometimes happens that, through ignorance, inadvertence or other reason, the holder of an instrument payable to his order will transfer it for value without indorsing it; and the question then arises, what is the effect of such transfer, and what rights does the transferee of an indorsable instrument take therein by virtue of its mere delivery to him for value, unindorsed?

Section 79 provides for such cases and enacts that the transferee acquires the transferer's title to the instrument, and, in addition, the right to have the indorsement of the transferer; but for the purpose of determining whether the transferee is a holder in due course, the negotiation takes effect as of the time when the indorsement is actually made. In other words, a transfer for value, but without indorsement of a negotiable instrument payable to order, assigns the title of the transferer thereto, but the instrument remains subject to such equities, if any there be, as affected it in the hands of the transferer. If there was a good defense to the instrument in the hands of the transferer, the same defense can be made thereto in the hands of the transferee, although it was delivered to him for value, before maturity, and he acquired it in good faith; whereas, if the instrument had been transferred by indorsement before maturity for value, the good faith transferee would then take not only the transferer's title, but also a right of enforcement of the instrument free from equities, not possessed by the transferer, assuming that it was subject to certain equities in his hands. Indorsement, then, of instruments payable to order is essential to their transfer free from equities. The law, it is seen, provides that the transferee for value without indorsement has the right to have the indorsement of the transferer, but where he obtains such subsequent indorsement his right to enforce the instrument free from equities as a holder in due course is determinable, not with reference to the time when he actually paid value for the instrument and received it by delivery unindorsed, but with reference to the time the indorsement is actually made. If, for example, he does not succeed in obtaining the transferer's indorsement until after maturity, the privilege of freedom from equities has ceased.

RE-ISSUE OR SECOND NEGOTIATION.

We come now to the concluding section of "Article 4—Negotiation of the instrument," which provides for the case of a re-issue or second negotiation of the instrument by a prior party thereto.

It is as follows:—

Section 80. When prior party may negotiate instrument. Where an instrument is negotiated back to a prior party, such party may, subject to the provisions of this act, reissue and further negotiate the same. Bue he is not entitled to enforce payment thereof against any intervening party to whom he was personally liable.

This section should be read in connection with sections 200-202, relating to the discharge of instruments by parties primarily and secondarily liable thereon. Under section 80 we see, when an instrument comes into the hands of some prior party, who has formerly issued or indorsed it away, it is not necessarily dead as a commercial instrument, but it may again be negotiated, subject to the provisions of the act. To more clearly understand this section conferring the power of re-issue and negotiation, we will look at various cases in which it might be applicable. A prior party may be a maker, an acceptor, a drawer, or an indorser. Let us take up each of these cases separately.

For example, the maker of a promissory note issues it, for value received, and, after passing through the hands of several indorsees, it is re-transferred to the maker for value given by him. Assuming that the re-transfer to the maker is prior to its maturity, the instrument is not necessarily discharged. Section 200, providing how an instrument is discharged, says it is discharged "(1) by payment in due course, by or on behalf of the principal debtor; (2) by payment in due course by the party accommodated, where the instrument is made or accepted for accommodation; (3) by the intentional cancellation thereof by the holder; (4) by any other act which shall discharge a simple contract for the payment of money; (5) when the principal debtor becomes the holder of the instrument at or after maturity in his own right."

In the event, then, that the maker of a negotiable instrument becomes its holder before maturity, not by payment of the same in due course, and makes no intentional cancellation thereof, he can, if he chooses, re-issue the instrument prior to its maturity, but, of course, all other parties whose names were on the instrument prior to its re-issue are no longer liable. If, however, the maker becomes the holder of the instrument at or after maturity, he cannot re-issue it. It is discharged, under subdivision 5 of section 200.

Likewise the acceptor of a bill of exchange which has been negotiated subsequent to his acceptance, who afterwards acquires it in the course of trade, before maturity may, although he is the primary debtor thereon, again put it out, or re-issue it before the time of its maturity arrives. An interesting case of this nature came before the English courts half a century ago (Attenborough vs. Mackenzie, 25 L. J. Ex. 244), in which the drawer of such a bill was held liable thereon to a bona-fide holder to whom the acceptor had re-issued it before maturity, notwithstanding the acceptor was the one primarily liable thereon. He was held to have the power of re-negotiation, and his acquiring of the bill before maturity was held to be a purchase, and not a payment, which would discharge the instrument and the liability of the drawer thereon. It will be instructive to state the facts and decision made in this case.

T owed £400 to M. M drew a time bill on T for the amount, payable to his (M's) order. T accepted the bill. Then M indorsed it and entrusted it to an agent to get discounted. The agent at first was unsuccessful, but finally procured a discount of the bill by T himself for £375. The agent turned over the proceeds to M, who remarked that as the bill was in T's hands, he (M) was thereby discharged.

This observation was not, however, communicated to T, who, before maturity, transferred the bill on discount to A.

The action was by A against M. as drawer, and A had judgment. M urged that payment by the acceptor discharges the drawer, to which the court answered that payment in due course, and as payment, would discharge him, but that here the money was paid before the bill was due and by way of discount, not payment. It was further urged that an acceptor cannot re-issue a bill after paying the amount, less the discount, in order to charge parties upon it to whom he himself will be liable. The court answered, not after paying in due course; but this was not payment, it was discount, and as regards discount, the acceptor is in the same position as any other person. It cannot be contended, said the court, that an acceptor or bona-fide holder of a bill, by discounting it before it is due, cannot re-issue it, although he is ultimately liable on it. Pollock, C. B., summed up the law governing the case, as follows:—

"When a bill has been created according to the custom of merchants, as a real commercial transaction, it is part of the general circulating medium of the country, and the acceptor, after its issue, stands with regard to a retransfer of it to him in the same position as any other person. He may, indeed, pay it to discharge it, but discounting it is not paying it; and if he discounts it he may re-issue it. Nothing will discharge the drawer but payment, according to the law merchant. Here the bill was not satisfied."

Of course, when the bill comes to the acceptor, at or after maturity, he being the primary debtor, cannot re-issue it. It is discharged. (Sec. 200.)

RE-ISSUE BY DRAWER OR INDORSER.

Having viewed cases of re-issue by maker or acceptor, let us take the case of re-issue by a drawer or an indorser. In this connection we must view section 202, which provides: "Where the instrument is paid by a party secondarily liable thereon, it is not discharged; but the party so paying it is remitted to his former rights as regards all prior parties, and he may strike out his own and all subsequent indorsements and again negotiate the instrument, except (1) where it is payable to the order of a third person and has been paid by the drawer, and (2) where it was made or accepted for accommodation and has been paid by the party accommodated."

This section, 200, is not altogether clear. Taking it in connection with section 80, let us first consider the case of re-issue by the drawer of a bill of exchange. A draws on B in favor of C, for value owed by B to A. B accepts, and C indorses to D, who transfers to A, the drawer. The bill has not been paid by B, the acceptor and primary debtor. Can A re-issue? Section 80 provides that when an instrument is negotiated back to a prior party such party may, subject to the provisions of this act, re-issue and further negotiate the same. But section 200 says that while, ordinarily, parties secondarily liable who pay the instrument may again negotiate it, yet where the instrument is payable to the order of a third person, and has been "paid" by the drawer, it cannot be again negotiated. It would seem, under this not very clear provision, that while A, the drawer, could enforce payment against the acceptor, he could not re-issue the bill. If, however, A should draw the bill upon B, payable to his own (A's) order, and after acceptance by B, should indorse it to C, who indorsed it to D, and A should afterwards re-acquire the bill from D, unpaid by the acceptor, there would be nothing in this case to prevent A's re-issuing the bill.

With regard to indorsers, the right to re-issue, after retransfer of the instrument to them, is clear under the provisions of section 80.

We shall go more fully into this question of re-issue or renegotiation in all its aspects when we come to consider sections 200 et seq. providing rules concerning the discharge of negotiable instruments.

ANOTHER INVENTION NEEDED

If the tireless messenger boy could only be added to the wireless telegraphy enough time would be saved to start a new series of leap years.—Saturday Evening Post.

SYSTEMATIC BOOKKEEPING FOR RETAILERS

The subject of a simple system of bookkeeping for retail stores, giving a comprehensive statement of condition as a basis for credit, has been under consideration for several years by the National Association of Credit Men. Several schemes have been submitted and investigated, but, up to the present time, nothing has appeared combining the essentials of simplicity, economy and clearness.

The growing importance of the matter elicited considerable discussion at the annual convention of the Association, at Cleveland, in June last, and the following resolutions were adopted:—

RESOLVED, That the Committee on Credit Department Methods be instructed to formulate a simple plan of bookkeeping for the use of the owners of retail stores, including a simple form of monthly statement showing in a comprehensive manner an analysis of resources and liabilities, purchases and collections, sales and the various expense accounts in detail, so that comparisons may be readily made month by month and year by year.

RESOLVED, further, that the members of the Association be requested to distribute copies of this plan among their customers and secure its adoption through that means.

To bring out, if possible, a system of bookkeeping which will answer the requirements of the situation the Board of Directors has arranged a competition in which a prize of $50 is offered for the best system submitted, and a prize of $25 for the second best system.

The competition has been placed in charge of a committee consisting of Mr. F. H. Meadow, of the Staver Carriage Co., Chicago, chairman; Mr. A. O. Kittredge, president of the Account, Audit & Assurance Company, Ltd., of New York, and Mr. Wm. A. Prendergast, national secretary of the Association. The conditions under which the competition is to be conducted are as follows:—

1. Plans submitted under this contest must be sealed and mailed to Mr. W. A. Prendergast, secretary of the National Association of Credit Men, 20 Nassau street, New York city, and bear a postmark not later than March 15, 1902.

2. The theory of each plan must be fully explained in typewriting, and must be accompanied by all necessary blanks and forms, with a sufficient number of entries thereon to exemplify the system. Explanatory matter must be typewritten on letter paper about eight inches wide and eleven inches long, such typewriting to be on one side of the paper only.

3. It is expressly stipulated that the National Association of Credit Men shall have the right to use all or any part of any plan submitted in this competition.

4. The decisions of the committee of award are to be final, that is without argument or appeal.

Contestants will be allowed the broadest latitude consistent with the requirements of the resolutions adopted by the National Association of Credit Men, upon which the competition is based. All essential particulars are presented above, and in justice to all competitors, no letters of inquiry will be answered other than to refer to what precedes.

CURRENCY FOR MAILING PURPOSES

The recent robbery of the Chicago postoffice and the possibility that the robbers will dispose of $74,000 worth of stolen stamps has called the attention to the need of some kind of subsidiary currency which can be sent through the mails, says the Washington correspondent of the Boston Transcript. It was never intended that stamps be used as money, yet the enormous growth of the mail order business has really brought that result about. The mail-order concerns accumulate large quantities of stamps, and to convert them into money often have to sell at a discount. Thus a "stamp trade" has sprung up which enables burglars to dispose of stolen stamps with little danger of detection. Congress will doubtless consider plans to print a limited amount of paper currency in denominations convenient for use in the mail.

Current Business Cartoons

The cartoons in the newspapers for the past month have been numerous and have dealt with a great variety of subjects. Lack of space makes it impossible to produce many of them in this issue of COMMERCE, ACCOUNTS & FINANCE. Prince Henry's prospective visit, the Boer war, the Philippine situation, the Isthmian Canal and the question of the relation of Cuba to the United States are perhaps the leading matters of interest before the public just now which the artists have attempted to portray.

And Still No End in Sight.—Chicago Inter Ocean.

The Boer war continues in its apparently never-ending career, and John Bull is worried in consequence. The cartoon which we reproduce from the Chicago Inter Ocean shows poor John examining his ledger at the end of 1901 with a very doleful face. As the reader knows, the ledger shows a decided loss. How better could the idea be expressed than by employing the symbolism of accounts?

Two Pictures of the Filipino, by Governor Taft and General Chaffee.—Chicago Record-Herald.

Prince "Hank Hohenzollern," as some irreverent Yankee has named him, is coming to pay this country an official visit, and we are presumed to be more or less upset in consequence. Among the various cartoons on this subject is a clever one from the pencil of Bush, of the New York World, whose salary, by the way, as we saw stated in an exchange the other day, is $15,000 a year. The cartoon in question is entitled "The Education of a Prince," and shows Emperor William pointing out to his brother the points of interest in a most awful caricature of Uncle Sam.

The Education of a Prince.—New York World.

Speaking of Princes, that Prince of the Steel Trust, Mr. Schwab, is now abroad on a pleasure trip, and all sorts of stories have been printed about his gambling at Monte Carlo. Perhaps he did gamble, and perhaps he did not; at any rate, the cartoon which we reproduce from the Chicago News is one of the cleverest shown for a long time. Note the expression of the three characters in the domestic drama.

The newly-elected President of Cuba has begun his Presidential work by recommending that schools be established throughout the island. It is a good work, and the seed that President Palma is sowing will certainly bring forth good fruit. . . .

Grandma Carnegie: "So you've been gambling? Deny it promptly, young man."—Chicago News.

Our little war in the Philippines still breaks out in spots, like the measles. Governor Taft thinks that the patient is recovering, and he paints the Philipino as a saint. General Chaffee, who is in a position to see the other side of the canvas, paints him as being a saint only when he is watched, and the direct opposite when no one is looking. McCutch-

The Sower.—Boston Herald.

eon, in the Chicago Record-Herald, has a clever cartoon on the subject, and we reproduce it.

tional Bank, Kansas City, Mo. The number is 4,251, series of 1882. The check number is A 330,250. It is signed by L. D. Cook, cashier, and F. W. Truman, president. It was issued on March 10, 1890. On the reverse side the figure C and 100 are plain. The number 4,251, in the center of the note, is printed upside down.

SAUCE FOR THE GOOSE

A farmer's wife bustled into a store in Washington county, Mass., says the Grocery World, the other day, and went for the proprietor with:—

"Mr. B——, I bought six pounds of sugar here last week, and when I got home I found a stone weighing two pounds in the package."

"Yes, ma'am."

"Can you explain the swindle, sir?"

"I think I can," was the proprietor's placid reply. "When I weighed your eight pounds of butter week before last I found a two-pound pebble in the jar, and when I weighed your sugar the stone must have slipped into the scales somehow. We are both growing old, ma'am, and I'm sorry to say that our eyesight isn't to be trusted. What can I do for you today, ma'am?"

For a moment the woman gazed at the tradesman over her brass-bound spectacles. Then she recollected herself and remarked that she had a dozen eggs which she wished to exchange for hooks and eyes.

GUARDING THE BANK OF ENGLAND

The Bank of England is guarded by a company of soldiers. The accompanying picture, reproduced from the Sphere and used here by courtesy of the New York Mail and Express, shows the guards entering the bank at night.

The bank was projected in 1694 by William Paterson, who was a Scotsman, as a joint stock association, with a capital of £1,200,000, which was lent at 8 per cent to the government of William and Mary. The bank therefore started as a servant of the government, and has retained this character throughout its career. It manages the national debt, holds the deposits of the government, and helps in the collection of the public revenue. The Guards (who sometimes march to the bank by the Thames embankment, and sometimes go by train) are on duty from 7 o'clock at night to 7 in the morning, and there are seven sentries on duty inside the building at the same time, each for an hour. The men get 1s. per night, and the non-commissioned officers 2s. 6d. The commissioned officer is entertained to dinner at the expense of the bank, and the men are also catered for.

HIS MAJESTY'S FOOT GUARDS ENTERING THE BANK OF ENGLAND AT NIGHT.

A TWO-FACED BANK NOTE

A freak $50 bank note caused W. H. Adams to miss his Christmas dinner, says the N. Y. Sun. Mr. Adams is a member of the firm of Adams & Smith, of Chicago, dealers in stocks and bonds. On Christmas eve, when the cashier tried to balance his books, he found he was $50 short, and Mr. Adams took it upon himself to try to find the shortage. He went to the office early in the morning and spent the entire day in counting the money and checking the books. Late in the afternoon he found a bill which had caused all the trouble.

It was a bank note, the face value of which was $50, but on the back of which was printed a $100 note. The note had evidently got out of the Government printing office by mistake. The face of the note bears the name of the Aetna Na-

WILLING TO ARBITRATE

"Are you willing to arbitrate?" asked the employer.

"Certainly,' replied the walking delegate, "provided I am given a reasonable assurance that the decision will be in accordance with our way of thinking."—Chicago Post.

Financial and Commercial Books

BANKERS' AND MERCHANTS' INTEREST TABLES. By Francis H. Coffin and David H. Moore. 13 x 9 1-2 inches. Bound in cloth. Leather back and corners. Cover and back title, gilt. Published by D. Appleton & Co. Price, $5.00.

The first impression received by the person examining this finely bound and printed book is the enormous amount of labor expended in its preparation. It contains, to quote from the title page, "Interest tables computed on the basis of 360 days per annum at 3 1-2, 4, 5 and 6 per cent, with an accurate calculation of interest on every sum from $1 to $1,000, and, by simple addition of two lines on every further sum, to $1,000,000." It also contains a 1 per cent one day table, on the basis of 365 days per annum, from which interest on daily balances can be computed at any time and on any sum.

There have been interest tables published before, but never, so far as we know, has so elaborate and comprehensive a set of tables been printed in book form. Each page of the book contains the interest for a given number of days, figured to a fraction of a mill, on sums of money ranging from one cent to $1,000. The amounts of principal are represented in boldface type and the interest calculation follows in a lighter face type.

To find the interest on $879 for 71 days at 4 per cent it is necessary only to turn to that department of the book devoted to 4 per cent interest, run down the 800 column to the given amount, and, in the next column, will be found the interest, $6.93. The interest on ten times $879 may be calculated in a moment by simply moving the decimal point one place to the right. Moving the decimal point one place further to the right gives the interest on 100 times $879, and so on.

A number of rules are given for finding interest at other rates than those given in the book, and in each case the volume is a very valuable time-saving adjunct.

The time table, which is printed in the beginning of the book, in black and red, is an aid in quickly finding the number of days between one date and another. The figures printed in black represent the days of the calendar month, those printed in red the days of the year. To find the exact number of days between one date and another, note the figures of each date, subtract the smaller from the larger and the remainder will be the required number.

As we said in the beginning of this article, the labor in preparing such a set of tables as this must have been enormous, and the value of the book to the merchant or banker must be correspondingly great. The volume has a thumb index, like that of an unabridged dictionary, and the table desired can be found almost instantly.

THE POLITICAL ECONOMY OF HUMANISM. By Henry Wood. 7 3-4 x 5 1-4 inches. 320 pages. Bound in cloth. Cover and back title, gilt. Published by Lee & Shepard. Price, $1.25.

Mr. Wood is well known as a writer on various economic and physiological subjects, and this book contains a series of able treatises written in his usual vein on the relation of the employer to the employed and the phases of the industrial question and their relation to socialism.

Among the questions considered are those of Supply and Demand, The Law of Competition, Labor and Production, Combination of Capital, Combinations of Labor, Employers and Profit Sharing, The Obligations and Privileges of Employees, The Unequal Distribution of Wealth, Money and Coinage, Tariffs and Protection, Industrial Education and Gold Production and Values. Every one of the subjects treated, and there are many others beside those named, is handled in a conservative spirit and with much common sense. The book is extremely interesting and one need not be a professor of political economy in order to understand and appreciate it. It is hard to see how any one can find much fault with the author's reasoning—only an extremist on either side will do so, we believe. With the reckless manipulator who "corners" the market on a staple article of general consumption Mr. Wood has no sympathy. With the great majority of the so-called "trusts" he is at variance, although he does not believe them to be the "soulless demons" that the extreme socialist loves to call them. On this subject he says in part:—

> Such combinations have been painted in lurid colors as dangerous monsters; but in reality, owing to natural limitations, no one but the stockholder need fear them. He is the victim of flaming prospectuses, unsound principles, and of an inordinate ambition to gain by a "short cut." The adverse experience of thousands, who have imagined that combination could override such an antique law as supply and demand, is very uniform. Many excellent financiers, so considered, have utterly over-estimated the power of combination, and realized loss through investment in trusts, instead of expected gain.
>
> But the trust principle may be employed in accord with natural law and the public interest. To increase production, cheapen processes and improve quality by systematic consolidation is lawful. A great university is an educational trust. Instruction in specialties, scientific experiment, and thorough research are all more exhaustive than would be possible in half a dozen small disconnected colleges. Likewise, factories, even though located apart, by becoming a unit may sometimes introduce new economics so as to better serve society in serving themselves.

Mr. Wood does not believe in too much of the so-called "higher education," that is to say, the university classical education. He believes that the youth should be educated for the occupation or profession for which he is best fitted, or, rather, for which he promises to be best fitted. He believes in the establishing of more manual training schools, more business colleges and the like, rather than the turning into the world of thousands of high school graduates, all educated upon the same level and all equally unready for any particular occupation in life.

The Political Economy of Humanism is a book the reading of which should benefit both the employer and the laborer. To be idealistic, life is too short for one human being to quarrel with the other, and, to be practical, such quarrels, when they occur in business affairs, are a waste of time, energy and money.

THE A B C OF BANKS AND BANKING. By George M. Coffin. 6 3-4 x 5 inches. 137 pages. Bound in cloth. Back title, gilt. Published by S. A. Nelson. Price, $1.25.

This little book seems to be exactly what its name would imply, that is, a presentation of the first principles underlying banking in the United States. The author in his practice says that it is designed to appeal to the reader outside as well as inside of a bank. It is by no means the last word or every word about banking. It may be said that it is a primer covering a field that has hitherto been somewhat neglected.

The chapter heads are as follows: Banking in General, Various Kinds of Banking, Capital Stock; Shareholders' Rights and Liabilities, Undivided Profits, Dividends and Surplus, Deposits; Checks; Lawful Money Reserve, Issuing Bank Notes, Borrowing Money, Loans and Discounts, Exchanges; Collections; Letters of Credit, Bonds, Mortgages and Stocks, Bank Reports, Examinations, Directors, Executive Officers, Their Powers and Duties, Internal Administration and Bookkeeping, and Other Suggestions.

The chapters are short and the book bears evidence of having been "boiled down" with a great deal of care. It is illustrated with a number of forms showing stock certificates, proxies, deposit slips, powers of attorney, lawful money reserve forms, and all the essential blanks and documents used in the modern bank. Some attention is paid to bank bookkeeping, although, of course, this complicated subject can not be treated at length in so short a space. Taken all together, the book seems to be just the sort of thing that a business man would like to have about his desk to solve any question concerning his banking affairs which may come up and to give him any facts on banking quickly and concisely.

THE KITE TRUST: A Romance of Wealth, by Lebbeus Harding Rogers. 7 3-4x5 1-2 inches. 475 pages. Bound in cloth. Published by the Kite Publishing Co. Price, $1.00.

Mr. Rogers has written a treatise, or, rather, a series of treatises, on economic subjects in the guise of a story. It is a wonderful story, too. Three American boys begin the business of manufacturing and selling kites on a capital of eight cents. That is the beginning of the story. At the end one of them, Micky Flynn, is President of the United States, and also President of the great Kite Trust, which is a combination of all the trusts in the country. There are 475 pages in the book, and the adventures of these boys is told in a lively and entertaining manner, and the fund of practical knowledge that may be gained from a perusal of the book is great.

The trust idea is explained, the fallacy of the silver question is made clear, an explanation of banking given, the greenback question is dealt with, Wall street and stock speculation are talked about, and the whole volume forms a well written manual on all sorts of business and financial topics. It ought to be instructive and profitable reading for "grown-ups," as well as boys. One wonders where Mr. Rogers acquired such a fund of common-sense information.

The book, while a good one to put into the hands of the boy just out of school, has also received favorable mention from some of the financial magnates of the country; and, though exciting, is a vast improvement on "Roaring Ralph Rockwood, the Reckless Ranger," and other classics of that sort.

THE BLAIR INK-MAKING FOUNTAIN PEN

There are so many kinds of fountain pens on the market that a newcomer in that line must have something strongly original to recommend it. The Blair fountain pen has the necessary originality in a marked degree. It differs from the ordinary fountain pen in that, instead of having a hollow chamber to be filled with ink obtained from an outside source, the chamber in this pen contains the material for making a supply of ink which will last from two months to a year with ordinary use. The ink material is contained in a small sack or cartridge which occupies a small space in the hollow reservoir, as shown in the accompanying cut. All that is necessary to do in order to write is to fill up the reservoir with water and refill as the mixture is exhausted by use. The ink thus formed is fluid, does not become muddy, and is said to be in every way as good as that obtained from the regular source. The advantage of this ever-ready supply of ink is apparent. Among the testimonials which the manufacturers of this pen proudly display is one from a soldier who served in our army during the Spanish War. He writes that he bought one of the ink-making security pens before starting for Santiago and used it during the entire campaign, in the trenches and out. He adds that for a long time it was the only pen in the whole regiment that was of service, owing to the general lack of ink. New ink cartridges may be had of the manufacturers for a small price. The new pen would seem to be not only handy, but extremely economical, for, as the makers, Blair's Fountain Pen Company, 163A Broadway, New York, say, "If a day's supply of ink is good, a year's supply is 364 times better."

THE BLAIR INK-MAKING FOUNTAIN PEN

FACTORY LOCATIONS AND RAILROAD FACILITIES

In this day of unexampled prosperity thousands of concerns in almost every branch of manufacturing are considering the question of better and enlarged quarters, cheaper facilities and changes in general that will give the business still better chances to grow and develop. Country locations are to be preferred above the crowded and expensive quarters of the great cities. Those who are looking for factory sites are confronted by various problems, one of the most important of which is the question of railway facilities. To go where transportation is expensive, where trains are few, where the railway officials are other than accommodating is of course a step in the wrong direction. There is no railroad running into New York that has as many different sites adapted for factories as the New York Central and there are no set of officials more able and willing to make it pleasant to the prospective manufacturer along its lines than are the officials of this road. We would suggest to everyone who is considering the question of a factory site to put himself in communication with the management of the New York Central lines. A letter addressed to George H. Daniels, General Passenger Agent, Grand Central Station, New York City, will be a step in the right direction. Maps descriptive of suburban towns, quoting rates, will be supplied, and thereafter the freight department will be glad to take up the question with respect to other points that will come up for discussion.

CONFEDERATE BONDS

If the following newspaper yarn is true, there are people with queer ideas living in England:—

It is surprising that there are in England many persons who still cherish the delusion that the bonds of the Southern Confederacy will be paid, reports the Atlanta Journal. Some of them are men who have been eminently successful in business. They have an organization known as the British Capitalist Association, and it had a meeting a few days ago. The secretary reported that the society had $40,000,000 of Confederate bonds and $25,000,000 of the bonds of the states of Virginia, Mississippi and Louisiana. The value of these securities was discussed, and several members declared their faith that they would be paid by the United States government. These Utopians are as wild as those who expect to get pay for their emancipated slaves.

Some years ago there was quite a demand for Confederate bonds. They were advertised for in many Southern newspapers, and brokers were commissioned to buy them. The last appearance of this craze was in 1880, we believe, and even then as much as $12 and $15 a thousand was paid for Confederate bonds. We know of several persons in Atlanta who sold large quantities of the bonds at that time. There was a wild rumor to the effect that several millions of gold which had belonged to the Confederacy had been found in London, and that the late Judah P. Benjamin had undertaken to obtain possession of it for the holders of the Confederate bonds. This was a fiction, but it gained very wide circulation, both in this country and England.

DIDN'T BELIEVE IN BANKS

All the imbeciles have not yet passed over into the fool's paradise. There are some yet left to furnish a means of living for those too strong to do honest work. An exchange says:—

"A Seattle firm which had more confidence in beans than banks, divided its money into two deposits, between a sack of beans and a sack of rice. A burglar drew on them for the entire amount, $156, and hereafter the correct business principle of using an old stocking will be pursued."

WHAT THE YANKEE IS DOING

The American match and the American watch are becoming more and more popular in the remotest corners of the globe. With American matches, and American oil, and American liberty, the irrepressible Yankee is doing a great deal of lighting and enlightening, and with his watches he is also marking time for the progress of civilization.

THE OFFICE CLOCK

No well-regulated business office exists at the present time in which there is not a timepiece of one form or another. The office clock, as a rule, is a conspicuous article of equipment, and, therefore, to be in keeping with other matters, should be of presentable appearance, and, of course, in the sense of standing for the integrity and reliability of the business firm or corporation, should be absolutely accurate. Every jeweler and dealer in timepieces stands ready to furnish an office clock according to requirements, and no doubt would greatly value orders from all the business men of his town or section of the city in which he is located, but something more is demanded by the business man than the ordinary dealer in clocks and timepieces is prepared to furnish.

Not only should a clock be absolutely accurate in its mechanism, and likewise presentable in appearance, but, further, it must have proper care and treatment in order to

FIG. 1. STANDARD PATTERN WITH CALENDAR

maintain its standing. There is, then, before the business man the necessity of selecting a clock with mechanism that can be depended upon and of an appearance that is in keeping with the other fittings of the office, and also the necessity of making arrangements of such care of the clock as will insure it always being in proper condition. This last requirement presents the opportunity of those who have exploited what is familiary described as improvements in clocks. The trade built up results in what may be described as time service systems.

At this time we are directing attention to the goods and the service offered by the Prentiss Clock Improvement Company, 49 Dey street, New York, one of whose instruments has directed the time movements of the employees of this publication ever since it was launched. In a sketch such as is now presented it is impossible to be exhaustive. It is about all that can be done to call attention to its leading features and thereby create a demand for the comprehensive literature sent out by the company.

FIG. 2. A 40-DAY MOVEMENT

FIG. 3. THE CALENDAR MOVEMENT

Where the office space demanded by a firm or corporation includes several rooms, as is now very frequently the case with leading establishments, not only is one clock necesary, but several others in addition. With a number of clocks it is, of course, demanded that they should all exactly agree in time. This brings in the question of synchronizing the movements. In other words, controlling them so that they shall always agree or shall always take their regulation from a single master clock. This is something of which the company mentioned makes a specialty.

In workrooms of all kinds, whether the work done is that

FIG. 4. AN OUTFIT OF SYNCHRONIZED CLOCKS

of a clerical nature or as in a factory of manual operations, the employees are prone to favor a clock which is slow at beginning time and fast at quitting time. Without casting aspersions upon any particular set of employees, we may mention that cases are on record where a clock has actually been changed so as to be from five to fifteen minutes slow at the beginning of a labor period and about the same degree fast at the quitting end. By this means the employees cheated their employers of from ten minutes to a half-hour's time, much to their delight, but, however, without profit to themselves in any degree. A clock that is regularly examined and adjusted and kept in order by some one outside of the regular force of the establishment is, of course, free from manipulations of this kind. Further, a clock that is controlled by proper electrical devices from a master clock is likewise free from such manipulations.

The Prentiss Clock Improvement Company offer to their patrons the choice of selection from a considerable number of designs. Some are of the simplest sort, showing nothing more than a dial in proper frame. Others include calendar adjustments. That shown in Figure 1 of the accompanying selections from the company's catalogue is described as the standard style. It has a twelve-inch dial, and is equipped with sixty to ninety-day movements. It is furnished both with and without the calendar attachment. The total height is forty-seven inches, and the width fifteen and one-half inches, and it is supplied in various woods to match the other office appointments.

In Figure 2 is shown a sixty-day movement, which illustrates in some degree the mechanism which is employed in the clock illustrated in the preceding figure. Technically the movement is described as follows: It is spring-wound, and though containing two springs, the winding is done on a single key arbor with a small crank key, which can be turned with ease and rapidity. This feature enables the makers to use long and heavy springs and still have a light, easy wind. The entire construction is described as being of the most substantial character, and one that will easily outlast the ordinary run of clocks. In a single winding it will run sixty days. In other words, a clock thus equipped requires attention only six times a year. The clock has a pendulum movement with wooden rod and heavy bob.

Figure 3 shows the calendar movement with which such a clock is equipped. This will interest many of our readers who are of a mechanical turn, because it shows the drop rod and release lever by which the calendar is started. The "21" is shown at the sight opening, and on the starting up of the mechanisms this card first drops down out of the way and lies close to the number "20," also shown in the cut. The further revolution of the card allows the "22" to drop into the position formally occupied by the "21." The regulator wheel and the month wheel are also to be seen on the left of the cut.

In this connection it should be stated that the calendar is a complete mechanism in itself, and is entirely separate from the clock movement. It has its own spring motor for driving it, and need not necessarily be directly connected with a clock. It may be set off mechanically by pulling a cord or pressing a knob, or electrically by touching a button, or connecting it by wire and battery with a distant clock. Whatever the method for starting, the stopping is always done automatically when the proper day and date has turned into position. This calendar is described by the manufacturers as not only perfectly automatic in its action, but is also perpetual, requiring no resetting or adjusting or re-starting after having once been started correctly. When the end of a short month is reached the "31" card simply passes by without stopping, and the "1" of the next month drops into place. The 29th day of February every four years is also provided for, and at the end of the year it is only necessary to wind up the main spring or motor, and the calendar is then ready for another year.

The last cut on this page illustrates a system of synchronized clocks. A synchronizer may be described as a separate electro-mechanical device used in connection with two or more clocks for controlling and regulating the time of each clock in such a manner as to compel all the clocks so connected to keep the same time. Any number of clocks may be so controlled from a single clock. The latter is called a master clock, and is usually the best clock of all.

The mechanism employed is so easily adjusted to requirements that the manufacturers make this assertion: Should the master clock require resetting, either backward or forward, it can be done without in any way interfering with the sub-clocks, and the latter will immediately begin to readjust themselves to the new standard of time as indicated by the master clock. This is a most desirable clock, as no resetting of the sub-clocks ever becomes necessary.

In closing we must be excused for offering a few words

naturally less expensive to make than sixty-day clocks, but clocks requiring winding once a week are expensive in use and soon consume all that has been saved in the purchase price. The very cheap grade of clocks cannot be made to keep time, and therefore clocks of this sort require constant setting ahead or backwards in order to serve, even approximately, the purpose for which they were intended. A good clock is a luxury, and comparatively few people realize the vital difference between a clock which can keep time and one which cannot.

with regard to using a clock for office purposes. As a rule low price in clocks means poor timekeeping qualities and cheap construction, while high price indicates superior workmanship and fine timekeeping qualities. With clocks, as with other goods, the best are not cheap in the sense of first cost, because they cannot be made cheaply. The best clocks are the cheapest in the long run, because of the long service which they render in comparison with the price paid for them. Clocks which require winding once a week are

With reference to timekeeping, correct time, it is to be said, is not to be had at any price. Clocks are in use which will run within two seconds per month, but even a clock which will do this cannot be depended upon to do it indefinitely, as there are many conditions which must be maintained if such a rate is to continue, and sometimes it becomes difficult to provide such conditions. When it comes to a question of so small a rate limit as two seconds per month, it also becomes a question as to how to obtain a standard which can be relied upon as being correct beyond dispute. Very much depends upon the position of the clock, the nature of the wall, if hanging, and the manner in which it is secured to the wall. Sudden and frequent changes of temperature, constant vibration of the building in which the clock is located, and poor regulation also cause large variations in its rate, so that it is always difficult to say beforehand just how closely a clock will run.

The company from whose catalogue, No. 282, these cuts have been selected, in addition to supplying clocks, also supply a time service and care of clocks to those patrons who are within convenient reach of their office. In addition to making office clocks, they also supply program or advertising clocks, which are in demand in many directions.

CLEAN MONEY

Is the eastern section of our country a land of clean money? A New York paper says it is, and tells the following yarn to prove its case:—

"Did you see the look of surprise on that man's face?" said the paying teller of a downtown bank, glancing toward a tall man with a slouch hat who had just walked away from the window, fumbling a roll of bills. "Well, he's from the West and that's the reason he is surprised.

"Of course I knew he was from the West because he was introduced here the other day. But I would swear he was from the West if this was the first time he had ever come here."

"How's that?" asked the man who was at the teller's window.

"Why, he was surprised to get a roll of crisp, clean bills. They're something almost unknown in most parts of the West.

"I don't know the exact reason, but they tell me it is because they keep the money longer in circulation out there. We couldn't do business with our people if we paid out the money that a western bank hands to its customers. Here people won't stand dirty money, and they will out West.

"You see it costs the bank 40 cents for every $1,000 of bills it gets redeemed at Washington. We don't find that much of a burden, and the banks in Boston, Washington, Philadelphia and the other big Eastern cities don't, but go out West and you'll hear the bank people kick.

"You'll also get your dirty money there—all you want—full of all sorts of reeks and odors, and torn almost into rags. But I suppose reform in this direction will spread as it has spread in other ways."

BRIEF MENTION.

A HANDSOME PAMPHLET of nearly one hundred pages, bearing the imprint of the Genesee Press, Rochester, N. Y., has been issued by the Yawman & Erbe Mfg. Co., whose New York office is No. 360 Broadway. It contains many matters of detail with respect to equipment of business offices that are of interest to our readers generally. It is entitled, "Suggestions." The cover page, bearing out the title which appears at the top, is suggestive to a marked degree. There is a fire in process in which bound books, such as ledgers, records, etc., are being consumed, while rising phoenix-like from the flame is a card index tray, thus representing that which has come to take the place of that which preceded it. The sub-title of the book is System in the Office, Card Index System, Credit System and Card Ledger System. It is something that every one of our readers will do well to obtain, and we are assured that it will be sent to all applicants who mention this notice. It contains illustrations of various forms of card indexes, with descriptive matter that is of importance. There are also shown the construction of trays, the method of holding cards in place and finally there are shown cabinets adapted for cards of different sizes. Various tables are inserted in the book, giving capacities of drawers and cabinets for cards ranging from 5 x 3 inches up to 8 x 5 inches. There is a cut showing how card indexes may be packed away in a safe. The illustrations in the book are nearly one hundred in number.

FAIRBANKS SCALES are known the world over. They have not only made this country famous in foreign lands, but they have in a special sense made St. Johnsbury, Vt., where they are manufactured, famous to many of our citizens who would otherwise know little or nothing of it. A hand book issued by the company describes not only the scales manufactured, from the simplest to those for special and scientific purposes, but also illustrates scales which are adapted for use under peculiar conditions, such as weighing coal into a furnace, weighing carcasses of beef and pork in cooling rooms, weighing freight trains, together with computing scales, postal scales, etc. There is no business that we can think of that does not need scales in one form or another, and accordingly the reader who sees fit to secure a copy of this company's catalogue, No. 322, which he can do by applying to the Fairbanks Company, 311 Broadway, New York, or to any of the other agencies of the company, will not fail to be serving his own best interests.

EVERY ONE WHO STARTS on a journey and who is of an observing habit must be impressed with the character of the advertising and the abundance of it which is done by the leading railway companies of the country. The equivalent of what cost the fathers and grandfathers of the present generation in the form of atlases, gazetteers and hand books of travel a very large sum of money is now furnished free by almost every railway company, so far as its own line is concerned. We have before us at this time a complete file of the folder advertising done by the Central Railroad of New Jersey, including its several divisions, giving time tables, maps and other details. The famous Royal Blue Line from New York to Philadelphia, Baltimore and Washington is included in what is presented. Any business man who wants to offer the young people of his household a good lesson in commercial geography could not do better than to become possessed of a set of circulars of this road, and, opening to the maps, commence discussing the suggestions therein offered. The Central Railroad of New Jersey, by its lines reaching from New York to Wilkesbarre and Scranton passes through a country that is unsurpassed for scenery. The person who, in winter time, for example, studies a folder as we have above suggested, would perhaps do well in vacation season to traverse the same route for the purpose of becoming familiar with the wonderful scenery and the natural advantages of the country covered. Still another folder before us describes the Seaside Routes operated by this road, and it likewise is pregnant with suggestions. "A Winter Vacation Among the Pines" is the title of an unusually attractive little pamphlet which is issued with the compliments of the Passenger Department of the Central Railroad of New Jersey, and is something that very one of our readers can afford to send for. We are assured by the Passenger Agent that it will be mailed free to anyone that applies for it mentioning this notice. Address General Passenger Agent Central R. R. of N. J., New York city.

WE ARE INDEBTED to the Kee Lox Manufacturing Co., corner of Nassau and Fulton streets, New York, for samples of typewriter paper of peculiar grades and qualities, which they are at present putting upon the market. The typewriter paper made by this company is adapted for various uses, from the heaviest manifolding down to ordinary typewriter requirements. Its distinguishing feature is that it is non-grease in character, that is to say it may be handled with impunity, does not smut, does not offset on the sheets of paper with which it comes in contact, and does not soil the fingers. The company is also putting upon the market a line of typewriter ribbons which they declare will wear longer, are less filling, are of brighter colors and will produce better impressions and stronger copies without blurring than any other articles of the kind ever made.

A VERY HANDSOME FOLDER done up in a red cover with a flap reaches us descriptive of the Elliott & Hatch Book Typewriter. The paper and printing are beyond criticism, and the whole get-up of the advertisement is so attractive to the eye as to make it a pleasure to examine it. The pamphlet contains illustrations of the machine in different positions, directions for use and specimens of he work of the machine in railroad lines. There are facsimile representations of way bills, one done in common penmanship and others on the machine with requisite duplicates. The book typewriter is a device that can be used to advantage in many offices. Its advent is of recent date in the business office, and the demand for it is likely to increase rather than diminish. Those of our readers who care to see a copy of the pamphlet above mentioned should write to the Elliott & Hatch Book Typewriter Co., Home Life Insurance Building, New York, mentioning this article.

WE HAVE BEFORE us various specimens of the advertising matter issued by the Fred Macey Company, of Grand Rapids, Michigan, and with branch offices at 293-295 Broadway, New York city. One of the pamphlets is entitled "Business System," and is devoted to illustrating card index adaptations. The Macey interpretation of card work employs a side locking rod. The company also fit up card indexes with the duplex or folding center-rods, and likewise with solid center-rods. The illustrations of card index work in the pamphlet are full size in fac-simile and in colors, and rank among the best and most attractive of their kind which it has been our good fortune to examine.

WHILE MANY OFFICES are supplied with electric lights at the present time, yet there are thousands which have no better facilities than those offered by ordinary illuminating gas. The gas may be all right, but its satisfactory use depends very largely upon the burner that is employed. With a purpose to meet requirements of this kind experienced by the business man, not only in his office but also in his house, the Kern Incandescent Gas Light Company, 18 Murray street, New York, has issued a series of circulars relating to the Kern Incandescent Gas Burner, which they assure us not only gives a great increase in illumination, but also actually saves on the gas bill. One of the circulars relates to the Kern Intensified Pony Arc, which, burning 5 1-2 cubic feet per hour, gives 300 candle power at a less cost than that of gasoline or electricity. A neat little circular in blue cover with a tuck flap discusses the general question of illumination, and sets forth the advantages obtained by the Kern Improvements. It contains various illustrations of the different burners and fittings which the company supplies, with quotations of prices. It is something that everyone who is not fully satisfied with present lighting facilities will be interested in examining.

RAPID AND PERFECT DUPLICATION is something that every business man requires sooner or later in connection with his schemes of publicity. It is frequently necessary to send out typewritten letters in large quantities, and, whenever this occurs, the work is wanted in a hurry. The facilities in an ordinary office are far exceeded, and it is necessary therefore to go abroad for the supply. Stegman & Pincus, Room 915, Park Row Building, New York, have issued a circular directing the attention of business men to their facilities in this regard, and also calling attention to the special machinery which they employ for such work, and which also is available for those who see fit to purchase for their own use. The printing machine referred to is called the Diagraph, and is something that is in extensive use in various directions, and giving good satisfaction. The firm mention their ability to duplicate typewritten letters at short notice, and state that the letters can be produced in any desired color of ink.

A PAMPHLET ISSUED by F. D. Belknap, publisher, 290 Broadway, New York, in the interest of the Rapid Addressing Machine Company, contains much matter which is of interest to all who are circularizing the trades. It is entitled "List O' Trades and How to Reach 'Em." It contains tabular statement of the number of persons, firms and corporations in given lines of business in the different states of the Union, bearing certain credit ratings in the Dun book. It enables any person who desires to circulate his advertising matter to determine the number of copies necessary to cover certain trades in certain territories, and likewise keeps the prices before him of addressing, folding, inserting, stamping, mailing, etc. Much work of this kind is ordinarily done in the individual office. At the same time the rates quoted by the Rapid Addressing Machine Company are such as to cause many persons to consider the expediency of a change in this regard.

THE INDUSTRIAL PUBLICATION COMPANY, 16 Thomas street, New York, are sending out a catalogue of books which they describe as "up-to-date and telling you how to do it." The works described include books upon such subjects as the Steel Square and its Uses, Stair Building Made Easy, Progressive Carpentry, Brick Laying, Everybody's Paint Book, The Modern Machinist, The Steam Engine in Theory and Practice, The Practical Draughtsman, Taxidermy, First Steps in Electricity, Wood Carving, Boiler Making and hundreds of others in various branches of the arts and trades.

THE COMMERCIAL VISIBLE TYPEWRITER, manufactured by the Commercial Visible Typewriter Company, 300 Broadway, New York, is a new claimant for favor among typewriting machines. A circular which the company has recently issued is printed in green, and illustrates the machine from various points of view, and withal gives a most excellent idea of the compactness with which the machine is constructed and its general adaptability for office use. The machine has the advantage of low price, compared with many others, and a very wide range of usefulness. It is fitted up not only for English, but also for various other languages.

A SPECIAL CLAIM MADE for the Blickensderfer Typewriter, supplied by the Blickensderfer Manufacturing Company, Stamford, Conn., with New York office at 325 Broadway, is the compactness of the device, and the fact that it can be readily transported as requirements may be. Some of the older typewriters in the market can only be taken from place to place as an article of special baggage, but the Blickensderfer, by common consent, can be put into a hand bag in a way to greatly please all who wish to take a machine with them on their travels, either for personal use or for the use of their secretaries. Several pamphlets which the company have issued show the device in a very attractive manner, and give the reader much information which is useful to him in determining his choice. The advantages of the machine, which are specially emphasized by the company, include the following: superior efficiency, paper easily introduced, quickly adjusted line space, noiselessness, interchangeable type, interchangeable ink rolls, writing always in sight, insertions and corrections readily made, clean print and direct inking. Many other points are mentioned in the pamphlets which the reader should send for on his own account, mentioning, when writing, the source of his information concerning the matter.

THE REMINGTON TYPEWRITER, which is perhaps more widely known throughout the world than any other machine of its class, has not relinquished the field in the least to its several energetic competitors. It seems to be abundantly able to keep up in the race, and every now and again announces some improvement in design or construction or in some labor saving attachment. The tabulating device which has recently been made available on models Nos. 7 and 8 is something that is greatly appreciated by all who have tabular work to do upon a typewriter. The circular describing the tabulating device referred to is obtainable by any of our readers mentioning this notice and addressing Wyckoff, Seamans & Benedict Company, 327 Broadway, New York.

A GOOD DICTIONARY should be an item of the equipment of every office as much as a good desk, a good safe or a good typewriter. The relationship of the dictionary to the typewriter is ordinarily recognized, using the term typewriter, of course, as the individual that operates the machine rather than the machine. As a rule typewriter operators are equipped with small and inadequate dictionaries. Nothing short of an unabridged dictionary will answer all of the questions that arise concerning the spelling and exact meaning of the various words that are employed. Webster's International Dictionary, the successor in direct line to Webster's Unabridged, and being a better interpretation of the unabridged idea than was the unabridged dictionary in its day, published by G. & C. Merriam Company, Springfield, Mass., is something exactly adapted to requirements. It is a royal quarto volume, with no less than 2,364 pages and upwards of 5,000 illustrations. Any of our readers mentioning this notice and writing to the publishers will receive some printed matter that will be of the greatest interest to them.

THE REPUTATION of Hall's Safes is not to be gainsaid. Their good qualities in resisting both the attacks of burglars and the ravages of the flames have been appreciated through more than two generations, and all that is to be said in comparing those of the present day with those that other generations used is that with the development of manufacturing, construction is improved, and those of the present, therefore, are better than those of an earlier date. The New York agents are Kinsey, Ranier & Co., 393 Broadway, and those of our readers who address inquiries to them will receive printed matter that is of the greatest interest.

BOOKS OF INTEREST TO BUSINESS MEN

BUSINESS LAW. By Thomas Raeburn White, B.L., LL.B. 5 by 7 1-2 inches; 323 pages. Bound in cloth. Back title gilt. Price, $1.50.

This is a neat, compact and handy book of business law for the use of students and business men. Among the subjects treated are Contracts, Sales, Partnerships, Corporations, Negotiable Paper and the like. The author's language is plain, and is understandable by any one having no previous knowledge of law. The book's clearness on the essential points of ordinary law should recommend it as a business book for the plain business man who has no time in which to consult a law library.

THE PHONOGRAPHIC DICTIONARY AND PHRASE BOOK. By Benn Pitman and Jerome B. Howard. 5 1-2 by 8 inches; 562 pages. Bound in cloth. Cover title and back title gilt. Price, $3.00.

This book is the most elaborate shorthand dictionary yet published, with the characters in fac-simile. It contains over 20,000 words, and for every one of these words there is a corresponding sign in the Benn Pitman system of shorthand. To the reporter, office or court stenographer, or any one writing the Benn Pitman system of shorthand, the book is invaluable. It is well made, tastefully bound, and is printed on a good quality of paper in clean, plain type.

THE LAWRENCE SYSTEM OF VOCAL AND PHYSICAL EXPRESSION. By Edwin Gordon Lawrence. 4 3-4 by 6 inches; 128 pages. Bound in cloth. Cover title and back title gilt. Price, $1.00.

The author says in the preface of this little book that his object has been to place in the hands of lawyers, actors and public speakers in general, a simple system of vocal and physical expression that will enable them to clearly convey thought by word of mouth and emphasize it by the proper action. To the man of affairs who is called upon for a speech on any subject, and who knows what to say but does not know how to say it, this book will be a great help.

BUSINESS LAW. By Alonzo R. Weed, LL. B., of the Boston Bar. 6 by 9 1-4 inches; 172 pages. Bound in cloth. Cover and back title red. Price, $1.25.

Mr. Weed calls his book "a manual for schools and colleges and for every day use." The titles of the chapters are as follows: Contracts, Principal and Agent, Partnerships, Sales of Personal Property, Bailments and Common Carriers, Negotiable Paper, Deeds, Mortgages and Leases, Collection Laws, Written Rates of Interest, Insurance, Patent Rights, Trade-Marks and Copyrights, etc.

The author does not waste words, and yet treats his subjects clearly and comprehensively. In short, he gives the law without the addition of wordy "trimmings."

BANKERS' AND MERCHANTS' INTEREST TABLES. By Francis H. Coffin and David H. Moore. 13 by 9 1-2 inches. Bound in cloth. Leather back and corners. Cover and back title gilt. Price, $5.00.

There have been interest tables published before, but never, so far as we know, has so elaborate and comprehensive a set of tables been issued in book form. "The volume contains," to quote from the title page, "Interest tables, computed on the basis of 360 days per annum, at 3 1-2, 4, 5 and 6 per cent, with an accurate calculation of interest on every sum from $1.00 to $1,000, and, by simple addition of two lines, on every further sum, to $1,000,000." It also contains a 1 per cent one day table, on the basis of 365 days per annum, from which interest on daily balances can be computed at any time and on any sum. There is a time table printed in black and red at the beginning of the book as an aid in quickly finding the number of days between one day and another. To a merchant or banker performing many calculations in interest this book is a great time saver. It is handsomely bound, finely printed, and has a thumb index.

POLITICAL ECONOMY OF HUMANISM. By Henry Wood. 7 3-4 by 5 1-4 inches; 320 pages. Bound in cloth. Cover and back title gilt. Price, $1.25.

Mr. Wood is well known as a writer on various economic subjects, and this book contains a series of able treatises, written in his usual vein, on the relation of the employer to the employed, and the phases of the industrial question and their relation to socialism. Among the questions considered and handled in a conservative spirit and with much common sense, are the following: Supply and Demand, the Law of Competition, Labor and Production, Combinations of Capital, Combinations of Labor, Employers and Profit Sharing, the Obligations and Privileges of Employees, the Unequal Distribution of Wealth, Money and Coinage, Tariffs and Protection, Industrial Education and Gold Production and values.

WEBSTER'S INTERNATIONAL DICTIONARY

NEW EDITION
NEW PLATES THROUGHOUT
Now Added **25,000 NEW WORDS**, Phrases, Etc.
Rich Bindings ✤ 2364 Pages ✤ 5000 Illustrations
Prepared under the supervision of W. T. Harris, Ph.D., LL.D., United States Commissioner of Education, assisted by a large corps of competent specialists.
The International was first issued in 1890, succeeding the "Unabridged." The New Edition of the International was issued in October, 1900. Get the latest and best.
Also Webster's Collegiate Dictionary with Scottish Glossary, etc.
"First class in quality, second class in size." *Nicholas Murray Butler.*
GET THE BEST

It's Good for You

To use our Typewriter Ribbons and Carbons, because they write better and last longer than the ordinary kind; they do not smut, blur nor fill the type, but they make fine copies.

No. 1 Ribbons, 75c. ea., $7.00 doz.
No. 1 Carbon, $3.00 pr. bx., 40c. doz.
Silkarbon, $4.00 pr. bx., 50c. doz.

We pay express or mail charges.

IMPERIAL MANUFACTURING CO.
289-297 Washington St., Newark, N. J.

STATIONERY

For business use. Embossed in color from Steel Dies—Nothing else. Capacity, 50,000 sheets daily. Samples and quotations gladly furnished.

THE AMERICAN EMBOSSING CO.
73 Lock St., Buffalo, N. Y

About a Pay Roll which proves itself, corrects all mistakes in figuring, divides up Pay Roll into several amounts needed to pay each person.

But let us send you a sample leaf, with circular, which tells the whole story.

BARLOW BROS., Grand Rapids, Mich.

PRENTISS CLOCKS.
SIX TIMES A YEAR
is all that is necessary to wind a Prentiss Clock. Why wind a clock every week when we can sell you one which will require winding but once in sixty days and will keep perfect time? Also Frying-pan, Program and Electrically synchronized clocks. Send for Catalogue No. 22.
THE PRENTISS CLOCK IMPROVEMENT CO.
Dept. 28, 49 Dey St., New York City

INTRODUCTION TO THE STUDY OF COMMERCE. By Frederick R. Clow, Ph. D. 7 1-2 by 3 3-4 inches; 224 pages. Bound in cloth. Back title gilt. Price, $1.25.

Mr. Clow's book is not intended as a complete text book on commerce. It is simply, as its title implies, an introduction to the study of commerce. It is intended as a text book for the use of teachers in schools or universities, or as a help to the student in his commercial training. Incidentally, it makes good reading for anyone interested in modern commerce, and particularly for the American merchant. The author begins by describing the Elements of Commerce; then follows a short essay on the Rise of Commerce, and then the Materials of Commerce are discussed. Foreign Commerce of the United States and of other countries is treated of, as is the Domestic Commerce of this country. The titles of other chapters are: Organization of Trade, Prices, Payments and How the Equilibrium is Maintained. We can heartily recommend this introduction to the Study of Commerce. It is a good book on a vastly important subject.

THE A B C OF BANKS AND BANKING. By George M. Coffin. 6 3-4 by 5 inches; 137 pages. Bound in cloth. Back title gilt. Price, $1.25.

This handy little volume is exactly what its name implies, that is, a presentation of the principles underlying banking in the United States. The author in his preface says that it is designed to appeal to the reader outside as well as inside of a bank. It is by no means the last word or every word about banking. It may be said that it is a primer covering a field that has hitherto been somewhat neglected. The chapter heads are as follows: Banking in General, Various Kinds of Banking, Capital Stock, Shareholders' Rights and Liabilities, Undivided Profits, Dividends and Surplus, Deposits, Checks, Lawful Money Reserve, Issuing Bank Notes, Borrowing Money, Loans and Discounts, Exchanges, Collections, Letters of Credit, Bonds, Mortgages and Stocks, Bank Reports, Examinations, Directors, Executive Officers—Their Powers and Duties, Internal Administration and Bookkeeping, and Other Suggestions.

Any book in this list will be sent to any address in the United States, Canada or Mexico upon receipt of price. If there is some special book that you require we shall be pleased to hunt it up for you. Address COMMERCE, ACCOUNTS & FINANCE, 25 Pine street, New York city.

C. W. HASKINS, C. P. A. E. W. SELLS, C. P. A.

HASKINS & SELLS

Certified Public Accountants

CABLE ADDRESS, "HASKSELLS." THIRTY BROAD STREET, NEW YORK

Accounts of Municipalities, Corporations, Firms and Individuals Inspected and Audited; Methods of Accounting Originated and Adapted to Conditions; Books of Accounts Opened, Regulated and Closed; Irregularities Discovered; Financial Situations Examined.

Experts under the Joint Commission of the Fifty-third Congress to Revise the Accounting System of the UNITED STATES GOVERNMENT.

BUSINESS NEEDS

Advertisements under this head one cent a word each insertion.

MY NAME IS SMITH—Smithy for short. I write advertisements, get up circulars, booklets, etc., with a "get-up" to them. Generally speaking, I am sort of a jack screw to lift things. Make the other fellow rubber neck to see what you have got. Need any jacks in your business? Write me for rights, rites, writes and wrongs. Yours for sledge hammer blows from Smithy. SMITH, care Commerce, Accounts & Finance.

INSURANCE, ASSURANCE AND RE-ASSURANCE.—Perhaps I can tell you some things that will save you money. There is a way of doing things even in the insurance business. Write me for blanket insurance, mill insurance or any old kind of insurance. I think I can talk interestingly. Address ASSURANCE, care Commerce, Accounts & Finance.

SECOND-HAND TYPEWRITERS can be repaired so that they can be used and produce work which is almost, if not quite, as good as from a new machine. I have the facilities for obtaining exceptionally good second-hand machines. I have a man who repairs them—a man that understands his business. These machines can be sold for 50 per cent discount from list price of the new machines. Does this interest you? If it does, address TYPEWRITER, care Commerce, Accounts & Finance.

POSITION WANTED.—A thoroughly competent office man, 33 years of age, familiar with up-to-date methods of bookkeeping and conversant with the use of card system, seeks a position. In making a change would prefer to locate in some small town or city rather than remain in New York. Can furnish highest testimonials as to character, capacity, etc. Address URBAN, Box 33, Commerce, Accounts & Finance.

BOY WANTED.—An intelligent, well-educated boy in office of a large corporation. One living in Brooklyn preferred. Address, with references, to Box 24, Commerce, Accounts & Finance.

A SALESMAN at present with a large mercantile house on the road, is eligible for some side line to represent through the middle and eastern states. Has a large and established clientele of customers, and can take up a new line to the advantage of both parties concerned. Address SALESMAN, care Commerce, Accounts & Finance.

ADVERTISING MANAGER.—I have been in the employ of one of the largest houses in the United States in the office as confidential clerk and secretary. The firm did a large amount of advertising, and accordingly I have had a very liberal education in the value of mediums used. I believe my services would be valuable to some out-of-town manufacturer. Address E. L., care Commerce, Accounts & Finance.

AGENTS WANTED.—Bookkeepers, clerks and others connected with firms having a number of employees can add something to their income every week without taking up any amount of time. Personality and acquaintance is all that is needed in introducing to the attention of your friends the matter which we ask you to take up as an agent. Investigate this and write for particulars to FINANCE, care of Commerce, Accounts & Finance.

NEW YORK UNIVERSITY

School of Commerce, Accounts and Finance

A college course in Higher Accountancy arranged in accordance with the requirements of the Certified Public Accountants' Act of the State of New York and fitting students for the Regents' Examination for the C. P. A. degree. The course in Accountancy is rounded out by instruction in finance, commerce and commercial law leading to the University Degree of Bachelor of Commercial Science.

NEW YORK UNIVERSITY

Washington Square NEW YORK CITY

Michigan University

Course in Higher Commercial Education

It is the aim of this course to give special training in the construction and organization of modern industry and commerce. While placing special stress upon what is technical or professional in a course preparatory to a business career, ample provision is made for instruction in history, language, science and other lines of study which contribute to a general education. This course is designed to provide an education equal in scope and mental discipline to any which the University offers.

Michigan University, Ann Arbor, Mich.

PACIFIC COAST REPRESENTATIVE.—I would like to establish connection with some large manufacturing industry which needs a representative on the Pacific Coast. I am 34 years of age, have the advantage of large and extensive travel, exceptional business experience, and possess executive ability. I am able to handle large undertakings. Highest class references. Address REPRESENTATIVE, care Commerce, Accounts & Finance.

OFFICE FURNITURE AND OFFICE FITTINGS.—My specialty is in discriminating where to buy and what to buy. I keep myself posted as to market rates and discounts. If you need anything in your office, files, desks, furniture or any office device, write me about it. I can save you time and money. Address CONFIDENTIAL, care Commerce, Accounts & Finance.

Leon Brummer, C. P. A.

Public Accountant and Auditor,

7 Pine Street, New York, N. Y.

"IF BUSINESS MEN ONLY KNEW."

If Business Men in general knew the real advantages of the Balance Sheet System of Accounting, our facilities, large as they are, would be vastly overtaxed. We could not meet the demand that would arise. As it is, we are faced by a large and growing business, requiring constant additions to our staff. We started the new year with more than twenty times as many people on our pay-roll as we had only three years before, and our arrangements are already well advanced for doubling the number. Our best advertisements are pleased clients, and we have lots of them who never miss an opportunity to tell their fellow business men of their satisfaction with our methods. If you want to know who some of them are, write us.

Every Business Man who becomes aware of the fact that the Balance Sheet System installed in his establishment will give him at all times as complete a statement of his affairs, including profit results to date, as is usually afforded by the annual or semi-annual closing of the books, and that, too, without extra clerical cost, at once negotiates for our services. We put at his command a going profit and loss statement, by which expenses are constantly contrasted with profits, and a going balance sheet, by which assets and liabilities are always correctly presented. If you want to know more about this, write us.

Every Business Man who inquires of us learns that we are in position to serve him in various ways:—

(a) We will receive his head bookkeeper or confidential man as a pupil for a time, drilling him while with us in all the details and routine of our methods, sending him back thus trained, equipped with a chart of accounts, a balance sheet ledger adapted to the special business, and a written specification covering every feature of the system to be installed.

(b) Or we will prepare the chart of accounts and balance sheet ledger, together with the specification illustrated by every blank and form of ruling that can be of use, and will send our own men to make the installation.

(c) For those at a considerable distance from our offices and who want a special drill in Balance Sheet Accounting, we have arranged a correspondence course of instruction adapted to the requirements of the business man's representative, and have similarly put ourselves in position to supervise the installation of complete systems at long range.

Balance Sheet Methods are not complex. Instead they are extremely simple.

The Balance Sheet System of Accounts is the first and only accounting system that the business man of average attainments has been able to understand and intelligently direct as a part of his office machinery.

The Balance Sheet Ledger is the first and only ledger the average business man has found any satisfaction in examining. It is attractive to him because it gives him what he wants to know about his affairs for intelligent planning and direction, in the way he wants to know it and at the time it will do the most good.

Address communications to

ACCOUNT AUDIT AND ASSURANCE CO., Ltd.

BOSTON:
502 Exchange Building.

NEW YORK:
25 Pine Street.

NEW YORK PUBLIC LIBRARY

COMMERCE ACCOUNTS & FINANCE

Volume 4 New York March 1902 Number 3

CONTENTS

Published Monthly by the Commerce Accounts & Finance Company Twenty-five Pine Street New York

KNICKERBOCKER TRUST CO.

234 FIFTH AVENUE, CORNER 27TH STREET
BRANCH OFFICES:
66 BROADWAY, AND 125TH STREET AND LENOX AVE.,
NEW YORK CITY.

CAPITAL AND UNDIVIDED PROFITS, $2,508,399.11.

LEGAL DEPOSITORY FOR STATE, CITY, AND COURT FUNDS.

Interest allowed on Time Deposits. Deposits also received subject to Demand Checks, which pass through the Clearing House as do those upon any city bank.

Authorized to act as Executor or Administrator of Estates, and as Guardian, Receiver, Registrar, Transfer and Financial Agent for States, Cities, Towns, Railroads, and other corporations, and to accept any other Trusts in conformity with the laws of any State or of the United States.

LETTERS OF CREDIT FURNISHED.
BUSINESS AND PERSONAL ACCOUNTS SOLICITED.

CHAS. T. BARNEY, - - - - - - - - President.
JOSEPH T. BROWN, - - - - - - 2d Vice-President.
JULIAN M. GERARD, - - - - Asst. Sec. and Asst. Treas.
FRED'K K. ELDRIDGE, - - - - - 1st Vice-President.
FRED'K GORE KING, - - - Secretary and Treasurer.
WM. B. RANDALL, - - - - - - - Trust Officer.

BOARD OF DIRECTORS:

JOSEPH S. AUERBACH, HARRY B. HOLLINS, JACOB HAYS, CHARLES T. BARNEY, A. FOSTER HIGGINS, ANDREW H. SANDS, JAMES H. BRESLIN, I. TOWNSEND BURDEN, HON. E. V. LOEW, HENRY F. DIMOCK, CHARLES F. WATSON, FREDERICK G. BOURNE, C. LAWRENCE PERKINS, CHARLES R. FLINT, AMZI L. BARBER, CHARLES T. COOK, JOHN MAGEE, HENRY A. MORGAN, HENRY C. BERLIN, CHARLES W. GOULD, FRED'K L. ELDRIDGE, HENRY W. DE FOREST, ALFRED B. MACLAY, HARRY W. McVICKAR.

C. W. HASKINS, C. P. A. E. W. SELLS, C. P. A.

HASKINS & SELLS

Certified Public Accountants

CABLE ADDRESS, "HASKSELLS." THIRTY BROAD STREET, NEW YORK

Accounts of Municipalities, Corporations, Firms and Individuals Inspected and Audited; Methods of Accounting Originated and Adapted to Conditions; Books of Accounts Opened, Regulated and Closed; Irregularities Discovered; Financial Situations Examined.

Experts under the Joint Commission of the Fifty-third Congress to Revise the Accounting System of the UNITED STATES GOVERNMENT.

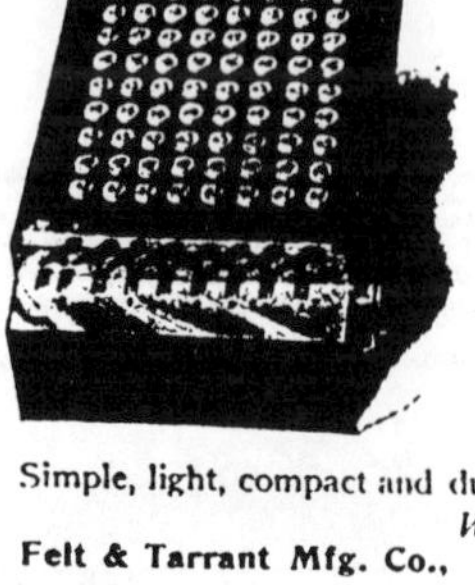

For **multiplication** the Comptometer is four times as rapid, and for **addition** twice as rapid as the most expert mental computer.

In hundreds of Railroad and Insurance offices it is saving the salary of several clerks for each Comptometer in service, and accounts are being kept which it would not pay to keep if the computation had to be done mentally.

Used by Accountants and Engineers in all lines of business.

In the United States Navy Department over 85 Comptometers are used on Engineering Computation.

Nearly one thousand manufacturing and commercial firms after buying one Comptometer have ordered a **second** one, and scores have purchased and use in their accounting rooms from 10 to 25 **each.**

It insures accuracy. No lever to operate; simply touching the keys does it all.

Simple, light, compact and durable. Many thousands in use.

Write for full description and sixty days' trial offer.

Felt & Tarrant Mfg. Co., 52 to 56 Illinois Street, Chicago.

Accounting for Cotton Mills—III.*

By GEORGE YOUNG

Under the inclusive term of General Expenses are commonly classed all items of expenditure which are general in their application in the sense that they cannot be applied, specifically, to lots nor classes of product.

It may be well to review, briefly, some of the arguments against the grouping together of costs and expenses.

DIFFERENCE BETWEEN COSTS AND EXPENSES.

Consider one phase of the subject. The mill superintendent is held accountable for costs; but he has no voice in the administration of the company's affairs, he has nothing to do with sales, it is no concern of his whether the product is sold at the mill door or delivered on the Pacific Coast, whether salesmen are overpaid or underpaid, whether commissions paid consignment houses are excessive or the reverse. It is obviously unfair to charge him with expenditures over which he has no control, to load mill costs with expenses of administration and marketing, which may be extravagant or economical, but which of a surety the manufacturing department cannot regulate.

Inward freights represent an investment of money necessary to the process of manufacturing, of converting raw material into finished goods, and cannot be considered as anything else than a part of the cost of the product; while outward freights do not enhance the value of the goods transported, but are rather to be considered as an offset to the selling price.

Again, the expenditure for taxes is essentially a cost of manufacture, an investment necessary to the production of goods; but interest is in no sense a manufacturing cost, it is rather a short circuit on profits. It is no fault of the manufacturing department that the company has not sufficient capital to run its business without borrowing. The manufacturing department produces goods at a certain cost, the sales department (referring to the two functions rather than to any physical separation) markets those goods at a certain net price, and the difference represents the profit on the transaction, which is in turn offset by an interest charge owing to the necessity of supplementing the company's capital with borrowed money; the net balance is the profit to the stockholders.

We might continue the discussion by a comparison of salaries of administrative officers, with those of superintendents; of salesmen, with those of foremen; of rent of sales office, with insurance on manufacturing plant, etc.

ACCRUING MANUFACTURING COSTS.

After establishing a rule that we will keep these two classes of expenditures entirely separate, the question arises as to the proper method of distributing or pro rating those general expenditures which we have classified under the head of Accruing Manufacturing Costs.

The distribution of these costs is a simple enough matter in the case of a mill producing one kind of goods; for example, print cloths; but when the product is diversified it becomes rather a complex proposition. The charges are of such varying incidence that the ratio of division between departments cannot be kept constant, nor can any one basis of distribution over product be established which will be strictly accurate.

Let us not forget, however, that we are not statisticians, but accountants; that we are not to see how finely we can theorize, and how nicely we can differentiate in the character and relationship of the different items, but rather to work always for practical ends; and in such a matter as this we should endeavor to find or devise a method which shall at once be economical in its operation, and sufficiently accurate for all practical purposes.

Let us examine the different accounts in this group. Taxes, insurance and depreciation properly distribute on the machine hour basis, that is, the basis of the running time made by the producing machines. It is true that these costs accrue whether the machinery is in operation or not, but all costs much be charged to product rather than to the machines themselves, and it would be altogether misleading to carry forward costs accruing against idle machinery, to be charged to the first product of those machines. Repairs, mill supplies, and heat, light and power might very properly be spread on the same basis as the foregoing items, since idle machines would not participate in these costs; and inward freights may be put in the same class, since the bulk of the items charged to this account will be freights on mill supplies. Superintendence would be distributed on the man hour basis, on the theory that it represents the cost of superintending the work of subordinates; and that portion of clerical labor which is properly chargeable to the cost of manufacture, such as pay roll and department clerks, might properly be spread on the same basis. The account entitled Miscellaneous Costs is intended only for those expenditures which are of too infrequent recurrence to warrant providing special accounts to carry them, and the amount involved in this class will be so slight as to be unworthy of consideration in a calculation made for the purpose of establishing a proper basis of distribution.

BASIS OF DISTRIBUTION.

It will be seen that, according to this analysis, only two bases are necessary to effect an equitable distribution of the items mentioned, viz: the machine hour and the man hour. Substitute for machine hours the hours of operatives of producing machines, multiplied by the number of machines operated, and you have reduced the whole to the one basis of the man hour.

There is one important item which we have not considered, viz: Non-Producing Labor. The basis established may be considered an equitable one for the distribution of wages of watchmen, oilers, etc. The cost of handling the raw material and the finished product by yardmen and teamsters, is in proportion to the pounds produced, and, therefore, properly chargeable on the pound basis; but this is a relatively small item, and no great injustice will result from the distribution of this cost on a basis which seems a proper one for the spreading of all other general costs of manufacture. Coming, now, to the non-producing labor within the departments, it will be seen that at least two bases are necessary to an equitable distribution of this labor. The wages of foremen and second hands represent the cost of supervising employees, and are properly chargeable therefore on the man hour basis; the labor of scrubbers, etc., is in proportion to the machinery operated, and this means distribution on the basis of machine hours, or of hours of operatives employed on producing machines; while the wages of doffers, creelers, filling carriers, etc., are chargeable on the pound basis, since the cost per pound of doffing, creeling and carrying is practically the same in yarns of all numbers.

The only real unfairness, then, resulting from a uniform basis of distribution seems to be in the matter of the departmental non-productive labor. This difficulty may be overcome by grouping the employees on the pay roll according to the different classes; those whose wages are applicable to product on the man hour basis in one group, and those who belong in the class chargeable on the pound basis in another, and dividing the wages of each group on its proper basis and including with the direct labor chargeable to the product of the department. This puts all the items gathered under the head of Accruing Manufacturing Costs on a single distributive basis, and renders possible a distribution of all at one operation, a most desirable end.

UNEQUAL PARTICIPATION.

It may be, however, that all of the machines in a given department should not participate equally in these costs; a

*An address before the Junior Class in Accounting, School of Commerce, Accounts and Finance, New York University, by George Young, Manager Textile Division of the Account, Audit and Assurance Company, New York and Boston.

mule room, for example, may contain mules of differing number of spindles, some occupying more floor space than others, requiring more power to run, etc., and yet each pair operated by the same number of employees. If we care to differentiate as carefully as this in departmental costs (and it is quite possible that we may wish to know the relative cost of the product of machines of different kinds in the same class) the desired result may be accomplished by dividing the machines of the department according to kinds, and treating each group, for example, all the mules of a given number of spindles, as a sub-department, and loading it with its pro rata of the total. Thus, though all the mules in the mule room should not be made to share, equally, in the total general costs of the department, with the mules classified according to kind, those in a given group would participate equally in the amount allotted to that group or sub-department.

Still another plan is that of establishing a table of factors of participation, using these machine factors in conjunction with the machine hours to ascertain the amounts chargeable to the product of different kinds of machines.

IDLE MACHINERY.

Distribution must always be made over product. Idle machines have no product, and therefore cannot participate in costs: and this means charging the product of machines run with all the general costs of the department, an arrangement which is perfectly proper under ordinary circumstances; but occasion may arise in which it would be altogether misleading to load product with costs properly chargeable to a large number of idle machines. In such a case these costs should be charged directly to Loss and Gain.

DIVISION AMONG DEPARTMENTS.

It will be necessary first to establish a proper ratio of division among departments. The extent to which we will departmentize these costs must be regulated by local conditions and the preferences of the management. In many cases it is deemed best to spread them over finished product only, rather than to make each preparatory process stand its pro rata, and under such an arrangement it is necessary to spread only at those points at which goods are produced for market. For example, in the case of a mill selling yarns and brown sheetings, and also bleaching a part of its output of sheetings in its own bleachery, it would be necessary to spread accruing costs in the spinning department in order that all the output of this department might bear its just proportion, whether sold as warps or hosiery yarns, or passed on through succeeding processes: in the weaving department in order that all woven fabrics might bear their proper pro rata of costs, whether sold in the gray or bleached: and again in the bleachery.

Allowing that we are to make these three divisions, it will be necessary to analyze each item of cost, and to include in the amount to be spread over the product of the spinning department the costs belonging to all of the preparatory processes from the opening of the cotton to the final process through which the sale yarn was passed; and in the amount to be pro rated over the product of the looms, the general costs belonging to all processes between the spinning and the weaving.

Taxes accrue on land, buildings and machinery; insurance, on buildings and the stock, raw, wrought and in process; and depreciation, on buildings and machinery. All of these may be divided among departments according to the floor space, and the proportion of values in departments to the total represented in all the producing departments of the mill. Heat and light might be divided according to the floor space. Power, according to the proportion of horsepower required to run each department to the total indicated horse-power of the mill. Repairs and supplies should be charged directly to the departments, and inward freights may be considered as coincident with these two accounts. Superintendence, clerical labor and non-producing labor (to which account we will charge only that non-producing labor which is common to all departments) may be divided on the basis of the hours of producers.

On this calculation a ratio of division between departments may be established. It has been already remarked that, owing to the differing incidence of these charges, the ratio cannot be kept constant. To effect a strictly accurate division it will be necessary to calculate the ratio each period; and yet the inequity will be slight, even if a ratio established by careful calculation under normal conditions be allowed to continue in force so long as the same general conditions prevail.

It is important, however, that the ratio be revised with each change of seasons, since some departments will use steam the year around, while others will use steam only during the winter months for heating purposes; and any similar change in conditions will suggest a revision.

The accruing manufacturing costs chargeable to the product of a given running period are those which have actually accrued during the period under review. Actual payment may have been made six months before or may not be due for six months to come, but that has no bearing on the case. Any item concerned in the cost of the output of the current period must be charged against that output without any reference whatever to dates of payment.

STOPPAGE OF PLANT.

Some of these costs will continue to accrue even though manufacturing operations may be temporarily suspended.

We cannot charge them to the costs of the period in which they have accrued, since that period has no production; and it would be obviously unfair to spread them over subsequent running periods. The proper method is to charge all general manufacturing costs which accrue during periods of suspension resulting from such causes as fires, strikes or trade depression, to General Loss and Gain, as a direct loss occasioned by the stoppage; never to Four-Week Loss and Gain, since that account is designed to show results from actual operations. Such an arrangement as this makes each period stand alone, a very decided advantage in comparing costs of different periods and of different mills, and it has the additional advantage of showing up the actual cost of stoppage.

Questions and Answers

SIMPLICITY NOT THE PRIME CONSIDERATION.

A. W. A., Cedartown, Ga., writes: "I have shown the paper to our cotton buyer, who is very much interested in the system which you outline for the handling of cotton, but he thinks there is rather too much theory about it."

Any explanation, either by word of mouth or on paper, covering every detail of such a system necessarily gives the impression of a very complex proposition. As a matter of fact, the cotton system as outlined is perfectly simple in its operation. The writer has in mind the office of a corporation using this system in which every junior clerk is thoroughly familiar with its workings, although it is no part of their duties to work on it.

It should not be forgotten, however, that simplicity is not the prime consideration. A simple business may get along well with simple accounting methods, but as the business itself becomes more and more complex the accounting must be modified to meet the changed conditions or else fall down.

The writer remembers very well when, as a junior clerk in a large cotton manufacturing concern, he used to be sent at intervals to the man in charge of the warehouse to find out the number of bales of cotton on hand. The mills used only one character of cotton, and though different grades were purchased there was little attempt at systematic mixing, the teamsters taking from the warehouses to the picker rooms whatever cotton was handiest. The warehouse man invariably qualified his statement of the number of bales on hand by adding, "If I hain't made no mistake.". It was quite apt to be found that he had made some mistake, and on more than one occasion when he was asked for a revision of his figures he looked in blank despair at the board on which he kept the tally, and said, "I've planed it off."

When this same company began to use several grades of Texas, Uplands, Sea Island and Egyptian cotton, simple cotton methods would no longer serve the purpose and had to be superseded by a system which was necessarily somewhat more complex, but altogether more satisfactory.

The writer also has in mind a recent case in which the cotton records of a mill failed absolutely to show even the gross number of bales on hand, to say nothing of the differences in grades and ownerships to be considered; it was necessary to count the cotton, no easy task, even with two thousand bales.

An application of the system outlined in the first paper of this series was made at this mill, and on another visit to the plant six weeks later they were able to make up in the office an inventory of cotton classified according to grades, ownership and location, in less than ten minutes.

MAY BE APPLIED TO SILK MANUFACTURING.

A. C. R., New York: Is the system advocated in your paper on cotton mill accounting equally adaptable to silk manufacturing?

The Proof-by-Balance Cost System can be applied to any manufacturing enterprise, and the Balance Sheet Ledger System of Accounts is adaptable to any business of whatsoever character. It has been successfully installed in almost every line of trade and manufacture, and in textile industries it is working satisfactorily, not only in cotton, but silk and wool as well. In silk manufacturing, owing to the value of the raw material, very accurate weighings are necessary at every stage of the process, and the accurate costing of product becomes a comparatively simple matter. The application of the Proof-by-Balance System simply means making proper use of the existing records and whipping the recorded facts into proper shape to give the desired results.

How Sovereign Nations Manage Collections

By RICHARD K. JARVIS

A great nation goes about collecting its debts, or what it assumes to be its debts, in much the same way as does an individual or a firm. It is true that the amount of pressure brought to bear upon the indebted nation is more or less heavy, according to the size and strength of that nation as compared to the one attempting to collect. The Sultan of Turkey is always in trouble, is always being sued for damages, so to speak, and never under, any circumstances, pays until the attorney—that is to say, the naval fleet of the collecting nation—is at his door. Then he cries, whines, delays matters as long as possible, and at length pays up.

The South American nations, being in a chronic state of war, are always treading upon the toes of other sovereignties, and consequently are always in trouble. Were it not for

Arranging matters.—St. Louis Republic.

Uncle Sam and his Monroe doctrine, South America would doubtless have been parcelled out long before this. But President Monroe's well-known creed is understood and respected by the large nations of Europe, and in consequence the republics to the south of us remain intact.

THE CASE OF VENEZUELA.

Venezuela is the latest nation upon which pressure has been brought to bear in the hope of collecting damages. There is a state of civil war in Venezuela and Colombia, and business affairs are much stirred up in consequence. If the prevailing accounts of his conduct and personality are true, President Cipriano Castro, of Venezuela, is a tyrant pure and simple, and in no sense the choice of the people of the so-called republic over which he rules. Consequently revolutions are common and Venezuela is very nearly bankrupt.

The causes that led up to the recent trouble on the Isthmus of Panama are curious and complicated. As Edward Emerson, Jr., in his article on "South American War Issues" in the Review of Review, says: "We are confronted with the anomaly of an apparent state of war between two sovereign states which the rulers of both countries unite in declaring no international war. First, large bodies of government troops, marching under their national flags and commanded by their regular officers, cross the frontiers and meet in pitched battle. The lists of casualties are appalling, and long strings of prisoners are marched into the interior. Captured flags and cannon are proudly exhibited at the capital. Then, instead of the long-expected declaration of war, come curiously worded diplomatic notes reaffirming that there is no war. Attention is drawn to the fact that the invaders of Venezuelan soil were led by a notorious Venezuelan rebel,

Uncle Sam to Germany: "Certainly, go ahead and collect your bill, only don't step on the dog."—Chicago Record-Herald.

and that, vice versa, the invaders of Colombian territory are led by Uribe-Uribe, the arch-rebel of Colombia.

"What cannot be denied are the actual ravages of war, with their inevitable consequences in the way of financial burdens and the ruin of trade. The sum total is bankruptcy on one side and national repudiation on the other. Colombia's only remaining currency, except at the Isthmus, is paper money. A Colombian dollar bill is worth three cents of our money. President Castro cannot pay the Venezuelan government's obligations to Herr Krupp and others in the Fatherland. Now a German fleet is knocking for payment at the Venezuelan customs ports. How can Castro be expected to pay up foreigners when he cannot pay his personal obligations to his own subjects? How can he be expected to withstand the foreigner when his own former financial supporters, backed by some of his best former officers and followers in the field, are moving to his capital to accomplish his downfall?"

The same writer goes on to say that he saw a whole army division of Colombian insurgents wearing Venezuelan uniforms and guarding Venezuelan territory; that he met gentlemanly exiles from Colombian universities and army schools serving under Venezuelan commissions. And so, too, he met Venezuelan gentlemen from the other side cheerfully fighting the battles of Colombia.

TROUBLE WITH OTHER NATIONS BOUND TO COME.

So, in the midst of this battle of Kilkenny cats, where much of the business interests are carried on by planters from the

Oh, no, Uncle Sam is not protecting Venezuela, he just happens to be on the ground, that's all.—Minneapolis Tribune.

United States, from England and from Germany, each one owing allegiance to his native country and not to Venezuela, some one's toes are bound to be trodden upon. Some German citizens got into trouble with the Venezuelan government troops; property owned by these German citizens was damaged, and the Germans thought the Venezuelan government should pay the damages. So a demand was made upon President Castro for payment. Venezuela, as we have said

Uncle Sam: "If you deserve a castigation, my friend, the Monroe Doctrine won't save you."—New York Tribune.

before, is pretty nearly bankrupt. President Castro is not supposed to be bankrupt, but what is the President's is not by any means the state's in South America. It may be added, however, that what is the state's very often eventually becomes the President's. So, in answer to the German demand for money, the Venezuelan government replied to the effect that no damage had been done to German citizens or their property, that no damages would be paid, and that Venezuela did not have any money, anyway. So Germany, following the usual custom, sent over a warship or two, not, of course, as a threat, oh, no! but merely to see that things were getting along nicely.

THE MONROE DOCTRINE.

And here comes in the delicate question of the Monroe Doctrine: "If Germany sends a fleet to Venezuela," says Uncle Sam, "to collect a just debt, all well and good; but if as the payment of that just debt she proposes to seize territory in Venezuela, that is an infringement upon the Monroe Doctrine and will not be tolerated." So Germany was given to understand the position of the United States in the affair, and Uncle Sam also sent a few warships to the Venezuelan ports. So matters stood for some time; the Venezuelan government backing and filling, making excuses, promising to pay one day, and appealing to the United States the next, for month after month. Uncle Sam kept his hands off, and the German government understood our country's views exactly. Now the question seems to be settled. Venezuela will, without doubt, pay damages. Small countries usually do this when big ones politely request, and in this case Germany's position is probably justified.

Just what will be the ultimate outcome of all these revolutions and wars in the South American republics is a question. They certainly hinder the development of what might be a commercially valuable part of the earth's surface. The resources of South America are great, and are developed only in the slightest degree. Probably the state of affairs

Prof. Peacemaker: "How can you expect anything but trouble with a head like that?

will work out its own salvation. Business men of all nationalities are interested in South America, and, with the Isthmian canal completed, the continent will develop faster.

GERMANY'S BUSINESS-LIKE METHOD OF COLLECTING.

Germany's manner of collecting indemnity of President Castro's government is, therefore, as we said before, not unlike that of any business house attempting to collect a bad debt. First, the business house sends its bill, then it writes letters, each letter being more and more urgent, and finally, after sending its own collector, it puts the whole affair in the hands of its attorneys and, generally speaking, the attorneys collect the debt. The South American republics are fortunate in having a strong neighbor like Uncle Sam, who looks out for them to the extent of keeping foreign rulers from stealing territory or taking the latter as a part of the damages demanded. If it were not for the Monroe Doctrine, there is little doubt that international damage suits would be much more prevalent in South America, for valuable territory would be the only medium by which a small nation would be allowed to settle a claim of a large European sovereignty.

We reproduce, in connection with this article, several cartoons from the American papers which illustrate in a humorous manner phases of the German-Venezuelan affair.

Ledger Rulings*

By A. O. KITTREDGE, C. P. A.

At the outset let us give brief consideration to those points which should be considered in an investigation of the ledger. Among them are the following: Dimensions of page, thickness of book, character of binding, quality of paper, ruling. Briefly, it may be asserted that so far as dimentions of page are concerned the book should be limited to the convenience of those who handle it, namely, on the one hand, the ledger clerks who do the posting; on the other hand, the credit men, collectors, heads of departments, etc., who have occasion to examine it from time to time.

With regard to binding there is enough to be said to warrant the consideration of that subject at another time. A whole evening could be devoted to a consideration of ledger bindings, spring backs, flat-opening schemes, loose sheet propositions, etc. Almost enough could be said on paper to warrant an evening devoted to that subject also. If our plans carry so far as this course is concerned we shall before the season is over have some one with us who is a paper expert and who, by means of samples of different qualities, tints or colors and makes of paper, will demonstrate to the class practically those matters which should be considered in selecting material for a first-class book.

That to which attention is especially directed this evening is ledger rulings, and we have put upon the blackboard some twelve diagrams which in a few moments we will briefly explain.

DEFINITIONS OF THE WORD "LEDGER."

Before considering the diagrams, however, let us give brief attention to definitions of the ledger with respect to its purpose and the manner of its use. If we turn to Webster's Dictionary we find the following definition of the ledger:—

A book in which a summary of accounts is laid up or preserved; the final book of record in business transactions to which the accounts from the journal, etc., are transferred.

In reading this definition I have been particularly drawn to the "etc." which appears after the word "journal." It seems to have gotten into place in this definition by some special saving grace, or else the definition would be badly out of date, for, as we all well know, the journal is conspicuous by its absence in most systems of accounts at the present time, for other things take its place. The "etc.," therefore, in the sense of describing posting mediums, is of more importance than perhaps the writer supposed when he penned this definition.

The word "ledger" by its etymology is found to have the meaning of a "laying down," also that of a "bed" or "couch." This reminds me to allude to the multitude of business transactions in which both hopes and fears have been mingled, which have ultimately found a bed or couch, in any event a final resting place in the ledger. If the ledgers of any given hundred business men should be thrown open for inspection how much would we find therein that has been in effect a lying down? In some cases the lying down has been obliterated, for the corpse of the transaction has been lugged off to the morgue, over whose doors is the legend, "Loss and Gain Account."

Still further inquiry into the origin and derivation of the word "ledger" shows that it has something about it of the nature of a nether millstone, which brings to mind the thought that many a business scheme has been ground to finest powder by the relentless logic of the ledger.

THE "CENTURY" DEFINITION.

In the Century Dictionary the following definition of the word "ledger" is to be found:—

The principal book of account among merchants and others who have to keep an accurate record of money and other transactions, so arranged as to exhibit on one side all the sums or quantities on the debit of the accounts and on the other all those on the credit.

*Abstract of a lecture before the junior class, School of Commerce, Accounts and Finance, New York University, November, 1901, by A. O. Kittredge, C. P. A., Professor of Theoretical and Practical Accounting.

In considering this definition I would call your attention to one or two peculiarities. First, it would seem to imply that the ledger is used only by those who have to keep accurate records. Again, it recognizes the two grand divisions of the ledger—namely, the debit and credit sides.

Referring to the third dictionary in general use among us at the present time—namely, the Standard, we find the following definition of the word "ledger":

The principal book of account of a business establishment in which all the transactions of each day are entered under appropriate heads so as to show at a glance the debits and credits of each account.

This definition will bear reading the second time, and the better it is understood the more satisfactory it becomes. Perhaps it is the best definition of the three so far presented, and yet, recalling modern methods, it is to be noted that it shuts the door entirely to monthly posting and to postings from summaries in general.

If we continue our investigation as to the meaning of the word "ledger" through the various treatises on bookkeeping we shall encounter some very striking statements. First, however, it should be stated that among the numerous text-books largely used in the schools there are a considerable number of volumes that do not define the ledger at all. It would seem that these authors have presumed on a general acquaintance with the book, for they at once proceed to show how it is to be opened, how it is to be kept and how it is to be closed, doing all this without telling what it is or what the word means.

"A RESERVOIR OF DEBITS AND CREDITS."

In Soule's "New Science and Practice of Accounts" we find the following:—

The ledger contains all the debits and credits of all the business transactions in a classified form. Things of a kind are brought together under their respective headings or titles, thus constituting accounts. The ledger is regarded as a reservoir of debits and credits and from it the business man may readily determine his financial relations with the persons with whom and the things with which he has dealings and also his net gain or loss and his capital or insolvency.

In considering this definition it occurs to me to remark that the word "reservoir" seems to be ill-chosen for the purpose in view. A reservoir, as the term is commonly used, designates an accumulated supply; a source from which something is to be derived. Now, as a fact, debits and credits do not flow from the ledger—that is, we do not go to the ledger as our reservoir of supply of debits and credits, but instead, debits and credits of transactions flow to the ledger, as streams to a pond or as rivers to a lake, and constantly accumulate in the ledger, the principal function of which is to retain them and keep them in proper order. We have then in the ledger the idea of accumulation in the sense of something that remains, rather than a reservoir, in the sense of something which gives forth more or less constantly a part of its contents.

Again, the author uses the words "debits" and "credits." Presumably, he had in mind instead those ascertained results which it is also a function of the ledger to show and which accumulate in the ledger as in a reservoir, for the use of the business man in determining his financial status.

Goodwin describes the ledger as follows:—

A book used to show the final summing up of all our business transactions and the standing of all personal and miscellaneous accounts.

Mayhew presents the following guarded and conservative definition:—

The ledger in double entry is a book to which entries recorded in the journal are transferred and so arranged as to present each account on a folio by itself.

I am at a loss to know what we would do under this definition if we happened to get several accounts on a single folio, and yet commercial ledgers are frequently ruled two, four, six and even eight accounts to the page. Again, where would this definition be with those who use no journal at all?

DUFF'S REMARKS ON THE LEDGER.

One of the pioneer authors of bookkeeping works in this country was P. Duff, merchant, of New York. Of all the text-books which came under my eye when I was a boy and after I stood at the desk as a bookkeeper, I value Duff's "North American Accountant" most highly. There is a certain verility about it, a certain business dignity withal, that commands attention. When it comes to the ledger, however, Mr. Duff talks about it and around it, instead of presenting a clean-cut definition, as witness the following:—

> All the other books used in business may be considered as tributaries to the ledger. Every transaction affecting our affairs must come to some account in the ledger for final adjustment. In the infancy of commerce the ledger was the only book used. The ledger is generally kept in

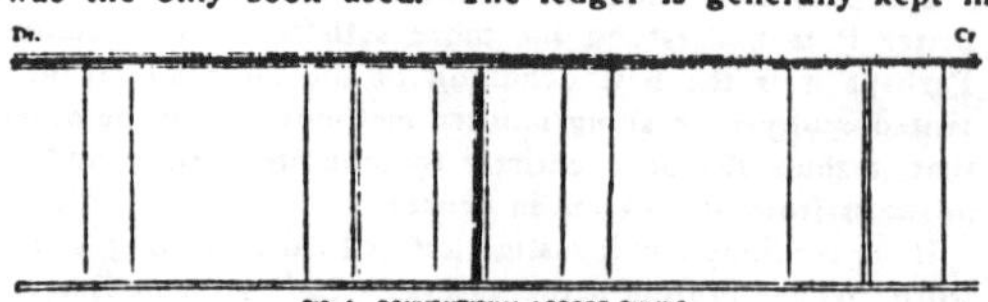

FIG. 1. CONVENTIONAL LEDGER RULING.

> folios of two pages to a folio. Of late years (1848) each page is made to serve for a folio by a dividing line down the middle.

Here is the history of modern accountancy condensed into a paragraph. In matters of metaphor and symbol the author presents all that Soule attempts and more.

I have on other occasions in the course of these lectures quoted from Thornton. Thornton is an author of the present day whose books are still fresh from the press. Thornton has a very happy way of clothing his ideas in words of comparison which causes them to remain in the memories of his readers. On a certain page of one of his more recent books he has the following to say about the ledger:—

> The ledger with its accounts may be considered as a sort of post office, with a vast array of properly arranged pigeon holes, each divided into two compartments.

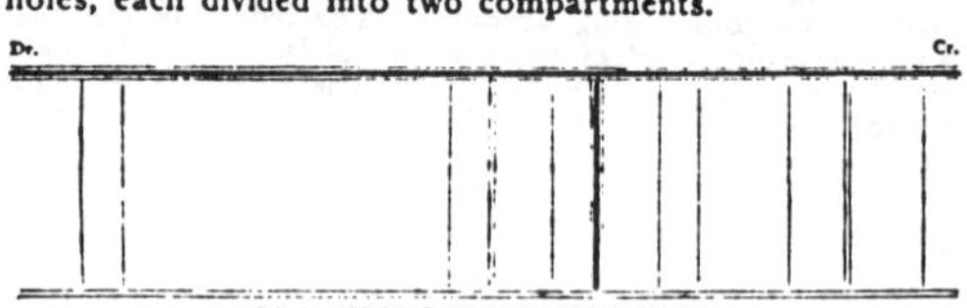

FIG. 2. MODIFICATION USED IN RETAIL STORES.

In another place this same author presents the following:—

> There are other books used in bookkeeping besides the ledger, but the ledger is the king of all. The ledger contains the final record of the facts of the business in the form best adapted to give useful information to its proprietors.

I like this definition, particularly the last clause in it: "The ledger contains the final record of the facts of the business in the form best adapted to give useful information to its proprietors." The ideal ledger, therefore, is that which is in the best shape to accomplish this result.

Speaking of ledgers now from the standpoint of rulings, printed heads, etc., I must admit frankly to you that I do not know how many forms are in use. I have been gathering samples for many years past and am constantly encountering something new. Underneath all of them, how-

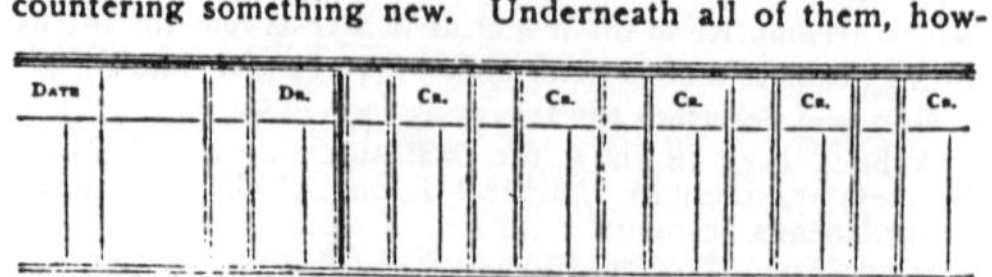

FIG. 3. FORM USED BY SOME INSTALMENT MERCHANTS.

ever, is the fundamental principle of debits contrasted with credits.

THE KIND OF LEDGER MOST USED.

You will recall in the definition that was given you a few moments ago, taken from Duff, that the ledger was originally kept in folios of two pages to a folio, and further, that he said of late years each page is made to serve for a folio by a dividing line down the middle. When it is recalled that Mr. Duff wrote these lines nearly sixty years ago the student has before him the reason why ledgers of the kind that Mr. Duff describes are not in conspicuous evidence at the present time. Great improvements in stationery goods have taken place in the time mentioned. Very few of us have seen in organized systems of accounts ledgers with

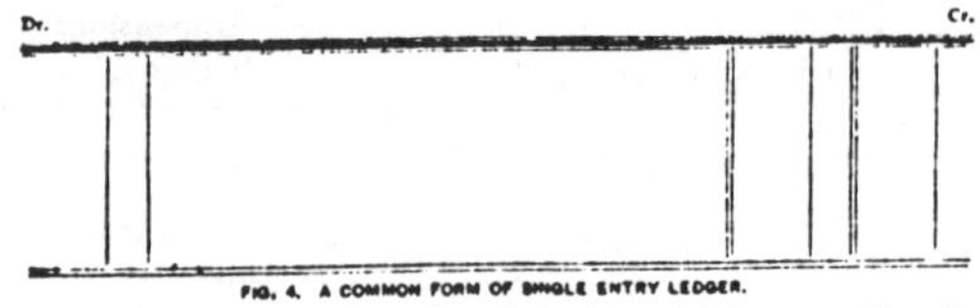

FIG. 4. A COMMON FORM OF SINGLE ENTRY LEDGER.

two pages to the folio. Instead, that which we ordinarily encounter is like that shown in Fig. 1, and this is described by Mr. Duff as a single page made to serve for a folio by a dividing line down the middle.

Here we have a column on each side of the middle division for dates, another for particulars, a third for journal folio or other posting reference and a fourth for the amount. This form of ledger, according to my own observation, is in use in a vast majority of cases. It is the kind of a ledger that every stationer is ready to furnish on demand and there are various advantages about it which cannot be gainsaid.

There are various modifications of this type, one of which is shown in Fig. 2, where in the item of particulars space on

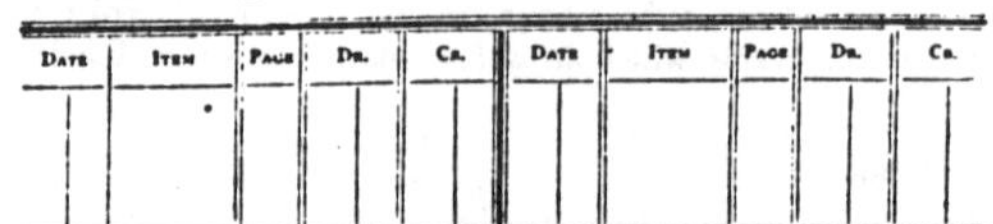

FIG. 5. LEDGER WITH TWO ACCOUNTS TO THE PAGE.

the debit side is greatly enlarged by giving to it what is saved by contracting the item space on the credit side. Such a ledger is frequently found in use in retail establishments, where all the items of the bills are transcribed on the face of the ledger to facilitate rendering statements. The space in the item division, therefore, is increased to accommodate the items, while the credit side, which is used only for the record of payments occurring with relative infrequency, is made smaller.

In some lines of business there is the occasion to record more credits than debits, as, for example, in the instalment business, where goods are sold in considerable blocks, to be paid for in weekly, fortnightly or monthly instalments covering a period of time ranging from three to thirty months. A form frequently found in use by instalment merchants is shown in Fig. 3. The debit side is contracted and the credit

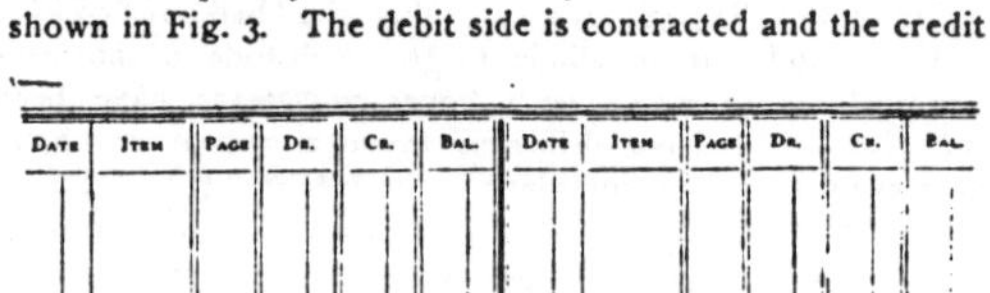

FIG. 6. DEBIT, CREDIT AND BALANCE LEDGER.

side increased by omitting unnecessary portions and devoting the entire space to columns for the notation of dates and the amount of payments or credit items.

A SINGLE ENTRY LEDGER.

In Fig. 4 is shown a form of ledger which is frequently designated as a single entry ledger and which, as you will perceive, is nothing more nor less in ruling than that which is commonly used for journal work. The date column and the items column are in common for the debit and credit amounts. I had occasion to use a ledger of this form very early in my experience in bookkeeping and found it very satisfactory in all respects. It is very possible that such use as I made of this form and the experience I had with it led me to favorably consider the form of ledger shown in three varieties in Figs. 5, 6 and 7—namely, the debit, credit and balance ruling. In Fig. 5 we have the style of ledger referred to in its simplest form, the balance column lacking and virtually the equivalent of that shown in Fig. 4, save only that two accounts are presented side by side on each page. In Fig. 6 the balance column is introduced, while in Fig. 7, in addition to the balance column there is presented a narrow auxiliary column in which may be noted the character of the balance—that is, designating it either as a Dr. or Cr. balance.

Date	Item	Page	Dr.	Cr.	Dr. or Cr.	Bal.	Date	Item	Page	Dr.	Cr.	Dr. or Cr.	Bal.

FIG. 7. DEBIT, CREDIT AND BALANCE LEDGER, WITH INDICATION COLUMN.

With a strict classification of accounts, getting all customers' accounts together by themselves and all purchase creditors' accounts together by themselves, the balance in a given volume or division of a volume would run regularly, either debit or credit, as the case might be. Wherever there is a variation, however, as, for example, in the case of a customer paying in advance for goods ordered, or the concern paying in advance for goods that it buys, the resulting balance in each account would be out of order. In such cases the form shown in Fig. 7 is very handy because it is a thing quickly done to write Dr. or Cr. against the balance, as the case may be.

If our requirements of space are such that in the construction of the ledger we cannot spare the space for this indication column then we may use satisfactorily that shown

Dr.	Cr.	Date	Page	Item	Dr.	Cr.	Date	Page	Item

FIG. 8. LEDGER WITH DOUBLE-ACCOUNTS REVERSED

in Fig. 6 by simply writing our irregular balances in red ink, or, preferably, by throwing a circle around the figures in black ink. There are objections to changing the pen very frequently in ledger work and therefore I am not favorable to a liberal use of red ink for any reason whatever.

The reason for the balance column should have attention in this connection. With the conventional style of ledger as shown in Fig. 1 and that which we have said is in more general use than any other, it is customary to keep the amount columns of the ledger footed in pencil and to throw the trial balance amounts out into the item column, also in pencil. There are comparatively few up-to-date bookkeepers who do not pursue some such method—namely, keeping columns footed, with an indication of balance at the date at which the footings are made. Now all that the balance column does is to afford a proper place for writing this bal-

Dr. Cr.

Date	Item	Page	Amount	Amount	Date	Page	Item

FIG. 9. TRANSPOSED-COLUMN LEDGER.

ance and the advantage of a place for everything and everything in its place holds good in bookkeeping routine as well as in other matters.

A DESIRABLE FORM OF LEDGER.

For such interest as it may have for you I would say frankly that my preference for ledgers for ordinary purposes centers very largely in Fig. 7. For ledgers for expense items, suspense items, reserve items, etc., I do not think any more satisfactory form could be devised. I also like it for customers' ledger and purchase creditors' ledger under various circumstances, although there are special forms for each of these not illustrated on the board but of which we have samples on the desk that are better under certain circumstances and conditions.

The ruling shown in Fig. 7 is the most economical of paper of anything that can be devised. It uses the paper up completely and does not leave whole half pages to be canceled by diagonal lines, as is frequently the case, using the form shown in Fig. 1.

In the matter of transfer from journal or cash book or from other posting medium to ledger, much may be said with reference to the order of the movements. Which should we write first in the ledger, the date, the journal page, the amount, or the item? Many bookkeepers argue, with some considerable show of reason, that the amount being the most important, it is expedient, as a mere matter of routine, to write it first and then let the other items be recorded in the ledger afterward. This leads to certain reverses and transpositions in columns in the rulings. In Fig. 8 is shown the ruling of a ledger with two accounts to the page with the order of the amounts reversed from that shown in Fig. 6. The argument for the use of this ledger is that if the amount is to be written first then the amount column should be in the first portion of the page reached by the hand carrying the pen. So, therefore, we have the

Date	Item	Page	Dr. Amount	Cr. Amount	Dr. Balance	Cr. Balance

FIG. 10. DOUBLE-BALANCE COLUMN LEDGER.

steps in this order: Amount, date, page, item, in each of the two rulings, making up a page.

AMOUNT COLUMNS SIDE BY SIDE.

Arguing from still another point of view, certain bookkeepers think that to have the two amount columns, debit and credit, side by side in the ledger, instead of somewhat remote from each other, would facilitate their work, first, by the footings of the two columns being side by side, more readily determining the condition of the account, and, second, in ruling off, making only one operation necessary on the center of the page as against two at the edges of the page as in some other rulings. A transposed-column ledger meeting these conditions is shown in Fig. 9.

Certain bookkeepers agreeing with the broad proposition that it is desirable to have a space in which to write the balance of an account, object to the forms shown in Figs.

Name	Monday		Tuesday		Wednesday		Thursday		Friday		Saturday	
	Dr.	Cr.	Dr.	Cr.	Dr.	Cr.	Dr.	Cr.	Dr.	Cr.	Dr.	Cr.

FIG. 11. A FORM OF BANK LEDGER.

6 and 7 and prefer instead two balance columns, one to take the debit balance and the other to take the credit balance. So we have as the result a double balance column ledger, as shown in Fig. 10. Here we have the two posting columns, debit and credit, side by side, and then two balance columns, debit and credit, side by side.

BANK LEDGERS.

On bank ledgers alone a lecture might be delivered. We shall give this division of the subject more attention upon some future occasion. A very simple form of bank ledger and one that is used by certain country banks, but which manifestly would be inadequate for a large city bank, is shown in Fig. 11. Here is a debit and credit column for each of the days of the week, the name of the customer being written to the left of the account rather than over it. There are various modifications of the general idea underly-

Date	Page	Purchases	Returns	Net	Date	Page	Goods Sales	Returns	Net

FIG. 12. LEDGER USED IN A DEPARTMENT STORE

ing this ruling, to which, as mentioned, attention will be given at some future time.

GOODS RETURNED.

Every one who has anything to do with a large retail business knows the annoyance that is experienced by goods sold being subsequently returned by the customer. Unless sales are diminished by returns the real facts of the business are obscured. It is necessary to subtract the returns from the amount of sales in order to get the net sales. If it is desirable to have this fact in the aggregate before the management then it is equally desirable to have the amount of net purchase of each customer similarly stated in his account for the purposes of the collection department.

On the other hand, the same general conditions prevail with reference to the goods that are purchased by the store to sell again. Certain articles sent by the sellers are returned and we want to know in settling accounts with them how much there has been purchased, how much returned and what the net amount is for which we are to settle.

A ledger that is intended to meet these requirements is shown in Fig. 12. The left-hand half shows the ruling that would apply to purchase creditors' accounts and the right-hand half that which would apply to customers' accounts. Referring to the latter, we have, first, the date, then the debit, entitled gross sales, and alongside of it a column for returns, and in turn the net. The other half of the page, as already explained, is devoted to the ruling that would be employed per contra with purchase creditors.

(In addition to the illustrations presented herewith, the speaker exhibited in working model form a safeguard ledger, a progressive ledger and several special rulings of real estate and insurance ledgers, all of which were carefully examined and criticised by the class during the recess interval. Incidental to the description of the ledgers were remarks concerning "back-posting" and proofs of correct posting. One of the class, by invitation of the lecturer, put upon the blackboard his plan of proving by casting out the 9's. Another explained the 11 check figure. Still another the 13 check figure. And still another the zero method of proof posting. Casting out the 17's was also referred to.)

LONDON'S NEW OFFICE BUILDING

Conservative London is to have a modern office building built on the American plan. It will not be a skyscraper like the towering business structures of New York and Chicago, but it will be, when completed, the largest office building in the world. While not low in reality—it is to be eight stories in height—it will present a somewhat squat aspect owing to its covering three acres of ground and having a front 750 feet long. The cut, which we reproduce from the St. Louis Globe Democrat, gives a fair idea of what this building will look like when finished. In the center will be a large court covered with a glass roof. In addition to the rooms for use as offices, the building will have Turkish baths, a club room, restaurant, cold storage chamber and safe deposit vaults. Seven banks have already applied for space and one man has made a bid for the bootblacking privileges in the basement. A considerable amount of American capital has been subscribed for this building, which is to be located in the Strand.

LARGEST OFFICE BUILDING IN THE WORLD.

COLLEGES AND THEIR DEGREES

Today there are 629 universities and colleges and 43 schools of technology in the United States. The total value of the property possessed by institutions for higher education amounts to $342,888,361, a gain of about $31,000,000 over the amount for the preceding year, says the Scientific American. The endowment fund amounts to $151,120,590. The total income of the year, excluding benefactions, amounts to $27,-739,154. The value of gifts and bequests during the years 1898-1899 amounted to $21,925,436. Some $2,500 is invested for each student who is now enjoying the advantage of any of the institutions of learning.

Classical courses claim by far the greater number of students—35,595 students out of the 147,164—while 21,860 were taking the general culture courses, 9,858 general science courses, 2,593 engineering, 2,550 in civil engineering and 2,329 in electrical engineering; 1,032 students were studying mining engineering, 627 architecture, 9,501 pedagogy and 6,-698 were taking business courses.

The number of degrees conferred during the year for work done was 15,087—10,794 on men and 4,293 on women. Thirty-eight different varieties of degrees were conferred, and in some cases only one candidate received a degree—musical doctor, for example. Seven hundred and thirty-five honorary degrees were conferred.

STRIKING ABBREVIATIONS

It isn't always just what is said; sometimes it is what is implied. School Education tells the following story. Let us hope its readers are not of too tender an age:—

A colonel of a British Regiment in South Africa who was repairing a railroad after one of General De Wet's many breakages, discovered a fine empty house, which he proceeded to occupy as headquarters.

When the news of the colonel's comfortable quarters reached Bloemfontein, he received a telegram which read:

"G. T. M. wants house."

The colonel was unable to make out what "G. T. M." meant, and inquired of officers, who translated it, "General Traffic Manager."

"All right," said the colonel. "If he can use hieroglyphics, so can I."

So he wired back:

"G. T. M. can G. T. H."

Two days later he received a dispatch from Bloemfontein ordering him to attend a board of inquiry. On appearing in due course he was asked what he meant by sending such an insulting message to a superior officer.

"Insulting," repeated the colonel, innocently; "it was nothing of the kind."

"But what do you mean," demanded his superior, "by telling me I can 'G. T. H.'?"

"It was simply an abbreviation," replied the colonel. "G. T. M. (general traffic manager) can G. T. H. (get the house)."

ONLY MEDIUM

"You are as good a medium as I ever saw," said the stranger at the close of the séance. "But you seem to be doing a poor business."

"Yes," sighed the other. "I am not a good advertising medium."

The Duties and Responsibilities of Auditors

By EBENEZER CARR

An Instructive Article by a Well-known Scottish Accountant

The Professional Auditor's position, whether in the case of a public company or of a private concern, is strictly a fiduciary one, his business being to safeguard the interests of each proprietor. In all his work he should be supremely matter-of-fact. He should take nothing for granted, but verify every item of liability and asset as to their existence and true value by the best evidence at his command, being careful that all liabilities, chargeable at the date of the balancing, are provided for, and that all wasting assets are properly written down.

In the exercise of his duties he should be guided by the highest principles of equity and commercial morality, with a determination to act independently and fearlessly, so that his work may be an example of rectitude and regularity.

An audit should be ideal in all points as to ability, method, thoroughness and integrity.

The first question that arises in the mind in considering this subject is:—

WHAT IS AN AUDITOR?

The Latin word "auditor" simply means "a hearer," and therefore does not in itself describe (except by use and association) the exact duties devolving upon him.

The answer to this question, to put it briefly, I think, Sir, is:—

One who by virtue of his appointment undertakes to:—

(a) Examine the correctness of the accounts under audit.

(b) Verify the liabilities and the present values of all assets.

(c) Present properly constructed accounts and balance-sheets to his clients.

(d) Certify such accounts and balance-sheets in strict accordance with facts, and where necessary report thereon.

Provided he faithfully performs these duties the auditor will comply with all the requirements devolving upon him in the detection not only of all clerical errors and errors of principle, but also, it may be, falsification of accounts and fraud.

It must be admitted, however, that the word "auditor," in the general acceptance of the term, has a somewhat elastic meaning, and I therefore now proceed to describe in a few words the accomplishments necessary for the proper fulfilling of all the duties devolving upon and required of the professional auditor.

Undoubtedly the higher his educational attainments the better, but, in addition to this, a special training for the varied nature of his duties and responsibilities is absolutely necessary. He should be possessed of a judicial mind with a thorough knowledge of bookkeeping in all its phases, and of all legal subjects relating to his duties, such as commercial law, including partnership and bankruptcy, company law, and the duties of liquidators and trustees.

All this may be acquired during the five years' training, the period which he has to serve under articles, as prescribed and necessary for qualifying, but this alone will not fit him for all his duties, he must also have a practical knowledge of the various customs of commerce and finance as essential to complete his qualifications.

Again, his qualifications must be of wide scope as he is frequently called upon to conduct the work in connection with the initial stages of company formation, which is of a specially technical character. It is also necessary for him to be conversant with the varied forms of bookkeeping in use and incidental to the various sections of trades, professions, societies, corporations and charitable institutions.

It is a true saying that "there are audits and audits," and I think societies, institutions and traders would do well to dispense with the too often perfunctory work of the amateur auditor, who, with few exceptions, has neither a clear understanding of his duties nor ability to perform them. I will not waste time by offering any further remarks upon this matter, suffice it to say that in all cases where the services of an auditor are necessary, a duly qualified professional accountant should be appointed. I venture to think that if this course were pursued much loss and consequent misery would be avoided.

Perfunctory audits in the commercial world, however, may be said to have practically disappeared under the improved regime established by the recognized bodies of professional accountants.

RIGHTS OF AUDITORS.

"The Companies Act, 1900," to some extent, defines the rights of auditors; although the provisions are not numerous they are far-reaching, and in effect are well known and understood by all members of the accountancy profession.

Sec. 23 of this act provides a satisfactory definition of auditorial powers, which have hitherto been somewhat uncertain, owing to the rights formerly given to company promoters either to adopt or modify the articles provided by Table "A" of "The Companies Act, 1862." The wisdom of clearly defining auditors' powers by enactment is, I think, undoubted, and must have a salutary effect on company formation and administration in the future, by arming them with rights to investigate all matters necessary for the full performance of their duties.

The following provisions in relation to this subject are contained in the two acts alluded to.

("The Companies Act, 1867," contains no provisions of this nature.)

Schedule 1. Table A. Articles 92 and 93 of "The Companies Act, 1862," relate to the rights of auditors as follows:—

Art. 92.—"Every auditor shall be supplied with a copy of the balance-sheet, etc."

Art. 93.—"Every auditor shall have a list delivered to him of all books kept by the company, and shall at all reasonable times have access to the books and accounts of the company; he may, at the expense of the company, employ accountants or other persons to assist him in investigating such accounts, and he may in relation to such accounts examine the directors or any other officer of the company."

"The Companies Act, 1900." Section 23 provides:—

"Every auditor of a company shall have a right of access at all times to the books, and accounts, and vouchers of the company, and shall be entitled to require from the directors and officers of the company such information and explanation as may be necessary for the performance of the duties of the auditors."

Before leaving this part of my subject, I wish to refer to the practice of some solicitors inserting in the clause in partnership deeds and other documents relating to the appointment of auditors, that the said office shall be filled by a particular class of accountant. This, I think, Sir, is decidedly wrong in principle, the effect being an undesirable imitation, and certainly it is not in the interests of clients. I am aware that it is frequently done in ignorance, but I also know that it is frequently done under undue influence. I hold that it is the duty of every incorporated accountant to let no opportunity slip of remedying this anomaly, as our society was formed with the object of preventing anything in the shape of a monopoly in the interests of the members of any body of accountants.

In the appointment of auditors the mention of "professional accountants" is sufficient to meet all requirements, and saves principals and others being bound to one section of the profession.

METHOD IN THE PERFORMANCE OF AUDITORIAL DUTIES.

This is a matter of very great moment—lack of method may cause trouble and inconvenience, and possibly the missing of important points.

An auditor, before passing from one section to another section of the work, should check every point in connection with the work upon which he may be engaged, and as regards the detail work performed by his assistants, it is a good plan to formulate this by supplying the senior audit clerk with written or printed instructions, to be kept in the audit note-book.

An audit note-book in columnar form should be kept for each audit, containing a list of all the books of account in use, and fully recording the extent of the examination on each visit, so that the audit clerk's principals can ascertain the exact state of the audit.

Audits should not be allowed to get in arrear, and where possible the practice of a continuous audit is advisable, e. g., monthly attendances in order to maintain a frequent check upon the clerks of clients.

On no account ought auditors to avail themselves of the assistance of their clients' clerks in the performance of their duties.

The extent of an auditor's work may be briefly summarized as follows:—

(1) To public companies under the Acts 1862 to 1900, and other bodies governed by previous acts and special acts.

(2) To private firms.

(3) To charitable institutions, hospitals, etc.

To whichever of the above divisions the accounts may belong upon which an auditor is engaged, his duties will be identical in many respects, but owing to the number of interests involved, and also to the conditions and restrictions imposed upon the management of public companies by the legislature, there are additional duties and more weighty responsibilities attaching to the position in the first division than is the case in the second group.

I may mention that by far the easiest audits to conduct, and generally the most satisfactory also, are those in which the proprietors or managers have, upon commencing the business, availed themselves of expert advice in instituting a system of bookkeeping which will provide for all the requirements of the case.

When an auditor is not fortunate enough to have had the direction of these matters from the first, I think he will find it well worth the trouble involved if he keeps a strict watch for opportunities to institute improvements, with the idea of gradually moulding the system into one which will record all the transactions clearly and accurately with the least expenditure of time and trouble; and while it may be argued that it is not the auditor's duty to either devise or regulate the system of bookkeeping, it is nevertheless the best means he can adopt of making sure that his work of checking will be both easy in operation and satisfactory when completed.

I will commence this subject by describing briefly the duties which are, with few exceptions, common to an audit of any description. To state these duties shortly they may be described as follows:—

(a) The scope of an auditor's examination.

(b) His duties in relation to the proprietors of the concern under audit.

(c) His duties in relation to the periodical final accounts and balance-sheet.

THE SCOPE OF AN AUDITOR'S EXAMINATION.

Opinions differ upon this; certainly he should not undertake an audit unless he has a free hand to do all that is necessary for presenting a fair and full representation of the position of the concern under audit; anything short of this is worthless, and recent events have proved the fallacy of incomplete and imperfect audits. I therefore emphasize the fact that such audits are a snare and a delusion, and possibly calamitous to the interest of proprietors generally.

It might even be contended that the calculations of all invoices of purchases, and entries of sales should be examined by him, but an auditor is rarely required to do this, and still more rarely paid for this work.

No hard and fast rule can be laid down, the auditor must be guided entirely by circumstances, the nature of the audit, and the scope of his instructions, but all these considerations should be governed by the principles of justice and integrity.

AN AUDITOR'S DUTIES IN RELATION TO THE PROPRIETORS OF THE CONCERN UNDER AUDIT.

He should see that interest on capital and drawings, and that all other matters are properly adjusted in accordance with the partnership articles, or, in the case of a company, that the provisions of the articles of association have been duly complied with.

He must also report acts of malfeasance of partners or directors.

It is an auditor's duty also to see that the directions of the minute book of a company are properly carried out by the managing director and secretary, and also ascertain that the instructions of the executive are strictly within the powers of the articles of association.

AN AUDITOR'S DUTIES IN RELATION TO THE PERIODICAL FINAL ACCOUNTS AND BALANCE SHEET.

He should adopt measures for ascertaining, to the best of his ability, whether there are liabilities other than those shown in the books, and if so, provide for same; also that a proper proportion is written off each wasting asset, and that all assets are taken at present value, provided they are not above cost, and in the case of the stock-in-trade at such prices as will realize the usual rate of profit.

HOSPITALS, DISPENSARIES AND CHARITABLE INSTITUTIONS.

As regards the two former cases the accounts and balance-sheet should be prepared in conformity with the requirements of the great hospital funds organized in various parts of the kingdom, which is necessary, in order for these institutions to obtain grants of money from said funds.

The accounts of other charitable and benevolent institutions should be presented in the form of a revenue account, and where circumstances render it necessary a balance-sheet should be furnished.

In all these cases it is necessary to institute a strict check upon collectors by the use of distinctive receipt forms in books in consecutive numerical order, the auditor's duty being to examine the counterfoils, in order to detect the abstraction of any forms, and to trace all moneys shown by these into the cash-book.

I will now proceed to give a brief description of the auditor's work of checking.

CASH RECEIVED.

Although I propose to deal with principles rather than details, this part of the subject deserves special mention because of its importance and the extreme difficulty, especially where cash is received in small amounts, of guarding against embezzlement by employees; so far as I am aware, no plan has yet been devised which is proof against a skilful operator, and I think an auditor must be considered to have performed this part of his duty if he has taken all proper precautions against dishonesty; as an example I may mention the case of book debts appearing on the balance-sheet as of a certain value, it does not seem reasonable for an auditor to be accused of neglect, should a portion of those debts turn out to be non-existent owing to their having been collected and embezzled shortly before the date of the balance-sheet, provided that he has gone through all the book debts with the principals, and that the same have been approved.

Provided also that, in cases where consecutively numbered forms of receipt in books are used, the moneys received are traced from the counterfoils into the cash-book.

However, Sir, it not infrequently happens that an auditor's duties do not extend behind the records of the cash-book.

CASH PAID.

When acting under instructions for a complete audit each entry should be compared with the receipt given by the payee; as regards petty disbursements, a separate voucher should be required for each payment signed by a principal or head of department where possible, but if this is impracticable the auditor will do well to watch this expenditure by comparing the various classes of expenses with corresponding periods in former years, and he should periodically review these with his clients.

Vouchers for payments should be initialed by the auditor so as to render it impossible for any receipt to be produced a second time for an improper purpose.

The audit of the cash-book is one of the most important duties of an auditor, and as such demands incessant care and attention.

PURCHASES AND SALES.

An auditor must ascertain the accuracy of the totals of these, and should insist on the production of an invoice for each item in the purchase book. Invoices should not be passed unless signed by the buyer of the department, and, if possible, countersigned by the principal or manager.

It is advisable that postings to bought and sold ledgers should be checked in detail where practicable, but where the postings are very numerous a satisfactory substitute should be adopted by raising accounts to test the accuracy of the bought and sold ledgers by summarizing the postings of each ledger, and periodically comparing the balances of these accounts with the schedules of balances abstracted from the ledgers.

By this system the records applying to trade debtors and creditors are focussed into two test accounts, viz., "Sundry Debtors" and "Sundry Creditors." This test upon the accuracy of the ledgers is so well known that it is unnecessary for me to take up any further time in describing the book-keeping form.

Having mentioned the principal points requiring special notice during the period of an audit, I will now deal with the matters requiring special attention when the books are closed for the preparation of periodical accounts.

FINAL ACCOUNTS AND BALANCE SHEET.

In the case of a private firm the auditor will probably be expected to prepare these, and he should take care to do so in such a manner as to afford all information possible for the guidance of his clients. It is very desirable that great care should be taken in deciding upon the form of the first accounts, and especially that the items of revenue account or profit and loss account, as the case may be, should be clearly described and sufficiently subdivided, so that comparison with subsequent accounts may not be impeded by changes in these respects.

The auditor to a public company expects to find the balance-sheet, etc., drafted in readiness for him, but it is quite within his province to require alterations to be made in the form as well as in the figures, and while clearness and simplicity are just as necessary for a company's accounts as for those of a private firm, I think an auditor may fairly take into consideration that there will probably be some persons amongst the shareholders present at the annual general meeting in whom the wish to criticise is more conspicuous than the ability to do so, and he should therefore avoid offering needless opportunities to this class of persons by displaying items separately unnecessarily.

I venture to think that this precaution is in no way inconsistent with the fundamental principle that an auditor should satisfy himself, not only that a balance-sheet is correct, but that it is also calculated to convey correct impressions.

The means an auditor may find it best to adopt for ascertaining that the figures on a balance-sheet represent facts vary of necessity to an enormous extent, and there are but few rules which will apply to all cases, the first step, however, viz., to ascertain that all liabilities and assets are in agreement with those shown in the books of account, may be considered universal; having satisfied himself upon this point, the auditor will proceed to test each item as follows:—

LIABILITIES.

(1) Mortgages or Debentures.—In the case of a private firm having a mortgage on property, instead of showing the charge upon the debtor side of the balance-sheet, it is generally advisable to deduct the amount of such charge from this asset, in order to show the asset at its net value only; but the debentures of a public company, which are usually a charge upon the whole of the assets, must be set out and clearly described among the liabilities; the description relating to mortgages should include:—

(a) Rate of interest.

(b) Whether a first, second or third charge.

(2) Sundry Trade Creditors, etc.—An auditor should make it his business to see that these are not only correct, but complete. Trade liabilities should be verified by comparison with stock-taking statements, and applications for these should be sent to all persons with whom the company or firm has had dealings during a reasonable period prior to the closing date, as well as to those having accounts still owing according to the bought ledgers.

In addition to trade liabilities there are various other charges for which there may be a liability at the closing date; some of these, such as rent, rates and taxes, lighting, etc., present no difficulty, and cannot well be overlooked; but others, e. g., legal expenses, commissions, etc., are easily omitted unless great care is exercised.

Debenture Interest.—It is perhaps hardly necessary to state that this is a direct liability, and must be included as such on the balance-sheet.

Reserve Fund.—A real as distinguished from a more or less fictitious reserve must be invested outside the business for which it is created, and the auditor should have the nature of such investment set forth on the balance-sheet.

Contingent Liabilities.—May be a very important item in certain cases. An auditor should take care that no unfair use has been made of this description by the inclusion of what are practically actual liabilities, from which the company has no reasonable chance of escape.

ASSETS.

(1) Freehold Property.—In the case of a company the original valuation or contract for purchase and sale of business must be produced, and in other cases the purchase price can be ascertained; in the absence of special causes for a decreased valuation an auditor would probably be justified in allowing the item to be shown at the purchase price, and it is his duty to see the title deeds of the property.

(2) Leasehold Property.—The leases must be produced and the auditor must see that sufficient is written off to extinguish the lease within the period for which it is granted, also making due provision for dilapidations and any unpaid ground rents.

(3) Plant and Machinery and Fixtures.—Depreciation in value must be provided for by writing off a proper proportion, usually from 5 to 10 per cent per annum, and care must be taken that cost of maintenance has not been added under the disguise of new fixtures or plant.

Owing to the difficulty of obtaining evidence that these items have been fairly dealt with, I suggest the necessity of a complete re-valuation at reasonable intervals, not only to insure that depreciation has been adequately provided for, but also to guard against the disappearance of certain properties altogether; this may happen in various ways, one of which is to enter plant sold as sales from stock, no credit being made to the account to which the transaction refers.

It is a good plan for the auditor to require production of all invoices for plant, machinery, fixtures and fittings.

(4) Stock-in-Trade.—Of all the items on the balance-sheet, the stock probably presents the greatest difficulty to the auditor, and I cannot but think his best course is to accept as little responsibility for the valuation as possible. I do not mean that he should not do his best to detect inflation by all means in his power, such as comparing rate of gross profit with former periods, or in any other way which may suggest itself, but it must be borne in mind that there are many trades where rate of profit varies to such an extent that his deductions from percentages at any fixed rate may be altogether wrong. Therefore it devolves upon him to have the stock book produced, duly signed as to the correctness of the calculations, also signed by managers of the departments and principals.

In addition to the foregoing I consider that he should obtain a certificate signed by the buyer and manager or principal, and in the following terms: "That the stock is taken at cost or under, and is of good value."

I think that having taken all reasonable precautions, and stated on the balance sheet at whose valuation the stock is taken, his duties in this respect may be considered at an end.

(5) Book Debts.—It should be ascertained that no bad debts are included under this heading and that they have all been transferred to bad debts account as a charge to profit and loss account, also that a sufficient reserve is made for doubtful debts.

A very useful means of criticising book debts is afforded by having the schedules ruled with several money columns for classification, and each debt entered under one of these according to the time it has remained unpaid; with the debts thus set out, and a knowledge of the custom in the particular trade as regards length of credit, the auditor will be able to obtain a fairly correct idea of the true value; in addition to this he should review every debt with his clients.

And finally the auditor should obtain a certificate from the principals in the following terms, viz.: "That all bad debts have been written off, sufficient reserve made for doubtful debts, that the debts as per schedules are in agreement with the ledgers, and taken down at the sum, or under, that they are expected to realize. And that the schedules of creditors are in agreement with the bought ledgers, and that all liabilities are provided for in the balance sheet."

Bills Receivable in Hand, Under Discount, etc.—The auditor must verify those in hand by careful inspection of each bill, and he should also make out a schedule of all bills under discount (if any). The asset in the latter case, of course, is included in the bank account, but it must be borne in mind that there is a contingent liability upon all immature bills which must not be overlooked, and should be properly provided for.

He must also inspect all bills deposited as collateral security against an advance, and indeed every other item of asset pledged or hypothecated which may form part of the business estate.

Debts Due from Directors or Officers of a Company.—An auditor should see that the amount of such debts is stated separately on the balance-sheet, and not included with the other book debts.

Investments.—An auditor's first duty in relation to these is to verify the existence of each investment by requiring the production of a share certificate or other evidence; he should then ascertain at what value each one is taken, whether at cost, present market price, or upon an estimate.

It would appear that in most cases the second of these, viz., present market price, is the proper basis to adopt, provided same is not in excess of cost; there are, however, various reasons why this is not always so, e. g., certain stocks are liable to fluctuate very considerably, and it might so happen that upon the date of the balance-sheet, the price, owing to temporary causes, was much above or below the normal, and the quotation very misleading in consequence.

Again, there are shares in various companies which, although valuable, are not quoted upon the Stock Exchange on account of the smallness of the capital. An auditor must therefore be guided by circumstances, but he should have it clearly stated upon the balance-sheet how these are taken; he should also see that the different classes of securities are properly distinguished, not allowing British Government stocks, for instance, to be grouped with speculative or comparatively worthless stocks, and the value stated in one sum.

In the case of banks it is the practice to write down their investments in Consols to panic or war prices, a prudential proceeding, which may well be followed by all financial companies in the case of assets on which they rely for speedy conversion into cash.

Inspection of Securities Relating to Stocks and Shares.—Method and thoroughness is essential in the examination of all bonds, scrip and certificates produced, and the auditor should retain all these securities until he has completed his examination of same. The reason for this must be obvious to everyone.

Bank Account.—In addition to the auditor verifying all the debits and credits with the bank pass-book, it is, as a rule, his duty to obtain the banker's certificate of the amount standing to the credit (or otherwise) on the date of the balancing, and which should be in agreement with the reconciliation balance.

Cash in Hand.—This must be counted as soon after the closing of the books as possible, and any irregularity reported at once.

GOOD-WILL.

I feel, Sir, that this is an extremely difficult subject upon which to offer any opinion; whilst it may not be the auditor's duty to advise upon this, at the same time having regard to the fact that good-wills may fluctuate as to their value to a very serious extent, I am of opinion that, in order to ensure a sounder basis for companies or trading concerns, steps should be taken either to write them down, or to create a sinking fund to provide for a decline of the business, which sooner or later, is inevitable, and I think this subject comes within the scope of his duties certainly to advise and report upon.

CERTIFICATES AND REPORTS.

The "Companies Act, 1900," Sec. 23 provides as follows:—

"The auditors shall sign a certificate at the foot of the balance-sheet stating whether or not all their requirements as auditors have been complied with, and shall make a report to the shareholders on the accounts examined by them, and on every balance-sheet laid before the company in general meeting during their tenure of office; and in every such report shall state whether, in their opinion, the balance-sheet referred to in the report is properly drawn up, so as to exhibit a true and correct view of the state of the company's affairs as shown by the books of the company; and such report shall be read before the company in general meeting."

The auditors' duties and responsibilities in these respects, I think, Sir, have been so well discussed that it is unnecessary for me to make any comment thereon, except to remark that he should clearly state in his certificate the extent of his examination, and the true position of affairs.

Section 28 of the same act makes it a misdemeanor for any person to wilfully make a false statement in a report or certificate, and as he may also be held liable to repay a dividend improperly declared upon the authority of his certificate, the fact of the auditor's interests being so intimately concerned in the matter should alone ensure the discharge of his duties carefully and to the best of his ability.

RESPONSIBILITIES OF AUDITORS.

An auditor's responsibilities differ according to whether he is acting for a private firm or a public company; in the first case he is the agent of the proprietor or partners only, and is to a large extent bound by their instructions; it would no doubt be part of his duty to point out to the principal any statements in the accounts which were in his opinion incorrect or misleading, and he would, of course, refuse to certify such accounts if requested to do so, but he has no power to require alterations to be made contrary to the proprietor's instructions.

The auditor to a public company is the agent of the shareholders, and he should never allow the expectation of losing the favor of the directors to influence him in the performance of his duties; the fact that his appointment sometimes depends upon the good-will of the board, and only nominally rests with the general body of shareholders, does not in any way affect his responsibility to the latter, and the Companies Act, 1900, makes it compulsory that he should report to them as well as state on the balance-sheet whether his requirements have been complied with.

The responsibility of an auditor does not extend, as Lord Justice Lindley pointed out in the case of the London and General Bank, "to giving advice either to directors or shareholders as to what they ought to do." "An auditor," said his lordship, "has nothing to do with the prudence or imprudence of making loans with or without security. It is nothing to him whether the business of a company is being conducted prudently or imprudently, profitably or unprofitably. It is nothing to him whether dividends are properly or improperly declared, provided he discharges his own duties to the shareholders. His business is to ascertain and state the true financial position of the company at the time of the audit, and his duty is confined to that. But then comes the question: How is he to ascertain that position? The answer is: By examining the books of the company. But he does not discharge his duty by doing this without inquiry and without taking any trouble to see that the books themselves show the company's true position. He must take reasonable care to ascertain that they do so. Unless he does this, his audit would be worse than idle farce. Assuming the books to be so kept as to show the true position of a company, the auditor has to frame a balance-sheet showing that position according to the books, and to certify that the balance-sheet presented is correct in that sense. But his first duty is to examine the books not merely for the purpose of ascertaining what they do show, but also for the purpose of satisfying himself that they show the true financial position of the company." You will also remember that in the Leeds Estate Building and Investment Company case Mr. Justice Stirling said that "the duty of the auditor was to be honest, i. e., he must not certify what he does not believe to be true, and he must take reasonable care and skill before he believes that what he certifies is true. What is reasonable care in any particular case must depend upon the circumstances of that case."

ERRORS OF PRINCIPLE.

Time will not allow me to enumerate examples, but having already referred to this subject, I content myself by emphasizing the importance of this part of an auditor's responsibilities, as any neglect might prove to be calamitous to the interest of the parties concerned, including the auditor himself, and consequently these are pitfalls which he should carefully avoid.

PAYING DIVIDENDS OUT OF CAPITAL.

The paying of interim dividends before the auditor has been consulted sometimes happens in cases where it is afterwards discovered that sufficient profit has not been made to warrant the payment of such dividends; in all such cases it is the duty of an auditor to report same to the shareholders.

Positions of trust always entail responsibilities and anxieties, but the conscientious professional auditor is prepared to accept the onerous duties devolving upon his acceptance of instructions, and to carry out his work thoroughly and with a single eye to safeguarding the interests of his clients.

FEES.

An auditor should be careful to fix his charges commensurate with the work and the importance of the audit; any deviation from this course, I hold, Sir, is an injustice either to his clients, in the case of his failing to do his work thoroughly in order to avoid being under paid, or to himself, and the profession generally, in the case of the fee being inadequate for the requisite duties which he may have conscientiously fulfilled.

In many instances an auditor is expected to do work, strictly speaking, outside his duties as auditor, it being a common experience of auditors to do all the clerical work connected with the private accounts, and to prepare the final accounts and balance-sheet. This, of course, must command an extra fee.

The growth of enterprise in commerce, the advancement in the administration of benevolent and social institutions, and the rapid strides in arts and sciences all tend to develop and increase the duties and responsibilities of the professional auditor.

THE FABLE OF BATWING

Oh ye, whose sons are growing up with yearnings for a college career, list to the fable of Batwing, whose story is told in Hide and Leather:—

An unlettered but eminently successful Shoe Manufacturer named Batwing, having toiled all his Life and struggled up from the Ranks to a position of Affluence determined that his Son and Heir should have the advantage of a College Education.

The Old Man didn't know how many parts ancient Gaul was divided into, and the Classic Heroes were nothing but names on Pullman cars to him. He could figure the cost of making a shoe without batting an Eye, but he passed up the higher mathematics. Trigonometry to him was something connected with Guns, and if he had run across the word Logarithm he would probably have guessed that it meant some strange French dish with queer Gravy on it.

Old Batwing didn't know the difference between Ibsen and Kipling. Browning and Annie Besant were Dope to him. He cut out the Occult, but when it came to knowing the kind of Shoe that would be a Seller next Season he was a Wonder from Wonderville.

Young Batwing carried a heavy handicap in Life's Race. He had Money in his Pocket that he had not Earned. He wore Long Hair and a Padded Suit, and butted his way through college. When he was too Old to stay longer without disgracing his Alma Mater, they handed him a diploma to get rid of him. His education was then Broadened by two years in Europe that cost the Old Man $10,000." The Young Gentleman, however, had nothing to show for it but some ill-fitting clothes made by a London Tailor.

Upon arriving at Home Batwing, Jr., discovered that his Father was dreadfully out of Style. The Senior wore Collars three sizes too large and four Seasons too late, and his Neckties were simply Impossible. This was a sore Trial to the Junior. There was nothing in the college curriculum that explained why a Man whose Checks are good at the Bank can't be induced to buy new clothes.

The firm name was now changed to Batwing & Son, and the Junior now began to go down to the Office each day. He stood about and got in busy people's Way from 10 till 12, and then went out to Luncheon. In the Afternoon he played Golf. One day a Girl wearing a scarlet coat and golf Socks met him on the Links and complained that he smelt of Leather.

After that he went riding every morning. Sometimes his clothes smelt Horsey, but the Girl said she liked that.

The Senior is getting Old and says he wants to sell out to a trust.

Moral: A little Learning is a dangerous Thing.

A THOUSAND DOLLAR STAMP

One of the rarest stamps ever put up at auction was recently sold at the opening day of the great sale of postage stamps by Messrs. Puttick and Simpson, says the London Mail.

Some idea of the scarceness and value of the specimen may be gained from the fact that the last of the used examples sold by the auctioneers realized £227. The one to be offered next month is, however, unused.

The stamp comes under the heading Roumania, and is, in fact, a Moldavian of 1854, 81 paras, blue on blue. To look at these rare stamps recalls very much a postmark, especially in photographs, where the colors are lost. They consist of a circle, within the circumference of which are a number of letters that do not read completely round. In the center is a bull's head in outline, between the horns of which is a five-rayed star, and below it is a bugle within the coils of which appear the number 81, 54 and so on, denoting the value of the stamp in paras.

REVIVAL OF AN OLD IDEA

Here is a bit of sarcasm from the Baltimore American: Jersey justice has struck again. It has decreed that a bank whose cashier is now in prison for wrecking it must make good his shortage to the customers, on the ground that if they had exercised proper vigilance his peculations and their losses could not have occurred. In other words, it has revived the obsolete doctrine that the purpose of directors is to direct.

COMMERCE ACCOUNTS & FINANCE

A Monthly Magazine of Higher Business Education and Practical Administration. Acknowledged Authority in the Profession of Commerce and Consistent Advocate of Methods Up to Date and Above the Table.

GEORGE E. ALLEN, Editor.

Published Monthly by the Commerce, Accounts & Finance Company, 25 Pine Street, New York. Subscription One Dollar a Year. Postage prepaid by the Publishers. In the absence of specific orders to stop at the end of the subscription term the paper will be continued and a bill sent. Entered at the New York Postoffice as Second Class mail matter.

* * *

We find in an exchange of recent date an article written over the nom de plume of "The Quiet Observer" and entitled "Some Random Thoughts," wherein the relationship of expert accountants and commercial teachers is more or less exploited. The writer says at the outset that he has just had a list of members of the American Association of Public Accountants of New York submitted to him, and he notices the name of but one person in the entire list who, to his knowledge, has ever been connected with a commercial school as instructor. After commending the Association as being perhaps the oldest and strongest in the United States, and stating that its membership is made up of accountants throughout the country, he asks, "Is it not surprising that not one of the commercial teachers of the country should be found on the list of membership of this fine Association?" He asks further, "Why are the names of the many commercial teachers throughout the country, who announce in their catalogues that they are expert accountants of more than local fame and reputation, not found on this list?" He concludes that for accountants of real ability the qualifications for membership demanded by the Association are very easily met.

*

Inasmuch as this article appears in what is recognized as the official mouthpiece of the commercial teachers, it has at least a semi-official significance. After reading it we are at a loss to know whether the writer is a bit sarcastic in asking why it is that commercial teachers are not found in this list or whether he is entirely earnest in his inquiry. Perhaps a little more intimate acquaintance with the men who compose the American Association of Public Accountants would reveal to this writer reasons why the average commercial teacher would be entirely out of place—outclassed, as it were—by being in the Association. The wonder is that even one of the teaching class has found it possible to become a member of the Association or agreeable to himself to retain that membership. If this writer is sarcastic, it means perhaps that the claims of certain commercial teachers to be public accountants of more than local reputation are ill-founded. Notwithstanding our somewhat extensive acquaintance with commercial teachers throughout the United States, we are unable to recall at the present time even one whose reputation as a public accountant is more than local or whose real qualifications would justify his membership in an organization like that of the American Association. Reading further into the article before us we find some excellent suggestions which it would be well for commercial teachers to carefully consider.

*

Certainly it would do a commercial teacher good to come in touch with those accountants who stand at the head of their profession. If the commercial teacher is not qualified for membership in such an association, it seems to us that he is not qualified to teach. Broadly, the commercial teacher who is not qualified for membership in this Association is not qualified to act as instructor in a first-class school. To this every accountant, and business man as well, can subscribe without equivocation. The trouble with the commercial teachers in the past has been that their standard has been entirely too low. The bright student of the class one year has become the teacher of the class the succeeding year. There has been a breeding in and in until "bookkeeping as she is taught" has become very, very different from "bookkeeping as she is practiced." Of accounting the commercial schools give little evidence of having any conception, and yet accounting is the scientific backbone of all bookkeeping.

*

This writer, as sensible as are his conclusions, errs before he gets through his article in that he confounds certified public accountants with the American Association of Public Accountants. The American Association of Public Accountants existed long before there was any such thing as an accounting law in New York State. As an organization it did much by way of co-operation in securing the passage of this law. Many of its members, although not all of them, along with other practising accountants, became certified public accountants after the passage of the C. P. A. act, and some of those who thus became certified public accountants later organized an association known as the New York State Society of Certified Public Accountants. We do not recall at this moment that there are any commercial teachers in the New York State Society of Certified Public Accountants, but if "Quiet Observer" had taken the trouble to inquire into the qualifications for membership in this organization he would perhaps have reached similar conclusions to those presented with regard to the American Association of Public Accountants. He could have drawn the same lessons with respect to those who undertake to teach young business men.

*

In another column of this issue our correspondent, Vannant, has something to say about commercial teachers and a convention which was held a few weeks since in one of the central cities of the country. We are far from endorsing all the conclusions which this correspondent reaches, and yet we are persuaded that the reader, even though a commercial teacher, will be interested therein. COMMERCE, ACCOUNTS & FINANCE has no quarrel with the commercial teachers. It does wish, however, that they had more practical qualifications for the work that they undertake, and that their teaching was more nearly in accordance with the practice of the best accountants in the country than it is at present. We know from observation and contact with the schools that they are steadily rising in their standards and that there is a better showing at the present time than has ever existed in the past. Perhaps some of this improvement has been due to such flagellations as Vannant and other writers of his ilk have administered in the past few years. We trust that Vannant's remarks will be taken without malice, and that, however pointed some of the paragraphs may seem, they will have the effect only of calling attention to matters that might be corrected to the advantage of the parties most in interest.

* * *

Sometime away back in the ages when man lived in trees and wore fingers on his feet, there was an ape who did not believe that the fist was the most effective weapon possible. He had a glimmering of mind, did this ape, and was not content to believe that because his great-grandfather and great, great grandfather had always fought with tooth and nail there was no better way of overcoming his fellow chatterers and gaining his share of cocoanuts and bananas. He looked at his fist and reasoned that if it was made to hold on to the limb of a tree it might be made also to hold a club. No doubt he suggested this idea to his brother apes, in whatever grunty and squeaky words his vocabulary possessed, and they laughed at him. They said, probably, that what was good enough for great grandpa gorilla was good enough for them, and they called the inventive ape a crank. But he put his thought into practical operation one day, and after these scoffers had been knocked heels over head by the new idea in offensive warfare, and had seen their inventive companion become lord of the roost, they, too. took to using clubs instead of the naked fist.

That inventive ape was an iconoclast. Webster's dictionary defines an iconoclast as "A breaker or destroyer of images or idols; one who attacks cherished beliefs; a radical." Galileo was an iconoclast. He believed that the earth moved around the sun, although every wise man and philosopher of his day declared that the thing was impossible: the sun moved around the earth because they could see it move. But, after a while, Galileo's theory was accepted as the truth, and the names of those old philosophers are now forgotten. So it is safe to say that iconoclasm is a good thing, provided that it is not overdone. We have seen men who took pride in being "breakers of idols," and therefore felt that, in order to live up to the name, they must antagonize everything that their fellow creatures believed, and that if, as it sometimes happens, their fellow creatures swung about, and came to believe as they did, they in turn must swing about and believe exactly the opposite. A weather-cock is not in it with this sort of an iconoclast. But, as we said before, to be an iconoclast in moderation is all right. The word means, when rightly applied, a man who does not take everything on trust; who tries to think for himself; who tries to invent new theories and new ideas and put them into operation in spite of popular opposition.

A business house that numbers a sane iconoclast among its managers is fortunate. This man will not be content to follow in the footsteps of his predecessors in business, if he sees a better plan for conducting affairs. The bookkeeper who is something of an iconoclast and who revolutionizes the old-fashioned methods of bookkeeping, in spite of the opposition of the old-fashioned bookkeepers about him, is doing a good work. "A safe conservative business" is all right so long as it continues to be safe, but when it is merely conservative, and the safety degenerates into old fogyism and lethargy, it stands about as much chance for success as would a hearse in a race with an automobile. This is the situation just now in the commercial world. America has always been somewhat iconoclastic; her business men have never believed a method or machine necessarily good simply because it was old. And this is why American manufacturers and American commerce are on top.

SCHOOL OF COMMERCE, ACCOUNTS & FINANCE

Diary of the Month's Work

Senior Class

RECORD FOR WEEK ENDING FEBRUARY 7, 1902.

MONDAY.
8-9 Lecture on Fire Insurance Law, by Mr. Stevens.
9-10 Lecture on Surrogate Accounting, by Mr. Jos. Hardcastle.

TUESDAY.
8-10 Lecture on Banking, by Prof. F. Johnson.

WEDNESDAY.
9-10 Lecture, by Dr. Webster, on History, Theory and Geography of Commerce.

THURSDAY.
8-10 Lecture on Accounting, by Mr. Conant.

FRIDAY.
8-10 Lecture on Partnership Law, by Mr. Walsh.

RECORD FOR WEEK ENDING FEBRUARY 14, 1902.

MONDAY.
8-9 Lecture on Fire Insurance Law, by Mr. Stevens.
9-10 Lecture on Surrogate Accounting, by Mr. Jos. Hardcastle.

TUESDAY.
8-10 Lecture on Banking, by Prof. F. Johnson.

WEDNESDAY. Lincoln's Birthday.

THURSDAY.
8-10 Lecture on the Auditing of a Stock Brokerage Business, by Mr. Dean.

FRIDAY.
8-10 Lecture on Partnership Law, by Mr. Walsh.

RECORD FOR WEEK ENDING FEBRUARY 21, 1902.

MONDAY.
8-10 Lecture on Fire Insurance Law, by Mr. Stevens.

TUESDAY.
8-10 Lecture on Banking, by Prof. F. Johnson.

WEDNESDAY.
8-9 Lecture on "A Systematic Education for Business Men," by Prof. C. A. Herrick, Director of the High School of Commerce, Philadelphia, Pa.
9-10 Lecture on the History, Theory and Geography of Commerce, by Dr. Webster.

THURSDAY.
8-10 Lecture on the Auditing of a Stock Brokerage Business, by Mr. Dean.

FRIDAY.
8-10 Lecture on Partnership Law, by Mr. Walsh.

RECORD FOR WEEK ENDING FEBRUARY 28, 1902.

MONDAY.
8-10 Lecture on Surrogate Accounting, by Mr. Jos. Hardcastle.

TUESDAY.
8-10 Lecture on Banking, by Prof. F. Johnson.

WEDNESDAY.
8-9 Lecture on "The Prices and Values of Railway Stocks," by Mr. T. F. Woodlock, Railroad Editor of the Wall Street Journal.
9-10 Lecture on the History, Theory and Geography of Commerce, by Dr. Webster.

THURSDAY.
8-10 Lecture on "Auditing a National Bank," by Mr. Dean.

FRIDAY.
8-10 Lecture on Partnership Law, by Mr. Walsh.

Junior Class

RECORD FOR WEEK ENDING FEBRUARY 7, 1902.

MONDAY.
8-10 Lecture on Money and Credit, by Prof. Jos. F. Johnson.

TUESDAY.
8-10 Lecture on Department Store Accounting, by Mr. H. M. C. Vedder.

WEDNESDAY.
9-10 Lecture on Transportation, by Mr. Eaton.

THURSDAY.
8-10 Lecture on Law of Contracts, by Mr. Bacon.

FRIDAY.
8-10 Lecture on Department Store Accounting, by Mr. H. M. C. Vedder.

RECORD FOR WEEK ENDING FEBRUARY 14, 1902.

MONDAY.
8-10 Lecture on "American Railway Evolution," by Mr. H. S. Newcomb, Editor of the Railway World.

TUESDAY.
8-10 Lecture on Department Store Accounting, by Mr. H. M. C. Vedder.

WEDNESDAY.
9-10 Lincoln's Birthday.

THURSDAY.
8-10 Lecture on Law of Sales, by Mr. Bacon.

FRIDAY.
8-10 Lecture on the "Profit and Loss Statement," by Prof. Kittredge.

RECORD FOR WEEK ENDING FEBRUARY 21, 1902.

MONDAY.
8-10 Lecture on "The Concentration of Railway Control," by Mr. H. S. Newcomb, Editor of the Railway World.

TUESDAY.
8-10 Lecture on Department Store Accounting, by Mr. H. M. C. Vedder.

WEDNESDAY.
8-9 Lecture on "A Systematic Education for Business Men," by Prof. C. A. Herrick, Director of the High School of Commerce, Philadelphia, Pa.
9-10 Lecture on Transportation, by Mr. Eaton.

THURSDAY.
8-10 Lecture on Law of Sales, by Mr. Bacon.

FRIDAY.
8-10 Lecture on Department Store Accounting, by Mr. H. M. C. Vedder.

RECORD FOR WEEK ENDING FEBRUARY 28, 1902.

MONDAY.
8-10 Lecture on "Federal Railway Regulation," by Mr. H. S. Newcomb, Editor of the Railway World.

TUESDAY.
8-10 Lecture on Department Store Accounting, by Mr. H. M. C. Vedder.

WEDNESDAY.
8-9 Lecture on "The Prices and Values of Railway Stocks," by Mr. T. F. Woodlock, Railroad Editor of the Wall Street Journal.
9-10 Lecture on Transportation, by Mr. Eaton.

THURSDAY.
8-10 Lecture on Law of Sales, by Mr. Bacon.

FRIDAY.
8-10 Lecture on Department Store Accounting, by Mr. H. M. C. Vedder.

Two Very Interesting Checks

An old check is always of interest to a banker. By an old check we mean a check drawn a number of years ago, before modern methods of business made commercial paper the comprehensive and artistic form that it now is. But a check becomes doubly interesting, not only to bankers but to the general public, when its signer is a man whose name is written large upon the page of history.

The editors of this paper take pleasure in presenting to their readers, upon this page, fac-similes of two very interesting checks. These checks are interesting both because they are old—each having been drawn at an early period of this country's history—and because they are signed by men of historical fame. The originals of the checks are in the possession of Mr. William Shanks, whose father was for years city editor of the New York Tribune. Mr. Shanks, Sr., received them from an old associate of his upon the staff of the Tribune, who was an ardent collector, and who had acquired them in some one of the ways by which collectors add to their store of treasures.

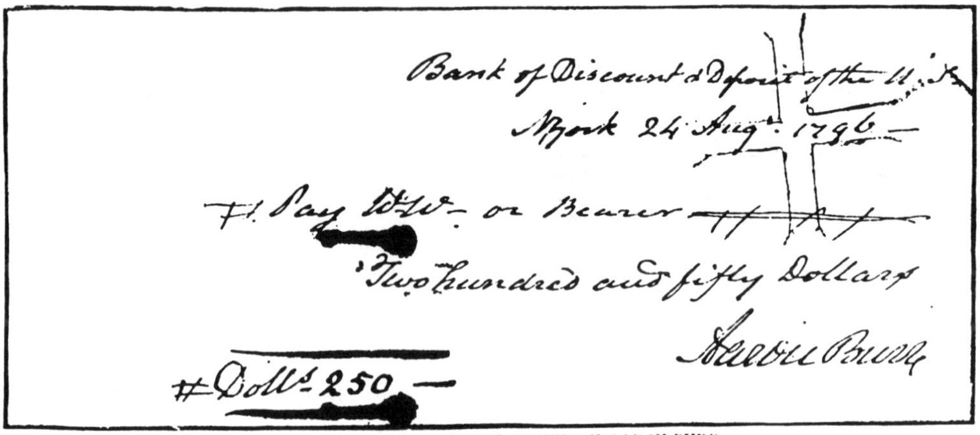
Bank of Discount & Deposit of the U. S.
N York 24 Aug. 1796 —
Pl. Pay W. W. or Bearer
Two hundred and fifty Dollars
Aaron Burr
Dolls 250 —

FIG. 1. FACSIMILE OF CHECK SIGNED BY AARON BURR.

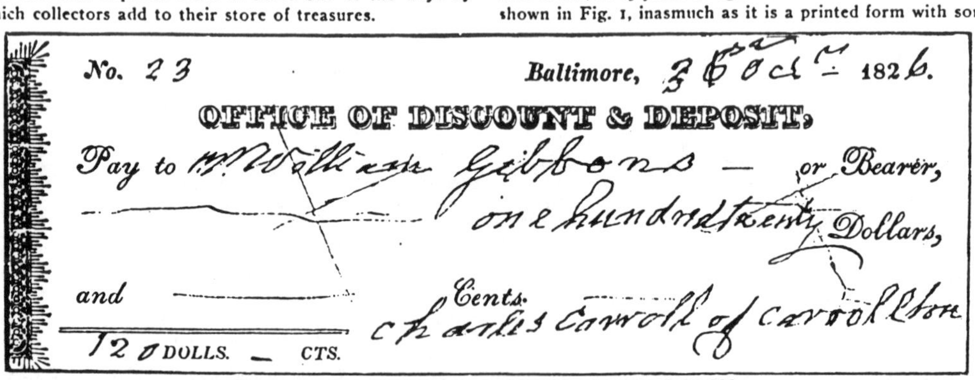
No. 23 Baltimore, 31 Oct. 1826.
OFFICE OF DISCOUNT & DEPOSIT,
Pay to Mr. William Gibbons — or Bearer,
one hundred twenty Dollars,
and Cents.
Charles Carroll of Carrollton
120 DOLLS. — CTS.

FIG. 2. FACSIMILE OF CHECK SIGNED BY CHARLES CARROLL.

The check shown in Fig. 1 is signed by Aaron Burr. It is dated at New York on the 24th of August, 1796. At that time Mr. Burr was forty years old. Eight years thereafter he fought the celebrated duel with Alexander Hamilton, in which he fatally wounded the latter, and, by so doing, wrecked his own political future and earned the hatred of the greater part of the American people.

The check is drawn on the Bank of Discount and Deposit of the United States. It is not filled in on any printed form, but is written upon a plain piece of white paper. The body of the instrument does not seem to be in Mr. Burr's handwriting. The reader will note that the initials only of the payee are given; who "W. W." may have been is a question; some of Mr. Burr's shady political friends, very possibly. The word "Dollars" is abbreviated to "Dolls.," where written at the lower part of the check. The dollar sign ($) had not been invented at the time this check was drawn. The method of cancellation indicated by the punched form in the upper righthand corner is very similar to that used in many banks today.

The check shown in Fig. 2 is also very interesting. Its signer was Chas. Carroll, of Carrollton, a signer of the Declaration of Independence. Mr. Carroll was born in 1737, and therefore was 89 years old at the time of drawing this check. He lived to the extreme age of 95, and was, just before his death, the only survivor of the signers of the famous Declaration.

Mr. Carroll's extreme age is apparent in his hand-writing, as shown on the face of the check, the said writing being shaky and very much off the line. However, there are not many of us, we fancy, who would write as well, or at any rate better, at 89 years of age. This check differs from that shown in Fig. 1, inasmuch as it is a printed form with some attempt at ornamentation. It is numbered also, which Mr. Burr's is not. It is dated the 31st day of October, 1826, about thirty years after Mr. Burr's check was drawn.

The dollar sign is not present on this check either. That convenient form did not come into use for some years after this date. The check was evidently placed on a common spindle file, as the perforations are plainly visible. A closer look at the date line seems to show that Mr. Carroll first wrote the date as "26 Oct.," and then changed it to "31st Oct." The paper in the original check is of fair quality, but rather porous. It does not compare favorably with the modern article. We are indebted to Mr. William Shanks for his courtesy in allowing us to reproduce these historical business papers.

The Negotiable Instruments Law*

By THOMAS B. PATON

Rights of Holder—Holder in Due Course—When Title is Defective

NOTE.—As enacted in New York, the Negotiable Instrument law is divided into nineteen articles as follows:—

1. GENERAL PROVISIONS (Sections 1—17)
2. NEGOTIABLE INSTRUMENTS: Form and Interpretation (20—42)
3. Consideration (50—55)
4. Negotiation (60—80)
5. Rights of holder (90—98)
6. Liabilities of parties (110—119)
7. Presentment for payment (130—148)
8. Notice of Dishonor (160—189)
9. Discharge (200—206)
10. BILLS OF EXCHANGE (210—215)
11. Acceptance (220—230)
12. Presentment for acceptance (240—248)
13. Protest (260—268)
14. Acceptance for honor (280—290)
15. Payment for honor (300—306)
16. Bills in a set (310—315)
17. PROMISSORY NOTES AND CHECKS (320—325)
18. Notes given for patent rights (330—332)
19. Law repealed: When takes effect (340—341)

The provisions of the law naturally fall under four general classifications.

a. General Provisions.
b. Negotiable Instruments in General.
c. Bills of Exchange.
d. Promissory Notes and Checks.

The text of the law is the same in all the states (with some slight exceptions which will be noted), but the numbering of the sections, and in some states of the articles, is not uniform. There is, however, the same continuity of articles and text, except that in some instances, "General Provisions" follow, instead of precede, the remainder of the act. By following this course of study with reference to the New York act, as above outlined, the reader in each state can apply the same to the law of his own state.

ARTICLE V. RIGHTS OF HOLDER.

In previous articles (1) certain general provisions as to negotiable instruments have been stated, (2) the requisites as to form of the instrument have been laid down and rules of interpretation provided, (3) the matter of consideration has been regulated, and (4) the law governing the subject of negotiation by indorsement or delivery set forth with particularity.

Following issue and negotiation, the next subject in natural order concerns the rights of the holder to whom a negotiable instrument has come, and the rules governing this subject are provided in Article V., which we are now to take up.

What every holder of a negotiable instrument desires is full payment. Whether he has a right thereto by reason of having taken the instrument under such circumstances as to constitute him a "holder in due course," or whether it is subject to partial or total non-payment in his hands, is defined with particularity in the sections embraced in Article V. The duties which devolve upon the holder of a negotiable instrument, concerning presentment for payment and notice of dishonor, so as to insure payment from parties only contingently liable thereon, are set forth in subsequent articles.

RIGHT OF HOLDER TO SUE.

The first section of the present article states the rule as to the right of a holder to sue for payment, and as to the effect of payment as a discharge of the instrument.

Sec. 90. Right of Holder to Sue; Payment.—The holder of a negotiable instrument may sue thereon in his own name, and payment to him in due course discharges the instrument.

Naturally, every holder of a negotiable instrument, unless born and bred in an atmosphere of pugnacity which begets a delight in lawsuits, would rather have payment voluntarily made by the debtor than forced from the latter by the judgment of a court of law. But where voluntary payment is refused there is no alternative but an appeal to the courts. And, recognizing this necessity, we have as the leading paragraph of Article V. a provision which makes plain just who can bring suit on a negotiable instrument and in whose name the suit can be brought.

There was a time in the early history of our law when the multiplication of lawsuits was looked upon with abhorrence, and in keeping with this sentiment the law prohibited the assignment of what are termed "choses in action," or rights to recover a debt, or money, or damages under a contract requiring an action for their enforcement. Then, in the progress of events, assignments of choses in action began to be made, and increasingly made, despite the law, and the courts, deferring to public necessity, would permit their enforcement in a suit by the assignee brought in the name of the assignor; and now in the present age, when the spirit of trade and transfer of property has become so general, this last impediment has been very largely removed by statutory enactments, providing that an assignee or a transferee of a right under a contract may sue in his own name.

At a very early period negotiable instruments, by reason of their nature and uses, were excepted from the general prohibition of assignment of choses in action and became freely transferable, nor was the holder subject to the requirement of bringing suit thereon in the name of the transferor. The promise to pay was to the payee "or order," and suits thereon were brought by the transferee in his own name. But while the indorsee or holder for value of a negotiable instrument can sue thereon in his own name, there has been a conflict of authority in some of the states whether an indorsee or holder "for collection" of a negotiable instrument, being a mere agent and not owner, could bring suit thereon, in his own name, in the event recourse to the courts became necessary. For example, in Minnesota, where the state statute provides that actions must be brought in the name of the real party in interest, it has been held that an indorsement of a note "Pay to A or order for collection," makes the indorsee merely agent for the indorser, to collect the note, but does not vest in him such title as to make him a proper party plaintiff in a suit upon it. (Bank vs. Hollister, 21 Minn. 385). In other states, to the contrary, holders of negotiable instruments indorsed to them merely "for collection" have been entitled to maintain suits thereon in their own names.

This much preliminary, we may better understand exactly what is meant by the first paragraph of section 90 that "the holder of a negotiable instrument may sue thereon in his own name." It will be observed the section does not say "holder in due course," which term comprehends acquirement for value, but merely holder. "Holder," we will remember, defined by section 2, "means the payee or indorsee of a bill or note, who is in possession of it, or the bearer thereof;" and, furthermore, looking back at section 67 we find that "a restrictive indorsement (such as "for collection") confers upon the indorsee the right to bring any action thereon that the indorser could bring."

It is therefore clear that in any state wherein the Negotiable Instruments Law has been enacted the holder of a negotiable instrument, whether he be owner or mere agent, can bring a suit thereon in his own name to enforce payment thereof, and when payment has been made to him "in due course" (that is, "payment made at or after the maturity of the instrument to the holder thereof in good faith and without notice that his title is defective." Section 148), the instrument is discharged.

We come now to the important section defining what constitutes a holder in due course.

HOLDER IN DUE COURSE.

Sec. 91. What Constitutes a Holder in Due Course.—A holder in due course is a holder who has taken the instrument under the following conditions:—

1. That it is complete and regular upon its face;
2. That he became the holder of it before it was overdue, and without notice that it had been previously dishonored, if such was the fact;
3. That he took it in good faith and for value;
4. That at the time it was negotiated to him he had no notice of any infirmity in the instrument or defect in the title of the person negotiating it.

In this section we have a full statement of the conditions under which an instrument must be taken in order to consti-

*Republished from the Banking Law Journal by permission. Copyright, 1899, 1900 and 1901, by T. B. Paton, all rights secured. To be revised and published in book form by the author.

tute the person acquiring it a holder in due course—or, in other words, a bona-fide holder for value, without notice—who is entitled to payment of its full face amount at all events, notwithstanding the instrument may, in the hands of any other holder, be non-payable by reason of want of consideration, fraud or other matter of defense between the original parties.

In the first place the instrument acquired must be complete and regular upon its face. In this connection it is well to bear in mind sections 33 and 34, treating of incomplete instruments delivered and not delivered, which were considered at length in previous issues of this paper. The substance of the law there stated is that where an incomplete instrument has been delivered by the maker, with authority to fill blanks therein and with the intention that it shall be a negotiable instrument, a bona-fide holder to whom the instrument is subsequently transferred, will be protected, although in filling up the blanks the authority has been exceeded; but where an incomplete instrument has never been delivered, but is stolen, filled up and negotiated, in this case, even bona-fide holders are not protected.

Next, the person acquiring the instrument must have become the holder of it before it was overdue.

Concerning the time when an instrument payable at a fixed or determinable future time is overdue, some authorities hold that a transfer upon the day of maturity is before the instrument is overdue, because the principal debtor has the whole of that period in which to pay; but other authorities hold that as payment of an instrument can be demanded at any reasonable hour during the day of maturity, one who takes it on that day takes it after it has in fact become due, and holds it subject to defenses. The Negotiable Instruments law does not provide a rule which settles this disputed point as to whether transfer on the day of maturity is, or is not, before the instrument is overdue.

Concerning instruments payable on demand, the only guide in the act as to when they become due or are overdue is in the provision (section 131) as to presentment: "Where the instrument is payable on demand, presentment must be made within a reasonable time after its issue, except that in the case of a bill of exchange presentment for payment will be sufficient if made within a reasonable time after the last negotiation thereof." "Reasonable time" is a very uncertain and elastic guide as to whether a demand instrument, transferred on a given day, is or is not, then overdue. The courts determine this question in view of the facts and circumstances of each particular case as it arises, with the result that in some cases certain periods of time from issue to presentment, such as two weeks, a month and the like, have been held unreasonable, while in other cases even longer periods have been declared reasonable. Each case, therefore, is, so to speak, more of a law unto itself than a safe guide for other cases. In some of the states statutes have been enacted in the interests of certainty, providing a fixed period, such as sixty days or four months, after which demand paper is overdue. In other states there is no other law of maturity than "reasonable time." The Negotiable Instruments Law goes no further than this. "Reasonable Time" is a very unsatisfactory regulation as to time of maturity in a system of negotiable instruments wherein certainty, and not guess-work, is the foundation stone. Therefore he who gives value for a negotiable instrument payable on demand and desires to be certain of full payment thereof, should take heed that it is still "fresh from the mint" of the issuer, and has not been sufficiently long outstanding to be declared overdue.

WITHOUT NOTICE OF PREVIOUS DISHONOR.

Furthermore, to be a holder in due course, the instrument must be taken without notice that it has been previously dishonored, if such is the fact. Thus if A gives his note, payable to order of B on demand and payment of the note is demanded of A and refused, the note is then dishonored. But if B thereafter negotiates the note for value to C, without informing him of the dishonor, C is a holder in due course, entitled to full payment from A, providing, of course, it was not "overdue" at the time C acquired it.

The next requisite to constitute a holder in due course is that he took the instrument "in good faith and for value."

What constitutes a holder in good faith? Carelessness is not the same as dishonesty, and the courts have settled that although a man may be negligent and omit to make the inquiry or take the precautions which a prudent man would have done, in acquiring a negotiable instrument, still he can enforce it as a bona-fide holder unless it can be proved that he actually took the instrument in bad faith. This is a matter to be determined from all the facts. Gross carelessness may be evidence of bad faith, but, at the same time, it may be consistent with good faith.

What constitutes a holder for value? We have already seen (sections 50 and 51) what constitutes value. It is any consideration which is sufficient to support a simple contract, and embraces an antecedent or pre-existing debt. For fuller exposition, our discussion upon those sections may be consulted.

The final requisite to constitute a holder in due course is "that at the time it was negotiated to him he had no notice of any infirmity in the instrument or defect in the title of the person negotiating it."

This is the "without notice" requirement of the common law, which provides that one entitled to payment of a negotiable instrument free from equities, must be a "bona-fide holder for value, before maturity, without notice." It is seen that there are two subjects, as to which the holder must take without notice of. They are (1) infirmity in the instrument, and (2) defect of title in the negotiator. Sections 94 and 95, presently to be considered, define with particularity when a title is defective, and what constitutes notice of infirmity in the instrument or defect in the title of the person negotiating the same.

We have now briefly reviewed the conditions under which an instrument must be taken to constitute the taker a holder in due course. The subsequent sections of Article V. amplify and particularize some of these conditions, state the rights of a holder in due course, state when an instrument is subject to original defenses, and provide as to when a holder is presumed to be a holder in due course, and when the burden of proof is on him to make proof thereof.

PERSON NOT HOLDER IN DUE COURSE.

Sec. 92. When person not deemed holder in due course. —Where an instrument payable on demand is negotiated an unreasonable length of time after its issue, the holder is not deemed a holder in due course.

This relates to the requisite that the holder must have acquired the instrument before it was overdue, which we have already discussed, particularizing same as to demand instruments. If a demand instrument is negotiated an unreasonable length of time after its issue, the taker is not a holder in due course. What is a reasonable time, and what is an unreasonable length of time? Scan the Negotiable Instruments Law from beginning to end, and no answer will be found. The answer rests in the bosoms of the judge and jury. There is no certainty here, only doubt and uncertainty. We have already criticised the weakness and incompleteness of such a requirement.

Sec. 93. Notice before full amount paid—Where the transferee receives notice of any infirmity in the instrument or defect in the title of the person negotiating the same before he has paid the full amount agreed to be paid therefor, he will be deemed a holder in due course only to the extent of the amount theretofore paid by him.

This section relates to cases where there is a piece-meal payment of consideration by the purchaser of a negotiable instrument. If part only of the consideration has been paid, and the purchaser then receives notice of infirmity or defect of title, his right to full payment, free from equities, is limited to the amount paid before notice; if he pays anything after notice, he is, as to such amount, merely a holder subject to defenses, not a holder in due course. An interesting question might not infrequently arise under this section whether a bank, which discounts a negotiable instrument for a customer and places the proceeds to his credit on deposit account, and then, after a portion of the deposit has been withdrawn, receives notice of defenses to the instrument, would have the right to rescind the balance of the credit and withhold its payment from the customer; or whether, after receiving such notice, if it allow the customer to withdraw the balance of the credit, it could enforce the instrument as a holder in due course, for the full amount?

WHEN TITLE IS DEFECTIVE.

Sec. 94. When title defective. The title of a person who negotiates an instrument is defective within the meaning of this act when he obtained the instrument, or any signature thereto by fraud, duress or force and fear, or other unlawful means, or for an illegal consideration, or when he negotiates it in breach of faith, or under such circumstances as amount to a fraud.

We have seen that one of the requisites to constitute a holder in due course is that he must have taken the instrument without notice of any defect in the title of the person negotiating it. In the above section we have a particularization of the matters which make a person's title defective, notice of any of which deprives the taker from such person of the rights of a holder in due course. They cover a wide range of unlawful and fraudulent acquisitions and negotiations of negotiable instruments, embracing frauds experienced by the commercial world in a multitude of detailed instances.

Sec. 95. What constitutes notice of defect. To constitute notice of an infirmity in the instrument or defect in the title of the person negotiating the same, the person to whom it is negotiated must have had actual knowledge of the infirmity or defect, or knowledge of such facts that his action in taking the instrument amounted to bad faith.

This section particularly defines what constitutes notice of an infirmity in the instrument or defect in the title of the person negotiating the same—for, to be a holder in due course, it must be taken without notice of such matters. This notice, we see, is either

(1) Actual knowledge of infirmity or defect; or

(2) Knowledge of such facts that make the taking of the instrument bad faith.

Actual knowledge of an infirmity or defect, of course, deprives the holder of the status of a holder in due course. As to what facts would make the taking of an instrument bad faith, this is a jury question under guidance of the court. Carelessness, negligence or imprudence in acquiring an instrument, or not following up suspicious circumstances by inquiry, are not necessarily the equivalent of bad faith or dishonesty.—a person may be perfectly honest, yet be careless and reckless—and the courts require evidence of actual bad faith, to defeat the title of one who claims as a holder in due course.

RIGHTS OF HOLDER IN DUE COURSE.

Sec. 96. Rights of holder in due course.—A holder in due course holds the instrument free from any defect of title of prior parties and free from defenses available to prior parties among themselves, and may enforce payment of the instrument for the full amount thereof against all parties liable thereon.

We have already stated in a general way, the rights or privileges of a holder in due course of a negotiable instrument. In the above section, his rights are legally and precisely defined. He is entitled to full payment from all parties liable thereon, notwithstanding there is a defect of title of prior parties, or defenses thereto, available to prior parties among themselves. Of course, his rights would not extend to collecting an instrument, upon which a prior indorsement, by way of transfer, had been forged. Here, there would not merely be a defect of title, but no title whatever in his transferor.

Sec. 97. When subject to original defenses.—In the hands of any holder other than a holder in due course, a negotiable instrument is subject to the same defenses as if it were non-negotiable. But a holder who derives his title through a holder in due course, and who is not himself a party to any fraud or illegality affecting the instrument, has all the rights of such former holder in respect of all parties prior to the latter.

In the first paragraph of this section we see that a negotiable instrument is subject to the same defenses as if it were non-negotiable in the hands of any holder other than a holder in due course. In other words the holder in due course is the only one who takes it free from equities and defenses. There is a conflict of decision as to what equities an instrument is subject to in the hands of one not a holder in due course. In some states only such equities as attach to the bill, can be asserted; while in other states equities between the original parties arising from collateral matters, may also be interposed as a matter of defense. The Negotiable Instruments Law does not regulate the law upon this point.

In the last paragraph of Section 97, a holder who derives his title through a holder in due course, and who is not himself a party to any fraud or illegality affecting the instrument, has all the rights of the holder in due course as against prior parties. To illustrate: A negotiable instrument is given by A to B under circumstances of fraud, which would preclude B's enforcement of it from A. But B negotiates it to C for value, before maturity, C knowing nothing of the fraud. C is a holder in due course, entitled to collect the full amount from A. C, however, negotiates the note to D, who has notice of the fraud by B upon A. Nevertheless, D can enforce the instrument against A as he takes all the rights of C, who is a holder in due course. Were it otherwise, C's right of negotiating or marketing the instrument would be crippled, if no one who knew of the circumstances surrounding the instrument could buy it from him.

WHO IS DEEMED HOLDER IN DUE COURSE.

Sec. 98. Who Deemed Holder in Due Course.—Every holder is deemed prima facie to be a holder in due course; but when it is shown that the title of any person who has negotiated the instrument was defective, the burden is on the holder to prove that he or some person under whom he claims acquired the title as a holder in due course. But the last-mentioned rule does not apply in favor of a party who became bound on the instrument prior to the acquisition of such defective title.

This, the concluding section of Article V, provides concerning the burden of proof when a negotiable instrument is brought into court for the enforcement of payment thereof. In the first place, the holder of the instrument is deemed, prima facie, to be a holder in due course. In other words, his mere possession or holding of the instrument, unless attacked, is sufficient to authorize his recovery without the necessity of making affirmative proof of all those requisites which are co-essential to constitute one a holder in due course. But when, in defense of payment, the fact is shown that the title of any person who has negotiated the instrument was defective (Section 94 particularizes the matters which make a person's title defective) then it becomes necessary for the holder to prove that he acquired the title as a holder in due course, or that some person under whom he claims, so acquired it. In other words, he must prove all the essentials to substantiate his, or his transferor's, status as a holder in due course. But the concluding paragraph of section 98 makes one exception. If the party sued on a negotiable instrument has become bound thereon prior to the acquisition of such defective title, then he cannot invoke the previously-mentioned rule in his favor; that is, he cannot upset the presumption that the holder is a holder in due course, and make him prove it. For example, A issues his negotiable note to B. B indorses it in blank, loses it and C finds it. C negotiates it to D for value, before maturity, without notice. D sues A. C's fraud is no defense to A, and D can enforce from A without proving that he is a holder in due course.

IN THE BUSINESS OFFICE

"Doesn't the everlasting rattle of the typewriters annoy you?"

"Their chatter, you mean."

Along the Highways and Byways of Business

By VANNANT

What is there in the business world that so much resembles comic opera, with, of course, the tuneful parts all omitted, as the labored efforts of commercial teachers discussing accounting? It is the custom of the proprietors of the so-called commercial colleges to get together semi-occasionally for the purpose of considering various matters of common interest. Papers are read and discussions are invited. Bouquet throwing comes in of course as an incidental pastime. All that they do, however, would be harmless if it was not published to the world. Unfortunately, however, for the good name of the profession, the proceedings of the conventions are published in full in the official journal, and thereby the practical, hard-fisted, common sense man of business is afforded additional arguments as often as these papers come out why he should discriminate against commercial college graduates whenever he needs more clerks. By these proceedings he is afforded a conception of the mass of misinformation with which the deluded youth of the land who go to these institutions are loaded, and which of course must be removed before they are worth anything to themselves or others in real business life.

* * *

Late in December last the National Commercial Teachers' Federation held its annual convention in St. Louis, Mo., and therein made a spectacle, the exact character of which is revealed to the world in the published reports which have recently been issued. Before considering specifically some of the comic stunts done by the doughty delegates, let us examine what the official reporter said by way of making himself solid for the next date:—

"First, as to the spirit of the convention: Perhaps no body of educators deserve more praise for the enthusiasm and broadminded views making for the uplift of human life than the commercial teachers of this convention. The spirit of the entire program evidenced an earnest of that desire to save young men and women from the useless and the unsuccessful. It was impressed that the whole energy of commercial teachers is as fully educational as that of any technical teacher can become. There was, moreover, that disposition of the times to grow constantly into ever larger courses of instruction, by adding to commercial courses whatever study or studies might appeal as practical and helpful."

Whatever may be said about the comparison that is fair between the energy of the commercial teachers and that of technical teachers, it still remains that the first qualification of the technical teacher is knowledge of his subject or practical familiarity with the topics under consideration. Chemistry, for example, is taught by experienced chemists, electrical engineering by those who are able to demonstrate their right to teach by performing practically the work required in the line mentioned, and architecture by those who have actually drawn the plans, specified the construction and superintended the erection of buildings. But where is the commercial teacher that is really wanted in the business office, or who could, in fact, hold his place in the practical work of business if perchance he once made his entrance therein?

* * *

However, this is not quite fair in the broad conclusion that might be reached. When it comes to teaching penmanship, the commercial schools do employ men who can write, and in the typewriting department they have those who can operate a machine. Cases are on record, even in the shorthand department, where teachers have been employed who could do practical shorthand work to the extent of reporting conventions, but such things are rare. When it comes to the accounting department, they occasionally have a man who knows the routine of simple bookkeeping, but beyond this they have never gone, and that is what makes the occasion so ludicrous when some member of this federation tries to tell what he does not know about accounting applied to business needs.

To give a more complete view of just what this convention did, the following is clipped from the official journal:—

"December 28th, 9 A. M., the business teachers' section was called to order as usual, President Hiner being in the chair. The topic for the hour, 'The Balance Sheet: What it Represents: How Made,' was championed by Dr. H. M. Rowe, Baltimore, Md., in a well prepared and enthusiastic paper. Discussion by Messrs. Chas. J. Smith, Enos Spencer, Eugene Moore, B. L. Merideth, D. W. Springer, G. W. Brown and Charles M. Bartlett. The next topic, 'Business Arithmetic: What and How Much Should Be Taught in the Commercial School,' had been assigned to Mr. W. N. Ferris, Big Rapids, Mich. The paper presented by Mr. Ferris needs no encomiums, as all know of his work along this line. This topic was discussed by Mr. R. M. Merideth, Zanesville, Ohio. This section was treated to a fine paper on 'Methods of Opening and Closing Corporation Books,' by Mr. Enos Spencer, Louisville, Ky. It was listened to with rapt attention. The usual discussion followed, participated in by Messrs. Moore, Dryden, Parish, Frye and others. On Monday, the first topic presented was 'Office Practice;' (a) 'Intercommunication,' led by L. W. P. Stiehl, of Uhricksville, Ohio; (b) 'Office Practice Combined with Barter Among Students,' led by Mr. J. F. Henderson, Oberlin, Ohio. These two papers were generally discussed with considerable animation. Mr. W. E. White, of Quincy, Ill., led and was followed by George P. Lord, Carl Marshall and A. S. Parish. 'Business Practice' was further considered in a well-written and interesting paper from a commercial high school standpoint, by Mr. J. B. Van Matre, of Omaha, Neb. Discussion followed. One of the important and timely topics was the 'Advantages and Adaptation of the Voucher System,' introduced by Mr. U. G. Frye, Chicago, Ill. The convention was well pleased, and the discussion showed much interest in this paper."

* * *

Space will not permit an examination into all these efforts, but brief inquiry into the paper on the Balance Sheet will repay the time spent. At the outset the author said:—

"There are two forms of the balance sheet with which all are familiar: the older form, which is made up by grouping the losses and gains, the resources and liabilities; and the later form, with separate columns for the debits and credits, losses and gains, resources and liabilities."

A pertinent fact which the speaker omitted to state is that, however familiar commercial teachers and authors of treatises on bookkeeping may be with these two forms of the balance sheet, neither of them is recognized in the business office. Neither of them comes within gunshot of what the business man requires. Here is still further quotation from the address:—

"As far as I can ascertain the older form of balance sheet was originally taken from the ledger after it was closed, and was intended mainly as an exhibit of the facts shown by the ledger at the time of closing and the sources thereof. It was really a transcript of the profit and loss account and of the old balance account, which has long since been dropped as a ledger account. The later form of the balance sheet doubtless had its origin in a desire to exhibit the results which would be finally shown by the ledger and as a guide preliminary to closing the ledger. I know of no other form to equal it, and it must often be supplemented by other statements. It is now a universal custom to make out a balance sheet, in whatever form it may take, before closing the ledger."

* * *

It is really unfair to this author to proceed with this criticism after this flat admission here made that he is discussing the balance sheet, not from the standpoint of requirements or business utility, but, instead, from a merely superficial survey of the annals of the commercial schools. In the few lines quoted the author shows that he does not know the difference between a balance sheet and a profit and loss statement, having confused and confounded the two. He cannot, evidently, conceive of a balance sheet away from a ledger, and yet business men are requiring every day in the year balance sheet statements of business in which, unfortunately, there has been no ledger maintained. As a fact, known to every man except commercial college teachers and authors of bookkeeping treatises balance sheets precede ledgers, follow ledgers, and are often constructed for the information of the embarrassed business man in spite of his ledger, or, in other words, "his ledger, to the contrary notwithstanding."

* * *

The paper from which the quotations have been taken and to which these remarks apply was illustrated by several forms, entitled, respectively, "Balance Sheet," "Merchandise Statement," "Sundry Account" and "Profit and Loss Statement," all of which fully bear out the conclusions already reached. Referring to the last form above named, I might, in justice to the author, quote his description:—

"The profit and loss statement is simply a reproduction of that account as it would appear in the ledger after the various accounts are closed and the profits adjusted as directed by the board of directors. A balance sheet similar in form and arrangement could be made up although the resources and liabilities are shown very plainly on the principal balance sheet."

Altogether this effort, I take it, will go thundering down the ages as an example of "business practice as she was taught (in the commercial schools) in the first years of the twentieth century."

* * *

In the course of his remarks Mr. Rowe paid his compliments to the balance sheet accounting as follows:—

"Several eastern accountants are promoting a system of accounting, which goes a step further, and exhibits at any time the cost value of the goods on hand. This is accomplished by recording the cost price, as well as the selling price, of each article as it is sold. The total of these cost prices, if deducted from the total cost of purchases, would, of course, give the inventory value of goods on hand, and if deducted from total sales would give the gross profit; but, except in a very few lines where goods are handled in large values, the plan is not practicable, and, besides, it attaches an importance to the value of the goods on hand which it does not possess. If the business manager knew, to a penny, the daily value of the goods on the shelves, it would be a unit of information of little consequence. What he does want to know in this connection is the goods that are moving rapidly, and those that are moving slowly, and the quantity on hand, so that he can anticipate the demand for the quick sellers, and push the slow sellers. The ordinary stock books give this information fully."

In other words, when a man, feeling the pangs of hunger, desires a square meal, console him by calling attention to the most excellent pair of shoes he is wearing, and assure him they are all he needs to keep the water out. Mr. Rowe evidently cannot conceive of the asset value of goods and the salability of goods as distinct matters. They are equivalents, apparently, to his mind.

* * *

The paper by Enos Spencer was entitled "Methods of Opening and Closing Corporation Books." There were no illustrations of either opening or closing books of the corporation variety or of any other sort, nor any description of these operations. There was talk of a desultory character about various matters more or less relevant to corporations, but to make possible the application of what this professor and author said would make necessary the use of the corporation laws of all the states in the Union. For a fact he did scatter awfully. Like various others, Mr. Spencer affects to see something involved and mysterious in corporation accounting. He gave himself "dead away" in this regard in his prefatory remarks, from which I quote:—

"In a single proprietorship and a partnership business there is only one set of books, the investment accounts of the individual investor or proprietors being kept upon the general or private ledger of the business. In a corporation the stockholders' or investors' names do not appear upon the general books as investors or proprietors. If they have any transactions with the corporation as employees, customers or creditors, their accounts will appear with the debtor or creditor class of accounts the same as those of any other individual's. For the purpose of keeping accounts with the stockholders as such, so that the number of shares held by each, the number of votes that each is entitled to at any stockholders' meeting, or for the purpose of paying dividends, or making assessments, a separate set of books is kept, known as the stock set or stock ledger. I prefer a stock ledger in which the name and address of every stockholder shall appear on his account, and in which he is credited with the number of shares held by him. The journal, or book of original entry for this ledger, will be the stub of the certificate of stock book or transfer book."

In view of the above I feel disposed to suggest to the professor that at the first opportunity he defines "set of books."

* * *

But it is only when we get to the "resolutions" adopted by the convention that we perceive the real fun of the combination. Here is resolve No. 1:—

"The National Commercial Teachers' Federation, in annual convention assembled, herewith voices its renewed confidence in commercial education as a means of fitting our youth for capability in the practical affairs of life, and for worthy citizenship in our matchless Republic."

"Matchless" is good, and, come to think, quite apropos. Among other respects it is matchless in that it is the only nation in which the commercial college has found root and grown, and the business public of which has allowed itself to be bluffed into supporting the institution in the belief that it was doing a good work. Here is resolve No. 6, the first sentence of which, read between the lines, seems to be of the nature of an honest confession—

"We hereby condemn the tendency that has sometimes been manifested in certain commercial schools to place the money-making feature of the school above its educational standing and responsibility. We affirm that a worthy commercial school should be something more than either a clerk factory or an intelligence office, and that it should be beneath the honor and dignity of any respectable school proprietor to increase his school attendance by misleading inducements that appeal to the cupidity of the student rather than to his honest desire for a genuine education."

Hereafter, if some one says "clerk factory," do not forget where he got the phrase. But what are we to think of resolve No. 7? Is it possible that the general government knows a thing or two about the commercial schools? Here is the declaration, which the reader may take for just what it is worth:—

"We herewith record our earnest protest against the recent arbitrary and ex parte ruling of the Attorney General of the United States, to the effect that the incorporated commercial schools of this country are not institutions of learning,' within the meaning of the United States laws, and which ruling unjustly deprives them of the benefit of a congressional enactment that was confessedly passed especially for their encouragement, and of which they have availed themselves for nearly eight years. The commercial schools of the United States do not ask for governmental aid in conducting their business, but they do demand the right to disseminate their educational literature through the agency of the United States mails at the same postal rates as those allowed to other educational institutions, and they especially insist that by the terms of the Manderson-Hainer act, of July 24, 1894, and which act has never been repealed, this right to send their periodical publications through the mails at the rates for second-class matter was especially conferred upon them, and that the interruption of this by an executive department of the government is unjust, arbitrary and illegal, and we hereby pledge our united efforts to secure not only our rights under the law, but the removal of the stigma that has been wantonly put upon our worthy profession by the arbitrary and uncalled for pronouncement of a government official."

In reading the first line of this, and also the first part of No. 1, I wonder if the word "herewith" was not intended to be "hereby"? However, rhetoric, we believe, is not in the commercial course. Evidently somebody's pocketbook is hurt. Why not allow all advertising matter, whether of commercial schools or butcher shops or dry goods stores, to go at second-class rates? So far as I have inspected the literature of the several industries mentioned, the dry goods stores are in the lead. What they send out is far more educational than that distributed by the commercial schools.

THEY NEEDED HIM

"I say," said the business man to the detective, "some fellow has been representing himself as a collector of ours. He has been taking in more money than any two men we have, and I want him collared as quickly as you can."

"All right; I'll have him in jail in less than a week."

"Great Scott, man! I don't want to put him in jail; I want to engage him."—Boston Transcript.

Current Business Cartoons

Newspaper cartoonists have been very prolific during the past month. There have been cartoons on all subjects now prominently before the public, and the standard has generally been high. The subject of reciprocity or tariff reform with Cuba has occupied the attention of the editorial

Ice bound.--Chicago Record-Herald.

writers to such an extent that it is natural that the cartoons should reflect the tone of the papers in which they appeared.

We reproduce three cartoons on the subject of Cuban tariff reform, from among the hundreds that have come to our desk. F. T. Richards, of the New York Herald, had

The latest Rough-Rider Charge.—New York World.

several well-drawn pictures on this subject, one of which we reproduce. It shows Congress as a giant, trampling upon prostrate Cuba, while Uncle Sam, evidently feeling much disgraced, watches the performance from a corner. The cartoon was inspired by a Shakespearean quotation.

As illustrating the similarity of ideas of two cartoonists in papers of distant cities, we reproduce two cartoons on the Cuban question, one from the Boston Herald and the other from the Chicago Record-Herald. The Boston paper's artist, Williams, shows the ship "Cuba Tariff Relief" becalmed in a smooth sea, with the sails hanging flat from the yards, and with no prospect of arriving in port. Uncle Sam is asleep at the tiller.

McCutcheon, in the Chicago Record-Herald, shows the ship "Cuban Reciprocity" ice-bound, with the flag union

Becalmed.—Boston Herald.

down at the foretop, the sails and rigging coated thickly with ice, and the ship's company trying to keep warm on the floes and bergs surrounding the vessel. The sugar trust,

"Oh, it is excellent to have a giant's strength; but it is tyrannous to use it like a giant."—New York Herald.

typified by a portly individual in fur-trimmed overcoat and silk hat, mocks the frozen vessel and her crew from a distant peak.

Columbia—Queen of Hearts.—Chicago Tribune.

"Eggs is riz," as the farmer says, and they were high enough before, as every householder knows. Bowman's cartoon in the Minneapolis Tribune is very clever. The hencoop is iron clad, and the farmer stands guard over it with a gun, while his wife, protected by a small boy, also armed, carefully carries one precious egg to the house.

Prince Henry's visit has been the subject of innumerable cartoons from one end of the country to the other. Of these we reproduce one from the Minneapolis Journal. The two eagles are as friendly as one could wish.

Speaking of kings and princes reminds us that Mr.

Eggs have gone up again. Minneapolis Tribune.

Schwab, whom the papers call the "Steel King," has returned from Europe. In his trips about the Continent and through England Mr. Schwab met with a very flattering reception, and, if reports are true, hobnobbed with royalty to a considerable extent. In the cartoon in the Brooklyn Eagle Mr. Schwab's triumphal reception by the crowned heads is pictured in exaggerated humorous fashion.

The Eagles in chorus: "Well, you are a bird!"—Minneapolis Journal.

When Attorney-General Knox, at President Roosevelts instigation, started his investigation of the subject as to whether merging of the railroad interests was constitutional, it was not thought that anything would come of it, but the Attorney-General surprised the country, and Wall Street in particular, by asserting that railroad merging was not constitutional. Bush, of the New York World, has one of his inimitable cartoons on this subject. We doubt if the

This shows the triumph of Republican institutions.—Brooklyn Eagle.

Attorney-General was much pleased with this picture, as it shows him bridled and saddled and ridden by the President, who has just dashed through Wall Street at full speed, leaving consternation on the bull side of the market.

The amusing discussion among the powers as to which

Uncle Sam: "Shut her off, old man; I've got enough!"—Denver Republican.

was the more friendly toward the United States during our war with Spain was cartooned extensively. We reproduce one of these cartoons, that from the Chicago Tribune. Each of the powers is presenting a valentine to Columbia.

An important part of the war tax has been done away with, Congress having taken action in the matter. The cartoon from the Denver Republican is illustrative of this subject. Uncle Sam has surplus enough, according to the artist, and does not need any more. Therefore he requests that the chute, down which the steady stream of gold has been flowing, shall be closed by Congress.

PHONETIC SPELLING

"How do you spell 'security'?" asked Badleigh Mildude, laboriously writing a letter to Andrew Carnegie to ask him for a loan of $50,000.

"With a 'c' an' a 'q,' of course," responded Tuffold Knutt. "Cain't ye tell by the sound of it?"—Exchange.

System in the Modern Office

Of all the improvements which progress has brought to the modern office, the system of filing business documents in get-at-able fashion is perhaps the greatest. The office man of the old days carefully tied his paid bills, used checks, etc., into bundles. These he then put away in boxes or chests, with the result that, when he wished to find a certain paper, he was practically sure that it would take him a week or more to find it. The paper was not lost, if we accept the old maxim illustrated by the story of the cook and the frying-pan, that "nothing is lost if you know where it is." The frying-pan, our readers will remember, was not lost, because the cook knew where it was,—it was overboard; and the business paper was not lost, because it was somewhere in one of the

FIG. 1. RAPID GUIDE CARDS.

thirty or forty chests; but the time spent in searching for it was lost.

Now, however, all this is changed. The card index system and adequate filing equipments are as much a part of the office of today as is the bookkeeper's desk. No firm doing a large business can get along without these aids to office system.

There are many kinds of filing devices, but perhaps one of the most complete is the system the appliances of which are manufactured and sold by Clarke & Baker, whose place of business is at 280 Broadway, New York City.

Clarke & Baker, who are selling agents of the Tucker Filing and Cabinet Co., of Ilion, N. Y., make a specialty of card equipments and office filing devices. In one of their several catalogues they said, concerning their special card equipment:—

"The value of any tool depends partly upon the quality of the material of which it is constructed. The quality of card

FIG. 2. DRAWER OF FILING CARDS.

used for filing and indexing is of the utmost importance. Consideration of the subject will show that the cards used must possess certain essential qualities if they are to prove efficient and satisfactory.

"The value of records may be temporary or permanent. And this fact must be borne in mind in considering the nature and quality of a card. In form and stock the card must be specifically adapted to accomplish the results desired.

"The first essential of a card system is that the card employed shall be made of paper stock manufactured with a view to the peculiar wear which such cards receive. Moreover, they must be cut by special machinery and cut with absolute accuracy, so that the dimensions in the same sizes will always be uniform and the edges square and true.

"Again, the surface of such cards must possess smooth fin-

FIG. 3. ANOTHER VARIETY OF DRAWER.

ish, taking ink readily and easily from the pen; and yet at the same time possessing good erasive quality, as minor changes in card memoranda are frequently required where it is needless to re-write the whole card.

"The stock of which the card is made must have snap and elasticity, so as to spring back into place under handling without becoming permanently bent or worn. This can be accomplished only by a card that will not wear down—a card made of the best stock and possessing superior resiliency.

"The above considerations have been impressed upon us by a careful study of and extensive experience in the needs of card users. Our card stock is especially made for us to accomplish these results. And we are confident that if the tests

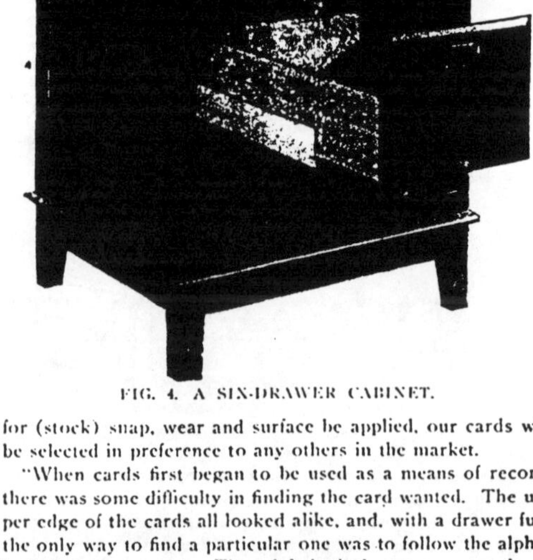

FIG. 4. A SIX-DRAWER CABINET.

for (stock) snap, wear and surface be applied, our cards will be selected in preference to any others in the market.

"When cards first began to be used as a means of record, there was some difficulty in finding the card wanted. The upper edge of the cards all looked alike, and, with a drawer full, the only way to find a particular one was to follow the alphabetical arrangement. The alphabetical arrangement is of course still followed, but improvements have been added. The latest, and perhaps the best, of these improvements is the Rapid Guide attachment, which may be readily adjusted to the upper edge of the card marking a division of the contents of the drawer, thus indicating the beginning of a department.

"This Rapid Guide, which is a special feature of the Clarke & Baker system, is equipped with metal projections in which the labels are removable and interchangeable at will. This guide possesses all the durability of metal without its weight, and is the only guide on the market having an interchangeable label. The Rapid Guide will not break or wear down, and the label does not become soiled or rubbed off. When a new label is desired, the old label is withdrawn and a new one inserted with no further trouble than the writing of the new title. For the filing of cards, checks and letters, and, indeed,

FIG. 5. SMALL CARD CABINET.

for all purposes requiring durability and facility, this is the best and most economical guide in use. In the end it always proves the cheapest."

Fig. 1 shows an assortment of these Rapid Guides, and in Fig. 2 and Fig. 3 the cards in the drawer are equipped with this handy adjunct. Fig. 2 and Fig. 3 also give a good idea of the card index system as perfected by this company. The cards of course may be made any size, but a number of regular sizes are kept in stock and are always on hand to meet the demand of customers.

When filing cards first began to be used it was at once seen that cabinets to contain the special drawers filled with cards were needed. The first cabinets made were somewhat crude and not to be compared with the elegant office furnishings now manufactured.

In Fig. 4 is shown a six-drawer card cabinet. It is made of quartered oak, has a desk top, and is in every way a beautiful piece of furniture.

In Fig. 5 is shown a small card cabinet, which may be placed on top of a roll-top desk or on a table. The front of each drawer in these cabinets is furnished with a metal pull, which is also a rack, meant to contain a typewritten or pencilled slip of paper describing the contents of the drawer.

The cabinets here illustrated are but two of the many styles manufactured by Clarke & Baker. This firm is prepared to equip an entire office with cabinets of all sizes and fitted for the systematic filing of all kinds of papers. They manufacture letter-file cabinets, in which the drawer containing an indexed letter-file tips forward and is held in a vertical position, so that the file may be consulted easily and without removing the drawer from the cabinet.

They manufacture document files for filing of folded papers. In one of their several catalogues, any or all of which will be sent to any one interested upon receipt of postage, is shown a photograph of the huge filing cabinets used in the London Assurance Corporation of New York City. This cabinet, which takes up the entire side of a large room, is equipped with book shelves below, and has rolling ladders on the side similar to those used in the modern shoe store, by means of which the files at the top of the cabinet may be reached. Another photograph shows the interior of the Corporation Counsel's office, New York City. The cabinet in this office contains 785 files.

To consult a catalogue such as Clarke & Baker's, or, better still, to see the goods themselves, is a revelation to the man unacquainted with the possibilities of a systematic filing system. A system such as this is but one of the many progressive steps which the American merchant has taken in the last twenty years and which have placed him where he is, in command of the commerce of the world.

A MECHANICAL ACCOUNTANT

Adding machines, or, to speak more correctly, machines by the aid of which the accountant can quickly and accurately add, multiply, subtract and divide, have been in use for some years, but to many they are still a novelty. Even to the initiated man, who has not only seen but is using a machine of this kind, its amazing possibilities and the number of uses to which it may be put, are a constant revelation.

The Comptometer, manufactured by the Felt & Tarrant Mfg. Co., of Chicago, is one of the best of these wonderful machines. After a little experience an operator on the Comptometer may, with little trouble and nothing like the expenditure of time required by the ordinary method, add, subtract, divide, compute interest and compound interest, figure discounts and even extract the square root.

The accompanying illustration gives a fair idea of what the Comptometer looks like. The machine is neat and compact, weighs nine pounds, is fourteen and one-half inches in

THE COMPTOMETER.

length, seven and one-half inches in width and five inches in height, and is an ornament to any office.

A large part of the work connected with accounting can be dispensed with entirely where the Comptometer is used. For instance: Items which are on different pages of a book, or on different sheets of paper, such as bills, checks, notes, time-tickets, etc., can be footed directly from the book or papers, while to be added the old way they would first have to be listed. Where there are a number of multiplications to be made and the products added, the multiplications can be made one after another without canceling, allowing the products to accumulate in the machine, giving as a final answer the sum of all the products. Many other kinds of work could be cited in which the machine enables one to dispense with half of the work and perform the other half twice as rapidly as it could be done by the old process. But do not get the idea that the utility of the Comptometer is confined to certain classes of arithmetical work. There is no class of arithmetical work connected with accounting or engineering on which it cannot be used, when skilfully operated, at a saving of from one-half to three-quarters of the time required by an expert mental computer; and by using the Comptometer there is in checking up a further saving of time, owing to the greater liability to error when doing the work mentally.

In offices where much adding of long columns of figures is done daily, a machine like the Comptometer becomes almost an absolute necessity. Particularly is this the case in banks, and bank men are fast realizing this fact.

Financial and Commercial Books

A MULTITUDE OF COUNSELLORS. By J. N. Larned. 8 1-2 x 5 3-4 inches. 500 pages. Bound in cloth. Cover and back title, gilt. Published by Houghton, Mifflin & Company. Price, $2.00.

This book is described on its title page as being a collection of codes, precepts and rules of life from the wise of all ages. It contains wise sayings, proverbs and good advice by the world's sages from Ptah-Hotep to Thoreau. This, of course, is a very wide range, but Mr. Larned has, with painstaking labor, covered the ground thoroughly. If in "A multitude of counsellors there is safety," the reader of this book should be tolerably safe when he has finished it. A selection from the precepts of Ptah-Hotep forms the second chapter, the first being an introductory essay on the ancient and modern knowledge of good and evil.

These precepts of Ptah-Hotep are taken from an ancient Egyptian papyrus, which, the introduction tells us, is the oldest book in the world. The author was a feudal lord of Egypt, under King Assa. Assa was a monarch of the fifth dynasty and he is believed by chronologists to have reigned at a period somewhere between 3700 and 3500 years before Christ. Most of the old Egyptian's precepts are as good advice to the young man of today as they were to the Egyptian stripling of 5600 years ago. He naively advises the avoidance of a quarrel with a bigger man, in the following language. "If thou findest a disputant while he is hot, and if he is superior to thee in ability, lower the hands, bend the back, do not get into a passion with him. He argues against idleness, shiftlessness and ill-temper, and advises all to respect knowledge and calmness of language.

Several chapters of this "A Multitude of Counsellors" are given up to quotations from the Old and New Testament, then follow chunks of wisdom from the Hindoos, the Persians, the "Seven wise men of Greece," the Buddhist Beattitudes, Confucius and so on, down to the comparatively modern sages like Thomas a Kempis and the Duke De La Rochefoucauld and on to Washington, Carlyle and Emerson. All this collected learning and wise thought is well worth reading and even better worth following. However, preaching the virtues is always much easier than practicing them, for as we know, some of these wise advisers were not the models they command others to be.

The book is a valuable reference library in itself, and to one wishing to find a proverb "to point a moral or adorn a tale" it should be very valuable.

INTRODUCTION TO THE STUDY OF ECONOMICS. By Charles Jesse Bullock, Ph. D. 7 3-4 x 5 1-2 inches. 581 pages. Bound in cloth. Back and title, gilt. Published by Silver, Burdett & Company. Price, $1.25.

This book, the author says, is designed for an introductory text book of economic science. The first three chapters aim to familiarize the student with an orderly treatment of some leading facts in the economic history of the United States. Throughout the book, economic principles are discussed with special reference to American conditions, and their workings are illustrated by frequent allusions to American experience.

The chapters of history treat of Westward expansion, land tenures in the United States, the growth of population, labor systems, the fur trade, etc.

The subject of economics is introduced with a chapter on the consumption of wealth. Then follow other chapters on the production of wealth and its various divisions, including labor and capital. There are chapters on the Theory of Exchange, Development of Metallic Money, Money and Credit, which includes the Theory of Banking, Monopolies, National Trade, and the Distribution of Wealth. Socialism, Taxation and Public Revenues are also discussed.

Mr. Bullock's book is an able introductory treatise to the study of economics and makes interesting and instructive reading. It is well printed on good paper and is neatly bound.

THE ANATOMY OF A RAILROAD REPORT. By Thos. F. Woodlock. 7 x 5 1-4 inches. 121 pages. Bound in cloth. Cover and back title, gilt. Published by S. A. Nelson.

This little book is uniform with the "A. B. C. of Banks and Banking," which we reviewed a short time since. The author disclaims any attempt at elaboration of his subject and says that he offers the book as a mere primer. It is intended for the use of those people who, while interested in railroad investments, are wholly unacquainted with railroad accounts. The book is divided into two sections, the first being the Anatomy of a Railroad Report, and the second being Ton-Mile Cost. It treats of phases of the railroad business concisely, but, so far as an outsider may judge, thoroughly and accurately. It is neatly bound and of a good, handy size.

NEW MANUAL OF THE CONSTITUTION. By Israel Ward Andrews, D.D., LL.D. 7 1-2 x 5 1-2 inches 431 pages. Bound in cloth. Cover title, gilt. Published by the American Book Company. Price, $1.00.

This is a new edition of this standard work and the book has undergone a thorough revision in order that it may be brought up to date. It is perhaps one of the best, if not the very best, treatise on the system of government of our country and each department of the governmental machinery is discussed thoroughly and impartially. The first few chapters are devoted to a history of civil government and its origin, and, more particularly, to a history of the government of the American colonies up to the time of the American Revolution. Then follows a number of chapters on the constitution of the United States, its framing, rulings and practical application. There is also a chapter devoted to state government. The Appendix contains a list of Vice-Presidents and Cabinet members who have held offices in this country since its beginning. The Appendix also contains the Declaration of Independence, the Articles of Confederation, the Constitution itself, etc.

HOW THE ESKIMOS TELL TIME

"How do the Eskimos tell time?" was the inquiry made by the New York Times of a man who has had considerable experience in North Greenland in connection with the Peary expeditions. He had just been telling something about the long arctic "day" with the sun circling around and around a short distance above the horizon, and the question was a natural one.

"They have two different methods," he replied, "according to the interval of time involved. For instance, if you are about to start on a journey and ask an Eskimo how long it will take, he will tell you 'three sleeps' or 'four sleeps,' corresponding to the number of days the trip will take, but he knows nothing about a day—only that every so often he has to stop to sleep. And, fortunately, the Eskimo finds it convenient to sleep about once in twenty-four hours, so that his 'sleep' means practically a day.

"On the other hand, I remember seeing Peary dispatching an Eskimo one morning with a message to a nearby settlement, and the explorer kept pointing to the sun, which at the time stood immediately above a rocky eminence across the bay. I wondered what it was all about, and asked Peary:

" 'I want that fellow to be back here to-morrow at this time,' he replied, 'and the only way to tell him is to call his attention to the position of the sun. He knows that he is to return when the sun has gotten around to that point again.'

"Sure enough, the next morning, when the sun had circled the horizon and was again above the point of rock, the Eskimo could be seen running across the bay in his kayak."

A MEMORY OF CHILDHOOD

Old lady (in shoe store)—"Have you felt slippers?"

Young gentleman clerk—"Very often, when I was younger."—Exchange.

BRIEF MENTION.

WHAT TEMPTING LITERATURE, especially at this season of the year, the circulars and booklets of the modern railway company make. We have just received an assortment of the advertising literature, issued by the Chicago, Rock Island & Pacific Railway, and we feel strongly tempted to drop everything and start for Colorado. The title of the booklets issued by this company are as follows: "Colorado, the Magnificent," "Manitou and the Mountains," "Winter Sunshine," "Fishing in Colorado," "Oklahoma Opportunity." We have received also several copies of the paper, The Western Trail, which the Rock Island Route issues for distribution among its patrons, or prospective patrons. The booklet "Colorado, the Magnificent," comes pretty near to being a work of art. It is finely printed on good paper, with wide margins, and is beautifully illustrated with marginal halftone cuts artistically arranged. These halftone cuts are reproductions from photographs, showing beautiful bits of scenery amid the Colorado mountains. The booklet "Manitou and the Mountains," is even more elaborate, being printed in tints with a colored cover, the front leaf of which represents sunrise on Pike's Peak, and the back a view of the town of Manitou, Colorado. There are photographs taken in the Garden of the Gods and along the cogwheel railroad to Pike's Peak. The quality of the literary work in these two booklets, and also in those entitled "Winter Sunshine" and "Fishing in Colorado," is fully in keeping with the beautiful illustrations. To the angler the little book "Fishing in Colorado" is good reading, and is tempting in the extreme. It is an account of an outing given by a party of city men, who spent their vacation in the trout-fishing region of Colorado. We advise every angler to read it. Such booklets as these would have been a revelation to the advertising man of twenty years ago. The printers' art and the art of the engraver have been measurably improved in that time, and, we may add, the art of advertising has improved along with them. This advertising matter of the Chicago, Rock Island & Pacific Railway Company is very beautiful, and is well worth not only reading, but keeping for its pictorial and literary worth alone.

THE TRUCK AND BARROW catalogue of the Howe Scale Company, of Rutland, Vt., has been sent to us, and we find it a very neat volume of 128 pages. In it are illustrated the various styles of factory barrows and trucks that this company manufactures. The casual reader will be surprised to find how many kinds of baggage trucks and factory trucks are manufactured. There are hotel trucks, made with broad wheels for running over carpets without injuring the latter. There are household trucks for carrying heavy articles about the house or barn, cotton trucks, baggage trucks, wheat trucks, longshore trucks and many others. There are trucks with two wheels, three wheels and four wheels; trucks made like boxes, and trucks made to run on tracks. The Howe Company also make light baggage wagons, for the hauling of baggage by hand in big city railway stations, and they make a variety of barrows, skids and other factory wheeled necessaries. What our fathers did by clumsy methods is now done by improved and easy methods, and in no branch of business is this improvement more apparent than in this carrying of goods from one department of the factory to another. We think any reader will be interested in the Howe Scale Company's catalogue, whether they may wish to buy a truck immediately or not. Page, Dennis & Co., 341 Broadway, are the New York agents.

WE NOTE with more than ordinary interest the booklet entitled "Trust Companies and Their Functions." The Knickerbocker Trust Company, of New York, has issued this booklet for the purpose of exploiting the advantages that the trust company is able to offer to its dealers. The enormous expansion of trade in the United States within the last few years has called into existence a large number of new financial and banking institutions. Business demands banking facilities. Circulation in the form of money is insignificant as compared with the check. The check is accepted without query in almost all of the transactions of business. This is based upon the stability of our financial institutions. Not so many years ago the case was a different one, and bank notes were an uncertain quantity, and checks were accepted more upon the credit of the firm issuing them than the banking house upon which they were drawn. The changing conditions in the field of trade relations have produced the trust company. The trust company, having broader rights under the terms of its charter, is enabled to facilitate these same trade relations and accord to the merchant assistance both financial and, we might say, in the way of credit which the bank cannot give. The booklet issued by the Knickerbocker Trust Company is a product of the printers' art which challenges comparison with the most artistic booklets that have been issued. As a treatise on the functions of a trust company, it is pointed, terse and tells its story in a way that is both impressive and convincing. Every merchant requiring a New York bank account will do well to read this pamphlet. A letter addressed to the Knickerbocker Trust Company will be sufficient to have one sent. We feel that the points taken in this pamphlet are particularly well taken. Commencing with the directory, we find the names of men connected with prominent business enterprises, who are known for their rigid honesty and ability. Money and credit are entrusted to the banking house. This trust is based upon the faith of the depositors in the ability and integrity of the directors. The statement of the Knickerbocker Trust Company shows resources of over thirty-two millions of dollars. The broader rights given trust companies by their charters enable them to pay interest upon their deposits. They are empowered to act as executors for administration of estates, as guardians, receivers, registrars and financial agents for cities, towns or corporations. Their facilities for making loans are exceptional, both in amount and in the length of time in the lending of the cash. New incorporations find in the trust company the greatest aid in organization and commercial consolidations. Freed from the restrictions imposed upon banks, the American trust company is beyond all question the best equipped monetary institution in the world—a fiduciary company empowered also to do a general banking business. In New York State alone, the extraordinary increase in the deposit account in the trust companies since 1897 has aggregated over five hundred million dollars. The Knickerbocker Trust Company makes collections on all foreign cash instruments in precisely the same manner that the bank does. It manages real estate, and acts as fiscal agent over a wide range of business affairs

THIS IS THE SEASON of the year when the householder begins to think about refrigerators, and the water-cooler becomes an important part of the office furniture. The McCray Refrigerator and Cold Storage Company, of Kendallville, Ind., send us a very handsomely illustrated catalogue of the refrigerators which they manufacture. The cuts in this catalogue are beautifully executed, and illustrate the various styles of McCray Refrigerators very handsomely. The old-fashioned zinc lined ice-box is put to shame by the handsome modern article, lined either with clean, dry wood upon which, says the catalogue, a match may be lit at any time, no matter if the ice-chamber be ever so full, or with smooth, handsome porcelain tiles. Regarding the keeping of drinking water in the refrigerator, the McCray catalogue says: "Open water coolers should never be located in the ice chamber, for the reason that if the refrigerators work properly all the evaporation from the product in the refrigerator should pass to the ice-chamber, where it is deposited on the ice, and runs off with the drip. With an open water cooler this evaporation is as liable to drop into the water as elsewhere; thus you would be drinking water which is tainted by the products in your refrigerator. It is far safer to keep the drinking water in a bottle, in one of the lower departments, than to have it in the ice-chamber. The modern water cooler is made by placing a coil of block tin pipe in the bottom of the ice-chamber, having one end attached to the city water works or other source of water supply, and the other end being supplied with a faucet out in front of the refrigerator from which to draw your drinking water. In this way you have the benefit of cold water for drinking purposes, without the dangers of the water in the ice-chamber being exposed to all the foul vapor from the product kept in lower departments of the refrigerators." To any one contemplating the purchase of a refrigerator, or templating the installing of a refrigerating plant in a hotel or private residence, we would recommend sending for a McCray catalogue. It is a thing of art in itself, and is alone well worth the trouble and postage stamp.

A GOOD DICTIONARY should be an item of the equipment of every office as much as a good desk, a good safe or a good typewriter. The relationship of the dictionary to the typewriter is ordinarily recognized, using the term typewriter, of course, as the individual that operates the machine rather than the machine. As a rule typewriter operators are equipped with small and inadequate dictionaries. Nothing short of an unabridged dictionary will answer all of the questions that arise concerning the spelling and exact meaning of the various words that are employed. Webster's International Dictionary, the successor in direct line to Webster's Unabridged, and being a better interpretation of the unabridged idea than was the unabridged dictionary in its day, published by G. & C. Merriam Company, Springfield, Mass., is something exactly adapted to requirements. It is a royal quarto volume, with no less than 2,364 pages and upwards of 5,000 illustrations. Any of our readers mentioning this notice and writing to the publishers will receive some printed matter that will be of the greatest interest to them.

THE REPUTATION of Hall's Safes is not to be gainsaid. Their good qualities in resisting both the attacks of burglars and the ravages of the flames have been appreciated through more than two generations, and all that is to be said in comparing those of the present day with those that other generations used is that with the development of manufacturing, construction is improved, and those of the present, therefore, are better than those of an earlier date. The New York agents are Kinsey, Ranier & Co., 393 Broadway, and those of our readers who address inquiries to them will receive printed matter that is of the greatest interest.

WE ARE IN RECEIPT of a very pretty little folder, with an artistically designed cover, advertising the Improved Beebe Indelible Check Protector. There are dozens of check protectors or check punches in the market, but the Beebe would appear to be one of the few that really protect the check drawer against alterations and frauds. The ordinary perforating and cutting machine, which at one time was considered to be an invaluable preventative, was found to be somewhat lacking in efficacy, because the cuttings might be cleverly replaced and a larger amount recut. The priting and embossing machines for a time seemed to be absolutely safe, but the clever swindlers found a way to remove the ink, the latter being on the surface of the paper only, and then restamping a large amount. The circular which describes the Beebe check protector, states that "the latter breaks and destroys the fibre of the paper, at the same time inserting a strictly indelible, acid-proof ink (specially prepared) into the fibre, which cannot be successfully removed by chemicals of any nature or otherwise. While the paper is thoroughly cut, nothing is taken away to give the forger a chance to fill in, as on the perforating or cutting machines." This circular makes very interesting reading, especially to the merchant or bank man using or handling a number of checks. Fac-simile samples of checks are enclosed with the circular, and these samples show how readily fraud may be perpetrated when some adequate means of precaution is not used. Most of us have had an idea that the safety ruled tinted or so-called "safety paper" was a sure protection, but this circular claims that this sort of paper is no protection, as any tints or colors which have been removed with acids in raising the check can be easily restored by water colors or crayons. A number of examples are also given of the raising of amounts on the face of checks, such as $100 to $600, $100 to $400, $200 to $500, and so on, each so cleverly done as to make detection most improbable. This circular of the Beebe Company makes very interesting reading, and we would advise any large check user to send for it. The company's offices are in the Sykes Block, Minneapolis, Minn.

IMPROVEMENT in duplicating processes keeps pace with the times. The old-fashioned gelatine pan for the duplicating of letters and business forms has given place to the Edison Oscillating Mimeograph, with its cylinder and its thousand copies in a few moments. The new catalogues and advertising matter of the A. B. Dick Company, of Chicago, manufacturers of the Edison Mimeograph, have just come to hand. These catalogues are neatly gotten up, and are so well written as to be very interesting to the casual reader. They are illustrated very neatly with halftone cuts of the various styles of mimeographs and other appliances, and the argument that they offer must appeal to any business man who requires a number of copies of one type-written circular or letter. The A. B. Dick Company also manufacture the Planetary Pencil Pointer and a neat and attractive little circular is enclosed with their other advertising matter. This circular of the pencil pointer is very snappily written, and certainly argues strongly for the purchase of the Planetary pencil-sharpening machine by every man who uses a pencil. The price of the Planetary Pointer is $4.50 but the booklet says "it is worth more, and you will say so when you use it."

THE PAMPHLET of the Manhattan Writing Machine is, we think, a durable one. It is strongly bound. The Manhattan writing machine is strong and, like the pamphlet, will stand wear and tear. The demand upon the typewriter today requires speed, clean cut impression of letters, absolute alignment and sufficient power in the blow from the type to produce well defined duplication. The mechanical perfection of the Manhattan Writing Machine has overcome the difficulties some other machines have experienced in the gradual disarrangement of the letters upon the type bar. The several mechanical devices connected with the shifting cylinder, the shift key and regulation of the length of the lines are constructed with a view towards mechanical perfection. Strength and rapidity is aimed at, and the facilities offered in this machine are self-evident to any one giving it a trial. Particular attention has been given to the tension of the finger keys, which is increased or diminished by turning an adjustable nut. The booklet devotes considerable space to information regarding the cleaning of the machine and the lack of attention that is too frequently found among persons who use typewriters. Emphasis is laid upon the fact that the typewriter, like any other piece of machinery, should be cleaned and well taken care of to produce the best results. The Manhattan Writing Machine is manufactured by the Standard Typewriting Company, of Newark, New Jersey.

BOOKS OF INTEREST TO BUSINESS MEN

BUSINESS LAW. By Thomas Raeburn White, B.L., LL.B. 5 by 7 1-2 inches; 323 pages. Bound in cloth. Back title gilt. Price, $1.50.

This is a neat, compact and handy book of business law for the use of students and business men. Among the subjects treated are Contracts, Sales, Partnerships, Corporations, Negotiable Paper and the like. The author's language is plain, and is understandable by any one having no previous knowledge of law. The book's clearness on the essential points of ordinary law should recommend it as a business book for the plain business man who has no time in which to consult a law library.

THE PHONOGRAPHIC DICTIONARY AND PHRASE BOOK. By Benn Pitman and Jerome B. Howard. 5 1-2 by 8 inches; 552 pages. Bound in cloth. Cover title and back title gilt. Price, $3.00.

This book is the most elaborate shorthand dictionary yet published, with the characters in fac-simile. It contains over 20,000 words, and for every one of these words there is a corresponding sign in the Benn Pitman system of shorthand. To the reporter, office or court stenographer, or any one writing the Benn Pitman system of shorthand, the book is invaluable. It is well made, tastefully bound, and is printed on a good quality of paper in clean, plain type.

THE LAWRENCE SYSTEM OF VOCAL AND PHYSICAL EXPRESSION. By Edwin Gordon Lawrence. 4 3-4 by 6 inches; 128 pages. Bound in cloth. Cover title and back title gilt. Price, $1.00.

The author says in the preface of this little book that his object has been to place in the hands of lawyers, actors and public speakers in general, a simple system of vocal and physical expression that will enable them to clearly convey thought by word of mouth and emphasize it by the proper action. To the man of affairs who is called upon for a speech on any subject, and who knows what to say but does not know how to say it, this book will be a great help.

BUSINESS LAW. By Alonzo R. Weed, LL. B., of the Boston Bar. 6 by 9 1-4 inches; 172 pages. Bound in cloth. Cover and back title red. Price, $1.25.

Mr. Weed calls his book "a manual for schools and colleges and for every day use." The titles of the chapters are as follows: Contracts, Principal and Agent, Partnerships, Sales of Personal Property, Bailments and Common Carriers, Negotiable Paper, Deeds, Mortgages and Leases, Collection Laws, Written Rates of Interest, Insurance, Patent Rights, Trade-Marks and Copyrights, etc.

The author does not waste words, and yet treats his subjects clearly and comprehensively. In short, he gives the law without the addition of wordy "trimmings."

BANKERS' AND MERCHANTS' INTEREST TABLES. By Francis H. Coffin and David H. Moore. 13 by 9 1-2 inches. Bound in cloth. Leather back and corners. Cover and back title gilt. Price, $5.00.

There have been interest tables published before, but never, so far as we know, has so elaborate and comprehensive a set of tables been issued in book form. "The volume contains," to quote from the title page, "Interest tables, computed on the basis of 360 days per annum, at 3 1-2, 4, 5 and 6 per cent, with an accurate calculation of interest on every sum from $1.00 to $1,000, and, by simple addition of two lines, on every further sum, to $1,000,000." It also contains a 1 per cent one day table, on the basis of 365 days per annum, from which interest on daily balances can be computed at any time and on any sum. There is a time table printed in black and red at the beginning of the book as an aid in quickly finding the number of days between one day and another. To a merchant or banker performing many calculations in interest this book is a great time saver. It is handsomely bound, finely printed, and has a thumb index.

POLITICAL ECONOMY OF HUMANISM. By Henry Wood. 7 3-4 by 5 1-4 inches; 320 pages. Bound in cloth. Cover and back title gilt. Price, $1.25.

Mr. Wood is well known as a writer on various economic subjects, and this book contains a series of able treatises, written in his usual vein, on the relation of the employer to the employed, and the phases of the industrial question and their relation to socialism. Among the questions considered and handled in a conservative spirit and with much common sense, are the following: Supply and Demand, the Law of Competition, Labor and Production, Combinations of Capital, Combinations of Labor, Employers and Profit Sharing, the Ob-

It's Good for You

To use our Typewriter Ribbons and Carbons, because they write better and last longer than the ordinary kind; they do not smut, blur nor fill the type, but they make fine copies.

No. 1 Ribbons, 75c. ea., $7.00 doz.
No. 1 Carbon, $3.00 pr. bx., 40c. doz.
Silkarbon, $4.00 pr. bx., 50c. doz.

We pay express or mail charges.

IMPERIAL MANUFACTURING CO.
289-297 Washington St., Newark, N. J.

A BUSINESS EDUCATION | FOR ...ONE... DOLLAR.

...THE PRACTICAL AGE...

A MONTHLY MAGAZINE full to the brim with helpful suggestions to young men and young women who are struggling successward.

THE BUSINESS HOUSE THAT JACK BUILT, an intensely interesting and highly instructive story of business life, and

APPLIED ENGLISH, an authority on writing and speaking the English language, which no young person can afford to be without, all for ONE DOLLAR.

If you have never seen THE PRACTICAL AGE, send for a free sample copy. Address,

THE PRACTICAL AGE,
Moline, Illinois.

ligations and Privileges of Employees, the Unequal Distribution of Wealth, Money and Coinage, Tariffs and Protection, Industrial Education and Gold Production and values.

INTRODUCTION TO THE STUDY OF COMMERCE. By Frederick R. Clow, Ph. D. 7 1-2 by 3 3-4 inches; 224 pages. Bound in cloth. Back title gilt. Price, $1.25.

Mr. Clow's book is not intended as a complete text book on commerce. It is simply, as its title implies, an introduction to the study of commerce. It is intended as a text book for the use of teachers in schools or universities, or as a help to the student in his commercial training. Incidentally, it makes good reading for anyone interested in modern commerce, and particularly for the American merchant. The author begins by describing the Elements of Commerce; then follows a short essay on the Rise of Commerce, and then the Materials of Commerce are discussed. Foreign Commerce of the United States and of other countries is treated of, as is the Domestic Commerce of this country. The titles of other chapters are: Organization of Trade, Prices, Payments and How the Equilibrium is Maintained. We can heartily recommend this introduction to the Study of Commerce. It is a good book on a vastly important subject.

THE A B C OF BANKS AND BANKING. By George M. Coffin. 6 3-4 by 5 inches; 137 pages. Bound in cloth. Back title gilt. Price, $1.25.

This handy little volume is exactly what its name implies, that is, a presentation of the principles underlying banking in the United States. The author in his preface says that it is designed to appeal to the reader outside as well as inside of a bank. It is by no means the last word or every word about banking. It

About a Pay Roll which proves itself, corrects all mistakes in figuring, divides up Pay Roll into several amounts needed to pay each person.

But let us send you a sample leaf, with circular, which tells the whole story.

BARLOW BROS., Grand Rapids, Mich.

R·I·P·A·N·S

There is scarcely any condition of ill-health that is not benefited by the occasional use of a R·I·P·A·N·S Tabule. For sale by Druggists. The Five-Cent packet is enough for an ordinary occasion. The family bottle, 60 cents, contains a supply for a year.

PRENTISS CLOCKS.
SIX.TIMES A YEAR
is all that is necessary to wind a Prentiss Clock. Why wind a clock every week when we can sell you one which will require winding but once in sixty days and will keep perfect time? Also Frying-pan, Program and Electrically synchronized clocks. Send for Catalogue No. 292.

THE PRENTISS CLOCK IMPROVEMENT CO.,
Dept. 28, 49 Dey St., New York City

may be said that it is a primer covering a field that has hitherto been somewhat neglected. The chapter heads are as follows: Banking in General, Various Kinds of Banking, Capital Stock, Shareholders' Rights and Liabilities, Undivided Profits, Dividends and Surplus, Deposits, Checks, Lawful Money Reserve, Issuing Bank Notes, Borrowing Money, Loans and Discounts, Exchanges, Collections, Letters of Credit, Bonds, Mortgages and Stocks, Bank Reports, Examinations, Directors, Executive Officers—Their Powers and Duties, Internal Administration and Bookkeeping, and Other Suggestions.

Any book in this list will be sent to any address in the United States, Canada or Mexico upon receipt of price. If there is some special book that you require we shall be pleased to hunt it up for you. Address COMMERCE, ACCOUNTS & FINANCE, 25 Pine street, New York city.

HALL'S Fireproof and Burglar Proof SAFES

Sold since 1840. Never fail to protect contents.

KNOWN EVERYWHERE

393 BROADWAY, N.Y.

Telephones: 3133-3136-307 Franklin.

BUSINESS NEEDS

Advertisements under this head one cent a word each insertion.

BUSINESS PICTURES—Do you want to illustrate your catalogue or booklet? Do you want a series of snappy pen and ink sketches to brighten your advertisement in the daily papers? Do you want a handsome wash drawing for your announcement in the magazines? If you do, write to me. I am a competent business artist, working in black and white and colors, and you see my sketches every week if you read the Sunday papers. My price is always a fair one. Address, PEN AND INK, Box 17, Commerce, Accounts & Finance.

SECOND-HAND TYPEWRITERS can be repaired so that they can be used and produce work which is almost, if not quite, as good as from a new machine. I have the facilities for obtaining exceptionally good second-hand machines. I have a man who repairs them—a man that understands his business. These machines can be sold for 50 per cent discount from list price of the new machines. Does this interest you? If it does, address TYPEWRITER, care Commerce, Accounts & Finance.

EXTRA WORK for extra hours. I want work for evenings. Am competent bookkeeper. Work must be in New York or Brooklyn. Address F. K., care Commerce, Accounts & Finance.

ACCOUNTANT AND BOOKKEEPER, 20 years' experience. Seeks permanent position as a bookkeeper or office manager. Highest credentials. Address C. B. L., Box 18, care Commerce, Accounts & Finance.

INSURANCE, ASSURANCE AND RE-ASSURANCE.—Perhaps I can tell you some things that will save you money. There is a way of doing things even in the insurance business. Write me for blanket insurance, mill insurance or any old kind of insurance. I think I can talk interestingly. Address ASSURANCE, care Commerce, Accounts & Finance.

OFFICE MAN AND BOOKKEEPER, thoroughly competent, and with 10 years' experience, desires to make a change. Is at present engaged with a firm of export commission merchants. Familiar with the real estate business, and desires to connect with some firm where knowledge of real estate and insurance will be of value. Address CARY, care Commerce, Accounts & Finance.

AGENTS WANTED.—Bookkeepers, clerks and others connected with firms having a number of employees can add something to their income every week without taking up any amount of time. Personality and acquaintance is all that is needed in introducing to the attention of your friends the matter which we ask you to take up as an agent. Investigate this and write for particulars to FINANCE, care of Commerce, Accounts & Finance.

PACIFIC COAST REPRESENTATIVE.—I would like to establish connection with some large manufacturing industry which needs a representative on the Pacific Coast. I am 34 years of age, have the advantage of large and extensive travel, exceptional business experience, and possess executive ability. I am able to handle large undertakings. Highest class references. Address REPRESENTATIVE, care Commerce, Accounts & Finance.

TYPEWRITING AND MANIFOLDING done well and cheaply, and in any quantity. Address COPYIST, care Commerce, Accounts & Finance.

WEBSTER'S INTERNATIONAL DICTIONARY

WEBSTER'S INTERNATIONAL DICTIONARY

NEW EDITION

NEW PLATES THROUGHOUT

Now Added 25,000 NEW WORDS, Phrases, Etc.

Rich Bindings ❧ 2364 Pages ❧ 5000 Illustrations

Prepared under the supervision of W. T. Harris, Ph.D., LL.D., United States Commissioner of Education, assisted by a large corps of competent specialists.

The International was first issued in 1890, succeeding the "Unabridged." The New Edition of the International was issued in October, 1900. Get the latest and best.

Also Webster's Collegiate Dictionary with Scottish Glossary, etc.

"First class in quality, second class in size." *Nicholas Murray Butler.*

GET THE BEST

G. & C. MERRIAM CO., Publishers, Springfield, Mass., U. S. A.

Will Make First-Class Book-keeper

of you in six weeks for $3 or RETURN MONEY; distance and experience immaterial; have placed THOUSANDS of pupils in PAYING POSITIONS, free of charge; perhaps I can do something for YOU, too! SAVE THIS AND WRITE, J. H. GOODWIN, EXPERT ACCOUNTANT, Room 887, 1215 Broadway, New York.

OFFICE FURNITURE AND OFFICE FITTINGS.—My specialty is in discriminating where to buy and what to buy. I keep myself posted as to market rates and discounts. If you need anything in your office, files, desks, furniture or any office device, write me about it. I can save you time and money. Address CONFIDENTIAL, care Commerce, Accounts & Finance.

A SALESMAN at present with a large mercantile house on the road, is eligible for some side line to represent through the middle and eastern states. Has a large and established clientele of customers, and can take up a new line to the advantage of both parties concerned. Address SALESMAN, care Commerce, Accounts & Finance.

"IF BUSINESS MEN ONLY KNEW."

If Business Men in general knew the real advantages of the Balance Sheet System of Accounting, our facilities, large as they are, would be vastly overtaxed. We could not meet the demand that would arise. As it is, we are faced by a large and growing business, requiring constant additions to our staff. We started the new year with more than twenty times as many people on our pay-roll as we had only three years before, and our arrangements are already well advanced for doubling the number. Our best advertisements are pleased clients, and we have lots of them who never miss an opportunity to tell their fellow business men of their satisfaction with our methods. If you want to know who some of them are, write us.

Every Business Man who becomes aware of the fact that the Balance Sheet System installed in his establishment will give him at all times as complete a statement of his affairs, including profit results to date, as is usually afforded by the annual or semi-annual closing of the books, and that, too, without extra clerical cost, at once negotiates for our services. We put at his command a going profit and loss statement, by which expenses are constantly contrasted with profits, and a going balance sheet, by which assets and liabilities are always correctly presented. If you want to know more about this, write us.

Every Business Man who inquires of us learns that we are in position to serve him in various ways:—

(a) We will receive his head bookkeeper or confidential man as a pupil for a time, drilling him while with us in all the details and routine of our methods, sending him back thus trained, equipped with a chart of accounts, a balance sheet ledger adapted to the special business, and a written specification covering every feature of the system to be installed.

(b) Or we will prepare the chart of accounts and balance sheet ledger, together with the specification illustrated by every blank and form of ruling that can be of use, and will send our own men to make the installation.

(c) For those at a considerable distance from our offices and who want a special drill in Balance Sheet Accounting, we have arranged a correspondence course of instruction adapted to the requirements of the business man's representative, and have similarly put ourselves in position to supervise the installation of complete systems at long range.

Balance Sheet Methods are not complex. Instead they are extremely simple.

The Balance Sheet System of Accounts is the first and only accounting system that the business man of average attainments has been able to understand and intelligently direct as a part of his office machinery.

The Balance Sheet Ledger is the first and only ledger the average business man has found any satisfaction in examining. It is attractive to him because it gives him what he wants to know about his affairs for intelligent planning and direction, in the way he wants to know it and at the time it will do the most good.

Address communications to

ACCOUNT AUDIT AND ASSURANCE CO., Ltd.

BOSTON:
502 Exchange Building.

NEW YORK:
25 Pine Street.

PUBLIC LIBRARY

COMMERCE ACCOUNTS & FINANCE

Volume 4 New York April 1902 Number 4

CONTENTS

Published Monthly by the Commerce Accounts & Finance Company
Twenty-five Pine Street New York

KNICKERBOCKER TRUST CO.

234 FIFTH AVENUE, CORNER 27TH STREET
BRANCH OFFICES:
66 BROADWAY, AND 125TH STREET AND LENOX AVE.,
NEW YORK CITY.

CAPITAL AND UNDIVIDED PROFITS, $2,508,399.11.

LEGAL DEPOSITORY FOR STATE, CITY, AND COURT FUNDS.

Interest allowed on Time Deposits. Deposits also received subject to Demand Checks, which pass through the Clearing House as do those upon any city bank.

Authorized to act as Executor or Administrator of Estates, and as Guardian, Receiver, Registrar, Transfer and Financial Agent for States, Cities, Towns, Railroads, and other corporations, and to accept any other Trusts in conformity with the laws of any State or of the United States.

LETTERS OF CREDIT FURNISHED.
BUSINESS AND PERSONAL ACCOUNTS SOLICITED.

CHAS. T. BARNEY, - - - - - - - President.
JOSEPH T. BROWN, - - - - - - 2d Vice-President.
JULIAN M. GERARD, - - - Asst Sec. and Asst. Treas.
FRED'K K. ELDRIDGE, - - - - 1st Vice-President.
FRED'K GORE KING, - - - Secretary and Treasurer.
WM. B. RANDALL, - - - - - - Trust Officer.

BOARD OF DIRECTORS:

JOSEPH S. AUERBACH,
HARRY B. HOLLINS,
JACOB HAYS,
CHARLES T. BARNEY,
A. FOSTER HIGGINS,
ANDREW H. SANDS,
JAMES H. BRESLIN,
I. TOWNSEND BURDEN,
HON. E. V. LOEW,
HENRY F. DIMOCK,
CHARLES F. WATSON,
FREDERICK G. BOURNE,
C. LAWRENCE PERKINS,
CHARLES R. FLINT,
AMZI L. BARBER,
CHARLES T. COOK,
JOHN MAGEE,
HENRY A. MORGAN,
HENRY C. BERLIN,
CHARLES W. GOULD,
FRED'K L. ELDRIDGE,
HENRY W. DE FOREST,
ALFRED B. MACLAY
HARRY W. McVICKAR.

It's Good for You

To use our Typewriter Ribbons and Carbons, because they write better and last longer than the ordinary kind; they do not smut, blur nor fill the type, but they make fine copies.

No. 1 Ribbons, 75c. ea., $7.00 doz.
No. 1 Carbon, $3.00 pr. bx., 40c. doz.
Silkarbon, $4.00 pr. bx., 50c. doz.

We pay express or mail charges.

IMPERIAL MANUFACTURING CO.
289-297 Washington St., Newark, N. J.

Use any pen and your own stationery. If your stationer does not keep it, write for free specimen of work. Beware of infringements. Address Dept.
Pen-Carbon Manifold Co., 145-7-9 Centre St., New York.

FREE--A PAIR OF SLEEVE PROTECTORS.

Do you want to know about our Loose Leaf Ledgers and office devices? They will save you time, trouble and money. To all bookkeepers in the States of New York, New Jersey and Massachusetts who write us for information about our systems we will send a pair of sleeve protectors. In writing mention size of cuff.

THE C. E. SHEPPARD CO.,
87 Maiden Lane, NEW YORK CITY.

C. W. HASKINS, C. P. A. E. W. SELLS, C. P. A.

HASKINS & SELLS

Certified Public Accountants

CABLE ADDRESS, "HASKSELLS." THIRTY BROAD STREET, NEW YORK

Accounts of Municipalities, Corporations, Firms and Individuals Inspected and Audited; Methods of Accounting Originated and Adapted to Conditions; Books of Accounts Opened, Regulated and Closed; Irregularities Discovered; Financial Situations Examined.

Experts under the Joint Commission of the Fifty-third Congress to Revise the Accounting System of the UNITED STATES GOVERNMENT.

The New Banking and Currency Bill*

By HON. CHARLES W. FOWLER

Chairman of the Banking and Currency Committee of the National House of Representatives.

Any commercial country must stand as a unit, and as a commercial government or country it must have a standard of value. If the country had no relation with other countries it would be comparatively immaterial what its standard was, but when it has a relation with one other or two other countries, or all the rest of the world, the question of what kind of a standard becomes just as important as the fact that it has a standard at all. Since we have a relation with all the rest of the countries of the world we should have the same standard as all of the rest of the countries of the world. If we do not, in all of the trade between this country and the rest of the nations of the world, there will be a discount and an exchange running against us sufficient to wipe out all the profits. Therefore we do not only want an unequivocal standard, but we want the standard of the civilized world, and that is gold.

HAVE WE A REAL GOLD STANDARD?

While we have had the gold standard in practice since 1879, and supposed that by law, on March 14, 1900, we had established it beyond a peradventure, it is doubtful whether that is true under all the circumstances, and that doubt rests in the fact that this government has outstanding today more than five hundred million silver dollars, one-half of which is mere fiat. There is no more moral obligation on the part of this government to redeem its United States notes in gold than that it should redeem the fifty-cent fiatism in the silver dollar. Morally it is identically the same proposition.

Now what is the situation with regard to these silver dollars? The silver dollar and the certificate that stands for the silver dollar are payable to the government for dues it receives, and therefore the government is receiving and redeeming by receiving all of the silver that it has outstanding, and yet, while by this indirection it is accepting the silver certificate and the silver dollar, it refuses to say that the Secretary of the Treasury shall pay out gold coin for silver dollars. But it is the settled policy of the government to maintain the parity, and the two last Secretaries of the Treasury—one a Democrat and the other a Republican—both declared that they would pay out gold coin for silver dollars if it was necessary to do so in order to maintain the parity. Therefore I say that, inasmuch as the government is constantly receiving the silver dollars and the silver certificates as dues, and the officers of the government who are responsible for the parity of its moneys have declared that they would pay out gold coin for silver dollars, the government ought to step forward and say if there is an ideal of honesty in the world, that ideal honesty is symbolized by the Stars and Stripes, and that there is no piece of money that it compels a citizen to take that is not worth gold coin. So much, then, for the standard.

THE RESERVE.

Having a standard, every country should have somewhere a reserve of that standard. Where should that reserve be? It should be immediately related, naturally related, to the commerce of the country which it is supposed that reserve will protect.

Let us inquire whether or no there is a reserve in the United States today. One person may suggest that the gold coin in the general fund of the Treasury of the United States is a reserve or part of a reserve, but that isn't a reserve, because, by appropriation bills, we could pay out every dollar of it tomorrow. Another person might suggest that the gold coin in the Issue and Redemption Division, represented by government certificates held by the banks, is a part of the reserve, but that isn't a part of a reserve, because tomorrow the banks may present the certificates and take that gold away. Another person might suggest that the gold today held by the banks is a part of the reserve of this country, but it is not a reserve in the sense that it is the reserve for the commerce of the United States, because, at the very first commercial flurry, every bank lies down on the government and hoards all the gold it has, and runs to the United States Treasury for more, and it does this because the banks are not compelled by law to prove their credits by the exchange of gold coin for any part of them.

Lastly, some one may say that the 150 millions in the Issue and Redemption Division is the reserve, the gold reserve in this country. The $150,000,000 began its reserve characteristic in 1879, when $100,000,000 was set apart for what purpose? To protect 346 millions of greenbacks, it being thought that about 30 per cent was a good reserve for a bank to hold against its debts. What happened? This $100,000,000 did not remain the reserve of the government to protect the 346 millions alone, but very shortly the whole commercial world of the United States began to look to this reserve and go there for support in times of crisis. It never was intended for reserve beyond the $346,000,000 until March 14, 1900, when it was extended to the treasury notes and made $150,000,000. If it had been a commercial reserve, instead of its being $150,000,000 now, it would probably be three or four hundred millions.

A reserve created in this country by the banks would grow as the commerce of this country grew from 1869 up to the present time, precisely as the reserves in the banks of France grew, and as the reserve in the Imperial Bank of Germany grew; as the reserve in the Bank of England grew in the last thirty years. Ours, however, is fixed by law. It cannot increase because it is limited by law. Therefore, I say, without any question, that there is not today anywhere in the United States a reserve to protect the commercial credits of the United States.

THE CURRENCY AND BUSINESS.

The next thought: It is important that the currency of a country, so far as it is paper currency, should be directly related to the business of the country, as checks and drafts are. A paper currency should spring into being and go to perform some special duty, with the same certainty that you draw a check to pay a debt. That is the quality of an ideal currency, and until we ourselves adopt a system that will develop that kind of a currency we will not have a proper paper currency.

Another essential of a proper financial and currency system is the complete mobilization of the loanable funds of the entire country, precisely as a bank in a community mobilizes the loanable funds of the particular community in which that bank happens to be located. It gathers the fragments of money from the hands of the masses and then loans that money to those who desire to borrow. Never will we have a proper financial system in this country until we get one which gathers the money in one section of the country where it is not needed, and loans it in another section of the country where it is needed, and it must flow from that section where it is not needed to that section where it is needed as easily, naturally and unobstructedly as the water flows into the North River from the ocean as the tide comes in.

CERTAIN ABSOLUTE PRINCIPLES.

Now, those are principles that are as absolute as the laws of gravitation, and must be recognized in working out the great problem confronting the American people. With these principles government ought to have, and can rightfully have, but little to do. What is the duty of this government? It is to establish by law a gold standard. It is to fix the measure of value by which transactions are to be car-

*Address delivered before the New York University School of Commerce, Accounts & Finance.

ried on, and then it should provide a system of currency, but should not itself carry on the business of the country. The government of the United States should be related to the business of the country just to the same extent and in the same way that New York City is related to the business of this country, and no other.

It should collect its revenues in the ordinary way and pay its debts in the ordinary way of a state or a municipality. All power exercised beyond this should be purely of a police character, seeing to it that no banking establishment abuses the rights that it exercises as a matter of law, and that the currency which goes to the people shall be redeemed in the standard of the country. That is a police regulation. The right to make a note is a natural right because it is the right to sell your credit, and that right is just as natural and inherent in a corporation as it is in an individual, but inasmuch as a corporation undertaking to do a banking business and issuing a bill that passes by delivery does a quasi public business, the government should step in and say it should so conduct this quasi public business as in no way to injure a citizen of this country.

Now, those are the principles that should lie at the foundation of a right system of finance and currency, and those are the duties of the government.

THE ACTUAL SITUATION.

Let us see, gentlemen, what we actually have in this country. I have pointed out to you what a right kind of a currency is. Have we such a currency today? Outside of the silver currency of this country, which ought to be regarded purely as token money or subsidiary coin, we have a bank currency. For all the purposes of this talk we shall treat gold certificates the same as gold, and I want to treat all silver certificates as subsidiary coin or token money. I should like to see all the silver of the United States coined into halves, quarters and dimes. It ought never to be considered in any other light than subsidiary coin, therefore the only paper currency that we have to consider in our system is our banking currency, outside of checks and drafts.

Now, have we in our present bank note system an ideal currency system? Let us see. How did it start? It started, in 1863, with these objects in view: of selling the bonds of the United States, of making a market for the bonds of the United States, not with a view at all of furnishing a currency for the people. They imposed a 10 per cent tax upon state institutions and then forced the banks to buy the bonds and issue the currency, the object being to sell the bonds, not to produce a currency. And there has never been an hour from the time that they passed the law, the object of which was to sell bonds and incidentally to produce a currency, that this currency has not been associated with these bonds and it has depended entirely upon the profit or loss of the bonds whether the notes continued in circulation or not.

The fact is that in 1879 we had $350,000,000 of these notes out. In 1888 we had $122,000,000 out—business increasing, notes decreasing. Twelve years after that we had $350,000,000 again. Will anybody tell me that that currency has any relation to business; that it comes into existence to perform some work and then retires when that work is done?

The banks today are trying to retire all the notes they possibly can; reaching the government limit of $3,000,000 each month. Is there any less need of money now than last year at this time, when they were increasing it? The only difference is, that now there no profit on the bonds to keep out the circulation. Then there was a profit, so that you have a currency in this country that depends upon the price of bonds for its existence instead of upon the business to be done.

A PECULIARITY OF OUR CURRENCY.

Another peculiarity about this currency that we have today is this: that in the city, where they do not need currency, it is a profit to have it out, but in the country, where they need a very great deal of currency and do not use checks, there it is unprofitable to keep it out. In a 4 per cent district these 2 per cent bonds net 60 1-100 of 1 per cent profit. In a 6 per cent district they net 51-100 per cent profit, and in an 8 per cent district they net 30-100 per cent profit, and I suppose, although I have not the data now, in a 10 per cent district there would be no profit at all. Now that is based upon the assumption that these notes are out all the time, but if the notes are out only half the time, or only half the notes out all the time, there is no doubt but that the banks are all losing money on the issues. So there is not any question of how much work these banks have to do, but simply a question of whether there is a profit in holding the bonds.

BOND DEPOSITS AND COMMERCE.

Another objection to the deposit of bonds to secure circulation. We have today about $325,000,000 of bonds deposited to secure circulation. What does that mean to the commerce of the United States? It means that you have taken $300,000,000 of money, property, from the channels of trade that otherwise might be added to the rest of the loanable funds and lower the rate of interest throughout the country. It means more than that. It means that if this $300,000,000 of property, that might be in gold coin or United States notes, were in the hands of the banks, it would be the basis of loaning five times as much as $300,000,000, or $1,500,000,000 to the people.

Now, you can imagine that if the banks should have $1,500,000,000 more to loan to the people of this country it would have a very depressing effect upon the rates of interest throughout the country, in which the producers of this country are very greatly interested.

A DESIRABLE CURRENCY.

I said to you that the currency ought to be as directly and naturally related to the regular transaction of business as checks and drafts are, and come and go with the same fluidity, simplicity and regularity as checks and drafts do, and when, like checks and drafts, it has performed its work, it should go back to the one who issued it, as a check comes back to the drawer. There never can be a currency panic in this country if there is always currency to do the work that currency ought to do, precisely as the checks do the work that checks can do.

Is a currency issued by the banks against their credit safe? The Bank of France has $800,000,000 of such notes out without any provision whatever in law with regard to a reserve to protect those notes, and the noteholder stands in the same relation to the bank as the man who has deposits at the bank, no preference of any kind being given. Yet the Bank of France has a small capital comparatively, only $35,000,000. The Bank of Germany has $330,000,000 of such notes out, pure credit currency. The banks of Scotland have $40,000,000 out. For 200 years the banks of Scotland have had a credit currency, and for 140 years there wasn't a deposit made in the banks of Scotland. The whole business was carried on by the banks giving the men who desired it a loan, taking their notes, and taking promissory notes of the men who desired to borrow; and notwithstanding the fact that they have had that system of currency for over two hundred years, there have never been more than three bank failures in Scotland, and no man who ever had a deposit in Scotland ever lost a dollar. Such a system of currency was issued for a long number of years by the Banks of New England, there being in the various states very little supervision; no railroads, no telegraph wires, the banks writing the notes out themselves or getting them printed at a tenth-rate printing office; and yet in the twenty years from 1840 to 1860, beginning with 300 banks in 1840 and coming up to 500 banks, the losses on the note issues in New England would have been paid by a tax of one-eighteenth of 1 per cent on the notes outstanding.

What made them so good? One thing: the fact that every day these notes found their way back to the place of issue and were redeemed in specie. This constant daily redemption in coin not only made these notes good, but it was a constant test applied as a touchstone to every credit in the banks' drawers.

AN INTERESTING COMPARISON.

Now compare that experience of twenty years with the forty years of national bank experience in the United States, much lauded by some people as being safe. I have just received from the Comptroller of the Currency an elaborate report, giving every year from 1863 down to the first day of January, which shows that if you had imposed a tax upon the notes outstanding to protect the notes of the failed banks every year, the tax on this much-lauded system would have been 22-100ths of 1 per cent, nearly double the amount that the banks of New England would have had to pay from 1840 to 1860. Why? With all of our facilities growing out of the telegraph, the railroad, uniform laws, uniform supervision and modern facilities, why is our system today proving less certain in its returns to the depositor and the noteholder than in the twenty years in that primeval time? Because we have no such thing as daily coin redemption of the notes of our banks and of the credits of our banks.

There is one thought in connection with the credit currency that I want to make very clear, and that is this: I said it should be a currency as directly and naturally related to the transactions of business as checks and drafts, but there is one peculiarity about a credit note properly protected that does not attach to a check or draft, and that is this: the better you make it the more it will tend to stay out in circulation. It passes by delivery. It is absolutely good. There is no tendency on the part of the man who gets it to send it in for redemption. Therefore, to offset this tendency to remain out because it is good, there should be a mechanism devised to force it back to its drawer or issuer; and when you have counterbalanced the tendency to remain out by a mechanism that sends it home, you have a system that is balanced and perfected and will bring every day the touchstone of redemption not only to the note itself, but to every credit that a bank gives.

THE PEOPLE AND THE BANKS.

So much for the credit note. Now as to the people and their relation to a credit note and to every accommodation at the bank. When a customer goes to a bank, whether he is in the country or in the city, he should have the option of saying to the banker what kind of a credit he wants, whether he wants a credit on the books of the bank to check against it or whether he wants the notes of the bank to use. Why? Because in the cities the people are accustomed to use deposits and pay out by check; in the country, where they are producing crops, like the great harvesting regions of the Northwest, or cotton plantations of the South, they want notes to use, and with no system in our country by which the notes can be issued as they are needed and in quantities as they are needed, we find that these people suffer very much for the means of carrying on properly the productive industries of the United States.

Barring laws that interfere with banking, whether people use notes or whether they use credit subject to check, depends entirely upon the habits of the people. How do we know that? In France they have $800,000,000 notes out issued by the Bank of France, but there is only $130,000,000 of deposits in the banks of France subject to check. In Germany there are $330,000,000 of notes out, and but $160,000,000 of deposits subject to check, showing that the people in Germany and in France prefer to handle notes to credit subject to check.

In Scotland, where for 140 years, as I said, they never had a deposit subject to check, in 1840 or about that time they began to deposit and check out against their credit. Today they have but $40,000,000 of notes, but I think something over $200,000,000 of deposits. So the people should have the opportunity in our country of using notes or credit subject to check, according to their requirements. The people in the far-off districts, away from the cities, who are unaccustomed to making deposits and checking out, should have bank credits in the form of these notes, a thing that is utterly impossible today, for every time they need any money in one of these remote districts they are compelled to call upon the New York market or upon the Chicago market to secure it. They ship the money away, use it a while, and ship it back again.

THE QUESTION OF ECONOMY.

Now, the question of economy comes up again with regard to these notes, and this is a matter of the greatest importance to the people. If you go to the bank today—this is a matter of the highest importance—and borrow $100, you lay down your note for six months, and the banker says, "What do you want that in?" "I want it in money, sir." He gives you $100 in bank notes. What has he given you when he gives you $100 in bank notes? Not the credit of the bank, but he gives you $100 in actual property, for he has put up government bonds to secure this $100 worth of notes, and when he hands you the $100 he charges you interest on the property and an insurance on the credit. If he had issued a bank note according to the French system, or according to the former New England system, he would have handed you $100 worth of notes: simply the credit of the bank, and he ought only to charge you for the insurance of your credit and not interest upon $100 worth of property.

That is a matter of the greatest importance to every borrower in this country, and to the extent that notes are used, bank notes, properly issued notes, it enters enormously into the cost of production in this country.

LOCATION OF BANKS.

A word with regard to the principle of banking that prevails in this country, whereby a bank is limited to its locality. A bank that cannot have a branch anywhere may be large or small, according to the locality where it is located. If in Wall Street, it may have a capital of $10,000,000, with $100,000,000 of deposits and do a profitable business. In a little country town it may have $25,000 capital and charge the people 10 per cent, and then not make any money. And so our banks all over the country have a capital that is proportional to the locality where they may be situated; and when the first strain comes, every small bank, conscious of its own weakness, conscious that every man in the neighborhood that has a dollar deposited with it knows of its own weakness, begins the struggle to get something to protect itself with, begins to feed upon every other small bank, begins to make every man pay that owes anything and refuses to pay out anything. As the manager of the Bank of France told me last summer, in a panic or in a crisis, small banks feed on commerce, but great banks feed commerce.

Ours is a purely individual system, with no point of contact or no principle of coherency anywhere. Therefore, it is a matter of the highest importance that banks should have an opportunity to establish branches in order that they may mobilize the funds in this country; that the bank that has some funds in one part of the country may by credit transfer it to some other part of the country where it may be needed at that particular time of the year; and then when not needed there can be sent back to the locality where it is needed at another time of the year.

Until we secure such a system of banking and acquire the habit of mobilizing our loanable funds, the rates of interest in this country will always be high because we are compelled to pay for the local organization of 12,000 institutions well organized, because the gentlemen who manage them are all honorable men, responsible men, high-priced men—president, vice-president, cashier, assistant cashier, secretary or assistant secretary, all getting salaries. So a little bank with $25,000 capital has to pay $15,000 or $20,000 in salaries, and hence the rate must be 8 per cent or 10 per cent or 2 per cent a month, as the case may be. Now it is a fact, contravened by no country in this world, that wherever you have the system of the branch banks the rates of interest are uniform throughout that entire country, plus the cost of transmitting currency from the central bank to its branches.

For more than two years in France, from the Mediterrancan to Paris, the rate was 2 per cent to everybody, everywhere, according to the credit that the man was entitled to receive. The little shoemaker who wanted $50 got his money for 2 per cent. The railroad magnate who wanted $100,000 got his money for 2 per cent. The little shoemaker was just as good a credit for $50 as the railroad magnate was for $100,000; and can any man tell me, give me any reason why a man in Texas who can offer government bonds for security should not get his money just as cheap as a man in New York City?

BETTER SERVICE FOR THE PEOPLE.

There is in the United States today in capital and surplus something like $2,000,000,000 of banking capital. I believe that half that capital, with a system of banks that would reach out everywhere all over this country, mobilizing the loanable funds, would serve the people vastly better than the whole $2,000,000,000. Who would be the gainer? If they are earning from 7 to 10 per cent on that extra billion—and I suppose they would average probably 10 per cent, probably $100,000,000—who would be the gainer? The borrowers, wouldn't they?

Further than that: I haven't any doubt but that the $10,000,000,000 debts owed by the people to the banks—and it is more than that—are taking out of the producers in this country an average rate of 6 per cent or $600,000,000 a year. And if we had a system of credit currency on the one hand and the right to establish branches on the other, the average rate of interest from one end of this country to the other, from the Atlantic to the Pacific, and from Canada to the Gulf, would not exceed 3 per cent. There would be an actual gain to the producers of the United States of at least $300,000,000 a year in their interest alone. This is a matter of the utmost importance for us to consider, because we are soon to meet the great productive countries of the world in the markets of the world, and the question of whether we are to pay 3 per cent all around throughout this country on our discounts, or 6 per cent, will determine whether we are to stay in the markets of the world or whether we are to leave the markets of the world.

INTERNATIONAL BANKING.

As supplemental to that thought, the bill which has been introduced covers also the subject of international banking, which is only an extension of the same principle to other countries beyond our borders and securing to American enterprise and American capital everywhere all over the world the same chance of controlling exchanges. I am satisfied that the country that controls the exchanges and loans the money to the people who hold the goods, also controls the bills of lading, and the men who hold the bills of lading can route the goods. And I assume, for I believe that it is absolutely true, that we will never have an American merchant marine until we have an international banking system that can route the goods over American ship lines.

Now, leaving these general topics for a moment, the object of the bill, which, I understand from Prof. Johnson, some of you, if not all of you, have read, is to bring about the very things that I have been discussing as ideal conditions, so far as the present complicated situation will permit. We hope by the measure to retire the demand obligations of the government and to compel the banks of the United States to maintain the gold standard. We expect to transfer from the government to commerce the question of the reserve. That will bring the reserve into immediate relationship with the commerce of the United States, and that reserve will rise or fall according to the amount of business done in the United States. It will not be fixed by law at $150,000,000, but the instincts of our great captains of industry will fix it at $200,000,000, $300,000,000, $400,000,000 or $500,000,000, as they determine from time to time. We believe that the bill will dispose of the bond-secured currency and give to the country a true credit currency issued by the banks to their customers where they want notes instead of a credit subject to check. Gold, by the bill, is made payable by the Treasury for silver dollars, but only after we take the precaution, on account of the unfortunate amount of silver that we own, of reducing the denominations to $5 and under, in order that this $600,000,000 of silver that we have today shall be kept and held firmly by the people for their daily work and by the banks for their change, thereby preventing any considerable portion of it going to the Treasury for redemption. In order to strengthen the position of the government, all other forms of money, bank notes, certificates of gold, United States notes, must be $10 and upwards, so that the whole field from $5 down—$3, $2 and $1—shall be occupied entirely by the silver dollar and the silver certificates representing them. Since the amount of the $1, $2 and $5 bills in the United States today amounts to $434,000,000, it is believed that this subsidiary coin and the silver dollar, together with the silver certificates of $1, $2 and $5, will be occupied all the time in doing the small work of the people of this country.

The Labor Question—Past and Present

By THOMAS B. HOPKINS

Illustrated by Current Cartoons

To attempt to compress within the limits of so short an article as this must be, the history of trade unions and their relation to the employer is quite beyond the bounds of possibility. It will be necessary therefore to merely sketch in the outlines and allow the reader to search for details among the many works upon the subject.

THE TRADE UNION IN HISTORY.

The average man is prone to consider the trade union as a comparatively modern association, but this view is erroneous. Labor combinations were active and powerful as far back as the Middle Ages, and the influence which they brought to bear upon commerce was most marked. Professor Thorold Rogers, the noted English political economist, says that the first intimation which he finds of labor combinations in English history is in Kingston in connection with the events of 1350 and 1381. He says further:—

"But I am convinced that it would be an error to conclude that these associations had no earlier existence. In London they were probably as old, at least, as the time of Longbeard, in the days of Richard I. It is certain that the city guilds were in existence as more less irregular associations long before the earliest charters which they possess. But prominence is given them in the earliest struggles between employers and workmen.

"The industrial life of England down to the Reformation, especially that carried out by Somerset, was one especially of trade combinations. The system was so powerful and so universal that the legislature was wholly unable to grapple with it. It broke down under a set of circumstances which have often been described, and was rapidly extirpated, under these new conditions, by the law of 1563. From that date to 1825 the trades union was effectually proscribed, and I am persuaded that the memory of the ancient system, once so universal and so vigorous, had entirely passed away, till at last an antiquarian economist, as I suppose I may call myself, rediscovered it, and traced it back to its early activity and efficiency. I will not say that what I found out entirely changed my views as to those relations of labor and capital which I have found in the earlier economists, but I gained an insight into bygone conditions in which a substantial deference to the claims of labor was, as I found, not incompatible with general and even national prosperity. The conclusions at which I arrived were by no means weakened.

as I followed up the consequences of the act of 1563, and traced the growing misery of the workman from the middle of the sixteenth century down to almost recent experience, long after the repeal of the old labor statutes, when the workman was left to the tender mercies of the judge-made law of conspiracy."

Since the year 1825 the trade unions of Great Britain have been powerful factors, many times working harm to the public in general, and oftener working for good. The harm which may be accomplished by an unprogressive trade union

Will it Pull Them Safely Out?—Philadelphia North American.

is vividly illustrated in Charles Reade's novel, "Put Yourself in His Place."

The British workman is conservative, and is likely to regard innovations like new machinery and labor-saving appliances as encroachments upon his privileges. The measures which he has taken to prevent progress in manufacturing facilities have acted as boomerangs, as such obstructive tactics are bound to act. It is safe to say that this attitude of certain British trade unions has hurt England in her most vital part, the one-time trade supremacy of the world. In the United States, I am glad to say, the labor combinations have not adopted this obstructive policy, and in consequence America now leads in the commercial race.

On the other hand, the trade unions of Great Britain have accomplished much in the way of benefiting their members and laborers in general. They have succeeded in getting the general rate of wages of skilled and unskilled labor throughout the country raised to a more adequate rate, and have enabled many poor working men and women to live in a respectable fashion. Prof. Rogers says: "I do not assert that all the improvement in the condition of workmen has come from the establishment of labor partnerships, but I do not know any other cause for a phenomenon in which, imperfect as it is, I feel a strong satisfaction."

UNIONS IN THIS COUNTRY.

The history of the trade unions of the United States is comparatively familiar to most of us. Prof. Ely, in his "Outline of Economics," says:—

"Labor organizations are not forced products. They have grown up almost spontaneously. They have arisen naturally out of the modern industrial conditions. Wherever capital is a separate factor in production, and is organized on a large scale, labor inevitably organizes itself sooner or later, in order that it may stand on an equal footing and make labor contracts advantageously for itself. Let us suppose one capitalist employs one thousand men. If these men are not organized, each man individually treats with all the capital in the establishment. All the capital is represented by one man, but one workman represents but a thousandth part of the labor force, and he is not in a position of equality. The workmen therefore unite their labor, and, speaking through one representative, place all the labor against all the capital. This is something that so naturally suggests itself that we find labor organizations in all modern lands.

"Labor organizations met at first with violent opposition, and it cannot be said that in their earlier stages, or even in their later growth, this opposition is by any means groundless. However, whatever bad traits naturally characterize labor organizations are aggravated so long as they are obliged to struggle for existence. Whenever the fact of their right to exist is frankly acknowledged, and employers, ceasing to persecute them or their officials, recognize the man who treats in the representative capacity for the sale of the commodity of labor as courteously as they would an agent for the sale of corn or wheat; finally, whenever courts cease to harass them with legal chicanery, they tend to become strong and conservative. The fact is undoubted that most serious abuses and outrages have attended the progress of labor organizations, but they have simply exhibited weaknesses of frail human nature and weaknesses which have been observed in more frightful manifestations in those other organizations, nevertheless excellent, which we call Church and State.

TWO CLASSES OF LABOR ORGANIZATIONS.

"Labor organizations may be divided into two classes, and, as a matter of fact, they are so divided today in the United States. These classes are the trade unions and the Knights of Labor. The trades unions are primarily organizations of skilled artisans. According to the old trades union idea, each craft should be organized by itself. The Knights of Labor are, according to their original idea, organizations of employees, both skilled and unskilled, regardless of trade. They aim to break down the barriers to common action found in differences of occupation. The Knights of Labor have also taken a broader outlook upon society, and have sought to accomplish greater things than the trades unions. The trades unions presuppose a difference of interest between employers and employed. They are, as it were, a fighting body. This divergence of interest exists, and fighting bodies often preserve peace. 'If you would have peace, prepare for war,' is an old maxim, and struggles between labor and capital have been most violent in Belgium, where no efficient organizations have existed. But the Knights of Labor have looked beyond a period of conflict to a union of productive factors which should be peaceful. They hope in some way to see labor and capital united in the same hands. The desire to make capitalists of wage-earners and to organize production on a co-operative basis. It is doubtless on account of this ultimate aim that they admit employers, of whom many are members, and also the professional classes, a considerable number of teachers, journalists and preachers being also members. The Knights of Labor are in so far a return to the principle of the old guild association.

"The Knights of Labor and trades unions have both modified their original programs. The trades unions have united in larger federal organizations, first in the central labor unions of our cities, and later in the national body, the American Federation of Labor. This national body has also made provision for the organization of unskilled work-

A Consummation Devoutly to be Wished.—N. Y. Tribune.

ingmen, and for local unions of workingmen of different trades where those engaged in each trade are too few for separate organization. The Knights of Labor have, on the other hand, organized separately a considerable number of trades in what are often called 'district assemblies,' and have thus recognized more largely than they were at first inclined to do the principle of federation with separate crafts as a basis.

"It has been estimated that at least a million workingmen in the United States are members of labor organizations. The number, of course, varies. A period of prosperity for the organizations is generally followed by one of reaction, and the present seem to be a period of recovery from the period of reaction which began early in 1886, perhaps in 1885, and continued for several years. Reaction always terminates in a new advance, and thus far in the United States each new advance has carried the labor organizations farther forward than ever before.

ORGANIZATION OF FARMERS.

"There are two powerful organizations of farmers, the Patrons of Husbandry and the National Farmers' Alliance and Industrial Union, the latter the more radical and more inclined to political action outside of the two old parties, especially the political action with the third party, called the Populist. These farmers' organizations are more like the old guilds in this, that they are organizations of independent producers designed to protect their interest against attacks from other social classes. Recent years have, however, witnessed an approach of labor organizations and farmers' organizations to each other for the attainment especially of common political aims."

STRIKES.

The strike is the great weapon of the trade union, and while it has accomplished much for the employee, it is a dangerous weapon—a two-edged sword that cuts both ways—and a prolonged strike works infinitely more harm upon the poor laborer than it does upon the rich employer. In most cases the laborer is depending upon his daily wage for his daily bread and cannot, therefore, afford to remain idle for weeks and, it may be, months. On the other hand, a rich employer will not long continue to be rich if his source of income is cut off, while his expenses go on. The violence that accompanies many strikes is their most disastrous feature. It is particularly disastrous to the strikers themselves, for it inevitably excites against them the enmity of the great public, and without the sympathy of the people at large no strike can succeed. It is not fair, however, to lay the blame for most of the violence accompanying strikes to the workingmen, for such a condition of affairs attracts the criminal classes, and they are responsible in most cases for the burning of buildings and the assaults upon property and person.

America has had several great strikes, and some of the greatest in the world have taken place in this country, notably the Homestead strike and the great strike in Chicago during President Cleveland's administration.

THE RECENT CONFERENCE IN NEW YORK.

But capital and labor are gradually getting nearer together, and it begins to look as though employer and employee were actually coming to a realization that the welfare of the one was necessary to that of the other. The noteworthy conference recently held in New York under the auspices of the National Civic Federation, to discuss the relations between labor and capital and to devise means for the peaceable settlement of disputes, was a great step forward.

Where can one find a more remarkable body of representative men than those gathered at this conference, to appoint a standing committee of three dozen members to settle disputes and prevent strikes. The newspapers have given much more space to the workings of this body, but I cannot resist printing the names of the members of the committee as appointed. Here they are:—

Welding Them Together.—Minneapolis Tribune.

ON BEHALF OF THE PUBLIC.

Grover Cleveland, Cornelius N. Bliss, Charles Francis Adams, Archbishop John Ireland, Bishop Henry C. Potter, Charles W. Eliot, president of Harvard University; Franklin MacVeagh, Chicago; James H. Eckels, John J. McCook, John G. Milburn, Buffalo; Charles J. Bonaparte, Baltimore; Oscar S. Straus, Ralph M. Easley.

FOR ORGANIZED LABOR.

Samuel Gompers, president of the American Federation of Labor; John Mitchell, president of the United Mine Workers; F. P. Sargent, Grand Master of the Brotherhood of Locomotive Firemen; T. J. Shaffer, president of the Amalgamated Association of Iron, Steel and Tin Worwers; James Duncan, secretary of the Granite Cutters' Association; Daniel J. Keefe, president of the International Association of 'Longshoremen; Martin Fox, president of the National Iron Molders' Union; James E. Lynch, president of the International Typographical Union; Edward E. Clarke, grand conductor, Brotherhood of Railway Conductors; Henry White, secretary of the Garment Workers of America; Walter MacArthur, editor of the Coast Seaman's Journal, San Fran-

THE NEW YO
PUBLIC LIBRA
ASTOR, LENOX A

cisco; James O'Connell, president of the International Association of Machinists.

FOR THE EMPLOYERS.

Senator Marcus A. Hanna, Cleveland; Charles M. Schwab, president of the United States Steel Corporation; S. R. Callaway, American Locomotive Works; Charles Moore, president of the National Tool Company; J. D. Rockefeller, Jr., H. H. Vreeland, Metropolitan Street Railway Company; Lewis Nixon, Crescent Shipyard, Elizabethport, N. J.; James A. Chambers, president of the American Glass Company, Pittsburg, Pa.; William H. Pfahler, president of the National Association of Stove Manufacturers, Philadelphia, Pa.; E. P. Ripley, president of the Atchison, Topeka & Santa Fe Railway; Marcus M. Marks, president of the National Association of Clothing Manufacturers; J. Kruttschnitt, president of the Southern Pacific Railway Company.

This committee has already done good work in compromising and settling several threatened strikes. It undoubtedly will do much more in the same line.

THE SOCIALIZATION OF CAPITAL.

As a contribution from a prominent man on the subject of the close relations of labor and capital, and as a view of the situation from the standpoint of the capitalist, I present the following, from an address by the Hon. Carroll D. Wright:—

Mr. Wright says:—

"I approach this subject neither as a political economist nor as a socialist, for I cannot claim to be either; but I have been in the habit, for almost a generation of studying social and industrial questions, and in studying them I have learned to respect most heartily and cordially that department of human knowledge which we call political economy. I have learned, also, to have no fear whatever of the word 'socialism.' I have learned to respect socialists as individuals, however much I might differ with them relative to their tenets. I believe that the socialists are doing a measure of good.

"It must be granted that industrial conditions constitute the basis of society, and that all social reform must hinge upon industrial conditions; and, therefore, the economic trend of these conditions toward what we popularly know as socialism constitutes a vital question.

"One of the great objects of socialism is to eliminate competition. We are having now, in this decade various combinations with the avowed purpose of eliminating competition. We are told of the competition among members of a single group; that each group has its own internal competition; that by consolidating all the members of that group into a great combination internal competition ceases. Then we should have the great groups competing with each other. Suppose, for instance, that under the modern industrial combination all the farmers should combine, and all the textile manufacturers, and all the iron and steel and the shoe and leather manufacturers, and so on down the list. In some degree these combinations destroy competition among the individual members of these groups; and then can these great combinations compete with each other? One of the most difficult questions of the trust discussion is found in that very matter. The socialists themselves feel that the trust, or the industrial combination which has come up since the trust, is an evidence of the power of combining to kill competition. These groups may become consolidated into greater groups, and finally into one group; and then the government takes the place of the combination. It is one of the tendencies of the times. It belongs to this trend. Whether it will ever be accomplished or not is another matter; but if it is accomplished it will come like all these other achievements of state socialism—as a matter of industrial evolution—and we shall find ourselves in the environment, and probably not quarrel with it. The trust means the socialization of capital.

"It so happens that there are 2,050 railroad corporations in this country. It is difficult to state just how many systems there are, but something like 800 roads or corporations run 2,050; and it is perfectly safe to say that ten men in the United States, whose names are familiar, control the whole 2,050 roads, either directly or indirectly. There are influential men outside of its group of ten powerful men—great railroad managers, able men, ornaments to the country—but, nevertheless, these ten men control the business of the United States, and nearly all of them live in the city of New York. This is a matter which, it seems to me, is worthy of our ~~consideration~~ when discussing the economic trend toward ~~state socialism~~. **The question might be asked whether it would not be just as well that instead of these ten men, who are in a way self-elective, the government itself should appoint ten commissioners in their place, and let us have that disinterested authorization of rates and that disinterested regulation of the traffic of the country which would come through such a board. The ten men are not subject to criticism. They are great men; they must be great men, and greater men that those that are called to conduct the affairs of the state itself. I know of no class of men that so thoroughly excite my admiration, my enthusiasm, as the men at the head of our great enterprises in industry, in transportation and in commerce; and I know, furthermore, that their interests are nothing, their profits nothing, unless they conduct their affairs in the interest of the public. Hence, there need be no fear of the socialistic trend. While it may reach farther than they think—it may reach so far as to take the whole control and management out of their hands—it cannot under any system reach, except temporarily, beyond the public interest itself.**

"The interstate commerce commissioners have said: "It is a matter of common knowledge that vast schemes of railway control are in process of consummation, and that the competition of rival lines is to be restrained by these combinations. If the plans already foreshadowed are brought into effective results, there will be a vast centralization of railroad properties, with all the power involved in such far-reaching combinations, yet uncontrolled by any public authority.'

"It's too heavy for either one, but between us we can carry it up any hill."

"This is a statement which will gradually and more rapidly, as time goes on, sink into the consciousness of this country; and when it sees that instead of ten men it is five, then instead of five it is three, and instead of three it is one man that controls all the railroad interests of the country, it will be found that public sentiment will not be afraid of the trend toward socialism.

"The great department stores in our large cities represent an economic trend toward state socialism, because they, more than any other modern development, really democratize business by absorbing the business of smaller stores and concentrating it under one great management. The socialist does not oppose the department store, for he sees in it the effort of the capitalist to socialize capital, to concentrate under one management many and varied interests.

"The chief element which is inducing the wage receiver to become a state socialist is machinery. Trades unions themselves are not socialistic organizations, although their members may in some degree be members of the socialist party. There have been some very sharp contests in the general meetings of the representatives of trades unions of this country by the socialist and anti-socialist elements. On the whole, socialism has been defeated in these contests; but here and there, among workingmen individually, the socialist trend is clearly perceivable, and it grows out of machinery, which is at the bottom of the movement. The workingman does not oppose machinery as such, for he recognizes that through it his wages have been increased, his productive power greatly enhanced, his comforts broadened and his work-day greatly reduced. Nevertheless, he believes with many economists that so far, the benefits arising from the application of power machinery have been equitably divided. He is willing that capital should have a large share in these benefits, but he thinks he ought to have a greater share than he now receives; and this belief leads him to the conclusion that he will not get the full benefit of the application of the invention until society shall become the owner of inventions.

"So there are three forces that we must recognize as involved in this economic trend toward socialism—the first, socialism itself, the weakest of the whole; the next strongest is organized labor; but the third and most powerful force that is driving this and other countries rapidly into state socialism is capital itself. And the capitalists, when you talk with them confidently, do not hesitate to say that this is inevitably the result of their combination."

Along the Highways and Byways of Business

By VANNANT

The newspapers of a few months since contained accounts of the discovery by a poor Mississippi River fisherman of a valuable pearl in a mussel shell. The fisherman, so it is stated, was plodding away at his daily grind, opening mussels, when his knife struck something hard. He threw back the upper shell, and, behold! "a pearl of great price"—of which price, I am obliged to admit, he received but a small percentage. I know how that fisherman felt when he made this discovery, for I also have found a gem in an unexpected and unlikely place, namely, amid the dreary waste of literature setting forth the claims of the so-called commercial schools and colleges of this country. My gem is a booklet of some sixty-five pages, and is neatly printed and prettily bound. It advertises an "Institute of Accounts" in the vicinity of New York, that, for educational advantages offered to its students, has only been equalled by the celebrated "Dotheboys Hall" in Yorkshire, presided over by Mr. Wackford Squeers.

* * *

The institution, the varied charms of which it is my desire to exploit for the benefit of the readers of COMMERCE, ACCOUNTS & FINANCE, is situated at a seaside resort not so very far from the metropolis. The gentleman who is principal and proprietor is also president of a "Practical Business College" in another part of the country. In the introduction to his pamphlet he says:—

"During the summer months of each year, that is to say from about June 1, until October 1, being sixteen weeks or four school months, I will take for that term, in New York City, a limited number of pupils and for a moderate sum, (as hereinafter stated) will give said students in return for said amount the following superior advantages: First—A thorough course of sixteen weeks in Practical Bookkeeping in all its branches. Banking, Business Arithmetic, Penmanship, Business Correspondence, Spelling, Grammar and Commercial Law, and all the necessary books, blanks and stationery needed during the term, or Shorthand and Typewriting with the above studies, exclusive of BOOK-KEEPING."

In the above, as in all other quotations from the booklet, I wish it distinctly understood that the spelling, composition, grammar and punctuation are the Professor's own.

* * *

The next item that the Professor offers is this: "I will board said students during the term in excellent and first-class style." This statement leaves no room for doubt. If the students were to board in "excellent style" alone we might feel some hesitation, but when the "first-class style" is added to the "excellent style," what more can one expect? Then, further, it is stated that—

Students will be instructed in forms and manners, viz.; Street, Table, Theater, Opera, etc. as well as in the forms of Book-Keeping, as a polished business man is always appreciated and respected.

I am strongly tempted to join the Professor's class. I confess that my theater manners, as distinguished from my opera manners, may be a trifle crude and lacking in elegance. I had not hertofore appreciated the distinction between the manners required at the theater and those required at the opera.

* * *

The Professor not only teaches "every day in the week, except Saturdays and Sundays, from 9 A. M. until 4 P. M.," but, as he so lucidly explains,

The Wednesday evenings or nights, as termed in the South, that occur, will be devoted to taking students to lectures and the very best theaters. Sundays will be devoted to visiting the churches, parks, trips on New York Bay, etc. I will, of course, accompany students on all trips, to theaters and everywhere they go.

This is kind of the Professor, very kind. The students will undoubtedly appreciate his company, for does he not say—

My references and testimonials should satisfy anyone that I am a gentleman, my integrity, moral character and ability unimpeachable, and in every way qualified to take charge of and educate young men in the branches herein named.

* * *

One section of the pamphlet is devoted to Manners and another to Dress. The Professor says:—

As at all times I wish my students to present a suitable apearance and to be correctly dressed, I will request that they have the following outfit:

One light business suit.

One square cut blue serge coat.

Several pairs white duck trousers.

One full dress suit or only a Tuxedo, and dress trousers and vest. (This latter is preferable and will answer all requirements). If students have both full dress suit and tuxedo it is well to bring both.

Note.—When attending the theatre, all students wear a tuxedo.

Necessary white and negligee shirts, no special number required.

Necessary clothing

One straw hat.

Gloves, ties, shoes, etc. ad lib.

It is optional with the pupil as to having an opera hat, but if he wishes to feel properly dressed and not feel out of place, but on the other hand feel correctly dressed at the theatre, opera, etc., he should by all means have one.

In the matter of dress it should not cost the student but very little, for the average young man who can avail himself of this opportunity will have all that is needed, except possibly the tuxedo and the opera hat, and both of these can be bought very reasonably in New York after he reaches there.

I have been a little puzzled concerning this last paragraph. It seems obvious that if it "should not cost the student but very little," that it should, therefore, cost him more than a very little, but the Professor is a teacher of grammar, and I am not.

* * *

The greater portion of the little book is made up of detailed itineraries of various Saturday and Sunday trips, on all of which, it will be remembered, the Professor will accompany his students.

The Art Museum and libraries, which the Professor calls "great institutions of Art and Curios," are visited. On the seventh Saturday the East Side, Five Points, Chinatown and the Bowery, the educational advantage of all of which is at once apparent, are visited, and the afternoon finishes by the party witnessing a game of baseball at the National League grounds. I cannot resist quoting the Professor's description of the trip which is to be taken on the ninth Saturday.

A trip to Canarsie and Bergen Beach, this is a trip of trips. We leave New York Friday afternoon and reach Canarsie about 7 P. M. This quaint old fishing town of Jamaica Bay, is much as it was one hundred years ago. Of all the places about New York none is more noted for its fishing and elegant fish and clam dinners than Canarsie. On arriving at Canarsie we indulge in one of these elegant fish dinners, and after dinner take a sail across the bay to Bergen Beach, spend an hour or so there and return to fisherman's headquarters, a celebrated place known as "The Yachter's Retreat" and put up for the night; by daylight we are up and off for the yacht which is anchored not far from our window, she is a beauty, about fifty feet long, on board is the skipper and several trained sailors, in a short time we are under sail and off for the briny deep, about 10 a. m. we are almost out of sight of land on the green waters of the Atlantic Ocean, and then out goes the lines for blue fish and soon the sport begins, and such sport! only those who have enjoyed it can appreciate this, as it beggars description. Time flies, soon it is time to turn our bow towards Canarsie and about 5 p. m. we are on our way home, leaving Canarsie behind us, but with pleasant recollections that are indellibly stamped upon our memories for life."

* * *

It will be noted that the principal of this all-embracing institution occasionally uses the word "elegant". We say occasionally, but this is a mild term, for "elegant" is used in at least twelve places to describe objects and things of widely varying kinds. We visit "elegant" churches, take "elegant" trips, eat "elegant" clam dinners and behave in an "elegant" manner. Is it any wonder that pleasant recollections are "indellibly" stamped on our minds?

Among the interesting and famous, not to mention "elegant" and "beautiful" institutions and places visited on Sundays, during the time occupied by the "course," are "Trinity Church and its old grave yard full of historic lore, the Moorish-Jewish Synagogue, the Crematory, where hundreds have been cremated, and the Morgue." The pleasant recollections should be even more "indellibly" stamped after having visited the two points of educational interest last named.

* * *

We have already quoted a portion of what the Professor has to say about himself, and the following bits culled from this garden of exotics will be of interest as still further setting forth his good qualities:—

I feel myself especially adapted to the work I undertake, for the following reasons: I am thoroughly prepared to teach the Business Branches, as my many years practical business experience, together with a good scholastic and college education, admirably fits me for same. I was born south, but virtually raised in New York, and then went South again, and now divide my time between the two sections, so I have the advantage of being perfectly familiar with the business methods and customs of the people in both the North and the South, and I might add the West, as I have spent many of my summers in Chicago and the West, and I am therefore thoroughly acquainted with that section in every particular.

The "good scholastic and college education" referred to was, according to the Professor's own statement, gained from attendance at public schools, a military institute, two colleges, a high school and two academies. The Professor says he "started to school at eight years of age, and went almost steadily until eighteen." I should feel some doubts as to whether he finally reached the school for which he started were it not that he says he attended the various institutions of learning above mentioned. "During vacations his father always put him to work in some business house or office."

* * *

There are fifteen pages devoted to testimonials concerning the Professor's good character and marvelous abilities. These testimonials are from various people in different walks of life. Some are from ex-students, and, as a matter of justice, it must be stated that they speak highly of their old instructor. Says the Professor again:—

"I could furnish numbers of similar letters but space forbids. If those I have given and the other matter in this book have not convinced the reader that I am qualified to undertake what I propose herein, then a volume of 1000 pages would have no effect."

Right you are, Professor, it would not. This booklet should convince any one; it has convinced me, and has furnished me more genuine enjoyment than would a dinner made of the most "elegant" clams that Carnarsie could furnish. I have followed your instructions to "Please read the contents of this book carefully, for every line is solid and worth reading," and I cheerfully agree that the statement is fact.

* * *

I have taken the trouble to quote from this booklet pretty extensively, and have done so because it is an illustration of what I have said before in these columns, namely, that parents who send their children to commercial schools should be very careful to choose a school of established merit, if any such can be found. Personally, I am not a believer in the commercial college as it exists at present, but I will not go so far as to say that there are no good schools in the country. The proprietor and principal of the "Institute of Accounts" claims to have taught thousands of students. What did those students learn? Manners? Perhaps. Business theories and practice? Possibly. The Professor, according to his own story, has had plenty of both, having occupied twelve different positions from 1871 to 1896, varying from office boy to teller and head bookkeeper of a bank, besides which it is stated, that at one time he "did" work at nights for the newspapers, among which were the Truth, Morning Journal and Dramatic News, and has constantly done newspaper work for newspaper people, both north and south, being at present correspondent at ——— ——— for the New York Clipper." But, even admitting him competent to teach bookkeeping and etiquette, what shall we say about the grammar, composition, business correspondence and spelling which he professes to teach? There is some bad spelling in the pamphlet, and numberless errors in grammar, not to mention faulty composition and ridiculous punctuation, and yet this commercial teacher claims to have taught thousands of students, and the price for his summer course, including board and lodging, tickets to theaters, etc., is $460. There was a wise man once, or at least I suppose there was, who stated that there is "a new sucker born every minute." That is not a refined expression, but unfortunately it seems to be true.

Isn't it time that some more rigid examination was imposed upon those who profess to impart commercial education to the young?

ALL RICH MEN NOT IDLERS

Young Cornelius Vanderbilt lectured in Boston, the other night, on the strictly technical subject of locomotive boilers, says the Philadelphia Bulletin, and crowds of people, who presumably neither knew nor cared anything about the theme of his discourse, were turned away from the doors of the building where the address was delivered. Yet, as a matter of fact, there is nothing new in the spectacle of a wealthy young American devoting himself to hard, practical work. The vague allusions of Anarchistic agitators to the existence of a class of rich idlers in this country have no real foundation. With few exceptions the possessors of American fortunes, whether they are young, middle-aged or old men, work systematically at their daily tasks. Probably a good many of them labor more hours out of each twenty-four than most of their employees.

WHAT THEY DID

The professor was lecturing on some of the habits and customs of the ancient Greeks to his class, says Tit-Bits. "The ancient Greeks built no roofs over their theaters," said the professor. "What did the ancient Greeks do when it rained?" asked Johnny Brown. The professor took off his spectacles, polished them with his handkerchief and replied calmly: "They got wet, I suppose."

A Detail Cash Book and Journal

From J. McL., Detroit, Mich.

I enclose herewith a specimen page of a cash book which,

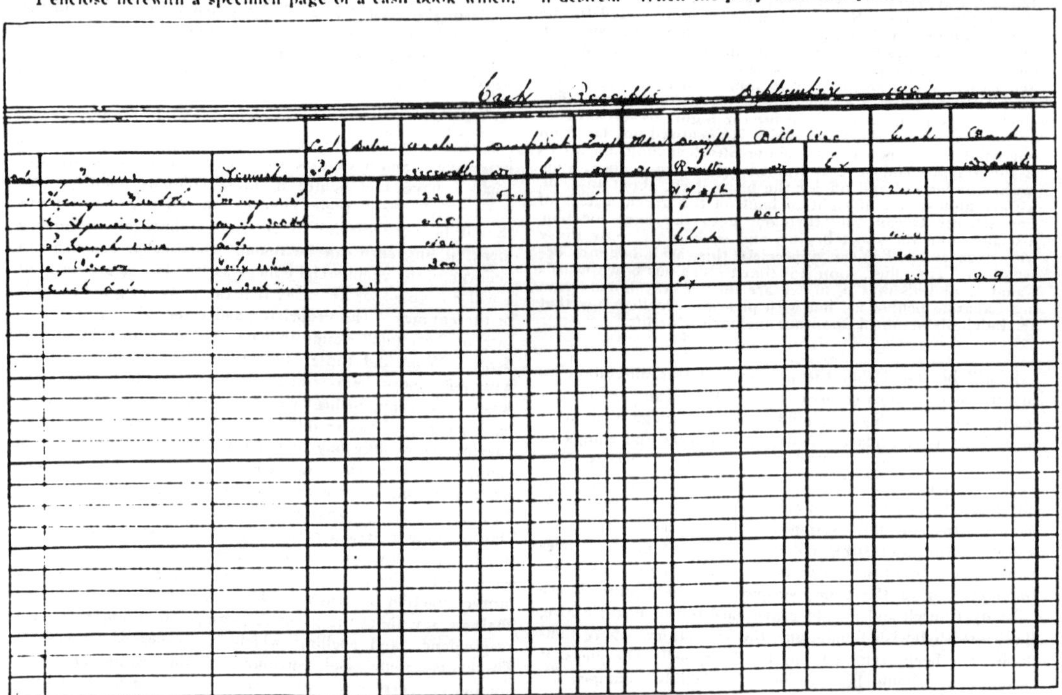

CASH BOOK, LEFT-HAND PAGE.

I think, in some respects, is new. In any event, I know that it is a time-saver. If you think it will be of interest to the readers of your paper, I shall be glad to have you present it for their inspection. I also enclose a page from my

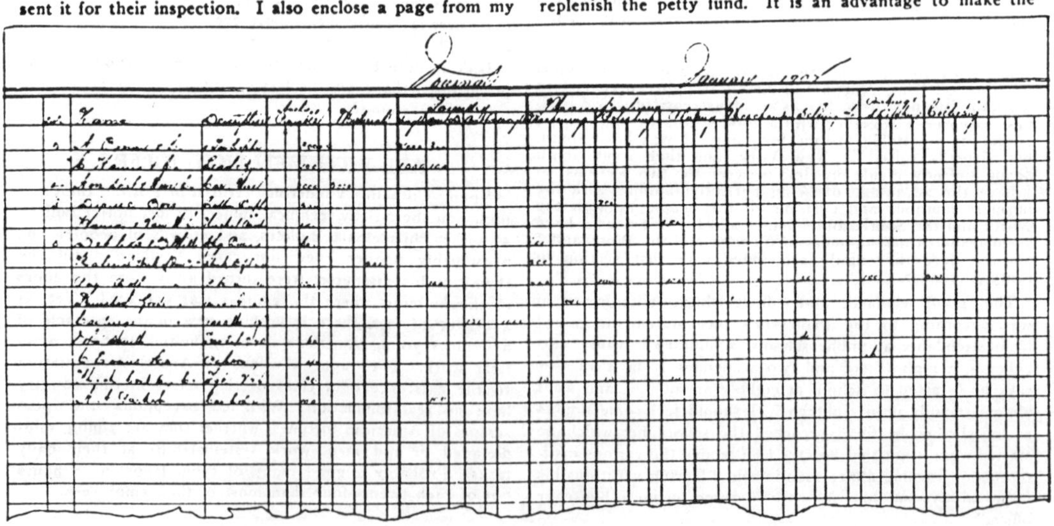

JOURNAL, LEFT-HAND PAGE.

journal, which is a companion to the cash book. These two are adapted, as you will perceive, to a manufacturing business.

When opening the cash book all moneys on hand should be deposited, and in subsequent deposits there should be included whatever has been received, even to the small amount in currency. Draw a check for cashier's use in hundreds, sufficient say for requirements for one week, or a shorter time if desired. When the petty cash thus provided has been depleted, make a voucher of the receipted bills paid out of this fund by the cashier and enter through the journal, making out a check the same as for any other voucher, and thereby replenish the petty fund. It is an advantage to make the voucher for this purpose on the last day of the week. A voucher index is necessary only when accounts payable are kept in one account in the ledger. The cash will always balance.

Referring now to the journal, I have written in a few entries such as might arise in a certain business, although the ruling shown is not limited to that exact business. It has been somewhat extended for the purpose of showing the principle and illustrating further applications. In any event, the ruling would have to be adapted to the exact business in hand, it being, on general principles, one thing in a manufacturing business and something else in a jobbing business.

The accounts payable are to be posted separately or to a single account, as may be preferred. The foundry account is for the purpose of getting the exact cost of castings, and is worth keeping, particularly when a cost book is kept. By it you can give the cost of the castings per pound, also the cost of making per pound, any time you wish to take inventory, which, of course, is a very short job in a foundry. Having the cost of making per pound for a period of, say, one year, you have the current cost of metal at all times and can figure at contracts accordingly.

The manufacturing account I have divided into three divisions. Some manufacturers may like it in this form, and some may prefer it in some other. I do not like it as well as to have a single column for manufacturing and to put the sub-accounts entirely on the right hand page. So in the present instance, with headings, Polishing Materials, Plating Material, etc., leaving the total amounts for a given time for any part of the manufacturing business when material is consumed, and also the wages for the same period. With this basis you can figure exactly when to add such material in keeping costs.

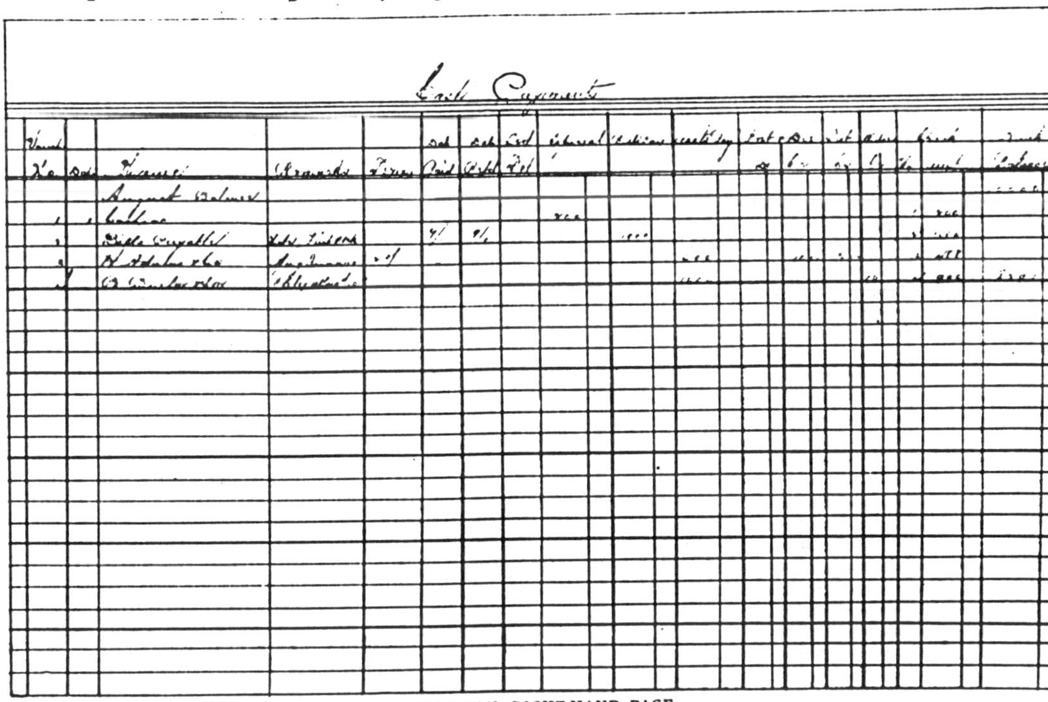

CASH BOOK, RIGHT-HAND PAGE.

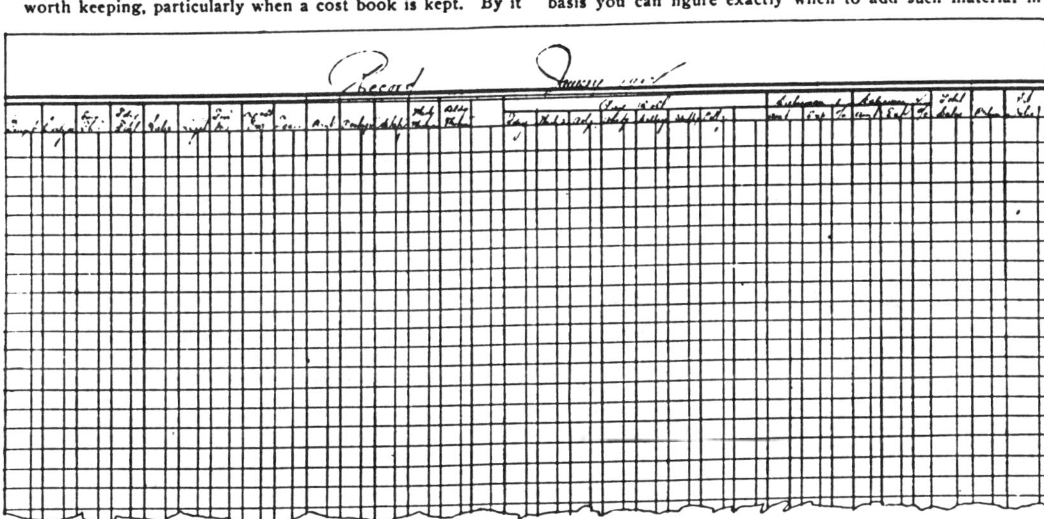

JOURNAL, RIGHT-HAND PAGE.

I might add that this latter is an item that is very generally guessed at, or, at best, estimated. When a cost book is kept, goods can be entered in Merchandise Account as soon as finished at exact cost. This saves guessing at inventory items. This is the account to show the profit or loss, and can be called Sales, or by any other name suitable. The

Material Account is merely for keeping track of material which cannot be charged up except when it is to be used. The columns entitled Selling, Shipping and Collecting do not require extension. The key to the book is this, everything that is to be paid for goes through this book and is put where it belongs and no expense account is to be kept. Charge salaries of superintendent and foremen and wages of mechanics to Manufacturing. All travelers' salaries and expenses and the cost of those in charge of orders and manufacturing goods in warehouses go to Selling Account. Charge the cost of bill clerks, shipping clerks, packers and teamsters to Shipping, and bookkeeper and treasurer to Collecting. Do this for six months or a year—that is, until an inventory is taken—and you will have the cost of your different items in a way to make estimates safe and reliable. There will also be revealed what particular branch of the business needs shaking up, and there will be presented facts upon which to base action.

The right-hand page is for keeping track of everything you want, say, at the yearly inventory. Carry the amounts over when you make entries in the journal, add up monthly and carry totals to last page of book, add up at end of year, and you have something useful. You have it correct, and you have it where you want it, not on pieces of paper or in memorandum books which cannot be found when wanted and are nearly enough correct to be misleading.

Note.—We have pleasure in presenting for our readers' consideration the cash book and journal forms so considerately contributed by this subscriber. Our readers will find them well worth studying. The critical observer will note at the outset that there is in the journal submitted a combination of journal and ledger principles. The footings of the columns give what ordinarily a ledger is depended upon to show. The columnarization affords a basis of classification which many bookkeepers will appreciate. At the same time the journal in a sense disappears, or, to put it otherwise, that which the beginner recognizes as a journal, namely, a classification scheme preliminary to postings, very markedly disappears in this extended classification.

The journal is a diminishing quantity in modern bookkeeping plans. It is less and less employed by those who have very complete systems in their charge. There is always, of course, the equivalent of the journal or the substitute for the journal. What our correspondent has submitted is a very extensive scheme of columnarization for statistical purposes. His object in view is to be commended in that costs are arrived at in such a way that results will be obtained calculated to influence the figures of estimates on contracts, etc.

This correspondent has set a most excellent example to the readers of this paper, and we trust that there are many who will follow his example and send us in specimens of their forms. A paper of this nature could be made extremely interesting and valuable by the free use of its columns for showing up different features of bookkeeping and accounting practice. We shall be glad to do our part if our readers will take initiative steps.

CHILDREN'S FUNNY MISTAKES

An English lecturer, Dr. Macnamara, M. P., has gotten together a collection of mistakes made by English schoolchildren, and, says the London Daily Mail, for an hour of uproarious mirth, few things can compare with them.

The question, "What is Parliament?" obtained the answer, "A place where they go up to London to talk about Birmingham." "Who was the first man?" an American boy was asked. On replying "Washington" he was reminded of Adam. "Yes," he said, "if you count foreigners." "What is a heretic?" was another question. "One who would never believe what he was told, but only after hearing it and seeing it with his own eyes." "Define Court of Chancery," said a teacher. "It is called this because they take care of property there in the chance of the owner turning up." "A vacuum," said another child, "is nothing shut up in a box." "An optimist," according to another, "is a man who attends to your head." A "pessimist" is a man who attends to your feet." Among musical instruments were included "funny bones," evidently intended for trombones. Fort and fortress had no difficulties for one little fellow. "Fort is a place for soldiers to live in. Fortress is where they keep their wives."

Questions in history drew forth the following information: "The fire of London, although looked upon at first as a calamity, really did a great deal of good. It purified the city from the dregs of the plague, and burnt down eighty-nine churches." "King James I. was very unclean in his habits and married Anne of Denmark." As for the hardships of the Salic law, we are told that Edward III. would have been King of France if his mother had been a man. "King Henry VIII. was a very good man; he liked plenty of money, had plenty of wives, and died of ulcers in the legs."

As for the marriage customs of the ancient Greeks, we learn that a man married only one wife, which was called Monotony. After that one can comprehend the definition of faith which is that quality which enables us to believe what we know to be untrue. How to sweep a room involves Herculean labors, according to one little maid who wrote "Scatter damp tea-leaves over the carpet, then carefully sweep the room into the dust-pan, and throw it out of the window."

The question, "What was the general character of Moses?" drew from one child the reply: "A gentleman." Not grasping the hang of the answer, the inspector asked why. "Please, sir, when the daughters of Jethro went to the well to draw water the shepherds were in the way, but Moses helped them, and said to the shepherds, 'Ladies first, please.'" Just before Christmas one teacher got her pupils to write letters to their fathers and mothers which they might take home. With the pathos belonging to poverty, a little girl of nine concluded: "And, please, ma, don't have a baby this Christmas; I do so want to have a happy time!" Wesleyans will appreciate the remark of the child who, when writing of the birds, said, "Do you know the swallows go away in the winter, but the sparrows belong to this circuit." Purity was the subject which occupied the pen of the child who ended her essay, "O, please, may I be pure, absolutely pure—like Epps' cocoa."

But, after all, the compositions read by Dr. Macnamara gave an even more intimate peep into the thoughts and imagination of the child than the isolated answer. Among reflections on a cow a boy revealed his belief that cream came only from the cow that was all white. In moralizing about politeness, another child ventured the remark that "some boys are rude over meals. You should not keep eating after you are 'tightening.' You should be very polite to girls, because their hair is long and they are pretty. Even if a girl scratches your cheek, or spits in your face, don't pinch her, don't tell her mother, but just hold her tight by the arms, to show her you could wallop her if you'd a mind."

THE TRUSTS AND PUBLIC OPINION

The period of indiscriminate trust denunciation seems passed. Some hold that the big trust in itself may be a pretty good thing, making for economy in production and consumption and thus comparable to labor-saving machinery, and that all the public needs to do is to protect itself against particular abuse, says the Des Moines Leader. Others, while still believing that the trust idea is all wrong, and that the competitive system of our forefathers is much better, realize that the tendency toward consolidation is so deeply implanted in modern business as to make it futile for any Government to attempt its suppression. A few years ago every one agreed on the broad proposition that trusts ought to be smashed, whereas now we have many who hold that they ought to be controlled, not smashed, and others who hold that they cannot be smashed. It may be predicted that public opinion is now veering strongly toward a national policy of trust control as distinguished from a policy of trust elimination.

HARD TO GET UP

"There is always room at the top," said the Good Adviser.

"Indeed, yes," answered the Unfortunate Person, "but the elevator is not always running."—Baltimore American.

The Negotiable Instruments Law*

By THOMAS B. PATON

Liabilities of Parties—Fraudulent Impersonation—Liability of Acceptor

NOTE.—As enacted in New York, the Negotiable Instrument law is divided into nineteen articles as follows:—

1. GENERAL PROVISIONS (Sections 1—11)
2. NEGOTIABLE INSTRUMENTS: Form and Interpretation (20—42)
3. Consideration (50—55)
4. Negotiation (60—80)
5. Rights of holder (90—98)
6. Liabilities of parties (110—119)
7. Presentment for payment (130—148)
8. Notice of Dishonor (160—189)
9. Discharge (200—206)
10. BILLS OF EXCHANGE (210—215)
11. Acceptance (220—230)
12. Presentment for acceptance (240—248)
13. Protest (260—268)
14. Acceptance for honor (280—290)
15. Payment for honor (300—306)
16. Bills in a set (310—315)
17. PROMISSORY NOTES AND CHECKS (320—325)
18. Notes given for patent rights (330—332)
19. Law repealed: When takes effect (340—341)

The provisions of the law naturally fall under four general classifications.

a. General Provisions.
b. Negotiable Instruments in General.
c. Bills of Exchange.
d. Promissory Notes and Checks.

The text of the law is the same in all the states (with some slight exceptions which will be noted), but the numbering of the sections, and in some states of the articles, is not uniform. There is, however, the same continuity of articles and text, except that in some instances, "General Provisions" follow, instead of precede, the remainder of the act. By following this course of study with reference to the New York act, as above outlined, the reader in each state can apply the same to the law of his own state.

Having heretofore considered those provisions of the Negotiable Instruments Law which relate to the form and interpretation of negotiable instruments, their consideration, negotiation, and rights of the holder, we come next to that branch of the law which provides the liabilities of the various parties whose names appear thereon. These parties—maker, drawer, acceptor or indorser—are responsible for payment to the payee or holder according to the various engagements which, as defined by the act, they have undertaken to fulfil by placing their names upon and delivering the instrument. And first, concerning the liability of the maker:—

LIABILITY OF MAKER.

Section 110. Liability of Maker.—The maker of a negotiable instrument by making it engages that he will pay it according to its tenor; and admits the existence of the payee and his then capacity to indorse.

Let us attempt to illustrate this section in the form of actual transactions. John Smith makes his negotiable promissory note, promising to pay to the order of William Jones $100, one month after date, which note he delivers to William Jones. When the month is up Smith must pay the $100 to Jones, providing the latter has given value for the note: and whether or not Jones has given value to Smith therefor, if Jones has indorsed it over to a third person for value, before maturity, Smith must pay the $100 to the holder at the end of the month, for by making it he has engaged "that he will pay it according to its tenor."

Smith, in making the note, further "admits the existence of the payee and his then capacity to indorse." What does this mean?

We will first take up the admission of capacity. Suppose Jones is a lunatic, or an infant, or otherwise incapacitated to make a legal contract, but, nevertheless, he actually indorses the note and it comes to the hands of some person who, barring any question of payee's incapacity, would otherwise have an enforceable title to the instrument. This person makes demand upon Smith for the $100 at maturity. Smith must pay. He cannot refuse on the ground of the incapacity of the payee to indorse, for by making the note payable to Jones he has admitted his capacity, and cannot call it into question against a holder in due course.

Then, concerning the maker's admission of the existence of the payee, let us suppose this case: There is no such person in existence as Jones, but some intermediary who claims to represent Jones in a proposed transaction between Smith and Jones makes Smith believe that there is, and Smith thereupon makes his note in Jones' favor, without value other than prospective, which he delivers to the intermediary to deliver to Jones. But, Jones being non-existent, the intermediary himself indorses it in Jones' name and finds somebody who will cash the note. Can the holder for value recover the $100 from Smith on the note, who, by making it, "admits the existence of the payee?" If not, what does the act mean when it provides that the maker, by making the instrument, "admits the existence of the payee?" If Smith issued the note payable to Jones, knowing there was no such person as Jones, then the holder could demand payment as upon a "bearer" instrument, for section 28, subdivision 3, provides, as we have seen, that "the instrument is payable to bearer * * * when it is payable to the order of a fictitious or non-existing person, and such fact was known to the person making it so payable." But the instrument is not payable to bearer, because Smith did not know that Jones was non-existing. Can the holder then, although unable to make title by delivery, claim an enforceable title through an indorsement which the maker is estopped to deny? Before the act, the weight of decisions governing such a case was to the effect that the indorsement by the intermediary, he not being the one to whom the maker promised or intended to pay, was a forgery, and conveyed no title; and we do not think the provision that the maker "admits the existence of the payee" was intended to cover such a case or change the law in this respect. We think that the holder in the case supposed could not make Smith, the maker, pay it.

What force and effect, then, is to be given to the provision that the maker "admits the existence of the payee?" for it certainly must have application to some cases where the payee's real existence is in dispute. For answer, we think its application is to those cases where the payee is dealing under a trade or assumed name. An illustration is afforded by the case of Jones vs. Home Furnishing Co., 9 N. Y. Ap. Div. 103. A promissory note was made payable to the order of the "National Publishing Company." This was a name assumed by one Joshua R. Jones in carrying on his business. Jones indorsed the note in this name to himself individually, and then sued the maker thereon. The maker claimed that the note was made payable to a company that had no existence, and therefore the instrument was fictitious, and that as the indorsement was fictitious and spurious, no title passed to the note. But the court held the maker was estopped from setting up that the note was made payable to a fictitious payee.

FRAUDULENT IMPERSONATION.

Then there are cases where one person assumes another's name, and receives an instrument made payable to him in the assumed name. That is to say, one whose name is in reality Robinson, impersonates Jones, and a note is made payable to Jones and delivered to Robinson, thinking him to be Jones. In this case, where Robinson has indorsed the name of Jones to the instrument and negotiated it, the courts have held that the indorsement, being by the precise party to whom the maker intended to make or order payment, is not forgery, and the holder has an enforceable title. The distinction between this case and the one where the note is made payable to Jones, non-existent, and delivered to an intermediary to deliver to the supposed Jones, is apparent. If the intermediary indorses as Jones, it is not an indorsement by the one to whom payment is intended—there being no such a one in existence—and the indorsement is a forgery. But where a note is made payable to Jones, and delivered to Robinson thinking him to be Jones, then Robinson is the real payee whom the maker has in mind to receive the money, although he falsely assumes the

*Republished from the Banking Law Journal by permission. Copyright, 189', 1900, 1901 and 1902, by T. B. Paton, all rights reserved. To be revised and published in book form by the author.

name of Jones; hence his indorsement of such name will transfer title.

In a promissory note, or instrument of like character, there are two original parties at its inception, maker and payee, and the language of the obligation is expressed in the form of a promise to pay, made by the maker to the payee or his order. In a bill of exchange, or instrument partaking of such a nature, there are three original parties, drawer, drawee and payee, and the language consists of an order by the drawer on the drawee to pay the payee, or his order. When such instrument is presented to the drawee and accepted by him, then the latter becomes an acceptor, and the primary debtor upon the instrument, as is the maker of a promisory note. Section 110, which we have just considered, provides the liability of the maker; section 111, to which we now come, the liability of the drawer, and the following section, 112, the liability of the acceptor.

LIABILITY OF DRAWER.

Sec. 111. Liability of Drawer.—The drawer by drawing the instrument admits the existence of the payee and his then capacity to indorse, and engages that on due presentment the instrument will be accepted and paid, or both, according to its tenor, and that if it be dishonored, and the necessary proceedings on dishonor be duly taken, he will pay the amount thereof to the holder, or to any subsequent indorser who may be compelled to pay it. But the drawer may insert in the instrument an express stipulation negativing or limiting his own liability to the holder.

Taking up this section in detail, we have already, under the last section, considered the nature and purport of the admission of the "existence of the payee and his then capacity to indorse." Besides making this admission to the commercial public, which he will not be permitted to controvert to their injury, he engages that on due presentment, the instrument will be accepted and paid, or both, according to its tenor, and that if it be dishonored, and the necessary proceedings on dishonor be duly taken, he will pay the amount to the holder or to any subsequent indorser who may be compelled to pay it.

This engagement of the drawer is not expressed in language in the body of the instrument itself; it is an engagement which the law fixes upon him because of his drawing and delivering the instrument; an engagement that if there is "due presentment" by the holder—and what constitutes due presentment is provided elsewhere in the act—the instrument will be "accepted and paid, or both." Some instruments do not require acceptance, and the obligation, it seems to us, would be better expressed by providing that the instrument "will be paid, or accepted and paid, according to its tenor;" but this is an unimportant defect. An acceptance not according to the tenor of a bill of exchange,—i. e., qualified—and its effect on the liability of the drawer will be considered when we reach sections 229 and 230 of the act. If the instrument is paid, that is the end of it. But "if it be dishonored, and the necessary proceedings on dishonor be duly taken,"—these proceedings are provided elsewhere in the act—then the drawer further engages that "he will pay the amount thereof (of the instrument) to the holder or to any subsequent indorser who may be compelled to pay it."

It is thus seen that the drawer is, at first, only contingently liable to pay the instrument, in the event the drawee dishonors it upon due presentment, and in the event dishonor is followed by the necessary proceedings, such as protest, or notice of dishonor, or both, to preserve his liability. This done, his obligation becomes an absolute one to pay the amount of the instrument to the holder, or to any subsequent indorser who has first been compelled to pay it.

It will be observed that the act does not in express terms provide the liability of the drawer to pay the notarial protest fees, where protest is either necessary or permitted; simply provides his engagement to pay the amount of the dishonored instrument. But, presumably, the protest, where necessary or authorized, is so much a part of the instrument as to make the fees of protest part of the obligation; and at all events, equally with the legal rate of interest, the general law attaches an obligation therefor.

This engagement of the drawer to pay in the event of dishonor, as has been said, is not expressed in the instrument itself, but is imposed upon him by the law under which he draws and delivers the instrument. But the Negotiable Instruments Law, it is seen, permits him to draw and issue a negotiable instrument, and by express terms therein, negative or limit his liability, if the instrument is dishonored. The closing sentence of section 111 provides: "But the drawer may insert in the instrument an express stipulation negativing or limiting his own liability to the holder." Clauses of this nature are occasionally seen in bills of exchange, as well as clauses or stipulations to the contrary purport, i. e., waiving some proceeding to which the drawer is entitled, as preliminary to his own liability, such as presentment or notice of dishonor, thereby making his liability more absolute from the inception of the instrument.

LIABILITY OF ACCEPTOR.

Section 112. Liability of Acceptor.—The acceptor by accepting the instrument engages that he will pay it according to the tenor of his acceptance; and admits:—

1. The existence of the drawer, the genuineness of his signature and his capacity and authority to draw the instrument; and

2. The existence of the payee and his then capacity to indorse.

When an instrument has been accepted by the drawee, the acceptor engages that he will pay it according to the tenor of his acceptance. His engagement is now analogous to the engagement of the maker. The maker engages to pay the instrument he has made according to its tenor, and the acceptor likewise engages to pay the instrument he has accepted according to the tenor of his acceptance. Later in the act we will come to provisions as to the kinds of acceptance, whether general or qualified, and the effect, upon the liability of the drawer or indorser, of a drawee qualifying his acceptance—that is, in express terms varying the effect of the bill as drawn. But so far as the acceptor is concerned his engagement or liability is according to the tenor of his acceptance, whether it is in accordance with the tenor of the instrument as originally drawn or not.

Beyond this engagement of the acceptor to pay he admits (1) the existence of the drawer, the genuineness of his signature and his capacity and authority to draw the instrument and (2) the existence of the payee and his then capacity to indorse.

We have already expressed the opinion that the provisions of the Negotiable Instruments Law that the maker "admits the existence of the payee" and that the drawer "admits the existence of the payee," were not intended to cover cases where there was a non-existent payee, unknown to the maker or drawer, so that the latter would be estopped, as against a holder through a forged indorsement of the name of such non-existent payee, from alleging that the indorsement was a forgery and not title conveying—basing this opinion on the weight of authority before the act to the effect that the maker or drawer was non-liable in such case, and upon the presumption that no change in the law was intended, and finding application for such a provision in cases of payees, non-existent by reason of assumed names, and the like. The same opinion holds with reference to the provision that the acceptor admits the existence of the payee.

But we now have the further provision of admission by the acceptor of the "existence of the drawer, the genuineness of his signature, and his capacity and authority to draw the instrument."

In this instrument, if we could suppose a non-existent or fictitious drawer, unknown to the drawee to be non-existent or fictitious, the drawee, accepting the instrument, would doubtless be liable thereon, providing there was a holder for value of the instrument, and the payee was not non-existent, as well as the drawer. The principle of liability of the acceptor upon an instrument bearing a fictitious drawer, unknown to him to be non-existent, is different from that applicable where the payee is non-existent, and that fact unknown. It rests upon the same basis as his liability upon accepting a bill bearing the forged signature of the drawer. The rule of the law merchant in this case is well known. We quote from one of the cases: "The drawee of a bill of exchange is presumed to know the handwriting of his correspondent; and if he accepts or pays a bill in the hands of a bona-fide holder, to which the drawer's name has been forged, he is bound by the act, and can neither repudiate the acceptance nor recover the money." The same reasons which make an acceptor liable to a bona-fide holder where he mistakes the signature of an existing person, which he supposes is genuine, apply where his mistake is of the existence of the drawer. In both cases the bona-fide holder relies upon the acceptance, which vouches for the existence and genuineness of the preceding signature.

Construing, then, the provision that the acceptor admits the existence of the drawer, the genuineness of his signature and his capacity and authority to draw the instrument, the acceptor cannot deny to a holder in due course that there is no drawer, although one is named; that the drawer's signature is a forgery; that the drawer had no capacity to draw the instrument, as where he is an infant, lunatic or otherwise legally incapacitated; or that the drawer had no authority from him to draw the instrument, as, for example, if the drawee had no funds of the drawer, and the drawing upon him was unwarranted and the acceptance a mistake.

Having briefly treated the respective liabilities incurred by makers, drawers and acceptors of negotiable instruments, we will, in the next number, take up the provisions defining an indorser, and providing the liability of irregular and general indorsers.

SCHOOL OF COMMERCE, ACCOUNTS & FINANCE

Diary of the Month's Work

Senior Class

RECORD FOR WEEK ENDING MARCH 7, 1902.

MONDAY.
- 8-9 Lecture on Fire Insurance Law, by Mr. Stevens.
- 9-10 Lecture on Surrogate Accounting, by Mr. Jos. Hardcastle.

TUESDAY. No lecture.

WEDNESDAY.
- 8-9 Lecture on Money, by Prof. Jos. F. Johnson.
- 9-10 Lecture on History, Theory and Geography of Commerce, by Dr. Webster.

THURSDAY.
- 8-10 Lecture on Auditing a National Bank, by Mr. Thos. B. Dean.

FRIDAY.
- 8-10 Lecture on Partnership Law, by Mr. Wm. F. Walsh.

RECORD FOR WEEK ENDING MARCH 14, 1902.

MONDAY.
- 8-9 Lecture on International Commercial Law, by Mr. Cleveland F. Bacon.
- 9-10 Lecture on Surrogate Accounting, by Mr. Jos. Hardcastle.

TUESDAY.
- 8-10 Lecture on Banking, by Prof. Jos. F. Johnson.

WEDNESDAY.
- 8-9 No lecture.
- 9-10 Lecture on History, Theory and Geography of Commerce, by Dr. Webster.

THURSDAY.
- 8-10 Lecture on Auditing a National Bank, by Mr. Thos. B. Dean.

FRIDAY.
- 8-10 Lecture on Partnership Law, by Mr. Wm. F. Walsh.

RECORD FOR WEEK ENDING MARCH 21, 1902.

MONDAY.
- 8-9 Lecture on International Commercial Law, by Mr. Cleveland F. Bacon.
- 9-10 Lecture on Surrogate Accounting, by Mr. Jos. Hardcastle.

TUESDAY.
- 8-10 Examination of class in Political Economy.

WEDNESDAY.
- 8-9 No lecture.
- 9-10 Lecture on Railroad Organization, by Mr. Arthur Hale, Asst. General Manager B. & O. R. R.

THURSDAY.
- 8-10 Lecture on Auditing a Manufacturing Business, by Mr. Thos. B. Dean.

FRIDAY.
- 8-10 Lecture on Partnership Law, by Mr. Wm. F. Walsh.

RECORD FOR WEEK ENDING MARCH 28, 1902.

MONDAY.
- 8-9 Lecture on International Commercial Law, by Mr. Cleveland F. Bacon.
- 9-10 Lecture on Rent Accounts, by Mr. Jos. Hardcastle.

TUESDAY.
- 8-10 Lecture on Banking, by Prof. Jos. F. Johnson.

WEDNESDAY.
- 8-9 Lecture on The New Banking and Currency Bill, by the Hon. Chas. N. Fowler, M. C. from New Jersey, Chairman of the Committee on Banking and Currency, National House of Representatives.
- 9-10 Lecture on History, Theory and Geography of Commerce, by Dr. Webster.

THURSDAY.
- 8-10 Lecture on Auditing a Manufacturing Business, by Mr. Thos. B. Dean.

FRIDAY. Good Friday (Holiday).

Junior Class

RECORD FOR WEEK ENDING MARCH 7, 1902.

MONDAY.
- 8-10 Lecture on Money and Credit, by Prof. Jos. F. Johnson.

TUESDAY.
- 8-10 Lecture on Department Store Accounting, by Mr. H. M. C. Vedder.

WEDNESDAY.
- 8-9 No lecture.
- 9-10 Lecture on Transportation, by Mr. J. Shirley Eaton.

THURSDAY.
- 8-10 Lecture on Law of Sales, by Mr. Cleveland F. Bacon.

FRIDAY.
- 8-10 Lecture on the Balance Sheet, by Mr. George Young.

RECORD FOR WEEK ENDING MARCH 14, 1902.

MONDAY.
- 8-10 Lecture on Money and Credit, by Prof. Jos. F. Johnson.

TUESDAY.
- 8-9 Lecture on the Balance Sheet, by Mr. George Young.
- 9-10 Lecture on The Pay Roll, by Mr. George Young.

WEDNESDAY.
- 8-9 Lecture on the Relation of Domestic Transportation to Foreign Commerce, by John Franklin Crowell, Expert on Internal Commerce, U. S. Treasury Department. (Bureau of Statistics.)
- 9-10 Lecture on Transportation, by Mr. J. Shirley Eaton.

THURSDAY.
- 8-10 Lecture on Law of Sales, by Mr. Cleveland F. Bacon.

FRIDAY.
- 8-10 Lecture on General Costs and Expenses, by Mr. George Young.

RECORD FOR WEEK ENDING MARCH 21, 1902.

MONDAY.
- 8-10 Examination of Class on Political Economy.

TUESDAY.
- 8-10 Lecture on Distribution of Manufacturing Costs, by Mr. George Young.

WEDNESDAY.
- 8-9 Lecture on Railroad Organization, by Mr. Arthur Hale, Asst. General Manager B. & O. R. R.
- 9-10 Lecture on Transportation, by Mr. J. Shirley Eaton.

THURSDAY.
- 8-10 Lecture on Law of Sales, by Mr. Cleveland F. Bacon.

FRIDAY.
- 8-10 Lecture on Department Store Accounting, by Mr. H. M. C. Vedder.

RECORD FOR WEEK ENDING MARCH 28, 1902.

MONDAY.
- 8-10 Lecture on Money and Credit, by Prof. Jos. F. Johnson.

TUESDAY.
- 8-10 Lecture on Distribution of Manufacturing Costs, by Mr. George Young.

WEDNESDAY.
- 8-9 Lecture on The New Banking and Currency Bill, by the Hon. Chas. N. Fowler, M. C. from New Jersey, Chairman of the Committee on Banking and Currency, National House of Representatives.
- 9-10 Lecture on Transportation, by Mr. J. Shirley Eaton.

THURSDAY.
- 8-10 Lecture on Law of Sales, by Mr. Cleveland F. Bacon.

FRIDAY. Good Friday (Holiday).

COMMERCE ACCOUNTS & FINANCE

A Monthly Magazine of Higher Business Education and Practical Administration. Acknowledged Authority in the Profession of Commerce and Consistent Advocate of Methods Up to Date and Above the Table.

J. C. LINCOLN, Editor.
FRIEND PITTS, Jr., Circulation and Advertising.
E. R. KITTREDGE, Business Manager.

COMMERCE, ACCOUNTS & FINANCE CO., Publishers,
25 Pine Street, New York.

Published Monthly. Subscription $1 a Year in the United States, Canada and Mexico. Other countries $1.50. Postage prepaid by the Publishers. In the absence of specific orders to stop at the end of the subscription term the paper will be continued and a bill sent. Entered at the New York Postoffice as Second Class mail matter.

* * *

The editors desire copies of the following issues of COMMERCE, ACCOUNTS & FINANCE: January 5, 12, 19, 26, February 2, 9, 16, 26, March 2, 9, 16, 23 and October 1, all of the year 1901. We will enter a two months' extension of the subscription of any reader sending us one or more copies of any or all of these issues. Copies must be clean and in a readable condition.

* * *

We print in this issue of COMMERCE, ACCOUNTS & FINANCE an address by the Hon. Chas. M. Fowler, of New Jersey, chairman of the Committee of Banking and Currency in the United States House of Representatives. Mr. Fowler's address is on a subject which is of great interest just at present, and one that is agitating financial circles and will have a great bearing upon the general business interests of the country. The currency system of the United States, as it now exists, is considered by many bankers and financial men to be unsuited for the growing interests of our great country. A number of arguments pro and con have been presented, and a number of systems looking toward the betterment of the national banking and currency system have been devised. Ex-Secretary of the Treasury Lyman J. Gage is said to be in favor of the establishment of a Central Bank—that is to say, a bank which shall not be directly controlled by the government, but to which each of the national banks of the country shall subscribe 5 per cent of its capital, thus providing a capital stock of about $50,000,000. Each constituent would be allowed to vote in proportion to the amount of stock held, say, a thousand dollars per vote. The directors will be elected by the stockholders, and the directors in turn will elect the officers of the bank. Each bank will have the power to establish branches throughout the country, something on the order of the system now in use in Canada. In time of emergency such a bank would have the exclusive right to issue notes to the extent of four times its capital, or about $200,000,000. The bank would supervise its stockholding members, and would have the power to make the examinations that are now made by the Comptroller of the Currency.

*

The establishment of such a bank as this would be has been advocated by many prominent men. Mr. Stickney, president of the Chicago Great Western Railway, in a notable address before the convention of the American Bankers' Association at Milwaukee, upon the subject of the reform of the currency and the establishment of a Central Bank, pointed out the defects of our present system. James B. Forgan, president of the First National Bank of Chicago, is a warm advocate of the asset currency system with a system of branch banks, and firmly believes that by the adoption of some such plan many difficulties and dangers would be removed. After speaking of the defects of our present currency system, Mr. Forgan says: —

First, there must be large capitalization of the individual banks that issue assets currency. This will be found to be the case in every country where it circulates. In the aggregate we have a very large banking capital in this country, unnecessarily large for the volume of business done, which is another extravagance of our system. Our policy has been to foster a large number of banks with small individual capitalization, by placing the smallest possible limit on the amount of capital necessary for organization.

Mr. Forgan goes on to say:—

First prepare the way now for assets currency sometime in the future by reorganizing our banking institutions so as to provide them with the essential requirements of such a system. Grant the banks more latitude and greater opportunity for development. Don't attempt to force anything. Just permit national banks to establish branches in the state in which they are organized, provided they have capital sufficient to warrant it. Then leave it to them to evolve systems of branch banks and amalgamation and consolidation with each other. No bank would sell out or surrender its own identity unless it was for the interest of its owners to do so, and competition would ensure their getting sufficient value for their investment and their vested rights. I suggest confining banks to the establishment of branches in the state in which they are organized so as to interfere as little as possible with the bank deposits in the reserve cities. Also for the organization of state systems of national banks. It seems to me that in some such way, out of our present system we might gradually evolve one which would be able to maintain a system of assets currency.

*

Other writers and thinkers upon this subject maintain that the government should organize a great Central Bank, to be run directly by officers appointed by the government. This bank could issue currency and carry on business on the plan of the Bank of England or the Bank of France, the German Reichsbank and other great government banks. The Second Bank of the United States, which went to smash under President Jackson's mailed fist, was an institution of this kind, and was prosperous up to the time that "Old Hickory" made it a political issue. It is only fair to say that politics, more than anything else, broke the Second Bank of the United States.

*

Mr. Fowler's address is interesting and very valuable. He has formulated a scheme that, while it may not meet with the approval of all bankers, will, we think, satisfy the majority. Out of the discussion will surely come some form of banking system that will meet the requirements of the financial world and business men in general. There is no subject now before the public that should be of more interest than this, for the step now taken will establish our financial status probably for centuries.

* * *

The late Cecil Rhodes was a man who made many enemies. These enemies, however, were not personal ones. They were enemies because they did not approve of Mr. Rhodes' empire building policy. Cecil Rhodes' one ambition was to found a great British empire in Africa, and he allowed this ambition, at times, to carry him too far: notably in the case of the Jameson raid. It will be remembered that he disclaimed responsibility for this disastrous raid, but it is generally believed that he was primarily responsible for it. Before this raid was attempted Cecil Rhodes was, perhaps, the most popular man in all Great Britain's possessions. After it his popularity waned somewhat. But, with his faults, and these faults were excusable from the imperialist point of view, Cecil Rhodes was a great man—a wonderful man. His clear-sighted vision saw that Africa was a great continent, rich and capable of development, and he believed that it should belong to Great Britain. He has been called an "Empire Builder," whose ambition it was to found a realm where he himself should rule, but it is only fair to state that this idea was erroneous. Mr. Rhodes was unselfish, and we think history will declare him one of the most unselfish great men that ever lived. He worked and fought and strove, not for the glory of Cecil Rhodes, but for the glory of England—the country that he loved.

*

His bequest of scholarships at Oxford University to students from Germany and the United States is an evidence of his broad minded and far-sighted thought. He believed, and said, that a union, or, at all events, an understanding, between Great Britain, Germany and this country would insure the peace of the world and do more for civilization and progress than anything else could do. It was undoubtedly with this idea in view that he bequeathed these scholarships. In the United States, each year, scholarships at Oxford are to be allotted, presumably by competitive examination, to two young men from each state and territory. These scholarships will undoubtedly benefit the young men, but they will also benefit Great Britain. The importation of young blood, and such young blood as this will be, from two progressive countries like Germany and the United States will undoubtedly help England and broaden English ideas. Mr. Rhodes' bequest is but another evidence of the progress of education and the interest that rich men everywhere are now taking in the subject. The average young man of a hundred years hence, it is safe to say, will be extremely well educated, particularly along technical lines.

* * *

The number of magazines and newspapers, annuals, monthlies, weeklies and dailies, published in the United States is very large. A list of the newspapers alone is surprisingly long. The number and variety of the periodicals shown on any of the big news-stands is surprising, and the trade, scientific, medical, labor and other special publications seem legion. The mind is scarcely able to grasp the significance of the numbers of such publications as enumerated by the newspaper directories. The total footings of circulation quoted spread out into such wide lines of figures that the wonder is how the people get time to read this mountain of literature. Do they read it? What do they read it for?

*

Every printed sheet of paper is issued and circulated with a reason. The cause of its existence may be found in a demand, or a supposed demand, on the part of a portion of the public for knowledge—knowledge of the subject, be it news, educational information or amusement. Life carries with it the right to strive, and the strife results in the survival of the fittest. Earth demands labor for her bounties. Men endowed with attributes of mind and muscle pay the world for the right of existence.

*

A publication's right of existence is based upon the requirements of demand. Does it meet these requirements? Does the demand demonstrate that its knowledge of the subject is that which the intelligence of the people require? Does its circulation show that its proportion of readers is as large as it should be among that contingent of people who desire to obtain information concerning the subject dealt with? The gross misrepresentation of circulation upon the part of many publishers precludes the possibility of analytical deductions from trustworthy standards. The dissemination of knowledge is the work of the publication. The merchant wishes to disseminate, through advertising, knowledge of the goods he has to sell to the public. The advertiser must discern what publications are reaching that portion of the people he wishes to educate. The right of existence of any individual advertisement should be considered. Does it enlighten and educate the persons seeking information upon the subject advertised?

*

A just discrimination, by the advertiser, not alone of the figures of circulation, but also of the proportion of circulation reaching the person that he (the advertiser) wishes to educate, is important. The discrimination is too frequently neglected, and the right of existence is not considered from the standpoint of the individual teacher, on the merits of goods exploited by him in advertising mediums.

AMERICAN ENTERPRISES ABROAD

Punta Arenas, in Tierra del Fuego, is the southernmost continental spot on the globe, but the modern lighthouse on that lonely coast is equipped with electrical machinery made in Schenectady, N. Y. The firm that manufactured it has also pushed electricity farthest north by installing dynamos at Hammerfest, in Norway, and, though it is a far cry from the deepest drifts of the Calumet and Hecla mine to Yanteles, in the Andes, 14,000 feet above the sea, two consignments recently left Schenectady, one for the deep mine, the other for the mountain.

By the very bedside of the Pope is placed every night an American flashlight apparatus in the form of a cylinder with an incandescent bulb in one end—in effect an electric candle, according to a writer in the World's Work. At Bagdad, Aladdin has been replaced by a New York concern. Lamps of fanciful patterns are sent from New York to a point on the Persian Gulf, and thence conveyed over some 300 miles of desert on camel back. They are then placed on rafts and towed 100 miles up the Euphrates and again loaded on camels and carried to their destination 200 miles from the river. These lamps decorate the palaces of the Sultan of Morocco, the Prince of Siam and several rajahs in British India, and they are also popular in Jerusalem.

From the Falls of the Couvery, one of the sacred rivers of India, to Kolar, in Mysore, American electrical engineers have recently set up an American transmission plant under somewhat remarkable circumstances. There are still wild elephants in Mysore, and there will always be white ants. But as a white ant will venture not more than five or six feet up a pole in search of edible wood, the steamer from New York carried out to India iron post-sockets seven feet high in which to set the poles, to the discomfiture of the ants. To disconcert the elephants and prevent grounding of the current through any behemoth that might venture to test the wires with his trunk, the engineers, after careful measurements, strung the wires just beyond reach of the biggest possible elephant standing on hind legs and groping.

"GOOD MORNINGS" OF THE WORLD

The following are the morning salutations of the various nations, according to one of our exchanges. The Spanish is, perhaps, the most picturesque; the Egyptian and the Chinese the most peculiar.

"How goes it?" That's German.
"How can you?" That's Swedish.
"How do you are?" That's Dutch.
"How do you stand?" That's Italian.
"Go with God, senor." That's Spanish.
"How do you live on?" That's Russian.
"How do you perspire?" That's Egyptian.
"How do you have yourself?" That's Polish.
"Thank God, how are you?" That's Arabian.
"May thy shadow never grow less." That's Persian.
"How is your stomach? Have you eaten your rice?" That's Chinese.

WHAT SPAIN TAUGHT THE FILIPINO

An American teacher in the Philippines writes that many geographies distributed throughout the islands represent Spain as the largest country on the map, and that it is almost impossible to change this false impression, says an Indianapolis paper. "Many of the native teachers," he says, "returned our maps and books, saying they were all wrong, as the United States was made to appear larger than the Philippines, or even than Spain." The rising generation of Filipinos will know better.

Balance Sheet Accounting—VI.

By GEORGE E. ALLEN

FACTS LOST IN FRILLS.

The word "system" as applied to accounting is getting to be greatly perverted. We hear much of the carbon system, the loose leaf system, the card system and other purely mechanical devices. Enterprising individuals have made certain adaptations of such devices and coupled their names therewith. We therefore have, for example, the Smith System, the Jones System and the John Doe System; the Richard Roe System, and various others.

In most of the so-called systems the essential facts of accounting are lost sight of in mechanical details. What the business man wants, regardless of the means resorted to for accomplishing that end, is an up-to-date statement of his assets and liabilities. When he gets this information as a foundation for the enterprise upon which he enlists, he wants a going statement of the additions thereto and the subtractions therefrom. When he asks for such facts, and in lieu thereof is given cases of cards or binders filled with ruled paper, or beautifully bound books, he naturally feels like the proverbial man who asked for bread and was given a stone.

The business man wants the facts about his affairs, and he wants them at such time and in such form as will enable him to make intelligent plans for future operations. It matters very little to him whether such facts are recorded in books or on cards or loose leaves, so long as the facts on demand are presented to him in proper shape, fully and accurately stated and always up to date.

The first essential of accurate and logical accounting is the distinct separation of asset and liability accounts. This has been sufficiently covered in what has preceded. Distinction must also be clearly made between expenditures properly chargeable to cost of product and expenditures connected with the maintenance and sale of the same. This has been somewhat discussed in chapters already presented, but a brief view of a certain class of facts connected therewith will be interesting at this time.

ESSENTIAL DISTINCTIONS.

The following letter from an esteemed correspondent is of interest:—

The object of this letter is to obtain information, not to criticise. Your contributor, Mr. George Young, states in his "Accounting for Cotton Mills," published in your March issue, that "Interest is in no sense a manufacturing cost." Very true! But should not interest be added to the cost of raw material?

My argument is as follows: The cost of raw material is the net amount paid for it laid down in my factory. Now, if the goods are billed "Net 4 mos. or 5 per cent off—30 days," I may elect to pay at the end of four months, for collections will then come in at a lively rate, and the cost of that invoice of material will be the face of the bill. If I have sufficient cash on hand and take the cash discount of 5 per cent in 30 days, that material costs but 95 per cent of the face of the bill. If, however, in order to take the discount, I am obliged to borrow at 6 per cent, the net discount on a four-months' net bill will be 4 1-4 per cent, increasing the cost of material from 95 per cent to 95 3-4 per cent of the face of the bill. Please point out the flaw in my argument.

The writer asks us to point out the flaw in his argument, and we will endeavor so to do. In the method of Cotton Mill Accounting referred to all discounts of purchases are deemed to be revenues. In the example given by our correspondent the cost of the bill of goods at the end of 4 months would be, as he states, the face of the bill. If the discount should be taken, the cost of goods would be the same, but there would be a revenue of 5 per cent which properly belongs to the earnings of capital available for such purposes. If money is borrowed for any purpose, the principal becomes a liability and the interest thereon a diminution of profits.

So far as this particular transaction or series of transactions are concerned, either way of figuring will reach the same result. Broadly, however, it is more logical to draw a distinct line between the cost of goods as invoiced and any discount that may be allowed thereon. To borrow money in order to obtain the benefit of a discount shows a certain union of motive, but the two transactions are separate and distinct nevertheless. It is more reasonable, while also essential to a carefully analyzed plan of accounting, to distinctly separate every phase of such a deal as is described by our correspondent.

While on the subject of the necessity of making proper distinction between various kinds of accounts, attention is called to certain expenditures which naturally appear under some similar names in accounts pertaining to manufacturing costs and accounts pertaining to commercial expenses. For instance, depreciation of manufacturing plant or machinery is properly regarded as a manufacturing cost, while depreciation of finished product must be regarded as a commercial expense. In like manner freight—in-bound—must be added to the cost of material or merchandise purchased, while freight —outward—is an expense connected with sales.

TWO OPTICAL ILLUSIONS

Optical illusions are always interesting, and here are two which, although not strictly new, may be new to some of our readers. In Fig. 1 the question is, Which is the longer distance, the distance between A and B, or between B and C?

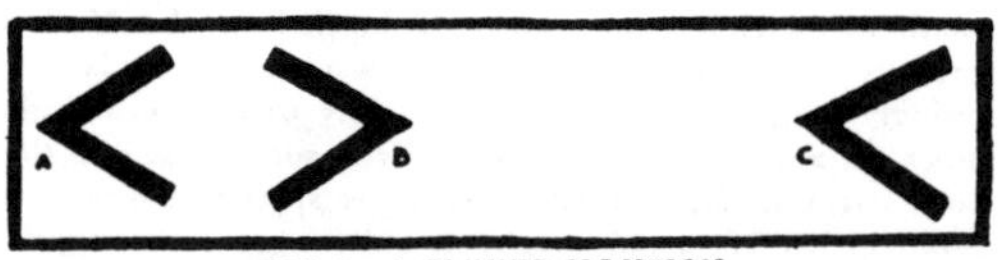

FIG. 1. A CLEVER ILLUSION.

The answer to this seems to be so apparent as to be absurd, but we would advise no reader to trust to his eye.

Fig. 2 is a series of circles, one within the other. If the reader will hold the page on which this diagram is printed,

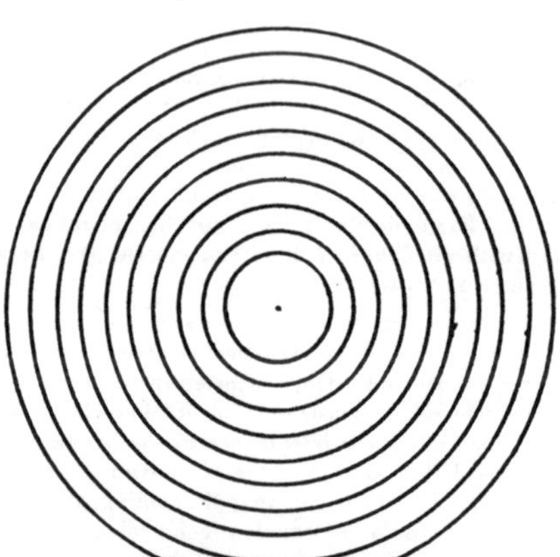

FIG. 2. THE CIRCLE THAT REVOLVES.

about a foot from his face and then revolve it at a medium rate of speed, he will presently see something that will interest him. Revolve from left to right first, and then from right to left.

THE ABSENT-MINDED PROFESSOR

"It's remarkable, Annchen," said the absent-minded old German professor, "I can't step more than a few inches at a time in my new shoes."

"No wonder: You've put them on, and they are still tied together as they came from the store."—Philadelphia Times.

Current Business Cartoons

Prince Henry has come and gone, and a fruitful subject for the cartoonist is therefore exhausted. The latter, therefore, turns once more to politics, to commerce and to the spring weather for inspiration, and has turned out a goodly group of pictures.

A Return Visit: "If you will not admit our pork, we in future will forbid the importation of German Princes."—Simplicissimus (Germany).

Speaking of Prince Henry's visit, it may be interesting to our readers if we reproduce a German cartoon showing how a portion of the German people regard the Prince's trip to the United States. Germany, by legislation, has practically excluded our pork products from the German market. The excuse for this is the supposed impurity of these products. To those of us who have been inside of a big pork-packing establishment and have seen the absolute cleanliness of every part of it, and have also seen a portion of the flesh of each animal inspected and tagged by government officials, Germany's fear seems ridiculous. However, we reproduce the cartoon in which Miss Roosevelt, dressed as a shepherdess, is espousing the cause of the injured pig and vowing retaliation.

Those who live in glass houses should not throw stones.—Brooklyn Eagle.

We reproduce another cartoon, from the Brooklyn Eagle, showing America's view of the situation. Uncle Sam is threatening to get even with the Germans by shutting out their delicatessen, beers, wines, etc. It is a poor rule that doesn't work both ways.

The dispute between the beet sugar interests and the advocates of tariff reform for Cuba has waged long and bitterly.

The Floating of Ship Subsidy.

"She moves, she starts, she seems to feel the thrill of life along her keel!"—Minneapolis Journal.

But tariff reform has at length triumped, in a measure. Richards, in the New York Herald, portrays this triumph in amusing fashion. The administrative forces have won the fight, but are in decidedly bad shape after the battle.

Cecil Rhodes opens two new roads for the invasion of England.—Chicago Record-Herald.

Those storekeepers and manufacturers who have been using the American flag for advertising purposes are warned to stop. The New York State Legislature recently passed a bill making it a misdemeanor to use the flag in this manner, and making the offense punishable by a fine or imprisonment. We believe this to be legislation of the right kind. The old flag is too sacred to be made a medium for posting the public on the merits of some one's cigarettes.

The Ship Subsidy Bill, the pet measure of Senators Frye and Hanna, passed the Senate by a vote of 42 to 31. Whether it will pass the House or not is another question.

Justice: "Halt! You must not desecrate it."—N. Y. Tribune.

The cartoon from the Minneapolis Journal is amusing and well drawn.

Cecil Rhodes had many enemies, but history will declare him, in spite of his faults, a great man, whose ambition was solely for the good of his country and his fellow-countrymen. His bequest of scholarships at Oxford for students

Stained Glass Window Design for Weather Bureau.—Chicago Record Herald.

from England, Germany and the United States is a measure that meets with the approval of every one. Competition for these scholarships will be keen, and, as Mr. Rhodes' strong mind readily foresaw, England will be benefited much by the importation, even for a limited time, of young blood from Germany and the United States. McCutcheon, in the Chicago Record, has one of his customary clever cartoons upon the subject.

We reproduce another funny cartoon from McCutcheon's pen, for which the cold weather—which, up to the time of

A Glorious Republican Victory!—N. Y. Herald.

writing, has lingered with us, even though the time for spring's arrival is long passed—has furnished the inspiration. The stained-glass window designed by the cartoonist, while not exactly a thing of beauty, might easily be a joy forever. Old Winter lingering in the lap of Spring, while the indignant young lady endeavors to get rid of him by hitting him with the horn of plenty, is a sight to behold.

WIPED SPECTACLES WITH BILLS

The observant man who is always aware of what is going on about him, and always alert to gather useful information, recently had an interesting experience in a Chicago hotel, says the Youth's Companion. His attention was drawn to an old man, a stranger, who sat next to him at the table.

"Excuse me," said the observant man, "but do you know what you are doing?"

"Yes, sir; I am wiping my eye-glasses."

"Do you know what you are using?"

"Yes. I am using a new two-dollar bill. I never use anything but a new bill for that purpose."

"But isn't it rather expensive?"

"It would be, perhaps, if I took a new bill every time I wiped my glasses and threw it away afterward; but it is just as good to spend when I am done with it. I don't do it for show, or to make a display of eccentricity; but I have found that there is nothing quite so good as a perfectly new bank note for cleaning glasses. It cleans them perfectly, and never scratches the surface of the glass. Make a note of it."

The other man did so, and in turn has passed the recipe on to his friends. It may be a new idea to many persons who wear spectacles.

A WOODEN JOKE

"Is it not true," said the Soulful Young Thing, "that there is something sadly poetical, and even musical, in the sound of a giant tree falling to the earth?"

"Yes'm," said the Michigan timberman. "I suppose there is what you might call a kind of logarithm about it."—Chicago Tribune.

THE REASON WHY

At a recent examination in an English school, the inspector put the question to a class of little girls: "Why is it that only the Queen's head appears on a penny?" "Please, sir, 'cos there isn't room for her feet."—Exchange.

FORCE OF HABIT.

Customer: I'd like a two-cent stamp.

Druggist: Just out; but we have "something just as good."

Customer: What's that?

Druggist: Two ones.—Cleveland Plain Dealer.

Duties and Responsibilities of the Public Accountant*

By ARTHUR LOWES DICKINSON

Chartered Accountant

The profession of public accountant, in the modern sense of the term, is a product of the nineteenth century, and owes its existence and progress to the great expansion of industry and commerce for which that period is remarkable, and in particular to the rapid growth of that form of partnership represented by the joint-stock company or industrial corporation.

The first public recognition of the importance of the profession dates from the royal charter granted in Scotland to the Scottish Institute of Accountants in 1856. Twenty-four years later a similar charter was given to the Institute of Chartered Accountants in England and Wales, a body formed by the consolidation of various pre-existing societies. Both the English and Scottish charters provided for a compulsory course of training prior to admission to either institute, comprising five years' continuous service in the office of a practicing chartered accountant, coupled with examinations in accounts, in certain branches of law and (in Scotland) in the elements of actuarial science. The growth of the profession in Great Britain since the date of these charters has been very great, and associates and fellows of the two societies are now to be found in every English-speaking community.

In the United States the development, while equally rapid, has proceeded on somewhat different lines. In place of granting special privileges to certain leading societies the Legislatures of the States of New York, Pennsylvania, California and Maryland have passed acts providing examinations for the degree of "Certified Public Accountant," commonly known as "C. P. A." The examinations comprise practically the same subjects as those in England and Scotland, but no period of service under a practicing accountant is required. In connection with the examination in the State of New York, a School of Commerce and Accounts has been organized in the University of New York, and is developing a very complete system of preliminary training, including bookkeeping and accounts, law, and the principles of economics. The importance to the profession generally of such an organized scheme for preliminary education cannot be overrated, and it is desirable that the educational authorities in other states should follow this example. There are also many local societies whose members are as a rule public accountants in practice; but no special qualifications attach to membership, and they have not adopted or required any special form of training. The principal of these societies are the following: Illinois Association of Public Accountants, New York Society of Certified Public Accountants, American Association of Public Accountants and the Incorporated Accountants of Massachusetts.

While at the present time there is here no obligation to serve an apprenticeship in the office of a public accountant, the great importance of this part of the education is generally recognized, and it may safely be stated that, with few exceptions, the members of the profession are all qualified both by the degree of 'Certified Public Accountant" or "Chartered Accountant," and, further, by a continuous practical experience extending over many years.

The experience gained in the period of training comprises not only all the branches of auditing and accounting, but also a general knowledge of the principles of commercial law, including the law of corporations and the law of bankruptcy, especially in so far as these laws have relation to accounts, the desire being that the accountant should have a sufficient legal knowledge to make him an intelligent client to his lawyer without in any way usurping the functions of the latter.

It is necessary to emphasize the fact that, while the bookkeeper or accountant or comptroller of a large corporation may have and should have a thorough knowledge of accounts, yet, from lack of the special training which can only be acquired by several years' practical experience in the office of a public accountant, he cannot be considered a member of the latter profession in the modern sense of the term. A public accountant is not merely a bookkeeper, a statistician or a man of figures, nor only a good man of business, but if he be successful in his profession he must combine all these qualifications, and in addition have a general knowledge of all industrial undertakings, of the forms of accounting most suitable to each, and of the general principles, both legal and economical, which govern them. The training referred to above is only the first step to the attainment of such a position, and must be supplemented by many years of practical experience as assistant or manager in the office of a public accountant, where, in the midst of innumerable problems in accounts calling for the exercise of skill and judgment, opportunities for acquiring efficiency in accounting in its highest sense can alone be found.

In addition to training and experience there are two most important principles upon which the position and reputation of the public accountant rest. The first is what may be called "the doctrine of personal responsibility." He alone is responsible to his clients for the results of his work; he cannot excuse himself by attaching blame to his subordinates, who are selected and trained by himself and imbued with his personality, and are thus qualified to act as his deputies in obtaining the information and statistics he requires. Being himself the absolute head, holding in his grasp all the threads of his business, subject to no control by directors, and free from all influence which might bias his judgment, he is in a position to accept, and does accept, the whole responsibility. His reputation and his success in his profession and his personal fortune are all dependent on his appreciation of the responsibility of his position and upon his continued endeavors to attain the high ideal at which he aims.

The second principle is that of absolute secrecy regarding all matters which may come before him in the course of his business. This rule is impressed upon his assistants from the earliest stages, and is recognized as so essential that breaches thereof are practically unknown; and the business community may feel thoroughly assured on this point when they avail themselves of the services of a member of one of the recognized bodies of public accountants.

DUTIES.

Having passed through his period of training and subsequently gained as an assistant or manager in the office of some senior member of the profession several years of general experience, the young accountant is qualified to practice on his own account, and his work may be classified under the following heads:—

First. The audit of accounts, entailing such examination as will satisfy him that the accounts laid before him are substantially correct and enable him to certify to this effect.

Second. The establishment of systems of bookkeeping and cost accounts, including such a system of internal checks between departments as will minimize, if not entirely prevent the possibility of frauds.

Third. The investigation of frauds.

Fourth. The supplying of trained assistants to help his clients in times of emergency in the keeping of their books and accounts.

Fifth. The investigation of the accounts of firms and companies with a view to certifying the profits or verifying the assets and liabilities on conversion of the same into public or private corporations, either by sale or by the consolidation of several concerns into one large corporation.

Sixth. The preparation of the accounts of assignees in

*Address delivered before the Illinois Association of Public Accountants.

bankruptcy, with special reference to the form in which the accounts have to be submitted to the court.

Seventh. Devising, opening and keeping books for executors' accounts, estate accounts and trust accounts.

Eighth. The investigation of claims for compensation.

Ninth. The calculation of sinking funds for repayment of loans or redemption of bonds, interest calculations and general problems in connection therewith.

A more detailed examination of the nature of the work of the public accountant and the responsibility which he is prepared to undertake is the object of the remarks which follow:—

THE AUDIT OF ACCOUNTS.

This may be divided into:—

(a) The continuous daily or weekly or monthly audit, in which all the details of the business will be examined and verified.

(b) The half-yearly or yearly preparation and audit of the balance sheet and profit and loss account, also involving a full, detailed examination of all the accounts.

(c) A financial audit of the accounts as prepared by the officials of the firm or company, not necessarily involving a detailed examination of all the transactions.

In small concerns where there is no special system of internal check a detailed audit would seem to be almost a necessity. The head of the firm, or the president and board of directors of the company, while naturally having a full knowledge of the methods of conducting the business, have neither the time, nor in most cases the requisite technical knowledge, to supervise the accounting department. This must necessarily be left to an official, whose work is often to a great extent unchecked, or only checked by his subordinates, who, in all questions involving the exercise of judgment, would hesitate to express an opinion at variance with that of their superior. Experience shows that where frauds occur they are in the majority of cases committed by men in a confidential position who have been implicitly trusted, but have abused the confidence placed in them. The head of a business owes a duty to his employees, as well as to himself, to see that there is such a check upon all the transactions of his staff as will obviate opportunities for wrongdoing; and no better means of exercising this check exists than a continuous verification of the accounts by an independent auditor. A public accountant filling such a position is an assistance to the heads of the business by ensuring accuracy, both in principle and detail, and a correct statement of profits earned; and by giving the benefit of his advice and experience on any difficult points that may arise. He is further of assistance to the head of the accounting department by means of his general supervision of the work of the subordinate officials, and because from his wider experience he can point out any weak points in the system, and the remedies therefor, and can frequently make suggestions for saving labor.

Some large employers have so recognized the advantage to themselves of an independent audit that they make arrangements for the daily attendance of one of the auditor's assistants to check up the cash transactions and to certify to the correctness thereof; but in the majority of cases a monthly or quarterly examination is considered sufficient. It may be noted here that the cost of such an audit is less than the salary of a permanent auditor as a member of the staff, at any rate, in all corporations of moderate size, and, in view of the comparative qualifications of the independent and salaried auditors the advantages to the employer must be largely on the side of the former.

In questions of foreign exchange, depreciation, valuation of inventories, reserves for bad and doubtful debts, the treatment of wasting assets and other problems of a like nature, the experience of the public accountant, gathered as it is from years of close contact with all kinds of business, should be invaluable, and the employer who has availed himself of these services continuously can feel that he has done everything possible to insure himself, not only against fraud, but also against errors of calculation and errors of principle in the accounting department of his business—errors which frequently result in serious overstatement of profits.

In certain concerns, when the principals do not consider the expense of a more frequent audit desirable, it is the practice to employ a public accountant only at the half-yearly or yearly balancing periods to conduct a complete audit of the transactions of the period and prepare the profit and loss account and balance sheet. While such an examination is not so effective a check as a more frequent one would be, especially in connection with possible frauds or errors in accounting resulting in loss to the employer, the same advantages would accrue in other respects, and the report or certificate of the independent auditor attached to the accounts is a guarantee of their substantial accuracy.

In the case of large corporations such a detailed audit as that outlined above is as a rule unnecessary even when the expense involved does not render it impracticable. The corporations referred to may be defined as those whose transactions are so numerous that they can employ their own staff to carry out the continuous audit described above, and, provided that a sound system is designed and (what is of equal importance) properly carried out, this is quite sufficient. It will, however, nearly always be found that the final preparation of semi-annual or annual accounts is left entirely to one official, who is checked only by his subordinates, and, like all other human beings, is liable to errors of principle upon points on which his subordinates' opinion would not be available. Here, too, therefore, appears the necessity for the independent auditor; firstly, to satisfy the general manager of the business that the system is as good as it can be; secondly, to test the system in varying ways, and to see that it is properly carried out; and, thirdly, to supervise the work of the corporation's auditor or comptroller by a verification of the final accounts, and, incidentally, to discuss and settle with him doubtful points, such as frequently arise, which can be settled better by two heads than one.

One incidental advantage of such an audit by a public accountant is that he has before him, by means of his trained staff, a complete view of the company's affairs in a condensed form, and can oversee the transactions as a whole more effectively than the corporation's officials, who deal with each point as it arises, and are necessarily involved more or less in a mass of details.

THE BALANCE SHEET.

Perhaps, however, the most important feature of the independent audit of the accounts of a corporation, large or small, is the verification of the assets and liabilities in the balance sheet, the determination of proper and adequate rates of depreciation, and of proper reserves for bad and doubtful debts. The experience of most public accountants goes to show that the estimates of managers are often too sanguine, and the auditor is able by inquiries into the status of the various book accounts, by a comparison of prices in the inventory with current market quotations, by a close examination of cost accounts, and in many cases by an actual test of quantities remaining on hand as compared with quantities purchased and sold, to satisfy himself whether the valuations both of book debts and of inventories are fair and reasonable, and frequently to suggest increased reserves which are generally justified by subsequent experience.

The modern practice of publishing monthly statements of net earnings which are necessarily based on approximate inventories renders the employment of an expert accountant even more desirable. The wisdom of the frequent publication of such statements which are necessarily only approximate inasmuch as they are published before there has been time to ascertain the absolute correctness thereof may be open to question, but so long as such statements are required, whether for publication or for the board of directors of the corporation, it is of the utmost importance that the basis upon which they are prepared should be accurate. Cases have occurred where from some mistake of principle in the calculation of an approximate book inventory, the statements so prepared have been utterly wrong, and the true facts subsequently ascertained by the investigation of an expert accountant have caused not only disappointment but loss to all concerned.

Accountants are often asked whether their periodical examination of the books of a concern will be an absolute safeguard against fraud. It is as well to make clear at once that it will not. If there is a bad system, frauds are comparatively easy, and, even with a good system, the collusion of two or more people may render it possible; but it may safely be said that the periodical examination of books and accounts by an independent auditor puts very much greater difficulties in the way of such frauds and renders their detection within a reasonable time of their commission almost a matter of certainty.

Reports are frequent of frauds which have remained undetected for long periods and have been discovered only on the temporary absence of the confidential clerk, trusted implicitly by his employers, and apparently wholly devoted to their interests, who has made himself invaluable by his constant attention to business, uninterrupted by any annual vacation. The large defalcations thus accidentally brought to light would be rendered almost impossible if the accounts were inspected in detail at regular or irregular intervals by a responsible public accountant. And it may be safely said that, if the large body of trusted officials of firms and companies, among whose ranks these comparatively few black sheep are found, would recognize the benefit to themselves of such a periodical detailed audit and urge it upon their principals as an additional safeguard, the number of these unfortunate incidents would be materially diminished.

THE ESTABLISHMENT OF SYSTEMS OF BOOKKEEPING AND COST ACCOUNTS.

The importance of employing the best possible systems of accounting must be admitted as an axiom. Without a good cost system, no manufacturing concern can expect to show the best results, and, although at first sight such a system may appear to some in the light of an expensive luxury, there can be no doubt that practical experience shows that the expense is amply compensated by savings in cost of manufacture. But while this is generally admitted by the leading manufacturers, there are many who either have no such system or such an incomplete one that it is of little, if any, use. One of the most important services which the public accountant can render to the business of the country is by urging upon his clients the importance of a proper cost system and employing his wide experience to establish it. The objects to be arrived at are, firstly, to ascertain not only the actual cost of any piece of work when completed, but also the cost of the different stages of manufacture. Secondly, to enable an approximate inventory to be taken at any time from the books without any physical valuation, thus enabling periodical statements of profits to be prepared, and, thirdly, to ascertain readily from the books the quantities of any class of stores or materials on hand, and to effect economies by taking advantage of the markets for replenishing supplies. It is claimed, and will, as a rule, be readily admitted, that the experience in all forms of cost accounts, suitable to all kinds of businesses, which the public accountant should have, renders his advice and assistance in these matters of the greatest value to his clients.

A good system of bookkeeping is of equal importance with a good system of cost accounts, and much unnecessary labor can be saved by adapting the books and accounts to the nature of the business and by suitable subdivisions thereof, so that work which, under one system, could hardly be done in the ordinary hours of business, is, under another and better one, easily accomplished. One essential of any system is that it should provide safeguards against fraud, and, as the records of such frauds show, even the largest institutions occasionally leave loopholes which the training and experience of the public accountant would, in all probability, have enabled him to detect and fill up. The practice of relying upon the honesty of individuals instead of a good system of bookkeeping is not to be commended.

The preparation of suitable forms of daily, weekly or monthly returns to show as concisely as possible the results of the trading with a summary of the most interesting detail contained therein is another branch of this important work. The information conveyed to directors by such statements is entirely dependent upon the shape in which they are presented, and it requires some skill to make it concise and yet at the same time complete in all important details. For such work the public accountant is eminently qualified.

THE INVESTIGATION OF FRAUDS.

The unraveling of fraud is a complicated piece of work, which can more satisfactorily be carried out by a public accountant whose business it is to know exactly where to put his finger on the weak spots than by the ordinary staff of the concern defrauded, who are as a rule wholly inexperienced in such investigations. If the defrauding official has to be prosecuted the evidence of the expert accountant will be required; his independent report will carry greater weight as a rule with a surety company than the report of the officials of the concern who are claiming against it; and there is the further advantage that such a report could be made by a public accountant without such interruption to the ordinary business routine of the office as would be involved if a greater part of the staff were engaged thereon.

THE SUPPLY OF TRAINED ASSISTANTS.

In an emergency, whether due to the illness or absence of a trusted accountant or bookkeeper, to the pressure of work or to other causes, the advantage to clients of availing themselves temporarily of the services of a confidential and skilled man will be appreciated by all who know what it means in such a case to have to depend upon the services of a more or less incompetent substitute. The public accountant always has in his employ trained assistants, competent to undertake any work of this class.

THE INVESTIGATION OF THE ACCOUNTS OF A BUSINESS FOR PURPOSES OF SALE, ETC.

This branch of the profession of accountancy is, perhaps, that which, up to the present, has been most in evidence in this country, and its importance can hardly be overrated. In every case of purchase and sale it is the desire of the seller, without necessarily any intent to defraud, to put the best complexion possible upon that which he has to sell. It is clearly to the interest of the buyer to know the exact facts about the business which he is buying, stripped of the gloss thrown over it by the views of the seller. An overstatement of profits or assets by the vendor may be deliberate or it may be due to ignorance or to mistakes of principle resulting in an honest belief on his part that his figures are correct; or the purchaser may only have to combat the sanguine views which a vendor is naturally inclined to take of the value of his own business. The position of the business, the nature of the assets and liabilities, the profits it has earned, and the distribution thereof (that is, whether they showed a rising or falling tendency), the existence of important future contracts not disclosed by the vendor, the omission of large liabilities under existing contracts which would materially affect the profits, the adequacy of the provision made for depreciation and bad debts; charges to construction account of expenditures on renewals and maintenance of plant, machinery and other fixed assets, which should properly have been charged against profits; all these, as affecting not only the profits, but the values of the assets, are matters of the greatest moment to the purchaser, who has probably neither the time nor the technical knowledge necessary to investigate the accounts for himself; and, unless he deliberately chooses to rely upon the vendor's statements, they can only be ascertained by an exhaustive examination of the books and accounts by a public accountant. As a new corporation, taking over either by purchase or consolidation one or more concerns, is frequently capitalized on a basis which will yield ten or twelve per cent on the capital stock of the new company, any error in the past profits forming the basis of the contract is multiplied in the same proportion in the capitalization of the new corporation.

THE ACCOUNTS OF ASSIGNEES IN BANKRUPTCY.

Much trouble and expense might be saved in all bankruptcy cases if a public accountant were instructed in the first instance to prepare the inventory of the firm in the form required by the courts, and to decide the manner in which the accounts of the estate should be kept. While the employees of the bankrupt firm may have a complete knowledge of its transactions, and be competent to keep its books, it should be remembered that the accounts which the assignee has to render are not such as would be required for a continuing business; and, if they are not kept in proper form in the first instance, they may have to be rewritten at a later date when the materials and information required are not readily available. A proper system started at the date of the assignment and written up concurrently with the books of the old firm and under the supervision of a public accountant will ensure the complete record of each transaction as it occurs in the form in which it is eventually required; and the final statements required by the courts are then readily compiled.

EXECUTORSHIP ACCOUNTS.

This is a branch of accounting of which it may be said that there is only one really correct and clear way of keeping the accounts, while there are many ways which are neither clear nor correct and yet are very generally adopted. The record of the transactions of a trust estate in a simple and complete form requires much skill and experience as well as a knowledge of the principles of law involved, and executors would be well advised if they relied upon the services of a public accountant to open the books of the estate and to audit them periodically. In fact, in many cases it would be found the most satisfactory course to leave the entire bookkeeping in the hands of the accountant, who would then be responsible for its accuracy.

COMPENSATION CASES.

The amount of compensation awarded in cases of personal injury generally depends, to a large extent, on the loss of income arising therefrom. For an accurate determination of the amount of such loss an examination of the accounts of the business or profession of the claimant is essential. His own statement of a decrease in profits or earnings subsequent to the injury should not be relied upon, partly because it is his interest to make it as large as possible and partly because the decrease may be due to quite other causes than the injury. An investigation of the accounts by a public accountant, for a period both before and after the injury, will bring together all the facts necessary to form a correct estimate of the loss sustained and the amount of compensation that should be awarded. Similar cases often arise of compensation for loss of trade or business resulting from other causes, and an investigation by a public accountant is equally necessary.

INTEREST CALCULATIONS.

Many public accountants have, and all should have, a thorough knowledge of this subject. Such calculations as sinking funds for redemption of leases, the instalments payable on car-trust obligations, amounts required to redeem bond issues or repay loans over a series of years, and other kindred points, are only a few of those matters of everyday occurrence in ordinary business affairs upon which a public accountant is generally qualified to advise his clients.

RESPONSIBILITY.

So far the subject of the utility of the public accountant has been considered from the point of view of assistance to principals who are responsible for or interested in the accounts either as partners in a private firm or as directors or managers of a commercial corporation. But there is a much wider responsibility which the public accountant is qualified and willing to undertake, and which it is becoming increasingly the custom to throw upon him—viz., responsibility to the general public who either as sleeping partners or as stockholders, or as creditors are interested in various undertakings as to the details of which they can necessarily have no knowledge.

The prospectus or invitation to the public to subscribe for stock in a corporation should always contain a certificate by public accountants as to the profits earned and the value of the current assets to be acquired. For their own purposes the promoters would obtain such a certificate, and in order to enable the public to judge for themselves of the value of the undertaking and the fairness of the purchase price, it is only reasonable that they should be furnished with a certificate of past results. If the large body of influential promoters of the undertakings which are offered for public subscription would adopt this practice they would materially aid in preventing the floatation of rotten concerns by unscrupulous speculators; for the absence of any certificate of profits would carry with it a warning to the public to be on their guard. The promoters would at the same time strengthen their own position by throwing a share of the responsibility for the statements contained in the prospectus upon those experts who alone can properly certify to their correctness.

It would seem to be a self-evident proposition that stockholders in a corporation are entitled to all the information in connection with its operations which can safely be made public without damage to its interests; and the most important part of this information is a full statement at regular intervals of the profits of the company and of its true financial position. As stockholders are for various reasons unable to verify such statements for themselves, it is natural that they should depute a representative to examine the books on their behalf and satisfy them by a comprehensive certificate that the accounts as stated to them present a true and correct view of the condition of the corporation's affairs. The only qualified body whose members are fitted to undertake this duty is that of public accountants, and there can be no doubt that, if such an examination were made compulsory by law or preferably adopted as a universal custom, stockholders would be more effectually protected against losses arising either from deliberate or accidental misstatements of fact. There can be little doubt that to all properly managed corporations a certificate to the annual balance sheet by an independent auditor would be of great value, and if public opinion insisted upon such certificates the losses arising from fraudulent, dishonest or badly managed corporations would be minimized.

It may be useful to state the position which public accountants claim to take up in giving their certificates. Accounts should show the actual facts, that is to say, the profits stated should be as far as possible the actual profits earned by the undertaking, and the wording adopted therein should be such as to truly and correctly describe the nature of the various items; the balance sheet should show the true value of the assets, or, where that is not possible or expedient in the interests of the stockholders, should state the basis on which the valuation thereof is taken, and the excess, if any, over actual value; and the wording adopted should be such as would explain to any reasonable business man the nature of the items included in each group of figures. The accounts are those of the directors, and they are necessarily the final arbiters of the form which they should take. But if the independent auditor objects to any of the items as not being properly described, or to the statement as a whole as not showing the true profits or the true values of any of the assets or liabilities, it will be his duty to qualify his certificate by embodying his objection therein. If, on the other hand, the auditor is appointed by the directors to assist them, his responsibility is to them alone; he can only advise and report to them, and has no discretionary power beyond the right to prevent the directors publishing his signature to any report or statement of accounts without his consent. If he were appointed by the stockholders it would be his further duty, in the event of the directors declining to affix his certificate to the accounts, to take the earliest opportunity of communicating his views directly to the stockholders. The reason of this attitude is that the corporation is the property of the stockholders and not of the directors as such, the independent auditor being, in this case, the representative of the stockholders to carry out fully that inspection of the accounts which, in a private partnership, each partner would undertake for himself. The directors, being appointed by the stockholders to manage the undertaking, are entitled to state the accounts in any manner they think fit before presenting them to the auditor. It is then the duty of the latter either to certify that the statement is correct and shows the true financial position of the corporation or to specify in what particular it fails to do so; the stockholders having appointed the auditor, are entitled to know his opinion as the result of his investigation, and he is therefore bound to report to them direct if the directors refuse to transmit his report.

PUBLICITY.

The subject of the regulation of trusts is now before the public, and the President's message to Congress suggesting some form of legislation requiring publicity, appears to be very generally approved. The large industrial undertakings can, without legislation, do a great deal in this direction by the publication of complete statements of account, certified by a public accountant appointed by the stockholders.

The United States Steel Corporation, the largest industrial undertaking in the world, has recently adopted this course, and if its example were followed by every honestly managed corporation the publicity thus attained would be of the best kind. It would be free from any governmental control, which is always to be deprecated in commercial affairs, and often leads to a false feeling of security; and it would entail an indorsement of the accounts by a member of a highly trained profession free from all suspicion of interested motives, whose reputation is bound up in his certificate. It may well be that legislation will eventually be necessary before complete protection is assured to the public. But all those who are against government interference with private enterprises, while desiring to compel reasonable publicity in the affairs of commercial undertakings, can direct this legislation into safe channels by using their influence to so firmly establish the principle of independent audits by public accountants that the state will merely have to make compulsory a course of action already adopted by the majority of well-managed enterprises. This has been the experience in Great Britain, where for many years the audit of the accounts of corporations has been a general practice, recommended, but not insisted upon by law. On the first day of the twentieth century this practice became compulsory by an act of Parliament, which laid down certain forms of certificate and report to be adopted by the auditors, and provided further that the accounts of every corporation must be examined and certified in this special manner by an independent auditor appointed by the stockholders.

If this short account of the status of the profession of the public accountant, of the duties which he is qualified to carry out, and of the responsibilities which he is prepared to undertake, may lead, in even a small degree, to their fuller appreciation by the public and to the greater protection of the large number of investors and others who are financially interested in commercial affairs, it will have served the purpose of its author.

A BOOK TYPEWRITER

A typewriting machine that, while capable of performing all the work of an ordinary typewriter, is also capable of writing directly upon the pages of a bound book, is obviously a very desirable equipment for many offices. The Elliott Book Typewriter does exactly this thing. It is so simple in its application and construction that in its movements of writing it resembles the pen more than a machine

Of course, for writing in a book, it is necessary that the writing point be brought to the paper, instead of the paper being fed to the keys, as in the ordinary typewriter, and in the Elliott machine the carriage is the writing mechanism; this moves back and forth and up and down over the paper as the work progresses. The writing space moves one space to the right every time the key is pressed. When a line is completed the writing is spaced down, instead of the paper being spaced up, as is the rule in common devices.

In a typewriter of the ordinary kind the surface upon which the paper lies, at the point where the type keys strike it, is cylindrical. In the book typewriter the paper lies perfectly flat. The flat surface therefore gives it added solidity, and this solidity is a great advantage.

Fig. 1. THE ELLIOTT & HATCH BOOK TYPEWRITER IN WRITING POSITION.

The original idea was to make a machine which would write upon the pages of books, but since the introduction of the Elliott Typewriter it has been found that it possesses many points of advantage over every writing machine, and that while it is unique in the accomplishment of its particular purpose, it is also excelled by none for manifolding, writing letters, or for any other purpose for which the typewriter is used.

With the ordinary machine it is impossible to handle writing material except it be of a certain size, limited to the length of the carriage, and of a certain thickness, to allow it to pass around the roller. With the Elliott machine the face is, as we said before, flat and smooth, and practically represents a table upon which any piece of writing material may be placed, whether it be a statement four or five feet wide, cardboard a quarter of an inch thick, a minute book or other form of record. In manifold work it is especially desirable, for the downward stroke of a steel type produces manifolding power greater than has heretofore been devised.

For the addressing of envelopes, for the writing of postal cards, tags, labels, etc., it is specially adapted, as these may be clamped exactly in place upon the flat surface of the machine and the typewritten lines will therefore be straight and uniform. It is possible with this machine not only to write correctly in a book, but to write upon a sheet of paper such as a form, bill of lading, etc., and at the same time make a copy directly upon a page of the book. This makes it especially desirable for railroad companies and banks. One railroad company uses over seven hundred Book Typewriters for way-billing freight, twelve or fifteen copies of these way-bills being required.

There is no elaborate and complicated mechanism to get out of order in this machine, and its simplicity especially recommends it to those who are unaccustomed to using the typewriter. It is equipped with a universal keyboard, and its key action is very easy. In speed it ranks besides the best typewriters made. The type bar is only about one-half the length of the bar of other machines and moves through a shorter arc. The depression of the shift key is less than one-half the depression of other machines, and is, therefore, quicker. The writing is always in sight. A device is provided which instantly throws the ribbon out of the line of vision, thereby revealing what has been written. There is an indicator which shows where writing is being done.

The Elliott Book Typewriter is a long step in the direction of the universal typewriter—that is to say, the typewriting machine that can be made to do all the writing necessary in a commercial office. It certainly will occupy a permanent position in every business office of the future where many records are to be kept.

The machine itself may be seen at the offices of the company, at 257 Broadway, New York City. Descriptive booklets may also be obtained there, and a practical illustration of the working of the machine given.

The illustrations which accompany this article show the Elliott Book Typewriter very well. In Fig. 1 the machine is shown with the carriage down and in writing position. In Fig. 2 it is shown with the carriage raised.

Fig. 2. THE ELLIOTT & HATCH BOOK TYPEWRITER, WITH CARRIAGE RAISED.

THE ADVERTISING MAN

It is the advertising man's business to make money for his paper, but we doubt if many advertising men would go as far in order to do so as did the specimen in the following story from the New York Weekly:—

Fussy Man (hurrying into newspaper office): "I've lost my spectacles somewhere, and I want to advertise for them, but I can't see to write without them, you know."

Advertising Clerk: (likely to be business manager some day): "I will write that ad. for you, sir. Any marks on them?"

Fussy Man: "Yes, yes. Gold-rimmed, lenses different focus, and letters L. Q. C. on inside. Insert in three times."

Advertising Clerk: "Yes, sir. Five dollars, please."

Fussy Man: "Here it is."

Advertising Clerk: "Thanks. It gives me, sir, great pleasure, very great pleasure, to inform you, sir, that your spectacles are on top of your head."

Fussy Man: "My stars! So they are. Why didn't you say so before?"

Advertising Clerk: "Business before pleasure, you know."

KNEW FROM EXPERIENCE

"This year will be the greatest in our history."

"How do you know?"

"Well, why shouldn't it be? Every other year has been."—Indianapolis News.

BRIEF MENTION.

THE TOWER Manufacturing & Novelty Company, 308 Broadway, New York, sends us an illustrated circular describing the Multiplex Punch and Eyelet Set which it manufactures. This Multiplex Punch, which seems to be about as complete as any office punch can well be, is a handy little machine for cutting paper, cardboard and what not, and inserting eyelets for fastening the various sheets together. The Tower Manufacturing Company's circular states that the Multiplex Punch is better than all others, because it is based upon scientific principles, and that it applies the power where most needed. The circular also says: "We desire to call attention to the fact that in the pliers on the market for the same work, the power at the termination of the closing movement bears a ratio of three to every unit expended upon the handles, measuring at the upsetters. The ratio obtained by the Multiplex at that time is 15 to 1." Judging by this circular and the illustration of the punch, we should say that the Multiplex Punch and Eyelet Set must be a very handy tool for the office man handling a great many files of papers.

WE HAVE BEFORE US a small circular containing an announcement made by Aiken, Lambert & Co., 19 Maiden Lane, New York City, of a certain fountain pen that they are telling the public about. This little folder informs us that the Mercantile Fountain Pen is all that a fountain pen should be. It is headed, "None Better." We have before us the pen, and we feel that the unsolicited praise, which has emanated from a large number of persons who are compelled to use a pen for many hours in a day, is no more of a recommendation than the merits of this particular pen is entitled to. The circular quotes from a number of letters, and we feel that the reading of what these people have to say about the Mercantile pen would be useful and valuable information for any one contemplating the purchase of a fountain pen. Messrs. Aiken, Lambert & Co. will, we feel sure, be glad to forward circulars to any one sending in their addresses.

"THE PROOF OF LEADERSHIP" is the title of an attractive pamphlet which is issued by the Columbia Typewriter Mfg. Co., setting forth the merits of the Barlock Typewriter. We examine with interest this pamphlet, which contains cuts of the various parts of the machine, together with a particularly well written description of its usefulness and the points of superiority which it possesses. The stenographer finds that a machine where the writing is visible at all times is a great advantage. Automatic line spacing is one of the points of the machine which has been given most careful attention. Left hand margin release together with an automatic margin recovery make this machine a particularly valuable one where tabulating work is essential. The machine is strongly made, and is guaranteed to stand wear and tear. Among other features is the placing of the keyboard with due and just proportions to the roller which carries the paper. This adjustment enables the stenographer to sit in a natural position, and does away with any eye strain resulting from an incorrect position while operating the keys. The details of construction, including the type bars, brackets, bearings and each and every individual part, are given the closest scrutiny before they are allowed to pass from the factory. This care results in an almost perfect alignment despite the roughest usage. Duplications, which are so necessary in present up-to-date business methods, are found to be exceptionally clear and distinct, owing to this care in the construction of the parts. We note that an improvement in the way of additional characters upon the keyboard is contemplated and under way. Some ninety characters in all are to be included, and with the aid of a shift key, the space occupied by the keyboard is not to be materially increased, while the ability to produce increased results is evident. The manifold copies from this machine are declared to be more numerous than from any other machine, as the type bars descend to the platen to make an impression. All parts are interchangeable, and a great variety of types may be attached to the type bars to meet the requirements that may be demanded by any individual business.

THE PRINTED MATTER emanating from the firm of the M. Hartley Company is always attractively gotten up. The headline of the pamphlet we have before us announces that the M. Hartley Company are successors to Hartley & Graham. The firm name of Hartley & Graham has been identified in the minds of all sportsmen as a sign for and a guarantee of integrity in the construction of sporting goods. It will seem strange to the eyes of the receivers of this catalogue to see the name of M. Hartley in place of Hartley & Graham. Marcellus P. Hartley died, and the firm has reorganized. The pamphlet issued covers everything from a cartridge to the highest priced shotgun, from a fly rod to a gang hook. Guns, pistols and even cannons of all shapes and sizes can be obtained at fair prices from this well-known firm, and every improvement in any way to the advantage of a firearm, is noted in the pages of their catalogue. In these the opening days of the fishing season, the sportsman thinks of his fly rod and of his fly hook. The murmur of running water comes to his ears, and he involuntarily dreams of a shady place by some stream, where the boiling riffle swirls between the rocks, and the wary trout lies deep. He longs for another cast upon those swirling waters, and wonders what fly the fish might rise to. The flies carried in stock by the M. Hartley Company are adapted to please the taste of the most fastidious trout, and the tackle may be depended upon to stand any strain that may be put upon it. In looking over this exceptionally well-printed catalogue one is impressed by the fact that it is a complete compendium of information, covering any and all points of information that a sportsman may find valuable.

ADVERTISING ON LEAD PENCILS is something rather new, and yet it is a clever way of gaining publicity. A lead pencil is something a man carries in his pocket until it is whittled away, and an advertisement printed on the side of a pencil, the latter to be given away, would seem to be something that should bring returns. The Pencil Exchange, whose place of business is at Boorem avenue and Forest place, Jersey City, N. J., manufactures pencils of superior grade in great quantities, and prints upon each pencil the name or advertisement of the customer. The pencils sold by the Pencil Exchange are of good quality, and compare favorably with any in the market. They are sold at $18 a thousand, or $1.80 a hundred, which price includes the printing upon each. This is a low price for so good an article. In the samples which we have seen, the name or advertisement is printed in gold letters, stamped into the wood of the pencil, and is very neatly done. Pencil ads., we have no doubt, will be popular.

ALUMINUM, which a comparatively short time ago was a new and untried metal, is now manufactured in a variety of useful and ornamental shapes. Its non-corrosive qualities and its lightness make it extremely desirable for certain purposes. Aluminum pens are something quite new, and yet entirely practical. A. N. Salomon, of 77 Broadway, New York, is manufacturing an assortment of pens of aluminum, and is advertising them as the "Aluminoid" pens. In Mr. Salomon's circular he says: "After fifteen years of continual service in pen-making, I have become convinced that the public was in need of a first-class pen that was durable, well-finished and non-corrosive. My past experience warrants the assertion that the enclosed samples are the acme of perfection and smoothness, and when made of aluminum are practically non-corrosive. Expert penmen, accountants and bookkeepers have endorsed the qualities of these pens. All first-class stationers carry them, or we can send you direct from the main office as many as you wish." The price of "Aluminoid" pens is $1.25 a box. One gross in a box.

THE HAMMOND TYPEWRITER CO. is now issuing two attractive booklets. One is entitled "The Hammond Typewriter," the other, "Ideal and Universal Keyboards." Both these booklets are credits to the printer's art. The covers are attractively printed with colored inks upon gray tones of paper, making a contrast which is pleasing to the eye. The description of the machine is printed in two colors of ink upon a heavy halftone paper, and the designs and halftones stand out so boldly and clearly that the pertinent points can be more readily observed than in most catalogues of this kind. The claims for the Hammond machine are numerous, and we think are deserving of the consideration of any persons contemplating changes from the machine that they may have at present in use, or who are desirous of purchasing a new machine. We are informed that the makers and sellers of the Hammond typewriter are never satisfied with their machine, no matter how perfect it may be, but are constantly striving to improve it in every way, in order to meet the requirements of any particular business or particular demand. The increasing use of carbon papers and duplications of original entry necessitate improvements in typewriting. Some lines of business require many duplications, and this necessitates a heavier impact from the type. This is a great strain upon any machine, particularly with regard to alignment. These points have been closely studied and the descriptions, as set forth in the catalogue, tell of the care which is given to every part, and are well worth reading. The study of Ideal and Universal Keyboards is particularly well exploited in the pamphlet. The matter is here dissected and analyzed. Terse and strong in its written descriptions, the pamphlet tells a story which cannot fail to be understood by the reader.

SILVER INK upon a black background announces boldly "Amberg Imperial Cabinets, the acme of perfection." The simplicity of this pamphlet commands attention at once, and in looking through the well-printed descriptions of the uses that the Amberg patent letter-files may be put to, the eye is pleased and curiosity excited. Send for a catalogue, look at its cover, and you cannot fail to at least glance through its pages. The advertising "suggestion" is particularly well thought out, and the cuts showing the various sections and construction of the Amberg file are interesting. The page under the heading of "Specimen Indexes" is so printed that it cannot fail to hold the eye. It looks odd, in fact the whole pamphlet as an advertisement is exceptionally well thought out. While the Amberg file is, we think, exceptionally well prepared, a number of new points are announced in connection with the manufacture of these files. The list of testimonials offered by this company must be sufficient guarantee to show that the merits claimed for the Amberg file have found endorsement in the minds of busy business men.

WE HAVE BEFORE US two circulars issued by the Pen Carbon Manifold Company, of 145 Centre street, New York. Both these circulars are gotten up in a most attractive form and with particular reference to holding the attention of the receiver of this piece of advertising literature. The character of the displayed announcement is such that it is almost impossible for one not to follow out the line of argument that it presents. Quoting from this little booklet, we find that the announcement is made that the Pen Carbon system is principally intended for those who use the pen for business purposes. The trouble and risk of rewriting or getting an imperfect copy is, by the use of carbon paper, positively eliminated. Through the use of carbon paper the copy book and the press are no longer required. The pen carbon stands in a class by itself. Those desirous of obtaining copies of pen and ink writing will find that the paper of the Pen Carbon Manifold Co. is particularly faithful in the duties that are required of it. It is particularly heavily charged carbon, and responds with a clear impression whether to the stroke of the pen, pencil, or type-stroke; be they light or heavy.| The impression is found to be free from smut and always sharply defined. The typewriter carbon paper manufactured by this company is found equally satisfactory, and the claim that this paper will make from five to fifteen perfect copies is, we think, one that has been amply demonstrated. The Ditmar's typewriter ribbon, manufactured by the Pen Carbon people, is claimed to be superior in every way. The statement is made that "The operator may rest assured that the copy is perfect. It is not the fault of the ribbon." The circular informs the reader that sample copies and price lists will be furnished on application.

WE NOTE with interest a sample of the carbon paper from the Empire Ribbon & Machine Company, 66 Beaver street, New York. The use of carbon paper has increased enormously within the last few years. The duplication of original entry and the substitution of a carbon copy for the letter-book copy has increased the necessity for these papers. Carbon paper is, as a usual thing, a very dirty substance to handle, soiling the fingers, and also everything else that it comes in contact with. The Empire Ribbon & Machine Company manufactures carbon paper that does not smut. This is an advantage which is apparent to all who have occasion to use carbon paper, provided that the impressions are as clear and clean as from other papers. The papers are to be used both on the typewriter and for duplication from the pen and pencil. The pen carbon is heavily charged, and produces clear and clean duplication. We are glad to note the improvement that has taken place in the manufacture of these papers. The important place they occupy in the business machinery of the office is constantly increasing the demand for them.

A PARTICULARLY ATTRACTIVE PAMPHLET is being issued from the office of the C. E. Sheppard Company, with address at 87 Maiden Lane, New York City. This pamphlet has a great tale to tell of the Tengwall File and Ledger Co. Various articles which are described in this pamphlet are all of interest to those who are looking for simplification of business methods and towards the saving of time in getting at any filed information required. The general discussion among thinking business men, on the question of the substitution of loose-leaf accounting records for bound books, is widespread. The Tengwall file is particularly well described, both by cuts, diagrams and by letter-press story. Persons contemplating any changes in their present office appliances for filing would do well to send for this catalogue. These Tengwall files are adapted to meet the requirements of a large variety of business enterprises. The catalogue quotes special binders for ledgers, transfer binders, invoice book binders, pocket price book binders, tariff file binders, music, map and other particular devices as may be required. These can be furnished with locks. Special attention is called, in a particularly well-printed circular, to the fact that some of the largest industrial enterprises of the country are using the Tengwall system. These include such concerns as the Carnegie Steel Company and the U. S. Steel Corporation. Still another special circular calls attention to a form of binder devised for the purpose of holding photographs, with a suggestion that such a binder would be particularly valuable to the salesman who carries with him the photographs of the articles which he has to sell, it being possible to remove the photographs from the binder almost instantly. The Tengwall system is adapted to meet the demands of any business, and the facilities at command of the C. E. Sheppard Company enable them to supply up-to-date forms requiring special ruling and meeting any and all requirements. Still another attractively-printed folder calls the attention of the writer, in bold type, printed in red ink, to "look at the prices." The price list and catalogue will be gladly furnished upon request.

BOOKS OF INTEREST TO BUSINESS MEN

BUSINESS LAW. By Thomas Raeburn White, B.L., LL.B. 5 by 7 1-2 inches; 323 pages. Bound in cloth. Back title gilt. Price, $1.50.

This is a neat, compact and handy book of business law for the use of students and business men. Among the subjects treated are Contracts, Sales, Partnerships, Corporations, Negotiable Paper and the like. The author's language is plain, and is understandable by any one having no previous knowledge of law. The book's clearness on the essential points of ordinary law should recommend it as a business book for the plain business man who has no time in which to consult a law library.

THE PHONOGRAPHIC DICTIONARY AND PHRASE BOOK. By Benn Pitman and Jerome B. Howard. 5 1-2 by 8 inches; 552 pages. Bound in cloth. Cover title and back title gilt. Price, $3.00.

This book is the most elaborate shorthand dictionary yet published, with the characters in fac-simile. It contains over 20,000 words, and for every one of these words there is a corresponding sign in the Benn Pitman system of shorthand. To the reporter, office or court stenographer, or any one writing the Benn Pitman system of shorthand, the book is invaluable. It is well made, tastefully bound, and is printed on a good quality of paper in clean, plain type.

THE LAWRENCE SYSTEM OF VOCAL AND PHYSICAL EXPRESSION. By Edwin Gordon Lawrence. 4 3-4 by 6 inches; 128 pages. Bound in cloth. Cover title and back title gilt. Price, $1.00.

The author says in the preface of this little book that his object has been to place in the hands of lawyers, actors and public speakers in general, a simple system of vocal and physical expression that will enable them to clearly convey thought by word of mouth and emphasize it by the proper action. To the man of affairs who is called upon for a speech on any subject, and who knows what to say but does not know how to say it, this book will be a great help.

BUSINESS LAW. By Alonzo R. Weed, LL. B., of the Boston Bar. 6 by 9 1-4 inches; 172 pages. Bound in cloth. Cover and back title red. Price, $1.25.

Mr. Weed calls his book "a manual for schools and colleges and for every day use." The titles of the chapters are as follows: Contracts, Principal and Agent, Partnerships, Sales of Personal Property, Bailments and Common Carriers, Negotiable Paper, Deeds, Mortgages and Leases, Collection Laws, Written Rates of Interest, Insurance, Patent Rights, Trade-Marks and Copyrights, etc.

The author does not waste words, and yet treats his subjects clearly and comprehensively. In short, he gives the law without the addition of wordy "trimmings."

BANKERS' AND MERCHANTS' INTEREST TABLES. By Francis H. Coffin and David H. Moore. 13 by 9 1-2 inches. Bound in cloth. Leather back and corners. Cover and back title gilt. Price, $5.00.

There have been interest tables published before, but never, so far as we know, has so elaborate and comprehensive a set of tables been issued in book form. "The volume contains," to quote from the title page, "Interest tables, computed on the basis of 360 days per annum, at 3 1-2, 4, 5 and 6 per cent, with an accurate calculation of interest on every sum from $1.00 to $1,000, and, by simple addition of two lines, on every further sum, to $1,000,000." It also contains a 1 per cent one day table, on the basis of 365 days per annum, from which interest on daily balances can be computed at any time and on any sum. There is a time table printed in black and red at the beginning of the book as an aid in quickly finding the number of days between one day and another. To a merchant or banker performing many calculations in interest this book is a great time saver. It is handsomely bound, finely printed, and has a thumb index.

POLITICAL ECONOMY OF HUMANISM. By Henry Wood. 7 3-4 by 5 1-4 inches; 320 pages. Bound in cloth. Cover and back title gilt. Price, $1.25.

Mr. Wood is well known as a writer on various economic subjects, and this book contains

NEW YORK UNIVERSITY

School of Commerce, Accounts and Finance

A college course in Higher Accountancy arranged in accordance with the requirements of the Certified Public Accountants' Act of the State of New York and fitting students for the Regents' Examination for the C. P. A. degree. The course in Accountancy is rounded out by instruction in finance, commerce and commercial law leading to the University Degree of Bachelor of Commercial Science.

NEW YORK UNIVERSITY

Washington Square NEW YORK CITY

About a Pay Roll which proves itself, corrects all mistakes in figuring, divides up Pay Roll into several amounts needed to pay each person.

But let us send you a sample leaf, with circular, which tells the whole story.

BARLOW BROS., Grand Rapids, Mich.

a series of able treatises, written in his usual vein, on the relation of the employer to the employed, and the phases of the industrial question and their relation to socialism. Among the questions considered and handled in a conservative spirit and with much common sense, are the following: Supply and Demand, the Law of Competition, Labor and Production, Combinations of Capital, Combinations of Labor, Employers and Profit Sharing, the Obligations and Privileges of Employees, the Unequal Distribution of Wealth, Money and Coinage, Tariffs and Protection, Industrial Education and Gold Production and values.

INTRODUCTION TO THE STUDY OF COMMERCE. By Frederick R. Clow, Ph. D. 7 1-2 by 3 3-4 inches; 224 pages. Bound in cloth. Back title gilt. Price, $1.25.

Mr. Clow's book is not intended as a complete text book on commerce. It is simply, as its title implies, an introduction to the study of commerce. It is intended as a text book for the use of teachers in schools or universities, or as a help to the student in his commercial training. Incidentally, it makes good reading for anyone interested in modern commerce, and particularly for the American merchant. The author begins by describing the Elements of Commerce; then follows a short essay on the Rise of Commerce, and then the Materials of Commerce are discussed. Foreign Commerce of the United States and of other countries is treated of, as is the Domestic Commerce of this country. The titles of other chapters are: Organization of Trade, Prices, Payments and How the Equilibrium is Maintained. We can heartily recommend this introduction to the Study of Commerce. It is a good book on a vastly important subject.

THE A B C OF BANKS AND BANKING. By George M. Coffin. 6 3-4 by 5 inches; 137 pages. Bound in cloth. Back title gilt. Price, $1.25.

This handy little volume is exactly what its name implies, that is, a presentation of the

R·I·P·A·N·S

There is scarcely any condition of ill-health that is not benefited by the occasional use of a R·I·P·A·N·S Tabule. For sale by Druggists. The Five-Cent packet is enough for an ordinary occasion. The family bottle, 60 cents, contains a supply for a year.

W. G. Mowat

Public Accountant

831 Ellicott Sq., Buffalo, N. Y.

Leon Brummer, C. P. A.

Public Accountant and Auditor,

7 Pine Street, New York, N. Y.

PRENTISS CLOCKS.

SIX TIMES A YEAR

is all that is necessary to wind a Prentiss Clock. Why wind a clock every week when we can sell you one which will require winding but once in sixty days and will keep perfect time? Also Frying-pan, Program and Electrically synchronized clocks. Send for Catalogue No. 22.

THE PRENTISS CLOCK IMPROVEMENT CO.,
Dept. 28, 49 Dey St., New York City

principles underlying banking in the United States. The author in his preface says that it is designed to appeal to the reader outside as well as inside of a bank. It is by no means the last word or every word about banking. It may be said that it is a primer covering a field that has hitherto been somewhat neglected. The chapter heads are as follows: Banking in General, Various Kinds of Banking, Capital Stock, Shareholders' Rights and Liabilities, Undivided Profits, Dividends and Surplus, Deposits, Checks, Lawful Money Reserve, Issuing Bank Notes, Borrowing Money, Loans and Discounts, Exchanges, Collections, Letters of Credit, Bonds, Mortgages and Stocks, Bank Reports, Examinations, Directors, Executive Officers—Their Powers and Duties, Internal Administration and Bookkeeping, and Other Suggestions.

Any book in this list will be sent to any address in the United States, Canada or Mexico upon receipt of price. If there is some special book that you require we shall be pleased to hunt it up for you. Address COMMERCE, ACCOUNTS & FINANCE, 25 [illegible] Street, New York city.

HALL'S Fireproof and Burglar Proof SAFES

Sold since 1840. *Never fail to protect contents.*

KNOWN EVERYWHERE

393 BROADWAY, N.Y.

Telephones: 3133-3136-307 Franklin.

BUSINESS NEEDS

Advertisements under this head one cent a word each insertion.

AUDITOR WANTED.—Thoroughly trained accountant competent to establish and manage auditing system for several large financial corporations. Address T. B. R., office of Commerce, Accounts & Finance, 25 Pine street, New York City.

SITUATION WANTED.—A young man of 33, experienced in modern accounting and system work, would like a position as accountant with a progressive firm—manufacturing preferred. Address SYSTEMS, Lock Box 650, Milwaukee, Wis.

$$ IN YOUR POCKET $$ in commissions. You can do the trick by writing letters to your friends. You will really confer a favor upon any one you ask to ————. Write me and find out what it is. It is honest and it is honorable. Address SURITY, care Commerce, Accounts & Finance.

I WANT BACK NUMBERS of previous volumes of Commerce, Accounts & Finance. I will gladly pay for them. Person having copies to spare please communicate with C. C. G., care Commerce, Accounts & Finance.

I AM AT PRESENT engaged in a large export commission business, and can furnish the highest testimonials as to efficiency of service rendered as a bookkeeper. Further advancement is barred by reason of the firm's personal dependants. Any firm or individual in need of an office man communicate with INDUSTRIOUS, care Commerce, Accounts & Finance.

BUSINESS PICTURES—Do you want to illustrate your catalogue or booklet? Do you want a series of snappy pen and ink sketches to brighten your advertisement in the daily papers? Do you want a handsome wash drawing for your announcement in the magazines? If you do, write to me. I am a competent business artist, working in black and white and colors, and you see my sketches every week if you read the Sunday papers. My price is always a fair one. Address, PEN AND INK, Box 17, Commerce, Accounts & Finance.

THOROUGHLY TRUSTWORTHY MAN, 30 years of age, wants to connect himself with some business house or person, where a knowledge of men, resulting from meeting people of all classes would be of value. Trained in office duties and accustomed to the management of the office force. Experienced interviewer and solicitor. Address ADAPTABLE, care Commerce, Accounts & Finance.

AM 35 YEARS OF AGE. Have spent eighteen years in a bank as bookkeeper and first teller. Am accounted an expert in the handling of money, and am a careful, rapid and correct bookkeeper. Excellent reasons for leaving the bank I have been with. Testimonials. Address IMPERATIVE, care Commerce, Accounts & Finance.

OFFICE FURNITURE, Files, Cabinets, etc.—I know a lot more about some things than you do. I have to—it is my bread and butter. You don't know the "cost" of a desk, a cabinet, filing devices and the hosts of other things you may want to use in your office. I do! I can save you money and make some myself. That is a good proposition for you to look in to. Try. UNITS, care Commerce, Accounts & Finance.

SECOND-HAND TYPEWRITERS can be repaired so that they can be used and produce work which is almost, if not quite, as good as from a new machine. I have the facilities for obtaining exceptionally good second-hand machines. I have a man who repairs them—a man that understands his business. These machines can be sold for 50 per cent discount from list price of the new machines. Does this interest you? If it does, address TYPEWRITER, care Commerce, Accounts & Finance.

EXTRA WORK for extra hours. I want work for evenings. Am competent bookkeeper. Work must be in New York or Brooklyn. Address F. K., care Commerce, Accounts & Finance.

INSURANCE, ASSURANCE AND REASSURANCE.—Perhaps I can tell you some things that will save you money. There is a way of doing things even in the insurance business. Write me for blanket insurance, mill insurance or any old kind of insurance. I think I can talk interestingly. Address ASSURANCE, care Commerce, Accounts & Finance.

OFFICE MAN AND BOOKKEEPER, thoroughly competent, and with 10 years' experience, desires to make a change. Address COMPETENT, care Commerce, Accounts & Finance.

A BUSINESS EDUCATION	FOR ...ONE... DOLLAR.

...THE PRACTICAL AGE...

A MONTHLY MAGAZINE full to the brim with helpful suggestions to young men and young women who are struggling successward.

THE BUSINESS HOUSE THAT JACK BUILT, an intensely interesting and highly instructive story of business life, and

APPLIED ENGLISH, an authority on writing and speaking the English language, which no young person can afford to be without, all for ONE DOLLAR.

If you have never seen THE PRACTICAL AGE, send for a free sample copy. Address,

THE PRACTICAL AGE,

Moline, Illinois.

ACTUALITIES OF BUSINESS

How We Are Training Young Men for Positions of Responsibility and Confidence

If Capitalists and Men of Affairs generally knew the course of training in business organization and administration we are in position to give their sons and nephews, and those whom they would like to have qualified for positions as private secretaries and confidential men, they would overwhelm us with their commissions.

We Take Young Men where the ordinary schools and business colleges leave them and give them practical training in the actualities of business. Our practice department includes the offices of the concerns for which we are working. The young men entrusted to our care, in addition to proper drill in theory in our lecture room, are sent out in real service under the supervision of our experts. They are made to perform the actual work that is to be done, and are even initiated in the art of controlling and directing others in the work.

A Large Number of Successful Graduates from this division of our work attests its usefulness. Inquiry of the young men themselves, or better, of those who were instrumental in putting them under our charge, will give facts sufficient to convince the most skeptical.

If the Bright and Aggressive Bookkeepers and office men of the country knew that Balance Sheet Accounting is now available to them in each of a large number of specified lines of business, both mercantile and manufacturing, at a very reasonable price, the instruction being by the correspondence plan, they also would make heavy demands upon us.

One Young Man who commenced under our training less than three years since has had his salary advanced during that time by reason of his attainments from $18 per week to $4,000 per year. Another has been so successful in building upon the foundation that we supplied as to have had an increase in salary every three months since the course was finished, with the result that today he has a handsome income. Numerous other instances might be cited. The pupil furnishes the native ability and aptitude and we do the training to his pecuniary advantage. Our own need of bright, well-trained young men alone affords numerous openings for those who become proficient in Balance Sheet Accounting.

It Will Be to the Advantage of the business man who reads this, whether young or old, no matter in what line engaged, to ascertain for himself what we have done in the past, as, for example, in reorganizing the accounting and administrative plans of some of the most prominent business concerns in the land, and equipping hundreds of smaller undertakings with up-to-date methods, and also to inquire into what we are doing just at present. We are busy, up to the capacity of the very considerable force we have gathered together, and inquire as you may, or call upon us when you can, you will be interested in what you will learn and see.

Correspondence Solicited.

ACCOUNT, AUDIT AND ASSURANCE CO., Ltd.

503 Exchange Building
BOSTON

25 Pine Street
NEW YORK

COMMERCE ACCOUNTS & FINANCE

Volume 4 New York May 1902 Number 5

CONTENTS

Published Monthly by the Commerce Accounts & Finance Company Twenty-five Pine Street New York

KNICKERBOCKER TRUST CO.

234 FIFTH AVENUE, CORNER 27TH STREET
BRANCH OFFICES:
66 BROADWAY, AND 125TH STREET AND LENOX AVE.,
NEW YORK CITY.

CAPITAL AND UNDIVIDED PROFITS, $2,508,399.11.

LEGAL DEPOSITORY FOR STATE, CITY, AND COURT FUNDS.

Interest allowed on Time Deposits. Deposits also received subject to Demand Checks, which pass through the Clearing House as do those upon any city bank.

Authorized to act as Executor or Administrator of Estates, and as Guardian, Receiver, Registrar, Transfer and Financial Agent for States, Cities, Towns, Railroads, and other corporations, and to accept any other Trusts in conformity with the laws of any State or of the United States.

LETTERS OF CREDIT FURNISHED.
BUSINESS AND PERSONAL ACCOUNTS SOLICITED.

CHAS. T. BARNEY, - - - - - - - - President.
JOSEPH T. BROWN, - - - - - - 2d Vice-President.
JULIAN M. GERARD, - - - Asst. Sec. and Asst. Treas.
FRED'K K. ELDRIDGE, - - - - - 1st Vice-President.
FRED'K GORE KING, - - - Secretary and Treasurer.
WM. B. RANDALL, - - - - - - - Trust Officer.

BOARD OF DIRECTORS:

JOSEPH S. AUERBACH,
HARRY B. HOLLINS,
JACOB HAYS,
CHARLES T. BARNEY,
A. FOSTER HIGGINS,
ANDREW H. SANDS,
JAMES H. BRESLIN,
I. TOWNSEND BURDEN,
HON. E. V. LOEW,
HENRY F. DIMOCK,
CHARLES F. WATSON,
FREDERICK G. BOURNE,
C. LAWRENCE PERKINS,
CHARLES R. FLINT,
AMZI L. BARBER,
CHARLES T. COOK,
JOHN MAGEE,
HENRY A. MORGAN,
HENRY C. BERLIN,
CHARLES W. GOULD,
FRED'K L. ELDRIDGE,
HENRY W. DE FOREST,
ALFRED R. MACLAY
HARRY W. McVICKAR.

C. W. HASKINS, C. P. A. E. W. SELLS, C. P. A.

HASKINS & SELLS

Certified Public Accountants

CABLE ADDRESS, "HASKSELLS." THIRTY BROAD STREET, NEW YORK

Accounts of Municipalities, Corporations, Firms and Individuals Inspected and Audited; Methods of Accounting Originated and Adapted to Conditions; Books of Accounts Opened, Regulated and Closed; Irregularities Discovered; Financial Situations Examined.

Experts under the Joint Commission of the Fifty-third Congress to Revise the Accounting System of the UNITED STATES GOVERNMENT.

Lackawanna Railroad

Address all communications to

C. W. TEN BROECK, Industrial Agent,
26 Exchange Place, New York City.

Do You Desire a Factory Site? The Industrial Department of the Lackawanna Railroad will aid you in finding one.

Are You Interested in Any Raw Product for Manufacturing Purposes? The Industrial Department of the Lackawanna Railroad will tell you if it is to be found along that road.

Does the Question of Power Concern You? The Industrial Department of the Lackawanna Railroad will tell you of good water power and of the proximity of fuel to points on that road.

Do You Want to Know the Usual Rate of Wages? The Industrial Department of the Lackawanna Railroad will give that information regarding any point on that road.

Do You Want to Know the Price of Gas, Water, Electricity? The Industrial Department of the Lackawanna Railroad will tell you.

Business Organization and Administration*

By A. O. KITTREDGE, C. P. A.

The subject that has been nominated in the notices of this meeting is one a good deal larger than any single lecture can do justice to. Business organization and administration as a proposition is just as large as is the business world at the present time. Go wherever business is and there is demanded plan and management of business.

I do not forget that many of those who are before me tonight are accounting students, and therefore it seems to me that the best way to treat this subject on this occasion is to consider it from the accountant's point of view.

It is my firm conviction, as well also as the conclusion of many others who have investigated the conditions under which business is transacted, that "accounting is the vital element of business." Without accounting no business can exist. Whether the factory is running or shut down, whether the store is opened or closed, still the accounting must be sustained.

A business can get along without lawyers, it can get along without salesmen, it can get along without various other adjuncts, but it cannot exist without accounts. Therefore it is entirely appropriate that we investigate business organization and administration from the standpoint of accounting, and, further, that we use accounting more or less as the foundation upon which we base our scheme and plan.

I conceive that the duties originally falling to the accountant—going way back, if you please, to the very beginning of the profession, or to the origin of what has since developed into the profession—were very much like those discharged by bookkeepers today. I suppose the early business man, not having skill at figures and perhaps not even being able to write, called in some one who was competent to make his calculations and write up his books of accounts. We are justified by the history we read in assuming that such was the case.

After a while, however, with the progress that was made in business and the large number who came to enjoy the benefits of education, the business man was able to have his own regular man for this purpose. Then commenced the development of the trade that is now known as bookkeeping. At the same time the accountant was promoted. Insetad of looking after affairs in the elementary way as he had formerly done, he now had the duty put upon him of supervising or revising the work of bookkeepers.

I am simply tracing the development of the accountant's work, proposing thereby to reach the standpoint from which the public accountant is viewed today.

THE ACCOUNTANT OF TODAY.

At present, as the accountant is called in to supervise or revise the work and calculations of bookkeepers, or, as it is commonly called, to audit, etc., he necessarily comes into very intimate relations with the business man, and thereby becomes more or less cognizant of his ambitions, his plans and his undertakings. Likewise he becomes acquainted with the business in its various details and the business man's methods of organization and administration.

In natural order therefore the public accountant of the present day, in addition to all the other duties that are put upon him, comes into very intimate relationship with various branches of business along the lines of organization and administration. Accordingly it is necessary that public accountants should take careful heed of that which goes to make a business successful in the best sense of the word.

Those who make a specialty of advising on business matters of this sort do along business lines work very similar to that which engineers do along mechanical lines. The man who lays out a system of business organization or a plan of business administration therefore is entitled to the term "business engineer" just as much as the man who designs a machine is entitled to the term "mechanical engineer."

THE FOUNDATION OF BUSINESS MANAGEMENT.

Referring now to the foundation of all successful business management, it seems to me that the one thing that the business man requires under all circumstances in order to use his own native talent to the best advantage is absolute knowledge at all times of his real position. Whatever the accounting plan may be employed, the foundation, or, rather, the real measure of usefulness, so far as service to the business man is concerned, is giving him the information that he needs in the form best suited to his requirements and at the exact time that he can make the best use of it. Therefore it seems to me, again, that we shall be entirely deficient in any plan that we may work out if we do not make an adequate accounting system our essential foundation.

We speak familiarly of the business manager as an individual. We very generally conceive of a business as being conducted or run by one man, and, as a fact, there are very few concerns nowadays, however organized, that are not in a sense at least run or adminstered by one controlling spirit. This dominant man becomes the business manager in the sense in which we are using the term. Yet there are a number of concerns in various branches of commerce and manufacture that are not run by one man alone, even though one man seems to be the officer of the day and in absolute charge. A careful inquiry into the facts of the case will show that he is backed by a council or cabinet of advisers. Whether you call it Board of Directors or by some other name, you will discover that as a fact he has the benefit of help and advice of several who are watching the situation very carefully. As the wisdom of several is superior to that of any one of the number, so is the strength of this man in coping with the situation greater than it appears.

In those organizations with which we are best acquainted in business at the present time, namely, corporations, we encounter various officers, such as president, vice-president, treasurer, secretary, business manager, managing director, and so on to the end of a considerable list. Sometimes the one man who voices the administration of the business is the president. In other cases, as we all know, the president is only a figurehead. Then, of course, he does not do the managing.

Take, for example, the typical New England cotton mill, than which there are few better administered institutions in the world; there, almost always, the man who puts into operation those plans which are decided upon is the treasurer.

Again, in certain other branches of business the vice-president has added to his title that of general manager. He is the vice-president and general manager of the business.

Where the management is almost personal, whether it be at the hands of president, vice-president, general manager or a man singled out as managing director, the business as a rule is of comparatively small dimensions. When we come to large organizations, for example, the so-called trusts, meaning always not trusts as defined in the law, but, instead, merely corporations with very large capital, there are various adjuncts to the management. In other words, there are various plans by which the opinions of a considerable number of able and interested men can be brought to bear upon every point of importance.

Primarily, in a corporation, whether large or small, the Board of Directors is charged with all the responsibilities of the management of the business. The Board of Directors promptly relieves itself of all detail work by electing officers and appointing committees, and specifying the duties of the committees. Very frequently there is provided an executive committee, which stands for the Board of Directors whenever the Board is not in session.

The Board of Directors in the proper discharge of its duties will elect a president, a vice-president, a treasurer, a secretary, and very frequently a chairman of the Board other

*An address delivered before the classes in Theoretical and Practical Accounting, School of Commerce, Accounts & Finance, New York University, March, 1902, by A. O. Kittredge, C. P. A., President of the Account, Audit & Assurance Co., Ltd., 25 Pine Street, New York.

than the president. This usually takes place where the president is a working man in the business, being a specialist either in the sense of financier, or inventor, rather than a mere capitalist. This plan gives the president in his capacity as specialist the opportunity to report to the Board when some impartial person occupies the chair.

From experience and observation I have reached the conclusion that in various corporations of considerable size, where some one is designated "general manager," it is virtually an admission that the regular officers are incompetent or derelict in duty. Such a course puts upon one person something that on the merits of the case belongs to several. It is a plan by which the Board of Directors, on whom all the responsibilities of the business should devolve, and which comprise those to whom the stockholders would naturally look for the real management of the company, are avoiding or escaping a share of that which they assumed when agreeing to act as directors.

The general manager in the execution of his functions over-rides, to a certain extent at least, all the other officers, and sometimes goes away ahead of anything the Board of Directors ever contemplated. There are undoubtedly exceptions to the rule, but I think the general officers of the company should discharge the duties of administration rather than turn them over to a hired man. If the individual called "general manager" is worthy of the position, make him president and constitute the Board of Directors his cabinet.

ADMINISTRATIVE COMMITTEES.

The management of business through committees, which is almost a necessity with very large organizations, is something that is of interest to consider in this connection.

I have already referred to the executive committee, which, in the majority of cases, is simply the Board of Directors reduced to a much smaller number, sometimes very much less than even a quorum of the Board of Directors.

Boards of Directors are often chosen for other reasons than the working qualities of the men so elected, and as the work must be done it sometimes transpires that a Board of Directors of fifteen or twenty-five members will have the quorum reduced to a very small number, simply to secure attendance at meetings of a working body. This plan puts the management into the hands of a comparatively small number. Again, there comes the resort to an executive committee, with the executive committee authorized to do in the place of the Board of Directors everything that the Board might do were it in session. It is certainly a creature of the Board of Directors, and therefore, in order to legalize its actions, they should be formally approved by the Board.

The finance committee is a very important committee in many large corporations. The duties discharged by it in many cases would only be those which are ordinarily undertaken by the treasurer in smaller organizations. It takes into its hands the general question of providing funds, and, as in the case with the United States Steel Company, such questions are brought before it as that of the conversion of a certain amount of preferred stock into bonds, etc.

Then there is the sales committee. It discharges for the larger organizations much of the responsibilities that would ordinarily fall upon the so-called sales manager of smaller concerns. Sales committees very frequently prove of great service, and often bring to light matters of vital importance which a single mind perhaps would never have dreamed to exist.

Under the sales committee would be the ordinary management of sales details at the hands of the general salesman and his subordinates, the order clerks, traveling salesmen, and so on to the end of the necessary equipment.

In large manufacturing concerns, where the office is located at one point and the factory some place else, a factory committee often becomes very useful. Take, for instance, several factories or mills, the product of which is sold through one general office, the factory committee is appointed to consider the question of equipment as affecting cost of product, and by considering the comparative costs of the several plants has the opportunity to become very useful indeed.

BUSINESS SYSTEM COMMITTEE.

That which has lately come into use in the way of a committee in certain large institutions is something at once novel and exceedingly useful, and that is a business system committee. It has come to be recognized that no business of size can run without an adequate business and accounting system. In a great many cases it is left entirely to the bookkeeper to decide that he will have such and such a blank, that he will use such a form of journal, that he will manage his cash in such a way, etc., and so on to the end of the list. But the business committee steps up and secures at the hands of a man competent for the purpose, namely, a business and accounting engineer, the outline of a complete business system, and then lays down the rule that the system shall be followed in its entirety and no changes made in it save only as good cause exists, and then only with the approval of that committee. I have watched with great interest the work of the business system committee of a number of important concerns, and I am more than pleased with the results they are achieving.

It seems to be the conception of each of a great many business men that he is entirely competent to devise his own accounting system and that if there is any one thing he knows all about, it is the designing of a necessary blank. The result is that the majority of establishments are long on blanks and short on the economical and scientific use of blanks, or to put it otherwise, they are long on bookkeeping and short on accounting. The one important thing the competent accounting engineer has to do with blanks as he finds them in use, is to throw out complication in form and duplication in work and get down to an economical and efficient working basis.

The business system committee can do a good deal along the lines of organization and administration which one individual could not accomplish as well because of its dignity on the one hand and its authority on the other. Take for example, a case that I am now thinking of, in which there are a considerable number of subsidiary companies acting as sales agents for the parent corporation. How important it is that all these subsidiary companies should be uniform in their methods, for comparisons of result in the home office! Without the business system committee possessing absolute authority this result would be very difficult of accomplishment.

One thing that I think all public accountants should advise against is that of allowing any young upstart who happens to sit on a bookkeeper's stool to devise a blank and bring it into use without first submitting the blank and the proposed plan of use to official scrutiny. Every blank properly considered is a part of the accounting and business system, but in itself there is no system in a blank. A great many think that if they could only get a copy of the blanks employed in a given business, they would have the whole system, but in this they are altogether mistaken. This is where the business committee of a large organization comes in for most excellent work in the directions of economy and efficiency.

In addition to the committees I have already named there are various special committees made necessary by the nature of the business, to which it is not necessary to refer. There is one thing, however, that should be mentioned in this connection, and that is the salutary influence of the minutes of meetings of committees, or in other words, of recorded conclusions. Let the committee on finance, or on factory management, or in fact any of the committees that I have named, get together and discuss the situation and have the proceedings of the meeting recorded in good style, putting a transcript in the general file for preservation. The effect of this plan is first, to fix responsibility, and second, to keep a diary of what takes place step by step in a way to convey its own important lessons.

DEFINITE RESPONSIBILITIES.

I am convinced of the great advantage of having proper

committees appointed, responsibilities allotted, minutes kept with conclusions recorded and revised by those who are still higher in authority. I might cite, by way of example, a manufacturing concern on a very important line of goods that established a subsidiary company several hundred miles away. The business at that point previously had been run as a branch office and was not satisfactory. On the new plan the old manager was made president of the subsidiary company, and his chief clerk was made treasurer. Both were given working interests in the company. They were advised to form a business committee and to put into effect no plan that this committee had not previously approved. The committee was to keep records, and it was also stipulated that copies of those records should be forwarded for consideration to the home office. The result was phenomenal. The expenses of the business in this distant town were reduced nearly 25 per cent in the first three months. Of course, you may argue that because these men had been given working interests in the business, they at once began to do better, but nevertheless I shall claim it was because they were given a better plan of business administration than they had ever had before.

Not long ago a case in Brooklyn of this general kind came to my attention. An establishment that was making money, and that was exceedingly liberal with its men, entered upon this plan of administering certain details very suddenly, and made up a business system committee out of the foreman of the shop and the leading office men. These men, in their new capacity, felt that it was up to them to do something, and they soon found where it could be done. They discovered ways of so administering the business as to effect a saving of no less than $40,000 per year. This was made up of economies which the president of the company who had previously administered its affairs unaided by cabinet or council had not been able to perceive or accomplish.

The time has gone by when it is expedient to put a man in a given place and let him work out his own methods without supervision. The best man improves under good advice and management.

Again returning to the question of accounting, it seems to me that accounting and business system must go hand in hand. It is impossible to separate them. The time was when an annual showing of results would answer the needs of a business man for planning, but with the rate at which business is moving at the present time no one can wait a year to correct a mistake or to put on more energy if the situation warrants it. There is no way of knowing what is being accomplished in a given place aside from the accounts. Mere physical inspection will not do; business is too complicated, the items are too many, the conditions are too varied for any one by mere intuition to know what should be done.

There is nothing that will meet the demands of the present day except properly kept accounts and the balances struck in them at frequent intervals. Nothing short of a showing of going results will serve to determine whether one man shall be kept or another discharged.

THE BUSINESS MACHINE AND ITS OPERATION.

Take another view of the subject: It seems to me that business organization, meaning now those facilities with which the business is conducted and managed, might very properly be likened to a machine. Speaking of organization in general, we are in the habit of using phrases such as "What a fine organization!" "What an able organization!" We even go so far as to comment upon organizations in political parties. Particularly is this the case just before election. We speak of the Tammany organization. Well if these remarks are appropriate with reference to political parties, why are they not equally true with regard to business? That business, other things being equal, which is the best organized certainly has the best chance for success.

We talk about organizations as applied to the militia. One regiment is contrasted with another, not alone by the personnel of the men, the officers and the privates, but as a whole, that is, as an organization. We say concerning the Seventh Regiment, for example, that it is well organized.

Again, we speak about educational organizations. The public schools, for instance, of one section of the country are far better organized than those of another section. We also speak in the same general manner about governmental matters at Washington, and even the Church of Rome.

Finally it comes to business organization. The factory of one concern may be excellently organized, another concern may excel in the organization of its sales department, etc.

If organization is the machine, then administration is the operation of the machine.

It makes no difference how excellent the machine may be for obtaining certain results, the goods produced derive a certain part of their quality from the skill of the man who operates the machine. So I argue that no matter how excellent the organization of the business may be, still the result will be measured more or less by the administration, by the capacity, or ability of the men who operate the organization.

Speaking of administration in the sense of operating the machine, we have various similes or comparisons. We have the administration of the government. Just at the present time the administration of the city government (New York) is being more or less discussed. Again, we have the administration of the national government, which is always in the public eye.

Again, if we have secured good organization, for example, in an army, there comes up immediately the question of administration. Some generals are aggressive and successful; others are dilatory and fail of results. Contrast one with another, the successive generals of the army of the Potomac during the War of the Rebellion. Contrast the aggressiveness of Grant and what he achieved with the little that McClellan accomplished. It is quite possible, however, that McClellan's organization contributed no small part to Grant's success in using the army actively.

From this and from other instances we derive the thought that some men can build in the sense of the organization, while other men are able to take the work where the builder left it and operate it, or manage and administer it.

Profit making may be defined as being the immediate object of all business. Profits may be further defined as the product of well-administered business organizations.

IMPORTANCE OF ADMINISTRATION.

My idea of the relative importance of business administration or management can be conveyed in a very few words. Let us say that five units compose the whole of a successful business undertaking. Then the idea, the invention, the mine, the patent, the claim, or the business that you have bought out, will stand for the first of these units. All the capital that is necessary to the business will stand for the second. Organization—meaning scheme, plan, method by which you are going to run the business—will, I think, represent another or the third one of the five; but administration or management will comprise the other two. I am disposed to give to management double the force, double the standing, double the importance of either of the other elements named. This seems to me about where business administration comes to and the importance that business management has in the business operations of the day.

No less an authority than former Speaker Thomas B. Reed has declared that the present age is distinctively the business age. He has said in a famous lecture, that has been widely quoted, that business men are now taking their position in the front rank, where, by rights, they belong; that business, in fact, is the living issue of the period. He goes on showing how in the past the soldier has had his day hewing the way for the lawyer and statesmen, who come next. Now, with constitutions and liberal laws upon the statute books, there is secured the freedom which makes business possible.

We know from history who were the captains of the soldiers who did the first great work in this onward march of progress. We know also who among the students of the law became great statesmen. We know likewise something of those in later days who are characterized as captains of industry, merchant princes, financiers, etc. The one trait in common among all of them has been great administrative ability.

But, says some one, no great thing at the present time is accomplished without capital, and that therefore we must not exclude capital in such a discussion as this. So it would seem at first blush, but let us inquire right here. Where was the capital at the outset with any one of the business leaders whom you can recall at this moment? Where was the capital with which the Astors, the Vanderbilts, the Goulds, Hill, of the Great Northern Railway; Huntington, of the Southern Pacific Railway; Standford, Mackay, Flood, O'Brien, and thousands of others who have made their marks in the business world, actually commenced? Where was the capital at the beginning of the career of the merchant prince, A. T. Stewart? Where was the capital at the beginning of the career of Carnegie of library fame? Capital is only a tool with which business is managed. It is a great convenience, to say the least, but the able manager does not find it altogether indispensable, for when he does not happen to have it he at once proceeds, like a mechanic lacking a tool for the particular work in hand, to construct it. For lack of it his progress is not arrested, it is only slightly retarded.

If you take the lives of the prominent men of industry, of finance, of commerce, of transportation, of mining, of insurance (and I am safe in including every division of business that can be mentioned) and go back to the beginning of their careers you will find in a majority of cases that capital has been created by the manager, instead of the manager having the capital put into his hands. After he has fully demonstrated his ability to create and to manage, then those who have capital, but who are unable to manage, freely pour it into the enterprises he espouses.

OPPORTUNITIES IN BUSINESS MANAGEMENT.

During a long trip to the Far West and Southwest, from which I have recently returned, I have had the opportunity to inquire somewhat carefully into the mining industry which is so alluring to a great many young men. I am moved to speak of this tonight because I have recently overheard several discussions between young men with reference to the expediency of quitting the East and going to the Far West, or to Alaska, or to Mexico, or even to Africa, to discover a rich mine. And so the question comes to me, Where is the mine of hidden wealth that the young man of the period can best work to his own advantage?

If we look carefully into the mining enterprises of the West we find that those who really succeed devote a long probationary period to trades or occupations of which the Eastern man knows very little. There are, for example, prospecting and developing, to say nothing of becoming accustomed to privations, that would soon prove fatal to a delicately reared young man. There is the need of certain knowledge of metallurgy. Finally, when he has located his mine and determined that he has a good thing, comes the question of necessary capital. Then arises the question of skilled labor to produce the metal in a marketable condition. All these elements enter into the real profitableness of the undertaking and serve to show how small a chance, at present at least, the adventurer from the East has of making a success in mining.

Could a rancher or a miner hope to succeed as merchant or manufacturer in New York? Could a cowboy hope to succeed in an office here in the East? These questions are no more preposterous than the other, Can an office man of the East become a successful miner?

It seems to me that the rule that we want to establish, and that which is the only safe rule, is, every one to the trade he knows, or to those new trades that are analagous to the ones he has already learned or is measurably familiar with.

It is true that there are mines in the West and Southwest of great richness and value, of gold, silver, copper, coal and various other metals and minerals. Shall the eastern boy of education and ability seek his fortune there? Yes, provided he knows the trade of mining, etc., or has the capital or requisite business skill. Otherwise, no.

But there are mines at home of still greater richness which the eastern boy can aspire to work to far better advantage and with far less privation and hardship. They are mines to the working of which his general education and training naturally tends. Let us make comparisons: A mine laborer, whether it be as mine helper or otherwise, gets only laborer's wages; a mine manager gets a salary commensurate with his ability; a mine owner with capital, combined with managerial ability, gets the fortune.

A bookkeeper gets wages—that is, whatever he is worth in the market—an accountant receives fees according to his ability and standing, and under favorable conditions builds up a profitable professional practice.

A business manager of skill, however able to successfully administer large undertakings, first proves himself indispensable to the industry with which he is engaged and then names his own terms. Secretary Gage, in the famous Denver address, said he knew of several positions of $25,000 each waiting for men who are able to fill them.

After the business manager has secured the large salary he is taken in on the various deals, and finally into the business as a partner, and then comes fortune.

This, gentlemen, is my idea of business organization and administration and the opportunities they offer to the ambitious and capable young man. In closing I would leave this thought with you,—there are mines in business organization and administration which, if you have the ability to work them, are worth more to you than all the gold mines or the silver mines of the West combined. In fact, the one may be made to include the other.

Defective Commercial Education

The May meeting of the New York Commercial Teachers' Association, held at the Packard School, was conspicuous for the attention given to the defects in commercial education as furnished by the commercial schools. This is a subject which is considered by many to be a special hobby of COMMERCE, ACCOUNTS & FINANCE, and it is a notable fact that in the two papers read and in the discussion which followed not a word was said by any commercial teacher in commendation of the product of the institutions which assume to turn out the business men of the day.

"VANNANT."

In the midst of the discussion one of the members present got the floor. He had in his hand a copy of COMMERCE, ACCOUNTS & FINANCE. Everybody knew what was coming. It was "Vannant." Some smiled and some scowled, but the gentleman who had the floor proceeded to read as follows:—

What is there in the business world that so much resembles comic opera, with, of course, the tuneful parts all omitted, as the labored efforts of commercial teachers discussing accounting? It is the custom of the proprietors of the so-called commercial colleges to get together semi-occasionally for the purpose of considering various matters of common interest. Papers are read and discussions are invited. Bouquet throwing comes in of course as an incidental pastime. All that they do, however, would be harmless if it was not published to the world. Unfortunately, however, for the good name of the profession, the proceedings of the conventions are published in full in the official journal, and thereby the practical, hard-fisted, common-sense man of business is afforded additional arguments as often as these papers come out why he should discriminate against commercial college graduates whenever he needs more clerks. By these proceedings he is afforded a conception of the mass of misinformation with which the deluded youth of the land who *go* to these institutions are loaded, and which of course must be removed before they are worth anything to themselves or others in real business life.

"We should all be willing to learn from just criticism."

said the reader of 'Vannant,' "but what I object to in this sort of thing is the fact that no remedy is suggested. I wish somebody would recommend a work on accounting adapted to the needs of commercial schools."

Nobody replied.

The reader then continued to quote from "Vannant" as follows:—

Whatever may be said about the comparison that is fair between the energy of the commercial teachers and that of technical teachers, it still remains that the first qualification of the technical teacher is knowledge of his subject or practical familiarity with the topics under consideration. Chemistry, for example, is taught by experienced chemists, electrical engineering by those who are able to demonstrate their right to teach by performing practically the work required in the line mentioned, and architecture by those who have actually drawn the plans, specified the construction and superintended the erection of buildings. But where is the commercial teacher that is really wanted in the business office, or who could, in fact, hold his place in the practical work of business if perchance he once made his entrance therein? However, this is not quite fair in the broad conclusion that might be reached. When it comes to teaching penmanship, the commercial schools do employ men who can write, and in the typewriting department they have those who can operate a machine. Cases are on record, even in the shorthand department, where teachers have been employed who could do practical shorthand work to the extent of reporting conventions, but such things are rare. When it comes to the accounting department, they occasionally have a man who knows the routine of simple bookkeeping, but beyond this they have never gone, and that is what makes the occasion so ludicrous when some member of this federation tries to tell what he does not know about accounting applied to business needs.

Several of the members present objected to the tone of "Vannant's" remarks, but nobody attempted to bridge the chasm which, according to "Vannant," exists between accounting as it is found in the business world and accounting as it is taught in commercial schools.

DEFECTIVE ENGLISH.

A. B. Darling, of the Centenary Institute, of Hackettstown, N. J., read an interesting paper on teaching the English language, in which he deplored the results usually attained by prevailing methods of instruction.

Mr. Darling's paper struck a responsive chord. One of the members of the association who is exceptionally successful in teaching shorthand declared that defects in English made shorthand acquirements comparatively worthless in a majority of cases so far as writing satisfactory letters was concerned.

Another member said the time usually devoted in commercial schools to teaching English was so short that very little could be accomplished. He suggested that pupils be familiarized with specific words used in business. As an instance of current ignorance, he mentioned one of his own pupils who was fairly proficient in shorthand, but who received in dictation the word "affidavit," and wrote it out "calves of David."

THE A B C OF ACCOUNTS.

A short extemporaneous address was made by George E. Allen of the Account, Audit & Assurance Company, Limited, a specially invited speaker, whose subject, according to the program, was "The A. B. C. of Accounts." Following is a synopsis of Mr. Allen's remarks:—

The first essential of teaching is clearness. The chief elements of clearness are simplicity and exactness. This is true of any kind of teaching, but it is particularly true of teaching the theory and practice of accounts. Too little attention to accounting principles and too much attention to bookkeeping details are two grave errors, each serious enough in itself, but doubly serious when they go together, as they frequently do.

In these days of huge industrial creations and consolidations, accounting becomes more and more a vital element. Comprehensive and up-to-date knowledge is essential to the intelligent management of any business, and in the construction of the modern edifice of accounting the work of a scientific architect is even more important than the work of skilful builders. It is only upon a solid foundation that a satisfactory superstruction can be erected. In accounting, as in architecture, foundation principles are few and fixed, although their application may be infinite. Let us consider briefly what may properly be termed the A. B. C. of Accounts.

Let us suppose that we go into some simple mercantile business in the usual way. Before we begin we must have money. At the outset we buy some goods. In so doing we merely change the form of our possessions. We also doubtless incur some indebtedness. Very likely we rent a store and perhaps we also buy goods on credit as well as for cash. It will therefore be seen that before we begin to make sales we have assets and liabilities. The statement of assets and liabilities is called the Balance Sheet.

Beginning with the Balance Sheet all subsequent bookkeeping is merely a record of the additions to or subtractions from assets and liabilities. It is evident therefore that there are four and only four fundamental classes of accounts, these are assets, liabilities, revenues and expenses. Assets and liabilities show the condition of the business. Revenues and expenses are the record of the operation of the business, and the net result thereof is periodically transferred to the Balance Sheet, thereby showing the periodical change of condition for better or for worse. Any other accounts are merely subdivisions of the four primary accounts specified, and should be distinctly subordinated thereto. It is failure to make this fundamental distinction that confuses the student of bookkeeping and leads the business man into disastrous complications.

EXACT CONFORMITY TO THE FOUR GRAND DIVISIONS.

Bearing in mind that the four grand divisions of accounts are asset accounts, liability accounts, revenue accounts, and expense accounts, the next essential of correct bookkeeping is exact conformity to this logical classification. Each subaccount must mean some separate and distinct thing. For example, the Merchandise Account must include merchandise only, and not attempt to cover merchandise sales. In the Merchandise Asset Account all goods should be carried at cost prices, and profits or losses shown in a separate account, which may be called the Merchandise Sales or Trading Account. The necessity for this plan may readily be demonstrated by supposing that some customer returns a bill of goods. To debit such returned goods to the Merchandise Account at selling prices, in accordance with the custom that largely prevails, leads to self-evident complications. Proper conception of fundamental principles would insure the avoidance of such errors.

Such in outline is the theory of mercantile accounts. In manufacturing the prevalent complication and confusion of ideas may be avoided by proceeding upon the theory that all processes and stages of manufacture are merely the transformation of assets from one condition into another. To raw material, which is the first transformation of condition from cash, must be added the cost of labor, superintendence, depreciation of plant, and everything that enters into the cost of product from the time when it is in the form of cash to the time when it is finished and ready for market. A sharp distinction should be drawn between costs of manufacture and costs of selling, and the subdivision of accounts should be limited as closely as possible to the showing of such facts as are necessary in planning future operations. Any up-to-date plan of accounting is conspicuous not only for what it contains, but for what it does not contain. Non-essentials are cumbersome and costly.

TIMELINESS.

Another important feature of modern accounting—a feature, moreover, which is destined to become general, if not universal—is timeliness. What the business man wants to know is the condition of his affairs up to date, so that he may make his plans of administration from the standpoint of the present instead of the standpoint of six months or a year ago. This result may be accomplished by shortening fiscal periods and giving to each short period the exact proportion to which it is entitled of any expenditure or revenue covering a greater length of time.

The fundamental principles of accounting apply with equal force to the corner grocery and the greatest corporation. The difference is solely in detail. The big trusts, with their numerous branches and departments, are merely a series of units—each a separate and distinct proposition—and to assemble the net results of the several units into one complete whole, is a simple mathematical computation. The first essential is a solid foundation. Any desired form of superstructure may then be built thereon and changes and additions made as circumstances may from time to time require.

In conclusion we must appreciate the fact that the present is pre-eminently the age of Commerce, and Commerce and Accounting are inseparable. In the history of the world there have been ages famous for war, famous for art and literature, and famous for music. Commerce now is king. In a measure the world appreciates its poets, its statesmen, its warriors, its scholars, and its philanthropists, but its sincerest worship is given to its financiers and captains of industry. Consequently it is not the teachers of Latin and Greek, not the teachers of science, and not the teachers of theology that have the greatest opportunities. It is the teachers of Commerce. The world demands more Morgans, more Rockefellers, and more particularly, additional thousands of well-trained young men to occupy confidential positions in business enterprises of the first magnitude. It is up to you, ladies and gentlemen, to produce them.

A PRACTICAL ILLUSTRATION.

The address of Mr. Allen was received with marked cordiality. "Mr. Allen is all right," said one speaker, "and the rest of us are all wrong. We forget foundational instruction and teach too many useless details." As an illustration, this speaker referred to a case which came under his own personal notice. A graduate of a commercial school obtained a position as bookkeeper for a manufacturing concern. This bookkeeper went on in his own way, until one day there was an unexpected demand for $10,000. Much to the surprise of the proprietors no such amount of cash was available, according to the books, and considerable embarrassment was felt until the discovery was made that a bank balance of $23,000 had been found beneath the rubbish of an elaborate system of accounts which purported to show everything, but really showed nothing.

The Commercial Teachers and Vannant

Our outspoken contributor Vannant has stirred up something of a hornets' nest by his recent sharp criticism of commercial schools and teachers. Commercial teachers all over the country are replying to Vannant's criticism, and some of the replies are printed below:—

A Reply from Chicago

From "A Commercial Teacher," Chicago, Ill.

There appeared in the March number of an eastern magazine an article, the author of which signs himself "Vannant." The writer is evidently a so-called professional accountant, and he has gone far out of his way to vent his spleen on business schools and teachers of business branches. The particular red rag that excited this champion of the arena was the report of the meeting of the Federation of Commercial Teachers' Associations, which was held in St. Louis in December last.

The article is raw and its animus is so apparently vindictive that even the editor feels called upon to offer an apology for it. The author takes exception to about everything that was said and done at that convention, to even the resolutions that were passed, and which could not have been of any concern to him in any event, but two of the papers read at that convention seem to have been singled out by this modern Ajax for his especial atttention.

HAS VANNANT A GRIEVANCE?

We have no means of knowing who Vannant is, but we venture the statement that he was in some way hit by something that appeared in one of these papers. Perhaps one of his pet forms or schemes was attacked, or it may be that a book he may publish is condemned by business teachers, and thus his pocket has been indirectly touched.

We have no intention of taking up the cudgel in behalf of either Mr. Rowe or Mr. Spencer in this controversy, as either of these gentlemen is able to take care of himself in a discussion of this kind, but it is to the covert attack on business teachers and schools generally and to the slurring tone of the article in general that we object. No one objects to friendly criticism when offered in a proper spirit, but even a dog will resent criticism of his actions when such criticisms are conveyed in unfriendly tones. Vannant evidently has a grievance. It may be well founded or it may not, but, no matter what it is, if he is the practical hard-headed man of business which he would have us believe, he should know better than to criticise the actions of any one in the spirit he does. He either does not understand human nature or he did not make his observations with the hope that they would be well received and his suggestions acted upon.

Hence we say Vannant has been hurt in some way and has taken advantage of the friendly cover of a nom de plume from under which he can shoot his darts (?) of sarcasm. We say sarcasm, for, if it be omitted, the article is as jejune as a last year's bird's nest. In no case does he resort to argument, and an analysis of his remarks, making as they do nearly two pages of matter, does not disclose a single convincing statement. He complains about almost everything business teachers do, as well as what they leave undone but he makes the following admission mirabile dictu:—

"When it comes to teaching penmanship, the commercial schools do employ men who can write, and in the typewriting department they have those who can operate a machine. Cases are on record, even in the shorthand department, where teachers have been employed who could do practical shorthand work to the extent of reporting conventions, but such things are rare. When it comes to the accounting department they occasionally have a man who knows the routine of simple bookkeeping, but beyond this they have never gone, and that is what makes the occasion so ludicrous when some member of this federation tries to tell what he does not know about accounting applied to business needs."

Vannant is evidently of that cult that believes unless a man is a member of the inner circle of his particular accountants' association he is a nobody and the truth is not in him. We would remind him that neither brains nor facts have yet been Morganized, even if it would seem that courtesy, modesty and money have been. The bold statement is made that beyond the mere routine of bookkeeping no business teacher has ever gone. He forgets that Col. Soule is the proprietor of a commercial school, and that he is the author of a well-known work, than which a prominent eastern public accountant told me he knew of none better in its line. Commercial teachers cannot be, as a rule, public accountants, because no man can serve two masters. If one attends to his school duties as he should, he can have no time to audit books. I always look askance at a commercial teacher who tells me he does public accounting, for I feel sure he must have an indifferent school.

CASE OF THE LATE DR. FIERCE.

The case of the late Dr. Pierce is in point. For years he had a large practice as a public accountant in Philadelphia, but what time he devoted to it was taken from his school. He told me himself that he finally concluded he would make more and give better service to those who employed him if he should confine his efforts to one business or the other. He chose the school, and he said from that day on his school advanced by leaps and bounds.

It is a well-known fact that professional men make poor teachers. Commercial schools in their endeavors to present the best possible courses have often called in successful practicing attorneys to give instruction in commercial law. The results have not generally met expectations. It is not so much what a teacher knows as what he can impart or the work he can get out of his class. It is not a fact, as Vannant would have you believe, that all technical subjects in schools of standing are taught by practitioners, specialists in their several lines. How many professors in the Harvard Law School or in the Ann Arbor Law School are practicing attorneys prominent in the profession? The University of Chicago is now organizing a college of law, but we have not heard that it was seeking the services of active practitioners for instructors.

BUSINESS SCHOOLS NOT PERFECT.

The business schools are not perfect, and no one is more aware of this plan than the business teachers themselves. Neither have we heard that public accountants were accused of knowing it all, even of those things that pertain to their particular profession. Modesty well becomes most of us. The reliable business schools of the country do not pretend great things, they simply profess to do a few things, but they do claim to be doing those few things well. That they are meeting the public's expectations in this regard is best determined by the generous and increasing patronage they are receiving each succeeding year. With all due deference to the judgment and superior acumen of our great and good friend Vannant we submit the public is undoubtedly a better judge of whether it is receiving value from these institutions.

Speaking again of public accountants, we happen to know a few ourselves. We can think of several who, if we may judge of a tree by its fruits, do not have sufficient hard-headed, practical business sense to successfully run a peanut stand. We know of one who had personal charge of a set of books. When he severed his connection with the house it cost the firm a pretty penny to audit his work and correct his mistakes. Yet that man for fifteen years has made his living as a public accountant. But to indict and convict without trial the entire profession of public accountants on the above statements would be paralleling our most wise and quissant friend (?) Vannant.

The Brooklyn Point of View

From "A Teacher," Brooklyn, N. Y.

The assaults of "Vannant" in the March issue of COMMERCE, ACCOUNTS & FINANCE upon the business schools and commercial teachers of the country are very interesting from several points of view. In the first instance the truth of the criticism upon the narrowness of the average commercial teacher's qualification must be admitted by all who are interested and are acquainted with the facts apparent in the conditions to which attention is called.

The commercial teacher has occupied, does now occupy, and will continue to occupy a unique position in the system of education existent in the United States. His place in this system is accounted for by the fact that business houses were demanding that degree of technical education and training which was not provided by common schools, nor by academic schools and colleges, at a time when our commercial expansion made it imperative that office help of an efficient character should be forthcoming as a product of some branch of the educational system. The demands of business houses were such that to maintain a quasi business school in connection with the business office, where young men might "grow into the business," was no longer desirable nor possible. Hence the advent of the commercial teacher and the origin of the business school.

From the time of its origin until the present day no reputable school of this class has found any difficulty in securing for its product, from the business community, ample recognition of its value and adaptation to business requirements. Thousands of young people of both sexes are taken from these schools annually and employed by business houses, which fact alone is sufficient to prove that the business school is fulfiling its mission, not alone to the business man who demands its product, but in a much larger way to the young man and young woman who, through this means, secure in a brief time that preparation which opens to them the opportunity for a useful career.

THE BUSINESS COURSE NOT AN END IN ITSELF.

There are very few commercial teachers who claim that the business course is an end in itself. All that is claimed for it is that it is a stepping-stone to thousands of young people who, before taking this course of training, are practically useless factors in the community. Some of these young men and young women have but a meager education, others are holders of high school diplomas, and not a few of the total number are college graduates. Is the work of transforming this present useless economic material into future usefulness a work to be deprecated? Let the young persons thus helped and the business men whom they are now serving, answer.

The business schools do not claim to be professional schools in any particular. Their courses of study are, therefore, limited both as to scope and as to time. That the reputable schools in this line are doing in a brief period of time all that they claim to do is beyond refutation. In this connection it is interesting to hear business school graduates who are now prominent men in the various forms of business activity bear witness to the fact that they learned more of practical "ready to use" knowledge in a few months spent in a business school than they did in any other equal period in any other school, whether high school or college.

SOME BUSINESS TEACHERS MEN OF LIMITED SCHOLARSHIP.

It is to be regretted that some business teachers are men of limited scholarship, but it must be remembered that the ability to teach, other things being equal, exists in the individual teacher either as an acquirement, through study and by experience, or as a "gift of God." "Vannant" has emphasized the necessity for expert technical ability as a part of the teacher's abiding qualification. It may be admitted that such qualification is necessary in the case of the teacher of chemistry, as "Vannant" cites, also in the case of the teacher of bookkeeping, but what is needed in the qualification of the teacher of shorthand, as, in fact, with the teacher of any subject in any school, is a thorough knowledge of the subject taught, together with genuine teaching ability.

The dexterity manifested by the court reporter who takes the liberty to construct for his own individual needs a system or revision of a system of shorthand is absolutely worthless as a part of a teacher's equipment, and it is a well recognized fact that teachers who possess this ability very often emphasize it to the detriment of good teaching. It should be remembered that the skill of the chemist is his power to analyze compounds and compound elements. Rapidity is not an element in his qualification. The same is true of the shorthand teacher. Among the shorthand teachers of this country there are many who were formerly court or news reporters. It is their testimony that teaching shorthand destroys their former speed as writers, but increases their technical knowledge of the subject, a condition to be desired rather than condemned.

The assertion of "Vannant" to the effect that there are few commercial teachers who are wanted, or who could do the work of a business office, seems very idle, insomuch as, even if true, it proves nothing. The teacher should be able to do the work of his subject without reference to speed as an element, and in addition to this his one great work is to teach. If his ability in these lines can be established, he is able to train and instruct his pupils for expert technical work. It is true of a large majority of experts in the various lines of business activity that they could not with all their technical knowledge and physical dexterity become successful teachers. This fact is not a criticism in any measure upon their usefulness in their respective spheres. But this charge of "Vannant" seems to lack the necessary facts to prove it. There are, as a matter of fact, numerous instances of supervising accountants in government and private enterprises who went into this work from the school room, having formerly followed the profession of teaching bookkeeping for many years.

A SUGGESTION FOR THE ACCOUNTANT.

As to the great bone of contention among accountants themselves, and especially between accountants and teachers of bookkeeping, it is suggested that some accountant who has settled to his own satisfaction and to that of his colleagues what a balance sheet really is, and from what sources it is obtained, should present a model with full explanations in order to dispose of a controversy which has become a veritable nuisance. Bookkeeping teachers claim that it is an arrangement of schedules setting forth assets and liabilities, and consisting of property on hand, unadjusted claims on personal accounts, accrued interest upon loans, notes or personal accounts, good will and patents, notes and bills on hand and outstanding, with a view to determine present net value of the business under consideration. In arranging this data due regard is had for a conservative appraisement of property values and discount allowances upon bad debts. The balances shown in the arrangement in the balance sheet will correspond with the respective accounts in the ledger according to the degree of truth as to present value of balances which said accounts exhibit.

In this very restricted sense the balance sheet may be obtained from the ledger. For all other values the balance sheet depends upon data collected without reference to the ledger. In other words, facts relating to the assets and liabilities of a business, from whatever source obtainable, are the material from which balance sheets are made. It is also understood by bookkeeping teachers that a balance sheet may be taken at any time in the history of a business by accumulating these facts from the sources above indicated. Profit and loss statements which may be desired as accompanying adjuncts to balance sheets may be made out at any time after the business has been in operation for a definite period of time. They depend upon the same conservative estimates of values obtainable from books, vouchers or appraisement of property that have been indicated as the sources of the balance sheet.

It seems most desirable from a professional standpoint that commercial teachers and expert accountants should have a better understanding of each other's work with due respect to the relative position and importance of the sphere, object and requirements of each in his respective calling. To this end may not the expert accountant lend professional aid of high value by way of kindly suggestion? The commercial teacher will gratefully accept such suggestions and apply them to his work to the end that the profession of teaching and the profession of practice may be mutually strengthened.

Rip Van Winkle Still Asleep

From E. E Gaylord, Beverly, Mass.

In the March number of COMMERCE, ACCOUNTS & FINANCE appeared an unfair, discourteous and intemperate attack on commercial schools and commercial teachers. The writer, under the nom de plume "Vannant," is nominally unknown, and thus safe from personal criticism, but the experienced woodsman needs only the trail to name the animal. Vannant's spoor, from the caption to the last derisive phrase, is perfectly plain. It is too bad that he had not the courage of his convictions. Suffice it to say that he is not a competent person to set himself up as a judge of the proper qualifications of a teacher.

OF MISINFORMATION.

"Vannant" says:—

> By these proceedings [of Commercial Teachers' Conventions] the common sense man of business is afforded a conception of the mass of misinformation with which the deluded youth of the land who go to these institutions are loaded, and which of course must be removed before they are worth anything to themselves or others in real business life.

Lyman J. Gage, speaking to the students of the Spencerian Business College, in Milwaukee, last October, said, referring to the commercial instruction he received from Mr. Robert C. Spencer:—

> No episode in my career, now stretching over a long period, do I regard as so valuable in itself as that period spent in the Chicago branch of the Bryant & Stratton educational institution. It taught me what I know about accounts; it gave me the power to analyze financial propositions; it taught me how to keep accounts myself, and when I passed away from the period of apprenticeship or clerkship to higher duties I was enabled by the education I derived in that school to determine the quality of those discharging similar functions over whom I had charge.

OF DISCRIMINATION.

"Vannant" says:—

> The practical, hard-fisted, common-sense man of business is afforded additional arguments as often as these papers [containing reports of Commercial Teachers' Conventions] come out why he should discriminate against commercial college graduates whenever he needs more clerks.

"Vannant" must have been asleep, lo, these many years. We are informed that the Packard School and the Long Island Business College, not to mention other well-known New York institutions, have standing orders from many of the foremost business concerns of the metropolis to send to them the bright graduates of these schools. The Chase National Bank has eighteen Packard graduates and the Fifth Avenue Bank has thirteen, while the officers of nearly a dozen of the great financial institutions of New York have recently sent, and are now sending, their children to get the training this school offers. What kind of discrimination is this? To quote further from "Vannant":—

OF "BLUFFING" BUSINESS MEN.

> It [the United States] is the only nation in which the commercial college has found root and grown, and the business public of which has allowed itself to be bluffed into supporting the institution in the belief that it was doing a good work.

Here are some of the commercial school graduates that have been thus "bluffed." Possibly "Vannant" may have heard of some of them:—

John A. McCall, President New York Life Insurance Company.
Timothy L. Woodruff, Lieutenant-Governor of New York.
James G. Cannon, Vice-President Fourth National Bank, New York.
S. S. McClure, publisher McClure's Magazine.
Frank A. Munsey, publisher Munsey's Magazine.
Herbert H. Swasey, Secretary Fifth Avenue Trust Company, New York.
Mr. Werner, publisher Modern Culture.
Warren F. Kellogg, Treasurer America Company, publishers New England Magazine.
Cornelius Doremus, President Germania Insurance Company, New York.
Jas. B. Duke, President American Tobacco Company.
Henry A. Patten, Cashier Astor Place Bank, New York.
Wm. B. Gennerich, President United National Bank, New York.
A. W. Teele, C. P. A., 30 Broad street, New York.
D. A. Keister, C. P. A., 88 Wall street.
F. N. Thompson, chief accountant U. S. Mint, Philadelphia.
Frank R. Blacklock, C. P. A., Baltimore.
Erastus Young, auditor Union Pacific Railway.
T. J. Foster, founder and manager of the International Correspondence Schools, Scranton, Pa.

COMMERCIAL TEACHING AND EXPERT ACCOUNTING.

But Vannant insists that commercial teachers are an ignorant, incompetent, superficial lot, because, presumably, they are not all members of the order of Certified Public Accountants. It is an outcropping of the spirit of jealousy that is present in every guild and profession. Simple matters are treated as if there were something occult about them. Arbitrary terms, such as "the going system," are used, and a fog of mysticism thrown about things not over-difficult for the average mind to grasp.

Teaching successfully in a good commercial school and serving acceptably as a public accountant are two entirely different professions, and few men have either the time or the peculiar combination of essential qualifications to excel in both these fields of laudable endeavor. But no doubt quite as many commercial teachers have succeeded as public accountants as there are public accountants who have become successful commercial teachers. The teacher in a commercial school must instruct his students in the elementary matters more or less directly related to the work of the public accountant, but primarily bearing upon the work of the prospective business man. These duties do not require an intimate nor even a general knowledge of the work of the public accountant. Nevertheless there are many commercial teachers who are more or less familiar with this work, and more are continually becoming familiar with it. But it is not from such men as "Vannant" that they are getting it. They willingly, gladly acknowledge their obligations to such men as Dicksee, Dawson, Norton, Whinney, Whatley, Lewis, Broaker, Haskins and Hardcastle; and they spend their hard-earned money freely for publications containing the writings of these men. But these men do not break forth into derision and contempt when they have occasion to speak of commercial schools and commercial teachers. They are sane, dignified, well-poised men who, as President Haskins, of the New York State Society of Certified Public Accountants, put it at their annual dinner recently, "mind their own business."

THE COMMERCIAL TEACHER IN BUSINESS.

"Vannant" says:—

> Where is the commercial teacher that is really wanted in the business office, or who could, in fact, hold his place in the practical work of business if perchance he once made his entrance therein?

Here are a few of him:—

Geo. B. Cortelyou, secretary to the President, formerly a teacher in the Walworth Business Institute, New York.

Edgar M. Barber, accountant in the office of the Appraiser, Port of New York (a member of both the American Association of Public Accountants and of the New York State Society of Certified Public Accountants), formerly for several years a teacher in the Packard School.

Theodore C. Search, for many years the able President of the Na-

PUBLIC LIB. ASTOR, LENOX AND TILDEN

tional Association of Manufacturers, formerly a teacher in the Quaker City Business College, of Philadelphia.

A. R. Haskin, auditor of the American Cigar Company, formerly for thirty years a teacher in the Eastman School, Poughkeepsie.

John R. Sparrow, C. P. A., chief expert in the Controller's Office, New York City, and one of the three state examiners of Certified Public Accountants—one of the most notable municipal accountants in this country—was for many years a teacher in the Long Island Business College, Brooklyn, N. Y. He received his commercial instruction and his start in public accounting from Mr. H. C. Wright, C. P. A., President of the Long Island Business College at the present time.

Mr. Sparrow says:—

I have your letter of the 14th inst. I spent fifteen years of my life in the work of commercial education, and left the school-room to pursue actively my profession. In the practice of it I have had a fair measure of success. I do not agree that commercial teachers are, as a class, impracticable. On the contrary, some, yes many, men of my acquaintance are filling honorable and responsible positions who are indebted for their early training to the commercial school.

The wide-awake, up-to-date commercial instructor and practicist, not a mere theorist, is the best mentor a youth can have. He can and frequently does arouse in the lad an interest in public and economic affairs by unfolding before him a view of the whole realm of commerce, which he can obtain in no other way. The lad studies and "does" business, and the great difficulty is to keep him restrained, so eager is he to get out and do battle for himself. It is not to be wondered at that bright men, whose lines were laid in the commercial schools, are to be found in the front rank in every walk of life throughout our broad land. So much for the boy. A teacher bright enough to fire a boy in matters commercial very often chafes at the confinement of the school-room and longs for larger worlds to conquer. It is not surprising then that many men prominent in business and the professions began life as commercial college instructors.

O. M. Powers, of Chicago; L. L. Williams, of Rochester; W. H. Sadler, of Baltimore; H. T. Loomis, of Cleveland; John R. Carnell, of Albany; E. P. Heald, of San Francisco; A. J. Rider, of Philadelphia, and H. E. Hibbard, of Boston, are a few, among many, well-known business school teachers who have won wealth and influence in business pursuits aside from the reputation they have made as eminent commercial teachers.

This is but an infinitesimal part of the evidence that might be adduced to show how unjust and baseless are the charges and insinuations contained in "Vannant's" malicious attack.

Agrees with Vannant

The May issue of the Practical Age has just reached us, and Vannant receives a liberal amount of attention in its pages. "Quiet Observer" gives two pages and a half to Vannant's criticism, and the article in general is, as might be expected, a refutation of that writer's argument. We regret that lack of space prevents our publishing this article, but we cannot resist quoting the following from it as showing that although "Quiet Observer" may, generally speaking, disagree with Vannant, he cannot help but agree with the latter's statement that commercial teachers are not fully equipped for the teaching of accountancy and bookkeeping:

From "Quiet Observer," in The Practical Age.

"On the other hand I am still of the opinion that commercial teachers should be more ambitious to equip themselves so that they would not be "out of place" in the company of professional accountants, but that they could enter into intelligent participation and appreciation of the professional work of higher accountancy. Both accountants and commercial teachers could find much of mutual interest and help from intermingling one with the other; and the exchange of information and the respect and esteem which would come to both parties from an appreciation of the work each is doing would be of incalculable benefit.

A New Orleans Critic

Mr. Geo. Soule, of New Orleans, La., the well-known writer on bookkeeping and accounting subjects, has the following reply to Vannant in the Practical Age:—

From George Soule, New Orleans, La.

I have read the article signed by "Vannant" in the March issue of COMMERCE, ACCOUNTS & FINANCE. I regret exceedingly the attack he has made upon a class of educational institutions so confessedly pre-eminent in good work as the commercial schools of the United States and Canada. The attack is aggravated by the fact that it is made under a nom de plume thus enabling the attacking party to secrete himself from view and to attack his victim from the rear. Surely, in this case, one of the two conditions must obtain. The writer of this article either must be profoundly and criminally ignorant of the facts of the subject about which he writes, or must state what he knows to be absolutely untrue, when applied to commercial schools as a class. In either case, his statements are ungenerous, unjust and malicious, if not libelous.

His criticisms of the views of particular parties, and of specified papers, are in order, as he has a right to discuss these matters; but even here, he should accord the professional courtesy that is due an honorable adversary.

I regret that I cannot command the time to consider all of the statements of "Vannant," relating to commercial colleges as a class. I will briefly consider two of his misstatements.

1. Referring to the publication of the proceedings of Commercial Teachers' Conventions, in the opening of his attack, "Vannant" says:—

Unfortunately, however, for the good name of the profession, the proceedings of the conventions are published in full in the official journal, and thereby the practical, hard-fisted, common sense man of business is afforded additional arguments, as often as these papers come out, why he should discriminate against commercial college graduates whenever he needs more clerks.

"VANNANT'S" ERRONEOUS STATEMENTS.

Regardless of the facts, and in violation of the divine injunction that, "Thou shalt not bear false witness against thy neighbor," "Vannant" has made the above erroneous statement, which is replete with libelous premises, and from which he deduces false conclusions. In its unqualified form, it is cunningly false, for the inference is that all business men are opposed to commercial schools and discriminate against their graduates when they need clerks and bookkeepers. Moreover, it implies that all students of all commercial schools are incompetent as clerks and bookkeepers. Notwithstanding the unjust statements of this writer, the truth is, that business men, by tens of thousands, do employ commercial school graduates as clerks and bookkeepers. And in many thousands of cases, they make direct application to commercial sechools for clerks and bookkeepers. Furthermore, many of the nation's most prudent and successful business men indorse and commend the properly-organized commercial schools. This they do, because of the efficient service of their employees who are graduates of these schools.

2. Let us again hear "Vannant". In the last sentence of his first "thunderbolt" he says, in referring to the publications of commercial college conventions:—

By these proceedings he is afforded a conception of the mass of misinformation with which the deluded youth of the land who go to these institutions are loaded, and which, of course, must be removed before they are worth anything to themselves or others in real business life.

With Shakespeare, I exclaim,

'Lord! Lord! how this world is given to lying."

It would indeed be difficult to make, in a sentence of equal length, more malicious misstatements than are contained therein. Under a nom de plume the writer of the sentence in question assassinates truth in every line, and malevolently attacks commercial schools as a class. For, be it remembered, the charge is made against all commercial schools and against all commercial school graduates.

With due respect, I asked with Cassius:—

"Now in the names of all the gods at once,
Upon what meat doth this our Caesar feed,
That he is grown so great?"

Were "Vannant" dogmatically to assert that the rose has no sweetness, that the rainbow has no color, his statements would be no more enigmatical than are his quoted declarations on the value of commercial school training. It is conceded by business men, presumably quite the equal in ability and integrity of "Vannant," that commercial schools are of practical commercial value. They are annually qualifying thousands of the young men and the young women of the country to perform good office work, in all the fields of business. With the knowledge acquired at the commercial schools the young people earn an honorable living, and, together with the increased knowledge gained by experience, they rise to higher positions in the business world. Thus commercial schools are not only serving the young men and the young women of our country, but they are at the same time serving the business community by supplying it with more competent employees than could possibly be obtained in any other way.

VALUE OF COMMERCIAL SCHOOLS.

Commercial schools as a class, occupy before the community the same position as the medical schools, the law schools, etc. None of the schools claim to teach all there is known, or to be known, in its respective field of knowledge. They do not claim that their graduates are renowned experts. Profound knowledge results from proper school training and from long years of study and experience. Commercial schools claim that they give a good course of study, involving the general principles of the business sciences, with many practical applications thereof. They claim that the course taught gives the student far more knowledge of bookkeeping commercial law, business arithmetic, correspondence, penmanship, etc., than he could possibly acquire in an equal time in the capacity of an apprentice or a clerk in business. The graduate of the commercial school, like the graduate of the medical school, or the graduate of the law school, is prepared to enter upon his chosen profession. And by continued study, by experience, and by the proper devotion to duty, he will rise according to his native ability, to the higher planes of accounting or to the rank of a successful business man.

It is well known that among all classes of schools in the various departments of education, there are some that are low grade, inefficient, and unworthy, in all respects. But this fact does not justify the indiscriminate anathematization that "Vannant" hurls upon the whole class of commercial schools.

"From the same soil the fairest flowers bloom and the foulest weeds grow." And thus it is that among the many good commercial schools, there are some of the unworthy kind. A poet, not "Vannant," tells us that,

> "Wherever God erects a house of prayer,
> The devil always builds a chapel there."

And because of the devil's action, "Vannant" would indiscriminately demolish both structures. And so, too, wherever there is evolved or projected anything that is good, there will arise the imitation and the counterfeit. Hence, again, the need of wide discrimination on the part of our unknown enemy, when discussing the merits or demerits of commercial schools.

There are several other points of "Vannant's" article equally as fallacious, unjust, and vindictive as are those I have considered, but I have not time to discuss them. The animus pervading the whole article, the direction given to the shafts of ridicule, and the application made of the many conclusions, evince the fact that there is something behind the man, in the dark. Something that is not seen on the surface. The wriggling of the writer is too vigorous to be accounted for except on personal interest. It seems clear that his desire is to injure the commercial schools of the country, but his motive for doing this is not so clear. For many years this nom de plume writer has been unfavorable to commercial schools and to college education. Does he wish to destroy the commercial schools and erect on their ruins a better class of schools? Or has he a school of his own that he wishes to benefit by misrepresenting other institutions of a kindred nature? These are pertinent questions which, I hope, will induce the unvaliant "Vannant" to come forth from his secret vantage ground and answer. If the standing of commercial schools in this country is to be decided from the viewpoint of "Aut Vannant aut nullis," I confess to a feeling of curiosity as to the identity of this self-heralded critic.

Business Subjects in Current Literature

The present may be defined as the magazine age. The number of periodicals is scarcely to be counted. The readers of the magazines are almost beyond estimate. To glance over a month's issues of the magazines of the world will give one a good idea first of what the thinking writers are investigating and considering, and second, of what the readers of the world are perusing.

Anyone who goes through a considerable number of the magazines which can be picked up at any news stand, or more especially anyone who loks through an index of the periodical literature of the month will be impressed with the amount of space that is given to what may be designated as business and financial subjects. Those who have made it a practice of examining the month's literature from this point of view, for some time past, cannot fail to be impressed with the increasing space and attention that are being devoted to what may be distinctively pointed out as business articles. If still another argument were necessary to prove that this is the business age it could be found in the mass of literature that is being devoted to business topics.

BUSINESS IN THE PERIODICALS.

For the moment we deal only with periodical literature. The same conclusion would be reached if we took up month by month the books which are brought out by the great publishers of the world. If we inquire into the book business we shall find that while romance, history and poetry are by no means being neglected, still the number of works which treat in a theoretical or practical way of business subjects are very numerous, and in fact that such volumes are becoming more and more numerous as time goes by. Name any business topic that you please, and strange indeed will it be if a number of magazine articles of recent date cannot be produced bearing upon it, and still stranger if a book by some competent author cannot be put in evidence, wherein the subject is ably if not exhaustively treated.

Somewhat in support of these broad assertions, but more particularly to give the reader a closer view of what is really going on in this direction, let us glance, by title only, at a few of the business articles which have appeared in the current literature of the month just gone. In presenting this view we shall not attempt to arrange the articles or their titles upon any definite basis, but rather to mass them for the reader's attention more in the sense of showing their quantity and the diversity of the subjects considered than for any other purpose. As we proceed it will be found that the subjects discussed which are of interest to the business man, and which, accordingly, may be classed as business literature, cover everything from the exploration of unknown countries to the exploitation of new branches of science. We shall find that some of the articles are written in a semi-popular style as though an apology were needed for introducing a business topic in a magazine. On the other hand, a very considerable number of the articles referred to bear no apology upon their face, but instead dive at once into the practical details of their subjects as though the reader were an expert. The one class of articles takes the reader as a beginner, the other approaches him as one who has had experience and therefore needs no coddling with respect to the subject discussed.

PRACTICAL PAPERS ON BUSINESS SUBJECTS.

In the Century Magazine H. Le Roux discusses "New Trails in Abyssinia." In Chambers's Journal, R. Thirsk presents an interesting article entitled, "Oil Rivers of West

Africa." In Country Life in America, W. T. Mann learnedly discusses, "Reclamation of a Barren Apple Orchard," thus giving to farmers and others something practical as well as profitable to think about. Emma Carleton, in the Century Magazine, discusses "The Making of Bottles," and A. Fisher, in the International Studio, presents an article, the third in series, upon "Enameling upon Metals."

The Bankers' Magazine of New York, as might be judged from its title, discusses various questions that are of importance to banks and the financial world, but many of its articles in their interest go beyond this comparatively narrow circle of readers. For example, A. M. Barrett tells in this magazine about "The Paying Teller of a Bank," and invests his subject with a peculiar interest. Another writer discusses "The Redemption of Bank Notes," therein bringing to the attention of the general reader various facts that are of interest to others than those immediately associated with the banking business. R. W. Jones, Jr., discusses "The National Banking System," while still another article, number six in series, takes up the question of "Banking Rules and Customs." Nor do we look alone to the periodicals distinctly banking in character for the discussion of banking subjects from the standpoint of the average business man. In Gunton's Magazine, G. Gunton discusses "Our Banking and Treasury System." In the London Banker's Magazine "Banking in Great Britain and Ireland during the year 1901" receives special attention.

In the American Review of Reviews, C. Snyder discusses "Captains of Industry" in a way to command the attention of every reader. The same author in Harper's Magazine presents a consideration of Fifty Years of Synthetic Chemistry." E. P. Watson, in the Engineering Magazine, discusses "The Modern Practice of Boiler-Making." In the Popular Science Monthly, F. Emory discusses "Our Foreign Commerce in 1901." In the North American Review, W. Wendlandt presents "A German View of the American Commercial Invasion." In the American Law Review, E. W. Moore presents an article on "Voting Trusts in Corporations," and thereby brings to the attention of business men various features of a question that is up for consideration at the present time in all directions.

In the World's Work "The Transformation of the Great American Desert" is attractively discussed by R. F. Hill. In Chambers's Journal appears an article entitled "The Practical Side of Commercial Education," in which points are presented that are of interest to all who are giving the least attention to educating the young man for business. In the North American Review, W. R. Harper discusses "The Trend of University and College Education." In Education, F. Waldo presents a number of ideas relating to the "Educational Use of the Typewriter."

G. H. Gibson, in the Engineering Magazine, presents an article treating on "High Tension Electric Power Transmission." In Cassier's Magazine, A. Reuterdahl discusses "Electric Storage Batteries." In the same periodical is an article by J. Wright, on "Electric Energy Direct from Coal."

In The Forum, from the pen of H. W. Horwill, is an article entitled, "Is England being Americanized?" In the Engineering Magazine K. Falconer discusses "The Factory Office as a Productive Department," and in so doing introduces many ideas of practical value to the manufacturer and to the superintendent of factories as well. In The Forum, J. P. Irish presents a question which is of more than ordinary interest at the present time to the people of certain localities of this country, "Shall the United States Lease its Grazing Lands?"

In the Contemporary Review E. J. Dillon discusses "The Commercial Needs of the Empire." In the Political Science Quarterly E. R. A. Seligman discusses "Economic Interpretation of History."

"New York's Comptroller, Edward M. Grout," is the subject of a carefully-prepared review from the pen of D. E. Fralick, published in the Anglo-American Magazine. In Munsey's Magazine G. E. Mitchell writes on "The Redemption of Our Dead Lands," a practical inquiry into the general question of irrigation. In The Forum W. A. Robertson discusses an "Amendment of the Interstate Commerce Act." In Gunton's Magazine the editor inquires "Is Labor Insurance Feasible?" In the American Review of Reviews G. H. Cushing presents "A New Factor in Lake Shipping." In Chambers's Journal is an article entitled "London's Great Landlords."

By way of reviewing a transaction which is soon to be celebrated in a great exposition, M. Farrand, in the American Historical Review discusses "Commercial Privileges of the Louisiana Purchase Treaty."

In Cassier's Magazine S. M. Vauclain presents thoughts on "Education for the Machine Trades." In McClure's Magazine H. H. McClure discusses "Marconi's Messages to Mid-Ocean." In Pearson's Magazine E. Mayo presents the "Story of Montana." In the Journal of Political Economy, A. D. Adams discusses "Municipal Gas and Electric Plants in Massachusetts." In Pearson's Magazine W. R. Stewart enlightens the public with regard to the "New York Subway." In the North American Review, R. L. Cutting discusses "Northern Securities Company and the Sherman Anti-Trust Law." In the National Geographic Magazine J. Page presents a very interesting article on the subject of "Ocean Currents." In the Pall Mall Magazine J. G. Leigh enlightens the public with respect to the "Panama Canal." In the World's Work, O. K. Davis presents "Results of the Pan-American Congress." In Harper's Magazine H. De Windt gives particulars of a "Land Journey from Paris to New York."

It is very natural as things are at present that the Philippines should occupy a prominent place in current literature. Thus we find in The Outlook, by F. W. Atkinson, and in the Arena, by A. R. Jurado, articles on "Education in the Philippines." In the American Catholic Quarterly Review B. J. Clinch discusses a "New Language Despotism." In the Century Magazine H. C. Rowland presents the "Seamy Side in the Philippines," and in the Political Science Quarterly C. C. Plehn discusses "Taxation in the Philippines."

THE LITERATURE OF PHOTOGRAPHY.

Photography, which is a branch of art or science making unprecedented progress at the present time, calls out a number of interesting articles from the pens of able writers in various magazines. Photography has an important bearing upon business in various directions, but we shall refer to articles on this subject by title only, simply giving the reader an idea of the attention that is being given to it without stopping to locate the articles or indicate their authors.

Among the literature of photography in the current month may be mentioned the following: "Architectural Photography," "Carbon Difficulties," "Verrill's Process for Producing Photographs in Colors," "Construction of a Dark Room," "Timing Development," "Deterioration of Lenses," "Reducing the Opacity of Negatives," and "Toning Bromide Prints." From this list it will be seen that the writers do not hesitate to take the general public into their confidence, they are not addressing their own class as experts, but, instead, are writing for general information.

In Outing, H. S. Babcock discusses "Manufacture of New Breeds and Varieties of Poultry." In the World's Work, M. G. Cuniff discusses "Social Clubs for Railroad Men." In the Political Science Quarterly, W. C. Ford discusses the "Economy of Russia." In Ainslee's Magazine, J. C. Speed writes of the "Development of Savings Banks." In Munsey's Magazine, H. W. Wilson discusses "The Race for Sea Power." In the World's Work, A. Goodrich presents a consideration of "Expansion of the American Shipyard." In the Engineering Magazine, C. U. Carpenter discusses "Money-Making Management for the Shop." In Gunton's Magazine, J. A. Baldwin discusses "Evils of Southern Factory Life." In the International Journal of Ethics, J. A. Ryan inquires into the "Ethics of Speculation." In the Anglo-American Magazine, E. Maxey writes concerning "Our Steel and Iron Industries." In the International Monthly, E. Steinbach discusses "Government Control of Trusts." In the Journal of Political Economy, R. R. Kuczynski discusses "Wheat Growing in Argentine." In the Popular Science Monthly, J. H. Gore gives particulars concerning "Draining of the Zuider Sea."

As remarked at the outset, this is not presented as a complete survey, nor yet has it been arranged with any other idea than of giving the reader a notion of what popular writers and popular magazine publishers are doing in the direction of bringing to the attention of the general reading public live business questions of the day. This attention to business at the hands of writers and publishers is a favorable sign, and one in which every business man should feel a deep interest. Business is the issue of the day, and the more the general public knows about business the better it will be for all business interests.

Convention of the National Municipal League

The eighth annual meeting of the National Municipal League and the tenth national conference for Good City Government opened in Boston on Wednesday, May 7, under auspicious conditions. There were present delegates from almost every part of the nation. A carefully prepared program had been issued, which included an attractive list of subjects to be discussed by men having national reputations in civic affairs. Provisions were made for meetings in both Boston and Cambridge, with a banquet at the Hotel Brunswick as the concluding number.

MR. CAPEN'S REMARKS.

The exercises were begun on Wednesday afternoon by an address of welcome delivered by Samuel B. Capen, chairman of the committee of arrangements. In the course of his remarks the speaker said, with regret, that the Boston Municipal League, which did such good work for many years, has not been efficient of late. Its neglect, however, was, in a sense, glossed over by the statement that much of what had been mapped out in its original constitution had since been carried forward by other organizations which had sprung into existence. Special reference was made to the work of the Twentieth Century Club, the Public School Association, the Citizens' Association and others. Continuing, the chairman said that while it is believed that Boston has long been the best governed of any of the large cities of the Union, and while that city has not had the great public scandals that have appeared in other places, yet, nevertheless, there is need in Boston of a quickening of the civic conscience, which is essential to all reform movements.

This opening address was followed by remarks by F. H. Myers on behalf of the Governor of the State, who was not present, and likewise by His Honor, Mayor Collins, who said he had snatched a few moments from a very busy day in order to say a word of welcome to an organization which has his most hearty sympathy.

A YEAR'S MUNICIPAL PROGRESS.

In the way of real business the first address was by Clinton Rogers Woodruff, of Philadelphia, secretary of the National Municipal League, entitled "A Year's Municipal Progress." In this address, which was of considerable length, the speaker rapidly traced what has been done in various directions. Specific mention was made of affairs in Boston, Philadelphia, Chicago, Cleveland, San Francisco and St. Louis. Attention was also given to what has been done in certain states, and mention was particularly made of the League's influence in the matter of the Alabama Constitution, and how certain of the League's recommendations have been accepted by the Virginia Constitutional Convention, which is now in session. The speaker asserted that the question of franchises to the public service corporations continues to absorb a large share of public attention. Special reference was made to the recent developments in St. Louis, also to the overwhelming vote in favor of municipal ownership at the Chicago election, which recently occurred. The speaker asserted that the work of establishing the merit system in cities proceeds with substantial, if not rapid progress. Taking the schools out of politics was also discussed at some length. In conclusion, the secretary said: "The concrete achievements of the past year have been more numerous and far-reaching than in any preceding year. In whatever direction we may look we see grounds for encouragement. Advances have been made in all quarters, and while the municipal problem is still a difficult one to solve, and calls for the exercise of the wisest statesmanship and the greatest public spirit, yet we are persuaded that it can be solved.

Other papers read at the first session included one by Edward J. Parker, Quincy, Ill., president of the American Park and Outdoor Art Association, on the accomplishments of that organization. Prof. Charles Zeublin, of Chicago, president of the American League for Civic Improvement, spoke on what had been accomplished by that association.

The second day's session was largely devoted to the franchise question and the referendum. Hon. E. A. Philbin, former District Attorney of New York, read a paper entitled "A Non-Partisan Administration." The Philadelphia situation was explained by Charles Richardson, of that city, vice-president of the Municipal League. The Boston situation was explained by E. H. Clement, editor of the Boston Transcript. The Chicago situation was covered by a paper read by George C. Sikes, of the Street Railway Commission of Chicago. Professor E. W. Bemis, superintendent of the Cleveland Water Works, described how the franchises and referendum are provided for in Cleveland.

UNIFORM MUNICIPAL ACCOUNTING.

In the afternoon session of Thursday a report of the Committee on Uniform Municipal Accounting and Statistics was presented by Dr. Edward M. Hartwell, chairman of the committee and statistician of the City of Boston. In the course of his remarks Dr. Hartwell traced the growth of the American city. He said: "It has emerged slowly and incompletely from the stage of development typified by the country town. American cities have multiplied rapidly in numbers and grown enormously in size. As a class American cities have been less successful than municipal corporations in some other parts of Christendom in adapting themselves to the demands of modern life. They appear to be suffering from retarded development." In the course of this speaker's remarks quotations were presented from some of the early works relating to municipal organizations, going back as far as 1649. He also quoted from the corporation act with regard to accounts, as follows:—

"Every city shall keep books of account. It shall also make stated financial reports to the State comptroller or other fiscal officer in accordance with forms and methods prescribed by him. Such reports shall be certified as to their correctness by said State comptroller, etc., or by some competent person appointed by him. They shall be printed as a part of the Public Documents of the State and submitted by the State comptroller or other fiscal authority to the Legislature at its next regular session. Such reports shall contain an accurate statement in summarized form and also in detail of the financial receipts of the city from all sources, and of the expenditures of the city for all purposes, together with a statement in detail of the debt of the said city at the date of said report, and of the purposes for which said debt has been incurred." The State comptroller or other fiscal officer is also authorized to examine into the affairs of the financial department of any city within the State, and is required to certify through his agents the correctness, after a special audit, of the reports of the several city comptrollers.

This address was followed by one on the "Application of Uniform Accounting," by Harvey S. Chase, of Boston. Mr. Chase's remarks included a description of the work done with regard to municipal accounts in Boston, Baltimore and in other cities. Reference was also made to the important work conducted by Haskins & Sells, of New York, under contract, for the City of Chicago.

THE CITY A BUSINESS CORPORATION.

Lawrence Minot, president of the Bureau of Statistics of Boston, spoke on "The City as a Business Corporation." In the course of his remarks Mr. Minot defined the foundation of government as follows: "To supply those things which are used in common and which must be paid for by general contribution." Emphasizing this, he said: "Some things fall inevitably into this class, and by government, good or bad, it is the only agency which can supply them. The majority of our wants, as, for instance, schools, water supply, bridges, libraries, hospitals, can be supplied in some measure by private enterprise. If the government is wisely and prudently administered, it can supply these wants far better and far more economically than private enterprise. Essentially, therefore, the city government is a labor-saving machine, an agency whose reason for being is the economy it affords." Concluding this train of thought, he said, "Good government lays at the foundation of our industrial activity and of our personal comfort."

At the evening session of Wednesday, Charles J. Bonaparte, of Baltimore, addressed the meeting on "Honest Government;" J. H. MacFarland spoke on "A Lesson to Smaller Municipalities." This address was illustrated with stereopticon views, and was local in character. The improvements of Harrisburg, as the speaker explained, were begun about a year ago as the result of a popular movement.

At the meetings on Friday addresses were delivered on the New York situation by Dr. Albert Shaw, editor of the Review of Reviews; on the "Pittsburg Victory," by George W. Guthrie, of Pittsburg, and on "Charter Legislation in New England," by Professor J. H. Beale, of Harvard University.

The election of officers resulted as follows:—

President, James C. Carter, of New York; vice-presidents, Charles Richardson, of Philadelphia; Samuel B. Capen, of Boston; Thomas N. Strong, of Portland, Ore.; H. Dickson Burns, of New Orleans, and Edmund J. James, of Chicago; secretary, Clinton Rogers Woodruff, of Philadelphia; treasurer, George Burnham, Jr., of Philadelphia; executive committee, Charles J. Bonaparte, of Baltimore (chairman); Geo. W. Guthrie, of Pittsburg; Frank N. Hartwell, of Louisville; George W. Ochs, of Philadelphia; Harry A. Garfield, of Cleveland; Hector McIntosh, of Philadelphia; William P. Bancroft, of Wilmington; William G. Dow, of Brooklyn; Dudley Tibbits, of Troy; D. L. D. Granger, of Providence; John A. Butler, of Milwaukee; Oliver McClintock, of Pittsburg; E M. Thresher, of Dayton; Joseph T. Alling, of Rochester; John Scudder McLain, of Minneapolis; Harrry B. French, of Philadelphia; Edward B. Warren, of Brookline, and the general officers named above.

THE WORRIES OF THE RICH

Those of us who are not overladen with the wealth of this world will take comfort from the following article. Bishop Potter recently addressed the Yale students on the subject of wealth and its cares. This is what the New York Mail and Express has to say about the address:—

"Bishop Potter, being a wise and appreciative man of his period, declares the new doctrine of justice to the rich. For a long while we have been wasting sympathy upon that camel with the needle's eye task. Some archaeologists tried to soften our sorrow by explaining that the eye in question was only the name of the narrower city gates, to pass which the ships of the desert had to reef sails to the extent of stooping and squeezing a little. That seemed a well-meant but far-fetched effort at consolation, and it did not soothe. We continued to feel it a duty to sympathize with any creature burdened with a difficulty as great as that of the rich man striving heavenward, even though the animal were that inane, hump-backed, loose-lipped brute known to Tommy Atkins by the appropriately foolish name of 'oont.'

"He can now go stick his silly head fast in the needle's eye as soon as he chooses. Since Bishop Potter has spoken we know that there is no Biblical denunciation of wealth—only the improper administration of great gains or inheritances. We shall not attempt to match texts with the noted prelate, who does not speak without the support of his ripe learning. His opening lecture to Yale students was an eminently practical recognition of present-day conditions, and if it jarred somewhat upon the non-millionaire layman's memories of Christ's teachings, that, in itself, may constitute a tribute to the superior clearness of Bishop Potter's vision.

"One thing no man doubts: Bishop Potter is sincere and courageous. He tells a blunt truth when he says in effect that the average of human happiness among slaves is sometimes higher than that of the average life of the city toiler. But he does not make that an argument for the re-establishment of what Carlyle called "the brass collar period." He knew well that in the case of slavery the practical advantages were far overbalanced by the ethical ills. We may be pardoned for believing that the same comment of incompleteness may be applied to his defense of the down-trodden and oppressed men of money.

"We need not worry to any alarming extent, however, in the effort to allot just the proper amount of sympathetic friendship to our little brothers of the rich. They will eke out a fairly enjoyable existence without our spiritual or material support. Any right-minded pauper who hears a strayed millionaire weeping in the wilderness will go cheerfully to the aid of his stricken brother. But he will do well to wait until he is asked. Meanwhile it is a comfort to be rid of that camel.

THE VALUABLE COW

It strikes us that the products of the American cow are being too abundantly vindicated. Everything about her is soaring. Her flesh goes up a cent or so every day now; her porterhouse steaks cost a dollar and a half. The milk which she yields brings, when carefully gathered by conscientious dealers, bottled in pretty glass jars, decorated with blue labels, and supplied to the consumer in such a way that all danger of contamination is scientifically prevented, about ten cents a quart, against the three and four cents that our good old pre-microbian milkman used to furnish it for, says the Mail and Express. Everybody knows that there is nothing like the leather that she, and more particularly her hopeful son, the calf, yield. And now her butter, established in its full rights by relief from competition with the oleomargarine product of her male relatives, has soared up to forty cents a pound, even at this genial season when she goes out to grass and increases her yield.

If the value of the American cow's produce continues to go kiting in this extraordinary fashion, there will soon be no living with her. Already, in her velvety pasture, she has adopted a high and mighty attitude toward the city dweller who strays her way. She refuses to recognize the right of the still more peculiar goddess of our worship, the American girl, to precedence, especially if the girl carries a red parasol. She takes the right of way herself. Gentility may go through the gate after she, the cow, has passed on, in imperial if not maiden meditation, fancy free. Is not she the queenly creature that all America bows down to?

There is no telling where the cow will land, if she continues her mad flight. Verily, the dictum of Mother Goose concerning her sky-vaulting accomplishments, is being justified.

NOT IN IT

Teacher—Johnny, hcw did you get your coat torn and your eye blackened? Now, tell me the truth; weren't you in a fight?

Johnny—No, teacher. There was a fight, but, honestly, I wasn't in it for a minute.—Exchange.

WAYS TO GET OUT

"I've got a grand scheme, old man, and I'll let you in on the ground floor."

"H'm! Are there any exits?"—Puck.

COMMERCE ACCOUNTS & FINANCE

A Monthly Magazine of Higher Business Education and Practical Administration. Acknowledged Authority in the Profession of Commerce and Consistent Advocate of Methods Up to Date and Above the Table.

J. C. LINCOLN, Editor.
FRIEND PITTS, Jr., Circulation and Advertising.
E. R. KITTREDGE, Business Manager.

COMMERCE, ACCOUNTS & FINANCE CO., Publishers,
25 Pine Street, New York.

Published Monthly. Subscription $1 a Year in the United States, Canada and Mexico. Other countries $1.50. Postage prepaid by the Publishers. In the absence of specific orders to stop at the end of the subscription term the paper will be continued and a bill sent. Entered at the New York Postoffice as Second Class mail matter.

* * *

That there is an art of teaching no one who has given even casual attention to the subject of education can deny. That those who are natural teachers or who have been drilled in methods of teaching, are better able to teach than those who have never acquired skill in conveying to others what they know, is something that very few would attempt to gainsay. That which is at all remarkable among the facts encountered in investigating the general subject of teaching is the intolerance that at once dominates the man who has taken a few lessons in the art of teaching or who has been a pupil of some school of pedagogy. His egotism even goes so far as to cause him, in some cases, to assert that a disciple of pedagogy is per se a better teacher than any one else ever can be, even though the said disciple has no real knowledge of the subject to be taught, while the other man may be overflowing with information concerning it.

*

Talking with such a one, it is found almost impossible to make him believe that a wide gulf exists between that which is taught and that which is practiced. When, for example, you assert that such is the case with respect to various office and business matters, he will look up into your face with all the guileless surprise of a blue-eyed child and say, "Why, of course, there is no such gulf, because we know how to teach, and as teachers we do not create a gulf." The practical man of business, however, well knows the existence of such a gulf, and therefore he intelligently and by habit carefully discriminates in hiring his office help, against the pupils of such teachers. When it comes to putting his own son at school he still further discriminates and selects, if perchance he can find such a place, a school wherein the teachers, whatever may be their pedagogic qualifications, are yet practically acquainted with the subjects that they attempt to teach.

*

The reader may think that all this is only opening up an old and threadbare subject, namely, the difference between theory and practice. Such, however, is not the case. As a fact, there is no difference between correct theory or science and correct practice. The one goes hand in hand with the other. On the other hand, there is a vast difference between the science or practice that is taught and that which prevails in the business world. Until teachers realize that no matter how able they are as teachers in the abstract, still it is essential to know practically that which they teach, there will remain the gulf above referred to, and further, as time goes on it will become wider and wider. Said such a teacher to the writer not long since, "Why, I am perfectly able to teach the game of football or the game of baseball, if required; but, to save my life, I couldn't play either of them." We can imagine the youth who is enthused over football or baseball, as the case may be, profiting by the teaching of this pedagogue! We can see the baseball and football men of the country running to this professor for expert assistance in winning the next match games!

*

How is it in the realm of surgery? How is it at a clinic? Does the man who teaches surgery successfully know nothing about surgery? Does he recognize any difference between surgery as it is taught and surgery as it should be practiced? Would he allow one of his pupils to go forth into the world, even though it is only into the hospital world, to practice surgery who had never seen an operation, and who had never studied the expert manipulations of the able surgeon in charge? Scarcely. Why then should business men in the education of their sons, private secretaries and clerks in general be held up by those who say: "You do not need a practical man to teach bookkeeping; you do not need an expert accountant to teach accounting. All that you do need is a teacher. Further, this teacher does not require a practical acquaintance with his subject. It is entirely sufficient if he is a teacher. Practical men cannot teach, and teachers do not need to be practical men. Indeed they would lose if they were practical." Such a one in the exuberance of his egotistical self-complacency will scarcely admit, what to every business man must be a foregone conclusion, that if the highest ability in teaching was combined with the largest fund of practical information and actual experience along the lines that are to be taught, the ideal would be reached. In reply to such a suggestion he says: "Stuff and nonsense! All that you need is a teacher. A real teacher can teach, whether he knows anything about his subject or not."

*

Some are born teachers. Others by hard effort acquire the ability to teach, and still others by stress of circumstances have teaching thrust upon them. Sorry is the lot of that youth, say we, who is placed under the instruction of a mere teacher, however great his ability at imparting information, who has no fund of practical knowledge to draw upon. The situation can be compared only to a pump located in a dry well. It may be a splendid pump, but work the handle as much as you will, there is no flow of water. Wind there may be, and therefore, completing the simile, we realize how, from the standpoint of practical men, many teachers are pumping wind when they should be pumping something else.

*

The reader may exclaim at this point, of what interest is all this to him. Assuming that the reader is a business man, the answer is easy. It is everything to him. The business man, to make use of a colloquial expression, is paying the freight. He is paying for the schools that are pumping wind when he should have, as the result of his expenditure, schools which impart real instruction. He is paying for the education of his son, his secretary or his clerks, as the case may be, the full, round price, and yet he is getting a service that is altogether inferior. The one who pays the bills is as a rule entitled to the goods which the bills call for. There is at present a non-delivery of the goods specified in the documents, not because those who run the schools are intentionally dishonest, but because in their blind egotism they are not able to discriminate between mere wind and something of real use. There has been a breeding in-and in among the pedagogues, and this physiological or mental sin has proceeded until their state of mind has become seriously abnormal, and yet the poor business man continues to pay the freight. It is high time he commenced to check his invoices and to demand the real goods, the notions of the pedagogues to the contrary notwithstanding. It is high time that business men asserted themselves in this most important matter of education and secured that which is justly their due and that for which they have been patiently paying all these many years.

The question of wage distribution is becoming almost as important as that of wage-earning. It is not enough, according to certain organizations among mechanics, that they shall have such and such hours and such and such rates of pay, but in addition the payment for work done must be made in certain ways and at certain hours, and always in the employers' time. In all that organized labor has so far done with regard to wage distribution it would seem that progress in method has been entirely ignored by the letter of the resolutions that have been passed, and by the efforts that have been made from time to time to secure legislation It would seem that the working man in conventions assembled fails to perceive that the world has moved and that business, for most excellent reasons, cannot be transacted at the present time as it was transacted in some of the days gone by.

*

An instance in particular is the controversy that has been more or less in evidence in one of the towns in central Massachusetts the past few weeks. In this case the workmen are objecting to the payment of their wages in the form of checks upon a local bank. So far as the facts of the case have reached us, it does not appear that there is any question as to the responsibility of the bank on which the checks are drawn, nor yet of the company whose checks have been delivered in payment of wages. Instead, the workmen merely assert that a check is not money, and that they must have money instead. On the face of it this is very plausible, but has any one who is a party to this discussion stopped to think how little real money we ever see in business transactions?

*

Take from your pocket, dear reader, the roll of bills that you have there, and examine them with the thought in mind that you are looking at money. As a fact you will find that the said bills are merely checks issued by the United States Government or some of the national banks. Bills issued by the United States Government read as follows: "The United States will pay to the bearer" five dollars or ten dollars, as the case may be. In the case of gold certificates issued by the government the language is as follows: "There have been deposited in the Treasury of the United States (twenty dollars) in gold coin, repayable to the bearer on demand." The currency issued by the national banks is also in the form of checks, and reads as follows: "The ——— National Bank will pay ten dollars to bearer on demand."

*

The checks issued by manufacturing concerns in paying their employees are, as a rule, made payable to bearer. Instead of being issued in denominations of five, ten or twenty dollars—that is, in amounts of even dollars—each one is made to cover an amount of weekly wages. In the community in which these checks are issued they pass current, and there is no difficulty in using one of them in the purchase of groceries or any article of family or personal requirements. It is asserted that it is no more difficult for the holder of such a check to obtain change for it than it would be to obtain change for a twenty-dollar bill, or of any other bill of a larger denomination than the amount of the purchase.

*

We have been particular in calling attention to these facts only in the sense of anticipating answers to some of the objections which are likely to be offered to the wage check proposition. One of these is as follows: "The ordinary workman feels that it is rather a mean proposition to ask any man to take a check in payment of goods or even to ask a friend to cash a check." As already shown there is no reason why this sense of meanness should be felt, except by the working man who would feel mean to present to a storekeeper a $10 promise to pay, signed by the treasurer of the United States or the president and cashier of a national bank, and ask change for it because a check of that kind is precisely what the working man would receive if he was not paid in real money, namely, in gold or silver.

*

That which is being entirely overlooked by those who object to the uses of checks even in wage distribution or in payment of any other kind, is that modern business demands the greater and greater improvement in forms of exchanging credits. About all that is done in business nowadays is to obtain a credit at some bank or other. The American people are not like others, namely, a money-using people. Instead we have learned to depend upon checks for practically everything except minor financial transactions, and the trend of events is in the direction of a still greater employment of interchanges of credits rather than a diminution of the custom. Wage earners in accepting checks only do what the tradesman has long been accustomed to doing. They get a credit at the bank in exchange for their labor, and this credit they are able to transfer to others as occasion arises.

*

In justice to the working men it should be mentioned that they have offered less objection to the plan of wage payments by checks than have others with whom they have come in contact. The professional labor agitator gets in his fine work as usual. It may not be quite as convenient to the retail dealers to take checks from workmen in payment of their accounts as it would be to receive from them government or bank bills. They, however, are not complaining, and their grievance, if they have any, is one of such slight proportions as to make it unworthy of the attention that is apparently being given it by those interested in stirring up contention. The suggestion in the case which we have quoted above is that a statute be enacted making it compulsory upon the part of employers to pay in money instead of checks. If such a measure should become the law the question would then arise, what is money and what is a check, for it might be that nothing short of gold and silver would be construed to be money under the terms of the bill, and this, we take it, is not what is really wanted.

* * *

Vannant does not contribute to this issue of COMMERCE, ACCOUNTS & FINANCE, but our readers must not think that he has ceased to contribute for all time. On the contrary, from what we know of Vannant and his personality, we feel sure we shall hear from him often and that what he says will be said plainly and will be very much to the point. His comments on the meeting of the Federation of Commercial Teachers' Association, which meeting was held in St. Louis last December, have been warmly, not to say hotly, received by commercial teachers in general. Vannant was not complimentary, and he aroused the wrath of the teachers, some of whom have already replied, and others, we understand, are preparing replies which, they believe, will confound their critic and upset his logic.

*

We publish some of these replies in this issue of COMMERCE, ACCOUNTS & FINANCE. They are worth reading, because the ideas of the other fellow are always worth reading, no matter whether we agree with him or not. The tone of the replies varies; some of them are written in a conservative and judicial spirit, others are tinged with a bitterness which would seem to indicate that the writers have been hit in a sore spot. Of one thing our readers may feel assured, that is, that Vannant will not sit silent under rebuke. He is a hard fighter, and when he reads these replies will undoubtedly reply in his turn. As we have said before, we do not always agree with everything that Vannant says, but we think that his comments deserve consideration, and think that all commercial teachers, good, bad or indifferent, may read them with profit. COMMERCE, ACCOUNTS & FINANCE aims to be fair, and is willing to publish the arguments of both sides, provided they are arguments and not mere vituperation.

* * *

Andrew Carnegie, who has recently sailed from New York to take up residence again at Skibo Castle, has, according to dispatches in the form of a press interview, undertaken to console Great Britain in the matter of the ship combine. Incidentally, he says that he has reformed by retiring from business. If we were to criticise this last statement we might be tempted to quote as apropos to the situation: "Satan finds some mischief still, for idle hands to do," and inferentially suggest that it were safer for this country, if not the world at large, that this man of affairs should remain in business than attempt reform at the terrible risk involved. However, what we set out to do was to present for the reader's consideration Mr. Carnegie's own words. Here they are, and they contain some ideas that will seem new to many who peruse them:—

"To combine the shipping traffic is a big order. There is free right of way on the ocean, and the tramp steamers are always with us. The merger may give regular daily sailings to passengers, which would be advantageous. I am not in the navigation syndicate, having retired from business and reformed, so I cannot advise you as to the exact character and bearing of the combination. But, in my opinion, the combine is purely a matter of money making. There is no question of patriotism in trade. It does not care a fig for a flag. It is dividends that count. Of course, every citizen worth a cent wishes his own country to be first in everything, and a peaceful, industrial victory is the only genuine one. Victory through war generally costs more than it is worth. If Great Britain continues her costly wars for shadowy ascendancy in distant parts, and the United States develops her industrial army, there can be only one result—Great Britain will have the shadow and the United States the substance. I think there is no prospect of early legislation permitting British-built ships to get American register. The Americans have resolved to become a maritime power commercially and will soon be able to build ships quite as cheap as Great Britain. At first the shipping combine will give the present owners higher returns, but regarding the latter prospects I do not care to prophesy. The people of the United States are in sympathy with the new trust. It seems to be a triumph for the flag and all patriotic Americans, which means all Americans, are naturally pleased. Besides, we have an idea that we can manage all things better than anyone else, and there is ground for this belief."

*

"Daily sailings," "dividends vs. patriotism," "industrial victory vs. war," and "American management" are among the suggestive items which this extract from the interview serves to make prominent.

* * *

A monthly paper issued ostensibly in the interest of the dry goods trade and which has reached the dignity of Volume 1, No. 8, presents in a recent issue what purports to be an interview with Mr. A. O. Kittredge, who is described as "Secretary of the American Institute of Bank Clerks," "President of the Account, Audit & Assurance Company, Ltd.," and "a lecturer" in connection with the New York University School of Commerce. The editor and proprietor of the paper is Max Jagerhuber. The article states that a reporter called to get Mr. Kittredge's views concerning the best manner of carrying forward the work of its credit office department. "The Credit Office," it should be remarked in passing, is the title of a department or division in the editorial pages of the periodical referred to. It would seem from the article referred to that Mr. Kittredge did not respond to the interview in a way to please either the editor or the manager of this department, and for this reason or some other he is given customary treatment. We quote:—

"In response to questions he—Mr. Kittredge—had the ready reply that 'it is not possible to make an issue of credit reporting,' the plain implication being that the matter is without public interest, and therefore does not contain news worthy of painstaking and thorough reporting. It was doubly plain that at least one professional expert had no facts to offer as to the best manner of achieving a better credit news organization, and our reporter turned away with a firmer conviction that the remedy cannot proceed from those who are unconsciously trading on a want without supplying it. The trouble with men like A. O. Kittredge is, that they see in the accounting and auditing field a means of livelihood only, and are unable to detect therein a moving principle whose application would set in order the entire credit organization, from the most trivial merchandise credit through to the bank clearing house, where the responsibility centers. Mr. Kittredge and others like him do useful work, each in his way, but a larger want is now compeling attention, and it can only be supplied by men who are able to grasp the fact that a credit news system has appeared whose various centers have to be brought into practical working relation through the method of co-operation. * * * Again, an increasing demand exists for a universal auditing center, whose audit will come to be as well known as the center from which the familiar postage stamp proceeds, but this auditing center will never be built up by men holding to the narrow viewpoint of A. O. Kittredge."

*

All this is interesting, and it gives us pleasure to present it to the readers of COMMERCE, ACCOUNTS & FINANCE, thereby assuring these sentences a wider circulation than would be possible for them to have in the pages of the paper from which they are taken. We are authorized by Mr. Kittredge to say that on the occasion referred to he declined to be interviewed, that he did say in answer to a single interrogatory that it did not seem to him possible that "credit reporting in a newspaper could be made an issue in which credit men and business men in general would feel a great interest." He still adheres to these views. What has been thrown into the article in the way of commenting upon Mr. Kittredge's engagements and connections is entirely gratuitous. It is news to him that he has ever aspired to the creation of a universal auditing center. He does admit that he is in the accounting business for the money there is in it, just as he supposes that Max Jagerhuber is publishing a paper for the money that can be made out of it. The motives of both gentlemen would appear to be commendable and in no wise opposed to public interests. Meanwhile we search in vain through the paper before us, and more particularly through the credit office department, for anything like up-to-date credit news or credit reporting.

* * *

The editors desire copies of the following issues of COMMERCE, ACCOUNTS & FINANCE: January 5, 12, 19, 26, February 2, 9, 16, 26, March 2, 9, 16, 23 and October 1, all of the year 1901. We will enter a two months' extension of the subscription of any reader for each copy of any or all of these issues sent us. Copies must be clean and in a readable condition.

THE CARNEGIE INSTITUTION

In the current number of Scribner's Magazine President Gilman, of the new Carnegie Institution, at Washington, details more fully than has previously been done the exact purpose of that enterprise. It is not to be a "university," he says, nor yet a memorial to George Washington. It will, however, we believe, put a pretty effectual stop to the purely sentimental movement that has had a Washington memorial as its object. It will, moreover, if the wishes of those entrusted with its development are carried out, meet the purpose of "the father of his country" in a much more generous measure than he could ever have dreamed. "Its chief function," says President Gilman, "is the encouragement of research," something in which this country has been a little backward as compared with some of the countries of Europe. "No branch of knowledge is to be excluded from the scope of the trustees." To this end they will "ask the counsel of the wisest of our countrymen. They will not all be famous men. Some are known only in very limited circles. They are the quiet men who are working out great problems free from the observation of all except those whose studies are kindred." Scholars, both in this country and in Europe, will be laid under tribute. "It will not be long before a group of astronomers are asked their advice in astronomy; of biologists in biology; of chemists in chemistry; of economists in economics—so on through the alphabet of the sciences." This will simply be the basis for subsequent arrangements, but the foundation is a broad one, the broadest perhaps yet reached in this country. The institution is intended to furnish the educational capstone for the country, not to fit scholars for finishing touches abroad, but to draw scholars from abroad over here.

The Negotiable Instruments Law*

By THOMAS B. PATON

When a Person is Deemed an Indorser—Liability of Irregular Indorser—To Whom is Indorser Liable?

NOTE.—As enacted in New York, the Negotiable Instruments Law is divided into nineteen articles as follows:—

1. GENERAL PROVISIONS (Sections 1—17)
2. NEGOTIABLE INSTRUMENTS: Form and Interpretation (20—42)
3. Consideration (50—55)
4. Negotiation (60—80)
5. Rights of holder (90—98)
6. Liabilities of parties (110—119)
7. Presentment for payment (130—148)
8. Notice of Dishonor (160—189)
9. Discharge (200—206)
10. BILLS OF EXCHANGE (210—215)
11. Acceptance (220—230)
12. Presentment for acceptance (240—248)
13. Protest (260—268)
14. Acceptance for honor (280—290)
15. Payment for honor (300—306)
16. Bills in a set (310—315)
17. PROMISSORY NOTES AND CHECKS (320—325)
18. Notes given for patent rights (330—332)
19. Laws repealed: When takes effect (340—341)

The provisions of the law naturally fall under four general classifications.

a. General Provisions.
b. Negotiable Instruments in General.
c. Bills of Exchange.
d. Promissory Notes and Checks.

The text of the law is the same in all the states (with some slight exceptions which will be noted), but the numbering of the sections, and in some states of the articles, is not uniform. There is, however, the same continuity of articles and text, except that in some instances, "General Provisions" follow, instead of precede, the remainder of the act. By following this course of study with reference to the New York act, as above outlined, the reader in each state can apply the same to the law of his own state.

We have, under sections 110, 111 and 112, considered the respective liabilities of maker, drawer and acceptor of negotiable instruments; and we now come to those sections which provide the liabilities of indorsers, as well as of those who negotiate an instrument by delivery.

The contract of a maker, drawer or acceptor, is one that is attendant upon the issue of an instrument, while that of an indorser is one that is connected with its negotiation. The subject of negotiation, it will be remembered, was considered fully under Article IV. We there learned that an instrument is negotiated when it is transferred from one person to another in such manner as to constitute the transferee the holder thereof; that if the instrument is payable to bearer it is negotiated by delivery; if payable to order, it is negotiated by the indorsement of the holder, completed by delivery. We also there learned how an indorsement is made; considered the two broad classes of indorsement, special and in blank, by which an "order" instrument is transferred; saw when an indorsement is restrictive, the purposes served by restrictive indorsements, and their effect; and also considered those classes of indorsement termed "qualified" and "conditional" and the nature of such special classes.

Negotiation by indorsement and delivery, or by delivery alone, according to the character of the instrument, having been thus provided for in Article IV., the sections to which we now come are designed to provide the contract and liabilities of those who indorse and deliver negotiable instruments by means of the various forms of indorsement, heretofore set out, as well as the liabilities of those who transfer negotiable instruments by delivery alone. In addition to those who transfer negotiable instruments by indorsement and delivery, or by delivery alone, there is another class of indorsements, known as irregular indorsements, which are made by persons who are neither makers nor payees, not for the purpose of transferring an instrument, but to give it additional credit. The nature of the obligation and liability assumed by such irregular credit signers, or backers, is also provided in the sections which we now approach:—

PERSON DEEMED INDORSER.

Section 113. When Person Deemed Indorser.—A person placing his signature upon an instrument otherwise than as maker, drawer or acceptor, is deemed to be an indorser, unless he clearly indicates by appropriate words his intention to be bound in some other capacity.

Here, we see, is the definition of an indorser, which is broad enough to include, not only those who, being payees or indorsees, indorse in the regular way for the purpose of transferring the instrument to another, but also all those persons who, not being payees or indorsees, place their names upon the instrument otherwise than as maker, drawer or acceptor, not for the purpose of transferring it, but to give it additional credit. Throughout the act the general policy has been to make all irregular parties indorsers; and, although an irregular indorsement is generally placed upon the back of the instrument, still, if a person, not maker, drawer or acceptor, should write his name across its face, he would under the provisions of the act be an indorser and incur liability as such. It will be observed that section 113 does not limit the contract of indorsement to the back of the instrument. It reads: "A person placing his signature upon an instrument otherwise than as maker, drawer or acceptor is to be deemed an indorser," not merely "upon the back of an instrument," but "upon an instrument" which includes both front and back. In connection with this provision we will recall subdivision 6 of section 36, prescribing rules of construction where the language of the instrument is ambiguous, which provides: "Where a signature is so placed upon the instrument that it is not clear in what capacity the person making the same intended to sign, he is to be deemed an indorser."

We thus see clearly the meaning of the provision of section 113 that "a person placing his signature upon an instrument otherwise than as maker, drawer or acceptor, is to be deemed an indorser." If a man signs as maker, drawer or acceptor, he is liable in those respective capacities; but if he places his signature otherwise upon the instrument, either front or back, he is an indorser and liable as such. In so placing his signature he may be (1) a regular payee or indorsee; or (2) not a regular party to the instrument, being neither maker, drawer, acceptor, payee or indorsee.

Speaking of irregular parties, we have already said that the general purpose of such signatures is to give the instrument the additional credit of those who sign. But sometimes a man, not a regular party, will sign his name upon an instrument with no intention to give his credit or to be bound thereon. For example, he may do so merely to identify an indorser. Nevertheless, under the act, his unexplained signature will obligate him as an indorser to any holder in due course, for section 113 does not deal with the motive underlying an irregular signature—the mere signing the instrument otherwise than as maker, drawer or acceptor, no matter what the motive, makes the signer an indorser, so far as the commercial world, which cannot look beyond the face into hidden motives, are concerned.

So far we have dealt with just a plain signature upon an instrument, otherwise than as maker, drawer or acceptor. We will now observe the concluding language of section 113 that by such a signature the person signing it is to be deemed an indorser "unless he clearly indicates by appropriate words his intention to be bound in some other capacity." In other words, if he does not desire to incur liability as an indorser, he may indicate by appropriate words in connection with his signature the nature of the obligation he does assume. If he should write above his signature "I guarantee payment of this note," he would then not be liable as an indorser, but as a guarantor, the nature of which contract is not defined by the Negotiable Instruments Law, but is determinable by the rules of the law merchant.

LIABILITY OF IRREGULAR INDORSER.

In the above we have seen what an indorser is under the Negotiable Instruments Law. We now come to Section 114, which defines in detail the liability of an irregular indorser:—

Section 114. Liability of Irregular Indorser.—Where a

*Republished from the Banking Law Journal by permission. Copyright, 1899, 1900, 1901 and 1902, by T. B. Paton, all rights reserved. To be revised and published in book form by the author.

person, not otherwise a party to an instrument, places thereon his signature in blank before delivery, he is liable as indorser in accordance with the following rules:—

1. If the instrument is payable to the order of a third person, he is liable to the payee and to all subsequent parties.

2. If the instrument is payable to the order of the maker or drawer, or is payable to bearer, he is liable to all parties subsequent to the maker or drawer.

3. If he signs for the accommodation of the payee, he is liable to all parties subsequent to the payee.

This section provides the law governing irregular indorsements. Such indorsements upon negotiable instruments are frequent in the world of commerce. A desiring money or credit from B, makes his note payable to B's order; but A's personal responsibility is, alone, insufficient to induce B to advance the money or credit to A. C, the friend of A, agrees to back him, and C's responsibility being sufficient, C will sign his name upon the back of the note which A has made to B. So signed, A will deliver the note to B and obtain the consideration desired. This is probably the most common form of the transaction. Sometimes it is B, the payee of a note already made and delivered to him by A, who desires credit from some one else, and the irregular signer will indorse his name to enable B, the payee, to negotiate the note; or the same thing, though more rarely, is true of an indorsee of the payee, who cannot further negotiate the note unless some friend, not a party, will also indorse it.

This transaction of lending credit to makers and payees of promissory notes by means of irregular indorsements has, in the past, come up before the courts of many states in numerous instances, and the judicial rules of liability of irregular indorsers which have been declared, have differed widely in different jurisdictions. In many states where C indorsed A's note payable to B, before delivering to B, C was held liable to B as a joint maker; in other states a guarantor; in other states he was liable to the payee as first indorser, requiring demand and notice; in still other states, a second indorser, not liable to the payee at all, unless the payee could prove that it was C's intention to be liable to him. It is unnecessary to pursue further the intricacies of conflict. The Negotiable Instruments Law, wherever it prevails, provides a uniform rule of liability of an irregular indorser, particularized according to the character of the instrument and transaction—that is to say, where a person, not otherwise a party to an instrument—that is, not maker, drawer, acceptor, payee or indorsee in the regular way—places thereon his signature in blank before delivery, he is liable as indorser. This is the general nature of the liability—indorser, not joint maker, not surety, not guarantor, but indorser.

TO WHOM LIABLE?

To whom is such indorser liable? And under what circumstances? Three specific cases are pointed out.

1. If the instrument is payable to the order of a third person, he is liable to the payee and to all subsequent parties. This is the case of a note made by A to the order of B, indorsed by C, and afterwards delivered to B. The indorsement in blank by C, we will remember, must be made "before delivery." In this case C is liable to B and to all subsequent parties as indorser.

2. The second case is where the instrument is made payable to the order of the maker or drawer, or is payable to bearer. Here he is liable to all parties subsequent to the maker or drawer. A draws a note payable to his own order, and indorses it. Before delivery to B, C indorses it. C is liable as indorser to B, and subsequent parties; he is not liable of course to A.

3. The third case is where A has made and delivered his note to B, the payee. Then, before B negotiates it, C signs for B's accommodation. Here C is not liable to B, the payee, although he may have indorsed it before B has indorsed it, but is liable to all parties subsequent to the payee. We will assume, further, the case of a note made and delivered by A to B, indorsed and delivered by B to D, and then indorsed by C for the accommodation of D. Here C would be liable only to parties subsequent to D. The condition "before delivery," upon which is based the liability as indorser of one "not otherwise a party to an instrument, who places thereon his signature in blank before delivery," we understand to mean "before delivery to the subsequent parties to whom such liability runs." An instrument might be delivered two or three times through successive hands before an irregular signer would indorse to enable the last holder to further negotiate it. The irregular indorsement at this stage would not be, of course, before the first delivery, but would be before delivery by the last holder or indorsee for whose accommodation the signature was made.

SECTION 115.

Section 115. Warranty Where Negotiation by Delivery or by Qualified Indorsement.—Every person negotiating an instrument by delivery or by qualified indorsement warrants:—

1. That the instrument is genuine and in all respects what it purports to be.

2. That he has a good title to it.

3. That all prior parties had capacity to contract.

4. That he has no knowledge of any fact which would impair the validity of the instrument or render it valueless.

But when the negotiation is by delivery only, the warranty extends in favor of no holder other than the immediate transferee. The provisions of subdivision 3 of this section do not apply to persons negotiating public or corporate securities other than bills and notes.

Having seen, by section 114, the liabilities of irregular parties to a negotiable instrument, we have, in section 115, provision for the liabilities of those regular parties who transfer an instrument by qualified indorsement, and of those persons who transfer an instrument by delivery. We learned by section 68 that a qualified indorsement constitutes the indorser a mere assignor of the title to the instrument; that it may be made by adding to the indorser's signature the words "without recourse," or any words of similar import; and, further, that such an indorsement does not impair the negotiable character of the instrument. Those who negotiate an instrument by a qualified indorsement, and those who negotiate an instrument by delivery, stand in a class peculiar to themselves with reference to their liability upon the instrument. General indorsers, as we shall presently see, must pay the instrument, if it is not paid by those primarily liable to pay it, providing the necessary steps are taken to preserve their liability; but there is no such obligation upon those who transfer an instrument by delivery or by qualified indorsement. They merely transfer title to the instrument which retains its negotiable character, and if it is a perfectly genuine and valid instrument they are not concerned whether or not it is subsequently paid. But such persons are liable if there is anything wrong with the title or genuineness of the instrument; and just what they are liable for, or warrant, and to whom they are liable, is provided in section 115, above set out.

In the first place, they warrant (1) that the instrument is genuine and in all respects what it purports to be; (2) that they have a good title to it, and (3) that all prior parties had capacity to contract. As general indorsers also warrant the instrument in these three particulars, we shall postpone a particular statement of what is embraced by such warranties for our discussion of the next section, 116, which provides the liabilities of general indorsers.

The person who transfers an instrument by delivery, or by a qualified indorsement, also warrants that he has no knowledge of any fact which would impair the validity of the instrument or render it valueless. What fact might impair the validity of an instrument? Well, it might be void, because of usury, even in the hands of an innocent holder. If the transferor by delivery or qualified indorsement knew this there would be a breach of his warranty and he would be liable. If he, himself, was ignorant of its invalidity because of usury, then he could not be held. What fact might render the instrument valueless? Suppose the maker of a promissory note becomes hopelessly insolvent, and the payee, knowing this, should transfer it by qualified indorsement "without recourse;" or if the note was payable to bearer, suppose the holder, knowing of the maker's insolvency, should transfer it by delivery. In so doing he would be breaking his warranty that he has no knowledge of any fact which would render the instrument valueless. But if he is ignorant of such fact, then his transfer subjects him to no liability, though the instrument is in fact valueless because of the maker's insolvency.

Taking up the next paragraph of section 115, we see it relates to the persons to whom the warranties of a qualified indorser, and of a person negotiating by delivery, extend; and here we find a difference between the two. When the negotiation is by delivery only, the warranty extends in favor of no holder other than the immediate transferee. When, on the other hand, the negotiation is by qualified indorsement, there is no such limitation of the warranty provided; it runs to all subsequent parties.

The concluding paragraph of section 115 limits the application of subdivision 3, that a person negotiating an instrument by delivery or by qualified indorsement warrants "that all prior parties had capacity to contract," so that it shall not apply to persons negotiating public or corporate securities other than bills and notes. This limitation is designed to protect those who deal in and transfer municipal or corporate securities, from liability where it turns out that the securities have been issued without proper authority. For example, the legislature of a state may pass a law authorizing the town or city of so and so to issue municipal bonds, the proceeds to be applied to certain specified purposes. The municipality thereupon proceeds, under color of law, to issue and market its bonds, executed by the appropriate officials. Then, after the bonds, apparently valid, are upon the market and in the hands of various holders, some question may be raised concerning the constitutionality of the law which authorized the issue, and the courts being appealed to may finally decide the act which purported to authorize the issue, unconstitutional, with the result that the bonds are void, and the officials who signed them had no capacity to contract. To make the transferor by delivery of such bonds responsible as warrantor for this would be too great a hardship; hence the reason of the provision that the warranty that prior parties had capacity to contract does not apply to persons negotiating public or corporate securities other than bills or notes. It puts upon the investor in all such securities the duty of safe-guarding his own interests by seeing to it, before purchasing, that municipal bonds have been duly authorized, and that there is no hidden defect by reason of unconstitutionality of authorizing law, or other defect of procedure under a constitutional law, which will render the issue invalid, and the officials who sign them, without authority or capacity to make such contracts.

In the next number we will take up section 116, upon "Liability of General Indorser."

Financial and Commercial Books

GRACE'S HANDY BOOK FOR MAKING RAPID CALCULATIONS. Size, 8 1-4 x 5 1-4. Bound in cloth. Title printed in silver. 65 pages. Published by Wm. Grace.

The full title of this book is "Merchants, Bankers & Brokers Handy Book for Making Rapid Calculations, in all Branches of Commercial Requirements, Weights, Measures and Moneys." The volume contains a series of tables for calculating the price of wheat, corn and oat bushels in decimals, for converting cubic meters to cubic feet and cubic feet to meters, meters to lineal yards, superficial feet or square feet to cubic feet, decimal tons to avoirdupois pounds, and the like. To the busy office man who has a great deal of calculating to do, and particularly to the clerk in an export house whose work it is to reckon in United States money the amounts named in foreign invoices, these tables should be very valuable. They are quite complete, and undoubtedly their use will save time.

We quote the following at random from the examples in the back part of the book to show how Mr. Grace sets about solving a difficult problem:—

EXAMPLE NO. 7.

What will 3759. cubic feet, 6 inches amount to at 47 shillings 6 pence per ton of 40 cubic feet.

```
See Table No. 7                  3759.      93.9875
         6 inches equals           50        2.375
                                 -------   ----------
                                 3759.50    4699375
See Table No. 32 Decimal 40        25      6579125
                                 -------   2819625
                                 1879750   1879750             £      s. d. 1000
                                 751900    ----------
                                 -------£223.2203125 equals   223.    4  4  875
                          Tons,  93,98750
                                   40
                                 -------
See Table No. 27                                Tons. Feet. In.
  40. shilling equals 2,  93.39.50000 equals     93    39    6
   7 shilling equals   35
   6 pence equals      025
   ----              -----
                     2.375
```

THE CASE FOR THE FACTORY ACTS. Edited by Mrs. Sidney Webb, with a preface by Mrs. Humphrey Ward. Size, 7 3-4 x 5 1-4. Bound in red cloth. Cover and back title printed in black. 225 pages. Published by E. P. Dutton & Co. Price, $1.00.

This book, which is an American edition of an English work, deals with the question of factory legislation and with the effort to improve the condition in English factories. The instances given of the employing of little children in English factories makes heart-rending reading. It is true, as Mrs. Ward says in her well-written introduction, that the factory workers' lot is much improved and that compared to what it was before the passing of the great reform bill in 1833, it is almost a paradise. To give an idea of what the lot of the children in the factory must have been prior to the passing of this act, we quote the following testimony from the book:—

Listen to the children: "I am fourteen. I was going seven when I first went to work at a mill. It was at Holling's I began to get crooked. I wrought two years at Holling's. It will be better than three years sin' I got crooked." . . .

"I am going eleven. I lug baskets upstairs with bobbins. It's that made me crooked. Can't read. I have wrought in a mill going for four years. We wrought from six to half-past eight for a year or more."

Or to the mothers: "No, sir, I hope the hours won't be reduced, because we have hard work to live as it is. Well, the children are tired at night. The first bell rings at half-past four by the factory clock. They have 'em in by about five or half-past. They let 'em out at nights at half-past six. No time for breakfast or tea. I have trouble to waken them up. Oh! no, sir, I never beg 'em off, our comings in won't allow it. We can't give way to what they would like. Their appetite is not always good; one in particular fails—eleven years of age—the youngest."

Or again to the voice of a father, as he looks painfully through the winter twilight for his children's home-coming. "They have been gone to work sixteen hours now. I have a deal of trouble to get them up in the morning. I have been obliged to beat them to get them well awake. It made me cry to be obliged to do it."

But, as Mrs. Ward further says:—

The great work is not complete. There yet remains the sweated trades whose miserable secrets were unveiled by the last labor commission; the trades which still prey like parasitic growths on the life of the nation, which destroy the tailoress, the shirtmakers, or the nailmaker, working in what she calls her home, beyond the present reach of law.

The body of the book is made up of a series of essays by prominent men and women socialists of Great Britain, and deals with Factory Legislation, The Historical Development of Factory Acts, The More Obvious Defects in the Factory Codes, Colonial Developments in Factory Legislation, and Some Current Objections to Factory Legislation for Women.

The case of the worker in some of our "sweat shops" and factories here at home is bad enough, but it surely must be worse in England. Any student of human nature and any broad-minded person interested in sane socialism will find this book well worth reading.

CAPE COD BALLADS. By Joe Lincoln. Size, 8 x 5 1-4 inches. Bound in yellow cloth. Cover design in brown and gold. Illustrated by E. W. Kemble. 200 pages. Published by Albert Brandt. Price, $1.25.

There is an element of humanity about Joe Lincoln's "Cape Cod Ballads" that captivates people who have souls. The author's heroes of the seacoast are creatures of flesh and blood—not posing statues, nor misty water-colors—and his lighter characters, with their quaint vanities, reflect the true spirit of provincial Yankee life. "Cape Cod Ballads" are full of natural music, appealing alike to old and young, to lettered and half-lettered, and are a valuable contribution to American verse.

The illustrations by E. W. Kemble are what one might expect from this talented character artist. They really illustrate the verses, and that, as everyone knows, is somewhat unusual.

SOME QUESTIONS OF LARGER POLITICS. By Edwin Maxey. Size, 8 x 5 1-4. Bound in red cloth. Cover and side title in gilt. 136 pages. Published by the Abbey Press. Price, 75 cents.

The author of this volume, who is a D. C. L. and an LL. D. and whose portrait is published as a frontispiece, discusses public questions from his point of view with much clearness and rather interestingly. Some of the questions of larger politics with which he deals are, "Race Supremacy in South Africa, Anglo-Russian Relations, Election of United States Senators, The Eight Hour Day by Legislation, and The Natural Right of Self Government." To give an idea of the author's style, we quote the following from his essay on The Eight Hour Day by Legislation:—

> Having shown that the eight-hour day is not only economically possible but economically desirable, we will consider the question from the standpoint of physical health; and upon this phase of the question I perhaps cannot do better than to quote Dr. Richardson, who has summed up the matter very briefly and forcibly in the following words: "Muscular as well as mental kinds of work demand limitation of hours. Among those of us who have studied this subject most carefully there is, I believe, little difference of opinion. Taking it all in all, we may keep our minds on eight hours as a fair time for work. We may consider justly that a person that works hard and conscientiously for eight hours has, for health's sake, done what is near the right thing; and in some occupations the eight-hour rule is absolute for health."
>
> While the case for an eight-hour day is thus extremely strong from the point of view of physical health, it is even stronger from the standpoint of social health. If you compel men and women to work so long each day that they have little time and energy left for thinking, they will remain unthinking animals. Wider education is, at once, cause and effect of the eight-hour movement. In fact, the real force that gives vitality to the movement is a spontaneous longing for a brighter, fuller life, and a deep conviction that shorter hours of labor will serve this end. Men and women who toil for wages are growing tired of being only working animals. "They wish to enjoy as well as to labor; to pluck the fruits as well as to dig the soil; to wear as well as to weave." On all sides there is an expansion of life. New possibilities of enjoyment—physical, intellectual, social—are being more and more realized by the masses. Among all classes of laborers the demand for leisure is becoming keener, because leisure means more to them. At present, part of the laborers are overworked and have not time for enjoyment and culture; and the other part have no work, hence neither the means nor the spirit for recreation or education. The former are working anxiously, almost frenziedly, lest they should be thrown out of employment, and the latter look longingly for employment. Shorter hours would accord better with the interests of industry and, what is far more important, with the betterment of mankind. I am inclined to think that we may safely assume that the majority will be willing to admit that the long hours so generally worked in many trades inflict serious injury upon the social health of a community.

The book is of a han[illegible] size and clearly printed, [illegible] the paper is somewhat i[illegible] and the binding hasti[illegible]

THE NIGHT SIDE OF NATURE. By Catherine Crowe. A new edition with [illegible] introduction by Thos. J. Hudson, Ph.D., LL.D. S[illegible] x 5. Bound in red cloth. Back title gilt. 4[illegible] pages. Published by Henry T. Coates & Co. Price, [illegible]

Do you like ghost stories? If you do, and enjoy what boarding-school young ladies call the "creeps," you should read this book. Miss or Mrs. Crowe's volume was originally published in the middle of the last century, but this is a new edition with an introduction by Prof. Hudson, whose connection with the Society for Psychical Research and writings on the Law of Psychic Phenomena are well known. Titles of some of the chapters are: Allegorical Dreams and Presentiments, Warnings, Apparitions, Troubled Spirits, Haunted Houses, and so on. Psychical research is now receiving much attention from scientists, and that is why, we presume, this book has been re-issued. No ghost story, it would seem, was too improbable for Miss (or Mrs.) Crowe to accept at its face value, and yet when we read some of the apparently authenticated records of the Society for Psychical Research, we find some of her most astonishing cases paralleled. Therefore, it does not pay to dismiss such stories with a sneer. At any rate, whether one believes in ghosts or not, he will find "The Night Side of Nature" interesting reading. It is well bound and well printed.

A GOOD FOUNTAIN PEN

A fountain pen that will write and write continuously without splutter and without catching is a desirable fountain pen. A fountain pen that will contain a sufficient quantity of ink to last for a reasonable length of time and which will distribute ink through the pen upon the paper evenly is a valuable adjunct to every busy business man's vest pocket machinery.

The Mercantile fountain pen, manufactured by Aikin-Lambert & Co. is made of the best Para rubber, fitted with a gold pen of the first quality, and is simple in construction, easily interchangeable and fully guaranteed. The successful working of a fountain pen depends almost wholly upon the quality of the gold pen with which it is fitted. The pens in the Mercantile fountain pen, made by Aikin-Lambert & Co., who for nearly forty years have been one of the largest manufacturers of gold pens in the world and who have established a reputation, a high reputation, for making fine goods. The ink is distributed from the fountain evenly, and yet always with sufficient flow to insure both a fine line and the heaviest stroke that can be made with a pen. Rapid writers or slow writers will find the ink always at the point of the pen and flowing smoothly.

THE MERCANTILE FOUNTAIN PEN.

The Mercantile fountain pen is made in various mountings, from the full silver or gold mounted No. 1, 16 carat pen at $4.50, to the chased barrels No. 1, 16 carat gold pen at $1.50.

Thirteen varieties of this fountain pen in various chasings and with vari[illegible] gold, silver or pearl ornamentation, are quoted on th[illegible] list within the range of the prices quoted. Each [illegible]ry fountain pen, no matter what its chasings may [illegible]ipped at its "working point" with a 16 carat gold p[illegible] is the result of forty years of manufacturing of go[illegible]

Messrs. Aiki[illegible]rt & Co., 1 Maiden Lane, New York, are exceptional[illegible]quipped with a full line of gold pens, penholders, pen[illegible]s, and a great variety of novelties in all makes of m[illegible] gold and silver plate as well as solid metal.

The high char[illegible] the house is shown by the guarantee that is given wi[illegible]en sold by them: "This pen is fully guaranteed, sub[illegible]xchange if not satisfactory."

Puzzles for Office Men

$20.00 IN PRIZES

Everybody likes puzzles. That is a broad statement, but it is pretty nearly true. Many a man coming home tired from

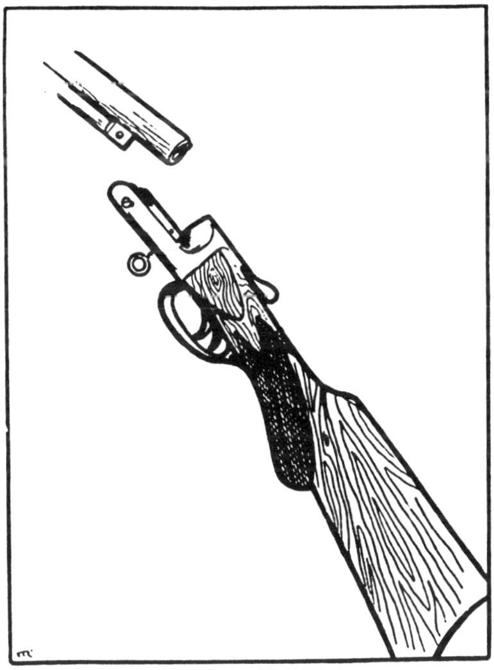

PUZZLE PICTURE NO. 1.

the day's work will spend an evening helping Johnnie decipher the cryptogram or solve the missing-word puzzle in

PUZZLE PICTURE NO. 3.

the current issue of the Children's Magazine. He may do this under the same pretext that he takes Johnnie to the circus, that of amusing the child, but in reality he does it because he enjoys it himself.

COMMERCE, ACCOUNTS & FINANCE, realizing that office men are much like other human beings, and therefore like puzzles, has arranged to publish a series of illustrated puzzles, beginning with this issue.

PUZZLE PICTURE NO. 2.

The puzzles will be printed in sets of four, and prizes will be awarded for essays upon the subjects which the puzzles represent. All the puzzles have to do with office work or

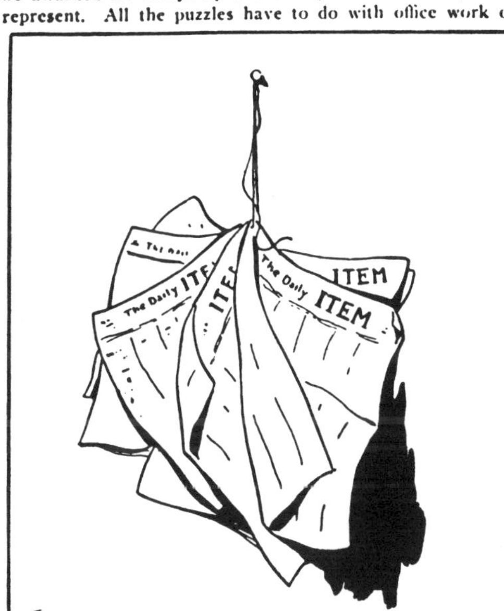

PUZZLE PICTURE NO. 4.

office fixtures. Those published in this issue are puns upon terms familiar to all accountants. For example, that in Fig. 1 is "Stock and Fixtures."

Each contestant is required, first, to correctly solve each

of the four puzzles; then he is required to write an essay, not exceeding two hundred words in length, upon the subject represented by each puzzle—that is to say, he must write four essays in all.

For the best set of essays a prize of ten dollars ($10) cash will be given. For the five next best sets yearly subscriptions will be given to THE BULLETIN, a semi-monthly magazine of the same size and general make-up as COMMERCE, ACCOUNTS & FINANCE, but devoted to the art and practice of banking. To any young man contemplating entering upon a business career THE BULLETIN is invaluable, being neither too technical nor too profound, but catering to the bank clerk rather than to the bank official. The regular subscription price of THE BULLETIN is $2 a year.

Each competitor in these contests will be required to enclose twenty-five cents for a three months' trial subscription to COMMERCE, ACCOUNTS & FINANCE. If the contestant is already a subscriber, this subscription will be sent to any non-subscriber named by him. Non-subscribers will, of course, send their own names. The twenty-five cents will not be applied to extend the subscription of one already a subscriber.

All communications must be addressed to the Puzzle Editor, care COMMERCE, ACCOUNTS & FINANCE.

School of Commerce, Accounts & Finance

Record of the Month's Work

Senior Class

RECORD FOR WEEK ENDING APRIL 4, 1902.

MONDAY. Easter Monday (Holiday).

TUESDAY.
8-10 Lecture on Banking, by Prof. Joseph H. Johnson.

WEDNESDAY.
8-9 Lecture on Business Organization and Administration, by Prof. A. O. Kittredge.
9-10 Lecture on History, Theory and Geography of Commerce, by Dr. Webster.

THURSDAY.
8-10 Review on Auditing, by Mr. Chas. B. Dean.

FRIDAY.
8-10 No lecture.

RECORD FOR WEEK ENDING APRIL 11, 1902.

MONDAY.
8-9 Lecture on The Relation of Finance to Accounting, by Dr. F. A. Cleveland, of the University of Pennsylvania.
9-10 Lecture on Surrogate Accounting, by Prof. Hardcastle.

TUESDAY.
8-10 Lecture on Banking, by Prof. Joseph H. Johnson.

WEDNESDAY.
8-9 Lecture on International Commercial Law, by Mr. Cleveland F. Bacon.
9-10 Lecture on History, Theory and Geography of Commerce, by Dr. Webster.

THURSDAY.
8-10 Lecture on Auditing, by Mr. Chas. B. Dean.

FRIDAY.
8-10 Lecture on Partnership Law, by Mr. William F. Walsh.

RECORD FOR WEEK ENDING APRIL 18, 1902.

MONDAY.
8-9 Lecture on International Commercial Law, by Mr. Cleveland F. Bacon.
9-10 Lecture on Surrogate Accounting, by Prof. Hardcastle.

TUESDAY.
8-10 Lecture on Banking by Prof. Joseph F. Johnson.

WEDNESDAY.
8-9 Lecture on The Commerce of the Pacific, by Hon. O. P. Austin, Chief of the Bureau of Statistics, United States Treasury.
9-10 Lecture on History, Theory and Geography of Commerce, by Dr. Webster.

THURSDAY.
8-10 Lecture on Auditing, by Mr. Chas. B. Dean.

FRIDAY.
8-10 Lecture on Partnership Law, by Mr. William F. Walsh.

RECORD FOR WEEK ENDING APRIL 25, 1902.

MONDAY.
8-9 Lecture on International Law, by Mr. Cleveland F. Bacon.
9-10 Lecture on Surrogate Accounting, by Prof. Hardcastle.

TUESDAY.
8-10 Examination on Banking, by Prof. Jos. H. Johnson.

WEDNESDAY.
8-9 Lecture on Government Bonds of the World, by Hon. F. A. Vanderlip, Vice-President of the National City Bank, Asst. Sec'y of the Treasury, 1897-1901.
9-10 Lecture on History, Theory and Geography of Commerce, by Dr. Webster.

THURSDAY.
8-10 Review on Auditing, by Mr. Chas. B. Dean.

FRIDAY.
8-10 Lecture on Partnership Law, by Mr. William F. Walsh.

RECORD FOR WEEK ENDING APRIL 30, 1902.

MONDAY.
8-9 Lecture on International Commercial Law, by Mr. Cleveland F. Bacon.
9-10 Lecture on Surrogate Accounting, by Prof. Hardcastle.

TUESDAY.
8-10 Lecture on Foreign Exchange, by Prof. Jos. H. Johnson.

WEDNESDAY.
8-9 Lecture on The United States Steel Corporation, by Dr. E. S. Meade, of the University of Pennsylvania.
9-10 Lecture on History, Theory and Geography of Commerce, by Dr. Webster.

Junior Class

RECORD FOR WEEK ENDING APRIL 4, 1902.

MONDAY. Easter Monday (Holiday).

TUESDAY.
8-10 Lecture on Manufacturing Accounts by Mr. George Young.

WEDNESDAY.
8-9 Lecture on Business Organization and Administration, by Prof. A. O. Kittredge.
9-10 Lecture on Transportation, by Mr. Shirley Eaton.

THURSDAY.
8-10 Lecture on Law of Sales, by Mr. Cleveland F. Bacon.

FRIDAY.
8-10 Lecture by Mr. H. M. C. Vedder.

RECORD FOR WEEK ENDING APRIL 11, 1902.

MONDAY.
8-9 Lecture on The Relation of Finance to Accounting, by Dr. F. A. Cleveland, of the University of Pennsylvania.
9-10 Lecture on Money and Credit, by Prof. Joseph F. Johnson.

TUESDAY.
8-10 Lecture on The Theory of Accounting, by Prof. A. O. Kittredge.

WEDNESDAY.
8-9 Lecture on Money and Credit, by Prof. Joseph F. Johnson.
9-10 Lecture on Transportation, by Mr. Shirley Eaton.

THURSDAY.
8-10 Lecture on Law of Sales, by Mr. Cleveland F. Bacon.

FRIDAY.
8-10 Lecture on Theory of Accounts, by Prof. Chas. E. Sprague.

RECORD FOR WEEK ENDING APRIL 18, 1902.

MONDAY.
8-10 Lecture on Money and Credit, by Prof. Joseph F. Johnson.

TUESDAY.

8-10 Lecture on Theoretical Accounting, by Mr. H. M. C. Vedder.

WEDNESDAY.

8-9 Lecture on The Commerce of the Pacific, by Hon. O. P. Austin, Chief of the Bureau of Statistics, United States Treasury.

9-10 Lecture on Transportation, by Mr. Shirley Eaton.

THURSDAY.

8-10 Lecture on Law of Sales, by Mr. Cleveland F. Bacon.

FRIDAY.

8-10 Lecture on Theory of Accounts, by Prof. Chas. E. Sprague.

RECORD FOR WEEK ENDING APRIL 25, 1902.

MONDAY.

8-10 Lecture on Money and Credit, by Prof. Joseph F. Johnson.

TUESDAY.

8-10 Lecture on Law of Sales, by Mr. Cleveland F. Bacon.

WEDNESDAY.

8-9 Lecture on Government Bonds of the World, by Hon. F. A. Vanderlip, Vice-President of the National City Bank, Asst. Sec'y of the Treasury, 1897-1901.

9-10 Lecture on Transportation, by Mr. Shirley Eaton.

THURSDAY. No lecture.

FRIDAY.

8-10 Lecture on Theory of Accounts, by Prof. Chas. E. Sprague.

RECORD FOR WEEK ENDING APRIL 30, 1902.

MONDAY.

8-10 Lecture on Accounting, by Mr. H. M. C. Vedder.

TUESDAY.

8-10 Class Review on Accounting, by Mr. Geo. E. Allen.

WEDNESDAY.

8-9 Lecture on The United States Steel Corporation, by Dr. E. S. Meade, of the University of Pennsylvania.

9-10 Lecture on Transportation, by Mr. Shirley Eaton.

Current Business Cartoons

The cartoonists have been more than usually busy the last month, and as politics are comparatively quiet, have devoted much of their skill to depicting in humorous fashion the hap-

Up to Congress.—New York World.

penings in the world of finance and commerce. The agitation against the so-called Beef Trust has been kept up to a high pitch by the press, and has resulted in President Roosevelt's asking Attorney-General Knox to investigate. There are arguments for both sides, but it seems to be the general complaint that the prices of meats are higher than they need to be and that some legislation controling these prices and the cornering of foodstuffs is necessary.

From the hundreds of cartoons on the subject of the war against the Beef Trust we reproduce three. The first is from the Chicago News, and pictures the Trusts as a bloated Goliath bearing a shield, upon which is depicted an octopus, charging forth to annihilate President Roosevelt, who, as David with his little sling, is prepared to give the giant what the original David gave the original Goliath. There have been several of these David and Goliath cartoons in the various papers.

The second of the Beef Trust cartoons is from the pencil of that veteran artist, C. G. Bush, of the New York World. No man in this country today is drawing better cartoons than is Mr. Bush. He hits the nail on the head every time, and, more than that, he knows how to draw. The ponderous weight of the Trust in this picture has crushed the retailer

This shows the careful attention the family cow will receive if beef continues to rise.—Chicago Record-Herald.

to the ground, and with one foot upon the Anti-Trust Law and with Competition chopped to pieces upon the block in front of him, the horned giant stands sharpening the knife of

Congress—"That's a very steep hill. Permit me to relieve you of this."—New York Herald.

greed and waiting for more victims. It is "up to Congress" to do something to curb his power.

The third cartoon is funny enough, and was drawn by Mc-

Cutcheon for the Chicago Record-Herald. The cow looks happy, as well she may. The family evidently regard her as their most valuable possession, and the old farmer and his son fan her with ostrich feather fans, while she feeds on the fat of the land, wears a crazy quilt blanket, sleeps on a mat-

A Modern David and Goliath.—Chicago News.

tress and has her portrait hung on the wall of the best parlor. For a really funny cartoon it is hard to beat McCutcheon.

The Cuban question—that is to say, the question of the reduction of the tariff upon Cuban goods—although partially settled, is still troubling the Cubans and the public men of this country. After a long and memorable fight it was decided to give Cuba 20 per cent reduction. This, the Cubans

Neptune Dethroned.—Chicago Tribune.

and their friends think, is too small, and Richards portrays their idea very cleverly and in his usual artistic manner. The polite gentleman, Congress, has relieved poor little Cuba of his very smallest burden, and leaves him to get up the hill with the balance of his load as best he can.

The announcement of the details of the consolidation of the Atlantic steamship companies, which consolidation was brought about by the wonderful Mr. Morgan, has of course afforded the cartoonists opportunity for many cartoons. Of these we reproduce two. The first, from the Chicago Tri-

John Bull "Seeing Things."—Minneapolis Tribune.

bune, shows Mr. Morgan emerging triumphant from the waves, placing the Sea God's crown upon his head and holding the trident in his hand. Poor old Neptune is dethroned and Mr. Morgan is ruler of the sea.

The second of the cartoons on this subject is from the

Shall it be a strike or back to the golf links.—Phila. North American.

Minneapolis Journal. The steamship consolidation has filled John Bull with alarm, and the British papers have given pages to the discussion of the subject and are "agin the government" for permitting the consolidation, which they regard as an absorption of British interests by American capital. John Bull is shown in the cartoon as "seeing things," and he certainly seems to be doing so.

The threatened trouble between the coal miners and the operators has of course been much cartooned, and of the clever pictures we reproduce one is from the Philadelphia North American. The cartoon, drawn at the time when "To strike or not to strike" was the all-absorbing question, explains itself. We are sorry to be obliged to add that, at the time of writing, war has been declared, and the strike is on.

A Businesslike Typewriter for Business Men

A typewriter that a business man uses in his daily work for the writing of his business letters and the typing of the literature of his office cannot be too good. It cannot be too well made nor can it work too smoothly. A cheap machine is too likely to get out of order, and the investment of even a small amount of money in such a typewriter is folly.

There are a number of good typewriting machines in the market and an investment in one of these is generally satisfactory, and a buyer feels, to use a popular expression, that he is getting his money's worth. This is particularly the case when he buys the Smith Premier typewriter. The desire of the Smith Premier Typewriter Co. always has been to make the very best typewriters offered on the market. In its catalogue the company says that it never has claimed perfection. Instead of claiming perfection it has been continually at work seeking improvement. Year by year the work is getting more difficult, because, in the late models perfection is well-nigh attained. It is the policy of the Company to have every department well officered, and every position in each department filled by a man expert in his particular line. A rigid system of part and machine inspection has been in force since the very early days of the Company's history. The aim has been high and continually increasing with the strong public approval.

Of course the essential and material part of the typewriter is its printing mechanism, and the printing mechanism of the Smith Premier machine is so good, so well made and so conveniently arranged as to be very near the perfection that the Company disclaims. It is almost indestructible, being made of the very best steel and hardened on all working points. It consists of a series of type bars in a circle, with the type at their free ends and so pivoted that they will all strike at a common printing point. Perfect alignment is thus assured. The type bars are mounted on hard steel conical bearings, 1 5-8 inches apart, and its type bar is the shortest ever used on a double-cased machine. Each type bar hanger is secured between an upper and lower steel ring with two perfectly-fitting rivets, which is a guarantee that it will always remain solid.

The line space mechanism of the Smith Premier machine is very convenient and is a very marvel of complete mechanism. The scale and proper feeding arrangement are unique, and the margin guides are adjustable and will automatically take in any width of paper, cards, envelopes and the like.

The keyboard of a Smith Premier is, so expert operators tell us, of the very best. The machine has a double keyboard, that is to say, it is unnecessary to press a shift key in order to strike a capital. The universal keyboard is used, as that by long experience has been found to be the best for practical use.

There is one device connected with this make of typewriter that recommends it to the operator perhaps more than any other, and that is the type-cleaning apparatus. There is no poking with a long brush between the bars of the machine and consequently no lost temper and irritation. When the type gets dirty, as even the type in as good a machine as the Smith Premier does get occasionally, it is necessary only to draw the platen forward, introduce the crank which resembles the handle of a carpenter's brace and bit, connect the lower part of this crank with the top of the circular brush, give this brush a few turns and your type is clean, your temper intact and your time not appreciably wasted. Although the brush is, generally speaking, a part of the machine, it may be easily removed by simply turning the wheel until its threaded shaft is disengaged from the bearing; then take out the brush.

The Company makes many varieties of machines for various branches of work. Some of its makes have wide carriages and some narrow. One, the Smith Premier No. 6, has a carriage that will permit the writing of a line sixteen inches in length, and will take paper eighteen and one-half inches wide. This, of course, is valuable where special forms are to be used. There are several varieties of type, each one neat and attractive in appearance.

The Smith Premier Typewriter Co. manufacture and sell a number of varieties of typewriter desks and cabinets. Some of the desks are made with a roll top and others are in the form of a library table with single or double banks of drawers. The prices of these desks and cabinets are as low

FIG. 1. PRINTING MECHANISM OF THE SMITH PREMIER TYPEWRITER.

as is consistent with good quality.

To the user of a typewriter—and who is not, in these days, a typewriter user?—such machines as the Smith Premier are to be recommended. They are fine pieces of mechanism, and if Horace Greeley could re-visit the earth it is safe to say that his fearful and wonderful handwriting would no longer puzzle the brains of compositors and correspondents. Horace was a good man but a bad writer. If he had owned a Smith Premier typewriter he would have been pretty nearly perfect.

We reproduce with this article two cuts. In Fig. 1 is shown the printing mechanism of the Smith Premier. In Fig. 2 is shown the process of cleaning the type with the crank brush. The catalogue says that every letter is cleaned in 15 seconds, and we see no reason for doubting the statement.

FIG. 2. TYPE-CLEANING APPARATUS OF THE SMITH PREMIER TYPEWRITER.

BANKING BY MAIL

Not a few progressive banks throughout the country are making a specialty of mail accounts—that is, accounts of customers who are not able by reason of their location to transact business with the bank personally. In these days of almost universal trolley connection, the average country bank is being brought into closer contact with its customers, but there are still many communities where, owing to lack of facilities, a trip to the bank involves both time and trouble, says the National Banker. This applies not only to individuals scattered through the adjoining territory, but to merchants and firms who do business at what might be termed cross-roads centers. Naturally the business man, no matter where located, must have a bank account, and almost without exception he does maintain one, but there is a great deal of possible business to be picked up in any community if the country bank will put forth the effort to obtain it. The postoffice department offers every inducement to this end. Rural free delivery is being extended in all directions. The farmer's mail not only comes to him promptly, but he is also able to register letters at his door, and to keep in constant touch with his nearest urban center. It follows that the necessity for a bank account, so far as he is concerned, is growing. Perhaps, if he is a progressive man, he already maintains one. As a rule, however, he does not. That he is a desirable customer goes without saying, and the proper effort put forth by any live country institution ought to result in a marked increase in this class of business. A little preliminary instruction is all that is necessary to put such an account in good working order. The new customer is taught that he can deposit cash or checks by mail quite as expeditiously as by a personal visit, and the bank will advise him promptly of the receipt of such remittances, and keep him posted as to the state of his account. Some banks have devised a number of ingenious forms by which business by mail is facilitated, and they report that success has followed every effort to extend their list of customers beyond the local boundary. In addition to widening the influence and profit possibilities of their institutions the men who are attempting this work are unconsciously conducting an educational campaign of great value, by making familiar to a very influential class many things which heretofore have been regarded from a hostile standpoint. Banking by mail should be encouraged in every possible way.

BRIEF MENTION.

TYPEWRITER RIBBONS and carbon papers are now indispensable adjuncts to the business office. Nobody who pretends to do business at all tries to do without a typewriter, and you cannot use the typewriter unless you buy typewriter ribbons. The Imperial Mfg. Co., of 289-299 Washington street, Newark, N. J., makes typewriter ribbons and carbons that, it is claimed, will write better than and will outlast the ordinary kind. The company claims, also, that its ribbons will not smut, blur nor fill the type, and that its carbons will make fine copies. The prices of the Imperial Mfg. Co.'s products are very reasonable, considering the high grade of goods manufactured, and it seems to us that the prospective buyer of this sort of material might do well to communicate with them. At any rate, their advertising is very attractive, and promises that the goods they manufacture and sell will be even more so.

DO YOU play Ping Pong? Of course you do; everybody does nowadays. But are you sure that you are playing real Ping Pong and not some other game advertised under that name? The genuine Ping Pong came originally from England, and although resembling in most respects its imitations, nevertheless differs in some important essentials. A little pamphlet issued by the Tower Mfg. and Novelty Co., 306-308 Broadway, New York, informs us that the said company sells the genuine Ping Pong. Now Ping Pong is a good game. It is one of the most interesting indoor games ever invented, and, unlike most indoor games, affords oportunity for a good deal of exercise. To the non-player this statement may seem ridiculous, but let him play three sets of Ping Pong against a strong adversary who sends the little celluloid spheres over the net with force, and he will agree at the end of the third set that Ping Pong affords exercise in ample quantity. The variety of styles of Ping Pong sets is wide and the prices vary accordingly. One may buy Ping Pong sets for $1.25, $1.70, $2.50, $3.75 and $5, and may, if he feels so disposed, buy finely appointed Ping Pong tables, lined as tennis courts are lined, for $18 or $20. If you play Ping Pong you want to play the real article, and the booklet issued by the Tower Mfg. and Novelty Co. convinces us that this company sells just what it advertises, namely, "the genuine Ping Pong."

ONE OF THE neatest little booklets that we have seen for a long time is that isued by the Title Guarantee and Trust Co., 146 Broadway, New York, and 175 Remsen street, Brooklyn, entitled "How We Bought Our House." It contains the story of a married couple that, after living in a rented house for a number of years, decided to buy a home of their own. When they set about buying such a house of course they felt it necessary that the title to the property should be securely guaranteed, and, feeling in that way, they wrote to the Title Guarantee and Trust Co., as that company, according to its advertisements, had the largest capital. The booklet goes on to describe the meeting with the representatives of the Title Guarantee and Trust Co., the manner in which the title was looked into and finally guaranteed by the company, the organization's complete arrangements for such work and the feeling of absolute satisfaction and security that the owners of the new home have felt since they acquired it. To any person contemplating the purchase of a new home the information which this booklet gives is invaluable. It is interestingly written also, and from a purely artistic standpoint is well worth securing and preserving, as it is beautifully printed and charmingly illustrated in color and with pen and ink sketches. We advise the readers of COMMERCE, ACCOUNTS & FINANCE to send a stamped envelope to the Title Guarantee and Trust Co. and ask for this little booklet. We feel sure that they will be repaid for tneir trouble.

MUCH OF THE FRUIT that comes to the markets of the great city is packed, as every one knows, in wooden baskets or crates; strawberries, peaches, grapes, plums and pears are so packed. Vegetables also are put up in this way, some of them. How few of us who see these baskets stacked in tempting array upon the stands of the fruit dealers stop to consider how the baskets are made. A booklet issued by the Mergenthaler-Horton Basket Machine Co., of New York City, with offices at 287 Broadway, tells us how the baskets have been made in the past, and also how they will, in all probability, be made in the future. The name of Mr. Mergenthaler is familiar, as he is the inventor of that wonderful machine, the Linotype, which sets type more accurately and much faster than can be done by hand. Now Mr. Mergenthaler has put the finishing touches to the apparatus known as the Mergenthaler-Horton basket machine. Fruit baskets were formerly made by hand, and the output was, in consequence, small in comparison with the demand. It is stated in the pamphlet before us that a surprisingly large proportion of the fruit crop of last year was allowed to rot, simply because of the scarcity of boxes in which to ship to the market. The Mergenthaler-Horton basket machines, photo-engravings of which are shown in the booklet, make complete strawberry boxes, grape baskets, peach baskets, etc., at a rate of speed and at a price which will put hand labor out of the running. Thin strips of wood are put into one end of the machine and the completed basket, ready to receive its filling of luscious fruit, is shot out of the other. The Mergenthaler-Horton basket machine stock is now on the market, and is to be supplied for a limited season to those desiring it at the rate of 70 cents a share, par value a dollar. In the booklet a prospectus of what the company intends doing and an estimate of its profits are given, and the figures will surprise and interest every investor. It will pay any one who has a little or much money for investment to write to the offices of the company for this little booklet.

TWO LARGE EYES look up at us through a pair of gold-mounted eye-glasses from the card advertising the business of Henry Kahn & Co., opticians and dealers in photo supplies at 189 Broadway, New York. Above these eyes is the pertinent question: "Do your eye-glasses fit like these?" The receiver of this card naturally turns it over and finds that Messrs. Kahn & Co. make "glasses to suit your face and sit on your nose," and also that modern methods are used in the examination of the eyes." Repairing of eye, field and opera glasses is done at reasonable prices, and the firm carries in stock a full line of thermometers, pyrometers, magnifiers, cameras, etc. Downtown business men of New York City may be glad to know that there is an up-to-date house doing business in their locality where eye-glasses may be repaired well and cheaply, and where new ones may be fitted by expert opticians.

LIKE A WHIFF from old ocean comes the booklet advertising the Ocean View House of Bay Head, Ocean County, N. J. On the cover is a picture of rolling surf and a sandy beach that makes one think of hot July and a bathing suit. The vacation season is coming and overheated city people seek the seashore. Bay Head, the pamphlet tells us, is situated on the New Jersey coast, with the ocean in front and Barnegat Bay behind. The drinking water used in Bay Head is from the purest artesian wells and comes from the solid rock 1,200 feet below the surface. Sounds cool, doesn't it? The Ocean View House, a photograph of which is shown, is situated overlooking the ocean, and has broad piazzas on all sides. There is a fine bathing beach directly in front of the hotel, and one may enjoy some fine boating among the picturesque creeks and winding inlets of Barnegat Bay. Lakewood, where George Gould's magnificent country home is located, is but eleven miles distant. Asbury Park is not so very far away. The Ocean View House, judged by the photographs, is cosy, cool and comfortable, and its rates are not exorbitant, single rooms being $10 or $12 per week, and double rooms $16, $18, $20 and $24. These prices include board, of course. There is but one trouble with the pamphlet—that is to say, one trouble from the standpoint of the weary and overheated business man—and that is that it makes him long to throw the ledger into the air and take the first train for Bay Head and the ocean breezes.

WE HAVE BEFORE US a copy of the pamphlet issued by the New York, Ontario & Western Railway, entitled "Summer Homes." It has been the custom of this railroad management for a number of years to issue a book descriptive of the hotels, boarding houses and places of resort along its line. From year to year the appearance of the book has steadily improved. The issue of this year is certainly worthy of the close attention, not alone of the person seeking a place for a summer outing, but of any individual who seeks ideas with a view to the issuing of literature for the purpose of announcing the advantages of any resort or summer hotel. This year's issue of Summer Homes is bound in heavy paper of a green tone, with a figure of a milkmaid impressed upon the paper and then dusted with gold. The background of the design is printed in silver ink. The back cover page uses the same color combination and announces "Summer Homes, N. Y., Ont. & Western R. R." The story the book has to tell is a story of the country. He who seeks for fishing may gain an understanding of where the trout, bass, pickerel and other fish are to be found. Those seeking rest and recreation will find a guide to point out to them the spots where beautiful scenery may be viewed and to inform them concerning hotel accommodation—cuisine and comfortable rooms—together with the whereabouts of golf links, tennis courts, polo grounds and the locations where similar amusements are provided for the visitor. The particular qualities of the air in the higher altitudes of Sullivan County are so widely known and have been so generally commended by physicians that it seems almost useless to dwell upon its beneficent effect. Certain towns and villages have possessed themselves of a proportion of health-seeking population so large that the entire community may be described as a sanitarium. The consumptive in the obnoxious stages of the disease is usually in a condition of health that necessitates his remaining close to his abiding place, so that we find the racking cough, which is so annoying to many ears, does not obtrude itself upon those people who visit Sullivan County for the magnificent sport that its streams offer. No persons breathing the salt air of the ocean can obtain a more lasting change for so small a consideration of dollars expended as by a visit to the wild, rugged and sometimes bleak hills of this range of mountains. The food, lodging and consideration shown to the visitor by the host are altogether surprising, considering the amount of board asked.

IS YOUR COPYING PRESS rickety and hard to work? If it is we would advise you to look at the Giant Cabinet Copying Press, a pamphlet advertising which is on our desk. This copying press is furnished in oak and mahogany finish, and contains a cabinet for all copying materials, a drawer at the top for blotters, shelves inside for copying bowl and brush, dip, blotter bath, etc. The door, which opens downward and has a solid support beneath it, makes a fine working table. The press proper is not worked with a wheel screw, like the old-fashioned kind, but is operated with a lever at the side, upon which a five-pound weight brings a pressure of 250 to 400 pounds to bear upon your letter. The pamphlet says "that's enough," and we should think it might be. As a finishing argument we quote the following from this breezy little advertisement addressed to the user of the old-style copying press:—

"Perhaps you keep letter-press copies of your letters. You probably have a $3 per week boy to look after this work, and with the material you furnish he does the best he can. "Johnnie," you say, "bring me the letter book and let me see a letter to John Jones." Johnnie gets the book, turns the pages back and forth, and finally, though the pages furnish no clew, he settles on one which he thinks is it. He brings it to you. You try to read; you smooth out the pages, lay white sheets under them; you swear at Johnnie, but all in vain—the copy is not clear."

The moral, however, is clear: buy the Giant Cabinet Copying Press.

THE LITERATURE emanating from the advertising department of the Equitable Life Assurance Society is, we think, as convincing as any similar reading matter that has passed under our eyes for a long period of time. The points taken are in all cases the results of actual occurrences. A clipping from a newspaper is reproduced, showing the death of an individual by some accident or sudden illness; from this groundwork of fact the argument is built up with the strictest adherence to the truth. We are always facing the calamity of death, and the insistence of poverty may be at any time meted out to our dependents by reason of accident, illness or death. The argument is, and again it is a true argument, that the average man will recklessly spend that money or surplus of money which could and should be placed in some fund where it might provide against the possible contingencies that must be reckoned with in life. The most strong-minded men will yield to the temptation to expend surplus money, even though they may fully realize that this proportion of their earnings should be set aside as a reserve fund. The imperative demand of a specific payment, which must be made, overcomes and precludes the possibility of this temptation. The claims made by the Equitable Life Assurance Society are that, irrespective of the wealth or poverty of the person assured, the magnificent organization, ability of its directing officers, soundness of its funded reserves and care included in all of its investments must reduce loss to a minimum. Surplus earnings of the individual cared for in this way are protecting those that are most dear to him.

The man becomes more of a man by reason of the knowledge that he has done all that lies within his power for those whose duty it is for him to protect. These arguments seem incontrovertible.

BOOKS OF INTEREST TO BUSINESS MEN

BANKERS' AND MERCHANTS' INTEREST TABLES. By Francis H. Coffin and David H. Moore. 13 by 9 1-2 inches. Bound in cloth. Leather back and corners. Cover and back title gilt. Price, $5.00.

There have been interest tables published before, but never, so far as we know, has so elaborate and comprehensive a set of tables been issued in book form. "The volume contains," to quote from the title page, "Interest tables, computed on the basis of 360 days per annum, at 3 1-2, 4, 5 and 6 per cent, with an accurate calculation of interest on every sum from $1.00 to $1,000, and, by simple addition of two lines, on every further sum, to $1,000,000." It also contains a 1 per cent one day table, on the basis of 365 days per annum, from which interest on daily balances can be computed at any time and on any sum. There is a time table printed in black and red at the beginning of the book as an aid in quickly finding the number of days between one day and another. To a merchant or banker performing many calculations in interest this book is a great time saver. It is handsomely bound, finely printed, and has a thumb index.

POLITICAL ECONOMY OF HUMANISM. By Henry Wood. 7 3-4 by 5 1-4 inches; 320 pages. Bound in cloth. Cover and back title gilt. Price, $1.25.

Mr. Wood is well known as a writer on various economic subjects, and this book contains a series of able treatises, written in his usual vein, on the relation of the employer to the employed, and the phases of the industrial question and their relation to socialism. Among the questions considered and handled in a conservative spirit and with much common sense, are the following: Supply and Demand, the Law of Competition, Labor and Production, Combinations of Capital, Combinations of Labor, Employers and Profit Sharing, the Obligations and Privileges of Employees, the Unequal Distribution of Wealth, Money and Coinage, Tariffs and Protection, Industrial Education and Gold Production and values.

INTRODUCTION TO THE STUDY OF COMMERCE. By Frederick R. Clow, Ph. D. 7 1-2 by 3 3-4 inches; 224 pages. Bound in cloth. Back title gilt. Price, $1.25.

Mr. Clow's book is not intended as a complete text book on commerce. It is simply, as its title implies, an introduction to the study of commerce. It is intended as a text book for the use of teachers in schools or universities, or as a help to the student in his commercial training. Incidentally, it makes good reading for anyone interested in modern commerce, and particularly for the American merchant. The author begins by describing the Elements of Commerce; then follows a short essay on the Rise of Commerce, and then the Materials of Commerce are discussed. Foreign Commerce of the United States and of other countries is treated of, as is the Domestic Commerce of this country. The titles of other chapters are: Organization of Trade, Prices, Payments and How the Equilibrium is Maintained. We can heartily recommend this introduction to the Study of Commerce. It is a good book on a vastly important subject.

THE A B C OF BANKS AND BANKING. By George M. Coffin. 6 3-4 by 5 inches; 137 pages. Bound in cloth. Back title gilt. Price, $1.25.

This handy little volume is exactly what its name implies, that is, a presentation of the principles underlying banking in the United States. The author in his preface says that it is designed to appeal to the reader outside as well as inside of a bank. It is by no means the last word or every word about banking. It may be said that it is a primer covering a field that has hitherto been somewhat neglected. The chapter heads are as follows: Banking in General, Various Kinds of Banking, Capital Stock, Shareholders' Rights and Liabilities, Undivided Profits, Dividends and Surplus, Deposits, Checks, Lawful Money Reserve, Issuing Bank Notes, Borrowing Money, Loans and Discounts, Exchanges, Collections, Letters of Credit, Bonds, Mortgages and Stocks, Bank Reports, Examinations, Directors, Executive Officers—Their Powers and Duties, Internal Administration and Bookkeeping, and Other Suggestions.

A BUSINESS EDUCATION | FOR ...ONE... DOLLAR.

...THE PRACTICAL AGE...

A MONTHLY MAGAZINE full to the brim with helpful suggestions to young men and young women who are struggling successward.

THE BUSINESS HOUSE THAT JACK BUILT, an intensely interesting and highly instructive story of business life, and

APPLIED ENGLISH, an authority on writing and speaking the English language, which no young person can afford to be without, all for ONE DOLLAR.

If you have never seen THE PRACTICAL AGE, send for a free sample copy. Address,

THE PRACTICAL AGE,
Moline, Illinois.

HAVE YOU READ
The Kite Trust?
If not, why not? Send $1.00 for a copy to W. O. Douglass, Treasurer of The Bank Clerks' Club of New York, care First National Bank, New York City.

About a Pay Roll which proves itself, corrects all mistakes in figuring, divides up Pay Roll into several amounts needed to pay each person.

But let us send you a sample leaf, with circular, which tells the whole story.

BARLOW BROS., Grand Rapids, Mich.

It's Good for You

To use our Typewriter Ribbons and Carbons, because they write better and last longer than the ordinary kind; they do not smut, blur nor fill the type, but they make fine copies.

No. 1 Ribbons, 75c. ea., $7.00 doz.
No. 1 Carbon, $3.00 pr. bx., 40c. doz.
Silkarbon, $4.00 pr. bx., 50c. doz.

We pay express or mail charges.

IMPERIAL MANUFACTURING CO.
289-297 Washington St., Newark, N. J.

R·I·P·A·N·S

There is scarcely any condition of ill-health that is not benefited by the occasional use of a R·I·P·A·N·S Tabule. For sale by Druggists. The Five-Cent packet is enough for an ordinary occasion. The family bottle, 60 cents, contains a supply for a year.

PRENTISS CLOCKS.
SIX TIMES A YEAR
is all that is necessary to wind a Prentiss Clock. Why wind a clock every week when we can sell you one which will require winding but once in sixty days and will keep perfect time? Also Frying-pan, Program and Electrically synchronized clocks. Send for Catalogue No. 22.
THE PRENTISS CLOCK IMPROVEMENT CO.,
Dept. 28, 49 Dey St., New York City

BUSINESS LAW. By Thomas Raeburn White, B.L., LL.B. 5 by 7 1-2 inches; 323 pages. Bound in cloth. Back title gilt. Price, $1.50.

This is a neat, compact and handy book of business law for the use of students and business men. Among the subjects treated are Contracts, Sales, Partnerships, Corporations, Negotiable Paper and the like. The author's language is plain, and is understandable by any one having no previous knowledge of law. The book's clearness on the essential points of ordinary law should recommend it as a business book for the plain business man who has no time in which to consult a law library.

THE PHONOGRAPHIC DICTIONARY AND PHRASE BOOK. By Benn Pitman and Jerome B. Howard. 5 1-2 by 8 inches; 552 pages. Bound in cloth. Cover title and back title gilt. Price, $3.00.

This book is the most elaborate shorthand dictionary yet published, with the characters in fac-simile. It contains over 20,000 words, and for every one of these words there is a corresponding sign in the Benn Pitman system of shorthand. To the reporter, office or court stenographer, or any one writing the Benn Pitman system of shorthand, the book is invaluable. It is well made, tastefully bound, and is printed on a good quality of paper in clean, plain type.

THE LAWRENCE SYSTEM OF VOCAL AND PHYSICAL EXPRESSION. By Edwin Gordon Lawrence. 4 3-4 by 6 inches; 128 pages. Bound in cloth. Cover title and back title gilt. Price, $1.00.

The author says in the preface of this little book that his object has been to place in the hands of lawyers, actors and public speakers in general, a simple system of vocal and physical expression that will enable them to clearly convey thought by word of mouth and emphasize it by the proper action. To the man of affairs who is called upon for a speech on any subject, and who knows what to say but does not know how to say it, this book will be a great help.

BUSINESS LAW. By Alonzo R. Weed, LL. B., of the Boston Bar. 6 by 9 1-4 inches; 172 pages. Bound in cloth. Cover and back title red. Price, $1.25.

Mr. Weed calls his book "a manual for schools and colleges and for every day use." The titles of the chapters are as follows: Contracts, Principal and Agent, Partnerships, Sales of Personal Property, Bailments and Common Carriers, Negotiable Paper, Deeds, Mortgages and Leases, Collection Laws, Written Rates of Interest, Insurance, Patent Rights, Trade-Marks and Copyrights, etc.

The author does not waste words, and yet treats his subjects clearly and comprehensively. In short, he gives the law without the addition of wordy "trimmings."

Any book in this [illegible] wil[illegible] sent to any address in the United States [illegible]nada or Mexico upon receipt of price. If [illegible] is some special book that you require we [illegible]all be pleased to hunt it up for you. Add[illegible] COMMERCE, ACCOUNTS & FI[illegible]ANC[illegible] 25 Pine street, New York city.

HALL'S Fireproof and Burglar Proof SAFES

Sold since 1840. Never fail to protect contents.

KNOWN EVERYWHERE

393 BROADWAY, N.Y.

Telephones: 3133-3136-307 Franklin.

BUSINESS NEEDS

Advertisements under this head one cent a word each insertion.

AUDITOR WANTED.—Thoroughly trained accountant competent to establish and manage auditing system for several large financial corporations. Address T. B. R., office of Commerce, Accounts & Finance, 25 Pine Street, New York City.

A YOUNG MAN of 30, eleven years experience in accounting and general office work, would like a position with a progressive house—wholesale or manufacturing preferred. Thorough investigation courted. Refer to present and former employers. Address S., 515 E. 14th Street, Des Moines, Iowa.

BUSINESS PICTURES—Do you want to illustrate your catalogue or booklet? Do you want a series of snappy pen and ink sketches to brighten your advertisement in the daily papers? Do you want a handsome wash drawing for your announcement in the magazines? If you do, write to me. I am a competent business artist, working in black and white and colors, and you see my sketches every week if you read the Sunday papers. My price is always a fair one. Address, PEN AND INK, Box 17, Commerce, Accounts & Finance.

NEW YORK UNIVERSITY
School of Commerce, Accounts and Finance

A college course in Higher Accountancy arranged in accordance with the requirements of the Certified Public Accountants' Act of the State of New York and fitting students for the Regents' Examination for the C. P. A. degree. The course in Accountancy is rounded out by instruction in finance, commerce and commercial law leading to the University Degree of Bachelor of Commercial Science.

NEW YORK UNIVERSITY

Washington Square **NEW YORK CITY**

I WANT BACK NUMBERS of previous volumes of Commerce, Accounts & Finance. I will gladly pay for them. Person having copies to spare please communicate with C. C. G., care Commerce, Accounts & Finance.

OFFICE FURNITURE, Files, Cabinets, etc.—I know a lot more about some things than you do. I have to—it is my bread and butter. You don't know the "cost" of a desk, a cabinet, filing devices and the hosts of other things you may want to use in your office. I do! I can save you money and make some myself. That is a good proposition for you to look in to. Try. UNITS, care Commerce, Accounts & Finance.

SECOND-HAND TYPEWRITERS can be repaired so that they can be used and produce work which is almost, if not quite, as good as from a new machine. I have the facilities for obtaining exceptionally good second-hand machines. I have a man who repairs them—a man that understands his business. These machines can be sold for 50 per cent discount from list price of the new machines. Does this interest you? If it does, address TYPEWRITER, care Commerce, Accounts & Finance.

I AM AT PRESENT engaged in a large export commission business, and can furnish the highest testimonials as to efficiency of service rendered as a bookkeeper. Further advancement is barred by reason of the firm's personal dependants. Any firm or individual in need of an office man communicate with INDUSTRIOUS, care Commerce, Accounts & Finance.

What Do You Do With Your Invoices?

When You Receive a bill for goods bought by you, what do you do with it? Do you hand it to your bookkeeper, who laboriously copies it, figure by figure, in a bulky invoice journal, from which the total amount is posted to the ledger?

When your Bookkeeper has wasted valuable time by the above process, what does he do with the invoice itself? Does he hand it to the office boy or the assistant bookkeeper, who places it in some compartment of a clumsy file along with a dozen other bills from the same house, each of which must be pawed over when this particular one is wanted again?

If You Are Wasting Time and Money by these antiquated methods, aren't you tired of doing so? Would you not welcome a system as far superior to them as the sun is to a kerosene lamp?

THEN USE THE

"Acx" System of Filing Invoices

Simpler, More Convenient and More Serviceable than any other. A time-saving application of elements more or less used in every up-to-date office.

What the "Acx" System Is.

A system of filing invoices by which (1) the copy of the order placed, (2) the record of the receipt of the goods, and (3) the invoices, are brought together on a sheet of the paper of a size and shape to be conveniently handled and preserved in any post binder file.

The "Acx" Invoice Filing Sheet is of manilla, 11 inches long by 8½ inches deep. The directions on it explain its use. Three lines of mucilage are in place on the sheet. The first of these (inside left hand) is entitled "Attach left hand of your order here." All orders should be filled out in duplicate, preferably by the use of carbon sheets, and the retained copy attached to the invoice sheet.

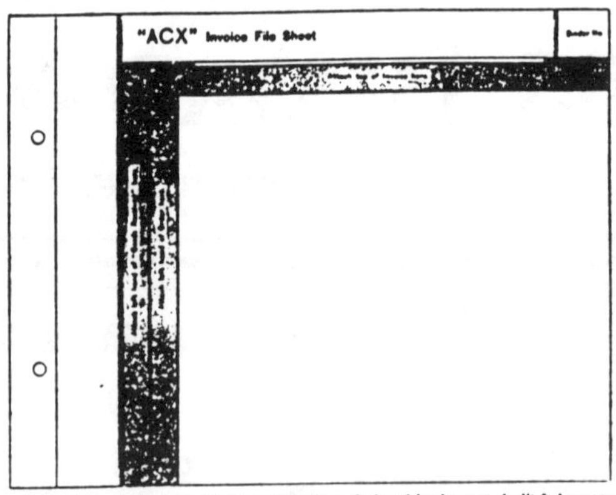

Reduced fac-simile of "Acx" Invoice File Sheet, designed by Account, Audit & Assurance Co., Ltd., 25 Pine Street, New York. Made by Self-Proving Account Book Co., New York. Patented February 8, 1898. Other patents pending.

When the goods for which the order is given are received, the count is made and entered upon a "Goods Received Slip," provided for the purpose. This slip is then attached to the Invoice Filing Sheet in the place marked "Attach left hand of Goods Received Here."

When the invoice is checked with the order and the "Goods Received Slip," its upper edge is moistened and laid against the mucilage on the Invoice Filing Sheet in the place marked "Attach top of invoice here." There are then superimposed upon this sheet (1) copy of the order, (2) record of the goods received, and (3) the invoice. The Invoice Filing Sheet is then paged in numerical order in its upper left-hand corner and is ready to be inserted in the binder; the latest invoice always being on top.

No Journalizing, no hunting for lost invoices, orders or goods received records. Order, receipt of goods and invoice all attached to one sheet of stiff paper, numbered and securely bound in a substantial binder, ready for instant reference. Post from this sheet direct to the ledger.

Price $6 a Thousand.

Address orders to

THE SELF-PROVING ACCOUNT BOOK COMPANY

86 Fulton Street, New York City.

THE NEW YORK PUBLIC LIBRARY

COMMERCE ACCOUNTS & FINANCE

Volume 4 New York June 1902 Number 6

CONTENTS

Published Monthly by the Commerce Accounts & Finance Company Twenty-five Pine Street New York

KNICKERBOCKER TRUST CO.

234 FIFTH AVENUE, CORNER 27TH STREET
BRANCH OFFICES:
66 BROADWAY, AND 125TH STREET AND LENOX AVE.,
NEW YORK CITY.

CAPITAL AND UNDIVIDED PROFITS, $2,508,399.11.

LEGAL DEPOSITORY FOR STATE, CITY, AND COURT FUNDS.

Interest allowed on Time Deposits. Deposits also received subject to Demand Checks, which pass through the Clearing House as do those upon any city bank.

Authorized to act as Executor or Administrator of Estates, and as Guardian, Receiver, Registrar, Transfer and Financial Agent for States, Cities, Towns, Railroads, and other corporations, and to accept any other Trusts in conformity with the laws of any State or of the United States.

LETTERS OF CREDIT FURNISHED.
BUSINESS AND PERSONAL ACCOUNTS SOLICITED.

CHAS. T. BARNEY, - - - - - - - - President.
JOSEPH T. BROWN, - - - - - - 2d Vice-President.
JULIAN M. GERARD, - - - - Asst. Sec. and Asst. Treas.
FRED'K K. ELDRIDGE, - - - - - 1st Vice-President.
FRED'K GORE KING, - - - Secretary and Treasurer.
WM. B. RANDALL, - - - - - - - - Trust Officer.

BOARD OF DIRECTORS:

JOSEPH S. AUERBACH,
HARRY B. HOLLINS,
JACOB HAYS,
CHARLES T. BARNEY,
A. FOSTER HIGGINS,
ANDREW H. SANDS,
JAMES H. BRESLIN,
I. TOWNSEND BURDEN,
HON. E. V. LOEW,
HENRY F. DIMOCK,
CHARLES F. WATSON,
FREDERICK G. BOURNE,
C. LAWRENCE PERKINS,
CHARLES R. FLINT,
AMZI L. BARBER,
CHARLES T. COOK,
JOHN MAGEE,
HENRY A. MORGAN,
HENRY C. BERLIN,
CHARLES W. GOULD,
FRED'K L. ELDRIDGE,
HENRY W. DE FOREST,
ALFRED R. MACLAY
HARRY W. McVICKAR.

C. W. HASKINS, C. P. A. — E. W. SELLS, C. P. A.

HASKINS & SELLS

Certified Public Accountants

CABLE ADDRESS, "HASKSELLS." — THIRTY BROAD STREET, NEW YORK

Accounts of Municipalities, Corporations, Firms and Individuals Inspected and Audited; Methods of Accounting Originated and Adapted to Conditions; Books of Accounts Opened, Regulated and Closed; Irregularities Discovered; Financial Situations Examined.

Experts under the Joint Commission of the Fifty-third Congress to Revise the Accounting System of the UNITED STATES GOVERNMENT.

Lackawanna Railroad

Address all communications to

C. W. TEN BROECK, Industrial Agent,
26 Exchange Place, New York City.

Do You Desire a Factory Site? The Industrial Department of the Lackawanna Railroad will aid you in finding one.

Are You Interested in Any Raw Product for Manufacturing Purposes? The Industrial Department of the Lackawanna Railroad will tell you if it is to be found along that road.

Does the Question of Power Concern You? The Industrial Department of the Lackawanna Railroad will tell you of good water power and of the proximity of fuel to points on that road.

Do You Want to Know the Usual Rate of Wages? The Industrial Department of the Lackawanna Railroad will give that information regarding any point on that road.

Do You Want to Know the Price of Gas, Water, Electricity? The Industrial Department of the Lackawanna Railroad will tell you.

Commercial Education

By ROLLIN JEFFRIES

There is in session at Saratoga at the time that copy for this issue of COMMERCE, ACCOUNTS & FINANCE is being prepared, a convention of the New York State Teachers' Association, at which several subdivisions of the Committee of Commercial Education will make important reports. I say "important" in the sense of the interest that they have for business and financial men. The Department of Commercial Education, of which Van Evrie Kilpatrick is chairman, has gone about its work in a commendable way, addressing questions to a considerable number of business men, and proposing to collate their answers in a way to give the convention the benefit of a concensus of opinion.

The questions proposed are presented under three general heads, as follows: (A.) Grammar School Training. (B.) High School Training, and (C.) General. A review of these questions, even at this late date,—for of necessity this will appear in print after the convention has adjourned,—cannot fail to be of interest to many readers.

SPELLING.

1. "Do boys who now enter your employ spell as well as boys formerly did?"

This is something that comes home to every business man, but, save from the vague impressions made upon his memory, it is one which he is unable to answer. As a rule, the "good old times" seem the best to us, and we of the departing generation therefore are sure that we never made the mistakes which our clerks make at the present time. In various circles the opinion prevails that education in the elementary branches is at present less thorough than it was formerly. We are apt to rail at every little deficiency that we discover, and spelling is one of these. We seem to forget, in business at least, that spelling is, comparatively speaking, a modern accomplishment, for we do not have to go very far back in the history of English literature to find an author, famous at present beyond comparison, who had the happy faculty of spelling his name in some seven different ways.

HANDWRITING.

The second question is as follows: "How is their writing (a) as regards legibility? (b) as regards speed?"

This evidently refers to the boys again, and very likely there is implied, although manifestly it is not expressed in the question, the same comparison that characterizes the first question, namely the old with the present. Most business men will say that the writing of the average boy of the period is not at all satisfactory. In some cases it is far more legible than it is speedy, although this is not the usual rule. Awkwardness seems to predominate, and yet there are remarkable exceptions to be noted. Many business men will discriminate against boys because they do not write satisfactorily, and will accept in their stead others whose writing passes muster, even though in other directions their qualifications are less satisfactory. Writing is a more important issue with the young man entering business than many teachers suppose.

The third question shows the object that was in mind in proposing that just quoted. It is as follows: "In school shall we emphasize speed or legibility "

Now, since business demands both, how is any one to answer this question satisfactorily? To have legibility at the expense of speed would result in a very slow office. To have speed at the expense of legibility would result in a condition of affairs that would be described by the correspondents of the concern as 'slouchy." Business demands a fair rate of speed and a high degree of legibility. The two must go hand in hand.

The next question is, "Do you favor vertical or slant writing?"

The average business man, I take it, would perhaps have to have explained to him the precise meaning of "vertical" and "slant" before he would be in position to answer this satisfactorily. Many a business man who has had his patience, and his eyesight as well, taxed with the peculiarities of Spencerian, welcomes what some of us have learned to call vertical, as a refreshing variation, but comparatively few have got so far into the technics of the case as to be able to answer this question without more or less preliminary investigation. From my point of view, I think the business man does not care a rap whether it be slant or vertical as long as it is legible and reasonably speedy in execution.

The fifth question is: "Reason for your opinion?"

Evidently in framing this question there was a doubt in the mind of the writer of the queries as to the kind of answers that would be obtained to No. 4, and therefore he asks the reason so as to be able to make up the concensus accordingly.

The sixth question gets right at the root of the matter: "Should the development of typewriting lead us to pay less attention in school to penmanship?"

Business men well know that there are most excellent typewriter operators in the market, whose accomplishments in penmanship are next to nothing. I have in mind a young man who, in spite of deficiencies in penmanship, has, through the use of shorthand and his ability to operate a typewriter, risen to a position of considerable responsibility, with very satisfactory compensation. If you should ask him for his name and address and he had no printed card handy, he would go at once to his typewriter in order to give you what you desired. If he attempted to write it by pen or pencil, I venture to say that you would require a translation then and there, for it is something that almost no one can make out. I cite this case because it is not altogether exceptional in character, and from my point of view it well illustrates what the introduction of the typewriter has brought about.

There has been a neglect of penmanship since the typewriter came into use. Very few stenographers are able to write satisfactorily, from the standpoint of the business man, in ordinary characters. The training in shorthand and typewriter work apparently has been at the expense of penmanship, and has cost the business world much in the way of general utility. Many business men today, and it is possible they may be described as old-fashioned in their notions, are insisting that their typewriters and their stenographers, as well as their bookkeepers, shall write legibly and with a reasonable degree of speed. I am not prepared to charge the lack of skill in penmanship manifested by many engaged in office work to the neglect of the grammar schools. The neglect is manifested in many other directions as well. What I am saying is intended only to emphasize what I conceive to be the business man's need, namely, helpers in the office better grounded in elementary branches, including very prominently in the list, penmanship.

ARITHMETIC.

The seventh and eighth questions of this division relate to arithmetic: "Are boys more or less accurate in arithmetic? Are boys more or less rapid in arithmetic?"

From the phrasing of these questions it is evident that there is the same comparison of dates maintained here as was suggested in the first question. Again I say the business man, save only from general impression, will find it impossible to answer these questions as they are proposed. He will be willing to tell you, however, his opinion of the arithmetical qualifications of the average young man in business. He will say at the outset that when boys enter the office there are a few of them who can add correctly; that there are a very few who can multiply and be sure of the result; that there are still fewer who, for example, can compute interest on a note and be certain of the accuracy of the result; and there are still less who know anything about averaging dates and various other special calculations demanded in the office.

A boy who offers himself at an office today, who is fairly accurate in arithmetic, quick to make proper application of rules to the problems that are presented, and who is fairly rapid in performing the calculations, is a veritable prize, and the average business man is glad to make arrangements for the employment of such a boy whenever he encounters him. Those who cannot do such work either accurately or rapidly are so numerous that the competent young man stands out markedly by way of contrast. I am of the opinion that many business men in attempting to answer these questions will have in mind, whether or not they put it upon paper, the special prominence that was given to arithmetic as long ago as when they were at school, and the large number of studies which have been brought to the attention of the modern youth that were never heard of in their school days. There will be in his mind the feeling that arithmetic, along with penmanship, has been buried under various matters which are in fact less essential than they are to business success. Some, perhaps, will go so far as to say that the "three R's" in modern education are sadly neglected. Nothing in the questions before us seems to refer even in a remote way to reading, and yet to be a good reader is in a sense a qualification for office work. The three R's, "reading, 'riting and 'rithmetic," as they have been familiarly put these many years, are just as much foundation stones for business success now as ever before, the schools would lose not one whit of their utility, from the business man's point of view, if they emphasized the three R's, even though some of the branches of studies coming later into the course were neglected, if not actually thrown out.

BOOKKEEPING IN THE ELEMENTARY COURSE.

Questions nine and ten are quite suggestive, to say the least: "Should bookkeeping be a part of the elementary course? If so, shall we teach single or double entry?"

I can imagine many a business man, after reading these two, laying down the sheet of questions in absolute despair. He will say to himself: "Everyone should know bookkeeping. The principles of debit and credit should be as much a part of elementary education as penmanship and arithmetic," and then he will pause, for whether bookkeeping should be a part of the elementary course as distinguished from some other portion of the general course covered in the public schools is something on which he is not so well informed. And then he will tackle the next question: "Single entry or double entry?" And if he be an up-to-date business man, he will very possibly say, "Is there such a thing in teachable shape as 'single entry' bookkeeping?" Many will answer that there is not. A few will take issue, and some will even go so far as to say that a well-administered single entry plan is far better than a poorly-administered double entry system, no matter how correct theoretically the latter may be. All this, however, depends upon circumstances. Would it not be better to have all instruction held to that which the business man recognizes as his only sure safeguard and dependence, namely "double entry"? Why should time be spent in the schools wandering around among the absurdities, inconsistencies and fallacies of so-called single entry? Why not define single entry once for all as being that which exists without method or system, and then proceed to lay down the method and system upon which the great business superstructure rests at the present time?

TYPEWRITING AND STENOGRAPHY.

The eleventh question is as follows: "In an eight-year course, would you favor the teaching of typewriting and phonography?"

If the business man had before him all that the eight-year course includes, he would be in better position to answer this question. Recognizing the importance of stenography and typewriting, it would be strange indeed if he did not see some part of the course through which he could draw a line, thereby obliterating certain unimportant things to make room for phonography and machine writing.

Certain banks at the present time make it a rule to employ no one, whether messenger, paying teller, receiving teller, bookkeeper, or clerk in some other department, who is not able to write shorthand. A bank president speaking to this point some time since, said: "It is not that we expect them to use the shorthand as a regular thing, but because we find that in addition to its being very handy to have, particularly when we are giving directions about work to be done, the young man who has acquired shorthand has had a mental discipline which the young man of equal ability who has not given attention to the study lacks."

There is another side to this question, however. It is that of the public schools becoming trade schools. If the public schools are to teach typewriting and phonography, which may be, for the purpose of this discussion at least, regarded as trades, or at least means of livelihood, why should they not teach carpentry, blacksmithing, bricklaying, sewing, garment cutting, millinery and a score of others? Where will you draw the line in the public schools when it comes to occupations or arts which serve to earn a livelihood?

ACTUAL BUSINESS TRANSACTIONS.

The twelfth and last question in this series is a clincher: "To what extent should actual business transactions be taught in school?"

The phrasing of the question shows the difficulty of the situation. Can "transactions" be taught? Is it not true, rather, that transactions properly reflected teach or impress their own lessons? Is it possible to teach business? Is it not true, rather, that the principles of business can be explained advantageously and that the application of those principles in individual transactions must be worked out by the skill of the man who engages in business? It would be interesting to see what is the conception of actual business entertained by the person who phrased this question. The question in itself is likely to tax the patience of many a business man who holds to the idea that at best teachers know very little business, and therefore that that which they would call business and proceed to teach would be so unlike the real article that the student would be harmed rather than benefited.

THE METRIC SYSTEM.

The second series of questions, as already indicated, refers to the high school. The first question is one which is suggested by much that is appearing in the daily press at the present time, not only in the way of stated articles, but also in reports of proposed legislative action: "Should the metric system be taught below the high school?"

This means, as I take it, "should instruction in the metric system be commenced in the high school, or should it have attention before the pupil reaches the high school?"

There is no doubt that the average youth should be instructed in the metric system in order to qualify him for the work that he will be called upon to perform in the average office. An effort is being made in various directions to supersede our time-honored inch, although illogically arranged, foot and yard, ounce and pound, square rod and acre, gill, pint and quart, by units, theoretically perfect, comprised in what is known as the metric system. The promoters of this plan are frequently quite intolerant, and lately they are demanding a law which they would use to abolish the old and install the new. From the standpoint of some of these men it would be wrong, after a while at least, to think feet, pounds, gallons and acres. In order to comply with the law of the land and be a good citizen a man would be obliged to get his mental faculties into such training that metre and kilo, gramme and litre would flow from his tongue as glibly and intelligently as did the older designations from the tongues of his father and grandfather. The promoters of the metric scheme seem to forget the utility of that which exists and would substitute that which is theoretically perfect, whether it has the full measure of utility or not.

However, this is an aside. It does not answer the question

NEW YORK LIBRARY

of where in the school course should commence consideration of the metric system. The average business man will say that since the metric system should be learned it should come in wherever is most appropriate. I would add to that as follows: The earlier that it is commenced the easier it will be, perhaps, for the pupil to assimilate its somewhat arbitrary features.

POWER OR MEANS OF LIVELIHOOD.

The second question is utilitarian in idea: "In a commercial course shall we emphasize those subjects which develop power, or those which tend towards a livelihood?"

In answering this we must consider the environment. In a "commercial course," shall one thing or the other be done? The average business man will ask, "What is a commercial course for? To round out without object the mentality of the student and afford him "culture," or to "fit him for business"? If it is to fit him for business, then certainly the answer is, that preference should be given to whatever tends in this direction.

LENGTH OF COMMERCIAL COURSE.

The next query bears on this same subject: "Do you favor a commercial course of three, four or five years in length?"

The business man, I take it, would say, "The length of time is not the essential element, but what does the course cover and what does it require on the merits of the case?" Reflecting upon what he really knows with regard to school courses, he will say that the tendency is to add non-essentials and to neglect that which is vital in the way of fundamental principles. Therefore he is afraid of long courses. Again, business is shortening up in its periods in all directions, and there are comparatively few of the great multitude of boys who are being fitted for business who can afford long school courses. They must get to work long before the course can be finished.

HIGHER EDUCATION.

The fourth question, "Is higher education as great a factor in business success as in other professions?" is an unfair one for the average layman.

What is "higher education," and how great a factor has it proven to be in "other" professions? Many a hard-fisted business man will be surprised at the relationship in which he finds himself as indicated by this question. He has been calling himself a "business man," and all at once he finds that he is a "professional" man. He evidently is credited with making a profession of business. Many a one who would be disposed to answer all these questions conscientiously will give this up in sheer despair.

For myself I am disposed to say that no element of education, properly considered, can fail to help the business man who has the faculty of making adaptations. Yet I know there are many who, by reason of their education, be it higher or otherwise in character, have been spoiled for business. There are men in the colleges and universities of the country today that are being educated away beyond any business opportunity that is open to them. On the other hand, there are business men, able in spite of all the over-education to which they have been subjected, who succeed as business men notwithstanding. Where you find a man over-educated, continuing the phrase for the benefit of the thought that it conveys, and who is successful in business, you will also find a man who is using to advantage every bit of the education that he has received.

It would seem that the attention given to typewriting and phonography in the question relating to the grammar school divisions should have exhausted that subject, but in No. 5 of this series they pop up again: "Should typewriting and phonography be optional or obligatory?"

If the students in the high school have got there by way of the grammar school, and if in the grammar school typewriting and phonography have been studied, why should the question of option come up in the high school division? It is true that in the question relating to this wide division in grammar school training the qualification of an eight-year course was brought in, but scarcely, we think, are eight years to be spent in the grammar school division.

After having been led to believe that the business man is a professional man by question 4, we have something else with respect to the business man's position thrust upon us by question No. 6: "Do you consider that lawyers, physicians and professional men generally should have some commercial training?"

Now, in all patience, let us get right down to business. Where is the lawyer, physician or other professional man that is the greatest possible success that does not bring to bear upon his profession the qualifications of a business man? Lawyers, physicians, professional men generally, make business out of their professions, and the more business instinct that a man has, other things being equal, and the more business training that a man has who devotes himself to a profession, the greater success will he make in that profession.

"But," says the practical reader, "there is a difference. You are talking about business training, and this question relates to business or commercial training as presented in the schools." There is a difference. Every physician, every lawyer and every professional man, even including the clergy, would be a better man in the narrow lines of his chosen calling if he had a business training. Whether he will profit by the somewhat colored instruction that he will get in the commercial division of a high school is altogether another question. It depends upon what the teachers who are employed know of real business and their ability to reflect what really appears in the business world, in their ability to reject what has been put into some of the books that pretend to treat of business subjects.

Modern languages are important subjects from the viewpoint of the managers of many branches of business. The next two questions in sequence touch upon this subject: "How many and what modern (foreign) languages should be taught? Which do you consider most important?"

The answer to this, as well as to some other questions in this series, might be, "It all depends." In some branches of business, and very prominent branches of business they are too, in some parts of the country, and in very important parts of the country as well, there is absolutely no demand upon the business man for any language except that of his own country. In other branches of business and in other sections of the country it would be greatly to the business man's advantage to be able to correspond, as well as converse, in any one of several foreign languages. In some parts of the country it would be French, in others German; in still others Italian, while the demand for Spanish on our southern border is very generally recognized. How can a general answer to such a question be given? The importance would turn naturally upon the business in which the one answering the question is engaged. If this question comes to the attention of some one doing business with Mexico, the West Indies or South America, we imagine that Spanish would have its importance particularly emphasized. If it were in an import or export business dealing with France or Germany, we imagine that either French or German would be similarly emphasized, but no such answer could apply broadly to the training that any given school should offer.

AGE OF THE BEGINNER IN THE STUDY OF BUSINESS.

And now to the final question in the high school division: "At what age should a boy begin the study of business subjects if he expects to complete a four-year commercial course in a high school?"

To this I might say, "Trot out your boy. Let me see of what timber he is built." Some boys are better able to comprehend business subjects at twelve and thirteen years of age than others are at seventeen to twenty-five years of age. Some boys are more thoroughly developed in their mental processes, as well as in their physical structure, at from fourteen to sixteen years of age than others who are several years older. A positive rule on this point would work hardship to some, while favoring others. A general average, it is true, might be obtained, but of what use are averages?

Finally we come to the last division, which, as already

mentioned, is entitled "General," and the first question in this series is inclusive in character: "Do you consider an applicant's school record as of value in the recommendation of a boy who wishes to enter your employ?"

Before answering that I should want to know something about the school and the ability of those conducting the school to reflect actual conditions by the records. I have a lively recollection of my own school record and of the school record of some of my classmates, and as memory serves me, those records would scarcely have reflected actual conditions in a way to be a dependence for the business man making selection. The brightest boy in the class and the one who has since made the greatest success in the business world did not show up well, so far as the record was concerned. He was too conscientious to secure that to which he was justly entitled. On the other hand, a dullard and a cheat succeeded in securing a magnificent record, so far as the school was concerned, and his business success since he left school is represented by a long row of ciphers. Seriously speaking, a boy's school record, if the business man ever cared a rap for it and took the trouble to examine it, would be worth something, the same as the character which his father and mother would give him, the same as his personal appearance as to neatness of clothes and cleanliness of body, but it is other points in the main that business men give prior consideration to.

IS PREFERENCE GIVEN TO GRADUATES?

The next question is suggestive in the extreme, particularly in the light of the codicil: "Are graduates given the preference over boys who have not finished the course?" And to this is appended the following parenthetical remark: ("If this could be done we believe it would be a powerful incentive to complete the course").

I would guess, if I were called upon to do so, that out of every thousand men in New York City, for example, who are employers of young men in their offices, there is not a half-dozen who have ever had brought to their attention whether or not an applicant had completed a high school course. If the question has been brought to the business man's attention, he has probably said: "A young man who has stuck to a thing until it is finished is worth more than one who has stopped midway." But he would no sooner have formed this opinion than perhaps the next applicant with whom he talked would show that by stress of circumstances he was compelled to leave the course before it was completed in order to do something for a livelihood. The business man would then say, perhaps, "Here is a fellow who has an incentive to action that is worth something, and, in any event, what they get at school is not half as important as what they learn in the office. I guess I will give him a trial."

CIGARETTE SMOKING.

The next question it would seem to be quite easy to answer: "Would the fact that a boy smokes cigarettes be a bar to taking him into your employ?"

Every clean, decent, moral man ought to answer that question emphatically. The line should be drawn at cigarettes, for a boy smoking cigarettes, no matter what his other qualifications are, is certainly objectionable in an office. The fact that he smokes, in the first place, should be reason why he should not be employed. The fact that he acquires the habit afterwards should be sufficient reason for his unconditional discharge, no matter what his attainments may be, or how great his usefulness in a general way.

LAST TERM OF SCHOOL LIFE.

"Do you favor a plan that the last term of the school life of a boy who does not intend to go to high school shall especially prepare him for a business career?"

Here comes in what is frequently manifested in educational matters, namely, the factory idea. All individualities, circumstances and peculiarities are left out, but as lumber is run through a planer so is the boy put through school, and the product is discussed as unconcernedly as though it were desks and chairs instead of muscle and brain. What is there in the whole common school course that cannot be properly regarded as preparation for business? What is there in the way of preparation for business that might be crowded into the last year of a course that is not of advantage on general principles? The business man, taking him far and near, regards the elementary instruction of schools, namely, that to which we have referred as comprised by the three R's, as of prime importance among the qualifications of the young men he hires. Next, he gives attention to their moral character, the circumstances of their surroundings, and incidentally takes stock of their natural endowments. There is always the mental reservation that no matter how good a boy may appear to be from the standpoint of this preliminary examination, to make him a really useful business assistant, he has got to be licked into shape by the practical work done in the counting-room and in the store. It is too bad for the teachers that they have to put up with these apparently arbitrary and unreasonable conditions which govern the business world, but such is the case and such would influence to a very large extent at least the answers to this fourth question. The fifth is very much like it:—

GRAMMAR SCHOOL OR HIGH SCHOOL?

"Do you prefer a grammar school boy or one who has had a high school training?"

To give my opinion of this question would be to repeat much that I have already said. With some boys that which has been obtained from the grammar school is of far greater utility than that which other boys have acquired by going through both grammar school and high school. So the answer to this would be: It all depends upon the boy and the circumstances of the case outside of the mere school training.

IN WHAT RESPECT MOST DEFICIENT?

"In what respect do you find boys who enter your employ most deficient?"

One line on the blank before me is provided for the answer to this question. The feelings and disappointments of the average employer of boys, which could be appropriately spread on paper in answer to this sixth question would require a small volume per boy, rather than a single line for all boys. Briefly, the most marked deficiency, after leaving out the questions of morality, integrity and personal habits, is ability in elementary matters. Reading, 'riting, 'rithmetic come in again, with special emphasis upon the writing and the ability to make simple mathematical calculations.

PREPARATION DEFECTIVE IN WHAT RESPECT?

The next question is personal in character: "As you look back over your school career, in what respect do you consider your preparation was defective?"

Again there is a short single line for all the answer that is wanted to this question. Is there a business man East or West, North or South in this great republic who feels that his preparation for his life's work as it has developed was sufficient? I think not. Is there a man who can point out in a few words the nature of the deficiency, beyond saying that he did not get enough of that which was really useful? This interpreted means writing, arithmetic, spelling, familiarity with certain branches of natural science, and with the laws of trade and finance, together with the minor arts of business. If he has been a progressive man in his business career, he has found it necessary practically to learn a new trade every week of his life, and very possibly he is saying to his own sons today: "Boys, it does not depend so much upon what you really learn or memorize at school as it does upon your acquiring the ability to learn things on occasion. The ability to study without a teacher, the ability to absorb and make applications would be worth far more to you than all that the schools can teach in a positive and dogmatic fashion."

A "SPLIT-UP" QUESTION.

The eighth question is split up in a somewhat remarkable manner: "Have you been pleased or displeased with boys in regard to the following: (a) Punctuality, (b) Manners, (c) Industry, (d) Truthfulness, (e) Cleanliness, (f) Ability to follow instructions, (g) Economy of time, (h) Economy of material, (i) Reliability, (j) Desire to advance?"

The answer to this might be safely put down as "Yes." I have been both pleased and displeased with different boys on every one of these points. Some have been punctuality personified, and have failed utterly in manners, truthfulness, cleanliness and reliability. Others have had magnificent manners, and have neither been industrious, nor yet able to follow instructions. Still others have followed instructions to the letter, and have been big fools when they were left to meet a situation upon which they had no instruction. All have desired to advance, but the general rule has been to measure advancement by wages, without regard to other considerations.

Finally, the last question of the list is: "Please state any other fact, opinion, or inference that your experience may suggest as being valuable along the line of this investigation. I have been scattering such facts, opinions and inferences along with the discussion of the numbered questions, and therefore there is left nothing for me to say in answer to it.

Balance Sheet Accounting

By GEORGE E. ALLEN

Fundamental Facts

From J. B. S., Chicago, Ill.

I am a new subscriber to COMMERCE, ACCOUNTS & FINANCE, and am not quite clear on several points of Balance Sheet Accounting. Would it be consistent for you to restate in a few words the essential features of your accounting plan, and also give an outline of your method of figuring manufacturing costs?

Under ordinary circumstances the foregoing letter would be answered by sending to the writer back numbers of COMMERCE, ACCOUNTS & FINANCE answering his first inquiry, and replying to his second inquiry in these columns. However, as the demand for COMMERCE, ACCOUNTS & FINANCE has exhausted the supply of extra copies, the writer takes the liberty of recapitulating what may be to some an old story. It is very simple, as all scientific laws when thoroughly worked out are simple.

The assets and liabilities of any business are all there is of it. The showing of assets and liabilities, commonly termed the Balance Sheet, is therefore all there is of accounting. Any business must begin with a Balance Sheet, and if it ever ends it must end with a Balance Sheet. The Balance Sheet is also the real thing at any intermediate date. Logical recognition of the all-importance of the Balance Sheet is Balance Sheet Accounting.

Beginning with the Balance Sheet the operating accounts of any business should be so constructed and conducted as to show in the simplest form the additions to and subtractions from assets and liabilities. To be of most value for administrative purposes, the Balance Sheet must be kept up to date. This is done by making fiscal periods short and by distributing equitably among the different periods such expenses and revenues as cover greater lengths of time. This is done by means of what are called Suspense and Reserve Accounts.

Such, in brief, is the theory of Balance Sheet Accounting.

MANUFACTURING COSTS.

The second inquiry of our correspondent pertains to a subject which has, more than any other, puzzled and confounded business men and accountants. The only theory of manufacturing accounts that stands the test of practical experience is the theory that any process of manufacturing is merely a change in the form or condition of assets.

The items that enter into manufacturing costs are materials, labor and factory expenses. Factory expenses comprise superintendence, clerical work in the factory and all costs pertaining to operating the manufacturing plant, including the depreciation thereof. A clear distinction must be preserved between raw materials in stock, finished product and goods in process of manufacture. To do this materials must be carried at cost through all stages up to the point where they are offered for sale in finished form. In addition to accounts covering goods in process, labor and factory expenses, an account may also be kept of special costs, which should include any expenditures incurred for work done outside of the concern. All manufacturing costs may be shown in the four accounts named. These four accounts, however, may be subdivided into such detail as may be desirable for purposes of management.

It will be readily seen that the account of goods in process is the one in which care and accuracy are most required. In many concerns claiming to keep accounts—concerns that watch pennies and postage stamps with a vigilance which would do honor to Sherlock Holmes—there is no systematic attempt to keep track of valuable material from the time when it is taken out of stock and delivered to the factory until the time when it assumes the form of finished goods. It is alleged by some that detailed factory accounts are too much trouble. Is counting cash too much trouble? Are assets of less value in the form of goods than in the form of money? Is not anything worth having worth keeping an account of? It is a significant coincidence that the people who take the negative of this proposition are largely the people who fail to succeed in manufacturing.

It is an error, however, to presume that factory accounts are either difficult or complicated. While individual pieces of material may be innumerable, the different classes of material are comparatively few, and the classification of material according to character and lots is usually natural and logical.

MONEY IN HAWAII

"Comparatively few persons in the United States are familiar with the financial conditions in Hawaii," said Mr. A. R. Serven, Chief Examiner of the Civil Service Commission. Mr. Serven paid a visit to the Pacific about a year ago, and he made a pretty thorough investigation of affairs there.

"Fewer still," he continued, "are acquainted in figures with the amount of coinage in circulation in Hawaii, says a writer in the Washington Star. In 1838 King Kalakaua bought up a lot of silver bullion and sent $1,000,000 worth to the San Francisco mint, where it was coined into dollars, half dollars, quarters and dimes of the same weight and fineness of American silver coinage.

"The money in circulation in the Hawaiian Islands is about $2,000,000. Silver passes at its full coinage value anywhere on the islands. Off the islands it is received at about 40 cents on the dollar. In paying debts outside the islands the Hawaiian people encounter all sorts of trouble as the result of this.

"Of the silver coined at the San Francisco mint there was $500,000 in dollars, $350,000 in half dollars, $125,000 in quarters, and $25,000 in dimes. The people of Hawaii, including many business men with whom I talked, were emphatic in their expressions that the Congress of the United States should recognize the silver currency of the territory at the same value as American silver, or should take it up and make the coin of the United States the medium of exchange throughout the islands."

WHAT HE WANTED

"Our company, sir," said the salesman keen,
"Has perfected a noiseless typewriting machine,
And no other house has done it."
The victim, he cackled in counterfeit glee,
"But say, can they furnish us, friend," said he,
"With a noiseless girl to run it?"

The Credit Department of a Modern Business*

By DORR A. KIMBALL

Credit Manager Marshall Field & Co., Chicago

During the last two decades our country has been undergoing a natural evolution in the development of both commercial and industrial life.

Many lines of modern business represent large investments of capital and great combinations of labor. The growth in this direction has been marvelous, so much so that certain good citizens appear to be alarmed and are anxiously inquiring what the future will bring forth.

About two years ago, in its search after truth, the Civic Federation of Chicago—a non-partisan organization—sent forth invitations to the ablest thinkers and most profound students of economies to be found throughout the United States, asking them to meet in a convention at Central Music Hall, in Chicago, to discuss what effect combinations of capital and combinations of labor have upon the general welfare of our people. At that meeting the University of Chicago was well represented, and four full days were devoted to the consideration of this subject, and very naturally a wide divergence of opinion was revealed. However, most of the speakers were in harmony on this proposition, that combinations of capital and combinations of labor have come to stay, being the successors of primitive conditions of trade rivalry, and if they can be properly organized and righteously conducted, then the dream of the brotherhood of man will begin to be realized, as their chief corner-stones will rest on the highest form of co-operation.

WONDERFUL CHICAGO.

Chicago is a most wonderful city. If the seven great wonders of the world were to be re-classified, I believe the phenomenal growth of Chicago as a city of commerce would deserve mention. No city is better known on the face of the globe. Our great fire in 1871 entailed severe hardship and untold privation, and yet, commercially speaking, it proved to be the greatest advertisement for Chicago, for the amount involved, that could have been made.

In many lines of business Chicago stands at the head. I was informed by a confidential man connected with one of our large packing house industries that during the year 1901 his establishment distributed upwards of $100,000,000 worth of beef. How many of us have any conception of the number of cattle $100,000,000 worth of beef represents? We are informed that "figures do not lie;" that may be true, but when figures are of large denominations sometimes they do not clearly convey the facts in a definite way.

Let me illustrate this in another manner. Imagine, if you please, a procession of cattle in "Indian" file stretching from Bunker Hill monument on the east to the Golden Gate of California on the west; but if I had $100,000,000 in cash, not only could I purchase that entire line of march, but I would have sufficient money remaining over to buy all the food this audience could consume during the remainder of the lives of its members.

The City of New York admits—reluctantly, however—that Chicago possesses the largest wholesale dry goods establishment in the world. The volume of business transacted on our Board of Trade annually is almost incomprehensible to the average man, and you will observe by the published reports of clearing houses throughout the United States, Chicago is frequently second to New York as a banking center, and yet men are still living who can remember when this western commercial and industrial metropolis was but a small village located in a mudhole in the midst of Indians. Surely the fairy tales of our childhood were no more marvelous than is the story of the phenomenal development of our own city.

I pride myself on being a young man, but apropos of the development of our city. I well remember going to the recorder's office to file for record a warranty deed running from Thomas Lyman to Mr. Marshall Field, by which Mr. Field acquired title, not only to all the ground occupied now by the University of Chicago, but, in addition, another large area between the Midway and Fifty-fifth street. I also recollect coming out from the city to this "far away" tract of land to make a plat of this purchase. Of course no university students then greeted me, but I never can forget the felicity with which I was received and the beautiful serenade tendered me on that day so long ago by a certain fraternal organization that seemed to be laboring under the delusion that it owned this whole neighborhood by virtue of the laws of pre-emption. The fraternity was composed of an innocent band of bullfrogs.

THE VALUE OF CREDIT.

Commerce and credit go hand in hand; they are inseparable. Practically speaking, the office or function of credit is to secure the willing transfer of capital from the possession of those who have it to those in need of it. Credit may be looked upon as an economic force of the highest importance, for in every civilized country credit has been absolutely necessary to develop great enterprises. Without it no nation, no state, no community can be strong; destroy a man's credit and you destroy the possibility of his making a success of his business.

Think for a moment what an important factor credit has been in our own country. During the dark days of our Civil War, to use a stock phrase, the United States was "short" on money, but, fortunately, "long" on credit, and credit gave to the promise of the government at Washington a power sufficient to bring into the treasury over three thousand millions of dollars, all of which was forever lost and swallowed up in the horrible vortex of cruel war; but if our nation had had no credit it would have ceased to exist, and you and I would have been left in a worse condition than Edward Everett Hale's "Man Without a Country."

Again, when Chicago was destroyed by fire scores of business men were thoroughly discouraged and utterly cast down, and many exclaimed, "We are ruined!" "Everything is lost!" "Poor Chicago is wiped off the map forever!" Those men were in no condition of mind at that time to appreciate the miraculous power of credit which soon brought new money to the work of reconstruction and made this city what it is today. Some one has pertinently said, "Credit is to business what mortar is to a brick wall—it is the adhesive material with which commerce is cemented."

A few years ago I was an eye witness of a great commotion at the corner of Adams and La Salle streets, where our great Illinois Trust and Savings Bank was then located. Men, women and children crowded into the office of the bank, and a line of depositors extended far out into the street. What was the matter? These people were alarmed; they had serious doubts as to the credit of that bank. Now the bank was perfectly good and remained open long after business hours to attend to the wants of its customers, and night after night the tellers remained at their posts, paying every depositor who called for his money, the result being that several hundred thousand dollars were withdrawn from circulation and locked up in safety deposit vaults as so much dead capital for the time being. Thus it will be noticed that all this disturbance and excitement was occasioned by a doubt as to that bank's credit. Panics originate in like manner—not for lack of money, not for lack of work, not for lack of trade, not for lack of food, but simply for lack of credit.

Credit is the legitimate offspring of confidence, and confidence is the rock—the great Gibraltar—on which the vast commercial interests of this world are resting. Annihilate confidence and immediately you destroy credit and commerce, and civilization with all its benefits will follow in the train of their destruction. Unless we can have faith and confidence in each other's honesty there can be no credit.

* Address before Chicago Chapter of the American Institute of Bank Clerks.

and without credit there can be but little business, as credit and confidence are inseparable.

CASH SALES VERSUS CREDIT SALES.

When a wholesale dealer sells goods he sells for cash or on credit. Some transactions are called cash transactions, when, in reality, they are purely matters of credit. To illustrate: A merchant residing in Nebraska visits Chicago to buy goods, he says, for cash, but sometimes he means this: When the goods are received at his store in Nebraska and the bills are checked off, then he will remit for them. Now, if the wholesale dealer agrees to this he makes a credit, i. e., he trusts that man at least a few days from the time the goods leave Chicago until the money is received according to this arrangement.

Buying and selling constitute trade, and if every trade were made strictly for cash, the merchant who could buy the most and sell the most to the best advantage would make the greatest success, but right here every dealer faces this fact, that most of the business of this world is done on credit; that is to say, the seller parts with his property and receives from the buyer a substitute, a promise of future payment, sometimes in writing, but frequently verbal, and I have known of occasions when that was all the seller ever did receive.

Now the fulfilment of this promise depends upon several things. First, the buyer's honesty; second, his ability; third, his experience and many other things. If the buyer is honest, the seller's safety depends upon the buyer's success, and the buyer's success is dependent upon his qualifications and other circumstances over which he may or may not have control. Every large wholesale house employs a person whose special work it is to look after the credits of that establishment, and he is called the "credit man," and if he proves a credit to his employers he will always trust the proper parties and decline credit to those unworthy of it. He should be careful, cool and courteous; not too hasty, but should possess sufficient courage to back up his convictions. He ought to be a good judge of faces, for often countenances are the index to the heart, and if he can detect quickly when a man is not telling the truth it is of great advantage. A dealer once said to me, "Beware of So-and-So"—naming a would-be purchaser—"when he tells you about his resources, it is always best to deduct 75 per cent from his statement, and if he makes it pretty large you would better take off 10 per cent extra, and the result will then be pretty near correct."

I am going to ask you for a few minutes to think with me of some of the fundamentals that a good credit man bears in mind when performing the duties of his occupation.

FUNDAMENTAL NUMBER ONE.

The very first point that a credit man wishes to settle in his own mind is that the party seeking credit is honest. "An honest man is the noblest work of God" is a very old maxim, but it is just as true today as when the words were first uttered. "Honesty is the best policy" is another truism which is thoroughly understood in every condition of life. From a purely commercial standpoint a man's reputation for honesty is the best asset he can have in his business. I know it is true that we sometimes hear men say facetiously that such old-fashioned adages about honesty sound very pretty, they are very nice sentiments; but really the up-to-date man of the twentieth century conducts modern business on new lines and has no particular use for maxims that should be consigned to a state of innocuous desuetude. Never was there a greater falsehood uttered. Not only do honest men believe honesty is the best policy, but dishonest men believe it too. Of course the latter class cannot speak from experience, but they learn by observation.

An old merchant of the David Harum type said to a young man just entering upon a business career: "See here, start right! Remember always this, honesty is the best policy; I know, because I have tried both ways myself." Ex-Secretary Gage, in an address, laid down this axiom, "All good men love the approval of the good, and all bad men are held in check in fear of a good man's reproach." When a man is known to be lacking in honesty no one wants to take any chances on him or have anything to do with him, and the credit man's happiness increases as he hears the sound of that man's footsteps receding in the distance.

FUNDAMENTAL NUMBER TWO.

After a man's reputation for honesty is settled in the mind of the credit man, very naturally he wants to know about the ability of his prospective customer to carry on his business successfully. Ability in the abstract is one thing, but ability in the special line of one's undertaking is quite another thing. Statistics are often cruel; they inform us that less than ten of every hundred men engaged in business are successful during their whole lives. Is not this a sad commentary on humanity? Something must be radically wrong somewhere.

One thing appears to be certain, there are too many "misfits" in life. I have known a first-class farmer to sell his farm and invest the money in a mercantile establishment and then make a failure. Why? He was a good farmer, but he had no experience in keeping a store. Many good lawyers would make poor physicians. A person should choose that profession or vocation which is suited to his particular ability, but too often the "round" men get into "square" places, or the "square" men get the "round" places, and the result is a misfit; but it is not discovered early enough to make the change, and I believe that some of the sad tragedies of life can be traced to this cause.

FUNDAMENTAL NUMBER THREE.

A man may be honest and possess great ability, but if he lacks application and industry, his chances of success are precarious. This age is one of push and of competition, and there is no place for lazy men. The merchants' path is not strewn with roses, no matter how attractive it may appear to the outsider. "Jacob, my son, take good care of your store, and by and by your store will take care of you!" This was the advice of a Hebrew father to his son. Application to business is a strong element towards success.

I heard a story the other day which may serve as an illustration. Mr. Rosenberg was teaching his son to be a clerk in his clothing store. While the father was absent at dinner the first day on which the boy began his service, the latter sold a suit of clothes, and naturally was quite elated. On the return of his father, the boy asked him if he did not think he was making splendid progress. The father, fearing his son might arrogate to himself undue importance on account of this transaction, said: "My boy, that man wanted a suit of clothes, didn't he?" "Of course he did!" exclaimed the boy, "and I was smart enough to sell him!" "Well," continued the father, "you still have many things to learn. When a man comes in this store and wants to buy a suit of clothes and you sell him, that is all right; but, my boy, when a man comes in this store and doesn't want to buy a suit of clothes and you sell him—Levi, that's business."

FAITH IN FELLOW MEN.

The modern up-to-date credit man should be like the Apostle Paul in this respect; he should be a man of great faith, faith in his fellow man. Paul's eleventh chapter of Hebrews is nothing more nor less than a statement of wonderful things accomplished by the use of faith. Paul says that faith is the substance of things hoped for—the evidence of things not seen. The credit man's definition is the same. I never look at a mercantile ledger which contains accounts against customers to whom credit has been given without thinking that ledger represents Paul's idea of faith, for in it will be found the substance of things hoped for—the evidence of things not seen. Therefore it can be truly said that just as the exercise of faith is required in all spiritual matters, likewise faith is the dominant element in commercial life.

CAPITAL.

I have thus far dwelt on the importance of things which in themselves alone do not pay bills—that is to say, no one can take one thousand dollars' worth of honesty, five hundred dollars' worth of ability and one hundred dollars' worth of industry and exchange these alone with a wholesale dealer for dry goods unless the applicant is possessed of a certain amount of capital. While it is true that absolute confidence in the integrity of the buyer is the great consideration for which credit is given, yet in most cases the dealer would also require for his safety that the buyer should possess some capital of his own, and the larger that capital the better it is for both debtor and creditor. The amount of capital required in any particular case to insure safety and success is an uncertain quantity, for the reason that some men have the faculty of making money under the most unfavorable circumstances, while others, even more favorably situated, can never make both ends meet; therefore the credit man is obliged to consider in every individual case the elements that go to make up a good business man.

To illustrate: Here is a certain young man just commencing business. He has been a clerk for many years and has had considerable experience in the kind of business he is now undertaking. He has been economical and has accumulated a few hundred dollars, saving it from his salary. Now every dollar of his capital has an enhanced value to him. In the first place, he earned it himself; and, secondly, by practice of rigid economy he has saved it, and, having both earned and saved, he understands the value of money as no one can who has done neither. Such a young man is worthy of confidence. But, on the other hand, here is another young man just commencing, with little ability and no experience whatever. Some kind, well-intentioned uncle or aunt has furnished him capital to start with, and the world smiles and says: "What a lucky young fellow; there is no end of money behind him!" But my observation proves, in about nine cases out of ten, the end of his money is seldom long in being reached. The credit man finds but little difficulty in handling a case of this kind, for if he sells this young man without the guaranty of his relative or some other responsible person he can blame no one but himself if he makes a loss.

Some merchants, however, are so anxious to sell goods they permit this desire to interfere with their better judgment in making a credit. If it were a question of loaning money, often times they would hesitate before making a loan to some they do not question when making a credit for merchandise. The trouble with this class of dealers is, they look upon merchandise as something that must be kept moving, and sometimes they find themselves in this predicament, that both their customer and the merchandise sold him on credit move so far away that they are never heard from again.

OBTAINING INFORMATION CONCERNING CREDIT.

The question naturally arises, How does the credit man obtain the necessary information to enable him to determine what is best to do? A personal interview always gives him an opportunity to learn from the would-be debtor what his condition is. Now, for a moment, please imagine that you are all credit men and that I am John Smith, a country merchant living in Wichita, Kan., and I come into your establishment for the first time, wishing to replenish my stock, and I inform the salesman to whom I am assigned that I desire to purchase goods on the usual credit terms. The salesman is very polite and says to me:—

"I am very glad, Mr. Smith, to see you, and our credit man, who passes on these matters, will also be glad to meet you. I will introduce you to him."

He presents me to you, and you in a kind and gentle way begin to question me in reference to my business affairs; perhaps something like this:

"How large a stock of merchandise have you on hand at present?" I reply, "Five thousand dollars."

You then ask if I sell my goods on credit or for cash, and I reply, "For cash."

"Have you any other resources?"

"Yes, I have cash on hand, i. e., on deposit in the First National Bank of Wichita, one thousand dollars."

"How much do you owe?"

"I owe nothing, having paid all my bills in full before coming to market."

"Do you carry any fire insurance?"

"Yes; four thousand dollars."

"How much rent do you pay?"

"Twenty-five dollars a month."

"How many goods do you sell a year?"

"About fourteen to fifteen thousand dollars' worth."

"How large a bill do you wish to purchase from us?"

"About two thousand dollars."

Now, Mr. Credit Man, during your interview with me you have formed your opinion of me from what I have said and from the way I look. If I have impressed you as a truthful man, an honest man, and if your judgment is not at fault, you would be perfectly safe in saying to me:—

"Mr. Smith, we will be pleased to extend the line of credit you ask, and hope this is only the beginning of many transactions which will prove mutually satisfactory."

Mr. Credit Man, if you will glance at this statement of my affairs you will perceive I am a first-class risk, provided I have been telling you the truth. In the first place, I have no indebtedness at present, and it is always what a merchant owes that gives him anxiety and trouble, and the same thing applies to the life of a university student.

Secondly, if my store should catch fire, I have the stock covered with four thousand dollars of insurance, and the chances are I would be able to save part of my goods; therefore the risk in this direction is very small. Thirdly, I am selling for cash, therefore I cannot lose anything in bad debts. Fourthly, my sales amount to over one thousand dollars a month, and therefore in sixty days I will have sufficient money to pay my bill to you, even if I did not have one thousand dollars cash now on deposit in my bank.

THE REPORT OF MR. HARDUP.

Now the next man who is presented to you, Mr. Credit Man, is Mr. John Hardup, from Oshkosh, Wis., and you proceed to interview in a like manner and elicit the following information:—

Stock on hand	$28,000
Trusted out	14,000
Cash on hand	very small
Total resources	$42,000
Liabilities.	
Owe bank	$7,500
Owe mdse. not due	15,000
Owe mdse. due	4,500
Total liabilities	$27,000
Net worth	$15,000

Carry $10,000 fire insurance; rent, $100 a month; sales, $35,000 per annum.

Now, Mr. Credit Man, if you compare these two statements it will be observed that Hardup thinks he is worth two and one-half times as much as Smith—fifteen thousand dollars as against six thousand dollars—and yet I do not believe that any one of you would trust Hardup for a dollars' worth of goods. Why? In the first place, his indebtedness is very large, and some of it is past due. Secondly, if fire should come, he has but ten thousand dollars of insurance on a stock worth twenty-eight thousand dollars, the difference being more than the amount he thinks he is worth. Thirdly, he is carrying altogether too large a stock for the business he is doing. His sales are less than three thousand dollars each month, and if he were unfortunate in collecting his outstanding accounts it would require many months' sales to cancel his present indebtedness. The only chance that I can see for Mr. Hardup to save himself from an inglorious failure is to have a "going-out-of-business sale" and reduce his stock, get a collector to collect his outstanding accounts as fast as possible and apply every dollar toward reducing his indebtedness, and then commence on a smaller scale in a more favorable locality.

TRUE AND FALSE INFORMATION.

I think I hear some one say: "How do you know the information you obtain by personal interview is true? The would-be debtor might deceive you!" Well, here is where the credit man has to exercise his judgment. It is usual for customers to give references to their banks and to other dealers with whom they have had an account, and by writing for this information it can be easily obtained. Then there are mercantile agencies who make it a business to collect information of the financial standing and responsibility of every one in trade, and they issue reference books which indicate the capital and credit of the parties reported, and by sending to them one can obtain a special report in regard to any particular party, and while these reports are not always infallible, yet, considering how much these agencies undertake to do, it is surprising that they render so acceptable service.

The credit man, to be successful, must give considerable attention to many other matters, to which the limit of this discussion will prevent even a reference. In closing, let us remember that when we make a credit we have parted with something of value, and for which value is to be returned at a future time, and so we take chances on what time may do. Of what it will do no one can be absolutely certain. There is then a degree of uncertainty which attaches to all credit transactions, but we need not be without our bearings. The sailor with his chart and compass may be in the middle of a tempestuous ocean, but he is not altogether "at sea." By making use of the aids at his command, and the experience of others before him in locating the danger spots, his risk is reduced to a minimum quantity, and this is the ambition of every credit man.

Along the Highways and Byways of Business

By VANNANT

I frankly admit that I greatly enjoyed the May issue of COMMERCE, ACCOUNTS & FINANCE. It was much more interesting than the March number that contained the poor screed from yours truly, which seems to have set all the schoolmasters humming. I doubt if the issue in which this is printed will be half as good, from my standpoint at least, as the last. However, the editor has said, "Vannant will not sit silent under rebuke," and again, "He is a hard fighter." Now that word rebuke struck me as particularly good. Who may "rebuke"? Certainly no one who is not master, or, at least, superior, by way of authority or position. A parent may rebuke a child; a teacher may rebuke a pupil. Does the reader follow my train of thought? What I am trying to say is that I do not at all feel rebuked. It is some other word that should have been used. Next, as to the fighting. I am not so sure the editor is right in that case, either. Suffice it for me to admit, however, that I have the courage of my convictions, and I am convinced that the facts of the case support me. If this is so, who is afraid?

* * *

But before I get my war paint and feathers in shape and my "tommyhawk" sharpened let us give a moment's attention to the questions at issue. What is the fight about, anyway? What are the contentions of the respective parties? I will state the case as I understand it, and if I err therein my critics can supply the deficiencies at some future time. First, however, let me say that this contest or "scrimmage," whatever it may best be called, is nothing new. In what I said in the March issue of COMMERCE, ACCOUNTS & FINANCE I only repeated, in substance at least, what has been printed from my pen at intervals during the past twenty years or more, as those who have files of The Bookkeeper (New York), American Counting Room, The Treasury, The Office and Business can readily verify. Particularly complete will my record in this regard be found in the pages of the two periodicals last named. My contention, stated in the briefest form, is that "those who teach should know." Unfortunately it is the fact, apparently, that the large majority of the teachers in the business schools do not know, experimentally or practically, that which they are pretending to teach. This would not be so bad if they dropped the misleading statements which their circulars issued to the public contain. The commercial teachers know and are able to teach many things which the youth of the land will profit by learning, and those of us who have come out of the schools into active business careers are never backward in giving proper credit for the same. It is that which the schools are unable to teach, because the teachers employed do not know and which, nevertheless, they assert in their advertisements they do teach, that is objected to; or, to put it otherwise, that subjects the school to ridicule on the one hand and their graduates to contempt on the other.

* * *

Now, my critics, old and new, are going to say that for a brief presentation of the question at issue the above is without good precedent, in that it combines argument with statement. However that may be let it stand for the moment. I have yet more to say. My critics are incensed at the style of my remarks. They say in effect "not so loud, or some one will hear you." And this reminds me of a story: A huckster drove into town shouting lustily from time to time, "Potatoes," "P-o-t-a-t-o-e-s." A man stepped up to the wagon and said, "Not so loud—you will disturb somebody." The potato man asked, "Do you want to buy some potatoes?" "No," said the citizen, "I only wanted to advise you against making so much noise. Why we can't do business for your incessant crying of 'potatoes.'" "Well, mister," said the huckster, "you see I wants to be heard 'cause I've got potatoes to sell." And he continued his way down street ever and anon calling "P-o-t-a-t-o-e-s, P-o-t-a-t-o-e-s." For many years past I have labored for and with the schools, and my one thought has been to get them on to the highest plane of utility by persuading them to tell the truth about themselves, and to cease pretending to do that for which they are entirely disqualified. I have shouted in the market places, or otherwise I should not have been heard. My pleadings, conversationally and in the ordinary form of writing have not been successful. A few loud words with the general business public to hear, by way of audience, have always served the purpose. More than once the late S. S. Packard, than whom the business schools never had a better champion, has gone up to the national gatherings of the commercial teachers with one of Vannant's screeds as the text for the masterful address he made. And perhaps as many as a hundred times has he told me in conversation: "I know we merit much that you say, but why not say it privately rather than before the public?" I met Prof. Packard and Dr. Pierce in the house of the latter, in Philadelphia, only a little while before the death of Dr. Pierce, for a conference with respect to measures that might be taken for the more practical training of young men for the business office and for the responsibilities of public accounting and auditing, and on that occasion the writings of Vannant came up for discussion. Both of the distinguished teachers with whom I found myself committed themselves to an indorsement of much that Vannant had written, but deplored the publicity of the thing. They freely admitted that many of the schools were overdoing the thing, that confounding bookkeeping with accounting, and talking about "business" when only penmanship and shorthand were really meant, was creating a sentiment of distrust among business men concerning the schools in general.

* * *

And now a word or two for my critics, whose communications of criticism and comment the editor has seen fit to print. I admire the editor's spirit, and cordially indorse the motto of hearing the other fellow's side. Col. Soulè swings off into poetry, and if only I had not lent my dictionary of quotations to a commercial teacher a few days ago I would try to reply in kind. Suffice it under the circumstances to suggest just one excerpt from the classics—

"Let the galled jade wince,"

or words to that effect. I disclaim an attack upon "a class of educational institutions so confessedly pre-eminent in good work as the commercial schools of the United States and Canada." I admit an attack upon the humbug part of all the commercial schools, wherever situated. As long as the schools do not attempt to teach anything which the teachers employed do not know practically they have my support. The more they get into their courses practically of what some of them now pretend to teach, and do not simply because the teachers do not know, the more they will merit the support of the business public and the plaudits of Vannant. Teach accounting, gentlemen, but employ real accountants to do the teaching. Teach business, if you will, but have practical and successful business men to do the instructing, not mere masters of penmanship and theoretical writers of shorthand. Teach only that which you know, and know practically, at the hands of your professors and teachers, everything your pretend to teach. That is all there is to it.

* * *

Col. Soulè, and others as well, insinuate that I attack the commercial schools because I have a school of my own "that I wish to benefit by misrepresenting other institutions of a kindred nature." Do they mean to judge my motives by their own? They apparently admit that their schools are hit—that is, injured—therefore mine must be benefited. Gentlemen, I have no school. I have never had as much as one cent invested in any school, and very probably I shall never have any connection whatever with any commercial school. Again Col. Soulè is curious, as are others also, about my identity. After saying, by way of reply to this point, that we can talk that matter over, as we have various others in the past, when next we meet, let me suggest that there is far more importance attached to the real facts of the case than to the humble instrument that makes them known.

* * *

My Chicago critic presents one or two excellent points. He must excuse me if I yield to his logic in part. He says: "Even a dog will resent criticism of his actions when such criticisms are conveyed in unfriendly tones." I should never have thought of saying dog, notwithstanding the barking. The figure of speech used by the editor in the introduction is "hornets' nest." As between stinging and barking, the latter really hurts the least. A "Chicago Commercial Teacher" continues: "Vannant evidently has a grievance." Further on he says: "Vannant is evidently of that cult that believes unless a man is a member of the inner circle of his particular accountant's association he is a nobody and the truth is not in him." To this I say, you have another guess coming to you. As to the grievance, there is none, as other parts of this article disclose. As to my standing with the accountants, I doubt if it is much better than with the commercial teachers. Several organizations to which it would be an honor to belong have never solicited my membership, and with certain others I could not affiliate under any circumstances. I quite indorse this writer when he says, concerning public accountants, that he knows some who "do not have sufficient hard-headed, practical business sense to successfully run a peanut stand." I know the same men, or possibly others of the same class.

* * *

But here is the gem of his whole letter. It is the truth, the whole truth and nothing but the truth. If it could be said of the majority of the schools, instead of a very few of them, Vannant would put up his fountain pen until such time as he found some other bit of humbug that needed to be effaced: "The reliable business schools of the country do not pretend great things; they simply profess to do a few things, but they do claim to be doing those few things well." I had the pleasure, some time since, of visiting a school in Chicago, being under the safe convoy on that occasion of one that, I almost guess, is the writer of the letter from which I have been quoting, and what I then saw and heard causes me in part so quickly to indorse what this critic has conceded in the controversy. We talked over at that time much that Vannant had been writing, only to agree mutually that, however true his assertions might be with respect to some schools, they did not appply to that school.

* * *

I have made a little calculation. Thirty-seven years ago I was a pupil in the leading commercial college in Podunk—the widely-known metropolis of one of the great states of this glorious Union. In that city, at the time, there were two other business schools, and the newspaper press, then, as now in other localities, proclaimed (in the advertising columns) each school as the only original and genuine, and from time to time in like manner offered warnings to the unwary lest they should by accident enroll in the wrong institution. In the towns north, south, east and west of us there were still other schools, none of which, as I recall the circumstances, was in the least backward in appealing to the public in the same general way. My curiosity led me to inquire at that time how many business schools there were in the entire nation. Unfortunately there was no Commercial Teachers Association in existence, and therefore no one really knew. Judging from facts which have since come to my notice I suppose there must have been three or four hundred of them. I am told now by those who are in position to know that for several years past there have been not many less than a thousand of these schools in existence The number of graduates per year per school is something I have not been able to ascertain with any degree of certainty. It is a very insignificant school, however, that does not turn out as many as fifty or seventy-five, while the larger schools, perhaps graduate ten times as many. Now here is the calculation I have referred to, and the figures are restricted to the time I have been connected directly and indirectly with the schools—say the space of a generation.

* * *

I assume that for the past thirty-seven years the commercial schools in number have averaged as many as 500, and that each school each year has averaged as many as 100 graduates. Then we have 500 x 100 x 37 or 1,850,000 graduates turned loose upon an inoffensive business world in that time. If we make ample allowance for the graduates who never go out of the schools further than the vestibule, being called back at that point to become teachers in the schools—even though they have never seen the workings of a business office—we still have left, say one million men per generation, who in the business world must acknowledge their obligations to the schools for their education, if, indeed, they do not reverse the matter and condemn the business schools for their lack of practical training and the vast amount of misinformation with which they were sent out. Now with one million men representing the schools the past thirty-seven years, is it strange at all that the handful, comprising such men as Lyman J. Gage, ex-Secretary of the Treasury; John A. McCall, President of the New York Life Insurance Company; James G. Cannon, Vice-President of the Fourth National Bank, New York; S. S. McClure and Frank A. Munsey, the publishers; T. J. Foster, founder of the International Correspondence Schools, and others who are mentioned by my critics, should exist as the exception to prove the rule? I venture to say for each of these men, that while he no doubt feels indebted to the school from which he graduated, for help in his course, still he is of the kind of timber that would have succeeded anyhow. The schools cannot have all the credit for the success of these men, for in abstract justice it belongs to the men themselves. They triumphed in their chosen courses, in spite of the misinformation and unwisdom of those who were their guides at the outset. Rather let the schools rejoice that there are a few who have escaped the swamps and jungles into which their preferred course of instruction not infrequently leads.

* * *

I have repeatedly read from beginning to end the earnest, truthful and common-sense letter from "A Teacher," Brooklyn. In my estimation it is correct throughout. Neither business man nor accountant, much less Vannant, can pick flaws in it. If all that I have written on this subject—one that I protest is close to my heart—had done nothing more than to produce this letter, the result would have justified the effort. This writer puts the schools where they can safely stand. He reads both teachers and accountants certain lessons they will do well to heed. He understands the situation perfectly. He has put the case far better than I have ever succeeded in doing, and therefore I thank him for his letter. Those of you who are "riled" at Vannant by reason of his style and general aggressiveness read this letter from "A Brooklyn Teacher," remembering the while that Vannant indorses it as being correct and complete. Perhaps then you can discuss the question before you without display of temper and without impugning motives.

* * *

There are various other assertions in the communications of some of my critics which I can likewise indorse. Mr. Sparrow says: "I do not agree that commercial teachers are, as a class, impracticable." For that matter Vannant does not so agree either. But has Mr. Sparrow really said what he means? Mr. Gaylord very justly says: "Teaching successfully in a good commercial school and serving acceptably as a public accountant are two entirely different professions." Everybody will agree to this. Again: "Quite as many commercial teachers have succeeded as public accountants as there are public accountants who have become successful commercial teachers." That is an exceedingly safe thing to say. It is true, for the line of promotion and advancement is in the other direction. Succeed as a teacher if you can, and then aspire to something higher and more remunerative.

* * *

It is an admitted fact that various commercial schools readily find places for their pupils. Some of the proprietors of these schools are so practical (so commercial, if you please) as to go among the employers of clerks, stenographers, bookkeepers and the like, in order to become acquainted with the real wants of the case and thereby be in position to train their pupils accordingly. Such commercial teachers are alive to the situation, and are doing a great good to both their pupils and the business world. These graduates are real helpers in the office. But there are others, one of whom called upon me not long since. "Now, Mr. Vannant, here is my diploma from the ——— college. By it you see I am qualified for any position your entire establishment has." "Have you ever done any real office work?" "No; I don't need to. I learned everything that is necessary at school. Prof. —— told me so." "What salary do you require?" "Not less than $2,500—" "Is not that steep for a beginner, particularly in view of the considerable number of experienced men who are looking for positions?" "Well, I might take a little less, but Prof. —— told me my ability would command that much." The only position we have open is that of assistant bookkeeper, and the salary is only—" I did not have the chance to name the salary. He cut me short. "Do you think I, a graduate of the ——— college, would take any position as mere assistant?"

* * *

I have been an employer of office labor upon a pretty extensive scale for over twenty-five years. My experience, owing to branch houses, etc., has been in several states covering a considerable part of the Union. I have encountered so many of the general class illustrated above that I have sometimes thought some of the schools were obtaining patronage under false pretenses.

* * *

For the good of the great cause of business education, I sincerely hope, and in the light of some of the letters before me I venture to believe that a considerable number of the schools of late see the situation in the correct light, and are, in fact, according to their ability and opportunity, arranging to serve the business man in the way he needs help, and at the time he requires help. If this is the case, Vannant will never need lift his voice, or even his pen, on this subject again. So mote it be.

Indorsers of Vannant

In the May number of COMMERCE, ACCOUNTS & FINANCE were published several letters from commercial teachers criticizing Vannant and his attitude toward business colleges and their methods of teaching. These critics and their sharp replies have apparently aroused the interest of those who believe that commercial schools are not all they should be, and the following letters contain some brisk arguments for the Vannant side of the question:—

Commercial School Graduates

From E. T. B., New York, N. Y.

It seems to me that there is one point against the commercial schools, as they exist today, that neither Vannant nor the opposition touch upon, that is, the kind of positions secured by graduates from the business colleges when they go out into the cold world to earn a livelihood. I am not referring just now to the students of shorthand and typewriting. I will admit, as does Vannant, that the commercial schools really do turn out stenographers and typewriters. I will admit this, but I want to add this comment; if the graduate of a grammar school knew as little about the study of arithmetic as some of the graduates of commercial schools know about the practical use of stenography, he never would be given a diploma. Ask any business man who employs stenographers if this isn't true.

But never mind the stenographers: How about the bookkeepers? When a young man leaves the business college, bearing with him his certificate of efficiency, what kind of a position does he secure? I maintain that, in nine cases out of ten, he secures no better position than does the young man just out of high school who has had no business education whatever. If he has no "pull" or influential connections, he starts at the foot of the ladder and works up, just as the high school, or even the grammar school boy has to do.

The commercial school people will say "Yes, that may be true; but after he has secured the position his rise will be much more rapid than the other boy." Will it? Let us see.

THE COMMERCIAL SCHOOL BOY AND THE OTHER.

He begins at the foot of the ladder, perhaps helping the bookkeeper; so does the other boy. He knows the principles of bookkeeping; the other boy does not. But neither boy knows anything about the peculiar system of bookkeeping used by that firm, and each has to learn it by actual experience. Now, I hold that while the boy who has not attended the commercial school is learning that particular system of bookkeeping, he is also learning the principles that underlie all bookkeeping, and learning them almost without effort, and from the best teacher—Practical Experience. At the end of a year, unless there is a radical difference in character and ability, one boy will hold as good a position as the other boy, and know as much about bookkeeping and office work.

But suppose the commercial college boy does get ahead faster—remember, I do not admit that he does, but for argument's sake we will suppose it—how much ahead is he? Not more than six months, surely. Even a commercial teacher will admit that, always understanding the natural abilities of the boys to be the same. But the commercial school boy has spent from one to three years to acquire his knowledge. This time is, in most cases, taken out of the time which might have been spent at high school or in actual work. If he had spent the two or three years in high school he would have had a better general education. If he had gone to work in a good, though subordinate, position, he would have learned more of actual business. What, therefore, has he gained by two or three years study and the expenditure of his money? He is six months ahead of the high school boy, but the latter knows more about general subjects and has not spent a cent.

BUSINESS MEN AND THE COMMERCIAL SCHOOL GRADUATE.

Many commercial schools, not all, perhaps, but many—claim to turn out young men ready and able to keep the books of a business house. They do not do this, and the graduate finds this out after bitter experience. Not one business man in a hundred gives the graduate of a commercial school a better position than he gives any beginner in his office. This may be bad judgment or prejudice on the part of the business man, but it is a fact nevertheless, and the average commercial school graduate will tell you so. If both boys go through high school and then one enters a commercial school while the other enters college or goes to work in an office, I think the second is the gainer. If he goes to college he has the advantage of the college education and associations. If he goes into business he gains just so much time. In either case I believe him to be ahead of the commercial school student.

From a Well-Known Accountant

From V. E. H., New York, N. Y.

I have read with considerable interest the criticisms of Vannant and the replies of those who have seen fit to take up the cudgels either for or against him. Some of the arguments on both sides have been lengthy, and when finished have not been conclusive either one way or the other. Others have been tinged with prejudice, which, of course, one expects to find in some slight degree in any criticism that may be made on any subject by those who are defending their own interests.

I myself am one who has, perhaps, no axe to grind. I also have had a commercial school education and believing myself thoroughly fitted by such education, have had the experience of seeking situations. Later, I have had experience in almost every phase of accountancy.

There is, perhaps, no doubt but that elementary instruction in bookkeeping, that is to say the elucidation of the principles of debit and credit and the instruction in the ordinary mercantile transactions, can just as well be imparted by those who have no specific training as can the teaching of the A, B, C's by a person who is not fitted for advanced teaching.

It must be noted that today the instructors in our common schools are required to pass certain examinations, and for the higher grades of instruction are required to possess a certificate from some normal school or other institution, certifying to their training in this field.

Coming along further to the instruction in the technical and professional schools, we find that in every case the instructors must be specially fitted for the degree, and certainly accountancy is a profession which requires, as much as any of the professions, careful training and instruction by experienced teachers.

The instruction that is given in the ordinary business school, so-called, I would liken to the instruction that a pupil in German might receive from an American instructor whose knowledge of the language has been acquired from the study of textbooks by English instructors.

In some branches the business schools undoubtedly have a field, but they certainly are not equipped today to fit a man for the profession of accountancy.

Hot Shot for the Commercial Schools

From P. F. J., Brooklyn, N. Y.

It is high time that some fearless and responsible periodical, or some writer like Vannant, took up the question of the so-called commercial schools. Most of these institutions being prolific advertisers, the eyes of editors seem blinded to the glaring impossibilities of promises artistically printed under the head of "Educational Announcements." At an astonishingly low price an education which guarantees a position of honor and high remuneration is offered for sale. Purchasers should beware of "gold bricks."

The majority of those entering upon the business of conducting a "Commercial College" do so to make money. For the purpose of attracting trade, promises of an alluring nature are made. Honors are frequently granted to those who are not eligible. Diplomas and positions are attractive baits, and are so often used as to throw discredit upon educational movements along these lines.

Thinking, brainy "Captains of Industry" hold it to be a mooted question whether the graduates of great universities make better business men than do those who have not been college students. The question has been argued pro and con through the press of the country, but still remains a question. These institutions, the great universities endowed with millions, are above mercenary motives. Can this be said of the commercial colleges?

Knowledge is power. "The man that knows and knows that he knows, he is wise, follow him." Does the commercial college impart knowledge? Is not the stuff taught "josh"? In the language of Omar Khayyam, "Their words to scorn are scattered, and their mouths are stopped with dust," many many times.

That Vannant should take up the question of education along these lines is a noble and plucky work.

No Theory Taught

From "Immune," Springfield, Mass.

I have read Vannant's articles in COMMERCE, ACCOUNTS & FINANCE, and some of his critics' replies thereto. Any one can see with half an eye that they—the critics—mean well, but what an awful stew the poor harassed commercial teachers seem to be in! Really it is too bad of Mr. Vannant to so harrow their sensitive feelings.

But maybe my point of view is too narrow and selfish. If the credulous public want the "education" the schools have to sell and are willing to pay the price, wish them luck and let them go ahead and buy it. If they get buncoed, why put it in the papers and make their humiliation greater? If they never find out the worth of the "gold brick," they are happy, and the commercial schools grow rich. We all must live, and teachers must make money somehow. Why do anything that tends to take bread from the mouths of the needy?

TEACHING IN THE COMMERCIAL SCHOOL.

But mine, I fear, is an exaggerated view of the case. I am prone to be sarcastic in proportion to what I think I have escaped by not being a graduate of a commercial school. I started out to make my own way in life comparatively early. I had kept books, learning how from my superiors in each case, in two or three establishments before I got a chance at the luxury, as I then thought it, of the "complete commercial education" offered by one of the most prominent "business colleges" in the country. Perhaps I was precocious, but I found that the teachers were prolific in directions to "do this this way," and to "do that that way," with never a reason why, except that, "that is the way it should be done," meaning the way laid down in the ——— manual. Practice—lots of it; no end of daily cautions, such as "Use a new pen"—meaning a special brand for that school, but reasons, principles or theory,—none at all.

So I quit, and bought books on the subject, Soulé, Dicksee, Thornton and a lot of others, and imbibed each author's theories, had a try at reconciling one with another, and relied on my efforts to earn my daily bread for the "practice" and exemplification of theory.

I am yet comparatively young, and perhaps my experience doesn't count, but I've worked along side of "business college" graduates, worked under them, hired them and fired them, and I never found one fresh from the "complete commercial education" factory that had any reasons for doing anything in the way he was taught to do it except "That that is the way they do it as So-and-So's college, and it must be right."

Of course, there must be exceptions, and some of the commercial schools are undoubtedly doing good work. But in the main, I am heartily in sympathy with Vannant's criticisms, and with the belief that there is the need of teachers who not only know how to teach, but what to teach and why.

Concerning "Teaching Ability"

From "Common Sense," Boston, Mass.

I read Vannant's somewhat peppery effusion in the March number of COMMERCE, ACCOUNTS & FINANCE, and when I had finished reading it I said "Hurrah!" and would have thrown up my hat had I been wearing one at the time. Vannant's remarks "hit me where I lived," as my fifteen-year-old boy would say. Whoever Vannant may be, his ideas on the "teaching" of the young by incompetent persons—that is, by persons who know only the superficialities of the subjects they profess to teach—are mine exactly.

The argument of Vannant's critics seems to be that "teaching ability" and a perfunctory knowledge of the subject to be taught are all that is necessary. Armed with "teaching ability" and a little knowledge, the pedagogue is not afraid of any lion in the path. If he cannot overcome it, he can, by a circuitous route, avoid it, and the youth whom he is leading doesn't know the difference. If this youth is studying bookkeeping and accounting, and, daring to think for himself and to allow his thoughts to stray from the hide-bound examples in the school text book, encounters a difficult problem—a question as to what should be done with a certain item under certain conditions—what follows? He asks the teacher, and that paragon of "teaching ability," not having the least idea what should be done with said item, replies: "Oh, that is a minor detail and irrelevant just now. Questions of that sort are usually settled by—ahem—er—circumstances and conditions. It isn't wise to cross a bridge until you get to it," etc., etc. Thus "teaching ability" emerges triumphant, and if the student isn't satisfied, why, he may as well be.

TEACHERS OF DRAWING.

The instructors in drawing in our grammar schools are generally speaking, graduates of normal art schools. They "know enough of the subject to teach." Their own drawing in many cases is mediocre at the best and bad at the worst, therefore they do very little drawing before their pupils and depend entirely upon the text books. The consequence is that the pupil in the grammar school cannot really draw at all. He can follow a copy after a fashion, but he can do little more. If he has any talent, it is not developed to any appreciable extent.

Now, who teaches the art students of Paris, the city to which, as every one knows, most aspiring artists go to seek a knowledge of painting and illustrating? In every case the instructor is himself an artist of renown and proved skill. He not only "knows enough to teach," he knows enough to paint, and to paint well He can tell the pupil where the latter's work is wrong, and, more than that, by practical illustration he can show him how to make it right.

HOW ABOUT THE DOCTORS?

Would you trust your own life, or that of a dear one, to a doctor who had received instruction in his profession from some one who possessed "teaching ability" and but a scanty knowledge of medicine? I don't believe you would. Then why should you trust the books—or even one important book—of your business to the care of a young man who has had no experience in office work, and who has been taught by a teacher who has little or no knowledge of accountancy but is long on "teaching ability"?

That there is such a thing as "teaching ability" I should be the last to deny, but that this is of such vast importance as to override all else and make knowledge of the subject taught a secondary consideration, I do deny most emphatically. Many first-class accountants would make poor teachers, but what of it? They do not pretend to teach. Now commercial teachers do pretend to teach office work and accountancy when, as some of the more candid ones admit, their knowledge of these things is, in so many cases, superficial and derived only from text books and not from practical experience

So this is why I said "Hurrah!" when I read Vannant's screed "pitching into" the commercial schools. I am not yet too old to have lost my interest in the practical education of the young, and I think I may honestly say that I wish the commercial schools well. But they will have to do better work than they are now doing before business men in general will accept the diploma of one of their graduates at its face value. By the way, Vannant uses a nom de plume, and some of his critics do the same. I also am going to avail myself of the privilege.

Business Subjects in Current Literature

Business is represented in the various issues of the magazines for the past month by an astonishing variety of articles. Various business subjects are treated by authorities, always in a thoroughly competent manner, and generally in a way that makes them very interesting reading, not only for one acquainted with the details of the special line of business described in the article, but for the casual reader of the magazine. Editors are fairly good barometers so far as indicating the trend of thought of their readers is concerned, and they give the public, through their magazines, only what it wants. The public today is interested in business, and consequently it gets business literature in vast variety. The readers of COMMERCE, ACCOUNTS & FINANCE must remember that in attempting to enumerate some of the articles on business subjects published during the past month, no attempt is made to give a complete list. That would be almost impossible. However, here are a few of the many interesting essays and stories from current periodicals.

GENERAL BUSINESS SUBJECTS.

E. H. Rydall, in the Era, writes of the "Ostrich Industry in California." H. Gannett, in the Forum, presents "Industrial Position of the United States." Henry George, Jr., writing for the Westminster Review, of London, gives us an article on, "The Next Depression in America." In Gunton's, G. E. Walsh discusses the "Value of By-Products." In the Overland Monthly, Joanna M. Kyle tells very interestingly of "The Humorous Side of the Patent Office." "A Business Talk on Yukon," by F. C. Wade, appears in the Canadian Magazine, of Toronto. P. Arndt writes of "Commercial Relations" in the International Monthly. An odd vocation and one little known is described by N. C. Hollister, in his paper on "The Wreck-Master's Work," in the Cosmopolitan.

"Life in Canadian Lumbering Camps" is described by M. Paterson, in the Canadian Magazine, and P. L. McGrath, in Frank Leslie's, gives us glimpses of the life of the sealers, in his paper, "Sealing off the Banks." "Foreign Trade Delusions" is described in Gunton's Magazine, and in the Engineering Magazine A. Willey writes of the "Modern Operation of a Grain Elevator."

No less a personage than Andrew Carnegie contributes to the North American Review a paper on "The Opportunity of the United States." In Gunton's Magazine, W. P. Wilson presents "Commerce as a National Peace-Maker," and "The Sugar Convention at Brussels" is discussed by T. Barth, in the Anglo-American Magazine. This subject is also discussed by G. Blondel, in the Revue Politique et Parliementaire of Paris, and "Sugar in 1902" is the title of an article by F. Dergauwen, in the Revue Generale, Brussels. In the World's Work, C. A. Smith attempts to answer the question, "Does Industrialism Kill Literature?" In Cassell's Magazine, H. Pettibone writes on "Gas Power Plants for Mining." An anonymous writer in the World's Work writes about the "World's Financial Center."

A writer by the odd name of Flamingo, in the Nuova Antologia, published in Rome, discusses "The Commercial Invasion in Europe by America." In the Fortnightly Review appears an essay on "British Shipping," by J. H. Schooling. In the Engineering Magazine, H. Emerson writes on the "Coal and Resources of the Pacific." In the National Magazine, C. H. Spencer writes of the "Mangingo Route, a Sea Level Canal." N. D. Scott, in the same periodical, has a paper on the "Merits of the San Blas Canal Route."

AGRICULTURE AND FORESTRY.

Agriculture, scientific gardening and subjects pertaining to forestry, farming, etc., have received attention from many writers. "American Forestry, a New Career," is the title of an article by J. R. Smith, in the Forum. C. C. Bovey, in the Review of Reviews, presents "The Fallacy of Exporting Beef." "Our Mountain Forests" are entertainingly described by C. P. Ambler, in Country Life in America. In this same magazine appears "The Art of Forestry, What is it?" by an anonymous writer. In the Forum, R. M. Barker writes of "Irrigation in the Arid Southwest." The contemporary Review, of London, contains an article on "Plant Sanitation," by J. B. Carruthers.

LABOR AND STRIKES.

It is but natural that the subjects of labor and the relations between employers and employees should receive attention in these days of strikes. B. O. Flower, in the Arena, discusses "Organized Labor and Direct Legislation." C. Warman, in the North American Review, has a paper on the "Way of the Workingman." "Wages in Municipal Employment" is the subject of an article by J. R. Commons, in the Quarterly Journal of Economics, and E. L. Bogart, in Bibliotheca Sacra, has the second of a series of articles on the "Steel Strike." In the Anglo-American Magazine, E. Gellender presents the second of his series of papers on the "Economic Aspects of Trusts." Among the articles on these subjects in foreign periodicals are "Labor Syndicates," by M. Dufourmantelle, and "Labor Prohibitions," by J. De Bruignac, in the Reform Sociale, Paris, and "A Pastoral Letter on Strikes," by Mgr. Bonomelli, in the Rasegna Nazionale, published in Florence.

BANKING.

Banking and financial subjects receive their usual share of attention. In the World's Work, W. J. Boies describes "New Banking Methods." "Supposed Necessity of the Legal Tender Paper" is discussed by D. C. Barrett, in the Quarterly Journal of Economics. In the North American Magazine, A. B. Martinez presents a paper upon the "Public Debt of the Argentine Republic." In the Bankers' Magazine, of London, F. E. Steele discusses "Banking Facilities and Import Trade," and this magazine also contains the fourth paper in a series on the "British Mint and Its Work."

GREAT MEN OF AFFAIRS.

There seems to be fewer stories than usual this month of great men who have succeeded in business. "Captains of Industry," the first instalment of a series, is published in the Cosmopolitan, and in that magazine also C. W. Price writes of "Thomas Alva Edison."

TRANSPORTATION.

There are many articles on the various kinds of transportation in this country and abroad, and among them are the following: "Street Railway Franchises in New York" are discussed in Municipal Affairs. In this magazine also appears an article on "Milan Street Railways," by E. Magrini. Cassell's Magazine contains a paper by J. F. Gairns, on "British Tank Locomotives." "New Forms of Locomotion" is what J. S. Montagu has to talk about to his English readers in the London Fortnightly Review. "The Bagdad Railway" is described by D. G. Hogarth, in the National Review of London. "Railway Development in South Africa" is the title of A. C. Key's contribution to the English Magazine. In the Canadian Magazine, W. D. Gregory writes on the "Folly of Railway Subsidies." In Cassell's Magazine there is an interesting description of "Railway Stations in England," by A. Sleveking and H. MacFarlane.

PHOTOGRAPHY.

As usual, photography and its various branches fill much space in our periodicals. In the Photographic Times, New York, appears a contribution on "Emphasis in Portraiture," by E. K. Hough, and one on "Intensification," by G. Hauber-isser. In the Times also G. A. Sawyer discusses "Photography in the Garden," and H. Edwards-Ficken presents "The Dark Room and its Fixtures." H. C. Dellery has his fourth contribution on "Architectural Photography," and the "Kallitype Process" is described by C. Roloff, in the same publication. In the World's Work, E. Meiklejohn writes of "Adventures in Wild Life Photography," and in Outing, R. W. Shufeldt tells of "Posing Wild Animals for their Photograph." Camera and Dark Room contains, "Improving the Negative," by W. J. Cotterell; "Artistic Landscape Photography," by F. Boiter; "Photographing of Interiors," by F. B. Hargett; "Handling Developing Papers," by M. D. Miller; "Positives and Transparencies," by A. J. Jarman, and "Orthochromatic Plates and Their Advantages," by L. A. Osborne.

ARCHITECTURE AND BUILDING.

Among the articles on Architecture and Building is the well-written one on "The Modern Tall Steel Building," by W. S. Smith, in Cassell's Magazine. A writer in the Architectural Record describes "General Work of the Contractor." There is a paper also in the Record upon the "Architectural Work of Ernest Flagg." S. G. Hilyer, in the Arena, presents "The Iconoclast as a Builder." Country Life in America has the second paper in the series entitled, "Making of a Country Home."

COMMERCIAL EDUCATION.

The subject of commercial education is receiving so much attention over here and abroad that it is but natural that much space should be given in current literature to its discussion. In the Educational Review, H. J. Rogers discusses, "Relation of Education to Industrial and Commercial Developments." H. W. Stebbins, in this same magazine, presents "Industrial Education as a Social Force." In the Atlantic Monthly, J. L. Loughlin writes on "Higher Commercial Education." "Industrial Art Schools in France" are entertainingly described by J. Schoenhof, in the Forum.

WOMAN IN BUSINESS.

"Woman, lovely woman," has her share in the business world today, and consequently her work should be and is written about in the magazines. Millicent Sutherland, in the North American Review, writes on "Woman and Her Sphere," and Lavinia Hart, in the Cosmopolitan, presents "Women as College Presidents." In the Arena, M. E. Carter has a legal paper on "Wives, Widows and Wills."

This brief notice of a portion of the business literature for the past month will give the reader of COMMERCE, ACCOUNTS & FINANCE an idea of the important part that commercial and industrial affairs are playing in our latter-day world. The list is not complete, but it will suffice, and may help the reader to find an article on some subject that is of particular interest to him.

KEEPS THEM AWAKE

Ping.—They say J. Pierpont Morgan is troubled with insomnia.

Pong.—Well, what if he is? The other fellows can't sleep of nights, either.—Chicago News.

MADE A DIFFERENCE

Schoolmaster.—Now, if your mother gave you a large apple and a small one and told you to divide with your brother, which apple would you give him?

Johnny.—D'you mean my big brother or my little brother? —Tit-Bits.

The Lawyer and the Accountant*

By STUART N. CLARKE

At this joyful meeting we can toast the lawyers with hearty good will, whether we look forward to work which we shall share with them, or cast a glance backward on our student days, already a memory.

Our studies have taught us that between the lawyer and the accountant there is much in common, and we know that the young accountant, before he thinks of taking a degree, has spent some years earning practical experience, a jewel which the young lawyer must dig for diligently after the glory of graduation.

In the near future we are likely to see the latter's shingle displayed in the window of his father's grocery; that imposing legend: "John Marshall Perkins, Attorney and Counselor-at-Law," will enliven the gloom of pop's undertaking shop, or will admonish the frivolous couples in the parental ice cream parlor

CLOSE RELATION OF THE TWO PROFESSIONS.

But from these limboes he will soon escape—he is clever, and is said to be a worker of the workers. We are sure to meet him again, to confer with him, have business relations with him; and this is a fitting moment to consider briefly, how it is that the way of the lawyer and the path of the accountant sometimes cross, or run parallel, and how the two professions dwell in sight of each other.

We can understand this better by throwing a searchlight on ourselves. A lady once said, dubiously, to an accountant: "I think yours is the queerest profession!" "True, madam, I'm a born querist," he replied. Indeed, the great seal of the brotherhood of accountants should be a question mark, a question mark, radiant, above a pile of books, opened and closed. It would symbolize the mind of the accountant, alert, filled with honest doubt, seeking always, under the apparent and the plausible, for the truth—the truth at all costs—and always at a reasonable profit to himself.

THE ACCOUNTANT'S THREE QUESTIONS.

In every case submitted to his skill the accountant's mind propounds three leading questions: What are the apparent facts? What the actual state of affairs? And, finally, Are these things according to law?

The first and second enigmas he answers readily by the exact science of his own profession. There stand its rules, like a range of mountains, unchanging and unchangeable. When he asks the third riddle: What is the law of the case? he must turn to face the open sea, advancing and receding, with tides and many currents, and laden with the tempest of conflicting judgments. He cannot leave his problem half unanswered—that is not his caliber—nor accept the opinions of others—that is still more foreign to his tendencies. No; by nature a discoverer, boldly he pushes off into the law to find out for himself.

MUST KNOW THE LAW.

It is part of his business to have no uncertain knowledge here. He fails in power and his clients cannot place their trust in him if he is not as fully aware of their legal rights as of their assets and liabilities. Therefore he must learn to navigate the ocean of the law; make a lawyer of himself to the extent his profession requires, and in his case, above other citizens, applies the mandate that all are presumed to know the law, because the demand for his services is based upon that presumption.

It must be an affair of everyday life to the accountant and the auditor to be able to discuss or look into any point in the laws of business or of ownership, to give a sound opinion, a valuable suggestion or a timely warning, either before or after legal advice is called for. Here, then, the two professions meet. And again, as it is part of the accountant's business to use the law, it is no less a part of the lawyer's necessity to know the outlines of accountancy, for the lawyer must also be guided by the coastline of our unchanging mountains.

In a word both professions are co-existing and closely related. Where the question is a commercial one there Accountics becomes law-giver to courts and attorneys, for the lawyer must always be a partisan, advocating one view, as opposed to its contra; but the accountant is never the advocate—he may not take sides. In the presence of the court he does not argue, but proclaims a conclusion of science, from which there is no appeal.

His position in a tribunal is as high as it is unique, and hence, to bring the argument home to ourselves, no pursuit is of more practical importance to us, outside the mechanics of accounting, than a constant study of the law, and a friendly association with the members of the bar.

THE VALUE OF THE SCHOOL COURSE.

It has been the extraordinary good fortune of the score of men sitting at this table that their education as accountants and auditors has included the imbibing of legal principles at their very fountain-head. We have argued and studied, have recited in the same class-room with men about to plead at the bar, and we may turn now to our own profession, assured that on legal questions we have learned to think as lawyers.

This was a happy accident; those who come after us in the school of Commerce, Accounts and Finance are denied this privilege in the fullness, perhaps, that we enjoyed it. We admired the scope and the grasp of the condensed courses given in our senior year, and I speak especially of Corporations and Partnership, as well as International Laws, yet we felt that it was not the same legal training that made our junior year so memorable and so beneficial.

It was then that we saw the lawyer being fashioned before our eyes; then that we were run into the same mould ourselves; as we sat together in the law classes it was a delight to behold several of our number not merely holding their own in argument, but surprising the men of law by a superior grasp and expression in their own subjects, and winning, by sheer force of merit, the assent and approval of their professors. These are memories to be cherished even above the possession of a sheepskin. We are justly proud of these victories; they have equipped us the better for our fight; moreover they have pointed out a new line of action. We must add to this armor and keep it bright. Systematic, persistent reading must continue to be one of our daily occupations if we are to reap any harvest from the good seed now planted. As Alumni, may we frequently renew the friendships of university days, and we cannot better reach our full growth as accountants than by debate and discussion, bringing out the fruits of our legal studies, that we may not forget, but constantly add to, our training among the lawyers.

*Address delivered at the dinner of the Graduating Class, New York University School of Commerce, Accounts and Finance, held at the St. Denis Hotel, New York City, June 7, 1902.

HE GOT THE TESTIMONIAL

An inventor, having produced a wonderful hair invigorating fluid, sent a case of bottles to a bald editor, with, says Collier's Weekly, a request for a testimonial.

He got it in these terms:—

"A little applied to the inkstand has given it a coat of bristles, making a splendid penwiper at a small cost. We applied the lather to a twopenny nail, and the nail is now the handsomest shaving brush you ever saw, with beautiful, soft hair growing from the end of it some five or six inches in length.

"Applied to doorsteps, it does away with the use of a mat; applied to the floor, it will cause to grow therefrom hair sufficient for a brussels carpet. A little weak lather sprinkled over a shed makes it impervious to the wind, rain or cold. It is good to put inside children's cradles, sprinkle on the roadside or anywhere that luxurious grass is wanted for use or ornament. It produces the effect in ten minutes."

COMMERCE ACCOUNTS & FINANCE

A Magazine of Higher Business Education and Practical Administration. Acknowledged Authority in the Profession of Commerce and Consistent Advocate of Methods Up to Date and Above the Table.

JOSEPH CROSBY LINCOLN, - - - Editor.
FRIEND PITTS, JR., - Circulation and Advertising.
E. R. KITTREDGE, - - - Business Manager.

PUBLISHED MONTHLY

SUBSCRIPTION $1 a Year in the United States, Canada and Mexico. Other countries $1.50. Postage prepaid by the Publishers. In the absence of specific orders to stop at the end of the subscription term the paper will be continued and a bill sent. Entered at the New York Postoffice as Second Class mail matter.

COMMERCE, ACCOUNTS & FINANCE COMPANY, Publishers
Twenty-five Pine Street, New York

Different readers will have different opinions of Vannant's response to his critics, to which we give space in another part of this issue. It may be held by some that Vannant is disposed to take himself too seriously even to be interesting. Others may point out that even when he has his opponent down, instead of pounding the floor with his head, as opportunity certainly offers, he merely holds him while he harangues the public, thereby presenting for the 'steenth time arguments supporting what every sane business man must agree is only common sense, namely, that teachers should not pretend to teach that of which they have no practical knowledge, and that teachers should be experimentally familiar with all that they attempt to teach. This general proposition has been discussed editorially in these pages quite recently, and nothing is necessary at this time in explanation of our own views of the subject. Vannant, while severe with some of his critics, has yet let others off very easy. As umpire we are forced to admit that he has done far less than exhaust the opportunities of the occasion.

*

We are disposed to prize Varnant among the contributors to COMMERCE, ACCOUNTS & FINANCE, if for no other reason, because his articles call forth comment. The reception of Vannant's diatribe, if such it is to be called, shows that this journal is being read, even though somewhat slowly, by a certain class. What appeared in the March issue called forth responses in May, and even at that we held the presses a whole week after the forms were complete to let some of our commercial teacher critics get into that issue. So long as a journal, trade paper, technical paper or what not, does only those things of which its readers approve, the editor hears never a word, but let a variation occur by which the sensibilities of some one are touched, or by which an error seems to be made, and letters from "Pro bono publico," "Oldest reader," "Veteran teacher" and others come pouring in. While approving of Vannant's aggressiveness we do not necessarily indorse his sweeping style. He says it is used only because otherwise attention would not be secured. However that may be, he has surely attracted attention this time.

*

Vannant's little calculation and the conclusions derived therefrom are original and suggestive as well. It is strange, is it not that with so many business men prominent in this generation of business successes, and, as Vannant estimates, with a million commercial school graduates in the field, that all of the successful men should not have come out of the ranks of the graduates? According to the schools, they had the inner track. It does gall West Point on occasion to find that a mere volunteer achieves success in tactics, strategy and administration. As the colonel says in the "Sultan of Sulu," the regular is a mere fighting man, and is prepared for nothing else, while the volunteer goes home at the end of the campaign and runs for Congress. Is it possible, after all the brave talk of the schools about "actual business," "practical accountancy" and other advanced planes of usefulness, that the graduates they turn out are in the main only plain plodders, like stenographers, typewriters, bookkeepers, entry clerks, stock clerks, telegraphers, time-keepers, etc.? Even if it is so the schools have achieved a great measure of usefulness, for where would the army be without the regulars? And where would business be without trained assistants in the minor arts of business?

*

Vannant's little calculation has reminded us of a story which we shall venture to tell, even though the moral suggested is not altogether complimentary to him. A man was up for horse stealing. The prosecuting attorney made out a very clear case against the accused by the testimony of two witnesses who saw him steal the horse. The lawyer for the defence was not in the least abashed, and proceeded to call fifty witnesses who did not see the horse stolen. Preponderance of testimony was on the side of the defendant. Vannant seems to claim the larger part of the million graduates from the schools in the past thirty-seven years as being able to bear testimony against the few who really have done something in the business world.

*

Much curiosity seems to exist as to Vannant's personality. Several have asked pointedly for his name and address. Such questions, of course, we cannot answer—save only with our contributor's permission. Otherwise we would be violating confidence. While Vannant has not yet removed restrictions entirely, he has yet committed himself to a picture scheme in which possibly all of our readers will be interested. We have suggested to him a page or double page as circumstances may warrant, to be entitled "Vannant and his critics." The center photograph would be of this old and time-tried critic of commercial education "as she is done," while arranged around would be the faces of those who have taken up the cudgels in defence of the schools and their ways. Vannant has cordially consented to the scheme. He has said, "I am not at all frightened by their letters, and I shall not be ashamed to be seen in their company. They all mean well—every one of them." So the plan is a go if the critics are agreed and will send us their photographs adapted to reproduction by the halftone process. We shall attempt to secure a picture of Vannant in a "customary attitude," and looking every bit the part he has played in the little drama that has occupied attention so long.

* * *

The office seems dismal and dusty
 And silent and sad as the tomb,
The ledgers look ragged and rusty,
 The desks are o'ershadowed with gloom;
The "old man" is testy and weary,
 The manager savage and glum;
The bookkeeper's draggled and dreary,
 The office boy's stopped chewing gum;
The mornings are cheerless and cloudy,
 The afternoons grimy and gray,
And this the reason,—'tis vacation season—
 The typewriter's gone away.

* * *

So called "standard time" of this country, as everyone knows who has traveled or even consulted a railway time table, is at present in belts, familiarly known as Eastern time, Central time, Mountain time and Pacific time. The way in which this standardizing of time was brought about is familiar to most of our readers. Before the railway companies came to an agreement with reference to these belts of time each individual company had a standard time of its own, and which was supposed to be an average of the sun time of the towns or communities through which the road ran. This resulted in a different standard for almost every road in the country, but comparatively little Inconvenience occurred until the roads began to be lengthened by consolidations and absorptions. Then the question of time became a matter of serious importance, for what would be correct at one end of the road was something very different at the other.

*

Whatever may be the standard time of a section of the country, so far as established by the railways running through it, there are still people in almost every community that for one reason or another prefer sun time, and who feel as though something was seriously out of joint when they are called upon to turn their clocks a few minutes backward or forward, as the case may be, to agree with so-called standard time. Instances can be cited wherein communities, ignoring the standard time of the railroads which enter them continue to conduct their local affairs upon the basis of so-called sun time. Factory whistles blow according to clocks set by sun time, and all social functions are similarly regulated. When it comes to getting ready to take a railway train in such a town the citizen or traveler, as the case may be, is obliged to go through certain rather complicated calculations. Standard or railway time is either fast or slow with respect to local time, but no one is exactly sure which it is, and therefore there is that delightful uncertainty overhanging the calculation which frequently causes people to miss connections.

*

Whether a given community is conducting its affairs with clocks set to railway time or by sun time, it becomes essential that whichever time is recognized shall be properly legalized, so that in the way of contracts there may not be the possibility of dispute. Little by little this question of standard time and legal time is getting into the courts for adjustment, and ere long there will be enough decisions, we dare say, to establish precedents and make it clear sailing for those who propose contracts of a character depending upon clocks and other indications of time.

*

By a decision recently handed down by the Ohio Supreme Court, bearing upon matters of this sort, it would seem that noon comes at 11.27 legal standard time at Akron, in that state. A citizen of that town took out a fire insurance policy some four years ago at 11.30 standard time, the policy being dated "noon" of the day it was issued. At the very minute the business man was getting the policy the business place which was being insured caught fire and was destroyed. By the Ohio law standard time is legal time, and the insurance company in this case refused to pay the insurance. The matter was carried through the courts up to the Supreme Court, which has now decided that "noon" meant the time the sun passed the meridian at Akron, which is 11.27 standard time. Inasmuch as by the admitted facts of the case the fire occurred a little later than this time, the court ordered the insurance company to pay.

* * *

Don't lose yer temper when yer meet a kicker.
Hard words don't help none in a business dicker;
Say what yer've got ter, but just say it smooth,
A leetle butter makes a crust go slicker.

—Rubaiyat of Obed Hayman.

* * *

The question of the metric system continues to be agitated in the daily papers. Certain scientific men, proceeding very possibly along purely theoretical lines, go so far as to suggest that the metric system ought to be made compulsory. Quite recently no less a scientific authority than Lord Kelvin has committed himself to this position. He is reported to have told the committee of the House of Representatives, before which he appeared, that while from political motives he would like to see Great Britain take the lead in an international adoption of the metric system, yet he would rejoice to have the United States take the initiative. So long as the desired end was accomplished he thought it did not really matter which of the Anglo Saxon countries moved first. This is undoubtedly very kind of Lord Kelvin, but after all it does not touch upon the merits of the question.

*

The reader is again reminded that all the agitation in favor of the adoption of the metric system is purely artificial. No doubt the scientific men are honest in urging the measure, but the decision is not to be theirs. It rightfully rests with practical men of affairs who in fact are the ones most concerned with the matters referred to. The wholesale merchant would no doubt profit by the adoption of the metric system. The small manufacturer, retailer, shopkeeper, farmer and the workman on the other hand would not profit by it. To these the metric system would be merely a nuisance, and to force it on them by legislation would be an outrage as well as an absurdity. It should not be overlooked that there is nothing to prevent exporters from using the metric system at present if they want to do so. Many are now so using it, and undoubtedly its use will gradually spread among those doing business with foreign countries in which the metric system has been established.

*

Right here it is interesting to consider what a representative body of business men think of the metric system. The National Association of Manufacturers, through its committee on resolutions, had the following to say concerning the proposition for making the metric system the legal standard in the United States: "It appears to this association, first, that the compulsory adoption of the metric system would probably affect the manufacturing interests of this country as follows: One-third who are exporters to European countries and dependencies would be benefited; one-third who do business in this country and all other countries would neither be benefited nor greatly injured; one-third who do business in this country and in England and dependencies would be seriously injured. For all this the expense and inconvenience would be very great. In view of these conditions and of the further fact that the metric system is already legalized for the use of those who find it profitable, this association recommends that no further action be taken on this matter at this time."

*

The preceding is a more complete statement of the pros and cons of this question coming from an authoritative source than perhaps has ever before been presented to the business public. Accordingly, it merits very careful consideration, and those who are thoughtlessly talking in favor of the metric system would do well to read it over every time they are tempted to say something on the subject. One thing should not be overlooked. Wherever a great change is contemplated in anything that exists, it is to be borne in mind whether the change is undertaken for the purpose of reform or for some other cause that there was some good reason at the outset for the plan that is found to be in existence. It is only fair to those who are using the present methods to let them continue until the reasons for their existence have been fully comprehended and the proposed measures have been shown to be practically better than the old. With all the theoretical completeness of the metric system the constitution of the human mind is such that it will far more readily think quarters, thirds, eighths, sixteenths, etc., than fifths, tenths and hundredths, and right here is a reason for the old and against the new which the advocates of the metric scheme apparently do not stop to consider at all.

The Negotiable Instruments Law*

By THOMAS B. PATON

Liability of General Indorsers—Missing Indorsements—To Whom Warranty Extends—Agent-Indorsers' Responsibility.

NOTE.—As enacted in New York, the Negotiable Instruments Law is divided into nineteen articles as follows:—

1. GENERAL PROVISIONS (Sections 1—17)
2. NEGOTIABLE INSTRUMENTS: Form and Interpretation (20—42)
3. Consideration (50—55)
4. Negotiation (60—80)
5. Rights of holder (90—98)
6. Liabilities of parties (110—119)
7. Presentment for payment (130—148)
8. Notice of Dishonor (160—189)
9. Discharge (200—206)
10. BILLS OF EXCHANGE (210—215)
11. Acceptance (220—230)
12. Presentment for acceptance (240—248)
13. Protest (260—268)
14. Acceptance for honor (280—290)
15. Payment for honor (300—306)
16. Bills in a set (310—315)
17. PROMISSORY NOTES AND CHECKS (320—325)
18. Notes given for patent rights (330—332)
19. Laws repealed: When takes effect (340—341)

The provisions of the law naturally fall under four general classifications.

a. General Provisions.
b. Negotiable Instruments in General.
c. Bills of Exchange.
d. Promissory Notes and Checks.

The text of the law is the same in all the states (with some slight exceptions which will be noted), but the numbering of the sections, and in some states of the articles, is not uniform. There is, however, the same continuity of articles and text, except that in some instances, "General Provisions" follow, instead of precede, the remainder of the act. By following this course of study with reference to the New York act, as above outlined, the reader in each state can apply the same to the law of his own state.

We now come to the section which provides the liability of general indorsers. It is as follows:—

Sec. 116. Liability of General Indorsers.—Every indorser who indorses without qualification, warrants to all subsequent holders in due course:—

1. The matter and things mentioned in subdivisions one, two and three of the next preceding section; and
2. That the instrument is, at the time of his indorsement, valid and subsisting.

And, in addition, he engages that on due presentment, it shall be accepted or paid, or both, as the case may be, according to its tenor, and that if it be dishonored, and the necessary proceedings on dishonor be duly taken, he will pay the amount thereof to the holder, or to any subsequent indorser who may be compelled to pay it.

In discussing this section let us first consider the nature of the warranty and engagement of the general indorser to subsequent holders in due course.

The warranty is (1) that the instrument is genuine, and in all respects what it purports to be; (2) that the indorser has a good title to it; and (3) that all prior parties had capacity to contract; also that the instrument is at the time of indorsement valid and subsisting.

These warranties, 1, 2 and 3, are the same that are made by any person who negotiates an instrument by delivery, without indorsement, or by a qualified indorsement "without recourse," as we have seen by section 115. First, the genuineness of the instrument is warranted. If it is a forged or bogus document, if the signature is spurious, the amount a forgery, or in other vital particulars it is not genuine, the warranty is broken. Not only must the instrument be genuine, but it must be in all respects what it purports to be.

"GOOD TITLE."

A further warranty is that the indorser has "good title." Title to negotiable instruments, we have learned, is passed or conferred in two ways; if the instrument is payable to bearer, by delivery; if payable to order, by indorsement completed by delivery. If a thief steals a bearer instrument and transfers it to an innocent purchaser for value, the latter acquires a good and enforceable title, though the thief had none. But where a negotiable instrument payable to order is stolen, the only method of transferring the instrument is by indorsement, and a genuine indorsement, by the true payee or indorsee, is an obvious impossibility. But by forgery of the necessary indorsement, some innocent purchaser may be deceived into acquiring it, under the belief that the chain of title to him, by genuine indorsement, is perfect. In this instance, however, no matter how innocent the purchaser may be, and no matter how much he has paid for the instrument, he in reality has no title; and if he himself transfers the instrument he renders himself liable to subsequent holders upon his warranty of "good title." Most of the cases involving a breach of the warranty of good title arise where there has been some forgery of indorsement under which no title has been conferred upon subsequent parties.

"PRIOR PARTIES."

The next warranty of the indorser is that "all prior parties had capacity to contract." The holder of a negotiable instrument, apparently good in every respect, may sometimes find, when he comes to obtain payment from the makers, or other parties who have promised or ordered payment, that by reason of some legal incapacity, such parties cannot be held liable upon the contract which they have apparently made. This is one of the matters covered by the warranty of the general indorser, as well as by that of the qualified indorser, or transferor by delivery, that all prior parties had capacity to contract.

These last two warranties, that the indorser has good title, and that all prior parties had capacity to contract, cover the numerous body of cases wherein some prior indorsement is either an out-and-out forgery or is made by some person without authority, or by some person legally incapacitated to make a contract of indorsement, the common law rule respecting which is to the effect that an indorser warrants the genuineness and sufficiency of the prior indorsements. Sometimes a prior indorsement is an absolute forgery; sometimes it is made by an agent, and a later holder is unable to know whether the agent was duly authorized; sometimes, again, there is a discrepancy in a prior indorsement, as, for example, a draft payable to "W. W. Owens," indorsed "W. W. Owen;" and still again, a prior indorsement may be by one legally incapacitated to contract. For the genuineness, sufficiency and title conveying power of these various defective indorsements a holder in due course is entitled to rely upon the warranty of the subsequent indorsers.

A more troublesome question is where a necessary prior indorsement is altogether missing. A negotiable instrument payable to order may be transferred, we have seen by section 79, without indorsement, but until properly indorsed it is subject to equities. Freedom from equities and payability at full face is, of course, the vital essential to a commercial purchaser, for no man wants to buy an instrument payment of which may be successfully defended. Is there any warranty, then, by an indorser to a subsequent purchaser that will relieve the latter against the possible consequences of such a defect in the chain of title? The indorser warrants that his title is good, but the purchaser takes the instrument with his eyes open to the fact of just what title the indorser has, namely, only the title held by the man who transferred without indorsement, together with the right to have his indorsement. But the latter's title might be subject to equities before such indorsement was made, and the instrument prove non-enforceable. Does the subsequent indorser warrant against this when he warrants "good title"—that is to say, is his warranty to be construed as "good title, free from equities," or merely what title the transferor without indorsement had? This is difficult to say. But, after all, it would seem that the subsequent purchaser would be protected by the indorser's engagement to pay, if on due presentation and notice, the payor did not.

Apart from the question of negotiation of an instrument with a missing indorsement, this defect sometimes confronts

*Republished from the Banking Law Journal by permission. Copyright, 1899, 1900, 1901 and 1902, by T. B. Paton, all rights reserved. To be revised and published in book form by the author.

a bank which is called upon to pay a check whereon one of the indorsements in the chain of title has been omitted. Of course there could be no indorser's engagement to pay the bank if the payor did not, for the bank itself is the payor in such a case; and if the bank paid such an instrument, its only protection, in case the payment proved unauthorized by reason of the missing indorsement, would be a right of recourse against the one who received payment, or upon the warranties of prior indorsers; providing, first, such warranties covered a missing indorsement, which, we have said, is difficult to determine, and, second, even if they did, depending upon a favorable determination of the question whether such warranties, under the language of the act, being only to "holders in due course," could be construed as running to the payor of the instrument, as they undoubtedly did under the law merchant. This question, to whom do the indorser's warranties under the act extend, we will take up presently.

MISSING INDORSEMENT.

Concerning the payment of checks and drafts in cases of missing indorsements, there is a mixed practice, so far as we have been able to ascertain, in the banking world. In some instances payment is refused until the instrument comes regularly to the bank. In other instances payment will be made where the last holder tenders the instrument to the bank, accompanied by some form of guaranty—e. g., "missing indorsements guarantied"—being virtually a warranty that the instrument is of the same legal effect as if it bore the missing indorsement. Among other questions which might arise in this connection is the one whether an incorporated bank would have power to bind itself by the guaranty of paper in which it had no interest. The entire subject of the payment of checks and drafts in cases of missing indorsements, and the basic question whether the bank should or should not pay such drafts, together with the effect and protection of express guaranties of missing indorsements, is one of interest and importance, but one which, at this writing, we cannot fully go into.

Returning from this brief digression, we resume our consideration of the matters and things which the indorser warrants.

The indorser further warrants that the instrument is at the time of his indorsement valid and subsisting.

The above, then, is the sum total of what the indorser warrants concerning the instrument, the parties and his title. In addition, he engages that on due presentment it shall be accepted or paid, or both, as the case may be, according to its tenor, and that if it be dishonored, and the necessary proceedings on dishonor be duly taken, he will pay the amount thereof to the holder or to any subsequent indorser who may be compelled to pay it.

This is the statement, in precise statutory form, of the well-known rule of the law merchant expressing the conditional liability of an indorser of a negotiable instrument. He is not the party primarily bound to pay the instrument. The promise or order of another to pay a certain sum of money at a stated time has come to him in due course of business, and he has passed it over by indorsement to still another. The presumption is that that is the end of the transaction so far as he is concerned. And it is the end, providing the promise or order to pay is fulfilled. But there is always the chance that the promise will not be kept, and to provide against this and to insure to the holder payment at all events it is always a part of the contract of the indorser that he will pay, if the maker does not, and the holder does his legal duty in the matter of presentment and in notifying the indorser of the dishonor. When this takes place, the conditional liability of the indorser becomes an absolute one, and he must pay and look for recourse to the prior parties liable on the instrument.

TO WHOM WARRANTY EXTENDS.

Having briefly considered the nature of the warranties and engagement of the indorser of a negotiable instrument, we will next consider to whom the warranty extends, and then it will be interesting to inquire just what indorsers are deemed to make such warranties and engagement.

To whom are the warranties of an indorser made? Section 116 provides, we see, that they are made "to all subsequent holders in due course." A holder in due course is defined, with particularity, by section 91. He is, in brief, one to whom the instrument is negotiated before due, without notice, in good faith, and for value; in other words, a bona fide purchaser for value, without notice, before maturity. But how about the payor of the instrument, the drawee or acceptor of a check or bill of exchange, for example? Is there no indorser's warranty of genuineness, capacity of parties and title to him? A draws his check payable to B. B's indorsement is forged, and the check is afterward indorsed by C, D, E and F, and is paid by the bank to F. Under the law merchant a party who transferred a bill of exchange by indorsement warranted the genuineness of all prior indorsements, and if any prior indorsement was forged, he was liable upon his warranty, not only to subsequent indorsers, but also to the drawee bank which paid the check, there being a two-fold principle upon which the bank could recover the money—first, from the immediate party to whom paid, irrespective of warranty, upon the principle that money paid under mutual mistake, without consideration, can be recovered; and, second, from any of the prior indorsers subsequent to the forged indorsements upon the principle of breech of their warranty of genuineness of all prior indorsements. But the Negotiable Instruments Act, strange to say, seems, in its terms, to confine this indorser's warranty to subsequent holders in due course, and to make no express provision of warranty to a drawee or other payor of a negotiable instrument. Literally interpreted, if a bank in the case supposed, paid to F a check upon which the payee's name had been forged, or whereon the amount had been raised, or where there had been any incapacity of prior indorsers, it would have no recourse upon any of the indorsers prior to F, and its only remedy would be against F alone, not upon his indorsement, but upon the principle of recovering money paid to him by mutual mistake, without consideration. This construction, we believe, is not in accord with the understanding of the commercial world, and possibly, if a case involving the bank's right to recover from C, D or E, as indorsers of a check upon which B's indorsement had been forged, came before the courts the warranty to "subsequent holders in due course" would be extended, by a liberal construction, to include the payor of the instrument. Of course there are certain things which, under the law merchant, the indorser does not warrant to the drawee who makes payment, and which he does warrant to subsequent holders in due course; for example, the genuineness of the drawer's signature. And again, the engagement of the indorser to pay, if the instrument is dishonored, naturally is not made to the payor, but only to subsequent purchasers. Unless it was the clear intention of the framers of the Negotiable Instruments Law to do away with all the warranties of an indorser to the payor which were established by the law merchant, and we shall subsequently see that it was not, it would have been better to have drafted, in addition to section 116, which covers an indorser's warranties and engagement to bona-fide holders, an additional section of indorser's warranty to payor, to embrace the genuineness of the instrument, except in the matter of signature, the genuineness of indorsements and capacity of indorsers, and that the indorser had a good title.

What we have just said whets the appetite for further light upon the meaning of section 116, rather than satisfies it. There are three main points to be considered:—

1st. The nature of the indorser's warranty and engagement, 2d, to whom it runs; and 3d, whether the warranty is that of indorsing owners only, or that of agents for collection, who indorse, as well.

We have already considered point 1, have entered upon a discussion of point 2, and have not, as yet, touched point 3. Going a little deeper into the subject, in a consideration of points 2 and 3, we reach the following conclusions, which, after statement, we will elaborate:—

1. That under the law merchant an indorser warranted to

bona-fide holders the various matters of warranty provided in section 116, as well as engaged to pay, if the principal debtor did not, upon due demand and notice; that, furthermore, the indorser warranted to the payor (such as a drawee) genuineness of the instrument, except in the matter of signature, genuineness and sufficiency of indorsements, and his title.

2. The warranty to the payor, under the law merchant, was only by an indorsing owner: an agent for collection, who indorsed, was not liable as warrantor of genuineness.

3. The framers of section 116 clearly intended to change the common law by making an agent who indorsed, as well as an indorsing owner, a warrantor of genuineness; and as an agent can only collect, but cannot sell, and any warranty of his must, necessarily, be only to the payor, the intention must have been to make section 116 provide a warrantor liability to payors, as well as to bona-fide purchasers.

4. But it is very questionable whether section 116 bears out such intentions, for it appears to provide a form of words, applicable to an indorsing owner warranting and engaging to pay to a purchaser for value, but not providing a warrantor liability to a payor, and hence, also, necessarily excluding any warrantor liability by an agent-indorser, as such can only run to a payor.

5. That this section, as it stands, is not clear as to its legal effect, and requires straightening out, either by the courts or the legislature

WHAT AN INDORSER GUARANTEES.

To amplify: The natural idea under the law merchant is that when ownership of paper is transferred from one to another by indorsement, or when value is paid therefor by the payor to the last holder, the owner indorsing to a purchaser for value, or collecting value from the payor, must naturally vouch, by his indorsement, certain things without which he could neither sell nor collect it. To the purchasing indorsee, he warrants genuineness of the instrument and of prior indorsements, capacity of the parties, that his title is good, and that he will pay it, if dishonored, after due proceedings by the holder. To the payor of the instrument, he warrants genuineness of instrument and prior indorsements, except concerning such matters as the payor is bound to know—for example, signature—capacity of parties, and his own title. The main idea of warranty, therefore, is in connection with the transfer or collection by an indorsing owner. But in addition to the indorsement of a real or apparent owner there may be an indorsement by one, who is not owner, but to whom the instrument has been indorsed, restrictively, "for collection." The indorsement by such a non-owner, or agent, obviously cannot be to a purchaser for value: the only value given for the instrument after such an indorsement is made, must flow from the payor of the instrument. Now, under the law merchant, the question several times came before the courts, where drawee banks had paid checks upon which prior indorsements had been forged, upon the indorsements of agents to whom the paper had been indorsed "for collection," whether the indorsement of the agent constituted a warranty to the payor of the prior forged indorsement? The courts held that it did not: that while the indorsement of an owner, really or apparently such, warranted genuineness to the payor, the agent's indorsement did not, and that he was not accountable for the money after its payment by him to his principal.

Such being the state of the law merchant when the Negotiable Instruments Law was enacted, the question arises whether that law changes the law merchant, so as to make, not only an indorsing owner, but an indorsing agent, a warrantor of genuineness and capacity of prior indorsements. That it was the intention of the framers of the law to make such a change is clear. In the original draft of section 116, the following provision appeared, which was omitted in the final revision:—

"But the provisions of this section do not apply to an indorser to whom the instrument has been indorsed restrictively, as agent only."

The striking out of this paragraph shows the intention of the framers to make agent-indorsers responsible as warrantors, equally with owner-indorsers. And as further evidence of this intention, the draftsman of the law, Mr. Crawford, in an explanatory foot note to section 116 in his published work on the law, says:—

"This section makes an important change in the law. The decisions have held that the indorsement of a bank to which paper has been indorsed for collection does not import a guaranty of the genuineness of all prior indorsements, but only of the agent's relation to the principal as stated upon the face of the paper, and that in such case the collecting bank was not liable after it had paid the proceeds to the principal, though the prior indorsement was a forgery. But the statute applies to all indorsers who indorse without qualification; and no exception is made of indorsers to whom the instrument has been indorsed restrictively. Hence, a bank indorsing paper forwarded for collection is liable in all respects as indorser, though the prior indorsement was for collection or for deposit, or otherwise restrictive."

INTENTION OF FRAMERS OF LAW.

Here we have clear evidence of the intention of the framers of the law upon two points:—

1. To change the law merchant, so as to make agent-indorsers warrantors equally with owner-indorsers.

2. To make the indorser's warranties stated in section 116 extend to payors, as well as to holders in due course; for obviously the payor is the only value-giver to whom the agent-indorser's warranty can extend—there can be no holder in due course from an agent authorized only to collect.

This being the intention of the law-framers, it is another question whether their production carries out such intention. In the first place section 116 expressly limits the warranty "to all subsequent holders in due course," and the law has elsewhere specifically defined a holder in due course in such terms as not to comprehend the payor; and unless the meaning of section 116 can be stretched to include payors of negotiable instruments as beneficiaries of the indorser's warranties, then there can be no case of an agent-indorser's warranty, for no holder in due course can take from such agent.

A critical diagnosis of section 116 leads to the conclusion that it is not, in all respects, a satisfactory rule of liability of indorsers upon negotiable instruments. While its framers evidently essayed, on the one hand, to provide a rule whereby indorsing-owners should warrant not only to purchasers, but to payors, the same things which they warranted under the law merchant, and, on the other, to provide a warrantor liability by indorsing agents to payors, not provided by the law merchant, what they have actually produced, is a rule of warrantor liability by indorsing-owners to holders in due course only. Payors, as parties to whom the warranties run, are not included; and not being included, of course, literally interpreting the law, there is no foundation for any warrantor liability by indorsing-agents. Furthermore, any attempt to read the law as providing what the framers intended but did not express, results in certain incongruities. For example, if we say they intended by this section to provide an indorser's liability, not only to holders in due course but to the payor, then we find the indorser not only warranting genuineness, title and capacity, but also engaging to pay, if the payor does not, which is absurd. Clearly, the intelligent constructionist will say, this provision was not intended to provide a liability of warranty by an indorser to the payor, but only to the holder in due course—that is the way it reads. But if we grant that, then we cut off the recourse of a payor upon indorsers as warrantors of the genuineness of a prior indorsement, and this is not politic; furthermore, it was not intended, for the framers had such a warranty to the payor in mind when they essayed to make the section provide a warrantor-liability of an indorsing agent. Then, again, if we attempt to construe the section according to the intention of the framers as creating a liability by all indorsers—indorsing agents as well as indorsing owners—we find the indorsing agent not only engaging to pay the instrument, if the payor does not—engaging with whom?—but also warranting, among other things, that he has a good title thereto.

We leave this section, in these particulars to the future construction of the courts. Construing it as a rule of warrantor liability and engagement to pay, by indorsing owners only, to subsequent owners in due course only, it is clear and consistent, but the attempt to read into it the indorser's liability to the payor as warrantor of genuineness of prior indorsements, of amount and of title, which should be provided for in a law of this kind, and also a provision making indorsing agents liable to the payor which the framers intended to provide, makes the section incongruous and of uncertain effect.

THE TALE OF THE MAN WHO ACQUIRED RICHES

By Joe Lincoln

And it was the one thousandth and second night, and Scheherezade, glancing into the mirror to see if her back hair was on straight, spake unto the Father of the Faithful and said:—

"Know thou, whose brilliancy is to the sun even as is the hotel clerk's shirt-stud to the porter's collar button, that in the days of Haroun-al-Raschid there lived a certain youth named Noureddin, who desired to become rich. And he communed with himself, saying:—

"'Lo, what is the chief end of man? Is it not to acquire the scads and grow weighty with the burden of the shekels? Behold him that hath flourisheth like unto the weed in the garden of the commuter; he cutteth the wide swath; he bosseth the Trust and runneth the steam yacht; while he that hath not loseth his job and becometh star boarder at the poorhouse.'

"And it came to pass that he swore by the beard of his grandsire, who had been of the tribe of the Populist, that he would seek the coin of the realm all his days and faint not. And he consulted the writings of the wise, hoping thereby to obtain wisdom. And in his seeking it came to pass that his eyes fell upon the words of the learned one, even of the Prophet, Rus-el-Sage, where it is written:—

"'Behold, let him who would amass the slippery spondulick, heed this law: Of each shekel that he earneth by the perspiration of his forehead, let him keep one-fourth thereof by the tightness of his fist. And so shall he become even as I am.'

"And the youth, having read this, leaped into the air and cracked his heels together three times, saying:—

"'Behold this is IT! I have struck it!' And he resolved all his days to abide by the law as it was written.

"And the sun shone and the moons came and went, and the youth grew older. And as he grew older, so his clutch upon the tin became tighter. And he was close, even with the nearness of an all-wool undershirt that hath been newly cleansed by the washing. And as he amassed the ducats so, of a verity, did he salt them down, taking care that the place of salting was heavy with interest.

"And it came to pass that when he was of the age of thirty he became enamored of a damsel whose grace was as the swaying pomegranate tree and whose voice was as that of the bulbul in the garden of the Prophet. And her sweetness prevailed upon him even to the spending of small blocks of lucre for the frozen cream and the uncooked bivalve. And each time that she worked upon him to shed thus, lo, his weepings and wailings kept the neighbors awake at night.

"And it came to pass that he took the damsel to wed, and their abode was in the kingdom of Musquash-up-the-Sound, where the rent was of exceeding minuteness and the sighing of the wind through the cracks in the roof was like unto the bellowing of the bulls of Bashan. And he allowed her two calico dresses a year, and she made over her wedding hat seven times.

"And behold, a son was born unto them, and Noureddin went without his noontide meat for the space of six months and bade his wife make over her hat for the eighth time because of the mighty expense. And the money which he loaned was put forth at 12 per cent instead of 10.

"And Noureddin grew rich and prospered, and his pile became great even as the Mount of Ararat, and the people spake of him as one who belonged to the tribe of Morgan. But as he grew richer his clutch upon the needful became tighter, for so long had he followed the law of saving that to spend a shekel had become like unto the yanking forth of a wisdom tooth, and to separate him from a shinplaster was even as the prying loose of the eternal foundations. And the getting of the camel through the eye of the needle would have been a lead pipe cinch compared to the getting of him to buy the yacht or to cut the swath of which he had dreamed in his youth.

"And the sun shone and moons waxed bright and faded, and it came to pass that the wife of Noureddin's bosom sickened and passed away. And the noise of Noureddin's mourning was loud in the land; and he wept exceeding sore and cast ashes upon his head, and would have rent his garments but that they were yet of a newness and had cost him eight and a half in the market place. And he buried his wife in the sandy side of the graveyard, where lots were to be bought exceeding cheap.

"And Noureddin became an old man and his years waxed long, and he called his son to him and said:—

"'Oh, son, thy father hath followed the rule of the Prophet and hath amassed much coin of the realm. I pray thee, when I am gone, continue in the same manner and spend no more than can be gotten out of thee by due process of law. And now I leave thee. Bury me beside thy mother, for, as thou knowest, by my shrewdness I secured two graves for the price of one.'

"And Noureddin turned his face to the wall and died and was buried even as he had desired.

"Then the son spake and said:—

"'Behold, my father is dead and his coin is mine. Lo, the old man lived like a vender of peanuts all his life and kept my nose exceeding close to the grindstone. Now is the time to square accounts. Verily, let us whoop her up!'

"And he bought himself a palace upon the Avenue that is called Fifth, and acquired a steam yacht that consumed many score tons of coal a week, even in strike time. And he said: 'Lo! the old gent had money to burn and did not even singe it; let me, his son, do my little best to heat up the atmosphere.'

"And the smoke of that burning is not yet dead in the land."

And Scheherezade paused and said unto the Father of the Faithful:—

"Oh, King, live forever! Behold the end of the tale is a question: Which of the two is the greater fool—the miser or the spendthrift?"

And the King pondered and said: "Verily, I know not, but it is certain that the spendthrift hath the more fun out of it. This is not my day for conundrums. Let us play ping pong."

And he bade the slaves put the leaves in the extension table.

WHAT HE REALLY SAID

Mrs. Buffers: "The teller at that bank says you are just the meanest, stingiest——

Mr. Buffers: "Great Scott! Wha—what is that? He says——"

Mrs. Buffers: "Well, he didn't say it in so many words, but that is what he meant, of course."

Mr. Buffers: "See here! What did the fellow say?"

Mrs. Buffers: "He asked me to indorse the check; and when I told him I hadn't the ghost of an idea of what he meant, he said he presumed I hadn't had much experience getting checks cashed—so there!—New York Weekly.

HIS OWN MEDICINE

St. Peter: "Who are you?" New Arrival: "I'm the paying teller of ——." St. Peter: "You'll have to get somebody to identify you."—Town Topics.

School of Commerce, Accounts & Finance

The New York University School of Commerce, Accounts & Finance was started through the instrumentality of the New York State Society of Certified Public Accountants. The primary motive of leading accountants in fostering such a school was to elevate the standard of their profession, and they have cheerfully borne the heat and burden of instruction, so far as accounting is concerned. The professional schools connected with New York University are conspicuous for their efficiency and success, and many of the friends of accountancy hoped that the new school would be wholly professional in character, especially intended to qualify students for the Certified Public Accountant's degree, and ultimately to secure an arrangement by which the school would confer this degree direct.

When the School of Commerce, Accounts & Finance was started the authorities of New York University saw fit to enlarge its scope so as to include various subjects in addition to accounting, and while accounting has been from the outset considered the central idea, a sufficient number of other subjects have been included to fully justify the triple name of Commerce, Accounts & Finance. The plan of the school, as outlined for the coming year, shows a commendable desire to strengthen the curriculum in every particular. Additional attention is given to accounting, and equal additions have been made to the studies pertaining more particularly to commerce and finance. Whether the enlarged scope of the school will add to the qualifications of students for the practical affairs of life and be more advantageous for both the students and the university than a course of study confined strictly to accounting, is something which only time and experience can demonstrate.

Judgment based upon results is certainly logical, and the first class graduated by the School of Commerce, Accounts & Finance is exceedingly creditable. At the graduation exercises of the University the students in the School of Commerce, Accounts & Finance certainly compared favorably with the students in the Schools of Law and Medicine. Many of the graduates of the School of Commerce, Accounts & Finance are men who have already attained some position in the business world, and their opinion of what the school is and what it ought to be is worthy of the serious consideration not only of the faculty of the school which has just graduated them, but of the general management of the University.

The graduating class, at their dinner, held at the St. Denis, Friday evening, June 7, in addition to the organization of an alumni association, appointed a committee to outline a plan of organization for an association on somewhat different lines than alumni associations usually follow.

Preliminary to the appointment of such committee, considerable discussion was had concerning the plan and scope of the school, its future, its objects, advantages, etc. The concensus of opinion was that the aim and object for carrying out that for which the school was originally started, namely, the training of students in higher accounting, and equipping them for obtaining the certificate of Certified Public Accountant, should be maintained to the utmost, and that there should not be allowed to creep in any side-issues which would tend to lead away from the accounting feature of the school; that inasmuch as there was a total lack of schools or institutions of any kind which were fitted to give a training in this line, this school would make a serious mistake if it in any way allowed its curriculum to make accounting a secondary feature. Of course, it was realized that accountancy is made up of more than instruction in accounts and the keeping thereof, and that commercial law and finance and commerce are all essential in the education of the trained accountant, and yet it was felt that perhaps too much could be made of these features and too little of the one important need which was the education in accounts at the hands of experienced and competent instructors.

The plan for the association above referred to was therefore to be one which will include within its scope the maintenance of the feature of accountancy in the curriculum of the school, the advancement of the interests of the school by co-operation with the faculty, and by any other means which may be expedient to aid and keep the school in the first rank of institutions of this class.

It was further discussed that the same recognition should be given to this department of the University by the state authorities in reference to accepting its diploma in lieu of other requirements that was accorded to the medical and other departments, and steps will undoubtedly be taken to effect this in the near future.

The efforts of the faculty and all others who had taken interest in the first period of this institution, were commended, and it can be said of the occasion that there was much brought out which was calculated to strengthen as well as to foster the growth of the institution.

The graduates of the first class are men who have reached years of discretion, and there was much brought out in the discussion which indicates the interest that they feel in the school and its future.

SCHOOL OF COMMERCE, ACCOUNTS & FINANCE

Record of the Month's Work

Senior Class

RECORD FOR WEEK ENDING MAY 2, 1902.

THURSDAY.
8-10 Examination and Review on Auditing, by Mr. Chas. B. Dean.

FRIDAY.
8-10 Lecture on Partnership Law, by Mr. William F. Walsh.

RECORD FOR WEEK ENDING MAY 9, 1902.

MONDAY.
8-9 Lecture on International Law, by Mr. Cleveland F. Bacon.
9-10 Lecture on Surrogate Accounting, by Professor Hardcastle.

TUESDAY.
8-10 Lecture on Foreign Exchange, by Prof. J. H. Johnson.

WEDNESDAY. End of School Year Examinations Begun May 9th.

FRIDAY.
8-10 Examination in International Law, by Mr. Cleveland F. Bacon.

RECORD FOR WEEK ENDING MAY 16, 1902.

TUESDAY.
7-10 Final Examination in Auditing, by Prof. Chas. W. Haskins.

THURSDAY.
7-10 Final Examination in Foreign Exchange, by Prof. Jos. F. Johnson.

FRIDAY.
8-10 Review on Corporation Law, by Mr. Wm. F. Walsh.

RECORD FOR WEEK ENDING MAY 23, 1902.

TUESDAY.
7-10 Final Examination in Corporation Law and the Law of Partnership, by Mr. Wm. F. Walsh.

THURSDAY.
7-10 Final Examination in Insurance Law, by Mr. Stevens.

FRIDAY.
8-10 Review on Surrogate Accounting, by Mr. Jos. F. Hardcastle.

MONDAY, MAY 26.
7-10 Final Examination in Surrogate Accounting, by Mr. Jos. F. Hardcastle.

Session for the School Year 1901-1902—Closed.

Junior Class

RECORD FOR WEEK ENDING MAY 2, 1902.

THURSDAY.
8-10 Lecture on Law of Sales, by Mr. Cleveland F. Bacon.

FRIDAY.
8-10 Lecture on Theory of Accounts, by Prof. Chas. E. Sprague.

RECORD FOR WEEK ENDING MAY 9, 1902.

MONDAY.	
8-10	Lecture on Money and Credit, by Prof. Jos. F. Johnson.
TUESDAY.	
8-10	Lecture on Accounting, by Mr. A. O. Kittredge.
WEDNESDAY.	
8-9	No lecture.
9-10	Lecture on Transportation, by Mr. Shirley Eaton.
THURSDAY.	
8-10	Lecture on the Law of Sales, by Mr. Cleveland F. Bacon.
FRIDAY.	
8-10	Lecture on Savings Bank Accounting, by Mr. Chas. E. Sprague.

RECORD FOR WEEK ENDING MAY 16, 1902.

MONDAY.	
8-10	Lecture on Money and Credit, by Prof. Jos. F. Johnson.
TUESDAY.	
8-10	Lecture on Savings Bank Accounting, by Mr. Chas. E. Sprague.
WEDNESDAY.	
9-10	Lecture on Transportation, by Mr. Shirley Eaton.
THURSDAY.	
8-10	Lecture on Law of Sales, by Mr. Cleveland F. Bacon.
FRIDAY.	
7-8	Review on Accounting, by Mr. H. M. C. Vedder.
8-10	Review on Accounting, by Prof. A. O. Kittredge.

RECORD FOR WEEK ENDING MAY 23, 1902.

MONDAY.	
7-10	Final Examinations on the Theory and Practice of Accounting, by Prof. A. O. Kittredge.
WEDNESDAY.	
7-10	Final Examination on Transportation, by Mr. Shirley Eaton.
FRIDAY.	
8-10	Final Examination on Savings Bank Accounting, by Prof. Chas. E. Sprague.

RECORD FOR WEEK ENDING MAY 30, 1902.

MONDAY.	
7-10	Final Examination on the Law of Agencies and Sales, by Mr. Cleveland F. Bacon.
WEDNESDAY.	
7-10	Final Examination on Political Economy and Money, by Prof. Jos. F. Johnson.

Session for the School Year, 1901-1902—Closed.

PUZZLES FOR OFFICE MEN

$20.00 in Prizes

In the May issue of COMMERCE, ACCOUNTS & FINANCE the first set of puzzles for which prizes were offered was published. The first set, as our readers know, were puns upon accounting terms. The second set is published in this issue. Fig. 1 is a term used to describe a process with which every bookkeeper and everyone dealing with long columns of figures is familiar. Fig. 2, Fig. 3 and Fig. 4 are the names of divisions of arithmetic with which every schoolboy, and certainly every bookkeeper is on speaking terms.

FIG. 1.

FIG. 2.

For the benefit of new subscribers and those who did not see the last issue of the magazine, we re-publish the conditions of the contest. Every reader of COMMERCE, ACCOUNTS & FINANCE should be able to solve these puzzles. They are not hard, in fact, this set is particularly simple. Send in your answers and essays. You may as well have one of the prizes as to let your neighbor get it. The conditions are as follows:—

Each contestant is required first, to correctly solve each of the four puzzles; then he is required to write an essay, not exceeding two hundred words in length, upon the subject presented by each puzzle, that is to say, he must write four essays in all.

For the best set of essays a prize of ten dollars ($10) cash will be given. For the five next best sets yearly subscriptions will be given to The Bulletin, a semi-monthly magazine of the same size and general make-up of COMMERCE, ACCOUNTS & FINANCE, but devoted to the art and practice of banking. To any young man contemplating entering upon a business career The Bulletin is invaluable, being neither too technical or too profound, but catering to the bank clerk rather than to the bank official. The regular subscription price of The Bulletin is $2 a year.

FIG. 3.

FIG. 4.

Each competitor in these contests will be required to enclose 25 cents for a three months' trial subscription to COMMERCE, ACCOUNTS & FINANCE. If the contestant is already a subscriber, this subscription will be sent to any nonsubscriber named by him. Non-subscribers will, of course, send their own names. The 25 cents will not be applied to extend the subscription of one already a subscriber.

All communications must be addressed to the Puzzle Editor, care COMMERCE, ACCOUNTS & FINANCE.

DOWN THE SCALE

It was a clear case of degeneration. The father, when in college, made an excellent record in mathematics. Twenty years later a son came under the teaching of the old professor; he was a fairly good student; a year later the youngest son arrived, says Current Literature. He was a sad case; knew absolutely nothing about the subject so far as the disgusted professor could ascertain. One day, after class, "Old Bill" had a short conference with him in regard to the work. In the course of the conversation the other members of the family were mentioned. "Your father," said the professor, "was one of my best scholars. Your brother was a fair student." Here was the opportunity for a master stroke, a grand combination of humor and mathematics—and the luckless youth seized it.

"Professor, it seems a case of a descending series, doesn't it?" "Hum," grunted "Old Bill," "rather seems like an assending series."

SHALL NEVER ABBREVIATE

One of the strict rules of the postoffice department is that the names of the following states and territories shall never be abbreviated in the directing of a letter, says the New York Press: Alaska, Hawaii, Idaho, Iowa, Ohio, Oregon, Samoa, and Utah. The reason is obvious. Ala. might be mistaken for Alabama; Id. for Indiana; O. for either Ohio, Oregon, or Oklahoma; Io. for Idaho, etc.

WHY NOT?

"Say, mamma," queried five-year-old Tommy, "am I really made of dust?"

"I suppose so, dear," was the reply.

"Then," continued the little fellow, "why don't I get muddy when you wash me?"

Current Business Cartoons

Strikes, combines, volcanic eruptions, peace between Boer and Briton and the doings of Congress have given the newspaper artists plenty to do during the past month.

The great coal strike is filling the paper with news at present. It is also depleting the pocketbooks of the consumers of coal. Lucky for us that the strike occurred in the summer, otherwise we might be chopping up the parlor furniture to obtain heating material. We publish one of Mr. Bush's cartoons on the coal strike, which appeared in the

The Big "Black Demon."—New York World.

New York World. The conception is very good indeed, whether we agree with Mr. Bush's view or not. The great, black, shapeless demon, Monopoly, is whirling down the public highway. The consumer, knocked headlong, will soon be beneath its wheels. The miner has put the rock "Strike" in its way, hoping thereby to stop its progress. Strikes are

The population of Chicago is increasing at the rate of 1,400 a week.—Chicago Record-Herald.

bad things. Bad for the striker, bad for the employer, and particularly bad for the public at large.

Chicago's population is said to be increasing at the rate of 70,000 a year. The city now has a population of over 2,100,000. That funny man, McCutcheon, has a cartoon in the Chicago Record-Herald which would seem to show that all roads lead to Chicago, as, in olden times, all roads led to Rome. New citizens are coming by all routes and by all conveyances, and it is possible that some day Chicago will be the greatest city in the United States. It will not do to tell

Mr. Fuel Oil from Texas arrives.—New York Tribune.

this to a New York man, however.

It is possible, perhaps probable, that a new fuel has been discovered which will help out the consumer by enabling

The rich man's plaything.

him to get along without coal. Texas oil, it is said, can be delivered in New York city at a low rate, and it is also said that it makes good fuel for all purposes. In the car-

The Insect—"You're next."—Philadelphia North American.

toon from the New York Tribune, coal is represented by a stout and wealthy gentleman who looks indignantly at Beaumont Texas Oil, the new arrival in the Panama hat and

Southern togs. Smoke coming from the factory bears the words, "Strikes—High Prices for Coal."

The automobile industry has had a big boom this season, and more horseless carriages have been sold than ever before. But automobiles are dangerous playthings sometimes, as the long list of accidents shows. Nelan has a cartoon in the Philadelphia North American showing the automobile as a great skull mounted on pneumatic-tired wheels dashing down the roadway killing all it passes.

Injunctions declared by several courts against the so-

Uncle Sam—"I could be happy with either, were t'other dear charmer away."—Ohio State Journal.

called "Beef Trust" have been surprises, not only to the meat packers but to everyone. In the Philadelphia North American the Chicago injunction is shown as a giant mosquito savagely stinging the Meat Trust on the back. The mosquito is saying to a curious looking quadruped which the artist has labelled, The Coal Trust, "You're Next."

"Hi, Gentlemen, step aside there!"—Cleveland Plain Dealer.

The debate upon the site of the Isthmian Canal is now raging in Congress. In the cartoon from the Ohio State Journal, which we reproduce, Uncle Sam is shown in a state of perplexity, besieged by the two young ladies, Panama and Nicaragua. He doesn't know which to choose, and is in trouble therefore.

The dove of peace that has hovered for so long over South Africa, has lit at last. The Englishman and Boer have shaken hands, and the fight is over. Everybody thinks it is high time, and in the cartoon from the Cleveland Plain Dealer, Uncle Sam, driving a truck with a tremendous load of commerce and trade, begs the erstwhile combatants to step aside and give him a clear road to South Africa.

THE OFFICE SAFE

In the old-fashioned days, when our great grandfathers were in business, the money and valuables belonging to the firm were kept in a so-called "strong-box" or small iron chest, and at night this strong box was carried to the bank where the firm deposited, and there left in charge of the cashier or teller for safekeeping until the next morning. This was the rule in many offices. In others the "strong-box" was more elaborate, and was a fixture of the office, being unlocked by several heavy and massive keys. In our grandfathers' time safes and vaults were used, but these safes were flimsy affairs, comparatively speaking, and the modern cracksman would have needed no more formidable tool than a can-opener to get at their precious contents. The vaults were quite pretentious, but were no protection whatever when compared with the complicated and enormous affairs of the present day. Our grandfathers opened their office safes or vaults with various queerly-shaped keys and wore out their pockets carrying these same keys to and from business.

The safes of our fathers were better, but they were not by any means perfect. The combination lock began to be used, although it was not as yet a very complicated affair. But it was considered a great step in advance of the key, as

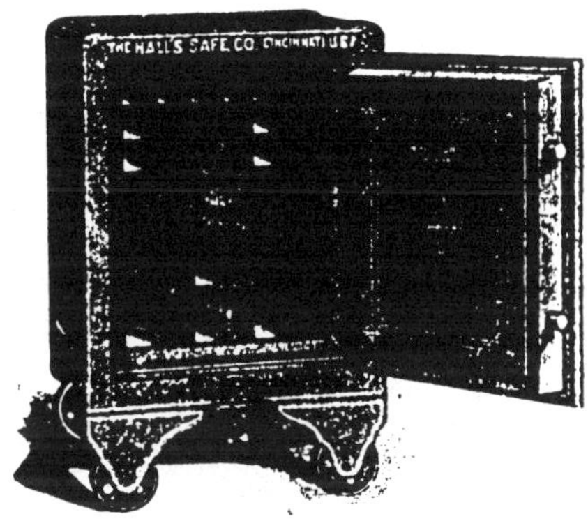

FIG. 1. SMALL OFFICE OR HOME SAFE.

indeed it was. The writer remembers working in a banker's office where an old-fashioned vault was built into the wall. The outer door opened with a sort of combination key arrangement, and to one clerk was entrusted the care of one section of this combination key, and to another clerk the remainder. It therefore took two clerks to open the safe. If one section of this combination was lost, trouble ensued. The inner door of the vault was opened with a long-shanked, eight-sided key, the carrying of which tended to make a small boy lop-sided.

But the office safe today is of a different breed. A visit to the salesroom of some great safe manufacturing concern, such as Hall's Safe Company, whose factory is at Cincinnati, Ohio, and whose products are sold in New York by Kinsey, Rainier & Thomson, at 393 Broadway, is likely to prove an eye-opener to those unacquainted with the possibilities of fire and burglar-proof office safes and vaults. Here one may see safes of all sizes and of many shapes. There are little baby safes for use at home or in a small office, and there are huge affairs with several sets of massive locking arrangements so complicated that it would seem no burglar working a lifetime could ever hope to overcome them. There are safes with small interior arrangements for the storing of office books and compartments for bills and cash, and there are safes within safes, where the shelves and compartments for books are above elaborate steel chests with massive doors which unlock with as much ceremony as do the outer doors. Here are coin safes with no compartments for the storage of books, but with shelves for the piling up of stacks of coin.

One peculiar-looking safe that is sure to attract the visitor's attention is, so the salesman informs us, the Hall's Company's Patent Screw-door Bank Safe. The door to this safe is a massive affair in the shape of a great screw that fits into a series of mammoth threads in the front of the safe. The body of this screw-door safe is three inches thick. The door is five inches thick, and the whole thing weighs 3,050 pounds, so one can readily see that it is not a plaything that a sneak-thief can put under his arm and run down the street with. The door is made to lock on the inside with time and automatic locks. There are no spindles or holes through the door. The door itself is rotated—screwed in and out—by a bronze hand wheel, and is made to operate easily by means of hardened steel roller bearings. It is ground to the safe, and is said to form a liquid proof and metallic fit.

In the catalogue of this Company, one finds illustrations of Bank Vault Vestibules and doors that are such beautiful pieces of mechanism as to be almost works of art. Instead of the old-fashioned homely inner doors, there are "day gates" or grills of Bessemer steel wrought and twisted into ornamental patterns. The bolt-work on the inside of the great door is covered with glass, and the bolt-work itself is either oxidized copper or shining nickel-plate. The company also makes express messenger boxes, beside which the old-fashioned "strong-box" of our grandfathers would look as flimsy as a tomato can. These messenger boxes are fire proof, made of continuous sheets of iron, with cement-filled sides. Safety deposit boxes for the fitting up of safe deposit vaults are shown. These are beautiful little affairs, made of 1-8 inch Bessemer steel, and put together, as some bicycle manufacturer used to say of his wheels, "like a watch."

It is necessary that the safe or vault of these days should be not only fire proof, but burglar proof, for the burglar industry has kept abreast of times, and the cracksmen of the day are clever rascals and expert mechanics. They have to be if they expect to succeed in their profession, and that they succeed so seldom is proof of the excellence of the modern safes. The officers of the Hall's Safe Company proudly show the following letter from a bank in Ohio. The letter needs no explanation:—

HALL'S SAFE CO., Cincinnati, Ohio.

Gentlemen.—On the morning of October 15, 1901, at about 1 o'clock a. m., a gang of six men, of the "Jesse James" type, and the most daring that ever terrorized northern Ohio, held at bay a dozen of our citizens while they attempted to rob our bank. Five or six charges of nitro-glycerine badly damaged the front of our building and blew off the outside and middle doors, then made several charges on our chest doors. But we are pleased to say, after so much talk through the newspapers of a heavy loss, the burglars did not get one cent, and the doors to the chest were opened by a representative of Hall's Safe Co.—by the combination—and all the money was secure.

We are, indeed, highly pleased with the Hall's Safe. So much so that we have just given our order for a new one near the same style.

We commend the Hall's Safe to the public.

The illustrations that accompany this article show two of the many styles of office safe manufactured by this company. In Fig. 2 is seen a double-door safe, for use in any fair-sized business office. Fig. 1 shows one of the "baby" safes, before referred to, for use in a private house or small office.

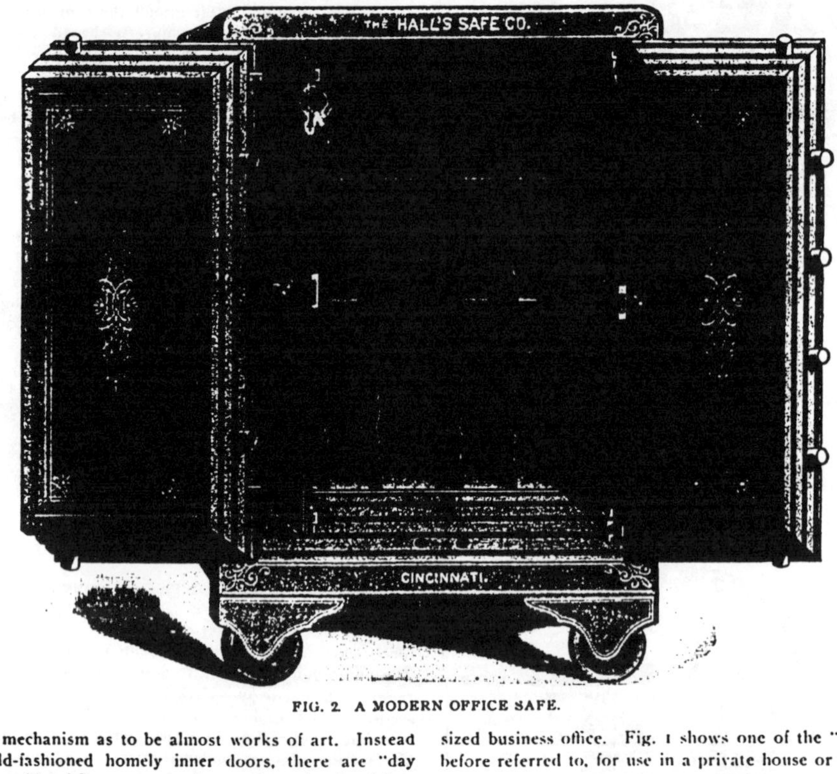

FIG. 2. A MODERN OFFICE SAFE.

MIXED GENDERS

Here is a story for which Pres. Hadley of Yale is said to be responsible:—

"A Frenchman called on the Mayor of Chicago, and as the visitor started to go he felt he must apologize for taking so much of the Mayor's time.

" 'I fear I have cockroached on your time, Mr. Mayor, and I extremely regret it,' he said.

" 'Oh, no, not at all, my dear sir. That word, though, my dear fellow, is henroached.'

" 'Pardon me, sir,' rejoined the Frenchman, as he shook hands with His Honor, 'I was mixed up in my genders.' "

BICYCLE "TERMS"

Madge—That old fellow I went to see about getting a place as stenographer in his bicycle store thought he had me on a question. He asked me if I understood bicycle terms.

Nelly—Why, of course!

Madge—Yes; I said, "Ten dollars down and two dollars a week till paid for," but even then I didn't get the place. —Exchange.

BRIEF MENTION.

THE BOOKLETS ADVERTISING summer resorts along the line of the Delaware and Lackawanna R. R. have come to hand, and, as usual they are artistic and interesting. One of them, the largest, is entitled "Mountain and Lake Resorts on the Lackawanna R. R." It is a handsome book of 128 pages, bound in a bright and attractive yellow cover, with an inviting little landscape in fac-simile of water-color on the front. It contains many beautiful halftone reproductions of photographs illustrating some beautiful spots reached by this railroad in New York, New Jersey and Pennsylvania. The reading matter is interesting also. There are one or two little stories, and the balance is descriptive matter relative to the various summer resorts. The distance from New York is given in each case, as is also the fare. The hotels and boarding-houses are listed with their prices for board and rooms. This larger booklet is well worth sending for for art's sake alone, but for anyone who intends spending the summer in the country it would seem to be very valuable. The Lackawanna also issues a little sixteen-page booklet giving the historical story of Richfield Springs, N. Y. Richfield Springs was once one of the most fashionable summer resorts of the United States, and still is visited by many people of rank and fashion. The little booklet contains several illustrations, three of them being curious old woodcuts that appeared in Harper's Magazine for June, 1859; the others are halftones, reproductions of photographs. The third booklet sent out by the Lackawanna R. R. describes Pocono Mountain and the Delaware Water Gap country. It begins with a pretty little story, entitled "Sculpture of the Elfs." It tells how the Elfin King prepared a beautiful spot for the site of his bride's court. The bride's name was "Beauty." The spot that the Elfs selected was in the vicinity of the Delaware Water Gap, and if any of our readers want to know how beautiful they made it, let them visit the Water Gap this summer and see for themselves. The booklet contains many little halftone illustrations, and judging by these, Delaware Water Gap and the Pocono Mountain must be picturesque and beautiful places for summer rest and recreation. Taken altogether, the advertising literature of the Lackawanna R. R. is well written, well illustrated and artistically printed.

THE CATALOGUE of J. Curley & Bro., manufacturers and importers of fine cutlery, is before us. The Curley Bros.' store is at No. 4 Warren street, New York City. The catalogue contains several hundred woodcuts, illustrating the various lines of cutlery, silver-plated ware, etc., manufactured by the firm, and shows this line to be very full and complete. Pictures of pocketknives in this catalogue are numerous enough to make the mouth of a small boy water. Besides the pocket cutlery, there are pictures of cigar cutters, oyster knives, skinning knives, and last, but not least, a combination knife-fork for the use of one-armed men.

WHAT BEAUTIFUL ADVERTISING matter the summer hotels are sending forth! Haddon Hall, a hotel on North Carolina avenue, Atlantic City, sends us a copy of its booklet for this season. The booklet contains little reading matter, but is made up of a series of handsome colored illustrations of views of Atlantic City and interior scenes in the hotel. Atlantic City, as every one knows, is the largest summer resort in the United States, having a transient population of from 150,000 to 200,000. Haddon Hall, the booklet tells us, fronts directly on the ocean, and is 50 feet from the board walk. It has a capacity of 450. It is heated throughout with steam and open grates, and has commodious sun parlors, fine halls, and is said to contain the finest collection of paintings in Atlantic City. The booklet is, as we said before, very handsome, and should be good advertising for the hotel.

A LITTLE FOLDER sent out by the American Bonding Co., of Baltimore, describes the work of the company and gives reasons why, in its own opinion, its plan of bonding is the best in the country. We quote the following as a sample of the plain talk to the prospective customer that is printed in this little folder: "Would you willingly encumber your estate with obligations for friendship's sake if you knew your family were to suffer on account thereof? Is it because you suspect you or your estate will never be called upon to pay such obligations that you obligingly acquiesce? Do you not know of instances where the unexpected happened and obligations were paid by the friendly sureties to the severe trial and reduction to penury of their families? When you sign a bond, you bind yourself, your "heirs, executors and administrators." As a rule the bond guarantees the holder against loss by dishonesty of the principal, and, in many cases, against the additional possibility of loss through his carelessness or errors of judgment, or through ignorance of the law's requirements. This is more particularly applicable in bonds given for administrators, executors, guardians and trustees. Are you dealing fairly with yourself, your wife, your children, to incur liability when the American Bonding Company will perform the services of surety for a reasonable compensation?" The folder argues well and makes interesting reading.

THE CATALOGUE of the Columbia, Hartford and Vedette bicycles, made in the Columbia factory at Hartford, Conn., is well gotten up and is in keeping with the artistic productions of former years. The line of bicycles shown in its pages is extensive, and we should think that every wheelman might find something to suit his taste among the many styles here shown. The prices of the bicycles are much lower than they formerly were, although, so the booklet tells us, the quality is "higher than ever." The Columbia people make bicycles for men and women, and make them with chains and without them

THE OLD-FASHIONED BINOCULAR, or marine glass, was a clumsy arrangement, although it was considered a wonderful affair by our fathers, but the little book descriptive of the Goerz Trieder Binocular shows us pictures of an instrument not one-half, no, not one-third the size of the old-fashioned variety, but which, the booklet says, will do all the old binoculars did, and much more besides. The interior arrangement of a Goerz Trieder Binocular is somewhat complicated, and appears to consist of an arrangement of magnifying prisms, and by this arrangement the field of the binocular is said to be greatly enlarged, while the magnifying power is also increased. The little book tells all this in an entertaining and interesting fashion and argues very convincingly. The binoculars are manufactured in a variety of sizes and styles, and the power varies according to price. The Goerz Trieder Binocular is manufactured abroad, but is sold by the Spencer Optical Manufacturing Company, 15 Maiden lane, New York City.

CHAS. J. GODFREY'S sporting goods catalogue for this season contains lists and pictures of almost every sporting implement known. There are cuts of shotguns, rifles, revolvers, hunting knives, hunting boots, decoy ducks, fishing rods, fishing lines, hooks, artificial bait, flies and many other things. This is the season of the year when the poor fish and partridge have nowhere to lay their heads, and the report of the shotgun and the tramp of the fisherman are heard in the land. It would seem, judging from the line of goods carried by Mr. Godfrey at his store at No. 4 Warren street, New York, that any sportsman might be fitted out there. The catalogue is printed on inexpensive paper, but the type is clear, and the woodcuts show the articles they picture very plainly.

WHEN WE OPEN the little booklet which Thos. Cook & Son, of 261 and 1185 Broadway, New York, send out to their prospective customers, we long to pack up and start for Europe. Cook's tours are known to everybody. In this booklet the synopsis of Cook's summer vacation tours to Europe is given, and the places visited by the tourists are entertainingly and invitingly described. Most of the tours in this book—by the way, the booklet will be sent to any one interested upon receipt of a stamp—are mainly sixty and seventy-day excursions to Gibraltar, Italy, Switzerland, Brussels, Paris and London. There are many halftone illustrations of noted places to be seen by the traveler, and altogether the book is very prettily made up.

THE MONARCH BICYCLES, manufactured by the American Bicycle Company, are sold at 152-154 Franklin Street, New York, and are pictured and described in the company's catalogue for 1902. Monarch wheels are made in a number of styles, with chains and without them, for the use of both ladies and gentlemen. In the catalogue much space is given to the description of the bevel gear chainless machine, which seems to be the company's special favorite for this season, and which also contains a cushion frame. This cushion frame, it is said, does away with the jarring of the ordinary wheel, and is therefore of great advantage. The coaster brake with which these machines are fitted is said to be a great help to the cyclers, as it makes wheeling safer. The catalogue, which will be sent to any one upon the receipt of a stamp, is prettily printed, with a colored cover, and contains sixteen pages of reading matter and illustrations.

REAL ESTATE IN NEW YORK is now worth so much money that it gives most of us a headache to think of it. The booklet issued by John Finck, dealer in real estate mortgages at 141 Broadway, New York, tells us a good deal about the increase of land values in the metropolis, and also a good deal about Mr. Finck's business. We are bound to say that it tells this in a convincing sort of way. The body of the booklet is made up of letters from Mr. Finck's customers, testifying to the satisfactory treatment that they have received in their dealings with him. Mr. Finck says in his booklet that his place of business is "The largest, finest and best equipped real estate mortgage office in New York."

ONE OF THE NEATEST CATALOGUES we have seen for some time is that issued by the Keuffel & Esser Co., manufacturers and importers of drawing materials and surveying instruments, whose factories are at Hoboken, N. J., and whose salesrooms are located in New York, Chicago, St. Louis and San Francisco. This catalogue is meant to be carried in the pocket, and is about the size of a fat pocketbook. It contains 482 pages, and on each page are illustrations of some of the goods made by the company. All sorts of artists' materials are pictured, and cuts of surveyors' instruments and mathematical instruments, India ink tablets and pencils are shown. It seems to us that this idea of a pocket catalogue is a good one. The architect, civil engineer or artist can carry a catalogue like this in his office coat without inconvenience, and, as there is an alphabetical index in the back, can almost immediately turn to the price list of the article which he happens to want.

THE OFFICE DESK today is not much like the office desk used by our forefathers. A first-class roll-top desk is now a handsome piece of furniture, and is put together with a great deal of care. T. G. Sellew, dealer in desks, whose place of business is at 111 Fulton Street, New York, is sending out a handsome catalogue, showing the kind of desks which he sells. The cuts in this catalogue are half-tones, and are extremely well done. The grain of the wood is shown in these pictures to perfection. The desks themselves appear to be as well made as they are good looking. Mr. Sellew says that this is the case, and that they "are massive and durable in construction, made with special regard to convenience and practicability, and are fully guaranteed."

THE ADVERTISING OF THE REGAL SHOE, manufactured by L. C. Bliss & Co., is always taking and unique, but the Regal Laundry List that the Bliss Company are sending out is a particularly clever conception. On each page of this laundry list is a blank form such as one sends with his soiled linen to the "Heathen Chinee" or the steam laundry. The regular laundry list form is followed, but at the side of each page and close to the list is a picture of either a style of Regal Shoe, a bottle of Regal Shoe Dressing, the Regal Shoe Polisher, or some other shoe "fixing" manufactured by the company. The advantage of this sort of advertising is that it is not read and thrown away, but is kept and used; consequently the advertisement of the Regal Shoe is always before the customer's eyes. A carbon sheet, for the making of duplicate copies of the laundry list is bound in the back of the book.

INK HAS ALWAYS BEEN a necessity of business. We say "always," although the ancient Babylonian merchants used to chisel their accounts on slabs of stone or scratch them on pieces of clay, which were afterwards baked in the oven. These were laborious processes, but they had the advantage of lasting. But ink has its advantages, which more than outweigh those of the forms just mentioned, and the catalogue and price list of the Thaddeus Davids Company contains some fine illustrations of the various styles of bottles and colors of ink that the company manufactures. Here are pictures of inks of all colors, put up in all kinds of bottles; also pictures of sealing wax, mucilage, paste bottles, and the like. The catalogue is very prettily printed, and the illustrations are among the best of the kind that we have seen, those in color being especially well handled, and showing the various shades of ink and forms of bottles very attractively. The Thaddeus Davids Company's New York warerooms are at 127 to 129 William Street.

BOOKS OF INTEREST TO BUSINESS MEN

BUSINESS LAW. By Thomas Raeburn White, B.L., LL.B. 5 by 7 1-2 inches; 323 pages. Bound in cloth. Back title gilt. Price, $1.50.

This is a neat, compact and handy book of business law for the use of students and business men. Among the subjects treated are Contracts, Sales, Partnerships, Corporations, Negotiable Paper and the like. The author's language is plain, and is understandable by any one having no previous knowledge of law. The book's clearness on the essential points of ordinary law should recommend it as a business book for the plain business man who has no time in which to consult a law library.

THE PHONOGRAPHIC DICTIONARY AND PHRASE BOOK. By Benn Pitman and Jerome B. Howard. 5 1-2 by 8 inches; 552 pages. Bound in cloth. Cover title and back title gilt. Price, $3.00.

This book is the most elaborate shorthand dictionary yet published, with the characters in fac-simile. It contains over 20,000 words, and for every one of these words there is a corresponding sign in the Benn Pitman system of shorthand. To the reporter, office or court stenographer, or any one writing the Benn Pitman system of shorthand, the book is invaluable. It is well made, tastefully bound, and is printed on a good quality of paper in clean, plain type.

THE LAWRENCE SYSTEM OF VOCAL AND PHYSICAL EXPRESSION. By Edwin Gordon Lawrence. 4 3-4 by 6 inches; 128 pages. Bound in cloth. Cover title and back title gilt. Price, $1.00.

The author says in the preface of this little book that his object has been to place in the hands of lawyers, actors and public speakers in general, a simple system of vocal and physical expression that will enable them to clearly convey thought by word of mouth and emphasize it by the proper action. To the man of affairs who is called upon for a speech on any subject, and who knows what to say but does not know how to say it, this book will be a great help.

BUSINESS LAW. By Alonzo R. Weed, LL. B., of the Boston Bar. 6 by 9 1-4 inches; 172 pages. Bound in cloth. Cover and back title red. Price, $1.25.

Mr. Weed calls his book "a manual for schools and colleges and for every day use." The titles of the chapters are as follows: Contracts, Principal and Agent, Partnerships, Sales of Personal Property, Bailments and Common Carriers, Negotiable Paper, Deeds, Mortgages and Leases, Collection Laws, Written Rates of Interest, Insurance, Patent Rights, Trade-Marks and Copyrights, etc.

The author does not waste words, and yet treats his subjects clearly and comprehensively. In short, he gives the law without the addition of wordy "trimmings."

BANKERS' AND MERCHANTS' INTEREST TABLES. By Francis H. Coffin and David H. Moore. 13 by 9 1-2 inches. Bound in cloth. Leather back and corners. Cover and back title gilt. Price, $5.00.

There have been interest tables published before, but never, so far as we know, has so elaborate and comprehensive a set of tables been issued in book form. "The volume contains," to quote from the title page, "Interest tables, computed on the basis of 360 days per annum, at 3 1-2, 4, 5 and 6 per cent, with an accurate calculation of interest on every sum from $1.00 to $1,000, and, by simple addition of two lines, on every further sum, to $1,000,000." It also contains a 1 per cent one day table, on the basis of 365 days per annum, from which interest on daily balances can be computed at any time and on any sum. There is a time table printed in black and red at the beginning of the book as an aid in quickly finding the number of days between one day and another. To a merchant or banker performing many calculations in interest this book is a great time saver. It is handsomely bound, finely printed, and has a thumb index.

POLITICAL ECONOMY OF HUMANISM. By Henry Wood. 7 3-4 by 5 1-4 inches; 320 pages. Bound in cloth. Cover and back title gilt. Price, $1.25.

Mr. Wood is well known as a writer on various economic subjects, and this book contains a series of able treatises, written in his usual vein, on the relation of the employer to the employed, and the phases of the industrial question and their relation to socialism. Among the questions considered and handled in a conservative spirit and with much common sense, are the following: Supply and Demand, the Law of Competition, Labor and Production, Combinations of Capital, Combinations of Labor, Employers and Profit Sharing, the Obligations and Privileges of Employees, the Unequal Distribution of Wealth, Money and Coinage, Tariffs and Protection, Industrial Education and Gold Production and values.

NEW YORK UNIVERSITY

School of Commerce, Accounts and Finance

A college course in Higher Accountancy arranged in accordance with the requirements of the Certified Public Accountants' Act of the State of New York and fitting students for the Regents' Examination for the C. P. A. degree. The course in Accountancy is rounded out by instruction in finance, commerce and commercial law leading to the University Degree of Bachelor of Commercial Science.

NEW YORK UNIVERSITY

Washington Square **NEW YORK CITY**

About a Pay Roll which proves itself, corrects all mistakes in figuring, divides up Pay Roll into several amounts needed to pay each person.

But let us send you a sample leaf, with circular, which tells the whole story.

BARLOW BROS., Grand Rapids, Mich.

INTRODUCTION TO THE STUDY OF COMMERCE. By Frederick R. Clow, Ph. D. 7 1-2 by 3 3-4 inches; 224 pages. Bound in cloth. Back title gilt. Price, $1.25.

Mr. Clow's book is not intended as a complete text book on commerce. It is simply, as its title implies, an introduction to the study of commerce. It is intended as a text book for the use of teachers in schools or universities, or as a help to the student in his commercial training. Incidentally, it makes good reading for anyone interested in modern commerce, and particularly for the American merchant. The author begins by describing the Elements of Commerce; then follows a short essay on the Rise of Commerce, and then the Materials of Commerce are discussed. Foreign Commerce of the United States and of other countries is treated of, as is the Domestic Commerce of this country. The titles of other chapters are: Organization of Trade, Prices, Payments and How the Equilibrium is Maintained. We can heartily recommend this introduction to the Study of Commerce. It is a good book on a vastly important subject.

THE A B C OF BANKS AND BANKING. By George M. Coffin. 6 3-4 by 5 inches; 137 pages. Bound in cloth. Back title gilt. Price, $1.25.

This handy little volume is exactly what its name implies, that is, a presentation of the principles underlying banking in the United States. The author in his preface says that it is designed to appeal to the reader outside as well as inside of a bank. It is by no means the last word or every word about banking. It may be said that it is a primer covering a field that has hitherto been somewhat neglected. The chapter heads are as follows: Banking in General, Various Kinds of Banking, Capital Stock, Shareholders' Rights and Liabilities, Undivided Profits, Dividends and Surplus, Deposits, Checks, Lawful Money Reserve, Issuing Bank Notes, Borrowing Money, Loans and Discounts, Exchanges, Collections, Letters of Credit, Bonds, Mortgages and Stocks, Bank Reports, Examinations, Directors, Executive Officers—Their Powers and Duties, Internal Administration and Bookkeeping, and Other Suggestions.

A BUSINESS EDUCATION | FOR ...ONE... DOLLAR.

...THE PRACTICAL AGE...

A MONTHLY MAGAZINE full to the brim with helpful suggestions to young men and young women who are struggling successward.

THE BUSINESS HOUSE THAT JACK BUILT, an intensely interesting and highly instructive story of business life, and

APPLIED ENGLISH, an authority on writing and speaking the English language, which no young person can afford to be without, all for ONE DOLLAR.

If you have never seen THE PRACTICAL AGE, send for a free sample copy. Address,

THE PRACTICAL AGE,

Moline, Illinois.

R·I·P·A·N·S

There is scarcely any condition of ill-health that is not benefited by the occasional use of a R·I·P·A·N·S Tabule. For sale by Druggists. The Five-Cent packet is enough for an ordinary occasion. The family bottle, 60 cents, contains a supply for a year.

Any book in this list will be sent to any address in the United States, Canada or Mexico upon receipt of price. If there is some special book that you require we shall be pleased to hunt it up for you. Address COMMERCE, ACCOUNTS & FINANCE, 25 Pine street, New York city.

HALL'S Fireproof and Burglar Proof SAFES

Sold since 1840. Never fail to protect contents.

KNOWN EVERYWHERE

393 BROADWAY, N.Y.

Telephones: 3133-3136-307 Franklin.

BUSINESS NEEDS

Advertisements under this head one cent a word each insertion.

WANTED, a thoroughly competent office manager; one familiar with the handling of a large clerical force and having ability to systematize work. We want a man who can infuse discipline, address and economy. Care of Commerce, Accounts & Finance.

BUSINESS PICTURES—Do you want to illustrate your catalogue or booklet? Do you want a series of snappy pen and ink sketches to brighten your advertisement in the daily papers? Do you want a handsome wash drawing for your announcement in the magazines? If you do, write to me. I am a competent business artist, working in black and white and colors, and you see my sketches every week if you read the Sunday papers. My price is always a fair one. Address, PEN AND INK, Box 17, Commerce, Accounts & Finance.

A CAREFUL, conscientious worker desires position as bookkeeper with some house where accurate work will insure advancement. American, age 31. Thirteen years' business training. Compensation moderate. Position outside of City of New York preferred. Address JUNIOR, care of Commerce, Accounts & Finance.

SECOND-HAND TYPEWRITERS can be repaired so that they can be used and produce work which is almost, if not quite, as good as from a new machine. I have the facilities for obtaining exceptionally good second-hand machines. I have a man who repairs them—a man that understands his business. These machines can be sold for 50 per cent discount from list price of the new machines. Does this interest you? If it does, address TYPEWRITER, care Commerce, Accounts & Finance.

I AM AT PRESENT engaged in a large export commission business, and can furnish the highest testimonials as to efficiency of service rendered as a bookkeeper. Further advancement is barred by reason of the firm's personal dependants. Any firm or individual in need of an office man communicate with INDUSTRIOUS, care Commerce, Accounts & Finance.

SALESMAN having a large line of retail customers in the eastern states among dry goods and gentlemen's furnishing stores desires to represent some line of goods that he can present in connection with the article which he now carries. Underwear manufacturers might do well to communicate with PERSONALITY, care Commerce, Accounts & Finance.

OFFICE FURNITURE, Files, Cabinets, etc.—I know a lot more about some things than you do. I have to—it is my bread and butter. You don't know the "cost" of a desk, a cabinet, filing devices and the hosts of other things you may want to use in your office. I do! I can save you money and make some myself. That is a good proposition for you to look in to. Try. UNITS, care Commerce, Accounts & Finance.

It's Good for You

To use our Typewriter Ribbons and Carbons, because they write better and last longer than the ordinary kind; they do not smut, blur nor fill the type, but they make fine copies.

No. 1 Ribbons, 75c. ea., $7.00 doz.
No. 1 Carbon, $3.00 pr. bx., 40c. doz.
Silkarbon, $4.00 pr. bx., 50c. doz.

We pay express or mail charges.

IMPERIAL MANUFACTURING CO.
289-297 Washington St., Newark, N. J.

PRENTISS CLOCKS.
SIX TIMES A YEAR
is all that is necessary to wind a Prentiss Clock. Why wind a clock every week when we can sell you one which will require winding but once in sixty days and will keep perfect time? Also Frying-pan, Program and Electrically synchronized clocks. Send for Catalogue No. [illegible].
THE PRENTISS CLOCK IMPROVEMENT CO.
Dept. [illegible], 49 Dey St., New York City

Leon Brummer, C.P.A.
Public Accountant and Auditor,
7 Pine Street, New York, N. Y.

What Do You Do With Your Invoices?

When You Receive a bill for goods bought by you, what do you do with it? Do you hand it to your bookkeeper, who laboriously copies it, figure by figure, in a bulky invoice journal, from which the total amount is posted to the ledger?

When your Bookkeeper has wasted valuable time by the above process, what does he do with the invoice itself? Does he hand it to the office boy or the assistant bookkeeper, who places it in some compartment of a clumsy file along with a dozen other bills from the same house, each of which must be pawed over when this particular one is wanted again?

If You Are Wasting Time and Money by these antiquated methods, aren't you tired of doing so? Would you not welcome a system as far superior to them as the sun is to a kerosene lamp?

THEN USE THE

"Acx" System of Filing Invoices

Simpler, More Convenient and More Serviceable than any other. A time-saving application of elements more or less used in every up-to-date office.

What the "Acx" System Is.

A system of filing invoices by which (1) the copy of the order placed, (2) the record of the receipt of the goods, and (3) the invoices, are brought together on a sheet of the paper of a size and shape to be conveniently handled and preserved in any post binder file.

The "Acx" Invoice Filing Sheet is of manilla, 11 inches long by 8½ inches deep. The directions on it explain its use. Three lines of mucilage are in place on the sheet. The first of these (inside left hand) is entitled "Attach left hand of your order here." All orders should be filled out in duplicate, preferably by the use of carbon sheets, and the retained copy attached to the invoice sheet.

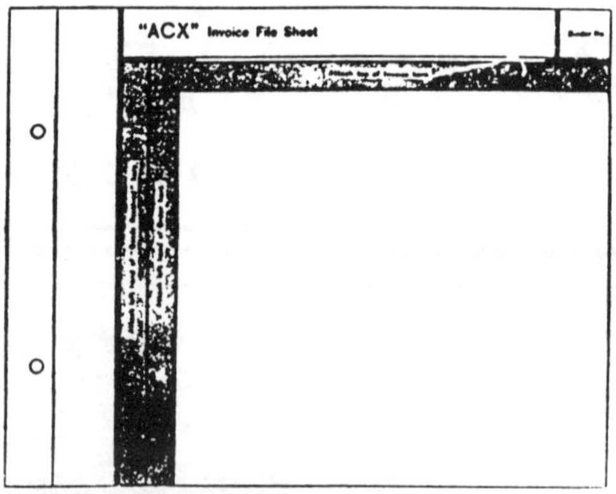

Reduced fac-simile of "Acx" Invoice File Sheet, designed by Account, Audit & Assurance Co., Ltd., 25 Pine Street, New York. Made by Self-Proving Account Book Co., New York. Patented February 8, 1898. May 20, 1902. Other patents pending.

When the goods for which the order is given are received, the count is made and entered upon a "Goods Received Slip," provided for the purpose. This slip is then attached to the Invoice Filing Sheet in the place marked "Attach left hand of Goods Received Here."

When the invoice is checked with the order and the "Goods Received Slip," its upper edge is moistened and laid against the mucilage on the Invoice Filing Sheet in the place marked "Attach top of invoice here." There are then superimposed upon this sheet (1) copy of the order, (2) record of the goods received, and (3) the invoice. The Invoice Filing Sheet is then paged in numerical order in its upper left-hand corner and is ready to be inserted in the binder; the latest invoice always being on top.

No Journalizing, no hunting for lost invoices, orders or goods received records. Order, receipt of goods and invoice all attached to one sheet of stiff paper, numbered and securely bound in a substantial binder, ready for instant reference. Post from this sheet direct to the ledger.

Price $6 a Thousand.

Address orders to

THE SELF-PROVING ACCOUNT BOOK COMPANY

86 Fulton Street, New York City.

THE NEW YORK PUBLIC LIBRARY ASTOR, LENOX

COMMERCE ACCOUNTS & FINANCE

Volume 4 New York July 1902 Number 7

CONTENTS

Published Monthly by the Commerce Accounts & Finance Company Twenty-five Pine Street New York

KNICKERBOCKER TRUST CO.

234 FIFTH AVENUE, CORNER 27TH STREET
BRANCH OFFICES:
66 BROADWAY, AND 125TH STREET AND LENOX AVE.,
NEW YORK CITY.

CAPITAL AND UNDIVIDED PROFITS, $2,508,399.11.

LEGAL DEPOSITORY FOR STATE, CITY, AND COURT FUNDS.

Interest allowed on Time Deposits. Deposits also received subject to Demand Checks, which pass through the Clearing House as do those upon any city bank.

Authorized to act as Executor or Administrator of Estates, and as Guardian, Receiver, Registrar, Transfer and Financial Agent for States, Cities, Towns, Railroads, and other corporations, and to accept any other Trusts in conformity with the laws of any State or of the United States.

LETTERS OF CREDIT FURNISHED.
BUSINESS AND PERSONAL ACCOUNTS SOLICITED.

CHAS. T. BARNEY, - - - - - - - - President.
JOSEPH T. BROWN, - - - - - - 2d Vice-President.
JULIAN M. GERARD, - - - - Asst. Sec. and Asst. Treas.
FRED'K K. ELDRIDGE, - - - - 1st Vice-President.
FRED'K GORE KING, - - - Secretary and Treasurer.
WM. B. RANDALL, - - - - - - - Trust Officer.

BOARD OF DIRECTORS:

JOSEPH S. AUERBACH,
HARRY B. HOLLINS,
JACOB HAYS,
CHARLES T. BARNEY,
A. FOSTER HIGGINS,
ANDREW H. SANDS,
JAMES H. BRESLIN,
I. TOWNSEND BURDEN,
HON. E. V. LOEW,
HENRY F. DIMOCK,
CHARLES F. WATSON,
FREDERICK G. BOURNE,
C. LAWRENCE PERKINS,
CHARLES R. FLINT,
AMZI L. BARBER,
CHARLES T. COOK,
JOHN MAGEE,
HENRY A. MORGAN,
HENRY C. BERLIN,
CHARLES W. GOULD,
FRED'K L. ELDRIDGE,
HENRY W. DE FOREST,
ALFRED B. MACLAY
HARRY W. McVICKAR.

C. W. HASKINS, C. P. A. E. W. SELLS, C. P. A.

HASKINS & SELLS

Certified Public Accountants

CABLE ADDRESS, "HASKSELLS." THIRTY BROAD STREET, NEW YORK

Accounts of Municipalities, Corporations, Firms and Individuals Inspected and Audited; Methods of Accounting Originated and Adapted to Conditions; Books of Accounts Opened, Regulated and Closed; Irregularities Discovered; Financial Situations Examined.

Experts under the Joint Commission of the Fifty-third Congress to Revise the Accounting System of the UNITED STATES GOVERNMENT.

Lackawanna Railroad

Address all communications to

C. W. TEN BROECK, Industrial Agent,

26 Exchange Place, New York City.

Do You Desire a Factory Site? The Industrial Department of the Lackawanna Railroad will aid you in finding one.

Are You Interested in Any Raw Product for Manufacturing Purposes? The Industrial Department of the Lackawanna Railroad will tell you if it is to be found along that road.

Does the Question of Power Concern You? The Industrial Department of the Lackawanna Railroad will tell you of good water power and of the proximity of fuel to points on that road.

Do You Want to Know the Usual Rate of Wages? The Industrial Department of the Lackawanna Railroad will give that information regarding any point on that road.

Do You Want to Know the Price of Gas, Water, Electricity? The Industrial Department of the Lackawanna Railroad will tell you.

Some Consequences of the Trust Movement*

By H. I. NEWCOMB

Three years ago, when the movement toward the concentration of the control of American industries had for the second time attained proportions which arrested the attention of the country, it was my privilege to lay before the American Association certain facts which seemed to me to show that the integration then in progress was but a step in the natural evolution of methods of industrial association. The process of combination, which at that time had assumed almost spectacular magnitude, has continued with undiminished momentum. The year 1901 saw the organization of the greatest of all industrial combinations, the United States Steel Corporation, with a stock and bond capitalization of almost one and a half billions of dollars, which is worth, at present market prices, about 83 per cent of that amount. During the first five months of the current year there were organized in the four states of New York, New Jersey, Delaware and Maine new companies, exclusive of all having less than one million dollars of capitalization each, with an aggregate par value of shares and bonds of $1,058,000,000. Unquestionably the organization of large corporations, in the United States, has been very greatly facilitated during the last three years by unprecedented domestic prosperity. The remarkable conditions which have recently placed within the control of American citizens an amount of capital never previously equaled and thus supplied a ready market for the flotation of securities cannot be expected indefinitely to continue. There are those to whom foreshadowings of the approaching end of the exceptional period seem already visible. However this may be, some retardation of the movement that has already continued over a period of unexpected duration may be predicted with certainty, and students of economic history will not be surprised if it is for a time wholly arrested. Three years ago the interpretation of the so-called trust movement as a step in the evolution of industrial organization had not won universal acceptance, but I submit that this interpretation is no longer the subject of reasonable controversy. Nowhere is the assertion that industrial integration is based on increased economic efficiency intelligently disputed. Some combinations have unquestionably been organized for the mere purpose of selling securities based on inflated valuations of the properties represented, and there is room for an honest difference of opinion as to the proportion in which the general movement has been pervaded by this form of fraud, but the licensed swindlers who have tainted commercial circles by their presence and influence have not attached their fraudulent purposes to a movement in itself vicious; nor has the folly of those whom they have beguiled consisted in mistaking the nature of a great economic tendency, but rather in failing to distinguish between the false and the real.

It is not my purpose, on this occasion, to seek to add anything to the discussion of the gain in productive power which may spring from bringing several establishments within the control of a single management. I presented that phase of the subject with some care in the paper already alluded to, and many contributions to the same subject from more accomplished students have appeared within the ensuing period.

THE BUSINESS CORPORATION AN ECONOMIC NEED.

When the leaders of industry discover a means of rendering labor and capital more productive which involves a different method of industrial association than that formerly in vogue, judicial science is compelled to assume the task of formulating a code of written or unwritten law which shall accord legal sanction and effect to the relations that are economically necessary among those who associate themselves according to the newly developed method. In the state of legal institutions which has persisted in English-speaking countries since the Common Law assumed a crystallized form and the power of rulers to devise new means of equitable relief from its unvarying terms fell into harmless disuse, this has ordinarily assumed the form of the adaptation of some pre-existing legal institution or concept to the new conditions. The business corporation, a purely legal institution, was the child of industrial necessity. The factory system, the railway and the steamship required new methods of capitalistic association. It was necessary in order that they might be developed that many individuals should unite in supplying capital, and that their aggregated investments should be employed subject to unified control and under a system of management permitting a fair degree of permanence. It was also necessary that each undertaking should be permitted to stand or to fall by itself, or, in other words, that there should be limited liability so that property not distinctly committed to an enterprise, although belonging to those sharing in it, should not be liable to attachment for its indebtedness should the undertaking prove unsuccessful. The factory system, the railway and the steamship do not exist today because the business corporation met these necessities. Industry declines long to pause at the mandate of obstinate political systems or unyielding legal rules or practice. The industrial imperative was happily met by the expansion of the legal concept of the corporation, but if it had not thus been met, law would have been forced to find some other way of meeting its requirements. About 1870, in the United States, the development of industrial relations made it necessary to combine under unified management numbers of productive establishments which had previously been separate. Various means of accomplishing this were attempted, none of which proved entirely successful, and only one of them now deserves attention. The early trust is entitled to a word, because it left its name as a legacy to popular discussion and its partial success as a lesson to the leaders of trade and commerce. At its best it was a scarcely satisfactory means of obtaining concentrated control. It was exceedingly vulnerable in law, and it speedily succumbed to legislative and judicial attacks which sprang partly from prejudice and partly from the immoderate demands and unwise policies of early trust managers. The trust of current popular discussion is nothing but a larger form of the business corporation exercising control over smaller corporations through its ownership of their securities. It has won its right to survival, in a struggle demonstrating its legal fitness, and its permanence is now as secure as that of the industrial aggregations with which it has come to be inseparably connected.

ECONOMIC SERVICES OF THE BUSINESS CORPORATION.

If I correctly apprehend the subject, the business corporation, in its enlarged form as in a smaller degree in its earlier form, serves well certain desirable economic ends. Primarily a legal institution and becoming allied to industrial institutions only that it might fix the relations among the participants in industry, it yet performs certain distinct and valuable producive functions. It is the producer of certificates of shares and indebtedness, the title to which passes readily from one individual to another, and these are commodities of marked utility and measurable value. The services which society receives from this form of capitalistic organization are that it provides an incentive to the accumulation of wealth; induces the owners of wealth to use it productively; that is, turns wealth into capital; and creates a tendency toward the general diffusion of wealth and comfort. The full possibilities of the business corporation in the performance of these services have by no means been realized. They are indicated, and it may be said established, tendencies rather than facts broadly accomplished.

*Paper read before the section on Economic and Social Science of the American Association for the Advancement of Science at its annual meeting at Pittsburg.

While admitting this and urging that it is necessary to exclude from present consideration those combinations which have been formed for purely speculative purposes or from an erroneous conception of the economic requirements of the industries affected, it is yet unhesitatingly affirmed that the rapid accumulation of American wealth since 1830, the present tremendous productive power of the people of the United States, and the current relatively high average of individual possessions and exceptional standard of living of this country have all largely been achieved by the aid of the business corporation. Even more than this, it is not too much to assert, that the more rapid gains, in all of these particulars, in the last three decades are partly attributable to the impetus arising from the further development of that useful legal institution.

AS AN INCENTIVE TO SAVING.

Mere productive efficiency will not suffice to account for the rapidity with which wealth has been accumulated. Accumulation is the difference by which production exceeds consumption. Just as the principal incentive to increased production is the desire for enhanced comfort so the primary impulse derived from the possession of a greater volume of commodities is to augment consumption. This impulse has not wholly been denied, nor should it have been, but neither has there been complete yielding. Millions of American homes as well as the never-ebbing tide of immigration testify to the increasing comfort that is the expression of augmented per capita consumption, but no more loudly than the multiplication of industrial establishments financed at home, and the rapid redemption of the securities of railways and factories that were originally constructed with capital borrowed from abroad, bespeak proper self-restraint. But abstinence from consumption is not a virtue that is its own reward. It will not be exercised unless there is a reasonable expectation of securing by present sacrifice a future gain of compensatory magnitude. Neither the much-abused economic man nor the individual of flesh and blood, unless his reason is distorted, expects to find this compensation in the mere contemplation of hoarded wealth. There are other incentives to saving, but it is impossible to deny the importance, almost exceptional, of that which arises from opportunity to invest what has been saved in such a way as to produce a regular income. This is the alluring prospect that is held out by the known existence of stable and reliable corporate investments. The farmer, artisan or laborer, who can live sufficiently within his income to accumulate less than seventy-five dollars, now has it within his power to become a part owner in the Pennsylvania railroad, which, with its affiliated corporations, controls approximately eighteen thousand miles of railway. He can make the investment through any banker in the United States, and it will bring him an income, proportionately much larger but scarcely less secure, than that to be derived from a bond of the United States Government or a British consol. If more adventurously inclined, he can become, with equal ease and an investment little more than half as great, a participant in the business of the United States Steel Corporation, with its mines and furnaces, and mills and railways scattered over almost half a continent, and he will receive, as long as present rates are maintained, an income of quite 10 per cent upon his investment. These are but illustrations of opportunities now open and daily being brought more forcibly to the realization of all American citizens. It is not sufficent to answer to this argument that the business corporation has existed, for seventy years, that its securities have always been marketable commodities, and that therefore the present movement affords no greater incentive to the accumulation of wealth than has long existed. There are two requirements which the smaller corporation did not meet that are fulfilled by the more comprehensive organization. The existence of the corporate investment must be generally known, and the risk involved must be as small as possible. It is difficult to say which of these is more important, the answer being special to each particular investor and governed by individual temperament. The opportunity must be known. The older type of corporation had its existence within a relatively limited area. The investors in its securities were usually local capitalists or their distant business associates. Changes in the ownership of shares were not very numerous, and they were usually the result of private and consequently almost secret negotiation. The large cities, of course, have maintained their stock exchanges for many years, but large classes of securities were long almost universally excluded from their lists, and it is impossible that they should be the scene of extensive trading in securities wholly dependent upon the special industrial conditions of small communities. Even in the case of railway shares it is only recently that some of the most important have become directly accessible to traders in the great American market, that of the Stock Exchange of the city of New York. The presence of a security in this great market gains for it a progressively increasing prominence that is, day by day through the public press and the ordinary agencies of finance, brought home to a steadily expanding circle of potential purchasers. Added to this the great corporation obtains a good deal of very effective advertising that is an incident of its size. Its officers and its operations are the subject of constant comment in the news columns of the great dailies and of the rural press. Its legions of employees usually enjoying incomes much beyond the average earnings of those with whom they are in daily contact, make its existence and its enterprise the subject of current discussion in every circle which they frequent. The great corporation is thus perpetually within the observation of nearly every citizen, and long before an individual has ceased to contemplate and wonder at its magnitude he is, if at all frugally inclined, apt to consider its attractiveness as a means of investment, and to inquire how he can make it a source of personal pecuniary gain. Stability is the especial attribute of the great corporation, although it is more difficult at once to perceive this than it would be if the perspective of the underlying circumstances of which great stability is the direct and certain consequence were not distorted by recent examples of the purely speculative creation of combinations. When an industry involving many establishments and covering a wide area is concentrated in the control of a great corporation there is a distribution of the risks of loss from purely local causes to which each separate establishment is subject. A local railway or a local mill may have its earning power greatly impaired during a season by the failure of agricultural production within the region tributary to it, by disturbed relations with its employees or between other employers in its vicinity and their employees, or by many other strictly local, and usually temporary, causes. Combination affords an effective form of insurance against losses of this character. Those of one district are distributed over the entire industry, and thus the earning power of the aggregation may be protected from perceptible impairment. Similarly the power of a great corporation to distribute temporary losses, although they cover wide areas, over longer periods of time is a means of insuring regularity in the returns to investors. The local capitalist who invests in a local enterprise is likely to insist upon the immediate distribution of all surplus earnings, and he is frequently unwilling to consent to the accumulation of a reasonable fund as a protection against future depression or losses from any cause. He has power to enforce his demands in this respect that does not lie in the hands of the investor who controls an interest having equal aggregate value in a larger enterprise.

SECURES THE USE OF WEALTH PRODUCTIVELY.

The manner in which the great corporation acts as an incentive to the accumulation of wealth and the way in which it impels the owners of wealth to its utilization as capital, that is to its dedication to production, are so inextricably intertwined and interrelated that it has been difficult to decide which function first to present. It will readily be understood that every incentive to save that has been discussed in this paper is also an incentive to the investment of the amounts saved. But it was expressly stated that there are incentives to accumulation other than those enumerated and yet differing from the mere desire to contemplate hoarded wealth. No greater error has ever been committed in the name of economic science than the assumption, which has received the apparent assent of many who ought to know better, that there is at any particular time in the possession of any community a definite amount of wealth which is utilized for productive purposes, and that this capital fund is fixed and inelastic. There are always those who will exercise a degree of abstinence from consumption, and some portion of their accumulations is always held aloof from investment. Hoarded wealth is a protection against certain ever-present contingencies which are realized with almost appaling force by many of the most intelligent among those whose ability to save, on account of their moderate incomes is least. This protection ought not to be diminished, but it is desirable from every point of view that means should be devised which, while leaving the protection in full force, will also secure the productive utilization of the largest possible proportion of aggregate wealth. It is scarcely necessary to show how the great corporation tends to draw this wealth into the industrial field or how the ready market for its securities guarantees the continuance of undiminished protection. In fact, here again the great corporation furnishes a form of insurance, averaging certain losses that fall upon every community with a substantial degree of regularity.

PROMOTES THE DIFFUSION OF WEALTH.

No one denies that the organization of the combinations which have characterized economic progress throughout the last few years has brought to certain industrial leaders enormous accessions of wealth. This enrichment of the leaders is the inevitable accompaniment of industrial progress and a necessary consequence of the fundamental principle of modern industrial organization which accepts the struggle of individuals to better themselves, under a regime of competition and free contract, as the best means of attaining general moral, social and industrial welfare. Wisely or unwisely, society has made individual gain the primary incentive to the exercise of industrial skill and foresight. Men of wonderful economic perception have led in the movement toward the concentration of industrial control. They saw, long before their fellows, the superior efficiency of enterprises conducted on a large scale, and they have devoted their tremendous energy and skill to the task of securing results which have now became visible to all men. They have provided America with an industrial organization of marvelous power; they have placed the products of its farms, its mines and its factories in the markets of every civilized nation, and they have almost demonstrated its ascendency in the domain of world finance. The greater portion of the accrued profit of these conquests has already been diffused among the people, but a tithe of it has sufficed enormously to enrich those under whose generalship the struggles were fought. It is so much easier to perceive the aggrandizement of the few than the more moderate gains which the diffusion of a greater aggregate has brought to the many that it is, perhaps, a little startling to be told that the movement is really toward the more general distribution of wealth. If what has already been accomplished were to be the end, it is possible that such a contention could not be supported. The movement must already have materially enhanced the average possessions of those who are not regarded as extremely wealthy, but the rewards of leadership have been so great that it need not be surprising should it be learned that the difference between average possessions and those of the most wealthy has been augmented during the last decade. That this is the case is by no means certain, as only general conclusions are possible, but its probability is sufficient to warrant its admission for the purposes of further discussion. It can be shown that the tendencies of the great corporation are toward the payment of better wages, toward greater stability of employment and toward the general amelioration of the conditions of labor. These things make for the diffusion of wealth, but not so strongly as the presence of a powerful incentive to saving, combined with recognized opportunities for investments from which satisfactory and stable returns may be anticipated. One has but to look at certain of the older communities of the United States, such as many which exist in Massachusetts and other eastern states, in order to realize how much has been accomplished in this manner with the relatively meager incentives and opportunities that have long existed. The outlook may be a long one. Its realization may point to a time when the methods of industrial association are in a less dynamic condition than at present, but the economic perception of the individual who cannot read in facts already accomplished the beginning of a movement that must result in an ultimate general diffusion of wealth among the people, in a great increase in average ownership and consequently in the average income and comfort, and in a considerable reduction of the difference between the average wealth and that of those whose possessions are greatest, is indeed imperfect. Savings banks, insurance companies, building and loan associations, societies for mutual relief and many other financial institutions which have attained high development in this country have tended strongly to secure the three desirable ends that have been suggested. They have aided in the accumulation, increased the productive utilization and fostered the diffusion of wealth, but I submit that they are now supplemented, and, in the course of progress already foreshadowed, will be still more powerfully reinforced by a greater force,—that of the industrial combination and its legal adjunct, the business corporation.

GREAT CORPORATIONS AND MORAL WELFARE.

Those who do not perceive that through the mutations of time an unceasing purpose works with continuous beneficence may be forced to admit all that has been said, but they will declare that economic welfare is not everything, and, perhaps, assert that, however desirable from the mere point of view of effective production it may be, the trust movement threatens the much more important moral and social welfare. The inquiry thus suggested is an important one and must not be avoided. It would be possible to approach it with the general question whether those who ask it have not conceded everything that is essential in admitting that there is a gain in productive efficiency. Certainly there are, from day to day, points at which the moral and the economic welfare of individuals are opposed to each other. This must be admitted, but those who see these difficulties most clearly are apt to take the more satisfactory philosophic view, which looks upon them as the merely temporary consequences of imperfect adjustments and as but disagreeable incidents of progress toward that ultimate form of social organization in which the highest economic condition shall be sanctioned by the best political organization, and shall become the means of attaining and the permanent basis of the most satisfactory ethical standards and moral practices. Such broad speculations are, however, too general to convince the doubting. It will be better to consider the specifications which are urged under the general charge that the movement is one to be feared.

GREAT CORPORATIONS AND DEMOCRACY.

It is said that these immense corporations are dangerous to a democracy, and that the tendencies of the movement are toward the creation of an aristocracy, or to use the word that appears generally to be preferred by those who speak from political platforms, a plutocracy. Certainly, an institution that tends strongly to the diffusion of wealth cannot be leading toward an aristocracy based on property unless there is some strongly counteracting tendency. The business corporation is a device by which the man of moderate means secures standing as a capitalist and adds to his income as a laborer the interest on his modest accumulations. It also gives him standing as a director of industry and as an entrepreneur, for, as a shareholder, he exercises the right of suffrage in corporate meetings, and, as a potential investor, his views are respected in the plans and prospectuses of promoters, and he is endowed with some negative power over their projects. The history of every corporation whose development has been attended by increasing stability shows that such progress is always accompanied by the diffusion of shareholdings and the multiplication of small investors. A meeting of the stockholders of the Pennsylvania railroad or of the New York, New Haven & Hartford differs from a town meeting principally on account of the greater precision of the methods of corporate management and the confidence in successful industrial leadership, which induces stockholders readily to delegate their rights of suffrage. Officers whose ability and fidelity has been demonstrated by the regular and prompt payment of interest and satisfactory dividends rarely have difficulty in obtaining the proxies of shareholders in sufficient number to provide for the perpetuation of their policies. Thus, while voting power in corporate meetings is proportionate to stockholding, and the officers represent the majority in interest rather than that in numbers, the progressive diffusion of ownership which is an incident of recognized stability, tends to make these terms approximately equivalent to each other. It is not to be overlooked that the direction of industry organized according to the corporate method is even now exercised in a representative manner, and that the accountability of its officers is much more perfectly enforced than that of political officers. All that is necessary then in order to create a real industrial democracy is that shareholding shall be diffused so that industrial citizenship is substantially coincident with political citizenship. This service is not beyond the power of the great corporation if its work is not unwisely impeded, and when it has been performed, political equality will have been placed upon the firm foundation of economic equality. It is, perhaps, a far glance into the distant future, but there is visible among the potentialities of the present movement, a time when every worthy citizen shall have become a capitalist with greater or smaller investments in the industry or industries which he prefers. The conception is that of a much truer industrial democracy than that contemplated by the Socialist, who crudely imagines that industrial equality can be achieved by making the direction of industry a political function.

THE RELATION TO INDIVIDUAL DEVELOPMENT.

It is frequently charged against the form of organization which industry is rapidly assuming that great combinations weaken individual character by increasing the proportion of employees to employers. Many who defend the movement on other grounds seem tacitly to acknowledge the correctness of this charge and to do no more than to urge that it is offset by other considerations. Such an offset would be impossible. Society cannot consent to the impairment of any of its individual members, and anything which may tend to produce that result must be disadvantageous even from a strictly economic point of view. But is there any such impairment? Under the form of organization which is disappearing, every industry was conducted in many separate establishments, each subject to independent direction. Production was more costly because its methods were limited by the capacity of the least competent among those who possessed such independent authority. Individual liberty of initiative in this aspect seems something very like freedom from responsibility. In the new order those who constituted the least capable in the old, or their successors, become employees charged with the direction of particular departments or branches of industry. The successful leader of a great corporation does not absorb the entire power of initiative in its affairs. The limitations of time and physical strength preclude such a course, and those who attempt it speedily give way to wiser men. Power to direct and opportunity to originate, in more or less restricted fields, are accorded to scores of employees, and both are exercised subject to the strictest accountability for results. The main differences between the old order and the new, therefore, so far as they affect the individual, are that under the new system he is given a broader view of the industry in which he is engaged, is brought into closer contact and competition with others in the same field, and is charged with a degree of responsibility which demands from him the highest industry and the most thoughtful application. There has never been a time when the industrial world offered greater opportunities for the development of individual power, or when the rewards of integrity and capacity were greater. The search for the exceptional man has attained an intensity that is without precedent.

THE MORAL ASPECT.

In the purely moral field there are also distinct elements of gain from the new method. The corporate means of association is not consistent with commercial secrecy, and this is increasingly true as corporations become larger and the numbers of their stockholders are augmented. The demands of the investing public are year by year obtaining more accurate and detailed reports from the larger companies, and as these become necessary, the practices which require secrecy are being abandoned. Nor is the corporation a thing devoid of ethical principles and soulless. It cannot perform with propriety the acts of charity and kindness which the individual may take upon himself, for the corporation cannot prefer one individual without making a victim of another. Its earnings are taken from the public and its gains belong to those whose capital it employs. Whatever it expends without obtaining an equivalent is either unjustly taken from the one or improperly withheld from the other. When it may justly obtain large profits for its shareholders, it places them in a position to perform, as individuals, those acts of beneficence which it is not privileged itself to undertake. But if the corporation has no right to be generous, it is more certain than the individual to be just. It has the combined integrity and moral responsibility of its officers, directors and shareholders. They perform their functions always in the sight of each other and often in that of the public, and no one doubts the answer to the inquiry whether men usually act more closely according to their ideals when subject to the scrutiny of their fellows than when the social imperative is lacking. There is nothing sinister or threatening in the development of this great factor in modern business that does not arise from human viciousness and that was not fourfold more sinister and threatening when the vicious human acted alone and independently.

Briefly, then, the great corporation is tending to create a broader and more substantial basis for moral, social and political welfare by increasing the productive power of mankind and securing the more general diffusion of the wealth which is produced and the more equal distribution of comfort. As an incident to progress in this direction, it is surrounding the individual by conditions which make more strenuous effort the condition of the especial success which it so abundantly rewards, and subjecting the conduct of business to methods that tend to elevate the standards of commercial intercourse.

OBSTACLES TO THE TENDENCIES DESCRIBED.

Much has already been accomplished in each of the directions indicated, but there is vastly more that may be done. The work of the business corporation has only begun, and its path has not yet been freed from obstacles that materially impair its efficiency. In the discussion which has preceded I have purposely presented the services of the business corporation in terms which, although they truly describe results already in some degree achieved, are better applicable to a condition in which progress is not hindered by certain impediments that are now but too apparent. In order to relieve my argument from frequent explanatory digressions, I have so far omitted reference to evils and abuses that are of such daily occurrence that to many they completely obscure the beneficent tendencies of corporate development. There are two principal reasons why the business corporation does not perform as completely as it might the great services which have been suggested.

FRAUDULENT COMBINATIONS.

One of these is that there are adventurers in industry and finance who have fastened themselves upon the new movement because it has provided them with opportunities to obtain illegitimate and largely fraudulent speculative gains. The successive recurrence of abundant harvests each supplemented by a notable export demand; the sudden expansion of the markets for American manufactures in foreign countries; and what may almost be described as the re-creation of the American railway system, but lately placed in the possession of the people of the United States an enormous aggregate fund, for which investments were sought. The presence of this fund forced down the rate of interest in every principal market; it led to the re-purchase of vast quantities of American securities which had remained for years in foreign vaults, and it permitted American financiers to subscribe liberally to loans desired by foreign nations. These operations, however, did not satisfy the investment demand. Its pressure raised the market prices of nearly all domestic securities, and, the supply of investments being still insufficient, there was a natural movement to increase it. Industry properly and automatically avails itself of such opportunities to make desirable modifications in its organization, and the supply of securities was speedily augmented by shares and bonds issued to provide for many very beneficial combinations, but from other quarters there came a flood of securities based on inflated valuations and representing combinations in which there was no economic advantage. Securities of the latter class were issued in large quantities merely to take advantage of a demand that was so great that the bonds and shares offered were not by any means invariably subjected to suitable scrutiny. The ordinary agencies of finance soon realized this fact, and in some degree have thenceforth protected private investors from deception. Protection of this sort, however, is only partial, and there is yet great opportunity to rob the unwary in this manner. Not the least serious aspect of this situation is that it arouses suspicion concerning all industrial securities, and by impairing confidence in their stability confines the economic services of the business corporation within narrow artificial limits. Speculation has not destroyed the efficiency of industrial combinations or of the corporate form of organization, for in doing so it would have destroyed itself; but it has seriously reduced the utility of both. Two things are clearly indicated as necessary to correct this condition. There should be reasonable publicity concerning the methods of organizing and conducting the business of industrial combinations, and corporation laws throughout the country should be uniform.

A NATIONAL INCORPORATION LAW NEEDED.

The independent right of every state in the Union to incorporate companies which, through state comity, are permitted to prosecute their enterprises all over the country, is an impassable barrier to uniformity and stability. A national incorporation law, even if applicable only to those corporations which are engaged in interstate or foreign commerce, supplemented by requirements imposing a proper degree of publicity, would draw a sharp line between the speculative and predatory corporation and that based on a real economic advantage and promoted and managed in the interest of investors. No single step is now indicated which would go farther in obtaining for the people the vast benefits that the business corporation can confer than the prompt enactment of a wise law providing for incorporation under the authority of the United States.

THE NEED OF MORE ENLIGHTENED LEGISLATIVE POLICIES.

Another cause which detracts from the utility of the great corporation is that it is still subject to an adverse public sentiment, which threatens the stability of many undertakings by exposing them to the danger of unjust legislation. Apparently there are many citizens who are so impressed by the visible accumulations of wealth which these corporations represent that they fail to see that they are really devices by which the man of moderate means may share in the profits and in the direction of great enterprises. If this fact were not lost sight of, it is scarcely possible that there would be any danger of unjust exactions in the form of taxation or of unwise legislative restrictions. There are many localities, however, in which enterprises of the same kind and making use of the same amounts of capital are taxed very differently if one of them happens to be conducted by an individual and the other by a corporation. The difference is always to the disadvantage of the corporation, and there is a marked tendency at present at work to accentuate the discriminations, although in the one case the enterprise represents a very wealthy individual, while in the other it may represent hundreds of men of very moderate means. Similar discrepancies are found in the regulative laws of many states. This situation need only be stated in order that it shall be perceived how seriously it must work to the disadvantage of those who would invest in industrial enterprises the small savings accumulated with difficulty from moderate incomes. If conditions in this respect are to be improved, it must be by the spread of enlightenment and the creation of a healthier public sentiment. This, too, will be fostered by giving greater publicity to corporate methods and by intelligent discussion of industrial conditions.

CONCLUSION.

As the advantages which great corporations offer to those who can, through their agency, become sharers in the profits of capital as well as recipients of wages are more completely understood, and as the public realizes the great truth that the necessities of industry must always supersede legislative decrees, it will be seen that the general welfare of society will best be served by eliminating the element of speculation as much as possible from corporate affairs, by withdrawing the threat of adverse legislation, and by the uniform definition of the rights of owners of corporate securities and the duties of corporate managers. America owes its present proud industrial position to the intelligence of its people, as expressed in the skill of its workmen and the foresight of those who have been called to positions of industrial leadership; to the fertility of its soil and the abundance of its mineral resources; to a form of government which applies to political problems the aggregated wisdom of its citizenship; and to a system of jurisprudence that is marvelously adaptable to changing conditions. Together, these things have led to industrial combinations and the great business corporation. The point attained is characterized by such startling departures from conditions that but lately existed that it is not strange that all are amazed and some are alarmed. Yet students of industrial history, who have traced human progress from the invention of the spinning jenny to the present time, will not concede that the steady process of moral and social improvement which has accompanied the progressive increase in economic efficiency is to cease at the point where productive power exceeds all precedent. They will seek among the conflicting consequences of a process of industrial re-adjustment for the never-failing trend toward general improvement, and among many losses and many gains will find the balance on the profit side. They will perceive that the beneficial tendencies of the present movement are permanent, while its evils and abuses are but temporary. They will ask that the good shall be held steadily in view and carefully conserved, and that the measures which are adopted for the correction of the evil shall be so carefully framed as not to destroy or hamper in any degree that which promises to be so broadly conducive to the general welfare.

WOULDN'T KNOW THE DIFFERENCE

Representative Patterson, of Pennsylvania, has a local railway pass for himself and wife. An Irish constituent recently came to him, smiling, and said: "Mr. Patterson, sor, as a favor, would you be after loaning me the use of your pass?" "But, Tim, everybody round here knows me, and they would know the pass wasn't yours." "Oh, bless ye, sor, I don't want it for meself at all. I want to let me ole woman feel sort of grand. Ye see, sor, no one would know me old woman from yours, and so I thought—" Patterson was paralyzed. But then the funny side of it struck him, and the Irishman thought he had been struck with ague, he laughed so.—Saturday Evening Post.

Bookkeeping in Its Relation to Commerce*

By JAMES MARTIN

Fellow and Secretary of the English Society of Accountants and Auditors

The subject upon which I have been invited to address you, "Bookkeeping in its Relation to Commerce," is a very wide one, which, if dealt with in any detail, would easily absorb several evenings instead of the short time which has been allotted to me to utilize to the best of my ability. You will, therefore, readily understand that I make no pretence to anything in the nature of exhaustive treatment. The dominant part of the title of this paper is "Commerce," for without commerce the science of bookkeeping would have remained dormant. The history of bookkeeping, therefore, is coeval with the history of commerce. Uncivilized people bartered one commodity for another by the method of direct exchanges, and with the limited trade they did there was not much necessity for accounts. This method of barter still, of course, obtains amongst people on the confines of civilization. The native tribes of South Africa exchange oxen for wives. Before the war, I believe, the father of a bride received four oxen from the bridegroom, but if the military authorities have been paying as much for oxen as they have for horses, I should think that wives and oxen were now interchangeable amongst native tribes at par value. The change from barbarism to civilization gave rise to commerce. Now what is commerce? It is the intercourse of nations in each other's produce and manufactures, in which the superfluities of one are given for those of another, and then re-exchanged with other nations to meet mutual wants. Strictly speaking, there is a distinction between commerce and trade, the former relates to our dealings with the British dominions beyond the seas and with foreign countries, and the latter is confined to mutual dealings at home.

The affairs of commerce are regulated by commercial law, of which our honorable director of studies, Mr. Montague Barlow, is the able exponent before this Chamber, and I heartily wish I were in a position to add to my knowledge by attending his course of lectures on the subject.

HISTORY OF BOOKKEEPING.

Bookkeeping, to which I will now direct your attention, has been aptly described by a writer as the handmaid of Commerce. What is bookkeeping? It is the science which enables one to ascertain the nature and extent of one's business and the amount of profit derived therefrom, or loss entailed thereby. The origin of bookkeeping is obscure, and time will not permit me to wander into that interesting era when civilization began to dawn, and the necessity of some method of accounting was slowly enforced. Archaeological excavations have brought to the light of day white stones used for recording receipts, and stones of a blue-gray color employed for denoting expenses.

Bookkeeping, as we now understand the term, took its rise like commerce from the shores of the Adriatic, and hence it is described by all early authors as bookkeeping according to the Italian system. I think it is generally agreed that the first person to write a treatise on bookkeeping was Lucas di Borgo, whose work was published at Venice in 1495. The first recorded work on bookkeeping in England which I have been able to discover is that of James Peele. It is styled "The Maner and Fourme how to kepe a perfecte notable accompte of Debitour and Creditour set foorthe in certain tables." It was published in London in 1553 by Richard Grafton. This author has a peculiar fascination for myself, as he became the Clerk of Christ's Hospital, on which ancient foundation I was educated, and with which my firm is now professionally connected. Peele also wrote "The Pathewey to perfectness in the accomptes of Debtour and Creditour," a work published by T. Purfoote, in 1569. Andrews in his continuation of Dr. Henry's "History of Great Britain," states that Peele taught the Italian method of bookkeeping in England. Before I leave this author I would like to say that I have seen Peele's books of account as Clerk of Christ's Hospital, which are carefully preserved by the authorities, and bear eloquent testimony after the lapse of three and a half centuries to Peele's skill and the faithful discharge of his duties.

The next author who claims a little attention is David Wedderburne, merchant of Dundee, who compiled "The Compt Buik," which is in the nature of a chronicle or diary of his own transactions from 1587-1630. The figures are largely Roman, and the descriptive matter is of a quaint and amusing character. Sir W. Wedderburn, Bart, formerly M.P. for Banffshire, is, I believe, descended from this author.

I pass along to John Mair, whose work came out in 1741, under the protection of the Right Hon. Charles, Lord Cathcart, to whom there is a most flowery dedication. This author depreciates the work of previous writers on the same subject, and considers that he has avoided their faults, supplied the defects complained of in other books, and earned the approbation of the public.

The next writer, William Webster, 1755, laid down a few plain rules, and made the practice easy by a variety of intelligible examples. He was evidently a more modest man than Mair, as in the preface he said: "I am very sensible that booksellers' shelves are already loaded with treatises on this subject." William Gordon, of Glasgow, brought out the "Universal Accountant and Complete Merchant," in 1763, and then we come to William Squire, in 1769, who says the reader should be expert in drawing out bills of parcels, transcribing and computing invoices and other precedents, which will yield him an entertaining and profitable exercise, and conduce in a great measure to his understanding the practice of bokkeeping.

At the close of the eighteenth century a Mr. Edward T. Jones received a patent under the hand of His Majesty King George III. for his "English System of Bookkeeping." This was in the year 1795. Mr. Jones was the forerunner of the race of modern professional accountants, and from him two of our present London firms trace their descent. Of the works of the nineteenth century I possess a list of over fifty, with which I do not propose to deal.

These lectures being in connection with higher commercial education, I am going to assume that you have more or less mastered the fifty authors of the nineteenth century, and are familiar with bookkeeping both in theory and practice. I would, however, like to say at this stage, from personal knowledge, what excellent work is being done in the bookkeeping classes formed in connection with the various polytechnics in and around London. The professors of bookkeeping conducting these classes have been very successful in passing candidates at the Chamber's examinations, and every advantage is offered to students of the art. I must not be taken to depreciate the efforts of private colleges and commercial schools, but I think it right to say what I know with regard to the London Polytechnics which are largely supported from public funds.

OBJECTS OF BOOKKEEPING.

Now let us examine the objects of commercial bookkeeping. They may be defined under two heads:—

1. To record the liabilities and assets, gains or losses of an individual, partnership, company or other corporation.

2. To enable the financial position of the foregoing to be placed before those interested either in the credit or capital of the concern.

How are these objects generally fulfilled? By means of the final accounts as prepared from the ledger balances and

*Lecture delivered before the London Chamber of Commerce, in connection with the Chamber's Higher Commercial Education Scheme. Originally published in the Incorporated Accountants' Journal.

known as trading and profit and loss accounts, and balance-sheet.

TRADING ACCOUNT.

I will take these accounts in order. The trading account is used for the purpose of arriving at the gross profit of a business. Let us consider what gross profit is. It is the difference between the cost of goods delivered at the place where they are to be offered for sale and the selling price. The cost may be made up of various items, differing according to the nature of the business. For example, in an ordinary retail concern it may simply be made up of purchases less returns, and carriage inwards, plus or minus difference in stock. More often than not the method adopted is to debit the starting stock on the one side of the trading account and credit the finishing stock on the other, but I think it is preferable to debit the starting stock and purchases and deduct therefrom the closing stock, thus showing clearly in one figure the cost price of the goods actually sold during the period. The debit side of the account then shows items of cost only, and the credit side sales less returns only. The advantage of this will be more clearly seen when we come to discuss the question of percentages later on.

In a manufacturing business some further items enter into the cost of the goods. Chief amongst these is manufacturing wages. Strictly speaking, rent and general upkeep of manufacturing premises and depreciation of plant and machinery should also be debited to the trading account, but for convenience they are sometimes charged to the profit and loss account. The rule to be applied for testing what constitutes a trading charge is this: Everything that adds to the cost of the finished article, in order to place it on the market, is a trading charge, and in dealing with a manufacturing business it will readily be seen that were the manufacturer to buy the goods complete instead of manufacturing them the manufacturing wages and the rent and upkeep of factory would disappear as distinct and separate charges, being already included in the cost price of the goods. These items must, therefore, be treated as part of the cost. Trade discounts should, of course, come off the cost price.

I have just stated that everything that adds to the cost is a trading charge; on the other hand, everything else is a charge against the second portion of the account—called profit and loss. In other words, the trading account shows the cost of buying and bringing to the market, and the profit and loss account shows the cost of selling and distributing, the balance in the first case being the gross profit, and in the second the net profit. If this rule is borne in mind no difficulty should be experienced in distinguishing between trading and profit and loss items.

In a large retail concern where there are a number of distinct departments, it is very advisable to keep a separate trading account for each department so that the proprietor may see how the departments individually are paying. This is usually done by having separate bought and sold day books and returns books for each department, or by having these books tabulated with departmental columns. The system to be adopted must be decided according to the magnitude and requirements of the business.

COST ACCOUNTS.

In the case of a manufacturing concern the question of obtaining separate results for departments necessitates the keeping of cost accounts, a branch of bookkeeping which merits a larger share of attention than I can possibly devote to it in this paper. I should like, however, to draw attention to the great importance—the great practical importance and pecuniary value to a manufacturer of knowing precisely where he is making profits and where he is incurring losses, for it is not at all unlikely that he may be doing both without being aware of the fact. If he keep the ordinary financial accounts only, he knows that he is making a certain margin of profit on his whole business, but he cannot tell whether the profit is a uniform one over the whole concern, or whether it is made up of the difference between a large profit in one or more departments and a loss in another. To say the least, he is quite in the dark as to where he is making the largest margin of profit, and may therefore be pushing his business with the greatest energy where it is the least profitable to do so. Now, if he knew precisely the percentage of profit in each section of his business he would be able to devote his energies to the best advantage, and would know exactly where and how far he could afford to modify his prices to meet the keen competition of the present day, both at home and abroad. Failure to work on scientific lines is one of the leading elements contributing to the ever increasing strain of foreign competition. Other countries have been keener than we have been to see the need for commercial education, and to supply it, and it is for you who, in time, will have to take your share in upholding the commercial supremacy of our nation, to so equip yourselves that you will enter the field without handicap whoever your competitors may be.

Costs accounts are really a separate and distinct branch of bookkeeping, and one on which you will find a very meager amount of information in books. In fact, costing is only in its infancy, and has undoubtedly a great future before it. It is therefore all the more necessary that you should endeavor to make yourselves acquainted with its fundamental principles and general application. I will endeavor to put before you a general idea of what must be aimed at, and rules of ordinary commercial bookkeeping will always be applicable in carrying it into effect. The cost of a manufactured article consists of three items, viz., material, wages and indirect charges (sometimes termed oncost). To take the simplest example, that of a factory with a number of departments, each department must be debited with the material supplied to it, and with the wages expended therein, and where the separate cost of individual articles produced in a department is required, the material and wages must be subdivided accordingly. This, as a rule, presents but little difficulty. The chief trouble is usually met with in correctly apportioning the indirect charges. The most important of these are rent, rates and taxes, heating, lighting, motive power, management and general expenses, including costs of sale and distribution. The object to be aimed at with regard to these is to first charge the expenses to departments and then apportion the departmental charges over the individual pieces of work in proportion to (1) wages, or (2) time, or (3) wages and material combined. The method of calculation must be decided according to circumstances.

Many of the departmental charges can be ascertained with absolute accuracy, and others such as rent, rates and taxes, heating, etc., can be so nearly gauged as to leave but little room for question. The remaining expenses, such as management and office expenses, travelers' and advertising, must be apportioned over the departments by way of a percentage, and the method of determining the percentage will depend largely on circumstances. For instance, if advertising be a heavy item, it may relate more largely to products of one department than those of another.

The total charges against the departments being thus ascertained, they are each credited with the value of the goods they turn out, and the difference represents the net profit or loss. As already pointed out, each department may be subdivided and the cost of individual contracts or orders ascertained. In doing this, wages and materials are usually charged to such contracts direct, and the indirect charges obtained from the departmental charges account.

Another important matter is that a check is provided against any misappropriation of stores. The stores accounts are debited with everything that goes into the storeroom and credited with all that is given out to the departments. The stock sheets at the end of the year should therefore agree with the balances in the stores ledger. Without these accounts a manufacturer has to trust almost entirely to the honesty of those who are handling his goods, having no means of knowing whether all his purchases have been properly accounted for.

THE PROFIT AND LOSS ACCOUNT.

As already stated, the profit and loss account starts with gross profit brought down from the trading account, that is, the profit after debiting only the costs of buying and bringing the goods to the market, including costs of manufacture, if any. We have now to deal with the expenses of sale and distribution. These consist chiefly of rent, rates and taxes, salaries, advertising, traveling, carriage outwards, cash discounts, depreciation of furniture, etc., office and general expenses, and the mode of arriving at them must be familiar to you all. Sometimes the gross profit from all the departments is brought into one profit and loss account, and the selling expenses debited against it without apportionment, the result being to show the net profit on the business as a whole. In certain circumstances this may be quite sufficient, but in other cases it is advisable to subdivide the selling expenses, and show the net as well as the gross profit on each department. This is particularly desirable where the gross profit in the different departments does not bear a uniform ratio to the turnover. For example, a department may turn over a large quantity of goods but show only a small percentage of gross profit compared with another department. Now the cost of sale and distribution will usually vary according to the quantity of goods handled, and it would, therefore, be misleading to treat the gross profit of such a department as a fair indication of its net result. It would undoubtedly be found that if it were charged with its proper proportion of selling expenses its net profit would show still worse than its gross profit in comparison with other departments of the business.

USE OF PERCENTAGES.

But to return to the trading account, I would like to say for one moment a few words on the question of percentages. If the figures are compiled in the way I have already indicated it will greatly facilitate this operation. The usual method is to calculate all percentages on the turnover, that is, on the sales. This is a custom which has come to be adopted chiefly, I think, on account of its convenience, as it will be found more strictly correct, for the purpose of comparing one year with another, to use the cost price as the basis. However, it is better in every case to continue the method (if any) which has been adopted in the past, otherwise the comparison with earlier years would be entirely misleading. Assuming, then, that we are to use the turnover as the basis of our calculations, the percentage of the gross profit on the sales should always be worked out and compared with that of past years. If the business is a manufacturing one, the percentages of the purchase—that is, the cost price of goods actually consumed in the period—manufacturing wages, and other items should likewise be ascertained, and any variations satisfactorily accounted for. Here will be seen the benefit of showing the stock in hand in the trading account in the way I have already recommended. With regard to the profit and loss account, every item of expense should be worked out in the same way. Any fluctuation in the ratio of the individual items can then be seen at a glance and should be carefully inquired into. In all these matters you should be able to render valuable service, and present figures in such a form that they could not fail to be at once intelligible, interesting and useful.

WHAT IS A BALANCE-SHEET?

Now I come to the balance-sheet. The term balance-sheet really means an account of the balances of an individual firm or company on a certain date. It is the product of double entry bookkeeping, and must not be confounded with the single entry statement of affairs. On the debit or left hand side of a balance-sheet appear the liabilities, capital, reserves, and unappropriated profits, and on the credit or right hand side the assets and any special expenditure not chargeable to profit and loss account, and a deficiency should there be one. In America a balance-sheet is generally termed "A Statement of Assets or Resources and Liabilities," the assets or resources appearing on the left hand or debit side, and the liabilities on the right hand or credit side, a method exactly opposite to that adopted here. A rising member of my profession, Mr. S. S. Dawson, of Liverpool, in a work compiled by him, states the position thus: "Some advocates of the English method contend that a balance-sheet is a personal account made out as against the proprietor of the business in question, and that he is, therefore, in credit to the extent of his assets, and in debit to the extent of his liabilities; on the contrary it is asserted that a balance-sheet is not an account at all, but is, as its name implies, a sheet or summary of balances as abstracted from the ledger, and as a consequence, such balances should appear on the same side on the sheet as they do in the ledger." Personally I incline to the American view of the matter, and in support of it I would point out that prior to 1860 all English authors of bookkeeping took practically the same stand. The alteration to the present English practice dates, I believe, from the Companies Act, 1862, in Table "A," of which we find a pro forma balance-sheet, containing on the debit or left hand side capital and liabilities, and on the credit or right hand side, property and assets. Now, although I think the American view more logical, yet we have to follow the English practice and consider the balance-sheet to mean that the proprietor of the business is Dr. to his liabilities and Cr. by his assets, but here we are met with another difficulty. I said just now that on the credit or right hand side appeared the assets, any special expenditure not chargeable to profit and loss account, and a deficiency should there be one. If I am correct the pro forma balance-sheet in the Companies Acts is wrong, as obviously the credit side can contain something more than "property and assets." Parliament is largely responsible, in my opinion, for a great popular error, which has had some mischievous results. As the matter is of importance I would quote what Mr. Francis W. Pixley, a leading authority, says: "The erroneous idea that a balance-sheet is necessarily a statement of liabilities and assets, of course, arose from the fact that as a matter of bookkeeping, the credit balances of the ledger which are transferred to the debit side of the balance-sheet must necessarily include all the liabilities, while in the same manner the debit balances (of the ledger), being transferred to the credit side of the balance-sheet, must necessarily include the assets. The fallacy, however, of the popular title is, of course, seen when attention is called to the fact that the credit side of the balance-sheet must also, by the same process, include all expenditure unrepresented by an asset. (I assume Mr. Pixley means expenditure not already charged to profit and loss account.) "Also all special losses or the general loss or deficiency to date brought forward from profit and loss account, while on the other hand the debit side necessarily includes the capital of the company or partners, also any reserve and any surplus from profit and loss account." If we are to be bound to consider all that appears an the credit side of a company's balance-sheet in the light of assets, we must subdivide these assets into three clases—Fixed, Floating and Fictitious. The fixed assets are represented by the permanent property for the acquisition of which the company was formed, the floating assets by the stock, book debts and cash, and the fictitious assets by such items as preliminary expenses and other expenditure not represented by property of value.

A bookkeeper who attempts to draw a company's balance-sheet ought to be fully acquainted with these technicalties, and must set about the work warily or he will come to grief. I would also point out that by the Companies Act, 1900, if any person in any balance-sheet wilfully makes a statement false in any material particular, knowing it to be false ,he is liable on conviction to two years' imprisonment. I may just add that it is not the duty of auditors of companies to draw balance-sheets, and I think it is a pity when Parliament was amending the Companies Acts in 1900, it did not obtain expert advice with a view to the issue of a more concise account and one more easily understood.

UNDERTAKINGS REQUIRING BOOKKEEPERS.

Having considered the final results of bookkeeping, as shown by the trading and profit and loss accounts and balance-sheet, I should like to enumerate the different undertakings for which the services of bookkeepers are required. I group them as follows:—

Manufacturers, merchants and traders.
Railways and shipping.
Banking and insurance.
Gas, water and electric light.
Mines.
Agriculture.
Municipalities and public undertakings.
Charities and public institutions.
Building and co-operative societies.
Hotels and clubs.
Estates.
Professional men.

I will not guarantee the list is absolutely complete, but I think you will find it long enough to retain in your memories. Now my advice to bookkeepers is to make themselves expert in some particular branch of accounts, and having mastered the technicalities of bookkeeping, to take up some trade or calling on which they can concentrate their knowledge and become of special value. The need of the day is for specialists, men with a good technical knowledge of some particular subject; there is getting less and less room in business life for general smatterers who are everything in turn but nothing long.

Balance Sheet Accounting

By GEORGE E. ALLEN

Suspense and Reserve Accounts

In previous articles of this series on Balance Sheet Accounting special attention has been called to the necessity of confining the Merchandise Account to the record of merchandise on hand at cost prices. Profit and loss should be shown in a separate sales account. By this method inventorying is reduced to the mere work of comparing goods in stock with the record of the same on the books. This may be done at any time, and in accordance with this plan fiscal periods may be made sufficiently short to secure a practically perpetual inventory.

With short fiscal periods—say monthly or weekly—and an inventory complete and up-to-date at the end of each period, all that remains to secure a complete record of going results is the equitable distribution among the different periods of such items of income and expense as do not properly belong to the single period in which they occur. Thus if $120 should be paid in January as a premium for insurance covering an entire year, and fiscal periods were monthly it would not be logical to charge the whole $120 to January expenses, but rather to charge $10 to each month during the year, so that each period would receive only its prorate of the total. Conversely, if an obligation were incurred to make a payment at the end instead of at the beginning of the year for something of continuous benefit throughout the twelve months it would be logical to divide such obligation equally among each of the monthly periods.

Expenses which are paid or incurred in one period, the cost of which in equity should be carried to another period or be pro rated over several periods are commonly called Items in Suspense. Provision for payments to be made at some future time for benefits received during the present or intermediate periods are termed Reserves.

Among the expenses requiring Suspense Accounts are insurance, traveling and advertising, which may be carried in a single Suspense account or subdivided to meet the requirements of the management. In making up the expense statement for any period such an amount is to be credited to each of these accounts as justly belongs to the expenses of the period under consideration. By this plan each period is made to stand its own proper share of expenses and the Suspense Accounts will in due season be closed out. It will thus be seen that pro rating expenses over the different periods to which they properly belong by means of Suspense Accounts is a very simple matter.

Reserve Accounts would be equally simple were it not for the fact that the amounts to be paid for certain purposes at some future date cannot be always determined in advance. An important Reserve Account, for instance, is the one which makes provision for bad debts. Losses from bad debts cannot be determined in advance, and to properly pro rate them over various periods requires that an estimate should be made of their probable amount based upon past experience. If, for example, experience has shown that bad debts amount to an average of 2 per cent, then as charges are made against customers 2 per cent should be carried to the debit of expense account and passed to the credit of the reserve account for bad debts. Reserve accounts are kept to provide for taxes, interest, repairs, depreciation, etc.

Depreciation of machinery in manufacturing is something which clearly illustrates the reserve principle. When we buy a piece of machinery we know that it will wear out in time. If we knew exactly how long it would last we could easily distribute its total cost over the intervening periods, but we do not know, and must therefore depend upon the best available estimate. In this connection attention is called to the fact that it is best to estimate on the safe side. Liberal reserves bespeak good management.

In manufacturing, depreciation of machinery is a cost of production. In the operation of a reserve account for depreciation of machinery therefore expenditures for replacements are debits, while the pro rate of the reserve for any period is the credit. The credit balance is the amount on hand available for maintenance without exceeding the reserve estimate.

To show the practical operation of a reserve account for the depreciation of machinery let us suppose that we have accumulated a reasonably large sum for such depreciation, and find that we must replace some of our old machinery with new, selling the old machinery as junk. We will suppose that our machinery account is debited with $10,000, which represents the original cost of machinery on hand. We have under the reserve plan been charging into the cost of manufactured articles an estimated amount to meet the depreciation which has amounted to say $5,000 duly credited to our reserve account. Machinery account is credited with what we take out of it based on original cost, which, in this case, we will say is $2,000. We also debit the reserve account with the $2,000. If we replace the old machinery with new, valued at say $3,000, we debit machinery account with $3,000. If that $2,000 of old machinery is sold for junk at say $100, we credit reserve with the amount. The $100 received for old machinery is therefore kept apart from loss and gain, which latter account represents the results of the operations of the period, and nothing else.

Under this plan the asset account is not arbitrarily depreciated, but a reserve account against it is provided, out of which the original value of the asset is maintained as fast as it may actually depreciate.

These examples are intended to show the operation of the principle of Suspense and Reserve, and its relationship to an up-to-date and continuous statement of business operation and condition.

The Accountant's Equipment*

By J. G. JOHNSTON, C. A.

A Practical Essay on the Functions and Education of an Accountant

The sphere of accounting is rapidly extending in all directions This is a financial and scientific age, and there is an increasing demand for men whose natural ability and professional training have fitted them to attack the new and difficult problems connected with the management of money which are constantly presenting themselves for solution, and to aid in conducting the commerce of the world by the practical application of the science of figures. When it is considered that all business transactions are represented by figures, the statement of which varies in intricacy in proportion to the complexity of the transactions themselves, and that few that have not had considerable experience can be trusted to manipulate figures so as to exhibit perfectly correct results, it is obvious that in a commercial community there is abundant scope for the exercise of the energies and talents of those who have been trained to the profession of accounting. On the other hand, seeing that confidence is the link uniting the man of figures to those who employ him, he who is ill equipped, and therefore unfit for responsibility, finds no room for himself in the earnest round of life. Recognizing, then, the importance that attaches to the duties of the accountant, we cannot but admit it is of the highest moment that his training should receive most careful attention.

The object of this essay is (1) To indicate the principal acquisitions and qualities of mind that it is essential for an accountant to possess in order to produce thoroughly good work, and (2) To refer briefly to the best practicable means for the attainment of these requirements. To this end we shall find it convenient to review the several spheres in which the accountant is employed.

In the practice of his profession, the accountant may be held to fulfil the following distinct functions: (1) Auditing, in all its branches; (2) Factorage, in its many forms; (3) Arbitration. There are, of course, specialties in all professions, which call for peculiar qualifications in those who practice them; but as we are now dealing with the case of the average accountant and his usual work, the above division will be found to answer our present purpose. To each of these functions pertains its own particular knowledge, in addition to the qualities of mind that should characterize the accountant in all his work. We shall therefore keep these distinct—considering the knowledge first, and the qualities afterwards.

First, then, as to the knowledge which the accountant must acquire. On reflection, it is obvious that the principle underlying all his professional work is representation. The conscientious accountant identifies his own interests with those of his employers, and acts as their representative. A distinct conception of this principle is essential to enable us to determine what his duties are in any particular instance. For example, we perceive it in the exercise of the first function named—

AUDITING.

The owner of money is desirous of being assured of the proper and bona-fide application of the funds that belong to him and that have been intrusted by him to the care of others. He cannot very well do the necessary work himself in person, and he accordingly deputes a man of skill and experience to carry out his wishes and report to him. This is the chief characteristic of all audits, and is a clear case of representative work. It is plain that the man of skill, so deputed, must have peculiar qualifications to enable him to carry out satisfactorily the intentions of his employer. The question is, What are those peculiar qualifications? In attempting to find an answer, we shall, as already indicated, consider first of all the acquired knowledge which is demanded of him.

It is a useful method to take a typical case, and from it to deduce general rules applicable to all cases. Let us suppose, for example, that an auditor is appointed to examine and report on the accounts of an executry, on behalf of the beneficiaries. This is, perhaps, as familiar a case as any that may be cited. Let us watch the accountant at work. At the outset he places himself, mentally, in the position of the beneficiaries, and sets himself the task of discovering if the funds belonging to them have been properly dealt with.

To this end he in the first place glances over the account submitted to him, and criticises its form. If it is drawn up in such a manner as to exhibit results intelligibly, he is satisfied on this point; but if not, he may find it expedient to recast the figures in a different form. To be able to do this properly, he must have a competent acquaintance with the art of stating figures clearly and logically. He then proceeds to inquire if all the funds to which the beneficiaries are entitled have been credited in the account, and that nothing has been charged against them for which they are not liable. Here, what may be termed "a knowledge of business management" is essential. In the next place, he demands evidence in support of the actual entries in the account, and when he receives it, he must be able to judge of its sufficiency. Perhaps heritable property, yielding rent, has been left by the truster, as well as bequests, of a positive character in the form of legacies, and of a negative character in the form of debts, arising chiefly from expenditure on his property. The matter of the former, legacies, is easily disposed of by a reference to the will; but the latter, and the rents, require calculation and careful treatment. The auditor is expected to assure himself that the proper legal principles of apportionment, as between heir and executor, have been applied in the case before him, and that they have been correctly worked out. He must, in fact, take care that the account would stand any test if called in question in a court of law.

Lastly,—and this is a matter of no small importance,—it is the duty of the accountant to ascertain that the funds forming the estate at the closing date of the account are actually in existence, and are legally invested. The investments may assume various forms, as, e. g., house property, shares of companies, heritable bonds, sums in bank. In support of each item the accountant first requires production of evidence that it stands in name of the proper parties, and then he inquires if the particular form of investment is either sanctioned by Act of Parliament or is permitted by the terms of the deed that the truster has granted. In some cases the scrutiny of an accountant has revealed that trustees have, inadvertently, exceeded their powers in this respect, and his firm refusal to pass the accounts without comment has resulted in the realization of investments, the existence of which has involved a serious responsibility upon the trustees. Accordingly, a knowledge of law, to a defined extent, is indispensable to the auditor. Upon being satisfied on all these points, and having ascertained that all calculations have been made correctly, he is in a position to report to his clients that the account is "accurately stated, and sufficiently vouched and instructed."

Looking back, now, upon the qualifications appearing to be needful in this simple instance, we can sum them up as embracing three kinds of knowledge: (1) of theoretical and practical accounting; (2) of business management; and (3) of law.

We pass on to consider another function of the accountant, viz.:—

FACTORAGE.

"Factorage" is a generic term, and includes all cases of representative management. The accountant may be called upon to exercise such management in four different capacities: (1) As a Judicial Factor—to take the place of trustees acting for beneficiaries; (2) as a Curator bonis—to manage the affairs of one who is legally incapable of transacting

*Originally published in the Accountants' Magazine, Edinburgh.

business; (3) as an Attorney or Commissioner—to represent, within defined limits, one who voluntarily deputes to him the guidance of his affairs; and (4) as a Trustee—to act for the benefit of the creditors of a debtor who cannot be trusted to do so himself. The first three of the above-named offices may be classed together as presenting common characteristics. Let us, as before, consider a typical instance, and learn from it some rules which we may apply in all similar cases.

An accountant is appointed, let us suppose, to take charge of an estate consisting of heritable and movable property—land and money. He enters into possession, and manages for the benefit of his client. Of the land he grants leases, uplifts rents, orders repairs, directs labor, and generally keeps matters going in the most efficient and economical manner. The funds he invests to the greatest advantage consistent with prudence. He not only has to beware of hidden legal pitfalls, lest he drag both his principal and himself into difficulties, but he must also possess a sufficient acquaintance with the means furnished by the law for effecting particular ends in management. Legal knowledge is in this case a more prominent feature than in previous instances. If the accountant would obtain and keep this class of business, which, from his knowledge of business management, he is otherwise qualified to undertake, he must be thoroughly grounded in law, so as to know how and when to use the machinery which it has at its disposal. Another feature we recognize as one already noticed—a knowledge of business management. To enlarge upon this part of the equipment would exceed our limits, and we must content ourselves with merely noting its importance.

Accountants have a fair share in the Fourth branch we have mentioned under this head—viz., Bankruptcies.

The working of a bankruptcy may be shortly described thus: A man finds that he cannot pay his debts. From the moment of his ascertained insolvency all his funds virtually belong to his creditors until the date of his discharge. In order to satisfy them that his estate will be properly realized and equitably divided among them, he appoints a trustee to represent both himself and them for this purpose, that is, under a trust-deed; or, if this course be not adopted, the creditors, through the court, themselves appoint a trustee, that is, under sequestration. The trustee in either case takes possession of the estate, keeps a careful watch upon the debtor in case he should make off with any of his property, and upon the creditors lest any of them should carry away illicit spoil. He must, amid clamoring duns, judge each debt according to the strict rules of law, and at the same time so conduct affairs as to obtain the utmost that can be extracted from the assets under his charge. His movements, under a sequestration, are no doubt to a great extent regulated by statute law, but a very great deal is left to his individual management; while under a trust-deed he is still more left to his own responsibility. The features in this phase of the accountant's duties are thus seen to be much the same as in ordinary factory management, but more marked. A knowledge of law, especially bankruptcy law, and the faculty of management, are absolutely essential qualifications of a trustee in bankruptcy.

A third class of business which we find undertaken by an accountant is

ARBITRATION.

In cases of dispute regarding figures which often come before our courts the judges are wont to avail themselves of the skill and experience of professional accountants, and to remit matters to them to judge between contending litigants, and to report their own opinion for the guidance of the bench; while extra-judicial contentions of a like nature are often amicably settled by a similar reference made by the parties themselves. The sphere of the accountant widens considerably when he undertakes this class of work; for, as a referee, he must not only be master of the rules of law regarding arbitration, but he must also be acquainted with the "surroundings," as it were, of the matters in dispute. For instance, to be in a position to decide as to profit-sharing between contending parties in a colliery business, he must know how coal profits are arrived at. Before he can condescend on a disputed fee, he must be able to appreciate at its true value the work performed. Moreover, the knowledge of theoretical accounting has to be extended so as to embrace the ability to unravel complicated statements, and to set forth results in a logical and luminous fashion. In defining the accountant's duties in this sphere, it will be seen that we have insensibly run upon the former lines of accounting, law and management, so that we may say that a system of training must embrace these three main divisions.

We have thus sketched, in broad outline, the accountant's chief duties and consequent requirements in practice. This outline might be filled in with many useful acquisitions, more or less needful; but we will only pause to notice, as of some importance, a knowledge of the elements of actuarial science. Questions relating to interest, annuities, expectancies, etc., are not of frequent occurrence; but the accountant, if not able to make simple calculations in the science when required, cannot but feel somewhat ashamed to have to refer to an actuary in a matter within his own province of figures.

Up to the present we have been dealing with what may be termed the "tools" of practical work, which are sufficiently patent. Those that we have now to consider are more difficult to describe: qualities of mind are less tangible than acquisitions of mind. Very much might be said on this subject, but we shall only refer to a few of the principal faculties that must be included in the accountant's "equipment." We have found that the best method of arriving at what is required by the accountant is to watch him at work. Let us try this plan again, and look on while he attacks a knotty problem in figures. His first difficulty lies in attempting to collect his thoughts. They persist in straying away from the subject in hand, and progress is slow and fatiguing. Inattention afflicts him. While this is one of the first symptoms of an over-wrought brain, it is likewise the sign of an under-wrought brain. The cures in the two cases are opposed to each other. The over-tasked mind must rest and be recreated, but the undisciplined organ must be stimulated to move briskly. Steady, hard work at subjects necessitating close attention is the only means of acquiring a habit of concentration, and no pains should be spared to gain it.

ABILITY TO THINK.

Supposing, then, that the student has mastered this difficulty, and is able to abstract his mind from wandering thoughts; another want becomes apparent. He is unable to think in an orderly fashion. His ideas have no logical connection with each other. He may see them clearly enough, and keep them steadily in his mind's eye, but there is no system in his thinking. He does not know where to begin his work, and he is always puzzled as to what to do next. This want, like the previous one, is only too common, and there are few who have not reason to lament it in themselves. The cure of the evil is more difficult than that of inattention. All minds are not alike in this respect, and where defects exist they are radical, and therefore not easily removed. Still, since the best work is impossible without "mental order," a proper system of training must include means for its cultivation.

Let us now suppose our tyro to have been trained to think attentively and logically. Up to this point he has gained nothing to distinguish him as an accountant, but a step further will place him in the territory of figures. He begins to calculate, but finds that he is at fault again; the mathematical faculty has not been educated. This faculty has commonly been called "a head for figures": a term that necessitates our drawing a useful distinction between two senses in which it is employed. There is a superficial sense, which may be designated as "technical facility." There is, at the same time, a deeper sense, which may be called "mental grasp." Between these two exists the greatest possible difference. The former is by no means to be disparaged, but where it exists without the latter, the owner may make an admirable servant, but not a competent master;

while the possession of "intellectual grasp" of figures goes far to fit a man for a position of prominence and responsibility in his profession. The truth of this will be readily perceived when we consider the meaning of the terms. By "technical facility" we understand a readiness in computation: "ready reckoning," in fact—a very useful accomplishment. On the other hand, an "intellectual grasp" of figures implies a thorough appreciation of their meaning. Numbers are essentially representative, and are used only to express the relations in which things stand to each other. If you doubt this, cut out from a balance-sheet the two rows of figures under "assets and liabilities," and see if you can make as much sense out of the numbers alone as out of the words which are left. The man of common sense attempts to realize, as far as he can, the actual state of affairs that is symbolized by the figures before him; and the true man of business, or methodized common sense, will, further, not rest satisfied until he is able to project before his mind's eye all the facts for which the figures are, by convention, made to stand. But behind facts lie ideas, and the grasp of these is at once essentially necessary and difficult. An illustration or two may help us towards a clear perception of this.

In the annual statement of a fire insurance company appears the amount of premiums receivable during the past year. There are the figures. The auditor examines the registers, etc., satisfies himself that the premium in respect of each policy on the books is included in the accounts. There are the facts. But, further, he questions himself as to the nature of premiums, and perceives that they represent chiefly the "office" value of risks borne by the company. Now, if all the premiums were charged at the beginning, and all the risks expired at the close of the year, the differences between the premiums receivable and the claims payable during the year would be profit. But, since premiums are usually charged quarterly, there must necessarily be at the close of the year a large amount of risks current, to meet which prudence dictates the setting aside of a proportion of each premium equivalent to the period during which the corresponding risk has yet to run, in order to form a reserve as against that risk, and to this point the auditor directs his attention. There is the idea behind the facts. The faculty exercised by him in following out the idea is the "mental grasp" of the true nature of the figures with which he is dealing.

A very familiar instance of the working of this faculty may be seen in the attempt to understand what a debtor balance on a cash book signifies. Here we say to ourselves: "The cash book represents the cash-keeper, or cashier; the cashier debits himself with what he receives, because he will have to account for it like a debt; thus, an excess of debit entries is a balance of debts or cash due by him—i.e., in his hands." In this simple act of reasoning we are distinctly conscious of the "grasp."

We left our would-be accountant in a state of suspense, unable to proceed for lack of "figure training." We may now imagine that he has made good his deficiencies to some extent at least, and is now fitted out for his peculiar business in life. Concentrated thinking, methodical thinking, a facility in the use of figures, and a grasp of their true meaning, form the only true foundation on which an average youth can hope to build a reputation for good and lasting work. There is, indeed, a form of genius that overleaps all tardy logical processes, and sees with preternatural vividness what most men have to toil up through a haze to behold. But its possession is very rare, and cannot always be depended on. We are thus compelled to take the utmost advantage of all means within our grasp to attain those faculties of mind that distinguish the able accountant.

PROPER USE OF FACULTIES.

At the same time, something must be done to direct the mind in the proper use of its faculties. For example, there is a mental conscience as well as a moral conscience, obedience to which enhances the intellectual powers, while a disregard of it often neutralizes their highest efforts. Against this conscience there are many sins possible. Two of the gravest may be alluded to. Want of thoroughness is in the forefront, as work partially done is practically not done at all, and therefore involves a waste of the powers employed in its execution. Thoroughness is a universally admitted virtue, and as such is commonly more an object of distant and respectful attention and contemplation than one of actual practice. There is thus but little use of speaking truisms on the subject: it is probably more to the point to remark that, on a rough calculation, for every minute supposed to be gained by "scamping" work, an hour has to be spent in the future in rectifying the errors that have inevitably been committed. A second fault is suggested by the first. It may seem strange to reckon it wrong either to force the mind beyond its natural speed, or to let it work habitually much within that speed, but it is so. Every mind has its own peculiar pace, at which alone it is possible to do good work; and although that pace may be to some extent gradually accelerated by careful training, yet if the mind be unnaturally pressed beyond its proper speed, demoralization and errors result. We see this truth evidenced when a slow-brained youth tries to get through his work as soon as his quick-witted neighbor. On the other hand, a habit of "taking things easy," as it is called, is equally bad; for the mind adapts itself by degrees to the slow pace at which it is usually worked, and when an occasion arises for a strenuous bracing of all its powers it refuses to exceed that pace.

We have now passed in review the principal mental acquisitions and qualifications of the accountant. Before dealing with the subject of his training we may with advantage mention two essentially different mental dispositions the extremes of which need to be guarded against. We have all noticed two dispositions that are the types of separate classes of minds. The one constantly tends to look at the broad outlines of work and the general principles that govern it, to the disregard of minor points; while the other as invariably fixes the attention upon details, oblivious of the structure. Each in excess is wrong, but it is rarely that a mind is found in which these tendencies are in equilibrium. In fact, the balance is to be attained only by discipline, for the tendencies we are considering constitute the character of the mental organization and cannot be eradicated. The only way of preventing them from leading into error is by artificially cultivating the contrary habit in each case.

MENTAL EQUIPMENT.

We come now to consider, very briefly, the means by which the accountant may be put in possession of the equipment that has been here indicated. To summarize the leading features of this equipment he is required to possess—

(1) A knowledge of theoretical and practical accounting in its various branches.

(2) An acquaintance with law and actuarial science (elementary).

(3) A familiarity with business management.

(4) A number of mental qualities—including, as chiefly requisite, (a) concentration; (b) mental order; (c) the mathematical faculty.

(5) A habit of using these properly.

Doubtless the ideal method of education would be an institution, or college, in which all branches of accounting were taught to the students by professors—theoretically, by means of lectures; practically, through actual work in departments: periodical examinations forming incitements to, and tests of work, and diplomas being granted to competent students at the close of their course. The practical means adopted by the societies of accountants follow pretty closely the lines of this ideal method. If we substitute "apprentices" for "students," and "masters" for "professors," the one answers, in the main, to the other. The societies form corporations which admit to their membership only those who have undergone a course of apprenticeship with their members. The binding nature of an indenture lasting for a specified term of years secures continuity of personal training. The obligation of the master to communicate, and of the apprentice to learn the work of the profession, is fitted to produce a thorough acquaintance with the various branches of practical business.

School of Commerce, Accounts & Finance

Graduating Exercises

The graduation exercises of the first class to graduate from the New York University School of Commerce, Accounts & Finance, were held in the Metropolitan Opera House, New York City, on the evening of June 5. At the same time were graduated the class of New York University School of Law, University and Bellevue Hospital Medical College, The School of Pedagogy, The Graduate School, and the New York-American Veterinary College. This occasion was the 70th annual commencement of New York University. A large crowd were present, the vast house being filled.

The graduates and instructors occupied seats upon the stage. The young men who completed their college course on that evening were an intelligent looking lot, and the graduates of the School of Commerce, Accounts & Finance were by no means the least intelligent. One by one the graduates came forward dressed in gowns and mortar-board caps to receive their diplomas from the hand of Chancellor McCracken, and as each name was called it was, of course, greeted with applause. The following were the graduates of the class of 1902, New York University School of Commerce, Accounts & Finance: Howard Lex Bain, William H. Boyd, Stuart N. Clarke, William H. Dennis, Robbins Gilman, Edward J. Gosford, Akiba Newstead, Samson D. Oppenheim, William H. Pickett, George A. Rowell, Marvin Scudder, George L. Seabury, Daniel J. Healy, Percy B. Jarvis, Everett S. Jarvis, Orrin R. Judd, Maurice S. Konheim Edward F. Lewis, Richard P. Tinsley, Harry M. C. Vedder, John A. Veit, Gustave J. Volckening, William A. Watson, Edward M. Williams.

The following are Honor men: Richard P. Tinsley, Orrin R. Judd, Everett S. Jarvis, Daniel J. Healy, Harry M. C. Vedder, Edward M. Williams.

DINNER OF THE GRADUATING CLASS.

A brief review of the work of the school was given in the COMMERCE, ACCOUNTS & FINANCE for June, and mention was made at that time of the dinner of the graduating class, held at the St. Denis Hotel, on the evening of June 7. This dinner was a very jolly affair, and the speeches were all interesting and more or less instructive. Mr. Clarke's speech was printed in the June issue of COMMERCE, ACCOUNTS & FINANCE, and our readers may judge from that sample the quality of the oratory. The menu was as follows:—

Little Neck Clams.
Celery. Stuffed Radishes.
Chicken Soup with Okra.
Kennebec Salmon, Cardinale.
Dressed Tomatoes.
Sweetbreads Larded, Bouquetiere.
Roast Spring Lamb, Mint Sauce.
Mashed Potatoes. New Peas.
Roast Squab.
Lettuce au Mayonnaise.
Strawberry Cake. Ice Cream.
Cheese. Coffee.

The list of toasts and those responding to them was printed on the menu card as follows:—

"WE" .... Mr. William H. Dennis

"No reckoning made, but sent to my ACCOUNT,
With all my imperfections on my head;
O, horrible."—Hamlet.

"US" .... Mr. Orrin R. Judd

"Wherein I spoke of most disastrous chances,
Of moving accidents by flood and field,
Of hair-breadth 'scapes . . . ."—Othello.

"WE STUDENTS" .... Mr. Gustave J. Volckening

"How doth the little busy bee improve each shining hour?"—Watts.

"WE PROFESSORS" .... Mr. H. M. C. Vedder

"I am Sir Oracle, and when I speak let no dog bark."—Twelfth Night.

"WE LAWYERS" .... Mr. Stuart N. Clarke

"O wise young judge, how do I honor thee!"—Merchant of Venice.

"THE LADIES" .... Mr. William A. Watson

"O woman, in our hours of ease,
Uncertain, coy and hard to please."—Scott.

Toastmaster, Mr. S. D. Oppenheim.
Nunc Plaudite.

The graduates are all ambitious, active young business men, who feel a keen interest in the University, and particularly in the School of Commerce, Accounts & Finance. They mean to continue to take an active interest in the future welfare of this school, and will do their level best to see that the high standard of its instruction is kept up. As has been said before in these columns, the outline of the school's work for the coming year shows a larger scope and a more thorough course of instruction. The School of Commerce, Accounts & Finance is bound to grow and become a power in the field of business education.

THE USEFUL MILLIONAIRE

There is a use for everything in this world, even for millionaires. Mr. Carnegie, himself a very useful millionaire, has the following to say about the uses of his brethren in his book, "The Empire of Business":—

The bees of a hive do not destroy the honey-making bees, but the drones. It will be a great mistake for the community to shoot the millionaires, for they are the bees that make the most honey, and contribute most to the hive even after they have gorged themselves full. Here is a remarkable fact, that the masses of the people in any country are prosperous and comfortable just in proportion as there are millionaires. Take Russia, with its population little better than serfs, and living at the point of starvation upon the meanest possible fare, such fare as none of our people could or would eat, and you do not find one millionaire in Russia, always excepting the Emperor and a few nobles who own the land, owing to their political system. It is the same to a great extent in Germany. There are only two millionaires known to me in the whole German Empire. In France, where the people are better off than in Germany, you cannot count one half-dozen millionaires in the whole country. In the old home of our race, in Britain, which is the richest country in all Europe—the richest country in the world save one, our own—there are more millionaires than in the whole of the rest of Europe, and its people are better off than in any other. You come to our own land: we have more millionaires than in all the rest of the world put together, although we have not one to every ten that is reputed so. I have seen a list of supposed millionaires, prepared by a well-known lawyer of Brooklyn, which made me laugh, as it has made many others. I saw men rated there as millionaires who could not pay their debts. Many should have a cipher cut from their $1,000,000. Some time ago I sat next Mr. Evarts at dinner, and the conversation touched upon the idea that men should distribute their wealth during their lives for the public good. One gentleman said that was correct, giving many reasons, one of which was that, of course, they could not take it with them at death."

"Well," said Mr. Evarts, "I do not know about that. My experience as a New York lawyer is that, somehow or other, they do succeed in taking at least four-fifths of it." Their reputed wealth was never found at death.

Under our present conditions the millionaire who toils on is the cheapest article which the community secures at the price it pays for him, namely, his shelter, clothing and food.

MAKES A DIFFERENCE

"A Virginia judge gave a man a year for stealing a straw hat," remarked the bookkeeper. "That's nothing," chimed in the clerk. "A man in Wisconsin got five years for taking an umbrella one day in a sudden rainstorm." "I thought that was justifiable larceny." "Ordinarily, yes; but this umbrella was the court's."—Exchange.

COMMERCE ACCOUNTS & FINANCE

A Magazine cf Higher Business Education and Practical Administration. Acknowledged Authority in the Profession of Commerce and Consistent Advocate of Methods Up to Date and Above the Table.

JOSEPH CROSBY LINCOLN, - - - Editor.
FRIEND PITTS, JR., - Circulation and Advertising.
E. R. KITTREDGE, - - - Business Manager.

PUBLISHED MONTHLY

SUBSCRIPTION $1 a Year in the United States, Canada and Mexico. Other countries $1.50. Postage prepaid by the Publishers. In the absence of specific orders to stop at the end of the subscription term the paper will be continued and a bill sent. Entered at the New York Postoffice as Second Class mail matter.

COMMERCE, ACCOUNTS & FINANCE COMPANY, Publishers
Twenty-five Pine Street, New York

The old saying, that once war was business but now business has become war, seems to be supported by the recent trend of events in whatever direction we may look. We regard the standing armies of the different nations of Europe as preparations for war, and certain ruling sovereigns are designated as war lords, and yet, so far as the nations themselves are concerned, there has been peace for quite a period of time. Just at present there is no anticipated outbreak of hostilities. On the other hand, there is an industrial or business war being waged by one nation upon another that is without parallel in history. A certain one of the war lords, a man who, according to popular representation, prides himself upon his kingly dignity and skill in warfare, and who has taken unusual pains to secure to his nation an efficient army and a well-equipped navy, all at once poses in a new light. Even his subjects seem to object to his new position in that he is disregarding the titular nobility and the wealthy class of the empire and is associating himself with mere industrial leaders. The king's favorite is declared to be among those who have long been engaged in industrial pursuits and who have won great success in their respective lines.

*

It is interesting to inquire into the details of the change which has occurred in this direction. When Emperor William of Germany succeeded to the crown he, on several occasions in the course of public speeches, gave expression to the conviction that his nobles constituted the principal bulwark of his throne. At the end of an eventful reign of fourteen years he is now giving numerous demonstrations of the fact that he looks upon the captains of industry and of trade as being a far greater source of strength to his empire than the aristocracy. The result of this policy is declared to be a democratizing of the empire.

*

Emperor William has ever been an interesting figure since he succeeded to the crown. He has managed in one way or another to command almost uninterruptedly public attention, not only at home, but abroad, where people enjoying a better perspective than can be obtained in his own dominions are able to form a more correct and impartial judgment of his personality than his own subjects. But, declares a correspondent of the Boston Evening Transcript, never has he been so interesting as at the present time, when divesting himself of all those prejudices among which he was reared, he places himself at the head of the German business world, bent on achieving for his people even greater pre-eminence in industry and trade than as a military power. It is the beginning of a revolution in Germany which, unlike other great popular movements of the same kind, will contribute to strengthen the foundations of the throne, instead of destroying them. The policy of the emperor will, in the first place, bring about the disappearance of those barriers of caste which have so long divided the aristocracy from the middle and lower classes. It will likewise tend to open the doors of the commissioned ranks of the army, and of the government administration to the bourgeoise, instead of continuing to restrict them to the nobility. Again, it will not only encourage but even compel men of birth to turn their attentions to trade and to industry, and to give up that foolish belief, according to which there are no other callings open to a nobleman than service of the Crown.

*

Further commenting on the situation, the same writer says that Emperor William's conversion to his present way of thinking was inevitable. When he came to the throne he had been taught to believe that his nobles were blindly obedient to his sovereign will, that they cared nothing for popular rights, nor for constitutional forms of government; in fact, that they resented the pretensions of the common people to have any voice in the administration of the empire. This impression had been carefully fostered in the Kaiser by Bismarck, who was never tired of publicly expressing his contempt for Parliament. For a time nothing occurred to modify these relations between the Emperor and his nobles or to impair his belief in their subserviency to his views. Finally the time came when he became alive to the necessity of introducing certain reforms, which the nobles believed would injuriously affect their financial interests. It was the Canal Bill which first brought about the conflict between the Kaiser and the aristocracy.

*

Nor is Kaiser Wilhelm the only reigning monarch who has appreciated the growing importance of business. Various monarchs of the old world are seeking the good will of the masses, sometimes at the expense of the nobility, and are one by one abandoning their former practice of identifying the crown with the aristocracy, as opposed to the middle and lower classes. This is especially true in the case of Italy, where young Victor Emanuel has placed the control of foreign affairs in the hands of a business man, whose principal title to fame is the success which he has achieved as the leading bicycle and sewing machine manufacturer of his country, and who is descended from a long line of merchant ancestors. Various statements along the same general line might be made with reference to England, Belgium, the Scandinavian nations and various other portions of Europe. Captains of industry and of trade are coming to be regarded at their true worth and are recognized by every monarch in Europe as infinitely more important factors in the welfare of his empire than the mere noble, no matter how blue the blood of the latter nor illustrious his lineage. In this connection it is to be remarked that the luncheon given at Sherry's, in New York, to Prince Henry of Prussia on the occasion of his recent visit to this country by leading business men is said to have interested Kaiser Wilhelm more profoundly and given him greater satisfaction than anything else connected with the memorable junketing tour. It was because it came from the business men of the nation.

* * *

This is the season of the year when the "sweet girl graduate" and the male graduate, whether sweet or sour, come forth from grammar school, high school and from the various universities and colleges to take up lifework in the world of business or among the various professions. With the college graduate this editorial may have little to do, although what we shall say applies to him to a large extent, but it is with the graduate of the high school or of the grammar school that we wish to deal. Let us take, for example, a young man graduating from a high school and about to enter a bank in a subordinate position. This young man has completed the courses taught in the school to the satisfaction of the authorities and has received a diploma certifying proficiency in his studies. He can write a fair hand, has a small knowledge of mathematics, can read a little Latin, and possibly less Greek; has a smattering of French and German; should know something about geography and physics, and has acquired some ideas concerning other branches of study. He has also studied English grammar and rhetoric. He enters the bank as, let us say, a messenger.

*

In the course of three, four or five years he rises to be assistant bookkeeper, or to fill some position of that nature. He has probably forgotten his Greek and Latin; also he has forgotten most of the studies not directly connected with his daily work. His penmanship has probably improved; he is cleverer at figures than he was formerly, and the smattering of bookkeeping lore he possessed when he left school has now given place to a fairly thorough knowledge of the subject. How is it with his grammar and his rhetoric? Can he write and speak the English language correctly and concisely? In most cases, we regret to say, the answer is, that he cannot do this, and yet to write and speak English correctly is a very essential qualification of a successful man. We do not mean to say that all men that the world calls successful speak or write correctly. Many do not; but if they have succeeded it is in spite of this fact, not because of it. To be able to write a good letter, to make a good speech and to express one's ideas thoroughly and grammatically is worth a great deal to every one engaged in business. It is stating no more than the bare truth to assert that the average young man in a bank or in a business house does not write or speak good English.

*

If any one doubts this, let him listen to the conversation of a group of young men, bank clerks, for instance. We venture to say that he will hear much bad English spoken. Let him examine a batch of, say, one thousand letters written by one thousand different young men and women employed in business offices. He will find that two-thirds of these letters are badly worded and contain mistakes in grammar, and sometimes in spelling. How is it with the average applicant for the position of stenographer? Every business man knows that more stenographers fail to give satisfaction because of lack of knowledge of English than because of deficiencies in the arts of writing shorthand or typewriting. The business colleges turn out thousands of stenographers and typewriters each year, and these graduates may be able to write from dictation at a high rate of speed and to pound out much copy on the typewriter, but it is only one in ten that knows enough about the rules of English grammar and rhetoric to correct a mistake when one is found in the notebook. The average young stenographer will embody the mistakes in the typewritten copy, regardless of the fact that it turns an otherwise understandable sentence into nonsense.

*

What is it that makes the average after-dinner speech so dreary? By the average speech we mean that made by the business man or the clerk who does not make speech-making a business. It is the lack of ability to express an idea as it should be expressed. The speaker may have good ideas in plenty, he may have valuable ideas on a given subject, but in many cases he tangles these ideas into a mass of hackneyed phrase and long syllabled mediocrity. He speaks of the "high road to success" and the "trump of fame" just as though public speakers since the time of William the Conqueror had not used the same old figures of speech. In consequence, a speech by an undoubtedly able man often becomes dreary and almost disgusting.

*

The same is true when a young business man endeavors to put his ideas on paper. Suppose he is asked to prepare an article on the duties of—well, the Janitor's Department of a bank. Does he tell us about the Janitor's Department in clear and orderly fashion? No, indeed, he doesn't. He begins by a long apology for writing the article in the first place. He says that he feels the honor that is conferred upon him, and trusts he may do his little best not to weary his readers. He fills two pages with this sort of thing and uses the old metaphors and figures of speech that thousands of men have used before him. Then he soars into lofty fields of imagination, and in so soaring makes an error in grammar occasionally. Perhaps he tells us a little about the Janitor's Department before he gets through, but he has so overloaded his information with what he hopes is "fine writing" that his readers learn little and care less about the subject.

*

In writing a business letter this same man will fill three pages with something that might be said in ten lines, and said better and much more to the point. He hurts himself and he gives his correspondent a poor opinion of the institution with which he is connected. Every business man and every thinking clerk knows that this is so, and that if he made the mistakes in his bookkeeping or his clerical work that he does in his English he could not hold the position that he now fills; yet he allows his grammar and his rhetoric to become slovenly and careless, simply because it is too much trouble to try and make them better.

*

It is a thorough knowledge of English that should be hammered into the students of the schools and business colleges rather than so many of the frills that are taught there. Only one man in a thousand uses his Greek after he leaves the high school, and the one thousandth can only use it by studying it more and more, because the little that is taught in the high school is next to worthless. Why not spend the time given to Greek and Latin in teaching the student the English language, and how to write and speak it?

NOTE BROKERS AND COMMERCIAL PAPER

From R. B. H., Ardmore, Pa.

Kindly give me some information as to the practice of note brokers in handling commercial paper as to charges. Do brokers handle the company's own paper, and if so, what indorsement do they require?

Answer. The question that our correspondent raises is one fundamental to the general system of selling paper through brokers. It is easily answered by saying that everything depends upon the security there is behind the paper and the habit that the makers have with respect to payments. If the security is adequate and the paper is taken up promptly when due, it is very easy to obtain a market for the paper either through note brokers or by direct application to some bank which handles commercial paper. Whether or not the paper is to be endorsed depends, as before intimated, upon the security there is behind it. If it is not well supported by assets, an endorsement may be required, but, as a rule, brokers, and bankers as well, would prefer to handle paper that is so well supported by assets as to require no endorsement.

The rate of brokerage depends entirely upon circumstances. The size of the line, the market and other conditions are always considered. The character of the paper, as to its support in the way of assets, likewise has an influence upon the brokerage charge.

Broadly, our correspondent should have no difficulty in disposing of paper at advantageous rates if the assets behind it are satisfactory.

"THAT" SIX TIMES

There is one word in the English language which can appear six times consecutively in a sentence and make correct English. To illustrate: A boy wrote on the blackboard, "The man that lies does wrong." The teacher objected to the word "that," so the word "who" was substituted. And yet it must be evident to the reader for all that, that that "that" that that teacher objected to was right, after all.—Four Track News.

The Negotiable Instruments Law*

By THOMAS B. PATON

Liability of Indorser Upon Paper Negotiable by Delivery—Order of Liability—Liability of Agent or Broker—Presentment for Payment

NOTE.—As enacted in New York, the Negotiable Instruments Law is divided into nineteen articles as follows:—

1. GENERAL PROVISIONS (Sections 1—17)
2. NEGOTIABLE INSTRUMENTS: Form and Interpretation (20—42)
3. Consideration (50—55)
4. Negotiation (60—80)
5. Rights of holder (90—98)
6. Liabilities of parties (110—119)
7. Presentment for payment (130—148)
8. Notice of Dishonor (160—189)
9. Discharge (200—206)
10. BILLS OF EXCHANGE (210—215)
11. Acceptance (220—230)
12. Presentment for acceptance (240—248)
13. Protest (260—268)
14. Acceptance for honor (280—290)
15. Payment for honor (300—306)
16. Bills in a set (310—315)
17. PROMISSORY NOTES AND CHECKS (320- 325)
18. Notes given for patent rights (330—332)
19. Laws repealed: When takes effect (340—341)

The provisions of the law naturally fall under four general classifications.

a. General Provisions.
b. Negotiable Instruments in General.
c. Bills of Exchange.
d. Promissory Notes and Checks.

The text of the law is the same in all the states (with some slight exceptions which will be noted), but the numbering of the sections, and in some states of the articles, is not uniform. There is, however, the same continuity of articles and text, except that in some instances, "General Provisions" follow, instead of precede, the remainder of the act. By following this course of study with reference to the New York act, as above outlined, the reader in each state can apply the same to the law of his own state.

The next section to be considered provides the liability of an indorser upon paper negotiable by delivery. It is as follows:—

Section 117. Liability of Indorser Where Paper Negotiable by Delivery.—Where a person places his indorsement on an instrument negotiable by delivery, he incurs all the liabilities of an indorser.

We have heretofore seen that there are two modes of transferring negotiable paper—by delivery, when payable to bearer; by indorsement of the holder, completed by delivery, when payable to order. Now it sometimes happens that a man holding a negotiable instrument payable to bearer will, unnecessarily, so far as an effective transfer is concerned, place his own indorsement upon it in the act of transferring it. Generally he will do this inadvertently or intentionally, but under a mistake as to the legal necessity therefor; sometimes he will make the indorsement by request of the one to whom he transfers it. However this may be, the liability which he thereupon incurs, as provided by section 117, is not alone the warrantor liability of one who negotiates an instrument by delivery, but the same liability as is incurred by one who indorses paper payable to order.

The general liability of an indorser, we have seen, runs to all subsequent holders in due course, but an attentive consideration of certain other sections of the act will make it appear that the indorser's liability provided by section 117, so far as it extends to all subsequent holders in due course, is incurred only by an indorser in blank of "bearer" paper, while one who indorses "bearer" paper by a special indorsement incurs an indorser's liability only to special indorsees who make title through his indorsement, and not to subsequent holders in due course who take title by delivery alone. This distinction is important to note.

That we may get at the exact legal effect of section 117, and of certain other sections of the act with which it may be appropriately grouped, let us here bring into view section 60, which provides that "if payable to bearer, an instrument is negotiated by delivery;" section 28, that an instrument "is payable to bearer (1) when it is expressed to be so payable; or (2) when it is payable to a person named therein or bearer; or (3) when it is payable to the order of a fictitious or non-existing person, and such fact was known to the person making it so payable; or (4) when the name of the payee does not purport to be the name of any person; or (5) when the only or last indorsement is an indorsement in blank;" and section 70, that "where an instrument, payable to bearer, is indorsed specially, it may nevertheless be further negotiated by delivery; but the person indorsing specially is liable as indorser to only such holders as make title through his indorsement.

CONCLUSIONS DRAWN.

Reading these four sections, 28, 60, 70 and 117, together, they lead to the following conclusions:—

1. An instrument is payable to bearer when it is payable in one of the five following ways: Bearer; A or bearer; fictitious or non-existing person, known to be such; payee not a person's name [i. e., a place or a thing); only or last indorsement in blank. (Sec. 28.)

2. If payable to bearer (i. e., in one of these five ways), it is negotiable by delivery. (Sec. 60.)

3. Where payable to bearer (i. e., in one of these five ways) and then indorsed specially, it is also further negotiable by delivery. (Sec. 70.) Amplifying this, bearer paper cannot be restricted or changed to "order" paper by subsequent special indorsement, but will still pass by delivery; e. g., (1) check payable to bearer, indorsed by A to B, lost by B, found by C, delivered to innocent D for value, gives D good title; (2) check payable to order of A, indorsed in blank by A, then indorsed specially by B to C, lost by C, found by D, negotiated by delivery to E for value, gives E good title. If it be said in this case that the instrument is no longer "bearer" paper, because the only or last indorsement is not in blank, but special, hence E cannot acquire good title by delivery only, the answer is, first, the last indorsement before the special indorsement was in blank, hence brings such instrument within the permission of section 70 of further negotiation by delivery, notwithstanding special indorsement.

4. Where a person indorses paper negotiable by delivery (i. e., paper payable to bearer in one of the five ways stated, or bearer paper which, though specially indorsed, is still negotiable by delivery) he incurs all the liabilities of an indorser. (Sec. 117.)

5. But above liability, so far as it runs to all subsequent holders in due course, is limited to an indorsement in blank, for where a person indorses bearer paper specially he is liable as indorser to only such holders as make title through his indorsement. Subsequent holders by delivery of such specially indorsed bearer paper cannot hold him liable as indorser (Sec. 170.)

ORDER OF LIABILITY.

We now come to section 118, which provides the order in which indorsers are liable.

Section 118. Order in Which Indorsers Are Liable.—As respects one another, indorsers are liable, prima facie, in the order in which they indorse; but evidence is admissible to show that as between or among themselves they have agreed otherwise. Joint payees or joint indorsees who indorse are deemed to indorse jointly and severally.

A negotiable instrument is not paid at maturity, and the holder who has taken the necessary steps to preserve their liability, thereupon calls for payment by the indorsers of the instrument. One of them pays it, and then he in turn wants reimbursement from some prior indorser. This brings up the question of the liability of indorsers as among themselves. The general rule of the law merchant is that where several persons indorse a bill or note in succession, they are liable to each other in the order in which they indorse; the indorsement imports a successive and several, and not a joint obligation, whether the indorsements be for

*Republished from the Banking Law Journal by permission. Copyright, 1899, 1900, 1901 and 1902, by T. B. Paton, all rights reserved. To be revised and published in book form by the author.

accommodation or for value received, unless there is an outside agreement different from that imported by the indorsements; but when the successive indorsements are for accommodation of other parties, the indorsers for accommodation may make an agreement to be jointly and equally bound, the burden being on the one who asserts such an agreement, to prove it. In the case of indorsements by joint payees or joint indorsees, however, here, under the law merchant, they are not regarded as successive indorsers, but jointly liable only.

The Negotiable Instruments law, in section 118, perpetuates the law merchant in the particulars above set out, except that it changes the law merchant which made joint payees or indorsees who indorse only jointly liable, by the provision making them jointly and severally liable. The exact effect of this change will be pointed out later.

Section 118 provides that "as respects one another, indorsers are liable, prima facie, in the order in which they indorse." The act, we see, makes no distinction between indorsers for value and accommodation indorsers. In the absence of an outside agreement, accommodation indorsers, as well as indorsers for value, are liable to one another in the order in which they sign the paper. This is a rule which two or more parties, signing for a friend, frequently do not heed, often to the sorrow of the one or ones who happen to sign first. Mr. A, for example, desires to raise money or extend a debt, and makes his negotiable promissory note for that purpose, which, if he can obtain thereon the indorsement of one or more responsible parties, will be acceptable to his creditor, present or prospective. He accordingly approaches Messrs. B, C and D, asking them to indorse for accommodation, which, out of pure friendship, do they, feeling that Mr. A will take care of the paper, and in the possible contingency that he does not, there will be three of them to shoulder the burden. But they make no agreement to that effect; they merely indorse as the paper is presented to them, Mr. B first, then Mr C, then Mr. D. Mr. A thereupon negotiates his paper, and at maturity fails to pay it. The holder thereupon looks for payment to Mr. D. He pays it, and under the law has recourse for the full amount upon both B and C, and if C pays it, he, in turn, can make B pay the whole amount to him. Instead, then, of each contributing one-third, the unfortunate Mr. B, who happened to indorse the paper first, must bear the whole burden; this because there was no contrary agreement between them, and because such is the liability imported from the order of indorsements alone. This has been the rule of the law merchant for a long while, and it is perpetuated by the Negotiable Instruments law. (See for an illustrative case the Banking Law Journal for April, 1897, pp. 175, 215.)

In view of this rule of law, the order in which two or more accommodation parties indorse negotiable paper is an important matter between themselves, showing the necessity in each transaction of this nature that they should make an agreement for contribution.

Such an agreement is provided for by section 118, which, after providing that, as respects one another, indorsers are liable, prima facie, in the order in which they indorse, continues: "But evidence is admissible to show that as between or among themselves they have agreed otherwise."

Of course, in the case of successive indorsers for value, there is no occasion for such agreements; each indorsee, paying value, expects to compel his indorser to pay him fully, if the instrument finally rests, uncollected, in his hands; it is only in the case of two or more parties, indorsing for accommodation of another, that the idea of contributing to pay the instrument, if the principal debtor does not, springs up.

The final clause of section 118 is as follows: "Joint payees or joint indorsees who indorse are deemed to indorse jointly and severally."

This changes the law merchant to the extent of making what was formerly a joint liability only, by joint payees or indorsees who indorse, a joint and several liability—that is to say, instead of the holder of a negotiable instrument seeking recourse upon such joint indorsers being compelled to sue all jointly, he can, at his option, sue any one of them severally. But so far as the liability between themselves is concerned, one of two joint and several indorsers who pays a negotiable instrument is entitled to contribution from his co-indorsers; his case is different from that of successive indorsers, for there the obligation is several and not joint.

LIABILITY OF AGENT OR BROKER.

Article VI., upon the liabilities of parties, concludes with the following provision:—

Section 119. Liability of Agent or Broker.—Where a broker or other agent negotiates an instrument without indorsement, he incurs all the liabilities prescribed by section 115 of this act, unless he discloses the name of his principal, and the fact that he is acting only as agent.

The liability prescribed by section 115, as we have seen, is the warrantor liability imposed upon those who negotiate an instrument by delivery or by a qualified indorsement, the warranty being that the instrument is genuine and in all respects what it purports to be; that the warrantor has good title; that prior parties had capacity to contract, except in the case of public or corporate securities, and that the warrantor has no knowledge of any fact which would impair validity or render the instrument valueless. When the negotiation is by delivery only, this warranty extends only to the immediate transferee.

By section 119 the same liability is imposed upon an agent or broker as upon an owner, negotiating an instrument, where the agent does not disclose the name of his principal and the fact that he is acting as agent.

This section covers the extensive business carried on by note brokers, who market commercial paper, and is the same liability as was imposed by the courts before the enactment of the Negotiable Instruments Law. To be free from personal liability, the note broker must disclose the principal for whom he acts in the sale of commercial paper and the fact that he is acting as agent, otherwise he will be understood to sell it as his own, and to warrant genuineness, title and the other matters of waranty set out in section 115.

ARTICLE VII.—PRESENTMENT FOR PAYMENT.

The payment or redemption of a negotiable instrument at its maturity, when the purposes for which it was brought into existence have been served, is the final essential in its history. It is with this end in view that it is issued, negotiated from hand to hand, and value given for it by each successive taker; or, if it is issued to the payee as a gift, its payment is what makes it worth the giving.

The contemplation of the parties is that this payment will be made by the principal debtor, or party primarily liable on the instrument; and if this is done, then the matter is ended. But, unfortunately, in numerous instances the principal debtor, for one reason or another, defaults or fails to make payment, and then, where the instrument has passed through more than one hand, and has, in addition to a primary debtor, other parties secondarily liable thereon, as is most often the case, it becomes necessary for the holder to look for payment to these other parties. But their liability, not being absolute, but contingent and conditional upon due presentment and notice to them of dishonor, the holder, as a pre-requisite to compelling payment by them, must have observed or complied with the requirements of the law governing these matters. If the primary debtor was the only party liable in the case, no such requirements would be needed. But to hold the parties secondarily liable, such as drawer or indorsers, the law merchant has established certain requirements as to presentment, and concerning notice of dishonor, which are now crystallized into statute and embodied in Article VII. and VIII. of the Negotiable Instruments Law, so that, complying with these requirements, the holder puts himself in a position to enforce payment from the parties secondarily liable on the instrument which the principal debtor has failed to pay.

WANT OF DEMAND.

The first provision of Article VII. relates to the effect of want of demand on the principal debtor. It is as follows:—

Section 130. Effect of Want of Demand on Principal Debtor.—Presentment for payment is not necessarily in order to charge the person primarily liable on the instrument; but if the instrument is, by its terms, payable at a special place, and he is able and willing to pay it there at maturity, such ability and willingness are equivalent to a tender of payment upon his part. But except as herein otherwise provided, presentment for payment is necessary in order to charge the drawer and indorsers.

This indicates, as we have already pointed out, that the requirement of presentment for payment is one made in view of there being parties on the instrument, in addition to the principal debtor, who are contingently liable to pay upon due presentment and notice, if the party primarily liable does not. The necessity of presentment has reference to looking for payment to such parties, if the instrument is not paid by the principal debtor. If there are no such parties contingently liable on the instrument, then there is no legal necessity for presentment. Take the case of a promissory note made by A to B. A is the primary debtor and B is the payee and owner. The only party liable to pay the instrument is A, the primary debtor, who has promised to pay B. In such case "presentment for payment (by B) is not necessary to charge the person primarily liable (A) on the instrument." Ordinarily, in such a case, where the instrument does not specify a place of payment, it is A's business to go to B and make payment, or, if the instrument is made payable at a particular place, to have the money at that place at the time fixed for payment; and if A fails to do this, B, without making any presentment, can immediately bring suit on the instrument to enforce payment by A.

PLACE OF PAYMENT.

Concerning specification of a particular place of payment, the act provides: "If the instrument is, by its terms, payable at a special place, and he (A) is able and willing to pay it there at maturity, such ability and willingness are equivalent to a tender of payment upon his part." Suppose, for example, A's note to B is made payable at the First National Bank of New York, and at the day of maturity A has funds on deposit in that bank sufficient in amount to pay the note. Under the Negotiable Instruments Law, as we shall see by section 147, "where the instrument is made payable at a bank it is equivalent to an order to the bank to pay the same for the account of the principal debtor thereon." A then has sufficient funds with his bank and has ordered the bank to pay the note to B. This is equivalent to a tender of payment of the note by A to B. If B presents the note at the bank, well and good. If he does not, what is the consequence? A is not discharged, for he is the primary and only debtor in the case we are considering. But if B brings suit against A on such an instrument, as he can, if he chooses, without making presentment, proof by A of his ability and willingness to pay at the place of payment—his having money in the bank at the time of maturity being equivalent to a tender of payment by A to B—will be a bar to B's recovery of interest on the note, or the costs of suit; all he will be entitled to will be the face of the note, and he himself will be obliged to pay the court costs. But in such a case not only must A have the money in bank at maturity of the note, but he must keep it there. In Hills vs. Place, 48 N. Y. 520, where a maker put money in bank sufficient to pay his note when due and gave instructions to pay upon presentation, but the note not having been presented at maturity, the maker thereafter withdrew the funds and did not bring the money into court, it was held, in a suit by the owner against the maker, that the former was entitled to judgment for principal, interest and costs.

NECESSITY OF PRESENTMENT FOR PAYMENT.

We see therefore that so far as the primary debtor on an instrument is concerned there is no necessity, in order to hold him liable, to present it to him for payment, except that where the instrument is made payable at a bank or other place, and the primary debtor has funds there with directions to pay it at maturity, it is to the holder's interest to make presentment at such place, as the easiest and most sensible and economical way of getting his money, for there is, in such case, a legal tender of payment staring him in the face, which, by non-presentment, he is refusing to receive, and forfeiting the interest which the money would otherwise earn from maturity; and if he adopts the alternative of enforcing payment through the courts he must himself pay the court costs. Furthermore, even where the instrument is not payable at a particular place, and assuming the principal debtor is the only party liable on the instrument, it is also to the holder's interest to make presentment to him for payment at maturity, and this is the general business practice. There are so many slips between the cup and the lip, and a commercial debtor is so often found solvent one day and bankrupt the next, that good business policy dictates, even though the law does not require, a presentment for payment to the primary debtor upon the day of maturity that the instrument may at once be satisfied and discharged, or, failing this, that prompt legal steps against the debtor and his property may be taken to save the amount to the holder before it is too late.

The non-necessity for presentment legally, even though it may be advisable commercially, is, as we have seen, confined to recourse upon the principal debtor. But where there are parties other than the primary debtor who are contingently liable on the instrument, which is the case in the large majority of negotiable instruments, it is not only to the holder's interest commercially to present the instrument for payment, but it is a necessity, legally, if he would afterwards look for payment to such other parties in the event of default in making payment by the principal debtor. As to this, the concluding sentence of section 130 provides:

"But except as herein otherwise provided, presentment for payment is necessary in order to charge the drawer and indorsers."

The drawer and indorsers are, as a general thing, the parties not primarily but secondarily or contingently liable to pay the instrument, if the principal debtor does not. To charge them, the general rule is, presentment for payment is necessary, and the provisions in Articles VII. and VIII., which we are about to take up, deal with the various details involved in this matter of presentment. There are some instances, of course, where presentment for payment is not necessary to charge a drawer or indorser, and these are covered by the words "except as herein otherwise provided." As we will see by section 139, presentment for payment is not required in order to 'charge the drawer where he has no right to expect or require that the drawee or acceptor will pay the instrument; by section 140 presentment for payment is not required in order to charge an indorser where the instrument was made or accepted for his accommodation, and he has no reason to expect that the instrument will be paid if presented; by section 142 certain cases are stated in which presentment for payment is dispensed with; and by Sec. 322, the rule of presentment for payment, so far as the drawer of a check is concerned, is modified to discharge him only to the extent of the loss caused by delay in non-presentment within a reasonable time after issue. All these exceptional matters will be taken up in regular course; here it is for us simply to observe the broad general rule that, except as otherwise provided, presentment for payment is necessary in order to charge the drawer and indorsers, and to proceed to the following sections of Article VII., which provide the detailed rules governing presentment for payment.

WHERE NOT PAYABLE ON DEMAND.

Section 131. Presentment Where the Instrument is Not Payable on Demand.—Where the instrument is not payable on demand, presentment must be made on the day it falls due. Where it is payable on demand, presentment must be made within a reasonable time after its issue, except that in the case of a bill of exchange presentment for payment will be sufficient if made within a reasonable time after the last negotiation thereof.

The Negotiable Instruments Law has separated negotiable instruments into two classes with reference to their time of payment—those payable on demand and those payable at a fixed or determinable future time (section 20), and has defined the instruments which belong to each class, section 23, providing when an instrument is payable at a determinable future time, and section 26, when payable on demand.

The section which we are now considering, 131, provides the rules governing the time of presentment for payment of instruments belonging to both of these classes. It first provides that "where the instrument is not payable on demand" (in other words, when it is payable at a fixed or determinable future time) "presentment must be made on the day it falls due." In a later section, 145, the time of maturity—i. e., the day the instrument falls due—is regulated by a provision that every negotiable instrument is payable at the time fixed therein without grace, and pointing out the day of maturity, when the time fixed by the instrument falls upon a Sunday or holiday. When we come to that section we will note certain exceptions to the rule that a negotiable instrument is payable without grace—exceptions which have been made in several of the states in the enactment of the Negotiable Instruments Law with reference to a particular kind of instrument.

After providing for presentment for payment where the instrument is not payable on demand, section 131 next provides for such presentment in the case of the remaining broad class of negotiable instruments—those which are payable on demand. Here the provision is that "presentment must be made within a reasonable time after its issue, except that in the case of a bill of exchange presentment for payment will be sufficient if made within a reasonable time after the last negotiation thereof."

Presentment for payment, then (except in the case of a bill of exchange), must be made within a reasonable time after issue. Concerning promissory notes, the rule in New York and some of the other states, prior to this act, was that a note payable on demand was a continuing security, not due until demanded, and on which an indorser remained liable until an actual demand. In this particular the Negotiable Instruments Law changes the common law of such states by the requirement that to charge the indorser presentment for payment must be made within a reasonable time after its issue.

BILLS OF EXCHANGE.

In the case of bills of exchange, however, presentment for payment, which is necessary to charge the drawer and indorsers, will be sufficient if made within a reasonable time after the last negotiation thereof. But this counting of reasonable time from last negotiation, instead of from time of issue, does not apply to checks, although a check is defined to be a "bill of exchange drawn on a bank payable on demand," for there is a special provision (section 322) that "a check must be presented for payment within a reasonable time after its issue or the drawer will be discharged from liability thereon to the extent of the loss caused by the delay." The rule of presentment for payment of checks, therefore, is the same as that provided for negotiable instruments generally—that is, a reasonable time after issue—and if not so presented, the indorsers will be absolutely discharged. But not so the drawer. His case is exceptional. To make him pay the check there must of course be a preliminary presentment for payment at some time, differing in this particular from the primary debtor upon a promissory note, who can be compelled to pay without any presentment, but mere delay in presentment does not ordinarily affect his liability. It is only where he suffers some loss or damage by reason of the delay and the non-presentment within a reasonable time after he has issued his check, as, for example, where the bank fails, and then he is discharged from liability only to the extent of the loss. To illustrate: A may issue his check to B, who holds it for two years without presentment at the bank. Then the bank fails before presentment and pays A 50 cents on the dollar of his money on deposit. To the extent of 50 per cent A is discharged from liability to B on the check; for the other 50 per cent B can hold him liable. If the bank should close up and pay A 100 cents on the dollar of his deposit, then there would be no loss or damage to A by reason of the delay in presenting the check, and he would have to pay the full amount. If, on the other hand, there should be a total failure of the bank in which A had his funds to meet the check, then he would be absolutely discharged.

We have now viewed the rule of presentment for payment to charge drawer and indorsers where the instrument is payable on demand, seeing the requirement is "within a reasonable time," either after issue or last negotiation, as the case may be. But the commercial holder of a negotiable instrument may be often puzzled to know what is a "reasonable time" within which presentment must be made in order to save his right of recourse, if need be, upon indorsers and drawer. This is a question upon which courts have differed widely, as special circumstances in the cases before them have led to the declaration of a longer or a shorter period of time being either within or without the limit; and the only rule upon which the courts have agreed is that, what is a reasonable time depends upon the facts and circumstances of each particular case. To remedy this uncertainty the legislatures in several states passed laws fixing a definite period for the presentment of demand notes, presentment within that period being within a reasonable time; after that period not. In Connecticut and Minnesota, for example, a four-months' period was fixed in Massachusetts and Vermont, sixty days. The Negotiable Instruments Law, however, adopts the old, uncertain and unsatisfactory "reasonable time" rule of the common law, and makes it supplant the fixed statutory period in those states which had established such periods, wherein the Negotiable Instruments Law has since been enacted. We are unable to see any merit in a rule of maturity of this character in a system of negotiable instruments wherein certainty is the chief desideratum, and think that a sixty-day or four-months' period, running from issue or negotiation, as the case may be, at the end of which time demand paper would be overdue and non-presentment within that period result in discharge of the parties secondarily liable, would be far more satisfactory and preferable.

Business Subjects in Current Literature

Although midsummer is close upon us, the magazine writers still continue to turn out in vast variety their grist of articles upon subjects pertaining to business. It used to be the fashion to make a midsummer magazine up out of lighter material, short stories, verse and general so-called light reading, but the magazines of today, with their special articles are as solid and meaty as are those of midwinter. There is no reason why this should not be the case, because, although business men go upon vacations, nevertheless it is a fact that the time given to these vacations is, in many cases, the only time that the hurried business man has in which to do much magazine reading.

COMMERCE, ACCOUNTS & FINANCE gives its usual partial list of articles on business subjects appearing in the magazines published in this country and abroad.

GENERAL BUSINESS SUBJECTS.

"Our Trade with Cuba" is discussed by C. R. Edwards in Annals of the American Academy of Polytechnic and Social

Science. F. B. Sanborn, in the Bookman, writes of "Boston Newspapers." A. Jamieson, in Chambers' Journal, published in Edinburgh, presents "Coal Resources and Coal Getting." In the Contemporary Review, of London, W. F. Ford discusses that topic of vital interest to both England and America, "The Commercial Invasion of Europe by America." In the Forum, H. O. Dwight writes of "Constantinople Book Shops." In the Architectural Record, "Modern Art and Jewelry" is written about by J. Schoffer. G. W. Osborn, in the World's Work, attempts to explain "Why the Price of Beef is High," and in the Cosmopolitan "Modern Bread Making" is described by H. S. Archer.

The third in a series of articles on the "Factory Office as a Productive Department," by K. Falconer, appears in the Engineering Magazine. "Duck Raising for Profit" is the odd title of an article by Frances Ellen Wheeler in Country Life in America. In the Anglo-American Magazine, T. Barth writes of "Germany and Her Commercial Treaties." In Gunton's Magazine, W. G. Irwin writes of the "Development of the Coal Industry." "The National Debt of Germany" is discussed by A. Wagner in the North American Review, and in the Fortnightly Review, of London, W. Bleloch writes of the "Fiscal Policy Regarding the Transvaal Mines." In the Fortnightly Review also appears a paper by P. Salmon on "The Business of Empire." In the Atlantic Monthly B. Fisher tells of the "Newspaper Industry." In the North American Review, L. A. Jones writes of "Land Title Registration in the United States."

An article on "Handling Ore in Blast Furnaces," by W. M. Cowles, appears in Cassier's Magazine. In the Methodist Review, Mrs. J. D. Drummond writes of "Southern Factory Problems." In Chambers' Journal, A. Jamieson has an article on "Aluminum." In the Engineering Magazine, W. M. McFarland writes on "Economy in Marine Engineering." "Our Trade with Porto Rico" is the subject discussed by O. P. Austen in Annals of the Academy of Polytechnic and Social Science. A French writer, L. Houllevigne, writes of the "Transport and Distribution of Energy" for the Revue Politique et Parlementaire of Paris. "The Triumph of American Bridge Building" is the title of a very interesting article by F. W. Skinner in the Century.

In the Missionary Review, of New York, there is an article on a business now, thank goodness, but little practiced, namely, "The Slave Trade in Hausaland;" the author is T. J. Tomkin. In the Forum, O. P. Austin writes of "Our Growing Dependence Upon the Tropics," and in Out West H. G. Maxwell has an article "On the Problems of Irrigation." In the Fortnightly Review, G. Marconi writes of the "Practicability of Wireless Telegraphy," and in the Monthly Review, another English Magazine, J. B. C. Kershaw discusses "The Promotion of Trade Within the Empire." In the North American Review, L. Springfield tells us of the "Tobacco War in Great Britain."

In the National Geographic Magazine are papers and articles on the "Coal Resources of Alaska." In Cassier's Magazine, H. Mason writes of "Heat, Light and Power from Alcohol."

An important article in the North American Review by J. D. Whelpkey is "England's American Food Supply." In Cassier's Magazine, H. Leffman writes interestingly concerning "Ancient Metallurgy." In Lippincott's, J. G. Speeds writes of "Tips and Commissions." In Brush and Pencil, of Chicago, "The Making of a Picture" is described by H. E. R. Fyffe, and the "Buying of Pictures" is the subject of an article by H. Quilter in Chambers' Journal.

In Gunton's Magazine, G. Gunton writes of the "Protective Tariff and the Warning from the Census." If thievery is a branch of business, then C. H. Deemis has a business article in Everybody's Magazine entitled "Science and Burglary."

"At the Trader's Station in Samoa" is the subject of L. P. Churchill's sketch in Lippincott's. In the North American Review, H. A. Castle presents "Defects and Abuses in Our Postal System." In Cassier's Magazine, F. A. Scheffler writes interestingly of "A Relic of Traction Engine History." In Harper's Magazine, R. T. Ely describes "An American Industrial Experiment at Pelzer, S. C." In the Art Journal, of London, "Coronation Weaving" is described by R. E. D. Sketchley.

In the North American Review, A. S. Dumont, the celebrated æronaut, writes upon "Air Ships and Flying Machines." In the Spanish journal, Espana Maderna of Madrid, J. P. de Gusman writes of the "Pan-American Congress in Mexico."

AGRICULTURE AND FARMING.

There are a few good articles on scientific farming in the magazines. "The Hills and Farms of Butte County, California," are described by Caroline M. Olney in the Overland Monthly. W. S. Harwood writes of "Agricultural Government Station Work" for Scribner's. "The Growing of Plants" is the title of an article in Country Life in America, and E. P. Lyle presents "Plant Growing in a Dutch Garden" in Everybody's. "Sugar and the Sugar Beet" are described by J. Waddell in the Popular Science Monthly.

GREAT MEN OF AFFAIRS.

Papers on great men who have succeeded in life are always interesting, and there are several of note in the current magazines.

F. H. Grooks, in World's Work, writes interestingly of Frank Vanderlip, ex-Assistant Secretary of the Treasury. In the Cosmopolitan, J. Ralph has an especially well written article on J. D. Rockefeller.

TRANSPORTATION.

Transportation by land and water and kindred subjects have more than their usual share in the magazines of the current month. A. Goodrich, in the World's Work, writes on the "Future of American Shipping." In the New England Magazine, R. Bergengren presents "Steel Ship Building in Massachusetts." "Motor Boats" is the title of an article by E. W. Roberts in the Emergency Magazine, and the same writer in the same publication describes "Motive Power of the Motor Launch." In the National Review, of London, E. R. Fremantle has an article on the "Outlook for the Merchant Marine," and in the Nineteenth Century, of London, R. E. Childers writes of the "Navigation Laws." In the Emergency Magazine, E. Bigwani has an article on "A Funicular Electrical Railroad." S. J. McLean, in the Forum, writes of "Railroad Rates and Regulations in Canada."

LABOR AND STRIKES.

In the North American Review, C. P. Wright has an article on "Strikes in the United States," and in the Fortnightly Review, of London, A. Miller writes of the "Labor Problem." In Reforme Sociale, of Paris, there is an article by L. Vanlaer on "Workman's Assurance," and in the same publication appears a paper upon the "Co-operative Movement in Denmark." In this publication, also, Dr. Haillot presents an article on "Labor Syndicates."

BANKING AND FINANCIAL SUBJECTS.

Banking and financial subjects are of more or less interest this month. In the Bankers' Magazine are a variety of papers. The following are some of the titles, with the names of their authors: "The Prevention of Bank Panics," by Mr. Newfang; "Notes on Foreign Exchange," by W. Graham; a paper on "The Bank Auditor" by J. C. Martine, and one on "City and Country Bookkeeping for Banks" by an anonymous author. In the same magazine also appears a well written article on "Bank Bookkeeping" by W. L. Day. The World's Work contains a paper on the "Bowery Savings Bank" by E. Lowry, and one on "The Consolidation of Banks," author's name not given.

In the Review of Reviews, of Melbourne, Australia, appears a paper upon the "Decimal System of Coinage Proposed for Australia," by R. T. Barlow. In the Westminster Review, of London, is an unsigned article on "Tory Finance Exposed."

PHOTOGRAPHY.

Among the articles appearing in Wilson's Photographic Magazine are the following: "Copying Prints," author's name not given; "Photography by Measure," by C. Jones, and "Exposure," by A. Watkins. In Camera and Dark Room, C. E. Fairman presents a paper on the "Manufacture of Dry Plates," and in the same publication appears "Platinum Printing," by W. J. Cotterell, and "Artistic Landscape Photography," by F. Voiter.

In the Photographic Times, C. H. Bothamay presents "New Methods of Intensification." E. F. Brun has a paper on "Theater Photography." In this magazine also are the following articles: "Masking Methods for Improving Prints," by P. Mathy, and "Selection of Subjects for Exposure," by W. Sprange.

ARCHITECTURE AND BUILDING.

In the Architectural Record is a very well written paper by G. Grohly on "Rich Men and Their Houses." In the Ladies' Home Journal an unsigned article appears, entitled "Country Homes from $500 to $600." In Country Life in America, B. Fleming presents his third paper in the series on the "Making of a Country Home." In the Architectural Record, F. Maade writes of "Art Noiveau," and in the same publication C. de Kay presents "A Villa in Capri."

TRUSTS AND CAPITAL.

There are several papers on the shipping combine in the publications of England. E. Robertson, in the Nineteenth Century, writes of the "Shipping Combine and the British Flag." In the Fortnightly Review is an unsigned paper on the "Ocean Trust and the British Policy." In the Monthly Review is an anonymous article entitled "The Profit and Loss of the Atlantic Shipping Deal." H. Michelson, in the North American Review, has a very well written article on "How to Curb the Trusts."

WOMAN.

There are but two articles on the woman in business in the magazines for the past month. One is by E. Flower, and appears in the Arena. It is entitled "Women in Business Positions." The other appears in Ainslee's Magazine and is by Lillian C. Paschell. The name of the article is "The Girl of the Future."

This partial list covers more or less completely the subject of business literature as it appears in the current magazines.

THE TALE OF THE HIRELING WHO DESIRED INDEPENDENCE

By Joe Lincoln

And it was the one thousandth and third night, and Scheherezade laid aside her chewing gum and spake unto the Father of the Faithful, saying:—

"Oh, thou who art the Whole and Real Thing, list to the recital of thy handmaiden.

"Behold, upon a time there lived a young man named Mustapha, who labored in the shop of a merchant. And the business done by the merchant was of a goodly size, so that the profits thereof might be discerned even with the naked eye, and because of these profits, upon the coming of every seventh day did the ghost up upon its rounds with a satisfactory promptness, and the youth received for his labors divers pieces of silver.

"And the duties performed by Mustapha were light, so that the greater part thereof was the holding down of the chair and the watching of the office clock, and the payment therefor was in proportion heavy. And his friends came unto Mustapha and said unto him:—

" 'Behold, Musty, old hoss, thou possesseth the good thing and revelleth in the soft snap. It behooveth thee to hang on to the same with the clutch like unto that of the Dread Destroyer upon the defunct Ethiopian.'

"But Mustapha heeded not these sayings, and bewailed his lot, saying:—

" 'Tell me, I pray thee, what am I, that am free born and of man's estate? Am I not even as the slave that men call Dago, that worketh upon the railroad? When the dial showeth the hour of nine do I not enter the door, and do I not remain within until it striketh five, always excepting the paltry hour or so that is given unto me for the partaking of my noon meat?

" 'When the old man saith "Go," do I not go? And when he saith "Come," do I not come, and that on the jump? When he maketh the goodly dicker and amasseth the extra profit doth he bestow a share upon me? Nay, rather doth he not pay me the same stipend yesterday, today and forever? Let me go forth and set up for myself, that I may be independent and hold up my head among men.'

"And he spake his thoughts unto the porter, even he that swept out the shop. And the porter, who had seen better days and was of the Tribe of the Has-Been, advised him, saying:—

" 'Verily, my son, be not too hasty. Cleave to that which is fair to middling and hanker not to become a Rockefeller the first crack out of the box. By the beard of the Prophet there are worse plagues in life than pay day, and rent day without pay day is one of them. I, myself, was independent once.'

"But the youth heeded not the sayings of the porter, but laid aside certain portions of his stipend, hoping thereby in time to amass a store of coin and open a shop of his own. And the porter noted these things, and, laying his finger upon his nose, closed his other eye with exceeding sadness.

"And the suns shone and the moons came and went and Mustapha added to his store of coin. And his longing for independence increased. And one day he sought the merchant and said unto him:—

" 'Take heed, oh tyrant, I, that was thy slave, am so no longer. I go to trade beneath my own emblem and to run thee out of business.'

"And the merchant said unto him: 'Go and be eternally condemned!'

"And Mustapha went.

"And he opened a shop upon the street that is called Straight, where the traders thereupon are called crooked. And the sign above his door was six cubits long, and was one of the sights of the city, like unto the Obelisk and the island that is called Coney. And he filled the shop with goods and sat him down to await custom.

"But behold, it came to pass that custom came not, and the only callers were the landlord and those seeking payment. And his store of coin became small, and he lay awake and worried, and when he returned home at night, taking the back streets to avoid creditors, the wife of his bosom waxed sarcastic because of the scarcity of shekels. And he became gray even as the aged rodent.

"And behold, he made an assignment, and his lawyer bade his creditors be of good cheer, for that of every shekel owed to them by Mustapha they were to receive one twentieth thereof when the estate was settled. And the creditors waxed wroth and blasphemed hugely.

"And it came to pass that Mustapha sat alone in his shop amidst his bills. And behold the aged porter came unto him and said:—

" 'Verily, oh friend of my bosom, did I not caution thee? Why didst thou throw up thy goodly and easy job?'

"And Mustapha answered and said unto him, 'Because that I desired independence.'

"And the porter spake again, saying: 'Well, thou hast it.'

"And Mustapha sighed and answered him yet again, saying: 'That's what.' "

And Scheherezade paused and said unto the Sultan:—

"Oh, King, live forever! Behold, again the end of the tale is a question. Is it better to be rich and a menial or poor and independent?"

And the King communed with himself for a space, and then answered her saying:—

"Surely independence is good, but it taketh money to pay the gas bill."

And he departed, seeking the trolley that beareth the populace to the baseball game.

Credit Viewpoints

By THOS. B. HOPKINS

Certain amiable people of both sexes are endeavoring with commendable energy to secure uniformity and universality in credit reporting. If credit could be based solely upon statements of assets and liabilities, and if all assets and liabilities were of the same value to all people, it might be possible to bring about something in the way of the millenium so fondly dreamed, but unfortunately foi the dreamers bases of credit must be judged largely from individual viewpoints.

The first essential of credit is honesty, and in the absence of established guilt in specific cases dishonesty is a matter of suspicion rather than conviction. Suspicion of dishonesty is something which any credit man may personally take into consideration, but it is something which for obvious reasons cannot be reported to others. Thus the most important factor in credit cannot be made common property.

BUSINESS ABILITY.

The second essential of credit is business ability. Until the success of any enterprise is fully achieved or until its failure has been demonstrated by experience this is also largely a matter of opinion. Certainly no conscientious credit man would care to place himself on record as prophesying the failure of any business concern on account of bad management until something had happened to demonstrate beyond the power of argument that such failure was inevitable. When such an unfortunate state of affairs had been actually brought about such a thing as credit would be out of the question, and credit reporting would of course be useless. On the other hand any credit man would be justified in declining credit where he suspected bad management, but he would not consider himself justified in putting such suspicions in the shape of a formal report. It will therefore be seen that the second essential of credit cannot be made common property.

It is easy for the credit man to deal with concerns possessing abundant tangible assets or to deal with concerns with no assets. Where the ability and value of the credit man comes in is in dealing with cases where there are some elements of doubt. Knowledge of human nature, intuition, and in many cases personal influence upon the business policy of the customer concerned, are part of the capital of the credit man. Such circumstances, however, are not proper subjects for anything like a clearing house of credit information.

TAKING CHANCES.

There are other ways in which any basis of credit must depend upon the viewpoint of the individual or institution directly interested in giving or withholding the same. Manufacturers of articles in which there is a margin of 50 or 75 per cent between manufacturing cost and selling price can afford to take greater chances than can dealers in money. Manufacturers of exclusive articles can also safely give credit under some arbitrary arrangement to secure prompt pay or cut off the suppiy of goods. Manufacturers possessing this source of strength, however, generally exercise such strength to the extent of requiring cash in doubtful cases rather than extending any credit at all.

It is also sometimes advantageous to give credit to dealers of more or less doubtful character for the sake of introducing goods in new territory. Where it is impossible to sell competitive articles to the best dealers in any city or town it is sometimes considered wise to establish business relationship with dealers less entitled to credit on general principles. Such cases must, of course, be decided according to the individual viewpoint of those most interested, and certainly it could scarcely be expected that information in regard to such dealings would be made common property.

Is it not therefore logical to conclude that there can be no universal or general basis of credit beyond the usual statement of assets and liabilties? Is it not true that in all doubtful cases the wisdom or lack of wisdom in giving credit depends upon individual circumstances? Furthermore, as doubtful cases must be decided not so much upon known facts as upon personal opinions and suspicions which cannot be made common property, what is there left to report that is worth reporting?

PUZZLES FOR OFFICE MEN

Twenty Dollars in Prizes

We publish in this issue of COMMERCE, ACCOUNTS & FINANCE the third and final series of the puzzles for office men, which have been so successful. This final series is as simple and yet as puzzling as have been those preceding it. To us, who know the solutions of the puzzles, there seems to be no reason why every reader of COMMERCE, ACCOUNTS & FINANCE should not solve them, but, no doubt, to many of those to whom the puzzles come unsolved, they seem to be rather difficult propositions.

The subjects in this final series are, of course, four in

FIG. 1.

FIG. 2.

number. That in Fig. 1 is a pun upon a process known to every bookkeeper who has anything to do with a ledger. Fig. 2, Fig. 3 and Fig. 4 picture articles used in every office.

For the benefit of our new subscribers, who may not have seen the preceding issues, we print again the conditions of the puzzle contest.

Each contestant is required first, to correctly solve each of the four puzzles; then he is required to write an essay,

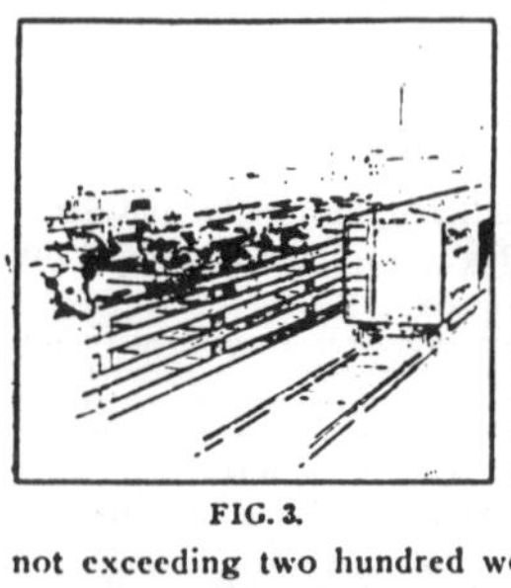

FIG. 3.

FIG. 4.

not exceeding two hundred words in length, upon the subject presented by each puzzle, that is to say, he must write four essays in all.

For the best set of essays a prize of ten dollars ($10) cash will be given. For the five next best sets yearly subscriptions will be given to The Bulletin, a semi-monthly magazine of the same size and general make-up of COMMERCE, ACCOUNTS & FINANCE, but devoted to the art and practice of banking. To any young man contemplating entering upon a business career The Bulletin is invaluable, being neither too technical or too profound, but catering to the bank clerk rather than to the bank official. The regular subscription price of The Bulletin is $2 a year.

Each competitor in these contests will be required to enclose 25 cents for a three months' trial subscription to COMMERCE, ACCOUNTS & FINANCE. If the contestant is already a subscriber, this subscription will be sent to any nonsubscriber named by him

Current Business Cartoons

England has been greatly stirred up about the combination of the Atlantic steamship lines, which combine was engineered by the indefatigable J. Pierpont Morgan. The

The latest American Do(d)ge weds the Atlantic with a "ring."—Punch.

British publishers have seen, or have pretended to see, the absorption of British shipping interests by the Americans, and their papers have been filled with articles and cartoons upon the subject. We reproduce two of these English car-

John Bull (humming drowsily)—"Rule, Britannia; Britannia,. ru"—. Father Neptune—"Wake up, John; wake up!"—Judy.

toons as being, perhaps, the best of those that have come to our notice. One of the cartoons is from Punch, and was drawn by Bernard Partridge, the celebrated artist. It is extremely well drawn, being in artistic merit far beyond the usual drawing of this kind. It is a caricature of the old Venetian ceremony, "The Marriage of the Adriatic." When Venice was a mighty sea power, one of the most imposing ceremonies, and one held each year, was the wedding of Venice to the Adriatic Sea by the Doge, who stood in the

He seems to prefer the Panama.—Minneapolis Journal.

stern of a ceremonial barge and tossed a ring into the water. In the cartoon, Uncle Sam, dressed in elaborate ceremonial robes, standing in the stern of a vessel bearing the American Eagle and a shield with the Stars and Stripes, is tossing a huge ring labelled "Shipping Combine" into the Atlantic ocean. It is a clever idea well carried out.

In the other English cartoon from Punch's mate—Judy—John Bull is shown asleep in a little boat, humming drowsily

Stingy Steve—"Not now, my lad; you must wait until he gets through."—Chicago News.

about Britannia's "ruling the wave." Father Neptune, appearing at the side of the boat, warns him to look out for a great steamer, Starred and Striped, typifying the American shipping interests. It is a little too late for John Bull to wake up, for America is already in the lead and will soon be the real ruler of the wave.

The artist of the Minneapolis Journal has used the prevailing craze for the Panama hat to advantage in his cartoon on the canal question in the Senate. At the time the cartoon was printed the Senate had just passed the bill giving President Roosevelt power to select the Panama route

The Hymn Universal.—N. Y. Tribune.

for the Isthmian canal. The bill has since been approved by the House, and the President has signed it. The cartoon explains itself.

Cuba, owing to opposition in the Senate, which opposition was led by Senator Elkins, must do without its tariff reduction, for this session at least. In the cartoon from the Chicago News, the sugar interest is typified by a huge hog which Senator Elkins is feeding. No doubt the question of tariff reduction for Cuba will be taken up with renewed energy in the fall.

The coal strike continues to furnish material for the newspaper artists, and in the cartoon from the Boston Herald the striking miners are typified by a masked figure with a shotgun, who, in firing at the homes of the non-union miners, has injured a woman. This woman represents the strikers' own cause. Of course, the idea is that violence

Only Injures His Own.—Boston Herald.

on the part of the strikers injures themselves much more than it does the operators.

Richards, in the New York Herald, has one of his well-drawn cartoons on the strike question. The miner in the rear is pushing forward the operator, who in turn pushes the dealer, who pushes the consumer, who pushes the wolf of starvation. Directly in front of the wolf are the women and children of the people at large. This cartoon emphasizes the fact that it is the women and children who suffer in strike times.

England, decked in flags and bunting, was awaiting the coronation with joyous expectation. With the suddenness of a flash of lightning came the news of the sudden and critical illness of King Edward. The whole world sympa-

The Real Sufferers.—N. Y. Herald.

thized with England, and in a cartoon which we reproduce from the New York Tribune, this idea was prettily expressed. "God Save the King," was in all hearts when the sad news was made public.

GREAT DISASTERS OF HISTORY

The interest aroused throughout Christendom by the terrible disaster in Martinique may make the following list of historical catastrophes interesting to BULLETIN readers. The list was originally published in World's Events:—

A. D. 63. Earthquake partially destroyed the cities of Pompeii and Herculaneum, killing legions.

A. D. 79. Eruption of volcano of Vesuvius, totally destroying the cities of Pompeii and Herculaneum, killing the entire population.

A. D. 526. Earthquake at Antioch, 250,000 killed.

1531. Earthquake at Lisbon, 30,000 killed, 1,500 houses destroyed.

1703. Yeddo, Japan, earthquake, 19,000 killed.

1716. Algiers, earthquake, 18,000 killed.

1731. Pekin, earthquake, 95,000 killed.

1731. Canton, earthquake, 100,000 killed.

1746. Lima, earthquake, 18,000 killed.

1754. Cairo, earthquake, 40,000 killed.

1755. Lisbon, earthquake, 50,000 killed in five minutes. Most of city destroyed.

1773. Guatemala, earthquake, 33,000 killed.

1783. Calabria, earthquake, 100,000 killed.

1797. Quito, earthquake, 41,000 killed.

1812. Caracas, earthquake, thousands killed.

1822. Alepho, earthquake, 22,000 killed.

1861. Mendoza, South America, earthquake, 12,000 killed.

1883. Krakatoa, volcanic eruption, 36,000 killed.

1883. Isle of Ischia, earthquake, 2,000 killed.

1888. Island of Mondo, Japan, earthquake, extent of casualties not yet known.

1902, May 8. Island of Martinique, volcanic eruption, 40,000 killed; entire city of St. Pierre destroyed, as well as many surrounding villages.

1902, May 9. Island of St. Vincent, volcanic eruption, La Soufriere casualties about 1,600.

ANCIENT ADVANTAGES

"That mediaeval armor must have been very uncomfortable," said a visitor at the museum.

"Yes," answered the man with darned clothes; "but there was one satisfaction about it. A man could always take down a suit of it in entire confidence that the moths hadn't got into it."—Washington Star.

ENGLISH AS SHE IS

"Why do you English people insist on calling an elevator a 'lift' and a pie a 'tart,'?" inquired the young woman.

"Really," answered the young man who came over to get married, "I can't say. I was about to ask you why so many people here call a lift an 'elevator' and a tart a 'pie.'"—Washington Star.

Something New in Typewriters

Solomon said, "Of making books there is no end." We of this latter day might say with equal truth, "Of making typewriters there is no end." There are typewriters galore, and they are of many names and of many shapes, but the same general principles underlie the great majority of them. In fact, so true is this statement that many of the more prominent varieties of typewriters are fitted with the same sort of keyboard.

FIG. 1. THE LAMBERT TYPEWRITER.

But it is only occasionally that something really new in the typewriting line is invented, and when it is invented it becomes at once an object of interest to business men and women. The Lambert Typewriting Co. seems to have invented something new and radically different in the way of a typewriting machine. The company manufactures the Lambert typewriter, and the Lambert typewriter is unlike any other typewriter on the face of the earth.

To begin with, this typewriter is small and compact. It is also said to be extremely simple in construction. Its general appearance is shown in Fig. 1, and by studying this illustration the reader will readily see how greatly this typewriter differs from all other machines. The keyboard shown in Fig. 2 is arranged in a circle. The spacer is the milled wheel in the center. The shift lever is the lever projecting at the side of the keyboard. The writer uses both hands, working the shift lever back and forth with the second finger of the left hand, and writing with the first and second fingers of that hand and the first, second and third fingers of the right hand. The keyboard being compact, the writing is said to be very easy and rapid. Pulling the shift lever downward to the position shown by the lower dotted line in Fig. 2 brings the small letters into writing position. The lever at the center means that the capitals will be printed, and pushing it upward into the position shown by the upper dotted line brings the type into place for punctuating. It is said by the makers of this machine that this working of the shift lever after practice becomes automatic, and mistakes are very infrequent.

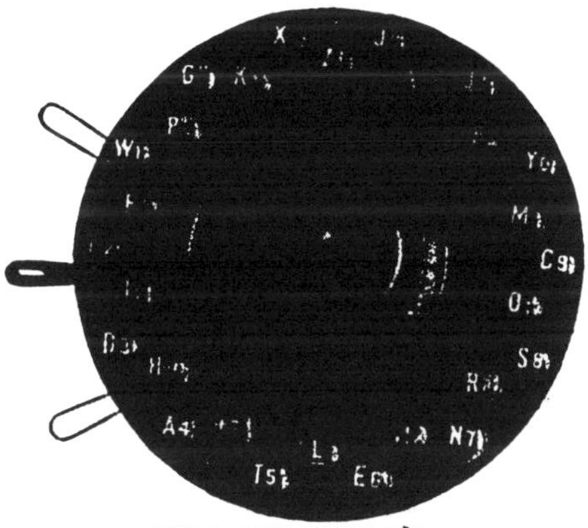

FIG. 2. THE KEYBOARD.

The writing mechanism of the Lambert typewriter is radically different from that of any other typewriting machine. To begin with, no ribbon is used, and writing is done by tilting the keyboard. From the interesting catalogue and instruction book we quote the following, as it describes better than we can the working mechanism of this machine:

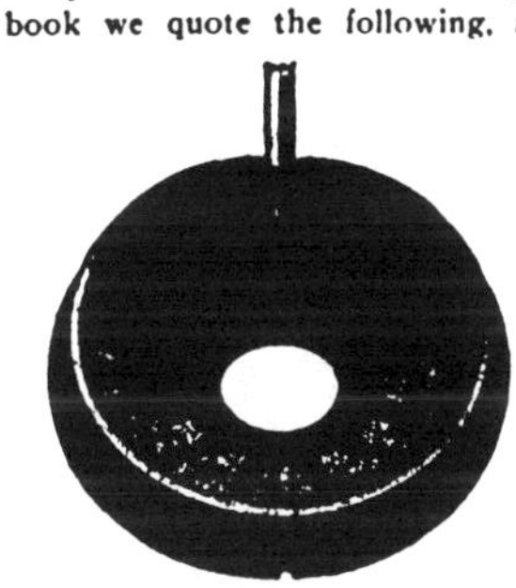

FIG. 3. TYPE-RING RIGHT SIDE UP.

The keyboard and type-ring one.—They are made one piece by the leg which connects them; they move as one. When you tilt the keyboard by pressing a letter, you bring that type in position to print. You must know the mechanical means by which this is done.

The keyboard is hung on a ball at its center. This plate has the function of as many different levers as there are distinct "positions" on it to touch. If the letters were on the flat plate, the positions so near together would not be distinct; they are made distinct by the knobs in this way: When you touch a letter you touch the top of the knob. Your touch is not exact, but the knob receives it on top. The effect is the same as if your touch were exact.

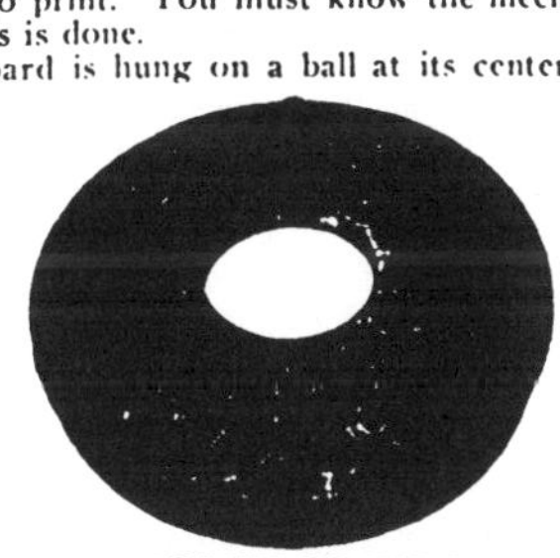

FIG. 4. TYPE-RING WRONG SIDE UP.

Again, the fulcrum is where the opposite side of the keyboard rises against the spacer. This also would be an uncertain position without some device to make it exact. The device is an alternation of hills and hollows all round the circle of contact between the keyboard and spacer. Opposite every knob is a hollow; the fulcrum is, therefore, the hills on both sides of that hollow.

These two devices together—the knobs to make a quick touch exact and two hills for the fulcrum—bring the type to exact alignment, although your touch is only somewhere near the right position.

The Type-Stop.—But the angle, at which you tilt, is not all; the tilting must stop at the right place. Inside the type-ring are three circles, like seats round the ring at a circus; and in the center of these three circles a cone, point down. This cone is the type-stop.

When you touch a letter and tilt the keyboard, that side of the type-ring is brought to the cone; and the cone takes one of the three seats directly under the letter you touch and

FIG. 5. TYPE SHIFT-LEVER.

over the type that prints it. The seat receives the cone, and the tilting stops with the type in exact position to print. These seats are in zigzag circles—three zigzag circles.

The type-ring shown in Fig. 3 and Fig. 4 has 84 types on the under face of it—26 capitals, 26 small letters, 10 figures and 22 points and symbols—arranged in three concentric zigzag circles. There is a type for every seat, and it is directly under the seat.

The inside zigzag circle is small letters; the middle zigzag circle is capitals; the outside zigzag circle is figures and points and symbols, with four exceptions.

So, with the least degree of tilt, you print the small letters; with the middle degree of tilt you print the capitals, and with the most degree of tilt you print the figures and points and symbols, with those four exceptions.

The type-shift lever, shown on Fig. 5, projecting leftward from under the keyboard, has on it a cam which raises and lowers the stop to the level of the seat that belongs to the type to print next.

We have said that no ribbon is used with this typewriter. Instead of a ribbon, an ink pad is used, and this ink pad can be re-inked, it is claimed, very easily by the use of a small brush. It is also claimed that this machine can be easily cleaned and oiled, that it will write as rapidly if not more rapidly than the ordinary typewriter, and that for clearness it is not equalled. Some of its fancy "stunts" are performed by turning the keyboard one way or another so that the letters can be made to run forward or back, thus making italics. By moving the milled-head lever to position straight back, after writing a line, and then re-writing the line, an outline letter is formed very ornamental and useful for titles and the like. Fancy borders, it is said, are easy to make when one understands this moving of the keyboard and the catalogue shows some very handsome combinations.

We think we have said enough to interest our readers in this odd and ingenious little machine. To those who are more interested we should recommend a call at the company's offices No. 1274 Broadway, and 86 La Salle street, Chicago, Ill. To those who cannot conveniently call, a catalogue will be sent upon receipt of postage.

DISTRIBUTION OF A BANK'S WORKING FORCE

The Bulletin of the American Institute of Bank Clerks has just issued one of the most interesting and unique publications ever put forth. It is a new departure in banking literature, as, in fact, is also the Bulletin. The Bulletin itself, as most of our readers know, is the organ of the American Institute of Bank Clerks, and this new publication is a premium for new subscribers; it is also on sale to the general public. It is a booklet tastily and neatly bound and printed, and is entitled "Charts of Bank Organization and Administration." It contains two pages of explanatory matter and seven charts showing the distribution of the working forces of the largest banks in this country. Besides showing the distribution of the forces, it is possible also, by the study of these charts, to follow the course of a note or any other paper through the bank, ascertaining which clerks handle it in turn and what finally becomes of it.

Let us take, for instance, Chart A. It is the chart of the First National Bank of Chicago. This bank employs nearly five hundred officers and clerks, and the duties of each of the officers and clerks is set forth in this chart, beginning with those of the president and ending with those of the office boys and the sealers and stampers of envelopes. To bankers outside of the great cities, to those about to organize a bank, to the bank clerk who is ambitious and who desires to know how the business is conducted in the great institutions, these charts must be invaluable. Certainly we have seen nothing in banking literature that seems to us to approach them for practical educational purposes.

To show how the course of each item placed in the bank for credit may be traced on the chart, we quote the following from the explanatory matter in the book:—

"We will suppose the city customer deposits $2,000, made up as follows: $1,000 in cash, a $600 check on one of our city accounts, and $400 check on New York. By referring to the receiving teller's department (7) we find that the credit ticket for $2,000 would go to the sorter in No. 4, to be sorted to the proper bookkeeper, and the figures $2,000 would be turned in at night to the general bookkeeper and entered by him under teller's city credits (12 C 1). On the other side we find the $600 item in one of our city accounts would go to the same department (12 A 1), the $400 item on New York would go to the general bookkeeping department (12) and the total would appear under New York (12 X 1). The $1,000 of cash would be the balance, and would be entered on the general proof under the head of 12 B 1. As the tellers all turn their cash into the paying teller, this amount would also appear in the ticket of the assistant paying teller (6) on the credit side (12 B 1), and would be used in this connection merely for proof."

The directions for following the course of an item from an out-of-town correspondent are similarly given. The Bulletin of the American Institute of Bank Clerks is to be congratulated upon having obtained, from sources to which it alone is accessible, the information set forth in these charts.

THE CONTRACTOR IN RUSSIA

A Russian correspondent sends us an amusing tale about an American contractor in Russia, says Commercial Intelligence. A few years ago the contractor in question cast eyes upon a certain contract on the Nikolaevsky Railway. Not being able to obtain it by fair means, he went on a beautiful cloudless day to the personage who had control of the contract, taking with him a huge umbrella. In reply to the personage's remark that there was no danger of rain, the Yankee contractor offered to bet 100,000 roubles that it would be pouring within half an hour. The offer was accepted. At the end of the half hour the sky was till cloudless, the sun was shining even more beautifully. The contractor therefore lost his bet—but he got the contract. Our correspondent adds that personally speaking he believes that the thing is usually done in a much simpler manner. Of course, such things are happily confined to Russia. It is a backward country.

NO MONETARY VALUE

"Remember," said the impressive person, "that your ancestors have left you an honorable name."

"Well," answered the titled youth ruefully, "it is all right on a visiting card; but it isn't much at a bank."

BRIEF MENTION

TWO OF THE NEATEST little booklets of their kind that we have seen for some time are those advertising the Bank of New York, doing business at 48 Wall street, New York City. One of these booklets is entitled "Early Days of the Bank of New York," and is an extremely well-written little historical sketch of this the second oldest banking institution in this country. The Bank of New York was, as most of our readers know, founded by Alexander Hamilton, and in this little booklet banking in the days just after the Revolution is described entertainingly and well. The names of the directors present at the first meeting of the bank are, many of them, well known today as names of patriotic and prominent citizens, whose descendants have obtained high places in the nation's administrative and financial circles. Among these names are those of Roosevelt, Low, Franklin, Verplanck, Seton and Cruger. The other booklet issued by this institution is entitled "Bank of New York National Banking Association." It also is a historical sketch, illustrated and very entertainingly written. In the back of the book is an article describing the bank and its branches as they now exist.

THE PAPERS OF LATE have contained many little items and editorial comments concerning the evils connected with the handling of tattered and dirty bank bills. In fact, so much attention has been given to the subject that many persons object strenuously to the idea of carrying about this sort of money and insist upon having clean and new bills given them at their banker's. The Real Estate Trust Company, of New York, whose banking rooms are at 30 Nassau street, have anticipated demands of this kind by sending out cards upon which the following notice is printed: "We would remind our depositors that we carry sufficient new money to cash counter checks." This is an innovation that will be appreciated by depositors of the Real Estate Trust Company, and will undoubtedly attract new business. The enterprise of this company is still further shown by another notice of this kind to the effect that the company is now prepared to return pass-books, written up and balanced to date, within twenty-four hours, or the same day if necessary. These evidences of enterprise should make good advertising for the Real Estate Trust Company.

FRANK C. CLARK, of New York, has issued a comprehensive little booklet describing his tours to the Mediterranean and the Orient. It contains a number of quaint pictures of scenes in the Far East which appeal particularly to people who desire to see the byways of the world.

ALBAUGH BROS., of Chicago, are advertising a clever automatic burglar alarm. Its mechanism is simple and seemingly effective, and it is claimed that it never fails to give an alarm the moment any door or window to which it is attached is moved in the slightest way. It is intended to serve as a bar to doors and windows, as well as an alarm, and appears simple and logical. No electricity is required, and the attractive little device may be carried in the pocket.

THE ERIE RAILROAD has created an industrial department which has been placed in charge of R. M. Parker, the Assistant General Freight Agent at New York. The object of the new department is to give all possible encouragement to manufacturers who may desire to locate anywhere along the lines of the Erie. The fact that this railroad taps the anthracite and bituminous coal fields of Pennsylvania and reaches harbors at New York, Buffalo, Cleveland and Chicago, affords facilities which the company proposes to thoroughly advertise. The industrial department is becoming a prominent feature of modern railway development, and is said to be much more influential in increasing revenue than the old-time method of manipulating rates.

THE CLINTON MANUFACTURING CO., of Clinton, Iowa, issues a map showing the unusual transportation facilities of that enterprising city. A particular advantage advertised is the fact that shipments in mixed cars can be readily made.

WHAT IS SAID to be the latest form of kerosene oil burning stove is advertised by the Hydro-Carbon Burner Co., of New York. They do not use in the construction of the burner a wick of any kind. The principle of operation is that the generator tube, as it is termed, is first heated with the alcohol flame. This initial heating is said to take about three minutes. When the tube is thus heated three kerosene oil is forced through it. As it passes through the generator it is converted into vapor. In this condition it passes into the neck of the burner, and in doing so draws air with it so as to make the combustion perfect, producing, it is claimed, a pure flame of great intensity, without smoke or odor, the same as in a gas flame. This burner is fitted with a patent self-cleaning needle valve, intended to keep the burner free and clear of carbon at all times. It, however, permits regulation of the flame in a manner similar to gas flames. The deposit of carbon has been a serious drawback to a perfect burner heretofore, which defect the new plan is intended to overcome.

THE SANITARY FIREPROOFING AND CONTRACTING CO., of New York, is on the market with office partition blocks which deserve brief mention. The blocks are made of plaster, steam, coal cinders and a secret chemical compound. They are held together by iron dowel pins and angles which are embedded in the blocks, and are thus protected from flames. The dowels being in short sections, their expansion by heat does not bulge the partition. It is claimed that such partitions cannot be broken on account of the dowels, and can be cut and altered without fear of collapse. They are very light in weight, and it is claimed that they are proof against fire and vermin.

IN ADVERTISING their letter files, Brower Bros. state that 96 per cent of all letters, though they must be kept, are not referred to after filing, and therefore the filing should be direct and without friction or waste of force on unnecessary details. Copies of letters sent, if loose, should not at once be filed with letters received. There should not be too much labor and waste of time in getting them together when so few are needed again, but they should be filed by themselves until wanted. Then only collated letters and answers are kept together in file with letters received. It is better to spend a few minutes in getting together the 5 per cent as wanted than hours on the 96 per cent that will never be looked at a second time. Brower Bros. claim that the horizontal way of filing is the better, for the reason that it is compact and keeps out dust and dampness, while the perpendicular method takes more room and invites dust and dampness. Modern business methods have greatly increased the amount of general correspondence, and letter filing is something to which every business man should give systematic consideration.

HEATING THE OFFICE is something which appeals to every business man, not only on account of his own personal comfort, but on account of the comfort and efficiency of his employees. Phelps Bros., of New York, claim to have a boiler which is up-to-date in every way. It is said to be properly rated, and they guarantee it to carry every foot of radiation that any of the sizes are rated to carry. The reams of tapping in each section that take the nipples are of the same taper as the nipples themselves, which is said to perfectly insure tight joints. The nipples are made of heavy cast-iron. The bolts which run through the boiler to hold it together do not run through the waterways, but through coreways, thereby protecting the bolts from water and at the same time giving the bolts the same amount of heat as the sections, thereby securing the same expansion and contraction as the boiler. In the smoke section they have a drop damper which works on a ratchet arrangement, with which is controlled the combustion according to the size of flue to which the boiler is attached. Around this drop damper there is a space of 1 1-2 inches, always insuring some combustion travel, even when the damper is shut. This damper, it is claimed, does not interfere with the regular automatic front and back dampers. The proprietors are very enthusiastic in presenting their boilers as an important factor in office heating.

THE BUTTLE PARQUET FLOOR CO. has issued two attractive booklets, one entitled "Hardwood Facts About Hardwood Floors," and the other, "Floor Culture by a Floorist." Flooring for offices is no different from the parquet flooring used in residences, with the exception, perhaps, that a tougher finish is used and the flooring has to be refinished a trifle oftener. The usual run of office floors are less expensive than those for home use. However, they have laid very attractive ones in the executive offices of the United States Steel Corporation, in J. Pierpont Morgan's office and in most of the offices of the World Building. In this last building tenants may have floors upon request, it apparently being the thought of the owner that his building will rent better if the offices are made attractive, and if kept attractive will hold the tenants.

THE BRITISH URALITE CO., of London, is out with a new fireproof and non-conducting material for building and other work. Uralite is composed of asbestos fiber and mineral substances only, and the novel process of manufacture results in the production, so it is claimed, of an absolutely fire-preventive material. The substance is a powerful non-conductor of heat, cold and electricity. It is practically water-proof, not being affected by hot or cold water, by atmospheric influences nor by such gases as will destroy galvanized iron. Uralite can be cut with a knife or saw. It can be painted, grained, polished and glued together like wood. It can be veneered to form paneling for walls or partitions for ships' cabins or for railway carriages. Such paneling, it is said, will not swell, crack or blister. Uralite does not split when a nail is driven through it. It is not affected when exposed to moisture or very great changes of temperature, and it can be impregnated throughout with any desired color.

SOME OF THE ADVANTAGES claimed by the Columbia Safety Door Co., of New York, for a door which they manufacture are that the wind cannot slam them as ordinary doors are slammed, with consequent breaking of door frame, glass and springs. In entering, the door cannot follow you beyond a point of safety for you. In passing out, the door swings from you. The opening of the doors slightly draws the warm air from the hall or corridor, instead of allowing cold air to pass in, thus holding the temperature at a desired degree. Drafts through the corridors and up the elevator shaft are stopped, and a great saving of coal results. They have no mechanism to get out of order. They operate with clock-like precision. Once adjusted, they can be taken down, or put up in ten minutes. They need not be removed in summer, but simply hooked to the walls, ready for instant use in dust storms and during any disagreeable weather. They require less than half the space needed for either revolving doors or doors which swing in both directions.

THE VETTER DESK WORKS, of Rochester, N. Y., are sending out a little book entitled "Business Pointers." These "Business Pointers" have mainly to do with the card system which the company manufactures. The company advertises that it is ready to send an entire outfit of this card system on approval, and the person receiving it may keep it long enough to test it thoroughly, and if found lacking in any of the advantages claimed for it it may be returned at the company's expense. The company also furnishes a rubber stamp outfit at what it claims is a very small cost. The main point of the Vetter system seems to be the use of tab cards, so called, to divide the records alphabetically and thus obviate the use of two files. The manufacturers claim that this alphabetical division in one file is unique with them. The Vetter Desk Works also manufacture all sorts of office furniture and appliances.

WE ARE IN RECEIPT of a booklet from the C. E. Locke Mfg. Co. describing the "Locke Adder," which they manufacture. This booklet describes an adding machine which appears to be small and convenient and which is sold at a price far below that of the ordinary adding machine. The capacity of this adder is said to be 999,999,999. It is claimed that the machine will not get out of order, and that it is already used by thousands of clerks and business men. The C. E. Locke Mfg. Co. also make a knife and eraser sharpener which it calls "A Novelty Hone." The hone comes in a little box shaped like a pillbox, and therefore can be carried in the pocket. It is claimed that by its use a knife or eraser may be sharpened in a few moments without trouble.

A SHOWY AND TAKING catalogue is that setting forth the merits of the Tribune Blue Streak Bicycle, manufactured by the Western Sales Department of the American Bicycle Co., at 497-501 Well street, Chicago. This catalogue is well printed and extremely well illustrated. The illustrations show sections of the forks and frame of the Tribune cycles, as well as hubs, tires, gearing and other "talking points." A special section of the catalogue is given to the Tribune Blue Streak Racer, which, so the makers assure us, is the choice of experts. There are pictures of some of the experts who have ridden the Tribune machine, and a fine view of the factory, which is located at Erie, Pa.

BOOKS OF INTEREST TO BUSINESS MEN

BUSINESS LAW. By Thomas Raeburn White, B.L., LL.B. 5 by 7 1-2 inches; 323 pages. Bound in cloth. Back title gilt. Price, $1.50.

This is a neat, compact and handy book of business law for the use of students and business men. Among the subjects treated are Contracts, Sales, Partnerships, Corporations, Negotiable Paper and the like. The author's language is plain, and is understandable by any one having no previous knowledge of law. The book's clearness on the essential points of ordinary law should recommend it as a business book for the plain business man who has no time in which to consult a law library.

THE PHONOGRAPHIC DICTIONARY AND PHRASE BOOK. By Benn Pitman and Jerome B. Howard. 5 1-2 by 8 inches; 552 pages. Bound in cloth. Cover title and back title gilt. Price, $3.00.

This book is the most elaborate shorthand dictionary yet published, with the characters in fac-simile. It contains over 20,000 words, and for every one of these words there is a corresponding sign in the Benn Pitman system of shorthand. To the reporter, office or court stenographer, or any one writing the Benn Pitman system of shorthand, the book is invaluable. It is well made, tastefully bound, and is printed on a good quality of paper in clean, plain type.

THE LAWRENCE SYSTEM OF VOCAL AND PHYSICAL EXPRESSION. By Edwin Gordon Lawrence. 4 3-4 by 6 inches; 128 pages. Bound in cloth. Cover title and back title gilt. Price, $1.00.

The author says in the preface of this little book that his object has been to place in the hands of lawyers, actors and public speakers in general, a simple system of vocal and physical expression that will enable them to clearly convey thought by word of mouth and emphasize it by the proper action. To the man of affairs who is called upon for a speech on any subject, and who knows what to say but does not know how to say it, this book will be a great help.

BUSINESS LAW. By Alonzo R. Weed, LL. B., of the Boston Bar. 6 by 9 1-4 inches; 172 pages. Bound in cloth. Cover and back title red. Price, $1.25.

Mr. Weed calls his book "a manual for schools and colleges and for every day use." The titles of the chapters are as follows: Contracts, Principal and Agent, Partnerships, Sales of Personal Property, Bailments and Common Carriers, Negotiable Paper, Deeds, Mortgages and Leases, Collection Laws, Written Rates of Interest, Insurance, Patent Rights, Trade-Marks and Copyrights, etc.

The author does not waste words, and yet treats his subjects clearly and comprehensively. In short, he gives the law without the addition of wordy "trimmings."

BANKERS' AND MERCHANTS' INTEREST TABLES. By Francis H. Coffin and David H. Moore. 13 by 9 1-2 inches. Bound in cloth. Leather back and corners. Cover and back title gilt. Price, $5.00.

There have been interest tables published before, but never, so far as we know, has so elaborate and comprehensive a set of tables been issued in book form. "The volume contains," to quote from the title page, "Interest tables, computed on the basis of 360 days per annum, at 3 1-2, 4, 5 and 6 per cent, with an accurate calculation of interest on every sum from $1.00 to $1,000, and, by simple addition of two lines, on every further sum, to $1,000,000." It also contains a 1 per cent one day table, on the basis of 365 days per annum, from which interest on daily balances can be computed at any time and on any sum. There is a time table printed in black and red at the beginning of the book as an aid in quickly finding the number of days between one day and another. To a merchant or banker performing many calculations in interest this book is a great time saver. It is handsomely bound, finely printed, and has a thumb index.

POLITICAL ECONOMY OF HUMANISM. By Henry Wood. 7 3-4 by 5 1-4 inches; 320 pages. Bound in cloth. Cover and back title gilt. Price, $1.25.

Mr. Wood is well known as a writer on various economic subjects, and this book contains a series of able treatises, written in his usual vein, on the relation of the employer to the employed, and the phases of the industrial question and their relation to socialism. Among the questions considered and handled in a conservative spirit and with much common sense, are the following: Supply and Demand, the Law of Competition, Labor and Production, Combinations of Capital, Combinations of Labor, Employers and Profit Sharing, the Obligations and Privileges of Employees, the Unequal Distribution of Wealth, Money and Coinage, Tariffs and Protection, Industrial Education and Gold Production and values.

INTRODUCTION TO THE STUDY OF COMMERCE. By Frederick R. Clow, Ph. D. 7 1-2 by 3 3-4 inches; 224 pages. Bound in cloth. Back title gilt. Price, $1.25.

Mr. Clow's book is not intended as a complete text book on commerce. It is simply, as its title implies, an introduction to the study of commerce. It is intended as a text book for

Public Accountants

ATLANTA, GA.—Ralph H. Brown, 318 Temple Court.

BOSTON, MASS.—Charles H. Fellows, 174 Summer; New England Audit Co., 45 Milk; J. S. Parsons, 214 Columbus Ave.; Safeguard Account Co., 53 Tremont; William Dillon, 502 Exchange Building.

BROOKLYN, N. Y.—Franklin Allen, Arbuckle Building, 371 Fulton.

BUFFALO, N. Y.—W. G. Mowat, 831 Ellicott Square.

CHICAGO, ILL.—Safeguard Account Co., 609-611A Merchants' Loan & Trust Building, 135 Adams; Haskins & Sells, 214 Dearborn.

DAVENPORT, IOWA.—J. C. Grabbe, McManus Building.

DETROIT, MICH.—N. A. Hawkins, 717-718 Chamber of Commerce; H. Naemansson, 496 Putnam Ave.

LONDON, CANADA.—Geo. F. Jewell, 361 Dundas.

NEW BEDFORD, MASS.—James L. Hathway, 72 Willis.

NEW ORLEANS, LA.—P. W. Sherwood, 904 Howard Ave.

NEW YORK, N. Y.—Patterson, Teele & Dennis, 30 Broad; Haskins & Sells, 30 Broad; Account, Audit & Assurance Co., Ltd., 25 Pine; Leon Brummer, 7 Pine; H. F. Searle, 45 Broadway; Hart Bros., Tibbits, Heiron & Co., 11 Broadway; Franklin Allen, Silk Exchange Building, Broadway, corner Broome.

PHILADELPHIA, PA.—Francis & Sterrett, Penn Mutual Building; Peter Ballingall, German-American Building; Charles W. Thomas, 409 Lippincott Building; Alfred L. Sellers, 1001 Chestnut.

PITTSBURG, PA.—John Vaughn, 5520 Claybourne; George W. Wood & Co., 341 Fourth Ave.

PROVIDENCE, R. I.—George R. Allen, 29 Weybosset.

SAN FRANCISCO, CAL.—Charles L. Lutgen, 218 California; Lester Herrick, 405 Montgomery.

TORONTO, CANADA.—F. H. Kidd, Bank of Commerce Building.

WINDSOR, CANADA.—F. H. Macpherson, 16 Sandwich, East.

WINNIPEG, CANADA.—Peter Thornton, 343 Main.

the use of teachers in schools or universities, or as a help to the student in his commercial training. Incidentally, it makes good reading for anyone interested in modern commerce, and particularly for the American merchant. The author begins by describing the Elements of Commerce; then follows a short essay on the Rise of Commerce, and then the Materials of Commerce are discussed. Foreign Commerce of the United States and of other countries is treated of, as is the Domestic Commerce of this country. The titles of other chapters are: Organization of Trade, Prices, Payments and How the Equilibrium is Maintained. We can heartily recommend this introduction to the Study of Commerce. It is a good book on a vastly important subject.

THE A B C OF BANKS AND BANKING. By George M. Coffin. 6 3-4 by 5 inches; 137 pages. Bound in cloth. Back title gilt. Price, $1.25.

This handy little volume is exactly what its name implies, that is, a presentation of the principles underlying banking in the United States. The author in his preface says that it is designed to appeal to the reader outside as well as inside of a bank. It is by no means the last word or every word about banking. It may be said that it is a primer covering a field that has hitherto been somewhat neglected. The chapter heads are as follows: Banking in General, Various Kinds of Banking, Capital Stock, Shareholders' Rights and Liabilities, Undivided Profits, Dividends and Surplus, Deposits, Checks, Lawful Money Reserve, Issuing Bank Notes, Borrowing Money, Loans and Discounts, Exchanges, Collections, Letters of Credit, Bonds, Mortgages and

A BUSINESS EDUCATION | FOR ONE DOLLAR.

...THE PRACTICAL AGE...

A MONTHLY MAGAZINE full to the brim with helpful suggestions to young men and young women who are struggling successward.

THE BUSINESS HOUSE THAT JACK BUILT, an intensely interesting and highly instructive story of business life, and

APPLIED ENGLISH, an authority on writing and speaking the English language, which no young person can afford to be without, all for ONE DOLLAR.

If you have never seen THE PRACTICAL AGE, send for a free sample copy. Address,

THE PRACTICAL AGE,
Moline, Illinois.

UNIVERSITY TRAINING
For Business

ACCOUNTING
BANKING
BROKERAGE

School of Comerce, Accounts and Finance.
Evening Sessions.
New York University, Washington Square, N. Y. City.

FALL TERM OPENS OCT. I.

Leon Brummer, C. P. A.
Public Accountant and Auditor,
7 Pine Street, New York, N. Y.

PRENTISS CLOCKS.
SIX TIMES A YEAR
is all that is necessary to wind a Prentiss Clock. Why wind a clock every week when we can sell you one which will require winding but once in sixty days and will keep perfect time? Also Frying-pan, Program and Electrically synchronized clocks. Send for Catalogue No. 292.
THE PRENTISS CLOCK IMPROVEMENT CO.
Dept. 28, 49 Dey St., New York City

Stocks, Bank Reports, Examinations, Directors, Executive Officers—Their Powers and Duties, Internal Administration and Bookkeeping, and Other Suggestions.

Any book in this list will be sent to any address in the United States, Canada or Mexico upon receipt of price. If there is some special book that you require we shall be pleased to hunt it up for you. Address COMMERCE, ACCOUNTS & FINANCE, 25 Pine street, New York city.

HALL'S Fireproof and Burglar Proof SAFES

Sold since 1840. Never fail to protect contents.

KNOWN EVERYWHERE

393 BROADWAY, N.Y.

Telephones: 3133-3136-307 Franklin.

BUSINESS NEEDS

Advertisements under this head one cent a word each insertion.

STENOGRAPHER—Man, age 30, thoroughly familiar with secretarial work, business, committee and association correspondence, desires position. Exceptionally well fitted by training and experience to act as private stenographer to business men who are called upon to handle funds as guardian or trustee, or who are secretaries for clubs, societies, committees, etc. Address SILENT, care Commerce, Accounts & Finance.

SECOND-HAND TYPEWRITERS can be repaired so that they can be used and produce work which is almost, if not quite, as good as from a new machine. I have the facilities for obtaining exceptionally good second-hand machines. I have a man who repairs them—a man that understands his business. These machines can be sold for 50 per cent discount from list price of the new machines. Does this interest you? If it does, address TYPEWRITER, care Commerce, Accounts & Finance.

DO YOU NEED BOOKS? Old books, new books, second-hand books. Agent for subscription books, and dealer in old and new books. Ask me for prices on books you want before you buy elsewhere. A. CROSS, care Commerce, Accounts & Finance.

I AM AT PRESENT engaged in a large export commission business, and can furnish the highest testimonials as to efficiency of service rendered as a bookkeeper. Further advancement is barred by reason of the firm's personal dependants. Any firm or individual in need of an office man communicate with INDUSTRIOUS, care Commerce, Accounts & Finance.

BUSINESS PICTURES—Do you want to illustrate your catalogue or booklet? Do you want a series of snappy pen and ink sketches to brighten your advertisement in the daily papers? Do you want a handsome wash drawing for your announcement in the magazines? If you do, write to me. I am a competent business artist, working in black and white and colors, and you see my sketches every week if you read the Sunday papers. My price is always a fair one. Address, PEN AND INK, Box 17, Commerce, Accounts & Finance.

SALESMAN having a large line of retail customers in the eastern states among dry goods and gentlemen's furnishing stores desires to represent some line of goods that he can present in connection with the article which he now carries. Underwear manufacturers might do well to communicate with PERSONALITY, care Commerce, Accounts & Finance.

OFFICE FURNITURE, Files, Cabinets, etc.—I know a lot more about some things than you do. I have to—it is my bread and butter. You don't know the "cost" of a desk, a cabinet, filing devices and the hosts of other things you may want to use in your office. I do! I can save you money and make some myself. That is a good proposition for you to look in to. Try. UNITS, care Commerce, Accounts & Finance.

DO YOU WANT A BOOKKEEPER who can tell you what you want to know? My experience in a large export business has taught me an accounting for small leaks. Address THIRTY-TWO, care Commerce, Accounts & Finance.

It's Good for You

To use our Typewriter Ribbons and Carbons, because they write better and last longer than the ordinary kind; they do not smut, blur nor fill the type, but they make fine copies.

No. 1 Ribbons, 75c. ea., $7.00 doz.
No. 1 Carbon, $3.00 pr. bx., 40c. doz.
Silkarbon, $4.00 pr. bx., 50c. doz.

We pay express or mail charges.

IMPERIAL MANUFACTURING CO.
289-297 Washington St., Newark, N. J.

R·I·P·A·N·S

There is scarcely any condition of ill-health that is not benefited by the occasional use of a R·I·P·A·N·S Tabule. For sale by Druggists. The Five-Cent packet is enough for an ordinary occasion. The family bottle, 60 cents, contains a supply for a year.

Working Plans of Leading Banks

Organization and Administration

Illustrated by

Charts

ONE of the original and fascinating features of the work of the American Institute of Bank Clerks is a collection of charts showing in a clear and comprehensive manner the arrangement of the working forces of several of the leading banks in different large cities of the country, together with an outline of the duties connected with each department.

These charts are a part of the correspondence course of study in Practical Banking, but they have created such general interest that the Institute has arranged to publish them in a handsomely bound booklet.

What the Charts Show

CHART "A" represents the First National Bank of Chicago, which has a very comprehensive plan of administration. The different departments of the bank are numbered in the chart for ready reference, so that the course of any item may be followed from receipt to final disposition. The main divisions of labor are clearly shown, and the duties of employees set forth in a clear and striking manner.

CHART "B" represents a prominent New York bank doing a large general business. The various departments and the duties of the different clerks therein employed are fully described.

CHART "C" shows the general plan of administration of one of the largest New York banks doing an extensive business with merchants and having a large number of correspondents throughout the country. An examination of the chart shows how this great business is handled.

CHART "D" represents in outline one of the largest and strongest banks in New York. An analysis of the chart shows that loans on collateral security are an important feature of the business transacted, although the bank's customers include numerous corporations of the first magnitude, and a desirable line of out-of-town banks.

CHART "E" represents a New York bank in the wealthy residence district, numbering among its customers many of the "400." The facilities afforded to ladies are a conspicuous and presumably very profitable feature of this institution.

CHART "F" shows the administrative plan of one of the leading banks of Philadelphia, doing a large general business and having numerous correspondents throughout the country.

CHART "G" is not intended to represent any particular institution, but rather to show the distribution of the working force of a typical New York bank of large size and progressive methods.

Terms and Conditions

While the charts are primarily a part of the regular educational work of the Institute, and were published separately only as an attractive premium for new chart-coupon subscribers, they are also esteemed of exceptional value to bankers generally and to others interested in up-to-date business organization and administration. To supply this demand for the charts which has come to us from all sources, they will be sent postpaid on the following terms:—

To new chart-coupon subscribers to the Bulletin,
as a premium, one copy each, ... Free
To the general public, per copy, . . - $2.00

Send order and make remittance payable to

American Institute of Bank Clerks

25 Pine Street, New York

NEW YORK PUBLIC LIBRARY

COMMERCE ACCOUNTS & FINANCE

Volume 4 New York August 1902 Number 8

CONTENTS

Published Monthly by the Commerce Accounts & Finance Company Twenty-five Pine Street New York

KNICKERBOCKER TRUST CO.

234 FIFTH AVENUE, CORNER 27TH STREET
BRANCH OFFICES:
66 BROADWAY, AND 125TH STREET AND LENOX AVE.,
NEW YORK CITY.

CAPITAL AND UNDIVIDED PROFITS, $2,508,399.11.

LEGAL DEPOSITORY FOR STATE, CITY, AND COURT FUNDS.

Interest allowed on Time Deposits. Deposits also received subject to Demand Checks, which pass through the Clearing House as do those upon any city bank.

Authorized to act as Executor or Administrator of Estates, and as Guardian, Receiver, Registrar, Transfer and Financial Agent for States, Cities, Towns, Railroads, and other corporations, and to accept any other Trusts in conformity with the laws of any State or of the United States.

LETTERS OF CREDIT FURNISHED.
BUSINESS AND PERSONAL ACCOUNTS SOLICITED.

CHAS. T. BARNEY, - - - - - - - - President.
JOSEPH T. BROWN, - - - - - - 2d Vice-President.
JULIAN M. GERARD, - - - - Asst. Sec. and Asst. Treas.
FRED'K K. ELDRIDGE, - - - - - 1st Vice-President.
FRED'K GORE KING, - - - Secretary and Treasurer.
WM. B. RANDALL, - - - - - - - Trust Officer.

BOARD OF DIRECTORS:

JOSEPH S. AUERBACH,
HARRY B. HOLLINS,
JACOB HAYS,
CHARLES T. BARNEY,
A. FOSTER HIGGINS,
ANDREW H. SANDS,
JAMES H. BRESLIN,
I. TOWNSEND BURDEN,
HON. E. V. LOEW,
HENRY F. DIMOCK,
CHARLES F. WATSON,
FREDERICK G. BOURNE,
C. LAWRENCE PERKINS,
CHARLES R. FLINT,
AMZI L. BARBER,
CHARLES T. COOK,
JOHN MAGEE,
HENRY A. MORGAN,
HENRY C. BERLIN,
CHARLES W. GOULD,
FRED'K L. ELDRIDGE,
HENRY W. DE FOREST,
ALFRED R. MACLAY
HARRY W. McVICKAR.

HASKINS & SELLS,
CERTIFIED PUBLIC ACCOUNTANTS.

204 DEARBORN STREET
CHICAGO

LINCOLN TRUST BLDG.
ST. LOUIS

30 BROAD STREET,
NEW YORK.

CABLE ADDRESS "HASKSELLS"

WILLIAMSON BLDG.
CLEVELAND, O.

30 COLEMAN STREET
LONDON, E.C.

Lackawanna Railroad

Address all communications to
C. W. TEN BROECK, Industrial Agent,
26 Exchange Place, New York City.

Do You Desire a Factory Site? The Industrial Department of the Lackawanna Railroad will aid you in finding one.

Are You Interested in Any Raw Product for Manufacturing Purposes? The Industrial Department of the Lackawanna Railroad will tell you if it is to be found along that road.

Does the Question of Power Concern You? The Industrial Department of the Lackawanna Railroad will tell you of good water power and of the proximity of fuel to points on that road.

Do You Want to Know the Usual Rate of Wages? The Industrial Department of the Lackawanna Railroad will give that information regarding any point on that road.

Do You Want to Know the Price of Gas, Water, Electricity? The Industrial Department of the Lackawanna Railroad will tell you.

Account, Audit & Assurance Company,

25 PINE STREET, NEW YORK.

Accounting Charts.

A chart of accounts bears the same relationship to the accounting system of a business that an architect's floor plans bear to a building. No one would think of commencing the construction of a building of any kind at the present day without first putting upon paper the dimensions of the building, the sub-divisions that it is to have and various other particulars. While putting it upon paper questions of arrangement, means of intercommunication, sources of light and of various conveniences and appointments would come up for discussion. It would be very strange indeed if in working out the floor plans there were not various alternative propositions brought up for consideration.

Just so with the accounting system of business. By the chart there is definitely established the accounts that are required for showing the business as it progresses, and in a way to meet the requirements of the management. Alternative propositions are presented in a way to be intelligently discussed.

What a queer building would result from the combined efforts of excavator, stone mason, carpenter, roofer, plumber and decorator without any controlling plan and without the oversight of a competent architect or engineer! The excavator would dig the cellar in any old shape he saw fit; the mason would proceed to wall it according to his own sweet will; the carpenter would put up the frame work as best suited his convenience, with scant attention perhaps to openings for light, ventilation, etc.; the plumber would put in his work where most convenient to him as a mechanic, regardless of all other considerations. Possibly the bath-tub would be in the parlor, if in neither the attic nor cellar. The roofer would cover the building in any way that suited him, while the decorator would give free rein to his pet fads in colors, etc.

You have seen some buildings that resemble work conducted under th conditions. You have seen hun' of buildings that were erected without plans, and at the hands of "builders" who were mere amateurs in putting material together. You never saw one of them you desired to own for either its beauty or yet its utility.

Is the picture at all overdrawn when we say that conditions of like kind underlie the most of the bookkeeping plans now in use? They are seldom arranged in the light of the purpose that they are to serve. While business men have long been in the habit of calling in architects to plan their store buildings, factories and residences, it is only recently that they have appreciated the advantages of calling in business engineers to plan their accounting and office systems. But as a fact, far more depends upon an adequately-planned accounting system than upon a well-arranged factory or a storehouse.

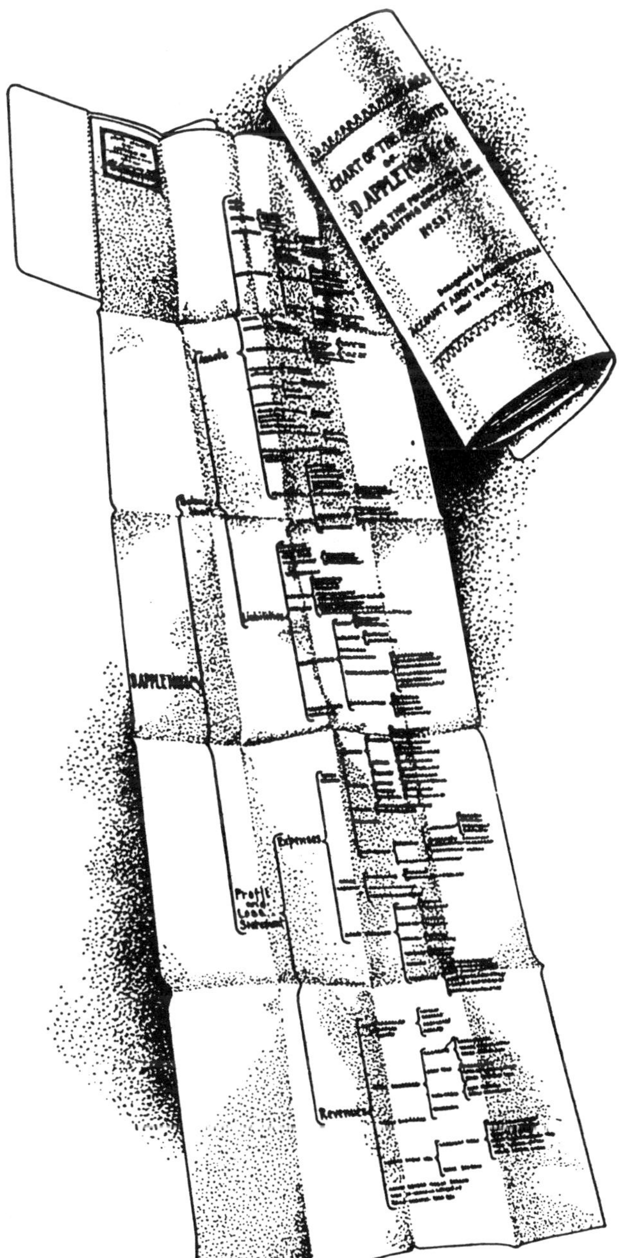

Fig. 1. Perspective View of a Working Chart. Sketch in upper right-hand corner shows same folded and in cover.

The usual rule in offices is to hire a "bright" bookkeeper and tell him to open the books. Or if the business is already running and the books are in operation and there occurs a vacancy, the most available man is put in place, and the work proceeds without any special regard to the accounts that are open or to be kept. Those who have the responsibility of examining and auditing books continually meet with surprises at the peculiar accounts that bookkeepers devise, and which, without

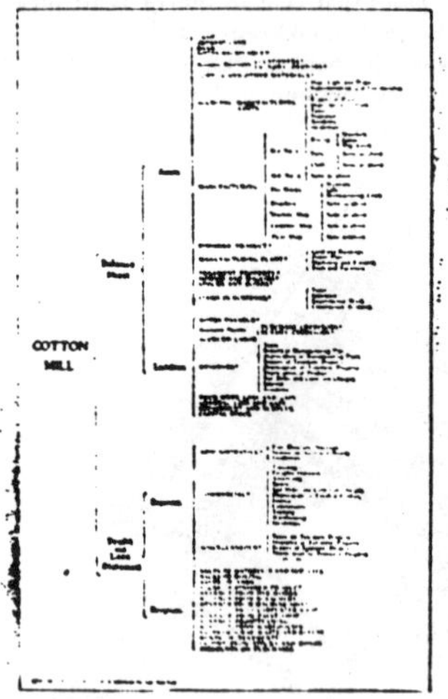

Fig. 2. Typical Chart of a Textile Business.

instruction or oversight, they frequently open and continue to conduct.

It is a well-known fact that the average business man detests accounts; that he has no particular love for his bookkeeper; that he never takes pleasure in examining the ledger of his business, and that in many cases he freely admits that he does not understand his bookkeeper's system. All this is an indication that the system is inadequately planned, improperly adjusted to the requirements of the business, and not at all scientifically administered.

On the other hand those business men whose accounts have been organized upon an adequate plan, and the work of whose accounting system proceeds upon a scheme that is adequate for the purpose, find great pleasure in examining their accounts, and really like to be on familiar terms with their ledgers. Every bookkeeper who is employed where such a system is in operation, instead of remaining a mere slave of routine, becomes an intelligent helper, able to give office work an impetus which it never before enjoyed.

A chart of accounts is a simple thing to get up by those who are accustomed to the work, and yet it is a very difficult thing to construct by those who have had no experience. Several examples of charts are presented on these pages. Fig. 1 is the picture of a chart as it is unfolded for use, and also as it is put up for ordinary preservation. Fig. 2 is a typical chart of a textile business, and Fig. 3 is a similar representation of the accounts of a street railway organization.

The object of charting accounts is to secure the foundation for a proper Profit and Loss Statement and Balance Sheet. Wtih accounts scientifically arranged upon this basis, a Going or Perpetual Profit and Loss Statement and Going and Perpetual Balance Sheet is not only possible, but within reach at no extra cost. You can have your accounts up to date just as well as not. There is no need of being thirty days to four months behind. Long fiscal periods like six months and a year are abolished, and instead, the business man for the purpose of planning and giving directions by way of administration, has facts before him up to date all the time.

With the accounts of a business correctly charted, and with a written specification showing how they are to be conducted, a bright bookkeeper is able to instal Balance Sheet Accounting without personal assistance and supervision. The work that we have been doing for some of the most prominent business establishments in the country, and that for which we have been paid very high prices in the past, thus becomes available to business concerns everywhere at a very moderate cost.

Among the lines of business for which we have already prepared charts accompanied by specifications may be mentioned the following:—

Printing, Book-binding, Electrotyping, Machine-manufacturing, Foundries, Planing-mills, Wood-working establishments, Agricultural-implements, Railways, Street-railways, Cotton-mills, Silk-mills, Warehousing Companies, Periodical Publishing, Department Stores, Banks, Telephone Companies, Telegraph Companies, Water-works, Copper-mines, Coal-mines, Stone-quarries, Hat-manufacturing, Hotels, Restaurants, Real-estate, Insurance, Commission, Brokerage, Book-publishing, Paper-making, Lithographing, Steam-engine Building, Builders' Iron-work, Contracting, Professional-business, Schools, Clubs, Sheet-metal Working, Carriage-manufacturing, Bicycles, Hardware, Dry-goods, Groceries, Furniture-manufacturing, Electrical-goods, Cigars, Breweries, Cold-storage, Advertising Agencies, Corset-factories, Thread-making, Shoe-factories, Rolling-mills, Stove-foundries, Plumbing, Tin-ware, and many others. Our experience to date is measured by several thousand undertakings of this character.

We are in position to chart the accounts of any business wherever located, and to send the same out accompanied by a brief specification at a very low price, and shall be pleased to correspond with everyone who is at all interested in the suggestion.

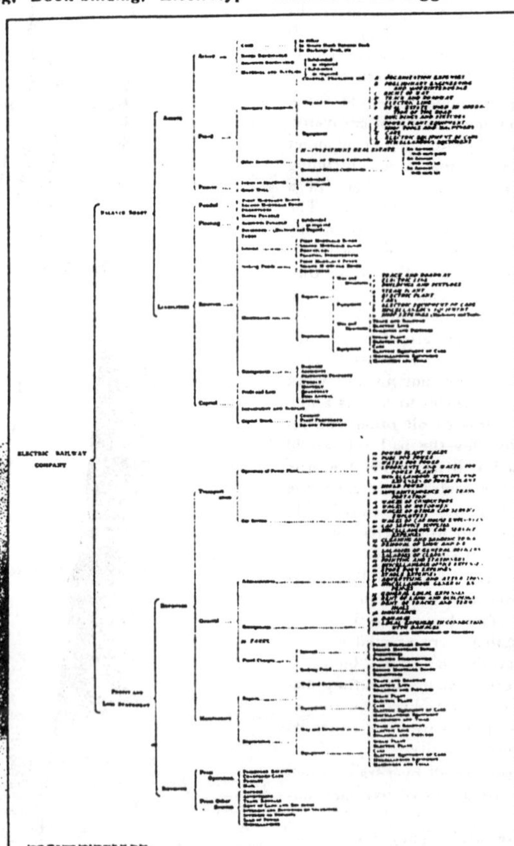

Fig. 3. Chart of the Accounts of a Street Railway Organization.

Address all communications to the **Account, Audit & Assurance Company, 25 Pine Street, New York.**

THE NEW YORK PUBLIC LIBRARY

The Reason Why*

By A. O. KITTREDGE, C.P.A.

[The Cananea Consolidated Copper Company operate extensive copper mines at La Cananea, Sonora, Mexico. The Company own not only the mineral rights, but also have acquired the surface rights of a very large area, and in the development of their enterprise have built extensive reduction works, including a narrow gauge road connecting the various mines with the concentrator and smelter. They have also built some forty miles of standard gauge railway, connecting La Cananea with the El Paso and South Western System at Naco, Arizona. Incident to the development of this enterprise also has been the establishment of a store, a bank, a hotel and a number of restaurants and lodging houses, a general supply department, electric light, telegraph and telephone systems, waterworks, etc. For the better accommodations of their employees a town site has been laid out in which lots are sold on liberal terms, and a street railway line connecting the reduction and mining divisions with the town site is in process of construction. Various other departments, more or less intimately associated with mining and reduction, the two grand divisions of the Company's undertakings, are also involved. The accounting with which the Company commenced its enterprise was that of the ordinary type, based largely upon what prevails in other mining and reduction enterprises in the southwest and more or less derived from the experience and practice of large railway corporations. The attempt was made from the outset to distinguish between "construction" and "operation." Early in the year (1902) an arrangement was made with the Account, Audit and Assurance Company to reorganize the entire accounting system of the Company with a view to putting the records of its affairs upon a solid and enduring basis and bringing its business routine up to the front of the very best that accounting engineers have devised. The work was undertaken under the general supervision of Mr. A. O. Kittredge, President of the Account, Audit and Assurance Company, and had the immediate attention of Mr. George Young, Manager of one of the divisions of the Company. Incident to the installation, and for the purpose of securing the very best co-operation at the hands of the considerable number of clerical employees of the Company, a lecture course was instituted and two nights in the week for a considerable period of time were devoted to practical instruction along the lines of balance sheet accounting. One of the last lectures of this series was delivered by Mr. Kittredge and bore the suggestive title given above, namely, "The Reason Why." In theory it was an explanation to the clerical employees of the Cananea Consolidated Copper Company of the reason for many of the various changes that were being made in the accounting routine of the Company and for instituting various new features of routine. On the occasion of this lecture the Cananea Consolidated Copper Company was represented in the person of Anson W. Burchard, Second Vice-President and Comptroller, and by John A. Campbell, Secretary and General Auditor. At the close of Mr. Kittredge's address, Mr. Burchard, in a few carefully chosen sentences, rounded out and enforced a number of the points that had been made and gave official indorsement to the plans which had been outlined. The installation in this case, as in all others at the hands of the Account, Audit and Assurance Company, was made upon the specification plan, with every feature of the work laid down by means of diagram and descriptive text. The duties of every employee were also outlined in what is known as the Code, corresponding somewhat to "general orders" in railway practice. To make the reader still further intelligent as to the work in hand, it should be stated that those divisions of the Company's business dealing with the outside public were given separate sets of accounts, while the general business of the Company, including a summary of results derived from the separate sets of books above mentioned, were presented in another set of books. Thus there is a separate set of accounts for the standard gauge railway division, another for the banking department and still another for the mercantile department, while the Company's books, being that which includes the results shown by these separate sets, carry the records of the mining and reduction works along with the various sub-industries more or less particularized above.]

What I propose doing this evening is to explain, in part at least, the reason why of various changes that are now being made in the bookkeeping and accounting routine of the company. It is one thing to have a plan and method outlined and thrown at you to follow, simply because it is ordered by the management, and quite another thing to have the plan and method explained not only as to its operation but also as to the reason why it is required. I am sure you will approve of discussion along these lines. With your assistance, in the way of asking questions, I will attempt in as few words as possible to get before you some of the reasons why various things in this regard are being done.

You do not need to be reminded that in an enterprise as extensive as that of the Cananea Consolidated Copper Company, spread over many square miles of territory as it is, and embracing numerous divisions, and still more numerous departments, covering practically everything from a mercantile proposition on the one hand to a rented tent on the other, and from the comparatively simple work of taking ore out of the hills to the operation of an up-to-date smelting apparatus and converter, going from the one extreme of a corral, with its complement of animals and vehicles, to the other extreme of the operation of a thoroughly-built railway, no man can carry the conditions of operation and the resulting facts in mind in a way to be competent to direct the undertaking without the assistance of accounts. At the bottom of all that we are doing is the effort to give the management the facts which are necessary to intelligent planning and directing.

PERSONAL ACCOUNTS.

Broadly, every one keeps accounts. The simplest form of an account is that between two individuals. Do I owe you or do you owe me? The first conception of accounts is that of personal accounts, but as business develops and as enterprises multiply the personal account becomes relatively of less importance, although actually it stands where it did at the outset. It becomes relatively obscure because there are so many other things that are of importance. As we get better acquainted with the needs of those who manage, we find that results of operations, statements of condition, and statistical comparisons are prime necessities, and therefore whatever the accountant does must accord prominent place to these features. A statement of condition necessarily includes all personal accounts, and in this view we find the real rank of personal accounts in modern business. They are simply an important sub-division.

THE CASH ACCOUNT.

If personal accounts are those which were first considered in the development of the accounting art and those which first come to mind when we think of accounts, then the next account that was probably thought of in progressive bookkeeping and that which naturally obtrudes itself upon our attention in getting up a plan of account keeping for our own purposes is the cash account. The moment that we consider the difference between a personal account and a cash account we have opened before us a view of that which serves to divide accounts into classes.

Without going into details it may be asserted that the cash account was probably the first asset account the need of which became apparent. A little later in the development of the science of accounting it is probable that merchandise as an asset account became a necessity. Perhaps at about the same time or a little later some one perceived the desirability of such accounts as real estate, buildings, factory equipment, etc. In any event, from such small beginnings, whatever they were, business accounting has gone on developing, and as it has progressed details have greatly multiplied.

Every year has seen the need of more and more account keeping, not alone in the sense of keeping track of personal relations already referred to, but more particularly with respect to the way in which the capital of a business is invested and the results of business operations. The prominent questions that are up for consideration whenever business men interested in a given enterprise get together, in-

*Abstract of an address delivered before the officers and employees of the Cananea Consolidated Copper Company, La Cananea, Sonora, Mexico, June 3, 1902, by A. O. Kittredge, C. P. A. President of the Account, Audit and Assurance Company, New York.

clude such as these: What are our assets and in what condition are they? What are our liabilities and in what shape are they? What are our expenses? Can they be reduced? What are our revenues? Can they be increased? In short, What is the real condition of the enterprise?

I take it that the best reason that can be found for account keeping, in a broad sense, is thereby to afford the business man what he needs to know, in the way in which he wants to know it, and at the exact time he requires the information to enable him to intelligently manage and direct his enterprise. I think the highest function of the accountant is to reflect to the business man the exact results of his operations to date. It is to be able to say: "Here, Mr. Business Manager, this is the result of what you have done."

SHOWING THE RESULTS.

As accountants we have nothing to say in the way of criticism of the way in which affairs are managed. The management of affairs belong to the business man. But as accountants, on the other hand, we have everything to say as to the showing of the results that have been accomplished.

It is the accountant's function to point out just where the enterprise is and to show the several steps that have brought it to that position. The relationship, therefore, of the accountant to the business man is clearly defined. The accountant merely holds up a mirror to the business man, showing him by way of accounts just what he has accomplished by his operations. If the business man is entirely satisfied with the way things are going, as reflected by the accounts, he will doubtless continue to drive ahead in that same direction. On the other hand, if the accounts show that the plan upon which he has been operating has not been producing satisfactory results, then, as an intelligent manager, he will no doubt change his plans. The accountant does not run the business but he does show the results of the running of the business by some one else.

In every new enterprise at the outset there is of necessity a lack of definiteness in the accounting system. There are various reasons for this, among which may be mentioned the absence of a definite object in the enterprise itself. The management in a general way desires to do about so, but as matters progress the plans of the management are materially modified. The physical condition of mines, the difficulties encountered in constructing a railway, legal and political conditions which arise and various other matters that might be mentioned, all have a modifying and qualifying influence. Instead of the scheme being conclusively and definitely outlined at the outset, and followed out consistently, as would be an engineer's plan, it is for a considerable period of time subject to amendment, and therefore there results the uncertainty in the accounts already referred to. In some cases the difficulties of the situation are further complicated by lack of definiteness in the actual method of the accounts themselves. As time goes on, however, and as the enterprise develops along its own lines, all these deficiencies can be remedied. The opportunity of bettering things soon appears, and the further the enterprise goes and the larger the amount of money invested the greater the need is of getting accounting affairs into the very best possible shape. As the enterprise grew, starting from nothing, it was necessary for the management to be patient in many things which would not demand patience if the enterprise had been older and better in hand, as a fact it has been necessary to be blind to a great many losses, and to much waste incident to the conditions under which the operations were proceeding, but the time has now come when all these deficiencies can be remedied, when various losses can be stopped, when numerous wastes can be ended and when things in general can be got into shape to manage on the merits of the case.

In my remarks thus far, all of which have been in general terms and not at all specific, I have, without so stating, given you the reasons why certain changes ought to be made in the account keeping of this company at the present time. If there has been anything allowed to go for the time being, not satisfactory in itself, but condoned because it was the best that circumstances would permit, and if circumstances have finally changed so that the business can now be taken in hand and thoroughly and adequately managed, then there is the need for abandoning those features of accounting which were employed in the past, but which for the future will be satisfactory in view of changed conditions. Again, if the enterprise has grown beyond what was contemplated in the early days, when the foundation was laid for that which is at present in operation, and if it bids fair to grow still further, then there is good reason why the accounting should be developed in proportion to the enterprise, and why adjustments all along the line should be made. The primary reason, as already stated, for all that is being done is to get the accounts into such shape that the management shall be furnished with the information that it needs for intelligently directing the enterprise, presented in the exact way that it will do the most good and come to hand at the very moment that it is needed for the purpose.

Let us go a little further into analysis. If you and I were going to start in business in any line whatsoever, we would very likely at the outset get together and take account of the capital that we have with which to operate. Perhaps the agreement would be that you were to furnish so much cash and that I so much in the way of goods, merchandise, implements, outfit, etc. Perhaps one or the other of us would be able to command a certain credit which would enable the firm to buy goods needed for the enterprise. Now such a statement as we would naturally draw up for mutual information at this time would be a statement of assets and liabilities. We would divest our personalities of the items that we had invested in the business, and therefore the statement made up would be neither that of your side, nor yet of my side, but instead of the business in which we were jointly interested. It would be a statement of the assets and liabilities of the business. It would show that the business had so much capital in such and such items, and that so much was owing in such and such directions. Such a statement, showing on the one side the assets and on the other side the liabilities, is, as all of you know who have had any experience whatsoever in account keeping, a balance sheet. A characteristic of the balance sheet is that it is always in balance. The debits exactly offset the credits, or rather the assets exactly counterbalance the liabilities. This result is accomplished by considering the net investment of the partners a liability of the business to the partners.

THE BALANCE SHEET.

Now if you stop to think the balance sheet of a business, or as it is sometimes called, the business statement, is the thing the business man is after at all times. It is impossible to open a set of books, no matter what the plan underlying the account keeping may be, without having as the foundation a balance sheet. In turn, if you stop to think of it, you will perceive that you cannot close a set of books except only as you have a balance sheet. If the fiscal periods are of considerable length, as for example, a year, that which the business man wants during the time as an indication of what progress the business is making, is a balance sheet. Thus it is that we are face to face with the balance sheet in the beginning, at the end and during the whole time the business is in operation.

Referring again to the assumed business that you and I have entered upon, we will assume that we go ahead and consummate various transactions. The result of our operations is that we either make or lose money. It is impossible for any business to stand still. The enterprise will either go forward or retrograde. We will make a profit if our revenues exceed our expenses, and we will lose more or less of our capital if our expenses are in excess of our revenues or earnings. After we have gone forward a month, three months or any other period, it would be very natural for either you or me to want to know just where the business stands, and so we would get together and take account of our affairs. By inspection of our records, however kept, we would find that our expenses have amounted to such and such a sum. On the other hand we would find that our profits or revenues or earnings, as the case may be, have amounted to such and such a sum. The difference between the profits or revenues on the one hand and the expenses of doing business on the other, would be either the profit or loss of the business. If the expenses are larger than the revenues, then we have lost. If the revenues are the larger, we have gained. Now what we would have made out between ourselves upon this plan is what is commonly known as a profit and loss statement. It is an account with the period of time giving it credit for what it has produced, and charging it what it has cost.

The declaration has already been made that any business will either go forward or fall behind. The profit and loss statement made out after the general plan inadequately described above will show that we have either added something to our capital or else we have impaired our capital. From this, without going into details, it is evident that the profit and loss statement is an essential part of the balance sheet. The balance sheet, as we described it a moment ago, showed by the difference between the assets and liabilities of the business the net amount of capital of the business, or that which the business owes the partners or investors. Now if the operations of the business have resulted in a profit, then at the end of the period the business owes us more than it did at the outset. On the other hand, if our management of the business has been such as to result in a loss, then there is less in the business, at this time, that is coming to us as partners or investors than there was before. In other words, the net capital of the business has been impaired or diminished. It seems to me that this principle is clear to all, and that therefore without dwelling upon it further, we may safely proceed to make the application in a larger way.

THE CANANEA COMPANY.

The Cananea Consolidated Copper Company occupies exactly the same position as the individuals who we imagined a little while ago formed a partnership and went into business. Its balance sheet will show what it has in the way of assets and what it has in the way of liabilities, including what it owes to its stockholders. Its transactions or operations are resulting in either a loss or a gain. It is either making money or it is losing money. Admitting all this, you still will say that its transactions are of so many kinds, its operations extend through so many departments, that altogether the problem is complicated and perplexing. This is very true, and it only emphasizes the need of careful analysis in the accounts. If it was desirable in the little business that we used for an illustration a moment since that you and I should know from time to time whether or not we were making money, how much more necessary is it for the management of a great enterprise like that of this company, employing, as it does, millions of capital, to know whether or not its operations are resulting in profit or making a loss?

The management should know at all times not alone that the enterprise is making or losing money, but it should know just where it is making or just where it is losing. It is fair to suppose in an operation as extensive as this, with as many divisions and departments as there is in this company, that some departments may be making money while certain others are losing. It may be good management to allow certain departments to continue to make losses, if thereby certain other departments are enabled to make a large profit. This is mentioned only for the purpose of emphasizing the necessity of having the statement so analyzed that the management is never in doubt as to the condition of the enterprise in any detail, or the results that are growing from any single subdivisions.

[At this point the speaker referred to an outline chart which had been spread upon the blackboard. This chart did not go into details, but gave simply the divisions of the Company's accounts, first, into Balance Sheet and Profit and Loss Statement, and, second, the division of the Balance Sheet into Assets and Liabilities and of the Profit and Loss Statement into Expenses and Revenue.]

THE TWO GRAND DIVISIONS OF ACCOUNTS.

The outline on the board is brought to your attention simply to show what there is in every set of accounts. All of the accounts of any business, irrespective of its kind, are comprised in two grand divisions, namely, the Balance Sheet and the Profit and Loss Statement. These two divisions are essential to any system, and in what I am calling your attention to now, there is nothing that is peculiar in what we are attempting to do here. The accounts comprised in the Balance Sheet subdivide into assets and liabilities. The accounts in the profit and loss statement are either expenses or revenues.

If you accept this broad proposition, that the company can have no other accounts than those which are embraced in one or the other of the four classes here shown, you will then admit that there is nothing left for us to do but to determine the accounts that by their naure should fall to each of these classes. First we must have a complete list of the asset accounts of the company; then we must have a complete list of the liability accounts of the company; next will be the list of accounts necessary to properly classify and show expenses, and finally must be a sufficient number of accounts to show the revenues of the company, so classified as to answer the questions which the management would naturally ask. As already stated, it is not sufficient to know that the company has made money. Instead, the management requires to know where it has made money.

[The speaker here unfolded for the inspection of his audience the completed chart of the accounts of the Company, as they had been worked out for and approved by the management. He explained that there was nothing in the chart that was not indicated in a general way by the simple diagram on the blackboard. The Company's chart simply had the blank spaces filled in to meet the requirements of the case.]

Among the assets of the company we have in the first place Cash; then following down in the order of their availability we have such assets as Notes Receivable, and Accounts Receivable, following which are the company's investments embraced in the mining division, the reduction division, the department of public service and miscellaneous.

On the liability side we have Notes Payable, Accounts Payable, the reserves which have been set aside for making good the company's wasting assets. Then come the Loss and Gain Accounts, showing in an analytical form either accretion or diminution of capital, and finally the Capital Account.

The Expense Accounts are subdivided for statistical purposes in a way to give the management at all times the statements that are needful to intelligent direction. In like manner, as already mentioned, the Revenue Accounts are subdivided for statistical reasons.

RESERVE ACCOUNTS.

I have referred to the matter of reserves as a liability, and have defined reserves as amounts set aside to make good wasting assets. On the broad proposition of explaining the reason why of various things that are being done, I shall attempt to give you further explanation of these reserve accounts. I shall attempt to make the application specific to the business in hand.

Without fear of contradiction I may assert that a large proportion of all the assets that this company has are of a wasting nature. For example, whatever may have been paid for the mines at the outset and what was a fair asset valuation of the mine when the books were first opened, becomes a diminishing quantity as the ore is taken out of the hills. Every ton of ore that is taken out of one of these mines leaves that mine so much poorer. While it is the proud boast of this company that its ore is practically inexhaustible, yet it is conceivable that in the course of time sufficiently prolonged, if operations are continued, it will be absolutely exhausted.

Let me make the application clear by taking a familiar illustration. Suppose that you and I pay $1,000 for a lot of coal, for example, 200 tons, and that we commenced using that coal to make steam. Suppose, for further illustration, that we consume under the boilers ten tons a day. Then in twenty days our coal would all be consumed, and that portion of our capital which the coal represented, namely, $1,000, would have gone up in smoke. We certainly would be doing ourselves wrong in keeping among our assets the cost of the coal when it had been consumed, or to particularize still further, it would be unfair in the way of a statement to have $1,000 in our assets representing coal on hand, when a quarter or a half or some other fraction of it had been consumed.

This is a fair illustration of a diminishing asset, and what we would do in this case, if we were good accountants, would be to charge into our expense of making steam an amount equal to the coal consumed day by day. Our asset account being credited with the amount thus consumed would diminish as the pile of coal diminished, until finally, when the last ton was put under the boilers, the last dollar in the asset account would likewise have disappeared. This is a clear and simple case of a wasting asset and the treatment that it is necessary to accord to it in good accounting. The illustration, however, has the advantage of definiteness of quantity, which does not exist in such a proposition as the mining which we are considering.

Whatever was paid for these mines must be spread over the cost of the bullion copper which results from the ore that is taken from the mines. Whenever the mines are exhausted the total cost by way of an asset should also be exhausted. Whatever the cost of the mines may have been, therefore, in the course of time becomes a part of the cost of the copper produced. Now this would be a very simple thing to accomplish, if only we knew just how many tons of ore there are in the mine as we knew a moment ago the number of tons of coal we had on hand. Given the cost of the mine divided back by the tons of ore and we shall have the price per ton of ore that should be figured into costs, but unfortunately no man can tell how many tons of ore the mines contain.

There are various surprises in mining matters, and the surprise to date in the case of this company, as it seems to me from examination of the records, is that the quantity of ore actually in the hills is greatly in excess of the fond hopes and rosy dreams of those who were connected with the original prospecting. With this uncertainty of amount existing we must resort to some plan to help us out with the company's account-keeping and statements, and yet still be upon a plan that will admit of such adjustments in the end as are necessary when the actual quantity of ore contained in the hills has been established. Instead, therefore, of crediting the asset account with a price per ton for each ton of ore extracted, thereby diminishing the asset, as we go along we let the asset item stand at the original figure and carry the credit to what is called a reserve account. We establish a price per ton as the value of the ore and charge into the cost of copper that price per ton on all the ore consumed, carrying the offsetting credit to the reserve account.

Now it is possible, in fact, very likely, that the price per ton thus established is in excess of the figure that would be produced by dividing the total number of tons of ore in the mines into the price that was paid for the mines. But of this we have no certain knowledge. So we continue this process of charging into costs the agreed upset price per ton and crediting to reserves the corresponding amount until such time as the reserve equals the amount paid for the mines. Now if the facts prove that when this stage has been reached that there are still many tons of ore in the mines, it will be so much to the advantage of the company from that time forward, for thereafter there will be no necessity of charging into costs the upset price per ton of ore for the purpose of reserves to offset the amount paid for the mines. This amount having been used in the costs to date, thereafter the stated profits of the company will be as though the ore cost nothing but the costs of extraction.

THE NARROW GAUGE RAILROAD.

This, however, illustrates only one of the reserve accounts which it is necessary to maintain for the purpose of keeping constantly before the management the actual facts of the situation. The Narrow Gauge Railroad running from the smelter and concentrator up into the mines has cost the company a very considerable amount of money. No matter how thoroughly repaired it may be kept, yet its entire value or cost will be sunk the moment that the ore in the hills has been exhausted, and there remains no more work for the railroad to do. It was built not as a commercial proposition but merely as an adjunct to the mining and smelting of ore. Its utility ceases whenever the ore is exhausted. Therefore the total cost of the railroad in addition to the cost of operation, must by rights be charged into the copper produced up to the time that the mines are exhausted. Now right here we have the same condition of uncertainty that we had in the previous illustration. We do not know how many tons of ore there are in the hills, and therefore we do not know over how many tons of ore we are to spread the cost of the road. We are under the necessity therefore of resorting to a reserve account charging into the cost of production as we go along whatever would seem to be fair under the circumstances, carrying the offsetting credit to the corresponding reserve account. When we have by this means taken up the entire cost of the road we have, of course, accomplished our object, and if there is still some ore left the company will be in position to make relatively a little more money than prior to that date, for the cost of the narrow-gauge road will no longer figure into costs of production.

The very expensive construction of the smelter and convertor and concentrator, including also the hoisting apparatus and other machinery about the mines, are still other examples of wasting assets. No matter how thoroughly each of these items is kept repaired the time will come, either by the exhaustion of the ore in the mines or because the art has advanced so that this machinery and these appliances are out of date and no longer economical in use, when all of it will be discarded. Accordingly their cost by rights should be spread over the work that they do during their lives. Here again there is the necessity of establishing a life period or other basis of calculation by which the costs shall be properly charged into production and credited to a reserve account, the reserve being held ready to pass to the credit of the asset account whenever the actual facts of the case have been ascertained.

SUBORDINATE INDUSTRIES.

In these items I am referring to features of accounting that in principle, but more particularly in detail, differ from that which has been employed in the accounts of the company to date, and which relate also to some of the principal undertakings of the company. This company is essentially a mining company, and therefore interest centers in whatever is done relating to mining or reduction, but incident to mining and reduction are various other industries which, although subordinate to these particular undertakings, yet require just as good accounting and just as careful analysis.

The management needs to know for the purpose of directing affairs, the details of each of these sub-industries and the results following from its operation as it does in other directions. For example, there is the necessity of such a scheme of analysis in the carpenter shop as will show costs of each particular order or lot of work as opposed to every other. For example, there were a lot of benches made last week and a lot of tables this week. The records should be so arranged that the benches will come out with their own particular costs, and the tables come out with their own correct costs. Each should bear its fair quota of general expenses, so that the total costs of all the different lots of work turned out shall equal the whole of the costs of the carpenter shop department. The same thing is to be said about the machine shop, about building construction, about repairs, about additions to the Narrow-Gauge Railroad or extensions to the Standard Gauge, and so on to the end of the list of all that the company is doing or may do.

THE "WORK ORDER" SYSTEM.

The rule is to let each tub stand on its own bottom. Let each undertaking, whether it be the production of a small article in the carpenter shop or of a ten-mile addition to the railway or of a number of houses on the town site, carry its own particular costs, not estimated costs but actual costs.

not partial cost but entire costs. To accomplish this analysis and secure these results we have started what is known as the "work order" system. There is absolutely nothing new about it. I might say by way of remark that in certain parts of the country ninety concerns out of every hundred have it in operation, and those that use it are among the best and foremost of their kinds. Everything that is done is to be carried along under a numbered work order. No labor is to be applied, no material is to be used except only the cost of that labor, and the cost of that material is charged to the work order to which it is applied. Accounts are maintained with all these work orders, and as they are finished they are closed out or credited with their costs by the transfer which is made to either the asset account to which the work rightly belongs or to an operating account, if the character of the work throws it in that direction.

On a moment's reflection it will be evident to every one that in making up the costs of any undertaking represented by one of these work orders upon the plan above described, there are other features of cost than those included in a mere statement of direct labor and materials consumed. There must be recognized the costs of superintendence, and clerical labor and the expenses of general administration, those of you who have come in contact with the blanks and forms which have been supplied will notice that provision has been made for these items as well as the others.

"CONSTRUCTION AND OPERATION."

Let me stop right here to give brief attention to certain terms that are in extensive use in connection with mining and railway enterprises throughout the country at large, and which sound so plausible that one would be led to suppose they cover everything, and that they are sufficient for all purposes. The terms referred to are "Construction" and "Operation." In every direction we find persons, whether they are capitalists and investors, or subordinates in the company, or mere employees, talking wisely about "construction" and "operation." Now these words and what they mean are all right as far as they go, but as I shall attempt to show you they are misleading in that they do not go far enough, and that their application is lost in the way of generalities without that specific quality which is necessary to intelligent direction and management. I am not impeaching the terms themselves, but am deprecating the use that is made of the terms. I am cautioning against the feeling of security that sometimes follows upon the use of the terms when as a fact much more is really necessary than the terms convey. Many of the disputes and discussions which arise among business men and among bookkeepers and others looking after records grow out of a misapprehension of the real meaning of these terms. For example, in railway work a new bridge is put in place of an old one. The superintendent or auditor in referring to this may call it a "replacement." Before long, however, the discussion will come up, is a replacement chargeable to construction or operation? A good many on the face of it, without stopping to think, would say that it is certainly construction; it is not operation for it is a new piece of permanent work. I think the most of you without very long reflection would decide that this is entirely wrong; that replacement is operation rather than construction, because operation had had the advantage of the use of the old bridge until it was worn out, and further, it could not be construction, in the sense of investment, because the new only takes the place of the old.

In some of the lectures in this course, to which you have already listened, attention has been given to the fact that much of modern business results only in the manipulation of assets. For example, this company had cash and bought mines. So far neither profit nor loss followed. Again, it had cash and paid for labor and materials, and thereby acquired the smelter, the convertor and the concentrator. Assuming that these last items are still worth what they cost, we have neither made nor lost by the operation, but we have converted our assets from the condition of cash into mines, smelter, convertor and concentrator. Again, we had cash and paid for labor, paid for the necessary mechanical appliances, and as the result have ore ready for the concentrator or smelter. We go a little further, operating the concentrator, smelter and convertor, and the result is finished product, in other words, bullion copper.

Now up to this time our assets have neither increased nor diminished, but in bullion copper we have an asset that is available in the market by which to get back cash or money, the recognized medium of exchange, and with the aid of which we shall be able to continue our operations. Profit comes into the calculation only when we get more for that with which we part, namely, bullion copper, than it cost us.

From this we derive the fact that there is no money made in mining in itself, no money made in concentrating or in the general process of reduction, but that in themselves profit is made when we sell the manufactured product for more than it cost us to produce it. As already shown our assets are wasting or are being consumed to the extent that we rob the hills of the ore that they contain. Having figured into costs just what this wasting of assets amounts to, profit appears when we get for the product more than we gave for it.

Now in these last sentences quite enough has been presented to show that construction and operation, however useful the terms are under ordinary conditions, do not go far enough. Daily operations may result in construction. Daily operations may result in marketable product. All that we have in the camp, therefore, from one point of view, may be considered operation, but after the operation has been completed it should be carried either into construction by which various asset accounts are commonly designated or into the costs of product, the need of which has already been explained.

In mining enterprises of this kind and in industrial undertakings in general, the accounts which are limited to construction and operation will be inadequate for the purpose. If operations meant cost of product only there might be some chance of solving that division of the problem by the elements named. If construction always meant an asset, the same result might be achieved in that division, but that which is constructed, as well also as that which at the outset is an asset, becomes sooner or later, as we have shown, a cost of product, and that which is operation at the outset very frequently is chargeable to construction, or rather is of the character of an asset.

This in brief is the reason why of the work order system already referred to and the reason why also for various details in the management of the work orders, the use of reserve accounts and other features with which you are more or less acquainted by the practical work that has been done on your desks. What we have accomplished by this plan is really simplification. Something is to be done; a house is to be built or a repair is to be made. Give it a work order with a number. Then the undertaking progresses without the necessity of our stopping to think whether it is construction or operation. It is duly charged with all the labor applied to it, with all the materials consumed, and with its pro rata of general expenses.

Finally the time comes for charging it out, that is, balancing the account. Then is decided the question whether it goes into the asset accounts or, as the old classification would call it, into construction or into costs of product, or, as the old classifications have it, into operation.

The statistical records that are left behind by this plan become adequate for answering every question that the management can ask. To attempt to decide in advance whether an item is construction or operation results in a congestion of details in a single account, an adequate analysis of which subsequently is a practical impossibility. The reason why therefore of the plans pursued is that it is cheaper to analyze as you proceed than to let items get cold and then try to sort them up on some agreed plan.

THE TIME BOOKS.

Now in closing let me make specific reference to certain details with which some of you are wrestling at the present time. Primarily there are the time books. The only difference between what was formerly in operation here, namely, an analytical pay roll, and that which is at present being introduced is the requirement to locate the labor performed by a given man on a given day against some work order number. As already shown it is not sufficient to charge labor against construction. It is far better to keep the cost of all construction items until they are done, and then make the transfer to the asset divisions of the accounts. By this plan we at all times give the management the analysis that is wanted for intelligent direction. The time books are arranged in such a way that a portion of the time of a man may be charged against any one of several orders during a given day. The scheme is sufficiently elastic and the blanks are so ruled as to meet any requirement in this regard.

Again there is the question of the issuance of materials. Materials as they come in are charged into Stores, or as it is more commonly described, into the Supply Department. They are issued by the Supply Department against numbered work orders. I neglected to say a moment ago that no labor hereafter will be paid for by the company except that which has previously been charged agains work orders, and here I should say that no materials can be issued hereafter except they are specifically charged to work orders. All the labor reported for payment must balance with the charges for labor made to work orders. A similar balancing is made between the amount of materials charged to the several work orders in progress and the total amount of materials issued by the Supply Department. There is a proof-by-balance at every step.

Some of you are asking. Does not all this involve more labor than the old plan? The answer to this is hard to make, conditions have to be considered. At the outset, yes. On the steady run, after things are in operation, no. With accounting alone compared upon the basis of things as they are, and things as they will be, yes; but with the total expense of the accounting department as things were compared with the expense of the accounting department as things will be, no. This last assertion may seem equivocal, but nevertheless it is true. The new plan means balancing up and proving correctness day by day without any back work to do. It carries all its costs as it goes along. Inventorying is done as things go out, with proof of correctness established at that date. The old plan was to let the accounts run upon whatever method was in vogue, and then prove up at long periods by inventorying and by long-drawn-out and extensive audits so-called. If the expense of inventorying and of the necessary corrections, reconciliations, etc., made also at large expense at the end of the period are taken into account as parts of the running costs of the accounting, then the new scheme is by far the cheaper.

But some of you are interested in knowing something else, almost personal in character. Will the new take more or less clerks? I might not be willing to answer that question so frankly were I discussing the affairs of an old-established institution in some other part of the country where steady employment is a matter of great importance to a very large number of people, who, in a special sense, are dependent upon the establishment for work. Here I can be absolutely frank, for from what I have seen the clerical labor here is something that comes and goes. There are very few of you here who are looking forward to long employment with this company. The most of you confessedly are here for short periods of time only. Now for my answer. I have reported to the management that there is 25 per cent to 40 per cent more clerical labor now paid for by the company than there is need of under the operation of a good system properly installed and economically administered. Some of you who are tenacious of the employment which this company affords at present may be alarmed at this statement, fearing instant discharge. To this I reply: those of you who are efficient in your work, and competent in your several capacities have everything to gain by the change proposed, and nothing to lose. Those of you, on the other hand, who are holding your positions merely by reason of favoritism or because you are pensioners, or for some other reason other than your real competency in the work involved have every reason to regret that changes are being made.

The Making of an English Accountant

By T. WHEELER MEATS, A. S. A. A.

[The editor of Commerce, Accounts & Finance desires to call the attention of its readers to the following article, which details the exhaustive system of study through which the aspirant for membership in the English Incorporated Society of Accountants and Auditors must pass in order to become one of the Society. The system is extremely thorough, and the student who passes successfully the final examination should, and does, know something about accounting.]

The final examination of the Incorporated Society of Accountants and Auditors being the final and complete test to which all who desire membership are subjected, in order, no doubt, to prove the thoroughness of the knowledge which they possess in regard to the science of accountancy and the usages of the commercial world, it follows that the field to be covered by this examination is a very wide one. It is divided into two distinct parts: —

Part I.—The accountancy subjects, embracing—

(a) Advanced Bookkeeping.
(b) Advanced Auditing.
(c) General Commercial Knowledge.
(d) The adjustment of Partnership and Executorship Accounts.

Part II.—The legal portion, with which I have no concern this evening.

The reason which prompts me to leave the legal subjects severely alone is not that they may be lightly treated by the candidates—far from it—indeed such an idea would hardly carry weight with one who has passed through the ordeal of those very trying legal papers, but that the legal mind is more able to deal with them from the point of view of the candidate, and were I to discuss them in a superficial manner I should not do justice to such an important class of study.

Before plunging into my subject, I will shortly refer to the ideas which primarily actuate the student, and to the various points of view from which he approaches the work of preparation which lies before him, the months of study, reading and bookkeeping practice, all absolutely necessary to give him any confidence in the success of his efforts, and to provide him with that success. The vast improvements in the system and method of bookkeeping taking place from time to time are the result of the demand made by the commercial world upon the skill of the professional accountant; consequently it is expected, and rightly so, of all those who are fully-fledged members of the profession that they should actually possess the knowledge which the said commercial world requires them to do, and that, therefore, the reputation of the expert accountant may improve and never suffer at their hands.

It sometimes happens that the candidate is generally so completely occupied until late in the evening that he is only able to devote five, or perhaps six, hours weekly to his entire studies, and often during busy times they have to be put on one side altogether. Under such circumstances it is not reasonable to expect as thorough a preparation as in the case where more spare time is available. I would suggest that where the candidate finds himself in such an awkward position as that which I have described, he should double the length of his period of preparation, and thereby prevent the possibility of his presenting himself for examination without being in a state of preparedness and without running the risk of either his law or accountancy suffering at the other's expense. Should, however, such a course of preparation be undertaken as is demanded by the Society, and by the requirements of the commercial community, the information obtained must be of extreme benefit to the after career of the candidate, and also carry him through the examination with success.

In order to present to you the work entailed in the preparation for the final examination of the Society in the short time which an evening allows me, and with a view to avoiding duplicating my remarks, I propose to divide the subject into the following parts:—

I. The Theory of Bookkeeping with Accountancy and Commercial Definitions.

II. The Construction of Accounts.

III. General Commercial Knowledge.

IV. The adjustment of Partnership and Executorship Accounts.

V. Auditing

VI. Program of Work.

I.—The Theory of Bookkeeping with Definitions

The study of the elementary portion of the theory of bookkeeping is included in the Society's intermediate examination, and it seems hardly likely, from perusal of past papers, that questions of such a nature will confront the "final" candidate, he no doubt possessing a complete grasp in this respect. Although this is the case, I do not consider that this, the basis on which the whole structure of bookkeeping rests, should be omitted entirely from the preparation of the final examination candidate, but that it should be taken together with the more advanced part of theoretical accountancy. Between the final and intermediate examinations a period of three years exists, and during this time much is learned of a practical nature, but much of the theoretical knowledge gained in the preparation for the intermediate examination is forgotten. I therefore suggest that during the month which precedes the strict course of study decided upon for the final examination, at least two or, if possible, three weeks be set aside for a renewal of elementary theory, and for a study of theory of an advanced kind, the effect of such a preliminary canter—if I may so term it—being to enhance the ability of the candidate to take the fullest advantage later on of the course which he has cut out for himself. I will now state—in the order in which I suggest that they should be studied—the points to which I would call your attention in regard to the theory of bookkeeping, again reminding you that such study should take place prior to the strict course of preparation.

(a) DOUBLE AND SINGLE ENTRY BOOKKEEPING.

This includes a definition of each system, the points of difference between them, the advantages of the double entry over the single entry system, how to remodel books kept by single-entry upon the double-entry system, and the application of the double-entry system to the progressive commercial ideas of the present day.

(b) BOOKS OF ACCOUNT.

A complete system of double entry bookkeeping, as contained in journal and ledger (with the cash book in a separate form from the ledger for the sake of convenience), the extension of each of the units mentioned, journal and ledger, into sections, with a subdivision of such sections as is often nowadays required. Special attention should be given to the journal and its position as recording the "first entry" of every transaction, either through the journal proper or through one of its sections or sub-sections.

(c) ACCOUNTS OF PROFIT AND LOSS.

Revenue account, income and expenditure account, trading account, manufacturing account, profit and loss account, the nature of the concerns to which these accounts severally are applicable, their definitions, the class of items of which each consists, and generally the treatment which each account receives from the time of its emerging from the trial balance (its origin) to the journal entries which close it.

(d) THE BALANCE SHEET.

Differentiate between the so-called single entry balance sheet, the statement of affairs, and the balance sheet resulting from the double entry system. Attention should be given to the order in which the liabilities and assets are stated, (1) in private concerns, (2) in the accounts of a limited company, (3) as necessitated by the double account system.

(e) ALLOCATION OF PROFITS BY WAY OF GENERAL OR SPECIFIC RESERVES. (RESERVE FUND, SINKING FUND, SURPLUS, RESERVE ACCOUNT.)

It is necessary that the candidate should be acquainted with the correct definition of each of these accounts, the exact meaning of each definition being clearly understood, as also should be the bookkeeping entries necessitated for each class of allocation from its origin to its conclusion. Particularly is this the case in regard to the making of provision for the repayment of loan capital by way of sinking fund; its protection by the investment of its equivalent, and the ultimate fate of the amounts set aside out of revenue. I am not suggesting that the candidate should plunge into that much-debated question, the constitution of a reserve fund, as I judge that with the preparation for this examination before him he will have other work to occupy his mind and will find the orthodox theories sufficient for his purpose.

(f) THE DISTINCTION BETWEEN CAPITAL AND REVENUE EXPENDITURE.

With particular attention to renewals, repairs and suspense accounts.

(g) ASSETS (FIXED AND FLOATING).

A consideration of each class of asset met with in the balance sheet, and the principle upon which its loss by way of depreciation is from time to time decided upon.

II.—Construction of Accounts

Under this head I propose to take into consideration the constitution of accounts generally, and it will be convenient to divide the subject of construction into three sections: —

Part 1. General Construction.

Part 2. Special Construction (arising out of General Construction).

Part 3. Statutory Construction.

To wade through the form of account employed by every kind of undertaking would be a task beyond the possibility of accomplishment, owing to the restricted amount of time which the accountancy student usually has at his disposal, but it will be seen that a detailed and complete study is obviated by a judicious classification or grouping, each group being the object of special attention. I have previously suggested to you that the principal aim of the Society's final examination is to cause such a course of study to be pursued by each candidate as to insure to him, should he successfully come through the ordeal, a thorough capability to meet any and every demand of an accountancy nature which may be made upon him, including the designing of a system of accounts suitable to any undertaking with which he is brought into contact. In view of the desirability of attaining this end I shall endeavor to cover as much ground as possible in dealing with the subject of construction.

Section I.—General Construction

I have made a classification of the accounts of undertakings which are likely to be met with, and the following grouping is the result:—

(a) The Accounts of Manufacturing Concerns.

(b) The Accounts of Merchants and Traders.

(c) Professional Accounts.

(d) Estate Accounts.

(e) Hotel and Club Accounts.

(f) The Accounts of Trustees and Executors.

(g) The Accounts of Charitable Institutions.

(h) The Accounts of Newspaper Proprietors, Printers and Publishers.

(i) Shipping Accounts.

(j) The Accounts of Banks and Financial Concerns.

(k) Agricultural Accounts.

(l) Mining Accounts.

(a) THE ACCOUNTS OF MANUFACTURING CONCERNS.

This group includes all concerns of a producing nature, and, as these vary a great deal, a study of one set of accounts will hardly give a knowledge of all, and a little sub-division becomes necessary. I would suggest the following as containing the most instructive information: Builders' and Contractors' Accounts, Factory Accounts, Brewery Accounts, and these also afford the greatest possibilities for the application of Cost Accounts, which will be referred to under the head of "Special Construction."

(b) THE ACCOUNTS OF MERCHANTS.

I would direct your special attention to the accounts of a merchant acting as agent to a foreign principal.

(c) PROFESSIONAL ACCOUNTS.

Under this head are included the accounts of solicitors, accountants, architects and auctioneers, and although it is not necessary for a candidate to make a complete study of each system, it is advisable that he should go roughly through them, and take notes of all points of an uncommon nature, paying particular attention to such leading features, and to the rulings which refer specially to the accounts of each profession, as he studies it.

(d) ESTATE ACCOUNTS.

(e) HOTEL AND CLUB ACCOUNTS.

(f) THE ACCOUNTS OF TRUSTEES AND EXECUTORS.

In this group the question is faced, Are estate books to be opened from the estate duty account by journalizing the assets and liabilities direct to capital account, thus necessitating a further journal entry to adjust the difference on realization, or shall the items be carried to a memorandum column, and shall the accountant refrain from journalizing either income or capital until realization? Advocates are to be found on both sides, but personally I prefer the latter method as the safer, and think a student will not suffer if he adopts it.

(g) THE ACCOUNTS OF CHARITABLE INSTITUTIONS.

Not very long ago a certain amount of dissatisfaction was expressed at the manner in which capital and income were mixed up in the accounts of some large charitable institutions, both as regards the receipts and payments, and a committee was appointed to inquire into the matter and to make a report. They did this; and in it they recommended that donations, legacies and subscriptions be shown distinctly, and that expenditure of a capital nature be distinguished from general maintenance. A perusal of this report will be useful.

(h) THE ACCOUNTS OF NEWSPAPERS, PRINTERS AND PUBLISHERS.

Special attention should be given to copyrights and royalties, including the bookkeeping entries necessary to record them. Many publishers print their own publications, and become therefore both printers and publishers; it also happens sometimes that the publication of a newspaper is included in the scope of the undertaking, and special bookkeeping arrangements are necessary to separately record, and to focus on to a private ledger, the work of each of these departments. Stock accounts periodically balanced, both in regard to raw material and works printed for the publishing department, and the valuation of the concluding stocks at balancing time, form important features.

(i) SHIPPING ACCOUNTS.

This refers more particularly to the accounts of a single-ship company.

(j) THE ACCOUNTS OF BANKS AND FINANCIAL CONCERNS.

I do not suggest the absolute necessity for a complete study of bank accounts, although this would by no means be work thrown away, but I would call attention to the example of branch and head office accounts, as provided by the general (or check) ledger of head office and general ledger of each branch, together with the incorporation of the branch trial balance in the head office books. A close acquaintance with the balance sheet of a bank and the method employed in regard to the dealing with interest on current accounts and bills is advisable.

(k) AGRICULTURAL ACCOUNTS.

These are not generally met with in examination papers, but they should not be omitted from the studies of a final examination candidate, who should pay special attention to cost accounts, showing the net profit made in each department of agriculture engaged in, and in conjunction therewith accounts of stock regularly verified.

Section II.—Special Construction

As I have previously mentioned, this will include bookkeeping of a special nature which arises out of, and is in advance of, the general construction of accounts, and the object of which is to deal with a quantity of details in such a manner as to facilitate the agreement of the books at balance time, and to aid the proprietor in ascertaining the cost of his manufactures and in other ways.

(a) SELF-BALANCING LEDGERS.

This system, having for its object the better control of the work of the ledger staff, and the more ready balancing of the books when required, is a great boon to those who have the responsibility of controlling the office staff of a large undertaking. It is probable that the final examination candidate will already be acquainted with the arrangement of the books necessary to record such a system, but in any case such knowledge should be taken to be an essential part of the final preparation. It is not sufficient to have a general idea; the whole of the bookkeeping entries necessary to keep the ledgers of a considerable concern under self-balancing principles should be quite understood.

(b) COLUMNAR BOOKKEEPING AND TABULAR LEDGERS.

One columnar method is used for the purpose of analyzing the total column, particularly in regard to petty cash accounts, bought and sold day books and cash books (where self-balancing ledgers are used), etc., and acts as a saving of time in regard to the posting of the ledgers by necessitating only the posting of the column totals.

Tabular ledgers are only applicable to undertakings the debits and credits of which are periodical and numerous, such as the accounts of laundries, building and friendly societies, bakers, gas and water companies; and the particular advantages obtained by the use of the tabular form of ledger is, that it is possible to apply the debits and credits in column totals to the commencing balances, and thereby prove each set of columns of the ledger separately as to the concluding balances, thus locating an error very quickly. The total of each column can be agreed with the actual book of first entry from which it is entered up.

(c) KAIN'S SYSTEM.

The candidate should be familiar with the ruling of the journal employed in this system.

(d) COST ACCOUNTS.

These accounts are applicable to all concerns of a producing nature, and they have for their object the institution of such method as will show the detailed cost of the productions to the manufacturer by way of estimate (rough cost book), and prove the correctness of such estimate by regularly kept and balanced stock accounts, without which, I suggest, that cost accounts may be a grave error. In relation to the accounts of contractors, brewers, factories and collieries, an example of which should be taken as containing the greatest amount of instruction on the subject, I particularly recommend the application of cost accounts. This is a system the importance of which, to the manufacturing community, it is impossible to over estimate, and upon which the candidate is certain to be tested in the examination; for both these reasons it deserves the most careful study at his hands. I would mention particularly that cost accounts, the composition of which (in regard to raw material especially) is not proved by the balancing of stocks, may be of a most misleading character.

Section III.—Statutory Construction

The following are the forms of accounts, as fixed by statute or prescribed by the Board of Trade, which I would recommend for the study of a candidate for the final examination:

(a) The Companies' Act, 1862, Form of Balance Sheet

ascertained in Table A.

(b) Life Assurance Companies Act, 1870, Form of Annual Accounts.

(c) Gas Works Clauses Act, 1871, Form of Annual Accounts.

(d) Regulation of Railways Act, 1868, Form of Annual Accounts.

(e) Building Societies Act, 1894, Form of Annual Accounts.

(f) Friendly Societies Act, 1896, Form of Accounts prescribed by Register.

(g) Form of Electric Lighting Accounts by the Board of Trade.

(h) The Statement of Affairs in Bankruptcy and Liquidation, together with the Deficiency Account, and the other Forms incidental to the Statement of Affairs.

III.—General Commercial Knowledge

This, the third section into which I divide my subject, embraces the entire field of information in regard to matters of commercial and of accountancy nature which are likely to be met with by the professional accountant of the present day, with the exception of what is otherwise dealt with here. It is impossible in this short paper to deal with every point which is included under this head, and upon which it is possible that the candidate will be tested, but I will endeavor to take into consideration as many of the leading features as possible.

(a) BILLS OF EXCHANGE AND THEIR TREATMENT IN ACCOUNTS.

This subject is one which is taken up considerably in the intermediate examination, and it may be presumed therefore that the final candidate has already a tolerable acquaintance with it; but, nevertheless, it is advisable that he should brush it up, particularly in regard to the forms of bills payable and receivable books, the stamp duties, etc. The legal aspect of this subject will be studied in mercantile law.

(b) CONSIGNMENT ACCOUNTS.

I would specially refer to the method of treating in the books of the consignor as to the issuing of the goods, the expenses on same, the remittances by the consignee and the valuation of the outstanding consignment upon stock-taking.

(c) EXCHANGE.

In these days, when so many English concerns possess foreign branches, a knowledge of the principles of exchange are essential to the preparation of the student of accountancy, and yet the final candidate can hardly afford to devote such time to a study of the subject as its importance warrants. Let it then be sufficient for him to understand—

1. The main principles governing the fluctuations in exchange values.
2. The basis upon which the items contained in the foreign trial balance are changed to sterling (the rates varying in the cases of fixed assets, floating assets and nominal accounts), and their incorporation in the head office accounts.

(d) THE ACCOUNTS OF A MERCHANT ACTING FOR A FOREIGN PRINCIPAL.

This includes a study of the procedure, and the accounts recording same, in reference to the following:—

1. The bill of exchange occasionally drawn by the foreign principal upon his agent in England against the consignment, and which is negotiated by handing over the bill of lading.
2. The arrival of the consignment, agent's procedure in regard to bill of exchange and disposal of the goods.
3. The brokers' accounts and remittances.
4. The account current, its form, and interest calculations.

(e) FIRE INSURANCE LOSSES.

Accounts for submission to fire offices. As you will be aware, an accountant is frequently instructed to prepare accounts with a view to arriving at the value of a stock-in-trade at the date of which the fire has taken place, and the candidate should be acquainted with the method employed for this purpose. It must vary according to the books which are saved from the fire; but presuming that none have been lost, the important point to arrive at is the percentage of gross profits on sales. After obtaining this, the preparation of the stock account is not difficult.

(f) LOSSES BY WAY OF DEPRECIATION AND BAD DEBTS.

The principal points which will require the attention of the candidate in reference to this subject are:—

1. The several causes from which depreciation may arise.
2. The manner in which general depreciation is calculated without interest being taken into consideration.
3. The method used when interest on the asset is taken into consideration.
4. The method of arriving at the basis upon which a reserve is made.

(g) STOCK ACCOUNTS.

There are several ways in which stock may be dealt with, and I will instance the following:—

1. Where each class of material used, and products obtained in a manufacture, are kept separate and form part of the D. E. system employed (cost accounts being used), the balance on the ledger stock accounts are presumed to agree with the actual stocks when taken.
2. Where cost accounts are not used and the materials are not classified.
3. In cases where the goods dealt in are of the nature of curios, or are valuable, but not very numerous, a form of stock book, known as a trading stock register, should be used, which provides information as to the history of each article, particulars of cost and selling price, and consequently a check is obtained upon the trading account. The verification of stock accounts at balance time is an important matter.
4. The stock accounts of wine and spirit merchants and bottlers provide much instruction and information, particularly as to valuation of goods in a process which is partly completed.

N. B.—I need hardly say that a basis of stocktaking once adopted should be maintained.

(h) INCOME TAX.

Accountants are brought into contact with income tax to a considerable extent, and candidates are likely to be required to deal with the subject at their final examination. An acquaintance with the laws relating to income tax is quite an undertaking, but it is necessary to read up a work upon the subject. I recommend candidates to run through a standard work and make profuse notes of the principal points which arise.

1. The schedules under which it is assessed and their application.
2. The basis of assessment referring to various classes of undertakings, and the reductions on account of abatement and exemption.
3. The preparation of accounts under schedule D, including the dealing with life assurance premiums, depreciation, and the items of expense which are not chargeable, the writing back of such items, and also of credits upon which tax has already been paid.
4. Appeals (a) against assessments recently made, and (b) to obtain a rebate of tax overpaid.
5. Income tax in relation to a partnership profit and loss account, and the deduction of income tax from certain payments on account of dividends, interest, ground rents, etc.

(i) THE USE OF PERCENTAGES.

In dealing with a matter, the utility of which has been discussed by this Society, a discussion which I have read with much interest, the difficulty seems to be to obtain a true relation of the percentage to the whole, and I confess that unless, as in the case of a manufacture, a standard value of the finished article can be decided upon and used for the purpose of the manufacturing account, it is hardly possible to obtain a sound basis to work upon. I think, however, that percentages, even when applied to items of cost on the one hand, and productions or sales at prices which vary on the other hand, will yield much useful information and bring a check, although not a perfect one, to bear upon the items contained in the accounts to which they are applied. I take it that the uses to which percentages are put are:—

1. To ascertain the variation in the expense of dealing with goods other than in manufacture, viz., in selling and

distributing.

2. To provide the manufacturer with a means of finding out whether the percentages used in his rough cost book for the purpose of estimating the cost to him of the articles, the selling price of which he is fixing, are in agreement with the actual percentages disclosed in his manufacturing account.

3. The percentage of gross profit to sales.

It is on these points that I submit the subject as one for the consideration of candidates.

N. B.—A difficulty sometimes arises in regard to percentages as applied to stock and materials. The stock at the commencement of the period under review should be added to purchases (less returns), and the stock at the close should be deducted, the result which should be shown in the trading account in one item, being the first cost to the manufacturer of the goods sold, and both the stocks are thus eliminated from the trading account.

(k) COMPANY WORK.

This subject will be considered under the head of "Auditing," and I shall treat it now from the standpoint of (a) bookkeeping, (b) the secretary, and (c) the directors.

1. The investigation on behalf of vendor or promoter.
2. The prospectus.
2. The issue of share capital, the application and allotment sheets, the share ledger, certificates, the minutes of allotment.
4. Forfeited shares and their re-issue.
5. The issue of debentures, both at a premium and at a discount, with provision for redemption at a fixed time.
6. The appropriation of profits by way of dividends, etc.
7. Transfer of shares and the issue of certificates.
8. The statutory books of account and record.
9. A comprehensive account of a secretary's duties.
10. The duties of directors at their first board meeting and afterwards.
11. Reconstruction.

(l) BANKRUPTCY WORK AND LIQUIDATIONS.

The statement of affairs in bankruptcy, and that referring to the winding up of companies, together with the accounts incidental to both, particularly the deficiency account, require a thorough study at the hands of the candidate; in fact, they should be entirely committed to memory, because if a question arises at the examination, the official form should be given exactly. The duties of trustees, liquidators and receivers will form part of the legal studies, and therefore are not dealt with here, but the forms of accounts to be kept should be noted.

(m) DEPARTMENTAL BOOKKEEPING.

The arrangement of a system of accounts to suit the requirements of concerns possessing several distinct departments is an essential study, and one might be assured of this, even without a perusal of the papers set in the past, in which departmental and branch accounts have been by no means overlooked. Nowadays the accountant is so often called upon to design such a system, owing, doubtless, to the existing tendency towards the creation of large businesses by the opening of a large number of branches, and the absorption of smaller concerns by larger ones, and because of the practice of adding departments to a successful concern. I would divide the designing of accounts to suit departmental and branch work as follows:—

First—A head office attached to a manufactory (or where goods are not manufactured, but the finished article purchased, a central distributing stores), the branches being supplied at selling prices. The branches may do a credit business or sell for "cash" only. They would be supplied entirely from headquarters, and the system which is recommended must provide an immediate and complete control of the whole working of each branch in the head office books.

Second—A large business divided into several departments, all in one building, such as (a) drapery, (b) furnishing, (c) tailoring, each department having a certain amount of self-control, but the head office, which is on the premises, maintaining a check upon the whole. In such work it sometimes happens that departmental monthly trading returns are required by the directors (and it is impossible to take stock more than once or twice a year), the work of preparing these returns often falling upon the auditor, and much care being required in their preparation in order that the gauging of the stock by percentage of gross profit may result in an agreement with the value of same when ascertained at stocktaking.

Third—A head office, working in conjunction with branches which are practically distinct, but the connection between which consists of a "remittance" account, and the periodical incorporation of the branch trial balance in the head office books.

Fourth—Departmental manufacturing accounts with cost accounts applied thereto. I have previously discussed under "Special Construction" the question of cost accounts, and will now consider only that portion of the same which carries the study of this important subject a step further and links with the departmental work of a factory the accounts necessary to record the cost of articles manufactured under each process through which they pass, so as to produce, simultaneously with the finished article, the account of its cost right up to its completeness in one sum, and also the distribution of such sum as between and over the various workshops through which the article has passed. To design a system which will provide the means whereby this end may be attained, and which will work in accord with the double entry basis upon which the accounts are constructed, is a task requiring considerable study and attention to detail and to the peculiarities of the situation, and this is so principally because it must be absolutely complete—each cost account being spread over the several departments, and the summary agreeing with the cost as definitely ascertained by the first portion of the profit and loss account.

The most important point to be considered is the proving of the rough cost book estimates as to each head of productive expense, by applying the same (in the case of materials) to the stock account, and comparing the balance of the latter with the stock on hand. The reliability of, and consequently the value of, cost accounts depends upon such a verification as this.

(n) THE HIRE-PURCHASE SYSTEM.

This method of purchasing goods is extremely popular in the present day, and entails the periodical repayment of such a sum as will, at compound interest, and at the conclusion of the repayments, amount to the selling price of the goods plus interest on the reducing balances of principal.

This class of transaction entails special bookkeeping entries in regard to:—

1. Apportionment of each instalment, as between principal and interest.
2. The rate and method of dealing with depreciation after taking repairs, which are sometimes (vide railway wagons) the subject of a yearly contract, into consideration.

There are several methods of dealing with the question of interest, and there are three bases upon which depreciation may be calculated, but, although I should much like to dwell upon these, I have to be content with recommending them to your consideration in the course of your studies.

IV.—The Adjustment of Partnership and Executorship Accounts

This will be divided into two portions:—

(a) Partnership.

(b) Executorship.

(a) The consideration of this subject commences at the balance of net profit, which is carried down to the third portion of the profit and loss account, and embraces interest upon drawings and upon capital, the adjustments and the distribution of the balance in the manner and proportion as agreed upon in the deed which governs the partnership. It is essential that the candidate should study this subject thoroughly, and a commencement should be made at the document mentioned—the partnership articles. The books will have been opened in accordance with the terms contained therein, and it is advisable that the candidate should make himself acquainted with the clauses which should usually be contained in such a document, in order that he may be able to advise, both in answering an examination question and in response to the inquiries of a client, as to the points which should be included, in order to lay a sound foundation for the protection of the financial relations of the partners generally. From the opening of the partnership books, I will move in one step to the conclusion of the first year of the partnership business, the books are balanced, net profit is ascertained, and the accountant—I am not now speaking of the auditor—has to consider—

1. The drawings of partners and the calculations of interest thereon.
2. The crediting of interest on capital and upon advances.
3. The adjustment of income tax in order that each partner shall bear his due proportion of same.
4. The closing of profit and loss account and partners' capital accounts, and the journal entries necessary to record the whole.

And also—

5. The accounts, on a dissolution of partnership, in regard to the adjustment of losses on realization.
6. The treatment of good-will in the partnership books.
7. The effect of the insolvency of a partner upon the concern, and the treatment of his overdrawn capital account.

(b) EXECUTORSHIP ACCOUNTS.

The duties which fall to the lot of the professional accountant in regard to this class of accounts vary very considerably, often commencing with the preparation of the estate duty account—although this is generally the work of the solicitor—and including the suggestion of the system to be employed by the executors or trustees, and the opening of the estate books. The adjustment of rents, dividends, etc., as between capital and income, the writing up of the accounts from time to time—perhaps the entire charge of them—and finally the closing entries upon the distribution of the estate also come within the scope of the accountant's work.

It happens rather more frequently, however, that the accountant is called in to advise as to the system upon which the accounts should be kept, and to open the books only and then to audit the accounts (a) at regular intervals, and (b) upon conclusion of the estate. I shall presume that the legal portion of executorship studies is being properly carried out, and that the matter relating to estate, legacy and succession duties, the order of the abatement of legacies, the apportionment of dividends, interest, rents, business profits, the list of authorized securities, the order of payment of debts, etc., all extremely important and likely to be met with in an examination paper have been given sufficient attention. In the first instance the candidate should commit to memory the leading headings of the estate duty account, and should also be well acquainted with the correct system necessary to open the estate account books, to record the estate transactions therein from time to time, and to make the closing entries upon the distribution of the estate. The candidate should also be well acquainted with the form of the residuary account.

I should advise that a text book on the subject of executorship accounts be studied, and the following points noted:

(a) Upon the death of testator the accountant is called in by the executor to act with his solicitor in regard to the preparation of the estate duty account, which entails a complete examination of the deceased's papers and a valuation of his assets.

(b) Upon probate being obtained, the accountant is instructed to open the books of the estate, and to lay down a system upon which they should be kept in future. He will here have to deal with the opening entries from the estate duty account. Under this the necessary account books should be studied.

(c) The periodical balancing of the books, and the writing up of capital and income and beneficiaries' personal accounts.

(d) The final adjustments, as between the beneficiaries, upon the conclusion of the estate or trust.

(e) The position of an executor in regard to the business of the testator.

It is needless for me to go further in this paper into the detail of this subject, as all necessary information will be contained in the text book which the candidate will read, and I have only mentioned the principal features as leading points to candidates who are just about to sit for their final examination, and who would do well to pay particular attention to them.

V.—Auditing

The next head under which I shall consider the studies of the "Final" candidate is that of "Auditing," and this is the most important class of work undertaken by members of the accountancy profession. The preparation of the candidate in Theory, Construction, General Commercial Knowledge and Partnership and Executorship Adjustments has tended to complete his bookkeeping training and to open the way to a study of the application of "expert" check to the subjects which have up to now occupied attention.

I have already suggested that during the month preceding the strict course which the student has mapped out for himself, there are certain studies of a perhaps rather elementary nature which he should undertake, and I would add to these the recommendation that during this month he should also read a text book dealing with Auditing; in fact, before the strict course commences he should have completed the reading of this book and should have supplied himself with profuse notes on the leading matter contained therein.

I do not intend to recommend a particular text book, but I am aware that the leading publications are to be found in your library. It has been my experience that the first study of a text book is the most difficult one, and to get it accomplished before the preparation commences in earnest is to remove a great obstacle from the course proper. I will divide the consideration of auditing into the following sections:—

1. Audit Procedure, (a) General, (b) Special.
2. Continuous Audits.
3. Statutes Relating to Auditing.
4. Investigations.
5. The Agreement of Trial Balances.
6. The Auditor's Certificate and Report.

1.—AUDIT PROCEDURE (a) GENERAL.

A study of the text book, together with the practical experience which the candidate has already gained, will doubtless have acquainted him with the usual method employed in the conduct of an audit; he will understand the drawing up of instructions as to the lines on which the audit is to be carried out, the method employed in calling over the books, and vouching in general, consequently it will only be necessary to complete the study of such matters by reading up each branch of the subject separately. I would recommend that the best subjects for special study are:—

(a) Vouching.

(b) The responsibilities of an auditor, with special reference to the Companies Act, 1900.

(c) The detection of fraud.

(d) The agreement of trial balances.

(e) Allocations of profit by way of "general" or "specific" reserves.

(f) The balance sheet—valuation of assets.

Included in (b) will be the question as to what profits are available for the payment of dividend, and on this subject the student cannot do better than read the lecture delivered by Mr. Beale, K.C., and which appears in the Accountant on December 1, 1900, entitled "Judicial Dicta and Legislative Restrictions as to the Payment of Dividends Out of Revenue."

The procedure necessary to the proper carrying out of an audit will, I need hardly say, vary in a manner dependent upon the class of the business and the nature of the system employed, but it is advisable to adopt a general rule as a basis (and that only) upon which the program of the work should be compiled. Therein should be included the general work which is common to nearly every audit, such as vouching cash book, examination of bank pass book, invoices, sales, stock, reserves for discounts and bad debts, and the adjustments necessary to bring the trading of the period into focus with the trading account, and to obtain a correct statement of the assets and liabilities in the balance sheet.

Such a general rule, which is intended to deal with ordinary work only, and is not so comprehensive as to include the whole of the audit work which necessarily would require special instructions, may be carried too far, and if so, have a very machine-like effect upon the audit work—a result which prevents the attainment of the real object of the audit, viz., to apply "expert" check to the accounts to be examined.

I would sum up my remarks upon the subject of "General Audit Procedure" by suggesting that the candidate should be prepared to submit to the examiners an audit program to suit any exigency, and be ready to take up systems of accounts, good, bad and indifferent, and to state how he would proceed to audit them. Much must therefore depend upon the thoroughness of the preparation, and perhaps a little upon the ingenuity of the candidate, although I am sure that the former will give the candidate more satisfaction, both at and after the examination, than any amount of the latter.

Genius is valuable, and if allied to thoroughness of study it is sure to attain to considerable success, but I think that to give a close application to the study in hand, and persevere in the preparation in an honest manner, will—if a sufficiently long course is taken—insure a most favorable result.

AUDIT PROCEDURE (b) SPECIAL.

In connection with the audit of accounts of every character, excepting private concerns owned by a single individual, the auditor has to make himself acquainted with the document which forms the basis of the undertaking:—

1. Executorship and Trust Accounts. The Will or Trust Deed.
2. Partnership Accounts. The Partnership Articles.
3. Joint Stock Companies' Accounts. The Memorandum and Articles of Association.

This is the first step in every audit, and following upon it comes the consideration of such statutes as have special reference to the concern in hand, and with which the auditor will of course be acquainted.

EXECUTORSHIP OR TRUST ACCOUNTS.

The rates and natures of the several duties, authorized investments, the apportionment of receipts between capital and income, the order of payment of debts and the abatement of legacies, are the principal points. I shall, perhaps, touch lightly here on those legal studies which directly affect the audit of accounts.

PARTNERSHIP ACCOUNTS.

The Partnership Act of 1890, which is practically the summary of the law governing partnerships.

2.—CONTINUOUS AUDITS.

This is an important subject, and has been frequently met with in the examination papers. In arranging a system for a continuous audit the great point which must be considered is the necessity for the auditor to retain in his hands a control over the books of the concern, as otherwise, the figures being liable to alteration after his visit, the very fact of the audit being of a continuous nature becomes a danger. In order that a system may be worth stating as an answer to an examination question, it should at least possess the above-mentioned qualification—it must give to the auditor the means of detecting any subsequent alteration of the figures which he has checked.

I would suggest that for the auditor to retain the private ledger in his own possession, and to write it up himself from time to time is the best protection with which he can supply himself, and if the totals of items posted are carried thereto immediately, the only danger appears to lie in alterations of a compensating nature in a particular ledger.

3.—STATUTES RELATING TO AUDITING.

The following statutes have direct reference to the audit of accounts:—

The Companies Act, 1862 (table A), which should be well studied, as it becomes ipso facto, the "Articles" of any company which does not frame special articles.

The Companies Act, 1879. This refers to the audit of banking companies.

The Companies Clauses Consolidation Act, 1845. This refers to Parliamentary Companies, excepting so far as they are governed by their special act.

Metropolis Water Act, 1871. Board of Trade appoints the auditor.

Railway Companies Act, 1867. Audit compulsory before a dividend can be paid.

Regulation of Railways Act, 1868. Makes audit compulsory.

Municipal Corporation Act, 1882. This provides for those three auditors—the Mayor's auditor and two elective auditors.

Building Societies Act, 1894. Accounts must be audited, and one of the auditors, at least, must be a person publicly carrying on the business of an accountant; and that is as far as we have got at present.

Industrial and Provident Societies Act, 1893. Audit by two members compulsory.

Friendly Societies Act, 1896. Two persons appointed by the society; audit compulsory. This is to be incorporated in the rules.

Companies Act, 1900. This, at any rate, makes an audit compulsory, and the candidate should be well acquainted with it.

4.—INVESTIGATIONS.

This is a subject possessing much interest, and is divided into a variety of heads.

1. Where fraud is suspected.
2. On behalf of vendors or promoters in regard to limited companies.
3. With a view to purchase of, or if financing an undertaking, or the purchase of a partnership in an undertaking.
4. On behalf of creditors.
5. On behalf of shareholders (popular nowadays).
6. With a view to the preparation of a statement of affairs.

In each of these cases different elements are introduced into the investigation, and the student should first make sure of the standpoint from which he approaches the matter, and the particular points to notice in the investigation. A very interesting and instructive paper upon this subject appears in the Incorporated Accountants' Journal for November, 1900—the author being Mr. Arthur E. Green, a fellow of this Society—and after perusing it with much interest, I strongly recommend it to candidates. Do not be content to deal with an investigation in a general sense, but go into the matter in detail and work out the effect of each manner of dealing with the assets and liabilities in the books of the concern.

5.—AGREEMENT OF TRIAL BALANCES.

Trial balances are often difficult to obtain, and considerable ingenuity has to be brought to bear in order to effect the necessary agreement of the debt and credit balances. There are several methods generally used for this purpose, prominent amongst them being—

1. Tabulating the ledgers.
2. Calling over the postings again, but first of all verifying the opening balances.
3. A system advocated by Mr. Craggs, F.C.A., which has for its leading feature that the clerk who is calling out shall enter the items on "slips" as he calls them, and so provide (a) a dissection of the book of first entry to (b) an adjustment account for each ledger.

The shortest course is, naturally, one to be adopted, and it is half the battle when each ledger or class of ledger has been made self-balancing by means of an adjustment account. Each of the methods named may be applied to advantage under different circumstances, and that is a matter for the consideration of the candidate.

6.—THE AUDITOR'S CERTIFICATE AND REPORT.

This subject should be read in conjunction with the Companies Act, 1900.

VI.—Program of Work

I have sketched a program of work for the final student,

as applying to the division of subjects as arranged in this paper, based on a six months' course, with an extra month for preliminary work, and it is as follows:—

Preliminary month—

Bookkeeping theory, definitions of commercial and accountancy terms, read through auditing text book. If it were possible, I would recommend that the text books referring to partnership and executorship accounts be read once in this month in order to get the first study of these three important text books over as early as possible. The selection of papers for study should also be included here.

SIX MONTHS' COURSE PROPER.

First month, four weeks—three evenings in each week.

Twelve evenings of two hours each.

(a) Construction of Accounts—

General construction should first be dealt with, and a paper should be looked up dealing with each type of accounts, say ten papers (or if a paper cannot be found referring to a particular subject, a book on that subject should be read), and these would occupy eight evenings. As each type is read up, such profuse notes should be taken of the leading features as to enable the candidate to fall back on such notes, and to thereby avoid further reference to the paper first studied. The other four evenings might be devoted to (a) special construction, three evenings; and (b) statutory construction, one evening. The two leading points in special construction are cost accounts and self-balancing ledgers, and to each of these should be devoted one evening.

Second month, say thirteen evenings, three per week, two hours each—

(b) Executorship Accounts—

Two evenings, read text book and compile notes.

(c) Partnership Accounts—

Three evenings, read text book and compile notes.

(d) General Commercial Knowledge—

This subject has been divided into thirteen distinct heads in this paper, and each one of them might, to advantage, be looked up in a paper read before one of the accountancy bodies referring to it, or in a bookkeeping text book. I think that these thirteen heads can be read up and exhaustive notes made as to each, in fourteen evenings, and seven of these should be undertaken in the second month. One evening in this month should be devoted to running over the profuse notes of the first month.

Third month, say thirteen evenings—nine of two hours and four of three hours each—

Nine evenings, reading (two hours each).

Four evenings, practice (three hours each).

Five evenings devoted to the study of the subjects comprised in General Commercial Knowledge.

One evening to Executorship Accounts notes.

One evening to Partnership Accounts notes.

Two evenings might be devoted to a consideration of the questions of "Good-will" and "Vouching."

The practice work should be of an all-round nature; a supply of questions may be obtained from past examination papers.

Fourth month (twelve evenings)—

Three evenings, reading (three hours each).

Four evenings, practice (three hours each).

Auditing Text Book, three evenings. To a thorough study of this book particular attention should be given, more especially to those subjects which have been alluded to in this paper.

General Commercial Knowledge, two evenings, to complete the first reading up of this subject. An evening should be given to "The Responsibilities of an Auditor" and "Defalcations."

One evening should be kept free to devote to special matters: instance, Book Debts, General Adjustments and Suspense Accounts, etc.

Fifth month (thirteen evenings)—

Eight evenings, reading (three hours each).

Five evenings, practice (three hours each).

One evening: Revise General Construction by running through the notes referring to each section.

One evening: Revise Special Construction by running through the notes referring to each section.

Two evenings: Revise General Commercial Knowledge by the profuse notes.

One evening: Revise Leading Legal Cases bearing on Auditing and take notes of same.

One evening: Study the Adjustment of Partnership and Executorship Accounts, and paying particular attention to Partnership Articles, the framework of which should be committed to memory.

One evening: To a study of the forms (which should be committed to memory) relating to Bankruptcy, Share Capital Accounts, Executorship Accounts, Statutory Forms of Account.

One evening for General Study.

Sixth month—

This month, being the concluding stage of the course, should put the finishing touches to the study which the student has undertaken, and will include:—

Eight evenings (three hours each), reading.

Five evenings (three hours each), practice in the writing of examination papers.

During the fifth and sixth months this practice should consist of one paper each evening, and the candidates would do well to observe examination conditions as far as possible, viz.: He should not read the questions until he commences to answer them; he should not hurry over the work unduly, but should be as neat and as exact as if he were sitting in the examination hall.

EIGHT EVENINGS OF READING.

The following is the work of the eight evenings to be devoted to reading in this month, the time to be allocated to each portion being dependent upon the special circumstances of each case:—

1. Auditing Text Book, notes, and a study of past examination questions.

2. Statutes relating to Auditing. Revise immediately before examination.

Leading Accountancy Cases. Revise immediately before examination.

3. General Commercial Knowledge. Revise the thirteen sets of profuse notes.

4. General Construction. Revise the eleven sets of notes.

5. Special Construction. Revise the four sets of notes.

6. Partnership and Executorship Accounts. Revise notes.

The method employed in obtaining systematic notes of each text book and "paper" studied is of much importance, and I rely upon it as a means of (a) saving the candidate the labor of wading through the original matter several times over: (b) of providing a bundle of documents which admit of a quick perusal without losing the sense of the matter contained therein.

I have adopted a six months' course because I believe this to be the minimum time in which a satisfactory preparation can be made by the average student, but I am quite prepared to admit that it is impossible to fix a definite period in an arbitrary manner, because the question of the capabilities of each candidate has to be considered, and whereas six months would enable one candidate to render a satisfactory account of himself, another might require double the time. I would advise that those who form the latter class (no doubt often owing to the smallness of time at their disposal for study) should lengthen the course of their preparation in proportion as their available time is curtailed. Above all, the candidate should avoid "cramming," which in itself defeats the main purpose of the examination, viz., the obtaining of a thorough qualification.

The papers which are set can, I think, be answered in the time given, provided that the candidate goes steadily ahead and does not hurry or waste time, and I suggest—you may not agree with me—that it is better to commence at the first question, answer it thoroughly, then take No. 2, and so on to the end. If a question is beyond you, do not waste time in dealing with it until you have answered the rest; then go back to it and do what you can. Candidates sometimes look their papers thoroughly over before commencing, and then answer the questions, beginning at the easiest and finishing with the hardest, but I am of the opinion that this course wastes about twenty minutes of valuable time and answers no good purpose that I can think of.

FINAL SUGGESTIONS.

May I make the following final suggestions to candidates:

1. Read the question which you are about to answer over very carefully; then read it over a second time, and if you grasp it thoroughly, commence to answer it. Do not be hurried by the racing pens around you (most trying to the nerves if you have any) when you are temporarily at a standstill yourself, but rely on just completing your paper in time.
2. Neatness of work—enter reference folios—rule off.
3. Always carry balances down.
4. Make use of the Journal, describe each entry fully.
5. In dealing with questions requiring long answers bring system and organization to bear on them as much as possible, not stating points as they occur to you, but in their natural sequence as they arise.

In concluding this paper, I would remind you that the suggestions which I have made form the framework only of the course of study necessary for the Society's final examination, and it remains to the student to fill in and build up the figure, exercising care and being thorough in the work of preparation, thereby earning a satisfactory position in the "Lists," and securing to himself a capability which will be of great use to him in his accountancy career.

Business Subjects in Current Literature

There are quite as many articles on subjects pertaining to business in the magazines for the past month as at any time during the year. COMMERCE, ACCOUNTS & FINANCE gives below its usual partial list of these articles.

GENERAL SUBJECTS.

In the North American Review, L. M. Haupt has a paper on the "Isthmian Canal,—Why is It Not Built?" H. Robins in Gunton's Magazine, writes of the "Rare Opportunity in the New South." In the Engineering Magazine, J. H. Hammond presents the "Transvaal Mines Under the New Regime." In the Strand, A. Inkersley tells us of the raising and gathering of "Pampas Plumes." "Perils of the Camphor Industry in Formosa," is the title of an article by F. H. Major in the Overland Monthly. In the same magazine is an entertaining article by G. W. Dickie, on the "Building of the Battle Ship." In the World's Work, D. Murray writes of "Cables and How They Unite the World." In the Arena, the question of the canal route is duscussed by E. Burwick, the title of his article being "Nicaragua or Panama."

W. Von Schierbrand, in the Forum, presents "Germany as a World Power." In the Engineering Magazine, W. W. Christie has a paper on the "Mechanical Economy of Stoking." In Scribner's, A. Heming, the artist, writes entertainingly on the "Abitibi Fur Brigade." In the American Review of Reviews appears an article on "Anthracite Coal Mines and Mining," by R. D. Rhone. In the New England Magazine is a very entertaining paper concerning an industry that is now almost dead, namely, "The Whale Oil and Spermaceti Trade of Nantucket," by Mary E. Starbuck. In Munsey's, D. Story has a paper on the "Art of the Needlepoint," which art is, of course, etching.

In the World's Work is a paper entitled "Revival of Skilled Hand Work," by C. Barnard. In the Popular Science Monthly, W. H. Burr writes of the "Panama Route for the Ship Canal." In Lippincott's, P. W. Hart tells of the "Work of a Cable Ship." In the Popular Science Monthly is an article by H. A. Miers, entitled, "Gold Mining in the Klondike." D. Murray, in Everybody's, presents the "Striking Story of Printing Telegraphs." In World's Work, W. Fawcett discusses the "President's Business Office at the White House." In the Engineering Magazine, C. U. Carpenter has the sixth in his series of articles, "Money Making Management for the Shop." In this same magazine appears a paper by A. L. Queneau, on the "Gold Sands of Cape Nome." In Outing, W. A. Stimpson discusses "Shad-Catching for the Market," and in Out West, T. Robinson has a well-written article on "Bananas."

R. S. Baker, in the Century Magazine, writes of "Irrigation in the Great Southwest." In the World's Work appears a paper—author's name not given—on "Wall Street; Making it Safe." R. P. Teele presents "Government Construction of Irrigation Works," in the Journal of Political Economy.

The foreign magazines contain a large assortment of entertaining papers on business topics, among them we note "England and Protection," by Y. Guyot, in the Contemporary Review, of London. Espana Moderne, of Madrid, contains a paper by J. P. Guzman, on the "Pan-American Congress in Mexico." In the Reforme Sociale, of Paris, "Lace Industry in Belgium" is described by B. Verhaegen. In the Revue Sociale, of Paris, L. Linnet presents Notes on Industrial Art. In the Young Man, published in London, M. Dumorat writes of "The Working Man in Japan." In the National Review, of London, E. R. Frementle presents "Cruisers and Commerce Protection." In Chambers' Journal, published in Edinburgh, "New York City" is described by an anonymous author. The Leisure Hour, of London, contains the fourth instalment of "Life on the London Press." J. B. Crozier, writing in the "Fortnightly Review, of London, tells "How to Ruin a Free Trade Nation." In the Revue des Deux Mondes, of Paris, appear a paper on the "Organization of the Coal Mining Industry." In the Monthly Review, of London, is a carefully-prepared article on "Trade and the New World," and in Chambers' Journal H. Quilter has the second in his series of articles on the "Buying of Pictures." In the Revue Politique et Parlementaire, of Paris there is a paper by A. Souchon, on "The Sugar Industry and the Conference of Brussels."

AGRICULTURE, FORESTRY, ETC.

As scientific farming and practical forestry are coming more and more prominently before the public, it is but natural that the magazines should contain a number of articles bearing upon these subjects. In the World's Work, C. H. Matson describes a "Giant Kansas Farm." W. R. Draper, in Ainslee's, writes entertainingly of our "Farmer Aristocracy." "Freight Rates on Argentine and North American Wheat" is the title of a paper by R. R. Kuczmiski, in the Journal of Political Economy. In Harper's appears a paper by O. W. Price, entitled, "American Private Forests." The only article on these subjects that we note in the foreign magazines is one on "Pioneer Farming in South America," in Chambers' Magazine.

ARCHITECTURE AND BUILDING.

Architecture and building occupy more than their usual share of space in the current periodicals. In the Architectural Record is an interesting paper by an unnamed writer, entitled, "The Old Church at Croscombe, England." "Formal and Natural Style" is discussed by G. F. Pentecost, Jr., in this same magazine. A. D. F. Hamlin presents in the Forum a paper on "Architectural Art." In the Catholic World, L. Gorham writes entertainingly of "Roman Catholic Church Architecture." Country Life in America contains the fourth of the series of papers on "Making of a Country Home."

BANKING AND FINANCE.

These important subjects are of course well represented. In the Bankers' Magazine, of New York, are several well-written papers on banking subjects. Among them are "Individual Liability of the Officers of a Bank," by E. T. Berger; "The Bank Clerk and Civil Service," by W. E. Stevens; "National Banks and Other Banks," by an unknown author; "Inertia of Congress Regarding Financial Legislation;" "Mystery of the Foreign Trade Balances," by W. H. Allen, and the fifth in the series of papers, "Bookkeeping for City and Country Banks." In the North American Review the "Debt of Prussia" is discussed by A. Wagner. A. D. Nois, in the Forum, presents a paper on "Financial Affairs." The Bankers Magazine, of London, contains an article on the "Financial Aspect of British Banking Amalgamations." The same periodical contains the second in the series of papers on "British Saving Banks." In the Nuova Antologia, of Rome, M. Ferraris presents "Agrarian Loan-Banks in Egypt," and in the Rassegna Nazionale, of Florence, Duoa di Cesaro writes of "Agrarian Banks and Sicilian Peasants."

PHOTOGRAPHY.

The summer season is the time for out-door photography, and it is but natural that the magazines should contain many articles on this interesting subject. In Wilson's Photographic Magazine appear the following: "The Aid of a Mirror," by W. J. Wrote; "Photographing Dogs," by G. Oliver; "Choice of a Reducer," author's name not given; "Persulphates and Their Use in Photography," by H. Marshall; "Various Methods of Intensification," by H. W. Bennett; "Photographic Permanence," by C. H. Hines, and a paper on the "Complete Elimination of Hypo." In the Photographic Times-Bulletin, G. Stratton-Porter writes of the "Universal Lens." J. Boyd, in the same magazine, has a paper on "Night Photography," and H. N. Johnstone, in the same periodical, tells us about "Pinhole Photography." H. C. Delery also presents the seventh in his series of papers on "Architectural Photography." Camera and Dark Room contains four well-written photographic papers. They are, "Success in Snapshot Photography," by A. J. Jarman; "Improvement of Negatives," by J. Hadden; "Trimming, Mounting and Framing," by W. J. Cotterell; and "Uranium Printing and Toning," by W. F. Thompson, in Blackwood's Magazine, of Edinburgh, there appears an article on "Celestial Photography."

PROMINENT MEN.

Andrew Carnegie and his writings form the subjects of two articles in this month's magazines. The first is a paper on "Andrew Carnegie," by C. S. Gleed, in the Cosmopolitan, and the second is "Andrew Carnegie; His Empire of Business," by M. W. Hazeltine, in the North American Review. In the Cosmopolitan, S. E. Moffat writes introducing Mr. Carnegie's lieutenant, "Chas. M. Schwab." In Ainslee's Magazine, R. Harlowe tells us about "F. Augustus Heinze, the Copper King." Julian Ralph, in the Century, has a carefully-prepared article about the "Marquis of Salisbury."

CAPITAL AND LABOR, COMBINES, ETC.

The great coal strike has called forth a number of articles on the labor question. N. G. Cunniff, in the World's Work, writes of "The Real Issue of the Coal Strike." G. Gunton, in Gunton's Magazine, presents "The Coal Strike and the Public." In this same magazine, the author has a paper upon the "Beef Trust." In the National Magazine appears an anonymous article on the "Public and the Packers." In the American Review of Reviews T. Williams presents "A General View of the Coal Strike." W. R. Draper, in the same magazine, discusses, "Solving the Labor Problem of the Wheat Belts." In the North American Review J. Handiboe writes of "Strikes and the Public Welfare." In this same magazine C. H. Cramp gives an article on the "Steamship Merger and American Shipbuilding." "Economics for Business Men" is the title of a paper in the Journal of Political Economy. In the same periodical is an article by W. E. Walling, entitled, "Collectivism and Industrial Development." In the Atlantic is an unsigned article discussing the "Shipping Combine."

In the Annals of the American Academy of Political and Social Science are three papers on the labor question. They are: "Factory Legislation and Inspection in the United States;" "The Child Labor Problem," and "Conciliation and Arbitration." In the Political Science Quarterly, A. F. Weber writes of "Accident Insurance for Workingmen," and in the International Journal of Ethics, J. Martin discusses the "Social Value of Trade Unionism."

Among the papers on these subjects in the Foreign Magazines may be mentioned the following: "The Shipping Combine from a Naval Point of View," in Blackwood's Magazine, of Edinburgh; "The Atlantic Shipping Trust," by O. Eitzbacher, in the Contemporary Review, of London; "The Shipping Combine," by P. de Rousiers, in the Revue de Paris; "Origin of Trusts and Industrial Combinations," by C. Cornelisen, in the Reforme Sociale, of Paris.

TRANSPORTATION.

G. G. Tunell, in the Journal of Political Economy, compares "American and German High Speed Trains." T. A. Edison, in the North American Review, presents a paper on the "Storage Battery and the Motor Car." That well-known writer on nautical subjects, J. R. Spears, has an ably-written paper in Outing, entitled, "Our Ships of the Sea." In the Engineering Magazine are three articles bearing upon railways. One is the "Effect of Waterways on Railways," by S. A. Thompson; the second is "Mechanical Engineering of an Electric Railway," by H. P. Quick. C. R. King also presents the second in his series of papers on "European Locomotive Construction." H. T. Newcomb, in the Review of Reviews, writes of "Anthracite Carrying Railroads."

In the foreign magazines are the following articles: "British and American Shipping," by B. Taylor, in the Nineteenth Century, of London; "Doomed British Shipping," by P. Barry, in the Westminster Review, of London; "Revolution in Railway Signalling," in the Pall Mall Magazine, by H. G. Archer. In this same magazine W. H. Y. Weber writes on "Transportation Improvements in London." In the Revue Politique et Parlementaire, of Paris, A. Charguetaud presents a paper on the "Canals and Railways of New York State," and in the Rassegna Nazionale, of Florence, J. Trochia discusses "Electric Railway Traction."

A STORY OF M'KINLEY

Before President McKinley served his term as President—in his lawyer days—he very often passed a pork butcher's shop on the way to his office and back home. In the morning he used to notice that sausages were twenty cents a pound always. The sign read:—

"Good Pork Sausages,
20 cents."

Sometimes they were 20 cents a pound in the evening, but more often 12. The sign might even read:—

"Fine Pork Sausages,
10 cents."

The thing, he used to say, worried him. Sausages were not of so perishable a nature that they would not keep until the next day. So he stopped one evening at the shop, said it looked like rain, and inquired about the price of sausages.

"Ten cents," said the storekeeper.

"But," said McKinley, "they were 20 cents this morning."

"So they were," said the unabashed sausage merchant. "So they were. Then I had 'em; now I haven't. Sausages at 10 cents is simply to get me a reputation for cheapness. See?"

The future President saw, and was in the habit of saying a great many reputations were made that way.—Furniture Journal.

A DIPLOMAT

The Boy—This isn't what she ordered.

The Grocer—I know it. Just tell her this is more expensive, but we'll let her have it for the same price.—Indianapolis News.

COMMERCE ACCOUNTS & FINANCE

A Magazine cf Higher Business Education and Practical Administration. Acknowledged Authority in the Profession of Commerce and Consistent Advocate of Methods Up to Date and Above the Table.

JOSEPH CROSBY LINCOLN, - - - - Editor.
FRIEND PITTS, JR., - Circulation and Advertising.
E. R. KITTREDGE, - - - - Business Manager.

PUBLISHED MONTHLY

SUBSCRIPTION $1 a Year in the United States, Canada and Mexico. Other countries $1.50. Postage prepaid by the Publishers. In the absence of specific orders to stop at the end of the subscription term the paper will be continued and a bill sent. Entered at the New York Postoffice as Second Class mail matter.

COMMERCE, ACCOUNTS & FINANCE COMPANY, Publishers
Twenty-five Pine Street, New York

The editor of COMMERCE, ACCOUNTS & FINANCE desires copies of the issues of March 9th, 30th, April 20th, and of June, 1901. For each of the copies of Commerce, Accounts and Finance bearing one of the above dates, returned to us in good condition during the next 30 days, we will extend the subscription of the sender six months without charge.

* * *

His Imperial Majesty, Edward VII, King of England, Scotland Ireland and Wales, Emperor of India, Defender of the Faith, and all the rest of it, is crowned. He has recovered from his very serious illness, has confounded the prophets of evil, who, basing their faith upon omens and portents, have assured us that he never would be crowned. Long live King Edward! We, of America, may join with our cousins across the water in the wish for the health and prosperity of the Sovereign of the British Empire.

*

But though we wish King Edward and his people all the prosperity that they can wish themselves, the King and our English friends must pardon us if we do not view the ceremony of the coronation with quite as much solemnity as do they themselves. To us, much of the quaint old ceremonies and the pompous old trappings verge closely upon the ridiculous. We cannot believe that because of them King Edward sits any more securely upon the throne of his ancestors, nor can we believe that the office of Head Groom of the Back Stairs is an honor to be sought after, and received with thanksgiving and pride.

*

King Edward is a "good fellow"; that is what most of his biographers say of him. They do not say that he is a great statesman; they do not say that he is a great general; they do not say that he has ever done anything to merit the wholesale gratitude and adoration of his subjects. He has been very prominent at social functions; has been much interested in athletic sports and racing, and has, during his life, behaved in general like a well-bred English gentleman. But he has done nothing that can be called great. Perhaps he might have done greater things had he not been Prince of Wales, and Heir Apparent. Perhaps if he had not been a member of the royal family, but had been merely an every-day, middle-class Englishman, he might have developed talents that would have put him among the list of those truly great men who achieve greatness, but his destiny was marked out for him in undeviating lines—he could be only the Prince of Wales and, later, the King.

*

After all, kings and emperors do not amount to much in this practical world of today. They act as ornaments and look pretty in the gilded chariots, behind the band, in the procession of progress, but the body of that procession is made up of the merchants, business men, inventors and scientists, who are doing things and not merely posing. It is the business men, merchants and tradesmen of Great Britain that have made the British Empire. The kings of Great Britain have not made it. Many of the nobles of King Edward's court would, perhaps, be ashamed to remember that some of their ancestors had been business men, but the ancestors themselves, if they were alive, would have more reason to be ashamed of their descendants. King Edward will, perhaps, be a good king, but so far as usefulness to the world in general is concerned, he counts for nothing. Cecil Rhodes did a thousand times more for England than Edward VII. can ever do. J. P. Morgan and Andrew Carnegie assist the progress of the world more than all the crowned heads on the earth are doing or can do.

*

In connection with this subject it is interesting to note the proof of the democracy of England, also of the democracy of King Edward. He has been crowned by his loving subjects, that is to say, his loving subjects have made him king and have placed the crown of empire upon his head. Yet King Edward believes, and his people are supposed to believe, in the divine right of kings. If King Edward is king by divine right, why is it necessary for his subjects to crown him? If he is crowned by divine command, then he is king anyway and it does not make any difference what his subjects do or say about it. Of course, if he is king merely on sufferance and because the English people permit it to be so, that is a different matter, and that is the way it really looks to "a man up a tree." But in order to be a real emperor, as King Edward undoubtedly aspires to be, it would seem as though one must believe in the divine right of kings, and in that case what is the use of being crowned by the people? Why not pick up the crown, fix it jauntily upon the royal head and say, "I am king, and don't you forget it." It seems to us that if we believed in the divine right of kings, that is about what we should do when we came to the throne.

* * *

The printing industry and the making of books have taken great strides forward in the last twenty-five or thirty years—yes, in the last ten years. The art of illustration has kept pace with the improvements in book-making, and books published during the Civil War, or just before it, look curiously antiquated and ridiculous. Nowhere is the improvement in book-making more apparent than in school text books. We picked up, at a corner book store the other day, a small book on accounting, which is a curiosity in its way, and over which we have had several good laughs. The book itself, so far as the text is concerned, is a handy little collection of business calculations, and contains interesting tables, methods for finding the square and cube roots, some exercises in geometry, examples in timber measurement, corn measurement, short rules for the mechanic, and the like. These rules are all modern enough, and if the book were printed and illustrated in up-to-date fashion, it would be of use to the business man and to the school boy, even now.

*

But the printing and illustrating are away behind the times. The printing is bad, being heavy, blurred and black, with many broken type faces and dropped letters. The binding is old-fashioned and the cover design, compared with the handsome designs of modern book covers, is very homely. But the illustrations are funny. They are rude wood cuts and are printed, for the most part, at the heads of the various chapters. For instance, under the head of "Banks and Banking," appears an illustration of the interior of what the sign tells us is the "Business College Bank." This interior is ornate, the bank people having, evidently, spared no expense nor bad taste in decorating their place of business. The walls are hung with curtains and pictures of apparently wooden men. There is a clock on the wall that is hung so near the very high ceiling that to reach it for the purposes of winding and the like one would have to use an extension fire ladder. The customers of the bank are queer creatures, with countenances made up of four dots—two dots representing the eyes, one the nose and the other the mouth. All these customers wear high hats and side-whiskers. Presumably, no one is allowed to deposit his money in the "Business College Bank" unless he wears a high hat and side-whiskers. In another illustration a gentleman about eight feet tall is explaining the mysteries of closing ledger accounts to a roomful of students, each one of whom has evidently taken an oath never to allow his hair to be cut. The back view of the group of heads looks like a panoramic view of a hay field, with the haycocks already piled up. Other pictures in the book are as ludicrous as these, and the country student deriving his ideas of city institutions from these illustrations must have gone woefully astray. The most astonishing part of the whole thing is that this book was copyrighted as late as 1877, and the edition, the copy of which we have, was published in 1884—only eighteen years ago. If such a book were put out now it would be hooted off the market. The world of business education is moving fast, and artistic ideas are moving with it.

WHAT THE CENSUS SHOWS ABOUT "TRUSTS"

In the Atlantic Monthly recently, Hon. William R. Merriam, director of the United States census of 1900, gave a valuable body of facts in regard to the "trusts" of the United States, taken from these our last census reports, says the Review of Reviews. This is an especially important phase of the last census returns, of course, because the ten years from 1890 to 1900 saw the birth of such a huge majority of the great industrial combinations now doing business. The Census office, in its investigation of "trust" statistics, considered that no aggregation of mills came under the head of an industrial combination unless it consisted of a number of formerly independent mills which had been brought together into one company under a charter obtained for that purpose. The census avoided the word "trust," too, although that highly illogical term has been sanctioned by popular usage, and adopted such phrases as "industrial combinations" or "industrial consolidations."

So far as can be ascertained from the data in the Census office, the number of these industrial consolidations is 183. They control 2,203 separate plants, scattered throughout the United States, 2,029 being active and 174 idle during the census year. For 56 of the idle plants, no returns could be obtained, making the total number of reporting plants 2,147. The 183 combinations extend to almost all lines of industry, producing articles of luxury, materials essential to the upbuilding and growth of the country, and even the very necessities of life. Fully 50 per cent of these combinations were chartered just prior to or during the census year; and it is noteworthy that the epidemic of industrial consolidation, so far as the so-called monopolies are concerned, has been practically confined to the past four years. It is evident, therefore, that the disease—if it be regarded as such—has spread very rapidly.

Even in 1900, before the final organization of the United States Steel Corporation and the extension of the boom in the iron industry, there were more industrial combinations engaged in making iron and steel than in any other field. Sixty-nine combinations, running 469 plants, with a capital investment of some $348,000,000, were what the census showed for iron and steel "trusts" two years ago. They employed 146,000,000 wage-earners and paid $81,000,000 in wages, besides $7,500,000 in officers' salaries.

It is a matter of vital interest to wage-earners and the public generally to know that twenty-three combinations are engaged in producing articles of food, their total annual output, $282,000,000, being second in importance to that of the iron and steel industry. The list includes such corporations as the National Biscuit Company, the American Sugar Refining Company, and the California Fruit Canners' Association. The number of reporting plants in this industry is 277, and the capital—by which is meant land, buildings, machinery, tools, implements, cash and sundries—is valued at $247,000,000.

There are twenty-nine combinations engaged in the production of beer, liquors and beverages. The total output is $93,000,000. These products cannot be considered as prime necessities of life. They are generally regarded, indeed, as mere luxuries. The number of reporting plants is 236, and the capital employed is valued at $120,000,000.

A division of combinations interesting to the general public is that of textiles. Seventy-two reporting plants engaged in this industry are controlled by nine of these corporations, and their capital is valued at $92,000,000.

Lumber and its allied industries are represented by eighteen combinations. There are sixty-five reporting plants, representing a capital of $25,000,000.

Six combinations relate to leather and its finished products. The number of reporting plants is one hundred, and the capital amounts to $63,000,000.

One hundred and nineteen paper-making plants were reported, which were under the control of eight combinations, and represented a capital of $59,000,000.

In the line of chemicals and allied products, there are 287 reporting plants, controlled by nineteen combinations, and having a capital of $187,000,000.

The clay, glass and stone industry, which includes cement and brick companies, and others of like character, comprises 201 reporting plants, controlled by seventeen corporations. The capital is $49,000,000.

Under the division of metals and metal products other than iron and steel are included the Amalgamated Copper Company, a brass company, a shot and lead company, a smelting and refining company, a metal, a lead and a zinc company—sixteen combinations, representing ninety-four reporting plants, with a capital of $120,000,000.

The tobacco industry includes five combinations, controlling forty-one reporting plants, with a capital amounting to $16,000,000.

Six combinations are interested in the manufacture of vehicles for land transportation. They control sixty-six reporting plants, which represent a capital of $86,000,000. Their manufactured output during the census year was also valued at $86,000,000.

Besides these, there was a census classification of thirty miscellaneous "trusts," operating 120 plants, and employing $45,000,000 of capital.

Mr. Merriam figures out that the 183 "trusts" had a total capitalization of $3,569,615, 808. The valuation of the land, buildings and other assets upon which this capitalization was based was $1,458,522,573. (This figure excludes the value of the property of two constituent companies in the United States Steel Corporation.) Mr. Merriam points to the rather startling fact that the total property value lacks $216,000,000 of equaling the value of the bonds and preferred stock, so that this sum, plus the value of the common stock, a total of not less than $2,018,000,000, seems to represent good-will, franchises and other intangible assets.

AGAINST THE RULES

"And say, boy."

"Yassir."

"Be sure you call me in case the hotel catches fire."

"Sorry, sir, but it's against de rules of de house."—Cleveland Plain Dealer.

Savings Banks Trial Balances

By WALTER E. HALLETT

The problems of savings bank trial balances are by no means so easy as the lay mind, unfamiliar with the questions involved, might imagine. Simple as the depositors' ledger seems to be in arrangement, and apparently without questions of complicated bookkeeping in practical operation, it is nevertheless, by reason of its very simplicity, the large number of accounts, and the multiplicity of transactions, a stumbling block to many an unwary bookkeeper; and the ingenuity of accountants has been taxed to devise schemes for the protection of the bookkeeper against himself, the author and finisher of his own undoing.

That the solution of the difficulty has not been as plain as the first three letters of the alphabet is proven by tne fact that as late as 1895 the report of the State Superintendent of Banking cited twenty banks whose proof of deposits was in error by greater or less sums.

While in the present year of grace the savings banks have substantially solved the question of accuracy, yet there is room for wide difference of opinion as to whether the other qualities desirable in a trial balance scheme, viz., simplicity, ease of operation and facility of analysis, are displayed as completely as possible in the plans in use by some of the larger institutions.

We have illustrated three schemes that may be considered as fairly representative of those in use in the large banks. These will serve to make clear the points raised in this brief discussion. In each case the trial balance proper is contained in the column at the right; what we have called the trial balance scheme is the whole page form by which the trial balance itself is worked out.

The first and last purpose of the trial balance is the elimination of ledger errors, and the various forms in use have been designed to discover such errors as persist in spite of the usual devices of posting and checking in different colored inks, proof by daily balance columns and so forth.

The medium of expression in bookkeeping, like that of other sciences, to be adequate must lend itself to the expression of all shades of meaning, simple or involved; and the savings bank trial balance scheme must often meet other demands upon it than the mere necessity of proving the total "due depositors." It must, perhaps, so arrange itself as to aid in the calculation of the interest in banks where the interest period and the trial balance date are coincident, as in Scheme 2; or it must prove the interest when calculated, as in Scheme 3, or prove the classification of all transactions with respect to their interest-bearing values, as in Scheme 3.

ELEMENTARY PRINCIPLES.

There are a few principles, however, that seem elementary and necessary to the trial balance scheme if it is to be a logical expression of the mathematical processes involved. The trial balance should always be separable into the elements that compose it. It may be regarded as a composite quantity, made up of the combination of several units, just as a chemical compound is made up of the chemical combination of two or more simple ingredients, and, like the chemical compound, should be capable of both quantitative and qualitative analysis.

In the simplest form of expression the trial balance is derivable from the algebraic equation $a + b = c$, with the algebraic quantities expressed in dollars and cents, and the members of the equation arranged in that linear and columnar phraseology which form the graphic formulae, as it were, of bookkeeping; and the simplest form of trial balance scheme is that which conforms most closely to this equation. The elements that go to make up the trial balance are four, viz., initial balances, deposits, interest and drafts; or, giving each an algebraic sign, $a + b + c - d = x$. That is, initial balance, plus deposits, plus interest, minus drafts, equals balance to be proven. This is exactly the form of Scheme 1, and is the simplest form of trial balance scheme. In Scheme 3 each of these elements is further classified into sums bearing six months', or three months', or no interest. In Scheme 2 this idea is not carried out, the first column being a composite quantity, consisting of balances from former trial balance modified by both drafts and deposits which affect six months' interest. This does not permit the analysis of the trial balance as above suggested.

The principle of subdivision is indispensable to the proper working out of any trial balance, and is in practice applied in a variety of ways. A ledger is generally considered as the unit of division, is charged with all deposits and interest and credited with all drafts. This makes each ledger an individual entity, and avoids the liability of the trespassing across the boundary line in error, as when an even number of accounts, say 5,000 or 10,000, constitute the unit of division. This principle may be carried out indefinitely. We know of one savings bank where every one hundred accounts form a separate division, but such an extreme subdivision is hardly possible in a bank having 100,000 or 150,000 accounts.

A study of the forms as described in the working plan appended to each will give an idea of their value as a workable proposition.

A study of the forms as described in the working plan appended to each will give an idea of their value as a workable proposition.

Scheme 1

Working Plan.—The trial balance dates are April 1 and

NUMBER	1 BALANCES OCTOBER 1, 1901		2 JANUARY 1, 1902 INTEREST		3 DRAFTS		4 DEPOSITS		5 BALANCES APRIL 1, 1902	
375001	470	00	8	22					478	22
2	39	25		43	14	23			25	43
7	1017	50	17	50	17	50			1017	50
8	621	00	10	50			37	50	669	
375012	14	28		24					14	52
3	4	19	0	00			75	00	79	19
4	147	16	2	57	150	57	148	00	147	16
7	840	02	14	27					854	29
375022	68			59	25		75	50	119	09
3	920	01	10	93	416	94	327		841	
7	117	13	1	75			100		218	88
8	808	75	7	29	65		65		816	04
375031	425		7	43	432	43			--	—
2	94	82	1	64			15		111	46
3	100			88					100	88
4	32	40		56			29		61	96
7	7	87	0	00	7	87			--	—
9	268	84	4	87	15	21			258	00
Total	5696	22	89	17	1144	77	872	00	5512	62
+	89	17								
+	872									
	6657	39								
—	1144	77								
	5512	62								

October 1. The balances are copied into column 5 as they stand at the trial balance date.

The total deposits on each account within the trial balance period are entered from the ledger into column 4, similarly the draft totals into column 3. Interest column has been filled out at the interest date. The total of columns (adding for deposits, deducting for drafts) work out the proof, as in the illustration.

Differences are brought out by horizontal addition, line by line. In case of a net difference in the ledger total, a recapitulation of drafts and deposits indicates where search for the error is to be made.

This form has been filled out to make the illustration clearer.

Scheme 2

Working Plan.—Periods, January 1 and July 1. Balances drawing six months' interest are copied into column 1; three months' sums and no interest sums are entered in their respective columns. These data furnish the material for calculating the interest directly into its own column without further reference to the ledger, and the balances entered into column 5 are derived from the other columns by horizontal addition, and then called back with the ledger for comparison.

A partial proof of the interest column total is made by adding together the interest on the total of columns 1 and 2, except that the cents which drew no interest must be dropped, and further, as the fractions of cents are not cal-

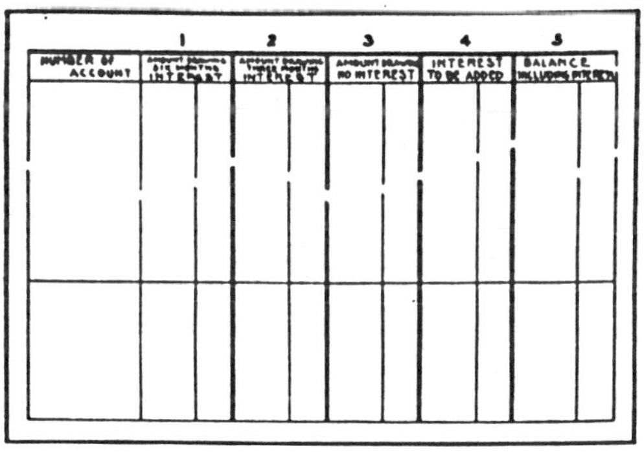

culated in the interest on each single account, there is always a total discrepancy for the page of several cents, so that this can hardly be considered academically a good proposition, although it is much depended on as a guide in the banks using this form.

No recapitulation of deposits or drafts is possible in this form. In case of net difference the balances are called back with the ledger until found.

Scheme 3

Working Plan.—Balance periods, January 11 and July 11. Balances are copied into the two right-hand columns, cents being always put in the o (no interest) column. Both deposits and drafts are classified with respect to their interest-bearing values, and are entered directly into their col-

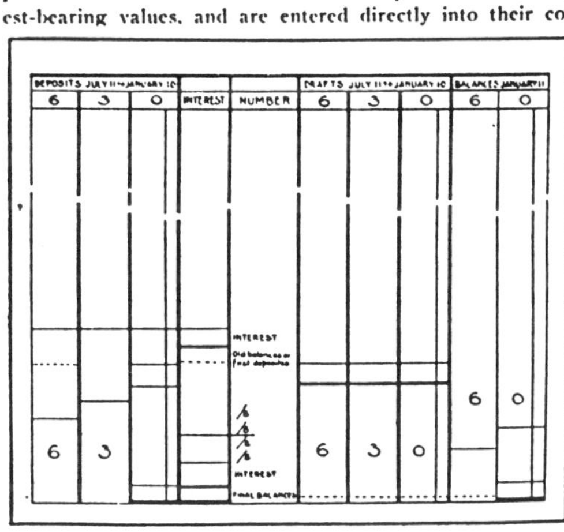

umns from the original draft or deposit tickets. The page proof is effected by deducting the total of draft columns from the corresponding deposit columns, adding previous balances and interest, to prove new balance, as in Scheme 1.

An absolute proof of the interest is made, the fractions of cents in each account being considered.

A comparative study of the three schemes shows in each case a different conception of the trial balance. In Scheme 1 deposits and drafts are treated merely as increments or decrements affecting the ledger balance; in Scheme 2 they are considered in their effect upon balances as interest-bearing values, while in Scheme 3 they are considered from both standpoints.

Each plan has its peculiar value in the general system of accounting of the bank making use of it. In Scheme 1 the date of the trial balance being distant from that of the interest, the advantage of a separation into interest-bearing classes is the least possible, while in Schemes 2 and 3 these dates coinciding, or nearly so, this feature gives the trial-balance scheme a constructive value in the general plan of bookkeeping that commends it to the student of accounts. On the other hand, Scheme 2 is defective in one of the qualities which we have considered as most desirable, viz., facility of analysis. Scheme 3 covers both of these points, perhaps at the expense of simplicity, but certainly very comprehensively.

In general, the handling of depositors' ledgers in the system of daily check and in the trial balance is subject to great variety of treatment, that being the best system which most completely avoids errors in the first place, and most thoroughly discovers them in the second, but until a generation of bookkeepers that never err arises, or a mechanical bookkeeping automaton is devised, capable of self-motion and initiative, we fear there will be need for checks and devices and trial balance proofs even to the end of the chapter.

CORPORATION BOOKKEEPING

From W. M. B., Kansas City, Mo.

Will you kindly give the opening entries for a corporation just beginning business; also the closing ones? I hope to have the pleasure of reading your answer to this question in an early number.

Answer. Our correspondent presents his question in such a delightfully indefinite form as to leave nothing to be desired in that direction. He does not tell us whether the corporation is to run a peanut stand or to control all the establishments in some leading industry. Closing entries, it is to be supposed, would depend in some measure upon the results of the business, but he does not tell us whether it is to be assumed that it has made a profit or has failed so disastrously in its undertaking that it is to be wound up. The easiest way in which to dispose of our correspondent's question would be to say frankly, We give it up.

This correspondent, as well as some others who have written us in the past regarding corporation affairs, seems to assume, as the foundation to his question, that there is some mystery in corporation bookkeeping or something special that exists in corporation work apart from ordinary business. This belief is, in a sense, common. We meet it in various directions, and certain book publishers have catered to the public along this line, for we find works advertised which play more or less upon the catching phrase of "corporation accounting" as though there was something in accounting of corporations different in principle or application from accounting in other directions.

If this correspondent, who, by the way, has all the facts of the situation, and of which we have none, will think of the business as a business and frame such entries, both opening and closing, as the business demands, he will get along without trouble; and this reminds us to say that modern accounting is business accounting, and not accounting of individuals, nor yet of firms nor of corporations. Adapt the accounting to the business, whether the business be owned by an individual, by a firm or by a corporation. Incidentally, adjust the account with capital to agree with the conditions of ownership. If it be an individual, that demands one thing; if it be a co-partnership, the demands will be different, and if it be a corporation, an account called Capital Stock will take the place of what in the first instance was the proprietor's name, and in the second instance accounts with the several partners.

ANCIENT AND MODERN FORTUNES

John D. Rockefeller told a friend a few days ago that he is unable to guess within $15,000,000 of the amount of his wealth. The world is worse off regarding Solomon, for in nearly three thousand years of figuring it is undecided whether the King of Israel was worth $5,000,000 or $100,000,000

Current Business Cartoons

COMMERCE, ACCOUNTS & FINANCE reproduces in this issue a curiously prophetic cartoon which originally appeared in

Uncle Sam.—"Stand clear there, all airth and ocean! My hands are free now, and I'm goin' to hyst a flag so big that it'll cover most o' the land and a good bit o' the sea!"—Published in Harper's Weekly in 1866.

Harper's Weekly shortly after the close of the Civil War. It was reprinted the other day in the Washington Star, and our readers will see when they look at it, how the artist's prophecy has already been, in a measure, realized. The drawing may have been made by Thomas Nast, the artist

The Relative Importance of News in Country Districts.—Chicago Record-Herald.

whose cartoons against the Tweed ring made him famous.

The corner in corn gave the papers a great deal to talk about during the past month, and kept the cartoonists busy. We reproduce three cartoons on the subject of the rise in corn. One from the New York Tribune shows a prosperous-looking "Bull" cheerfully fanning himself as he stands

The Poppers and the Popped.—Boston Herald.

over a small stove filled with steaming ears of 90-cent July corn. The grief-stricken bear is hungry, but the corn is out of his reach. In the cartoon from the Boston Herald the

Mr. Bear will have to "shell out" to get any of the hot corn.—N. Y. Tribune.

"Shorts" are represented as popcorn in a large popper. Flames beneath the popcorn form the words "90-Cent Corn." The "Bulls" sitting on the handle of the popper are cool and

No gentlemen, that is not another volcanic eruption; it's just Uncle Sam digging the Panama Canal.—N. Y. Times.

comfortable, and the poor "Shorts" are having a hard time of it. McCutcheon, in the Chicago Record-Herald, shows another side of the corn question. Although the farmers have displayed before them bulletins setting forth the doings of

King Edward and President Roosevelt, likewise those of Mary Maclane, nevertheless, the crowd is around the bulletin on which is lettered, "The Latest News About Corn."

Emperor William invites Mr. J. Pierpont Morgan to Luncheon.—N. Y. World.

The canal question is now in the hands of President

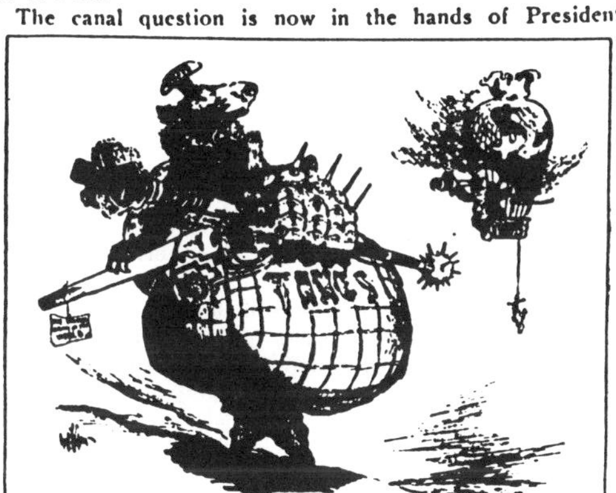

From the Balloon.—"What's he Growling at? He's Old King Trust himself.—Boston Herald.

Roosevelt. If France's title to the Panama route is proven

If the cost of living continues to increase we shall be obliged to go back to first principles.—Chicago News.

good, why the Panama canal it will be. In a cartoon from the New York Times the powers are shown gazing across the water at an eruption of rocks and earth that they fear may be volcanic, but is in reality only the United States digging with great strenuosity the Panama canal.

J. P. Morgan was recently invited to dine with Emperor William, and Bush, who is the clever cartoonist of the New York World, pictures this dinner. Everything movable is secured to the table or floor. Even "grandfather's sword" is nailed securely to the wall, as is also Prince Henry's high-

Silk Mill Owner to Workman.—"Take that beast to the pound first, then I'll talk to you."—Philadelphia Times.

chair. The Emperor evidently fears Mr. Morgan's well-known habit of acquiring anything that he fancies. We do not mean that he acquires these things dishonestly, but the Emperor, in the picture, evidently is taking no chances.

To Cut the Ropes is Suicide.—N. Y. World.

Strikes, labor troubles, food combines and the like play the dickens with the poor consumer, and in a cartoon from the Chicago News is shown what we may come to if the cost of living continues to increase. Bradley, the artist, evidently thinks we shall return to the custom of Mother Eve, and dress in fig leaves, which will be cheap, if rather airy.

The Czar of Russia recently invited the other European

powers to a conference in which it was proposed to take some measures against the American trusts. Williams, who draws the cartoons for the Boston Herald, gently intimates that Russia with her taxes, her despotism, censorship and mighty standing army is the greatset trust in the world.

The coal strike continues, and it seems to be no nearer the end than it was a month ago. In a cartoon which we reproduce from the New York World, the coal miner is shown swinging in the shaft in a buckét, entitled, "Miners' Union." It is evident that he intends cutting loose from his soft coal contracts. The World says that to do this is suicide.

Down in Paterson, N. J., a city in which there appears always to be something lively going on, they recently had a strike which resulted in a riot. The anarchists led this riot, and the industrious and well-meaning working men suffered because of their leadership. In the Philadelphia Times the situation is depicted very clearly. The mill owner refuses to confer with the workman until the bulldog of anarchy is taken away and shut up.

THE TALE OF THE SUBURBANITE WHO LIVED UP TO HIS NEIGHBORS

By Joe Lincoln

AND it was the one thousandth and fourth night, and the King spake unto Scheherezade, saying:—

"Oh, thou, beside whom the mighty Munchausen would have appeared even as an 'also ran,' get, I pray thee, busy. Else how shalt thou earn thy six per?"

And Scheherezade heard the command of the Father of the Faithful, and spake unto him thus:—

"Know, O Illustrious, that in the City of Bogullop, which is in the Land of Dingbat, which is over against Goop, there lived a man who toiled daily. And behold the name of the man was Abdallah, and the wife of his bosom was fair to look upon, and his children were as blossoms in the gardens of Paradise. And their abode was adjacent to the housetop, being even in the seventh flat, and happiness reigned therein.

"And it came to pass that the wage of Abdallah was increased, and raised yet again, and the teller at the savings bank gave him the glad hand when he called thereat. And there was no shine upon his coat sleeves, and he sent three shirts to the laundry each week.

"But the suns shone and the moons came and went, and the wife of Abdallah's bosom waxed unhappy and longed for higher things. And she spake unto her husband, saying:

" 'Oh, light of mine eyes, why stay we in this six by nlne, in which to make up the bed must I climb out even upon the fire-escape? Let us, O my husband, seek the suburbs, where the automobiles slay not and the sweet chirrup of the bulbul is heard in the land.'

"And Abdallah harkened unto the voice of his wife, and answered her, saying, 'Do even as thou wilt.' And she spent many days and shekels upon the railroads seeking an abiding place.

"And it came to pass that at the end of her searching she sought Abdallah and said unto him:—

" 'Oh, thou who payeth the freight, harken unto the voice of thy better seven-eighths. Behold, the day of deliverance is at hand! After grievous toil I have discovered a place of abode at beautiful Whangdoodle on the Marsh. Lo, a house hath been offered unto me, wherein are twelve rooms and a bath, hot and cold water, steam heat, fireplace in the library, cozy corner for the cook in the kitchen, and all the modern annoyances. And about it are spacious lawns and flower beds until one cannot rest. Of a surety the entire shooting match is beyond the range of vision. And the rent is but eight simoleons per month more than we are now giving up.'

"And Abdallah pondered for a space, and then said unto her:—

" 'May the blessing of the Prophet be with the spacious lawns and the cozy corner, but oh, partner of my joys and spender of my income, hath it not come to mine ears that Whangdoodle on the Marsh is the abiding place of them that are cutters of ice in the world of fashion and whose doings fill the Sunday papers? Can we, I ask of thee, trot in the class of such?'

"And she answered him, saying: 'Of a surety. Dost thou not receive three thousand pieces of silver each year? By the beard of my grandmother, who was the Bearded Lady in the sideshow, is it not our move?' And Abdallah answered her, 'Yea.' And they moved.

"And it came to pass that, after a space, the wives and daughters of the dwellers in Whangdoodle on the Marsh called upon the wife of Abdallah, and their raiment was as that of the peacock, and the flashing of their jewels put the sun to shame. And when Abdallah returned home on the 5.30 unlimited, the wife of his bosom met him with tears, begging for new and costly robes of silk and golden bracelets, that she might go fittingly to return the calls of her neighbors.

"And the men of Whangdoodle called upon Abdallah, and the cut of their garments was of the latest, and the smoke of their cigars was even as the scent of myrrh and frankincense. And Abdallah buried his cob pipe in the backyard and bought copiously of Manuel Garcias for their entertaining.

"And it came to pass that Abdallah and his wife became members of the Whangdoodle Pedro Club, and when the club met at their abode the walks and spacious lawns were overhung with canopies, and the bill for the banquet was of the length of the Brooklyn Bridge. And there was no discount for cash.

"And Abdallah and the wife of his bosom worshipped at the First Reformed Tabernacle, on the Main street of Whangdoodle, where the collection was taken up on golden salvers, and the father of the flock spent his summers in Europe. And each time that Abdallah was asked to dig up for the filling of the salvers and the paying of the European bills, he wept full sore.

"And the companions of his evenings were bank presidents and promoters of oil companies, and the three thousand that had looked so large in the seventh-story flat became but as a widow's mite in his sight.

"And because that the oil promoter's children attended the private school, so also were the children of Abdallah placed therein, and there received they the higher education, which is as nothing compared to the height of the fee therefor. And the pile in the savings bank waxed low and dwindled, and became even as a hole. And there was naught wherewith to fill it. And the sellers of cigars and foodstuffs became clamorous and demanded lucre, and Abdallah feared to answer the doorbell.

"And it came to pass that Abdallah and his wife and his children left Whangdoodle on the Marsh and went none knew whither, and the place knew them no more. And the time of their moving was the hour of darkness, and the wheels of the wagons were muffled. And in all Whangdoodle none mourned save only the sellers of cigars and foodstuffs."

And Scheherezade paused and said unto the Sultan:—

"Oh, King, live forever! Behold, as is customary, the end of the tale is a question. Is three thousand a year a good salary?"

And the King answered and said unto her:—

"Verily, the Rooster is Lord of the Barnyard, but in the cage with the Bird of Paradise he roosteth low."

And he commanded his harpers to play "Good Morning, Carrie."

Stationery Manufacturing Company

318 BROADWAY, NEW YORK

Multi-Bank Check Register.

There are comparatively few business concerns at the present day which do not find good reason for maintaining a deposit account in more than one bank. Houses with branches in various cities

Fig. 1. General appearance, closed and partly opened. Goes in safe like a Demy-book.

frequently find it expedient to have a bank account in each place, if for no other reason than to receive daily deposits of collection wherever a branch is located. Large organizations frequently find it desirable to have several bank accounts, even in the one city in which their principal office is situated. All financial institutions have numerous correspondents variously located.

The Multi-Bank Check Register, which is illustrated on these pages, is a device which makes possible the employment of as many banks as desirable, whether one or one hundred, and which consolidates the record of all of them into a single book or holder. Further, it permits the analysis of the items according to the accounting system employed, in a way to permit the direct posting of all individual amounts, and at the same time the total postings (footings of columns) according to classification. It is also adapted to keep the accounts with the banks apart from the record of the checks drawn, thus restricting the knowledge of receipts and balances on hand, to the one person who has the register in charge. Further, it permits the check record to be used as a posting medium detached from the accounts with the banks. Even though a dozen ledger clerks perform the work of posting from the check record, still none of them gains any information as to details of the financial situation.

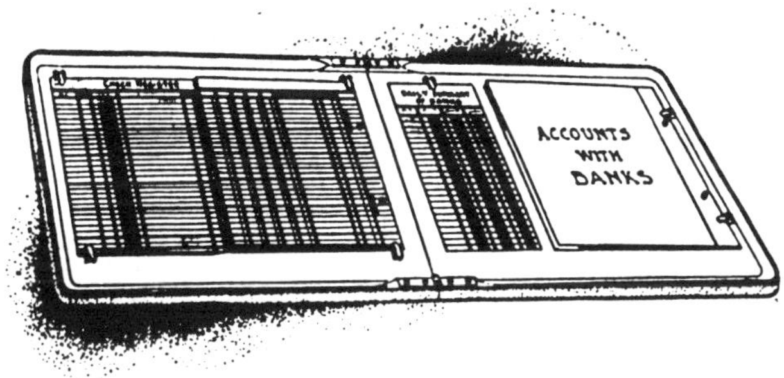

Fig. 2. Check Register wide open, as in use. (Patent pending.)

When the Multi-Bank Check Register is closed, Fig. 1., it is of the shape and size of a thin Demy-book, and goes into the safe as any regular book would be put away.

When it is spread open for use, as in recording a check drawn, it presents the appearance shown in Fig. 2.

The record, that is the part which takes the place of the conventional stub of checks drawn, is in the form shown in Fig. 3. The bottom or wide page of this pad receives the usual particulars of the check, such as, "what account," "date," "amount," "number" and designation of the particular bank on which it is drawn. The narrow leaves of this record, which are made more or less in number as the requirements of the case may be, are columnarized according to the general accounts to which totals would be posted.

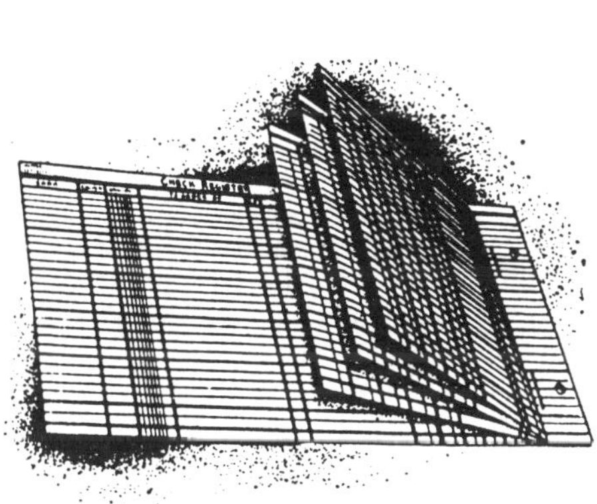

Fig. 3. Removable Register of Checks. Serves as Posting Medium in detail and in totals, and files in a Post Binder. (Patented.)

For example, if a check were to be drawn to the order of John Smith in payment of a bill that had been passed to his credit on the books among Purchase Creditors, we would want to debit John Smith with the amount, and we would also want to debit in our general ledger our account with Purchase Creditors as a whole. From the body of the register, Fig. 3, the posting would

Fig. 4. Accounts with banks. Perpetual ledger plan—indexed. Filled sheets file in Post Binder.

be made directly to John Smith's account. The amount of Smith's Check would be extended in the column devoted to Purchase Creditors, and the total of this column in regular course would be posted to the general ledger account with Purchase Creditors.

The same routine occurs where checks are issued in payment of expense bills. In such cases it is the footing of the column "Expense" that is posted, and not the item itself. In brief, the register of checks here shown is equivalent in feature of use to a columnar journal or columnar cash book. Those who are familiar with the columnar principle and the classification which it facilitates and with total postings by column footings will require no further explanation.

Fig. 4 shows the details of the accounts with banks. The contained sheets are of the form of ledger pages, the construction is virtually a loose-leaf or perpetual ledger with the leaves placed between index sheets. In the use of the device after checks have been recorded in the register proper, Fig. 3, they are posted to the accounts with banks, at the right of the holder. Whenever the sheets carrying the accounts with banks have become filled, they are removed to a transfer binder and are there also filed between index sheets.

Fig. 5 is a further detail of the ac-

Fig. 5. Ruling of an Account with a Bank.

counts with banks, and shows the ruling employed. It also indicates the way in which the lines are numbered, for recording the numbers of the checks drawn. There are fifty lines to the page, and two sets of pages are furnished. Without laboriously inserting

Fig. 6. Detail of Daily Summary.

the check numbers and without the use of a numbering machine, with only the work of placing an indication of the correct number of hundreds at the top of the sheet, the account with a given bank may commence with any check number. For example, if in introducing the use of this Multi-Bank Check Register numbers have reached 1525, and the first check to be drawn on the new plan is 1526, all that is necessary to do is to place 15 at the top of the sheet shown in Fig. 5, and then to use line 26 for recording the check.

In Fig. 6 is shown a detail of the daily summary of transactions with banks. This is a slip supplied in duplicate, put up in pads and adapted to carry the cashiers' summary at the close of each day's business. The list of banks printed down the side is the same as the bank accounts in the ledger already described (Fig. 4). The total of checks

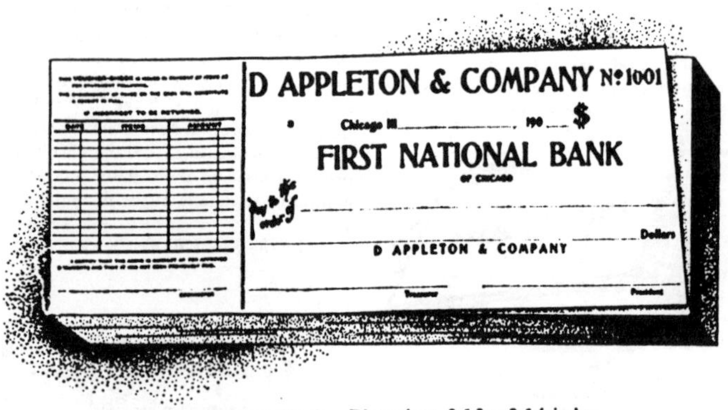

Fig. 7. Face-Voucher Check. Dimensions, 8 1-2 x 3 1-4 inches. Everything on its face, and no folding. (Patent pending.)

drawn upon the bank is extended in like position, and finally the balance of each bank is extended in the column at the extreme right. The total of deposits, including balance brought forward less the total of checks drawn, would of course be the total of the balance on hand, and this is equal to the total of the individual balances extended as above.

This summary slip is supplied and used in duplicate with carbon, first to provide a convenient report to the

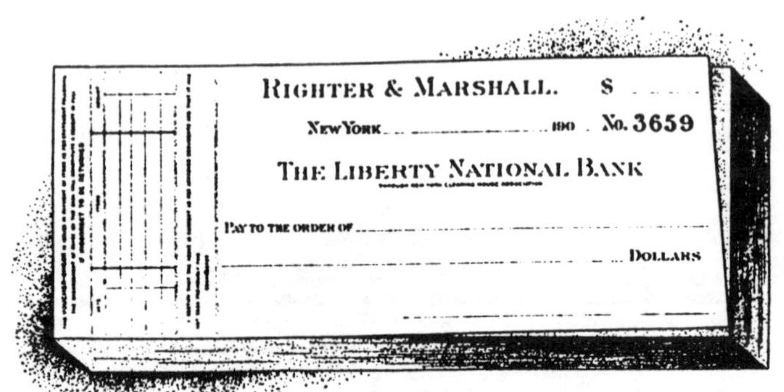

Fig. 8. Another form of Face-Voucher Check, with the voucher part differently located. (Patent pending.)

president, treasurer or other officer of the company supervising financial operations, and second, for leaving with the cashier such a summary of bank transactions as may be convenient for posting to the Balance Sheet Ledger, or to the other volume carrying the general cash record.

We are furnishing for use with the Multi-Bank Check Register, Face-Voucher Checks of the general forms shown in Figs. 7 and 8. The two checks illustrated differ only in the position of the voucher part on the face of the check. We invite careful attention to this design of check, which has already received the cordial approval of various leading banks throughout the country. It overcomes fully all the objections raised to the usual forms of voucher checks.

Notice what precedes and follows the voucher form. The voucher itself is drawn in such a way that the indorsement of the check makes it a receipt for the amount, thus avoiding the necessity of stipulating special receipts, and the expense later on of filing them. In the process of issuing the check, the bookkeeper or ledger clerk first certifies to the correctness of the amount for which the check is drawn. Thereafter follows the signature of the firm or the officers of the company, as the case may be.

Referring again to the devices shown on the first page it is to be remarked that the removable register of checks, Fig. 3, may be adapted to a daily, weekly or monthly time schedule, as may be the preference of the management. Paper is admittedly the cheapest material that is used in an office at the present time, and however much it may appear to cost in the form of stationery, it is still very much cheaper than labor. In ordinary practice it is found an economy to use one of the removable registers daily, qualified, of course, by making it more than one whenever the business is sufficiently extensive to require more checks per day than the number of lines on a register page (25). For very small businesses the removable registers may be ruled so as to have more than one day on a single page, with the days separated by proper ruling.

Attention is called to the following price list:—

PRICE LIST.

Multi-Bank Check Register, Demy size, finished in Russia, each	$7.50
Removable Register, one single narrow leaf, per hundred	5.00
Removable Register, two narrow leaves, per hundred	6.00
Removable Register, three narrow leaves, per hundred	7.00
Set of Index Sheets, "Accounts with Banks," specially tabbed, 1 to 30 banks, as required	2.00
Bank Account Sheets, numbered 0-49, per hundred	1.00
Bank Account Sheets, numbered 50-99, per hundred	1.00
Face Voucher Checks on Safety Paper, numbered and padded, (plates extra), first thousand, $10.00; in lots of 10,000, per thousand	6.00

SPECIAL INTRODUCTORY OFFER.

We make the following special offer to those desiring to avail themselves of the Multi-Bank Check Register without delay. The stationery referred to below will be printed with the name of the firm or company ordering, and the classification of accounts in the Register arranged in accordance with the scheme which may be supplied by the purchaser.

1 Multi-bank Check Register Holder, Demy size, finished in Russia	$7.50
300 Removable Register Pads, with 1 or 2 narrow leaves, as required, at $6	18.00
1 Set of Index Sheets and Covers, Accounts with Banks, tabbed as required, not exceeding 30 in all	2.00
100 Bank Account Sheets, numbered 0-49	1.00
100 Bank Account Sheets, numbered 50-99	1.00
2,000 Face Voucher Checks, type printed or lithographed (one bank)	16.00
500 Sets in duplicate Daily Summary of Transactions with Banks	5.00
	$50.50

The above would constitute an outfit for many establishments for more than a year. For the succeeding periods only supplies would be required.

We offer the lot delivered to any express company for $35 net, or omitting the checks, for $20 net. You can use the register with your present stock of checks if you prefer.

For cash with order we will include, without extra charge

1 post binder for filing Register Checks, 8½x14, regular price	$1.50
1 post binder for filing "Accounts with Banks," 8½x11, regular price	1.00

The device above described is only one of a large number of Working Units of the Balance Sheet System of Accounts, of which we are the exclusive manufacturers under contract, and which we are prepared to furnish the public upon most advantageous terms. We solicit correspondence. Address communications,

Stationery Manufacturing Company,
318 Broadway, New York City.

BRIEF MENTION.

"SIMPLICITY" IS THE TITLE of a little booklet sent out by the Eastman Kodak Co., of Rochester, N. Y. Its cover bears a very dainty design reproduced from a photograph, and the booklet is illustrated with many halftone cuts of the various makes of cameras which the Eastman people turn out. The word "kodak" has become a part of our language, but, as everyone knows, it was originated by the Eastman Co. This little booklet is interestingly written and finely printed. We think it well worth a 2-cent stamp to any one interested in amateur photography.

ANOTHER CATALOGUE SENT OUT by the Eastman Kodak Co. is entitled "Kodak: The Growth and Triumph of an Idea." Its cover, printed in green and gold, shows a large tree, amidst the foliage of which is the word "Kodak" in gold letters. The roots of this tree are entwined around acorns enclosing rolls of kodak film. The catalogue is finely illustrated with halftone cuts, and it is surprising to see how many kinds and shapes of cameras are manufactured by this company. There are cameras with portrait attachments; cameras for the pocket, for the hand, for the satchel, and to be carried on bicycles. There are also Panoram-Kodaks, so-called, which are said to widen the scope and interest in landscape work, and to be of special value in taking vertical pictures of high waterfalls and mountain peaks, and broad stretches of landscape. The catalogue contains a price list of kodaks, films, chemicals and the like.

A SMALL FOLDER advertising the filing systems and card and document files manufactured by the Yawman & Erbe Manufacturing Co., whose New York office is at 360 Broadway, has been received at this office. The folder shows many forms of office filing cabinets, all very neat and attractive, and, to judge by the pictures and text, well suited to the purposes for which they are designed. The Yawman & Erbe Co. make a great many different varieties of these filing cabinets, and their catalogue should be interesting to any up-to-date business man.

THE MALLMAN ADDOGRAPH CO. are sending out pamphlets printed on heavy cardboard, and advertising their adding machines. The first page has a halftone reproduction of the Addograph machine, and the inside pages of the folder state that the Mallman Addograph for adding and figure writing is the handiest, the quickest and the easiest to operate, besides much more to the same effect. The offices of the Mallman Addograph Co. are Sheboygan, Wis.

THE NEW YORK STENCIL WORKS, with factories and salesrooms at 98-100-102 Nassau street, New York City, have issued a large catalogue showing the various styles of stencils which they manufacture. It is interesting to see how many stencils of all sorts and sizes are made and kept in stock by this company. The catalogue is plainly printed, although the paper is rather cheap.

A VERY HANDSOME BOOK advertising the Premo Camera comes to us from the Rochester Optical Co., Rochester, N. Y. The halftone reproductions of photographs in this book are works of art, and the subjects chosen are beautiful. The Premo Camera is made in many shapes and styles, and for all sorts of work. If the photographic reproductions shown in this book are fair samples of the work done by the Premo, it must be a very fine camera. The Rochester Optical Co. manufacture carrying cases, developing trays, printing rollers and all sorts of photographic appliances. They are all described in this book, which is well worth sending for because of its artistic worth, if for nothing more. One particularly fine photograph is that entitled, "A Summer Day in the Country," which shows a farm wagon drawn by two horses, coming along a dusty road shaded by arching trees. Some of the pictures are quite worth cutting out and preserving.

A FINELY-PRINTED CATALOGUE is that of the Standard Tool Co., whose New York offices are at 23 John street, and whose manufactory is at Cleveland, Ohio. This catalogue is a handsomely-bound book of over 200 pages, and of a size to fit the pocket. The Standard Tool Co. are manufacturers of twist drills, reamers, chucks, taps, milling cutters and special tools, and their output is well known by the users of such articles. The catalogue shows cuts of various drills and tools manufactured by this company, and contains a price list and cable code. It is a neat-appearing catalogue, such as one might suppose a manufacturing company of the size and reputation of the Standard Tool Co. would issue.

THE DELAWARE & LACKAWANNA Railroad Co. have issued two more neat little books advertising their road and the summer resorts reached by it. The first booklet is descriptive of the Pocono Mountain Special, which carries passengers to the lake and mountain resorts on the Lackawanna road. The text is in the form of a story, and there are some beautiful halftone illustrations. The other booklet is entitled, "A Romance of the Rail," and is illustrated with halftone pictures accompanied by jingling verses. For instance, a picture of an attractive young lady in white, just boarding a train, is accompanied by this rhyme:—

"This is the maiden all in lawn,
Who boarded the train one early morn
That runs on the 'Road of Anthracite,'
And when she left the train that night
She found to her surprise and delight—
Hard coal had kept her dress still bright."

The pamphlet says that hard coal is used exclusively on all trains of the Lackawanna Railroad; hence the name, "Road of Anthracite."

THE APPLIANCES of the modern office would make the eyes of our grandfathers, who had to get along with clumsy and inadequate filing, and copying devices, stick out. The Tengwall File and General Ledger Co., whose main offices are at 90 Illinois street, Chicago, have just issued a general catalogue describing the Tengwall system of files, ledgers, etc. The Tengwall Company manufacture transfer ledgers, loose-leaf ledgers of several kinds, transfer binders, pocket price books, and many files, holders and binders. The ledgers are all loose-leaf ledgers, and the Tengwall device for holding the leaves in place is pictured in many cuts. The catalogue is well printed, very neatly gotten up, and describes the Tengwall system in readable and convincing fashion. It also contains the price list of goods manufactured.

ANOTHER PHOTOGRAPHIC pamphlet is that sent out by the Manhattan Optical Co., of New York City, describing their Vera Stigmat lens for cameras. Great things are claimed for this lens, and the pamphlet is mainly made up of testimonials from various amateur and professional photographers.

THE CHICAGO BINDER and File Co., of 334 Dearborn street, Chicago, are sending out circulars and catalogues describing and illustrating their loose-leaf ledgers, and "Champion" and "Perfect" loose-leaf files. The company also manufacture post binders, clip holders and other bookkeeping and office filing devices. The circular describing the Multiple Lock, Expansion Back, Perpetual Loose-Leaf Ledger shows the ledger to be a substantial affair with a heavy back, evidently locking with a key. In the circular are testimonials from the users of this ledger, and the following descriptive matter: "Having a multiple automatic lock which opens only with a special key, and locking every 32d of an inch, it will bind any number of sheets so firmly that no one of them can be taken out without tearing and leaving stub, or mutilating the perforations. The entire back is covered with leather, giving it the neat and true appearance of a bound blank book, and leaving no exposed metal parts to become corroded and rusty by dampness, and at the same time furnishing a good lettering surface. It lies down close to the desk, and opens out flat." The circular also advertises the M-L Ledger Transfer, which is a post file, and for which many good points are claimed.

A LITTLE BROWN PAPER FOLDER has come to our desk, bearing on its title page this curiosity-exciting legend: "Why My Photographs Are Bad." One is rather at a loss to know whether or not this means to give the reasons why the reader's portraits are bad, but on opening the folder it is seen to be an advertisement of a book bearing the above title, and written by Chas. M. Taylor, Jr. The book is said to be of great value to the amateur photographer, as it describes and illustrates common errors of photographers, tells how they may be avoided, and gives specific directions as to the taking and developing of really good photographs. There are six testimonials in the folder from the heads of photographic departments of large stores, from dealers in photographic supplies and from prominent amateur photographers. The book is published by Geo. W. Jacobs & Co., 103 South Fifteenth street, Philadelphia.

THE ILLUSTRATED CATALOGUE of steel pens manufactured by the Esterbrook Steel Pen Co., whose warehouse is at 26 John street, New York, is before us. It is a 24-page booklet containing cuts and descriptive matter illustrating and describing the various makes of pens which this company manufacture. The Esterbrook pens are well known, but it may surprise the average business man who receives this catalogue to see how many and how various are the styles of pens turned out by this large house. Fine pens and coarse pens, stub pens and pens with needlelike points, pens for text writers, oblique pens and pens of various queer shapes and sizes. One pen is called the "Poet's" pen, another the "Elbow" pen, because it has a crook in the shank like the human elbow. Then there is the Mammoth Falcon pen, which is the big brother of the well-known Falcon pen, and is big enough in all conscience. There are ruling pens, for which many good qualities are claimed. The little booklet is good pen literature, and although not in the least ornamental, should be found useful by the business man.

BOOKS OF INTEREST TO BUSINESS MEN

BUSINESS LAW. By Thomas Raeburn White, B.L., LL.B. 6 by 7 1-2 inches; 222 pages. Bound in cloth. Back title gilt. Price, $1.50.

This is a neat, compact and handy book of business law for the use of students and business men. Among the subjects treated are Contracts, Sales, Partnerships, Corporations, Negotiable Paper and the like. The author's language is plain, and is understandable by any one having no previous knowledge of law. The book's clearness on the essential points of ordinary law should recommend it as a business book for the plain business man who has no time in which to consult a law library.

THE PHONOGRAPHIC DICTIONARY AND PHRASE BOOK. By Benn Pitman and Jerome B. Howard. 5 1-2 by 8 inches; 552 pages. Bound in cloth. Cover title and back title gilt. Price, $3.00.

This book is the most elaborate shorthand dictionary yet published, with the characters in fac-simile. It contains over 20,000 words, and for every one of these words there is a corresponding sign in the Benn Pitman system of shorthand. To the reporter, office or court stenographer, or any one writing the Benn Pitman system of shorthand, the book is invaluable. It is well made, tastefully bound, and is printed on a good quality of paper in clean, plain type.

THE LAWRENCE SYSTEM OF VOCAL AND PHYSICAL EXPRESSION. By Edwin Gordon Lawrence. 4 3-4 by 6 inches; 128 pages. Bound in cloth. Cover title and back title gilt. Price, $1.00.

The author says in the preface of this little book that his object has been to place in the hands of lawyers, actors and public speakers in general, a simple system of vocal and physical expression that will enable them to clearly convey thought by word of mouth and emphasize it by the proper action. To the man of affairs who is called upon for a speech on any subject, and who knows what to say but does not know how to say it, this book will be a great help.

BUSINESS LAW. By Alonzo R. Weed, LL. B., of the Boston Bar. 6 by 9 1-4 inches; 172 pages. Bound in cloth. Cover and back title red. Price, $1.25.

Mr. Weed calls his book "a manual for schools and colleges and for every day use." The titles of the chapters are as follows: Contracts, Principal and Agent, Partnerships, Sales of Personal Property, Bailments and Common Carriers, Negotiable Paper, Deeds, Mortgages and Leases, Collection Laws, Written Rates of Interest, Insurance, Patent Rights, Trade-Marks and Copyrights, etc.
The author does not waste words, and yet treats his subjects clearly and comprehensively. In short, he gives the law without the addition of wordy "trimmings."

BANKERS' AND MERCHANTS' INTEREST TABLES. By Francis H. Coffin and David H. Moore. 13 by 9 1-2 inches. Bound in cloth. Leather back and corners. Cover and back title gilt. Price, $5.00.

There have been interest tables published before, but never, so far as we know, has so elaborate and comprehensive a set of tables been issued in book form. "The volume contains," to quote from the title page, "Interest tables, computed on the basis of 360 days per annum, at 3 1-2, 4, 5 and 6 per cent, with an accurate calculation of interest on every sum from $1.00 to $1,000, and, by simple addition of two lines, on every further sum, to $1,000,000." It also contains a 1 per cent one day table, on the basis of 365 days per annum, from which interest on daily balances can be computed at any time and on any sum. There is a time table printed in black and red at the beginning of the book as an aid in quickly finding the number of days between one day and another. To a merchant or banker performing many calculations in interest this book is a great time saver. It is handsomely bound, finely printed, and has a thumb index.

POLITICAL ECONOMY OF HUMANISM. By Henry Wood. 7 3-4 by 5 1-4 inches; 320 pages. Bound in cloth. Cover and back title gilt. Price, $1.25.

Mr. Wood is well known as a writer on various economic subjects, and this book contains a series of able treatises, written in his usual vein, on the relation of the employer to the employed, and the phases of the industrial question and their relation to socialism. Among the questions considered and handled

TITLE GUARANTEE AND TRUST COMPANY

Does each year an increasing proportion of the whole business of examining titles and making mortgage loans in New York City. Last year it loaned

Over Thirty-Five Million Dollars

on real estate in New York City. When you buy real estate, or borrow on it, come to this company. Fees moderate and uniform.

Capital and Surplus, $6,000,000

146 Broadway, MANHATTAN. 175 Remsen St., BROOKLYN.

R·I·P·A·N·S

There is scarcely any condition of ill-health that is not benefited by the occasional use of a R·I·P·A·N·S Tabule. For sale by Druggists. The Five-Cent packet is enough for an ordinary occasion. The family bottle, 60 cents, contains a supply for a year.

in a conservative spirit and with much common sense, are the following: Supply and Demand, the Law of Competition, Labor and Production, Combinations of Capital, Combinations of Labor, Employers and Profit Sharing, the Obligations and Privileges of Employees, the Unequal Distribution of Wealth, Money and Coinage, Tariffs and Protection, Industrial Education and Gold Production and values.

INTRODUCTION TO THE STUDY OF COMMERCE. By Frederick R. Clow, Ph. D. 7 1-2 by 3 3-4 inches; 224 pages. Bound in cloth. Back title gilt. Price, $1.25.

Mr. Clow's book is not intended as a complete text book on commerce. It is simply, as its title implies, an introduction to the study of commerce. It is intended as a text book for the use of teachers in schools or universities, or as a help to the student in his commercial training. Incidentally, it makes good reading for anyone interested in modern commerce, and particularly for the American merchant. The author begins by describing the Elements of Commerce; then follows a short essay on the Rise of Commerce, and then the Materials of Commerce are discussed. Foreign Commerce of the United States and of other countries is treated of, as is the Domestic Commerce of this country. The titles of other chapters are: Organization of Trade, Prices, Payments and How the Equilibrium is Maintained. We can heartily recommend this introduction to the Study of Commerce. It is a good book on a vastly important subject.

THE A B C OF BANKS AND BANKING. By George M. Coffin. 6 3-4 by 5 inches; 137 pages. Bound in cloth. Back title gilt. Price, $1.25.

This handy little volume is exactly what its name implies, that is, a presentation of the principles underlying banking in the United States. The author in his preface says that it is designed to appeal to the reader outside as well as inside of a bank. It is by no means the last word or every word about banking. It may be said that it is a primer covering a field that has hitherto been somewhat neglected. The chapter heads are as follows: Banking in General, Various Kinds of Banking, Capital Stock, Shareholders' Rights and Liabilities, Undivided Profits, Dividends and Surplus, Deposits, Checks, Lawful Money Reserve, Issuing Bank Notes, Borrowing Money, Loans and Discounts, Exchanges, Collections, Letters of Credit, Bonds, Mortgages and Stocks, Bank Reports, Examinations, Directors, Executive Officers—Their Powers and Duties, Internal Administration and Bookkeeping, and Other Suggestions.

Public Accountants

ATLANTA, GA.—Ralph H. Brown, 318 Temple Court.

BOSTON, MASS.—Charles H. Fellows, 174 Summer; New England Audit Co., 45 Milk; J. S. Parsons, 214 Columbus Ave.; Safeguard Account Co., 53 Tremont; William Dillon, 502 Exchange Building.

BROOKLYN, N. Y.—Franklin Allen, Arbuckle Building, 371 Fulton.

BUFFALO, N. Y.—W. G. Mowat, 831 Ellicott Square.

CHICAGO, ILL.—Safeguard Account Co., 609-611A Merchants' Loan & Trust Building, 135 Adams; Haskins & Sells, 214 Dearborn.

DAVENPORT, IOWA.—J. C. Grabbe, McManus Building.

DETROIT, MICH.—N. A. Hawkins, 717-718 Chamber of Commerce; H. Naemansson, 496 Putnam Ave.

LONDON, CANADA.—Geo. F. Jewell, 361 Dundas.

NEW BEDFORD, MASS.—James L. Hathway, 72 Willis.

NEW ORLEANS, LA.—P. W. Sherwood, 904 Howard Ave.

NEW YORK, N. Y.—Patterson, Teele & Dennis, 30 Broad; Haskins & Sells, 30 Broad; Account, Audit & Assurance Co., Ltd., 25 Pine; Leon Brummer, 7 Pine; H. F. Searle, 45 Broadway; Hart Bros., Tibbits, Heiron & Co., 11 Broadway; Franklin Allen, Silk Exchange Building, Broadway, corner Broome.

PHILADELPHIA, PA.—Francis & Sterrett, Penn Mutual Building; Peter Ballingall, German-American Building; Charles W. Thomas, 409 Lippincott Building; Alfred L. Sellers, 1001 Chestnut.

PITTSBURG, PA.—John Vaughn, 5520 Claybourne; George W. Wood & Co., 341 Fourth Ave.

PROVIDENCE, R. I.—George R. Allen, 29 Weybosset.

SAN FRANCISCO, CAL.—Charles L. Lutgen, 218 California; Lester Herrick, 406 Montgomery.

TORONTO, CANADA.—F. H. Kidd, Bank of Commerce Building.

WINDSOR, CANADA.—F. H. Macpherson, 16 Sandwich, East.

WINNIPEG, CANADA.—Peter Thornton, 313 Main.

UNIVERSITY TRAINING For Business

ACCOUNTING BANKING BROKERAGE

School of Comerce, Accounts and Finance. Evening Sessions. New York University, Washington Square, N. Y. City.

FALL TERM OPENS OCT. I.

Any book in this list will be sent to any address in the United States, Canada or Mexico upon receipt of price. If there is some special book that you require we shall be pleased to hunt it up for you. Address COMMERCE, ACCOUNTS & FINANCE, 25 Pine street, New York city.

HALL'S Fireproof and Burglar Proof SAFES

Sold since 1840. Never fail to protect contents.

KNOWN EVERYWHERE

393 BROADWAY, N.Y.

Telephones: 3133-3136-307 Franklin.

BUSINESS NEEDS

Advertisements under this head one cent a word each insertion.

The Manufacturer HE Pays the Freight.

BOOKKEEPERS who have books to keep and papers and letters to file should be interested in all devices that may assist them in keeping things in order. Do you study the catalogues, watch the improvement in filing devices, binders and all the helpful little accessories to office work? I do. Write and tell me what annoys you in the office, perhaps I can help you. Address COMMISSION AGENT, care of C. A. & F.

BOOKKEEPER. First-class man wants to make a change; familiar with all methods of keeping accounts; able to devise books for special purposes; expert at foreign exchange, shipping and figuring in general; wages, $25. R. T., care Commerce, Accounts and Finance.

SALESMAN having a large line of retail customers in the eastern states among dry goods and gentlemen's furnishing stores desires to represent some line of goods that he can present in connection with the article which he now carries. Underwear manufacturers might do well to communicate with PERSONALITY, care Commerce, Accounts & Finance.

SECOND-HAND TYPEWRITERS can be repaired so that they can be used and produce work which is almost, if not quite, as good as from a new machine. I have the facilities for obtaining exceptionally good second-hand machines. I have a man who repairs them—a man that understands his business. These machines can be sold for 50 per cent discount from list price of the new machines. Does this interest you? If it does, address TYPEWRITER, care Commerce, Accounts & Finance.

PRENTISS CLOCKS.
SIX TIMES A YEAR
is all that is necessary to wind a Prentiss Clock. Why wind a clock every week when we can sell you one which will require winding but once in sixty days and will keep perfect time? Also Frying-pan, Program and Electrically synchronized clocks. Send for Catalogue No. 28.
THE PRENTISS CLOCK IMPROVEMENT CO.,
Dept. 28, 49 Dey St., New York City

Leon Brummer, C.P.A.
Public Accountant and Auditor,
7 Pine Street, New York, N. Y.

SALESMAN WANTED. Experienced traveler, by large Eastern house; have exceptional proposition for capable, energetic salesmen, with clear road record; men who can sell best general store trade can make permanent connection on salary, expense and commission basis; want well dressed men, 25 to 35 years, single preferred; must furnish unquestionable reference. Address TRADE, care Commerce, Accounts and Finance.

DO YOU NEED BOOKS? Old books, new books, second-hand books. Agent for subscription books, and dealer in old and new books. Ask me for prices on books you want before you buy elsewhere. A. CROSS, care Commerce, Accounts & Finance.

HAVE YOU NOW under consideration the issuing of any new bit of advertising matter? Such, for instance, as a little Catalogue, Booklet or Folder, or a new Circular to replace some former one not "up-to-date." If I have happened to diagnose your case correctly, why not write me, and if you have anything that you would like bettered, why not slip a copy of it in your letter to me? F. COOK, care Commerce, Accounts and Finance.

A BUSINESS EDUCATION	FOR ...ONE... DOLLAR.

...THE PRACTICAL AGE...

A MONTHLY MAGAZINE full to the brim with helpful suggestions to young men and young women who are struggling successward.

THE BUSINESS HOUSE THAT JACK BUILT, an intensely interesting and highly instructive story of business life, and

APPLIED ENGLISH, an authority on writing and speaking the English language, which no young person can afford to be without, all for ONE DOLLAR.

If you have never seen THE PRACTICAL AGE, send for a free sample copy. Address,

THE PRACTICAL AGE,
Moline, Illinois.

MAN WITH EXECUTIVE ABILITY and extensive dry goods experience, capable buyer and manager, is open for engagement; position in city or progressive town desired. Address PROGRESSIVE, care Commerce, Accounts & Finance.

Working Plans of Leading Banks

Organization and Administration

Illustrated by

Charts

ONE of the original a[illegible]scinating features of the work of the American Institute of Bank [illegible]s is a collection of charts showing in a clear and comprehensive manner the arrangement of the working forces of several of the leading banks in different large cities of the country, together with an outline of the duties connected with each department.

These charts are a part of the correspondence course of study in Practical Banking, but they have created such general interest that the Institute has arranged to publish them [illegible] a handsomely bound booklet.

Wh[illegible] the Charts Show

CHART "A" represents the [illegible]ional Bank of Chicago, which has a very co[illegible]ve plan of administration. The different [illegible]ents of the bank are numbered in the chart f[illegible]erence, so that the course of any item may [illegible] from receipt to final disposition. The main [illegible]ns of labor are clearly shown, and the duties of e[illegible]oyees set forth in a clear and striking manner.

CHART "B" represents a pro[illegible] New York bank doing a large general business. [illegible]e various departments and the duties of the diffe[illegible]lerks therein employed are fully described.

CHART "C" shows the general plan of administration of one of the largest New York banks doing an extensive business with merchants and [illegible]ving a large number of correspondents throughout the country. An examination of the chart shows how th[illegible] great business is handled.

CHART "D" represents in outline one of the largest and strongest banks in New York. An ana[illegible] of t[illegible]e chart shows that loans on collateral securit[illegible] a[illegible] important feature of the business transacted. [illegible] the bank's customers include numerous corp[illegible]s of the first magnitude, and a desirable li[illegible] [illegible]f-town banks.

CHART "E" represents a Ne[illegible] [illegible]k [illegible] the wealthy residence district, numbering among its customers many of the "400." The faciliti[illegible] afforded to ladies are a conspicuous and presumably very profitable feature of this institution.

CHART "F" shows the administrative plan of on[illegible] of the leading banks of Philadelphia, doing a large general business and having numerous correspondents throughout the country.

CHART "G" is not intended to represent any particular institution, but rather to show the distribution of the working force of a typical New York bank of large size and progressive methods.

Terms and Conditions

While the charts are primarily a part of the regular educational work of the Institute, and were published separately only as an attractive premium for new chart-coupon subscribers [illegible]y are also esteemed of exceptional value to bankers generally and to others interested in up-to-date business organization and administration. To suppl[illegible]emand for the charts which has come to us from all sources, they will be se[illegible] postpaid on the following terms:—

To new chart-c[illegible]pon subscribers to the Bulletin, as a premium, one copy each, ...	*Free*
To the general public, per copy, . . .	*$2.00*

Send order and make remittance payable to

American Institute of Bank Clerks

25 Pine Street, New York

THE NEW YORK PUBLIC LIBRARY
ASTOR, LENOX AND TILDEN FOUNDATIONS.

COMMERCE ACCOUNTS & FINANCE

Volume 4 New York September 1902 Number 9

CONTENTS

Published Monthly by the Commerce Accounts & Finance Company Twenty-five Pine Street New York

The Stationery Manufacturing Company,

318 BROADWAY, NEW YORK

The ACX System of Filing Invoices

ACX sheets have been before the public for several years. During the period of their introduction they have been perfected in various details of manufacture, and now are offered with the assurance of being just what intelligent and progressive office men require.

Briefly described, ACX sheets are the loose leaf principle applied to invoice books. This description, however, is hardly sufficient, because certain new features impossible with the old scrap-book used to contain invoices are brought into play.

The ACX sheet carries the copy of the Order, the Goods Received slip and the Invoice. Each of these, whatever may be the system, has to be filed. To file them together is an idea in the abstract that finds favor. But since when one is wanted for subsequent inspection, the others are wanted also, the filing together becomes a point of considerable advantage.

Many concerns record goods received in a book. Others make no separate record, but, instead, "check the invoice." The latter is at best a slip-shod method—one that frequently amounts to nothing, and one that, for various reasons, ought to be abandoned.

It is the simplest thing in the world to look at a lot of goods and then put a check mark against the corresponding item on the invoice. Counting, weighing, measuring, etc., whatever is necessary to prove the correctness of the invoice, is neglected. Contrast with this the plan of giving the receiving clerk nothing but a blank form, or the form with a skeleton invoice inserted, and requiring of him the insertion of the proper figures.

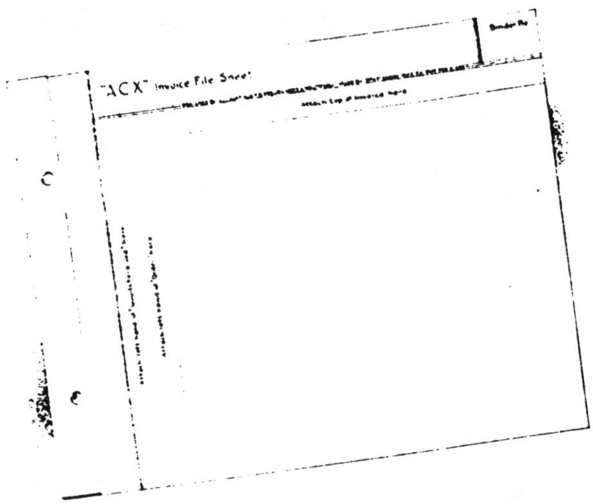

FIG. 1. AN ACX SHEET.

Most concerns at the present day ledgerize the accounts of their purchase creditors, whether they pay upon the voucher plan or otherwise. The invoice for this use becomes of prime importance and should be held in the office, rather than entrusted to the receiving clerk and others. When the Goods Received slip comes in, check the invoice by it. The copy of the order having been first attached to the ACX sheet, put the Goods Received slip over it, and finally the invoice over the two, as per the directions on the face of the sheet. (Fig. 3.)

Ledgerizing the accounts of purchase creditors is one of the best ways of indexing them alphabetically. If the goods are price-marked and the number of the invoice goes on the tag, the goods become the living indexes of the invoices and the accompanying papers. If the ACX sheets are put away in the file in chronological order, or very nearly so, we have still another plan of finding anything we are looking for.

To recapitulate: First knowing the name of the seller, we turn to the ledger index and there find reference to the invoices he has supplied. Second, seeing an article in stock, the number it bears refers us to the invoice, and, third, knowing approximately the data, reference to the ACX file gives us the Invoice, the Goods Received slip and the copy of the order.

The ACX sheet in itself (Fig. 1) is a piece of manila paper, thickened or reinforced at the left-hand end, to compensate for the thickness of the superimposed sheets put upon the body. There are two spaces covered with gum along the left-hand end, one for receiving the end of the copy of the Order and the other for the Goods Received slip. There is also one space of gummed surface along the top of the panel for receiving the Invoice. The copy of the Order, the Goods Received slip and the Invoice are attached by moistening the backs and laying against the gummed surfaces.

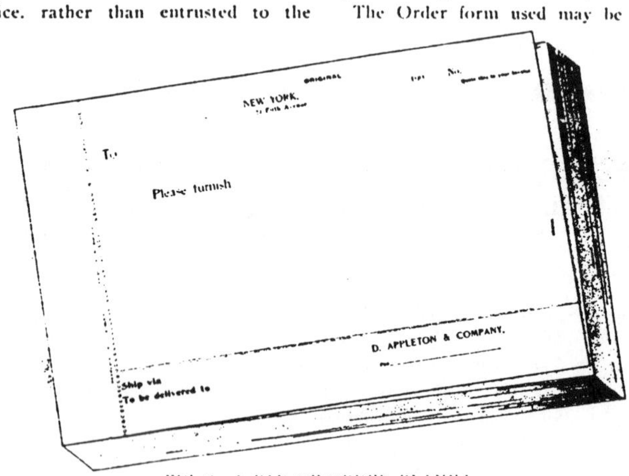

FIG. 2. A PAD OF ORDER BLANKS.

The Order form used may be anything that is conven[illegible] [illegible] the purpose. Preference, [illegible] should be given to something [illegible] duplicate of which is in fac-simile [illegible] for example, by the carbon proc[illegible] [illegible]urther, preference should be g[illegible] [illegible] something the dimensions of [illegible] within the outlines of the p[illegible] [illegible]e make an order form, carb[illegible] [illegible]ation (Fig.

2), to which the reader's attention is directed. See also price list.

The same general remarks apply to the Goods Received slips. It should be of appropriate dimensions. If long invoices are common, more than one size will be desirable, the long one being arranged to fold. A form of Goods Received slip supplied by us is shown in Fig. 4.

It is occasionally expedient to have more than one copy of the order. In large establishments, more or less departmentized, as many as four are frequently required, as follows:—

1. To the seller.
2. To the bookkeeper.
3. To the department to which the goods will be delivered.
4. For the purchasing agent's file.

In the same manner more than one copy of the Goods Received slip are likewise desired upon occasion, as follows:—

1. To the bookkeeper for the ACX file.
2. To the bookkeeper for prices.
3. For the receiving clerk's file.

The proper cost marking of goods in merchandising and supply departments demands that the price applied shall carry freights, duties (when the goods are imported) and the cost of handling. All these can be best figured in the office. The same amount wants to go on the goods as goes to the debit of the goods account. Hence the second copy of the Goods Received slip going to the office to receive the prices.

The ACX sheet, with its burden of papers attached, goes upon a post binder, forming a book, as shown in Fig. 5. The posting is done directly from the invoice to the credit of the Purchase Creditor's account. The offsetting debits are gathered up weekly or monthly on summary sheets (Fig. 6), and from them are posted to the Merchandise Purchase Account, Expense Account and other accounts affected. The summary sheets fasten in place upon an ACX sheet and go into the file at the exact points up to which they have served.

In every office there are a number of petty invoices every month, so unimportant in detail as to make it seem ridiculous to attach each one to an ACX sheet. For such we supply an ACX envelope, adapted to receive and hold a number in a way to maintain the system, while also avoiding unnecessary expansion. The faces of the envelopes (not here illustrated) are adapted to receive a summary of the invoices placed within them. The items may be posted to the ledger accounts, either in detail or in lump, as may be preferred.

Samples of the various supplies for the ACX System of Filing Invoices, ACX Sheets, ACX Envelopes, Purchase Orders, Goods Received Slip and Summary of Invoices will be sent free upon application to prospective buyers, and low prices will be quoted upon receipt of information as to quantities, etc. Letters of inquiry will be cheerfully answered.

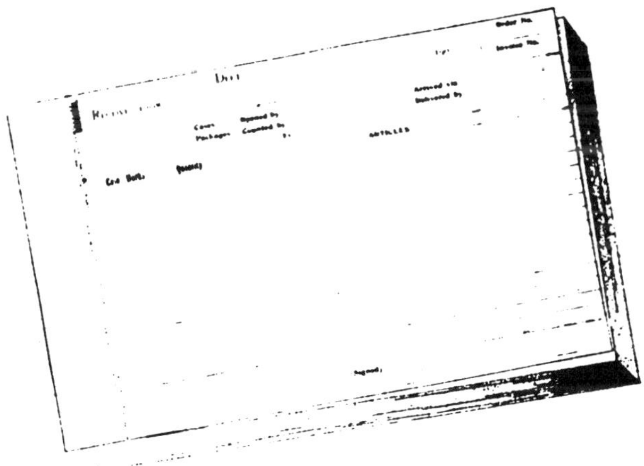

FIG. 4. A PAD OF GOODS RECEIVED SHEETS.

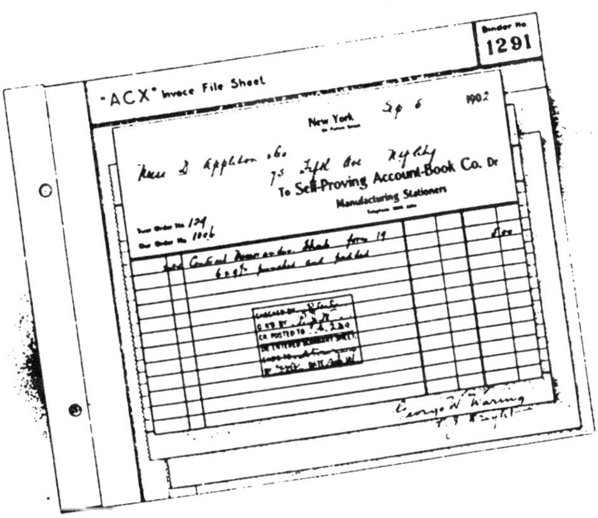

FIG. 3. AN ACX SHEET WITH DOCUMENTS ATTACHED.

The ACX Stationery Record

Various special applications of the "ACX" principle are made, among which we may mention at this time the "ACX Stationery Record." This is a plan for keeping stock of the stationery equipment of an office, showing the sources of supply, cost and various other details.

The supplies for the "ACX Stationery Record" are (1) "ACX Stationery Record Envelopes," (2) "Purchase Order Cards," (3) Post Binder, (4) Form No. Register.

The "ACX Stationery Record" Envelope is a specially made manila envelope, $8\frac{1}{2}$ x 11 inches, opening at the right hand end. The other end is reinforced to compensate for the thickness of the papers filed in the envelope and is punched for post binder. Upon the face of the envelope is printed "ACX Stationery Record," "Number of Form," with a blank beneath for filling in the form number, which number also serves as the page number of the book formed by the envelopes in the binder, and carefully arranged directions as to the contents of the envelope and the use of the system.

The use of the ACX Stationery Record may be briefly described as follows:

When it is desired to make a change in a certain form of stationery, the copy for the new form should be prepared in duplicate by the use of carbon paper, or by a hand-made copy of the original. Upon both original and duplicate the correct form number should be written. This form number should also be entered in the Form Number Register, a book kept for the purpose.

In ordering the stationery from the printer, the latter is given the original of the copy, and the duplicate is placed in the envelope bearing the same form number.

The printer is required to send two

proofs, one to be marked and returned and the other proof is placed in the envelope. Thus the person or firm ordering has always a complete showing of its stationery orders in progress.

If the contract price is made on a certain quantity of stationery, a notation of the same is made on the Purchase Order Card. When the printer delivers the new stationery it is carefully checked up with the original copy and with the proof. If it is found satisfactory the copy and proof are removed from the envelope and a sample of the new form is substituted, after marking it, either with rubber stamp or pen, as "Master Sample." If changes or improvements are made in this form a new "Master Sample" is required for each change. It is well to file and retain all old "Master Samples."

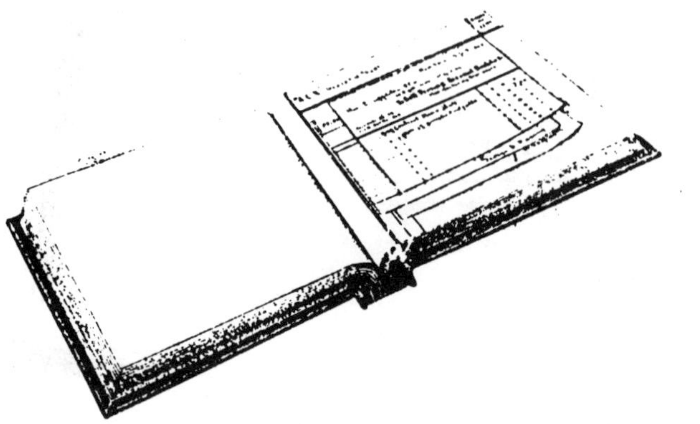

FIG. 5. A FILE OF ACX SHEETS.

All old forms of stationery should also be filed, and if they were in use before the adoption of the "ACX Stationery Record" system, and, therefore, have no form numbers, numbers should be arbitrarily given "Master Samples" of each, and these samples should be put in envelopes and the numbers entered in the Form Number Register.

These old forms, if they have been superseded by new and improved ones, should be destroyed with the exception of the "Master Samples." On the Purchase Record Card the fact of the change should be recorded, and also the date of the destruction of the stock of old forms, and by whose order they were destroyed. A new number should always be given to a new form. A number should not be used more than once unless the change made in the form is very slight.

Where forms are put up in pads the fact should be noted on the "Master Sample," so also if the stationery is in sets, duplicate, triplicate, etc. It is best, in cases like these, especially if the sheets in the set are of different colors, to use a complete set for the "Master Sample." A bound book should be known by its form number and by the title on its back. If it is thought best, a page cut from the back of the book may go into the file as representing the form number, and entries may be made upon it, describing the binding of the book, and the style and wording of the lettering on the back and side. Some large houses assign a form number to each style of pencil, eraser and penholder used, and specimens are placed in envelopes as "Master Samples." If desired, the record of the form of every style of mucilage bottle, inkstand, waste-paper basket, etc., may be kept in the "Stationery Record" by simply attaching a catalogue picture of the article to a sheet of paper, marking on this sheet the price and other particulars, and inclosing this sheet in a "Record" envelope.

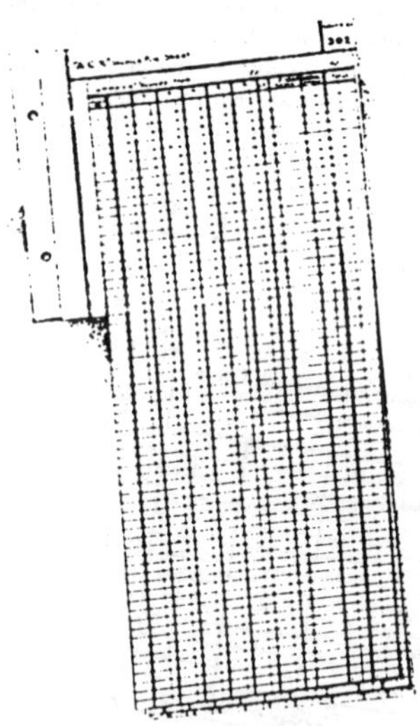

FIG. 6. SUMMARY OF INVOICES.

The value of the "ACX Stationery Record" to a house using a great deal of stationery and many varieties of office supplies is apparent. The waste in the ordinary stationery department of an office is great unless some such system as this is used. Further particulars will be cheerfully given upon request.

Address all communications to
Stationery Manufacturing Company, 318 Broadway, New York.

A BUSINESS EDUCATION | FOR ...ONE... DOLLAR.

...THE PRACTICAL AGE...

A MONTHLY MAGAZINE full to the brim with helpful suggestions to young men and young women who are struggling successward.

THE BUSINESS HOUSE THAT JACK BUILT, an intensely interesting and highly instructive story of business life, and

APPLIED ENGLISH, an authority on writing and speaking the English language, which no young person can afford to be without, all for ONE DOLLAR.

If you have never seen THE PRACTICAL AGE, send for a free sample copy. Address,

THE PRACTICAL AGE,
Moline, Illinois.

TITLE GUARANTEE AND TRUST COMPANY

Does each year an increasing proportion of the whole business of examining titles and making mortgage loans in New York City. Last year it loaned

Over Thirty-Five Million Dollars

on real estate in New York City. When you buy real estate, or borrow on it, come to this company. Fees moderate and uniform.

Capital and Surplus, $6,000,000

146 Broadway, MANHATTAN. 175 Remsen St., BROOKLYN.

HAVE YOU READ

The Kite Trust?

If not, why not? Send $1.00 for a copy to W. O. Douglass, Treasurer of The Bank Clerks' Club of New York, care First National Bank, New York City.

Ralph H. Brown
Public Accountant and Auditor,
318 Temple Court, Atlanta, Ga.

KNICKERBOCKER TRUST CO.

234 FIFTH AVENUE, CORNER 27TH STREET
BRANCH OFFICES:
66 BROADWAY, AND 125TH STREET AND LENOX AVE.,
NEW YORK CITY.

CAPITAL AND UNDIVIDED PROFITS, $2,508,399.11.

LEGAL DEPOSITORY FOR STATE, CITY, AND COURT FUNDS.

Interest allowed on Time Deposits. Deposits also received subject to Demand Checks, which pass through the Clearing House as do those upon any city bank.

Authorized to act as Executor or Administrator of Estates, and as Guardian, Receiver, Registrar, Transfer and Financial Agent for States, Cities, Towns, Railroads, and other corporations, and to accept any other Trusts in conformity with the laws of any State or of the United States.

LETTERS OF CREDIT FURNISHED.
BUSINESS AND PERSONAL ACCOUNTS SOLICITED.

CHAS. T. BARNEY, - - - - - - - - President.
JOSEPH T. BROWN, - - - - - - 2d Vice-President.
JULIAN M. GERARD, - - - Asst. Sec. and Asst. Treas.
FRED'K K. ELDRIDGE, - - - - 1st Vice-President.
FRED'K GORE KING, - - - Secretary and Treasurer.
WM. B. RANDALL, - - - - - - - Trust Officer.

BOARD OF DIRECTORS:

JOSEPH S. AUERBACH,
HARRY B. HOLLINS,
JACOB HAYS,
CHARLES T. BARNEY,
A. FOSTER HIGGINS,
ANDREW H. SANDS,
JAMES H. BRESLIN,
I. TOWNSEND BURDEN,
HON. E. V. LOEW,
HENRY F. DIMOCK,
CHARLES F. WATSON,
FREDERICK G. BOURNE,
C. LAWRENCE PERKINS,
CHARLES R. FLINT,
AMZI L. BARBER,
CHARLES T. COOK,
JOHN MAGEE,
HENRY A. MORGAN,
HENRY C. BERLIN,
CHARLES W. GOULD,
FRED'K L. ELDRIDGE,
HENRY W. DE FOREST,
ALFRED R. MACLAY
HARRY W. McVICKAR.

HASKINS & SELLS,

CERTIFIED PUBLIC ACCOUNTANTS.

204 DEARBORN STREET
CHICAGO
—
LINCOLN TRUST BLDG.
ST. LOUIS

30 BROAD STREET,
NEW YORK.

CABLE ADDRESS "HASKSELLS"

WILLIAMSON BLDG.
CLEVELAND, O.
—
30 COLEMAN STREET
LONDON, E.C.

Lackawanna Railroad

Address all communications to

C. W. TEN BROECK, Industrial Agent,
26 Exchange Place, New York City.

Do You Desire a Factory Site? The Industrial Department of the Lackawanna Railroad will aid you in finding one.

Are You Interested in Any Raw Product for Manufacturing Purposes? The Industrial Department of the Lackawanna Railroad will tell you if it is to be found along that road.

Does the Question of Power Concern You? The Industrial Department of the Lackawanna Railroad will tell you of good water power and of the proximity of fuel to points on that road.

Do You Want to Know the Usual Rate of Wages? The Industrial Department of the Lackawanna Railroad will give that information regarding any point on that road.

Do You Want to Know the Price of Gas, Water, Electricity? The Industrial Department of the Lackawanna Railroad will tell you.

BOOKS OF INTEREST TO BUSINESS MEN

BUSINESS LAW. By Thomas Raeburn White, B.L., LL.B. 5 by 7 1-2 inches; 323 pages. Bound in cloth. Back title gilt. Price, $1.50.

This is a neat, compact and handy book of business law for the use of students and business men. Among the subjects treated are Contracts, Sales, Partnerships, Corporations, Negotiable Paper and the like. The author's language is plain, and is understandable by any one having no previous knowledge of law. The book's clearness on the essential points of ordinary law should recommend it as a business book for the plain business man who has no time in which to consult a law library.

THE PHONOGRAPHIC DICTIONARY AND PHRASE BOOK. By Benn Pitman and Jerome B. Howard. 5 1-2 by 8 inches; 552 pages. Bound in cloth. Cover title and back title gilt. Price, $3.00.

This book is the most elaborate shorthand dictionary yet published, with the characters in fac-simile. It contains over 20,000 words, and for every one of these words there is a corresponding sign in the Benn Pitman system of shorthand. To the reporter, office or court stenographer, or any one writing the Benn Pitman system of shorthand, the book is invaluable. It is well made, tastefully bound, and is printed on a good quality of paper in clean, plain type.

THE LAWRENCE SYSTEM OF VOCAL AND PHYSICAL EXPRESSION. By Edwin Gordon Lawrence. 4 3-4 by 6 inches; 128 pages. Bound in cloth. Cover title and back title gilt. Price, $1.00.

The author says in the preface of this little book that his object has been to place in the hands of lawyers, actors and public speakers in general, a simple system of vocal and physical expression that will enable them to clearly convey thought by word of mouth and emphasize it by the proper action. To the man of affairs who is called upon for a speech on any subject, and who knows what to say but does not know how to say it, this book will be a great help.

BUSINESS LAW. By Alonzo R. Weed, LL. B., of the Boston Bar. 6 by 9 1-4 inches; 172 pages. Bound in cloth. Cover and back title red. Price, $1.25.

Mr. Weed calls his book "a manual for schools and colleges and for every day use." The titles of the chapters are as follows: Contracts, Principal and Agent, Partnerships, Sales of Personal Property, Bailments and Common Carriers, Negotiable Paper, Deeds, Mortgages and Leases, Collection Laws, Written Rates of Interest, Insurance, Patent Rights, Trade-Marks and Copyrights, etc.

The author does not waste words, and yet treats his subjects clearly and comprehensively. In short, he gives the law without the addition of wordy "trimmings."

BANKERS' AND MERCHANTS' INTEREST TABLES. By Francis H. Coffin and David H. Moore. 13 by 9 1-2 inches. Bound in cloth. Leather back and corners. Cover and back title gilt. Price, $5.00.

There have been interest tables published before, but never, so far as we know, has so elaborate and comprehensive a set of tables been issued in book form. "The volume contains," to quote from the title page, "Interest tables, computed on the basis of 360 days per annum, at 3 1-2, 4, 5 and 6 per cent, with an accurate calculation of interest on every sum from $1.00 to $1,000, and, by simple addition of two lines, on every further sum, to $1,000,000." It also contains a 1 per cent one day table, on the basis of 365 days per annum, from which interest on daily balances can be computed at any time and on any sum. There is a time table printed in black and red at the beginning of the book as an aid in quickly finding the number of days between one day and another. To a merchant or banker performing many calculations in interest this book is a great time saver. It is handsomely bound, finely printed, and has a thumb index.

POLITICAL ECONOMY OF HUMANISM. By Henry Wood. 7 3-4 by 5 1-4 inches; 320 pages. Bound in cloth. Cover and back title gilt. Price, $1.25.

Mr. Wood is well known as a writer on various economic subjects, and this book contains a series of able treatises, written in his usual vein, on the relation of the employer to the employed, and the phases of the industrial question and their relation to socialism. Among the questions considered and handled in a conservative spirit and with much common sense, are the following: Supply and Demand, the Law of Competition, Labor and Production, Combinations of Capital, Combinations of Labor, Employers and Profit Sharing, the Obligations and Privileges of Employees, the Unequal Distribution of Wealth, Money and Coinage, Tariffs and Protection, Industrial Education and Gold Production and values.

INTRODUCTION TO THE STUDY OF COMMERCE. By Frederick R. Clow, Ph. D. 7 1-2 by 3 3-4 inches; 224 pages. Bound in cloth. Back title gilt. Price, $1.25.

Mr. Clow's book is not intended as a complete text book on commerce. It is simply, as its title implies, an introduction to the study of commerce. It is intended as a text book for the use of teachers in schools or universities, or as a help to the student in his commercial training. Incidentally, it makes good reading for anyone interested in modern commerce, and particularly for the American merchant. The author begins by describing the Elements of Commerce; then follows a short essay on the Rise of Commerce, and then the Materials of Commerce are discussed. Foreign Commerce of the United States and of other countries is treated of, as is the Domestic Commerce of this country. The titles of other chapters are: Organization of Trade, Prices, Payments and How the Equilibrium is Maintained. We can heartily recommend this introduction to the Study of Commerce. It is a good book on a vastly important subject.

THE A B C OF BANKS AND BANKING. By George M. Coffin. 6 3-4 by 5 inches; 137 pages. Bound in cloth. Back title gilt. Price, $1.25.

This handy little volume is exactly what its name implies, that is, a presentation of the principles underlying banking in the United States. The author in his preface says that it is designed to appeal to the reader outside as well as inside of a bank. It is by no means the last word or every word about banking. It may be said that it is a primer covering a field that has hitherto been somewhat neglected. The chapter heads are as follows: Banking in General, Various Kinds of Banking, Capital Stock, Shareholders' Rights and Liabilities, Undivided Profits, Dividends and Surplus, Deposits, Checks, Lawful Money Reserve, Issuing Bank Notes, Borrowing Money, Loans and Discounts, Exchanges, Collections, Letters of Credit, Bonds, Mortgages and Stocks, Bank Reports, Examinations, Directors, Executive Officers—Their Powers and Duties, Internal Administration and Bookkeeping, and Other Suggestions.

Any book in this list will be sent to any address in the United States, Canada or Mexico upon receipt of price. If there is some special book that you require we shall be pleased to hunt it up for you. Address COMMERCE, ACCOUNTS & FINANCE, 25 Pine street, New York city.

Public Accountants

ATLANTA, GA.—Ralph H. Brown, 318 Temple Court.

BOSTON, MASS.—Charles H. Fellows, 14 Summer; New England Audit Co., 45 Milk; J. S. Parsons, 214 Columbus Ave.; Safeguard Account Co., 53 Tremont; William Dillon, 502 Exchange Building.

BROOKLYN, N. Y.—Franklin Allen, Arbuckle Building, 371 Fulton.

BUFFALO, N. Y.—W. G. Mowat, 831 Ellicott Square.

CHICAGO, ILL.—Safeguard Account Co., 609-611A Merchants' Loan & Trust Building, 135 Adams; Haskins & Sells, 214 Dearborn.

DAVENPORT, IOWA.—J. C. Grabbe, McManus Building.

DETROIT, MICH.—N. A. Hawkins, 717-718 Chamber of Commerce; H. Naemansson, 496 Putnam Ave.

LONDON, CANADA.—Geo. F. Jewell, 361 Dundas.

NEW BEDFORD, MASS.—James L. Hathway, 72 Willis.

NEW ORLEANS, LA.—P. W. Sherwood, 904 Howard Ave.

NEW YORK, N. Y.—Patterson, Teele & Dennis, 30 Broad; Haskins & Sells, 30 Broad; Account, Audit & Assurance Co., Ltd., 25 Pine; Leon Brummer, 7 Pine; H. F. Searle, 45 Broadway; Hart Bros., Tibbits, Helron & Co., 11 Broadway; Franklin Allen, Silk Exchange Building, Broadway, corner Broome.

PHILADELPHIA, PA.—Francis & Sterrett, Penn Mutual Building; Peter Ballingall, German-American Building; Charles W. Thomas, 409 Lippincott Building; Alfred L. Sellers, 1001 Chestnut.

PITTSBURG, PA.—John Vaughn, 5520 Claybourne; George W. Wood & Co., 341 Fourth Ave.

PROVIDENCE, R. I.—George R. Allen, 29 Weybosset.

SAN FRANCISCO, CAL.—Charles L. Lutgen, 218 California; Lester Herrick, 405 Montgomery.

TORONTO, CANADA.—F. H. Kidd, Bank of Commerce Building.

WINDSOR, CANADA.—F. H. Macpherson, 16 Sandwich, East.

WINNIPEG, CANADA.—Peter Thornton, 343 Main.

About a Pay Roll which proves itself, corrects all mistakes in figuring, divides up Pay Roll into several amounts needed to pay each person.

But let us send you a sample leaf, with circular, which tells the whole story.

BARLOW BROS., Grand Rapids, Mich.

W. G. Mowat
Public Accountant
831 Ellicott Sq., Buffalo, N. Y.

R·I·P·A·N·S

There is scarcely any condition of ill-health that is not benefited by the occasional use of a R·I·P·A·N·S Tabule. For sale by Druggists. The Five-Cent packet is enough for an ordinary occasion. The family bottle, 60 cents, contains a supply for a year.

PRENTISS CLOCKS. SIX TIMES A YEAR
is all that is necessary to wind a Prentiss Clock. Why wind a clock every week when we can sell you one which will require winding but once in sixty days and will keep perfect time? Also Frying-pan, Program and Electrically synchronized clocks. Send for Catalogue No. 282.
THE PRENTISS CLOCK IMPROVEMENT CO., Dept. 28, 49 Dey St., New York City

Leon Brummer, C.P.A.
Public Accountant and Auditor,
7 Pine Street, New York, N. Y.

The Utility of Reserve Accounts*

By A. O. KITTREDGE, C. P. A.

The penny-wise and pound-foolish policy is nowhere more strikingly demonstrated than in the crippled physical condition of certain railroads. The payment of dividends at the expense of maintenance has brought several of the great steam railway systems to bankruptcy, and even in these days of general prosperity numerous street railways are failing to provide for the stormy days that are bound to come. The depreciation of plant and equipment is something which must be duly considered in railway accounting, and the maintenance of adequate reserve is, therefore, a matter of vital consequence.

THE PRINCIPLE OF RESERVES.

The principle of reserve accounts may, perhaps, be most clearly illustrated by considering them in connection with their antitheses, commonly called suspense accounts. A suspense account is a record of expenses paid or incurred in one fiscal period, the cost of which in equity belongs to one or more subsequent periods. For example, insurance premiums are usually paid yearly in advance. Any business conducted on the plan of monthly fiscal periods would, therefore, not charge the entire premium to the first month, but prorate it over the twelve months of the year. In other words, a suspense account, called Insurance Premiums, would be opened, which would be debited with the whole amount of the premium paid. Thereafter, this account would be credited each month with the periodical pro rata, which amount would be charged into current expenses.

Reserve accounts are the antithesis of suspense accounts and are maintained to receive periodical credits offsetting payments made at some later date. If the amount of such later date payments could be definitely determined in advance, reserve accounts would be as simple as suspense accounts, being merely a matter of prorating over two or more fiscal periods; but as reserve accounts are largely matters of estimate, opportunity is offered in connection therewith for the highest type of business judgment.

The operation of the reserve principle may be shown in the matter of taxes, which are usually paid at the end of each year. It would be manifestly unfair to any business to have the taxes for a whole year charged to the individual month in which payment is made. The logical plan is to charge each month, assuming again that the business is conducted on the plan of monthly fiscal periods, with its pro rata of the year's taxes. Since no bill is rendered, nor can one be obtained until the taxes are due, it is necessary to estimate the amount in the light of experience and to charge the proper pro rata monthly to general expenses, and credit the same to the reserve account provided for taxes. When the time comes for the actual payment of the taxes thus provided for, an amount will have accumulated equal to the amount of the taxes, and the tax reserve account hitherto credited with such accumulation is thereupon debited with the payment made.

ESSENTIALS OF MANAGEMENT.

In the foregoing remarks it is presumed that the business is conducted on the plan of short fiscal periods—preferably monthly in the case of a railroad—as on no other basis can be brought before the management the facts essential in formulating plans of operation. Accounting statistics must be up-to-date in order to be of any practical value, and comparisons are most earnestly desired with the business of the month immediately preceding and with the corresponding months of previous years. Such information can only be obtained through the maintenance of reserve accounts, which fact gives added value and interest to the form as well as the substance of this feature of accounting. The continuous wear and tear of machinery and equipment which will ultimately result in considerable outlay for repairs and final replacement must, therefore, be added to costs of operation. Wear and tear are cumulative costs which begin the moment power and equipment are put in motion. The time of making repairs may be early or late, as necessities determine, but depreciation begins at the very beginning, and substantial provision should be made accordingly. Reserves for repairs and ultimate replacement are, therefore, primary considerations, and in any plan of accounting intended to furnish facts essential to management, such reserves should be separate and distinct, complete and up-to-date at the end of each monthly period, and at all times and under all circumstances liberal.

RESERVES FOR REPAIRS.

Reserves for maintenance naturally divide into two general classes, reserves for repairs and reserves for depreciation or replacement. These two general accounts may be subdivided as much or as little as may be desired for purposes of management. Repairs are not always or even generally made when the wear and tear actually occur, but rather during some moderation of business, or when the wear and tear have progressed to such an extent as to render further postponement of repair work impossible. In some cases repairs are put off for financial reasons. The necessity for repairs, however, beginning with the introduction of any new building, or piece of machinery, or equipment and increasing in a progressive ratio, is an ever present operating cost, and it is only fair that each fiscal period should be charged with its due proportion of this accruing expense. A charge for repairs should, therefore, go into each period from the outset, based upon an estimate of the actual wear and tear of the property.

In the subdivision of reserve accounts for repairs where different classes of motive power are employed, it is desirable to maintain separate and distinct records of each. It is, likewise, desirable to maintain a distinction between repairs of track and roadway and repairs of equipment. Buildings, fixtures and various other forms of plant may also be entitled to separate repair accounts, and reserves should be maintained accordingly. An examination of the cost of repairs in the past will afford a basis for the respective reserve accounts. Subsequent observation of actual costs for repairs, as contrasted with the reserve amounts provided therefor, will show whether the estimate, as provided, is too large or too small.

RESERVES FOR DEPRECIATION.

In addition to repairs, provision must also be made for the ultimate replacement of most of the physical assets of a railroad. No matter how much they may be repaired, the time comes, sooner or later, when they must be replaced by something more modern, and sufficient money should be periodically set aside to meet the inevitable expense of replacement when it comes. A story is told of an old lady who insisted that she never needed any new stockings, for the reason that she knitted new feet upon her old ones every fall and new legs upon the old feet every spring. Such a theory of repairs may be applied for years to street railway buildings, tracks and roadways, but radical inventions and changes of methods will some day require new feet and legs at the same time. The displacement of cable systems by underground trolleys is a case in point. Such a change scarcely comes under the head of repairs.

In equipment inevitable change is even more conspicuous. From bobtail horse cars to the ponderous electrical vehicles of modern systems is a radical change, but it is an evolution as well as a revolution. The history of street railways during the last ten years abundantly illustrates the necessity of liberal reserves for maintenance, and who will venture to say that the next ten years will record any less degree of material progress? Progress is a good thing, but mighty expensive, as many can testify.

If the life period of power plants, tracks and cars were

*Article contributed to the Street Railway Journal by A. O. Kittredge, C. P. A., President of the Account, Audit and Assurance Company and Professor of Theoretical and Practical Accounting in the School of Commerce, Accounts and Finance, New York University.

positively known in advance, it would be an easy matter to write off at the end of each fiscal period a sufficient amount to balance the account at the end of the time limit. The fact is, however, that such life periods can only be estimated. Some estimates will be too long, others too short.

LIFE AND REPAIR HISTORY.

While the life period of any individual piece of machinery or equipment is uncertain, this very uncertainty is worthy of record in the light of its duration and cost of repairs. Depreciation and repairs are taken care of through general reserve accounts, made up of classes of units rather than the individual units themselves, yet it is often desirable to maintain subsidiary accounts for the purposes of management. Therefore, the record of the life and repair history of important machinery in power plants and the similar history of cars or classes of cars becomes of considerable importance. This can only be done through a reserve account for each article or class of articles. The first entry in the account of life history would be the inventory value, which would, of course, be a debit. The credits would be the reserves for depreciation. In the repair record the credits would be the periodical reserves for repairs, and the debits the actual costs of repairs as made. Similarly, in the depreciation record the credits would be the reserve for depreciation, and the debits the cost of actual replacements as made.

RESERVES FOR EMERGENCIES.

While reserves for repairs and depreciation must be based upon estimates, the facts are obtainable to make such estimates sufficiently exact for practical purposes. There are other expenses, however, in the nature of emergencies, which cannot be estimated with very satisfactory approximation, but which must, nevertheless, be taken into account. Accidents and damage suits are something which every railroad must, sooner or later, face, and it is the part of wisdom to make due provision for such emergencies. From the viewpoint of logical accounting, it would be manifestly unjust to charge to any single period the cost of a destructive accident, or to charge to subsequent individual periods the expenses of any damage suits that might happen to be decided therein against the railroad. Such a course would derange the statistical history of the company for purposes of comparison and management.

The more reasonable and satisfactory way of providing for emergencies is through a reserve account which would be credited month by month with such an amount as might be deemed sufficient to meet such extraordinary expenditures. The offsetting charge would be to operating expenses. According to this plan proper charges to the expenses of operation would be made as time passes and a fund thereby accumulated with which to make good the value of property when destroyed by accident, and also to pay claims for damages as adjusted.

The very idea of an accident is that it is something unexpected, and while any estimate covering such emergency must of necessity be vague, due provision must be made therefor. The disastrous Johnstown flood was certainly not anticipated in any specific way by the Pennsylvania Railroad. There could scarcely be a better illustration, however, of the wisdom of the Pennsylvania's policy in maintaining large emergency reserves, for the enormous expense resulting from the Johnstown disaster had no appreciable effect upon the resources of the railroad.

Cost Accounts*

By A. E. SHOWELL, A. S. A. A.

You will, I am sure, all admit that my subject is a very wide and important one, and one to which we cannot direct too much attention. Perhaps it may be said that it is not a matter that so directly affects the professional accountant as many others; still, it is quite possible that some of the student members may find themselves called upon to advise in the starting of manufacturing concerns, or even obtain appointments as accountants to such, and for that reason it is my wish to deal briefly with the general run of a system leading up to the obtaining of accurate Cost Accounts, rather than with any special system which might be suitable to one business and not to another.

The importance of the subject is very much increased by the redoubled efforts of foreign countries to capture our trade. If we are to retain our trade we must not only maintain our reputation for quality by keeping up our standard of excellence, and by taking full advantage of the labor-saving appliances and other such economies, but we must also be prepared to cut things very fine in the matter of selling price; and, in order that we may discover where economies can be effected and where we can cut down to meet competition, it is essential that great care should be exercised in ascertaining the cost of production.

PRIME FACTORS.

The two prime factors in almost all costs are Labor and Material. I therefore propose to deal with my subject under those two main heads.

LABOR.

The first point to consider is the drawing up of a system for accurately recording the time made by the workman.

RECORDING TIME.

The one which I believe is most usually adopted is the check, or tally system. The workman, on arrival at the works, passes a time office, and there receives from the foreman or timekeeper a metal tally with his number, which is taken from a board bearing the corresponding number.

From this board the timekeeper enters up his time sheets, recording by a mark those whose tallies have been applied for.

In case of labor paid by time, and where the workpeople do not take meals on the works, the tallies should be deposited in a box each time on leaving the works, and then re-sorted by the timekeeper in readiness for their being applied for on the return from the meals, and the recording process again repeated.

There are also systems of automatic time-recording machines, such as the Bundy, Day, Llewellyn, etc., which are very effectual, and in some instances are to be preferred to the above-mentioned.

PREPARATION OF WAGES SHEETS.

At the end of the week the timekeeper will total up the time made by each employee, and will fill in the rate of pay against each. This he will ascertain from a book which should be kept, wherein is a record of each employee, showing date of engagement, rate of pay and each successive variation in rate, after which he will make the calculations and sign the sheets as having prepared same and made the calculations. The various foremen or overlookers should then examine the sheets or book, and sign the same as being correct as regards time and rate for the employees under his control. The sheets or book will then be sent to the counting house to be checked by an independent clerk, and in order that any deductions, such as rent, sick fund, etc., may be made, and a check for the net amount drawn; or, as in many cases it is preferable, the check is drawn for the gross amount of the wages, and the sums deductible paid over to the cashier, and treated as ordinary receipts.

It might be well, in this connection, to warn you of the provisions of the Truck Acts, regulating the question of making any such deductions from wages, and to remind you of the necessity, in all cases where deductions are permitted by the acts, of getting an agreement signed by each employee, from whom such deductions are made, authorizing the same

Where a workman is employed exclusively upon piece-

*Lecture delivered before the English Incorporated Society of Accountants and Auditors, and first published in the Incorporated Accountants' Journal.

work, or even is paid day wage, and is solely occupied upon one process or class of article, it is a very simple matter to correctly charge off his time to that process of class of article; but where he is employed in various branches—take, for instance, an engineer, who, during one day may have done (a) repairs to the machinery pertaining to one process in the morning, and has been occupied (b) fitting up shafting for driving some new machinery upon the works in the latter part of the day; or, again, has been engaged until dinner time (c) upon repairs to a locomotive which has suddenly broken down, and for the remainder of the day upon work connected with (d) the manufacture of some article for stock, then very careful apportionment of the time spent will have to be made, so that the correct amount may be charged against each of the following: (a) Maintenance of plant relating to the particular process; (b) the work's order relating to the cost of erecting the new plant; (c) the locomotive repairs account, and (d) the stock order number relating to the particular article.

In cases of this nature the employee must be provided with time boards or slips, whereon to record, at the completion of each job, or when employed upon one job the whole day, then at the end of the day, the nature of the work, or where there is one, a works or stock order number (to both of which I will refer later) and the time occupied. This should be initialled by his own foreman or by the foreman of the department where the work has been done.

In the case of overtime, where higher rates of pay obtain, special record will have to be made of time thus spent upon the particular job. This is important, not merely from the point of view of the preparation of the wages sheets, but in order that a record may be made of the extra expenditure incurred, so that the principal may be able to judge as to the real necessity of such addition to the cost.

ANALYSIS OF WAGES.

These time boards or slips will be collected each day and entered up by the clerk whose duty it is to prepare the analysis, either on rough sheets, or, for preference, in a waste book ruled across with money columns, using a page, or portion of a page, for each separate process, branch of manufacture, works order or stock number to which the items are chargeable, the cross columns being used for the different classes of workmen employed upon it.

WAGES ANALYSIS SUMMARY.

The time clerk will, at the end of the week, i. e., the end of the period for which wages are made up, after casting the analysis, enter the same either on loose sheets, which can be press-copied in order that he may retain a record, if he has to send same from outlying works, or in a ruled book if the works are concentrated. The gross total of these sheets will, of course, agree with the amount of the weekly wages paid.

Where the nature of the business requires the cost books to be entered up weekly, the summary of analysis sheets can be used for the purpose of posting direct to the prime cost ledgers, being either pasted into guard books or filed in some convenient manner; but when monthly, quarterly or half-yearly statements of cost are sufficient, much labor may be saved by entering the sheets up week by week in a wages journal, with printed heading down the side for all constant accounts, such as maintenance of plant, repairs and renewals to buildings, locos, wagons, etc., and with the necessary space for expenditure upon works order numbers, stock numbers, and then five, thirteen or twenty-six money columns for the weekly amounts, a total column, ledger folio and remarks.

I now turn to the other principal factor in Cost Accounts, viz.:—

STORES.

It is of equal importance that there should be a system for the accurate recording of all transactions, whether requisitions, orders, prices, consumption or stocking of stores.

Assuming that there are several sections or branches connected with the works, each of which has its separate stores department, it will be the duty of the chief of each section or department to make out periodically, say weekly, a requisition to the head office for his estimated requirements, sufficiently far ahead to enable their being purchased, in case no stock is on hand at the chief stores. The forms are most convenient, I find, bound in books, paged and perforated, with manifold copying sheets interleaved.

The forms should show in columns, in addition to full description of the article or material, the quantity required, the purpose it is required for, when required by, and also for the guidance of buyers, the date of last supply, and by whom supplied, and a column for remarks.

In some firms the requisitions themselves are put before the principals, but to my mind it is more convenient to have them entered up in a requisition book, and especially if several of the departments and branches are using similar materials; by so doing the various classes of materials can be grouped in entering up the requisition book, and the principal or buyer can see at a glance the total quantity of each commodity required throughout the whole works.

The requisition book therefore should have additional columns, showing firm goods are to be obtained from, number of order, quantity ordered, rate, date received and reference to invoice.

STORES ORDERS.

The goods having been ordered, manifold order books being used, the number of the order and other details will be entered up in the requisition book.

STORES INVOICES.

In cases where the Cost Accounts for each works, branch or department are kept separately by them, it will be advisable, and, in fact, necessary, to obtain separate invoices for the quantity of goods sent to each, as much inconvenience and delay would be occasioned by sending an invoice from one department to another for them to mark off their portion.

If the Cost Accounts, however, are all kept at the head office, one invoice is quite sufficient; but it will be necessary for the branch storekeeper, on receipt of goods, to send in an advice form to the head office, giving quantities, and with any remarks as to quality and condition. When the invoice clerk at the head office has marked same off, he will fill in the blank columns on the advice form, the invoice number, firm supplying, rate and value, and return the advice for the departmental storekeeper to complete the necessary entry in his stores received book.

STORES INVOICE BOOK FOR HEAD OFFICE.

When the inward invoice clerk first receives the invoice from the vendors, he will number it, and enter the name and amount of same, after deducting trade, but not cash discounts, in a column for "amount of invoice as received" in the stores invoice book. After the advices have come to hand from the various departments that have received the goods, and the various quantities traced and agreed, and the rates and extensions checked, he will enter the amount for which the invoice is passed in a column for that purpose. This may or may not agree with the "amount as received" column, according to whether there has been any correction made in the invoice.

This amount will be posted to the credit of the individual firms, and to the debit of a general stores account in the commercial ledger. It may be a convenience to have the right hand side of the opening ruled with analysis columns, so that the amounts relating to each works or department may be entered in separate columns as a check on the departmental stores account, and to facilitate the localization of errors in the works books.

STORES RECEIVED BOOK FOR DEPARTMENT.

This book should be ruled with columns for recording the date, number of invoice, firms supplying, description and quantity of goods, rate, amount, and also stores ledger folio.

The amounts will be posted from this book to the debit

of the account in the stores ledger for the particular material.

STORES LEDGER FOR DEPARTMENT.

This ledger is much the same as the commercial ledger, save that the accounts are with the different classes of materials instead of individuals. Both sides of the account should be ruled for description of goods, rate and amount, whilst the debit or "received" side will, in addition, have space for name of firm supplying goods.

If the material is received by transfer from another department, or from the chief stores, or if it is material which has been previously issued and returned for any reason, or if it is material recovered from plant, then, instead of name of firm supplying, the transfer or returns advice number (which I will deal with later) should be entered.

ISSUE OF STORES.

I will now deal with the issue of stores by the storekeeper. No goods should be allowed to be issued except on a written order from the foreman or manager of the department or branch requiring the same. These orders should be numbered consecutively, and a duplicate retained by the foreman ordering the stores. When the stores are issued, the storekeeper must obtain the foreman's signature to the order form as having received the goods. The order should state distinctly for what purpose the stores are required, i. e., for some process of manufacture, maintenance of plant, buildings, works order number, or stock order number, as the case may be. Cases may arise where stores issued for one purpose are eventually used, for some special reason, for another purpose altogether. In such instances the foreman must immediately advise the storekeeper, who will enter such to the credit of the account which was originally debited, and debit the account for the job to which the material was actually applied. Every effort should be made to reduce such cases to a minimum, or errors will creep in.

STORES ISSUED BOOK FOR DEPARTMENT.

The storekeeper will record in his stores issued book the full details of the material issued, and from this book he will post the quantity and value to the credit of the account in his stores ledger for the particular material so issued.

STORES ISSUED ANALYSIS.

He will then prepare a periodical analysis, according to the requirements of the business, and to coincide with the period for which the wages analysis is prepared, and send the same to the head office for filing and posting to the prime cost ledgers; or the foreman's orders themselves, with the acknowledgment of receipt of goods duly signed, after having been dealt with and initialled by the storekeeper, may be sent to the head office and used as the source from which the debits to prime cost arise. In the former case, where the analysis of the stores issued is prepared by the storekeeper, the door is perhaps rather left open to the storekeeper to so adjust his summary of analysis as to cover any irregularities that may have been going on, and it would be desirable, in fact necessary, to periodically test the accuracy of his analysis.

WORKS ORDERS FROM HEAD OFFICE.

It is most advisable that a fixed rule be made that no general expenditure, such as maintenance or repairs, alteration or addition to plant, exceeding a certain sum, say £25 or £50, should be put in hand by the foreman or departmental manager without the preparation of an estimate which should be submitted to the principal, and when approved by him a works order, bearing a distinctive number, should be issued for the work to be done. As I mentioned just now, in dealing with wages, and again with stores, all expenditure on account of that job should be booked by the storekeeper or wages clerk to that particular number.

STOCK ORDERS FROM HEAD OFFICE.

In works where articles such as boilers, cranes, wagons or such like are manufactured, or with smaller articles where a certain number are being made for stock, a stock order should be issued by the principal or manager to the department or departments, to make the same, and for the purpose of ascertaining the actual cost of the particular article, part or group of articles, all wages expended, or stores issued for the same should be booked to the stock order number.

PROCESSES.

In the case of works, where processes are continuously carried on, such as chemicals, glass, salt, iron and such like, the wages and stores will be charged off to the particular process, quality, section of work or other sub-division which the nature of the business requires.

STORES TRANSFERS, ETC., USED BETWEEN DEPARTMENTS.

It may be well to mention here that stores issued by the chief stores department to departmental stores should be merely treated as transfers. The storekeeper issuing such should enter the quantities and values in his stores issued book (or if the transactions are frequent, in the case of departments, a separate book for transfers may be kept), and post to the credit side of his stores ledger. He should also send to the department receiving the goods a stores transfer, with full details of quantities and values. After verifying same, the receiver should enter in his stores received book, or transfer book, in the same way as if the goods had been received from outside merchants, but quoting stores transfer number in place of the name of the merchant, and then return the transfer, signed and dated, to the issuing department. These transactions being merely departmental, need not be recorded at the head office unless, as before stated, all the clerical work is done there.

RETURNED STORES.

There will also arise cases, even in the most carefully prepared estimates, when an excess of material is applied for, and a rule should be made that the surplus must in all cases be returned to the storekeeper. There will also be in many trades scrap material and unsuitable or spoiled articles or material which must be returned to the stores; or, in the case of scrap, come under the control of the storekeeper, although not actually deposited in stores. A form similar to the stores transfer should be sent by the foreman, returning such to the storekeeper, giving particulars of the job for which the material was originally issued.

SCRAP.

With regard to scrap, the question of pricing presents, at times, a difficulty. But the system I find most effective is to fix a standard for all the usual classes of material, which can be revised periodically by the head office, as the market for such fluctuates. In such cases the storekeeper must enter the quantities and values in his stores received book in the same manner as in the case of transfers, and after having made such entries send the form to the head office, so that it may be correctly dealt with by the costs clerk, or the advices themselves may be sent to the head office direct and treated as quite distinct from ordinary stores.

FUEL AND RAW MATERIAL.

There are, of course, cases where wages and stores are not the largest factors in cost of production. Take, for instance, the works with which I am connected, where fuel is the largest, and consequently one of the most important items in the cost of production.

In such cases it is necessary to have a complete system whereby the coal, or other raw material, received in bulk, and which cannot therefore be passed through stores, is charged off to the particular set of works where it is to be used.

FUEL OR RAW MATERIAL RETURNS.

Returns must be sent in to the head office, giving the name of sender, name of vessel or number of truck, gross tare and net weight, remarks as to quality, etc. If any portion is used for other purposes than the actual process of manufacture—say, for instance, coal for locomotives, steamers, offices, cottages or other distinctive purpose—a periodical return must be made to the head office, so that the same may be dealt with in the proper manner.

FUEL OR RAW MATERIAL REGISTERS, FOR BOTH DEPARTMENT AND HEAD OFFICE.

A register of fuel—or other raw material, whatever it may be—will have to be kept, with columns for date advised, date received, number of advice, name of colliery or merchant, number of wagon or name of boat, weight advised, weight received. The book for the head office will, in addition, require columns for pit price, railway rate, delivered price, and then also analysis columns for weight and value, with headings for the various branches, departments or processes.

FUEL OR RAW MATERIAL INVOICE BOOK.

The fuel invoices will be entered in a book, similar to the stores invoice book already described, with analysis columns.

The total of the fuel invoice book will be posted periodically to the debit of the fuel account for each works, or to a general fuel account, which account will be relieved by the analysis of the fuel received book, the amounts, and if necessary, quantities, being charged off to the various processes in the prime cost ledger or to the expenses accounts, such as locomotive running, craft working, offices, etc., in the impersonal ledger.

PRIME COST.

Having dealt with the main items which go to make up prime cost in most factories, up to the time of the receipt of advices by the head office, where I am assuming the Cost Accounts are being kept, and with the necessary books for recording these advices, I will endeavor to explain in a general way the method of dealing with the same in the prime cost books.

First of all, let me submit to you suggested rulings for prime cost ledgers. The rulings suitable for one trade are, of course, not necessarily applicable to another; but, speaking generally, one or other of these forms will be a guide, with certain modifications in most cases.

(1) For works where an article or number of articles or parts are made to a stock order number.

(2) In works where processes are being carried out and material being manufactured.

Firstly—The wages, after having been dealt with as already described, will be posted, either weekly direct from the analysis sheet sent in by the various departments, or periodically from the wages journal, to the debit of the accounts to which its items relate, and under the various subheadings showing the different classes of workmen, if deemed necessary, in the prime cost ledger. The total will, of course, be posted to the credit of wages account in the impersonal ledger, and per contra the wages checks which will have been posted to the debit of that account. In the case of general items, such as maintenance of plant, repairs to buildings, etc. (except when chargeable against a process or the manufacture of some regular and exclusive output), will not be posted to the prime cost ledger in the first instance, but to separate accounts in the impersonal books (which can be ruled to record, if necessary, on the self-analyzing principle), afterwards to be dealt with by apportionment over the various stock orders, etc.

Secondly—As in the case of wages, the debits for stores used can be posted to the prime cost ledger, either weekly direct from the stores used analysis sheets (or the stores orders themselves), or these analysis sheets may be summarized in a stores journal similar to the wages journal and posted periodically (monthly, quarterly or half-yearly), as the circumstances of the trade would indicate to the debit of the respective accounts in the prime cost ledger, and the total to the credit of the general stores account.

The transfer forms relating to returned stores or scrap will have to be journalized, and the items posted to the credit of the various accounts to which they relate, in the prime cost ledger. The debits will be posted to the general stores account; or, if a separate account is kept, then scrap will be posted to the debit of such in the impersonal ledger.

The expenditure upon works orders (i. e., special expenditure upon works, for which an estimate has been prepared and passed by the principal) should be very closely watched and totalled up week by week, and when the amount is approximating the total authorized by the works order, the principal should be informed by the costs clerk.

Thirdly—Fuel or other raw material, received in bulk and not passed through stores, is treated as separate and distinct from ordinary stores, and will be posted to the prime cost accounts periodically, in the same way, from the fuel or raw material received book or from the invoice books themselves, if kept on the self-analyzing principle. In such cases it is advisable to post the quantities as well as values, so that the consumption of coal, or other raw material, per ton of the manufactured material produced, may be ascertained. This is of course a most important point.

Fourthly—Maintenance and other expenses not directly or exclusively connected with and chargeable to the cost of particular articles will have to be apportioned over the various stock orders, etc.

In the case of processes, the actual cost of the maintenance of plant, repairs to buildings, and such like, can usually be ascertained, as a distinct set of buildings, or part of building, and separate and special plant are usually employed. But in cases where several classes of trade are carried on under one roof, and the same plant is being used for various stock orders, etc., the apportionment of the cost of upkeep and running must be approximated.

It is impossible to lay down any rule as to the best method of apportioning indirect charges, it being a very much debated point, and one which in itself would require more than the limits of this paper to give anything like adequate consideration. As a rule, however, one or other of the following bases are usually employed:—

Sales value of articles produced.
Sales quantity of articles produced.
Wages expended on articles produced.
Wages and stores expended on articles produced.
Time employed on articles produced.
Estimated life and value of machinery employed in producing.

Similar bases may be adopted in apportioning the wages of foremen, timekeepers, etc.

"STOCK ORDERS" PRIME COST LEDGER.

In the case of my specimen ruling for prime cost ledger that relating to stock orders and articles for stock, as distinct from processes or bulk goods, the finished articles will be credited to the account when transferred from works and taken into stock at warehouse, as distinct from stores.

Stock and stores must be kept quite distinct, and must not be confused. When completed articles are sent into warehouse, whether they have been manufactured for a special order or for general stock, a warehouse transfer form should be made out by the departmental foreman, giving the full particulars as to weight, etc. The rate and value will then be filled in by the prime cost clerk, and the transfer sent to the warehouseman, who will allot a warehouse number (as distinct from stock order number) and will be entered in the stock books.

The costs clerk will enter the goods and value to the credit of the account for the particular stock order number, or the account for the particular class of article in the prime cost ledger, recording also the warehouse number allotted.

PROCESSES PRIME COST LEDGER.

In the other case, it is practically only a debit ledger, the space at foot for credits being merely for adjustment of overcharges in wages, returned materials, and so forth.

The real credits for sales are, in this case, better abstracted from the sales journals, which should be ruled on the self-analyzing principle, giving quantities, as well as values, of each material. In abstracting the sales it must, of course, be borne in mind that the stocks at the commencement of the period will require to be deducted, and the stock at the end of the period added, in order to ascertain the make to which the figures in the prime cost ledger apply.

COST SHEETS.

These can be compiled at intervals, as the exigencies of the particular trade demand, columns being ruled for the average cost per ton of each part of the process, which can be subdivided to any extent, according to the detail posted to the prime cost ledger from the subsidiary books. Columns may, if thought advisable, be also provided for the standing and general charges, rents, rates, management expenses, travelers, bad debts (estimate), advertising and carriage, if included in selling prices. These items will be taken from the various accounts in the impersonal ledger; but as they are mostly of the nature that are unaffected to any appreciable extent by the volume of business done in any particular period, there is no real reason for considering them in comparative costs.

There is just one other matter which I would call attention to, and that is the system in vogue at some factories, what I might call the

ESTIMATE COST SYSTEM.

It is adaptable to works where there is a regular steady output of certain articles, packets, boxes, etc. The principal prepares a very carefully detailed estimate, which he enters in an estimate book.

Assume the estimate is for 100,000,000 cigarettes in packets of ten. He heads his estimate book with this quantity. The book has columns for tobacco, paper, packets, boxes, each with weight or number, rate and value; also columns for the various classes of wages and expenses, and total prime cost. He calculates exactly the weight of tobacco which will be required for making this quantity, and prices the same at the rate then ruling, or makes allowance for a probable rise or fall in market during the period of manufacture. The same applies to the other material.

If the wages for the various processes of tube making, cutting, machining, boxing, etc., are paid piece work, the calculations for them will be simple; but, if day wage, he will have to make a careful estimate of the probable output of the person or persons engaged in each process, per hour or per diem.

These estimates are totaled on a cost sheet as the quantity under each estimate is produced.

The sales are also abstracted from the sales journal periodically, giving quantities and amount. A column is provided for estimated average discount and the average net amount realized.

To the costs, as per the estimate, is added the miscellaneous expenses, estimated on the same lines as I referred to just now in dealing with the processes costs sheets. The total cost (estimated) is then ascertained, and the net profit or loss shown.

These cost sheets are periodically summarized in the form of a trading account, and a comparison of these will often lead to the detection of error, either in estimates or in the account.

In preparing the trading account for comparison, care must be taken as to adjustment of stocks.

In conclusion, gentlemen, let me thank you for the very patient manner in which you have listened to what is, I am afraid, a very imperfectly prepared paper; but if it only has the effect of drawing your attention more seriously to the country generally, of keeping enormous importance, not only to us accountants and to manufacturers, but to the country generally, of keeping Cost Accounts, it will not have been time wasted.

The Negotiable Instruments Law*

By THOMAS B. PATON

What Constitutes Presentment for Payment—Payable at Bank—Payable at Business Office—Illustrative Cases

NOTE.—As enacted in New York, the Negotiable Instruments Law is divided into nineteen articles as follows:—

1. GENERAL PROVISIONS (Sections 1—17)
2. NEGOTIABLE INSTRUMENTS: Form and Interpretation (20—42)
3. Consideration (50—55)
4. Negotiation (60—80)
5. Rights of holder (90—98)
6. Liabilities of parties (110—119)
7. Presentment for payment (130—148)
8. Notice of Dishonor (160—189)
9. Discharge (200—206)
10. BILLS OF EXCHANGE (210—215)
11. Acceptance (220—230)
12. Presentment for acceptance (240—248)
13. Protest (260—268)
14. Acceptance for honor (280—290).
15. Payment for honor (300—306)
16. Bills in a set (310—315)
17. PROMISSORY NOTES AND CHECKS (320—325)
18. Notes given for patent rights (330—332)
19. Laws repealed: When takes effect (340—341)

The provisions of the law naturally fall under four general classifications.

a. General Provisions.
b. Negotiable Instruments in General.
c. Bills of Exchange.
d. Promissory Notes and Checks.

The text of the law is the same in all the states (with some slight exceptions which will be noted), but the numbering of the sections, and in some states of the articles, is not uniform. There is, however, the same continuity of articles and text, except that in some instances, "General Provisions" follow, instead of precede, the remainder of the act. By following this course of study with reference to the New York act, as above outlined, the reader in each state can apply the same to the law of his own state.

Having considered the cases in which presentment for payment is necessary, and the rules governing the time for presentment, both when an instrument is payable on demand and when it is not so payable, we now come to the section which provides the rules to govern the sufficiency of presentment for payment.

SUFFICIENT PRESENTMENT.

Section 132. What Constitutes a Sufficient Presentment.—Presentment for payment, to be sufficient, must be made:—

1. By the holder, or by some person authorized to receive payment in his behalf;
2. At a reasonable hour on a business day;
3. At a proper place as herein defined;
4. To the person primarily liable on the instrument, or if he is absent or inaccessible, to any person found at the place where the presentment is made.

Here, we see, are four co-requirements (1) who must make presentment, (2) time of day, (3) place and (4) to whom presentment must be made.

The provision as to the person who must make presentment is that it must be made by the holder, or by some person authorized to receive payment in his behalf. The "holder" is defined by the act (Sec. 2) to be "the payee or indorsee of a bill or note, who is in possession of it, or the bearer thereof." The instrument to be presented may be one either originally payable to order and indorsed in blank, or in terms payable to bearer, or it may be one payable to order. Where the instrument is payable to order, the holder is the payee or indorsee who is in possession of it. If the possessor of such an instrument is not the payee or indorsee, he is not the holder entitled to make presentment and receive payment, and payment to such possessor will not be valid, unless he has been authorized to receive payment in behalf of the holder. But mere possession of the instrument by one not the payee or indorsee is not, of itself, sufficient evidence of the possessor's authority, or right to payment. In the case, however, of an instrument indorsed in blank, or in terms payable to bearer, then any one in possession of it is the holder, entitled to make presentment and receive payment, for in this case the mere possession is sufficient evidence of the possessor's right to payment, as the bearer; and payment to such person will be valid, unless the payor knows that he acquired possession wrongfully.

The next requirement is that the instrument must be presented "at a reasonable hour on a business day."

We have already seen that instruments not payable on demand must be presented for payment on the day they fall due; while instruments payable on demand must be presented within a reasonable time after their issue, or (in case of bills of exchange) after their last negotiation. These provisions, as well as those of section 145, fixing the time of maturity,

*Republished from the Banking Law Journal by permission. Copyright, 1899, 1900, 1901 and 1902, by T. B. Paton, all rights reserved. To be revised and published in book form by the author.

have to do with the day of the year on which presentment is to be made. That matter being regulated, the present requirement governs the time of the day for presentment. The provision is that it shall be made "at a reasonable hour."

Let us, then, proceed to consider what is a reasonable hour of a business day at which to present an instrument for payment. When the instrument is made payable at a bank, the act itself provides a definition, in section 135, which we here quote:—

WHERE PAYABLE AT A BANK.

"Where the instrument is payable at a bank, presentment for payment must be made during banking hours, unless the person to make payment has no funds there to meet it at any time during the day, in which case presentment at any hour before the bank is closed on that day is sufficient."

The course of legal decision underlying and leading up to the above epitomized rule will be found set forth at length in an article by the editor in the Banking Law Journal for April, 1898, at page 196, in which we discussed the sufficiency of a demand after banking hours to hold indorsers on a note payable at a bank. It is there shown that in the years 1806 and 1813 cases first came before the courts of England where acceptances, payable at banking houses, had been presented there after the doors were shut and everybody gone home. The presentment in such cases was held insufficient, and the drawer or indorsers discharged. Then the general rule came to be recognized that in order to charge the indorsers of a note payable at a bank, the note should be presented at the bank on the day of maturity during its customary banking hours, and if the holder goes to the bank after those hours and finds it closed, he can make no valid demand and the indorser will be discharged. Afterwards cases arose where the maker had no sufficient funds in the bank during the day, and although demand was not made during banking hours, the holder thereafter gained admittance and found a person authorized to answer; and in these cases the presentment, after banking hours, was held sufficient. What these decisions have held is just what is now provided by section 135. Presentment to be sufficient must be made during banking hours, except in the single case where the payor has had no funds in bank to meet the instrument at any time during the day, when presentment at any hour on that day before the bank is closed is sufficient, for the holder would not have obtained payment even if he had presented the instrument during banking hours. But a presentment after banking hours, while the bank is yet open, in a case where the maker had sufficient funds in bank to pay the instrument during the day would be, obviously, insufficient, for it is incumbent on the holder to make presentment at the proper time for receiving payment at the bank—during the banking hours which the institution has fixed for its payments to the public—and if he goes there out of due time, when he might have obtained the money by going at the proper time, it is his own fault.

WHERE PAYABLE AT BUSINESS OFFICE.

We have seen above what is a reasonable hour of the day for presentment when the instrument is payable at a bank. We must now consider, what is such reasonable hour for presentment when the instrument is not so payable—that is, where it either specifies a business office or a residence as a place of payment, or where, without such specification, it merely gives the address of the person to make payment, or where neither specification of place of payment or address of payor is given in the instrument. In all these cases the only provision made by the act for the enlightenment of the holder as to the time of day at which he can sufficiently present his instrument for payment, is that it must be done "at a reasonable hour;" and for the holder's further guidance as to how he can sufficiently satisfy the law's requirements in this respect in the presentment of each particular negotiable instrument that comes to his possession, he is left to consult the law merchant.

Let us, then, consult the law merchant and see if we can come to a proper understanding of what is a reasonable hour of the day at which to present a negotiable instrument for payment when it is not made payable at a bank.

It is just about one hundred years ago that questions as to the time of day—and of night, we must add—for sufficient presentment began to come up for decision before the courts of England. Where instruments were made payable at banking houses, as was most frequently the case, the hours for presentment were fixed by the courts, as we have already shown. But often acceptors of bills of exchange would make them payable at their own places of residence, or places of business, and questions as to sufficiency of the hour of presentment in these cases also came before the courts. In the early case of Barclay vs. Bailey, 2 Campb. 527, an acceptance was made payable at the acceptor's residence. It was presented there about 8 P.M. on the day of maturity. The house was open, a servant being there. The hour was held reasonable, and the presentment sufficient. In the later case of Wilkins vs. Jadis, 2 B. and Ad. 188, decided in 1831, an acceptance was likewise made payable at the residence of the acceptor. It was presented there between 7 and 8 P.M. In this case the house was shut and no one answered. The presentment was also held sufficient, the fact that there was nobody to answer making no difference. In this case the court stated the following as its understanding of the law:—

"As to bankers, it is an established rule that presentment out of the hours of business is not sufficient; but in other cases the rule of law is that the bill must be presented at a reasonable hour. A presentment at 12 o'clock at night would be unreasonable, but presentment between 7 and 8 o'clock is reasonable."

A MASSACHUSETTS DECISION.

In an early Massachusetts case, Farnsworth vs. Allen, 4 Gray, 453, where the holder of a note had to first ascertain the maker's residence, and then drive nine miles out in the country on an evening in August, where he made presentment at 9 P.M., routing the maker out of bed, the court held that presentment, under the circumstances, was at a reasonable hour and sufficient. It expressed its view of the law thus:—

"No fixed rule can be established by which to determine the hour beyond which a presentment, in such case, will be unreasonable and insufficient to charge an indorser. Generally, however, it should be made at such hour that, having regard to the habits and usages of the community where the maker resides, he may be reasonably expected to be in a condition to attend to ordinary business. In the present case, taking into consideration the distance of the place of residence of the maker from Boston, where the note was dated, and where it was held when it became due; the means that were taken to ascertain the residence of the maker, and the season of the year at which the note fell due, we are of opinion that a presentment at 9 o'clock in the evening was reasonable and sufficient. It is quite immaterial that the maker and his family had retired for the night. The question whether a presentment is within reasonable time cannot be made to depend on the private and peculiar habits of the maker of a note not known to the holder; but it must be determined by a consideration of the circumstances which, in ordinary cases, would render it seasonable or otherwise."

But in a case in Maine (Dana vs. Sawyer, 22 Me. 244, year 1843), where the holder went to the maker's residence between 11 and 12 in the evening, called him out of bed and presented the note to him, which he did not pay, the court held that this was an unreasonable hour, and not sufficient to hold the indorser.

From these cases, involving presentment at residences, we do not think it would be safe for any holder to defer presentment after 8 o'clock in the evening.

A CASE FROM MAINE.

Let us now look at cases where the presentment was at places of business. First we will cite an interesting case from Maine (Lunt vs. Adams, 17 Me. 230), involving an early morning presentment. The holder went to the maker's country store at 8 o'clock in the morning, accompanied by a sheriff with a writ of attachment, and making presentment, had the sheriff immediately levy on the maker's goods, because payment was not then made. The court, under the circumstances of the case, held the presentment was not at a reasonable hour, and that the attachment suit was premature. It reasoned as follows:—

"There may be little difficulty in towns and cities, where there are business or banking hours, in deciding that a payment shall be made during those hours. But in places where no particular hours are known for making and receiving payments, there is more difficulty in determining what would be a reasonable hour for this purpose. It may often happen that the party having a payment to make would appropriate the earlier part of the day to obtain the means, either by collecting or by procuring a loan from a bank or from some person in a neighboring town. To establish a rule that would deprive him of that opportunity and subject him to a suit, and that would render him liable to have his business broken up while thus employed, might justly be regarded as unreasonable. The general rule being that the party has all the day to make his payment, that in relation to bills and notes should not be so varied as to prevent his having a fair opportunity to make arrangements and provide the means of payment before he is subjected to a suit. In this case the demand was made at an hour so early as to deprive him of that opportunity; and it was not, therefore, made at a reasonable hour."

It is to be noted concerning the above case, that the question of sufficiency of hour of presentment was not decided with respect to the liability of an indorser, or other party secondarily liable; but the action was against the maker of the note, and the real point involved was whether it had been prematurely brought, having been commenced by attachment immediately after the presentment at 8 A.M. on the day of maturity.

Looking at other cases involving sufficiency of the hour of presentment at a place of business: In 1825 the case of Triggs vs. Newnham, 1 Car. and P. 631, arose. A solicitor made an acceptance payable at his office, which was also his place of residence. It was presented there at 8 P.M. The court said that "presentment at an attorney's office at 8 o'clock in the evening is within a reasonable time." We hardly think, however, that such a ruling would be made where a man's office was at a place different from his residence. The case is really one of a presentment at a residence, wherein the courts have held, in several cases, that 8 o'clock P.M. is not too late.

AN OLD ENGLISH CASE.

In the old English case of Morgan vs. Davison, 1 Starkie, 114 (year 1815), a bill of exchange was made payable at the counting house of the acceptor. It was presented between 6 and 7 P.M., at which time there was no one at the place but a girl left to take care of it. The presentment was held sufficient. "The hour," the court said, "was not an improper one. The holder might reasonably expect to find the party in his counting house at that time." But we hardly think this would be said of business offices in large cities such as New York and Chicago. There are, in truth, some decisions involving presentment at places of business wherein the view is taken that business hours range during the whole day down to bedtime in the evening; but we think these decisions afford an unsafe guide for presenting instruments at business offices, and that it is only when presentment is at a residence that the time is extended to the bedtime hour. We will, however, cite two of these cases, one from New York and one from Illinois.

In Cayuga County Bank vs. Hunt, 2 Hill, 635 (year 1842), an acceptance of a bill, mentioning no place of payment, was presented at the office of the acceptors, No. 4 Wall street, New York. The office was closed and no one was there. The hour of presentment was not mentioned in the notary's certificate, which recited presentment on the third day of grace. But the court held that, prima facie, and unless controverted (which was not done), the certificate imported presentment during the proper hours of business. "These," said the court, "except where the paper is due from a bank, generally range through the whole day down to bedtime in the evening."

In Skelton vs. Dustin, 92 Ill. 49 (year 1879), a draft was accepted at Indianapolis, no particular place of payment being stated. The only evidence as to the time of day the acceptance was presented was the notary's certificate that after the close of banking hours he presented the draft at the office of the acceptors and demanded payment. The court held the certificate was prima facie evidence of presentment during the proper hours of business. "These," said the court, "except where the paper is due from a bank, for the purpose of presenting a note or bill for payment, range through the whole day down to bedtime in the evening."

The quoted language of these last two cases, so far as they relate to presentment at a place of business as distinguished from a place of residence, seems absurd, for how many business offices are kept open until bedtime? We think the rule of law is more correctly stated by Mr. Daniel, at section 603 of his work on Negotiable Instruments, as follows:—

"When presentment is at the place of business it must be during the hours when such places are customarily open, or at least while some one is there competent to give an answer. It is only when presentment is at the residence that the time is extended to the hours of rest."

IN MISSOURI.

In the Banking Law Journal for June 1, 1893, was reported a case before the Supreme Court of Missouri (Clough vs. Holden) wherein the liability of an indorser upon a note depended upon the determination of the question whether 5.20 P.M. is after business hours in the city of Chicago. The point involved was whether, upon a note payable at the maker's place of business in Chicago, the notary's call for payment at 5.20 P.M., at which time the office was locked, was a sufficient presentment for payment to hold the indorser. The trial court had ruled that 5.20 P.M. was within business hours and that the indorser was liable, and it refused to allow evidence offered by the indorser to prove the custom in Chicago as to business hours and that presentment for payment at 5.20 P.M. was not made in the usual business hours of office men and business men in the city. The Supreme Court reversed the judgment, holding the trial court was wrong in excluding this evidence. It said: —

"We take it that 5.20 P.M. is not such an unusual hour that this court would be justified in holding, as a matter of law, that it was not within business hours in Chicago. . . . The notary's certificate that the note was presented for payment in business hours is only prima facie. . . . When the presentment is at the place of business it must be during the hours when such places are customarily open, or at least while some one is there competent to give answer. It is only when presentment is at the residence that the time is extended to the hours of rest. Daniel, Neg. Instr., section 603. . . . We have examined Skelton vs. Dustin and cannot find anything in conflict with the view we have taken of the law. That case holds that the notary's certificate was prima facie evidence that the note was presented during the proper hours of business. In that case the defendant relied upon the objection to the certificate. In this case, when that objection is overruled, defendant offered to show affirmatively that the presentment was not within business hours. No such proof was offered in Skelton vs. Dustin. Nor do we question that in different communities 'business hours range during the whole day down to bedtime.' It is for this reason we think it is competent and proper to allow the indorser to show what range they took in the city of Chicago at the time this presentment was made or attempted to be made."

"DURING BUSINESS HOURS."

In this case, we see, the court adopts Mr. Daniel's rule that presentment at the place of business must be during the hours when such places are customarily open, or if after that time, at all events while some one is there competent to give answer; and that it is only when presentment is at a residence that the time is extended to the hours of rest. It explains away the language of Skelton vs. Dustin, and Bank vs. Hunt, which we have criticised, by saying it does not question that, in some communities, business hours extend down to bedtime; but it holds that the range of business hours in any particular place is a matter of special proof; hence refuses to hold, as matter of law, that 5.20 P.M. is or is not after business hours in Chicago, holding the proper tribunal to decide such a question of fact is a jury of American citizens.

In the foregoing we have attempted to bring out the main points in the decided cases which have dealt with what is a reasonable hour at which to present paper, not payable at a bank, for payment. A negotiable instrument, says the act, must be presented for payment "at a reasonable hour on a business day," and there it stops, having provided by section 7 that "in any case not provided for in this act the rules of the law merchant shall govern." Nothing very satisfactory or positive in the way of a fixed limit of time of day for presentment can be gathered from these cases. Each case has its own special circumstances as to place of presentment, locality and other matters. Where the instrument is presented at a residence, the rule seems to be that it may be presented at any time down to the hours of rest, and in several cases 8 P.M., and in one special case 9 P.M. was held not too late, while between 11 and 12 P.M. was not at a reasonable hour. Proof would be doubtless admissible as to the habits and usages of the community where the payor resides in determining the reasonableness of the hour. Where the instrument is presented at a place of business, the customary business hours of the locality will govern. These, in any case, may depend upon special proof. In addition (we have not cited cases on this point), although presentment may be after business hours, it will not be considered unreasonable if any person, competent to answer, is at the place and gives an answer refusing to pay.

Banking as a Profession for Young Men*

By JAMES R. CHAPMAN

To my mind the choosing of a career is one of the serious problems of life, and it is to be deeply regretted that so many young men seem to give it little thought, leaving to chance its solution, whether they shall become butchers, bakers or candlestick makers. It has always been my contention that a man must love his calling in order to be successful in it, but if he has not enough decision to choose one above others he will quite likely drift, drift, contented to be on any old pay roll, and exhibiting energy only twice a month—when he draws his salary.

Of course these statements are subject to modifications, for many boys and young men, through circumstances and family misfortunes, are thrown upon their own resources very early in life and are almost forced to accept the first position which offers itself; others by adaptability discover their calling and become successful men.

You have heard it said that every man finds his place; every place does not always find the man, and the "misfit" is often distressing. Sooner or later the incumbent is exhibiting himself in a second-hand store, selling below cost, or maybe he has joined the army of professional promoters, those financial vultures, from which class of so-called bankers "good Lord deliver us." I believe very little in fatality, and about as much in heredity. "Find a way or make one" is a much more hopeful motto to take along with us when we start out to conquer the business world.

A great many boys come to my desk every year with the question, "Want a boy, mister?" but when one of them says, "I want to be a banker," he has my attention.

You will pardon me for giving my own experience. From earliest childhood a bank has always been an object of attraction to me. My father was a banker before me, and it was one of my delights when a small boy to spend a day in this wonderful institution with its vaults full of money. When schooldays were ended it seemed perfectly natural for me to apply for a position at a bank, so one fine morning, twenty-five years ago, found me starting out with my pocket full of drafts, a messenger boy in the bank of a New England city which was then my home. During this period of time banking has been my continuous profession, and I attribute whatever success it has been my fortune to attain largely to the fact that I knew what I wanted to do, and have always been mighty glad I did it.

INDUCEMENTS TO THE BEGINNER.

Few vocations offer so many inducements to beginners as banking; short hours, numerous holidays, good salaries, social standing, agreeable companionships, these are advantages not often secured. There is also a fascination connected with the business that cannot be resisted; there is a charm in the handling of money to the on-looker; and when the novice enters a banking room, seeking employment, and sees his fortunate brother—all the "show" positions are in sight—surrounded by money, he gets the impression that what appears so plentiful must be easily earned, and his mind is made up; he determines to be a banker. He does not see the many steps to be taken before he can fill the high positions; he knows nothing of the weary hours to be spent at the desk unsnarling errors, nor the sleepless nights, when worse combinations than 4-11-44 will be holding high revelry in his tired brain. This is not to discourage, for, after all, every business has its peculiar experience; this is a work-a-day world, and we must expect some hard knocks climbing up the business ladder. Banking is certainly as honorable a calling as one could choose, for probably no other commercial business has developed so many men of influence and high standing, and bankers are the men to whom the nations look in times of panic and depression.

The business itself is founded on confidence and faith in mankind; the successful banker must possess the confidence of the public, and in return is entitled to that of his customers. Next to the clergyman and physician, he is man's closest adviser, and even this order is often reversed. He ought to be a good judge of human nature; he should be quick to commend the good and condemn the bad points of business methods and enterprises; he should avoid speculative schemes; he should have decision enough to say "No," and he should remember always that he is a public servant holding a position of trust with heavy responsibilities.

SHOULD BE A BROADMINDED MAN.

The banker should be a broadminded man; he has the opportunity of becoming familiar with almost every kind of business through acquaintance with his customers, and is often invited to assume control of the finances of other large corporations in other lines of trade. He must watch the ticker every day, for he has many loans on stocks and bonds; he must note the fluctuations in wheat, corn, oats, barley and rye; he must know the price of picnic hams, tierces of lard, barrels of pork, of eggs, butter, cheese, dried fruits and fresh fruits, nuts, and bales of tobacco; he must know the value of cattle, sheep and hogs, and many other things which he constantly carries as collateral and security for his loans. He should have a general knowledge of real estate values, and know something of commercial law. Of course he should be a good credit man, know how to pick a statement to pieces, eliminate the good-will, patents, unexpired insurance, treasury stock and office fixtures until he has the "quick assets" and liabilities before him.

Sometimes 'tis true the customer leaves his banker with the feeling that he hasn't much left, but I've no doubt many a disaster has been averted by this kind of a searching investigation. Lastly, but not least, a banker should be a man of strictest integrity and honor, always a courteous gentle-

*Paper read before Chicago Chapter of the American Institute of Bank Clerks by the Vice-President of the American Trust & Savings Bank, Chicago, Ill.

man. How gruff and harsh and angular we are; how we push and scramble in the race for fame! If you cannot be successful, you can be polite; if you cannot be rich, you can be kind; a sour man will never make a popular banker. I have often heard it said that much of the success of the president of our largest trust company and savings bank has been due to his geniality and invariable courtesy. These are some of the business qualifications the young banker should be seeking to cultivate, so far as he can, during the period of his clerkship. I believe a college education unnecessary for the equipment of a banker, and that the four years can be spent to better advantage in the office. Few, comparatively, of our bank presidents have attended college, but have begun as office boys, working their way up step by step.

PROMOTION IN BANKS.

Promotion in banks is rapid in the large cities, but slow in towns and smaller cities. In the New England Bank there has been but two changes since the writer graduated from it twenty years ago, and five years ago a Milwaukee cashier celebrated his fiftieth anniversary. The clerks in a large city bank are continually going through a sifting process, the incompetent ones being shaken out from time to time, the good ones being promoted. While this is true in all kinds of business, yet shortcomings are overlooked in the store or office that cannot be passed by indulgently in a bank. From the time a boy enters a banking house he becomes under the influence of discipline and system; the public are continually passing in and out; his department is exposed to their gaze, and he is expected at all times, for his own sake and the comfort of those about him, to be quiet and orderly. In those positions in which he comes in contact with customers he should cultivate a pleasant address and a spirit of accommodation, and should never lose his temper, although subjected often to great annoyances by unreasonable persons. While this may seem trivial, it may have much to do with the general reputation of the institution. Begin your career in a small bank, rather than in a large one, if possible. The smaller institution gives one more opportunity to learn and to become familiar with the various departments, and is by far the better training school. The routine work in a large bank is not beneficial; there is too much of it; it blunts the ambition and narrows the horizon.

Banking, like all other business, finds its greatest development in the money centers of the world. The country banker may be an autocrat in his little community and often accumulates a large fortune, but his horizon is limited. The banker in a city of fifty to one hundred thousand has an easy time usually—about six hours work, which might be packed into three; plenty of time for golf, the ball game long drives in the country, a winter in Florida or California, a summer in Europe, nothing to worry about, for the stockholders are satisfied with 6 per cent dividends, and the directors likewise, if a little is left over after paying expenses. But in cities like London, New York and Chicago, the banker has room to expand; he is on his mettle all the time, eight or nine hours every day. His clearest thought, his most critical judgment are drawn upon at sight from a hundred sources; it is a strenuous life, surely, and let no young man think, when he enters the banking profession in a large city, that he is going to have many idle moments.

VOLUME OF BUSINESS IN A LARGE BANK.

The volume of business in a large city bank in these days of prosperity is appalling when we see the figures before us. In the bank with which I am connected, and it is far from being one of the largest in the city, the important transactions show the following figures for last year:—

Sent to Clearing House	$309,000,000
Loans made	47,500,000
Number of checks paid by paying teller	67,976
Amounts paid by paying teller	17,600,000
Number of checks paid by bank	1,488,381
Total deposits received	596,401,000

Multiply these figures by the business of all the other banks and the result would be beyond comprehension. You and I contribute our quota to this vast total, and I am inclined to believe that you can get more information regarding the composition of this total in a banking office than in any other business office in the world.

While, possibly, business opportunities are greater than ever just at present, it is also true that lines of business are restricted; it is no longer safe for two young men to start off in business together with small capital in a large city; the greater department stores have swallowed up the little shops; combinations, mergers, are the talk of the day, and the work of absorption steadily continues; it has even spread into the banking circle of late to an almost alarming extent. The survival of the fittest is the new commercial watchword. Thousands of young men who, if conditions had not changed, might have been preparing themselves to conduct small enterprises of their own, are forced to seek other fields of employment, and have to be contented with a salary rather than a share of the profits of their own business. The banks are educating large numbers from this class, and, judging from what I know of the fraternity, we are giving to the world many sagacious men of affairs. The banker is a public educator and is continually called upon for advice. He spends a good many hours teaching people business methods, especially the gentler sex, who usually class banks in the same category with mice and snakes.

A WOMAN'S IDEA OF A BANK ADVERTISEMENT.

Occasionally, however, you meet with an exception. I recall a young woman of this city, well known for her poetical effusions, who not long ago came into the bank to open an account. After having received considerable assistance in the making out of deposit tickets, writing checks, etc., she came to show an interest in the banking business, and one day informed me she understood a bank advertisement in the paper and thought she could improve on it and asked for an opportunity. This was granted, with the following result:—

THE AMERICAN TRUST AND SAVINGS BANK.

Is the best place of its kind in Chicago. You give us the Savings—we give you the Trust.

Interest is allowed on all deposits of $1 and over. This accumulates so rapidly that there is no need to wait. This is why there are no chairs in the bank except for those who own it. There is no charge for checks unless you buy a book full. If you go in and ask for one, you get it—with a Pleasant Smile thrown in.

Classes in addition are held daily. The Head Cashier will personally teach addition to all women under thirty who do not stop clocks. Men, children and clock-stoppers are taught by the Policeman farther down.

If you are very nice and polite to the Head Cashier he will make out your checks, but you have to pass them in yourself. This is the only unpleasant part of Banking Business.

If you have money in the Bank at Interest the bank will have great Interest in you. This is different from other Institutions that imitate us and claim to be Real Banks.

Nobody need be afraid in our Bank. The dangerous people are all in cages—with a policeman to watch them. If they seem suspicious it is not their fault.

The Crowd on La Salle Street is composed of Happy People, who Bank with us. Get in Line early and Avoid the Rush.

The mucilage on our Revenue Stamps is flavored with Chocolate. Choice of Huyler's or Allegretti's.

Let no bank clerk think his education is completed even after many years of service; new questions are continually coming up to be solved, and the clerk can often be of great benefit to his bank and help himself by keeping posted; numerous periodicals are always at his disposal, containing valuable information pertaining to banking law and methods of business, and the odd moments can be well employed if he has the inclination.

MAKING AND SAVING MONEY.

I have left one of the most interesting and important questions for the last. Why do we go into business? Oh! to make our reputation; to become influential—successful. Yes, to a certain extent, but primarily we go into business to make money, and we do not become successful business men unless we do. What opportunity does banking afford for fortune making? You will have to begin in the old-fashioned way, namely, "save your money." Salaries paid in banks are, as a rule, more liberal than those paid in wholesale or retail houses, but bank clerks are an extravagant class of young men and are not money-savers. They are doubtless made so by their surroundings; money is the theme of conversation, and is always before them in large amounts; it therefore becomes common and loses its value in their eyes. The "settling down" time comes later to the bank clerk than to any other, and I would advise the spendthrift to seek some other employment. On the other hand, the economical clerk, by careful saving and judicious investments, which are often brought to his attention through his relation with the bank, finds himself at twenty-five with a comfortable bank account, a good foundation for that fortune he is seeking. Later, when he becomes an official, opportunities for making money increase. While bank officers are not usually immensely wealthy, they are a prosperous body, made so largely by taking advantage of information which naturally comes through their business relations. So if you are in a bank and do not like it, resign at once; we will not begrudge what we have taught you, but we prefer not to have you stay. But if you enjoy the work, keep at it, and remember that there is always room at the top.

MAKING A BASEBALL

Many business men know how to play baseball, but perhaps some of them do not know how a baseball is made. Hardware says that the production of a baseball is an operation almost as unknown to the public as its use is familiar.

Yet nearly four million balls a year, or about 12,000 a day, are manufactured by one Pennsylvania factory alone, and for a great many of these $1.50 apiece is paid.

A remarkable amount of skill and fine workmanship is needed to turn out a ball that will stand, even for a short time, the powerful batting of the big players or will come up to the requirements for league work.

The various steps in the manufacture of a first-class baseball are briefly as follows:—

It is first a solid ball of Para rubber just an inch through. The ball is placed in a machine by a boy tender and is automatically wound with a strong, pure woolen yarn. The winding is done with an evenness that no human fingers could equal, and the thick, blue-mixed wool forms a perfectly uniform covering for the core.

This layer is made just an inch thick. When the right amount of yarn has been wound on it the machine stops automatically, the ball, now two inches thick, is removed and another core set.

The partly finished balls are next dipped. That is, they are dropped into a transparent fluid called "plastic composition," which is really a kind of cement. This fluid is very adhesive, and when it enters the wool covering there is a solidification that prevents the ball from ever being knocked out of shape. So certain is this, in fact, that the company guarantees to replace all balls that are so injured.

The balls are next wound again—this time with a certain definite thickness of three-ply white yarn. This is covered with a three-ply blue yarn until it has reached the requisite size of nine inches in circumference. All of these winding processes have been automatic, and the balls appear of exactly the same size and weight. But no chances are taken, and each is weighed several times during the final winding, so that accuracy may be assured.

After being dipped in the cement again the ball is ready for covering.

The covers are alum-tanned horsehide, which is as soft and fine as the best white kid. For the best balls only eighteen covers can be got out of one hide, as only the very choicest parts can be used.

The hide is first knee-staked. That is, it is stretched backward and forward over a knee-high stake by a strong boy till it will stretch no more. The cutting is done by machinery. The cover is in two pieces, each the shape of the figure 8. A machine cuts out these pieces and perforates them ready for sewing. These machines are wonderfully accurate and very rapid.

The balls are placed for covering in dampers of wood, and the covers are fastened first with brass staples and then with strong cotton thread of the best quality. It takes about fifteen minutes to sew the cover on a ball. This requires considerable muscle, and only men are employed on the work.

The ball is still rough on the seams. It is rolled by hand and a few hours later by machinery, whence it emerges the completed article, ready for packing and selling.

The market for baseballs is entirely in this country, with the exception of a small and recent demand that has developed in Cuba and the Philippines.

OUR NEW POSTAGE STAMPS

The Bureau of Engraving and Printing is at work on a set of new designs for the series of 1902 of United States postage stamps. There will be some notable changes, including the incorporation of a 13-cent stamp to facilitate foreign registered letter business, says a Washington dispatch to the New York World.

A new border is being designed for the entire set of stamps. The design as accepted by the Third Assistant Postmaster-General contains an arch over the picture in the center. In the upper right and left hand corners are eagle heads gracefully arranged above an artistic scroll. The words "United States of America" will supplant "United States Postage." Under the picture will appear the words "Postage," and "Four Cents" or "Six Cents," as the case may be.

The picture of Grant will be on the 4-cent stamp, instead of Lincoln, which will be on the 5-cent blue stamp in place of Grant. On the new 8-cent lilac-colored stamp, which now bears the head of Sherman, will be a likeness of Martha Washington, the first woman to be thus honored by the American Government. On the new 13-stamp, which probably will be one of the first issued, will be a picture of the late Benjamin Harrison from a portrait furnished by his widow. There will be one other change in the regular series. The head of Commodore Perry on the one-dollar black stamp will be supplanted by the head of Farragut.

The rest of the series will have new borders of uniform character, but the persons represented will remain unchanged.

These stamps will be as follows: 1-cent, Franklin, green; 2-cent, Washington, carmine; 3-cent, Jackson, purple; 6-cent, Garfield, magenta; 10-cent, Webster, light brown; 15-cent, Clay, olive green; 50-cent, Jefferson, orange; $2, Madison, sapphire blue; $5, Marshall, gray-green.

The special delivery stamps will also be changed in design and color. Instead of the running messenger boy they will bear a picture of a messenger on a bicycle on the left-hand side, and will be bright red.

A STORY OF GRANT

Ex-Gov. George S. Boutwell, who began life as a grocer's clerk, in his reminiscences tells a good horse story, says the N. E. Grover. President Grant was attracted by a horse owned by a Washington butcher, and he bought it for $500. Subsequently he took Senator Conkling out to ride behind his new acquisition, and the President asked the senator what he thought of the animal.

"It strikes me," said the senator, "that I would rather have the $500."

"Well, that's what the butcher said," remarked the President.

NEW BANKS

Mr. Ridgely, the Comptroller of the Currency, is said to have made the following statement recently at Washington: "During the year ended June 30, 1902, there were added to the national bank system 437 national banking associations, with aggregate authorized capital stock of $30,407,000, and with bond deposits as security for circulation of $6,012,750."

COMMERCE
ACCOUNTS
& FINANCE

A Magazine of Higher Business Education and Practical Administration. Acknowledged Authority in the Profession of Commerce and Consistent Advocate of Methods Up to Date and Above the Table.

JOSEPH CROSBY LINCOLN, - - - Editor.
FRIEND PITTS, JR., - Circulation and Advertising.
E. R. KITTREDGE, - - - Business Manager.

PUBLISHED MONTHLY

SUBSCRIPTION $1 a Year in the United States, Canada and Mexico. Other countries $1.50. Postage prepaid by the Publishers. In the absence of specific orders to stop at the end of the subscription term the paper will be continued and a bill sent. Entered at the New York Postoffice as Second Class mail matter.

COMMERCE, ACCOUNTS & FINANCE COMPANY, Publishers
Twenty-five Pine Street, New York

We believe it is claimed by the friends of commercial education "as it is taught" that commercial teachers are a highly paid class of men and that the compensation that they receive is in keeping with the valuable knowledge that they impart. We think we have seen this stated at least once in the last six months. Judge of our surprise, therefore, when, in looking over one of the leading papers of a great city the other day, we chanced to come upon the following advertisement:—"Wanted.—Gentleman teacher of bookkeeping, all commercial branches and grammar, for day and evening school. Salary, $15.00 per week."

*

Our commercial teaching friends will, we believe, agree with us that $15.00 a week is not a large salary, as salaries go. It is better than the ordinary street laborer receives, but it is not by any means the equal of the wage paid the bricklayer or the mason. Then, too, the bricklayer has to do but one thing, namely, lay bricks. But this commercial "teacher" who is "wanted" must teach bookkeeping, all the commercial branches and grammar for less money than the bricklayer receives. The bricklayer works only during the day, or if he does work at night, he receives extra pay for so doing. Our commercial "teacher" must teach both day and evening and gets no extra pay for the evening work. Now to teach bookkeeping alone, and to teach it well, would seem to us to be worth at least $15.00 a week. In fact, we think to teach bookkeeping as it should be taught is worth several times $15.00 a week. When you add to this grammar, which is itself a study of no small importance, and then tack on all the commercial branches, we can not help but feel that $15.00 a week is at least 50 cents short of what it should be.

*

But the advertiser—commercial school proprietor or whoever he may be—evidently expects to get a teacher for that price. Now, if he does get someone to undertake the task for this salary, what sort of a teacher will the someone be? Obviously he will be one who has made a dismal failure of everything else that he has undertaken. He will be one who cannot keep books well, because he could get more than $15.00 a week for keeping them. He will be one who cannot write shorthand well, because he could get more than $15.00 a week for writing shorthand if he was a competent stenographer. Male stenographers are usually paid more than $15.00 a week if they are competent. If a man is competent to teach grammar, he should be able to write the English language well and clearly, and if he is able to do this he should be able to earn more than $15.00 a week. But this advertiser expects to get someone to teach bookkeeping, penmanship, shorthand, typewriting—these being commercial branches—and grammar for the said $15.00. Well, perhaps he will get someone. We fear he will. But how about the pupils whom this "teacher" will teach? What sort of instruction will they get? What will they know about bookkeeping after being taught by one who knows next to nothing about it himself? Will they not be inclined to feel that their tuition fee has been wasted, and will they not be tempted to say, as other disgruntled students have said before, that "all commercial schools are frauds"? This is a question we leave to our commercial teaching friends to answer.

* * *

What a number of preaching magazines and periodicals are now on the market. By preaching magazines we do not mean religious publications. We mean magazines and periodicals whose chief aim seems to be to give the young man good advice, and to teach him how to succeed in life. If preaching were all that were necessary it would seem as though every young man who can read ought to succeed, for there are more articles published about "The High Road to Success" and "The Pathway to Prosperity" than one can shake a stick at. Preaching is so much easier than practice. The periodicals in which these articles appear do not in every case bear the earmarks of success, but they preach to the young man just the same and expect him to follow their advice.

*

It is a question whether all this preaching does much good. One grows tired of hearing of the "High Road to Success," and sometimes wishes it were possible to go across lots. The "Pathway to Prosperity" is so covered with verbal slush that, in order to traverse it, it would seem necessary to put on rubber boots. Then, too, the aspiring young man is apt to say, "If the effects of prosperity make the successful man talk and write such slop as this, then I prefer to be a failure." The trouble with all these preaching articles seems to be that they do not give practical advice, but simply talk along in the same old round of wornout phrases and threadbare metaphor. What the young man really needs is common-sense advice and helpful words of warning from those who have been through the mill and know where the mistakes in life are likely to be made. There are articles of this kind published every month in the magazines, but there are more of the preachy, mushy kind. It is, as we said before, so easy to preach and so very hard to practice.

UNFORTUNATE WAITER

"Another new waiter has come and gone," said the veteran of the 15-cent restaurant to a reporter of the Philadelphia Record, as he deposited a beef stew in front of the favorite customer. "What was the matter with him?" asked the favorite customer. "Well, it wasn't exactly his fault," explained the veteran. "You see, the second day he was here a customer comes in and asks for a brace of frankfurters. 'Sausage is all out,' says the new waiter, 'but if you wait awhile I think I can get you some.' He was so eager to be obliging that he was going to send across the street for 'em.

"Well, sir, as he went through the door into the kitchen he happened to tread on the dog's tail. The dog set up a howl and the customer yells: 'Hey, there! Never mind that sausage. I guess I don't want it!' Then he puts on his hat and goes out. The boss saw the whole thing, and that night the new waiter was paid off and quit. Pretty tough, wasn't it?"

A NEW VARIETY

"I thought all brides were women."

"They are; why?"

"In my geography lesson it tells about Hebrides."—The School Bulletin.

Municipal Bond Issues in Ohio*

By FRANK H. SHAFFER

If without warning a trump should sound and the seals be removed from the many safe deposit vaults in this city, humanity would stand aghast at the resulting disclosure of wealth. And most of this is represented by municipal bonds. What is true of this city, noted for its thrifty German-American citizens, is equally true of all the large cities of the United States. The entire indebtedness of the United States could be many times liquidated by this hoarded wealth, and the vast mass is being constantly increased by the incessant issue of additional bonds.

The subject of municipal bonds is therefore a most interesting one, and to persons connected, as are the members of this chapter, with the institutions which play a large part in the investment and distribution of municipal bonds, the subject is also most important. The general subject, viewed from the standpoint of the law, is too broad for the confines of a paper such as I am asked to read to you tonight. I shall not attempt to go into the technicalities of the subject, and shall confine myself as nearly as possible to matters of local interest connected with municipal bonds in Ohio.

A MUNICIPAL CORPORATION.

A municipal corporation, as we all know, is an involuntary organization of the inhabitants within certain local confines, of all ages, sexes and conditions, under the direction of the legislature, by which they are clothed with a corporate character for the purposes of local government. The term "municipal corporations" in Ohio properly applies only to cities and villages. Counties, townships, school districts, road districts are more properly called quasi corporations, which, for purposes of civil administration, are vested with a few corporate functions. Nevertheless, the term municipal bonds has come to have a broader signification than that of bonds issued by a city or town. In the common ordinary acceptation of the word the term now covers all securities issued by any of the agencies of local government.

A municipal corporation differs in many respects from a private corporation. In the first place it is an involuntary association. The inhabitants need not accept their charter or accede to its terms; yet they are bound by it. The charter may be dissolved, amended or changed at will, at the pleasure of the legislature. No contract is involved between the state and the corporation, the state and the members nor between the corporation itself and its members. Its members are not shareholders. They need have no property interest in it, and their voice is not proportioned to their interest. It is formed simply and solely for the purposes of local government. The opposite is true in each of these respects in private corporations.

A municipal corporation, therefore, is a creature of the legislature, and has such powers and only such powers as are granted expressly by the charter, or are necessarily implied from its terms in order to carry out the purposes of the organization.

The Constitution of Ohio (Article XIII., Section 6) provides that the General Assembly shall provide for the organization of cities and incorporated villages by general laws. What we mean, therefore, when we refer to the charter of a city or village is that code of general laws which grants certain powers to or restricts certain acts by local organizations of the respective classes. Other state constitutions do not all contain this limitation. In some states, especially in the South, each municipal corporation derives its powers from a special act which applies only to itself. In such states, as may be imagined, the volumes of yearly laws are of unwieldy proportions. The tendency, without exception, in the recently-adopted constitutions is toward requiring municipal legislation to be enacted by general laws.

The construction courts put upon corporate power is a strict construction. The power to do an act must be expressly granted or necessarily inferred. The power to issue negotiable bonds is a power that must be expressly granted; it will not be inferred. The United States Supreme Court held, in the case of Merrill vs. Monticello, 138 United States Reports, page 673, by Justice Lamar, that:—

The implied power of a municipal corporation to borrow money to enable it to execute the powers expressly conferred upon it by law, if it exists at all, does not authorize it to create and issue negotiable securities, to be sold upon the market, and to be taken by a purchaser freed from the equities that might be set up by the maker.

In this case the town of Monticello, in the year 1869, issued $20,000 of bonds to pay for the building of schoolhouses. In 1878, when these bonds matured, they were paid by an issue of funding bonds. The statutes of Indiana did not in express terms confer upon towns the power to fund such an indebtedness and issue bonds for that purpose. The bonds were therefore declared void, although in the hands of a bona-fide holder for value.

In this case, if I am rightly informed, although the refunding bonds themselves were declared void, nevertheless the owner was allowed to sue the town of Monticello and recover upon the original bonds or upon the obligation represented by the original bonds on the theory that the town, having received the money and applied it to a municipal purpose, was bound to account for it.

NEGOTIABILITY.

The attribute of negotiability is the most important quality possessed by municipal securities. As men connected with the business of banking, you are especially qualified to appreciate this statement. When one purchases a valid municipal bond in the open market without notice of any infirmity, he takes it free from all claims or equities that might be enforced against the former owner. The bond may have been found upon the street; it may even have been stolen, yet the purchaser in good faith secures an absolute title to it.

This quality of negotiability has established municipal securities in their present position at the head of savings investments. To be negotiable, bonds must contain words of negotiability—that is, like promissory notes, they must provide for the payment of a sum certain, at a definite time, and to the order of a person named or to bearer. In fact, a municipal bonds is a municipal promissory note, issued generally under the seal of the corporation, and containing, in addition, certain recitals referring to the authority under which they are issued and to the formalities and proceedings leading up to their issue. As a general rule, the absence of a seal is not a fatal defect unless the law under which they are issued specifically requires such a seal. The recitals in a bond are not an absolute necessity, yet from the standpoint of a purchaser they are often of the utmost importance, as I shall later on explain.

In Ohio municipal improvement bonds must state upon their face the purpose for which they are issued and under what ordinance. A failure in this respect would probably affect the negotiability of the bonds. This is generally accomplished by stating the title of the ordinance and the date of its passage.

As the validity of municipal bonds involves the construction of ordinances, statutes and constitutional questions, an invariable custom prevails among those who deal in municipal securities to have these questions and the regularity of all proceedings leading up to the issue of the bonds passed upon by members of the bar; and this branch of the law has become almost as much of a specialty as patent law or criminal law. A certificate of validity is issued, and is depended upon by the purchaser of the bonds just as the purchaser of real estate relies upon the examination of title and certificate of the real estate examiner.

INVESTIGATIONS CONCERNING LEGALITY.

When a lawyer is called to pass upon the legality of an issue of bonds his employment generally begins by the

*Address before Cincinnati Chapter of the American Institute of Bank Clerks.

submission to him of a transcript of the proceedings taken by the legislative or executive body upon whom is devolved by law the authority of issuing them. If the issue is by a city or town, the transcript is prepared and certified to by the city or town clerk. If the issue is by a county, the transcript is by the county auditor. The transcript is required to state in detail all action and proceedings taken by the board, from the inception of the undertaking to the final issue and execution of the bonds.

The first question investigated is whether the resolution or ordinance has been properly passed. The statutes prescribe the formalities required, and the transcript furnishes the evidence. When this question has been settled in the affirmative the examiner then investigates the question of the authority of the board to issue the bonds. This authority is found in the charter or code of laws relating to municipal corporations.

Municipal corporations, like private corporations, act through agents; the statute will, therefore, designate the officers, board or tribunal upon which is devolved the power and duty of executing and issuing the municipal securities. As the construction of such statutes is strict, every person in his dealings with municipal corporations is conclusively charged with knowledge of the character and extent of the authority, not only of the corporation itself, but of the officers and agents through whom it acts. If authority is not given by the statute the bonds are absolutely void even in the hands of innocent purchasers.

The legislature, in granting authority, frequently imposes terms and conditions which must be complied with before the authority can be execised. For example, a petition of taxpayers or a vote of the electors.

CONSTITUTIONALITY OF THE STATUTE.

After the regularity of the proceedings has been determined the question of constitutionality of the statute is to be inquired into.

Most state constitutions now limit the amount of indebtedness to a certain percentage of the tax duplicate. There is no such limitation in Ohio. But we have in our present Constitution certain provisions restricting or regulating corporate action, which, though positive and definite in their terms, have at different times received such different constructions by our Supreme Court as to leave the mind of the examiner in doubt and in suspense as to their proper meaning, or, to be more explicit, what the court will construe the proper meaning to be in a given case.

A dozen years ago Erie avenue, Columbia avenue and a great many thoroughfares in the eastern part of the city and county were improved under mandatory laws at the expense of the abutting and continguous property owners. Proceedings were taken in each case to contest the constitutionality of that part of the laws which compelled the public boards to make the improvements and left them no discretion. This provision was sustained by the courts, but so many similar laws were passed and the evil of such legislation became so oppressive that finally our Supreme Court sustained the objection, and mandatory laws became a thing of the past. It was a favorite method of the old street railway company to have streets improved at the expense of the property owners and irrespective of their own ideas on the subject. Article XIII., Section 1, provides that: "The General Assembly shall pass no special act conferring corporate powers." It has been claimed by some of our ablest lawyers that this provision was intended by the framers of our constitution to apply only to private corporations. Our Supreme Court held otherwise. To evade the effect of this provision the General Assembly resorted to the classification of cities according to population, and has been accustomed to pass acts which, though general in their terms, were, in fact, special in their effect.

For example, Cincinnati is a city of the first grade, first class; Cleveland a city of the first class, second grade. Our Supreme Court held that classification according to population was constitutional and that these acts, although special in their effect, were valid if the form was such that they did not exclude any other city from coming into the class, and did not apply only to the existing member or members of the class. This holding has been sustained in a long line of decisions. Under this construction the legislature has for many years been authorizing the various cities in the state to construct their local improvements, and, as a necessary accompaniment, to issue bonds. The amount of these bonds is in the hundred of millions of dollars. All the improvements in this city have been constructed under such laws.

The Southern Railroad, the Eggleston avenue improvement (involving over two million dollars), our granite paving (involving probably ten millions), the Eighth street viaduct, the city hall, the purchase of our parks, the six-million-dollar water works and countless other improvements and purchases have been constructed and acquired under just such acts. Under the pressure of such legislation, and to restrict the authorization of improvident expenditures by special act, our Supreme Court drew another distinction about eight years ago in what is called the Hixson-Burson case, 54 O. S. 470.

Section 26 of Article II of the Constitution provides that all laws of a general nature shall have uniform operation throughout the state. In the case referred to, Athens County, through its county commissioners, was authorized to improve its turnpikes, issue bonds for that purpose and levy taxes to pay the same. The issue of bonds was limited to $300,000.

Our Supreme Court had many years before decided that an act providing for the improvement of a designated county road was local in its nature and not in conflict with the Constitution. Relying on this construction, the legislature had passed many such laws, and the yearly volumes of state laws were full of similar legislation.

SUIT AGAINST COUNTY COMMISSIONERS.

A taxpayer of Athens County brought suit to enjoin the county commissioners from selling the bonds. The decision was against the taxpayer in both of the lower courts and the cause was dismissed. In the Supreme Court, however, to the surprise of the bar, these holdings were reversed and the former decision of the court on the subject overruled. The principle was established that the subject of roads was not of a local, but of a general nature, and that therefore all laws relating to roads should have uniform operation throughout the state. In other words, when the legislature desired to authorize a county or township to improve its highways it could only do so by an act that applied equally or uniformly to each and every county or township in the state alike.

Since this decision the court has held that bridges also are matters of a general nature and can only be provided for by general laws. Crematories and court houses and county buildings, and nearly every other kind of public improvements, have since been included in the list of matters of a public nature.

The decision in the Hixson-Burson case put a stop to all special laws granting power to county commissioners to make these improvements. The legislature, however, relying upon the numerous decisions of our Supreme Court sustaining the classification of cities, continued to enact laws authorizing cities and towns to make street improvements, street extensions and viaducts.

During the past three months the court has decided that the Harrison Avenue Viaduct Act, authorizing the issue of $300,000 of bonds; the Street Repair Act, authorizing the issue of $100,000 of bonds each year for four years, and the Delta Avenue Viaduct Act, involving a large bond issue, were null and void. These decisions were rendered without report—that is, without an extended opinion giving the reasoning of the court in reaching the several conclusions. Upon the 18th day of March of this year our Supreme Court finally and squarely decided that an act conferring power upon certain cities under the general classification, upon a subject matter of a general nature, was special legislation, and therefore void.

Under this final construction I may safely say that not one-tenth of the large improvements in the cities of this state have been constructed under constitutional laws.

The laws, being constitutional and void, it would follow logically that all bonds issued under these laws are void. The courts, however, have a well-established doctrine that the reversal by the Supreme Court of a state of a principle of law therefore declared by it, will not be permitted to operate to the injury of those who put faith therein and regulated their conduct thereby. The settled judicial construction of a statute at a time a contract is made enters into and becomes a part of the contract made upon the faith of it. A subsequent judicial determination by any court will not affect the rights secured on the faith of the prior adjudication. All contract rights are to be adjudged by the principles established by the judiciary at the time the contract was entered into. All bonds, therefore, issued before our Supreme Court declared these recent constructions of our Constitution will be sustained under this principle, and the holders of these bonds need not fear about their validity. All bonds issued thereafter must be under laws that conform to the present construction of the constitutional provisions or they will be void.

The result is that special legislation upon general subjects will not again be resorted to by our legislature. To lawyers who have investigated the subject, there can be no doubt that the final determination of these matters by our court of last resort is the logical and correct one. The policy of the court in changing its position upon matters that have been considered settled, and in reversing its decisions within a period of so very few years, is not calculated to increase the reverence of the laity for the unerring wisdom of our courts or cause them to feel that the law is an exact science.

And, after all this effort on the part of the courts to bring about a reformation in this matter of legislation, what has been accomplished?

THE LONGWORTH BILL.

Bowing to these decisions, the present legislature has passed what is called the Longworth bill. This bill is general with a vengeance. Pressed upon the legislature by the demand of our local political authorities, and not called for nor required by cities generally, not only Cincinnati, but all municipal corporations in the State of Ohio are authorized to issue bonds for any municipal purpose each year for a period of four years, to an amount equal to 1 per cent of the value of the tax duplicate. The tax duplicate of this city is a little over two hundred millions of dollars. During the next four years the board of legislation, not the board of public service, may increase the bonded debt of this city to the extent of eight millions five hundred thousand dollars. This, if I am rightly informed, does not include the two million dollars authorized for water works purposes.

The effect in the state at large is to authorize municipal corporations to increase their bonded debt during the next four years to the extent of nearly one hundred millions of dollars. And this, too, without requiring the question of bond issue to be submitted to the voters. The Longworth act authorizes a further increase of 4 per cent in the bonded indebtedness of each municipal corporation, provided that in each case the question is submitted to the voters and is ratified by a two-thirds vote.

Other states are protected from such legislation by constitutional provisions limiting the indebtedness that each town or city may incur. As I have remarked before, Ohio has no such limitation.

It is not within the province of a paper such as I am reading to you tonight to characterize such legislation as the Longworth bill. Every thoughtful man must have his own opinion of it.

The decisions of our Supreme Court to which I have called your attention have been those relating to cities, towns and counties. In respect to school districts, too, the trend of the decisions has been in the same direction, and there is no doubt that school buildings will also be held to be of a general nature, and to be provided for by general and not special laws, as heretofore.

ARMORY BONDS.

An interesting subject also is the issue of Armory Bonds. In the year 1893 the commissioners of Cuyahoga County, under authority of an act of the General Assembly, issued bonds in the sum of $225,000, and expended the proceeds in building an armory for the Ohio National Guard. The bonds were sold to an eastern insurance company. In the year 1898 the Supreme Court held that the act under which they were issued was void, because it authorized the levy of a tax upon the property appearing on the duplicate of the county instead of upon all the property in the state. The bonds were therefore declared void. In order to enable the county of Cuyahoga to pay these bonds the legislature passed an act providing that where a county has issued bonds and has expended the proceeds in buildings which it still owns, and afterwards the law is declared unconstitutional at the suit of a taxpayer, the county commissioners are authorized to issue bonds to refund the void bonds. The constitutionality of this last act was upheld by the United States Circuit Court of Appeals, and the bonds were paid.

In the year 1890 the commissioners of Hamilton County issued $100,000 of Armory Bonds and $15,000 in Armory Furnishing Bonds. A suit to restrain the commissioners of this county from levying taxes to pay these bonds and to declare the bonds themselves void was tried before Judge Rufus B. Smith during the past year, and he, following the decision of the Supreme Court in the Cuyahoga County case, held the bonds void. The holders of the bonds will lose nothing, however, and the bonds will be refunded under an enabling act similar to that provided for Cuyahoga County.

Franklin County—Columbus—has had a similar experience with her armory bonds.

RECITALS IN BONDS.

I have referred to the importance of recitals in the bond form. These are statements contained in the bond itself as to the existence of important facts or the performance of necessary acts or conditions leading up to the issue. Recitals are made for the purpose of influencing the purchaser, and the courts have decided that purchasers may rely in certain cases upon their truth.

An interesting case showing the application of this principle of estoppel by recitals is Village of Kent vs. Dana, decided by the United States Circuit Court of Appeals of this circuit, upon February 12, 1900. The facts of this case are as follows:—

In the year 1892 the council of the Village of Kent, Ohio, desiring to induce the location of a glass factory within its limits, agreed to donate the sum of $80,000 for that purpose. The plan met with the approval of the citizens, and the only obstacle was the fact that villages in Ohio are without power to make any donation in aid of a manufacturing company, such purpose not being municipal or public in its nature. It would have been impossible to issue salable bonds for the purpose of raising this $80,000 if the public had any idea of the real object of the issue.

The council of the village accordingly passed an ordinance entitled, "An ordinance to provide for issuing bonds of the village of Kent, Ohio, for the purpose of extending the time of payment of certain indebtedness, which, from its limits of taxation, said village is unable to pay at maturity." The bonds were issued as refunding bonds, and finally came into the hands of The Rutland Savings Bank, of Rutland, Vermont. The interest on the bonds was paid until 1896, when the village defaulted. Suit was instituted on the coupons over due, in the United States Circuit Court for the Northern District of Ohio. The decision of the Circuit Court was in favor of the plaintiff, and the case was carried to the Court of Appeals by the village. This court held:—

A municipal corporation having the power to issue bonds for the refunding of its indebtedness, and having exercised that power by passing an ordinance directed for that purpose, and by issuing negotiable bonds in due form, reciting that they are issued in conformity to the statute, and that all the requirements of the law have been duly complied with, and all the conditions precedent exist, cannot deny its obligation as against a bona-fide holder who purchased such bonds for value before maturity, and defeat the recovery thereon, by showing that the recitals are false, and were made for the purpose of enabling the corporation to market the bonds, which were in fact issued for an unauthorized and illegal purpose.

In the course of the opinion Judge Severens says:—

It must be admitted that the scheme of issuing the bonds of the village for the purpose of promoting a glass factory is unlawful, and the device of exercising an unquestioned power of the council of the village to give its obligations the appearance of validity was in point of law a great abuse of authority. But it is evident enough that the electors of the village, as well as the members of the council, were involved in the conspiracy to gain an unlawful end, by professing an honest and lawful purpose, and using the means permitted for such purpose. It would be an utter perversion of justice if, by such an exploit, the result finally worked out should be that the public, who have confided in the good faith and integrity of the representations of those who sent the bonds into the market, should be made to pay the intended bonus to the glass factory, while the promoters of the scheme reap the benefits which were expected to result therefrom.

The validity of the bonds was sustained.

REFUNDING BONDS.

The city of Wooster, Ohio, in the year 1892, desired to build a freight and passenger railroad passing through its limits, and to own and control the same. An enabling act was passed by the General Assembly, and bonds to the amount of $76,000 were issued under its authority. Of this amount the city authorities were able to sell only $16,000, as the object of the issue was so outrageously unconstitutional as to frighten off all except the most reckless purchasers. The council thereupon, as in the Kent case, passed an ordinance to issue $76,000 of refunding bonds. The bonds were described as Refunding Bonds, and, among other recitals upon their face, was the statement that they were issued by the city of Wooster for the purpose of refunding and extending the time of payment of a certain like amount of its outstanding legal and subsisting indebtedness, which, from its limits of taxation, the city is unable to pay at maturity. Judge Day, of the United States Circuit Court for the Northern District of Ohio, before whom the matter finally came, in the course of his opinion, said:—

The original indebtedness was contracted under an unconstitutional law, and that the action of the city in passing the refunding ordinance and issuing the bonds themselves was for the purpose of bringing them ostensibly within the statutes, and that the real intent was to carry into effect the illegal and unconstitutional legislation under which the city of Wooster was to build and acquire a railroad. All of this may be true, but the bonds and ordinance were studiously drawn so as to bring them within the terms of the law, and to lead a purchaser to believe that the city was acting within its legal power and authority, and was seeking in good faith to provide for a valid outstanding legal indebtedness. The recitals were carefully drawn to bring them within the terms of the statute, and to certify on the face of the bonds that the law had been complied with. In such case, the authorities, as well as the reason of the law, will not permit a city or municipal corporation to deny the truth of recitals which are drawn for the purpose of entrapping innocent purchasers of the bonds, who had a right to rely upon the good faith of the council acting within the powers conferred upon it by law. The law has entrusted to the city council a determination of the facts which permit it to exercise the power conferred by the statute, and when it has found such facts and recites them upon the face of the bonds which are placed upon the market, the city is estopped from disputing the truth of the recitals.

IMPORTANCE OF RECITALS IN BONDS.

By these two cases the importance of recitals in bonds is impressively shown. In the absence of such recitals the bonds would not have been worth the paper upon which they were engraved. The following are some instances where recitals have been the means of saving the innocent bondholder:—

A recital that "the total amount of this issue does not exceed the limit prescribed by the Constitution."

A recital that the bonds were duly sold, when in fact they were donated.

A recital that the bonds were issued for municipal purposes when in fact their purpose was illegal.

A recital that the bonds were issued under authority of an election duly held, when the election was irregular and void.

The United States Supreme Court has never decided that the recital on the face of the bond that it was issued under authority of an election duly held, when in fact no election at all was held, would estop the municipal corporation from making this defense. Yet there is no doubt, in the opinion of authorities on this subject, that in a proper case the Supreme Court would so hold.

The two questions involved in each case is, first: Has the corporation a general authority to issue the bonds for the purpose for which they purport to be issued? and second, Have the officers making the recitals the authority to represent the corporation in making them? If these two questions are answered in the affirmative, the bonds in the hands of innocent holders will be sustained in spite of the falsity of the recitals.

CERTAINTY OF VALUATION.

In view of the uncertainty of the law, persons interested in the purchase and sale of bonds have suggested that some plan should be adopted by the state to have the validity of bond issues determined before they are put upon the market and get into the hands of innocent purchasers. The absolute certainty of validity is an important element in regulating the price of bonds, and the city itself is frequently the sufferer on account of the doubt that at times may be aroused as to the validity of the issue.

Two Southern states have provisions on the subject that might be considered with profit.

In Texas it is made the duty of the Attorney-General of the state to examine all proceedings connected with the issue of bonds by cities, towns and counties in the state, and before any bonds are sold he shall furnish a certificate of validity. The bonds are then registered with the Comptroller of the state, and a copy of the certificate is indorsed on each bond. Thereafter such bonds are valid against any defense except fraud.

In the state of Georgia, where no bonds can be issued without a vote of the electors, it is made the duty of the Attorney-General of the state or the Solicitor-general—an officer corresponding in certain respects to our county solicitor—within a certain number of days to file a petition in the Superior Court of the county in the name of the state, setting forth the proceedings of the corporation and describing the bonds. The corporate authorities are notified to appear and show cause why the bonds should not be validated and confirmed. An early hearing is provided for, and any resident may, if dissatisfied, appear and contest the validity of the issue. The decision of the Superior Court, or, if the case be appealed, that of the Supreme Court, confirming and validating the issue, is forever conclusive, and the validity of the bonds shall never be questioned in any court. On each of the bonds there must be written or stamped the words: "Validated and confirmed by judgment of the Superior Court," specifying the date and court. Notice of the hearing is given by two publications in a newspaper. All costs are paid by the corporation.

Provisions such as these, if enacted in Ohio, would have the effect of protecting innocent holders of bonds; they would also have the effect of putting a stop to the perpetration of such frauds as those involved in the Kent and Wooster cases. They would also materially enhance the value of bonds and thus benefit the cities themselves.

The present Constitution of Ohio was ratified over fifty years ago. Several important amendments are to be submitted to the electors of the state at the next annual election. The growth of the state during the past half century, the enormous increase of corporate power and combined capital, the changes in condition both social and commercial that have occurred since the present Constitution went into effect, suggest the importance of a constitutional convention in this state in the immediate future.

It is to be hoped that its provisions will be so clear that our courts will not be called upon to change their constructions, when, after deliberation, they have announced their decisions. It is evident that the most important provision of the next Constitution of Ohio will be one limiting the indebtedness of municipal corporations.

The Tale of the Merchants Who Monkeyed with the Law

By JOE LINCOLN

AND it was the one thousandth and fifth night, and Scheherezade, resting from her labors at the typewriter, spake unto the Father of the Faithful, saying:—

"Oh, thou mighty one, condescend to harken to the voice of the meanest of thy slaves."

And the King commanded her, saying:—

"Tell thy tale, I pray thee, for I am weary and would fain sleep."

And Scheherezade obeyed and spake thus:—

"Know, oh illustrious, that in the days before the goodness of the great Haroun Al Raschid became as a chestnut, there lived in the city of Raggbhag two merchants. And the name of the one was Ahmed and of the other Abdou. And behold, their shops were adjacent unto one another and the trade done by each was of a goodly size. And the merchants were friends and each was as the apple of the other's eye. And behold, when a stranger had bought of the goods of Ahmed until he would buy no more, then would Ahmed conduct him unto the shop of Abdou, and the latter took what was left.

"And it came to pass that on a day as Ahmed sat at ease before his door, behold, there came unto him a certain man of law. And the man of law winked at Ahmed and whispered unto him, saying:—

"'Of a verity thou art a wise one. He that getteth across the tape ahead of thyself must arise several hours before he retireth.'

"And Ahmed was amazed and questioned him, saying, 'What the sulphurous abode of torment?'

"And the man of law winked yet again and said:—

"'Surely it is a wise stroke to allow the sign of thy shop to project over thy neighbor's premises. The stranger passeth and seeth the sign and saith unto himself, "Of a surety this man hath acquired the shop of his neighbor. Verily he is owner of a Trust."'

"And the man of law winked yet again and shook his head with exceeding sageness, and, having bought a shekel's worth of postage stamps, he went upon his way. And Ahmed, who had previously given no thought to the projection of the sign, pondered deeply until the setting of the sun and chuckled much at his own shrewdness.

"And it came to pass on the following day that a man of law called at the shop of Abdou. And behold, he was the friend of him who had visited Ahmed. And he gazed upon Abdou with exceeding sadness and shook his head as one who sorrows. And Abdou said unto him:—

"'Why shakest thou thy head like unto the automaton in the cigar dealer's window?'

"And the man of law shook his head yet again and said, as one who pities, 'Verily, it saddeneth me to gaze upon such an easy mark. Of a surety thou art the prize good thing.'

"And Abdou was angry and questioned him, saying, 'What art thou gratuitously bestowing upon me?'

"And the man of law pointed to the sign of Ahmed and said, 'Why dost thou allow thy neighbor's sign to crowd thee off the premises? Does thou not know that he is making merry at thy expense? It behooveth thee to compel him to move the sign and also to pay thee much coin for damages. If he will not do these things, there is the law which will compel him. And if thou desireth the real thing in lawyers, I am thy persimmon.' And he left his business card upon the desk and went away. And Abdou pondered deeply.

"And Abdou the next day went unto Ahmed and commanded that the sign be moved. And Ahmed would not, for he said, 'Hath not the sign been as it is for, lo, these many days? Hath thy kick been delayed on the road that it is so long in coming?'

"And the sign remained as it was and a coldness grew between the two merchants and each sent no more custom to the shop of the other. And a day came when Abdou said unto Ahmed:—

"'By the chin draperies of the Prophet, if that sign is not moved by the going down of the sun, then will I appeal unto the law, and thou shalt pay me much damage.'

"And Ahmed answered and said, 'Appeal.'

"And it came to pass that Abdou sought out the man of law who had called at his shop and put the case in his hands. And Ahmed sought the man of law who had called at his shop, and commanded that he defend him, Ahmed, against the suit of Abdou. And the two merchants spake no more the one to the other, but the two men of law shook hands and smiled hugely, forasmuch as the sheep had been delivered into the hands of the shearers.

"And the suit went through the Civil Court and the Uncivil Court and the Superior Court and the Inferior Court and the Court of Appeals and the Supreme Court, and behold, when it had completed the circuit, it took a fresh start and began again. And the suns shone and the moons came and went, and the merchants became older, and, by reason of excessive reaching down in their garments for the wherewithal to pay the men of law, did their arms ache.

"And behold, the day came to pass when there was no more in the pockets of the said garments, and the men of law came unto the merchants and said, 'Where is the coin that thou still owest us?'

"And the merchants replied unto them, saying, 'Thou hast expressed our own thoughts with great exactness.'

"And the men of law seized the shops of the two merchants as part payment for their services. And the merchants were cast forth into the street.

"And it came to pass that as they sat upon the curbstone, Ahmed spake unto Abdou for the first time in many years, saying:—

"'Oh thou, who was once the friend of my bosom, behold, I have been thinking and the process is exceedingly painful. The removal of the sign by a carpenter would have cost me two shekels. And I have spent, lo, these many shekels and I have moved first. Verily in all the world there is no fool like unto myself.'

"And Abdou answered him and said:—

"'Oh brother, thou errest. There is one greater and his name was as mine own, but is now Dennis.'

"And they continued to think."

And Scheherezade said unto the Father of Faithful, "Oh King, live forever! once more there is a question. Are lawsuits profitable?"

And the King answered her "Yea."

And she was astonished and said, "To whom, I pray thee?"

And he answered her yet again, saying, "To the lawyers."

And he turned his face to the wall and wept.

Charts of Bank Organization and Administration

What the Papers Say About Them

The Charts of Bank Organization and Administration, offered as premiums for new subscribers to the Bulletin, the bright banking periodical published by the American Institute of Bank Clerks, have been most favorably received by bank men. The financial papers have also spoken very highly of them, and on this page we reproduce two notices from prominent New York financial publications, and one from a large news bureau. The notices follow.

Under the head of "Bank Organization and Administration" the Financier, of New York City, says:—

"The American Institute of Bank Clerks has issued its first premium number, containing "Charts of Bank Organization and Administration." The charts represent the plan of organization and administration of a number of the prominent banks in the United States, the scope of the various departments being clearly shown and the duties of the officers and employees of the bank comprehensively described. The first chart represents the First National of Chicago, and by reference to the same it can be seen just how business is done by this large institution, each transaction being followed down through the various departments from president and cashier to the humblest messengers, who do nothing but get the mail from the postoffice. The second chart is of a prominent New York bank which does a large general business. The third chart shows the general plan of administration of a bank in New York doing an extensive business with merchants, and with a large number of correspondents throughout the country. The fourth chart gives an outline of a New York bank whose most important feature is its loans on collateral security, although the banks' customers include numerous corporations of the first magnitude, and a desirable line of out-of-town banks. The fifth chart explains the workings of an institution in the residential part of New York offering extra facilities to ladies. The sixth chart shows the administration plan of one of the large Philadelphia banks, doing a large general business. The last chart represents no particular institution, but shows the distribution of the working force of a typical New York bank of large size and progressive methods. The supplement is certainly valuable and interesting, as it shows at a glance the responsibilities and exact duties of the various officers and employees in representative institutions."

CHART BOOKLET WITH ONE CHART UNFOLDED.

The Commercial and Financial Chronicle, of New York, says concerning the charts:—

"The American Institute of Bank Clerks has issued a quarto pamphlet of 'Charts of Bank Organization and Administration,' the object being to show graphically the distribution and arrangement of regular routine work in large banks. The largest chart, about five times the size of a Chronicle page, represents the organization of the Chicago First National; the last one represents that of a typical large bank; the other six represent actual large banks, each of which constructed its own chart, but preferred to remain anonymous. The method used is that of subdivision again and again subdivided into increasing minuteness and number of branches, in the familiar family-tree manner. The Chicago chart-tree has so many twigs that it cannot be intelligently represented in words. Taking a simpler case, a chart sets forth the routine duties of the paying teller and the several assistants directly under him; the receiving teller and his assistants, the note teller and his, the mail teller and his, the loan and discount clerks and theirs, and so on through the list, the entire number being under the several vice-presidents and cashiers, who in turn are responsible to the president, who includes the whole. One chart, by the way, is of a New York bank in the wealthy residence district, and here we find separate ladies' paying and receiving tellers and assistants, a stationery clerk, a front-office man, an 'outside man,' who attends at carriage doors, and a ladies' maid—all of which is entirely correct and businesslike. The American Institute of Bank Clerks, which issues this collection of charts, is a special organization, of course unknown to the general public. Its officers and trustees are bank officers, and the banks assist in its support financially, but the several chapters manage their own affairs, under the general direction. The object is the good one of aiding the members—by lectures, by a school of correspondence, by conducting examinations and issuing certificates, and otherwise—in self-improvement and general advancement in the banking calling."

In one of its news sheets, the New York News Bureau, under the heading, "Valuable Pamphlets for Students of Banking," compliments the charts, as follows:—

"The American Institute of Bank Clerks has issued its 'premium number one' giving exceptionally complete charts of bank organization and administration. The charts are drawn from the actual working plans of the largest and best-known banks in the United States. The scope of the various departments is clearly shown, and the duties of officers and employees are comprehensively described. To bank clerks and all students of banking the work should be exceedingly valuable. The publication is one of a series intended to apply to an educational scheme in banking."

SOME FACTS ABOUT CHECKS

Bank checks possess many advantages for the conduct of business, and are used to a proportionately great extent. They are in nature but orders for the payment of money, and are payable in the order in which they are presented, not according to that in which they are drawn, says C. E. Locke in an exchange. As given in the usual course of business, they do not constitute payment of the indebtedness for which they are given until paid. Nor will the concurrent receipting of the debts for which they are given change this. If they are not paid on proper presentation, resort may be had to the original claims. The rule is different in this respect as to certified checks. So the having of checks certified constitutes payment as to the persons drawing them.

Checks should be dated. If not dated at all, and they do not contain any statement as to when they are to be paid, they are never payable. They may be ante or post-dated, as well as dated on the day of delivery. By being ante-dated they may be made to cover prior transactions, and in a measure determine the relative rights of the parties to them, provided that no fraud is intended or done. Post-dating in the main determines the date of payment.

When post-dated so as to fall due on Sunday, they are payable on the following Monday. Checks post-dated or maturing on legal holidays should be presented the day following. When post-dated checks are paid before the dates mentioned, the money paid on them can be recovered. If blanks are left for the date, the holders of checks are thereby authorized to insert the true dates of delivery, but no other dates, and if they insert any other date it makes the checks void. Changing the date of checks without consent of the drawers will do the same.

The presumption is that when checks are drawn, funds wil be provided at the banks on which they are drawn to meet them, but presentation for payment must be made within a reasonable time. If not so presented, the holders will be charged with any consequent loss. When persons receiving checks and the banks on which they are drawn are in the same place, they should be presented the same day, or, at the latest, the day after they are received. Where they are in different places, the checks must be mailed to some bank or person at the place where payable before the close of the day following any receipt, and the latter must present them before the close of the banking hours on the day following the receipt there; no extra time will be gained by holders depositing checks in their own banks for collection.

After duly presenting checks, it is also the duty of the holder, if they are not paid, to notify the drawers before the close of the next secular day following the presentation and dishonor. No particular form of notice is required. It may be written or verbal. The principal case in which losses occur from failure to use due diligence in the collection of checks is where the banks on which they are drawn fail in the meantime. If the banks continue solvent, the drawers will remain liable to pay their checks for months at least after they are drawn. Presentation and notice of dishonor will also be dispensed with where there are no funds to pay checks, and where the banks on which they are drawn suspend payment before they can be presented, using proper diligence. After receiving checks, they must be presented for payment, unless such presentation would be useless before the original claims can be sued on, for, by accepting checks, there is an implied agreement to use that method of procuring the money for which they are drawn.

When checks are negotiable and pass by indorsement or delivery, the same degree of diligence will be required of each person to whom they are indorsed, in order to hold those indorsing them, as is required of original payees to hold original drawers of checks. But by putting checks in circulation, the liability of the drawers cannot be prolonged. They must be presented within the same time by indorsees as by payees.

OUR FIRST PARENTS AND THE APPLES

The author of the article printed below is unknown. Presumably he was hanged long ago. His crime, which appears in an exchange is as follows:—

How many apples did Adam and Eve eat. Some say Eve 8 and Adam 2—a total of 10 only. Now we figure the thing out far differently. Eve 8 and Adam 8 also—total 16.

And yet the above figures are entirely wrong. If Eve 8 and Adam 82, certainly the total would be 90.

Scientific men, however, on the strength of the theory that the antediluvians were a race of giants, reason something like this: Eve 8-1 and Adam 8-2—total 163.

Wrong again; what could be clearer than if Eve 8-1 and Adam 8-1-2, the total was 893.

If Eve 8-1-1st and Adam 8-1-2, would not the total be 1,623?

I believe the following to be a fair solution: Eve 8-1-4 Adam before Adam 8 1-2-4 Eve—total 8,938.

Still another calculation is as follows: If Eve 8 1-4 Adam, Adam 8-1-2-4-2 oblige Eve—total 82,056. We think this, however, not a sufficient quantity. For though we admit that Eve 8-1-4 Adam, Adam if he 8-0-8-1-2-4-2 keep Eve company—total, 8,082,056.

All wrong. Eve, when she 8-1-8-1-2 many, and probably she felt sorry for it, but her companion, in order to relieve her grief, 8-1-2. Therefore Adam when he 8-1-8-1-4-2-40fy Eve's depressed spirits. Hence both ate 81,896,864 apples.

BELOW COST

"Do you really sell below cost?" inquired the curious individual.

"Certainly," replied the great merchant.

"Below the cost to you?"

"Oh, no. Below the cost to the customer before we marked the goods down."—Chicago Post.

Current Business Cartoons

The Trust question and Coal Strike have been the marks against which most of the cartoonists have pointed their pencils during the past month. There have been cartoons on the strike question in great quantity and on the Trust question in even greater.

COMMERCE, ACCOUNTS & FINANCE publishes in this issue two cartoons on the Coal Strike selected from the multitude. One, by Richards, of the New York Herald, is extremely apt and, as is customary with this artist's work, is very well

"Hit harder, Theodore!"—N. Y. World.

drawn. It shows the figure of Common Sense pointing to the settlement, by arbitration, of the threatened strike on the Manhattan Elevated Railroad as an object lesson for the benefit of the fighting mine operators and miners. This

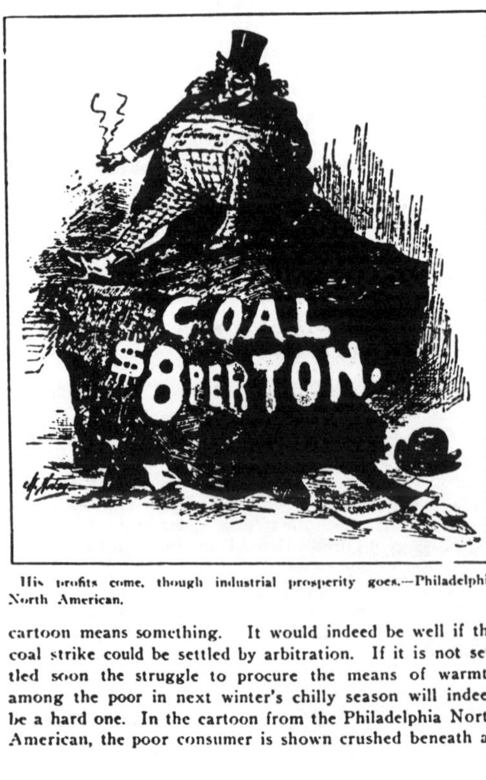

His profits come, though industrial prosperity goes.—Philadelphia North American.

cartoon means something. It would indeed be well if the coal strike could be settled by arbitration. If it is not settled soon the struggle to procure the means of warmth among the poor in next winter's chilly season will indeed be a hard one. In the cartoon from the Philadelphia North American, the poor consumer is shown crushed beneath an enormous lump of coal, labeled "Coal $8 per ton," upon which sits the affluent operator, who apparently is having

"Gentlemen, stop long enough to look at that!"—N. Y. Herald.

all the fun there is in the situation.

Among the many cartoons on the Trust question the one drawn by Bush, in the New York World, stands out

Uncle Sam—"That's What knox!"—Minn. Journal.

prominently. It shows Uncle Sam with his fingers caught in the split of the log "Monopoly" and begging President

A Strenuous Vacation.—N. Y. Herald.

Roosevelt to strike harder upon his wedge, "The Law." In the cartoon from the Minneapolis Journal the Trusts are apparently being knocked over the ropes by Attorney-General Knox, whose recent injunctions against some of them have certainly been body blows. The Trust question is practically certain to be the leading issue in the next presidential campaign.

The Czar of Russia has recently interested himself in the "Trust" question to the extent of sending out a note to the various powers asking for a European Convention which

When that European Anti-Trust convention meets.—Chicago News.

shall take measures to curb the power of the American industrial combinations. Bradley, in the Chicago News, has a funny cartoon illustrating this convention as it may be held. The hall is divided into two sections, one for the Russian delegation and the other for the Morgan, or "Trust" delega-

After Wu Ting Fang introduces American methods.—Chicago Record-Herald.

tion. King Edward, Emperor William, the Sultan of Turkey and apparently all the other crowned heads are on the Morgan side, wearing the Morgan badges, while the Czar sits in solitary state upon the Russian side. He does, indeed, look lonesome. Bradley also has an extremely ludicrous cartoon illustrating President Roosevelt's attitude towards the "Trusts." President Roosevelt has been, as every one knows, spending his vacation at Oyster Bay, L. I., and in this cartoon the Trust octopus is shown as having wan-

Uncle Sam—"Say, sonny, how soon do you think you'll want to get in the big boat?"—Chicago Record-Herald.

dered into the bay where President Roosevelt is taking a swim. The President's strenuous appearance alarms the octopus, who looks worried.

By the way, speaking of the President's vacation, it has not been entirely restful. A small army of office-seekers and politicians have been rushing to Oyster Bay, and Mr. Roose-

The Octopus—"Wh-what's that? Help!"—Chicago News.

velt has been kept busy almost every moment of his stay. The New York Herald cartoon pictures the situation there cleverly. The President of the United States does not have the most restful time in the world even on vacations, and after two terms there are a few men, no matter though they be energetic as the present incumbent, who do not leave the Presidential chair weary and glad to give up the cares of office.

Minister Wu Ting Fang is going back to China. He has been superceded by another influential Chinaman, who will represent his country at Washington. But Minister Wu has been a very up-to-date minister. He has seemingly come to the conclusion that America's progressive ideas are just what is needed to send China ahead. McCutcheon, in

Where the cream goes.—Chicago News.

the Chicago Record-Herald, shows what may be expected in the Yellow Kingdom after Mr. Fang's American ideas are adopted over there.

Cuba is having all sorts of trouble in its endeavor to run things on its own hook. The failure of Congress to make satisfactory tariff concessions has been a heavy blow for

Mr. Morgan in his latest role. Chicago Record-Herald.

the Cuban interests, and in the Chicago Record-Herald's cartoon its situation is illustrated. Uncle Sam, leaning over the rail of the Ship of State, is calmly inquiring how soon distressed Cuba, in his leaky boat, will be willing to climb aboard. Cuban annexation is bound to come sooner or later.

Mr. Gates and his various "plunges" and speculations have filled the columns of the papers to a large extent, and the question of speculation has been much discussed. In a cartoon from the Chicago News the tired worker is shown outside the window, pausing in his toil to wipe his forehead, while the fat and sleek cat "Speculator" is lapping up the profits of his labor. Let us hope that no one turns on the Panic tap.

Mr. Morgan is, by long odds, the leading figure of the commercial and financial world today. He is, perhaps, the most famous citizen of the United States, bar none. In the Chicago Record-Herald appears a cartoon, which we here reproduce, showing him as an international pawnbroker, loaning money to bankrupt governments everywhere for all sorts of purposes.

THE LIGHT OF OTHER DAYS

When the Romans invaded Britain and settled in many quarters, says an exchange, they used small clay lamps, some open like a shell, others covered, with only a small hole left to allow of the lamp being filled with oil. Open clay cups with two hollows were also common, one hollowing being provided for the wick, the capillary attraction drawing the oil from the other.

Many beautiful bronze lamps are discovered in the ancient Roman camps, illustrating by these simple domestic articles the perfection to which art had been carried when nothing was considered too ordinary to be beautiful. Dr. Hill Burton, referring to the beauty of design and decoration on the commonest articles of Roman manufacture, says: "They afford traces of decoration sufficient to show an elevation in the ornamenting of common articles which the pottery of the present day is only now reaching, and that rather by slavish imitation than by original development." The same historian also records that "a good many terra cotta candelabra or lamps have been found of that particular form which has in a manner become canonical through its matchless grace and simplicity, and has hence, ever since it existed in its purity, been contorted into ornamental service."

The origin of the cruse has been found among Roman antiquities, and, strange to relate, this simple lamp appears to have been adopted wherever the Roman settled with his conquering legions—France, Italy and northern Africa producing them with little variation from the Roman originals.

BANKING CRISIS IN RUSSIA

"That the Russian peasantry are in deep distress is beyond dispute," says a prominent London financial paper. "They have gone through a long succession of bad harvest, taxation is heavy, and the country is passing through a serious commercial and banking crisis. If that were all, however, we might hope for a change. The harvest this year is expected to be good. But although a single good harvest, of course, cannot restore prosperity, it is something gained, and let us hope that it will be followed by other good years. Unfortunately the impression is very widespread in Russia, as well as elsewhere, that the poverty of the peasantry is not due to bad harvests alon, but that the whole agricultural system of Russia is in a bad way.

"On the other hand, matters are decidedly improving in Germany. At the liquidation going on there lately money is abundant and cheap, and there is reported to be a good demand for investment. Apparently therefore the crisis is drawing to an end. Of course it cannot be expected to terminate completely just yet, but the period of alarm and apprehension is past, and the saving classes are once more beginning to invest. Matters look more promising likewise in Austria-Hungary.

A HORSE IN THE SADDLE

A warrior, who is also a politician, has just been welcomed back to Canada with effusion, says the London Globe. The opening speech put the case in a nutshell. "We rejoice," said the chairman, "to see the old war horse back again in the saddle, ready once more to help us guide the ship of state." The returning hero was apparently an equine jockey with sea legs, a fine combination.

HALL'S Fireproof and Burglar Proof SAFES

Sold since 1840. Never fail to protect contents.

KNOWN EVERYWHERE

393 BROADWAY, N.Y.

Telephones: 3133-3136-307 Franklin.

BUSINESS NEEDS

Advertisements under this head one cent a word each insertion.

The Manufacturer HE Pays the Freight.

BOOKKEEPERS who have books to keep and papers and letters to file should be interested in all devices that may assist them in keeping things in order. Do you study the catalogues, watch the improvement in filing devices, binders and all the helpful little accessories to office work? I do. Write and tell me what annoys you in the office, perhaps I can help you. Address COMMISSION AGENT, care of C. A. & F.

STENOGRAPHER AND TYPEWRITER wanted.—Young man about 20. Willing to make himself generally useful about the office and in doing confidential errands. Applicant must be of good address and capable of following orders. Address, "PROMOTION," care Commerce, Accounts & Finance.

I SELL FILES. Vertical files, sectional files, pamphlet files, card index files and every conceivable kind of a file that may be needed to hold office memorandums or papers. I sell files cheap, not cheap files cheap, but files cheap. Write "FILES," and ask for prices. Address, care Commerce, Accounts & Finance.

SECOND-HAND TYPEWRITERS can be repaired so that they can be used and produce work which is almost, if not quite, as good as from a new machine. I have the facilities for obtaining exceptionally good second-hand machines. I have a man who repairs them—a man that understands his business. These machines can be sold for 50 per cent discount from list price of the new machines. Does this interest you? If it does, address TYPEWRITER, care Commerce, Accounts & Finance.

AN ACCOUNTANT REQUIRES the services of a young man of intelligence. One who is not afraid of hard work and long hours,

UNIVERSITY TRAINING

For Business

ACCOUNTING BANKING BROKERAGE	School of Comerce, Accounts and Finance. Evening Sessions. New York University, Washington Square, N. Y. City.

FALL TERM OPENS OCT. I.

may look forward to advancement. Address with age, reference, salary wanted and full particulars. "EXPERT," care Commerce, Accounts & Finance.

A BOOKKEEPER. Age 30; highest credentials; familiar with up-to-date systems in filing devices, wants to make a change. Is at present in the Export Commission business. Address, "J. B.," care Commerce, Accounts & Finance.

A CAPABLE, EXPERIENCED BUSINESS man, expert accountant, manager, worker, is looking for employment where his services can be made profitable to both parties; present employer retiring; guarantee thoroughly satisfactory services or no pay; New York city preferred, but location immaterial; highest New York references; interview solicited. "G.," care Commerce, Accounts & Finance.

HAVE YOU NOW under consideration the issuing of any new bit of advertising matter? Such, for instance, as a little Catalogue, Booklet or Folder, or a new Circular to replace some former one not "up-to-date." If I have happened to diagnose your case correctly, why not write me, and if you have anything that you would like bettered, why not slip a copy of it in your letter to me? F. COOK, care Commerce, Accounts and Finance.

Use any pen and your own stationery. If your stationer does not keep it, write for free specimen of work. Beware of infringements. Address Dept.
Pen-Carbon Manifold Co., 145-7-9 Centre St., New York.

FREE--A PAIR OF SLEEVE PROTECTORS.

Do you want to know about our Loose Leaf Ledgers and office devices? They will save you time, trouble and money. To all bookkeepers in the States of New York, New Jersey and Massachusetts who write us for information about our systems we will send a pair of sleeve protectors. In writing mention size of cuff.

THE C. E. SHEPPARD CO.,
87 Maiden Lane, NEW YORK CITY.

DO YOU NEED BOOKS? Old books, new books, second-hand books. Agent for subscription books, and dealer in old and new books. Ask me for prices on books you want before you buy elsewhere. A. CROSS, care Commerce, Accounts & Finance.

A THOROUGHLY-COMPETENT, well-educated, fully-experienced, aggressive and capable office manager, expert bookkeeper, fluent correspondent and traveling representative; aged 35; excellent address, personality, bearing, credentials, desires permanent position here or elsewhere, in any or all of above capacities. "P. J. L.," care Commerce, Accounts & Finance.

YOUNG MAN, about 20 years old; must be good stenographer; one having some knowledge of bookkeeping preferred; must furnish the very best of references; salary small to begin, but excellent chances of advancement; applicants must state age, references and salary expected. "WHOLESALE HARDWARE," care Commerce, Accounts & Finance.

Account, Audit & Assurance Company,

25 PINE STREET, NEW YORK.

Accounting Specifications

After a set of accounts has been charted, as explained in these columns last month, there remains to be prepared a specification of the way the accounting structure is to be managed in order to make it produce the promised results. The work in this regard is analogous to that performed by the architect after the plans of the building have been made. He puts before the builder, by means of the specification, the kinds and qualities of materials to be used, and frequently gives important advice as to the methods to be employed in combining them in the structure.

An accounting specification may be described as written directions concerning the management of the accounts. The various forms and blanks to be employed are illustrated and described, the different accounts to be opened are explained, not only in words, but also by means of a diagram of each account showing what goes on the debit side of the account, what goes on the credit side, and what the balance, debit or credit, as the case may be, really shows.

Balance Sheet Accounting, as the reader may have apprehended last

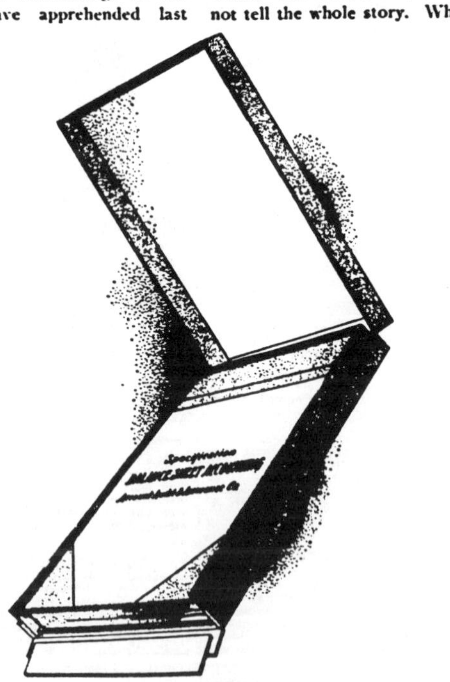

FIG. 1. THE ACCOUNTING SPECIFICATION AS IT GOES OUT IN A BOX.

month, differs from the usual application of double entry in that there is first instituted a scientific inquiry as to the accounts really necessary to open for properly showing the transactions of the business. This results in the

FIG. 2. THE SPECIFICATION REMOVED FROM THE BOX, SHOWING THE INDEX.

Chart. The chart alone, however, does not tell the whole story. What is lacking is supplied by the specification.

Many of the results achieved by Balance Sheet Accounting would be impossible of achievement, or, at least, unreasonable in expense, were it not for the considerable number of "Working Units" which have been devised to go along with the system. So many of these as are necessary to the work in hand are covered in the specification, being illustrated by models or forms, and their use fully set forth in the descriptive text.

Wherever a change in accounting is to be made there is more or less installation work to do. The object of the specification is to reduce such labor

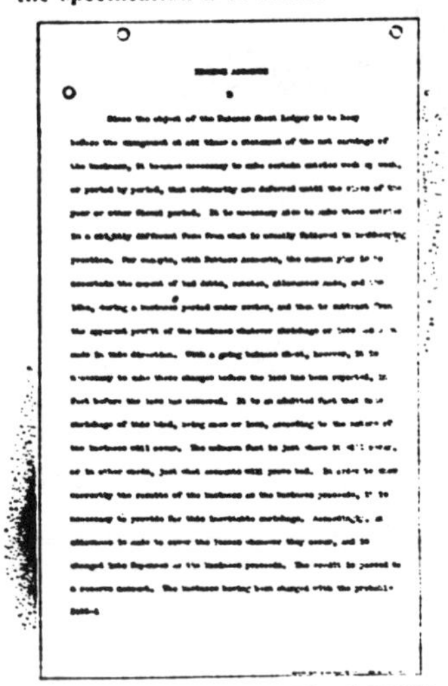

FIG. 3. SPECIMEN PAGE OF TEXT.

to a minimum; in fact, to overcome the need of it entirely in all cases where there is an interested man on

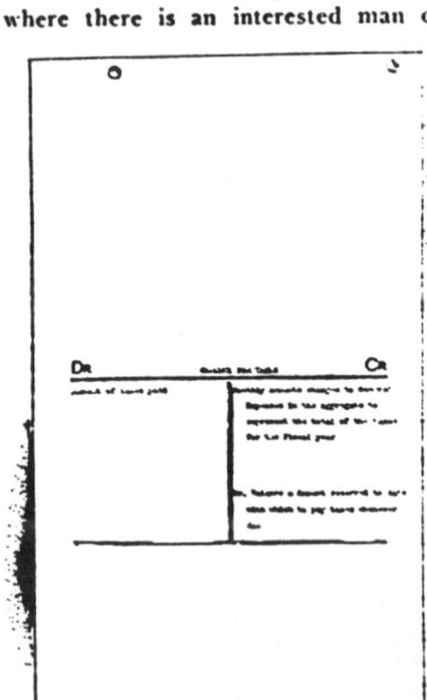

FIG. 4. SPECIMEN OF ACCOUNT FORM.

the ground to take hold of the work practically. The specification explains how every part is to act, and therefore saves the need of traveling expenses and the sojourn of a man in the office for a considerable period of time.

It pays to have a set of accounts charted and specified, even where there are no changes to be made. The Specification secures uniformity of work and avoids those jars in the administration of routine where changes in employees take place. The Specification becomes the ready means of explaining to the new man just how things are to be done and the reason why for doing them in that particular way.

Business statistics, to be of the greatest possible value, demand continuity of method. There is no better plan of securing this than to have the accounting system Charted and Specified. First, there must be intelligent investigation as to the requirements of the business, and based thereon will be the best method to pursue, fully described and set forth in the Specification.

The average office is "long" on bookkeeping and "short" on accounting. The Specification serves to cut off all superfluities, and with modern methods frequently makes one writing serve where several were required before. The object ever in view in preparing a specification is to economize labor, while yet giving the business man just what he wants to know about his business in the way he wants to know it, and at the time it will be of the greatest service to him in planning and management.

The Specifications of Accounting Systems which we prepare are all upon the Balance Sheet plan—that is, they show how to keep a set of books in an economical manner, and yet in a way to keep constantly before the management a Balance Sheet and Profit and Loss Statement of the business. The Balance Sheet and Profit and Loss Statement are going parts of the accounting system, and not results worked out by inventorying at the end of long fiscal periods.

For further particulars address

Account, Audit & Assurance Company, 25 Pine Street, New York.

BRIEF MENTION.

THE OFFICE WATER COOLER has become a necessity where formerly it was considered a luxury; many offices now cool their drinking water all the year round, therefore, a little folder issued by W. H. Dimond, of 120 Broadway, New York, advertising the water coolers manufactured by the Hale & Kilburn Mfg. Co., makes timely reading even at this autumnal season of the year. The Hale & Kilburn Co. make the "Favorite" Water Cooler in several styles and sizes. These coolers are made with polished hardwood cases, porcelain-lined wells and nickel faucets The woodwork is finished in oak and mahogany. It is claimed that the porcelain lining of the well prevents contamination of the water, and that the scientific construction decreases the consumption of the ice and prevents sediment from passing through the faucet. The Company also manufactures polished hardwood stands for their various coolers.

ANOTHER HANDSOME SPECIMEN of photographic literature has been sent to us by the Rochester Comera & Supply Co., of Rochester, N. Y., makers of the Premo camera, whose booklet we have described elsewhere on this page. This last product of the Rochester Company's good taste in advertising enterprise is descriptive of the Poco camera, and is a handsome piece of advertising. There are dozens of beautiful halftones; the printing is well done; the paper is good, and in general the catalogue is an artistic creation. The Poco camera in all its styles is described, so also is the Snappa camera, and the Cyclone and Cyclone, Jr. Like the other advertising outputs of the Rochester Camera Co., this catalogue is worth sending for and preserving, whether one wishes to purchase a camera or not.

THE CHICAGO, ROCK ISLAND & PACIFIC Railway is sending out a little booklet the title of which is "Items of Interest." It is printed in simple form and is not illustrated, but it gives special excursion rates and general information for tourists. Excursion fares and special round trip rates are contained in the booklet, and much valuable information is given for the benefit of the excursionist who may intend visiting points in the Rocky Mountain country and the far West and Southwest.

AN EXTREMELY HANDSOME little book is that issued by the International Navigation Company, whose New York office is at 73 Broadway. The Company also has offices in the principal cities of the country. The bool is tastefully bound in gray paper and contains descriptions of the new twin-screw steamships "Vaderland" and "Zeeland." The text is as interesting as a story, and this, and the reproductions of photographs of the various cabins, dining saloons and smoking rooms, makes the casual reader long for an ocean trip on one of these fine boats. The colored illustrations are as fine as any we have ever seen, and the whole book reflects credit upon the designers and printers. Such a book as this is expensive to produce, but must be good advertising.

ANOTHER BOOK, issued by the International Navigation Company, advertises the fine steamers of the American and Red Star Lines. The illustrations are in color and are beautifully made. The art of color-printing has advanced rapidly in the last few years, and these books are fine examples of the art. The text is well written and clearly printed, and whether one is contemplating a trip abroad or not, the books are well worth sending for. They will be sent to any one interested upon receipt of postage.

THE FALL GUNNING SEASON is just beginning, and, therefore, the catalogue of guns and sporting goods manufactured by the H. & D. Folsom Arms Co., 314 Broadway, New York, makes timely reading. Here are pictures of guns galore. Pictures of double and single-barrel shot guns, rifles, repeating rifles, pocket rifles and air guns. Here are pictures of revolvers of all shapes, sizes and prices. Also gun cleaners, cartridge holders, holsters and gun cases. The Company sells, likewise, hunting jackets, caps, canvas leggins and money belts. To one who contemplates a gunning trip this fall, the catalogue should be of great value.

THE PACIFIC MONTHLY has issued a special Columbia River edition, which is intended to exploit the beautiful scenic resorts in the far Northwest, and it is a credit to editor, publisher and illustrator. The illustrations are beautiful halftones of mountain and river scenery. It may open the eyes of some who think that beautiful scenery is only to be found on the other side of the ocean, to send for this number of the Pacific Monthly, look at these magnificent views and read the text accompanying them.

THE MERCANTILE SAFE DEPOSIT CO., whose offices are in the Equitable Building, New York, is distributing a pretty little pocket memorandum book, advertising their business. The memorandum book contains the storm signals, a list of feast days and legal holidays and a calendar for the current year. There are a number of blank pages for jotting down casual notes. The little book is very neatly bound and well printed.

A YELLOW COVERED FOLDER, issued by the Union Pacific Railroad, bears on its cover page these words, "Reach your destination quickly." Of course, the way to accomplish this, as set forth in the folder, is to travel by the Union Pacific Road. The folder contains an alphabetically arranged list of the towns and cities on the Union Pacific, Oregon Short Line and Oregon Railroad and Navigation Roads. This list gives information regarding each town and city, giving the number of its population, and describing its principal features and its hotels. The folder also contains maps of the country traversed by the various roads, and a few halftone illustrations of scenes along the way.

A VERY HANDSOME CATALOGUE is that issued by Crouch & Fitzgerald, of New York. Messrs. Crouch & Fitzgerald are makers of trunks and bags, and have stores in various parts of New York, their downtown depot being at 161 Broadway. The catalogue is bound in flexible cloth, and is illustrated with some fine halftone cuts of the various trunks and bags which the company makes and sells. One interesting trunk is called a "Rod and Gun Trunk" and is made with partitions and blocks for the convenient storing of fishing rods, a shot gun and a rifle. There are also sole leather trunks, steamer trunks, army trunks, trunks made with drawers like a bureau, and hat trunks that should delight the souls of the fair sex. All sorts of handbags, suit cases and hat boxes are illustrated and described in this catalogue. This, as we have said before, is one of the neatest catalogues of the kind we have ever seen.

OTIS H. KEAN, the advertising expert, whose office is at 140 Nassau Street, New York, is distributing a handsome 12-page book, setting forth the merits of his work as an advertising writer. The book is beautifully printed on heavy-coated paper, and the illustrations in color, which show samples of Mr. Kean's work, are really fine. From an advertising expert we, of course, expect good advertising literature, and this appears to be just that.

ANOTHER NEW TYPEWRITER is on the market, and it is manufactured by the Fox Typewriter Co., of Grand Rapids, Mich. The catalogue of the Fox typewriter, which has just reached our desk, shows the machine to be compact in appearance, and, judging by the description, to have some taking mechanical points about it. There are several models manufactured by the company, and we see no reason why the new typewriter should not become a favorite. Those interested in typewriters may find it to their advantage to send for the Fox catalogue.

THERE ARE A GREAT MANY varieties of loose-leaf ledgers and filing devices in the market, and the Sieber & Trussell Manufacturing Co., of St. Louis, Mo., have issued a small catalogue, well illustrated and printed, describing the S. & T. loose-leaf ledgers, price books, hand punches, transfer and lock binders, and the various presses which they manufacture. Judging by the illustrations, the loose-leaf books manufactured by this company are exceptionally neat in appearance, and are not clumsy. This company seems to make a specialty of punches and punch presses. The catalogue contains a price list.

THE FORT HALL INDIAN Reservation, of Pocatello, Idaho, was opened to the public on June 17th and July 17th of this year. The Oregon Short Line Railroad Co. is distributing a folder describing the lands of this Reservation as being ideal for the home-seeker. The folder describes the founding of the Reservation, and there are maps showing the various building sites contained within its borders. It is illustrated with halftone reproductions of photographs, the subjects of these illustrations being, for the most part, portraits of good looking bucks and squaws.

A VERY FINE EXAMPLE of railway advertising literature is that sent out by the Chicago, Rock Island & Pacific Railway entitled, "Under the Turquoise Sky." The text is by Henry P. Phelps, and describes the beautiful scenery and the beautiful climate of Colorado, where, as some one has said, "for more than three hundred days in every year the unclouded, friendly sun shines in a turquoise sky." The halftone illustrations in this book are well executed, and the subjects are chosen with care. The preparation of railway literature has become an art in itself. A great deal of money must have been expended in the preparation of this particular example of the art, but it seems to us that it must have been judiciously expended. The book is really beautiful when one considers that it is intended to be given away. As advertising matter for the bringing of business to the Rock Island Railway it would seem that it must be a success.

ANOTHER BOOK, issued by the Mercantile Safe Deposit Co., Equitable Building, New York City, is entitled "The Safe Deposit, Its Inception, Growth and Present Importance." It contains a history of the hiding place of treasure from the Stone Age to the present time. Each step in the history of the safe deposit for money and valuables is illustrated in an amusing way. The cave man is shown hiding his primitive treasure in a hole in the floor of his den. An ancient Egyptian is pictured placing his box of jewels under a slope in the floor of the Pyramids. The dwellers in Troy and in Rome are pictured concealing their treasures. So, also, is the Goth, the Baron, the old-time King, the Puritan and the Revolutionary hero. Finally, as the climax of development, the modern safe deposit vaults—presumably those of the Mercantile Safe Deposit Company—are depicted with their array of vaults, bars, time-locks and uniformed watchmen. The book is a very clever advertising conceit, containing much humor and common sense. We understand that it will be sent to any one interested if postage is enclosed in the letter of inquiry.

Working Plans of Leading Banks

Organization and Administration

Illustrated by

Charts

ONE of the original and fascinating features of the work of the American Institute of Bank Clerks is a collection of charts showing in a clear and comprehensive manner the arrangement of the working forces of several of the leading banks in different large cities of the country, together with an outline of the duties connected with each department.

These charts are a part of the correspondence course of study in Practical Banking, but they have created such general interest that the Institute has arranged to publish them in a handsomely bound booklet.

What the Charts Show

CHART "A" represents the First National Bank of Chicago, which has a very comprehensive plan of administration. The different departments of the bank are numbered in the chart for ready reference, so that the course of any item may be followed from receipt to final disposition. The main divisions of labor are clearly shown, and the duties of employees set forth in a clear and striking manner.

CHART "B" represents a prominent New York bank doing a large general business. The various departments and the duties of the different clerks therein employed are fully described.

CHART "C" shows the general plan of administration of one of the largest New York banks doing an extensive business with merchants and having a large number of correspondents throughout the country. An examination of the chart shows how this great business is handled.

CHART "D" represents in outline one of the largest and strongest banks in New York. An analysis of the chart shows that loans on collateral security are an important feature of the business transacted, although the bank's customers include numerous corporations of the first magnitude, and a desirable line of out-of-town banks.

CHART "E" represents a New York bank in the wealthy residence district, numbering among its customers many of the "400." The facilities afforded to ladies are a conspicuous and presumably very profitable feature of this institution.

CHART "F" shows the administrative plan of one of the leading banks of Philadelphia, doing a large general business and having numerous correspondents throughout the country.

CHART "G" is not intended to represent any particular institution, but rather to show the distribution of the working force of a typical New York bank of large size and progressive methods.

Terms and Conditions

While the charts are primarily a part of the regular educational work of the Institute, and were published separately only as an attractive premium for new chart-coupon subscribers, they are also esteemed of exceptional value to bankers generally and to others interested in up-to-date business organization and administration. To supply this demand for the charts which has come to us from all sources, they will be sent postpaid on the following terms:—

To new chart-coupon subscribers to the Bulletin, as a premium, one copy each, ... Free
To the general public, per copy, . . . - $2.00

Send order and make remittance payable to

American Institute of Bank Clerks

25 Pine Street, New York

OCT

THE NEW YORK PUBLIC LIBRARY

COMMERCE ACCOUNTS & FINANCE

Volume 4 New York, October 1902 Number 10

CONTENTS

Published Monthly by the Commerce Accounts & Finance Company Twenty-five Pine Street New York

Account, Audit & Assurance Company,

25 PINE STREET, NEW YORK.

A Pleased Customer is the Best Advertisement

The above heading is the expression of a truism. What we want to do at this time is to make the application.

We have been hammering away for a long time, and, while we have realized that we have many pleased customers, it is only recently that we have secured from a number of them expressions of their opinions of what we have been doing for them. In what follows we shall attempt to get before the reader the point of view of our customers.

If we have succeeded in pleasing the many hundreds for whom we have been working, then it is fair to suppose that, with opportunity, we shall succeed in pleasing you and others.

The original letters from which the following excerpts are made are on file in our office, and we shall be pleased to show them to any one who desires to verify our statements. For reasons which must be obvious, we omit names and places in what is now presented.

To the Advantage of Every Business Man

A Connecticut manufacturing concern, producing a line of goods which has been made famous the world over, wrote some time since:—

> "We take pleasure in testifying to the fact that by the use of the Balance Sheet Ledger we have been able to make periodical statements of our business for some time past, which have been much more satisfactory than anything that we have previously been able to produce. In our case, these statements are being made monthly, but they might as well be made daily or weekly. We thoroughly believe it is to the advantage of every business man to adopt Balance Sheet Accounting, for by so doing, with a slight rearrangement of certain bookkeeping details, the standing of the business at any date can be instantly determined."

A Barometer of Trade

The proprietor of a New England department store, writing one of our clients whom we had referred to him, said:—

> "Balance Sheet Accounting was installed in my store in August last, and in the interval has given entire satisfaction. Our accounting system previous to that date had been the usual double entry plan. I thought it was as satisfactory as could be evolved, although I was never entirely pleased with it. There was a good deal of bookkeeping about it, but very little information of tangible value. I felt disposed to cling to the old method, however, and was rather skeptical concerning the Balance Sheet system. I must confess, however, that my prejudices were soon overcome. By the Balance Sheet System of Accounts I can now tell every day just where I stand in each of the several departments, and to a certainty."

Works Splendidly

The treasurer of a mercantile concern in Pittsburg writes us as follows:—

> "Balance Sheet Accounting is giving us entire satisfaction. The system seemed more or less difficult and complicated at first, but now, I am happy to state, it is working splendidly. The office force is systematized, and the work passes through the regular channels daily. The essential feature of this system is the results which are obtained. It is certainly most gratifying to have a complete balance sheet and profit and loss statement on one's desk at the end of each four weeks, showing results both in detail and grouped, thus enabling one to tell at a glance whether or not we are making or losing money in any of our various departments. It enables us to locate and stop a leak before any serious damage has been done. It is also very gratifying to be able to take off this balance sheet without going through the ordeal of taking an inventory of the merchandise. While the outlay at first seems large, we feel that the system is well worth the initial cost and the work of installation. It gives us in return the four-weekly results above referred to, which are invaluable to an up-to-date business house."

Favorable to Statistics

The treasurer of a mercantile concern in New York writes as follows:—

> "It gives me a great deal of pleasuure to express my high appreciation of the accounting system which has been installed for this company by you. The system is sufficiently elastic to permit the keeping of all necessary accounts for statistical purposes, and enables us to show at short notice the actual condition of our business at any time in all of its various branches. The going inventory feature, which enables us to see at all times the condition of our Merchandise Account, is exceedingly desirable."

Feeling of Security

The president of a prominent merchandise distributing concern in Chicago, writing us recently with respect to the Balance Sheet Accounting System which we installed for his company some time ago, says:—

> "We have found Balance Sheet Accounting excellent in every respect. We realize fully that before the installation of your system we were considerably like a ship at sea without a rudder. Since we adopted it, we feel that we know at all times our exact financial situation. I assure you that the feeling of security to be derived from this knowledge is of great asistance to us in our business."

Superior to Traditional Methods

The secretary of a manufacturing company, with offices in New York and factory in Connecticut, writes us:—

> "During the past three years our company has used Balance Sheet Accounting, as installed by you. We desire to say that the system has proved eminently satisfactory, and we consider it far superior to the traditional methods of bookkeeping commonly prevailing."

A Safe Guide

The secretary and treasurer of a manufacturing concern in New York, making a line of street railway specialties, writes:—

> "We deem it but just to inform you, without waiting for solicitation, that with the installation of the Balance Sheet System of Accounting in January last, there came to us a most valuable guide and helpmate. Immediately we found material benefit, which has increased as time went on. We feel now that in making business calculations we have a safer guide than ever before, because we base calculations upon what we know to be a true record of the past."

Recommended to All

A prominent firm of miners and shippers of coal, with office in New York, writes as follows:—

> "Referring to the installation of the accounting system which you have recently made for us, we are glad to inform you that the same has met with our entire approval, and we are getting along very nicely under the new order of things. We recommend your methods to all who desire an up-to-date plan of accounting. Under the system you have given us, we are able to make up a statement of our affairs on very short notice and at any time."

Cheaper Clerks Can Perform the Work

The president of a big distributing

concern located in one of the New England cities writes us:—

"We are perfectly satisfied in every respect, and have only words of commendation to say in regard to the workings of our accounting department. We were anticipating the necessity of employing extra people to handle the system, but we find that the routine is so perfect and simple that cheaper clerks can perform the work as well as more expensive bookkeepers under the old plan. The total expense of our accounting department is in reality less than it would be by other methods."

The Actual Condition of Business Always Known

The treasurer of a mercantile concern located on the Pacific Coast says:—

"I am pleased to inform you that the accounting system which you installed for this company some months ago is proving very satisfactory. By following the plan outlined in the specification, the officers of our company are now in position to observe the progress of the business from day to day, and ascertain its actual condition at any particular period of time."

Can Make No Mistake

A prominent bank officer of New York wrote one of our prospective clients some time since in answer to an inquiry as follows:—

"I consider the Balance Sheet System of Accounts an excellent one, and I think you will make no mistake if you arrange to have it put into your establishment."

Abreast with 20th Century Ideas

The general manager of a mercantile concern in Boston says:—

"Balance Sheet Accounting certainly seems to be abreast with twentieth century ideas and keeping pace with progress in other lines of mercantile and manufacturing business. It is certainly a satisfaction to feel that we have the most effective and modern system of bookkeeping extant."

Saving of Labor

The auditor of a street railway company in one of the Southern cities wrote us some time since as follows:—

"I desire to express my complete satisfaction with the Balance Sheet System of Accounts which you have just installed for us. The results obtained far exceed my expectations. We now have a balance sheet every month with less labor than was required under the old system to simply keep our books. Our statements are now obtained the day following the close of the month, and under the method inaugurated are absolutely correct. I consider the system a perfect one for street railways, and especially adapted to every accounting department that aims at perfection. It is accurate, simple, labor and time saving, and worth much more than it cost."

Decided Improvement Over Old Methods

The manager of a New England agency of a large publishing concern writes as follows:—

"The system of accounting which your office recently installed to cover our home office and its agencies is a decided improvement over our old methods of bookkeeping. What strikes me forcibly is the fact that the home office can control business at far distant points, obtaining results promptly at any date. The forms, blanks and summaries at first seemed to me to involve a good deal of detail, but I now realize their value. . . . As far as this agency is concerned, things are moving more smoothly, and when I am at the home office to discuss with the management the four-weekly loss and gain statement, it is very gratifying to have the results of this business so clearly placed before us."

The System is O K

A firm operating in both Detroit and Toledo wrote us a short time since:—

"As you know, we have not yet installed the Balance Sheet Accounting System in our Detroit office. So far it is at work only at Toledo. . . . The system is O. K. and worth all that it cost. If properly established, it is a safeguard that few business men can dispense with."

Would Not Be Without It for Ten Times Its Cost

A company in a Southern city, manufacturing a line of electrical supplies, for whom we installed the Balance Sheet System of Accounts some time since, writes after a thorough trial of the system:—

"We find no words adequate to express our estimate of its value. Appreciating it as we do, we would not take tenfold the amount paid for it and be without it."

With Burdens Lightened

The vice-president and general manager of a large corporation in this city, the business of which is conducted through agencies and subsidiary companies, wrote us some time since as follows:—

"Before leaving on an extended trip West and South, during which I propose to visit our several sub-companies and agencies, it occurs to me that I should drop you a line to express my pleasure at the continued success of the accounting system and business methods that your company has installed for this corporation. It is a matter of much surprise to me that in the complicated business of such a concern as ours, with its large departments and with subsidiary companies established in all principal cities, we are able at the end of each four-weekly period to know just how our business is being conducted. I have with me, in a consolidated report, the business statement of our company for the last six months, with the ups and downs clearly shown at the end of each four weeks. I am thus thoroughly equipped to meet our managers and treasurers, go over their business with them, and advise them as to what their future conduct should be. . . . Thus, having lightened my burdens and equipped me to meet the several propositions that I am obliged to face on my tour, you can understand my desire to express to you my satisfaction and personal gratification."

A Satisfied Receiver

A prominent lawyer in New York, who served as the receiver in the readjustment of the affairs of a very large corporation of this city, writes as follows:—

"During my receivership, your company was employed to prepare the necessary accounts of the business and forms of reports. It undertook for me the work of systematizing the business and substituted up-to-date methods for those which prior thereto had been in use for the corporation. It gives me pleasure to state that these improved methods were applied promptly and with efficiency and success. In fact, to the happy outcome of the receivership and to the success in a business way of the new corporation, the work of your company has, in my judgment, largely contributed. I shall take great pleasure in advocating the employment of your company wherever better business methods are to be installed."

Prosperity Attributed to Balance Sheet Accounting

The proprietor of a large instalment house-furnishing concern in Toronto wrote some time since as follows:—

"It affords us much pleasure to highly recommend Balance Sheet Accounting. Previous to the introduction of this plan, our bookkeeping was to a large degree unsatisfactory, although we tried hard to have it right. It was inaccurate and incomplete. A balance sheet was not possible oftener than once a year. Sometimes it was not taken then, because of the dread of the very considerable undertaking. The result of the balance sheet, when declared, was unsatisfactory and disappointing, because we always felt that our condition was better than it actually was. With nothing to guide us or indicate our real position, we continued along, month after month, in a blind manner, only to realize in the end that the facts were entirely different. . . . Our bookkeeping to-day is in such a position that our manager knows every detail of the financing and merchandising. He has this information daily. The actual conditions of transactions, inward and outward, are always before him, any and all necessary details or information are constantly at his command.

"We have a balance sheet weekly; in fact, we always know the actual condition of our affairs. If we are losing, we know just how much it is, and where the loss occurs. If we are making a profit, we know how much, and can trace the cause. The cost of maintaining this happy condition of affairs in our office is no greater than were the old methods under equal conditions of trade. We attribute a good portion of our prosperity and progress of the past twenty-one months to this system of accounting. There is nothing that could induce us to go back to our old methods of bookkeeping; such a step would be retrograding, and fatal to our success."

The Most Complete—Yet the Simplest

The general manager of a machine manufacturing concern in Rhode Island writes us:—

"Balance Sheet Accounting has been in operation in our factory since July a year ago. It has proven a very satisfactory system in use, requiring a surprisingly small amount of labor to carry it on, considering the results obtained. We find it especially valuable in securing costs of production. . . . Considered as a whole, I do not hesitate, after having had experience with other systems, to recommend yours as one of the most complete, and yet the simplest, of any I have used."

Saves Time and Labor

A prominent business concern in Montreal writes us:—

"Last February, the Balance Sheet System of Accounts was introduced into our business. We are more than pleased with the results of the system. It not only saves time and labor, but gives much clearer results than the plan which we previously used. We cannot speak too highly of it, and have no hesitation in recommending it to every one. We believe it will be adopted by every progressive business man as soon as the system becomes better known."

Has Given Full Satisfaction

A mercantile concern which has had Balance Sheet Accounting in its office for a year past, wrote us a short time since as follows:—

"It gives us much pleasure to write you regarding the success of the Balance Sheet System of Accounts which you installed for us some time ago. It has given full satisfaction, and we are pleased to recommend it to any who are interested in making a change. The method has fulfilled our anticipations."

A Going Balance Sheet

The proprietor of a manufacturing concern located in Ohio, making a number of specialties, wrote us some time since as follows:—

"We are pleased to say that Balance Sheet Accounting is proving invaluable to us. What we like about it especially is the 'going' balance sheet, which shows completely the condition of our business from month to month, instead of but once a year, and releases us entirely from the task of closing and reopening the books at the end of each year, as has been our custom in the past. Another important point is that the system requires cost entries in connection with each sale, and thus the matter of profit or loss is kept constantly before us. . . . We are pleased to say that we have greatly enjoyed the written instructions or specification for the self-installation of the system, instead of the verbal instructions, which, of course, would necessitate the presence of a high-priced expert. . . . We would add that the relative labor-cost of administering the Balance Sheet System is no more than that of the method which it superseded."

Well Satisfied

The president of a company operating a department store in one of the New England cities wrote us as follows:—

"We are very well satisfied with Balance Sheet Accounting as it was inaugurated for us about a year since. It is practical, simple and easy to get at. We think it is one of the best systems now before the public."

A Wonderful System for Managing Large Enterprises

The treasurer of one of the largest copper companies in the United States, operating works in Mexico, and for which Balance Sheet Accounting was installed a short time since, writes us:—

"I have carefully studied the entire code prepared by you, and under which the management of our mines in Mexico are now operated. It is the most wonderful system of managing a large enterprise that has come within my experience. It controls all departments of the company, and these are not small, since we employ six thousand people constantly. The transactions of nearly fifteen thousand inhabitants must go through the books of our company in one way or another, whether it be the bank, the general store, the blacksmith shop, the railroad, the factory, or the hospital. I congratulate the management of any company which is operated under your system and supervision."

Cannot Commend the System Too Highly

The treasurer of a large concern in Boston, manufacturing a line of specialties, wrote us a short time since as follows:—

"We have had Balance Sheet Accounting in operation in our establishment for a number of months, and are perfectly satisfied with it. Previous to the introduction of this plan we were keeping our books double entry, and were doing a great deal of work which not only did not show us any results, but which also kept us in the dark as to our losses or gains until we took an inventory. The Balance Sheet of our affairs, which we now have each month, and the facts shown us by the monthly profit and loss statement have been invaluable to us in conducting our business. Each of our directors has a copy of this monthly balance sheet and profit and loss statements, which keeps them fully informed of our condition and progress. We cannot commend the system too highly, and believe the facts shown by it will enable any concern to conduct its business to better advantage and make more money than they could under any other system."

A Good Thing in Case of Fire

The head bookkeeper in a department store in one of the New England cities wrote us a short time since concerning the Balance Sheet System of Accounts as follows:—

"Personally, I like the system very much, and am greatly pleased with the results which we are able to arrive at by its use. . . . You doubtless heard of the big fire we had a few weeks since. It was in connection with this that I came to appreciate the system more than ever, and to feel compensated for whatever extra work it has made me. Had it not been for the fact that we were able to explain to the satisfaction of the insurance inspectors that the stock shown on our books was correct, we would have been obliged to take an inventory of the stock on hand, which, as you know, would be a very big undertaking."

For further particulars address

Account, Audit & Assurance Company,
25 Pine Street, New York.

What Is Money?*

By J. SHIELD NICHOLSON, M.A., D. Sc.

In a very able address on the "Constitution and Course of the Money Market," delivered in 1888 by Dr. Charles Gairdner, late manager of the Union Bank of Scotland, the introductory sentences are as follows: "The money market of the United Kingdom is an institution of great importance and of some complexity. It has gradually grown to enormous proportions, and embraces a fund almost equal in amount to the sum of the National Debt. This fund is held by the banks, is practically at call, and is repayable in gold; and yet ninety-five per cent of it is engaged in promoting the industries and material interests of the country and the world, while only five per cent is actually held in coin." If you consider carefully the meaning of this statement, it must strike you that, in spite of your familiarity with the state of things described, it is a very extraordinary statement. The fund of money of the money market is, on this calculation, over £600,000,000 in amount; 95 per cent of it is apparently not in the market at all—that is to say, not in the banks by which it is said to be held; and only 5 per cent is actually in coin. It may be added also that the total amount of coin in the United Kingdom is only about one-sixth of the total money of the money market as given by Dr. Gairdner, and it is not in any sense under the control of the banks, but is being circulated from hand to hand.

Since, then, the greater part of the "money" of the money market is not metallic money, the question is, "What is it?" It is, no doubt, something very real, for, as we all know, the abundance of scarcity of "money" affects the rates charged by banks for advances and discounts, and in that way affects the whole trade of the country. When the scarcity of money becomes extreme, we have indeed a commercial crisis, and for the time being all the trade of the country is thoroughly disorganized. And we know also by experience that at times of crisis the amount of metallic money, or money material, held by banks is of the most vital importance. In the words of Walter Bagehot, the author of "Lombard Street," and a banker and an economist of the first rank, "All our credit system depends on the Bank of England for its security. On the wisdom of the directors of that one joint stock company it depends whether England shall be solvent or insolvent." And if the precise method of stating the truth seems rather overstrained, there is no question of the central fact. Once the real gold reserves available for banking purposes get below a certain level—which again is variable according to circumstances—the whole monetary system of the country becomes clogged and for the time almost unworkable.

The subject I propose to discuss in this lecture is the meaning and nature of the term "money."

MEANING OF THE TERM "MONEY."

In dealing with the question "What is money?" we may begin by a rapid survey of the various "things" that have been in the past or are in the present actually called "money." You will find in the book on "Money," by the late Professor Jevons, an interesting account of a great variety of primitive kinds of money—e. g., cattle, slaves, tobacco, dried fish, straw mats, skins, and many others. You will also find in the very remarkable and learned work of Professor Ridgeway on the "Origin of Currency and Weight Standards" excellent illustrations of the beginnings of the evolution of "money." In the course of progress the metals gradually displaced other substances; in the struggle for monetary existence among the metals, silver and gold were the survivors; next, in the duel between gold and silver, for centures silver held the supremacy; and it is only in the last quarter of a century that gold has obtained the position of being practically the world standard for material money.

Long, however, before the battle of the standards had become critical, some of the most important "money" functions had come to be performed by other "things," these other "things" being embraced by Jevons under the comprehensive term "representative" money. The substance of all these things, if it can be called substance, is in effect credit; and although for certain purposes bank notes seem to have more of the nature of metallic money than do bills of exchange or checks, as a matter of fact, in the money economy of the present day bills of exchange, and especially checks, are of far greater importance than bank notes. You might, without much inconvenience, abolish bank notes and carry on all internal trade and all foreign trade by coin, checks and bills of exchange, but without checks and bills, or something of the same kind, our present monetary system would be impossible. These various instruments—these credit documents—perform most important monetary functions; of this fact there can be no doubt. The latest return of the London Bankers' Clearing House gives nearly 10,000 millions sterling as the amount of checks, bills, etc., for the year 1901.

THE ONE-POUND NOTE.

I have said that bank notes are now of relatively small importance, but it was not always so. The history of Scottish banking, in particular, shows of what vital importance were the one-pound notes, and by no one has this importance been better brought out than by Sir Walter Scott in his famous letters on the Currency to the editor of the Edinburgh Weekly Journal, under the pseudonym of Malachi Malagrowther. The publication of these letters, it may be said, preserved for Scotland its one-pound note. The one-pound note—this is the sum of Sir Walter's argument —"converted Scotland from a poor, miserable and barren country into one where, if nature has done less, art and industry have done more, than in any country in Europe, England herself not excepted." And here, if you will allow me, I will interject a general remark on the study of economics. It is necessary, in the first place, to get a real grip of economic methods, and especially of the method of abstract analysis. If you start at once with what you are pleased to call facts, you will make no progress whatever; you might as well hope to understand botany by taking at random a barrowful of weeds and making your own classifications and dissections, without reference to the science of the subject. You must in economic science in general, and in monetary science in particular, get firm hold of leading principles, or, if you prefer, of guiding hypotheses; you must not be afraid of abstract reasoning. Thorold Rogers, who collected an invaluable mass of materials in his great work on the history of "Six Centuries of English Prices," fell into the most serious errors in his commentaries and deductions, simply because he despised and failed to understand the abstract theory of money and prices. The corresponding work for France, also for six centuries, by Vicomte d'Avenel, is in this respect far superior to that of Rogers, because the author has taken the trouble to make himself a master of theory. You must, then, begin with theory—abstract, hypothetical theory.

But it is equally important to observe that you must end with facts and with history; your theory is only preliminary. And in dealing with historical facts you must not expect to find them all nicely cut and dried, and ready to be ticketed with some particular form of some particular theory. Real facts are never isolated in this way; they are intermingled with all kinds of other facts, and that is why you require your analytic methods to make the separation. And, moreover, facts of one kind being so intertwined with facts of other kinds, you must be prepared to search in very unlikely places. Most of you will not look naturally

*Lecture delivered before the Society of Accountants, in Edinburgh, by the Professor of Political Economy in the University of Edinburgh.

to Sir Walter Scott for the history of Scottish banking, but on the important phase to which I referred he may rank as an authority; and I may say incidentally, that there is more economic history—that is to say, history dealing with the real life of the people—in the novels of Sir Walter Scott than in any general history with which I am acquainted. I apologize for the length of this digression, and turn again to my abstract theories.

Seeing, then, that in actual usage the term money is so variable, it is hopeless to begin with the so-called facts; we must take our monetary system to pieces to discover the working; in other words, we must consider separately the various functions of money. We shall then find that the reason why it is so difficult, if not impossible, to frame a definition of "money" which shall include all the "things" actually called "money"—the reason is that some of the functions of money are best performed by some things and others by other things. This is true even of the so-called primary functions, and only when we have examined these primary functions shall we be able to determine if a simple definition of money is possible.

FIRST GREAT FUNCTION OF MONEY.

The first great function of money is to provide a general medium of exchange. It is usual to begin an account of this function by reference to the inconveniences of barter, as in the example of the prima donna on a voyage round the world, who, in exchange for her songs in the Society Islands, was to get a third of the receipts. When counted, her share consisted of three pigs, twenty-three turkeys, forty-four chickens, four thousand cocoanuts, and large quantities of bananas, lemons and oranges. The only method of saving his wealth was to set the live stock to devour the fruit, and although this may be called a primitive form of banking it is highly inconvenient.

After some such preliminary statement of the inconveniences of barter, and the insinuation that barter is only proper for savages, it is usual again to drag up barter from these lowest deeps and to set it on the highest pinnacle of civilization. We are told that all exchange is in reality barter, that commodities pay for commodities, and that money is only an intermediary. That trade is incapable of development when confined to direct barter, and also that all trade is in the last resort barter, are both truths of the highest importance. And both propositions being true, the appearance of contradiction must be an appearance only. All the difficulty would be avoided if it were stated that all exchange is ultimately barter, but that "money" is in general a necessary intermediary. To describe money as "only" an intermediary is to suggest at any rate that it might be dispensed with. And if by "money" we mean exclusively metallic money, that is perfectly true; but if we mean that the monetary function, as performed by some representative of this metallic money, can be eliminated and dispensed with, that is perfectly false.

You can only realize the fundamental importance of this primary monetary function by tracing the stages of industrial progress. The gradual substitution of exchange by money for exchange by barter has been one of the greatest agencies in civilization. Without money in its simplest form—that is, in the shape of cattle or skins or some material thing generally desired and acceptable—trade would have been strangled in its infancy. And without money in its most highly developed form—that is, in the form which it assumes in banking—modern industry would be impossible. In any just analysis banks are as necessary to production as are ships, railways or factories.

But before leaving this primary function of money, that is, as a medium of exchange, we may go one step further. It is not necessary in modern commerce that some credit document, such as would be taken by a banker, should directly represent so much coin at every transaction. Besides checks and bills, there are book credits, and even book credits are not necessary. It is sufficient that the commodities to be exchanged shall be expressed in terms of money, and in this case a relatively small balance—if any—of money need be transferred. In the case of international trade, indeed, we often have cases in which commodities are directly exchanged for commodities without the intervention of any form of credit. In this and similar cases, however, the monetary function passes into that of a measure of values. Both sets of commodities are measured in terms of money, and this is very different from simple barter.

A STANDARD MEASURE OF VALUES.

It is time to observe then, secondly, that money is required not only to furnish a common medium of exchange, but to provide a standard measure of values, or common measure in which all values can be expressed.

The necessity for a common measure of values appears very early in history. Thus in the early medieval period, when rents were actually paid in the shape of so much labor or so much produce, it became customary to measure the values in terms of money. And in our own times, valuations are made for all kinds of purposes, as well as for actual exchanges. Thus, historically and actually, we may separate the function of money as a measure of values from the function as a medium of exchange. But the two are so closely connected that, though there may be measurement without exchange, there cannot be exchange without measurement, that is, in the ordinary course of modern trade.

In spite of this close connection, however, it is important to observe that the actual medium may not itself be the standard measure; it is enough if it is related to the standard as multiples or sub-multiples, or in any exactly determinate way. At present, in the United Kingdom, the sovereign is the standard unit of value; all values are measured in numbers, or in parts of sovereigns or pounds sterling. But the actual payments may be made by bronze, silver, notes, checks or entries in books. And the unit of value which itself constitutes or determines the standard measure need not itself be a coin at all. Thus, in most European countries, the standard unit of value was originally the pound of silver, but there was never a coin of that magnitude or ponderosity. In fact, for centuries in England, though the standard measure was the pound of sterling, the only coins of any importance were silver pennies; the table, twenty pennyweights one ounce and twelve ounces one pound, shows the original relation of the penny coin to the pound measure—the pennyweight was literally a penny weight.

If all transactions and exchanges were effected immediately, anything that is universally accepted would serve as a standard measure of values. Thus, for example, inconvertible bank notes, at any particular moment, will effect exchanges just as well as convertible notes or coins. If others accept the notes at the same valuation in any market, that is suf-

MORE TROUBLE COMING.

The People—"And now Jack Frost is about to take a hand in the game."—From the New York Herald.

ficient. But as soon as we consider the production of things we pass from a moment of time to a more or less prolonged period of time.

STANDARD FOR DEFERRED PAYMENTS.

It is this element of time which gives rise to a third primary function of money, namely, to provide a standard for deferred payments. Both theoretically and practically this function of money presents the greatest difficulties. The real meaning of any monetary contract is liable to be disturbed by fluctuations in the value of the monetary standard. Here, again, the best and most easy example is inconvertible paper. Suppose the notes were constantly changing in value, and that in the course of a week or a year you had to pay for every new purchase twice as much in notes, while for your old contracts, including your income, you only receive the old amount of notes, obviously you would be deprived of half the purchasing power of your money. That is the essential evil of inconvertible paper; it fluctuates in value, and vitiates the real meaning of contracts. In extreme cases it ceases to fulfil this function of money altogether, and monetary bargains are made on some other basis in spite of legal prohibitions and penalties.

Now what is true of inconvertible paper in a magnified form is true of every standard for deferred payments in a greater or lesser degree. You make a contract on a gold basis—you will no doubt receive so much gold, or what represents so much gold, when the contract matures; but what the value of that gold will be depends entirely on the course of prices in the meantime. And, as a rule, if you take any selection of representative commodities there is some movement in prices; that is to say, so much gold purchases more or less of various things and services.

So long as the conditions of production and of demand are liable to change, it is impossible to get any standard with absolute stability of value, and the utmost we can aim at is relative stability of value. To attain this end we may eliminate certain common causes of fluctuation. Thus, for example, as regards supply, it is quite clear that if you have a very large durable stock, the variation in the annual production will be of minor importance. The annual supply of gold, for example, is always small relatively to the total world's supply, unlike the annual supply of wheat. Thus, so far, gold is a better standard than wheat. Again, for some things there is a fluctuating demand, and for others relatively a steady demand; and here again gold has the advantage compared with other substances that at different times have been used as money.

At first sight, it seems as if the want of stability of value in the standard itself is a very terrible thing; but in this world there is perhaps nothing practical which attains the perfection of theory, and fortunately, within limits, this want of perfection is, under ordinary conditions, of no practical importance. Your yard measure expands and contracts with every change in temperature, but for ordinary purposes this is of no importance. In the accurate measurement of time, however, such contraction and expansion must be allowed for, and you have great skill displayed in making compensations in chronometers; and similarly in certain astronomical observations and calculations, an error in the instrument of the smallest degree may vitiate the result, and incidentally send a big ship to the bottom of the ocean. Fortunately, as regards value, no such precise measurements are required for practical purposes—everything is, as a rule, done within reasonable margins. It is only occasionally, with very great change in the conditions of demand or supply, that serious changes occur in the value of the money material that constitutes the standard. On such occasions there may be a very real disturbance of the meaning of monetary contracts and a very real disturbance of the distribution of wealth. Even in this case, however, the evil ought not to be exaggerated. The loss of one is the gain of another in any monetary disturbance, and the evil only becomes serious where the uncertainty actually dominates the volume of trade and production.

A STORE OF VALUES.

To the three primary functions of money already considered we may add a derivative function. Money may be used as a store of values. In its elementary form this function is extremely simple—it consists simply of hoarding so much actual metal. But in the course of development this function of money has also become much more difficult of comprehension. To pay money into a bank by means of a check is very different from putting—according to the French idiom—little sous into a big stocking. In the case of the check, the only material difference consists as a rule in the change of a few figures in the books of one or two banks. And yet we speak as if the money were "stored" in the bank.

Thus, again, we are led back to the original question propounded as the problem of this lecture, namely, What is "money"? What is this "money" that I put in the bank when I pay in a check, and what does the bank do with the "money"? We may indeed ask not only What is the "money," but Where is the "money"?

The answer to the question "What is money?" which serves to cover most of the popular usages, is the answer given in the late Professor Walker's book on Money—"Money is that money does"—or, in other words, anything which performs the functions of money may be classed as money.

But then all the difficulties of the definition reappear when we ask the further question: In order that a thing may be classed as money, must it perform all the functions, or only one or two of these functions? Take, for example, concrete cases: In this country, for practical purposes, the gold coinage only fulfils all the functions. Gold only is compulsory legal tender under all conditions for the fulfilment of monetary contracts; Bank of England notes, for example, are not legal tender by the bank itself, and other bank notes are still more restricted as regards this function; even the other coins made of silver and bronze, though popularly classed as money, have only a limited acceptance—they are, indeed, "token" money, and legally on the same footing as bank notes except for small payments.

The sovereign again is, in this country, the only standard measure of values; it is so, however, simply because the law has so determined. When a country is obliged to resort to inconvertible paper it very often prohibits the use of gold as a standard, and by penalties tries to make its notes the standard. If we refer back to history, we find examples of what is called the double standard, or better, the alternative standard, of gold and silver—that is to say, at the option of the debtor a monetary contract might be met by so much gold or so much silver, the rate being in general determined by law. On various grounds economists have proposed other standards, as, for example, an amalgam of gold and silver, or notes representing so much gold and silver.

Again, in this country gold is the standard for deferred payments. Take the National Debt: it is repayable in gold, though it may not be repaid for centuries. Similarly as regards many perpetual debentures, the interest is payable in pounds sterling—that is to say, gold. But when we take very long periods, changes in the value of the standard may be of practical importance. In this case we have all the difficulties connected with appreciation and depreciation, some of which will be considered in connection with the "Foreign Exchanges." To remedy these difficulties some economists have proposed a tabular standard. In effect, this is a composite standard composed of a number of representative commodities. It is assumed that the debtor will covenant to pay not so much gold, but so much purchasing power, and thus the amount of gold money to be paid would vary with the course of prices.

Finally, when we consider the function of money as a

store of value, the most important store is, in this country, the reserve of gold in the Bank of England. Most of the rest of the money that is deposited or stored in our banks is only "representative" money; it is only supposed to be repayable in gold. As a matter of fact, if all the so-called money which is supposed to be repayable at call were demanded at the same time, only a very small percentage could be paid. But although all this "bank" money could not be changed into gold at any particular time, and although it only represents gold in the highly conventional sense that it is repayable in gold if demanded, it is not to be considered as in any sense unreal or intangible. The funds of the banks which are not represented by gold are represented by other forms of property—as, for example, by the produce and manufactures against which bills are drawn and are taken to the banks for discount, and also by the government and other securities, which are really mortgages over the property of the nation or of companies or of individuals.

It was said by Sir James Steuart, a great writer who preceded Adam Smith, that any form of property could be melted down into bank money. But the aggregate amount of this "bank" money must always depend partly on the amount of the real reserve available, and partly on the nature of the demands likely to be made on this reserve. The progress of banking in one important respect is shown by the diminution in the proportion of gold reserve to liabilities which it is necessary to keep, and this again depends partly on the demands for gold for circulating purposes—including transmission abroad—and partly on the credit of the banking system as a whole.

It would obviously be absurd to say that only the gold of the money market is money, and still more absurd to go to the other extreme and say that the other forms of property pledged directly or indirectly to the banks are money. If, then, for the last time, we put the question: What is "money"?—As the result of our inquiry into the monetary functions, the only satisfactory answer appears to be that we must recognize that there are various kinds of money, and that the definition must vary according to the monetary function that we are considering. In reality, instead of trying merely to frame a verbal definition, we ought always to make clear the different monetary functions. And a good practical rule is, as in other similar cases in economics, to use qualifying adjectives indicating the kind of money or the kind of monetary function to be considered.

The standard of value in any country is exactly determined by the law of that country, and this definition governs the interpretation of all monetary contracts. How far the use of such a standard is compulsory is also a matter of law, and how far the law can be carried out depends partly on public opinion. As a matter of fact, at the present time most commercial contracts in this country are expressed in terms of "money," that is to say, in terms of the pound sterling; but if people so desire, there is nothing to prevent them making bargains to make payment according to a tabular standard or any other standard. But, as a matter of history, in the course of time the governments of all countries beyond a certain stage have adopted as their standard some definite amount of gold or silver (and in some cases an alternative at a certain rate). At the beginning of last century England formally adopted the gold standard, and in the last thirty years the gold standard has been adopted to such an extent that it may now claim to be the commercial standard of the world. The gold moneys of the different countries are in this way related according to the amount of fine gold they contain. In certain countries, however, silver is still the standard, and in others there are various legal standards which are only indirectly or partially on a gold basis, as, for example, the rupee in India. These other standards, however, for the purposes of international trade may be reduced to terms of gold at any particular time.

THE MEDIUM OF EXCHANGE.

The medium of exchange in any country which people must accept in satisfaction of a debt when offered by the debtor is also a matter of law, and how far its compulsion can be extended to future contracts is a matter of government and public opinion. How far, as a matter of fact, people may and do accept other means of settlement in place of legal tenders is a matter of habit and convenience, and how far such acceptance is final or irrevocable is a matter of law. These various "things," which locally and temporarily so far fulfil the function of money as a medium of exchange, may be said to represent, or to be based upon, standard money—that is, in most countries, gold, directly or indirectly. Thus gold in gold-standard countries may also be said to be the fundamental medium of exchange, though in some cases the foundation may be in bulk and value relatively small compared with the superstructure. The actual use of gold may be economized to a marvelous extent by the use of "representative" money, but it cannot be dispensed with altogether, any more than the foundations of a building.

Gold, then, under present conditions, certainly fulfils all the monetary functions to a degree that is not true of anything else. But, to raise one last difficulty for purposes of illustration, gold itself is not money, but only money material, and therefore so far only representative of "money." At the time of the great Australian gold discoveries, in the early 'fifties, gold in South Australia is said to have fallen to 45s. an ounce, and in Victoria to 60s., as compared with the mint price of £3 17s. 10½d. Of course, with open mints and no charge for coinage such a difference could not arise, although even in London at the present time there are on occasions slight differences between the mint price and the market price of gold. But this last

THE OTHER FELLOW GETS IT ALL.

Fisherman—"They say the fishing is good, but I don't seem to catch much."—From the Brooklyn Eagle.

difficulty is not raised for purposes of explanation, but of illustration. The point is, that for certain purposes the money material—even gold itself—must be distinguished from money.

In conclusion, then, we can only reaffirm the position already laid down: For various reasons the term "money" is used in various senses, which are best indicated by qualifying adjectives. Thus we may speak of metallic money, both "standard" and "token"; of paper money, including convertible and inconvertible bank notes; of "representative" money, including not only bank notes, but various forms of bankers' credits; we may speak of "national" money and of "international" money; of money in active circulation, or of money in passive reserve; of money as legal tender and of money as the currency in practical use; we may speak of the value of money, meaning thereby the rate of interest, or of the value of money, meaning thereby its exchange value, as determined by the level of prices; and thus, finally, we are led to consider the appreciation and the depreciation of money, and the relative values of different forms of money and money materials.

Accordingly, when we are dealing with monetary problems, it is generally necessary to lay down at the outset the meaning to be attached to the term "money" in the course of the argument—a precaution of special importance in dealing with the "quantity theory of money." Otherwise, if we do not take this precaution, it is hardly possible to escape confusion. And this habit of constantly looking into the meaning of money has its practical advantages. The whole business of banking consists in estimating the demand for money of different kinds for different purposes; in some cases a demand for money may mean no more than a change of figures in bankers' books; but in other cases it may mean that the Bank of England is obliged to borrow, as on certain historical occasions, actual gold from the Bank of France.

Items in Suspense and Reserves*

By A. O. KITTREDGE, C. P. A.

We observe a business from three points of view—the past, the present and the future. The business man wants to know about the present. He cares very little for the past, because that is done and settled and he could not change the conditions if he tried. If we take care of the present, the future will take care of itself. If we pay something today for which we get no benefit at the present, but do get benefit next month, we do wrong if we charge the expense to the present day. If the present period gets the benefit of something which we must pay at some future date, then we do the present period wrong unless we take into account that expense which we have to pay.

Some men have stated that they do not owe anything because their bills were not yet due. If, for example, taxes are paid at the end of a period and the bills are sent in at the end of a year, we do not owe any taxes, because they are not yet due, but if our taxes are to be paid at the end of the year, surely the expense of taxes is a part of the expense of every day of that year.

In the case of bonds which are issued, interest payable at intervals of six months, the expense should not be charged to that period in which it is paid, but as an expense of every day of that six months. Depreciation of street railway tracks, replacing of new ones, the wear that makes new ones necessary, certainly is not an expense of the day that the new rails are paid for and laid. The cost of these expenditures has existed every day in the period, whether it be a month or a year.

Repairs of machinery you take care of as a part of the cost manufacture. The repair is made when the machine actually breaks—the break does not occur by reason of what happened today, but the machine has been getting ready for that break the whole time it was in use. Therefore to charge into the cost of manufactured goods of the present period the repair which we make today is wrong. Each day's use of that machine has worn it out to a greater or less extent. A reserve should be accumulated to provide a fund out of which to pay for the repair.

DIVISION OF EXPENSE.

We have, in the period preceding the present interval, certain things that effect the present interval, and we shall have in intervals succeeding the present interval things which really belong to the present period. This brings us against the principle of suspense on the one side and reserves on the other. If we pay out January 1st $120 premium for insurance policy running for one year, we certainly do not want to charge up that $120 into the expense of January. We will assume, for the case of argument, that we are running our business on a monthly basis, then only 1-12th of that $120 belongs to the expense of January and the remaining 11-12ths should be divided into the remaining eleven months of the year. One-twelfth being charged to each month.

If on the first of January we make a contract for some money, we to have the use of that money for the year, but the interest not to be paid until the end of the year, we get the benefit of that money every month of the year. It certainly is not fair to the business and it would not be a correct statement to allow that expense to effect the last month of the year only, the month in which it is paid. If the interest, for example, is $120, then certainly $10 should be charged into the cost of each month and credited to a reserve, as we call it, there to accumulate with other items of its kind, of the succeeding months, until at the end of the period we have reserved out of the business enough to meet this obligation which becomes due the last day of the year.

It is customary in some lines of business to declare profits first and make reserves afterwards. They go through the profit and loss statement and say that they have made so much money, and from it they will reserve a certain amount and pass the balance to surplus, out of which to pay dividends, etc. This makes use of terms in a way that they do not tell the whole truth. When I see the word profit applied to a sum of money, I am led to believe that it is a profit, not a profit mixed up with something else, and not an amount that must be debited by something or other. Instead of getting at profits first and taking a portion of the so-called profits to set aside as a reserve, it seems to me far better to keep the reserves going, and to charge into expense the cost of manufacture, thus producing your result in the way of profit that is profit, the reserves having all been made.

You have been advised that the business man wants a continual statement, a perpetual balance sheet, a perpetual profit and loss statement, and that the nearest that can be brought to perpetual is to make the fiscal periods very short. I recommend in most cases periods of four weeks, and in some cases periods of one week, and in extreme cases daily periods. Now, if our fiscal periods are going to be short, the old standpoint of getting our profits first and taking our reserves after scarcely would work.

BALANCE SHEET MUST TELL THE TRUTH.

The balance sheet is the essential element of accounting, but what is the use of the balance sheet unless it tells the truth? The business man wants to know actual facts. There is no reason why we should not have suspense on

*Extract from an address before the Students in Accounting, School of Commerce, Accounts & Finance, New York University, by A. O. Kittredge, C. P. A., Professor of Theoretical and Practical Accounting.

ENOUGH FOR ALL.

Uncle Sam—"Yes, boys, I have grain enough to supply the world."—From the Philadelphia North American.

the one side and reserves on the other. The balance sheet should certainly tell the truth, and yet how are balance sheets regarded by the public? I listened to a lecture a short time since, in which the speaker said that there were three kinds of lies—lies, damn lies, and balance sheets.

If we had accumulated a reasonably large sum for the depreciation of machinery and then discovered that we had to throw away a certain amount of our machinery and buy new, and the old machinery is sold for junk, how shall we enter that on our books? We have a machinery account, which we have debited with $500,000, the cost of the machinery we have in factory. Now, since depreciation is part of the cost of goods, as we go along and our machinery depreciates, we charge into the cost of goods an estimated amount to equal the depreciation, which in this case we will say has amounted to $200,000, which amount we have credited to reserves. Machinery account is credited with what we take out of it, which in this case we will say is $75,000. If that $75,000 worth of machinery is sold for old junk, for $5,000—we credit reserve with the $5,000 we receive for it. We also debit the reserve account with the $75,000 machinery discarded. Now, if we replace the machinery with new, which costs us $125,000, we debit the machinery account with $125,000. I do not think the $5,000 we received for old machinery belongs to loss and gain, particularly if we treat loss and gain account as being the results of the business transactions of the period. I think whatever we get for that machinery is something that stays on hand in reserve for future contingencies.

Never depreciate the asset account, but provide a reserve against it. If you want to know what you have got in that account, subtract the reserve from it.

The American accountant regards reserves from the standpoint of the business, while the English accountant from the standpoint of the stockholder.

A HELPFUL CHART.

Below is a chart which will be a material help in understanding the principles of items in suspense and reserves.

Suspense.	Period.	Reserves.
Items paid in advance.	Expenses paid in period prorated from suspense pro-rated to reserve.	Items that are to be paid at some future time.

Expenses are comprised in three general heads—those which are specifically paid in the period, those which are pro-rated out of suspense, and those which are pro-rated to reserve.

There is a difference between the American and English accountants in the matter of reserves. You may have noticed that almost every year the English stockholders of the Pennsylvania Railroad say that the dividends are too small compared with the earnings. The answer is that they have large allowances in reserve for future contingencies. Take, for example, the Johnstown disaster, in which hundreds of miles of rail were destroyed, and owing to the fact that their reserves were large, they did not have to call on their stockholders for one cent.

On the other hand, English accountants think that all the earnings of a business belong to a stockholder. For example, a large steamship company in England owned twelve ships, and they were in the habit of paying all their earnings to the stockholders, never thinking of setting aside a reserve for an accident. After a while, one of the ships sank, and it had to be replaced with a new one. Now, since they had no reserve accumulated for that purpose, and since they could not take the amount out of the dividends, the stockholders were obliged to go down into their pockets and pay for a new ship.

In contrast with this we will take, for example, a large corporation in the North which goes South and buys timber, with no other purpose in view than cutting the timber and shipping it to New York. Sometimes they have no money, and have to issue bonds. Bonds payable demand a reserve to be put up against that mortgage. If mortgage is $100,000, and there are 100,000 feet of timber to be cut, there is $1 per foot to be set aside.

ILLINOIS ACCOUNTANTS

The Illinois Association of Public Accountants, which was incorporated in 1897, is officered the present year as follows: President, George Wilkinson; vice-president, Ernest Reckitt; secretary and treasurer, J. Porter Joplin. The total membership of the organization is thirty-three, of whom twenty-three are fellows, and ten associates. A perusal of the by-laws indicates that the requirements for admission are quite severe, including, among other things, the condition that no accountant who has not been in practice on his own account at least three years is eligible.

The Work of the Professional Accountant

By JAMES L. SELKIRK

An Interesting Address by the Secretary of the Scottish Society of Accountants and Auditors

Accountancy, as a distinct profession, organized and equipped for public service, is of comparatively modern growth. It can hardly be said to date farther back than to a period within living memory. The nineteenth century, in many respects the most remarkable and eventful in history, witnessed the gradual rise and development of what may be regarded as, in a real and special sense, an important branch of the legal profession, possessing, however, distinctive features of its own. At the present day it has attained a position and an influence in commercial and official life commensurate with the highly onerous and responsible duties which it is called upon to discharge.

A variety of circumstances, interesting and important in themselves, has undoubtedly produced this gratifying result. The progress of education, of the arts, of science and special culture, the development of invention—by which locomotion, as well as manufactures and industries of every kind, have been thoroughly revolutionized, and time, cost and energy enormously economized—the amendment of the laws of the country in order to adapt them to the requirements of the rapidly changing conditions of commercial enterprise, the extension of trade and commerce to all parts of the habitable globe, with its immense reciprocal advantages—these and other more or less important agencies have been continuously at work contributing to the development of natural resources and the creation of wealth in a manner and to an extent undreamt of in earlier times.

This marvelous progress, with its accompanying prosperity, necessarily led to the introduction of an immense variety of new machinery, by means of which the requirements of the day were suitably and sufficiently met. It was under circumstances such as have been indicated that the accountancy profession gradually emerged, and gave definite shape and form to skilled methods by which were carefully and accurately recorded the immense variety and complexity of business transactions taking place throughout commercial circles. It is not at all surprising, therefore, that the demand for trained professional assistance quickly became quite phenomenal. Not only did this spring from established undertakings of every name, but each new enterprise, from its inception to its completion, sought the experienced help and guidance of the public professional accountant. His position and sphere came to be as distinctly recognized as those of the solicitor. At every step in the formation of companies and business concerns generally, his skill and experience as an expert in figures and accounts were in requisition and were fully appreciated.

From time to time special circumstances gave impetus to the profession, and in due course the entire business community came to recognize it as an important factor in the development of sound commercial prosperity. The passing of the Companies Act of 1862, and of the subsequent acts amending the same, may be regarded as, in some respects, the beginning of a new era in accountancy. It gave an enormous stimulus to auditing as a special department of professional work—a department which has ever since occupied a foremost place in the accountant's range of duties, and at the same time has led in numerous cases to appointments as secretary, for which his special training rendered him well fitted.

In like manner, though not to the same extent, the various Acts of Parliament regulating the accounts—numerous, important and diversified as they usually are—of municipal and other corporations and public companies, as well as of public bodies of every description, have, by their fuller recognition of the necessity for a professional audit, done much to raise the accountant and his work in the estimation of the entire commercial and trading community.

Besides these, there are numerous other branches falling within the range of an accountant's work, which may properly be referred to more or less fully here. Prominent among these the following fall to be mentioned:—

THE BANKRUPTCY ACTS.

Reference is obviously limited to those applicable to Scotland. These acts were consolidated under the important act of 1856, which, notwithstanding sundry defects, chiefly of a minor nature, is a most valuable statute, and has proved an immense boon to the mercantile community of Scotland. It reflects infinite credit on its authors for the comprehensive and judicious manner in which the interests of all parties—and especially of creditors—are recognized and dealt with. Members of the society practicing in England will kindly pardon the reference, but it seems to be freely allowed that the Scottish act is, in certain important respects, superior to the English act of 1883. This is hardly the place to discuss the relative merits of these acts. The outstanding features of the Scottish act are its completeness, its provision for economical working, its absence of officialism, and its giving the absolute control of the bankrupt estate to the general body of creditors, who are empowered to elect the trustee, as well as a committee of their number—designated commissioners—to act with and advise him as to the realization of the estate. The trustee is not necessarily an accountant, though he almost always is so, especially in the larger centers, and this is most convenient and suitable, as no one else is so well qualified to discharge the varied and responsible duties of the office. It not only requires a thorough knowledge of bankruptcy law, but an accurate acquaintance with legal procedure incident to the office of trustee.

TRUST DEEDS.

This is a process of voluntary liquidation peculiar to Scotland. Recourse is usually had to it when an insolvent debtor is unable to make a satisfactory settlement with his creditors, and when circumstances are specially favorable to an expeditious and economical winding up, particularly where the estate is a small one and free from possible complications. Except in the preparation of the deed conveying the estate to a trustee for the general behoof, the assistance of a solicitor is not usually required, though questions do arise now and again calling for legal guidance. While this method of liquidation has its advantages, it has also its drawbacks. For example, although the deed is a voluntary assignation, on the part of the debtor, of his whole means and estate in favor of a trustee for behoof of his creditors, the latter are not usually bound to accede to it, though they many, and generally do, rank on the estate and draw their dividends, reserving the right to sue for the balance of their respective debts. For this reason insolvent debtors are, as a rule, unwilling to grant such a deed, preferring sequestration, especially because under it they have the prospect sooner or later of obtaining a complete discharge of their whole debts, with or without composition, for which the Bankruptcy Act makes full provision. This leads me to remark on this branch of an accountant's work, that some of the best qualities of the public accountant are usually exhibited in connection with the handling of an insolvent's affairs, with a view, particularly, to the carrying through of a private settlement. From first to last he (the accountant) is called upon to make clear to the creditors, not merely his special knowledge of how best to submit a complete and reliable state of affairs, but so to present it as to satisfy them that the course he recommends to be followed—if he does submit a recommendation—is, in all the circumstances, the best. His case is, however, seldom free from difficulty, and much will often depend on the prudent and judicious advice which he may be prepared to offer, as representing, in some sort, both parties. The conduct of the insolvent not infrequently determines the action of the creditors, especially when it is ascertained that he has not kept regular books, and is unable to furnish satisfactory explanations as to how his insolvency has arisen. By familiarizing himself beforehand with all the facts of the case, the accountant may do much to guide the creditors at a critical juncture, and to facilitate the proper course of action. Where the insolvent is desirous of making an offer of composition, the accountant should be able to advise both as to the amount, as well as the terms of it, and thereafter, without delay, to take steps to carry it to a satisfactory completion. There are few directions in which a professional accountant will find more scope for the exercise of those qualities which go to make a successful professional man than in the discharge of this particular duty. It may, at the same time, be truthfully said that it is generally discharged with tact, discrimination and ability, and if success does not always attend the effort to carry through the proposed arrangement, the failure to do so may safely be attributed to other causes than those for which the accountant is responsible.

If he errs at all, it is usually in this respect—that he has not taken reasonable precautions to insure that in the event of arrangement falling through his fee shall, nevertheless, be paid or provided for. Why, it may be asked, should such a point be emphasized? Because the accountant, in the discharge of this duty, requires to give it immediate and personal attention; everything else he may have on hand must, for the most part, stand aside, and for weeks together, between correspondence and personal calls, his attention is closely engaged. Nor is this all. Although his best efforts may be put forth to accomplish his object, he may find at last that certain creditors, for reasons of their own, refuse to accede to the proposal, which consequently falls through, leaving him in the position of ranking on the estate—which meantime has gone into bankruptcy—for the professional fee which he has fully earned.

COURT APPOINTMENTS.

There is another very important branch of accountants' work which falls to the profession, and which calls not only for an accurate and intelligent knowledge of the different forms of accounts, but the utmost painstaking carefulness in their preparation. I refer to the various court appointments, which include Judicial Factors, Factors on Trust estates of various kinds, Curators bonis, etc. They also embrace remits of various kinds, with reference to accounting, for the guidance of the court in determining disputes as to partnerships, joint adventures, and contracts generally. These involve a thorough knowledge of figures, of the principles of correct bookkeeping, of the preparation of states, and generally the adjustment of accounts over which disputants have failed to see eye to eye, and have sought the assistance of the court.

The liquidation of public and private companies furnishes another important class of work for the public accountant, which is closely allied to the winding up of estates in bankruptcy. Whether the appointment of liquidator is by the creditor, the shareholders or by the court, it is universally felt that it should be in his favor as the person who, by training and experience, is the person best fitted for the position.

In this connection, as well as in bankruptcy, expedition in winding up and in declaring a dividend are matters upon which shareholders and creditors set great store, and they are sometimes at a loss to understand why there should be so much delay. There may be room for this complaint, but before judgment is passed on the liquidator or trustee, inquiry should be made of him as to the cause of it, and if this is done it will generally be found that some assets have been specially difficult of realization, or some claims have been of a doubtful character, and that until every asset has been recovered and doubtful claim disposed of the liquidation or sequestration cannot properly be closed. Sometimes, too, it is found necessary to take a debtor into court, if the matter is of sufficient importance to warrant such a course. Accountants who have had some experience of litigation will always be slow to enter upon it, for the simple reason that creditors rarely appreciate it, and prefer to take a smaller dividend promptly paid, rather than wait a year or more in the expectation of getting a somewhat larger one. The liquidator or trustee, with the advice of the law agent and committee of creditors or commissioners, will always carefully weigh the whole circumstances, and will only go into court if he is clearly of opinion that it is his duty to do so.

ARBITRATION.

One of the most important and responsible duties which the accountant is called upon to undertake is that in regard to arbitration, which in a special degree calls for the exercise of the highest professional qualities, combined with exceptional business sagacity. The combination is, no doubt, unique, but the duties of the office of arbitrator demand more than ordinary qualifications in order that absolute confidence in the integrity, ability and impartiality of the gentleman to be appointed may be secured. Happily, there are not a few in our profession who are, in all essential respects, eminently fitted to discharge most efficiently these duties, difficult and often delicate as these are.

SECRETARIAL.

The accountant is not infrequently chosen to fill the secretary's chair, for which his training and experience abundantly qualify him. This applies to the post in public companies, public associations of every kind, including those connected with trade, charity, education, literature and kindred bodies, where the field is wide, and there is ample opportunity for intelligent activity as well as valuable and useful training. The profession is also laid under tribute to furnish specialists for various public offices, such as clerks and treasurers to school boards and public and private trusts, city accountants, city and town chamberlains, city registrars, factors of landed estates and managers of banks, insurance companies, etc.

There is yet another field in which the profession may find room for the exercise of active energy. I refer to the vast and interesting field of insurance in its numerous branches and developments. Not only are many of the most important positions in the great insurance world filled most efficiently by experienced and trained accountants, but almost every member of the profession finds insurance a legitimate as well as a remunerative department of his business.

It will be observed that in this paper little more has been done than to outline the subject. The purpose in view will, however, have been served if I have succeeded, however imperfectly, in deepening the conviction, which I feel sure is entertained by every member of the society, that our profession is eminently fitted to fill a useful and honorable place in all our industrial communities. There, in a special degree, the guidance and assistance of the public ac-

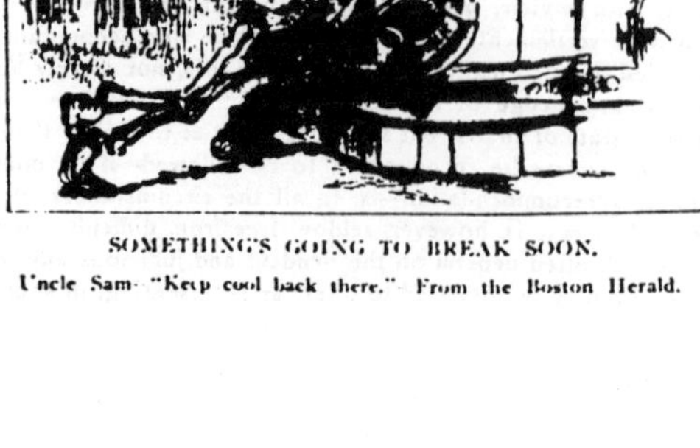

SOMETHING'S GOING TO BREAK SOON.

Uncle Sam—"Keep cool back there."—From the Boston Herald.

countant will be fully appreciated, and will be in constant requisition.

THE FUTURE OF THE PROFESSION.

Notable as has been the development in many directions, during recent years especially, of professional accountancy, it is in the highest degree probable that the future has still greater things in store for it. Progress is the great law of Nature, and as trade and commerce continue to make rapid strides, the profession may be relied upon not only to keep pace with it, but to contribute its full share to the general prosperity, until it receives more distinct and formal official recognition.

With a view to greater efficiency and usefulness, the profession has been steadily organizing itself, until the various institutes and societies now embrace within their membership a large proportion of the entire practicing members of the profession throughout the United Kingdom, besides many others holdng important official positions. The examinations prescribed by these various bodies sufficiently attest the high standard of qualification aimed at, and furnish a guarantee that candidates who pass successfully will prove an accession of strength and efficiency to their membership.

There is, however, an obvious drawback, which ought sooner or later to be remedied. Under existing circumstances there is nothing to hinder any one, no matter what his antecedents may have been, to begin business as an accountant, leaving the impression on the public that he is a thoroughly qualified practitioner, when, in point of fact, he may have been unsuccessful in some mercantile pursuit, and only fallen back on the accountancy profession when every other avenue seemed closed.

Such a state of matters is most unsatisfactory, and is injurious alike to the profession and to the mercantile community. We do not allow any one to practice law or medicine who has not undergone certain prescribed examinations, received the necessary certificate of qualification, and been duly enrolled as a qualified practitioner. Why, then, should not a similar regulation apply in the case of persons seeking to enter upon the accountancy profession, which confessedly requires a lengthened and severe course of training and study in order to thorough equipment for the discharge of its varied and responsible duties? This can only be satisfactorily done by legislation under which the names of all who passed the prescribed examinations would be entered on a register, and all others debarred from practicing who proposed to commence business as accountants after the passing of the act.

There could be no greater hardship in such a case—if hardship it could be regarded—than exists in connection with the professions of law and medicine, to which reference has already been made, and in regard to which there is universal satisfaction. To this end public opinion seems steadily tending, and, meantime, every step taken to promote professional efficiency, and thereby to impress the general business community with the claims of accountancy, will serve to bring about such changes as have been indicated, to the advantage alike of the profession and of all who have business relations with it.

CENTS AND NICKELS

At the Treasury Department they say that the cent is the barometer of business conditions. A heavy storm or sudden coming of cold weather—anything, in short, that keeps the penny-spending part of the population at home—is accurately reflected in the falling off of the cents coming to the sub-treasuries for exchange, says an exchange. During periods of dulness cents accumulated at sub-treasuries, but when trade revives they begin to circulate rapidly again.

The United States Treasury, during the fiscal year which has just ended, manufactured 79,611,143 cents and 26,470,213 nickels.

The cent-making machines in the mint at Philadelphia are constantly turning out pennies all the year round.

Up to date, Uncle Sam has turned out 1,100,000,000 cents, 240,000,000 nickes, 100,000,000 dimes, 200,000,000 quarters and 150,000,000 half-dollars.

AMERICAN DIPLOMACY.

The key that opens China to the world's commerce.—From the Denver Republican.

Somewhere in the world are 119,000,000 big copper pennies. What has become of them is a mystery, for, barring a few in the hands of collectors, they have disappeared, no one knows where.

Many years ago the government issued 4,500,000 bronze 2-cent pieces, and of those over 3,000,000 are still outstanding.

The same is true of the nickel 3-cent pieces, of which nearly 2,000,000 are unaccounted for.

Slot machines have greatly increased the demand for coppers, and so also have the penny newspapers and the odd prices made popular in dry goods shops.

The "life" of a cent is only four or five years, because it changes hands ten times for once that a half-dollar is moved from one person's pocket to another's.

All worn-out pieces are melted for recoinage, and on every $1,000 thus reminted the government loses nearly $30.

Cents are subject to more accidents than any other coins. Being of such small value, very little care is taken of them.

MORGAN'S TIPS

"My tips to servants on the Oceanic 'amounted' to $13," said a traveler who came over with J. Pierpont Morgan, according to the Detroit News. "The rule is to give $2.50 to the table steward, $2.50 to the bedroom steward, $1 to the bathroom steward, $2 to the check steward, $2 to the smoking-room steward, $1 to the shoeshine steward, and $5 to the chief steward in case he has performed special courtesies. As these special courtesies were wanting on my trip, I cut the chief steward out and gave the deck steward $4, because he took excellent care of me, reserving the best place for my steamer chair, etc. I saw Morgan give the chief steward $100, and it was generally understood among the help that all would fare in proportion. I guess he gave the table steward $50."

NAME WAS FAMILIAR

In a Philadelphia kindergarten a teacher was telling the little children about a clock. "Now, this," she said, "is the pendulum—this thing that swings back and forth. Did any of you ever hear the word 'pendulum' before?" A child put up her hand. "Yes, teacher," she said. "Pendulum Franklin. I've heard it often."

MIND READER NEEDED

Old Gent (dictating indignant letter)—Sir, my stenographer, being a lady, cannot take down what I think of you; I, being a gentleman, cannot think it; but you, being neither, can easily guess what my thoughts might be.

Systematic Advertising

Every business man of the present day is more or less of an advertiser. In this assertion we use the term advertising in its broad and most expanded meaning, embracing all kinds of publicity. Newspaper advertising is included as a subdivision or a mere department, as is likewise the advertising done by means of circulars, pamphlets, catalogues, etc. While every man is more or less of an advertiser there are a few, who, by reason of the kind of business in which they are engaged, have forced upon them the necessity of becoming large advertisers. They have forced upon them the necessity of spending considerable sums of money each year in the introduction of the goods they are making, or in sustaining the markets already opened to those goods.

The art of advertising has been expounded by many writers, but for the most part the instruction has been from those who were discussing advertising for no better purpose than to direct the attention of the public to themselves as experts, either in the art of phrasing advertisements, or in typographical embellishments, or appropriate illustrations, or some other minor division of the work. The opportunity still remains for some one to discuss the art of publicity in a scientific and unprejudiced way.

Systematic advertising will be an important division of such a work as the able author who undertakes to discuss advertising in the broad sense shall attempt to produce for the benefit of the public. We imagine one of the illustrations he will employ in this book will be drawn from the work of some of the railway companies which maintain systematic advertising—just as they sustain train schedules, always on time and up to date.

There is no better illustration of this particular class of advertising than that found in the work of George H. Daniels, general passenger agent of the New York Central & Hudson River Railroad, and exemplified in what has been familiarly named "The Four-Track Series." This, according to the catalogue before us, had reached, up to a few months ago, the respectable number of thirty-five different titles, not including the "Monthly Magazine of Travel and Education" known as "The Four-Track News." Further, eight etchings, executed by photogravure process and printed on heavy plate paper, 24 by 32 inches, and ready for framing, are also among the work referred to, but not included in the catalogue count.

We risk nothing in saying that for general information there is far more in this collection than in what comprised the entire library of our grandfathers, who were able to get over the country only with the meagre comforts of the old-time stage coach. It is a liberal education in itself to go through what has been gathered together under this head, and more and more does the wonder of the reader increase when he realizes that all that has been presented is not simply for his edification, but to impress upon him the moral, "When you travel, go by the New York Central lines."

In an article like this we cannot even give all the titles of the good things before us, much less describe them in detail. Suffice it, then, that we take up one or two at random as an indication of what the general lot comprises.

We are all interested in Asia and the Chinese Empire, and where shall we find a map of these important localities, as they are today, equal to that now offered to view? Four-Track Series No. 28 contains just such maps as we want for the purpose, and far better than are ordinarily to be found in most up-to-date cyclopaedias and atlases. They are accompanied by a carefully prepared article, entitled "China and the Chinese," as they appear to an American who spent twenty years in the "Flowery Kingdom," written by Guy Morrison Walker.

Perhaps some of the most effective advertising that is done anywhere is accomplished by sharp contrast. What then must be the effect upon the readers' mind when, right in the midst of a paragraph on the antiquity of China, to have thrust upon his attention an elegant photogravure of a view in the Mohawk Valley, with four parallel tracks in the foreground and a rapidly approaching train in the distance? Again, returning to the text, he reads on, and after he gets fully engrossed in the subject of Foreign Intercourse, wherein is explained how the first great traveler to reach China was Marco Polo, what must be his feelings when there is thrust upon his attention a magnificent view of the new Central-Atlantic type locomotive hauling the through passenger trains of the New York Central lines? This we take to be the secret of the strength of the advertising in the Four-Track Series. There is given something that the reader wants to know. It is given freely and without stint, and of a quality beyond comparison, but at the same time he is never allowed to forget that it is with the compliments of the New York Central, whose railroad and railway equipments are of the best, that the thing is put into his hands.

Following the able article by Mr. Walker is a paragraph with respect to the pronunciation and meaning of various Chinese names. The next page is devoted to some hotel advertisements, including the Iroquois, of Buffalo, and the Grand Union, of Saratoga Springs. The other pages of the outside of the folder are taken up with general information regarding China, being an alphabetical list of prominent persons and places frequently referred to in dispatches from the Orient. The sandwiching in this part contains portraits of the captains of various steamships reaching New York who are also agents for the New York Central road, and who meet passengers on the pier on their arrival in port. There is likewise a magnificent view of Niagara Falls and some minor advertisements.

The map side of the folder contains, first, a finely engraved map of the Chinese Empire, including Japan and Korea, prepared by Rand, McNally & Co.; and, second, a general map of Asia to smaller scale from the same map publishers. The maps are in colors, and, as before stated, are superior to what ordinarily appears in atlases and encyclopaedias. Some of the auxiliary information presented is a list of treaty ports, with the estimated Chinese population, and the value of imports and exports, a table of distances in American miles by the common routes of travel between various prominent points in China, etc.

Of course, the New York Central, in putting out an article of this kind, the cost of which must have necessarily been a considerable sum, does not fail in all appropriate ways to impress upon the reader that in any globe-trotting scheme the New York Central is a very important link, and that therefore it should not be forgotten in marking the route that is to be followed.

To show how thoroughly up to date, as well as systematic, is the advertising managed by George H. Daniels, general passenger agent of the New York Central lines, we have only to refer to what is called Census Booklet No. 1, and which was compiled from advance sheets of the twelfth United States census, and which has become No. 13 of the Four-Track Series. It is devoted particularly to the urban population of the country in the year 1900. Among the tables presented in it is one showing the cities in the United States with more than 100,000 inhabitants, each arranged according to rank. In order to emphasize the ultility of the New York Central lines, those which are reached by these lines are printed in full-faced type, and one is surprised to see the large number of full-face names that it contains. There are 38 cities in all mentioned with a total population of upwards of 14,000,000. Of these no less than 19 are touched by the New York Central lines, and these 19 contain a population of upwards of 9,500,000.

Another table shows the cities and towns in the United

States with more than 8,000 population, giving a comparison of the census of 1900 with that of 1890, and likewise distinguishing those which are on the New York Central lines and those which are located elsewhere in the United States. Of the entire number of towns thus enumerated those having a population of 12,645,000 are reached by New York Central lines, while all the others have a population of only 12,120,000. There next appears in the folder a map of the United States, including Mexico and the West Indian Islands, with a red-line space marked out showing the territory dominated by the New York Central, with various statistical deductions drawn from it. The principal map in the pamphlet, being this red-line space enlarged, shows places of over 100,000 inhabitants by a certain form of mark, and places from 8,000 to 10,000 by another mark. This map only accentuates and emphasizes what is shown by the table of statistics above referred to. Other pages of the folder contain various advertisements more or less pertinent to the New York Central lines.

As before mentioned, it will be impossible to do justice to the entire series in such an article as this. By way of conclusion, therefore, we can only give very briefly the names of some of the others. One that we pick up is entitled "Three Ways to Go to New York." The first of these is via the New York Central, and by what precedes it would seem that a very large proportion of the people of the United States in going from their homes to the metropolis would not have to go far out of their way to travel by the New York Central lines. The second way is by water in sunlight, that is, down the Hudson River by daylight. And then for the third there is the alternative of going down the Hudson by night. All of these various ways are amply illustrated by photo-views showing the places of interest, steamers, etc.

"The Railroad and the Dictionary" is the title of another of the booklets before us. In this the compiler has borrowed from the Century Dictionary various words and terms relating to railway construction and travel, and has arranged in attractive form the definitions and illustrations that apply to the same. Any one who takes this little book with him to read while en route will learn more of what makes his trip safe and pleasant than would otherwise be easy to accomplish.

"The Luxury of Modern Railway Travel" was the first of the Four-Track Series put out, and still holds its own by way of favor. It shows by exquisite illustrations the standard New York Central passenger engine, a view in a buffet and cafe car, the interior of a sleeping-car, the interior of a compartment-car, the interior of a drawing-room car, the interior of a dining-car, and the interior of an ordinary passenger coach. There are still other illustrations, all of a general character, including a number of views of buildings, and a folded diagram illustrating a complete vestibule train made up of the different cars above enumerated.

No. 6 of the Four-Track Series is entitled "The Adirondack Mountains." No. 20 is entitled "The Adirondack Mountains and How to Reach Them." They are in nowise competitors in contents, but are both useful to any one who has a fondness for wild scenery, hunting, fishing, etc. They are companions, and should be taken together.

"Real Rapid Transit," being No. 23, shows how people patronizing the New York Central lines reach ninety suburban towns out of New York. This pamphlet is of particular interest to those who are looking not only for homes in the suburbs, but for factory sites as well. The local fare is quoted, with nomination of excursion rate, monthly commutation rate and the price of the family ticket.

"American Railroads, Their Relation to Commercial, Industrial and Agricultural Interests," being a reprint of an address by George H. Daniels, general passenger agent of the New York Central lines, before the International Congress of Philadelphia, in October, 1899, is also in the series. It contains just such common sense talk, supported by statistics and arguments of the strongest logic, as one would expect from such an eminently practical business man as is this orator and manager.

We reluctantly put aside, as being too many for this notice, pamphlets bearing such titles as "America's Winter Resorts," "Sailings of Ocean Steamships," "To Ottawa, Ontario, via the Rideau Lakes and Rivers," "America's Summer Resorts," "The Thousand Islands," "Two Days at Niagara Falls," "Race with the Australian-London Mail," "Round the World by Way of New York and Niagara Falls in 60 to 80 Days," only to give attention to one which, perhaps, the reader has already seen and appreciated, namely, that famous reprint of "A Message to Garcia," by Elbert Hubbard, editor and publisher of the "Philistine." The copy before us is one of the second half-million edition. We have never learned just how many copies of this most excellent essay were printed and circulated by the New York Central, but that they were numerous is evident by the figures above, and still more by the fact that almost everybody has through this means read this famous bit of instruction and advice. It is more than a sermon. It is a standard treatise; it is a code; in short, it is something that every young man should have. It is something that every proprietor and business manager should see that his clerks read and comprehend.

Most of the Four-Track Series are sent only on receipt of from five to ten cents each for postage and mailing, but this particular item, being No. 25 of the series, is sent free, postpaid, to any address in the world. We suggest that the reader, if he has not already had a copy, apply for the same. Address George H. Daniels, general passenger agent, Grand Central Station, New York, mentioning this notice.

OLD FROSTY'S SALUTATION.

"Good morning; have you got in your winter's coal?"—From the Cleveland Plain Dealer.

A NEW EXPERIENCE

It is told of the late P. D. Armour that on one occasion he made a present of a suit of clothes to each of his employees in a certain department. Each man was told that he might order his own suit and send the bill to Mr. Armour, no restrictions being made as to price. In order to avail himself fully of this liberality, one young man ordered evening clothes costing $80. When the bill was sent in, Mr. Armour sent for the clerk to vouch for its accuracy, and, finding it right, assured the man it would be paid. As the clerk was leaving, however, Mr. Armour said to him: "I wish to say to you that I have packed a great many hogs in my time, but I never dressed one before!"

THE UP-TO-DATE KAISER

In pursuance of Emperor William's desire to adopt good American things, the Prussian railroad minister has ordered the adoption of the American baggage check system.

COMMERCE ACCOUNTS & FINANCE

A Magazine of Higher Business Education and Practical Administration. Acknowledged Authority in the Profession of Commerce and Consistent Advocate of Methods Up to Date and Above the Table.

JOSEPH CROSBY LINCOLN, - - - - Editor.
FRIEND PITTS, JR., - Circulation and Advertising.
E. R. KITTREDGE, - - - Business Manager.

PUBLISHED MONTHLY

SUBSCRIPTION $1 a Year in the United States, Canada and Mexico. Other countries $1.50. Postage prepaid by the Publishers. In the absence of specific orders to stop at the end of the subscription term the paper will be continued and a bill sent. Entered at the New York Postoffice as Second Class mail matter.

COMMERCE, ACCOUNTS & FINANCE COMPANY, Publishers
Twenty-five Pine Street, New York

We sometimes hear men of middle age, when discussing their own affairs and prospects, expressing the regret that they were not bred to a profession. "I wish I had a profession," says one, meaning thereby that at present he is only a business man. It seems to us that no one who has a proper appreciation of business, and the opportunities which business presents, and the recompense which business affords, can wittingly give expression to such ideas. The contra inquiry would be, Why not make a profession of business? It must be from an inspection of the smaller offices of business that any one is lead to express a wish such as appears above, for whoever inspects the work of a business man who has the higher responsibilities resting upon him, must know that in the exercise of those functions he brings to bear a broader education than many so-called professional men have as their equipment. The question then arises, Why not make a profession of business, or of some department of business—as, for example, a profession of selling, a profession of buying, a profession of management, or a profession of administration? Business is progressive, and of late has been progressing at a rate that few have comprehended. It is demanding more and more in the way of education and specialization and peculiarity of ability. The profession is there, although it is to be admitted it is not marked by any three letters after the name if any one chances to look for it.

* * *

Among the correspondence, which appears in another part of this issue, is a letter written by an old commercial school man, who calls up the echoes of the controversy in which Vannant was engaged in these columns a few months since. Our correspondent's special reason in writing at this time was to answer something that was said in our last number about the compensation offered for a teacher of bookkeeping, etc. We are glad to publish his letter for various reasons. It is evidently sincere, and it gives expression to views which we are sure are held by a very large number of those who are engaged in commercial education. Our correspondent, after making due allowances for the heated controversy and the things that were said upon the subject under such conditions, admits for the most part that the contentions have been based upon facts. This is admitting quite enough, and is a fitting way of bringing the controversy to a conclusion. COMMERCE, ACCOUNTS & FINANCE has no object to gain in all that it publishes except to serve the business public. It is not opposed to the schools, but instead is very much in favor of them. It does not believe in humbug or misrepresentation, but does believe in a square fight in the open field.

*

As long ago as when there was appearing in these columns a controversy between Vannant on the one side and the commercial teachers of the country on the other, a desire was expressed by several to have the identity of Vannant revealed. As many of our readers will recall, the proposition was made at that time to publish a composite picture, with Vannant in the center and his critics arranged around, and we solicited photographs from those who had been engaged in this controversy for the purpose, having first exacted from Vannant the promise to put in his exhibit. The offer has been standing all these months without a single response, and we have just returned to Vannant that which he offered us, and pen these lines for the purpose of declaring the matter closed and the offer withdrawn.

THE 1804 DOLLAR

The immortal 1804 dollar crops up in a new guise. The Central Government would make the rest of the world feel easy if it would issue an official history of this much-discussed coin and set at rest forever the numerous versions of the story of its minting, circulation, distribution, recalling and ultimate destruction, says the New York Press. The latest fiction is that only 1,900 of these dollars were coined, and that all were recalled except four. Referring to the report of the director of the mint, I learn that the actual number coined was 19,570. The belief of most numismatics is that the number in existence is from seven to nine. The value is from $600 to $4,500. Captain Abbott of the Treasury Secret Service, recently found a long-lost one in Lima, Ohio, which is worth $3,000 if genuine. A German is said to have received it as pay in South America, many years ago.

There are numerous counterfeits bearing the date of 1804. They are generally made of the 1801, which bears a close resemblance to the coveted 1804, by cutting out the "1" and inserting a "4" in its place. Any scratches or depressions about the date are sure indications of falsity. There are also re-strikes, made with the original dies, but at a later date, and as they did not have the collar, the lettering around the edge is irregular, as it was put on by hand afterward. An old friend of mine is in possession of a perfect specimen of this dollar—so far as the design is concerned. The metal, however, is lead. He acquired it under peculiar circumstances.

In an article on coins, this friend said that no successful counterfeit of the 1804 dollar had been made. In reply, he received by mail a packet containing the lead one, accompanied by a letter from an anonymous correspondent. The handwriting was exquisite and the phraseology that of a person of education and taste. After going into a complete history of the original coin, the writer closed as follows: "I send this to you as a token of esteem and a sign of friendship. Keep it for my sake. Remember that it comes from one whose freedom would hardly be encouraged were his name and vocation to become known, therefore the name I sign is a fiction. I present it on condition that you never publish what I have written." As death usually is regarded as lifting the embargo, my friend permitted me to read the letter and to publish the foregoing extract, for he learned recently that his anonymous acquaintance is dead.

The genuine 1804 dollar has on the obverse side the head of Liberty turned toward the right; flowing hair tied back with a ribbon in a large, loose knot; "Liberty" above, "1804" beneath; seven stars on the left and six on the right, around the edge. Reverse: The customary E Pluribus Unum, eagle and shield; "United States of America" around the edge; thirteen stars clustered between the eagle and the scroll work under "States of." It is a strikingly handsome coin.

The Stock Broker and His Customer

By THOMAS B. PERKINS

In looking over the columns of this paper I have noted inquiries from various readers, said readers being located in small cities and towns far from the great centers, begging to be enlightened as to the method by which stock dealing is carried on by the broker and his customer. The readers who have written these letters live where there are no great stock exchanges, and yet where in the syndicate pages of their daily or weekly papers they see daily reference to "panics in Wall Street," "great booms in industrials," "slumps," "puts," "calls," and so on.

It is not my purpose in this article to give in detail the methods of dealing between brokers on the floor of the stock exchange, but merely to reprint a magazine article published some years ago, the writer of which narrates in an interesting way the manner in which a small buyer of stocks buys and sells on a margin in the average broker's office. The quotations and illustrations have been brought up to date, and I think many readers will find the article as interesting as I found it.

In nearly all the buildings in the vicinity of Wall Street, New York, are scores of brokers' offices, in which six days in the week, year in and year out, thousands of dollars are risked in stock speculation. Some of these offices are luxuriously furnished, with private apartments for special customers, while many others are bare, save for the few fixtures necessary for the rapid transaction of business. Some of the customers who frequent these brokers' offices are wealthy men, who daily invest thousands of dollars in stocks. Of them, however, we shall have nothing to say, preferring to describe the dealings of the "little fellow," the confirmed stock dabbler of comparatively few dollars, but large hopes. Nearly all the trading done by the last named is on a small margin, of from five to ten dollars per share, and in consequence the small capitalist is often enabled to derive the profit from a considerable block of stock with relatively but a small investment. As the clock on the broker's wall nears ten, the circle of chairs, facing a huge blackboard, begin to fill with the habitues of the office, who are ready to buy or sell, as their judgment dictates.

In one corner of the room is the "ticker," which reels off the tape recording the sales made on the Stock Exchange, and from which the quotations on the blackboard are copied.

NEW YORK STOCK QUOTATIONS

	C.&O.	MO.P.	READING	SO.P.	WIS.CT.	WEST.UN.TEL.	PENN.R.R.	MAN.EL.	UNION P.	ERIE	AM.SUG.	LOUIS.&NASH.	MET.ST.RY.	BALT.&OHIO	U.S.STEEL
CLOSED	54	121⅞	73⅞	78⅛	30⅝	95⅞	167	136	110⅞	41	130⅞	162⅞	145⅞	114¼	40⅞
OPEN...	52⅞	120⅞	73⅜	77⅞	28⅝		166⅞		109⅜	41⅛	130	163⅞	145⅜		40½
HIGH...	53⅜	121½	74	79	30½						130¼	163⅜			
LOW...	51⅞	120⅞	72⅜	77⅞	28⅜										
	52⅞ 52 51⅞ 53 [illegible]	120⅞ ⅞ 121 [illegible]	73⅞ ¼ [illegible] 74 73⅜	77⅞ 78 [illegible] 79 78	30⅛ ¼		166⅞		109⅞ 110 ⅞	41⅝ 40 ⅞	130⅛	162⅞ ¼ ⅞	145⅜ ¼ ⅜ ½		40¼ ⅞
HIGH...	56	122	74⅜	79	28½	96	167	135½	110⅛	41⅛	131⅛	164½	147	116¾	41
LOW...	53⅞	119⅞	72⅜	77⅞	28⅞	94	166	134	108⅞	40⅜	129¼	162⅞	146	113⅞	40⅜

STOCK QUOTATIONS, AS SHOWN ON THE BLACKBOARD.

At five minutes to ten the broker bids his customers "good luck," and leaves for the floor of the Exchange to execute their orders, which are either given before the Exchange opens, or by means of the private telephone which connects the broker's office with the floor of the Exchange. The boy who chalks the quotations on the blackboard has been busy placing at the top the closing quotations of the day previous, and at the bottom the highest and lowest quotations recorded "yesterday." The young man in charge of the office has stationed himself near the private telephone, and exactly as the clock strikes ten, the first, or opening, quotation comes out on the "ticker." The boy calls out "C. & O., 200 shares at 52½," and chalks the figures in the space marked "open" near the top of the blackboard. The "ticker" rapidly reels off the sales, and before the first quarter-hour has passed tens of thousands of shares have been bought and sold with a rapidity which is bewildering to a novice in stock speculation.

AN ILLUSTRATIVE SPECULATION.

As each sale is noted by the "ticker," the boy calls out the price, and if it varies from the last quotation he chalks the price upon the blackboard in the division reserved for that particular stock.

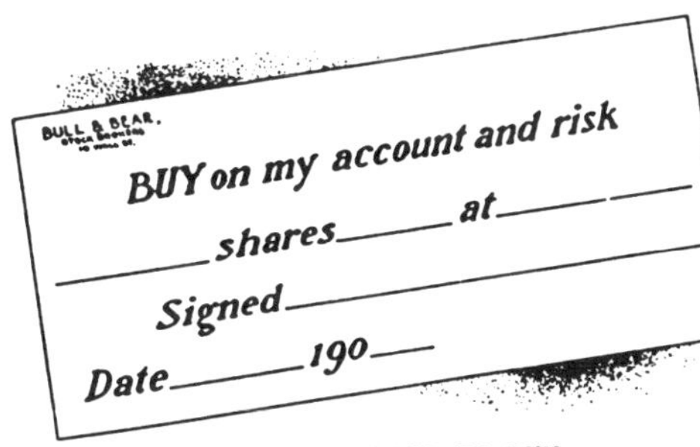

CUSTOMER'S ORDER TO BUY.

Just for the sake of illustration, suppose we are sitting facing the blackboard, and feel an inclination to "try our luck." The first thing to do is to step up to "the Captain's office," as the cashier's desk is called, and hand over, say, two hundred dollars as a deposit against our transactions. The cashier takes our money and gives us a receipt, and we resume our place and carefully watch the blackboard to determine whether it is safer to buy or to sell. Quite likely we decide that "C. & O." is remarkably cheap at 52½, and thereupon we instruct the young man at the telephone to "Buy twenty shares of C. & O. at market or better, one per cent stop loss."

The order has been instantly wired to the broker on the floor of the Exchange, and while we are waiting for the purchase to be effected we watch the blackboard for such fluctuations as may be announced over the "ticker." A moment later the telephone bell rings, and the attendant calls out, "Bought twenty C. & O. at 52⅝, sell at 51⅝." We note that the purchase was effected at an advance of ⅛ per cent over the blackboard quotation, which, however, is to be accounted for from the fact of twenty shares being "a fractional lot," and therefore not obtainable at the same figures as one hundred-share lots, which represent the quotations.

Our deposit with the broker was but two hundred dollars, yet we have purchased twenty shares of stock at $52.62 per share, or a total value of $1,052.40. The two hundred dollars we deposited is therefore the "margin" on the stock, which in this case was ten dollars a share, as it is called on the Exchange, "ten per cent margin."

We do not propose, however, to risk more than twenty dollars on the transaction, and therefore we stated in giving our order, "One per cent, stop loss," which means that in case the price drops one dollar below what we paid, which would be 51⅝, our stock is to be at once closed out at market price.

OUR INTERESTED NEIGHBORS.

The blackboard now begins to deeply interest us, as we have made a venture, and we watch the rise and fall of quotations in "C. & O." with the closest of attention. We also watch the quotations on the other stocks, as there is a sort of sympathy in stock quotations, which is common to the condition of the market. Perhaps our neighbor in the next chair is a "bear," and nearly frightens us out of a year's growth by his remarks about the low earnings of Western railroads and the general depression in business. But he is a "bear," and these well-known Wall Street animals view all things with a dubious eye, and thrive on panics and reports of failures. Quite likely this particular "bear" is "short" of "C. & O.," and is trembling in his boots for fear the price will advance before he can safely unload.

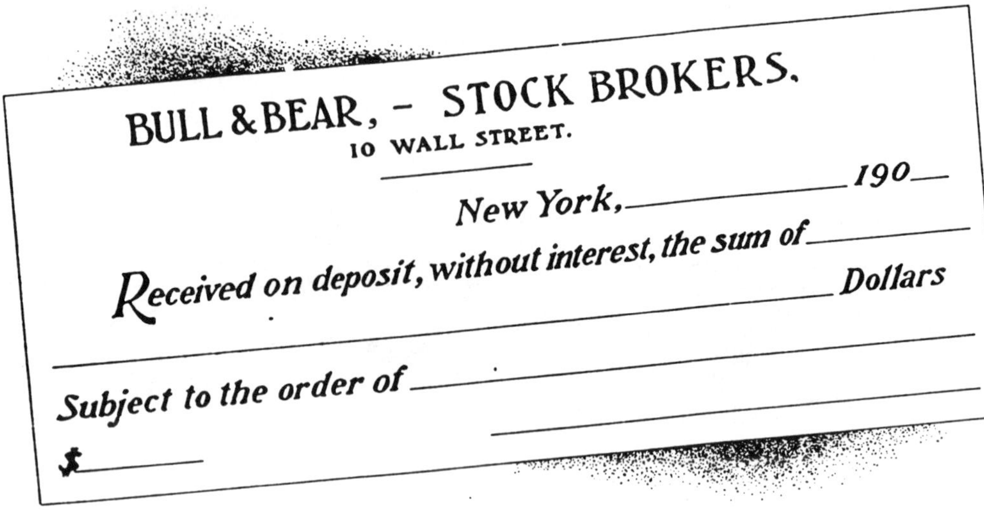

BULL & BEAR, - STOCK BROKERS.
10 WALL STREET.

New York, ______ 190__

Received on deposit, without interest, the sum of ______ Dollars

Subject to the order of ______

$______

BROKER'S RECEIPT FOR CUSTOMER'S CASH DEPOSIT.

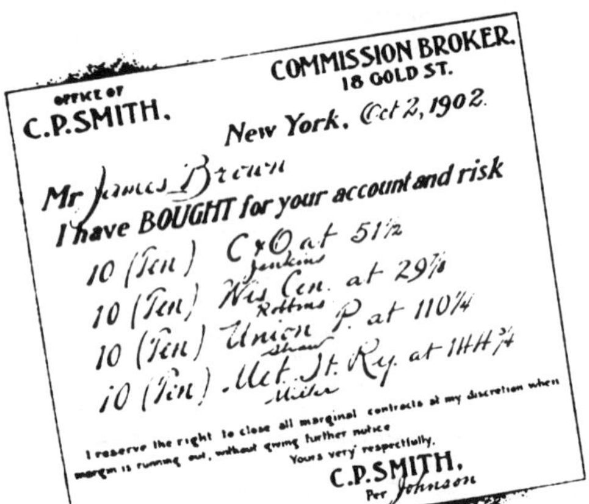

OFFICE OF C.P.SMITH. COMMISSION BROKER. 18 GOLD ST.

New York, Oct 2, 1902.

Mr James Brown

I have BOUGHT for your account and risk

10 (Ten) C & O at 51½ Jenkins
10 (Ten) Wis Cen. at 29⅞ Robbins
10 (Ten) Union P. at 110¼ Shaw
10 (Ten) Met St. Ry. at 144¾ Miller

I reserve the right to close all marginal contracts at my discretion when margin is running out, without giving further notice.

Yours very respectfully,
C.P.SMITH,
Per Johnson

BROKER'S NOTIFICATION TO CUSTOMER OF STOCKS PURCHASED.

Our neighbor on the other side may be a sanguine "bull," and feels confident that every stock on the list is selling for just half its value. "C. & O." will go far in ten days, in his opinion. If we listen with our left ear, the market is on the verge of a panic; if with our right ear, there is to be a boom in stocks which will cause our modest twenty shares to take on an air of importance which is exceedingly fascinating. However, we will not plan for spending the profits just yet, for stocks, like women, are "mighty unsartin."

The cashier hands us a little slip of paper to sign, acknowledging the purchase we have made and the price at which to sell in case the market should decline. Should the price advance before declining to our stop order, we might take such profit as we deemed advisable, not having placed any limit to the amount of profit at time of giving the order. We can also cancel the "stop loss order" before the market turns 51⅝, and place it lower or higher as we may think best; but in any event the broker will sell out the stock should it decline to within a fixed percentage of one per cent. of the amount on deposit. This precaution on his part is necessary to secure him from loss, as he is carrying the difference in the total cost of the stock and the amount deposited, which represents an investment on his part of over eight hundred dollars.

The "ticker" continues to record the sales, and the boy industriously chalks them on the board, quite regardless of the immense amounts of money which the fluctuations represent. Presently there is a movement in the quotations of "C. & O.," and the price begins to tumble from 52⅝ to 52½—52—51⅞, and there remains steady for awhile at the last-named figure. Our hopes of profit are now very feeble, for the market is three-quarters of a per cent below the figure at which we purchased, and dangerously near the "stop loss order" point.

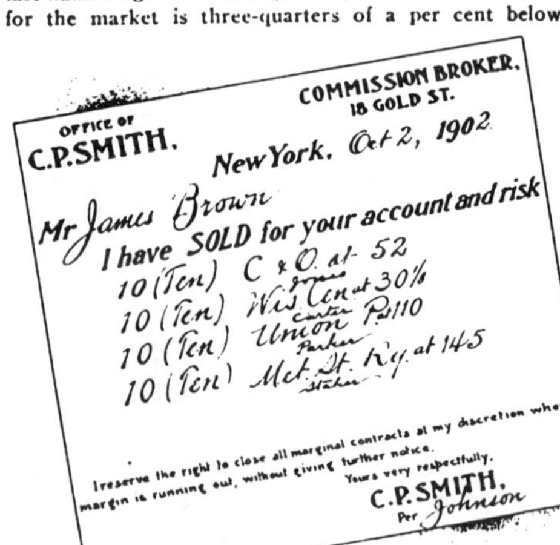

OFFICE OF C.P.SMITH. COMMISSION BROKER. 18 GOLD ST.

New York, Oct 2, 1902

Mr James Brown

I have SOLD for your account and risk

10 (Ten) C & O. at 52 Jones
10 (Ten) Wis Cen at 30⅛ Carter
10 (Ten) Union P. at 110 Parker
10 (Ten) Met St. Ry. at 145 Stokes

I reserve the right to close all marginal contracts at my discretion when margin is running out, without giving further notice.

Yours very respectfully,
C.P.SMITH,
Per Johnson

BROKER'S NOTIFICATION TO CUSTOMER OF STOCKS SOLD.

ANXIOUS MOMENTS.

A rumor goes around the room that "C. & O." is going

to heavily decline, because some thousands of shares have been suddenly thrown on the market. Our "bear" neighbor begins to feel in his element, and says he knew "C. & O." was altogether too high for a safe purchase. While we are considering the advisability of ordering our stop order placed still lower, the boy calls out "C. & O., five hundred shares at 52," and the bubble in the thermometer of hope rises again. Another rumor now goes the rounds to the effect that there are a number of speculators heavily "short" of "C. & O.," and that they are bidding up the stock in their efforts to "cover." This seems to be apparently true, for the quotations continue to advance by $\frac{1}{8}$ and $\frac{1}{4}$ per cent, until $53\frac{3}{4}$ is reached, when the market is without life, and no sales are reported for ten minutes. The "bull" neighbor on our right hopefully states that "C. & O." will reach 75 before three o'clock, and wants to bet a silk hat that it will touch par before it declines to 50. No one seems to care for the hat, and his confident assertion apparently worries the "bears" in the room, who have sold the stock in anticipation of a sharp decline.

Believing that "a bird in the hand is better than two in the bush," we do not wait for further advance, but order the young man at the telephone to "sell twenty C. & O. at market and cancel stop order." The report comes back that our stock has been sold at $53\frac{7}{8}$, or $\frac{1}{8}$ per cent above the last sale noted on the blackboard. The stock having cost us $52\frac{5}{8}$, the net profit, after deducting the broker's commission of $\frac{1}{8}$ per cent each for selling and buying, is 1 per cent, or for the twenty shares $20.

Our balance with the broker is now $220, which we can either draw out in part or whole, or continue to speculate. In any event, we are objects of envy for some of the others in the room, for the winners of this huge game of chance are comparatively few. The ghosts of fortunes lost and their one-time owners hover around with a persistency pitiable in their hopeful hopelessness, but the man who daily increases his balance, and finally withdraws with the profits of a child of fortune with few brothers.

GOING "SHORT."

The operation known as "going short of the market," or selling stock with none on hand, in the expectation of buying at a lower figure when called upon to deliver, is not favorably considered by the outside public who occasionally "dabble in Wall Street," who, as a rule, prefer to "bull" the market.

The professional stock trader, however, is inclined to sell stocks before purchasing, and by his sales is often able to depress the market temporarily a few points until the timid public closes out its stock at the lowest point, and then puts the difference into the pocket of the professional "bear" trader. The method of selling stocks is conducted on the same plan as buying, the amount deposited with the broker being the margin between the price at which the stock is sold and the quotations on the Stock Exchange. If the price of the stock advances after the sale, and the margin deposited becomes exhausted, the broker buys in the stock to protect himself from loss. On the contrary, should the price of the stock decline, after the sale the customer can take his profit by buying in the stock at a favorable moment.

A number of speculators, and occasional investors in stocks, have one or more rules for buying or selling, upon which they place great reliance, but the only method known which will insure a profit with certainty is to "buy when they are down and sell when they are up"—but the "when"; aye, there's the rub.

The Negotiable Instruments Law*

By THOMAS B. PATON

Place of Presentment—Where Place of Payment is Specified—Where it is General—Where Debtor is Dead—Presentment to Joint Debtors

NOTE.—As enacted in New York, the Negotiable Instruments Law is divided into nineteen articles as follows:—

1. GENERAL PROVISIONS (Sections 1—17)
2. NEGOTIABLE INSTRUMENTS: Form and Interpretation (20—42)
3. Consideration (50—56)
4. Negotiation (60—80)
5. Rights of holder (90—98)
6. Liabilities of parties (110—119)
7. Presentment for payment (130—148)
8. Notice of Dishonor (160—189)
9. Discharge (200—206)
10. BILLS OF EXCHANGE (210—215)
11. Acceptance (220—230)
12. Presentment for acceptance (240—248)
13. Protest (260—268)
14. Acceptance for honor (280—290)
15. Payment for honor (300—306)
16. Bills in a set (310—315)
17. PROMISSORY NOTES AND CHECKS (320—325)
18. Notes given for patent rights (330—332)
19. Laws repealed: When takes effect (340—341)

The provisions of the law naturally fall under four general classifications.

a. General Provisions.
b. Negotiable Instruments in General.
c. Bills of Exchange.
d. Promissory Notes and Checks.

The text of the law is the same in all the states (with some slight exceptions which will be noted), but the numbering of the sections, and in some states of the articles, is not uniform. There is, however, the same continuity of articles and text, except that in some instances, "General Provisions" follow, instead of precede, the remainder of the act. By following this course of study with reference to the New York act, as above outlined, the reader in each state can apply the same to the law of his own state.

We come now to the next provision of Section 132, providing the requirements for sufficiency of presentment, relating to the place at which presentment must be made.

"Presentment for payment to be sufficient, must be made . . . 3. At a proper place as here defined."

In this connection we must consider Section 133, which defines such proper place:—

Sec. 133. Place of Presentment.—Presentment for payment is made at the proper place.

1. Where a place of payment is specified in the instrument and it is there presented;
2. Where no place of payment is specified, but the address of the person to make payment is given in the instrument and it is there presented;
3. Where no place of payment is specified and no address is given and the instrument is presented at the usual place of business or residence of the person to make payment.
4. In any other case if presented to the person to make payment wherever he can be found, or if presented at his

THE FARMER IS SATISFIED.

"I don't see nothin' to grumble at!"—From the Cleveland Plain Dealer.

*Republished from the Banking Law Journal by permission. Copyright, 1899, 1900, 1901 and 1902, by T. B. Paton, all rights reserved. To be revised and published in book form by the author.

last known place of business or residence.

INSTRUMENTS WHERE PLACE OF PAYMENT IS SPECIFIED.

Let us take up these provisions in detail. First, we have those classes of instrument which specify therein a place of payment. For example, a promissory note drawn by A to the order of B, and made payable "at the First National Bank, New York"; or "at my office, No. 1 Broadway, New York"; or a bill of exchange drawn by A upon B to order of C, payable at a particular bank, or place of business, and accepted by B according to its tenor; or a bill drawn upon B generally, but accepted payable at a particular place. To charge the drawer and indorsers of a bill of exchange, or the indorsers of a promissory note, so payable, presentment for payment must be made at the place so specified in the instrument. It will not do to present the instrument at any other place. As said by the Supreme Court of the United States in Cox v. Bank, 100 U. S., p. 712, speaking of a bill of exchange: "Cases arise where the drawer of a bill of exchange designates in the instrument the place of payment, and the decisions are that in such a case both the drawer and the indorser will be discharged unless the bill be there presented for payment at maturity."

An early case in North Carolina, Smith v. McLean, 2 Taylor, 72, will illustrate the rule as to the indorser of a promissory note, and show from what an early date it has been recognized in this country. The action was by the holder against the indorser of the following promissory note:—

> \$1,930. Fayetteville, N. C.
> 9th Nov., 1811.
>
> Six months after date I promise to pay to Mr. Hugh McLean, or order, one thousand nine hundred and thirty dollars, for value reveived, payable at the State Bank. D. Anderson.

At maturity, the holder presented this note to the maker at Fayetteville, who replied that he could not pay it then, and that it was unnecessary to present it at the bank, as there were no funds there to discharge it. The note was not presented at the bank, and the indorser was held discharged. The court said:—

"The note was made payable at the State Bank. The holder of a bill, payable at a particular place, must present it there when it falls due; otherwise the drawer is discharged. As between the holder and indorser, a promissory note payable at a particular place is precisely like a bill payable at a particular place, as between the holder and drawer. It is a part of the contract that the note should be presented at bank. Here, indeed, Anderson dispensed with such presentment. But that shall not affect McLean. His contract is that payment of the note should be demanded at the bank. Those terms must be complied with by the holder, else he cannot look to the indorser."

PRICE OF STOCK EXCHANGE SEATS.

Still marching onward and upward.—From the New York Tribune.

Of course, so far as the primary debtor, the acceptor of a bill or the maker of a note, is concerned, the effect of non-presentment is different. The nature and extent of their liability was fully discussed under Section 130.

ADDRESS GIVEN IN THE INSTRUMENT.

We next have to consider the place of presentment with reference to that class of instruments where, although no place of payment is specified in the body of the instrument, the address of the person is given in the instrument, and it is there presented. For example, where the address of the maker of a promissory note is added after his signature; or in the case of a bill of exchange, where the address as well as the name of the drawee is placed upon the bill, which is thereafter accepted without specification of a particular place of payment. Here, equally as in those cases where the place of payment is specified in the body of the instrument, presentment at the address given is necessary to charge the drawer and indorsers, or the indorsers alone, as the case may be. The law, we see, is peremptory: "Presentment for payment, to be sufficient, MUST be made . . . at a proper place as herein defined," and "presentment for payment is made at the proper place . . . where no place of payment is specified, but the address of the person to make payment is given in the instrument, and it is there presented." The address given, therefore, would seem to be the only proper place for presentment, and seemingly this is so, even though the maker or acceptor may have changed his address and located elsewhere in the interim between the execution and maturity of the instrument, or in cases where the address on the instrument is not, and never was, the correct address of the maker or drawee.

On this point the case of Cox v. Bank, 100 U. S., 704, is illustrative. The following bill of exchange was involved:—

> \$5,000. Hopkinsville, Ky.
> August 2, 1875.
>
> Eighty days after date pay to the order of J. C. Whitlock five thousand dollars, value received, and charge to account, renewing a bill for same amount and names due August 3, 1875.
>
> Merritt Cox.
>
> To Messrs. Cox & Cowan,
> New York, N. Y.

Written across the bill was:—

"Accepted: Cox & Cowan."

The bill was thus drawn and accepted at Hopkinsville, Ky., where all the above parties resided, both at the time of its date and maturity. The payee indorsed the bill to Wright & Co., of New York, who indorsed it to the bank. At maturity, the bank's notary made diligent but unsuccessful inquiry for the acceptors in New York City, and then protested the bill, and mailed notices to the drawer and payee at Hopkinsville. The question was whether presentment was at the proper place so as to make drawer and payee liable to the holder, and the court held that it was; that the bill was, in law, payable at New York City, and the presentment was sufficient. The court said that the bill having been addressed to the drawees at the city of New York, and they having accepted the same without qualification, explanation or condition, the bill became payable in that city, even though no mention was made of any dwelling, store or place of business where the bill should be presented.

WHERE PLACE OF PAYMENT IS GENERAL.

The provisions so far considered apply to instruments wherein the place of payment is particular—that is, where a particular place of payment is specified in the instrument itself, or where the particular address of the person to make payment is likewise specified. We now come to consider the provisions governing instruments wherein the place of payment is general—that is, where no place of payment is specified and no address of payor is given in the instrument. Presentment in such cases is governed by subdivisions 3 and 4 of Section 133.

"Presentment for payment is made at the proper place . . .

"3. Where no place of payment is specified and no address is given and the instrument is presented at the usual place of business or residence of the person to make payment.

"4. In any other case if presented to the person to make payment wherever he can be found, or if presented at his last known place of business or residence."

These provisions provide the general rules as to place of presentment where no place or address is specified in the instrument. In this connection it may be said that the date of a note at a particular place does not necessarily make that the place of payment, or at which payment should be demanded for the purpose of charging the indorser. While the date is presumptive evidence of the maker's residence at such place, if his actual place of business and residence is known by the holder to be elsewhere, payment must be demanded at the maker's place of business or residence, and not at the place where the note is dated. Various cases have arisen and been decided at common law, growing out of the maker's removal to another city or State or country, between the time of execution and of maturity of a promissory note, as well as cases where a maker resides in one city or State and gives his note dated at another. The detailed rules announced by the courts in all such cases supplement and amplify the general provisions of the Negotiable Instruments Law above set forth.

WHERE PERSON IS ABSENT.

We have now considered (1) by whom, (2) time of day, and (3) proper place at which presentment for payment, to be sufficient, must be made, as provided by Section 132. The final requisite of sufficiency, as therein set forth, concerns (4) to whom. The provision is:—

"Presentment for payment, to be sufficient, must be made . . .

"4. To the person primarily liable on the instrument, or if he is absent or inaccessible, to any person found at the place where the presentment is made."

Unless absent or inaccessible, presentment for payment must be made to the person primarily liable on the instrument. Who is such person? By Section 3 we have seen, "the person primarily liable on an instrument is the person who, by the terms of the instrument, is absolutely required to pay the same." In the case of a promissory note, therefore, this would be the maker. In the case of a bill of exchange, accepted by the drawee, it would be the acceptor. But how about a bill of exchange that does not require acceptance, but simply needs to be presented for payment—a bill payable on demand, or at sight, or on a day certain? To whom should such a bill be presented for payment? Do you say the drawee? Yes, that is the rule under the law merchant, but Section 211 of the act provides that "the drawee is not liable on the bill unless and until he accepts the same," and the act, as we have seen, requires that presentment for payment "must" be made "to the person primarily liable on the instrument," which the drawee is not, until he accepts it. Of course, the drawee is the only person to whom to present a bill of exchange not requiring acceptance for payment, but the authority for this is the law merchant, for the Negotiable Instruments Act fails to so provide. Subdivision 4, as it stands, is incomplete. It should have an additional clause making provision that presentment for payment of a bill of exchange, not requiring presentment, must be made to the drawee. The provision that presentment for payment

TO THE BUSINESS MAN.

The modern sword of Damocles.—From the Chicago News.

must be made to the person primarily liable does not cover such a case.

If the drawee, acceptor or maker is absent or inaccessible at the time of presentment, then the act gives the holder the option to comply with the requirement of sufficiency by making presentment to any person found at the place where the presentment is made.

MUST EXHIBIT THE INSTRUMENT.

We now reach the point where the holder of a negotiable instrument at a reasonable hour on a business day upon which the instrument is due, is at a proper place to make presentment for payment, and is about to make such presentment to the drawee, acceptor or maker, as the case may be, or in the absence or inaccessibility of such persons, to any other person there found. What must the holder then do to gain payment or to charge the indorser if payment is refused? He must exhibit the instrument, and if paid, must deliver it up. This is provided by

Sec. 134. Instrument Must Be Exhibited.—The instrument must be exhibited to the person from whom payment is demanded, and when it is paid, must be delivered up to the party paying it.

This provision is based on the rule of the law merchant that, except in special cases of lost notes, it is necessary, to constitute a valid demand, that the note must be produced and ready to be surrendered on payment. The rule has been thus stated in a Massachusetts case (Arnold v. Dresser, 8 Allen, 435: "No valid presentment and demand can be made by any person without having the note in his possession at the time, so that the maker may receive it in case he pays the amount due, unless special circumstances, such as the loss of the note, or its destruction, are shown to excuse its absence."

One of the national banks in New York City once lost recourse upon the indorser of a collateral note by failure to observe the spirit of this rule. It seems that a promissory note, secured by certain railroad bonds, had been indorsed to the bank and the collaterals transferred. At maturity, the bank's notary took the note, without the collaterals mentioned in it, to the maker and requested him to pay it. The maker demanded the production of the collaterals, and refused to pay without, informing the notary he would pay on the production of the collaterals. Thereupon the notary protested the note and gave the indorser notice, and this procedure was followed by an action by the bank against the indorser (Ocean Nat. Bank v. Fant, 50 N. Y., 474). The bank took the ground that the note was simply a negotiable promissory note, that its provisions respecting the collaterals did not change or modify its character, and that the demand was good without a tender of the collaterals. But the court held that the indorser was discharged. It said that an agreement to restore the collaterals to the maker on payment of the note was to be implied from the transaction as stated in the instrument itself, and that the acts should be simultaneous. The right of the maker to receive the collaterals when he should pay the note stood upon the same footing as his right to the surrender of the note itself, and that it would be most unreasonable to require the maker to pay such a note in the absence of the collaterals, which frequently consist of negotiable securities, and to trust to his legal remedies against the holder to recover them.

Upon this subject of production and exhibition of the instrument it has been held, however, that demand of payment without actual exhibition of the note is sufficient to hold the indorser in a case where the maker does not demand to see the instrument, but refuses payment for lack of funds. (Legg v. Vinal, 165 Mass., 555.)

An interesting speculation may here be indulged whether, if a bank holding an indorsed note for collection, should call the maker up over the telephone, describe the note and demand its payment, and the maker should reply that he had no funds and could not pay, without asking to see the instrument, this would be sufficient presentment to bind an indorser. We will not discuss this now.

WHERE DEBTOR IS DEAD.

We now approach Section 136, having considered Section 135 in connection with a previous section:—

Sec. 136 Presentment Where Principal Debtor Is Dead.—Where the person primarily liable on the instrument is dead, and no place of payment is specified, presentment for payment must be made to his personal representative, if such there be, and if with the exercise of reasonable diligence he can be found.

This section has relation to Subdivision 4 of Section 132, providing to whom presentment must be made, and covers presentment of instruments where the makers and acceptors are dead, which do not specify a place of payment. We have seen that where the person primarily liable is absent or inaccessible, presentment for payment can be made to any person found at the place; and not only does this rule apply in cases where the maker or acceptor is alive, but also in cases where, though dead, the instrument specifies a place of payment and it is there presented. But where the maker or acceptor is dead, and the instrument does not specify a place of payment, then it will not do to make presentment at the acceptor's or maker's former residence, if he has a personal representative who can, with reasonable diligence, be found, but presentment must be made to such personal representative. If, however, none has been appointed, then presentment for payment can be made to any person found at the maker's former place of residence.

The two next following sections also have relation to Subdivision 4 of Section 132, providing to whom presentment must be made. They cover cases where there is more than one person primarily liable on instruments wherein no place of payment is specified. Section 137 makes provision where such persons are partners, and Section 138 where they are joint debtors, not partners.

PERSONS LIABLE AS PARTNERS.

Sec. 137. Presentment to Persons Liable as Partners.—Where the persons primarily liable on the instruments are liable as partners, and no place of payment is specified, presentment for payment may be made to any one of them, even though there has been a dissolution of the firm.

In this case of partnerships as makers or acceptors of negotiable instruments, it is seen that it is optional with the holder to make presentment to any one of the partners, and that he is not obliged to make presentment to all; and that he has this option, even though there has been a dissolution of the firm prior to maturity of the instrument. This section embodies the common law rule, which is to the same effect. (See Gates v. Beecher, 60 N. Y., 518.) Under the law merchant, partners are but one person in legal contemplation, and a demand of one partner is regarded as equivalent to a demand of all. But with joint makers or debtors, not partners, the case is different. The following section embodies the rule of the law merchant as to presentment to joint debtors, not partners:—

Sec. 138. Presentment to Joint Debtors.—Where there are several persons, not partners, primarily liable on the instrument, and no place of payment is specified, presentment must be made to all.

The following extract from the opinion of Folger, J., in Gates v. Beecher, shows clearly the reasons why demand in the case of partners is sufficient if made upon one, and in the case of joint debtors, not partners, why it must be made upon all:—

"There is a distinction taken between the case of a note of joint makers who are not partners and a note of partners who are still partners at the maturity of the note. That distinction rests upon the fact that partners are but one person in legal contemplation; that each partner, acting in such capacity, is not only capable of performing what all can do, and of receiving and paying out that which belongs to all, but by such acts necessarily binds them all; that, as incident to such joint relations, all of the partners are affected by the knowledge of one. These things do not pertain to the relation of joint makers who are not partners. Hence, while a demand of one partner is equivalent to a demand of all, a demand of one of joint makers not partners is not. And so a demand upon one partner is sufficient, because he represents the firm, and a dishonor by one is a dishonor by all, and each is presumed to have authority to act for the others; while in the case of a note of joint makers not partners, the indorser has a right to rely upon the responsibility of all and each, and may insist upon a dishonor by each."

After showing that after dissolution each of the partners still continues to have a common interest and a common liability in the past transactions of the partnership, the judge says:—

"It being so, that the act of one of the former partners in relation to a valid subsisting liability of the late firm does affect the others, and is taken as their act, and his knowledge thereof as their knowledge, there seems no reason why a refusal of one to pay, on demand, a note of the partnership, should not be deemed to be a refusal of all, and all be chargeable therewith. And then, a demand of payment made to one is a demand of payment made to all, and is sufficient upon which to give notice of non-payment to their indorser. And further, in aid of this idea, it is to be remembered that the contract of the indorser of a promissory note of a co-partnership is that he will pay if the co-partnership does not, while that of the indorser of the note of joint makers is that he will pay if neither of them does.

"One joint maker, not a partner of the other, may not be able to speak for the other as to his ability or disposition to protect his promise and to save his indorser from liability, while one partner, though the firm has been dissolved, is supposed to know and care as much as the other for its ability and willingness in those respects. Again, the purpose of demand and notice to the indorser is that he, being made known of the failure to pay by the co-partnership, may be put at once on his guard, to save himself, if may be, from loss. This end is achieved when one of the former partners has refused to pay, as when all have. Taking all the reasons for the distinction made by the law between the case of a note of joint makers who are partners and of that of joint makers who are not partners, and all the reasons requiring a demand of payment of the maker and notice thereof and of refusal to the indorser, in order to charge him, we are of opinion that the rule that a demand of one co-partner is sufficient, applies as well where the co-partnership has been dissolved as where it has not."

The Tale of Him Who Fain Would Have Grown Rich Hastily

By JOE LINCOLN

AND it was the one thousandth and sixth night, and the King spake, saying, as one who sorrows:—

"Yea verily, it is true that I grow old and long for the things of old. 'Give me,' saith the wise man, 'old books, old friends, old wine, old jokes and old shoes.' Tell me, oh Scheherezade, one of thy tales."

And Scheherezade, laying aside the scroll which she was reading,—the same being "The Beautiful Dishwasher, or Lord Basil's Bride"—spake unto the Sultan thus:—

"Know, oh thou whose wealth exceedeth even the price of coal, that in the days of the good Caliph there lived a youth whose name was Hassan, and who sold goods over the counter of the shop of a merchant. And each day there came unto him the fair ones of the city and with them he held converse after his own fashion, saying:—

" 'Verily, it is a most excellent match. Nay, not the exact shade, but as near akin to it as is the mosquito of Jersey akin to his brother of Long Island. One cubit, sayest thou? It is well. C-a-s-h!'

"And for his services the stipend received by Hassan was small and although he wasted not his substance in riotous living, nevertheless the shekels which he laid by for the coming of the rainy day were as hard to find as are the molars of the barnyard fowl. But he complained not and was in a measure content.

"And it came to pass that a maiden aunt of Hassan died and was buried and unto her nephew left she her store of lucre, which was of the value of one thousand pieces of silver. And Hassan wept full sore and cried with a loud voice, forgetting not, however, to reach out for the one thousand pieces.

"And after he had been paid the same, he communed with himself, saying:—

" 'By the Burnsides of my father, this is an unhandy sum! If the principal be spent where am I better off than I was before? If I put it in the bank to grow great with compound interest I may have enough to live upon by the time I am ninety and then shall I be dead. I am possessed of too much coin to continue to measure tape, and of too little to do anything else. Of a surety the situation beats the home of the eternally lost.'

"And he grew discontented with his employment and unto the fair ones who came to his counter he dispensed no more the sweetness of his smile. And at the home of his abiding did he growl loudly at the cakes of flannel and the chopped meat, and the landlady gave him the frosty glare and the chicken neck.

"And upon a day there came unto him a friend and the same was arrayed in purple and fine linen and bore upon his breast a precious stone that caused his shirt bosom to smoke. And Hassan was amazed and questioned him, saying:—

" 'Hast thou married a daughter of the late Shiek Gou'd or art thou a Coal Baron?'

"And the friend answered not, but winked sagely and placing in Hassan's hand a scroll, departed.

"And Hassan read the writing upon the scroll and the same told of the Gettrichezee Investment and Trust Company, in which one desiring gain might place his shekels and receive upon the end of each month one hundred per cent in interest therefor. And the writing upon the scroll told yet again of the method by which this was accomplished,—how upon the rising of each day's sun did the wise ones, the Sultans of Finance, come unto the officers of the Gettrichezee and give them the quiet hunch as to which stocks were that day to blow the top out of the market. And the good officers made haste to get aboard, that their investors might share in the cutting of the melon.

"And Hassan read the scroll and shouted and was exceedingly glad forasmuch as he had chanced upon the good thing and might be numbered with the elect. And he hastened to the bank and drew therefrom the thousand pieces of silver and carried it to the officers of the Gettrichezee Investment and Trust Company, and the offices were splendid to look upon and the number of clerks was legion.

"And all that month from the rising of the sun to the going down thereof did Hassan figure in his mind the fruit of his investment. For he saw plainly that at the end of the period he would receive as interest one thousand pieces and, by reinvesting, four thousand at the end of the second period, and so on yesterday, today and forever, until he might buy the everlasting sea for a bath-tub and toss golden coins across it to see them skip.

"But it came to pass that on the twenty-ninth day of the month did the officers of the Gettrichezee Company place their apparel in their chests and flit by night. And with them flitted also the coin of the investors, and when Hassan visited the offices which had been so fair to look upon he found them filled with the minions of the law. And the minions of the law scoffed at Hassan when he begged for his thousand pieces of silver, and laughed scornfully and bade him hie hence for a good thing and an easy mark and be careful not to blow out the gas.

"And Hassan departed sorrowfully and communed with himself, saying:—

" 'Now see I plainly the meaning of the name of the Company. One was to invest with It and trust to Allah.'

"And he returned to his counter."

And Scheherzade paused and said unto the Father of the Faithful.—

"Oh King, live forever! Can one become rich in haste and without toil?"

And the King answered her, saying: "Sure."

And she was amazed and questioned him yet again, saying: "How?"

And he answered her:—

"By running a Get-Rich-Quick Company."

And he winked unto his steward and commanded that the latter bring him a flagon of sarsaparilla all red and no white.

The Bookkeeping of Industrial Concerns

By J. FRED BIANCHI

Of Volmer & Co., Accountants, Amsterdam, Holland

Thanks to the accountant profession, times are past in which the bookkeeping of every concern was organized in the same way, without keeping in view the object with which the administration in different concerns is kept. Nowadays every concern has its own system of administration, which is especially fitted to that particular concern.

However, without infringing upon the principles that have been laid down in the preceding lines, it is possible to give some general rules for the administration of a particular branch of business—rules that must always be kept in view when the bookkeeping of a company of that kind is being organized.

The detailed deviations, which must be indicated by an able expert for every concern particularly, do not put aside the general principles, which always remain intact.

The bookkeeping of industrial concerns is particularly apt to be resumed in a general scheme. The object, always to be kept in view with the organization of an administration of any of those concerns, is to get a clear statement of the cost price of the article made.

COST PRICE.

The cost price of the product must be clearly demonstrated in the books in every detail, so that the manufacturer may have a sound basis for the regulation of his selling prices.

The elements of which the cost price of an article is composed are:—

a. The prices of the raw materials.
b. The wages and costs of steam power.
c. The depreciation of machines and buildings.
d. A proportionate part of the general expenses.
e. The interest on the capital employed.
f. The value of the waste.

The first two elements are clear, and need no further explanation.

DEPRECIATION OF MACHINERY.

In order to fix a percentage of depreciation of the machines it is not sufficient to take into consideration the wear and tear, but also:—

1. The possibility of new inventions, which depreciate the old machines very rapidly.
2. Economical causes, i. e., when the success of an article depends upon a temporary fashion.

To have the general expenses subdivided into several accounts may be of much use. For instance, it may arrive that an offer is made for a considerable lot of the products, in connection with which the selling expenses are reduced to a minimum.

The manufacturer must be able to see in his books if it is possible to execute that order without loss.

The interest on the capital employed is a factor of which many a non-professional man often loses sight in his calculations. It must not be forgotten that a large capital stock means a considerable loss of interest.

WASTE.

Subdivision f. is so important a factor that in connection with it the administrations of industrial concerns may be divided into three separate parts:—

1. Those for concerns where only one article is manufactured without producing any waste.
2. Those for concerns where several secondary articles are the result of the fabrication of the principal article.
3. Those for factories where several articles are made.

In all these classes of concerns the cost price of the articles manufactured must be stated in the books, but it is demonstrated in different ways.

With concerns of the first class it is relatively simple; a trading account may give every detail. But with the second the price to be obtained for the accessory products is of the greatest importance for the purpose of fixing the price of the principal article.

So it was some years ago with cacao manufactories. The principal product of these manufactories was, of course, cacao, but after an enormous rise in the price of cacao-butter, that secondary product became the principal product and cacao is now only an accessory product.

Here the cost price of a certain quantity of principal and secondary products must be diminished with the selling price of the secondary products in order to find a minimum price for the principal article.

With concerns manufacturing several articles it is necessary to have a separate account or card for every work, in order to be able to see how much is earned or lost on every work delivered.

Every work must share for a proportionate part in the general expenses—in proportion to the wages paid for the particular work—depreciation, etc.

I should go beyond the limits of this article to give here a detailed scheme of the bookkeeping of those concerns. Let it be sufficient to say that the system is in use by iron works and other manufactories of that kind. A description of the several subsidiary books will open no new views to the reader.

The object of this article is only to lay down some general rules which may be of practical use to my colleagues at the other side of the ocean when framing the bookkeeping of an industrial concern.

GREAT SHIPMENTS OF GOLD

"I notice that the newspapers have recently spoken of the carrying of $7,000,000 of bullion to a foreign country by one of the ocean liners as the greatest amount ever transported," said a man who has been with the navy for years to a reporter of the Washington Star. "It is entirely wrong. In 1885 there was brought from the mint in New Orleans to the treasury in Washington $11,000,000, and it was brought in a steamer.

"The government decided to transport $15,000,000 from New Orleans. It was first thought best to bring it by rail, but this was assuming a great risk. The cabinet discussed the matter carefully and it was finally decided that the safest way would be by water. The members of the cabinet saw that there was a chance for a hold-up if the money was brought by train.

"The United States ship Swatara was first designated to carry the money, but it was found she would be inadequate to transport the whole amount, so the wooden sailing steamer, Yantic, was pressed into service to help out. We removed from the Swatara her magazines. The shells from the shell-room were removed, as were also the sails from the sail-room, so that all available space was utilized for packing the coin. The only weapon of defense was a Gatling gun.

"The money was conveyed from the mint to the vessels in wagons. A squad of secret service officers watched the work. The two vessels were in tow, and the trip from New Orleans to the Washington navy-yard occupied a little more than four days. Considerable wind was encountered off Hatteras, but otherwise the trip was without incident. The money was carried from the navy-yard to the treasury by an express company.

"The money was in boxes of $2,000 each, and in bags. My recollection is that the money was in silver dollars, or the greater part of it, for, while unloading at the navy-yard, one of the bags, rotten from being in storage so long, gave way and a large number of silver dollars were scattered about the wharf.

Correspondence

Sales Book Systems

From S. W. S., Philadelphia

In most up-to-date methods of bookkeeping for houses carrying many retail accounts, by what stages are credit sales passed up to the ledger? Do many concerns still run the antiquated sales book, posting therefrom monthly to the credit of merchandise or sales account? If not, what simple method is employed?

Answer.—Numerically speaking, there are still many concerns who run the antiquated sales book, posting therefrom daily, or at most weekly, to the debit of the customers' accounts in their ledger, and posting therefrom monthly to the credit of the merchandise account. Such concerns, however, are not up to date, and are not entitled to rank with progressive concerns. Those concerns which are up to date, and which are entitled to the name of progressive, use for the most part duplicate methods, by which a transcript of the invoice, or rather carbon copy, of the invoice becomes the sales book.

There are various ways in which these copies are prepared, some of them employing typewriters, and others being done by hand. The latter process is greatly to be preferred, on account of being the most expeditious, and withal the most economical. That plan which was in vogue in some concerns a few years ago, and which we are persuaded has not yet fully gone out, taking business as a whole, necessitated several hand copies of each sale transaction. The first charge was made on a slate; from the slate it was copied into the blotter; from the blotter it was copied into a sales book, and from the sales book into the journal, and from the journal it was posted to the ledger. Incidentally, a transcript of the sales book was made out in the form of a bill for the customer.

Single Entry

From B. J. R., Philadelphia.

Do many firms use single entry?

Answer.—In a question of this kind we feel obliged to ask a preliminary question: "What is single entry?" After years of experience we have failed to appreciate the existence of anything that is entitled to a scientific standing that is called single entry. There are various approaches to double entry, lacking more or less that which constitutes double entry, and which are called single entry. Some of these plans are more or less expounded in the text books, and many of them are in use. If our correspondent means, "Are there many concerns which do not keep their books by double entry?" we would say, Yes, a great many. And some of them keep their books so thoroughly by schemes approaching double entry, but which lack the corner-stone of double entry—namely, proof by balance—that we are compelled to take off our hats to them. There is no such thing as single entry as opposed to double entry. There are various approximations to double entry, and, as before remarked, there are a very large number of books that are kept which are not provable by balance methods.

Management of the Bank Account

From B. J. R., Philadelphia.

What is the prevalent method of keeping the bank account? Is it customary to keep the account in the ledger?

Note.—The answer to this question depends altogether upon the standpoint from which the ledger is regarded. What is the ledger? As a fact, there are ledgers and ledgers. We can have the customers ledger and the accounts payable ledger and the employees ledger, the purchase ledger, the general ledger and the balance sheet ledger. If the ledger in the mind of this correspondent in asking this question is a book containing accounts representing the condition of the business, then, for the sake of consistency, the bank account, or the cash account if the bank account is a subdivision of that account, should be included. This, however, does not necessarily mean that all the items of the bank account should be posted from the pass book and check book to an account in the ledger called Bank Account. It is quite sufficient to take the balance from the Bank Account as it is kept on the stubs of the check book and include it in the monthly or weekly statement, as the case may be.

Discussions on Commercial Education

From A. S. O., Rochester, N. Y.

I was asked a few months since to write an article for the purpose of refuting certain statements made in your journal on commercial education, and in reply I stated that in my opinion the statements criticised were in the main true. There has been, however, an undertone or between-the-lines tone of criticism that has been necessarily very distasteful to those of us who have given the most of our lives to this work. Little good, it seems to me, usually results from public printed controversies, where each contestant, lawyer-like, attempts to exploit his own ideas and belittle the opponent. In such cases both say what they would otherwise leave unsaid, and possibly some of these bitter replies to various articles which have appeared in your journal may partly account for the editorial paragraphs which appear in the current number. The spirit is not good.

If you are a bookkeeper, as I assume you are, there may have been a time when you would have sought a position as teacher of bookkeeping at even $15 per week. It is quite possible that you could have accepted this pay with a clear conscience and have given value received in teaching elementary bookkeeping and other elementary commercial subjects to perhaps twelve or fourteen year old children, or even older students, who needed to be taught the subject from the very beginning, and with whom the knowledge of the most competent expert accountant in the city of New York could not be made valuable until they had been taught how to journalize and post and make a simple trial balance. Is not this a fact, and is not this the other side of this question? Some one had to do this work; it has not been high nor advanced, but it has been necessary, and I, for one, am glad that there are now higher and more advanced courses for those who care to take them.

I have read COMMERCE, ACCOUNTS & FINANCE from the very first number, and with all the severe things it has said about business colleges I am glad the journal has been printed, and sincerely hope it will continue to thrive. We have it on file and are willing that our students, even, should read the severe things which are occasionally said about us.

Form of Balance Sheet

From B. J. R., Philadelphia

What is the prevalent form of balance sheet in the United States?

Answer.—The form of balance sheet used in this country does not differ essentially from that used in others, if we except Great Britain, where the point of view with some of the chartered accountants seems to vary. In the United States, the assets are usually placed first, and in the order of their availability, and the liabilities second. Capital is always considered a part of the liabilities, and is the element which makes a balance sheet of the two statements.

BABYLON HAS FALLEN

Ancient Babylon was anything but a city of stately palaces and hanging gardens, according to men who have been looking into things.

Two big Bromley rugs would have covered the gay banquet room where Belshazzar saw the "handwriting on the wall." It was only 50 or 60 feet long, says an exchange. The hangings all depictions show to have been costly and rich. Explorations show no trace of a room in the "kase" which would be deemed large enough for a lady's boudoir, except the historic banquet room above mentioned. Nothing but a monotony of burnt bricks and mud bricks is disclosed at Babylon, while at Agra white marble and red sandstone seems to have been used.

KNICKERBOCKER TRUST CO.

234 FIFTH AVENUE, CORNER 27TH STREET
BRANCH OFFICES:
66 BROADWAY, AND 125TH STREET AND LENOX AVE.,
NEW YORK CITY.

CAPITAL AND UNDIVIDED PROFITS, $2,508,399.11.

LEGAL DEPOSITORY FOR STATE, CITY, AND COURT FUNDS.

Interest allowed on Time Deposits. Deposits also received subject to Demand Checks, which pass through the Clearing House as do those upon any city bank.

Authorized to act as Executor or Administrator of Estates, and as Guardian, Receiver, Registrar, Transfer and Financial Agent for States, Cities, Towns, Railroads, and other corporations, and to accept any other Trusts in conformity with the laws of any State or of the United States.

LETTERS OF CREDIT FURNISHED.
BUSINESS AND PERSONAL ACCOUNTS SOLICITED.

CHAS. T. BARNEY, - - - - - - - - President.
JOSEPH T. BROWN, - - - - - - 2d Vice-President.
JULIAN M. GERARD, - - - Asst. Sec. and Asst. Treas.
FRED'K K. ELDRIDGE, - - - - 1st Vice-President.
FRED'K GORE KING, - - - Secretary and Treasurer.
WM. B. RANDALL, - - - - - - Trust Officer.

BOARD OF DIRECTORS:

JOSEPH S. AUERBACH,
HARRY B. HOLLINS,
JACOB HAYS,
CHARLES T. BARNEY,
A. FOSTER HIGGINS,
ANDREW H. SANDS,
JAMES H. BRESLIN,
I. TOWNSEND BURDEN,
HON. E. V. LOEW,
HENRY F. DIMOCK,
CHARLES F. WATSON,
FREDERICK G. BOURNE,
C. LAWRENCE PERKINS,
CHARLES R. FLINT,
AMZI L. BARBER,
CHARLES T. COOK,
JOHN MAGEE,
HENRY A. MORGAN,
HENRY C. BERLIN,
CHARLES W. GOULD,
FRED'K L. ELDRIDGE,
HENRY W. DE FOREST,
ALFRED B. MACLAY,
HARRY W. McVICKAR.

HASKINS & SELLS,
CERTIFIED PUBLIC ACCOUNTANTS.

30 BROAD STREET,
NEW YORK.

CABLE ADDRESS "HASKSELLS"

204 DEARBORN STREET
CHICAGO

LINCOLN TRUST BLDG.
ST. LOUIS

WILLIAMSON BLDG.
CLEVELAND, O.

30 COLEMAN STREET
LONDON, E.C.

Lackawanna Railroad

Address all communications to
C. W. TEN BROECK, Industrial Agent,
26 Exchange Place, New York City.

Do You Desire a Factory Site? The Industrial Department of the Lackawanna Railroad will aid you in finding one.

Are You Interested in Any Raw Product for Manufacturing Purposes? The Industrial Department of the Lackawanna Railroad will tell you if it is to be found along that road.

Does the Question of Power Concern You? The Industrial Department of the Lackawanna Railroad will tell you of good water power and of the proximity of fuel to points on that road.

Do You Want to Know the Usual Rate of Wages? The Industrial Department of the Lackawanna Railroad will give that information regarding any point on that road.

Do You Want to Know the Price of Gas, Water, Electricity? The Industrial Department of the Lackawanna Railroad will tell you.

BOOKS OF INTEREST TO BUSINESS MEN

BUSINESS LAW. By Thomas Raeburn White, B.L., LL.B. 6 by 7 1-2 inches; 322 pages. Bound in cloth. Back title gilt. Price, $1.50.

This is a neat, compact and handy book of business law for the use of students and business men. Among the subjects treated are Contracts, Sales, Partnerships, Corporations, Negotiable Paper and the like. The author's language is plain, and is understandable by any one having no previous knowledge of law. The book's clearness on the essential points of ordinary law should recommend it as a business book for the plain business man who has no time in which to consult a law library.

THE PHONOGRAPHIC DICTIONARY AND PHRASE BOOK. By Benn Pitman and Jerome B. Howard. 6 1-2 by 8 inches; 662 pages. Bound in cloth. Cover title and back title gilt. Price, $3.00.

This book is the most elaborate shorthand dictionary yet published, with the characters in fac-simile. It contains over 20,000 words, and for every one of these words there is a corresponding sign in the Benn Pitman system of shorthand. To the reporter, office or court stenographer, or any one writing the Benn Pitman system of shorthand, the book is invaluable. It is well made, tastefully bound, and is printed on a good quality of paper in clean, plain type.

THE LAWRENCE SYSTEM OF VOCAL AND PHYSICAL EXPRESSION. By Edwin Gordon Lawrence. 4 3-4 by 6 inches; 128 pages. Bound in cloth. Cover title and back title gilt. Price, $1.00.

The author says in the preface of this little book that his object has been to place in the hands of lawyers, actors and public speakers in general, a simple system of vocal and physical expression that will enable them to clearly convey thought by word of mouth and emphasize it by the proper action. To the man of affairs who is called upon for a speech on any subject, and who knows what to say but does not know how to say it, this book will be a great help.

BUSINESS LAW. By Alonzo R. Weed, LL. B., of the Boston Bar. 6 by 9 1-4 inches; 172 pages. Bound in cloth. Cover and back title red. Price, $1.25.

Mr. Weed calls his book "a manual for schools and colleges and for every day use." The titles of the chapters are as follows: Contracts, Principal and Agent, Partnerships, Sales of Personal Property, Bailments and Common Carriers, Negotiable Paper, Deeds, Mortgages and Leases, Collection Laws, Written Rates of Interest, Insurance, Patent Rights, Trade-Marks and Copyrights, etc.

The author does not waste words, and yet treats his subjects clearly and comprehensively. In short, he gives the law without the addition of wordy "trimmings."

BANKERS' AND MERCHANTS' INTEREST TABLES. By Francis H. Coffin and David H. Moore. 13 by 9 1-2 inches. Bound in cloth. Leather back and corners. Cover and back title gilt. Price, $5.00.

There have been interest tables published before, but never, so far as we know, has so elaborate and comprehensive a set of tables been issued in book form. "The volume contains," to quote from the title page, "Interest tables, computed on the basis of 360 days per annum, at 3 1-2, 4, 5 and 6 per cent, with an accurate calculation of interest on every sum from $1.00 to $1,000, and, by simple addition of two lines, on every further sum, to $1,000,000." It also contains a 1 per cent one day table, on the basis of 365 days per annum, from which interest on daily balances can be computed at any time and on any sum. There is a time table printed in black and red at the beginning of the book as an aid in quickly finding the number of days between one day and another. To a merchant or banker performing many calculations in interest this book is a great time saver. It is handsomely bound, finely printed, and has a thumb index.

POLITICAL ECONOMY OF HUMANISM. By Henry Wood. 7 3-4 by 5 1-4 inches; 320 pages. Bound in cloth. Cover and back title gilt. Price, $1.25.

Mr. Wood is well known as a writer on various economic subjects, and this book contains a series of able treatises, written in his usual vein, on the relation of the employer to the employed, and the phases of the industrial question and their relation to socialism. Among the questions considered and handled in a conservative spirit and with much common sense, are the following: Supply and Demand, the Law of Competition, Labor and Production, Combinations of Capital, Combinations of Labor, Employers and Profit Sharing, the Obligations and Privileges of Employees, the Unequal Distribution of Wealth, Money and Coinage, Tariffs and Protection, Industrial Education and Gold Production and values.

THE A B C OF BANKS AND BANKING. By George M. Coffin. 6 3-4 by 5 inches; 137 pages. Bound in cloth. Back title gilt. Price, $1.25.

This handy little volume is exactly what its name implies, that is, a presentation of the principles underlying banking in the United States. The author in his preface says that it is designed to appeal to the reader outside as well as inside of a bank. It is by no means the last word or every word about banking. It may be said that it is a primer covering a field that has hitherto been somewhat neglected. The chapter heads are as follows: Banking in General, Various Kinds of Banking, Capital Stock, Shareholders' Rights and Liabilities, Undivided Profits, Dividends and Surplus, Deposits, Checks, Lawful Money Reserve, Issuing Bank Notes, Borrowing Money, Loans and Discounts, Exchanges, Collections, Letters of Credit, Bonds, Mortgages and Stocks, Bank Reports, Examinations, Directors, Executive Officers—Their Powers and Duties, Internal Administration and Bookkeeping, and Other Suggestions.

Any book in this list will be sent to any address in the United States, Canada or Mexico upon receipt of price. If there is some special book that you require we shall be pleased to hunt it up for you. Address COMMERCE, ACCOUNTS & FINANCE, 25 Pine street, New York city.

Public Accountants

ATLANTA, GA.—Ralph H. Brown, 318 Temple Court.

BOSTON, MASS.—Charles H. Fellows, 114 Summer; New England Audit Co., 45 Milk; J. S. Parsons, 214 Columbus Ave.; Safeguard Account Co., 53 Tremont; William Dillon, 602 Exchange Building.

BROOKLYN, N. Y.—Franklin Allen, Arbuckle Building, 371 Fulton.

BUFFALO, N. Y.—W. G. Mowat, 831 Ellicott Square.

CHICAGO, ILL.—Safeguard Account Co., 609-611A Merchants' Loan & Trust Building, 135 Adams; Haskins & Sells, 214 Dearborn.

DAVENPORT, IOWA.—J. C. Grabbe, McManus Building.

DETROIT, MICH.—N. A. Hawkins, 717-718 Chamber of Commerce; H. Naemansson, 496 Putnam Ave.

LONDON, CANADA.—Geo. F. Jewell, 361 Dundas.

NEW BEDFORD, MASS.—James L. Hathway, 72 Willis.

NEW ORLEANS, LA.—P. W. Sherwood, 904 Howard Ave.

NEW YORK, N. Y.—Patterson, Teele & Dennis, 30 Broad; Haskins & Sells, 30 Broad; Account, Audit & Assurance Co., Ltd., 25 Pine; Leon Brummer, 7 Pine; H. F. Searle, 45 Broadway; Hart Bros., Tibbits, Heiron & Co., 11 Broadway; Franklin Allen, Silk Exchange Building, Broadway, corner Broome.

PHILADELPHIA, PA.—Francis & Sterrett, Penn Mutual Building; Peter Ballingall, German-American Building; Charles W. Thomas, 409 Lippincott Building; Alfred L. Sellers, 1001 Chestnut.

PITTSBURG, PA.—John Vaughn, 5520 Claybourne; George W. Wood & Co., 341 Fourth Ave.

PROVIDENCE, R. I.—George R. Allen, 29 Weybosset.

SAN FRANCISCO, CAL.—Charles L. Lutgen, 218 California; Lester Herrick, 405 Montgomery.

TORONTO, CANADA.—F. H. Kidd, Bank of Commerce Building.

WINDSOR, CANADA.—F. H. Macpherson, 16 Sandwich, East.

WINNIPEG, CANADA.—Peter Thornton, 343 Main.

R·I·P·A·N·S

There is scarcely any condition of ill-health that is not benefited by the occasional use of a R·I·P·A·N·S Tabule. For sale by Druggists. The Five-Cent packet is enough for an ordinary occasion. The family bottle, 60 cents, contains a supply for a year.

A BUSINESS EDUCATION | FOR ...ONE... DOLLAR.

...THE PRACTICAL AGE...

A MONTHLY MAGAZINE full to the brim with helpful suggestions to young men and young women who are struggling successward.

THE BUSINESS HOUSE THAT JACK BUILT, an intensely interesting and highly instructive story of business life, and

APPLIED ENGLISH, an authority on writing and speaking the English language, which no young person can afford to be without, all for ONE DOLLAR.

If you have never seen THE PRACTICAL AGE, send for a free sample copy. Address,

THE PRACTICAL AGE,

Moline, Illinois.

PRENTISS CLOCKS.

SIX TIMES A YEAR

is all that is necessary to wind a Prentiss Clock. Why wind a clock every week when we can sell you one which will require winding but once in sixty days and will keep perfect time? Also Frying-pan, Program and Electrically synchronized clocks. Send for Catalogue No. 282.

THE PRENTISS CLOCK IMPROVEMENT CO.,
Dept. 28, 49 Dey St., New York City

Leon Brummer, C.P.A.

Public Accountant and Auditor,

7 Pine Street, New York, N. Y.

UNIVERSITY TRAINING

For Business

ACCOUNTING
BANKING
BROKERAGE

School of Comerce, Accounts and Finance.

Evening Sessions.

New York University, Washington Square, N. Y. City.

FALL TERM OPENS OCT. 1.

The Stationery Manufacturing Company,

318 BROADWAY, NEW YORK

A New Line of Note Books

The ordinary note book, as furnished by the stationery trade, is essentially a single entry book. Concerns using advanced accounting systems require a double entry book.

The ordinary note book affords no opportunity to strike a balance, either as a whole or for a definite period, for example, a month. The users of advanced accounting systems and managers of businesses that are thoroughly systematized demand statements from time to time, both of notes receivable and notes payable, not alone as to the total outstanding, but also as to maturities month by month. There should be provided in every office such a construction of note book as will facilitate these statements.

The line of note books to which we call attention at the present time provides a complete register of all notes issued and taken up, showing at all times the total amount outstanding, the amount in gross and in detail due each month, the amount of demand notes, the amount of the notes falling due beyond the current year, and a record of indorsements and collateral.

These note books in dimensions are similar to the ordinary note books sold by the stationers. The stock size, from which the accompanying illustrations were made, measure 8¼ inches vertical depth by 12 inches right to left.

These note books are known under the general head of "3-A Notes Payable Records" and "3-A Notes Receivable Records." The Notes Payable Record is illustrated herewith, and the Notes Receivable Record is its exact antithesis.

Fig. 1 of the illustration shows a Notes Payable Record opened in a way to indicate the character of the leaves. Fig. 2 shows the book likewise open, but lying flat. Fig. 3 shows the details of the page in each signature for notes falling due beyond the current year, for demand notes, and for the record of indorsements and collateral.

These books are of the long and short leaf variety. The projecting edges of the long leaves are thickened or reinforced to offset the thickness of the narrow or short leaves, thereby providing an even surface wherever the book is opened. For example, referring to Fig. 2, it makes no difference whether writing on the left-hand page or the right-hand page, there is always an even surface.

Still further referring to Fig. 2—the first page of each signature provides space for the record of the person's name in whose favor the note is drawn and where it is made payable. At the left of these columns is a space for noting the amount of the notes issued and also the amount of the notes paid. Still further to the left is a column for the due date, the time to run, and the date of the note. These particulars are thrown out to the left, so as to be free of the edge of the narrow leaves as they are turned over.

Again referring to Fig. 2, it will be noticed that each face of the narrow leaf is devoted to two months of time, and is provided with a column of issued, another column of paid, with date due and date paid in connection therewith. Three of these intermediate or narrow leaves, carrying four months each, cover the year.

The final wide page of each signature is ruled as shown in Fig. 3. This is divided into three spaces—one for recording notes falling due beyond the current year, and the second for recording demand notes, while the third space receives the record of indorsements and collateral.

In the space devoted to notes falling due beyond the current year, it will be noted that there are two money col-

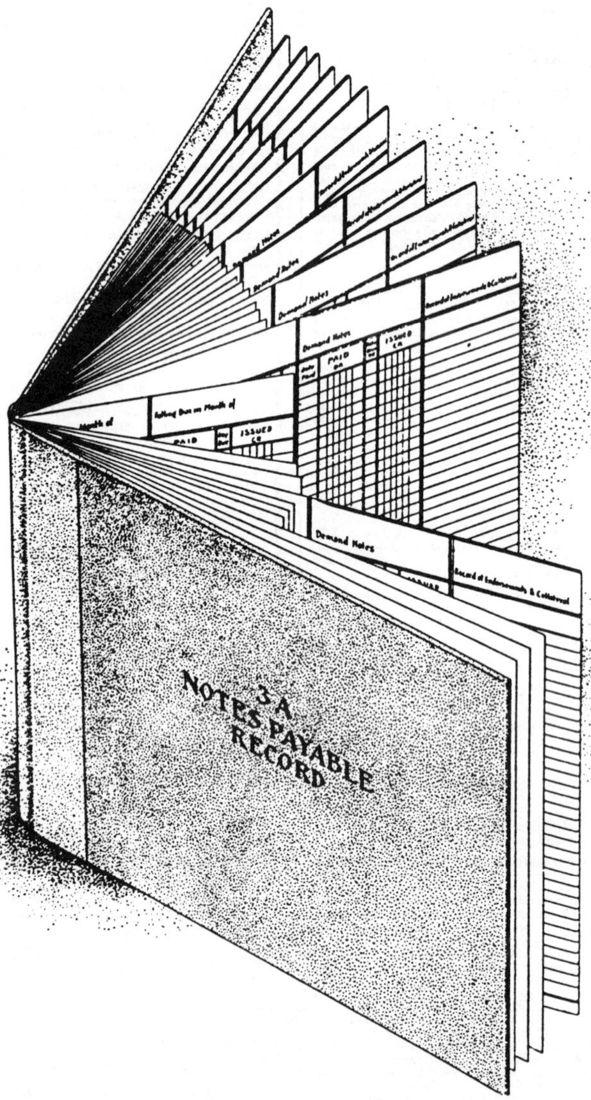

FIG. 1. GENERAL APPEARANCE OF A 3-A NOTES PAYABLE RECORD.

umns—one for paid and the other for issued—and that there are likewise two money columns for paid and issued in demand notes.

In the use of this book, the particulars concerning the notes are recorded on the first left-hand wide page, as shown in Fig. 2. There is entered, first, the date of the note, next the time to run, following which is the due on the left-hand page, shown in Fig. 2, falls due in February, then the amount, in addition to being entered under the head of "Notes Issued" on the left-hand page, is entered in the money column entitled "Issued" in the February space. In turn, if the next note to be entered falls due in April, in the same way it is entered in the April space on the narrow pages, and so on. charges for all notes taken up. Then a balance between these two columns at any date would show the notes outstanding.

In the same manner, using the monthly columns, the difference between the paid and issued under each month on the narrow pages would show the amount outstanding or falling due during the month.

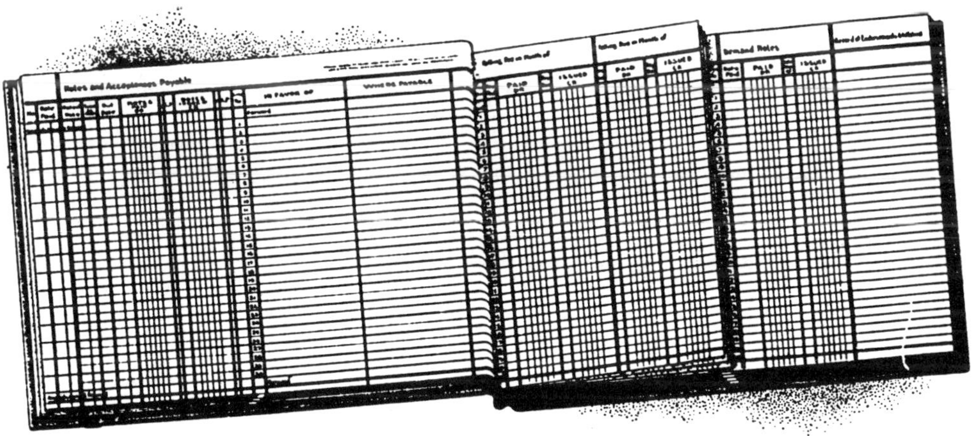

FIG. 2. A 3-A NOTES PAYABLE RECORD, OPENED FLAT, SHOWING EVENNESS OF WRITING SURFACE.

date. Then, in the second of the money columns, namely, in that entitled "Notes Issued," is entered the amount of the note. In the columns entitled "In Favor of" and "Where Payable" are entered these essential particulars.

The book is so ruled that two lines are devoted to each note. The first line, being 1 and 2 of those shown on the left-hand page in Fig. 2, is devoted to the issuing of the note, and the second line to the paying of the note. When it comes to the paying of the note, the entry is made in the same way as the issuing of it, using the second line in the panel.

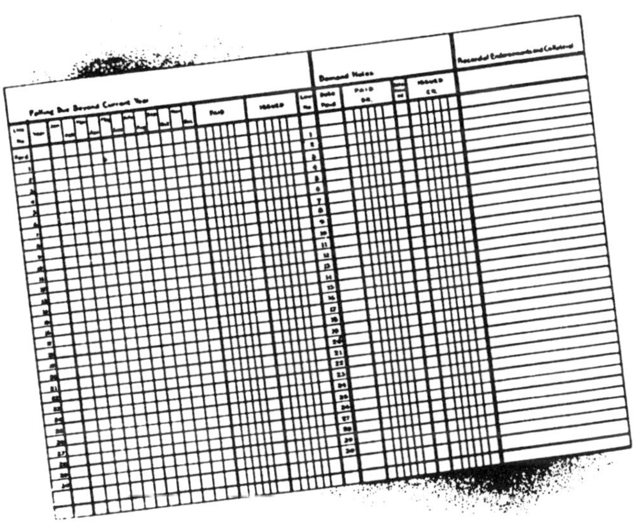

FIG. 3. RULING OF SECOND WIDE PAGE IN EACH SIGNATURE.

Assuming that the entries in this book commence with the first month in the year, then the first half of the first narrow page would be named for January, the second for February, and so on through, until successive spaces have covered the twelve months of the year. If the first note that we enter

By this plan the credit column, or "Notes Issued," on the left-hand page in Fig. 2, receives the amount of all notes sent out, and the debit column, entitled "Notes Paid," receives the

As already alluded to in what precedes, those notes falling due beyond the current year are recorded on the second wide page, while demand notes likewise find a space upon the second wide space. To prove the book, therefore, it is necessary to take the balance of each of the narrow pages, plus the balance of notes falling due beyond the current year, plus the balance of the demand notes, and compare this total with the balance in the money columns on the first wide page; in other words, the left-hand page in Fig. 2.

There are various ways in which this note book may be used. The items shown in it may or may not be ledgerized, at the option of the bookkeeper in charge. The book may be used as the book of original entry, as well also as of final entry. If the items are ledgerized, they may be posted directly from this book to the ledger, for which purpose two L F columns are provided. Or the original entry may be made in the book, and from this book the items may be journalized, and thence posted to the ledger. Preferably, however, the book is used as the sole and final record of notes, the balance in the book being taken in the preparation of the monthly trial balance.

When the items are posted from the first left-hand wide page to the monthly spaces in the narrow pages, the column alongside of the L F, indicated in the head by a check mark, is used for keeping the tally. As the items are posted, the check mark is put in place opposite the same.

The last column on the second wide page of each signature, entitled "Record of Indorsements and Collateral,' is intended to receive memorandums of the indorsements which are upon the notes before delivery, and also of the collateral which is deposited with the notes as security for their payment.

In case a note is taken up by issuing a new note, the old one is to be recorded as paid, upon the plan which the record provides, and as previously described. The new note, in turn, should be recorded in its proper place according to the date at which it is issued.

The line numbers printed down the center of the two wide pages and on the narrow margin of each right-hand narrow page are for helping the eye across the page and avoiding the necessity of closely following the ruled lines when making an entry. For example, if on the first wide page a note is entered on line 15, and its due date falls in the month of June, the position of the entry on the June page is determined by referring to line 15 on that page, instead of laboriously tracing along the lines from the wide page across the narrow page.

Notes recorded in this register may or may not be designated by number, as the preference of the user may determine. A number column is provided at the extreme left-hand margin of the first wide page.

The Notes Receivable Record, as already stated, is the exact counterpart in all respects of what is here shown. The two books are alike in binding, and as manufactured, each is capable of containing the business of an ordinary concern for one or more years. Each signature is complete in itself, and the signature that ends with December is the one for which forwarding entries would be made to a succeeding signature commencing with January of the new year. The book is adaptable to fiscal years commencing with any month.

Each book is provided with a title page and with a preface or introduction containing full directions for use.

The books, either Notes Payable or Notes Receivable, will be sent postpaid to any address in the United States for $1.25 each. Address

Stationery Manufacturing Company, 318 Broadway, New York.

BRIEF MENTION

WE WONDER WHO INVENTED the first folding chair. "Camp stools" they used to be called in the days when the seats were made exclusively of carpet, and when they broke down with alarming regularity. Now, however, made as they are of finished wood and in neat and durable fashion, they are called "portable chairs," and are really ornamental as well as useful. In the folder issued by the Andrews School Furniture Co., with offices at 9 West Eighteenth Street, New York City, a number of styles of these folding chairs are shown, and they are certainly very attractive in appearance. The chairs are made singly or in sections of two or three. According to the folder, the chairs may be folded into very small compass and packed away until the time for their use. In the folder also are several reproductions of photographs showing halls and Sunday-school rooms fitted with chairs manufactured by the Andrews Company. One of the most notable of these illustrations is that showing the hall of the Northern Liberty Market Association of Washington, D. C. This hall is said to be seated with over 4,000 of the Andrews portable chairs. There are folding chairs made for schools, churches, halls, etc., and the variety of styles is surprising. The company also manufacture book boxes for the holding of hymn books in church pews.

THIS COUNTRY OF OURS is continually developing new industries. A comparatively short time ago all the wine used in the United States was imported from abroad. Then, a little later, California began to manufacture wine, and the business has developed to an extraordinary extent. Within the last ten years, however, much good wine has been manufactured in the Eastern States, particularly in Central New York. The Empire State Wine Co., of Penn Yan, N. Y., is sending out some very attractive advertising matter. A card issued by them shows a lady and gentleman seated at dinner, with a bottle of "State Seal" champagne between them, and the printed matter on the card tells why every one who drinks champagne at all should drink "State Seal." The Empire State Wine Co. claims that this wine is as good as the best manufactured anywhere in the world, that it is absolutely pure, and is prepared and bottled by skilled labor, from the finest selected grapes. Prices, it is also claimed, are away below those charged by foreign dealers for the same quality of wine. In another circular issued by the company, the wine cellars and vineyards at Penn Yan are shown in attractive half-tone reproductions of photographs.

THE H. & D. FOLSOM ARMS CO. have been sending out a little leaflet advertising the celebrated Morris canoe, which they sell at their warerooms, 314 Broadway, New York. The Morris canoe is described as being made on the old Indian model, with full, easy lines, and being very graceful in appearance. The canoe is said to be very rigid in the water, and therefore safe for the carrying of ladies and children. It is made of canvas, with ribs and siding of cedar, and with all woodwork oiled, shellacced and varnished. Many other points of excellence are claimed for this canoe, and by sending to the Folsom Company for the little leaflet, any one interested may acquire further information. The canoe is made in a variety of sizes, and prices vary accordingly.

THE SOUTHERN PACIFIC RAILWAY CO. issues some interesting little primers for children and grown-ups. The particular primer which we have in hand is a little booklet describing the big trees of California. There are a number of illustrations of some wonderfully big trees in the Yosemite National Park, and the printed matter accompanying the illustrations is in primer style, being printed in large type, and with the ideas expressed in the simplest terms. The primer gives a great deal of information about the big trees that will interest older people as well as children, and it seems to us that the little folder is well worth sending for.

PIPES MAY COME AND PIPES MAY GO, but the meerschaum pipe goes on forever. It still remains the "real thing" to the pipe smoker, and to possess a good meerschaum and to color it himself would seem to be the height of the said smoker's ambition. Wm. Birnbaum, whose warerooms are at 80 Nassau Street, New York, manufactures all sorts of meerschaum pipes as well as amber and briar smoking goods. The advertising matter issued by Mr. Birnbaum states that he makes a specialty of repairing, boiling and mounting of pipes in the best manner and at low prices. To the smoker, Mr. Birnbaum's establishment should be interesting.

THE "INDIAN GIRL" is the attractive name of the canvas-covered canoe manufactured by J. H. Rushton, of Kenton, N. Y. Mr. Rushton sends out a very pretty little folder exploiting the "Indian Girl" canoe and setting forth, by illustration and well-written text, the merits of the little craft. The folder states that Mr. Rushton hires a skilled builder from Maine, a man of fourteen years' experience in this class of work, to superintend the construction of the canoes, and that this builder's experience, together with Mr. Rushton's twenty-eight years' sojourn in the same line, accomplishes results that appeal to canoe lovers. The folder states also that Mr. Rushton manufactures rowboats, sailboats, as well as paddles, oars, etc., and that he issues an eighty-page catalogue, which he will be glad to send to those interested.

A REPORT of the proceedings of the thirteenth annual meeting and convention of the Minnesota Bankers' Association has been embodied in a very pretty paper-bound book issued by the association and distributed by its secretary, Jos. Chapman, Jr., of Minneapolis. The book is printed in two colors, on good paper, contains a report of each day's proceedings, the speeches of the delegates in full, with many half-tone illustrations. The convention itself was held at Crookston, Minn., on the 24th and 25th of last June.

"BUSINESS SYSTEM IN THE SALES DEPARTMENT." That is the title of the handsome catalogue issued by the Perine & Mosely Co., 358 Dearborn Street, Chicago. The catalogue illustrates and describes what the originators call "The Commercial Routine System," and this system, to quote from the text, "consists of a series of drawers of cabinet or desk form, each drawer containing a map of a city, State or country, the name of each city, State or country being cast in the polished brass handle with which each drawer is fitted. The Commercial Routine System," so says the catalogue, "is distinctly a system for the sales department, and affords the best advantages for thoroughly and systematically caring for the trade, keeping track of customers, agents, etc. It is a geographical chart of business interests and movements of traveling salesmen, showing at a glance where customers or agents are located, the territory allotted to each, where you have prospective trade, inquiries, correspondence, contracts, collections, etc." The system is intended to appeal to firms having a large number of salesmen on the road, and, judging from the catalogue, must be very complete. The Perine & Mosely Co. manufacture a number of desks, both roll and flat top, containing the index drawers with the maps and other paraphernalia, and they also manufacture wall cabinets, folding drawers, a progressive card index system, and so on. The catalogue is well printed and finely illustrated in color. It is a credit to the engraver, printer and the house issuing it.

THE RAZALL MANUFACTURING CO., of Milwaukee, Wis., have issued a booklet entitled, "Systematic Accounting." The book is an advertisement of the loose-leaf system perfeted by this house. It contains descriptions of the various accounting and bookkeeping devices and systems which the Razall Co. are ready to sell or to install. With the booklet come small folders advertising Edison's Mimeograph and Ward's Asbestos Copying Bath. This copying bath, it is claimed, is made of the best galvanized aluminum and brass, thus preventing all rust or corrosion. The pan is filled partially, and the cover entirely, with specially-prepared asbestos, which absorbs and retains a large quantity of water, and thus moisture is always distributed evenly through all the cloths laid between the cover and the blotter. By this means, it is said, any number of cloths desired are always ready for copying.

WE ARE INDEBTED to the First National Bank of Chicago for a copy of a very handsome book, which it has recently issued, entitled "The History of the First National Bank of Chicago," by Henry C. Morris. This has been published under the authority of the President and the Board of Directors. As many of our readers know, the institution in question is now engaged in the erection of the largest and finest banking building of the great West. A steel plate from the architect's drawings, showing the appearance of this building, is used as the frontispiece to the book. The history of the First National Bank is preceded by some account of early banking in the United States, especially in the West and at Chicago. Other illustrations appearing in the book are a portrait of Edmund Aiken the first president; another of Samuel M. Nickerson, the second president; also one of Lyman J. Gage, ex-Secretary of the Treasury and third president, and of James B. Forgan, the fourth and present president. There are also pictures of the first, second and third or present building of the bank, a pyramid diagram showing at different dates the relative position of the different items reported by the First National Bank of Chicago, a chart showing the growth of the bank, and a chart of Business Organization and Administration. The latter was supplied by the American Institute of Bank Clerks and is a duplicate of that which is used in one of the study courses of the Correspondence School of Banking. Among the appendices are a list of members of the Board of Directors from the establishment of the bank to date, a list of officers from the establishment of the bank to date, and a statement showing dividends declared from its foundation to date, also statements of condition at different periods from 1863 to 1902.

HALL'S Fireproof and Burglar Proof SAFES

Sold since 1840. Never fail to protect contents.

KNOWN EVERYWHERE

393 BROADWAY, N.Y.

Telephones: 3133-3136-307 Franklin.

BUSINESS NEEDS

Advertisements under this head one cent a word each insertion.

STATIONERY SALESMAN WANTED—One thoroughly conversant with the file and binder business. Only such as can command a good personal trade need apply. Salary and commission. Excellent chance for the right man. Address BINDER, care Commerce, Accounts & Finance.

SECOND-HAND TYPEWRITERS can be repaired so that they can be used and produce work which is almost, if not quite, as good as from a new machine. I have the facilities for obtaining exceptionally good second-hand machines. I have a man who repairs them—a man that understands his business. These machines can be sold for 50 per cent discount from list price of the new machines. Does this interest you? If it does, address TYPEWRITER, care Commerce, Accounts & Finance.

A FIRST-CLASS BOOKKEEPER wants to make a change of employers. I have been with the house where I now am for seven years, and am not satisfied with my prospects for promotion. Can refer those interested to my present employers, and to other reliable merchants and financiers. I solicit an interview. Address H. B., care Commerce, Accounts & Finance.

I SELL FILES. Vertical files, sectional files, pamphlet files, card index files and every conceivable kind of a file that may be needed to hold office memorandums or papers. I sell files cheap, not cheap files cheap, but files cheap. Write "FILES," and ask for prices. Address, care Commerce, Accounts & Finance.

YOUNG MAN WANTED to sell an office novelty on commission. Liberal terms. Address LAMP, care Commerce, Accounts & Finance.

OFFICE AND BANK FITTINGS. Having been connected with a large office furniture manufacturing company for years, I am now in business for myself. I can save you money on your office furniture, desks, chairs, counters and the like. Let me figure on the fittings for your new office. To fetch me, drop a line to OAK, care Commerce, Accounts & Finance.

SALESMAN WANTED—One who can really sell. Salary and commission. References required. Address J. M. S., care Commerce, Accounts & Finance.

A GENTLEMAN OF EXPERIENCE in business desires a position as bookkeeper, manager our outside man. Salary not the only object: future chances a big item. References given on request. QUILL, care Commerce, Accounts & Finance.

WHERE ARE YOU HAVING YOUR ENGRAVING DONE? I haven't the largest plant in the world, but my machinery is of the newest and best and my workmen are skilled. Also, and this may interest you, my prices are away below the big fellows'. Give me a trial. Representative will call. Address CUTS, care Commerce, Accounts & Finance.

HAVE YOU NOW under consideration the issuing of any new bit of advertising matter? Such, for instance, as a little Catalogue, Booklet or Folder, or a new Circular to replace some former one not "up-to-date." If I have happened to diagnose your case correctly, why not write me, and if you have anything that you would like bettered, why not slip a copy of it in your letter to me? F. COOK, care Commerce, Accounts and Finance.

DO YOU NEED BOOKS? Old books, new books, second-hand books. Agent for subscription books, and dealer in old and new books. Ask me for prices on books you want before you buy elsewhere. A. CROSS, care Commerce, Accounts & Finance.

HAVE YOU READ

The Kite Trust?

If not, why not? Send $1.50 for a copy to W. O. Douglass, Treasurer of The Bank Clerks' Club of New York, care First National Bank, New York City.

TITLE GUARANTEE AND TRUST COMPANY

Does each year an increasing proportion of the whole business of examining titles and making mortgage loans in New York City. Last year it loaned

Over Thirty-Five Million Dollars

on real estate in New York City. When you buy real estate, or borrow on it, come to this company. Fees moderate and uniform.

Capital and Surplus, $6,000,000

146 Broadway, MANHATTAN. 175 Remsen St., BROOKLYN.

Charts of Bank Organization and Administration

ONE of the original and fascinating features of the work of the American Institute of Bank Clerks is a collection of charts showing in a clear and comprehensive manner the arrangement of the working forces of several of the leading banks in different large cities of the country, together with an outline of the duties connected with each department.

What the Charts Show

CHART "A" represents the First National Bank of Chicago, which has a very comprehensive plan of administration. The different departments of the bank are numbered in the chart for ready reference, so that the course of any item may be followed from receipt to final disposition. The main divisions of labor are clearly shown, and the duties of employees set forth in a clear and striking manner.

CHART "B" represents a prominent New York bank doing a large general business. The various departments and the duties of the different clerks therein employed are fully described.

CHART "C" shows the general plan of administration of one of the largest New York banks doing an extensive business with merchants and having a large number of correspondents throughout the country. An examination of the chart shows how this great business is handled.

CHART "D" represents in outline one of the largest and strongest banks in New York. An analysis of the chart shows that loans on collateral security are an important feature of the business transacted, although the bank's customers include numerous corporations of the first magnitude, and a desirable line of out-of-town banks.

CHART "E" represents a New York bank in the wealthy residence district, numbering among its customers many of the "400." The facilities afforded to ladies are a conspicuous and presumably very profitable feature of this institution.

CHART "F" shows the administrative plan of one of the leading banks of Philadelphia, doing a large general business and having numerous correspondents throughout the country.

CHART "G" is not intended to represent any particular institution, but rather to show the distribution of the working force of a typical New York bank of large size and progressive methods.

These charts are a part of the correspondence course of study in Practical Banking, but they have created such general interest that the Institute has arranged to publish them in a handsomely bound booklet, and to use the same as a premium for new subscriptions at $2.00 each.

To each new subscriber to The Bulletin at $2.00, as a premium, one copy Free

Send order and make remittance payable to

American Institute of Bank Clerks

25 Pine Street, New York

NOV 18 '02
THE NEW YORK PUBLIC LIBRARY
ASTOR, LENOX AND TILDEN FOUNDATIONS

COMMERCE ACCOUNTS & FINANCE

Volume 4 New York November 1902 Number 11

Correspondence School of

Business Organization and Administration

"ACCOUNTING IS THE VITAL ELEMENT OF BUSINESS."

In response to the urgent demands of our friends throughout the country, we have arranged to extend to the business world at large what we have for many months past been doing for a very small and select circle. We accordingly take this means to announce the "Correspondence School of Business Organization and Administration," into which we shall be pleased to receive pupils wherever situated.

This school has not been hastily organized. As a fact, nearly three years of hard work have been spent upon preparation for it. As the result, practical business training is offered the like of which can nowhere else be procured.

The lesson courses are arranged in two series: Preparatory and Advanced. The legend on the banner is "Accounting is the Vital Element of Business." Every effort is made, therefore, to get the pupil fully conversant with accounting principles as the foundation of his work and then building thereon to instruct him in Organization and Administration along selected lines.

Each student upon enrolment is subjected to a preliminary examination to put upon our office records the facts of his elementary training. Notation is also made of various personal facts connected with his history, such as age, experience in actual business, references, etc. So far we have found remunerative employment for every one who has been under our charge, and at present the applicants upon our rolls for intelligent help are in excess of our ability to supply. Every one who entrusts himself to our care is assured of a good position on completion of either one of the advanced courses of training.

PREPARATORY COURSES

- A English Grammar, Composition and Business Rhetoric $25 00
- B Business Correspondence 15 00
- C Shorthand and Typewriting 25 00
- D Comm'l Geography $15 00
- E Financial and Commercial History 15 00
- F Business Arithmetic 15 00
- G Double Entry Bookkeeping 25 00
- H Commercial Law . 25 00

Special courses arranged in the light of particular requirements.

ADVANCED COURSES

Accounting, Business Organization and Administration of

1. Machine Shop with Foundry $100
2. Cotton Mill (Textiles in General). 100
3. Street Car Line 100
4. Department Store . . . 100
5. Country Bank 100
6. Large City Bank . . . 100
7. Book Publishing House 100
8. Periodical Publishing Concern $100
9. Mercantile Business (wholesale) . 100
10. Mining 100
11. General Manufactur'g 100
12. Installment Merchandising 100

The prices preceding are for single payments with the order. Under proper conditions, and at a slight advance over these rates, we are prepared to concede monthly or quarterly payments.

Time unlimited. Students may enter at any time, and proceed with their work rapidly or slowly as suits their convenience.

The Lesson Courses are all sectionalized. A second section will be forwarded only when proficiency has been shown in the first.

All examination questions will be printed in Commerce, Accounts & Finance, a subscription to which is included in the price of each course. "Collateral Reading" and "Talks With Students" will also be features of the periodical.

ACCOUNT, AUDIT & ASSURANCE COMPANY 25 PINE STREET NEW YORK

Published Monthly by the Commerce Accounts & Finance Company Twenty-five Pine Street New York

The Stationery Manufacturing Company

318 BROADWAY NEW YORK

IMPREST CASH SYSTEM.

We did not originate the imprest cash system. In fact, we do not know who did originate it. Our impression is that, like some other good things in accounting and business details, it originated in Great Britain. We have, however, done mu·h to perfect the details and to put it into working shape, and the object of this article is to call attention to one plan, at least, by which the scheme can be made effective.

Tickets in the cash drawer are an offense suffered by many cash systems. There would seem to be a propensity upon the part of those having to do with cash to defer entries for the time being and substitute therefor a ticket in the drawer. It was, perhaps, this propensity upon the part of the persons in charge of the cash that led to the invention of the imprest system, for to a certain extent the ticket scheme is made use of:

First for the facts. Fig. 1 shows the voucher or ticket as employed by this system. In actual use it is 5½ inches wide by 8½ inches long. It is printed with the name of the concern, and down the left hand half with the names of the accounts to one or the other of which a petty cash disbursement might be charged. Opposite each item is a number which refers to the number of the column in the voucher summary, as shown in Fig. 2. Right here it should be remarked that the voucher summary here shown does not correspond with the voucher, the two fragments of systems being introduced to give greater variety to this description.

In the column succeeding the number column is space for a check mark, thus making it possible to indicate by the simplest stroke of the pen or pencil to which account the item which the ticket or voucher represents should be charged.

The right hand half of the voucher contains space for items and particulars, below which is room for certification as to correctness, formal approval by, and a record of entered on summary by, thus giving the whole history of the transaction from beginning to end. Across the bottom of the voucher is space for receipt, the receipts to be filled in in all cases where the transaction is of any importance.

The imprest cash system has as its foundation the setting aside or the "impressing" of a specified sum of money for a purpose, in other words, for disbursements for petty items. As the expenses are paid, a voucher of the kind just described is filled out for each and this voucher is dropped into the drawer or cash box, as the case may be. After a while, when the imprest amount has been so far depleted as to make a replenishment desirable, the vouchers or tickets are taken from the drawer and listed and summarized on a sheet such as is shown in Fig. 2, and thereby demand is made upon the treasurer for a check for the replenishment of the fund.

As these vouchers are made up, they are fastened together in a bundle and the summary sheet is folded and put over them after the fashion shown in Fig. 3. The back of the summarizing sheet contains space for date, numbers of vouchers taken up, the inclusive amount, the formal approval by the officer of the company in charge, and a record of the check

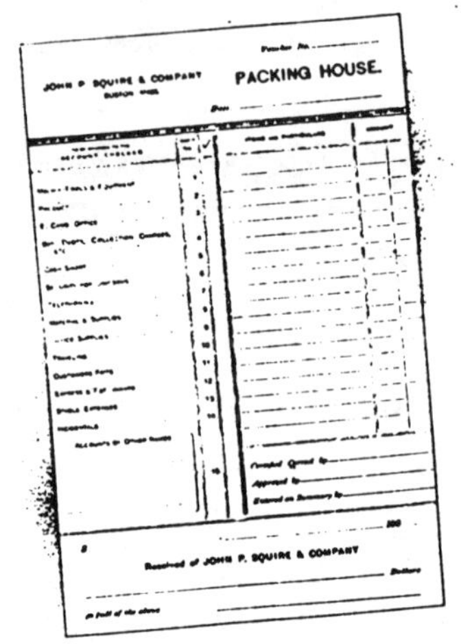

Fig. 1. Reduced Fac-Simile of Imprest Cash Voucher. Actual Size, 5½x8½.

which was used for lifting the vouchers. Referring to Fig. 3, it will be seen that vouchers 2732 to 2752 inclusive, amounting to $85.96, approved by Charles A. Smith, were taken up and paid by check No. 2497 on the Hanover National Bank.

The voucher summary shown in detail in February 2 has its surface divided into columns corresponding to the expense analysis of the business to which it is devoted, and also summary. The folding of the summary is such that these two columns are always exposed. The summary and vouchers underneath it are fastened together by wire staples, eyelets, McGill fasteners, or other suitable devices.

The voucher summary serves as the posting medium to the expense accounts in the ledger. The footings of the expense columns on the voucher summary become the amounts to be carried to these accounts. It will be noticed in Fig. 2 that there are two lines at the bottom of the summary, one entitled "Footings" and the other "Postings." "Footings" is, of course, as its name indicates, for the footings of the amounts in the columns, while "Postings" is virtually an L. F. space and shows below the item the ledger page to which it has been carried.

In addition to the expense columns, there is provided at the extreme right hand of the voucher summary, "Other Accounts by Name," so that the imprest system may be extended to any degree desirable. Whatever is paid out of the imprest system can be entered upon this summary and thereby carried to the ledger in regular course.

Some of the advantages of this system are apparent without enumeration, but brief reference to the same will not be without interest to the reader. In the first place, it makes necessary every disbursement of cash, being evidenced by a check on the bank. The replenishment of the imprest fund is in effect payment of the vouchers or tickets in the drawer which have accumulated, and for this purpose, as in the illustration shown in Fig. 3, a check of a certain number on a specified bank is drawn.

In the general statement of the company's business, the imprest amount is always a fixed quantity. There is so much cash on hand in

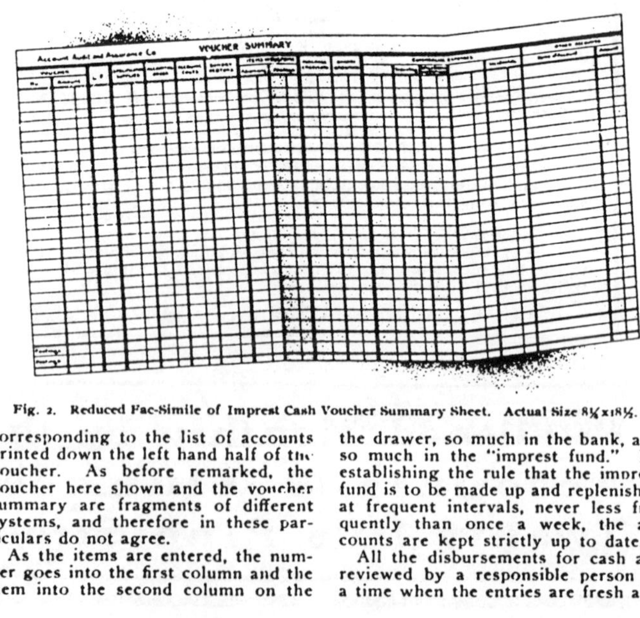

Fig. 2. Reduced Fac-Simile of Imprest Cash Voucher Summary Sheet. Actual Size 8¼x18½.

corresponding to the list of accounts printed down the left hand half of the voucher. As before remarked, the voucher here shown and the voucher summary are fragments of different systems, and therefore in these particulars do not agree.

As the items are entered, the number goes into the first column and the item into the second column on the the drawer, so much in the bank, and so much in the "imprest fund." By establishing the rule that the imprest fund is to be made up and replenished at frequent intervals, never less frequently than once a week, the accounts are kept strictly up to date.

All the disbursements for cash are reviewed by a responsible person at a time when the entries are fresh and before the items have been forgotten. There is a constant cash audit in progress, greatly to the advantage of the integrity of the cash account.

By insisting upon the certification being filled out, provided for in the voucher shown in Fig. 1, and the formal approval of some one else in the proper position for the purpose, likewise provided in the space on the voucher, there follows that no amount is paid out without the co-operation of at least two persons.

The filing away of vouchers in this form puts them in most convenient shape for reference where any occasion to go to them at a subsequent date arises.

By posting from the voucher summary as above described, the bookkeeper's labor is reduced to a minimum. No disbursing cash book is required. Each disbursement of a considerable amount will be made, of course, by check and will be posted straight from the check book or check register. Small disbursements

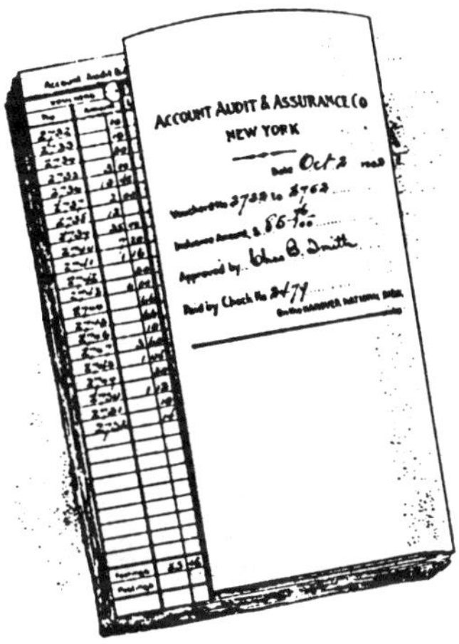

Fig. 3. Bundle of Imprest Cash Vouchers and the Summary Sheet as finally made up.

will be posted straight from the voucher summary here shown.

We are prepared to supply the stationery equipment of the imprest cash system here illustrated at the following very low prices:

Vouchers as per Fig. 1, printed to agree with the classification of accounts that may be communicated to us, and with the name of the concern, $4 per thousand. Discount on large quantities.

Summary sheets, the equivalent of Fig. 2, being 8½ by 18½ inches, columnarized to agree with the items in Fig. 1, $10 per thousand. Discount on large quantities.

Other sizes of summary sheets at proportionate prices.

Address communications to

Stationery Manufacturing Company, 318 Broadway, New York.

BRIEF MENTION.

A LITTLE BOOKLET advertising the Star Safety Razor is sent out by O. H. Wilmarth, 40 Nassau street, New York. The booklet is illustrated with cuts of the Safety Razor and its attachments, and is very neatly printed and well worded. The user of the ordinary razor may be astonished to know that over five million people are using the Star Safety Razor, which, by the way, does not look like a razor at all. The booklet contains directions for using the razor, and pictures of many fine cases filled with razors, extra blades, strops, etc.

THE WORDS "DON'T SWEAR," printed in red, confront the reader of the folder advertising the Century Inkstand. The printed matter on the folder commands the reader not to swear at high ink bills, inky fingers, or when he finds mud where the ink should be. The reasonable course is to buy the Century Inkstand, which, so the folder assures us, is everything that an inkstand should be. It cannot wear out, the ink does not evaporate and is always pure and free from dirt and dust. What more can one expect from an inkstand, and in these soft coal days, too?

THE QUESTION OF HEAT is a vital one just at present, and, therefore, the folder advertising the Miller Oil Heaters makes timely reading. The Miller Heaters are made in various shapes, with nickel or Japan finish, and are sold at various prices. They are said to be simple of construction, easy to rewick and made so that they cannot smoke. When so many people are falling back upon oil as a means of producing heat, this heater booklet should be worth sending for.

THE STANDARD PAINT COMPANY, with offices at New York, Chicago, Hamburg, London and Paris, are issuing a handsome booklet extolling the P. & B. water-proof system of insulation. The book contains half-tone reproductions of photographs illustrating many interiors of cold storage companies using the P. & B. paper. It also contains reproductions in fac-simile of letters from many large firms using the P. & B. papers and speaking highly of them. In the book, likewise, are quotations from several technical journals and from newspapers describing the use of insulated papers and of the P. & B. paper in particular. Taken, all in all, this book should make good advertising for the Standard Paint Company.

AN ODD FOLDER has reached our desk, coming from the Egry Autographic Register Company. The title of the folder is "New and Valuable Ideas That Will Save Money," and pictures of stacks of coin and piles of greenbacks help to attract the reader's attention. The Egry Autographic Register and Manifolders are described in the pages of this pamphlet, and the various uses to which it may be applied are set forth in an alluring manner. "By the Egry system," says the pamphlet, "three or more copies of each Bill of Lading or Shipping Receipt are issued at one writing without the handling of sheets or changing of carbon, as both stationery and carbon are on rolls, and by the use of the Register an automatic feed is gained. The Register is ever ready for action, and by its complete arrangement the operator may issue the instruments with the greatest rapidity. All copies are clear and distinct, as the stationery is automatically carried over a rigid writing surface."

THE TRUST COMPANY OF THE REPUBLIC, whose offices are at 346 Broadway, New York City, are issuing a neat little folder advertising its general banking business. The pamphlet is very artistically printed and decorated, contains a list of the officers and directors, and, also, a map showing the possessions of the United States, wherever situated.

"THE WESTERN TRAIL" is the title of an illustrated paper issued monthly by the Chicago, Rock Island and Peoria Railway, and sent without charge for a year to those interested. Its pages, of course, are principally given up to the exploiting of the farm lands traversed by the Rock Island route. In the specimen copy before us there are beautiful half-tone pictures of farms and ranches in Kansas and New Mexico, and the farmers and ranch owners shown in these pictures certainly look prosperous. This is a big country of ours, and such publications as the "Western Trail" help to bring this fact to the casual reader's notice.

WE ARE IN RECEIPT of a catalogue of the Pierce School, bearing upon its face "38th Year." This organization, which is housed in the Record Building, 917-919 Chestnut street, Philadelphia, is one of the institutions of the Quaker City. The book before us gives the general information concerning the school that is usually contained in college year books. The corps of teachers, the faculty, the calendar for the current year, some particulars concerning the different courses, together with the proceedings of the last commencement day, with addresses, etc., are presented. An indication of the localism of the school is furnished by the table of recapitulation of students, published near the end of the book. Last year there were entered in the school 1,627 pupils. Of these, 1,381 came from Pennsylvania, 200 from New Jersey; Maryland contributed 8 and Delaware 9. Other states, to the extent of 19, contributed from 1 to 3 each.

THE HISTORY of the famous Missisquoi Springs and its wonderful cures is issued by the Missisquoi Mineral Springs Company, of Sheldon, Vt. According to the information contained in this booklet, the water from the Missisquoi Spring is nature's own cure for all kinds of troubles. A description of the various diseases suffered by those who have visited the Spring in the hope of cure is somewhat gruesome, but the description of the marvellous manner in which they were cured of these diseases and sent upon their way rejoicing is inspiring; but the names are given in almost every instance, and often they are those of prominent men and women, so the testimony would seem to be authentic and convincing. If the reader is troubled with rheumatism, or gout, or cancer, or almost any other bodily ailment, let him send for this book and be happy.

RUBBER TIPS FOR CHAIR LEGS are what Geo. W. Berrian, of 29 Maiden Lane, New York, manufactures and sells in large quantities. These rubber tips are intended to be placed upon the legs of the ordinary office chair, and they prevent noise and the scratching of the floor. Mr. Berrian also sells rubber goods of every description, but it is the rubber chair tip that he is specially advertising this fall and winter.

BOOKS OF INTEREST TO BUSINESS MEN.

The A B C of Banks and Banking.—By George M. Coffin. 6¾ x 5 inches; 137 pages. Bound in cloth. Back title gilt. Price, $1.25.

This handy little volume is exactly what its name implies; that is, a presentation of the principles underlying banking in the United States. The author in his preface says that it is designed to appeal to the reader outside as well as inside of a bank. It is by no means the last word or every word about banking. It may be said that it is a primer covering a field that has hitherto been somewhat neglected. The chapter heads are as follows: Banking in General, Various Kinds of Banking, Capital Stock, Shareholders' Rights and Liabilities, Undivided Profits, Dividends and Surplus, Deposits, Checks, Lawful Money Reserve, Issuing Bank Notes, Borrowing Money, Loans and Discounts, Exchanges, Collections, Letters of Credit, Bonds, Mortgages and Stocks, Bank Reports, Examinations, Directors, Executive Officers—Their Powers and Duties, Internal Administration and Bookkeeping, and other suggestions.

Business Law.—By Alonzo R. Weed, L. L. B., of the Boston Bar. 6 x 9¼ inches; 172 pages. Bound in cloth. Cover and back title red. Price, $1.25.

Mr. Weed calls his book "a manual for schools and colleges and for every day use." The titles of the chapters are as follows: Contracts, Principal and Agent, Partnerships, Sales of Personal Property, Bailments and Common Carriers, Negotiable Paper, Deeds, Mortgages and Leases, Collection Laws, Written Rates of Interest, Insurance, Patent Rights, Trade Marks and Copyrights, etc.

The author does not waste words, and yet treats his subjects clearly and comprehensively. In short, he gives the law without the addition of wordy "trimmings."

Introduction to the Study of Economics.—By Charles Jesse Bullock, Ph. D. 7¾ x 5½ inches. 581 pages. Bound in cloth. Cover and back title gilt. Price, $1.25.

This book, the author says, is designed as an introductive text book of economic science. Throughout the volume economics are discussed with special reference to American conditions, and their workings are illustrated by frequent allusions to American experience. There are chapters on the Consumption of Wealth, the Theory of Exchange, the Development of Metallic Money, Money and Credit, and the like.

Political Economy of Humanism.—By Henry Wood. 7¾ x 5¼ inches; 320 pages. Bound in cloth. Cover and back title gilt. Price, $1.25.

Mr. Wood is well known as a writer on various economic subjects, and this book contains a series of able treatises, written in his usual vein, on the relation of the employer to the employed, and the phases of the industrial question and their relation to socialism. Among the questions considered and handled in a conservative spirit and with much common sense, are the following: Supply and Demand, the Law of Competition, Labor and Production, Combinations of Capital, Combinations of Labor, Employers and Profit Sharing, the Obligations and Privileges of Employees, the Unequal Distribution of Wealth, Money and Coinage, Tariffs and Protection, Industrial Education and Gold Production and Values.

The Kite Trust, A Romance of Wealth.—By Lebbeus Harding Rogers. 7¾ x 5½ inches; 475 pages. Illustrated. Price, $1.

This is a treatise or series of treatises on economic subjects in the guise of a story. The tale itself concerns three American boys, and is very interesting as well as instructive. The trust idea is explained and an explanation of banking is given. The greenback is dealt with, as are also Wall Street and stock speculation.

Business Law.—By Thomas Raeburn White, B. L., L. L. B. 5 x 7½ inches; 323 pages. Bound in cloth. Back title gilt. Price, 50 cents.

This is a neat, compact and handy book of business for law for the use of students and business men. Among the subjects treated are Contracts, Sales, Partnerships, Corporations, Negotiable Paper and the like. The author's language is plain, and is understandable by any one having no previous knowledge of law. The book's clearness on the essential points of ordinary law should recommend it as a business book for the plain business man who has no time in which to consult a law library.

The Phonographic Dictionary and Phrase Book.—By Benn Pitman and Jerome B. Howard. 5½ x 8 inches; 552 pages. Bound in cloth. Cover title and back title gilt. Price, $3.

This book is the most elaborate shorthand dictionary yet published, with the characters in fac-simile. It contains over 120,000 words, and for every one of these words there is a corresponding sign in the Benn Pitman system of shorthand. To the reporter, office or court stenographer, or any one writing the Benn Pitman system of shorthand, the book is invaluable. It is well made, tastefully bound, and is printed on a good quality of paper in clean, plain type.

Grace's Handy Book for Making Rapid Calculations. 8¼ x 5¼ inches. Bound in cloth. 65 pages. Title printed in silver. Price, $1.

The full title of this book is "Merchants', Bankers' and Brokers' Handy Book for Making Rapid Calculations in all Branches of Commercial Requirements, Weights, Measures and Moneys." The volume contains a series of tables for calculating the price of wheat, corn and oat bushels in decimals, for converting cubic meters to cubic feet and cubic feet to meters, meters to lineal yards, superficial feet or square feet to cubic feet, decimal tons to avoirdupois pounds, and the like. To the busy office man who has a great deal of calculating to do, and particularly to the clerk in an export house whose work it is to reckon in United States money the amounts named in foreign invoices, these tables should be very valuable. They are quite complete, and undoubtedly their use will save time.

The Lawrence System of Vocal and Physical Expression.—By Edwin Gordon Lawrence. 4¾ by 6 inches; 128 pages. Bound in cloth. Cover title and back title gilt. Price, $1.

The author says in the preface of this little book that his object has been to place in the hands of lawyers, actors and public speakers in general, a simple system of vocal and physical expression that will enable them to clearly convey thought by word of mouth and emphasize it by the proper action. To the man of affairs who is called upon for a speech on any subject, and who knows what to say but does not know how to say it, this book will be a great help.

The Anatomy of a Railroad Report.—By Thomas F. Woodlock. 7 x 5¼ inches. 121 pages. Bound in cloth. Cover of back title gilt. Price, $1.

This little book is intended for the use of those people who, while interested in railroad investments, are wholly unacquainted with railroad accounts. The book is divided into two sections, the first being the Anatomy of the Railroad Report and the second being Ton-Mile Cost. It treats of phases of the railroad business in concise fashion, but thoroughly and accurately.

Any book in this list will be sent to any address in the United States, Canada or Mexico upon receipt of price. If there is some special book that you require we shall be pleased to hunt it up for you.

Address **Commerce, Accounts & Finance, 25 Pine street, New York City.**

About a Pay Roll which proves itself, corrects all mistakes in figuring, divides up Pay Roll into several amounts needed to pay each person.

But let us send you a sample leaf, with circular, which tells the whole story.

BARLOW BROS., Grand Rapids, Mich.

W. G. Mowat
Public Accountant
831 Ellicott Sq., Buffalo, N. Y.

FREE--A PAIR OF SLEEVE PROTECTORS.

Do you want to know about our Loose Leaf Ledgers and office devices? They will save you time, trouble and money. To all bookkeepers in the States of New York, New Jersey and Massachusetts who write us for information about our systems we will send a pair of sleeve protectors. In writing mention size of cuff.

THE C. E. SHEPPARD CO.,
87 Maiden Lane, NEW YORK CITY.

KNICKERBOCKER TRUST CO.

234 FIFTH AVENUE, CORNER 27TH STREET
BRANCH OFFICES:
66 BROADWAY, AND 125TH STREET AND LENOX AVE.,
NEW YORK CITY.

CAPITAL AND UNDIVIDED PROFITS, $2,508,399.11.

LEGAL DEPOSITORY FOR STATE, CITY, AND COURT FUNDS.

Interest allowed on Time Deposits. Deposits also received subject to Demand Checks, which pass through the Clearing House as do those upon any city bank.

Authorized to act as Executor or Administrator of Estates, and as Guardian, Receiver, Registrar, Transfer and Financial Agent for States, Cities, Towns, Railroads, and other corporations, and to accept any other Trusts in conformity with the laws of any State or of the United States.

LETTERS OF CREDIT FURNISHED.
BUSINESS AND PERSONAL ACCOUNTS SOLICITED.

CHAS. T. BARNEY, - - - - - - - - President.
JOSEPH T. BROWN, - - - - - - 2d Vice-President.
JULIAN M. GERARD, - - - - Asst. Sec. and Asst. Treas.
FRED'K K. ELDRIDGE, - - - - - 1st Vice-President.
FRED'K GORE KING, - - - Secretary and Treasurer.
WM. B. RANDALL, - - - - - - - Trust Officer.

BOARD OF DIRECTORS:

JOSEPH S. AUERBACH,
HARRY B. HOLLINS,
JACOB HAYS,
CHARLES T. BARNEY,
A. FOSTER HIGGINS,
ANDREW H. SANDS,
JAMES H. BRESLIN,
I. TOWNSEND BURDEN,
HON. E. V. LOEW,
HENRY F. DIMOCK,
CHARLES F. WATSON,
FREDERICK G. BOURNE,
C. LAWRENCE PERKINS,
CHARLES R. FLINT,
AMZI L. BARBER,
CHARLES T. COOK,
JOHN MAGEE,
HENRY A. MORGAN,
HENRY C. BERLIN,
CHARLES W. GOULD,
FRED'K L. ELDRIDGE,
HENRY W. DE FOREST,
ALFRED B. MACLAY
HARRY W. McVICKAR.

HASKINS & SELLS,

CERTIFIED PUBLIC ACCOUNTANTS.

204 DEARBORN STREET
CHICAGO

LINCOLN TRUST BLDG.
ST. LOUIS

30 BROAD STREET,
NEW YORK.

CABLE ADDRESS "HASKSELLS"

WILLIAMSON BLDG.
CLEVELAND, O.

30 COLEMAN STREET
LONDON, E.C.

Lackawanna Railroad

Address all communications to
C. W. TEN BROECK, Industrial Agent,
26 Exchange Place, New York City.

Do You Desire a Factory Site? The Industrial Department of the Lackawanna Railroad will aid you in finding one.

Are You Interested in Any Raw Product for Manufacturing Purposes? The Industrial Department of the Lackawanna Railroad will tell you if it is to be found along that road.

Does the Question of Power Concern You? The Industrial Department of the Lackawanna Railroad will tell you of good water power and of the proximity of fuel to points on that road.

Do You Want to Know the Usual Rate of Wages? The Industrial Department of the Lackawanna Railroad will give that information regarding any point on that road.

Do You Want to Know the Price of Gas, Water, Electricity? The Industrial Department of the Lackawanna Railroad will tell you.

HALL'S Fireproof and Burglar Proof SAFES

Sold since 1840. Never fail to protect contents.

KNOWN EVERYWHERE

393 BROADWAY, N.Y.

Telephones: 3133-3136-307 Franklin.

PUBLIC ACCOUNTANTS.

Atlanta, Ga.—Ralph H. Brown, 804 Empire Building.
Boston, Mass.—Charles H. Fellows, 174 Summer; New England Audit Company, 45 Milk; J. S. Parsons, 214 Columbus Ave.
Brooklyn, N. Y.—Franklin Allen, Arbuckle Building, 371 Fulton.
Buffalo, N.Y.—W. G. Mowat, 831 Ellicott Square.
Chicago, Ill.—Haskins & Sells, 214 Dearborn.
Davenport, Ia.—J. C. Grabbe, McManus Building.
Detroit, Mich.—H. Naemansson, 496 Putnam Ave.
London, Canada.—Geo. F. Jewell, 361 Dundas.
New Bedford, Mass.—James L. Hathway, 72 Willis.
New Orleans, La.—P. W. Sherwood, 904 Howard Ave.
New York, N. Y.—Patterson, Teele & Dennis, 30 Broad; Haskins & Sells, 30 Broad; Account, Audit and Assurance Co., Ltd., 25 Pine; Leon Brummer, 7 Pine; H. F. Searle, 45 Broadway; Hart Bros., Tibbits, Heiron & Co., 11 Broadway; Franklin Allen, Silk Exchange Building, Broadway.
Philadelphia, Pa.—Francis & Sterrett, Penn Mutual Building; Peter Ballingall, German-American Building; Charles W. Thomas, 409 Lippincott Building; Alfred L. Sellers, 1001 Chestnut.
Pittsburgh, Pa.—John Vaughn, 5520 Claybourne; George W. Wood & Co., 341 Fourth Ave.
Providence, R. I.—George R. Allen, 29 Weybosset.
San Francisco, Cal.—Charles L. Lutgen, 218 California; Lester Herrick, 405 Montgomery.
Toronto, Canada.—F. H. Kidd, Bank of Commerce Building.
Windsor, Canada.—F. H. Macpherson, 16 Sandwich, East.
Winnipeg, Canada.—Peter Thornton, 343 Main.

TITLE GUARANTEE AND TRUST COMPANY

Does each year an increasing proportion of the whole business of examining titles and making mortgage loans in New York City. Last year it loaned

Over Thirty-Five Million Dollars

on real estate in New York City. When you buy real estate, or borrow on it, come to this company. Fees moderate and uniform.

Capital and Surplus, $6,000,000

146 Broadway, MANHATTAN. 175 Remsen St., BROOKLYN.

A BUSINESS EDUCATION | FOR ...ONE... DOLLAR.

...THE PRACTICAL AGE...

A MONTHLY MAGAZINE full to the brim with helpful suggestions to young men and young women who are struggling successward.

THE BUSINESS HOUSE THAT JACK BUILT, an intensely interesting and highly instructive story of business life, and

APPLIED ENGLISH, an authority on writing and speaking the English language, which no young person can afford to be without, all for ONE DOLLAR.

If you have never seen THE PRACTICAL AGE, send for a free sample copy. Address,

THE PRACTICAL AGE,

Moline, Illinois.

Use any pen and your own stationery. If your stationer does not keep it, write for free specimen of work. Beware of infringements. Address Dept. —

Pen-Carbon Manifold Co., 145-7-9 Centre St., New York.

The Procedure in the Complete Audit of the Accounts of a Commercial Firm*

By H. MORGAN.

THE importance of a complete audit of the accounts of all business men has been demonstrated so often and so conclusively, that it is a matter of surprise how often one hears the question, "What is the use of having accounts of private firms or individuals audited?" Such a question could be answered by almost any successful business man, nearly every one of whom would ascribe his success in a very large degree to the advantage of having had his accounts kept on a good and correct system, by means of which he has been enabled to have prepared correct and reliable accounts, showing the course of his trading and his financial position from time to time. The conditions under which practically every business is carried on in these days, are such that no one can hope to successfully compete with his fellow traders unless he is regularly supplied with correct accounts, showing the conduct of every part of his business. In addition to this, except in the case of very small businesses, it is necessary for the principals to devote the whole of their time to the superintendence of their business, which renders it necessary for them to leave the keeping of their accounts and the handling of the cash to clerks and cashiers.

This, then, brings us to the chief objects of a complete audit, which may be stated to be—

(1) The supplying of a check on the honesty and accuracy of subordinates, and

(2) The preparation of a balance-sheet and trading and profit and loss accounts.

Audits may be stated to be of two kinds, viz., "completed" and "continuous." The former kind of audit, in which the auditor is called in when the accounts are completed, and he is only required to investigate them and affix his certificate, is seldom met with except in the case of public companies, and therefore does not concern us here.

In the case of commercial firms, it is almost the invariable custom for the audit to be of a "continuous" nature, in which the auditor makes periodical visits and superintends the keeping of the accounts, checks the cash in hand, &c., and finally prepares trading and profit and loss accounts and balance-sheet.

Now, then, as to the procedure, I will suppose that the auditor is required to commence his duties at the time when the firm commences business. He will probably be requested to devise the system and indicate the manner in which the accounts shall be kept. First of all as to the books. The chief ones that will be required will be: private ledger, general (or expense) ledger, bought ledger, sold ledger, cash book, petty cash book, bill book, bought and sold day books, and journal. Special attention should be given to the ruling of the cash book, and separate columns provided for the cash posted in the bought and sold ledgers. For every ledger an adjustment account should be opened, which will enable each ledger to be balanced separately. In large businesses it will be found necessary to have several bought and sold ledgers, in which cases there should be separate cash books, only the totals being entered in the general cash book. The petty cash book should be ruled with dissection columns. In addition to the above-mentioned books, the special nature of a business may require others. For instance, in a retail drapery business there should be kept a stock and profit book, salary ledger, &c., but as they would be only subsidiary books, it is not necessary to discuss them here. I feel sure that an auditor will find himself well repaid by devoting a little extra time and attention to the rulings of the books and the system on which they shall be kept.

The Deed of Partnership.

Having got the books, the auditor would call for the deed of partnership, this being the foundation of the accounts. In the majority of cases he will have to make the opening entries, which require a certain amount of knowledge and skill, outside the capabilities of the ordinary book-keeper, and they demand very careful consideration. Partnership deeds are nearly always drawn up by solicitors, without the auditor being consulted or being shown a draft of the deed, with the result that they are generally very complicated and even obscure as regards most of the matters relating to the accounts. For instance, if a man in business takes into partnership someone who has to introduce so much capital you will probably find a clause in the deed reading something after this style: "The capital of the firm shall consist of the good will, plant and machinery, book debts and stock-in-trade, of the business formerly carried on by the said 'So-and-so,' which shall, for the purposes of this partnership, be valued at £——, &c., &c." Nothing at all is said about the value to be placed on each separate item. Now you cannot, for obvious reasons, open an account headed "Good will, plant and machinery, book debts and stock-in-trade," so the auditor would have to ascertain the value of the various items. There would almost certainly be a valuation of the stock-in-trade and, perhaps, of the plant and machinery; if not, all the partners should agree as to the value to be placed upon it. The auditor would probably be handed a list of the book-debts, showing the actual amount, but it would very likely contain several that were, at any rate, doubtful. The partners should also agree as to the value to be placed upon these, and the difference between the actual amount and the agreed value will be placed to the credit of "reserve for bad and doubtful debts." Having now obtained the values of plant and machinery, stock-in-trade and book-debts, the balance of the sum mentioned in the deed of partnership will be good will.

The matter of the liabilities also requires special attention. It will very often be the case that the old partner (or partners) undertakes to pay all the liabilities, and, if so, it should be seen that he is charged with rates, rent, gas, &c., &c., accrued due at the commencement of the partnership; also that the new firm is not charged with any goods delivered before that date. The auditor should inspect with especial care all invoices, receipts, &c., for the first few weeks of the partnership.

Having now seen that all the books are properly opened, he will proceed with the ordinary course of his audit, and will pay periodical visits. The first book that will have his attention each time will be the cash book. All postings of cash and discount should be called, and although this is to a certain extent mechanical, it cannot be too carefully done. The terms allowed to or by each customer should be entered at the head of his account, and if discount in excess of the usual rate has been deducted, a satisfactory explanation should be called for and furnished. Having seen that all the items are duly ticked, the cash book should next be vouched. I may here mention that an auditor should always impress upon his clients the importance of making payments wherever possible, by cheque, payable to "order" and crossed, even though they may be only for small

*Prize Essay, read before the Incorporated Accountants' Students' Society of London, by the successful competitor.

amounts. This method of payment renders it very much more difficult for a cashier to be dishonest, and it affords an additional check as to a payment being bona-fide. Receipts should be obtained for all payments and placed on a file in the order in which they are entered in the cash book. By this means the vouching of the credit side of the cash book can be very easily and quickly done. The auditor should be careful to see that each voucher is effectively cancelled; and for this purpose a rubber stamp marked "Audit" is very useful. Some accountants cancel vouchers by initialling them with a thick colored pencil, but it is very much easier to erase a pencil than an ink mark, and there is thus a possibility of the voucher being put in a second time. It will be found that even in the best regulated offices vouchers will occasionally be missing, and where this is so, the returned cheque will generally be sufficient evidence of the payment.

Payments for Wages.

Payments for wages require very particular attention. A cheque should, where possible, be drawn for the exact amount, and the list be signed by the foreman or person in authority. The better check, however, on the accuracy of the payments for wages, lies in the adoption of a good system of making the payments. Payments to regular employes at a fixed rate per week or per month present little difficulty, but where the amount is reckoned by the time worked, or piece-work done, the wages sheet should be certified by the foreman, the calculations checked by an office clerk and the payments made by a third party. The persons performing these duties should be changed periodically; there is thus, so to speak, safety in numbers.

The auditor should satisfy himself that all cash receipts have been duly entered on the debit side of the cash book. The means of doing this can be best provided by the use of numbered counterfoil receipt books. The giving of a receipt on a form other than the firm's ordinary one should be prohibited. Should any counterfoil be left blank or any numbers be missing a satisfactory reason should be given. Receipts from ready money sales should also be carefully checked. In nearly all places of business where these are of material amount, some "check" system is in use, and the auditor should see that it fulfils its purpose. Equally important as the making of all payments by cheque is that all receipts, however small should be paid into bank. These payments into bank should be carefully checked and ticked

Gov. Stone—"I can't stop it! I've got my hands full!"—Chicago Record-Herald.

off against the pass book, and it should be seen that they are duly credited.

Having vouched the cash book the additions should be checked, and also the cash-in-hand and the floating cash balances, if any. The bank account should then be agreed, the cheques being ticked off against the pass-book. The cash-book being finished, the calling of the ledgers should next be done. I will suppose the bought ledger is first taken in hand. Most of the debit side, being chiefly cash and discount, will already have been ticked off with the cash book. The credit side, which will be all, or nearly all, goods, will then be called into the purchase book, and the few unticked items on the debit side—returns and allowances—called into the returns and allowances book. The additions of the purchase and returns and allowances books should be checked, and the totals posted to the debit and credit respectively of the general ledger adjustment account. A journal entry should be made to incorporate these totals in the general ledger, the bought ledger adjustment account being credited, and purchases account being debited, with the total of the purchases, and the same accounts being debited and credited respectively with the totals of returns and allowances. The sold ledger will be ticked off and checked, and the totals posted to the adjustment and nominal accounts, in a manner similar to the bought ledger. One of the chief difficulties which an auditor will have to guard against is the possibility of a clerk altering or erasing a figure after it has been ticked. A very good method to adopt is, when calling the ledger, to use a slightly different tick wherever there has been any alteration or erasure. By this means it can be seen if a correction has been made after the item has been called.

The auditor should at each visit check and vouch the petty cash book. Many of the payments will be of such a nature that it is impossible to get a voucher for them from the person to whom the payment is made; but where this is the case, the person making the payment should write out a voucher himself and get it initialled by someone in authority. The monthly totals of the petty cash account in the general ledger, and the totals of petty cash payments should be posted to the credit of the dissection columns to the debit of their respective nominal accounts.

Items charged to plant and machinery, or fittings and fixtures, should be carefully examined to see that they are properly chargeable to those accounts, and that nothing in the nature of repairs or renewals is included. In businesses where the expenditure on plant and machinery is considerable, very great care should be exercised in the treatment of it in the accounts. In my opinion, the best method is to open in addition to the plant and machinery account, a renewals and replacements and a repairs and alterations account, the amount charged to profit and loss by way of depreciation should not be credited to plant and machinery account, but to a separate "reserve for depreciation account," the plant and machinery thus remaining at its original amount. The sum standing to the debit of renewals and replacements account should be transferred to the debit of the reserve for depreciation account, as renewals should not be written off in addition to depreciation, because the plant and machinery is improved to the extent of the amount expended on renewals. Repairs and alterations, however, are a dead loss, and should be written off in the profit and loss account.

Expenses.

With regard to the treatment of expenses, unless the items are numerous, they can be posted direct from the cash book to the nominal accounts in the general ledger, but if the number of items is large, it is advisable to have an expense journal with dissection columns headed "rent," "rates and taxes," "repairs," "renewals," &c., &c., and post the various items to the credit of the personal

THE NEW YORK PUBLIC LIBRARY ASTOR, LENOX AND TILDEN FOUNDATIONS

accounts and the totals to the debit of the nominal accounts in the general ledger.

Before concluding my remarks on the auditor's duties between the times when the accounts have to be balanced and the profit and loss account and balance-sheet drawn up, I would mention that unless the nature of the business demands it, his visits should not be made on special days or at regular intervals. It is of advantage that they should, if possible, be in the nature of surprise visits, as in addition to keeping the book-keepers up-to-date in their work, the auditor is more likely to discover any wilful discrepancy or dishonesty on the part of a book-keeper or cashier, if he has no notice of the auditor's visit and no time to prepare for it.

I now come to the time when the trading and profit and loss accounts and balance-sheet have to be prepared. First of all, it should be seen that the adjustment accounts in the general ledger agree with the respective accounts for the bought and sold ledgers. This being done, trial balances of the various ledgers should be taken out, and this often proves a long and tiresome job. Should the trial balance not agree, the auditor would first of all go through the items, and may find that he has entered one on the wrong side. Then, again, the amount of the difference will often be a guide as to where the mistake is most likely to be; thus, if it is an even sum, it is probably due to a mistake in an addition, while if it be an odd amount, he is more likely to find it in an unposted item or a balance which he has omitted to take out.

Profit and Loss Account.

Having obtained his trial balance, the auditor will next set about making out the trading and profit and loss accounts. The trading account will be debited with the stock-in-trade at the commencement of the period and the balance of the purchases account, also with any expenses that directly affect the price of the goods, such as productive wages, carriage, &c. On the credit side will appear the sales and the stock-in-trade at the close of the period. I may here mention that an auditor will often find that in certain businesses, such as furnishing, engineering, building, &c., it is the custom to supply the firm's fittings, fixtures, plant, or machinery out of stock, just as though it were a transaction in the ordinary course of the firm's business. Where this is done, it should be seen that no profit, but only cost price, is charged, and that purchases, and not sales account, is credited with the amount. The balance of the trading account will be carried to the credit of the profit and loss account, unless, as occasionally happens, there is a loss on trading.

To the debit side of the profit and loss account will be transferred the debit balances on the nominal accounts, depreciation, &c. When closing the nominal accounts the most important thing is to see that all outstanding liabilities have been debited. More particular care should be directed to such items as rent, rates, gas, electric-light, and to cases where accounts are only rendered at certain periods. In these cases the amount accrued due since the last payment or since the last statement was rendered, should be calculated or ascertained, and carried down on the nominal account as a liability. It is a very good practice to journalize these entries, as by so doing there is less risk of and omission to bring down a balance, and it is a guide in making up the accounts at the next period. Where the benefit of a charge or payment has not been exhausted, such as rent, or rates paid in advance, insurance, or where there is a stock on hand such as stationery, postages, &c., the amount should be credited and brought down as an asset on the nominal account. Some accountants prefer to leave no balances on the nominal accounts, but to transfer them to a suspense account. This, however, requires the items to be re-transferred at the beginning of the next period, and from such experience as I have had, I have been able to see no objection to bringing the balances down on the nominal accounts.

Special features will present themselves in connection with some of the nominal accounts. With regard to rent, where portions of the business premises are let off, it is advisable to open separate accounts for rent paid and rent received. On the profit and loss account, rent should be shown on both sides, or else the amount paid should be placed in an inside column, and the rent received deducted, the net amount being carried out. By showing it in this way, if during any period, any part of the premises usually let off is unoccupied and the amount charged for rent thereby increased, the reason can be readily seen. It is the usual custom to debit rent with the cost of the telephone; this is always payable in advance, so the value of the unexpired period will be carried down. Income Tax, Schedule A, being deductible from the rent, will also be debited to rent account. Should the time when the accounts are closed fall just after this tax has been paid, and before it has been deducted from the rent, it must be treated as a payment in advance on account of rent.

I think discount given and discount received should be shown on the debit and credit sides respectively of the profit and loss account, and not the balance shown as a single item. A reserve should be made on both the bought and sold ledger balances at the average rates. These rates can easily be arrived at by reckoning the total amounts of goods, for which payment has been made or received, and comparing them with the totals of the discount received or given. Discount should also be reserved on bills payable and bills receivable, according to the time when they become due.

All debts that are bad should be transferred to the debit of the bad debts account. It is a good plan, where the bad debts are numerous, to keep a subsidiary ledger, into which are entered all debts written off, as although they are written off they should not be lost sight of, and efforts should be made to recover them.

An item which will always be of the greatest interest to auditors is the audit fee. If the fee has been agreed upon, it should be charged against the period in respect of which the charge is made, although it often is not taken into account until it has been paid.

With regard to law costs, charges incurred in connection with the recovery of debts should, I think, be debited to bad debts account, and it is the usual custom to charge the costs in connection with the acquisition of freehold or leasehold property to the real account.

Depreciation.

The question of depreciation is usually a very knotty one, and demands very careful consideration. In the case of leasehold property, if the term is a short one, not more than six or eight years, it will suffice to write off a proportionate part each period, but if it is a long lease another method should be employed. An account headed "leases depreciation fund" should be opened, and a certain sum added to it each period. The effect of adding to this fund is that the floating assets are increased accordingly, and it thus supplies additional working capital to the business. I think, therefore, that it is fair to reckon interest on the amount standing to the credit of the depreciation fund at the same rate as is allowed to the partners on their capital. To arrive at the amount to be credited to the fund each year, the auditor would consult his compound interest tables and find the amount of an annuity, which will, in the number of years in the term of the lease, amount to the sum at which the lease stands in the books. In addition to adding this sum to the fund each year, the fund must be credited and interest account debited with interest on the amount standing to the credit of the depreciation fund. The result will be that when the lease expires, the fund will equal the sum at which the lease stands.

Depreciation of plant and machinery is a very important matter. As to the rate the auditor will, to a certain extent, be guided by his experience in the audit of businesses of a similar nature, and also by the special circumstances of the case. Where plant and machinery is a large item, it is often advisable to have a revaluation after a few years, which will show whether the rate of depreciation has been correct. The usual rate, however, is generally from 7½ to 12½ per cent. per annum.

When a firm possesses live stock, such as horses, there should be a revaluation each period, as their value will vary so considerably by reason of losses, accidents, &c., that it is unsafe to write off depreciation at a fixed rate.

The interest account, in addition to any amounts paid to outside parties, will also be debited with interest on capital and on advances made by any of the partners in excess of the capital agreed to be subscribed by them. As to the rates at which it is to be reckoned, the auditor will consult the partnership deed, in which it should be set out.

Having completed the profit and loss account, the balance thereof, either profit or loss, will be apportioned amongst the partners, in accordance with the terms of the partnership deed. In addition to capital accounts, it is advisable to have a current or drawing account for each partner. Should the deed provide that each partner is to be entitled to draw the whole of his share of profit (if any), the full amount will be transferred to the credit of his current account, but if it stipulates that he can only draw a part of his share, that part only will be credited to his current account, and the balance transferred to his capital account.

It is a good plan when the profit and loss account is completed, to compare it with that for the previous period (if any). Where there is any material alteration in the proportion of any of the items, it should be seen that the reason can be accounted for.

The drawing up of the balance-sheet is undoubtedly the most important part of the auditor's duties. In doing it, he must bear in mind that although he is employed by the firm and is acting for them, there rests upon him a certain responsibility for third parties, who, relying on his certificate, may enter into extensive engagements with the firm. A firm may, and often does, submit its balance-sheet to its bankers or some of its creditors, with a view to obtaining credit or an extension of credit, or someone may, on the strength of the balance-sheet, be induced to acquire an interest in the business. It is, therefore, the auditor's duty to ensure that the balance-sheet is a fair and full one, and accurately sets forth the position of the firm.

Chief Items in a Balance Sheet.

I will now touch upon the chief items which may appear in a balance-sheet, and the means which I think an auditor can and should adopt to verify their accuracy. First of all, I will take the debit or liabilities side:

Sundry Creditors on Open Account.—It is the usual custom amongst business men and firms at the time when their accounts are being made up, to send a circular letter to each of the customers on the bought ledger, asking for a statement of his account, for the purpose of "stocktaking." By means of these statements, the ledger balances can be easily checked. The total amount of the creditors should be set out in the inside column, and the amount of discount reserved on the bought ledger balances deducted, the net amount being carried out.

Creditors for Rent, Rates, Taxes, &c.—These I have already mentioned when speaking of the profit and loss account.

Bills Payable.—This item can be verified by an inspection of the bill book. It is hardly likely that there will be a wilful mistake here, as if a bill is not entered, the amount of the creditor's ledger balance will be accordingly increased, and the only effect of the omission

Corps of Archaeologists investigating the books of the County Treasurer's office at Chicago.—Chicago Record-Herald.

would be to transfer the liability to the heading "sundry creditors" instead of "bills payable."

Mortgages on Freehold or Leasehold Property or Advances on Securities.—These items are very easily checked. The assets on which they are charged will appear on the assets side of the balance-sheet, to verify which the auditor would ask to be shown the title deeds, the agreement for the lease, or the securities. In the event of a charge having been created, the deeds, leases or securities, would have been deposited with the mortgagee or party making the advance, and the auditor would see, instead, a copy of the mortgage deed or the receipt for the documents given by the party making the advance. He will thus, so to speak, kill two birds with one stone, by verifying the existence of the asset and the amount of the charge upon it at the same time.

Reserve for Bad and Doubtful Debts.—I shall refer to this item when dealing with "sundry debtors."

Reserve for Depreciation of Plant and Machinery and Leases Depreciation Fund.—These items I have previously dealt with.

Partner's Capital and Drawing Accounts.—The balances on these accounts should be set out in the names of each partner respectively.

The Credit Side.

I now come to the credit or assets side of the balance-sheet.

Cash in Hand.—This will include the balance of cash as shown in the cash book, the petty cash balance, and the floating cash balances, if any. The amounts will be verified by production of the cash, or if the date of the accounts has gone by, the auditor should check the cash, petty cash, and floating cash balances accounts up to the date of inspection, and count the cash. He should also see that it does not include any I O U's or post-dated cheques. It is, however, desirable that the amount of cash on hand should be as small as possible, and the auditor should therefore request the cashier to pay in all his cash on the date to which the accounts are made up or early the following morning, and care should be taken to see that it is duly credited.

Cash at Bank.—In my opinion, the most preferable plan to check this item is to apply to the bankers for a certificate as to the balance, and I think this is becoming a very general practice amongst accountants.

Sundry Debtors.—I mentioned when dealing with the profit and loss account that all bad debts should be written off the ledger, but in addition to these there will almost certainly be some which, though not bad, are doubtful, and in respect of which a reserve must be made. In order to ensure that the reserve is adequate, the auditor should go through the personal accounts with one of the partners or a person in authority, whose attention should be specially drawn to anything that is irregular in an account, such as a cheque being dishonored, a renewal of a bill, or a delay in payment. Such an irregularity is a sign of weakness, and unless there is some good and satisfactory reason for it, a reserve should be made according to the circumstances of the case. Where a customer has become bankrupt, or has entered into an arrangement with his creditors, particulars of the estate should be entered on the account, from which the auditor will be able to estimate how much the debt is likely to realise.

Bills Receivable.—These should be produced to the auditor, and if any of them have been negotiated since the date to which the accounts are made up, he should trace them in the books.

Plant and Machinery and Fixtures and Fittings.—Where these items are of large amount, it is desirable that an inventory should be made, which can be compared with the previous one. Changes should be noted, and it should be seen that they are accounted for in the book. It is advisable that the item be so worded that it is made clear on what basis the amount has been arrived at, thus "at cost" or "as per valuation made by so-and-so."

Stock-in-Trade.—I do not think it is part of an auditor's duty to check the taking of the stock, but it is certainly desirable that he should satisfy himself as to the basis on which the valuation has been made, and he should also check the extensions and additions. In businesses where values are not subject to material fluctuations, the stock should certainly be taken at cost price, but in the case of trades where the class of goods dealt in is subject to any considerable fluctuation, it should be calculated on the selling price, less the usual percentage of profit, obtained in that particular class of business. The auditor should see that the stock-sheets are duly signed by the managers or principals.

Work in Progress.—This can be verified in the same way as stock-in-trade, but should always be valued on the basis of "cost."

Freehold and Leasehold Property.—I have already mentioned these when dealing with mortgages and advances. If they stand in the books at their original cost, the items should be worded accordingly.

Investments.—It will generally be found that in the books of commercial firms, these remain at cost, and are not re-valued every time when a balance-sheet is drawn up. Where this is so, the stocks or shares should be set out in detail (if possible) and the words "at cost" added.

Lastly, the auditor should not omit to add a foot-note stating the amount of the firm's contingent liability on bills discounted.

Work That May be Dispensed With.

I have now given my idea as to what constitutes a complete audit of the accounts of a commercial firm, but I think the question that would suggest itself to an accountant is this:—"Can any of the work be dispensed with and the audit still be considered an effectual one, as although an accountant would be only too pleased to check every addition, every posting, and every invoice or voucher, clients are not often willing to pay such a fee as will admit of the work being so minutely done as I have set forth?" Yes, I think that a large part of it can be dispensed with, and although it may not be exactly a complete, it would be an effectual audit.

I think that the calling of all items of cash and discount in the way I have mentioned, should always be carefully done. The calling of the items of goods into the bought and sold ledgers, however, is a matter of considerable detail, and in many cases involves a very great deal of work. The balancing of an ordinary bought or sold ledger does not as a rule require a very large amount of skill, and is within the capabilities of most ledger clerks, and if a clerk is given to understand that he will have to balance his ledger, it will most likely have the effect of making him more careful in his work. Here, then, the value of keeping an adjustment account for each ledger comes in, as by its means the auditor is supplied with a check on the accuracy of the book-keepers, and it enables him to dispense with the calling of the goods and the checking of the additions in the ledgers. The auditor himself should write up the adjustment accounts, which should be kept in the general ledger, or, if the bought and sold ledgers are numerous, in a separate "balance" ledger, which should have a lock, and thus be, so to speak, in the custody of the auditor. It is advisable that the book-keepers should have different ledgers allotted to them each period.

This brings me to the conclusion of my essay. The extent of it has not allowed of my going into many matters that are peculiar to special classes of trade, and has only permitted me to touch upon the general principles which I think should be followed in the complete audit of the accounts of a commercial firm.

Bank Wrecking and Salving*

By CHAS. G. DAWES.

NATIONAL banks in the United States are managed, as a rule, with marked ability, conservatism and integrity, and insolvent national banks are the rare exception. Again it should be remembered that only the most picturesque incidents in connection with this peculiar phase of bank management have sufficient novelty to make them entertaining to readers outside the ranks of those who study this problem from a professional viewpoint. With these points in mind a glimpse at this page of banking history may be had without unconsciously gaining a false impression that "bank wrecking" is a common practice, and that banking is anything less than the most cautiously conducted business of the country. And in attempting to point out the weak spots in general banking methods, with suggestions of safeguards which would tend to diminish the number of national banks forced into insolvency, the point that I have just emphasized should not be lost sight of or forced into the background.

In attempting to realize the nature and extent of the task which confronts a Comptroller in managing the affairs of all the national banks of the country which are in process of liquidation owing to insolvency, it is necessary to recall the relation of the bank to the public which it serves.

It is, so to speak, the financial switchboard of the entire business community. All the live commercial wires centre at the bank. There is scarcely a monetary transaction of any moment in any community which does not in some manner record itself at the bank—and generally the attitude of the bank toward any enterprise of importance is vital.

This implies that as the manager of the insolvent national banks of the country the Comptroller of the Currency finds himself charged with the direct control of a great variety of enterprises which are among the assets

*Bank Wrecking and Salving by Chas. G. Dawes, Ex-Comptroller of the Currency. From the Saturday Evening Post, September 20, 1902.

Secretary Shaw to the Rescue.—Philadelphia Press.

of the liquidating bank. Thus, at the same time, the Comptroller becomes at once the responsible manager of scores of farms, stores, factories and other examples of the more common forms of investment. In addition to this he is never without a choice list of novelties in his collection of bank assets. One Comptroller, for example, acquired, in his capacity as custodian of bank assets, a small herd of buffaloes, and in discharge of his duties was obliged thoroughly to post himself on the demand for buffaloes on the hoof. However, he managed this peculiar enterprise well and made the most of his shaggy herd.

The Comptroller a Wholesale Business Manager.

There is seldom a time when the Comptroller has not under his management several mines of various kinds: properties which must be handled with good judgment in order to avoid great sacrifice. Frequently this official has an opportunity to demonstrate his ability as a railroad manager, for in one or another part of the country some insolvent bank is almost sure to count a street railroad among its assets. Occasionally a larger intramural road of first-class importance, with all its complicated traffic and legal problems, gets into this class, and the task of making it "pay out" without heavy shrinkage is a serious undertaking of no small magnitude. Of this class the Chicago Calumet Electric Road, in which over three and one-half million dollars of the money of the depositors in the defunct National Bank of Illinois is invested, is the most important example.

To all practical purposes the Comptroller of the Currency finds himself in the position of the private capitalist who has scattered his investment in a wide variety of enterprises. His lieutenants are the Receivers who are appointed directly to administer the affairs of each insolvent bank, and to these men are left the details of making the most of the assets in their charge. But the Comptroller must keep a vigilant eye upon all those diverse properties and know that his policy regarding each is being faithfully carried out.

Naturally many insolvent banks have one asset of major importance, upon the management of which largely depends the success of the liquidation. In one instance this is a street railway, in another a mine, a ranch, a manufactory, a plantation, a theatre, a newspaper, or an electric and gas plant. In the history of the Comptrollership hundreds of mines and several breweries have been administered.

Invariably many curious and interesting situations arise in the management of so diverse a collection of properties. Among the main assets of the Chestnut Street National Bank which became insolvent were the securities of the Philadelphia Record. In its politics this journal was opposed to the National Administration of which the Comptroller was an appointee. There was, of course, no tampering with the politics of the journal, although, in one sense of the term, it was, through the Receiver of the national bank, indirectly under the management of the Administration. Its policy was consistently maintained, and its editors, reporters and other employes were as little disturbed as if the journal had not come under the Receiver's influence. As a consequence, it earned as high as $250,000 a year and finally sold for about $2,800,000. But at intervals through the period of the Receivership it faithfully criticised the Administration. The credit for this splendid financial outcome is principally due to George H. Earle and Richard Y. Cook, of Philadelphia.

A Capitalist's Fine Sense of Honor.

One of the most pleasant experiences in connection with my administration of the office of the Comptroller of the Currency that I now recall is an episode which is well calculated to increase confidence in the integrity of human nature.

A capitalist whose name is widely known in railway circles met me in Chicago to discuss the affairs of a certain national bank. He said:

"You have just been appointed Comptroller of the Currency and the course of action which you propose to pursue in relation to this bank will largely determine my own action. I was elected a director without my own knowledge in the bank which, though not closed, is insolvent, and have continued in that official position under protest. My holdings of stock amount to $1,000, and double that amount, of course, is the limit of my liability under the law. But the fact remains that I did allow my name to be used as that of a director of the bank and this may have influenced some persons to become depositors. Because of that possibility I have determined to step in and save the depositors and other creditors from loss, provided the other shareholders, without expense to them, will consent to arrangements necessary to an equable execution of this plan. And now, with this explanation of the situation, I desire to learn what is your official view of the matter."

Though I knew this man to be of large fortune he was not classed among the multi-millionaires, and the plan which he proposed involved the immediate use of a very large amount of ready money—not far from $500,000. Before he was through with the project, as I recall it, he voluntarily took upon himself the actual losses of others to the extent of nearly $1,000,000, and all because his fine sense of personal honor would not let him see depositors suffer loss by the failure of an institution with which, even without his knowledge, at first, his name had been associated. The gentleman who did this has not expected, asked or received public credit for his action, and some years have now passed since these occurrences. He is a modest man and no doubt has found his full reward in the consciousness of duty well done. But I hope he may read this and know that in the annals of the Comptroller's office there has been no more conspicuous instance of fidelity to a semi-public trust, and that among the few of us who knew how he had voluntarily taken upon himself the losses of hundreds of people of slender means he stands and shall always stand as one of Nature's true noblemen.

There are many specific causes besides the general one of financial panic that are prolific of disaster to banking enterprises. Foremost among these must be placed that of unsafe loans to officers, directors and employes of the bank making the loans. As the most useful thing that could be said on the subject of bank wrecking would be the statement of some rule to prevent it, a word on this point is not inappropriate.

Beginning with Mr. Lacey, in 1891, every Comptroller of the Currency has made some recommendation for the passage of a law restricting the making of loans by a bank to its own directors or officials. The problem is to devise such restrictions for the safety of the depositors as will discourage improper loans to directors and officers while not injuring the depositors by discouraging to too great an extent the assumption of bank directorship by the active and responsible members of the business community. My own recommendation was, in substance, that it should be made illegal for an officer or director of a bank to borrow from it without the written approval of at least two other directors.

Up to the year 1900 there were 370 failures of national banks, and of these sixty-two were clearly due to excessive accommodations to officers and directors. At that time the Comptroller made an investigation which showed that of the 28,709 directors of national banks in this country, 18,534 were, directly or indirectly, indebted to the banks under their control. These borrowing directors and 2,279 officers and employes (not directors) owed their banks $202,287,441. This sum was 32.55 per cent. of the capital stock of all the national banks doing business in the country at the time. It is not to be inferred that all these loans were necessarily an abuse of privilege. On the contrary, many of them were among the safest loans of the banks in question. In fact, one of the cities in the country wherein ninety per cent. of the capital of its national banks was borrowed by their directors, officers and employes has been notably free from failures and scandals.

Then there is a clear and tangible danger of going to the other extreme of placing too severe restriction upon official borrowing—the danger of driving from the directorships of national banks the live, active and progressive men of the community. Naturally, strong and forceful men, with large and diverse interests, will not consent to serve as bank directors when that official position involves tying their own hands, to the point of hardship, as borrowers in the money market of their communities. But restrictions which will be both reasonable and effective are needed, and the National Banking Act should be so amended by Congress as to provide them.

The Efficient Work of the Bank Examiners.

Putting "all the eggs in one basket" is another prolific source of banking disaster. I recall one instance which strikingly illustrates the criminal and fatal results of this practice. A national bank in a large city had in the neighborhood of $12,000,000 assets, its credit was of the best, and its stock was quoted much above par. Suddenly the Comptroller closed its doors, and the cashier of the institution took his own life. Three times the amount of its capital had been invested in a single enterprise! As each stockholder was held for a 100 per cent. assessment, the suffering caused by its liquidation was something not soon to be forgotten by the community involved. Direct defalcation on the part of officers and employes is, of course, a source of bank failures. Often quick and clever action on the part of the Bank Examiners prevents heavy loss and sometimes saves liquidation. The banks whose failure is prevented through the supervision of the National authorities and their checking of dangerous tendencies are not known to the public, but there is generally full discussion of the question of thoroughness and competency of Bank Examiners when a failure does occur. As a rule, a high degree of efficiency exists in the conduct of the Bank Examinerships of the country.

Once, when visiting a friend in one of the suburbs of Philadelphia, I received a message from a Bank Examiner who had been at work in another city. He insisted that I come at once to Philadelphia. Arriving there I found him in company with the president of a large bank in that city where he had been prosecuting his duties. A few moments disclosed the fact that there had been a defalcation to the amount of at least $600,000. As a result of the Examiner's decisive action a large part of the defalcation had been recovered before the board of directors had become aware that there was any trouble in their institution. Later, through this defalcation and the depreciation of certain securities, this bank was compelled to close. Infraction of the law in the extension of credits through the certification of checks sometimes results in the wrecking of banks which are otherwise in good condition.

Throughout the entire history of bank liquidation runs a depressing strain of tragedy. Three suicides, in quick succession, followed the closing of as many banks in my own official experience, and I never ordered the appointment of a Receiver without the apprehension that perhaps I was unwittingly pushing another man to the last desperate extremity of those too proud to face the results of their own crimes.

Always the two objects first in the purpose of a Comptroller of the Currency in the liquidation of an insolvent bank are to close up the transaction with as little delay and expense as possible and to realize the maximum amount from the assets. Often it is difficult to accomplish speedy settlement without heavy sacrifice of securities, and frequently the only way in which to prevent material shrinkage is to take sufficient time to protect the enterprises in the list of assets.

The records show, however, that the cheapest liquidation of insolvent enterprises is that of national banks. This is to be in part accounted for by the fact that in this phase of his duties the Comptroller is unhampered by red tape and has free authority over the institutions under his management.

From the beginning of the Comptrollership up to 1899, for example, the amount of nominal assets liquidated was $235,636,788. Of these $101,618,174 was actually collected, with $40,000,000 nominal assets still on hand. The percentage of total expenses was only 7.15. The percentage which the creditors of these national banks received was 75.03, and this has not materially changed in subsequent years.

In that year (1899) investigation was made regarding the cost of collections under Receivers for State and private banks appointed under authority of the State courts. Information was had concerning 283 such banks which paid dividends of 42.97 per cent. The cost of administration was 16.3 per cent. of the total collections, or over twice the percentage of expense of liquidating national banks.

Of late years the plan of consolidation in the administration of insolvent banks which have reached an advanced stage of liquidation has been followed by Comptrollers with decidedly economical results. Some thirty different banks, for example, were placed under one receiver and a small force of office assistants at Washington, with the result that the cost of the management was reduced to an average of only $427 a year for each bank.

ECONOMICAL TO THE LIMIT.

The native pointed out to the stranger an old man who was passing. "That man," said the native, "beats the world on close figuring.'

"Makes a little money go a long ways, does he?"

"Well, rather. Last winter he put revolving doors into a big building that he owns, and he never took them out again all summer."

"Pure matter of economy?"

"Exactly."

"Rather small and mean, I should think. The cost of taking out and putting back the revolving doors ought not to be great, and he's giving his tenants and their patrons a lot of unnecessary trouble."

"That's just it," explained the native. "He's making them work for him for nothing. Why, he stores up the power generated by those doors and uses it to run the elevators. Why, the man is so close that he doesn't get mad, because he thinks his anger would cause him to give out heat that he'll need in the winter."—N. E. Grocer.

The Foreign Exchanges*

By J. SHIELD NICHOLSON, M.A., D.Sc.

IN attempting to give in a single lecture an account of the theory of the foreign exchanges, it is obvious that the attention must be mainly devoted to general principles. Those who require practical details may be referred to Tate's "Cambist," or to the A B C of the Foreign Exchanges by Mr. George Clare. That the general theory requires careful statement, and is not so obvious as is sometimes assumed, is evident from Mr. Goschen's standard work, which is still of the highest value on account of its principles, although most of the examples are altogether out of date.

I shall first of all explain the meaning of the terms and the extent and limits of the fluctuations, and then I shall notice, so far as time permits, some of the important indirect effects on banking and trade of certain kinds of fluctuations in the exchanges.

International Debts.

The term foreign exchanges refers to the settlement of international debts. Accordingly, in the logical treatment of the subject, we ought to begin with the analysis of international indebtedness. The first element to be considered is the amount of the exports and imports. It is a commonplace of economic theory that imports are paid for by exports. And if there were no other elements in international indebtedness imports could be paid for in no other way. Either the value of the exports must equal that of the imports, or else the trade must cease. A country that does not itself produce gold could not go on paying for imports with money; it must replenish its money supplies, and it could only do so by selling exports abroad. Suppose that a country had an excess of imports which it could only pay for by sending money or money material. As the country was denuded of its money prices would fall; it would become a good country to buy from and a bad country to sell to; and thus exports would be stimulated and imports would be checked until the adverse balance was reversed. In practice, in modern societies, long before the country was denuded of its money, there would be, through the drain on the reserves of the banks, such a check to credit that prices must fall. But the principle is still the same: Provided exports and imports are the only elements in international indebtedness, prices must be so adjusted that exports and imports balance or else the trade must diminish or cease.

The operation of this principle is hidden by various conflicting circumstances. As Adam Smith pointed out long ago, it is practically impossible at any time to say what is the balance of trade between any two countries. What is sometimes called the "real" par of exchange in the sense of an equality of indebtedness, is much better called an "ideal" or hypothetical par—a useful assumption in certain kinds of reasoning. It is altogether different from the "mint" par or "nominal" par, which expresses a definite concrete fact, as is explained later on.

Again, for simplicity of reasoning, we say that one country—England—trades with another country—France—just as if the two countries were run by a gigantic trust on each side, and as if the state of account were reckoned up and published every day. Nothing, of course, could be further from the truth. It was well said by Ricardo, who spent most of his days in making money on the stock exchange and his nights in making fame in economic theory, that every transaction in commerce is an independent transaction. The trade between France and England is not run by two trusts, but by a multitude of independent merchants.

The reconciliation between the two positions is found in the course of prices. The merchants have to make their bargains in terms of prices, and prices are influenced not only by particular relative causes, but by general causes. And amongst such general causes are the terms on which bills can be discounted or advances from banks obtained. And, as will be shown presently, the rate of discount depends inter alia on the course of the foreign exchanges, which again depends inter alia on the balance of exports and imports, or rather on the payments that have to be made on account of trade transactions.

There are, however, other elements in international indebtedness as well as exports and imports on account of which payments have to be made. These elements I shall only enumerate, as I must in some way economise my limited time. You will find them very clearly stated in Mr. Goschen's second chapter; and in the page that forms the frontispiece to Mr. Clare's little book you will see a debtor and creditor statement for London of international transactions.

Other Elements.

Besides exports and imports, we have to take account of payments in connection with freights, the purchase or sale of stock-exchange securities, the advance of loans, the interest on loans, the expenses of governments abroad, the expenses of foreign residents, the obligations incurred by banks, the profits of commissions of various kinds, and other minor elements. You will find it useful, I think, to translate all these various elements into the language of exports and imports; that is to say, to consider what would be the effect on the state of indebtedness if these various obligations were equivalent to or expressed by a corresponding increase of exports or imports, as the case might be. This, indeed, is not only a good practical rule, but is a necessary procedure when we seek to explain the course of international trade—why, for example, year after year, the imports into the United Kingdom exceed the exports by many millions. This undoubted fact does not show that the imports are not paid for by the exports, but only that some of the exports are not in the form of material commodities. Thus, for example, a freight has been well called an "invisible" export; the advance of a loan—i. e., the capital sum—is, so to speak, an import of securities from the foreigner, and we must pay for the securities by exporting more commodities; the interest on the loans, on the other hand, acts from this point of view like another invisible export—now we export, so to speak, the coupons and receive payment in the shape of so much additional imports; the expenses of government or of absentees abroad may be regarded as if we actually were obliged to pay for additional imports to that extent, the imports being consumed on the way; and, finally, foreigners have to pay us by sending us something of value—that is to say, really by adding to our imports—on account of our commissions in settling international transactions of various kinds.

It appears, then, that not only are exports and imports the principal elements to be considered in international indebtedness, but that other elements may also be likened to them and expressed in terms of exports and imports—and, indeed, they have a precisely similar effect on the balance of indebtedness.

We are justified, then, in dealing with international indebtedness, in taking exports and imports as typical or representative, and in that way simplifying the central problem.

If, however, it may be taken as axiomatic that the exports are paid for by imports, in the extended use of those terms, it is equally certain as a matter of common observation that the producers of these exports are paid for them in the money of their own country, and the producers of the corresponding imports are also paid for

*Lecture delivered before the Edinburgh Society of Accountants by the Professor of Political Economy in the University of Edinburgh.

them in the money of their country. It is all very well to say that the coal exported by England is paid for by the wine imported from France, but it is pretty certain that the English colliers do not drink the French wine, and the French wine-growers do not burn the English coal. The English colliers eventually receive English money, and the French wine-growers French money, for their respective productions. Accordingly, if we carry out the same reasoning as regards all the other exports and imports, we see that the settlement of this international indebtedness involves the conversion at some point or other of French money into English money, and conversely. The French consumers of English coal in some way or other have to pay for it in English money, and in some way or other to pay this money in England. The way in which this is done is explained by the theory of the foreign exchanges. "The foreign exchanges," to quote the old standard work, "are transfers from the money of one country to that of another effected by the operation of Bills of Exchange."

Transfer of Money Power.

It may of course happen that different "foreign" countries have identical currencies, but the terms of the definition do not exclude this case; the essence is the transfer of money power from one country to another. The French consumer, through suitable agents or intermediaries, is obliged not only to change his francs into sovereigns, but the sovereigns must be paid in England. If, however, every independent transaction of commerce were settled independently, we should have a multitude of parcels of coin or bullion constantly flowing in about equal streams from and to every country. England would be receiving money for exports and sending away money for imports. But the resources of very early civilizations were equal to avoiding this source of waste, and the foreign bill of exchange may be traced back, at any rate, to the middle ages.

For simplicity, it is convenient to assume that in this method of the settlement of the indebtedness one country is altogether active and the other altogether passive—i. e., that one always draws and the other accepts. Suppose, for example, that American merchants export corn, cotton, etc., to England, and draw for the value on the corresponding English importers or purchasers. The bills being drawn on London entitle the drawers to receive money there from the acceptors. But so far they would be no better off, for they would have to fetch the corresponding gold from London. But suppose, further, that other American merchants buy from London piece goods of the same value as this exported corn. They can, of course, settle their debts by sending gold, but they can settle them equally well by buying these bills from the exporters and sending them to London, where they will be paid by the acceptors. By the intervention of these bills the remittance, to and fro, of bullion is avoided, and the American exporters of produce receive American money and the English sellers of piece goods receive English money.

It is clear, however, that the bills being payable in pounds sterling, and being sold for dollars, the first element in determining the price of the bill is the relative value of the pound sterling and the dollar. This again depends on the amount of fine gold each contains, and what is called the mint par of exchange tells us how much of the other country's currency contains, according to its law, the same amount of pure metal as is contained in our standard coin, according to our law. The mint par is deduced from the legal definitions of the respective standard coins. If we take the pound sterling as fixed, or as the basis, the mint par with U. S. A. is 4.866 dollars, with France 25.2215 francs, with Germany 20.43 marks.

If the foreign coins were being exchanged at the same spot in order to be melted down, this mint par would also give the actual rates of exchange. But the term foreign exchanges refers primarily to a transaction in which a bill (say) for pounds payable in London is sold for dollars received in America, and it is this difference of place which accounts for the fluctuations in the rates of exchanges, or, as it is called, the rise and fall in the exchanges.

Causes of Fluctuations.

I proceed then next to notice the principal causes of these fluctuations and the limits to their rise and fall. It is better now to pass from the simple case of one kind of export and one kind of import, and to include all the elements in international indebtedness, and, inter alia, the invisible exports, and, if I may coin a similar phrase, the "intangible" obligations.

Suppose, then, at any particular time a number of people in New York have to make remittances to London, and that a number of other people in New York are anxious to sell various credit documents, bills, drafts, etc., which entitle the holders to receive money in London. If the demand exceeds the supply, the price of these bills (or other documents) will rise. But the limit of the rise will be given by the point at which it will be just as cheap for the American debtor to send actual gold to London. This is the outgoing gold point from New York, and it may be taken as £1 or $4.89½; conversely, if the supply of bills exceeds the demand the price falls, and it may fall to such a point that it would be just as profitable for the owner of the bill—the American creditor—to send for the gold. This is the incoming gold point to New York, and may be taken as £1 or $4.83½.

To resume: The mint par is just $4.866 or £1. If the rate rises to $4.89½ it generally pays to send us gold, if it falls to $4.83½ it generally pays to take gold from us. These gold points, or specie points as they used to be called, for export and import cannot of course be fixed with absolute precision, as they depend on the cost of transmitting the gold, but the average or normal is approximately certain, and it is only under exceptional conditions that these limits are exceeded.

If you refer to Mr. Clare's book you will see a diagram showing the course of the exchange at New York per cable transfer on London for the year 1891. In January, to begin with, the rate is low—$4.85½, and it rises to the

Europe thinks of Disarming.—St. Louis Globe-Democrat.

maximum (the outgoing gold point from New York) in March—viz., $4.89½. It remains high till the end of June, when there is a fall to the minimum of $4.83½—the incoming gold point for New York. The general course of the fluctuations in this case is determined mainly by trade influences. The States, as a rule, ship to us large quantities of corn, cotton, etc., in the autumn, and from August to December the exchanges are therefore generally favorable to the States, and, conversely, unfavorable to us. During the rest of the year the balance is in our favor and against America. In this particular year, however, it also happened that London was selling in America large quantities of American securities in the spring, so that there was an extra demand for remittances from New York to London.

The difficulty of giving actual concrete cases for the purpose of illustrating the theory is that we cannot in this way take the theory in parts and in order of simplicity; the concrete cases generally require for their explanation the whole of the theory and some practical qualifications besides. And in this example which I choose to illustrate the effect of exports and imports on the exchanges between New York and London, I have introduced two terms not yet explained—namely, the term favorable and the term cable transfer.

Favorable or Unfavorable.

What, then, is the meaning of the expression that the exchanges are favorable or unfavorable, or for or against a country? The use of the terms may be explained in two ways—one partly historical, and the other very real at the present time. If we take our former illustration and consider the case of the American importer, if the exchange is below par he is able to buy his remittance for so much less—he gives fewer dollars for a hundred pounds payable in London. Thus it looks as if American currency fetched more of English currency. In former times there was always much anxiety about the actual exchange of currencies, and this is one historical meaning of the term favorable—i. e., to obtain more foreign currency than usual for the native money. There is, however, a deeper meaning—also historical. When the exchange is favorable to a country it shows, so far—that is, omitting other elements of indebtedness—that the exports have exceeded the imports. Under the old ideas of the mercantile system this was considered a favorable state of trade. "Sell much and buy little" was considered the chief rule of the national trade economy. It is not necessary, again, on the one side, to expose the fallacy, or on the other to indicate the element of truth contained in this maxim.

It is plain that, so far as any advantage was obtained from the state of the exchanges by way of trade, if the exchange was favorable to the importer or the buyer of the bill it was so far unfavorable to the exporter or the drawer of the bill. Probably the idea was that the exporter would transfer any loss to his foreign debtor. This usage, however, of the terms "favorable" and "unfavorable"—namely, as supposed to indicate the balance of trade—is now, or at any rate ought to be, only of historical interest.

But, I hasten to say, there is a sense in which the terms, favorable and unfavorable exchanges, may still be used with a very real meaning. Gold is a commodity which, for many purposes, is very different from any other commodity. The gold held by the Bank of England is of far greater importance to the United Kingdom than is indicated by its monetary value. If, owing to any cause, we exported suddenly twenty or thirty millions more of commodities than was usual at that period of the year—if, for example, owing to the outbreak of war between China and Japan we exported a mass of materials suitable for the mutual destruction of these friendly States, there might be some political protests and some interesting law-suits, but, on the whole, the trade of this country would revive, and possibly leap and bound. But if, on the other hand, these wily Orientals were able suddenly to withdraw from the Bank of England twenty or thirty millions of gold, which also is very useful in time of war, our trade, instead of leaping and bounding, might very possibly suffer from the depressing influence of a commercial crisis.

Passage of Gold From One Country to Another.

It is the passage of gold from one country to another that gives the principal general interest to the foreign exchanges. To the great mass of the people of this country who are engaged in business of various kinds the course of the foreign exchanges is in general of no interest whatever, except in one particular—namely, if there is a rise or fall, in consequence, in the rate of discount. That they see and feel. For one business man who considers the course of the foreign exchanges a thousand consider the movements of the bank rate. There are also, it is true, other indirect influences which occasionally have far-reaching consequences and call for careful examination. In general, however, especially in this country, the principal interest of the foreign exchanges is in connection with the rate of discount.

And this leads me to notice the other term which arose in my New York illustration—namely, cable transfer. In itself this term requires no explanation, but it leads up to a point of importance—namely, the difference between the short exchange or exchange at sight, and the long exchange or after so many days' notice. This distinction also, it will be found, is closely connected with the rate of discount.

The typical instrument for settling international indebtedness is, as already pointed out, the bill of exchange, which arises from an actual trade transaction. If, then, this bill of exchange is not payable at sight, but, say for simplicity, after three months, its present value is subject to three months' discount. Accordingly, if in New York a cable transfer on London could be bought, say at par—i. e., if for one pound payable at once in London 4.866 dollars would be given, then for a pound payable after sixty days the discount must be subtracted. Thus, referring to the foreign rates of exchange in London quoted in the "Economist" at the date of writing, the New York cable transfer on London is £1 or $4.87½, while the long exchange at sixty days is $4.84⅜.

It may be worth while to consider this case with an example in which a remittance is sent from London (say) to Paris. If the London debtor can purchase for a pound a cheque for so many francs payable on demand, he will require for his pound so many more francs in a bill which must be discounted, and how many more francs will depend on the rate of discount in Paris. Thus, in the same number of the "Economist," I find in the London course of exchange Paris cheques are quoted at 25.12 1-3, which happens to be very nearly the gold point against us, and bills at three months are quoted at 25.32½. The principal cause of the difference is the rate of discount in Paris.

Rate of Interest.

In certain cases, moreover, the rate of interest, or rather the relative rate, in the country which draws the bills may be of importance in influencing the course of exchanges. Suppose, for example, that the rate of discount in Paris is much lower than in London, or suppose that the Bank of England raises its rate and that the conditions of the London money market are such that the market rate in London rises to the same extent, or it may be even more. What would be the effect on the exchange between Paris and London? One natural and obvious result would be that Paris bankers would wish to send money for investment in London at the more profitable rate, and thus the exchange would turn—so far—in our favor. This natural and obvious effect would be more intensified by a less obvious cause. Bills drawn on London by Paris, having their present value calculated at the London rate, would be a good investment for Paris bankers. Thus they would compete for these bills—not for remittance but for investment. This extra demand, however, must so far turn the exchanges in our favor still more, or at least make the movement more speedy. It is, of course, the difference in the rates in the two places which must be considered in this connection.

As I indicated before, as regards this country, the movement in the exchanges is generally only of interest in connection with the bank rate. If the exchanges turn against this country so that gold is exported, or even if a drain is anticipated, the bank rate is raised, and directly or indirectly this rise may operate on mercantile advances generally.

The foreign exchanges may also be affected by the state of credit in both the countries considered. This is obvious from the fact that the documents used for remittance are credit documents, and our typical bill of exchange depends ultimately on the credit both of the drawer and the acceptor. The intervention of banks also has become of late years of more and more importance, and all banking rests on credit. The rate of exchange between any two centres, say London and Paris, will also be affected by the rates subsisting between these centres and other centres with which they have transactions. The principles applied, however, are the same, and indeed for purposes of theory we may regard the rest of the world as one great foreign country.

Similarly the operations of banks in adding stability to the exchanges by creating paper for remittances to pay for imports, which are really paid for by exports at a later date—those operations present no theoretical difficulty.

Depreciation of Currency.

It seems to be otherwise, however, when we come to the case of the depreciation of currency and its effects on foreign trade. The problem is simple enough so far as the actual premium on gold is concerned. If a sovereign will buy so many francs at the rate of the mint par, and if the francs are depreciated, the sovereign must obtain so many more to the extent of the depreciation. If the depreciation is considerable, it may be said that the apparent course of the exchanges depends mainly on the extent of the depreciation. The other causes of fluctuation are still there, but they are altogether hidden by the premium on gold. There are also in this case no limits to the nominal or apparent rise in the exchange—that is, taking the sovereign as fixed and the depreciated currency as variable.

So far the reasoning is obvious. There is, however, a point involved which is by no means simple in theory, and is yet of very great practical importance. The question is this: Suppose the currency of a country, which was formerly on a gold basis, becomes depreciated owing to excessive issues of inconvertible notes, will this depreciation of itself tend to encourage exports or diminish exports (and, conversely, of imports), or will it have no real effect? I believe that the correct answer to this problem is, that the effect will depend altogether on the way in which the depreciation takes place, and that the answer must be different in the different cases.

First, take the case in which the notes become discredited almost as soon as they are issued—that is to say, suppose that long before there are such abundant issues as to cause an inflation of prices through the increase in the quantity of currency a premium on gold arises. What will happen as regards exports and imports? People exporting to the country in question, and selling for the inconvertible paper which is, we may suppose, practically the only currency, will only receive about the same price as before, but, owing to the premium on gold, they will not obtain the same amount of gold to take back or send back to their own country.

Therefore, exports to the country with the depreciated notes will be checked. Conversely, exporters from that country will sell for the old prices reckoned in gold in other countries, and with this gold they can purchase more currency at home, and thus there will be a stimulus, so far, to exports from the country in question.

But take now another case. It might happen that prices in the country considered rose more than was indicated by the premium on gold. The Government might make its issues with great prudence, and float a mass of this paper and gradually inflate prices before any danger of inconvertibility was suspected, and thus without any premium on gold arising, and later, for a time at any rate, the inflation of prices might exceed the premium on gold.

In this case exports to this country would be stimulated and exports from it would be checked, and the final result would be that the adverse balance must be met in gold; then, as gold left the country the premium would rise, and ultimately it is quite possible that the effect of the depreciation might come to be exactly the opposite.

Take now a third case. If all the parties concerned were practically to ignore the depreciation, and conduct all their exchanges on a gold basis, there would be no stimulating influence either way. But it is very doubtful if this theoretical result is ever attained in practice. The people who really pay for the imports are the consumers in the country with the depreciated paper, and the people who must eventually receive the money for the exports from this country are the producers there, and both consumers and producers in the country concerned are in general obliged to use this depreciated paper.

The foreign trader may insure himself against risk by making his bargains on a sterling basis of exchange, but he cannot prevent the depreciation affecting the conditions of demand and supply in the internal markets of this country, and these markets are influenced by the extent and by the mode of the depreciation, and thus indirectly the foreigner also must be affected.

Inconvertible Paper.

The use of inconvertible paper is of very frequent occurrence, and has important indirect consequences. In recent years, also, the fluctuation in the rates of exchange between gold and silver have been of even greater interest and importance. The same principles must be applied, mutatis mutandis, as in the case of inconvertible paper. It would, however, be hopeless at the end of a lecture of this kind to tire your attention by trying to show the way in which the principles must be applied, or to discover to which of the three cases of depreciated paper the depreciation of silver may be likened. To those who wish to work at a good monetary problem I can heartily recommend the subject of the effect (if any) of the depreciation of silver on the prices of commodities in gold-using countries.

As the subject treated in this lecture is necessarily both technical and complex, it may be useful if, in conclusion, I restate briefly the principal positions.

The term "foreign exchanges" refers to the settlement of international debts. These debts are expressed in the moneys of the respective countries. Accordingly, the first thing is to find out the relative values of these moneys according to the fine gold they contain. This gives the mint par.

Next, we note that the consumer in one country must in some way pay the producer in the other—that is, he must remit money or something that will command money—in the typical case, a bill of exchange. The price of these bills varies with the demand and supply, and the limits of the fluctuations are given by the cost of sending gold or of sending for gold. This gives the gold points or specie points.

In most cases these fluctuations in the exchanges are only of interest to merchants directly engaged in foreign trade, and, being within narrow limits, are of little importance. But whenever the course of the exchanges is such that a drain of gold sets in, or is feared, there is a rise—and it may be a sharp and a great rise—in the bank rate. Such a movement may affect trade generally, and in extreme cases lead to a commercial crisis.

Another case is also of general importance. If the currency of one country becomes depreciated, the premium on gold will rise to the extent of the depreciation, and there are practically no limits to this rise. The British dealer with the foreign country which has the depreciated currency may make himself safe by making his bargains on a sterling basis, but he cannot avoid the indirect effects of this depreciation. Under various conditions the depreciation of the currency of a country mav stimulate or may diminish its exports. It really depends on the way in which the depreciation arises.

A similar argument may be applied when one country has a silver standard and the other gold. The effect of the depreciation of silver upon the silver-using countries depends on the causes and methods of the depreciation. The assertion that the depreciations of a currency acts as a bounty on exports may be true in some cases; in others, however, it would act as a tax on exports, and in any case these effects tend to disappear in time.

An Instance of Profit-Sharing*

By SAMUEL CABOT.

TO any one who looks at the present industrial situation from either a utilitarian or a humanitarian point of view there must be mnch that seems most lamentable in the attitude of employer to employed, and still more in that of employed to employer. As the writer intends to give a short description of his own experiences and efforts, there are obvious reasons why he should pass by the humanitarian aspect of the question and lay chief stress upon the advantages from an economic point of view, both to labor and capital, of a more cordial co-operation.

Any one who has really watched the work of the operatives in a textile mill or print works from within, and for any considerable period of time, must be impressed with the conviction that if their work were for their own individual benefit, the amount accomplished would certainly in many cases reach 30 per cent. more, and in most at least 20 per cent. In addition to this, the economies of material and the saving of machinery would also be much greater. If the work is paid by the day, and not by the piece, this difference would of course be more marked, but even in piecework the gains possible for an interested operative as contrasted with an uninterested one may easily exceed the estimate above.

The writer, having worked in such a mill, had these truths early "proned inter him," as the negro philosopher, Uncle Remus, expresses it. It thus became a settled purpose in his mind that he would try—in case he ever had occasion to run a factory of his own—to make the employees interested in economy and thrift on their own account. This he has now been able to do; and as it has been carried on for a period of fifteen years, the plan may be said to have passed the experimental stage.

The arrangement is a very simple one. Each operative who wishes to take part in the profit-sharing is required to sign a paper agreeing to give a notice of sixty days before leaving, and also to do all in his power to save expenses; and, in short, to render the business successful. In consideration of this a certain proportion of the net profits—known only to the proprietor, but always the same proportion—is divided among the profit-sharers pro rata, according to their wages, during the period just elapsed. In the writer's case the profits are calculated every six months. The profits are paid—one-half in cash to the participant, and one-half is placed in a savings bank by the proprietor as trustee for the employee. If the employee dies in the service, his heirs are at once entitled to the accumulated fund in the savings bank, with interest.

If the operative desires to leave the works, and gives the required sixty days' notice, the fund remains at interest two years in the bank, and is then handed over to the operative, provided he has not sold the secrets or formulas he may have learned in the course of his employment in these works.

In case the employee should not keep his part of the agreement—should, for instance, organize a strike, stopping work without the required notice of sixty days—his accumulated profit, which is only contingent upon his adherence to the promises made to the employer, does not come back to the latter, but is divided into two equal parts, one of which is apportioned in cash among the operatives who have adhered to their bargain, and the other is added pro rata to their funds in the savings bank. It seems to the writer that it is of greater importance that the money once divided should never come back to the employer again, as otherwise it would give room to suspicion that men were discharged in order to obtain their accumulated savings. If a man is discharged for cause, the employer has the right to turn his accumulation over to the faithful men who have kept their promises. There has been—in the writer's experience—but one attempt to systematically break this agreement, an attempt early in the arrangement to organize a strike. The result was a loss on the strikers' part of a considerable sum of money and the division of that sum among those who respected their promises. The strike lasted two days, and has never been repeated, the strikers begging to be taken back on the old terms.

And now in regard to the results. It is, of course, obvious that absolute tabulated figures are impossible in such a case, as much of the effect must be too subtle to be chronicled in dollars and cents. It is, however, the firm conviction of the writer that his men have given him a return upon the investment made fully equal to that which one ought to expect. The earnestness and diligence of the workmen seem much above the average, and, moreover, the thousand-and-one economies which are so important in an industrial plant are more than usually observed. In fact, from careful observation, it seems unquestionable that the advantages far outweigh the cost.

The class of workmen is not above the average of those in a silk or print works, yet the savings in the bank reaches already $500 in many instances, and much more in a few.

The profits distributed among the thirty-five to forty shares averages a little over 14 per cent. of the total wages they earn, and a considerable number of them have already received more than $1,000 apiece in profits.

Although the sum distributed has been over $25,000, the writer believes that the immunity from strikes for so long has been well worth the expenditures, leaving the much-increased industry and economy as a profit to the employer.

In many instances this system might be modified to advantage, as, for example, by allowing the operative, after a term of years, to mortgage his bank savings to the employer. He could in this way be encouraged and enabled to build a home at an earlier date than he could otherwise hope to do. Such an arrangement would be also an advantage to the employer by increasing the number of permanent workmen of experience in the neighborhood of his establishment. But many other modifications will doubtless occur to the reader, and it is not the purpose of this paper to dogmatize upon the subject, but merely to state facts and results.

*Originally published in the "American Monthly Review of Reviews."

The Tale of the Man Who got Hunk

BY JOE LINCOLN.

AND it was the one thousand and seventh night and Scheherezade sang blithely for that her heart was glad. And her song was one that had been issued as a supplement to the Sunday paper and the sweetness of her voice was as the rasping of a file upon a hoop of iron.

And the King hearkened for a space and then spake unto her saying:

"Break away, I pray thee! Hath not Kibosh, the prince of physicians, declared that I have a weak heart? Saith the wise one, 'Of two evils choose that which may be borne without anaesthetics.' Tell me a tale and keep thy song for the ears of the mothers of my wives.'

And Scheherezade obeyed and said unto the Father of the Faithful,

"Know, oh Mightiness! that in the city of Hing, which is in the pleasant vale of Gobswat, there lived a man who was poor. And the name of the man was Mahmoud and he had many kinsmen. And in the days of his adversity he sought these kinsmen saying,

"'Verily, I am up against it even unto the uttermost; wilt thou not, out of the kindness of thy heart, help me to the getting of a position that I may earn the wherewithal to exist?'

"And the kinsmen, each in turn, gave him the refrigerating stare and the marble heart, bidding him get hence and hustle for himself. And when he pleaded for a bite they turned him over to the dog.

"And Mahmoud was exceeding wroth at his kinsmen and vowed vengeance against them, saying,

"'By the tomb of the prophet, some day will I get even with these my relatives, yea, even to the extreme of squareness.' And he repeated the vow upon the rising of each day's sun.

"And it came to pass that Mahmoud chanced to do a kindness for a great man of the city who was a politician, and the great man was grateful and obtained for him a position upon the police force. And after a space he became a captain of the force and began to amass riches after his kind.

"And the suns shone and the moons came and went and the size of Mahmoud's pile increased and he bought a mansion upon the Avenue that is called Fifth and rode to and from the same in the carriage which no horse draweth. And the people of the city spake often of his riches but when strangers asked from whence the riches were gathered they winked deeply and answered naught.

"And the day came when Mahmoud lay upon his deathbed and he sent for all his kinsmen, yea, for all those which had wronged him in the days of his adversity. And when they were gathered about him, he said,

"'Oh beloved, I am about to be taken from you, and to be gathered unto my fathers. Unto you, therefore, do I leave my gear, my monies and my lands, to be divided as ye may see fit. And it is so written in my will."

"And the kinsmen were amazed, forasmuch as they had known of Mahmoud's vow of vengeance against them, and they fell upon their knees and blessed him for his exceeding kindness.

"And Mahmoud smiled sweetly as one whose aim is accomplished. And he turned his face to the wall and died.

"And it came to pass that the kinsmen set to work to divide the goods of Mahmoud among themselves. And the dividing thereof was as the poet hath written,

"'Verily, there shall be babel of tongues and much trouble in the house,
Yea, trouble unto the uttermost even to the pulling of the hair and the rending of the garment,
And each shall agree with neither and neither shall agree with both.'

"And the days passed and the nights came and went and the kinsmen of Mahmoud were as nigh unto agreement concerning the division of the inheritance as they were at the beginning.

"And they took unto themselves counsellors of law and sought justice in the courts and there fought they yesterday, to-day and forever. And the estate of Mahmoud passed unto the pockets of the counsellors and after it passed also the estate of each of the kinsmen.

"And the day came when the kinsmen sat at porridge about the supper board of the almshouse and the eldest among them spake unto the others, saying,

"Verily, it occurreth to me that our late lamented relative kept to the letter of his vow and hath got exceeding hunk.'

"And the others answered him, saying,

"'It is as thou hast said.'

"And they kicked themselves in secret."

And Scheherezade paused and said unto the Father of the Faithful,

"Oh King, live forever! What thinkest thou of the vengeance of Mahmoud? Was it not hidden and yet plain?"

And the King answered her, saying,

"It was a dead give away."

And he bade his slaves bear him to the minstrel show that he might learn another joke of the same age.

COMMERCE ACCOUNTS & FINANCE

A Magazine cf Higher Business Education and Practical Administration. Acknowledged Authority in the Profession of Commerce and Consistent Advocate of Methods Up to Date and Above the Table.

JOSEPH CROSBY LINCOLN, - - - Editor.
FRIEND PITTS, JR., - Circulation and Advertising.
E. R. KITTREDGE, - - - Business Manager.

PUBLISHED MONTHLY

SUBSCRIPTION $1 a Year in the United States, Canada and Mexico. Other countries $1.50. Postage prepaid by the Publishers. In the absence of specific orders to stop at the end of the subscription term the paper will be continued and a bill sent. Entered at the New York Postoffice as Second Class mail matter.

COMMERCE, ACCOUNTS & FINANCE COMPANY, Publishers
Twenty-five Pine Street, New York

NOW that the vacation period for the year has closed, we can, we presume, introduce a discussion into these columns of vacation practices without fear of offense. The vacation idea is unquestionably an excellent one, but, like many other excellent things, when carried to extremes it works other than with entire satisfaction. Many a concern has gone crippled through the summer for no other reason than because this clerk, that clerk and the other one were away on vacations. The profitableness of business has been diminished, if not entirely lost; principals who have been at home trying to manage business have been driven to desperation, and all simply because vacations must be taken, and the rule has come to be established that the warm season of the year is the vacation period.

*

We know of one concern that is so thoroughly disgusted with its experience in this regard the present year that for another season it contemplates one of two things, either to abolish vacations entirely among its clerks or to absolutely shut up the establishment for two weeks during one of the summer months, meanwhile hanging out a card, as they do in certain classes of restaurants, "Closed for repairs." There is more reason than rhyme in this last suggestion. The business referred to is largely profession in character, and while, for several years past the business in question has been more active in the summer months than in certain other portions of the year, still less inconvenience and less loss, it is believed, would occur from absolutely waiting two weeks until the entire force got back from mountain and seaside than has occurred the present year by having a number of them away for a short time during the whole of the summer and the whole concern being crippled.

*

Some of the large banks insist upon their clerks commencing the vacation period immediately after the 1st of January. The total number of clerks is counted, and, allowing two weeks as the vacation period, the total number is divided by twenty-six, the number of two-week periods there is in the year. This indicates the number of clerks to be absent at one time. The clerks are thereupon classified, and the number, whether it be two, five or twenty, in each class, is given its two weeks and is expected to occupy them for vacation purposes and to be on hand the balance of the time. There is reason in this, for the bank's business, like Tennyson's stream, goes on forever. Each clerk gets his vacation, and yet at no time is the business of the institution necessarily stopped or delayed. The practical working out of the scheme is that the bank must employ as many extra men as those who are away.

*

Where there are a few large institutions that can thus arbitrarily divide the year and fit one condition into the other in a way to keep up its working force at all times, there are hundreds of small concerns which are unable to do this, and which accordingly suffer the crippled condition through the hot weather first referred to in these paragraphs. Again it transpires, as we happen to know by experience, that the clerks themselves have something to say, and that in some instances, at least, they do not feel that they are getting their just deserts to have their vacation in January instead of in the summer time, when everybody else is having a vacation. So, regard the case as you may, there you are. On the one hand there are the intricacies of business and on the other there are the personal preferences and prejudices of the class to be benefited.

*

Again referring to the proposition of the establishment above alluded to, which has suggested for another year absolutely closing its doors for two weeks during the vacation period and all going off for a "hurrah, boys," at the same time, we would say that we think, in its case, the suggestion a good one, and we should not be at all surprised if the concern undertakes to put the proposition into operation. It is not, however, a conclusive solution of the vacation difficulty. While it may be able to close in this way, by reason of its business, which, as before mentioned, is professional in character, there are hundreds of others who cannot close. There are many firms that cannot close, on the one hand, and others, on the other extreme, that cannot divide their employees into classes and begin the vacation periods at the beginning of the year. Altogether it is hard to decide what to do. Perhaps some of our readers have given this subject thought and will be interested in taking it up for discussion through our correspondence columns. There is plenty of time just now for matters of this class.

*

NO WORRY.

"Have you had any more duns?" inquired the Sultan of Turkey.

"A few," answered the court official.

"Well, let me have them."

"I hope Your Majesty is not going to allow yourself to be personally worried by these importunate—"

"Not at all. The pearl of the harem wants them. She is making an autograph collection."—Washington Star.

A MATCHLESS OBSERVATION.

"Have you a match?" asked the chronic bore who had dropped into the busy man's office for a chat. "My cigar has gone out."

"It seems to have the advantage of you," remarked the busy man.

"How's that?" queried the c. b.

"It knows its place," replied the b. m.—Chicago News.

IT CERTAINLY IS.

Mortified Bridegroom—You told me your father's wedding present would be a check for four figures.

Blushing Bride—Well, isn't eleven dollars and thirty cents four figures?—Chicago Tribune.

The Negotiable Instruments Law*

By THOMAS B. PATON.

Presentment Not Necessary to Charge Drawer—Circumstances Excusing Delay in Presentment—When Presentment May Be Dispensed With.

Note.—As enacted in New York, the Negotiable Instrument Law is divided into nineteen articles as follows:

1. GENERAL PROVISIONS (Sections 1-17).
2. NEGOTIABLE INSTRUMENTS: Form and Interpretation (20-42).
3. Consideration (50-55).
4. Negotiation (60-80).
5. Rights of holder (90-98).
6. Liabilities of parties (110-119).
7. Presentment for payment (130-148).
8. Notice of Dishonor (160-189).
9. Discharge (200-206).
10. BILLS OF EXCHANGE (210-215).
11. Acceptance (220-230).
12. Presentment for acceptance (240-248).
13. Protest (260-268).
14. Acceptance for honor (280-290).
15. Payment for honor (300-306).
16. Bills in a set (310-315).
17. PROMISSORY NOTES AND CHECKS (320-325).
18. Notes given for patent rights (330-332).
19. Laws repealed: When takes effect (340-341).

The provisions of the law naturally fall under four general classifications:

a. General Provisions.
b. Negotiable Instruments in General.
c. Bills of Exchange.
d. Promissory Notes and Checks.

The text of the law is the same in all the States (with some slight exceptions which will be noted), but the numbering of the sections, and in some States, of the articles, is not uniform. There is, however, the same continuity of articles and text, except that in some instances "General Provisions" follow, instead of precede, the remainder of the act. By following this course of study with reference to the New York act, as above outlined, the reader in each State can apply the same to the law of his own State.

IN considering the provisions of Article VII we have seen that while presentment for payment is not legally necessary to charge the person primarily liable on the instrument, it is necessary, except where the act otherwise provides, in order to charge the drawer and indorsers. We have also seen when the instrument must be presented where it is payable on demand, and when not so payable; and also what constitutes a sufficient presentment with reference to the requirements as to who must present, time of day, proper place, and to whom presentment must be made.

We now come to those sections which provide under what circumstances presentment for payment, ordinarily necessary to charge drawer and indorsers, is either entirely dispensed with, or delay in making the same beyond the time fixed by the act is excused. First we have a provision applicable to the drawer alone—that is to say, providing the circumstances under which presentment is not necessary to charge him.

To Charge the Drawer.

Sec. 139. When Presentment Not Required to Charge the Drawer.—Presentment for payment is not required in order to charge the drawer where he has no right to expect or require that the drawee or acceptor will pay the instrument.

For example, a man draws and issues or negotiates a draft on another without any right to do so, or without any reasonable ground to expect that the drawee will honor it. Presentment is not necessary to charge him with liability. He has either committed a fraud, or a piece of folly in undertaking that the drawee would honor the bill when he had no reasonable ground so to expect it, and is not entitled to a presentment. Considerable discussion has been had whether in every case where there was a lack of funds of the drawer in the hands of the drawee, this fact alone would dispense with the necessity of presentment; but the courts have declared that even though the drawer has no funds, if it can be shown that he had a reasonable expectation that the draft would be accepted and paid, presentment would be necessary to hold him. As pointed out by the Supreme Court of the United States in Life Insurance Company v. Pendleton, 112 U. S. 708, there might be an agreement between drawer and drawee that the latter would pay the former's drafts, or a course of dealing between them in which the drawee was accustomed to pay drafts of the drawer without reference to the state of their mutual accounts, which would authorize a reasonable expectation by the drawer that his draft would be honored, even if he had no funds with the drawee, and entitle him to presentment. As said by Mr. Daniel (Sec. 1,074 Neg. Instr.), "the true criterion of the right to require due demand and notice is, not whether the drawer had funds in the drawee's hands, but whether or not the drawer had a right to expect or require that the drawee would honor his bill."

Again, if a bill has been accepted for the mere accommodation of the drawer, and he has undertaken to supply funds to meet it, presentment to the acceptor would not be required to charge the drawer.

Indorser's Right.

Coming next to special circumstances affecting the indorser's right to presentment; circumstances affecting the indorser's right alone.

Sec. 140. When Presentment Not Required to Charge the Indorser.—Presentment for payment is not required to charge an indorser where the instrument was made or accepted for his accommodation, and he has no reason to expect that the instrument will be paid if presented.

Ordinarily, we know, the indorser is not the primary debtor, and does not expect to be called on for payment, except in the contingency that the primary debtor defaults, and he is looked to, the legal requirements being observed, to make it good. But sometimes an instrument is made or accepted expressly to accommodate the indorser by enabling him to get the money on it for his own benefit. John Smith, for example, desires to raise money, so he induces Peter Jones to make a promissory note to his (Smith's) order, which he indorses and discounts at the bank, using the proceeds in his business. In this case, of course, as between Jones, maker, and Smith, indorser, Smith is the man to make the note good at maturity. Section 140 covers such cases, and dispenses with a presentment for payment which, from the nature of the case, is unnecessary.

We have seen that where the drawer has no right to expect or require that the drawee will pay the instrument, he is not discharged by non-presentment. But the indorser of the instrument, it is readily seen, is not on the same footing with the drawer in this respect. Presentment of such an instrument is necessary to preserve his liability, for, ordinarily, he is not aware of the drawer's fraud or folly, and has no reason to suppose the bill will not be honored. But if he participates in the fraud of the drawer, or if he is guilty of fraud on his own account, then he can be held without presentment. An instance of the latter kind is suggested in the Missouri case of Moody v. Mack, 43 Mo. 213. An indorser purchases a

*Republished from the "Banking Law Journal" by permission. Copyright, 1899, 1900, 1901 and 1902, by T. B. Paton, all rights reserved. To be revised and published in book form by the author.

draft or check to his order, and sells it for value. Before its presentation he obtains a duplicate from the drawer, which he indorses and collects. This defeats payment of the first draft. In such a case he could not escape liability thereon by alleging non-presentment.

In the two sections last above considered we have seen rules providing under what circumstances presentment is not necessary to charge the drawer, or to charge the indorser, regarding each independently. We now come to sections which, looking at both drawer and indorser together as parties to be charged by presentment, provide the circumstances which will either (1) excuse a delay in making presentment, or will (2) dispense with presentment altogether.

Sec. 141. When Delay in Making Presentment is Excused.—Delay in making presentment for payment is excused when the delay is caused by circumstances beyond the control of the holder and not imputable to his default, misconduct or negligence. When the cause of de lay ceases to operate, presentment must be made with reasonable diligence.

Following we enumerate some general circumstances which have been held by the courts to excuse delay of presentment for the period during which such circumstances operate.

General Circumstances Excusing Delay.

1. Breaking out of war or hostilities between country of holder and country where instrument is payable, or the prohibition of commercial intercourse between such countries, excuses delay in presentment during continuance of hostilities or public prohibition of commerce and intercourse.

2. If parties in same country, but public enemy invades so as to make intercourse between parties dangerous or impracticable, same principle applies.

3. Where riot, insurrection or other political disturbance takes place, interrupting and obstructing the ordinary negotiations of trade, the same principle controls as where commercial intercourse between the parties is interrupted by military operations or interdictions of commerce.

4. Where a malignant, contagious or infectious disease is prevalent in the locality of payment, so extensive as to cause a suspension of business and making it hazardous to enter the infected district, this excuses delay during the prevalence of such disease.

5. Overwhelming calamity or unavoidable accident, such as the carrying away of bridges by freshets and the destruction of means of communication; or the obstruction thereof by heavy snow storms; or the devastation caused by tornadoes and earthquakes, rendering commercial intercourse impracticable for the time being, likewise excuses the delay which such circumstances occasion.

6. An accident, miscarriage or default in the postal service, without any negligence on the holder's part, where he has intrusted the instrument to the mail for transmission to the place of payment, excuses the delay of presentment thereby caused.

Special Circumstances Excusing Delay.

In addition to the above general circumstances, there are certain special circumstances which excuse delay of presentment until such circumstances cease to operate. Among these are the following:

1. Where two joint makers of a note not payable at a particular place live so far apart that presentment for payment to both cannot be made on the same day, the delay for the necessary time required to present to the second, after presentment to the first, is excused.

2. The sudden illness or death of, or accident to, the holder or his agent very near the time the instrument becomes due, which renders it impossible or impracticable to present it precisely at maturity, excuses the delay necessarily caused thereby.

Having seen when delay in making presentment for

Brought face to face for the good of the Nation—Philadelphia Press.

payment is excused until the cause of delay ceases to operate, we will, therefore, at once proceed to consider the cases when presentment for payment may be entirely dispensed with.

When Presentment May Be Dispensed With.

Having seen when delay in making presentment for payment is excused until the cause of delay ceases to operate, we now proceed to when presentment may be entirely dispensed with.

Sec. 142. When Presentment May Be Dispensed With. —Presentment for payment is dispensed with:

1. Where after the exercise of reasonable diligence presentment as required by this act cannot be made;

2. Where the drawee is a fictitious person;

3. By waiver of presentment express or implied.

The first class of cases in which presentment for payment is dispensed with is where after the exercise of reasonable diligence presentment as required by this act cannot be made. We have already viewed in detail the requirements as to presentment, and it is not necessary to enumerate all the conditions or circumstances, which would dispense with presentment. For example, if the maker of an instrument not payable at a specified place should die before maturity and there was no personal representative to whom the instrument might be presented, this would be one case in which presentment would be dispensed with. Then the various conditions which might arise from the maker of an instrument, not payable at a specified place, having absconded, or having moved to another country, or to another State, or whose whereabouts could not be ascertained with reasonable diligence suggest the question whether, as at common law, no presentment would be necessary, or whether the requirement in subdivision 4 of section 133 that "in any other case," presentment to the person to make payment is sufficient if made "at his last known place of business or residence," would require presentment at such place, if known.

Drawee A Fictitious Person.

Next, presentment for payment is dispensed with "where the drawee is a fictitious person."

This provision, it is seen, relates to bills of exchange. If a man draws a bill on a fictitious drawee, of course there is no person in existence to whom to present it, or who can make payment. Of course, therefore, there is no requirement of presentment. As to notice of dishonor, we will see later, that it need not be given to the drawer of such a bill, nor to the indorser if he was aware of the fiction at the time he indorsed the instrument; but an innocent indorser would be entitled to notice of dishonor.

The final provision as to when presentment for payment is dispensed with, relates to those cases where there is a "waiver of presentment express or implied."

Sometimes a waiver of presentment is embodied in the instrument itself; as where it contains the words "presentment and protest waived;" or "the drawer and indorsers severally waive presentment for payment, protest and notice of non-payment;" or many other forms of language of similar import. In such cases the waiver enters into the contract of every party who signs the instrument, whether as drawer, maker, acceptor or indorser. Sometimes the waiver is not embodied in the instrument, but is written over the signature of one of the indorsers. In such case, there is a conflict of authority over the proposition whether the waiver is the individual waiver of the indorser over whose signature it appears, or whether subsequent indorsers are bound thereby. The safest view to take is that it is the individual waiver of the one indorser only. The practice of attaching "no protest" slips to drafts has given rise to much controversy and difference of opinion as to its effect as a waiver of presentment, protest and notice. There is a dearth of judicial decision upon this point, and the banking practice is varied. Some bankers disregard the slip altogether while others give heed to it, to the extent of omitting formal protest and notice, but not dispensing with presentment. So far as presentment for payment of a draft having a "no protest" slip is concerned, the general practice is to make presentment, whatever differences of opinion may exist as to the necessity of subsequent steps.

Sometimes an indorser, at the time of making his indorsement, will make a verbal promise to pay the instrument absolutely, or to pay it if the maker does not. Some authorities hold that such verbal promises may be proved as waivers by the indorser of the necessity of presentment and notice; while on the contrary it has been held that the policy of the law requires that an instrument shall tell its own story, and that presentment is not waived by such a verbal promise.

Other Waivers.

It has been held that the expressions "accountable," "eventually accountable," "hold ourselves responsible for payment," and the word "holden," imply a waiver of demand and notice. The following words have also been held a waiver of demand and notice by an indorser: "I assign the within note to J. T. and hold myself responsible for the payment of the same, the maker to have two years to pay the same, unless he prefers to pay sooner—interest on the same to be paid annually."

Not only may a waiver be written on the instrument by a party at the time he signs it, but it may be done at any time before maturity, and no new consideration will be necessary to support the waiver.

In addition to express written and verbal waivers, a waiver may be implied by any act, course of conduct or language of a drawer or indorser calculated to induce the holder not to make demand or give notice, or to put him off his guard in that respect. Eighteen months before maturity of an instrument, a party told the holder not to protest it, as it would be paid at maturity. This was held a waiver of demand and notice. Where an indorser informs the holder that the maker has absconded, and requests forbearance, this is a waiver; and if the drawer or the indorser tells the holder that the bill will not be paid, or that he cannot pay it when due, this likewise is a waiver of demand and notice by him. So if the indorser tells the holder to let it run, and he will pay it when called for. Other instances which have been held waivers by indorsers are as follows:

Indorser writing holder before maturity that the maker has failed, acknowledging liability, and asking indulgence until funds can be realized.

Indorser, upon being informed before maturity that maker wanted note to run another year, replying that he is willing.

Indorser, being informed that maker has failed, replying there would be no trouble about it, and he would pay it.

Indorser, before maturity, saying that he will pay it, or arrange it, or using equivalent expression.

Indorser telling holder to give himself no uneasiness, that note would be paid at maturity; that he is collecting money for the maker and will see it paid.

Indorser, after maturity, agreeing with maker to take up note, to give back to him the property for which note was given, and to return note without further consideration.

Indorser, obtaining possession of note before maturity and holding it until after that time.

Indorser agreeing to extension of time for payment.

Promises, or acknowledgments of continued liability, to pay, after maturity, with knowledge that the usual steps of demand, protest or notice, were not taken, also constitute waivers of the necessity of such steps, by the party by whom the promise or obligation is made. Also part payment by a drawer or indorser, after maturity, with such knowledge, has like effect.

SYSTEM.

IS there any word in the vocabulary used by business men more thoroughly overworked at the present time and more ridiculously applied on occasion than the word system? We meet a business man who is somewhat impressed with his own capabilities in devising ways and means to meet the smaller emergencies of office routine, and he tells us that he has invented a "system" for this or a "system" for that. We go among dealers in office appliances, ranging from the printer on the one hand to the manufacturers of office furniture on the other hand, and we are assured with all seriousness that they have a "system" for this and a "system" for that. We are approached by salesmen who call our attention to their "systems." We meet men who are going about the country telling about their "systems," and there is also a periodical called "System" which month by month puts forth schemes that have been devised for the use of cards, etc.

The word system has come to mean, in the way in which it is used, nothing more nor less than plan, or method, or scheme. It is a misuse of the term, for there is about the word "system" when considered in the full sense which the word conveys, a completeness. It is equivalent to a circle. It starts from a given premise and reaches a foregone conclusion, and yet in the way in which the word is commonly applied we find it tacked on to infinitesimal elements of method, all of which are distinguished by some such term as system.

We presume that no protest that we can utter against the misuse of this term will make a particle of difference to the people who are devoted to the wrong use of the word. We presume that no objection that we can offer will make any difference in the use of the term upon the part of men who are employing it in describing the trifling changes which they make from time to time in office routine. Still we are disposed to call attention to the facts as presented above with the mild suggestion that it would be well to stick closer to truth and draw less upon imagination in the use of the word.

If there is any one that has a system, meaning something that is complete, rounded out, that reaches from premise to conclusion, let him use the word system. Let others, on the other hand, who have a mere fragment of a system, a mere item in office management and development, let them use some such term as plan, method or scheme

The Bonus System of Rewarding Labor*

By H. H. GANTT.

AWARDING extra compensation for extra work has long been the practice in successful manufacturing; but the particular method of awarding a bonus above referred to is of recent origin and fills an important need in modern systems of management.

It may be briefly described as follows: Alternative ways of doing a piece of work are carefully investigated by the most competent expert available and the results recorded. The best method is determined and taught to an ordinary workman, who is awarded extra compensation in addition to his day's pay for doing the work in the time and manner specified.

This method of compensation was the outcome of an attempt to introduce in complicated work equitable piece rates determined as nearly as possible by scientific methods.

To understand the subject thoroughly it is necessary to become familiar with the work of Mr. Fred W. Taylor, who was the first to apply the scientific method to the investigation of ordinary labor problems, for this system was a direct outgrowth from his work.

Mr. Taylor, the Pioneer Investigator.

In the early eighties, Mr. Taylor, then in the employ of the Midvale Steel Company, became convinced that the scientific method of investigation was the only means of finding the best solution to the various problems with which he found himself confronted; and whether the problem was that of managing a machine shop or of shovelling coal, he remained firm to his conviction, and did his best to obtain his conclusions by that means. Conscious that his method was correct, he maintained his faith in the results, no matter how much they differed from previous ones, and often had the satisfaction of accomplishing what had been declared impossible.

The fact that Mr. Taylor combined the knowledge and methods of the scientist with the experience of a practical mechanic, enabled him to bring to bear the scientific method on ordinary mechanical problems in a most efficient manner, and his experiments to determine the laws that govern the cutting of metals is most noteworthy, inasmuch as he not only had to investigate a problem having a large number of unknown quantities, but had to develop a method of investigation of a problem which had been declared by engineers and mathematicians alike incapable of solution. That the problem has been solved, at least in part, is evidenced by the fact that slide rules embodying the laws of cutting steel have been in practical operation for more than two years.

The Output of Machine Shops Doubled.

This investigation has had, aside from its main object, a most important result, for it has developed a method of making in a few hours a scientific determination of the value of a tool steel for any given purpose; this very important art has in the past been so imperfectly understood that as a rule tool steel has been sold more by the merits of the salesman than by its own. With the new ideas this condition will before long be a thing of the past and opinions will give place to facts. Again, the application of the scientific methods to the investigation of ordinary mechanical problems has often disclosed facts previously unsuspected. Most notable among these was the discovery made by Messrs. Taylor & White in testing tool steel, that certain kinds of self-hardening steel had an important property previously unsuspected. By taking advantage of this property, and making use of it under a proper system of management, it is possible to practically double the output of a majority of the machine shops in the world.

The Scientific Study of What a Man Can Do.

The value of scientific knowledge to engineering and industry has long been recognized, and the great advances that have been made in this country and in Germany are due largely to the fact that such knowledge has been applied; but the idea of making a scientific study of what a man or a machine could do was new, and so complicated that few looked upon it with favor.

A workman was allowed to do the best he could with the appliances he liked, and a machine or a tool was expected to do what its builders claimed for it. An effort to get more work out of a man or a machine had been made by paying for the amount of work done instead of for the time taken; in other words, by the introduction of piecework in place of day-work; but the knowledge of how much a man or a machine could do was so vague that piece prices set by records or "judgment" were invariably found to be wrong, and the attempt to change them has caused more labor trouble than all other causes combined.

Eliminating, then, the method of setting piece rates by "judgment" and by previous records, the method of investigation or experiment was the only one from which anything could be hoped. No two men worked exactly alike, and few used exactly the same tools. The capacity of a machine and the best method of operating it were seldom what its maker stated. That there is a best method of doing a piece of work, or that there is a best method of operating a machine, and a maximum capacity for that machine, are not doubted, but the problem of determining them was something for which there was no guide except the general principles of scientific investigation.

A Greater Output, and Greater Reward, of Labor.

Believing firmly that if piecework is to be permanently successful the rates must be properly fixed in the beginning, and not "cut," Mr. Taylor undertook to determine by the above method the amount of work to be expected, and fixed his piece rates accordingly. with the result that men provided with the proper appliances, educated in the best methods, and given a piece rate that was permanent, have produced a greater output at much less cost than under the old method, at the same time earning larger wages.

The difficulty about this method is that the investigation is often long and tedious, for no permanent rate should be set until we know the best method of doing the work, and the exact time it will take a good man to do it.

For financial reasons it is frequently impossible to wait for a complete scientific investigation of every condition before fixing a rate of pay, and the need of a means of making use of a partially completed scientific investigation, or of what knowledge we have, has long been felt. Piece-work will not do it satisfactorily, for it is not desirable, or even feasible, to change rates frequently, as the workman never feels settled, and is continually afraid of having his wages reduced. This unsettled feeling, which always accompanies the old-fashioned method of rate setting, is the source of the opposition to that type of piecework, and the reason why so many men prefer day-work at smaller wages.

The first requirement, then, of any system aiming to take advantage of a partially completed investigation is that, no matter what other changes are made, the workman's weekly pay shall not be reduced.

The Laws Governing the Output of Labor.

It is a well-established fact that a man who is working at day's wages never does work to his maximum capacity, but will do so if he can be sure of earning a commensurate additional compensation. If the work is light, and does not require much physical effort, this additional amount

*Originally published in the "American Monthly Review of Reviews."

La Belle France—"Now my dear Philander, have patience."—Chicago Inter-Ocean.

may be as low as 30 per cent. of his day rate. If, however, the work is hard labor, and he becomes physically tired at the end of the day, he requires 50 per cent. additional to make him put forth all his energies; and if, in addition to the physical strain, the conditions under which the work is done are unpleasant, such as severe heat, he requires 70 or 80 per cent. additional to make him do his best.

The Working of the "Bonus System."

These facts, which have been established by history, enable us to take advantage of the results of a partially completed investigation; for, if we set for a day's work such a task as our investigations prove can be done, and offer for its accomplishment the proper premium or "bonus," in accordance with the facts just stated, we shall find a very large proportion of men ready and willing to do the work in the manner and time specified in order to earn the increased pay. This, then, is the "bonus system," which was first introduced by the writer in the works of the Bethlehem Steel Company. It consists of teaching an ordinary workman to do a piece of work by the best methods we can devise and asking him to do it in the time it would take a good workman. If he accomplishes this task in the time set, he is given the wages of the good workman; otherwise, he gets simply his own day rate. Aside from the educational effect, which is most marked, the result of this is that many ordinary workmen, who lacked only incentive, promptly take their places among those that naturally have more ambition, and the general moral tone is elevated.

When we write out a set of instructions according to the results of a partially completed investigation, the remaining information will, in the long run, generally be found out either by the expert who is making the investigation or the workman. In the first case, a new set of instructions is made out in accordance with the additional information and the proper bonus set. In the second case the same thing should be done, but in addition the workman discovering or devising the improved method should be given a cash compensation commensurate with the value of the improvement which should thereafter belong to his employer. By such a system the workman is encouraged to be something more than a machine, for he is first taught the best knowledge available, and paid for learning more.

The Advantages to Workmen and Employer.

Add to the satisfaction that comes with increased wages honestly earned, increase in quantity, and, as experience has shown, improvement in quality of work at a lower cost, and we have a condition that rapidly tends toward prosperity for all concerned.

As in any manufacturing establishment, it is important to obtain the maximum output from the plant, it is very essential that the maximum product should be gotten from every machine, and the fact that a man loses his bonus when he fails to get out this maximum product is a very big factor in accomplishing the desired result, for he learns to take care of his machine or tools, and complains promptly if his work is interfered with.

Again, those who are indirectly connected with the output, such as foremen, men who supply material and appliances, and those who repair machines, all should receive a bonus in proportion to the number of men that produce the maximum output, and the whole makes a system that is as nearly automatic as is possible; for what is for the good of one is for the good of all, and a man who will not do his duty soon finds that he is in the wrong place.

Exact Bookkeeping for Laboring Operations.

This description of the principles on which the bonus system is founded gives but little idea of how it is carried out, but a very little thought shows that proper appliances for doing the work and a complete and exact system of time and record keeping are the first essentials. Thanks to the recent advances made in the art of doing such work, an exact system of keeping time, records and costs can to-day be made a source of economy by preventing the errors and waste which always go with those methods which depend upon verbal reports and memory.

It has long been the custom to keep a daily record of cash, which must balance to a cent. Modern methods require that we shall keep a daily record of labor and material, and the bonus system in its best development compels a modern system of management in that it requires that we shall at all times know the work done and to be done and the means for doing it. Such a system requires that work for men and machines should be laid out as fully as possible the day before, which has a strong tendency to do away with delay and idleness, which are expensive alike to the manufacturer and the bonus workman.

That such a system requires more organization than the ordinary shop possesses is not denied, but few realize how little such organization costs, and how many times it pays for itself in the course of a year.

Output of the Bethlehem Company Doubled.

The principles above outlined were applied during the spring and summer of 1901 to the ordnance and armor-plate machine shops of the Bethlehem Steel Company and resulted in a short time in more than doubling the output of those shops. The system is still in use substantially as introduced, and the superintendent, Mr. Archibald Johnston, in his testimony before the House Committee on Labor, February 13, 1902, makes the following statement regarding it: "This arrangement has worked very satisfactorily, both to the men and the company, for it has enabled us to get work out more quickly, and to add to the producing capacity of our invested capital; while for the men, it has been a great benefit, as we have many instances of employees who have bought homes for themselves principally from their extra earnings on the bonus system, and from overtime work. The system has been a stronger incentive to industry than any other we have been able to put into effect in our plant."

The cause of this result is not hard to find, for the men, realizing that their interests are being cared for, give their co-operation.

JUST THE REVERSE.

"He looks as prosperous as a trust promoter. Is that his line?"

"Oh, no; quite the contrary."

"What do you mean by that?"

"He doesn't promote trust; he limits it. He's the credit man of a big wholesale house."—Chicago Post.

Business Subjects in Current Literature

THE magazines for the past month were filled with a great variety of the so-called "special" articles, and these special articles were, in the majority of cases, written concerning some peculiar phase of business. It is quite evident that magazine readers desire this sort of thing, and that editors find that it pays them to print business articles. Below the reader will find the usual partial list of such articles and the names of the magazines in which they appear.

Articles on General Subjects.

In the "World's Work" J. Blethen writes of "A Typical Irrigating Community." J. Dowd, in "Gunton's Magazine," discusses "Negroes as Cotton Manufacturers." In the "International Monthly," E. Mead writes learnedly respecting "The Growth of Property Rights in Water." "Census of Manufacturers" is the title of an article by S. M. D. North in the "American Review of Reviews." C. M. Harger in "Outing" presents "Modern Methods in the Cattle Industry." O. P. Austin, the authority on such matters, discusses "Our National Foreign Markets" in his article in the "World's Work." Booker T. Washington has an article in "Everybody's" entitled "Work With the Hands." In the "Political Science Monthly," of Boston, B. H. Meyer tells us about "The Interstate Commerce Commission." "The Distribution of Land Values in Cities" is discussed by R. M. Hurd in the "Yale Review." "Irrigation on the American Frontier" is presented by E. E. Sparks in "The Chatauquan." M. Summerville, in "Harper's," writes of "Epochs of Gem Engraving." "Teaching by Correspondence" is the title of an article by R. Doubleday, which appears in the "World's Work." E. W. Mayo, in "Ainslees," writes of "The City of St. Louis." In "Pearson's," H. C. Fyfe has an article on "The Symplon Tunnel." R. P. Bolton, in "Cassier's Magazine," presents an article with the alluring title, "The Engineer in the Kitchen." W. M. McFarland writes of "The Naval Engineer of the Future," his paper appearing in "Engineering Magazine." In the "Bookman," W. L. Andrews tells of "Early American Book-binding." "Beauty in Advertising Illustration" is the title of J. B. Walker's article in the "Cosmopolitan."

The "Overland Monthly" contains a paper by J. S. Cannon on "Commercial Rubber Plantations." In the "Engineering Magazine" "The Mining Industry and Mineral Resources of British Columbia" are discussed by W. M. Brewer. W. H. Page, in the "World's Work," gives us "An Intimate View of Publishing," and in the same periodical "England, as Seen by an American Business Man" is described by A. Goodrich. In the "Strand," F. Westbury has a very interesting article on "Sponges," and G. F. Kunz, in the "North American Review," writes of "The Management and Uses of Expositions." "Politics and Business Prosperity" is discussed by G Gunton, in "Gunton's Magazine," and in "Cassier's Magazine," C. O'Neill writes of "Armor-Plate Making in the United States." In the "Engineering Magazine" appears a paper on "Production and Industrial Investment" by W. D. Ennis, and in the same magazine "The Doom of the Naval Engineer" is predicted by C. M. Johnson. In "Everybody's," "Life in the Mining Regions" is very interestingly described by F. Morris.

In the foreign publications appear these articles: "Possibilities of Wireless Telegraphy," by C. Bright, in the "London Monthly Review." "Letter to the Working Classes," by J. H. Schooling, in the "Fortnightly Review." "New Designs for Wall Papers," by A. Vallance, in the "Art Journal," of London. In the "Revue Politique and Parliamentaire," of Paris, D. Bellet writes of "Commercial Education in England," and in the "Revue de Paris," V. Berard writes of "Foreign Commercial Relations."

Architecture and Building.

The "Architect Record" contains its usual number of articles pertaining to architecture and kindred trades, among them being the following: "The New York Stock Exchange," by M. Schuyler; "Reinforced Concrete Construction," by G. Hill, and the second in the series of papers by A. Melani on "Modern Italian Architecture." In "Cassier's," P. Kreuzpointner writes of "The Testing of Structural Materials."

Banking and Finance.

Articles on financial and banking subjects have been a trifle less numerous than usual. In the "Banker's Magazine," of New York, C. A. Conant discusses "Intervention of the State in the Banking World." In the same magazine an anonymous writer presents a paper on "Discounts, Loans and Investments," and in this periodical, also, appears an unsigned article on "The Redemption of the Credit Currency." In the "World's Work," a paper entitled "A New Era in Financial Real Estate" is presented. H. White, in "Gunton's," discusses "The Economics of Branch Banking," and in the "Ladies' Home Journal" "The Work of the Chief Clerk of the Treasury Department" is described by C. Howard.

The English magazines contain the following articles: "Financial Policy of British Railway Companies," by C. H. Grunling, and "Business Education in England," by an anonymous writer, both in the "Banker's Magazine," of London. "National Solvency and Banking Credit," by E. E. Gallander, in the "Westminster Review." G. Bing, in the "Fortnightly Review," discusses "Fiscal Problems of To-Day," and W. H. Williamson, in "Chamber's Journal," of Edinburgh, tells us about "Bulls and Bears on the Exchange."

Farming and Forestry.

C. H. Matson, in the "World's Work," writes of "World-wide Lessons From Kansas Farms." In the "American Review of Reviews," H. C. Adams has an article on "The Diffusion of Commercial Prosperity." W. R. Draper, in the "American Review of Reviews," presents "The Farmer's Balance Sheet for 1902," and in "World's Work," W. S. Harwood tells of "Breeding New Kinds of Corn."

Photography.

Whether it is that the summer season has stirred up the enthusiasm of the amateur photographers or not, it is certain that the magazines contain an unusual number of articles concerning photography. "Wilson's Photographic Magazine," for August, contains the following: "Street Photography," by J. Bartlett; "Negative Density," by an anonymous writer; "Natural History Photography," by E. W. Konard; "Photographing Domestic Animals," by J. H. McFarland; "Stains," by F. Graves; "Improvement of Negatives by Masking," by P. Mathy; "Ascetone as a Developer," by J. Bardwell; "Platinotype Process," by an anonymous writer; "Residues," by G. W. Webster; "Plates in the Tropics," by R. Dellont, and "Mounting and Framing Photographs," by H. Kingsborough. In the "Photographic Times-Bulletin" are papers entitled "Carbons on Porcelain," by W. H. Dunham, and the ninth article in the series on "Architectural Photographing," by H. C. Deleny. P. Lowell, in the "Popular Science Monthly," writes interestingly concerning "Areography." There is an article also in "Badminton," published in London, on "Bird-nest Photography."

Transportation.

The automobile, of course, occupies its usual front seat in the current magazines, but as most of the articles are not written from the point of the business man, a list of them is not given here.

In "Cassier's Magazine," J. F. Gains writes of "British Tank Locomotive Types"; in the same periodical F. H. Mason has an article on "Electric Railways in Berlin." Mexico's "Isthmian Railroad" is described by H. Eliot in "Ainslees," and C. Hovey, in the same publication, has some interesting stories of "Special Trains." In "Cassell's Magazine," of London, "Metropolitan Underground and Overhead Railways" are discussed by D. T. Timmns. In the Pall Mall Magazine, "British and French Express Trains" are written of by H. G. Archer.

Capital and Labor.

It is, no doubt, owing to the great coal strike, but whatever the cause, the articles on trusts, labor unions, strikes and the like, are more than usually numerous this month. M. G. Cunniff, in the "World's Work," writes of "Labor Unions From the Inside." "The Control of Organized Labor and Capital" is discussed by an anonymous writer in the "Banker's Magazine." D. Strong, in "Munsey," tells of "Labor Days of History." E. H. Mullin, in "Cassier's Magazine," presents a paper on the "Organization of an Industrial Unit." In the "Arena," G. F. Spinney discusses "Humanity's Part in the Labor Problem," and W. A. Wyckoff, in "Scribner's," has a paper entitled "Among the Wage Earners." B. O. Flower, in the "Arena," presents "Child Labor in the United States," and in "Harper's," R. F. Ely writes of "Industrial Betterment." In the "Catholic World," R. Cartwright gives us "An Economic Study of the Miner as He Is," and in "Gunton's Magazine," G. Gunton asks and attempts to answer the question, "The Coal Strike, Is It a Conspiracy?" H. L. Gantt, in the "Review of Reviews," tells of the "Competitive System of Rewarding Labor," and in the same periodical S. Cabot gives an instance of "Profit Sharing." "The Political Science Monthly" contains an article by E. A. Sayons entitled "Early Trusts in Holland," and a paper by J. Martin, "Do Trade Unions Limit Output?" The "Educational Review" presents an article by A. Shaw on "The Outlook for the Average Man in a Non-Competitive Society," and S. McReynolds writes of "New Jersey, the Home of Trusts," for "World's Work."

In the foreign periodicals appear the following: the "Pall Mall Magazine" contains a paper by E. Robertson on "The Atlantic Shipping Combine." C. Benoist, in the "Revue de Deux Mondes," of Paris, writes on "The Organization of Miners.' The "Revue de Socialistic" contains the second in the series of articles by G. Sorel on "Industrial Syndicates and Their Significance," and in the "Revue Politique et Parliamentaire" M. Bellew writes of "The Labor Congress at Dusseldorf."

Woman.

In "Everybody's," Bessie Van Vorst writes of "The Woman That Toils." In "Ainslees," Marghatita S. Gerry tells us about "The Woman's Commonwealth of Washington." In the "Westminster Review," of London, appears a paper entitled "Early Writers on the Woman Question."

The Puzzle Competition

THE puzzles for office men, published in "Commerce, Accounts and Finance" for May, June and July, attracted a good deal of attention, and a number of solutions were submitted. Strange to say, however, no one of the competitors exactly fulfilled the conditions of the competition: either one or more of the answers was incorrect or the contestant omitted to enclose the 25 cents necessary to fulfill the conditions. This is to be regretted while it is, nevertheless, a fact. Some of the contestants merely sent the answers and did not write out the essays; others, as we have stated before, sent the essays but did not solve the puzzles correctly. The Editor of "Commerce, Accounts and Finance," therefore, does not feel justified in awarding the prize to any contestant.

As samples of the answers and essays received in the puzzle competition we print two sets, both concerning the last series of puzzles published in the July number.

A Chicago Man's Answers.

W. W. Cooley, of Chicago, prefaces his series of answers with the following original introduction:

Puzzles for Office Men, July, 1902.

Answer 1—Posting.
" 2—Ruler.
" 3—Pen.
" 4—Safe.

State the Acceptance of the Tender. Trusting to Secure the Assets without Depreciation, we assume the Liabilities for this Article and ask Credit. It is a "Safe" Statement that, if the Pen has a Careful Guide, the Posting to the Ledger will Dictate and be the "Ruler" of the Trial Balance, Discounting the necessity of a Check—a Proof and Index that no Loose Leaf was omitted. The Typewriter gives its Impression in a Pressing manner as an Endorsement which, Filed in a Vertical or upright way, is a Record or Journal of the Day—presenting a Balance Sheet that is a Voucher in favor of Careful Posting—Perfect Ruler—Clean Pen and Safe.

Mr. Cooley follows this screed with these short essays:

Posting.

Perfection in posting is an essential condition for the securing of the trial balance. Too much attention cannot be given to this work. While none of us is absolutely correct in all things, by careful attention to details we lessen our troubles, trials and tribulations at the end of the month. With many, too much reliance is placed on "checks" rather than on their own efforts. This causes carelessness which is a plant of wondrous growth and speedy development. Would you enjoy the comforts of a home rather than the suroundings of an office at late hours, give attention to your posting.

Ruler.

I met a ruler of an office who said the "ruler was a useless expense," and ruled the ruler out. When such a ruling is made by the ruler the rule is very offensive to the ruled, and the ruled, as a rule, have no rule of respect for the ruler, which, in such cases, is the two-legged ruler and not our friend who is sometimes round, and, if treated right, is straight.

Pen.

There are different kinds of pens—gold pens, steel pens, hog-pens and penitentiaries. Some penmen have a penchant to steal gold pens. Later they become pensive and penitent when penned in the penitentiary free from penetration of the penetrating gaze, yet with no pension for penace. The penalty, penury, is usually pendant. Penitential moods penetrate the solitude of the penman's penal pen.

Moral: Don't steal gold pens.

Safe.

A good safe is a convenience that is a benefit to any office, but the miserable pie boxes that are offered for sale

Uncle Sam.—"Hey, there! Pull together!"—From the New York Tribune.

under the alias "Safe" are both a nuisance and encumbrance. For safety a galvanized ash barrel is better. It offers about the same protection from fire and water, while it is not an object of suspicion to the midnight toiler who would otherwise spoil the ornament that adorns the office under the cognomen of "Safe." The greatest safeguard to the safety of a safe of this character is to leave it under the watchful eye of the maker or never lock the door.

ANOTHER SET OF ESSAYS.

J. A. Hiner sends the following essays, which the reader will note are to be considered as solutions of the same set of puzzles.

The Trial Balance.

A trial balance is the signboard to every bookkeeper's pathway, and without it he is simply groping along in the dark, liable to miss his road or fall into some dangerous chasm. In fact, the trial balance enables the bookkeeper to give an analytical statement of the firm's business, and shows by what means and by what cause certain results have been produced. The trial balance is an abstract of the ledger, and not only shows that the ledger is in balance, but it also shows the open amounts of the various accounts as they appear upon their respective pages. Now, supposing, of course, that accounts have been systematically classified in the ledger, it is an easy matter for the bookkeeper to make a balance sheet from his trial balance, and show the resources and liabilities, losses and gains of the business, giving a summary of all business transacted during a certain period. Should the bookkeeper prefer, he may take his trial balance by balances, and while he is more liable to make errors by this process, yet when he has completed his trial balance by this method he practically has a balance sheet at the same time.

The Ruler.

The ruler is an indispensable article in every well-regulated office; it not only aids the bookkeeper in drawing straight lines, but may also be used incidentally by the "Old Man" to straighten out the office boy. In either case it keeps things in line about the office, and is the emblem of authority when in the hands of the "Boss." The office ruler is not unlike other rulers, in that some are more intelligent than their companions; that is to say, some are graduated, of course, from the factory in which they are made, while others are more polished and claim a higher intrinsic value. This class would like to pose as the "Exalted Ruler" of the office, but there is the other class that is always flat against everything. Again, we would say that the life of the office ruler is parallel with that of other rulers, from the fact that they are short-lived and their future is uncertain. However, a good ruler in an office is always an index to the style and grade of work which the bookkeeper places upon his books and statements.

Pens.

Of all the office implements the pen plays the most important part. By its use the history of the business and important data is placed upon record. It is the medium by which the clerk or bookkeeper conveys to the pages of various books the transactions and dealings of a business. The pen not only serves a great and good purpose in the counting room but when placed in the hand of an educated person useful thoughts and ideas are reduced to writing and are given out to the world as the product of a fertile and cultivated brain. By the aid of the pen the author and the editor alike transmit to the public at large a continuous flow of useful information which enlightens the reader, both old and young; thereby giving to the world the noble deeds of eminent men, which shed their usefulness over coming generations. Through the use of the pen the boy or girl may acquire the art of writing and become proficient in penmanship, which is a golden key that never tarnishes or loses its value. The

At Last!—Philadelphia Press.

pen unlocks the doors of great business houses and lets the applicant in, and with its silent touch, as if by magic, the broad gates of success open before them.

The Safe.

The safe is symbolical of economy and thrift. It indicates that its owner has in a marked degree been a financial success. The safe is also the most essential as well as the most useful piece of office furniture in any establishment. As a means of protection for money and other valuables it is indispensable. In fact, the safe serves as a repository for everything about the office of an intrinsic value, and no one would think of conducting a business of any magnitude without a receptacle of this kind. Security is one of the fundamental principles of every successful business enterprise, and the safe serves as the "Grand Protector" of all the firm's interests, and all the compensation it requires for this service is a little corner of the office.

POINT OF VIEW.

The farm boy gazed on the gray cashier,
And thought, as entranced, he lingered near;
"Land! would that I that job could hold—
To stand all day and just count gold."

The gray cashier, from his dull employ,
Viewed the tan-brown cheeks of the awkward boy,
And mused: "It would be my dearest wish
Could I be that boy and go off to fish."
—Chicago Record.

WHAT HAPPENED THEN?

Client—I called to employ you to argue a case for me before the court of appeals. Briefly stated, it is this: I hired a cab from the—

Lawyer—Excuse me, but I never argue dead issues.

Client—Dead issues?

Lawyer—Certainly; isn't this a carcase?—Richmond Dispatch.

ECONOMY OF LABOR.

A thin man and a fat man started out on the East side the other day to sell lemons. The thin man was energetic and impressed one as being a hustler; the fat man was indolent, as fat men are apt to be, says the New York Times. Gathering himself together, the thin man would yell:

"Lemons n-i-c-e l-e-m-o-n-s, two for five, five for ten, twenty for a dozen, sixteen for a quarter."

After he was through the fat man said:

"Here too."

A New Work on Accounting

A MANUAL OF BOOKKEEPING

By J. THORNTON

THIS attractive volume, comprising over 500 pages, with numerous illustrations, is one of the clearest and most concise surveys of the principles of accounting which has recently appeared. While its illustrations are given in terms of English money the bookkeeping principles discussed are universal.

The work is divided into two leading parts, the first of which is "LAWS AND PRINCIPLES," and the second "APPLICATION."

LAWS AND PRINCIPLES

In the first part there are discussed the Principle of Exchanges, the Principle of Debit and Credit Accounts, the Principle of the Classification of Accounts, the Principle of Ledger Entries, the Principle of Proving, the Principle of Transfer from Preparatory to Final Record, and the Principle of Balancing and Closing the Ledger.

APPLICATION

Under the head of Application the following chapters are presented: Rules and Tools, What Capital Consists of, Capital in Cash, Capital in Bills, Capital in Debts, Capital in Goods, Fixed Capital, Profit and Loss, Capitalist's Accounts, Company Bookkeeping, Errors, and Non-Capitalistic Bookkeeping.

Several chapters are arranged in the form of lessons, following which are questions for class purposes, arranged in such a way, however, as not to detract in the least from the value of the book in the hands of the general reader. A comprehensive index, together with answers to exercises completes the work.

Price, $2.50.—Sent Postpaid to any address in the United States on receipt of price.

Address COMMERCE ACCOUNTS & FINANCE CO.

PUBLISHERS AND BOOKSELLERS - 25 PINE STREET, NEW YORK

BUSINESS NEEDS.

Advertisements under this head one cent a word each insertion.

OFFICE AND BANK FITTINGS.—Having been connected with a large office furniture manufacturing company for years, I am now in business for myself. I can save you money on your office furniture, desks, chairs, counters and the like. Let me figure on the fittings for your new office. To fetch me, drop a line to "Oak," care Commerce, Accounts & Finance.

WHERE ARE YOU HAVING YOUR ENGRAVING DONE?— I haven't the largest plant in the world, but my machinery is of the newest and best and my workmen are skilled. Also, and this may interest you, my prices are away below the big fellows'. Give me a trial. Representative will call. Address, "Cuts," care Commerce, Accounts & Finance.

HAVE YOU NOW under consideration the issuing of any new bit of advertising matter? Such, for instance, as a little catalogue, booklet or folder, or a new circular to replace some former one not "up-to-date." If I have happened to diagnose your case correctly, why not write me, and if you have anything that you would like bettered, why not slip a copy of it in your letter to me? Address, F. Cook, care Commerce, Accounts & Finance.

DO YOU NEED BOOKS?—Old books, new books, second-hand books. Agent for subscription books, and dealer in old and new books. Ask me for prices on books you want before you buy elsewhere. Address, A. Cross, Commerce, Accounts & Finance.

SALESMAN WANTED.—Salesman of ability is wanted by a novelty house to sell a desk lamp. The lamp itself is a good one and catches the busy man's eye. Liberal commission. Address "Lamp," care Commerce, Accounts & Finance.

OLD BOOKS ON ACCOUNTING SUBJECTS.—I want to know about any curious old books on accounting which you may wish to sell. I will pay liberal prices for such books if they are what I desire. Address, "Librarian," care Commerce, Accounts & Finance.

SAFES.—A large safe dealer has on hand fourteen second-hand safes of various sizes and makes—some great bargains among them—and all will be sold away below half price. Address, "Safe Dealer," care Commerce, Accounts and Finance.

SUPERINTENDENT.—Man of thirty-six years desires a position of responsibility in some large house. Has been superintendent of an office force of seventeen people for the last twelve years. References given. Address, "A. G. B.," care Commerce, Accounts & Finance.

POSITION WANTED—By a strong willing man as shipper in a mercantile house. Good habits, experience and general ability. References given. Address, "Porter," care Commerce, Accounts & Finance.

PEN, INK AND PAPER.—I sell all three and I sell them cheaper than most dealers. If I have not what you want in my stock, I will get it for you. Let me make your account books. I make such books well and do not charge de luxe prices. Address, "Stationer," care Commerce, Accounts & Finance.

UNIVERSITY TRAINING

For Business

ACCOUNTING
BANKING
BROKERAGE

School of Comerce, Accounts and Finance.
Evening Sessions.
New York University, Washington Square, N. Y. City.

FALL TERM OPENS OCT. I.

STATIONERY SALESMAN WANTED—One thoroughly conversant with the file and binder business. Only such as can command a good personal trade need apply. Salary and commission. Excellent chance for the right man. Address, "Binder," care Commerce, Accounts & Finance.

I SELL FILES.—Vertical files, sectional files, pamphlet files, card index files and every conceivable kind of a file that may be needed to hold office memorandums or papers. I sell files cheap, not cheap files cheap, but files cheap. Write "Files," and ask for prices. Address, care Commerce, Accounts & Finance.

Account Audit & Assurance Company

25 PINE STREET NEW YORK.

REMARKS CONCERNING BALANCE SHEET ACCOUNTING.

We have had extensive experience with the accounts of manufacturing establishments in various lines, as well as with mercantile institutions, and in the light thereof we unhesitatingly guarantee for your special business, whatever it may be, every statement that our circulars contain. You can depend upon the Balance Sheet System doing for you all that it has done for others, and that they are fully satisfied is attested by numerous letters from users that we have on file, extracts from some of which have already appeared in these columns.

The Balance Sheet Accounting System will do all that is set forth in our circulars and much more. It will operate at less expense relatively than any other accounting plan now before the public. It is one that no business man would think of parting with after he has once become familiar with it. This is amply attested by the statements of numerous users.

Our plans are scientific in method, correct in detail and labor-saving in effect.

A page inserted in the specification which we would like to prepare for you will contain our assurance to the effect that we will stand by the system for any reasonable length of time, supplying, without cost to you, any additional information that you may find you need, and at any time explaining anything in the specification which may appear to be obscure.

Always Made to Order.

The Balance Sheet Ledger is always made to order. We carry in stock absolutely nothing in this regard. We can, however, produce in a very brief space of time a Balance Sheet Ledger that is exactly adapted to your requirements. We require, as a preliminary, the opportunity of taking your measure and working it out according to requirements. The Balance Sheet Ledger is simply an accompaniment to the specification and is something absolutely useless, save only as the whole accounting plan is adjusted to it. A chart of the accounts, a specification of the system, and the Balance Sheet Ledger, are inseparably associated.

A specification of the Balance Sheet System of Accounts is always made to order, in view of the special conditions of the business to which it is being adapted and in the light of facts which we carefully ascertain in advance. It gives careful directions for everything that is to be done, all so phrased as to be readily understood by any one who is accustomed to bookkeeping details.

The Balance Sheet System is not a mere bookkeeping method embodied in blanks and forms, and ready for delivery on call, but instead is a carefully devised plan of accounting, worked out in each case to meet the requirements of the business stated.

Cheaper than Ordinary Bookkeeping.

The operation of the Balance Sheet System is cheaper than that of ordinary bookkeeping methods. While in a few details a little extra labor is required, the saving in all other directions is more than enough to counterbalance it.

Among the results that you will have before you at all times are a statement of your exact financial condition and a showing of your profits to date. You will be relieved from dependence upon an annual inventory for a statement of your condition.

The conclusion of all that we do is a "going" balance sheet and a "going" profit and loss statement. You have the results of your business constantly before you, without waiting for the end of a fiscal period and without the tedious and expensive preliminary work of inventorying.

You Know What Changes Are to be Made Before They Are Undertaken.

No changes will be made in your establishment until after the specification, etc., has been delivered complete. You will then have the opportunity of seeing on paper exactly how the system will work, and that too before any part of your present system is changed. When it comes to actual installation, the work proceeds somewhat upon the plan that is pursued by a railway company in rebuilding a bridge, and yet running trains over it every day. One part at a time is adjusted. There is nothing revolutionary in our methods, nor the way in which they are installed.

Our Delivery.

Our delivery consists (a) of the Balance Sheet Ledger, which at once is your private ledger and the going statement of the business; (b) a scientific chart of your accounts, upon which the Balance Sheet Ledger is based and which also is the foundation for the management of the accounting work; and (c) a specification, showing just what is to be done, who is to do it, and how it is to be done. This specification is the embodiment of all the instructions that you require and is illustrated by diagrams of accounts, rulings of books, forms, blanks, etc. It is a complete exposition of the best interpretations of office details. In some cases there is also (d) a code of rules for the government of your employees.

Inventorying Systemized.

Inventorying, in the ordinary sense of the term, is done away with. Whatever counting of stock is undertaken after the system is in operation will be merely that which is required in order to verify the book accounts. The necessary counting of stock can be done at any time, and in any department, independent of all other departments.

The Balance Sheet System will afford you a "going" balance sheet of your business and a "going" profit and loss statement, without an increase in clerical labor over that which is usually required to keep accounts by the best plan in common use.

Results Assured.

The Balance Sheet System of Accounts will give the following results: A statement of your resources and liabilities at all times; likewise a statement of your profits and losses; and a perpetual inventory, so that you will know at all dates the value of your stock on hand. It does away with the necessity of inventorying and closing the books at the end of a given period, in order to ascertain whether the business has been profitable or not.

Mode of Procedure.

Where we enter into a contract our first step in the performance is to secure, through some one who can answer our questions, an idea of the exact condition of the accounts at the present time, and how the various details of office work are being managed. This we do in order that we may properly contrast therewith what we recommend to be done. Next we chart the accounts, thus exhibiting the skeleton of the system and graphically showing the relation of one part to another. The specification follows, in which all the bookkeeping details are set forth and illustrated. You make no changes in your methods or office routine until after we have submitted the specification and you have had the opportunity of examining it from beginning to end. Finally, you start the installation, commencing where the interruption will be felt the least, and proceeding therefrom, step by step. We ordinarily want from two to four months to complete our undertaking. These figures will vary according to the nature of the business.

Labor of Maintenance.

The work of maintaining the system, after it is inaugurated, is considerably less than that which applies to ordinary double entry. Various labor-saving devices are used, which lessen the expense in various directions, to an extent that more than makes up for the little extra that is required in certain special details. The net result is a considerable saving of labor to the bookkeeper and a reduction of cost to the proprietor.

In addition to an ideal accounting system, we secure to the office every labor-saving device, every improved form, and every up-to-date method of simplifying work.

For further information address

Account, Audit and Assurance Company, 25 Pine street, New York.

PRENTISS CLOCKS.
SIX TIMES A YEAR
is all that is necessary to wind a Prentiss Clock. Why wind a clock every week when we can sell you one which will require winding but once in sixty days and will keep perfect time? Also Frying-pan, Program and Electrically synchronized clocks. Send for Catalogue No. 2d.
THE PRENTISS CLOCK IMPROVEMENT CO.
Dept. 28, 49 Dey St., New York City

R·I·P·A·N·S

There is scarcely any condition of ill-health that is not benefited by the occasional use of a R·I·P·A·N·S Tabule. For sale by Druggists. The Five-Cent packet is enough for an ordinary occasion. The family bottle, 60 cents, contains a supply for a year.

INVENTORY SHEETS

Stock Taking Made Easy

Simplify Your Methods! *Economize Your Work!*

OUR INVENTORY SHEETS

are now in general use by mercantile houses, as the employment of them provides the **simplest and most economical method of Taking Stock.**

As soon as a sheet (one or more) has been filled, it can be returned to the office for pricing and extensions.

The loose sheets are used temporarily in our **PATENT HOLDERS** with **Special Smooth Insides** for Inventory work.

When Inventory is finished, it is bound **Permanently** in our Patent Automatic Binder. As this Binder will hold some 1700 sheets, it can be used to retain the inventories of successive years.

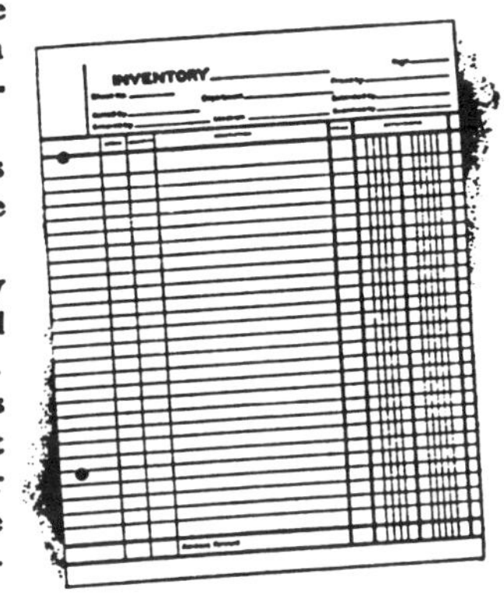

PRICES

100 Sheets, tableted	$ .75
300 Sheets, tableted	1.75
500 Sheets, tableted	2.75
1000 Sheets, tableted	5.25

PRICES

Safety Holders, Size No. 2, each	$1.20
Eclipse Holders, Size No. 2, each	1.35
Automatic Binders, Size No 2, each	2.50

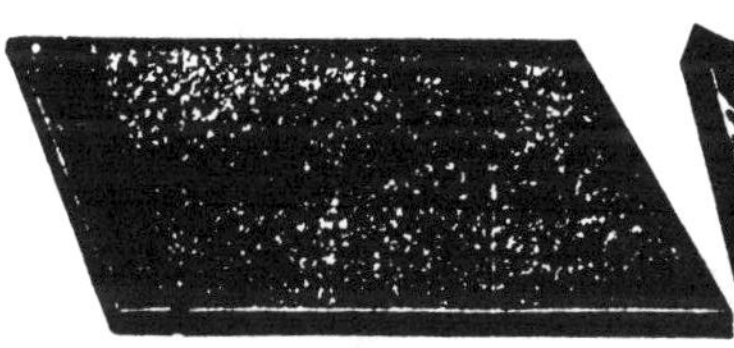

SAFETY HOLDER

HOLDS 1 TO 25 SHEETS

Finely Tempered Steel Spring, Nickel Plated.

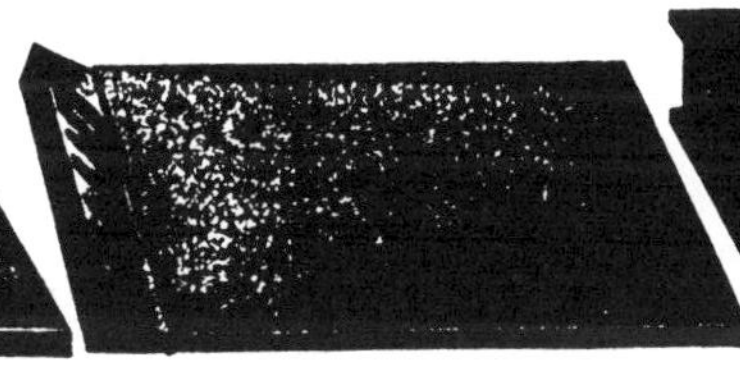

ECLIPSE HOLDER

HOLDS 1 TO 120 SHEETS

Finely Tempered Steel Spring, Nickel Plated.

AUTOMATIC BINDER

MADE TO HOLD 100 to 1700 SHEETS

Correspondence solicited regarding, Order Blanks, Holders and Binders.

STATIONERY MANUFACTURING CO.

318 BROADWAY - - NEW YORK

Account, Audit & Assurance Company

25 PINE STREET NEW YORK

WHAT BALANCE SHEET ACCOUNTING DOES.

I.—Initially, it provides an adequate analysis of the accounts of the business, thereby securing a proper representation of the transactions upon the books.

II.—It classifies the daily details of transactions in a way to show "going" results.

III.—The assets of the business are correctly and completely represented at all dates.

IV.—The liabilities of the business are correctly and completely represented at all dates.

V.—The gross profits on goods sold are always shown and there is presented in contrast therewith the total costs of doing business, thereby revealing net profits.

VI.—Among the assets, in the case of a manufacturing business, there are always shown the cost value of the materials and supplies on hand, the cost to date of the work or orders in progress, and the cost of the finished product on hand.

VII.—All this is presented without the preparation of a physical inventory. Inventorying, like counting cash, is resorted to, only for the purpose of verification and proof.

VIII.—The usual fiscal period is abolished. Net profits to date are shown daily (as in department stores), weekly (as in a mercantile business) or once in each four weeks (as in the case of a manufacturing business), according to the time schedule adopted.

IX.—The work of annually or semi-annually closing the books is abolished. The books are always closed and at the same time are always open. Results to date can be easily read from the Balance Sheet Ledger at any and all times.

X.—The labor of maintaining Balance Sheet Accounting, when the system is once in operation, is no greater than that of ordinary double entry. In many cases it has proven to be considerably less.

XI.—The Proof-By-Balance System of Cost Accounts, a constituent element of the Balance Sheet plan, gives the exact cost of goods produced in a factory. There are no estimates. The results are always definite and exact.

XII.—Factories are run at "even keel." The entire cost of the manufacturing department for a given period is balanced by the aggregate of the cost of the individual lots of goods put through.

XIII.—The Balance Sheet System provides that no payments to workmen (pay-roll) shall be made until the amount of their time has been charged to an order in process. Accordingly there is no time paid for that is not accounted for. Charges to orders in process offset the payroll amount. Non-productive labor is handled by prorating its amount over the orders in process.

XIV.—Balance Sheet Accounting is the only system of accounting ever introduced. It is complete. From established premises it reaches definite and exact conclusions.

XV.—Balance Sheet Accounting is eclectic in its elements, and uses as its component parts in the way of ledgers, blanks and forms, various items that are adapted to the purpose in view without reference to their source or origin.

XVI.—Balance Sheet Accounting begins with a balance sheet, ends with a balance sheet and maintains a balance sheet between times.

XVII.—Balance Sheet Accounting facilitates business management. It shows shortages and neglect wherever the same occur. It definitely fixes responsibility. It necessitates order and method in accounting affairs.

XVIII.—Balance Sheet Accounting improves the bookkeeper's position by enabling him to keep all his work up-to-date and by defining a day's duties.

XIX.—In Balance Sheet Accounting there is no back work. Instead, everything is finished as it proceeds.

XX.—The Balance Sheet Ledger upon the business manager's desk in the morning, among other interesting and valuable particulars, gives him the following:

Amount of cash receipts of the preceding day.
Amount of cash disbursements.
Balance on hand and where located.

Amounts charged to customers.
Amounts credited to customers.
Balance owing by customers.

Amounts credited to Purchase Creditors.
Amounts charged to Purchase Creditors.
Balance owing to Purchase Creditors.

Amount of goods (merchandise) taken in.
Amount of goods sent out.
Balance on hand.

Amount of goods sold.
Cost of goods sold.
Gross profit.

Expenses of doing business (viz. clerk hire, rent, advertising, insurance, etc.)

XXI.—Similar facts as to receipts, disbursements and balances are afforded of Notes Receivable and Notes Payable. Sundry Debtors, Sundry Creditors, etc.

XXII.—Balance Sheet Accounting is not "ready made." Instead, it is always "custom made," and made to fit the business after the most careful measurements have been taken. The preceding epitome of Balance Sheet Ledger showings is to be accepted as typical and not as specific.

XXIII.—The Balance Sheet System adapted to your business will give you the exact showings you require, presented in the way you want them and at the time they will be most serviceable to you in planning and managing.

XXIV.—Balance Sheet Accounting is scientific. All its provisions are based upon an accurate and adequate "chart" of the accounts.

XXV.—Balance Sheet Accounting is installed upon the specification plan. A carefully prepared specification, based upon the chart of accounts, is prepared, which stands to the accounting system very much as an architect's specification stands to a building about to be erected.

XXVI.—Each specification is illustrated by drawings of the rulings, blanks and forms required, and by diagrams showing the relationship of the different parts one to the other.

For further particulars, address

Account, Audit and Assurance Company, 25 Pine street, New York.

COMMERCE ACCOUNTS & FINANCE

THE NEW YORK PUBLIC LIBRARY

Volume 4 New York December 1902 Number 12

Published Monthly by the Commerce Accounts & Finance Company Twenty-five Pine Street New York

Account, Audit & Assurance Company

25 PINE STREET NEW YORK

WHAT BALANCE SHEET ACCOUNTING DOES.

I.—Initially, it provides an adequate analysis of the accounts of the business, thereby securing a proper representation of the transactions upon the books.

II.—It classifies the daily details of transactions in a way to show "going" results.

III.—The assets of the business are correctly and completely represented at all dates.

IV.—The liabilities of the business are correctly and completely represented at all dates.

V.—The gross profits on goods sold are always shown and there is presented in contrast therewith the total costs of doing business, thereby revealing net profits.

VI.—Among the assets, in the case of a manufacturing business, there are always shown the cost value of the materials and supplies on hand, the cost to date of the work or orders in progress, and the cost of the finished product on hand.

VII.—All this is presented without the preparation of a physical inventory. Inventorying, like counting cash, is resorted to, only for the purpose of verification and proof.

VIII.—The usual fiscal period is abolished. Net profits to date are shown daily (as in department stores, weekly (as in a mercantile business) or once in each four weeks (as in the case of a manufacturing business), according to the time schedule adopted.

IX.—The work of annually or semi-annually closing the books is abolished. The books are always closed and at the same time are always open. Results to date can be easily read from the Balance Sheet Ledger at any and all times.

X.—The labor of maintaining Balance Sheet Accounting, when the system is once in operation, is no greater than that of ordinary double entry. In many cases it has proven to be considerably less.

XI.—The Proof-By-Balance System of Cost Accounts, a constituent element of the Balance Sheet plan, gives the exact cost of goods produced in a factory. There are no estimates. The results are always definite and exact.

XII.—Factories are run at "even keel." The entire cost of the manufacturing department for a given period is balanced by the aggregate of the cost of the individual lots of goods put through.

XIII.—The Balance Sheet System provides that no payments to workmen (pay-roll) shall be made until the amount of their time has been charged to an order in process. Accordingly there is no time paid for that is not accounted for. Charges to orders in process offset the payroll amount. Non-productive labor is handled by prorating its amount over the orders in process.

XIV.—Balance Sheet Accounting is the only system of accounting ever introduced. It is complete. From established premises it reaches definite and exact conclusions.

XV.—Balance Sheet Accounting is eclectic in its elements, and uses as its component parts in the way of ledgers, blanks and forms, various items that are adapted to the purpose in view without reference to their source or origin.

XVI.—Balance Sheet Accounting begins with a balance sheet, ends with a balance sheet and maintains a balance sheet between times.

XVII.—Balance Sheet Accounting facilitates business management. It shows shortages and neglect whenever the same occur. It definitely fixes responsibility. It necessitates order and method in accounting affairs.

XVIII.—Balance Sheet Accounting improves the bookkeeper's position by enabling him to keep all his work up-to-date and by defining a day's duties.

XIX.—In Balance Sheet Accounting there is no back work. Instead, everything is finished as it proceeds.

XX.—The Balance Sheet Ledger upon the business manager's desk in the morning, among other interesting and valuable particulars, gives him the following:

Amount of cash receipts of the preceding day.
Amount of cash disbursements.
Balance on hand and where located.

Amounts charged to customers.
Amounts credited to customers.
Balance owing by customers.

Amounts credited to Purchase Creditors.
Amounts charged to Purchase Creditors.
Balance owing to Purchase Creditors.

Amount of goods (merchandise) taken in.
Amount of goods sent out.
Balance on hand.

Amount of goods sold.
Cost of goods sold.
Gross profit.

Expenses of doing business (viz., clerk hire, rent, advertising, insurance, etc.)

XXI.—Similar facts as to receipts, disbursements and balances are afforded of Notes Receivable and Notes Payable, Sundry Debtors, Sundry Creditors, etc.

XXII.—Balance Sheet Accounting is not "ready made." Instead, it is always "custom made," and made to fit the business after the most careful measurements have been taken. The preceding epitome of Balance Sheet Ledger showings is to be accepted as typical and not as specific.

XXIII.—The Balance Sheet System adapted to your business will give you the exact showings you require, presented in the way you want them and at the time they will be most serviceable to you in planning and managing.

XXIV.—Balance Sheet Accounting is scientific. All its provisions are based upon an accurate and adequate "chart" of the accounts.

XXV.—Balance Sheet Accounting is installed upon the specification plan. A carefully prepared specification, based upon the chart of accounts, is prepared, which stands to the accounting system very much as an architect's specification stands to a building about to be erected.

XXVI.—Each specification is illustrated by drawings of the rulings, blanks and forms required, and by diagrams showing the relationship of the different parts one to the other.

For further particulars, address

Account, Audit and Assurance Company, 25 Pine street, New York.

KNICKERBOCKER TRUST CO.

234 FIFTH AVENUE, CORNER 27TH STREET
BRANCH OFFICES:
66 BROADWAY, AND 125TH STREET AND LENOX AVE.,
NEW YORK CITY.

CAPITAL AND UNDIVIDED PROFITS, $2,508,399.11.

LEGAL DEPOSITORY FOR STATE, CITY, AND COURT FUNDS.

Interest allowed on Time Deposits. Deposits also received subject to Demand Checks, which pass through the Clearing House as do those upon any city bank.

Authorized to act as Executor or Administrator of Estates, and as Guardian, Receiver, Registrar, Transfer and Financial Agent for States, Cities, Towns, Railroads, and other corporations, and to accept any other Trusts in conformity with the laws of any State or of the United States.

LETTERS OF CREDIT FURNISHED.
BUSINESS AND PERSONAL ACCOUNTS SOLICITED.

CHAS. T. BARNEY, - - - - - - - - President.
JOSEPH T. BROWN, - - - - - - 2d Vice-President.
JULIAN M. GERARD, - - - Asst. Sec. and Asst. Treas.
FRED'K K. ELDRIDGE, - - - - 1st Vice-President.
FRED'K GORE KING, - - - Secretary and Treasurer.
WM. B. RANDALL, - - - - - - Trust Officer.

BOARD OF DIRECTORS:

JOSEPH S. AUERBACH,
HARRY B. HOLLINS,
JACOB HAYS,
CHARLES T. BARNEY,
A. FOSTER HIGGINS,
ANDREW H. SANDS,
JAMES H. BRESLIN,
I. TOWNSEND BURDEN,
HON. E. V. LOEW,
HENRY F. DIMOCK,
CHARLES F. WATSON,
FREDERICK G. BOURNE,
C. LAWRENCE PERKINS,
CHARLES R. FLINT,
AMZI L. BARBER,
CHARLES T. COOK,
JOHN MAGEE,
HENRY A. MORGAN,
HENKY C. BERLIN,
CHARLES W. GOULD,
FRED'K L. ELDRIDGE,
HENRY W. DE FOREST,
ALFRED B. MACLAY
HARRY W. McVICKAR.

HALL'S Fireproof and Burglar Proof SAFES

Sold since 1840. *Never fail to protect contents.*

KNOWN EVERYWHERE

393 BROADWAY, N.Y.

Telephones: 3133-3136-307 Franklin.

ANNOUNCEMENT EXTRAORDINARY!

A LIBRARY OF PRACTICAL BOOKS FOR THE STUDENT, THE ACCOUNTANT AND THE BUSINESS MAN

What Shall Be Its Name?

A COMPETITION WITH THE BOOKS FOR PRIZES

COMMERCE, ACCOUNTS & FINANCE has pleasure in announcing to its readers and to the business public in general that at great expense it has bought the manuscripts, titles and copyrights of the five volumes illustrated in the accompanying cut. It proposes to use them in furthering the interests of this periodical.

Books Composing the (?) Library

The books will be published one at a time, but our arrangements are so advanced that we feel warranted in promising the complete set in a reasonable length of time.

Each book is to be set from new type, illustrated by original engravings, printed on paper specially made for the purpose, and handsomely bound in cloth with gilt back and side titles. Each book will be upwards of 500 pages in extent, and nothing in the bookmaker's art will be spared to get them up in excellent shape, at once attractive to the eye and convenient for use.

PUBLICATION COMMITTEE,

The set of books will be produced under the direction of the following Publication Committee:

W. H. Grace, chairman, President Commerce, Accounts & Finance Company.

Friend Pitts, Jr., secretary, Treasurer Commerce, Accounts & Finance Company.

A. O. Kittredge, author, President Account, Audit & Assurance Company.

H. M. C. Vedder, Specialist in Accounting and Auditing.

George Young, Textile Accounting and Industrial Operations.

H. W. Courter, General Merchandise and Installment Accounts.

J. A. Cave, Manufacturing Accounts.

J. V. Palmer, Printers' and Publishers' Accounts.

C. H. Sumwalt, of the Correspondence School of Banking.

Advisory Councils.

This committee will be supplemented by sub-committees or advisory councils on special topics, the chairman of each of which is a specialist in his own particular branch. These sub-committees will co-operate with the general committee by way of suggestions as to the manner of treating specific topics, the choice of illustration and matters of similar character.

WANTED—A NAME.

The set of books here announced will constitute a library desirable at once for the desk of the business man, the study table of the student and the shelf in reach of the bookkeeper and the clerk while engaged in their daily work. It will also be invaluable to the professional accountant, but **what shall it be called? By what name as a library shall it be introduced to the public?**

We want the most appropriate name as well as the most striking name for this library. It should be something that will give force and character to the several million copies of the announcement which we shall circulate. Who can suggest the right name for the purpose?

There is always wisdom in a multitude of councilors. Therefore, we constitute every one who reads this paragraph a member of our special council on names. Out of the multitude of suggestions thus to be offered we have reason to expect the right idea will come to the top. Just to make it interesting, we propose a friendly contest with prizes.

COMPETITION.

To the person suggesting the name that we finally adopt for this library, we will present a com-

plete set of the books (five volumes). The set so given shall be one of the first off the press and each volume will be properly inscribed over the autograph of the author. To each of ten others who suggest good names, the same being deemed the next best of those we receive, even though we are unable to make use of what they offer, we will give a single volume of the library similarly inscribed over the autograph of the author. Each successful contestant is to have the right of selection.

A subscription for one year to COMMERCE,

The First Volume of the (?) Library to be Issued

ACCOUNTS & FINANCE goes with each volume sent out as a prize.

This competition will close at 6 o'clock P. M., May 1, 1903.

All entries are to be addressed to LIBRARY NAME COMPETITION, care of COMMERCE, ACCOUNTS & FINANCE, 25 Pine street, New York.

Each competitor is privileged to make as many suggestions of names as he pleases, but only one prize will be awarded to any contestant.

The decision in this competition will be announced in COMMERCE, ACCOUNTS & FINANCE at as early a date as circumstances permit.

EXCLUSIVELY FOR SUBSCRIBERS TO COMMERCE, ACCOUNTS & FINANCE.

The books here announced will not be sold through the trade. The sale will be limited to the cash subscribers to COMMERCE, ACCOUNTS & FINANCE, or to put it otherwise, each volume of the set carries with it a yearly subscription to this periodical.

If you are already a subscriber to COMMERCE, ACCOUNTS & FINANCE, your subscription will be extended for one year for each volume that you purchase.

NO DISCOUNTS TO ANY ONE.

Books will not be sent out on any other terms than those quoted below. The only way to get an advantage in price is to order in advance of publication day.

PRICES.

Either volume, including therewith one yearly subscription to COMMERCE, ACCOUNTS & FINANCE, cash with order, $5.

The set of five volumes, including therewith five yearly subscriptions to COMMERCE, ACCOUNTS & FINANCE, or a single subscription for five years, cash with order, $25.

INSTALLMENT PAYMENTS.

Subscribers, with approved references, may order the set of five volumes at $30, payable $5 with order and the remainder in five monthly installments of $5 each, the title to the books remaining with the publishers until full payment has been made.

Nothing less than a whole set will be furnished on the installment plan.

ADVANCE ORDERS.

Orders in advance of publication will be accepted at the following specially reduced rates:

The set of five volumes, including five yearly subscriptions to COMMERCE, ACCOUNTS & FINANCE, or one subscription for five years, cash with order, $20. Single volumes, including the subscription as above, $4 each.

ORDER OF PUBLICATION.

The arrangement of the volumes in the illustration indicates the order in which they will be produced. "TOOLS OF BUSINESS" will be the first of the set to go to press, following which will be "ELEMENTS OF BOOKKEEPING," "BALANCE SHEET ACCOUNTING," "AUDITING," and "BUSINESS ORGANIZATION AND ADMINISTRATION," in the order named.

The date of publication cannot be named at this time, but the books will be pushed through as rapidly as circumstances make possible. The manuscript for the entire set is in a very forward condition at the present time.

NO ADVERTISING.

There will not be a line of advertising in any of the volumes from cover to cover. Manufacturers' cuts will not be used, but instead new engravings are being made throughout. On the other hand, provision is made, as indicated in the foregoing, for a copy of this periodical to go with each volume. Its advertising pages are open to the business world at reasonable rates, and afford an unequalled opportunity of reaching the very public the advertiser is after.

"TOOLS OF BUSINESS."

The first volume to be brought out as announced above will be "TOOLS OF BUSINESS." This name is to be construed liberally and taken to mean everything from a pen holder to a typewriter, from a chair to a desk and from a method of screening the office window to systems of heating and ventilation.

In this work the author takes up his subject analytically and presents one after another of the several subjects discussed in a most attractive fashion. The scheme of the book is a cyclopedia of office equipment, or a dictionary of those things which

every business man needs to know about in equipping and arranging his business office.

Typewriters, for example, are described analytically and critically. They are divided into classes according to the principles underlying their operation and after these principles have been fully explained, illustrations of different interpretations of those principles are brought forward. The differences between the leading typewriters is clearly defined and the advantages, as well as the disadvantages of some of the cheaper machines are fully set forth.

The office floor is carefully treated, the discussion extending from rugs and mats and carpets to the treatment of the wood of which the floor is composed.

Desks are discussed with respect to the conveniences which they offer, their size, the space occupied and the work to be done. Letter files and cabinets are correspondingly handled. In a similar manner blank books, like ledgers and journals, are discussed with respect to the ends to be accomplished and the materials of which they are composed. Card indexes, loose leaf ledgers, binders and other office appliances are similarly treated.

In future numbers of COMMERCE, ACCOUNTS & FINANCE we shall take pleasure in laying before our readers the personnel of the Sub-Committees or Councils upon whom the Publication Committee depends for advice with respect to details of arrangement, etc. We shall also present in the course of early numbers a complete outline of the contents of this volume.

Address all communications to

COMMERCE, ACCOUNTS & FINANCE COMPANY, 25 PINE STREET, NEW YORK.

BUSINESS NEEDS.

Advertisements under this head one cent a word each insertion.

STATIONERY SALESMAN WANTED—One thoroughly conversant with the file and binder business. Only such as can command a good personal trade need apply. Salary and commission. Excellent chance for the right man. Address, "Binder," care Commerce, Accounts & Finance.

SUPERINTENDENT.—Man of thirty-six years desires a position of responsibility in some large house. Has been superintendent of an office force of seventeen people for the last twelve years. References given. Address, "A. G. B." care Commerce, Accounts & Finance.

POSITION WANTED—by a strong, willing man as shipper in a mercantile house. Good habits, experience and general ability. References given. Address, "Porter," care Commerce, Accounts & Finance.

SALESMAN WANTED.—Salesman of ability is wanted by a novelty house to sell a desk lamp. The lamp itself is a good one and catches the busy man's eye. Liberal commission. Address "Lamp," care Commerce, Accounts & Finance.

BOOKKEEPER WANTED.—A competent bookkeeper is wanted by a mercantile house. Fair salary and a good chance for advancement. Address, "B. J.," care Commerce, Accounts & Finance.

Safe Investments

ON

Bond and Mortgage

may be made on desirable property in the

POCONO AND BLUE RIDGE MOUNTAINS OF PENNSYLVANIA

the great natural resort section on the

Lackawanna Railroad

Hotel proprietors are seeking to enlarge their quarters in time for next season's business. They need money for the work. The Lackawanna Railroad has compiled a list of desirable opportunities for placing money in these enterprises, and full particulars may be obtained by addressing

C. W. TEN BROECK, Industrial Agent LACKAWANNA RAILROAD

26 Exchange Place, New York City

TITLE GUARANTEE AND TRUST COMPANY

Does each year an increasing proportion of the whole business of examining titles and making mortgage loans in New York City. Last year it loaned

Over Thirty-Five Million Dollars

on real estate in New York City. When you buy real estate, or borrow on it, come to this company. Fees moderate and uniform.

Capital and Surplus, $6,000,000

146 Broadway, MANHATTAN. 175 Remsen St., BROOKLYN.

FREE--A PAIR OF SLEEVE PROTECTORS.

Do you want to know about our Loose Leaf Ledgers and office devices? They will save you time, trouble and money. To all bookkeepers in the States of New York, New Jersey and Massachusetts who write us for information about our systems we will send a pair of sleeve protectors. In writing mention size of cuff.

THE C. E. SHEPPARD CO.,
87 Maiden Lane, NEW YORK CITY.

Columnar Bookkeeping*

By CHARLES DYER CHASE.

A FEW weeks ago, having had occasion to devise four account books on the columnar system, and reserving as usual my original draft, with several loose sheets of the printed work for future reference, it occurred to me that perhaps they might be interesting to the members of our association.

The ordinary city bookkeeper, accustomed to the common text book methods of keeping accounts, and seeing those about him using nearly the same systems, naturally believes that all the bookkeeping of the country is kept in practically the same manner. Few realize that there is more bookkeeping done, or attempted to be done, in a slipshod, unmethodical manner, by no recognized system, than there is in a systematic way.

I believe that more than half of the persons keeping accounts in the United States use but a single book for that purpose. Usually this is but a mere memorandum book, in which transactions are entered chronologically only, never being gathered in classified form till put upon a bill for presentation to a customer. As most accounts so kept are usually paid without the formality of a bill, they are then merely concelled by drawing one or more Xs across their face on the book.

Retail Bookkeeping.

Sometimes, when some petty shopkeeper suddenly realizes, as he is making out a bill in a hurry, how convenient it would be to have all the charges against each customer gathered in one place under the name of that customer, or has seen in other hands a ledger in which this is carried out, he waxes ambitious and attempts the same thing. He takes a book, and writing the name of a customer at the top of each page, either posts t › it from his daily memorandum, or makes his entries directly on the ledger without the interposition of any other book.

This is probably his first improvement in the science of accounts, and it is a veritable advance, containing in it the germ of all classification of accounts. I do not believe that a half of the bookkeepers of the United States go beyond this. The ordinary grocer, butcher, baker, or other small shopkeeper, knows nothing better; and as the volume of his business transactions is small, he is able to learn of his profits and losses, his assets and liabilities, by other means than the ones usual to the systematic user of the double-entry methods.

Few bookkeepers realize, and the petty shopkeeper probably never learns, that the double entry system of accounting can be carried out in a single book—the ledger. The cash book, the sales book, the journal, and others, are simply conveniences, not essentials. They are means of classifying entries before placing them upon the ledger, the reservoir into which all the records of the business finally flow. The entries can be made in the same classified form upon the pages of the ledger direct, and with the same final result.

I need not explain to you the disadvantages of this method of accounting, the greatest of which is the difficulty of assuring correctness of double entries, or of discovering and correcting wrong entries when made. It has its advantages as well; and that it can be used by large concerns of a certain class is shown by the adoption of West's system by many of them.

The little shopkeeper before alluded to, if he has attended strictly to business, has perhaps become so prosperous that his little ledger does not now answer the many questions regarding his position that are continually coming up in his mind. Heretofore he has kept accounts with individuals only. He does not know how much cash he has received or paid out, or what has been the amount of his sales. By counting the cash in his pocket he learns what he has on hand, and this with an inventory of his merchandise and a totalling up of the amounts due him by his customers tells him what he is worth.

Cash Account and Sales Account.

Probably the second improvement he makes in his method of accounting is to open a cash account and a sales account in his ledger, to which he will post cash and sales transactions from his book of original entry, and which I will call a journal—"a record of an account of daily transactions."

As our petty shopkeeper, owing to a limited capital, is obliged to hold chiefly to cash transactions in his business, entries of cash will be the most frequent on his journal and occupy the most of his time in posting to the ledger. After posting a great many of such items, and seeing page after page overflowing with them, it may perhaps occur to him that by adding a couple of extra columns to his journal, into which to pass all cash transactions, adding them up and carrying totals forward from page to page, he would save all necessity for posting them to the ledger at all, except in monthly totals; in fact, the cash ledger would be transferred bodily from the ledger to the journal, the two columns still remaining, however, in their essence, a part of the ledger The details of the account would be looked for on the journal, and the totals of his monthly and yearly transactions in cash on the ledger.

As almost the whole of his remaining entries on the journal will be purchases or sales, he has only to add a couple more columns for these, and there will

Teddy's Touchdown

"That's right, Uncle, cheer! you would have growled long enough if he had failed."—Minneapolis Tribune.

*Address delivered before the Boston Bookkeepers' Association.

be few remaining items for what we will now call the two sundries columns of his journal.

I will not take up your time by any explanation of the different methods of keeping the purchase or sales accounts, a subject in itself sufficient for an evening's discussion, but confine myself to the varying use of the columns for them. If the purchases of merchandise are comparatively few in number there is no necessity of having a debit column for them, as the additions on each journal page and the carrying forward of footings from one page to another through the month might prove to be more than would the posting of each purchase in detail to the account in the ledger. One of the main objects of the extra column is to save time and labor, not to increase them. Of course some bookkeeper may think that the having of a small and compact merchandise purchase account in the ledger with but twelve monthly entries to it in the year, instead of a the journal and he has it.

Perhaps the first thing he desires to know is how much is owing him by his customers. He may want to know this frequently, and perhaps at almost a moment's notice. It is a long and tedious job to go over his ledger and balance each account every time he wants the information. Why not stick in a couple more columns, which will then always show in their balances the net amount due him from his customers almost instantly at any time. The thing is done; and now, when he needs a little additional money in his business and hustles to his banker to get a small note discounted, he is able to answer immediately the question as to how much he has out on book account.

Accounts Payable.

Perhaps he also wishes to know what he is himself owing others for goods purchased of them. If he buys frequently and in small amounts, making

CONFECTIONERY SALES		CHOCOLATE SALES				SUNDRIES		DEALERS		SUNDRY MDSE. PURCH.	SUNDRY EXPENSES	OWNER'S PER. ACCT.
DR.	CR.	DR.	CR.	DR.	CR.	DR.	CR.	DR.	CR.	DR.	DR.	DR.

Combined Cash, Sales and Journal (Right Hand Page)

much larger one with perhaps a hundred or more entries, is in itself worth the extra labor involved in the addition and carrying forward of the column accounts. Here is where the individual idiosyncrasy of the bookkeeper comes in.

Addition of Columns.

After our now busy bookkeeper has filled up page after page of his ledger with itemized charges to expense account, perhaps he comes to think that what is good for his cash and merchandise accounts ought to be equally good for his expense account, and he sticks in one column—a debit one only—for this; to his great relief when he hurriedly at the end of the day falls to posting up his books, neglected in the rush of his daily work.

Our intelligent bookkeeper has by this time dis- many entries in the course of the month, he may devote a credit column to them as well; but if his purchases are few in number, and of relatively larger amounts, it might prove to be more work to foot up the columns and carry the totals forward than it would to post each individual amount. Of this each bookkeeper must be his own judge. If his purchases are frequent and of one house, or if a branch store and receiving all goods from the parent house, then he may devote a credit column to that one house. If the rebates and returns of merchandise from himself to his dealer, or from his customers to himself, are comparatively few in number, it would not pay to have a column devoted to them, so far as the saving in time and labor is concerned, although the pages of his journal and ledger might be more

DATE	ACCOUNTS	ACCOUNTS	ITEMS	L. PAGE		CASH		DISCOUNT	CUSTOMERS	
	DR.	CR.		DR.	CR.	DR.	CR.	DR.	DR.	CR.
			Brought forward							
			Carried forward							

Combined Cash, Sales and Journal (Left Hand Page)

covered that this column business is capable of indefinite expansion, and with almost equally good results. If there is any particular information he desires, as to any class of accounts, he has only to stick in one or two more columns for catch basins and the thing is done. In these receptacles the items are held until the end of the month, when in one amount they are emptied into the reservoir of the ledger account. If at any time during the month the owner wishes to know what the amount is up to that particular day, he has only to add up that one or two columns on the last page of entries in symmetrical and complete by their addition.

If he is obliged to take many notes from his customers in payment for goods sold them he may if he wishes devote a couple of columns to the bills receivable account, the balance of which will then always show him at any moment the amount outstanding on account of notes due him.

The foregoing examples are simply typical ones. Other accounts can be kept in the same manner, and the extent to which this is carried by railroad, insurance and other large corporations would astonish many of those present—perhaps.

Merchandise account may be subdivided into several classes of merchandise, each with its special column or columns; or each such class may be again subdivided into purchases and sales of that class.

As I have already shown, it is not always necessary or desirable to have two columns—a debit and credit one—for each account, although some bookkeepers seem to think so. If the entries are mostly or entirely to one side of the account devote a column to that alone. If there happens to be a few entries to the other side they can be passed through the sundries column and posted in detail; or, as I often do, wait until the end of the month and then make an abstract of the contents of the sundries column, posting only the totals of each class of items found in it. This saves some work and also some room in the ledger, and makes the ledger accounts more compact, there being but twelve postings to each side of the account. The same thing may be done with the contents of the expense column by making an abstract, posting the totals only of each division of expense items.

From what I have already said I think you will see that a pair of columns in the journal is simply a page transferred from the ledger into this book, so that the posting of items, instead of involving a rewriting of the date, item, amount and page references, is simply a transferring of the amount alone into a column on the same folio of the same book, the date and all explanations of the transactions having already been written in making the original entry. This takes much less time, and, being so simple and easy a matter, the most careless and negligent bookkeeper is likely to have every account represented by columns in the journal posted up to date, and the information therein therefore ready for instant use.

Proving.

One of the greatest advantages derived from the use of the columnar journal is that of being able to prove the correctness of the work on each folio of the journal before passing to a new one. The columns are added up, and on a loose sheet of paper the total of the debit columns compared with the total of the credits; if they agree the column totals are carried to the top of the next folio, and not before. This proves the work so far as equal debits and credits and the additions are concerned, but does not detect the posting of items into the wrong debit or credit column. The making of a monthly abstract of some of the columns, such as sundries, expenses, etc., will detect wrong posting in these, probably the ones where the fault is the most likely to exist.

When a pair of columns is used for a class of accounts, such as accounts receivable (customers) or for accounts payable (dealers), such a section of the monthly work of the bookkeeper may be proved to the exclusion of the rest. This is a great advantage, as it may be that the information is wanted immediately regarding this particular class of accounts, and there is no delay from the unnecessary posting of all the work that is waiting, or from time lost in selecting the items wanted from the many others mixed with them that can wait a more convenient moment. If all entries are made on the one journal the simple addition and carrying forward of two columns on each folio gives the information desired at once.

Another advantage is the subdivision of the bookkeeper's trial balance work into distinct sections; in the case mentioned, four. Here the bookkeeper, instead of having all his proof work come at one time in the month, and that time the one when he ought to be and usually is occupied in making out and sending statements of account to his customers, is enabled to do one-fourth of it each week in the month, with breathing intervals between.

Limitations.

By the time that the bookkeeper has employed all the columns already mentioned, he has no doubt found that he must restrain his desire for them and put up with much less than he would like to have, for the size of the book he is using is limited. In my own experience I do not remember of ever having as many columns as I would have liked, and I believe that experience to be the common one.

Where the business is small, the transactions comparatively few in number, and the accounting work easily within the power of one person, one book for the entry of all transactions is sufficient, and on the score of simplicity is I think to be desired. If in such a case the bookkeeper desires more columns, then he can use an additional book. When, for that reason or because the work is too much for one person, the one book of entry becomes insufficient, probably the first move will be to take from it the two cash columns, giving them a book by themselves, and enabling the bookkeeper to subdivide his cash transactions still further by means of additional columns in his new cash book. These columns will probably be for merchandise accounts, accounts with customers, and a more complete subdivision of the expense accounts.

For lack of time I have not referred to many things, the omission of which will at once be noticed by those familiar with columnar bookkeeping.

It would be the easiest thing in the world for me to talk for hours on the subject of columnar bookkeeping, for like the card-index principle it is capable of almost illimitable extension and use, and the subject is so intertwined with that of general bookkeeping methods that it is difficult to draw a line between them, or to know where to stop.

Practical Applications.

Having thus roughly outlined what I may call the evolution of columnar bookkeeping, and which is already well-known to some of you, I will now bring forward some examples of the work as I have used it lately. I have here a draft, on one sheet, of the ruling and lettering for four account books, the

POSTAGE	TELEGRAMS	EXPRESS	OFFICE SUPPLIES	SALARIES	SUNDRY EXPENSES		SUNDRIES		"A" SALES	"B" SALES	"C" SALES	
DR.	DR.	DR.	DR.	DR.	DR.	DR.	DR.	CR.	CR.	CR.	CR.	CR.

Cash Book (Right Hand Page)

The Lamb and the Wolf; or Latter-Day Financiering.—Philadelphia North American.

ruling of all being of the colors and shades desired in the finished books. I have also brought sample sheets of the books as made, together with one filled in as it might be in actual work by what I may call a shorthand or abbreviated method of making entries.

As an example of the combined cash, sales and journal, which I will call simply a journal, I will take the first example, designed for a confectionery manufacturer, and which was started and kept by a young woman who had never before kept regular account books, and who hardly knew what double entry was. The only serious difficulty she had was caused by making entries or corrections on the face of the customers' ledger without passing them through the columns of the journal, thereby causing the balance of customers' account in the general ledger to differ from the true balance in the customers' ledger. After she was put to a great deal of trouble and tribulation in tracing out and adjusting these transactions she had no further difficulty. With a realizing sense of the many hours that it had taken to trace out and correct an error made in a moment, she was careful thereafter to put nothing on the ledger save through the journal. One lesson was sufficient.

Commencing with the left-hand edge of the book, the first column is for the day of the month. The next column—a very wide one—is for the written entry, with explanation; and I subdivide this column with two faint vertical lines for convenience in writing in the debits and credits of the entries. The next column is for check marks or page numbers, subdivided into two, for debit and credit checks. Next come a pair of cash columns, then a single discount debit column, and finally a pair of columns for customers' accounts. This arrangement of the left-hand page is one that I very often use in drafting journals for different classes of business.

You will notice that the ruling for the four books before you is very much alike, although two are combined cash, sales and journal, one a cash book, and one a combined sales and journal. It would take too long to explain why this should have happened to be the case, but it is simply the result of an extended experience in designing such account books, during which I made many variations from the common and accepted practice. These changes often puzzled good bookkeepers at first, simply because it was new and they had never before seen anything of the kind. When the special reasons for the change were given, usually to save time or the amount of work, it was often accepted with gratitude, and sometimes perhaps with a feeling that they were just a little better than other bookkeepers in having an uncommon account book.

The right-hand page is the one where the greatest variation in ruling is made, and it is seldom designed twice alike. It is varied with every class of business, and even with the same business—at different periods of its growth. A change in a man's method of conducting his business, or of his method of paying his bills, or contracting liabilities—these and many other things, almost without number, would cause a change in the number, size, or arrangement of columns on the right-hand page of the journal. The example before you was designed for this particular business, and for this particular bookkeeper. If the bookkeeper had been different I should have varied the arrangement to meet what I thought the different capabilities or requirements of another bookkeeper rendered desirable.

Subdivision of Merchandise Account.

Before proceeding further I will here state that I believe merchandise account should always be subdivided into merchandise purchases and merchandise sales. If merchandise is itself subdivded into different classes, then each class should have its purchase and sales account. I believe I have had more arguments with other bookkeepers on this point alone than on all others combined. Most bookkeepers will confess that it is a good idea for a single merchandise account, but fear its apparent complexity when subdivided into several classes.

In this instance merchandise sales was divided but once, into confectionery sales and chocolate sales. The first pair of columns on the right-hand page was given to confectionery sales, for the reason that the entries to that account were more frequent than to any other, and consequently it should be brought the nearest to the item and explanation column of the left-hand page. The next two columns were given to chocolate sales, and the next two were left blank for another class in case the owner should later decide (as it was suspected he would) to divide still further. Until that time it would answer finely to keep account temporarily of some new confection, to be closed at the end of the month into the regular confectionery sales account.

As this manufacturing confectioner was in the habit of purchasing his supplies frequently during the month, and of several dealers, the next two columns were entitled dealers, through which was passed all personal accounts payable. The next two columns were for sundries, a word or a condition which it seems impossible to get rid of on any such account book, however complete it may be. The next column was given to sundry merchandise purchases, the next to sundry expenses, and the last—also a debit column—to the personal account of the proprietor, given the extreme position to the right because it had the fewest entries to it each month.

There was no single sundry expenses account in the general ledger, but at the end of each month an abstract was made of the contents of this column, classifying it into whatever subdivisions of the expense accounts was thought best, and charging each such account with the monthly total of its items found in the column. The same thing was done with the contents of the sundry merchandise purchases column, which was subdivided into several classes. The word sundry was attached to the title of each of these columns so as to imply by the word that the contents of the column was passed to sundry accounts and not to one alone.

A Variation.

I will refer to the second example of journal ruling (not illustrated in this article) only to note a variation introduced to meet a peculiarity of business practice on the part of the proprietor. In the case of the confectioner, whenever a customer paid his account the only debits were to cash and discount. In this new example, however, customers were often allowed the freight or express charges in addition, and to save the time and room taken in writing an explanation of that in the item column this class of expenses was taken from the others and given a special column by itself, into which the insertion of an amount, on the same horizontal line with the credit to a customer, was sufficient to say that that customer was credit for the amount on freight or express account, as well as for the cash and discount, also entered on the same line in their appropriate columns. As many petty customers also paid their accounts in postage, a column was opened for this, which was debited on the same line for the amount of postage credited to the customer.

We will now suppose either that the business has increased to such a point that one bookkeeper is no longer able to do all the work necessary in keeping the accounts, or that even if he is able to do so the increased volume of transactions renders an increased subdivision advisable. To subdivide still more, an increased number of columns is desirable, and for this an additional book will be required. As very much the larger proportion of entries is of cash and sales transactions, the additional book will no doubt be devoted to one of these, we will say the cash.

The ruling and printing for the left-hand page of the cash book will be precisely the same as for the combined cash, sales and journal. It will contain two columns for cash entries, two for customers' entries, and a discount debit column. The ruling for the right-hand page will depend upon the character of the business. In the one in view the expense items were many during the month, much greater in number than the cash sales, and most of them were paid in cash. For these reasons the expense columns are brought nearer the fold of the book than are the sales columns. The left half of the right-hand page is therefore given up to expense debit columns, then comes a pair of sundries columns, and the right half of the page is filled with merchandise sales columns, according to whatever subdivision of merchandise is used.

Planning New Books.

In opening or designing a new book for a business with which you are not already wholly familiar, or which is changing in its character from time to time, it is not always well to map out too closely and sharply just what all the columns at your disposal shall be devoted to. A class of transactions which you now expect to have a large number of entries may, later on, be largely reduced in extent, owing either to some change in the character of the business or to the proprietor's method of conducting it. For this reason, unless I am very much pushed for space for necessary columns, I like to have a pair of extra ones—a debit and credit—for whatever use may turn up afterward.

The first five columns on the page in question are devoted to the postage, telegrams, express, office supplies and salaries accounts, in the order named, which is also about the order in which they have the largest number of entries in the business for which the book was designed. The next column is entitled sundry expenses, and the contents of it is abstracted at the end of each month, precisely as stated of the similar column in the previous journal. The next column is a spare one, for any debit account that turns up unexpectedly afterward; or for temporary use in separating out and holding during the month any class of debit items desired, for the purpose of gaining a knowledge of their total, and which is at the end of the month closed into the account from which it has been temporarily divorced for this purpose. Next comes the two sundries columns, then three merchandise sales columns, and finally another spare column, in this case a credit one.

American Cities of To-Day*

By GEORGE B. WALDRON.

THE heart of modern life is the city. With the scores of splendid cities that adorn our continent it is difficult for us to appreciate the radically different conditions under which our grandfathers lived. When the nineteenth century opened there were only three cities in the country whose population exceeded twenty-five thousand. New York, even then the American metropolis, had 60,515 people; next came Philadelphia, with 41,220, and then Baltimore, with a population of 26,504. Only six cities altogether had above eight thousand people, and only eighteen, including these six, had more than four thousand. Where Chicago now stands was unbroken prairie. The rich western cities of St. Paul, Minneapolis, Omaha,

*Originally published in "Mahin's Magazine" and here used by Permission.

Kansas City, Denver, Portland, Seattle and San Francisco were yet undreamed.

Mammoth New York.

To-day, New York City, with her 3,437,202 people, stands, next to London, the largest city in the world. She exceeds Paris by nearly a million people, and has almost twice as large a population as Berlin. Include the teeming populations of New Jersey and New York State that border on the metropolis, and there are over 4,500,000 people whose interests center on New York Bay.

Even we Americans find it difficult to comprehend the vastness of these numbers. Within the 308 square miles that comprise Greater New York there are crowded more people than are contained in twelve of our great northwestern states and territories. These twelve commonwealths possess 1,178,000 square miles of area, thirty-nine per cent. of the home territory of the nation, and enough to carve out 3,800 cities the size of Greater New York.

There are sections within the metropolis more densely crowded than any other spot on earth. Sanitary District A of the old Eleventh Ward in 1894 had an average of 986 persons to every one of its thirty-two acres. There are single blocks within the city each of which contain more than three thousand people.

Other Big Cities.

Proud as Americans are of their metropolis, they

Comparative size of the World's Great Cities.

do not overlook their other great cities. There is ambitious Chicago, with 1,698,575 people, and staid old Philadelphia with 1,293,697. Then there are the three cities of St. Louis, Boston and Baltimore, each with a population of over half a million. Five cities more are above the three hundred thousand mark, eight others have over two hundred thousand, and nineteen more have above one hundred thousand. The following table shows how our population is distributed according to sizes of cities in which they live:

Population of Cities.	Number of Cities.	Population.	Per Cent*
Over 1,000,000	3	6,429,474	8.4
200,000 to 1,000,000	16	5,366,335	7.0
100,000 to 200,000	19	2,412,538	3.2
50,000 to 100,000	40	2,709,338	3.6
25,000 to 50,000	82	2,800,627	3.7
8,000 to 25,000	384	5,234,581	6.9
4,000 to 8,000	613	3,419,499	4.5
Urban population	1,157	28,372,392	37.3
Semi-urban	...	8,208,480	10.8
Rural population	...	39,413,703	51.9
United States	...	75,994,575	100.0

*Per cent of total population.

According to this classification, the urban population—those living in cities and towns of above four thousand people—number over thirty-seven per cent. of the nation. Add those who live in villages and centers large enough to be considered semi-urban, and they include forty-eight per cent. of the people. This leaves fifty-two per cent., or a little more than half the nation, in the rural districts. The wide-awake salesman does not need to be told of the marked differences between the wants of our city and country citizens.

Wide disparity appears among the states in the proportion of urban population. Fifty-one per cent. of the people of Pennsylvania and Ohio live in cities of above four thousand. Connecticut cities contain sixty-six per cent. of her people, those of New Jersey sixty-eight per cent., and those of New York seventy-one per cent. There are eighty-seven in every hundred of the population of Massachusetts in her cities, while the percentage in Rhode Island reaches ninety-two—highest of any state. At the other extreme stands Indian Territory, with only two and one-half per cent. of her people living in cities. Oklahoma, Mississippi and North Dakota have five per cent., New Mexico and Idaho six per cent., Arkansas and South Dakota seven per cent., while North Carolina has eight per cent. of her people living in cities.

Broadly speaking, three-quarters of all the people in the North Atlantic States live in cities and villages; the like is true of half the people of the North Central and Western States. In the South, conditions are radically different, for there three-quarters of the people live on the farms and only a quarter in the cities and villages.

Our Foreign-Born Citizens.

The cities have peculiar wants growing out of the dense crowding of the people. There are also peculiarities because of race differences. Of the ten million American citizens born outside the United States, more than half are living in cities of over twenty-five thousand people. In other words, the foreign born are relatively nearly three times as numerous in these cities as in the rest of the country. Including these ten million foreign born, there are 26,198,939, or thirty-four and three-tenths per cent. of the entire population, who are of foreign parentage—and their home is peculiarly in the city. New York, Chicago and Detroit have as many as seventy-seven per cent. of their population of foreign parentage—more than double the proportion for the entire country. Milwaukee has nearly eighty-three per cent. But the most marked congestion of foreign blood is found in some of the Massachusetts manufacturing towns. Holyoke and Lawrence have over eighty-three per cent., and Fall River above eighty-six per cent. who are of foreign parentage. Here are the figures for our nineteen leading cities, showing the total population, those of foreign parentage, and the percentage to the entire population of those with foreign blood:

	Total Population.	Foreign Parentage.	Per Cent.
New York	3,437,202	2,643,957	76.9
Chicago	1,698,575	1,315,307	77.4
Philadelphia	1,293,697	710,200	54.9
St. Louis	575,238	350,777	61.0
Boston	560,892	404,999	72.2
Baltimore	508,957	104,223	38.2
Cleveland	381,768	288,491	75.6
Buffalo	352,387	260,185	73.8
San Francisco	342,782	257,784	73.8
Cincinnati	325,902	197,896	60.7
Pittsburg	321,616	205,247	63.8
New Orleans	287,104	108,010	37.6
Detroit	285,704	221,281	77.5
Milwaukee	285,315	235,889	82.7
Washington	278,718	58,371	20.9
Newark	246,070	167,950	68.3
Jersey City	206,433	145,647	70.6
Louisville	204,731	77,253	37.7
Minneapolis	202,718	139,952	69.0

Note the low percentage of foreign blood in some

of the southern cities, such as Baltimore, New Orleans and Louisville, with about thirty-eight per cent., and Washington, D. C., which excels all our large cities in the proportion of native stock, having only twenty-one per cent. born of foreign parents.

The Germans.

Coming to specific nationalities, there are 7,832,681 Germans in the United States, and 809,624 of these, or more than one in every ten, are in New York City. This makes our metropolis the second largest German city in the world. New York has nearly half as many Germans as Berlin, the Kaiser's largest city, and more by over one hundred thousand than Hamburg, the second largest city of the empire. There are 439,758 persons of German birth or immediate descent living in Chicago—a quarter of her entire population. St. Louis has 207,554 Germans, Philadelphia 199,650, and Cincinnati 139,810. The German population of Milwaukee numbers 151,045, which is fifty-three per cent., or more than half her entire citizenship.

The largest Irish city in the world is not on the Emerald Isle, but in America. New York City has 743,198 citizens of Irish descent—twice as many as Ireland's chief city, Dublin. Philadelphia stands

Foreign Born Citizens of New York.

second in this country as an Irish city, with 284,576. Then comes Chicago, with 237,478. The Irish comprise one-third of the population of Boston, numbering 191,638. San Francisco has 78,819 of Irish descent and St. Louis 69,376.

John Bull is also well represented in our cities. There are 177,089 of English parentage in New York City, 91,210 in Philadelphia, 82,272 in Chicago, and 33,569 in Boston. Of the Scotch, 58,032 live in New York, 34,017 in Chicago and 15,059 in Boston.

The largest Scandinavian city in the country is Chicago, with 173,981. New York has 79,084, and the Twin Cities of St. Paul and Minneapolis 94,759. New York city has 220,900 Italians, more than the Italian city of Florence, 255,280 Russians, 57,215 Poles and 178,260 Austro-Hungarians. There are 35,145 French in New York and 17,744 in New Orleans. Chicago ranks first for Bohemians, with 78,821. New York has 31,595 Bohemians and Cleveland 30,489.

Colored Population.

If we draw the color line, the city with the largest population of negro blood is Washington, D. C., with 86,702. Baltimore has 79,258 people of color, and then follows New Orleans with 77,714. Philadelphia numbers 62,613 negroes among her citizens, and New York 60,666. Chicago has but 30,150, fewer than Charleston or Richmond. Jacksonville leads all the cities in the proportion of colored population, having fifty-seven per cent. Next stand Montgomery, Charleston and Savannah, more than half of whose citizens are people of color. At the other end of the list are Milwaukee and Fall River, only a third of one per cent. being colored. Other cities with a negro population of less than one per cent. are Buffalo, Rochester, Syracuse, Worcester, Scranton, Minneapolis and San Francisco.

The Far West, as might be expected, leads in Chinese population. San Francisco is first with 13,954, and Portland second with 7,841. New York

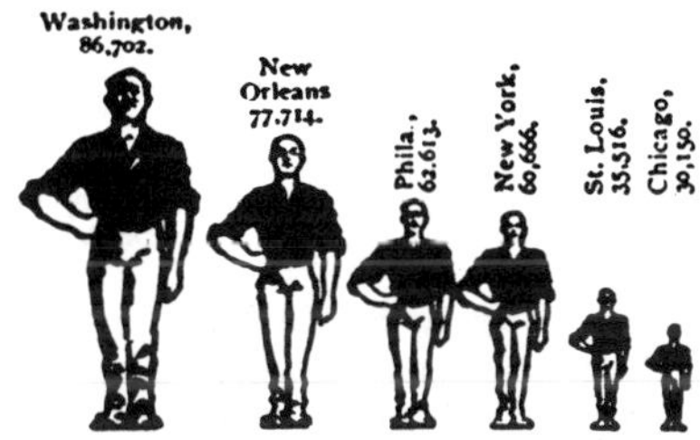

The Colored Population of Our Cities.

City has 6,321 Chinese and there are 2,111 at Los Angeles. Seattle is the largest Japanese city in America, with 2,990. San Francisco contains 1,781 and Portland 1,189.

City People's Money.

How much money have city people to spend? The question can be answered in part only as yet, and for but a few of the large cities. The city of Chicago has 262,621 of her citizens at work in factories. The combined wages are $131,065,337, an average of $499 each. In the factory offices are 35,003 salaried officers and clerks, and their salaries average $982 a year. Among the Chicago wage-earners 210,687 are men, and their average wages are $553. There are 44,961 women earning an average of $294, and 6,973 boys and girls under sixteen years of age whose earnings average $190 a year. Below are the facts as to wages of factory workers in twenty-nine of the cities of over one hundred thousand population for which the figures have been published. Officers and clerks on salary are not included.

	Wage Earners.	Wages.	Average.
New York	462,763	$245,021,881	$529
Chicago	262,621	131,065,337	499
St. Louis	82,672	38,191,076	462
Boston	72,142	39,184,191	543
Cleveland	58,810	27,892,689	474
Buffalo	43,422	19,915,817	459
San Francisco	41,978	22,037,527	549
Cincinnati	63,240	27,189,069	430
Milwaukee	48,328	20,240,656	419
Newark	49,550	23,999,442	484
Jersey City	19,499	9,126,042	468
Louisville	29,926	10,945,720	366
Minneapolis	26,608	12,708,523	478
Providence	42,693	19,998,312	469
Indianapolis	25,511	10,882,914	426
Kansas City	15,381	7,783,652	506
St. Paul	17,593	7,669,805	436
Rochester	33,408	13,832,122	414
Denver	10,926	6,824,003	625
Toledo	15,383	6,845,687	445
Columbus	17,066	7,718,824	452
Worcester	25,593	12,894,784	504
Syracuse	14,917	6,735,177	452
New Haven	20,536	10,016,571	488
Paterson	30,190	12,812,538	424
Fall River	32,780	11,739,129	358
St. Joseph	7,429	3,109,647	419
Ohaha	7,422	3,755,816	519
Los Angeles	8,044	3,992,733	496

The general average of wages, it will be noted, range between $400 and $500 a year. Yet wages in Denver are $625, while in Louisville they drop to $366. Figures so far given out seem to confirm the rule that wages generally are lower in the South and higher in the Far West.

Another tendency is noteworthy. Workers in the large cities get higher returns than do those in the country districts. Take the state of Illinois, for example. The average wages paid in the factories of the large cities of the state are $497, while outside the cities and towns the average is but $423. Even more marked is the difference in Missouri. Wages in the large cities average $466, against $361 in the country factories, less by over $100.

And so we come back to the opening statement that the heart of modern life is the city. There dwell nearly half the people of the nation, there are most of its factories and its wage-earners. There are earned the largest wages with the consequent power to supply a wider and more costly range of wants.

Happy is he who knows how to reach the pocketbook of the workingman of the city.

The Credit Man

By A. G. HAHN.

THERE is probably no person connected with business enterprises who receives as many criticisms and raises as much spleen as the poor credit man.

The nearer he adheres to the line of duty the more he is liable to be censured by both salesman and purchaser, all of which is exceedingly unjust. The credit man is the watchdog of his employer's property, as the treasurer is of its money. He has no more right to let the merchandise of his employers go out on a known uncertainty than the treasurer would have to put up its money on a game of poker or a horse race.

Many concerns have been ruined by credit men who "run chances" with its goods, but the honest man who has the keeping of another's property can do nothing else than to watch with the utmost vigilance and refuse to let it go out of his hands without a reasonable assurance that its equivalent will be forthcoming according to the contract made at the time of sale.

Friendship on the part of the salesman for the purchaser, general appearance on the part of the latter, a reputation for honesty in the community, and a thousand other things that tend to promote confidence, but are not evidences as to responsibility and will not move the credit man if he is true to his trust. Credit is a will-'o-the-wisp; to-day it flourishes as the grass, and to-morrow it withereth and is cast into the oven.

A man may be good to-day and the next year may be absolutely unworthy of credit. Many a man whose credit in '93 would have been questioned, was bankrupt in '94, and that through no fault of his own, nor because of any dishonest intention or practice.

The credit man must be of a judicial turn of mind, and, like justice, must be blindfolded to all sentiment and judge solely from conditions and not theories. It is not just to sell a man on his past record only, or because he paid his bill two or three years ago. A few hundred dollars' margin may be wiped cut by a few months' illness, or by trusting out goods injudiciously, or by loss of trade, increased competition or hard times, a consequent loss of profit, and the eating up of all the capital in the living. Hence the credit man must look to present facts and not dwell in the past.

Sources of Information.

His sources of information are varied. First is the salesman, whose judgment is to be discounted by his interest in making the sale, by his temperament, whether sanguine or pessimistic, by his experience, and by the credit man's experience with him. If he is a new man on the road he naturally believes any representation made. He takes all for granted, and feels that the credit man questions his honor if he questions his judgment, but he learns better as the bills become due, and his faith is proven unfounded.

Another source of information is the buyer's acquaintances. These are often pressed by the traveler as the best of evidence, whereas they are in reality of slight value, excepting as a straw which shows which way the wind blows. The butcher and grocer may say he pays them, but it is very easy to pay dollars at home where hundreds are owing abroad, and it is a matter of pride for the buyer to keep up his local credit.

The landlord is a rather prolific source of information to the inexperienced salesman, and almost invariably says that the merchant is "all right," but what does he know about it?

The banker may say he carries him for as high as $500 or $1,000, but he may have a lien on everything the man has.

A fellow traveler for another house may say, "he is all right; my house sells him," but he very seldom knows how much he is owing his house, so that these sources of information are varied and they are not sufficient to prove that a man who is asking credit is financially responsible.

Another conspicuous and glaring evil is the pernicious system of long-term credit which now prevails. It is an old and truthful adage that "short credits and prompt payments make long friends." As the financial worth of many people is subject to sudden variation—when monetary responsibility goes up and down like mercury in a thermometer—and under the system of long credits we sometimes find that persons to whom we are selling with the fullest confidence have ceased to be worthy of accommodation. Another and chief source of information is through the mercantile agencies. This source is ridiculed and like all human institutions is doubtless defective, and at times grossly unreliable. As good as these agencies may be, they should only be a mere factor in determining credit.

Some lay much stress upon the desirability of a full knowledge of detail and nicety of construction of a statement, the manner in which it is made up, etc., as indicative of good business. This shows its effects in determining credit, but is a mere factor. "The bird with the handsomest plumage does not always sing the sweetest."

From the above will be seen that the credit man has considerable of a burden to bear. In fact, the nervous strain placed upon him because of the responsibility incident to his position is greater than on any other class of employees.

If he asks for a property statement give it cheerfully. Keep nothing back. If you are worthy of credit you have, stand the consequences like a man, and not try to put the credit man in a position where he is liable to be censured by his employers, or perhaps lose his official head.

"Credit never knocks at the door of the indolent, never lingers under the shadow of indecision, never smiles on good intentions that are barren of results."

THE TALE OF THE PHILANTHROPIST WHO BECAME A GOOD THING

BY JOE LINCOLN

And it was the one thousand and eighth night and the King spake unto Scheherezade, saying:

"Oh thou, who tortureth the language of the realm upon the rack of thy typewriter, tell me, I pray thee, one of thy sweetly familiar tales that I may dream of home and mother."

And Scheherezade, swallowing in haste the last gumdrop from her box of Hilah's, obeyed the command of the Father of the Faithful and spake unto him thus:

"Know thou who alone art It, that in the days of the only original package in Caliphs there dwelt in a far city a man who had toiled much by proxy and had by this means laid by much store of coin, so that to him the coming of rent day was devoid of terrors and he feared only the assessor and the reporter for the saffron journal. And the name of the man was Sakhar and he communed with himself, saying:

"'Verily, sad is the lot of man born of woman. To-day he scorcheth in the auto and to-morrow he meandereth in the hearse. To-day he is hot stuff and to-morrow he is cremated. Of a surety I grow old, the creaking of my bones is heard in the land, and the undertaker measureth me with his eye when I go forth upon the ways of the city. Truly, the weight of my dividends is heavy upon me. When I die, shall I leave my store of dust to found an orphan asylum or a home for the indigent rich? Nay, is it not better to hand out the same in chunks while I am yet alive, that the fame of my good deeds shall be spread abroad and I may read my praise in the papers?'

"And he resolved to become a philanthropist.

"And it came to pass that he sent for the gleaners of news, even for those that are as buttons on the switchboard for the turning on of the power of the press. And to them he laid bare his heart, bidding them print his intentions in the papers of the city and to state therein that he proposed to gratuitously dispense the contents of his barrel.

"And the reporters salaamed before him and exalted him to the skies, and, after each had touched him for a five or a ten in order that he might get his hand in, they left him and went on their way rejoicing.

"And in the journals of the next morning was it set forth in letters of the redness of the noonday sun, that the mighty Sakhar was become a philanthropist and that he desired assistance in the matter of ridding himself of his simoleons. And behold the assistance came in full measure.

"For it came to pass that the Bungtown Swedenborgian Chapel desired a new chapel and the Pumpkin Hollow Literary Association wished a library, and the Bungstarter's Social Syndicate would fain acquire a clubhouse, and the Society for the Relief of Tired Travellers yearned for a sinking fund. And so on and so forth without rest or ceasing.

"And behold the mail of Sakhar was delivered each day in wagons and in that mail came letters from needy ones with suffering children and hungry mothers-in-law and starving grandparents. And the inventors of the Self Propelling Baby Perambulator and the Automatic Hash Chopper desired funds, and the publishers of the World's Reformer wished cash wherewith to bring out the next installment of reformation, and the United Missionaries to Clink clamored for transportation. And Sakhar hired secretaries to open the mail and stenographers to answer it. And over the first week's wails he wept full sore in sympathy, but over those that came thereafter he waxed profane. But he continued to give.

"And it came to pass that crowds waited before his door in the morning and howled grievously during the day. And when he went forth upon the street his progress resembled the parade of a district leader. And supplicants for his bounty broke his windows in the daytime and hid under his bed at night.

"And there came a day when he sent again for the gleaners of news and to them he made proclamation, saying:

"'By the whiskers of all my ancestors, not to mention those of the Prophet, I bid ye harken to me. Let it be spread abroad in letters forty cubits long, upon the first page of the six P. M. extry-extra that is issued at ten in the morning, namely this, to wit: "The Graft is Played Out!" "The Bank is Broke!" "There is Nothing Doing!" For behold, I have closed out the philanthropic business and am no longer a mark. Verily, it may be a crime to die rich, but it is a condemned sight bigger one to undertake to make everybody else die that way.'

"And he changed his will so that all his property was left to the Home for the Feeble Minded, and in that Home lived he the balance of his days."

And Scheherezade paused, and said,

"Oh, King, live forever! Is it a crime for a man to die rich?"

And the King answered her and said:

"It is—for the other man."

And he departed to the poolroom to bet on the football game.

COMMERCE ACCOUNTS & FINANCE

A Magazine of Higher Business Education and Practical Administration. Acknowledged Authority in the Profession of Commerce and Consistent Advocate of Methods Up to Date and Above the Table.

JOSEPH CROSBY LINCOLN, - - - Editor.
FRIEND PITTS, JR., - Circulation and Advertising.
E. R. KITTREDGE, - - - Business Manager.

PUBLISHED MONTHLY

SUBSCRIPTION $1 a Year in the United States, Canada and Mexico. Other countries $1.50. Postage prepaid by the Publishers. In the absence of specific orders to stop at the end of the subscription term the paper will be continued and a bill sent. Entered at the New York Postoffice as Second Class mail matter.

COMMERCE, ACCOUNTS & FINANCE COMPANY, Publishers
Twenty-five Pine Street, New York

"What is luck?" is a question that a writer in "Everybody's Magazine" for October asks and attempts to answer. In answering this question he calls to his aid successful men all over the world. Opinions differ, of course, but the general consensus seems to be that there is no such thing as luck. It is true, of course, that the successful man—the man who began with little or nothing and has acquired much of everything—does not like to admit that his rise was due to good fortune rather than work, energy and his own talent; but, nevertheless, although there are times when one is tempted to believe in luck, it is pretty safe to say that no great and lasting success is attained by luck alone.

*

Charles W. Schwab, president of the United States Steel Corporation, is quoted as saying, "I believe there are lucky men. I have made it a rule in my life to surround myself with lucky men and to have no other kind in positions of importance that I control." This sounds like an indorsement of luck, as luck is commonly defined, but it appears that Mr. Schwab when further questioned, meant by "lucky men" men who had achieved success in what they undertook, that is, men who would not be beaten but worked indefatigably, were forehanded and far-sighted and succeeded by their own efforts. They were no more lucky than was the man who climbed the Matterhorn after dozens of others had made the attempt and failed. He went about it the right way, that was all, and was not easily discouraged.

*

James J. Hill says, "Luck is opportunity. And opportunity? It is of a man's making largely. There is no doubt that to some few men very little opportunity comes, but even in their cases if they sought further, refusing to be satisfied with that which is, they would find better opportunity. No substitute for hard work has ever been discovered. Certainly the substitute is not luck." Perhaps there is something in opportunity, but there is also something in seizing of the opportunity when it comes, and if one knows enough to recognize it when it comes and does seize it, it is not because he's lucky. Henry Ward Beecher did not believe in luck. Richard Cobden did not, neither did Voltaire, neither does Russell Sage nor Mrs. Hetty Green. Mrs. Green says, among other chunks of wisdom, "Don't live high." We suppose there is a good deal in that. The infallible rule for getting rich, for which the guileless individual sent his dollar, was, our readers will remember, "Work like Hades and don't spend a cent." If one acquired wealth in that way, it certainly would not be because of his luck.

*

Baron Rothschild is about the only person of prominence who is quoted as having believed in luck as the dictionary defines it. He wrote to one of his sons, "Never have anything to do with an unlucky place or an unlucky man. I have seen many clever men—very clever men—who had not shoes to their feet. I never act with them; their advice sounds very well, but they cannot get on themselves, and if they cannot do good to themselves, how can they do good to me?" The Baron's argument seems rather weak to us. The men may have been clever but they certainly lacked some other qualities besides luck, or they would have had, at least, shoes. We venture to say, that if any one had entered the Baron's office and had told the great man that he was great simply because he was lucky, the remark would not have been accepted with enthusiasm nor would it have remained long uncontradicted.

THIS AGE OF HUSTLE.

To point to the hurry and stress of modern town life as the cause of half the ills to which flesh to-day is heir has become almost a commonplace in aetiological diagnosis, says the "Lancet," of London. The old-fashioned complaints might almost excite a medical man's pity, so much do they seem to be crowded out by those active widespread young fellows, neuritis, neurasthenia, and a whole young family of nervous illnesses, the offspring of the strained existence of to-day. A chain is as strong as its weakest link, and to-day it appears that the nervous system is the weak link of the organism. The weakness is not natural. It is acquired because the strain upon this link is so often almost constant and out of proportion to the wearing power of the material. Whether as generations advance, individual nervous systems will more easily bear the labors asked from them or not, at any rate it may fairly be assumed that in the early days of any new style of life the generations born under an old regime have the worst of it. Their children cope more easily with the new necessities. They are earlier confronted with them, and new arrangements which perplexed and worried their parents become habits easily borne and therefore not to be reckoned among the trying elements of existence.

Thus we may imagine future generations perfectly calm among a hundred telephones and sleeping sweetly though airships whizz among countless electric wires over their heads and a perpetual night traffic of motor cars hurries past their bedroom windows. As yet, it must be sorrowfully confessed, our nervous systems are not so callous. Some of us still start at the telephone ring and find the irregularities of the instrument a source of irritation and worry. Many of us are actually nervous at the sudden appearance of a motor car round the wrong side of a London street corner. The result of countless repetitions of these trials, small though they may be singly, is not to be lightly estimated.

Fortunately, the very causes of nerve exhaustion, so far as improved rapidity of locomotion may be counted one of them, provide one important counteracting feature of town life at the present day. We are alluding to the facility with which those whose week days are spent in city toil may spend the seventh in breathing the fresh air and beholdng the innocent joys of the rustic. To the hard-working Londoner the value of the week-end properly used is hard to overestimate. From the eager broker and worried business man to the stifled seamstress and toiling artisan there are few who cannot find further or nearer from the metropolis some fresh and open spot where they may replace the evil atmosphere of the office or the factory. Without trains, electric tramways and motor cars, such a wholesome change of scenery and surroundings would be scarcely possible in the limited time available.

National Federation of Accountants

THE week beginning October 27 was a big week for the profession of the Public Accountant. Indeed, it probably is no exaggeration to say it was the biggest week for the profession in the history of this country. During the week there was formed at Washington the "Federation of Societies of Public Accountants in the United States of America." A long name, but an appropriate one—appropriate because the Federation is to be composed of societies of Public Accountants from Back Bay to the Golden Gate.

Every existing society of Public Accountants in the United States was represented by delegates. The feeling as to the necessity and utility of such an organization was unanimous, and the question was discussed and the whole matter settled in twenty-four hours.

The officers elected are:

President, Mr. Charles W. Haskins, C. P. A., of New York.

Treasurer, Mr. Robert H. Montgomery, C. P. A., of Pennsylvania.

Secretary, Mr. George Wilkinson, of Illinois.

The presidents of the societies composing the Federation are its vice-presidents.

It was through the action of the Illinois Association of Public Accountants that the Convention was called, and to that Association are due the credit and honor of elaborating the plans. Last July Mr. George Wilkinson, the president, read a paper to the Illinois Association, in which he set forth the need of a national body and suggested the lines for its organization. A committee was then named to carry out the plan, and the Convention at Washington and its accomplishment are the results of that committee's work.

Drafting a Constitution.

The committee at once drafted a pro forma constitution and by-laws which were sent to the various societies of Accountants organized under state laws. The committee set forth its views of the necessity of a national Federation, and suggested that a convention be held on October 22d, and asked each society to send delegates. The matter was thoroughly canvassed, and the date having been made a week later, the result of the committee's work was the presence in Washington of nearly thirty prominent Accountants representing every existing society in the United States.

The Convention was called to order Tuesday morning at the New Willard Hotel. Upon motion Mr. A. Lowes Dickinson, M. A., F. C. A., of New York, took the Chair. Mr. Wilkinson was elected secretary of the meeting. A Credential Committee was appointed, and their report showed delegates present from Massachusetts, New York, Maryland, New Jersey, Pennsylvania, Michigan and Illinois—as said before, every existing society was represented.

The convention made the organization permanent by electing Mr. Harvey S. Chase, of Boston, chairman, and Mr. Wilkinson, secretary, and proceeded at once to the consideration of the constitution. The name was adopted as stated above, particular attention being given to having it indicate the wide extent of the organization and that it is a combination of societies and not of individuals. The objects as stated in the Constitution are:

Its objects shall be (a) to bring into communication with one another, the several associations and societies of public accountants, organized or to be organized under the laws of the several states of the United States of America; (b) to encourage the formation of state associations of public accountants in states where they do not exist; (c) to encourage state C. P. A. legislation on uniform lines; (d) to secure Federal recognition of the profession of the public accountant; (e) to facilitate and assist the training of young members of the profession, and to establish a uniform standard of efficiency in federated societies; (f) to disseminate throughout the United States a general knowledge of the objects of the federation and of the utility of the public accountant in the industrial and financial development of the country; and (g) to further the interests of the profession generally.

A Committee on By-laws was then appointed and the convention adjourned to await its report. This committee was composed of one delegate from each society, the presidents of the societies who were not delegates being invited to join the committee in an advisory capacity. An evidence of the deep interest the delegates felt in the matter is shown by the fact that the committee held a continuous session, lasting nine hours, not adjourning for a moment until the By-laws were complete and the report ready for the Convention. In the By-laws are fifteen articles, some with several sections, which, it is believed, completely cover the situation. The convention made some few changes and adopted the By-laws substantially as they were reported.

Address of President Haskins.

The election of officers was the next business, and the unanimity of feeling was shown when but one nomination was made for each office. Mr. Haskins, who is the first president, has been prominently connected with every movement of moment made in the interests of the profession of Public Accountant in America in the last five years. In taking the Chair Mr. Haskins said in part:

Gentlemen, and Delegates present, I need not tell you that this is one of the greatest honors that has ever come to me. I have not had many, but I consider it one of the greatest I have had because personally I have taken more

He Finally Found the Key.
Uncle—"Much obliged, boys; I guess I won't need you after all!"
—Philadelphia Record.

interest in the profession of accountancy than I could have possibly taken in any other thing. My heart has been in it and I have given my best work to it. I have not always worked, perhaps, to win the approval of all the accountants, but still I have done the very best that I could do, and I hope to do better; and I think that this opportunity which we have now gives us a wider and a broader field. There are opportunities which, it seems to me, will come to us from such a Federation as the one we have organized, opportunities for developing this profession and establishing ourselves stronger with the people, in addition to the fact that we may get some of the Federal recognition that we have been talking about to-day.

I think that a very great deal of credit and thanks should be given the Illinois Society for the formation of this Federation. They have certainly done hard and creditable work, and I do not think we can thank the Illinois Society, and Mr. Wilkinson especially, enough for the hard work that has been done.

I want to thank the delegates again for the honor conferred on me and to say I will do the best I can. (Applause).

Mr. Robert H. Montgomery, in nominating Mr. George Wilkinson for secretary, said:

This afternoon when we were analyzing the duties of Secretary, which I believe is the next office to be filled, some one remarked that the Secretary's office would be what the gentleman who happened to occupy that position made it. Now, I believe there is in the Secretary's office of this Federation the opportunity to do great work, and coming as I do from Pennsylvania, I am prepared to name a gentleman who is not from Pennsylvania, but whom we believe is of Pennsylvania to a certain extent, who is well known there, and we think a great deal of him, and I believe after the work of this Federation is over that all of us will have that same high degree of respect and regard for him that those who have known him so long entertain. I have the pleasure of nominating Mr. George Wilkinson.

There were several seconds, and the full vote was cast for Mr. Wilkinson. In acknowledging his election, he said:

Secretary Wilkinson's Remarks.

Gentlemen, you are very kind indeed to express, as you do by this applause, your approval of my election as secretary.

As you know, this movement had its inception in a paper I had the honor to read at a meeting of the Illinois Association of Public Accountants; it was acted upon unanimously at that meeting, and the president was given authority to name a committee, which he did. When the committee had prepared a draft plan, the society unanimously voted to join the Federation, without any "ifs" or provisions at all, and we are here. Then I took up the matter with the other associations by correspondence, and interest in the matter has not been allowed to lag. It was not until I came back from England a week ago, however, that we succeeded in getting the societies definitely in line. I think to-day's meeting shows you that very nearly all the Public Accountants of the United States are in earnest in this matter, and when we have laid before them what we thought to be a very important matter they have responded most nobly, by their presence here, and by the work they have done and by the untiring devotion they displayed in a continuous session of nine hours' solid work—they have shown you very clearly that they are in earnest, and I am sure it augurs very well for

"Whoa!"—Washington Star.

the success of the Federation. I do not believe any such day's work has ever been put in in the interest of the profession of Public Accountants, here or in any other country, as has been put in to-day by the several gentlemen who have come here and, at their own personal inconvenience and loss of time, have devoted their energy to this movement.

I thank you, gentlemen, for the very kind way in which you have received my election.

Mr. Robert H. Montgomery, of the Pennsylvania Institute of Certified Public Accountants, was elected treasurer.

The delegates to the convention, deeply sensible of the untiring energy devoted to the cause by Mr. George Wilkinson, and the debt the profession owes him therefor, made their feeling and appreciation a part of the record of the convention. Mr. E. L. Suffern, C. P. A., of the New York State Society, moved a vote of thanks to Mr. Wilkinson, saying: "I move that we express our thanks to our secretary, who has managed the business and affairs of the convention entrusted to him in the efficient manner for which he is noted."

A delegate from each state spoke in support of that motion and it was vigorously carried.

A vote of thanks was also accorded Mr. Harvey S. Chase for the able manner in which he had presided over the convention.

The business of the meeting being finished, the delegates listened attentively to papers read by Mr. John Alexander Cooper, of Illinois, and Mr. Max Teichmann, C. P. A., of Maryland.

The convention adjourned soon after 10 P. M.

Summary of the Work Accomplished.

Summarized the work accomplished is: The complete organization of the Federation of all the Accountant societies in the United States, including Constitution, By-laws, election of officers, Executive Board and committees.

Many expected this work would take two days for its accomplishment, but it was completed in one.

It is confidently believed that the membership of the Federation will be increased very shortly by the admission of a number of societies to be organized in the West.

November—Coal Baron: "Carry it in for Ye, Mister?"

The Rate of Interest*

By J. SHIELD NICHOLSON, M.A., D.Sc.

IT was shown in my lecture "What is Money?" that the term "money" is used with a variety of meanings. If, then, we take the term "interest" in what seems the most simple and obvious sense—namely, as the price paid for the use of a loan of money for a time—in order to get at the real or underlying meaning we must decide what is to be understood by "money" in this connection. We find on the first inspection that very often in these loans the "money" is merely an intermediary, and that what is really lent and borrowed—when the whole transaction is complete—is so much "capital." Take, for example, the common case of the conversion of some private manufacturing concern into a limited company. The company, in effect, borrows so much money from the investors and pays in return so much interest of various kinds and under various conditions. But this interest is only earned by converting the money into various forms of productive "capital." The money in this case is only, to begin with, a medium of exchange, and the essence of the loan is "capital."

What is Capital?

In other cases, however, the primary object of the loan is not to obtain capital for extending production, but to obtain "money" in the sense of legal tender, or at least in some form that will be accepted as such—the object being to meet some prior monetary obligation. In times of financial crisis, for example, many houses may be perfectly solvent if only time is allowed for realization, but they fail simply because they cannot meet in money their monetary obligations. Accordingly most recent writers on the principles of economics have drawn a sharp distinction between interest on loanable "capital" and interest on loanable "money," although unfortunately writers on money articles constantly use the terms "money" and "capital" as interchangeable.

In an examination of causes and principles the distinction is fundamental, and it is so also as a rule in practical business. If we take the Bank of England rate as typical or representative of the rate charged for loanable money as such, and the rate on first-class securities or debentures as typical or representative of the interest on loanable capital, we find that there is often a considerable difference between the two rates. Whilst interest on capital is relatively very steady—the yield to consols not varying perhaps one per cent in fifty years—the bank rate may sometimes be above and sometimes below, and the changes are often very frequent and occasionally violent, oscillating in the same period between 2 and 10 per cent. The differences are not to be explained by any difference in security or in risk. In both cases the security for all practical purposes may be considered perfect. I propose then to deal separately with these two kinds of interest, and to notice later on the interaction there may be between the two rates.

I have used the expression interest on capital, but a very slight application of economic analysis shows that capital itself is even more difficult of definition than money. It would be hopeless, by way of introduction to a subject sufficiently complex already, to enter into all those difficulties, but by way of illustration I may mention the two most popular meanings. Some people—and they may quote the authority of Adam Smith—look on capital as wealth that yields a revenue; others—and they may quote J. S. Mill—regard capital as wealth used in production. In some cases those differences of definition are of no practical importance, because the "capital" yields revenue by being used in production, but in other cases there might be great differences between capital and non-capital according to the definition. The recent war loan, for example, yields a revenue to the lenders, and, for all we know, may yield a revenue for centuries; but the corresponding capital has been used for the most part in the destruction of life and property, and it would be too severe a strain on language, even with a plentiful use of those convenient terms "indirectly" and "fructifying," to include destruction by war under the term economic production,—and cases might be multiplied indefinitely. Take, again, the borrowings of various local authorities on the security of the rates. The loans will yield a revenue and so far rank as capital to the creditors so long as the cities and towns yield sufficient rates; but it is quite possible that, considered from the point of view of production, the "capital" will very soon melt away altogether. Those examples show that the terms "loanable capital," and consequently "interest on loanable capital," are by no means so simple as they appear at first sight. And the deeper we carry the analysis, whether in theory or in practice, so much greater do the difficulties become. Recently the highest legal talent of the country has been exercised in determining what is the nature of capital and how capital is related to dividends.

In whatever way we regard it, the answer to the question "What is capital?" presents difficulties in theory, in business, and in law. These difficulties may be partly surmounted, and the nature and meaning of "capital" and "interest on capital" made clear by taking different cases. Capital, like money, has different functions.

The interest on capital as such, in which the money is only used as an intermediary, may be

The "Motley Fool" of the Day—New York World.

* Lecture delivered before the Society of Accountants in Edinburgh, by the Professor of Political Economy in the University of Edinburgh.

divided first of all into two great classes which we may call profit-interest and loan-interest.

Profit-interest arises in this way. The owner of any form of capital who employs it in production will expect to gain certain gross profits. He will expect something in the form of reward for his labor and enterprise, which economists call wages of management or superintendence; he will also expect on the average of a mass of transactions or over a period of time to cover all sorts of depreciation of his capital—his gross profit must provide for insurance against risk; and besides these two elements he will expect something by way of interest. The three elements are best distinguished in the case of a joint-stock company. In this case the wages of superintendence appear in the shape of directors' fees and salaries; the insurance against risk is represented by the reserve fund, or it may be by actual insurances under that name; and the balance which goes in dividends to the shareholders represents the interest on their capital. This interest again differs according to the security—e.g., debentures, various preferences, ordinary shares, &c.; but after all allowances there remains an element which may be called pure interest—that is, interest on capital in which there is practically no risk and no trouble of management, although the interest is, so to speak, produced in the business. If any industry gets into a depressed condition it is quite possible that the gross profits may not yield any interest after allowing for management and depreciation, and of course the capital may disappear altogether; but over a period of years it may be said that the "productive capital" of the country yields on the whole a certain rate of pure interest besides the other elements in gross profits.

Loan Interest.

Loan-interest on capital is considered from a point of view in which direct production is of secondary or it may be of no importance. People may be unable or unwilling to employ their capital themselves, and they lend it to others, receiving so much interest for its use. In this case it is indifferent to the lender what use is made of his capital,—it may be wasted by an extravagant landlord or by an improvident government; but so long as the interest is obtainable from other funds at the disposal of the debtor this makes no difference. The interest on large amounts of capital is paid out of the produce of rates and taxes, and cannot be considered as earned by the productive employment of the capital concerned; and in other cases the interest is really paid out of other capital belonging to the debtor.

If, however, we leave out of account for the present the case of foreign investments and consider one country in isolation, it is plain that all this interest obtained on loans must itself in some way be produced in the country. The loan-interest may in some cases be a simple transfer of profit-interest, as in the case of various companies or of private firms, so far as they work with borrowed capital. This case is simple; but the loan-interest may also come, as already indicated, from other sources,—from the general income of the tax-payers or from the gradual dissipation of other forms of capital. Loan-interest of this kind—whatever form it may assume, that is to say if it is not obtained from the productive employment of the corresponding capital—is of the nature of a tax upon productive capital and industry; and if all the capital of a country were advanced in unproductive loans of this kind the country would speedily be ruined.

If the capital is sent for investment in foreign countries, the case is in some ways similar to loans for unproductive purposes at home. In this case, only the interest is received by the lending country; and thus from the national standpoint there is so far a reduction of income as regards the profits and wages which arise from the employment of capital in home industries.

Consider now the causes that determine the direction of the employment of loanable capital. It is clear that after allowing for security, facility for investment, and other conditions, the rate of interest on all kinds of capital must tend to equality.

Accordingly there must be a constant interaction between loans for productive and for unproductive purposes. If trade is flourishing, and gross profits, including profit-interest, are advancing, capital is directed towards industrial concerns; and conversely, with a depression of trade and profit-interest declining, capital is turned to non-industrial loans or to advances to foreign states on which the yield is a little better.

Interest for many purposes is best regarded as the price paid for the use of capital. And if interest is once looked on as a price, it comes under the general principles determining prices. In the course of progress the tendency of prices is to come under the influence of competition. And if we take a rapid glance over the actual history of industrial progress we find that one of the most striking results is the substitution of the principle of competition for the principle of monopoly in the determination of interest. In old societies interest was usually regarded as immoral and sinful, because in most cases it represented what was extracted by the usurer from the absolute necessities of the borrower. Under modern conditions the rate varies principally with the security that is offered, and not according to the particular necessities of the borrower. The borrower might be willing for his purposes to pay 10 per cent a-month; but if the security is satisfactory he may have to pay less than 5 per cent a-year.

Wider Markets and Prices.

Another principle that becomes prominent in the course of industrial progress is that prices are determined more and more by wider and wider markets. In older societies there were numbers of local markets, and prices were mainly determined by the local conditions affecting demand and supply. Under present conditions for many "commodities"—using the term in an extended sense—there is a world-wide market. The prices of wheat, of cotton, of silver—to take but three instances—are determined by the conditions of demand and supply all the world over. A striking example was afforded by wheat in the year 1879. That year was the coldest of which there is any instrumental record in these islands, and there was a great failure of the harvest. So easily, however, was the deficit met, that the price of wheat only rose to 53s. 6d., as compared with 51s. as the average of 1871-1880. Even at the beginning of the nineteenth century such a deficiency in the harvest might have doubled or trebled the price.

The point of the illustration is this, that the price of loanable capital—that is, interest—in the course of industrial progress has also come to be subject to conditions of demand and supply all the world over, and no longer depends on local or even national markets. The rate of interest on loanable capital in this country depends, to say the least, very largely upon the rates that may be obtained in other countries; and with every development of the means of communication, including the diffusion of knowledge or the extension of publicity in the world's

Uncle Sam—"Say, young fellow, these periodical jags are getting monotonous".

great markets—with every increase in the security afforded by the advance of international law, and of the recognition by individuals and by governments of the sacredness or the compelling force of contracts—loanable capital will come more and more under these great world-influences.

I proceed, now, to notice very briefly some of the principal causes affecting, first the supply, and next the demand, for loanable capital as distinguished from "money."

As regards the supply of capital, the causes may be divided into two groups. First, there are all the causes which tend to increase production or to diminish cost. A given amount of labor and also a given amount of coal will, with appropriate machinery, produce more than ever before, and, in all probability, this increase in the powers of production will continue. Again, the great improvements in transport, in security, and, I may add, in knowledge, have opened up abundant new sources for supplies of various forms of raw material, including the raw material of food. This process seems also likely to continue, and man's power over nature to be further extended to a great degree. There is also to be considered the continuous utilization of waste products, and the adoption and extension of multitudes of economies. And perhaps the greatest cause of all—if we are to consider the world's supply of capital—is the advance of all the other nations on the roads made by the pioneers of civilization. China may follow Japan, as Japan has followed the West.

But whether this enormous increase of wealth will be turned into "capital," or will be consumed directly and unproductively, depends on a second group of causes. These causes are mainly moral and intellectual, but they are equally real and important. Such, for example, are the causes which are summarized under the phrase the "effective desire of accumulation." There can be no doubt that, taking a wide survey, these causes tend to increase in force. The people in civilized states look further into the future and they make more provision for the future. This is shown not only by the growth of all forms of insurance, but by the growth of education and of morality, and by the desire to rise in the social scale. The better members of the lower social classes strive more and more to rise into the higher, and one potent means is by saving a certain amount of capital.

But it is not so much on the moral as on the intellectual side that the creation of capital is affected by modern progress. People are willing to wait longer and to take more roundabout methods to secure their ends, and in the last resort that means they put more and more wealth into the form of capital.

Security.

The great cause affecting the accumulation of capital that always appears in every part of the inquiry is security. Security to enjoy or to dispose of the fruits of saving is a necessary condition to the creation of capital. Under present conditions the increase of security as affecting the accumulation of capital may be specially observed in two ways. First, in the countries that are in the van of progress more and more undertakings are conducted on a sound basis. We are apt to lay too much stress on striking failures or gigantic frauds, but there is no question that relatively the losses of business are less than ever before, or the losses that occur are more easily repaired. The ordinary increase of capital in this country is now estimated at 200 million pounds per annum.

But, secondly, the influence of the increase of security is still more noticeable in backward and new countries. More and more countries are offering security for the creation of capi al, and with the growth of security there is at once an increase in productive power. Thus, from whatever point it is regarded, there is no question that, as far as supply is concerned, the tendency is for a continuous and considerable increase of capital.

Demand.

Let us now consider demand, and, in the first place, the demand on the part of unproductive consumers. Amongst these the most important are the governments of the world, both national and municipal. The national debts of the world are said to have a par value of about 6000 millions sterling, and have mainly been incurred for unproductive purposes, especially for war or for armaments, and accordingly the interest is not derived from the productive employment of the original capital. Local debts to a greater extent represent productive capital, but still in this case also a large part is unproductive—that is to say, the loans do not produce their own interest. On the other hand, however, a large part of this expenditure, though classed as unproductive, in reality adds greatly to the efficiency of a nation as regards production, and also adds to those moral and intellectual qualities of the people which lead them to provide more and more for the future—that is, to create capital.

But, secondly, the demand for capital may be directly for productive purposes, and this demand has increased enormously of recent years through the growth of joint-stock companies, which now in this country exceed in importance private firms. The spread of companies gathers together masses of capital which was formerly wasted or kept idle for want of facilities for investment, and accordingly this increased demand largely creates the corresponding supply.

And as regards the demand, for productive purposes generally, it may be observed that every new demand on a sound basis implies a certain surplus in the future—that is to say, the ultimate effect of borrowing for production is a further increase of supply.

It appears, so far, that the supply of capital is likely to outstrip the demand, and that the rate of interest on capital will tend to fall. And this general conclusion is strengthened by another consideration, the influence of which is not at first sight so obvious. There is to be considered the growth of population. Of the great civilized nations it is only in France that there appears to be an absolute diminution in the sense that the deaths exceed the births; but in other countries the rate of increase has fallen off, and the eminent French economist and statistician, Leroy-Beaulieu, has plausibly maintained such a decrease is the natural result of democracy. If, however, capital increases faster than population, the natural result is for wages to rise and interest to fall.

On the other hand, there is the possibility of a great war, which would directly increase the demand for capital and also tend to diminish the supply. It would also indirectly, by the shock to security, tend to raise the rate of interest. The subject, however, is too problematical for present consideration. I venture to observe, however, that the recent fall in the price of first-class investments, or, what is the same thing, the rise in the yield, has been too readily ascribed to the South African war. The effects of that war, whether as regards the demand or the supply of capital or any shock to security, do not seem of sufficient magnitude to account for the rise in interest. It is difficult to see why the Boer war should have so great an effect whilst the Franco-German war had relatively none.

I am inclined to think a more potent factor is the greater industrial demand and the widening of the field for investment. The gilt-edged securities have lost part of their monopoly or their scarcity value, and there has been a displacement of old capital and an investment of new in all kinds of undertakings which formerly were not available.

Thus loan-interest has moved in sympathy with profit-interest, and the rise is due not to any abnormal increase in the demand for unproductive wars, but to the increase in the yield of productive capital. The last four years have been years of unexampled prosperity.

Loanable Money.

I have dealt at such length with the rate of interest on "capital" that I have little time to consider the case of interest on loanable "money." For the present it must suffice if I indicate very briefly the leading ideas; for a fuller statement and for technical illustrations you have Bagehot's "Lombard Street," and Mr. Clare's "Money Market Primer," and, I may add, the admirable little book of Professor Dunbar on Banking.

We may begin by saying that the value of money, in the sense of the rate charged for advances of money, depends on the supply and the demand. But the term "money," as we saw in the first lecture, is a very variable and elastic term, and we must always consider the particular monetary function or functions involved. The "money" we are now concerned with must be either legal tender or by custom or habit it must have the force of legal tender. The special function of the money of the money market is to provide means for settling bargains made in terms of money. The money that is strictly legal tender is far too small in amount to make these settlements. The whole stock of legal tender in the United Kingdom, including Bank of England notes issued against securities probably does not exceed 126 million pounds. Of this, again, more than half is in actual circulation from hand to hand, leaving some 50 or 60 million pounds for banking purposes, and of this amount generally more than a quarter is held by the Bank of England. At the date of this calculation the sum due by the banks of the United Kingdom on deposit and current accounts was 650 million pounds—that is, ten times the amount of the legal tender available. This is what is meant by saying that "bank" money consists for the most part of credit; it is based on legal tender, it represents legal tender, and on demand it is convertible into legal tender; but it is not itself legal tender, and the possibility of banking rests on the fact assured by experience that the demand for legal tender in the ordinary course of things will be relatively small, and can be calculated. Accordingly, the banks keep in the way of till money just as much legal tender as they think will be required; and just as the proportion of the kinds of legal tender required—silver, gold, notes—is known by experience, so also is the total amount.

It is only putting the same fact in another way when it is said that in most trade transactions payments are made by cheques or bills. In the words of Mr. Clare, "Cheques and bills form the principal currency of this country." A reference to the Clearing-House Returns shows the magnitude of the transactions, and these returns furnish the best test of the activity of trade.

But although legal tender forms only a relatively small part of the currency, it is an absolutely essential part. A certain amount is necessary for wages, retail transactions, railway fares, and various payments for which cheques—at least ordinary cheques—are not available. In ordinary times, as I said, the amount of legal tender required can be readily calculated and readily obtained, but as soon as the ordinary conditions change there is a change in the demand for legal tender. Thus an increase in the volume and activity of trade increases the demand directly, and any shock to credit by diminishing the use of cheques and bills indirectly increases the demand. In extreme cases an internal drain of this kind may lead to a commercial crisis.

Foreign Demand.

It will be seen, then, that whilst the supply of legal tender is practically limited and inelastic, the demand is liable to variations, even if we consider only internal trade. But the principal demand for legal tender, or rather for the gold on which it is based, is the foreign demand. A foreign demand may arise suddenly in the most unexpected way, and it may be such that it can only be met by the export of gold. It is in this connection, as already pointed out, that movements in the foreign exchanges are of general importance. The Bank of England seeks to protect itself, and also to attract gold from other countries, by raising its rate. And since the Bank of England practically holds the only available reserve of gold for foreign demands, the proportion of its reserve to liabilities is a factor of the greatest importance in determining the rate.

For simplicity, I have spoken as if there was at any time only one rate charged for advances of money. It is hardly necessary to point out that the bank rate may differ from the market rate, and that in practice there are great differences in market rates—according to the security offered, the class of business, the condition of the loan, and other circumstances.

Although the rate of interest on capital as such is best distinguished from that on money as such, there is an interaction or a sympathy between the two rates. If the rates obtainable for money are low, purchases of first-class securities are increased, partly for the better interest and partly for the probable rise. A low rate also specially stimulates speculation for the rise on the Stock Exchange, if other conditions are favorable. But a rise in the price of securities, with fixed interest, is the same as a fall in the rate of interest. Conversely, with higher rates for money as such, securities are sold, and the fall is again hastened by Stock Exchange speculation. Still, it is evident that a large part of the holdings of banks is of the nature of a documentary reserve, and although speculation on the Stock Exchange, whether for the rise or fall, is generally affected by the bank rate, it depends much more on other influences. Thus for long periods there may be a considerable difference between the two rates —namely, the interest on capital, and the interest on money as such.

The Production of Gold.

I will conclude with a brief notice of one point of special interest at the present time. We have seen the fundamental importance of the gold reserve in the Bank of England, and of the effects of movements in that reserve on the rate of discount. It might then, at first sight, be thought that the annual supply of gold from the mines would be of fundamental importance, so that with a falling off in supply discount rates would rule high, and with an increase there would be a fall. There is, however, no such simple or necessary connection. We may take for illustration the recent changes in the production of gold.

During the last quarter of a century the supply of gold has doubled, and it is quite possible that during the next quarter in may again be doubled. The question is, What will be the probable effect on the rate of interest on loanable money? The answer, I think, depends on the way in which the supplies are used. If a large part of the new gold were constantly added to the money market, so far the increase of supply would tend to lower rates. But the further question arises, Who is to keep the gold in the market? The gold of itself is as barren a metal as ever it was, and it is also as heavy and as inconvenient for large payments. The banks, including the Bank of England, will not be at the expense of keeping more gold than they require as reserve, and people will not use more than they are accustomed to as currency. Thus the new gold must be forced into circulation, not necessarily in this country but in some part of the commercial world. The natural effect will be to raise prices, and in that way to stimulate trade. This stimulus to trade may again lead to a rise in the rate of discount.

Similarly, a falling off in the supply of gold tends to lower prices, and so to depress trade, and in that way indirectly a diminution in the production of gold may lower the rate of interest, as was the case twenty-five years ago. There are, no doubt, as in all these monetary questions, other counteracting and disturbing elements. The depreciation of silver had very great effect, in my opinion, in lowering prices, and also in promoting the useless hoarding of gold by France and other countries. It is quite possible, now that silver has lost its monetary influence, with the increase in the natural supplies of gold, there will be also some unlocking of these great hoards, and thus a still greater rise in general prices. Such a fall, however, in the exchange value of gold as is indicated by a rise in general prices, may be accompanied by a rise in the rate of interest, unless counteracted by the other causes indicated.

Argument.

In conclusion, this case may be used to illustrate the general argument of this paper.

At first sight nothing seems more natural than to say: Interest means the price paid for the use of money; gold is money, and therefore if the supply of gold is increased, the supply of money also is increased, and therefore the rate of interest will fall. This argument, however, which at first sight seems so simple and plausible, on analysis is full of difficulties, not to say full of fallacies.

We must first of all distinguish between interest on "capital" and interest on "money." If we take account of all the capital of the world on which interest is paid, the gross total must be reckoned by thousands of millions sterling. This interest arises in many ways: it may be definitely earned in production or in the case of industrial companies, or it may be paid out of taxes, as in the case of the interest on national debts. But as the result of competition, what may be called the pure interest—that is after allowing for risk, depreciation, management, &c.—the pure interest on all these multitudinous forms of capital tends more and more to equality, or the differences become less and less throughout the commercial world.

Suppose, then, that the amount of gold is increased by 50 million pounds a year, what is this 50 million pounds added to these thousands of millions? It is evident, then, that the argument, from the increase of the supply of "capital," falls to the ground.

If, however, we carefully separate "capital" from "money," it is no doubt true that the amount of loanable money is of much smaller dimensions. But even loanable money embraces more than legal tender, and legal tender includes more than gold. The advances made by banks consist of a relatively small amount of legal tender and a still smaller amount of gold itself.

Why, then, should an addition to the supplies of gold from the mines lower the rate of interest on loanable money? It is well known that during the last twenty-five years the Bank of England rate has been for months together at the official minimum of 2 per cent., and the corresponding market rate has been lower still. And it is noteworthy that the rates were lowest when the annual production of gold was lowest. No doubt the adequacy of the ultimate reserve of gold held by the Bank of England is of the greatest importance to our credit system; but the amount of that reserve has very little connection with the annual production of gold, and the annual production of gold has still less connection with the rate of interest.

. Two Thinkers,—Ohio State Journal.

Financial and Commercial Books

THE LAW OF BANKS AND BANKING, Including Acceptance, Demand and Notice of Dishonor Upon Commercial Paper.—By John M. Zane. 9¾ x 6⅞ inches. 852 pages. Bound in law sheep. Published by T. H. Flood & Co. Price, $3.

The aim of the above treatise, as stated by the author in the preface, is "to present all the law that can be properly considered as applicable to the business of banking." This does not mean, of course, that the book presents all the law which the banker may find to his interest to know, but it treats fully of the law applicable to the main operation of banking. The topics treated include: Banks, their organization and proof of existence; the right to carry on banking and legislative regulations of banking; who may be stockholders in banking companies, liabilities of stockholders, right to transfer stock, etc.; duties and liabilities of bank officers and agents, and their power to bind the bank; powers of banks and effect of usage on powers; rights and liabilities of banks and depositors, including here a large number of topics, such as rights of banks to apply deposit to own claim, liability of holder of check and for overpayment and wrongful payment, etc., liability for collections, for negligence of corresponding clerk, etc., loans and discounts; the law of acceptance and of demand of payment, notice of non-payment and of protest of collectible paper; powers of banks to issue notes; dissolution and insolvency of banks. There are also two chapters devoted to Savings Banks and Clearing Houses, and in an appendix the federal statutes in regard to National banks are collected.

The book is written as well for bankers as for lawyers. In statement it is clear and concise, and the whole work bears evidence of great care to attain the utmost accuracy. An ample index affords a ready key to every subject treated.

APPLIED ENGLISH.—By Isaac Wesley Lucia. 7½ x 5⅛ inches. 129 pages. Bound in cloth. Cover title gilt. Published by J. W. Warr. Price, 75 cents.

There is a great deal of good sense boiled down in Mr. Lucia's little book. Also, there are some things, it seems to us, not quite so sensible, for instance, when the author tells us that we should not say, "May I go down stairs?" but that we should say, "May I go below stairs?" Below stairs is, undoubtedly, correct according to the strict letter of the law, but "May I go down stairs?" is, also, correct, for long usage by cultivated people has made it so. But, aside from some hair-splitting of this nature, "Applied English" is a good book, well worth buying and studying.

STATISTICAL STUDIES OF THE NEW YORK MONEY MARKET.—By J. P. Norton. 9¼ x 6 inches. 108 pages, with folding chart. Bound in slate-colored paper. Cover title in silver. Published by the Macmillan Company. Price, $1.

This handsomely printed book is one of the publications of the Department of Social Sciences of Yale University. Professor Norton says in his preface:

> In the following pages an attempt is made to apply the mathematical methods of interpolation and correlation to the financial statistics of discount rates and banking items as published weekly by the financial journals.
>
> In studying correlation, the methods of Professor Karl Pearson have been of very great use. Although Professor Pearson's writings have been largely in connection with the biological problems of evolution, his statistical methods have been found to apply satisfactorily to the problems presented under the theory of money and credit. I have tried as far as possible to subordinate the mathematical side of the work, and when for clearness it was necessary to introduce some mathematical formulas, I have tried to state the logic of the formulas also in words and to express the meaning of the tables graphically by charts.

It would seem that Professor Norton has been successful in the attempt, as above set forth, and to the financial man and particularly to that financial man who is interested in cause and effect, this book should be very valuable.

The titles of some of the chapters are, "Brief Analysis Under the Theory of Money and Credit," "Statistical Studies in the New York Money Market," "The Statistics of the New York Associated Banks," "The Growth Element," "The Percentage Deviations" and "Periodicity in the Reserve Deviations."

The subjects are treated in scholarly fashion and the book is filled with illustrated tables. It also contains a large folded chart, which chart shows the movements of the weekly averages of the total reserves, loans and deposits of the New York Associated Banks from 1879 to 1900, with their respective growth axes; also, percentage deviations of the total reserve, loans and deposits, ratios of reserve to deposits, and the discount rate on call loans at the Stock Exchange.

EVERY DAY ENGLISH, BOOK ONE.—By Jean Sherwood Rankin. 8 x 6 inches. 232 pages. Bound in cloth. Ornamental cover design. Educational Publishing Company. Price, 75 cents.

This is a text book for intermediate grades in public schools. It appears to be just what its name indicates. The author attempts to teach the child to speak and write our language correctly, and does not attempt to burden him with too many rules of scholastic grammar. The book reads like an interesting story rather than a dry text book. It contains many poems and quotations from celebrated authors, and should interest the young scholar at once. Any book calculated to get rid of the dry-as-dustisms of ordinary grammar should be welcome, and the author of "Every Day English" deserves a vote of thanks.

MAN AS AN INVESTMENT.

The Hon. Lyman J. Gage, Ex-Secretary of the Treasury, is a great believer in young men. In the course of a recent magazine article he said:

"The public appreciates more and more the importance of investing money in men, not buildings. When I hear of large gifts to erect magnificent halls at our colleges, I think what greater good would be accomplished if that money were used to help a number of deserving young men and women through their college courses. When these young people have finished their work in the world, they may each and all be able to erect $50,000 buildings for their alma maters. A certain generous-minded man once said to me: 'I have given money quite freely to help the distressed, to soften the bitterness of helpless age and to alleviate the condition of the unfortunate, but there was little or no inspiration in it. When, on the other hand, I have helped a bright boy to secure for himself a good education, my imagination has become affected. I have seen my dollars—won by hard application in sordid ways—transmuted into intellectual agencies powerful to affect the thoughts and feelings of generations which will live when I am dead.' This sentiment is becoming prevalent among the thoughtful men of America."

THE REASON WHY.

"Tell me frankly, count, how much you owe."

"Really, sare, your question covers me wiz confusione."

"That's all right. Confide in me. If you are to marry my daughter I want you to be open and honest. How much do you owe?"

"Nossing."

"Nothing! You owe nothing?"

"Alas, eet ees too true. Nobody weel trust-a me."

SMALL BOY FOR HIS AGE.

The druggist leaned over the counter and asked the little girl in the soiled gingham frock what she wanted, says the New York "Times." She handed him up a crumpled note which read:

"Give the girl a dose of quinine for an eight-year-old boy in a capsule."

"Say, you tell your mother she wants to get that kid into a museum without delay," remarked the druggist, as he filled the order.

Business Subjects in Current Literature

THERE were a great many articles dealing with social questions in the magazines of last month, and this fact may be due to the recent coal strike. This great strike stirred up the entire community, and many writers on subjects dealing with political economy obtained space in the current periodicals. There were the usual number of articles on general business topics. The following is a partial list of the same:

Articles on General Subjects.

"Commerce and Tariffs in the Phillipines" is the title of an article by C. C. Plehn in the "Journal of Political Economy." A. O. Norton, of the "Kindergarten Review," writes of the "History of Education in the Training School." "Early American Bookbinding" is discussed by W. L. Andrews in the "Bookman." I. A. Hourwich in the "Journal of Political Economy" writes of "Production and Consumption of the Precious Metals." "Leslie's Monthly" contains an interesting paper on the "Production of Beef" by E. Mayo. "Mineral Resources of British Columbia" are described by W. M. Brewer in the "Engineering Magazine," and in the same periodical J. F. Meigs discusses "Ordnance Engineering as a Mechanical Industry." In the "World's Work" F. Matthews writes of the "New York Chamber of Commerce," and in the same periodical appears a paper on "Life Insurance Companies and How They Use Their Enormous Surplus." In the "School Review," of Chicago, appears a well-written paper by C. W. Irish on "Commercial Studies in the High School." In "Popular Astronomy," a magazine published at Northfield, Minn., J. Morrison tells us about the "Source and Maintenance of Solar Energy." In the "Engineering Magazine" W. H. Booth writes of "The Draughtmen in the Workshop." In "Gunton's Magazine," H. W. Wilber presents a paper on the "Conditions Which Affect Beef Prices." In the "Overland Monthly," A. Inkersley describes the "Log Rafts of the Pacific." In "Munsey's" F. C. Perkins writes of "Coaling Warships at Sea." In the "Overland," also, Carrie Williams writes of "Silk Culture in California." "Foundations of the American Iron Industry" is the title of A. Brown's article in the "Engineering Magazine." In "Pearson's," G. Kobbe tells the "Story of New York City." In the "World's Work," J. McDowell describes "The Life of a Coal Miner." Our renowned friend, R. P. Hobson, in the "North American Review" has a paper on "America, Mistress of the Seas." In "Gunton's Magazine," W. G. Davis gives a "Statistical View of American Cities." "Limits of Electrical Power Transmission" are written about by A. D. Adams, whose paper appears in the "Engineering Magazine." In "Cassier's Magazine," H. W. Howe presents "Progress in Iron and Steel Metallurgy." In the "Atlantic," Edward Atkinson discusses "Commercialism."
"Commercialism."

In the foreign magazines appear the following articles: "Paradox of the English Business Man," by R. E. Vernede, in "MacMillan's Magazine"; "Iron Mines on Lake Superior," by W. S. Harwood, in the "Pall Mall Magazine"; "Chicory Cultivation in Belgium," by J. E. Whitby, in "Chambers' Journal," Edinburgh; "The American Industrial Peril," by C. C. Townsend, in the "Contemporary Review"; "Fire Risks Resulting From Electricity," by A. T. Stewart, in "Chambers' Magazine"; "Tooled Book Bindings," in the "Art Journal," of London; "Book Illustration," by E. F. Brewtnall and L. F. Day in the same publication; in the "Magazine of Art," London, is a paper by W. S. Sparrow on the "Leek School of Embroidery and Its Work"; in the "Gentlemen's Magazine," of London, the second paper dealing with the "Life of Phineas Petts, Naval Constructor," by E. W. Williams, appears; in the "Revue de Deux Mondes," of Paris, is an article on "Coal Mines" by C. Benoist; in the "Deutsche Revue" of Stuttgart, F. Lampe has a paper on "Germany and the Panama Canal."

Farming, Forestry, Etc.

E. F. Cook in the "Popular Science Monthly" has a paper on the "American Origin of Agriculture." In the "Journal of Political Economy" is an anonymous paper on the "Prosperity of Agriculture." Alice J. Graveson in the "Leisure Hour" writes of the "Day Harvest in the High Alps."

Architecture and Building.

Articles on architecture and buildings have been rather numerous. Among those published in the magazines are the following: "The Flat Iron, or Fuller Building of New York City" is described in the "Architectural Record." In the same periodical G. A. F. Middleton has a paper on "English Farmsteads." P. J. Henrick in the "Atlantic Monthly" tells of the "Limitations to the Production of Sky Scrapers." "Landscape Architecture" is the title of a paper in the "Art Interchange." In "Munsey's" F. D. Ardnett writes of "Doorways of New York."

Banking and Finance.

Among the papers dealing with financial subjects are the following: "Recent Developments in Finance," by A. D. Noyes, in the "Forum"; "Currency: Circulating Medium During the Civil War," by W. C. Mitchell, in the "Journal of Political Economy"; J. L. Laughlin in the same periodical has an article on "Prices and the International Movement of Specie."

The "Banker's Magazine," of London, contains two interesting financial papers, one on "The Amount of Gold in the World," and the other on the "American Monetary Position."

Capital and Labor.

As we have stated, articles on social questions are many. Among them we have noted:

"Labor Unions Restrictions of Industry," by M. G. Cunniff, in the "World's Work"; "A Fixed Wage—Is It Just?" by G. Maxwell in the same periodical, and one more in this interesting magazine, namely, a paper on the "National Negro Business League," by Booker T. Washington. In "McClure's," R. M. Easley writes of "Organized Labor, What It has Learned." In the "National Magazine," J. B. Clark writes of the "Latest Phase of the Trust Problem." In the "Arena" G. F. Washburn has a paper on the "Trust Problem and How to Meet It Through Co-operation." In the same magazine, Leonora B. Ellis writes of the "Movement to Restrict Child Labor," and in this periodical also W. E. Copeland has a paper on "Co-operative Brotherhood." In the new "Church Review" Lydia F. Dickinson discusses "Ethics of Pecuniary Dependence." In the "North American Review," R. E. Van Cortlandt presents "Social Conditions and Business Success." In the "Green Bag," H. E. Montgomery discusses the "Control of Trusts." In the "Methodist Review," "Economic Theory of Wages" is treated of by F. W. Moore. "Conciliation in Labor Disputes" is the title of W. F. Clowes' paper in the "Anglo-American Magazine." In "Scribner's," W. A. Wyckoff has the second in his series of articles about "London Wage Earners."

In the foreign publications the following articles are specially interesting: "Accidents to Workingmen," by E. van der Smissen, in the "Revue Generale," Brussels; "Labor Organization in the United States," by C. D. Wright, in the "Contemporary Review," and the "Influence of Trusts and Monopolies on the Market," by C. Cornelisse, in the "Revue Socialistic."

Photography.

The articles on photography, while not any more numerous than usual, have been scattered through many magazines. In "Wilson's Photographic Magazine" appear four papers, the first being "Practical Points on Back-Grounds"; second, "Telephotography"; the third, "Photographers' Association of America," and the fourth, "Copying Daguerreotypes," by J. A. Tennant. In "Camera and Dark Room," W. Ide has a very interesting paper on "Portraiture at Home." F. Voiter writes of "Four Tray Developments," and B. D. Underhill discusses "Portraiture and Copying by Lamplight." J. Haddon also has a paper in this magazine dealing with the "Ozotype." In the "Overland Monthly" are three papers on photography: W. E. Dassonbille writes of "Individuality in Photography"; W. N. Brannan presents a paper on "Scientific and Freak Photography," and M. Backus discusses learnedly "Expert Photography as Applied to Forgery." In the "Century," A. Steiglitz has an article on "Modern Pictorial Photography," and in the "Art Amateur" E. Luchesi writes "How to Make Sensitized Postal Cards." In "Blackwell's Magazine," of Edinburgh, "The Artist and the Camera" appears.

Prominent Men.

The only article dealing with prominent business men in the magazines for the past month was that by J. H. Bridge, in the "Cosmopolitan." Mr. Bridge writes of "Henry Clay Frick."

Transportation.

The locomotive, the steamboat and the motor-car come in for their usual share of attention. In the "Annals of the American Academy of Political and Social Science," H. A. Millis presents a paper on the "Present Street Railway Situation in Chicago." A. Ruhl, in the "Century," writes very entertainingly on the "Building of the New York Subway," and in the same publication F. W. Skinner presents a paper on the "Difficult Engineering in the Subway." In the "National Magazine," W. A. Bancroft writes of "Street Railways and the Public." "Ocean Steamships" is the title of L. Perry's article in the "World's Work." In the "Engineering Magazine," the "Lighting of Railway Trains in Europe" is described by G. Guerne. J. F. Flannery writes about "Liquid Fuel for Ships" in "Cassier's Magazine." In the same magazine the "Costs of Electric Power Transmission," by A. D. Adams, appears. An interesting article is that of W. Ogden, in "Everybody's," on "Old Steamboat Days on the Missouri." "Twentieth Century Types of Ship Building" is the title of a paper in the "American Review of Reviews."

Correspondence

Cartoons and Comments.

From R. L. L., New York.

I desire to refer to one feature in Commerce, Accounts & Finance which perhaps would improve the paper by its omission. I refer to the cartoons. Others besides myself have felt that it would be possible to use the space which they now occupy to much better advantage. I will suggest a substitute: Why not take up the first section of the C. P. A. examination questions each month and have them answered by members of your staff or other leaders in the profession? Of course, it would be necessary to disclaim any responsibility, and I believe your readers would accept the matter in the spirit given. Such a scheme would go through the eight numbers and the remaining four could be employed equally as well in some other direction.

I hardly believe this proposition is new to you, but in the position of an accounting student now and having been a casual reader of the journal since its beginning, I can speak of the appreciation of at least one for this valuable feature.

NOTE.—We fear that this correspondent does not appreciate the appearance in these columns of business in cartoons and comments to the extent that many others do as indicated by various complimentary notices which we have received. It would be hard indeed to publish a journal to meet the wants of everybody at all times, and accordingly there is left before the editor the necessity of meeting the views of as many of his readers as possible.

It is not a new suggestion to us to print the examination questions of the C. P. A. Board and discuss them. We have attempted to do this once or twice, but have failed to realize our expectations in various details, and therefore in a measure have dropped the matter. As a fac , in a great many instances the questions are nonsensical. In some cases they are trick problems, and we could hardly discuss them before a miscellaneous audience in a way to do the general cause of education any good. This said, however, we may mention that we have a series of questions relating to accounting which we expect to publish in the near future and which perhaps would be of some assistance to this student and others.

Position of the Bookkeeper.

From J. C. E., New York.

Reading from time to time the very able articles which appear in Commerce, Accounts & Finance on the profession of Accounting, its past, present and future, I have been struck by a total absence of consideration for the claims of the professional bookkeeper, "the man with the hoe," so to speak, who does the labor while others theorize and perform experiments.

So far as I have been able to ascertain from the publications of the New York University, the honors and titles awarded by the School of Commerce, Accounts and Finance are only available to inexperienced young men, unhampered by responsibilities or either family ties or onerous business duties, whose qualifications have been the ability to plank down a one-hundred dollar bill and the leisure to devote their afternoons to theoretical studies in the School of Commerce, Accounts and Finance. Please do not take it that I am sneering at the theory of accounts, but where, may I ask, do I, the professional bookkeeper, with a record of twenty-five years of English and American accounting, where do I come in on this scheme, by which is denied the honors of my calling and the goal of my ambition to all but inexperienced and impractical college boys?

I say the honors of my calling, for twist and turn it how you will, the C. P. A. was born and nurtured on the office stool of a common bookkeeper. Without the practical experience that begot it, the title, in nine cases out of ten, will most likely be awarded to brainless memorizers, fresh from the hands of the professional grinder. Has the professional bookkeeper no place in the economy? I refer to myself, the man who exists now at the present moment, the man they are shutting the gate on, not the man of the future.

ANSWER.—Our correspondent encloses a very handsomely engraved card. Along the center of the card appears his name. At the lower right-hand corner is the name of the business with which he is connected, while conspicuously in the lower left-hand corner is, not bookkeeper, but accountant. We ask, paraphrasing his own language, "where, oh where, is the bookkeeper?" Evidently he is ashamed of the word bookkeeper and prefers to hide behind the title accountant.

There are several points in our correspondent's letter to which replies should be especially made. As to the School of Commerce, Accounts and Finance of the New York University being patronized solely by inexperienced young men, unhampered by responsibilities, etc., it should be noted that those who so far have taken the course offered are quite the contrary from inexperienced young men. They are men employed in the daytime, many of them in responsible positions, some perhaps as bookkeepers, and quite a number of them as assistant accountants in professional accountants' offices. Far from being college-bred men, cramming for a degree, they are practical men endeavoring to improve their equipment for their chosen calling.

It would be as well for our correspondent to ask with respect to the American Society of Mechanical Engineers, where is the man with the shovel and pick, who dug the tunnel, who did all the hard work? Why should he not be honored instead of the professional engineer? The answer to this question would be nothing more than a laugh.

Bookkeepers we must have, and men who are content to be bookkeepers will be bookkeepers. Accountants we must have, and some bookkeepers rise above their position on the office stool and reach the dignity of accountants. Some accountants are made by the drill and discipline of bookkeeping in the office. Other accountants acquire their skill in a professional way by careful training in the responsibilities of accountancy. It goes without saying that every accountant must understand bookkeeping, but it does not follow that even the best bookkeepers are accountants. There is a sharp line between bookkeeping and accountancy, and as time goes on in business this is being more and more recognized.

Among intelligent bookkeepers, go where you will, you will find men who are earnestly striving to reach beyond their present positions. You will find bookkeepers who are ambitious to become accountants, bookkeepers who are studying accountancy, bookkeepers who recognize that in bookkeeping there is only what may be termed a manual trade, while in accounting there is something over, above and beyond mere manual work.

Taking our correspondent's letter just as it reaches us, we are justified in assuming that he has no ambition to become an accountant, but is quarreling with fate that the bookkeeper is not loaded with accounting honors. If that be his position, then there is no answer to make him, except to say that he is barking up the wrong tree.

BRIEF MENTION.

THE AUTUMN RAINS make us think of umbrellas, and in this connection the attractive circular sent out by Hermon August, of 428-430-432 Broadway makes interesting reading. Mr. August manufactures umbrellas, and in his circular a handsome young lady is pictured holding aloft one of this season's styles in those useful articles. In the circular it is stated that every umbrella from the August factory has those little touches of superiority which give the umbrella department a reputation. It is the "Riverside" umbrella that Mr. August manufactures.

THE PEN CATALOGUE of Joseph Gillott & Son is out, and Henry Hoe, sole agent for J. Gillott & Son, whose office is at 91 John street, New York, is making a specialty of the sale of these pens. In the catalogue are wood cuts of pens of all sizes, shapes and descriptions, fine pens, coarse pens, stub pens, oblique pens, pens with tilted tips and the so-called "crow quill" which has a point so fine that the lines it makes look like hairs. Any one needing pens should send to Mr. Hoe for this catalogue.

THE GUNNING SEASON is upon us, and Mr. George P. Finnigan, proprietor of the Finnigan Lodge, at Greene, N. Y., is sending out circulars setting forth the attractions of this lodge as a home for sportsmen during the woodcock and partridge season. The circular is illustrated with a large half-tone photograph of the lodge and a portrait of Mr. Finnigan and two of his dogs. It is stated that the lodge is in the very heart of a 100,000 acres of the best woodcock and partridge cover in America, and that about 2,000 of these birds were killed in that vicinity last year. Mr. Finnigan furnishes horses, wagons, guides and dogs to those who patronize his house.

AMONG THE MANY CATALOGUES of artists' materials sent out by dealers in these specialties, that of F. W. Devoe & C. T. Raynolds Company, with offices at Fulton and William streets, New York, and 176 Randolph street, Chicago, is notable. Tre catalogue is a copiously illustrated book of 110 pages, tastefully bound in grey-blue paper. In the catalogue are pictures and price lists of oil and water color paints, easels, campstools, brushes, burnishers, china kilns, ink bottles, drawing utensils and the like. There is an index at the back and the prices of each article in its various sizes are printed below the illustrations. The book is a good example of what a catalogue should be.

S. ROEBUCK & COMPANY, with offices at 172 Fulton street, New York City, are advertising Roebuck's Elastic Weather Strips. These strips, so the company's circular declares, are warranted when properly applied, to exclude cold, wind, snow, rain or dust from rooms in all sorts of buildings.

SOME BEAUTIFUL ADVERTISING MATTER comes from the Dennison Manufacturing Company, whose offices are in Philadelphia, Boston, New York, Chicago, Cincinnati and St. Louis, setting forth the merits of the Dennison Crepe paper. One booklet, beautifully illustrated in half-tone and colors, explains how the crepe paper may be used for show window and interior decorations. Many fine half-tone pictures of show windows decorated with the paper are displayed in the pages of the booklet, and it is really surprising to see into how many shapes, ornamental and beautiful, the various colored papers may be cut and twisted. An office interior is shown in which the wall decorations, portieres, ceiling panels, and even the sofa pillows are made of this paper. Another handsome booklet explains how the crepe paper may be used for table decorations; fine half-tones accompany the text. Both of these Dennison booklets are splendid examples of up-to-date advertising in which the sparing of expense has been of secondary importance compared with the obtaining of the effect desired.

THE STANDARD OIL COMPANY is sending out to dealers in stoves and to hardware dealers in general a little folder advertising the Perfection Oil Heaters, which are made in a variety of styles and sold at various prices. The Perfection Heaters appear to be beautiful little stoves, and, as most people know from experience, an oil heater in the season when furnace fires are too warm and no fires at all are not warm enough, is a great convenience.

ASBESTOS HAS BEEN PUT to a number of practical purposes the last ten years, and the asbestos and magnesia products manufactured by the H. W. Johns-Manville Company are tastefully advertised in the folders sent out by that house. The Company's main offices are at 100 William street, New York, although there are salesrooms in almost all of the large cities of the country. The folders the Asbestos Fire Felt Pipe Covering. This Fire Felt is a fabric of fibrous asbestos, and is made in cylindrical sections for pipes, sheets for boilers and rolls for heaters. The prices of various sizes of pipe covers are quoted in this folder, which is very tastefully printed. In another small sheet issued by this Company the Mobiline Sheet Packing for gas and gasoline engines is advertised. The Company also manufactures roofing and building materials of asbestos, fire-proofing cements and all sorts of asbestos products.

A VERY BEAUTIFUL BOOK, advertising the Snappa camera, has been sent us by the Rochester Optical and Camera Company, of Rochester, N. Y. Most camera literature is good, but this seems to us to be especially fine, being beautifully printed upon good paper and having a very attractive cover design. There are many illustrations, most of them being reproductions of photographs taken by the Snappa. They are printed in tints, and each page of the booklet is surrounded by an ornamental border in color. Altogether, the Rochester Optical and Camera Company has reason to be proud of its advertising literature, and the Snappa booklet should be a strong factor in selling Snappa cameras.

THE BOOK OF INSTRUCTIONS for the use of writers operating the Columbia Bar-Lock Typewriter has come to our desk. While not an elaborately printed affair, yet it describes in what seems to be clear and business fashion the method of operating the Bar-Lock machine. It is illustrated with woodcuts of various parts of the typewriter.

THE BAUSCH & LOMB OPTICAL COMPANY, of Rochester, have offered $3,000 in awards for the best photographs taken by photographers using the company's lenses and shutters. The particulars of this competition, which closes January 1, 1903, are given in a booklet, which may be obtained by sending one's name and address, accompanied by a stamp, to Hastings & Miller, 118 Nassau street, New York. This booklet is well printed and is extremely well written, evidently by some one used to such work. All amateur photographers should be interested in a contest of this kind, and therefore we recommend that they send for the booklet.

"FIREFLY PENS," so says a leaflet that has come to our desk, "are made of a new incorrodible metal as flexible as gold. They are oblique pointed, and are especially adapted for rapid writing." The pens are manufactured by Ormiston & Glass, Limited, London, England, but the sole manufacturers for the United States are Henry Bainbridge & Co., 99 William street, New York City.

MANUFACTURING COST — HOW TO OBTAIN IT—We are indebted to E. J. Forney, of the North Carolina State Normal and Industrial College, Greensboro, N. C., for a copy of a little pamphlet which he has recently issued entitled "The Manufacturing Cost—How to Obtain It." It is a book of only twenty pages, and yet is replete with information of the greatest importance to manufacturers everywhere. In the letter accompanying the pamphlet the author says: "I have been a student of yours (Commerce, Accounts & Finance), as you will see, and I take this opportunity to say that the benefit to me of the paper has been incalculable. It strikes directly at the practical—the thing we need. The paper has not covered the entire field. Therefore you will probably be interested in some of my details." The author takes up first producing one line of goods and discusses the accounts under such heads as raw material, supplies, labor, fuel, insurance, taxes, non-producing labor, impairment and betterments. Incidentally he brings in four-week loss and gain, dividing the business year into thirteen periods of four weeks each. Following this he takes up the question of making two or more lines of goods. The text is supplemented by various forms, including a "material ticket," "workmen's time ticket," "assembling ticket," etc.

Correspondence School of Business Organization and Administration

"Accounting is the Vital Element of Business"

In the November issue of COMMERCE, ACCOUNTS & FINANCE we presented a general announcement of the CORRESPONDENCE SCHOOL OF BUSINESS ORGANIZATION AND ADMINISTRATION. At this time we shall give particulars concerning some of the lesson courses.

The instruction in advanced lines is made specific. Accounting is the foundation of everything done, but instead of accounting being taught in the abstract, it is taught in the applied sense. The student elects the line in which he desires to be instructed and receives instruction in that line with the illustrations limited to the specialty.

1.—Machine Shop With Foundry. $100.

In this case the student is supposed to have some machine shop and foundry in mind. If he has the run of the office of such an institution, so much the better. His instruction commences with the charting of the accounts, and is continued, with full explanation of the details which go to make up the accounts. The entering of orders, the analysis of orders, the conveyance of the order to the foreman or superintendent, are each described. Incidentally the methods of handling cash, including petty cash and the bank account, are worked out in all necessary detail. Items in suspense, matters in reserve, and the handling of the different accounts composing the Balance Sheet Ledger are carefully exploited.

After the accounting foundation has been thus broadly laid, the question of the business organization and administration of the shop is undertaken. Various examples are presented, ranging from a very small shop to one of considerable size. The question of business matters as distinct and different from those of shop details is presented, and the relation of one department to another is carefully discussed. The question of a code for managing and operating these several divisions is introduced and illustrated.

2.—Cotton Mill Work. $100.

This subject is intended to cover textiles in general. The accounting foundation is laid broad and deep, covering everything from entering the order and the purchase of material, together with the time keeping and payment of employees, to the final adjustments in the balance sheet. All details are gone over carefully.

On the accounting foundation thus established there is then introduced the question of general organization at the mill, including the business head (president or treasurer as the case may be), the superintendent, the foreman, the overseers. The arrangement of the offices, the duties assigned to each of the occupants thereof, the correspondence, and all other details are carefully gone over.

If the student has the run of a cotton mill or other textile institution, he is encouraged to bring into his work illustrations derived from the actual practice of the establishment under view. His instruction will be so complete as to enable him to take charge of the work and carry it through.

4.—Department Store. $100.

In no line of business is proper organization and efficient administration more necessary than in the department store. In no branch of merchandising does the going balance sheet and profit and loss statement develop to better advantage than in this. There is perhaps no line of business extending more rapidly throughout the country than the department store.

In this course, as in others, the student at the outset is drilled in the accounting and then upon the foundation so laid is given instruction in the matter of arrangement and management.

The accounting taught is made to include every ticket and slip, no matter how insignificant, and the details are so handled that there is no rewriting or copying. The best use of modern devices for economizing labor is carefully pointed out, and the results are displayed in the balance sheet ledger and profit and loss statement, which in this case are made to give their results daily. The margins of profit in the department store are not large. They frequently depend upon the cashing of bills. All these matters are discussed in exhaustive detail.

11.—General Manufacturing. $100.

The student in this course, as well as in others, is drilled first in the principles and practice of the accounts, that which is to be accomplished in this direction being first worked out in chart form.

After the accounting has been thoroughly covered, there is taken up the general question of the purchase of supplies, the care of supplies, the entry of orders in the factory, the relationship of the superintendent to the general office, the relationship of the foreman to the superintendent, with illustrations and provisions for taking care of these several functions.

Where the student has access to a factory, he is encouraged to bring into the work practical illustrations drawn from the methods under view, and at completion he is left in such shape as to be competent to administer the

[res]ponsibilities of the es[tablishm]ent, or to introduce im[provem]ents in routine in different [depart]ments as circumstances permit.

[H.]—Installment Merchandising. $100.

Special interest attaches to the sale of goods upon the installment plan, involving as it does various principles in accounting and various methods in business management not current outside of this division of trade. The student in this course is carefully grounded in the principles of accounts, with special application to this branch of business, and upon this foundation the peculiar details of the business in hand are explained and illustrated. The merchandise account, the cost of goods contrasted with the selling price, the reserves as against excess commissions and returns or countermands, and various other features are carefully illustrated and impressed.

In the end the student is left competent to engage in any division of the business, to organize the accounts of such a business, to serve as a superintendent of such a business, or to reconstruct and simplify various details of establishments in this line.

Preparatory Courses.

One of the greatest difficulties that we have encountered in the instruction that we have been giving in this line the last few years is the lack of thorough grounding in fundamental principles. We have been approached by those desiring instruction as accountants who were deficient in the elements of bookkeeping. We have been approached by those who desire to be drilled as secretaries and amanuenses, who were deficient in ordinary English. For this reason the preparatory courses mentioned in the announcement of this school have been most carefully prepared. They embrace:

A. English Grammar, Composition and Business Rhetoric $25
B. Business Correspondence $15
C. Shorthand and Typewriting $25
D. Commercial Geography.. $15
E. Financial and Commercial History $15
F. Business Arithmetic...... $15
G. Double Entry Bookkeeping $25
H. Commercial Law......... $25

We also arrange special courses in the light of particular requirements.

In each of these courses the student is given practical instruction from the outset. All that which is superfluous from the standpoint of every-day, hard-fisted business is relegated to the background, and only that is taught which is applicable to the requirements of business transactions. The illustrations employed are eminently practical and are derived from actual going business.

For further particulars address **ACCOUNT, AUDIT & ASSURANCE COMPANY, 25 Pine street, New York.**

PUBLIC ACCOUNTANTS.

Atlanta, Ga.—Ralph H. Brown, 804 Empire Building.
Boston, Mass.—Charles H. Fellows, 174 Summer; New England Audit Company, 45 Milk; J. S. Parsons, 214 Columbus Ave.
Brooklyn, N. Y.—Franklin Allen, Arbuckle Building, 371 Fulton.
Buffalo, N.Y.—W. G. Mowat, 831 Ellicott Square.
Chicago, Ill.—Haskins & Sells, 214 Dearborn.
Davenport, Ia.—J. C. Grabbe, McManus Building.
Detroit, Mich.—H. Naemansson, 496 Putnam Ave.
London, Canada.—Geo. F. Jewell, 361 Dundas.
Montreal, Canada.—George Gontheir, 11-17 Place D'Armes Hill.
New Bedford, Mass.—James L. Hathway, 72 Willis.
New Orleans, La.—P. W. Sherwood, 904 Howard Ave.
New York, N. Y.—Patterson, Teele & Dennis, 30 Broad; Haskins & Sells, 30 Broad; Account, Audit and Assurance Company, 25 Pine; Leon Brummer, 7 Pine; H. F. Searle, 45 Broadway; Hart Bros., Tibbits, Heiron & Co., 11 Broadway; Franklin Allen, Silk Exchange Building, Broadway.
Philadelphia, Pa.—Francis & Sterrett, Penn Mutual Building; Peter Ballingall, German-American Building; Charles W. Thomas, 409 Lippincott Building; Alfred L. Sellers, 1001 Chestnut.
Pittsburgh, Pa.—John Vaughan, 5520 Claybourne; George W. Wood & Co., 341 Fourth Ave.
Providence, R. I.—George R. Allen, 29 Weybosset.
San Francisco, Cal.—Charles L. Lutgen, 218 California; Lester Herrick, 405 Montgomery.
Toronto, Canada.—F. H. Kidd, Bank of Commerce Building.
Windsor, Canada.—F. H. Macpherson, 16 Sandwich, East.
Winnipeg, Canada.—Peter Thornton, 343 Main.

UNIVERSITY TRAINING

For Business

ACCOUNTING
BANKING
BROKERAGE

School of Comerce, Accounts and Finance.
Evening Sessions.
New York University, Washington Square, N. Y. City.

FALL TERM OPENS OCT. 1.

W. G. Mowat
Public Accountant
831 Ellicott Sq., Buffalo, N. Y.

Leon Brummer, C. P. A.
Public Accountant and Auditor,
7 Pine Street, New York, N. Y.

About a Pay Roll which proves itself, corrects all mistakes in figuring, divides up Pay Roll into several amounts needed to pay each person.

But let us send you a sample leaf, with circular, which tells the whole story.

BARLOW BROS., Grand Rapids, Mich.

Use any pen and your own stationery. If your stationer does not keep it, write for free specimen of work. Beware of infringements. Address Dept.

Pen-Carbon Manifold Co., 145-7-9 Centre St., New York.

HAVE YOU READ

The Kite Trust?

If not, why not? Send $1.50 for a copy to

Commerce, Accounts & Finance,
25 Pine street, New York City.

BOOKS OF INTEREST TO BUSINESS MEN.

The A B C of Banks and Banking. —By George M. Coffin. 6¾ x 5 inches; 137 pages. Bound in cloth. Back title gilt. Price, $1.25.

This handy little volume is exactly what its name implies; that is, a presentation of the principles underlying banking in the United States. The author in his preface says that it is designed to appeal to the reader outside as well as inside of a bank. It is by no means the last word or every word about banking. It may be said that it is a primer covering a field that has hitherto been somewhat neglected. The chapter heads are as follows: Banking in General, Various Kinds of Banking, Capital Stock, Shareholders' Rights and Liabilities, Undivided Profits, Dividends and Surplus, Deposits, Checks, Lawful Money Reserve, Issuing Bank Notes, Borrowing Money, Loans and Discounts, Exchanges, Collections, Letters of Credit, Bonds, Mortgages and Stocks, Bank Reports, Examinations, Directors, Executive Officers—Their Powers and Duties, Internal Administration and Bookkeeping, and other suggestions.

Business Law.—By Alonzo R. Weed, L. L. B., of the Boston Bar. 6 x 9¼ inches; 172 pages. Bound in cloth. Cover and back title red. Price, $1.25.

Mr. Weed calls his book "a manual for schools and colleges and for every day use." The titles of the chapters are as follows: Contracts, Principal and Agent, Partnerships, Sales of Personal Property, Bailments and Common Carriers, Negotiable Paper, Deeds, Mortgages and Leases, Collection Laws, Written Rates of Interest, Insurance, Patent Rights, Trade Marks and Copyrights, etc.

The author does not waste words, and yet treats his subjects clearly and comprehensively. In short, he gives the law without the addition of wordy "trimmings."

Introduction to the Study of Economics.—By Charles Jesse Bullock, Ph. D. 7¾ x 5¼ inches. 581 pages. Bound in cloth. Cover and back title gilt. Price, $1.25.

This book, the author says, is designed as an introductive text book of economic science. Throughout the volume economics are discussed with special reference to American conditions, and their workings are illustrated by frequent allusions to American experience. There are chapters on the Consumption of Wealth, the Theory of Exchange, the Development of Metallic Money, Money and Credit, and the like.

Political Economy of Humanism.—By Henry Wood. 7¾ x 5¼ inches; 320 pages. Bound in cloth. Cover and back title gilt. Price, $1.25.

Mr. Wood is well known as a writer on various economic subjects, and this book contains a series of able treatises, written in his usual vein, on the relation of the employer to the employed, and the phases of the industrial question and their relation to socialism. Among the questions considered and handled in a conservative spirit and with much common sense, are the following: Supply and Demand, the Law of Competition, Labor and Production, Combinations of Capital, Combinations of Labor, Employers and Profit Sharing, the Obligations and Privileges of Employees, the Unequal Distribution of Wealth, Money and Coinage, Tariffs and Protection, Industrial Education and Gold Production and Values.

The Kite Trust. A Romance of Wealth.—By Lebbeus Harding Rogers. 7¾ x 5½ inches; 475 pages. Illustrated. Price, $1.50.

This is a treatise or series of treatises on economic subjects in the guise of a story. The tale itself concerns three American boys, and is very interesting as well as instructive. The trust idea is explained and an explanation of banking is given. The greenback is dealt with, as are also Wall street and stock speculation.

Business Law.—By Thomas Raeburn White, B. L., L. L. B. 5 x 7½ inches; 323 pages. Bound in cloth. Back title gilt. Price, $1.50.

This is a neat, compact and handy book of business for law for the use of students and business men. Among the subjects treated are Contracts, Sales, Partnerships, Corporations, Negotiable Paper and the like. The author's language is plain, and is understandable by any one having no previous knowledge of law. The book's clearness on the essential points of ordinary law should recommend it as a business book for the plain business man who has no time in which to consult a law library.

The Phonographic Dictionary and Phrase Book.—By Benn Pitman and Jerome B. Howard. 5½ x 8 inches; 552 pages. Bound in cloth. Cover title and back title gilt. Price, $3.

This book is the most elaborate shorthand dictionary yet published, with the characters in fac-simile. It contains over 120,000 words, and for every one of these words there is a corresponding sign in the Benn Pitman system of shorthand. To the reporter, office or court stenographer, or any one writing the Benn Pitman system of shorthand, the book is invaluable. It is well made, tastefully bound, and is printed on a good quality of paper in clean, plain type.

Grace's Handy Book for Making Rapid Calculations. 8¼ x 5¼ inches. Bound in cloth. 65 pages. Title printed in silver. Price, $1.

The full title ofthis book is "Merchants', Bankers' and Brokers' Handy Book for Making Rapid Calculations in all Branches of Commercial Requirements, Weights, Measures and Moneys." The volume contains a series of tables for calculating the price of wheat, corn and oat bushels in decimals, for converting cubic meters to cubic feet and cubic feet to meters, meters to lineal yards, superficial feet or square feet to cubic feet, decimal tons to avoirdupois pounds, and the like. To the busy office man who has a great deal of calculating to do, and particularly to the clerk in an export house whose work it is to reckon in United States money the amounts named in foreign invoices, these tables should be very valuable. They are quite complete, and undoubtedly their use will save time.

The Lawrence System of Vocal and Physical Expression.—By Edwin Gordon Lawrence. 4¾ x 6 inches; 128 pages. Bound in cloth. Cover title and back title gilt. Price, $1.

The author says in the preface of this little book that his [illegible] been to place in the hands of actors and public speakers in a simple system of vocal and expression that will [illegible] clearly convey thought by word of mouth and emphasize it by the proper action. To the man of affairs who is called upon for a speech on any subject, and who knows what to say but does not know how to say it, this book will be a great help.

The Anatomy of a Railroad Report. —By Thomas F. Woodlock. 7 x 5¼ inches. 121 pages. Bound in cloth. Side and back titles gilt. Price, $1.

This little book is intended for the use of those people who, while interested in railroad investments, are wholly unacquainted with railroad accounts. The book is divided into two sections, the first being the Anatomy of the Railroad Report and the second being Ton-Mile Cost. It treats of phases of the railroad business in concise fashion, but thoroughly and accurately.

Any book in this list will be sent to any address in the United States, Canada or Mexico upon receipt of price. If there is some special book that you require we shall be pleased to hunt it up for you.

Address **Commerce, Accounts & Finance, 25 Pine street, New York City.**

A BUSINESS EDUCATION | FOR ...ONE... DOLLAR.

...THE PRACTICAL AGE...

A MONTHLY MAGAZINE full to the brim with helpful suggestions to young men and young women who are struggling successward.

THE BUSINESS HOUSE THAT JACK BUILT, an intensely interesting and highly instructive story of business life, and

APPLIED ENGLISH, an authority on writing and speaking the English language, which no young person can afford to be without, all for ONE DOLLAR.

If you have never seen THE PRACTICAL AGE, send for a free sample copy. Address,

THE PRACTICAL AGE,

Moline, Illinois.

PRENTISS CLOCKS.

SIX TIMES A YEAR

is all that is necessary to wind a Prentiss Clock. Why wind a clock every week when we can sell you one which will require winding but once in sixty days and will keep perfect time? Also Frying-pan, Program and Electrically synchronized clocks. Send for Catalogue No. 2C.

THE PRENTISS CLOCK IMPROVEMENT CO.,
Dept. 28, 49 Dey St., New York City

A New Work on Accounting

A MANUAL OF BOOKKEEPING

By J. THORNTON

THIS attractive volume, comprising over 500 pages, with numerous illustrations, is one of the clearest and most concise surveys of the principles of accounting which has recently appeared. While its illustrations are given in terms of English money the bookkeeping principles discussed are universal.

The work is divided into two leading parts, the first of which is "LAWS AND PRINCIPLES," and the second "APPLICATION."

LAWS AND PRINCIPLES

In the first part there are discussed the Principle of Exchanges, the Principle of Debit and Credit Accounts, the Principle of the Classification of Accounts, the Principle of Ledger Entries, the Principle of Proving, the Principle of Transfer from Preparatory to Final Record, and the Principle of Balancing and Closing the Ledger.

APPLICATION

Under the head of Application the following chapters are presented: Rules and Tools, What Capital Consists of, Capital in Cash, Capital in Bills, Capital in Debts, Capital in Goods, Fixed Capital, Profit and Loss, Capitalist's Accounts, Company Bookkeeping, Errors, and Non-Capitalistic Bookkeeping.

Several chapters are arranged in the form of lessons, following which are questions for class purposes, arranged in such a way, however, as not to detract in the least from the value of the book in the hands of the general reader. A comprehensive index, together with answers to exercises completes the work.

Price, $2.50.—Sent Postpaid to any address in the United States on receipt of price.

Address COMMERCE ACCOUNTS & FINANCE CO.

PUBLISHERS AND BOOKSELLERS - 25 PINE STREET, NEW YORK

BUSINESS NEEDS.

Advertisements under this head one cent a word each insertion.

LESSONS IN BOOKKEEPING.—A competent commercial teacher of long experience will give lessons in bookkeeping to a few pupils Wednesday and Friday evenings during the winter. Address, for terms, etc., "Teacher," care Commerce, Accounts & Finance.

DO YOU NEED BOOKS?—Old books, new books, second-hand books. Agent for subscription books, and dealer in old and new books. Ask me for prices on books you want before you buy elsewhere. Address, A. Cross, Commerce, Accounts & Finance.

LIVE MAN WANTED to solicit subscriptions for a high-class business journal. Liberal commission. Address, J. P. D., care Commerce, Accounts & Finance.

SEVEN SAFES LEFT.—Seven of those second-hand safes are left out of the fourteen that I advertised last month. Various sizes and makes. Prices astonishingly low. Address, "Safe," care Commerce, Accounts & Finance.

OFFICE AND BANK FITTINGS.—Having been connected with a large office furniture manufacturing company for years, I am now in business for myself. I can save you money on your office furniture, desks, chairs, counters and the like. Let me figure on the fittings for your new office. To fetch me, drop a line to "Oak," care Commerce, Accounts & Finance.

HAVE YOU NOW under consideration the issuing of any new bit of advertising matter? Such, for instance, as a little catalogue, booklet or folder, or a new circular to replace some former one not "up-to-date." If I have happened to diagnose your case correctly, why not write me, and if you have anything that you would like bettered, why not slip a copy of it in your letter to me? Address, F. Cook, care Commerce, Accounts & Finance.

SALESMAN WANTED.—We want to hire a man who knows the stationery, office file and binder business. We want to hire him to sell our binders, files and account books and we will pay a man who can really sell a good salary. Address, "Accounts," care Commerce, Accounts & Finance.

WHERE ARE YOU HAVING YOUR ENGRAVING DONE?—I haven't the largest plant in the world, but my machinery is of the newest and best and my workmen are skilled. Also, and this may interest you, my prices are away below the big fellows'. Give me a trial. Representative will call. Address, "Cuts," care Commerce, Accounts & Finance.

Some Men Pay $10,000 for an expert to manage their advertising. There are others who pay **$5.00** for an annual subscription to **Printers' Ink** and learn what all the advertisers are thinking about. But even these are not the extremes reached. There are men who lose over **$100,000** a year by doing neither one.

For sample copy send 10 cents to PRINTERS' INK, No. 10 Spruce St., New York City.

EVENING WORK WANTED.—An experienced bookkeeper, now employed by a large manufacturing house, will take extra work evenings, to be done either at home or at office of employer. Address, "Expert," care Commerce, Accounts & Finance.

OLD BOOKS ON ACCOUNTING SUBJECTS.—I want to know about any curious old books on accounting which you may wish to sell. I will pay liberal prices for such books if they are what I desire. Address "Librarian," care Commerce, Accounts & Finance.

PEN, INK AND PAPER.—I sell all three and I sell them cheaper than most dealers. If I have not what you want in my stock, I will get it for you. Let me make your account books. I make such books well and do not charge de luxe prices. Address, "Stationer," care Commerce, Accounts & Finance.

INVENTORY SHEETS

Stock Taking Made Easy

Simplify Your Methods! *Economize Your Work!*

OUR INVENTORY SHEETS

are now in general use by mercantile houses, as the employment of them provides the **simplest and most economical method of Taking Stock.**

As soon as a sheet (one or more) has been filled, it can be returned to the office for pricing and extensions.

The loose sheets are used temporarily in our **PATENT HOLDERS** with **Special Smooth Insides** for Inventory work.

When Inventory is finished, it is bound **Permanently** in our Patent Automatic Binder. As this Binder will hold some 1700 sheets, it can be used to retain the inventories of successive years.

PRICES	
100 Sheets, tableted	$ .75
300 Sheets, tableted	1.75
500 Sheets, tableted	2.75
1000 Sheets, tableted	5.25

PRICES	
Safety Holders, Size No. 2, each	$1.20
Eclipse Holders, Size No. 2, each	1.35
Automatic Binders, Size No 2, each	2.50

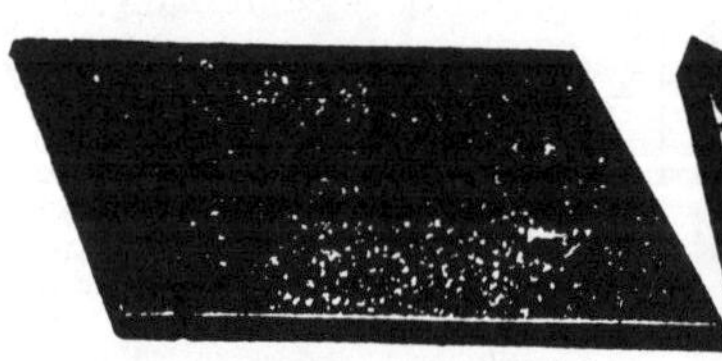

SAFETY HOLDER

HOLDS 1 TO 25 SHEETS

Finely Tempered Steel Spring, Nickel Plated.

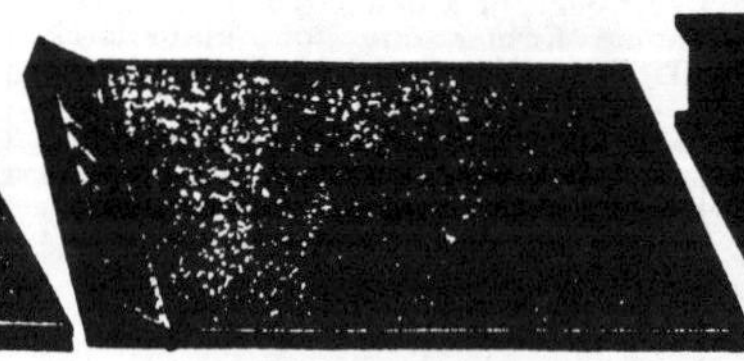

ECLIPSE HOLDER

HOLDS 1 TO 120 SHEETS

Finely Tempered Steel Spring, Nickel Plated.

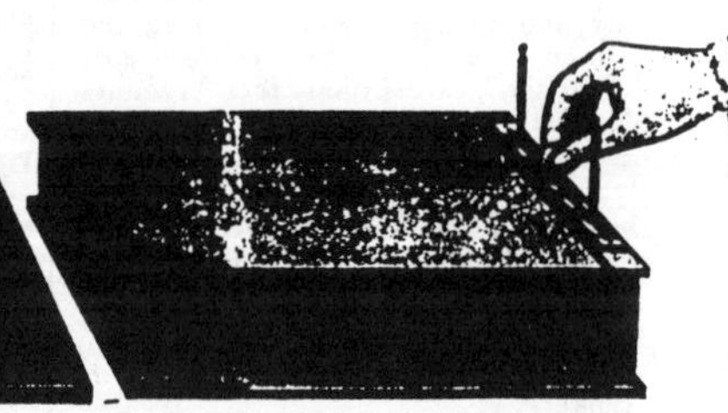

AUTOMATIC BINDER

MADE TO HOLD 100 to 1700 SHEETS

Correspondence solicited regarding, Order Blanks, Holders and Binders.

STATIONERY MANUFACTURING CO.

318 BROADWAY - - NEW YORK

Volume V
Nos. 1-4, January-April 1903

297013

ASTOR, LENOX AND TILDEN FOUNDATIONS.

COMMERCE ACCOUNTS & FINANCE

Volume 5 New York January 1903 Number 1

THE NEW YORK PUBLIC LIBRARY 297013 ASTOR, LENOX AND TILDEN FOUNDATIONS R 1904 L

CONTENTS.

Published Monthly by the Commerce Accounts & Finance Company Twenty-five Pine Street New York

ANNOUNCEMENT EXTRAORDINARY!

A LIBRARY OF PRACTICAL BOOKS FOR THE STUDENT, THE ACCOUNTANT AND THE BUSINESS MAN

What Shall be Its Name?

A COMPETITION WITH THE BOOKS FOR PRIZES

COMMERCE, ACCOUNTS & FINANCE has pleasure in announcing to its readers and to the business public in general that at great expense it has bought the manuscripts, titles and copyrights of the five volumes illustrated in the accompanying cut. It proposes to

Books Composing the (?) Library.

use them in furthering the interests of this periodical.

The books will be published one at a time, but our arrangements are so advanced that we feel warranted in promising the complete set in a reasonable length of time.

Each book is to be set from new type, illustrated by original engravings, printed on paper specially made for the purpose, and handsomely bound in cloth with gilt back and side titles. Each book will be upwards of 500 pages in extent, and nothing in the bookmaker's art will be spared to get them up in excellent shape, at once attractive to the eye and convenient for use.

PUBLICATION COMMITTEE.

The set of books will be produced under the direction of the following Publication Committee:

W. H. Grace, chairman, President Commerce, Accounts & Finance Company.

Friend Pitts, Jr., secretary, Treasurer Commerce, Accounts & Finance Company.

A. O. Kittredge, author, President Account, Audit & Assurance Company.

H. M. C. Vedder, Specialist in Accounting and Auditing.

George Young, Textile Accounting and Industrial Operations.

H. W. Courter, General Merchandise and Installment Accounts.

J. A. Cave, Manufacturing Accounts.

J. V. Palmer, Printers' and Publishers' Accounts.

C. H. Sumwalt, of the Correspondence School of Banking.

ADVISORY COUNCILS.

This committee will be supplemented by sub-committees or advisory councils on special topics, the chairman of each of which is a specialist in his own particular branch. These sub-committees will co-operate with the general committee by way of suggestions as to the manner of treating specific topics, the choice of illustration and matters of similar character.

WANTED—A NAME.

The set of books here announced will constitute a library desirable at once for the desk of the business man, the study table of the student and the shelf in reach of the bookkeeper and the clerk while engaged in their daily work. It will also be invaluable to the professional accountant, but **what shall it be called? By what name as a library shall it be introduced to the public?**

We want the most appropriate name as well as the most striking name for this library. It should be something that will give force and character to the several million copies of the announcement which we shall circulate. Who can suggest the right name for the purpose?

There is always wisdom in a multitude of councilors. Therefore, we constitute every one who reads this paragraph a member of our special council on names. Out of the multitude of suggestions thus to be offered we have reason to expect the right idea will come to the top. Just to make it interesting, we propose a friendly contest with prizes.

COMPETITION.

To the person suggesting the name that we finally adopt for this library, we will present a com-

plete set of the books (five volumes). The set so given shall be one of the first off the press and each volume will be properly inscribed over the autograph of the author. To each of ten others who suggest good names, the same being deemed the next best of those we receive, even though we are unable to make use of what they offer, we will give a single volume of the library similarly inscribed over the autograph of the author. Each successful contestant is to have the right of selection.

A subscription for one year to COMMERCE,

The First Volume of the Library to be Issued.

ACCOUNTS & FINANCE goes with each volume sent out as a prize.

This competition will close at 6 o'clock P. M., May 1, 1903.

All entries are to be addressed to LIBRARY NAME COMPETITION, care of COMMERCE, ACCOUNTS & FINANCE, 25 Pine street, New York.

Each competitor is privileged to make as many suggestions of names as he pleases, but only one prize will be awarded to any contestant.

The decision in this competition will be announced in COMMERCE, ACCOUNTS & FINANCE at as early a date as circumstances permit.

EXCLUSIVELY FOR SUBSCRIBERS TO COMMERCE, ACCOUNTS & FINANCE.

The books here announced will not be sold through the trade. The sale will be limited to the cash subscribers to COMMERCE, ACCOUNTS & FINANCE, or to put it otherwise, each volume of the set carries with it a yearly subscription to this periodical.

If you are already a subscriber to COMMERCE, ACCOUNTS & FINANCE, your subscription will be extended for one year for each volume that you purchase.

NO DISCOUNTS TO ANY ONE.

Books will not be sent out on any other terms than those quoted below. The only way to get an advantage in price is to order in advance of publication day.

PRICES.

Either volume, including therewith one yearly subscription to COMMERCE, ACCOUNTS & FINANCE, cash with order, $5.

The set of five volumes, including therewith five yearly subscriptions to COMMERCE, ACCOUNTS & FINANCE, or a single subscription for five years, cash with order, $25.

INSTALLMENT PAYMENTS.

Subscribers, with approved references, may order the set of five volumes at $30, payable $5 with order and the remainder in five monthly installments of $5 each, the title to the books remaining with the publishers until full payment has been made.

Nothing less than a whole set will be furnished on the installment plan.

ADVANCE ORDERS.

Orders in advance of publication will be accepted at the following specially reduced rates:

The set of five volumes, including five yearly subscriptions to COMMERCE, ACCOUNTS & FINANCE, or one subscription for five years, cash with order, $20. Single volumes, including the subscription as above, $4 each.

ORDER OF PUBLICATION.

The arrangement of the volumes in the illustration indicates the order in which they will be produced. "TOOLS OF BUSINESS" will be the first of the set to go to press, following which will be "ELEMENTS OF BOOKKEEPING," "BALANCE SHEET ACCOUNTING," "AUDITING," and "BUSINESS ORGANIZATION AND ADMINISTRATION," in the order named.

The date of publication cannot be named at this time, but the books will be pushed through as rapidly as circumstances make possible. The manuscript for the entire set is in a very forward condition at the present time.

NO ADVERTISING.

There will not be a line of advertising in any of the volumes from cover to cover. Manufacturers' cuts will not be used, but instead new engravings are being made throughout. On the other hand, provision is made, as indicated in the foregoing, for a copy of this periodical to go with each volume. Its advertising pages are open to the business world at reasonable rates, and afford an unequalled opportunity of reaching the very public the advertiser is after.

"TOOLS OF BUSINESS."

The first volume to be brought out as announced above will be "TOOLS OF BUSINESS." This name is to be construed liberally and taken to mean everything from a pen holder to a typewriter, from a chair to a desk and from a method of screening the office window to systems of heating and ventilation.

In this work the author takes up his subject analytically and presents one after another of the several subjects discussed in a most attractive fashion. The scheme of the book is a cyclopedia of office equipment, or a dictionary of those things which

every business man needs to know about in equipping and arranging his business office.

Typewriters, for example, are described analytically and critically. They are divided into classes according to the principles underlying their operation and after those principles have been fully explained, illustrations of different interpretations of those principles are brought forward. The differences between the leading typewriters is clearly defined and the advantages, as well as the disadvantages of some of the cheaper machines are fully set forth.

The office floor is carefully treated, the discussion extending from rugs and mats and carpets to the treatment of the wood of which the floor is composed.

Desks are discussed with respect to the conveniences which they offer, their size, the space occupied and the work to be done. Letter files and cabinets are correspondingly handled. In a similar manner blank books, like ledgers and journals, are discussed with respect to the ends to be accomplished and the materials of which they are composed. Card indexes, loose leaf ledgers, binders and other office appliances are similarly treated.

In future numbers of COMMERCE, ACCOUNTS & FINANCE we shall take pleasure in laying before our readers the personnel of the Sub-Committees or Councils upon whom the Publication Committee depends for advice with respect to details of arrangement, etc. We shall also present in the course of early numbers a complete outline of the contents of this volume.

Address all communications to

COMMERCE, ACCOUNTS & FINANCE COMPANY, 25 PINE STREET, NEW YORK.

BRIEF MENTION.

THE AMERICAN TYPE FOUNDERS' COMPANY are sending out some beautiful advertising literature. "The Bookman" is the title of a circular in magazine form, printed on fine paper and with a handsome cover. The Bookman is devoted to exploiting the various old style letter types manufactured by the American Type Founders' Company. Some of these types, as shown by the examples in the Bookman, are artistic in the extreme, printed as they are in colored inks with the nicest care in composition and press work. The examples shown are a delight to the eye. It seems to us that this publication must be the best sort of advertising, for it shows not only the styles of the artistic types, but demonstrates by fine printing the beautiful results that may be obtained by their use.

THERE ARE VARIOUS styles of patent binders in the market. One that has recently come to our notice is that advertised by the Barrett Bindery Company, of 180-182 Monroe street, Chicago, Ill. The "Emerson" binder is the name of the Barrett Company's product, and in their advertising matter they say that it holds papers in a vise and that they cannot be jerked out. The Barrett Company's advertisement also says that the Emerson binder has been greatly improved recently, that new patents have been allowed and that every purchaser gets his money's worth.

THE PERFECT SCRAPBOOK, the Perfect Bill File and the Perfect Pocket Wallet are advertised in the little folder sent out by Montross, Clarke & Emmons, of 51 Nassau street, New York City. The scrapbook appears, from the illustration, to contain on pockets, each page which, the circular says, are of double thickness of stout manila and designed to withstand hard use. The size of the page is said to be 9 x 11, and there are three pockets to each page, each pocket being 9 inches long and 3 inches deep. No paste is used, but the clippings are put in the various pockets of the scrapbook. The Perfect Wallet and Book File also contain pockets for the reception of clippings, letters or bills.

JANUARY IS THE SEASON when one turns over a new leaf and begins a new diary. The Tower Manufacturing and Novelty Company, of 306 Broadway, New York City, manufacture diaries of all kinds and descriptions. Their advertising literature calls attention to the fact that their diaries have a page for each day in the month and that their "Monthly Diaries" for 1903, which are sold in sets of twelve, have a book for each month of the year.

JAMES SHEA, STATIONER, PRINTER and engraver at 75 Nassau street, New York City, is sending out an attractive little book containing samples of typewriting papers. All colors and qualities of typewriting papers are shown in the little book, and from it a judicious selection may be made. Upon each page is printed the style number of the paper and the price per ream.

SEPARATE LEAF PRICE BOOKS are something new. They are made to open at the side or at the end, and each book is said to contain seventy-five white leaves and twenty-five buff index sheets. The white leaves may be removed, and when a supply is exhausted fillers containing a hundred more leaves may be substituted. Montross, Clarke & Emmons, of 51 Nassau street, New York City, are the manufacturers of these price books.

AMONG DUPLICATING MACHINES the Edison Mimeograph is well known. The A. B. Dick Company, of Chicago and New York, are the manufacturers of the Mimeograph and a variety of circulars from their office have reached our desk. The company manufacture the Edison Oscillating Mimeograph, which is a machine for rapid duplicating and which is claimed to be the best of its kind. Beside the Oscillating machine the A. B. Dick Company manufacture and sell the Diaphragm Mimeograph, a less expensive apparatus and which, although slower in its operations, is said to be very satisfactory. To those who intend purchasing a duplicating device we should think that the booklet called "The Little Red Book," published by A. B. Dick Company, would make interesting and profitable reading.

MOST OF THE LETTER PRESSES used in the offices of the country have the old-fashioned screw device. The Cabinet Letter Press Company, of Detroit, Mich., in their catalogue describe the "Giant" copy press, which works with a lever and, so the catalogue claims, puts from 350 to 400 pounds pressure on the copy book. There is a picture in the advertising matter sent out by the company showing a small child operating the lever of this "Giant" press. Beneath the picture is this legend, "Any child can pull a pound. That gives seventy-two pounds pressure on your letter-book if you use the "Giant."

IN CATALOGUE No. 2 sent out by the Joseph Dixon Crucible Company, of Jersey City, N. J., the Dixon stenographic pencil is advertised. This pencil, the catalogue says, is made in three grades of hardness or softness, and is round, light and does not fatigue the hand.

J. A. MIDDLETON WAS ELECTED assistant to the president at a recent meeting of the board of directors of the Lehigh Valley Railroad Company. Mr. Middleton's office will be at 26 Cortlandt street, New York City.

THE WATERMAN FOUNTAIN PEN COMPANY have been calling attention to their wares by some unique advertising. Some of this advertising is in the shape of handsomely illustrated posters and circulars. The company has been advertising for the Christmas holidays a certificate, which is a beautiful affair, printed, or, rather, engraved in four colors and gold. The certificates are intended to be given instead of the pen so that the recipient may afterwards call at the Waterman store and choose the pen he or she prefers. Of course, the certificates are not really engrossed by hand, but are fac-similes made by the engraving process from the original engrossed copy.

The Investigation and Audit of Trust Companies*

By A. O. KITTREDGE, C. P. A.

MODERN conditions demand regular and systematic investigation and report or audit in all divisions of business. The trust company, which, in the short time that it has been before the public, has been exempt from various rules, should be no exception in this regard.

Trust companies and banks are in the same general class, and in a sense the same business rules would apply to the two. Banks are systematically examined or audited under provisions of the law, and while trust companies are occasionally examined by representatives of the banking departments of the different states under which they are organized, at the same time regular and complete audits are with them the exception rather than the rule.

Banks, upon the basis of natural selection and long experience, have reached a basis that might be described as uniformity in accounting. That is, the features of their accounting systems are so much alike that the examination of one bank is a fair preliminary study for the examination of various other banks. On the other hand, trust companies are yet so new that in various directions their account-keeping is crude. Their methods, if not experimental, are yet in a condition not thoroughly worked out or reduced to definite form.

If any excuse were necessary for obtruding upon the attention of this assembly at this time some remarks about the investigation and audit of trust companies, the same is contained in the preceding remarks.

In every modern business venture or organization for business purposes a very considerable part of the undertaking rests upon the basis of credit and upon the intelligence or care with which its managers conduct the business. Accordingly, in the prospectus of various trust companies we find paraded at the head of the list, from twenty to twenty-five men who are the directors or trustees of the organization and whose high standing in the community it is supposed gives credit to the company with which they are connected.

The public does not stop to think that at best a very small number of men stand for the actual transactions and policy of a company doing business. Such, however, is the case, and the trustees, high-minded men as they very generally are, require the services of an expert examiner from time to time in order that they may know that those put in immediate charge of the affairs of the company are not mismanaging their trust. On the other hand, the stockholders and the public at large have rights likewise in this regard.

Scope of a Trust Company's Business.

A trust company may be described as a corporation authorized by law to undertake every kind of trustee work, and, in addition to it, to do a general banking and financial business. A trust company has a wider business scope than a bank. While it can furnish its customers with every facility which the bank can supply, it can render them a great many services which the safest and best equipped bank in the country cannot place at their disposal.

A bank cannot offer its customers the facilities which a trust company offers, because from the special character of its business and its close relation with trade, it has always been hedged around by law with restrictions deemed necessary in case of purely commercial undertakings.

Trust companies exemplify enlarged banking powers adapted to the ever growing requirements of modern business. They do not compete with nor usurp the places of banks, but in themselves use the banks, while with their transactions they go over and beyond anything for which banks were created.

The functions of a trust company are numerous and far reaching, comprising various matters from the management of estates to ordinary trusteeships, and from a banking department on the one hand to an underwriting syndicate on the other. They include, in addition to ordinary banking, the following among others: trustee under mortgages to secure bond issues; trustee for married women with respect to their separate property; guardian, receiver, or trustee of the estates of minors; executor or trustee under wills; committee of estates of lunatics, idiots and persons of unsound mind; administrator, trustee, guardian, executor, receiver, and assignee of insolvent estates; manager of estates of every kind during the temporary or permanent absence of the owners, or for persons advanced in years, or for persons wishing to place the care and management of their property in the hands of a capable agent; collection of rents, interest, dividends, etc.; registrar and transfer agent of the capital stock and bonds of corporations; general agent for non-residents and invalids; general agent for foreign municipalities, corporations, etc., for the transaction of approved financial business; the general execution of legal trusts, and many others both general and special.

Laws Under Which Trust Companies Exist.

Trust companies exist under and by virtue of state laws. The laws in the several states do not agree and some of them are more favorable to trust companies than others. All of them demand reports from the trust companies annually and in some cases more frequently. In most of the states there is provision for occasional examination of trust companies by representatives of the state banking department.

The official bank examinations by national bank examiners throughout the country are frequently characterized as being insufficient and in many cases unsatisfactory. The pay allotted to bank ex-

More Gateways than One.—New York Herald.

*Address delivered before the Trust Company Section of the American Bankers' Convention, New Orleans.

aminers is notoriously small and the time in which the examination of a bank is ordinarily made is altogether too short. There is no basis of comparison between the examination of a bank as commonly conducted and that of a trust company as circumstances demand. There is an entirely different class of talent required in the examination of a trust company.

As with banks so with trust companies. We find different organizations doing a different class of business, and yet the range of differences with banks is very much less than the range of differences with trust companies. We find one trust company specially organized to take care of the financial interests of a certain clique of wealthy men, or to look after the investments of a certain circle of men. We find along side of it another trust company doing the same thing for another set of men. While in the one case, railroads and street car lines may be the principal features, in the other it is industrial operations, including perhaps real estate matters.

No Two Trust Companies Working Exactly Alike.

However we approach the subject, we find no two trust companies, speaking within limits, doing exactly the same kind of business. There is an individuality about each, and therefore we come back to the previous conclusion that the examination of a trust company must proceed upon original lines; that it cannot be based upon work done for other trust companies, or, rather, that it cannot be done after a general pattern supposed to fit other trust companies.

It would seem to be the opinion of some of those who are giving but brief consideration to the subject, that it is possible to devise a plan or scheme of trust company investigation and examination that should be at once very simple in its elements and at the same time very comprehensive in its results. I have been urged to present on this occasion a blank that might be used by examiners of trust companies. As already stated, a single blank is inadequate. It does not begin to reach the case, and if we are to take any individual trust company and in the light of complete knowledge of its affairs prepare a blank or set of blanks by which its periodical examination should be conducted, we would find that this blank or set of blanks would not apply to any one of the numerous trust companies working side by side with that to which the first set of blanks was devoted.

The examiner of a trust company must become familiar with the different undertakings of the several departments of the company. He will approach each as a new proposition. He will bring to bear in his work all the experience that has accrued in the investigation or various industrial and mercantile operations, and he will proceed with his undertaking cautiously and ever with an eye looking out for the unexpected.

Division Into Departments.

First will be the division of the trust company into its several departments. These are more or less numerous according to circumstances. Each of them is more or less developed likewise according to circumstances.

He first takes up, for example, the department devoted to individual trusts and the management of estates, including such matters as executorships and trusteeships under wills. In this division he must follow out each individual trust and examine it on the merits of the case and not from the standpoint of any fixed rule.

Next, for example, he takes up the question of administration, and in this department considers the company from the standpoint of administrator, trustee, guardian, receiver, or assignee, as the case may be. Here again each individual undertaking must be examined from beginning to end in order to put into the report that which he is expected to present.

Again, he takes up the question of trusteeship under mortgages issued by corporations or municipalities. Here there is the inquiry along specific lines to be assured that the company is not making mistakes and is not abusing the confidence reposed in it. And so we might go through all the different divisions of a trust company's business, including membership in underwriting syndicates, guardianship, managers of estates in the absence of owners, agencyship for the collection of interest, rents, etc., general financial agents, registrarship, etc.

Since a trust company's functions are so various and so numerous, an examination into its affairs for the purpose of certifying as to its condition is other than a simple matter. No rule expressed in few words can be laid down for the purpose. No single blank or form will meet the exigencies of the case, but the examiner must patiently check up each of the several departments of the trust company and in each department follow out each of the several undertakings laboriously and carefully, until a definite conclusion is reached.

Origin and Rise of Trust Companies.

The examiner who approaches a trust company for the purpose of audit and investigation should know something of the origin and rise of these corporations in order to be in position to judge of their operations. What is there about trust companies that enables them to enter a field to all appearances fully occupied and in a period of less than a quarter of a century to succeed to the prominence which they at present hold?

This has been answered by one writer on the basis of the theory of natural selection. According to this writer, a gradual change in our financial conditions and the increase in our national wealth has led to corresponding changes in the structure of our monetary institutions and resulted in the formation of establishments suited to our changed environment, in the form, on the one hand, of trust companies with large capital and surplus to conserve, and on the other hand, of banks solidified and amplified by amalgamation in order to be better able to handle the growing volume of our enormous trade. It was inevitable that the great stream of our bankable wealth, which has enormously increased of late years, should sooner or later become divided in this way, in order to separate that portion which was actively engaged in trade from our invested capital; and the extraordinary development of the trust companies already formed and the new life infused into banking show how beneficial to both the change has been under the new classification and division.

The whole design of banking is to further and facilitate trading operations, in which, as a rule, two-thirds of its resources are directly employed in the form of discounts, and so unavailable for any other purpose. Trust companies, on the other hand, instead of using their capital in the way of discounts of personal obligations, keep it in hand for other uses. Trust companies are not concerned with trade risks. Accordingly, they are not shackled by restrictions imposed to guard against trade risks. The trust company of to-day, combining as it does every function of financial business, stands with respect to the financial world as the department store stands in the commercial world.

A Trust Company's Balance Sheet.

One or two general directions may be given in closing: What the examining auditor must do in order to prepare a complete report of the affairs of a trust company can be determined by measuring the affairs of the trust company by a balance sheet and profit and loss statement. It is customary with trust companies, as well as with banks, to put forth from time to time a statement of their affairs. This statement approximates a balance sheet, but is not complete. On the other hand, a complete balance sheet, or the outline of a complete balance sheet, will give the standard by which the affairs of a trust company may be judged.

Let us consider just what these broad statements mean. The affairs of every trust company, as well as of every other business institution, are susceptible of statements in balance sheet form. What are the assets and what are the liabilities? Preliminary to any balance sheet statement must be a profit and loss statement. What are the expenses? What are the revenues? The profit and loss statement closed into the balance sheet statement makes the latter complete.

At the outset, then, let the executor lay down broadly the accounts that to him seem necessary to constitute a balance sheet of the business. A balance sheet can contain nothing but assets and liabilities. What are the names of the accounts necessary to correctly represent the assets of the company? What are the names of the accounts necessary to correctly show the liabilities of the company?

In this analysis he must not be content with generalities, but instead must enter into details. The resulting statement will be very much more extensive than that in the form given to the public, and yet its footings will be identical with the footings of the published statement, provided, of course, that the latter is correct.

It will not be sufficient to put down in this balance sheet, for example, so many bonds of such and such an issue and then close that division of the account by saying "Other Stock Investments." Instead, the other stock invesiments must be laboriously and completely listed.

It will not do to put down Bonds and Mortgages, but instead Bonds and Mortgages must be extended in detail. It will not do to put down Other Outstanding Accounts. Instead, these accounts should be completely and correctly listed. It will not do to put down Cash on Hand. Instead, there should be shown so much cash in the vault, so much in this bank and so much in another bank, as the case may be. Again, on the liability side, it will not do to put down Amount Due Depositors, without the preparation of a complete list of depositors showing in detail what makes up the total. And so we might go on through the entire list.

Suspense and Reserve.

There are always matters pending in trust company affairs which among the assets should be covered by some such account as Items in Suspense. Insurance paid in advance, and various expenses which have been anticipated and which are to be pro rated out as the months pass by, should come under this head. Items in Suspense is a very proper entry in every balance sheet and yet there are comparatively few balance sheets which show the same.

On the other hand, there are various accrued expenses which are not yet paid which should go on the liability side of the balance sheet under the head of Reserves. Taxes have accrued upon a certain piece of property and yet are not due for three months to come. The accrued taxes to date should be placed under this head. Interest has accrued on money borrowed, but is not payable for some time to come. In charging into Expense the expenses which occur, Reserve for Interest should be credited. In turn, when it comes to the payment of interest the Reserve Account is debited. Again referring to Suspense, the reverse interest charge is to be managed in the same way.

The thought underlying this suggestion is that the auditor who sets out to establish a correct balance sheet of a trust company thereby has pointed out to him the direction in which his investigations should extend, whereby he becomes cognizant of all the facts of the company and whereby he gets into a position to certify to the correctness of the statement he may prepare.

The "Poor" Farmer Yesterday and To-day.
In the past, ignorance and isolation. In the present, intelligence and information.—Chicago Tribune.

THE COSTLY BUG.

In "Harper's Weekly," Dr. H. C. McCook, in an article, "Insects and Civilization," gives some startling statistics as to the amount of destruction done annually in this country by insects of various sorts. Here are his figures:

"The chinch bug caused a loss of $30,000,000 in 1871, upwards of $100,000,000 in 1874, and in 1887 $60,000,000. The Rocky Mountain locust or grasshopper, in 1874 destroyed $100,000,000 of the crops in Kansas, Missouri, Nebraska and Iowa, and the direct loss was probably as much more. For many years the cotton caterpillar caused an annual average loss in the Southern states of $15,000,000 while in 1868 and 1873, the loss reached $30,000,000. The fly weevil, our most destructive enemy to stored grains, particularly throughout the South, inflicts an annual loss in the whole country of $40,000,000. The coddling moth, the chief ranger of the apple and pear crops, destroys every year fruit valued at $30,000,000 to $40,000,000. The damage to live stock inflicted by the ox bot, or ox warble, amounts to $36,000,000.

"These are fair samples of the enormous money losses produced in one country by a few of the pigmy captains of pernicious industry, whose hosts operate in the graneries, fields, stock farms, and the stock yards of our country. What is the grand total? In 1899, E. Dwight Sanderson, after careful consideration of the whole field, put the annual loss in the United States from insects at $409,000,000."

MEAN ENOUGH.

"Grouch is the stingiest man in the office."

"Yes, he's mean enough to take the beam out of his own eye, if he thought he could sell the timber."

Federation of Societies of Public Accountants

In our last issue we gave particulars of the meeting at Washington late in October, at which was organized the Federation of Societies of Public Accountants of the United States of America. It appears that the American Association of Public Accountants is not satisfied with the result, possibly because it seems like transferring to another what it has proposed in the past to undertake to do itself. At the meeting of the Board of Trustees November 26 the following resolution was passed:

In view of the fact that certain of our members have sent to the individual members of the association a printed circular advocating the joining of the association with the Federation, and that those views do not agree wth the consensus of opinion of the Board of Trustees,

"Resolved, That the views of this board as expressed in the following objections to the American Association of Public Accountants joining the Federation be conveyed to the members of this association; to the members of the New York State Society of Certified Public Accountants; to the National Society of Certified Public Accountants of the United States; to the Incorporated Public Accountants of Massachusetts; to the Pennsylvania Institute of Certified Public Accountants; to the Maryland Association of Public Accountants, Baltimore; to the Illinois Association of Public Accountants, Chicago; to the Society of Certified Public Accountants of the State of New Jersey; and to the Incorporated Michigan Association of Public Accountants."

On the vote:—Nine members of the board voted "aye"; one member, Past President Conant, of the firm of Haskins & Sells, desired to be placed on record as voting "no."

Following the above in the report that is sent out to the several organizations mentioned is the following:

"The American Association of Public Accountants, after careful consideration of the constitution and by-laws enacted at the Washington Conference, creating the "Federation of Societies of Public Accountants in the United States," and also the report of their representatives of the proceedings of that conference, regret that they cannot become a member of the "Federation" for the folowing reasons:

"First—That instead of a federation pure and simple, it is virtually a central organization, to be governed by an executive board, who in the language of the by-laws 'shall be responsible for the conduct of the affairs of the federation,' and who in turn may delegate their powers to an executive committee composed of five of its members.

"Second—That a fixed place, viz., Washington, is designated as the annual meeting place, unless otherwise ordered.

"Third—That no provision is made for the calling of special meetings of the federation.

"Fourth—That an annual subscription of five dollars is assessed upon every society for each of its members.

"Fifth—That while no headquarters is positively arranged for in the by-laws, the executive board has full power to establish one.

"Sixth—That instead of each society at the annual convention being allowed to cast the entire vote allotted them, only delegates present can vote, thus destroying the unity of the society as an entity, and making each delegate an individual factor.

"Seventh—That the representation and taxation of the societies are unequal, a society with seven members being entitled to one vote, paying thirty-five dollars, while a society with two hundred members has only four votes and pays one thousand dollars.

"Eighth—That the whole spirit of the by-laws is not that of a federation, but an organization of a dominating central body.

"Ninth—That owing to the limited powers granted to the United States General Government in the Constitution, with the express limitation that all powers not so granted are inherent in the sovereign states, and that the various accountant societies are incorporated under the laws of several states and are subject to those laws, a general society, such as that constituted, would be of doubtful utility.

"Tenth—That while a federation or congress of delegates from the various state societies might meet together from time to time to secure as far as possible uniform legislation, placing all certified accountants on the same plane as regards professional experience, knowledge and requirements, a solidified body or association such as the one proposed is unnecessary and would involve an outlay entirely uncommensurate with its utility.

"Eleventh—On the basis as proposed the Federation does not offer anything more than this association now does.

"Twelfth—That Article X, section 1, of federation by-laws may lead to great confusion and injustice, as members that more properly affiliate with other societies to which they belong may elect to be identified with the American Association, and so improperly increase our quota of dues.

"Thirteenth—That a federation on the lines of the one approved by our association at the meeting of October 14 is all that is required.

T. CULLEN ROBERTS, C. P. A.,
Secretary.

We have no idea that the Federation will cease because the moribund organizations put forth this plea. It still remains to be shown, however, just what real good can be accomplished by the Federation. Getting accountants together is worth a great deal, but the announced object has legislation in view. The question of result turns largely upon what is possible in this regard.

BONDS AS AN INVESTMENT.

Do the readers of Commerce, Accounts & Finance ever stop to consider what an enormous quantity of bonds of all descriptions are issued each year in the United States? The number of bonds is legion, but many of us know comparatively little about them for the reason that we have invested nothing in them, or if we have done so have done it through the advice of our banker, in whom we place implicit trust. Mr. Joseph Hardcastle, a well-known authority on the subject of bonds, has written concerning them as follows:

"If one should judge by the immense volume of business in the purchase and sale of bonds, one would naturally conclude that the investing public would have a fair knowledge of the nature of a bond. I venture to say, however, that the public, in general, know little of the nature of a bond, of the rate per cent. it yields less; and still less of the method of keeping a bond account when held as an investment.

"As to the nature of a bond: The holder of a bond is entitled by that instrument to receive, say, quarterly; or half-yearly, a fixed sum from the issuer of the bond, for a certain number of years, and at the end of that time to receive another fixed sum of money. The fixed sum receivable at the maturity (as it is called) of the bond, is generally $100, $500 or $1,000, and the bond is then known as a $100 bond, $500 bond or a $1,000 bond. The sum to be received during a year, whether payable quarterly or half-yearly, often gives the name to the bond, being quoted at a certain per cent. on the sum to be received at the bond's maturity. The price paid for a bond, in the open market, is called its market price, the price quoted daily in the newspapers. In the following illustration, it is not expected that the reader will understand how the set of numbers used are obtained until he has read this paper in its entirety. If I pay $110.42 for a $100 bond, the bond having five and one-quarter years to run, the said bond paying 4½ per cent. yearly, in half-yearly installments, on its maturity value, this $110.42 is the equivalent of ten and one-half installments each of $2.25, payable at the end of each half year, and $100 additional at the end of five and one-quarter years. As an investment, which yields us 2⅜ per cent., at compound interest, compounded half-yearly, the present value of the annuity is $22.08, and the present value of the $100, whose payment is deferred five and one-quarter years, is $88.34, i. e., the two privileges—that of receiving an annuity and

His Biggest Game.—New York Herald.

of receiving a sum deferred—are, at the time of purchase, together equal to $22.08 and $88.34, or $102.42. We here see that two future sets of payments have their present equivalent payment.

"The rate per cent. a bond yields its owner? The answer to this question has been in part anticipated. We have seen that the present value of a sum payable at the maturity of the bond and of the present value of an annuity. It is not difficult to understand how to obtain the present value of $100, whose payment is deferred for a number of years, interest being at a certain rate per cent. per annum, compounded, say, half-yearly. This present value is simply such a sum as will amount to $100 in the given time, at the given rate per cent. per annum, compounded semi-annually. And its value may be found by dividing $100 by the amount of $1 at compound interest for the given time at the given rate. With interest at 3 per cent. per annum and payable semi-annually, the following table gives, for three years, the present value of $100, whose payment is deferred.

Years.	Present Value.	Years.	Present Value.
½	$98.5222	2	$94.2184
1	97.0662	2½	92.8260
1½	95.6317	3	91.4542

This table is obtained on the principle of dividing $100 by the amount of $1 for the given time, the compounding being half-yearly, or, otherwise expressed, by dividing the $100 by 1, plus the compound interest, at the given rate for the given time.

"To pave the way for a solution of the question under consideration let us analyze the following transaction: A loans B $100 for three years at 3 per cent. per annum, interest payable semi-annually. A, on his part, gives to B $100. B, on his part, gives to A the right of receiving an annuity of $3 per annum, payable semi-annually for three years, and at the end of that time the further right of receiving $100. Since the $100 given by A is the equivalent of the two rights granted by B, it follows that one of these rights equals $100, less the other, or that the present value of the annuity equals the difference between $100 and the present value of the deferred sum ($100). But by the table the present value of $100, whose payment is deferred three years, is $91.4542. Hence the present value of the annuity equals the difference between $100, and $91.4542 or $8.5458. A, therefore, pays $8.5458 for the privilege of receiving the annuity, and $91.4542 for the privilege of receiving the $100 at the end of three years.

"But let us suppose that B offers $4 instead of $3 per annum, what should A now give for the two rights which he purchases, other conditions of the question remaining the same? The value of the $100 deferred would be the same as before, viz., $91.4542, but the value of the annuity would be greater than before, in the ratio of 4 to 3, i. e., it would be 4-3 of $8.5458, or $11.3944. And A would have to pay for these two rights the sum of $91.4542 and $11.3944, or $102.8486. The solution we have given is a solution of the following question: What should be given for a $100 4 per cent. bond maturing in three years, interest payable half-yearly, so as to realize 3 per cent. per annum? Answer, $102.8486.

"How should the bond account be kept when bonds are bought as an investment? To begin, the bond account should be debited with the cost of bond, and the interest account credited with the coupons, as they are cashed. But at the end of the half year the bond has decreased in value. How much? It is evident that we can find the present value of the same bond having two and one-half years to run, and paying, as before, 3 per cent. on our investment. It will be found to be $102.3913. This last amount we will call the "effluent" cost, i. e., the cost which naturally flows from the original cost, a proper allowance being made for depreciation. The difference between the original and effluent costs is the depreciation of bond in case, $0.4573. This represents a portion of our original investment returned, being included in the coupon paid. In this case, $2 is the coupon paid for the half year, of which $0.4573 represents a portion of the investment returned, and the difference, $1.5427, the interest on our original investment for six months, 3 per cent. per annum, showing that our bond yields us 3 per cent. per annum. To repeat, debit (as below) the bond account with the original cost; credit interest account with maturing coupon. Find the depreciation as above. Credit bond account and debit interest account with depreciation; balance bond account by crediting it with effluent cost. Bring down effluent cost. Continue the operation during the life of the bond, and the final balance will be $100. Credit account with $100, paid at redemption of bond, and the account will have no longer an existence."

Bond Account.

Original cost....	$102.8486	Depreciation	$0.4573
		Effluent cost.....	102.3913
	$102.8486		$102.8486
Effluent cost.....	$102.3913		

Interest Account.

Depreciation	$0.4573	Coupon	$2

"It seems to me that while the effluent cost is the proper quantity which should determine the resolution of the coupons into their two elements, assets returned and interest earned for the purpose of declaring dividends, ascertaining earnings, incomes, revenues or profit—that the market price of the bond should determine the status of an institution for the purposes of a public statement."

SCIENCE IN SHOVELS.

A recent issue of "Engineering" gives some interesting data of steps taken by the Bethlehem Steel Company to reduce the cost of common labor employed in shoveling coal, ore, etc., and several highly trained specialists were engaged to study the problem. It was found that the time taken to insert a shovel into a pile was shorter if it were shoved into the top instead of the bottom of a pile. It also varied with the material, taking longer for coke than sand, and, of course, with the man also, a powerful laborer taking 22 pounds at each shovelful, while the average was not more than 12 to 14 pounds. As a result of this investigation, new sets of shovels, specially adapted to different kinds of work, were used, and instead of sending a man out in the morning with a shovel and allowing him to carry it all over the premises and use it indiscriminately on coke or ore, shovels of different sizes and shapes were used for different materials. The result of the study of this problem has been that the staff of common laborers, which average 400 or 500, at wages of $1.15 per day, has been cut down, and the work is now done by 85 men, who are paid at the rate of $1.85 per day.

GOOD AT FIGURES.

"Is he good at figures?"

"Well, rather. He can make almost anything out of nothing. Why, he's the man who takes a city directory and figures out a population half again as large as the government census gives."—Chicago Evening Post.

Nature of Credit*

By HON. LYMAN J. GAGE, Ex-Secretary of the Treasury.

I THINK if I had been putting it down in your programme, I should have called these words of mine, not "an address," but an informal talk on the nature of credit, its philosophical origin, how it is availed of, the forces that make it effective, how it is operated in the field of commerce, and how it can be more broadly applied than it now is.

I suppose if somebody were to ask you "What are the three greatest material elements or forces in human society?" you would probably say, first, 'Production in some form yielded by the soil, the forest, the field, the mine and the sea"; and if you were to be asked "What is the next great force operating for the human family?" you would probably say "Transportation," for that is the force and power which distributes the product of man's labor far and near, and makes production profitable and available for human uses. If somebody were to ask you, "What is the third?" I think you would have to answer and say, "Credit," for according to my best thinking, credit is only second to transportation in operating the great field of productivity and transferring the products of human labor from man to man and distributing them to the blessing of all. Every ship and every train of cars that carries the product of human labor to market, or from the factory to the farm, is represented, with scarcely an exception, by some evidence of ownership resting somewhere in the field of credit, as through bills of lading, bills of exchange or promissory notes, negotiated with and carried by the banker.

The Nature of Credit.

What then is the nature of this thing we call credit—this powerful operating force in human society? In the first place, it is a sentiment in the mind; a sentiment which renders the possessor of property or values of any kind willing to transfer that property or those values to another, without immediate payment, resting upon the promises of the purchaser for his reimbursement later on. That is a tremendous force when you think about it, but many are willing to do that thing, to part with the ownership of what they possess with the expectation of getting its value back again with some gain or reward for its use in the meantime.

Of course, such a sentiment as that, operating in the human mind charged with all these great possibilities, could not have existed in a raw and barbaric state of society. Civilization had to make many conquests before men were willing to do this thing. The sentiments of probity, integrity, the principle of the Golden Rule, had to permeate society more or less, and even beyond that laws had to be instituted, provisions made for the collections of obligations from the debtor, should he become unwilling to meet his just debts.

Well, we need not trace very minutely the progress of human society by which this sentiment of the human mind became so operative as it now is. Let us rather ask by what method it became so efficient for human uses, as we now perceive it to be?

Through a period of evolution, reaching not so very far back in the distant past either, there was developed what we now call in its ripeness and full fruition the machinery of banking, and it is banking which makes the tremendous force to which I have alluded available to human uses.

The Bank and Credit.

How does the bank do it? I am undertaking here in fifteen or twenty, or not more than thirty minutes, to sketch what I suppose a political economist of the first order would require at least two volumes to adequately explain—he would have chapters and sub-chapters. I will have to skip all reference to the function which bills of exchange perform in our international trade, vast and important as they are. I will have to pass all that by, and consider the bank in its domestic relations only. How does the bank make credit effective? It makes it effective by giving its own credit, which is good or ought to be good and well known, in exchange for the credit of the individual who ought also to be good, but who may be very little known, not so well known as to make his obligations powerful in the exchanges of the community, while the banker's credit is powerful for the exchange of commodities in the community. It is, therefore, the province of the banker to exchange his credit for the lesser known credit of the members of the community with whom he deals.

How does he do it? Generally speaking, and in a large degree, he evidences the fact that he has given credit to his customer by passing up to his credit on his books—the banker's books—the amount for which his credit has been exchanged with the dealer. This credit then becomes the subject of the individual's check or draft. That is to say, the individual has acquired the right to draw money from the bank, and now there works out a very interesting and very influential chain of consequences which I wish you to keep track of. You will all recognize that this right to draw money is in all ordinary times preferred by the man who possesses it to the money itself. He does not draw his money from the bank, although he has that right. His check on the bank is as effective for the payment of goods that he buys or for bills that he pays, as would be the actual money. He passes his check, then, to another. That is to say, he passes his right to draw money, but this second party, the recipient of the check, finds himself in the same state of mind as the man from whom he receives it. He has the right to draw money, but he does not care to exercise that right; he prefers to reserve the right and then transfer it to another, and not handle the actual money.

The second party, if he takes a check from the first party, may deposit it in the same bank on which it is drawn, in which case it is simply a transfer of bank credit, or he may deposit it in another bank, but it then becomes a credit at rest in the second bank, subject to future transfer. Thus you will see in these rights to draw money there is built up a vast system of credits, consisting of rights on banks for money, and these are made the subjects of transfer and retransfer, and retransfer again and again, in buying and selling between man and man, in payment of accounts, in settlement of notes and all the purposes for which money is supposed to be necessary.

The banker has indeed to look out and see that he is in a position at all times to meet the requests of

*Address delivered before New York Chapter, American Institute of Bank Clerks. Reported by Robert Hockey, Secretary New York Chapter.

such as may perchance prefer the money, then to continue to forbear the right to use it; but experience has shown, and very well demonstrated, that the banker with reasonable cash reserves, say twenty-five per cent., and good counterclaims on the community, is able and always will be able to meet whatever requests are made upon him for absolute cash. Do not, however, fail to notice that there has been an enormous expansion of deposits in this process by these credits created through loans. There is a popular idea that deposits consist of money put in the bank, and if a man puts money in the bank he has got "money in the bank." That is all well enough for a popular idea, but nothing could be more erroneous. When a man puts money in the bank he parts with his money absolutely and completely. He has exchanged it for a right to draw money. When a man puts his note in the bank and it is put to his credit on the banker's books, he is exactly in the same situation as the man who has put in his money; he has a right to draw money, and as the deposits of money will swell deposits on the right side of the bank ledger, so the deposits of bills of exchange and promissory notes or whatnot for which the individual gets credit will also swell the deposits on the bank's books, and when the notes or loans are paid off by the application of credit balances thereto, deposits are reduced.

Loans and Deposits.

I think that is a fact very largely lost sight of. Really, loans and deposits are almost corollary terms—when deposits rise, loans rise, or rather, to put it in the other way, when loans rise, deposits rise; when loans decline, deposits decline. The application of the deposits to the liquidation of a debt in the bank reduces by that amount the "deposits."

The vice-president of a large institution to-day said to me: "Bank deposits have gone down alarmingly. Where has all that money gone?"

"Money gone?" said I.

"Yes; sixty to seventy millions fall in deposits. Where has the money gone? Who has it?"

"Nobody has it."

"Well, deposits have gone off sixty or seventy millions," he declared.

"Yes, but loans have gone off forty-five or fifty millions also."

"Yes, that is so."

"Well," I said, "with the exception of the comparatively small amount of money which has gone to the West to move the crops, the banks have substantially the same amount of money that they had six weeks ago."

"I do not understand that."

"Well, I am not going to set up for a schoolmaster, but if you have one hundred thousand dollars to your credit over there in the Merchants' Bank, and I owe the National City one hundred thousand dollars, and the National City calls upon me to pay, and I sell my securities to you, and you give a check on your bank, and I take your check and pay the National City Bank my loan, your deposit will go down one hundred thousand dollars, and the loans in the National City Bank would go down one hundred thousand dollars, would they not?"

"Yes, I see how it works."

A New York Illustration.

My attention was called three or four years ago to a movement here in New York which illustrates the thought I have just been trying to express. There was a sum of twenty-three millions of dollars in money which in the course of six weeks went from the banks elsewhere. The larger part of it undoubtedly went to the West and South to move the crops. It touched that vital point, the reserves, because the only money that the banks had on hand or could in any way issue or invent were legal tender notes or gold, and on this foundation, or in the relation of one to four, one of money to four of deposits, the situation rested. The movement of money to the West and to the South was the most natural and healthy movement imaginable. It was all that we needed to bring bread to the seaboard and to give the sons of the soil power to labor; but drawing twenty-three millions of reserved money from the banks caused a forced liquidation of loans. The banks had to call in money from their debtors; that is what they call it, "calling money." I do not think as a whole the bank got much money by calling it; they get "liquidation." They had all the money to start with. No one has any money to amount to anything. The banks have it. There is little money resting outside of the banks anywhere.

And this is what resulted: To get the banks in a position again so that their reserves would bear the relation of one to four to liability: this actually took place—figures show it—they called in ninety-two millions of loans, substantially four times the money they parted with. Ninety-two millions of dollars of liquidation in loans brought the deposits down by the application of credits belonging to somebody which I describe in the case of the one hundred thousand dollar loan, so that deposits fell and loans fell ninety-two millions of dollars, and when the loans had fallen ninety-two millions of dollars you can see that what we have is their reserves on hand, although their actual cash is twenty-three millions of dollars less than before. The reduced volume of cash was then an effective and lawful reserve against their liabilities, reduced as they were in the sum of ninety-two millions.

But that is a pretty expensive process; in order to part with twenty-three millions of dollars in money for the country's use. Expansive for the trading community, whether they be speculators, merchants, manufacturers or holders of investment securities.

Expansion of Credit.

The expansion of loans will expand deposits, and as Mr. Vanderlip showed in a late address in Wilmington, deposits have increased within three and a half years in the United States about three billions of dollars. Imagination fires up on that statement, and people look at those figures and say, "How rich we are getting; look at the money in bank; three side of the ledger, you will see that loans have risen three billions of dollars; that is, there has been an expansion of credit, and the right to draw on these credits that the bankers have made constitute an effective floating currency, as effective for all the purposes of trade as if they were five hundred, one thousand or five thousand dollar bank notes in active circulation. Can't you all see they are? They certainly are. The cash on hand in the banks during that same period of time has not risen five millions of dollars. The banks had a surplus reserve at the beginning of the expansive movement, and that surplus reserve has served to swell the tide of credit, the tide of deposits, which I have said are corollary terms—to an enormous extent. This is affecting all the banks as a whole, national, state and others, with a feeling of some anxiety; but to whatever of danger from over-expansion the banker and the community is exposed, it still remains true that credit, the machinery of banking, the instruments which credit has devised, is in about the degree of third in importance the most influential and useful factor employed in the service of modern commercial and industrial life.

Next to production and transportation it is the most powerful and beneficent influence operating in human society.

Another Device of Credit.

Now I come to another point in my talk which relates to a device of credit which used to exist, and in other countries does now exist, but which has been destroyed with us, much to the harm, in my opinion, of the general body politic. There is no difficulty now in going to the bank and obtaining a credit on its books in exchange for a good note, the proceeds to be checked against it in the ordinary way; that is to say, to acquire the right to draw checks on the bank for cash; there is, I say, no difficulty in doing this, provided the bank has a little more than its legal reserve on hand. But there are uses of life for which if credit is to be utilized so as to cover these other uses, some device of credit must exist other than bank books, checks and drafts. Checks will not pay cotton-pickers in the southern cotton fields. There is no place for the cotton pickers to go and realize the money on them, and it is money or what will circulate as money that he wants. Checks will not pay the lumberman in the northern woods; they will not pay the lumberman in the pineries of Washington or Oregon, nor the salmon fisherman in Alaska, nor the coal miners of Pennsylvania, Kentucky or Indiana, nor the great army of harvesting hands that gather the grain in the Far West. No; but are not these needs of life as worthy the facilities of credit from the bank as are the needs of Wall street operators, or the dealers around Sixth avenue, Twenty-third street, Thirty-fourth street, or any other street? Certainly, they are, for these uses to which I have referred lie at the very foundation of our prosperity.

I have pictured to myself as illustrating this particular point, a man going to a bank—three of them—one saying, "I want to borrow ten thousand dollars, Mr. Banker."

"Yes, what do you want to do with it?"

"I want you to pass it to my credit. I shall be checking against it in the course of my business."

The banker says to himself, "I have a little surplus over the legal reserve, I will take my chance with him."

All right. The banker thus adds to his liabilities ten thousand dollars by crediting the borrower with the amount of the loan. Number two comes along; he makes the same request. He is treated in the same way.

Number three comes along and says, "I would like ten thousand dollars, Mr. Banker. I see you have accommodated my two friends. I hope I am not too late."

"What do you want to do with the money?" is the banker's question.

"I am establishing a number of stations down Pamlico Sound for the purchase of fish and sea food of various kinds; I want to distribute money because these people must have the cash in their hands when they come in with the boat-loads of fish or oysters."

"Oh, so you need cash?"

"Yes."

"Well, I cannot accommodate you."

"You accommodated these two men."

"Yes, but you want the money."

"No, I don't want money, not real money; your notes will answer my purpose perfectly."

"Well, I have no notes of my own on hand."

"But, Mr. Banker, I notice by your published statement that you have a right to issue notes? I will pay the money back before the notes come back for redemption."

"But," says the banker, "you ask me for something rather worse than if I were to give you the cash, for I have to invest eleven thousand dollars of my money in United States bonds in order to get ten thousand dollars of my notes which you want to borrow. That I cannot afford to do, and I need the cash as reserve for the loans I just now made."

So you see by a currency system as costly as capital, the benefits of credit as operated by banks are positively denied in a large number of cases, and handicapped at all times and everywhere, because the banker has no way of extending to the borrower through his notes what he effectively extends to all the other members of the community who can use checks and drafts.

Talk With a Banker.

I asked a banker awhile ago with whom I was talking and who seemed to be rather set in his views on this subject, a series of questions. I will repeat them here:

I said to him, "Do you think credit is an efficient agency operating to the advantage of the human family?"

"Yes, I do," he replied.

"Do you think that the development of banking is the most efficient aid to the operation of credit?"

"Yes."

"Do you think that books of account and checks and drafts effectively reach the needs of all the larger members of the community who desire the use of credit, and who can avail themselves of that machinery?"

"Yes."

"Do you think that bank credits, checks and drafts supply the machinery to cover all the uses of life?"

Well, he didn't know, and I sketched to him the outlying interests which I have described to you. "No," he finally replied, "checks certainly do not meet such needs."

"Well, then," said I, "if credit is a useful thing and serves the purposes of human society in a degree only three removes in the order of production, transportation and credit—if credit is such a useful thing, and the machinery of credit operated by the banks is legitimate, give me a reason, if you can, why the banker's credit should not be made effective also through the use of his notes in the smaller

President Castro.—"Do you know, I rather like the idea of a war, why we haven't one for nearly two weeks, and it's been getting terribly dull!—Chicago Record-Herald.

THE NEW YORK PUBLIC LIBRARY ASTOR, LENOX AND TILDEN FOUNDATIONS

spheres of labor, and in remote sections of the country."

Well, he said he would admit they should.

"Can you think of any other form," I continued, "by which bank credit can be utilized for these general uses unless by bank notes of convenient denominations?"

He said he could not.

"Then, have you not any objections to the issue of what is called credit currency?"

Well, he said, he thought it was a useful and a necessary addition to the machinery by which credit is made applicable to the purposes of society; "But," he added, "I think the notes ought to be made safe in the hands of the holder."

I said, "We agree exactly; we stand now upon the same platform as to the desirability of things, and now all you and I have to do, or all we should have to do if the power were allowed us to introduce this new machinery of credit notes, would be to so arrange that the banks would be limited in their issues within the lines of safety, and that wise provisions be made to secure the notes against loss in the hands of the holders. Will you join in that effort?"

He said, "I don't believe I will."

"Why not?"

He said, "I believe it is better for me as it is now. I believe we will make more money under the present system than we would under that. It may be better for the country, but I believe it is in the interest of the New York banks to keep as we are."

Then I asked him this question: "When do you think the banker flourishes best, when the country is safe and prosperous, everybody is employed, credit is safe, no great war rumors shaking the country? Or is the banker better off when vicissitude and losses and stoppage of industries and bankruptcies ensue?"

"Well," he replied, "I think we are all members one with the other, and everybody is better off on the whole when everybody is prosperous."

And there we left the argument.

The Fowler Currency Bill.

You were addressed, I think, last year by Mr. Fowler on his bill. His bill is a sweeping measure. It carries an element of betterment, which I think is necessary and for which you see the argument. His bill, however, is too sweeping, it goes too far for the temper of the people at the present time. He has excited the opposition of a large number of diverse interests which will coalesce in opposition. He proposes branch banks, large banks with numerous branches. These banks may perhaps be desirable in themselves, and much may be said in favor of such arguments, but he has twelve thousand opponents in the twelve thousand banks who are jealous of their own particular rights and who are not going to have them interfered with, if they can prevent it. Then he has in opposition to him the general prejudice of the community against large banks with branches. He also aims to cure what I think—but which I have no time to discuss—a radically wrong principle in our system of finance: that is, the greenback. He eliminates that by a careful and gradual process which would be safe, easy, and nobody would ever notice the change if it could be introduced; but against it also he will raise a multitude of objectors who forget that the greenback, serviceable as perhaps it may have been in the time of our civil struggle, is yet a costly instrument, and that it fell to forty cents on the dollar when measured by gold in 1864-65. But the community has become used to that form of money and think it safe. They call it "battle-scarred and time-honored," the "poor man's money"; and against these he has to make headway if he carries his bill through as a whole.

Some measure, however, either the one proposed by Mr. Fowler, or one more simple still, looking to the use of a credit currency properly limited and safe-guarded, is but a question of time. Such a currency is an essential addition to the banking machinery, which operates to make banking effective for human uses.

BOOKKEEPING IN RHYME.

Some of the older readers of this column perhaps had their geography inflicted upon them, when at school, in sing-song fashion, and perhaps some still recall a jingle with respect to rivers, or rather to the capital cities of the different states, almost all of which are located on rivers, which runs something as follows:—

"State of Maine, Augusta,
On the Kennebec River."

and so on, to the end of a long list. In Thornton's little handbook, entitled "Easy Exercises in Bookkeeping," we find a page of mnemonical rhymes, which, so far as memory serves us, is the first instance of bookkeeping reduced to jingle that we recall. As likely to interest our readers, we reproduce the different rhymes in this connection, and suggest that many of our readers would profit by committing the same to memory:—

Real Accounts.

1. You cannot well go wrong, if you Think what you're about;
For you Debit what comes "In," and Credit what goes "Out."

Personal Accounts.

2. Debit all "Receivers," who receive—no matter what,
Services, or Goods, or Cash—the smallest little jot.
Credit all the "Givers": those who give you "Any" Thing,
Or Favor or Advantage to the house of business bring.

Balance Sheet.

3. Assets are Debits; keep "that" very clear:
All Liabilities Credits appear.

Profit and Loss.

4. Debit your "Losses," and credit your "Gains";
Errors avoiding by Thinking and Pains.

Subsidiary Accounts.

5. "Balance" and carry to Profit and Loss;
Always remember to carry across.

How to Balance Goods.

6. (1) Enter Stock Value on Creditor Side.
(2) Balance by Rules, that are given as Guide.
(3) Goods carry "down" to begin the next year.
(4) Profit in P. and L. ought to appear.

How to Prove.

7. If the Books are "Proved," as they always ought to be,
Capital and Balance Sheet will certainly "Agree."

Discounts.

8. With "Discounts or Bad Debts" remember well
That "After" Cash (or Bank) comes P. and L.

Discounts. (Add or Substract?)

9. When B. R. you pay in Discount away,
Or "less 5 per cent."—"Subtraction" is meant.
But in most cases "Add," or your work will be bad.

Discounting Bills.

10. Both the Discount and Bank (or Cash) debited are
When you "Discount a Bill." But you credit B. R.

Bills.

11. "Debit the Drawer" (if not drawn by "Me,"
And then it's the Bill that must debited be).
"Credit Acceptor" (but credit B. P.
Whenever the Bill is accepted by "Me").

Bills Paid or Dishonored.

12. When Bills are duly "Paid"—no entry for the "Man";
But Cash and Bill alone is the only proper plan.
"Debit the Man" for a Dishonored Bill;
Credit B. R., for its value is "Nil."

Bad Debts.

13. "Composition is not "Loss." Perhaps the cash you'll see.
In one or several "Dividends," just as the case may be,
The "Balance" ("After" these are paid) you carry to B. D.

THE TALE OF THE ONLY ONE AND THE HIGHER EDUCATION

BY JOE LINCOLN

And it was the one thousand and ninth night and the Father of the Faithful was troubled. And he spake unto Scheherezade, saying:

"'Hearken, slave, to the conundrum of the Boss! If it taketh eighty times one hundred weight of coal per day to heat this Palace of Delights, and if coal is sold by the bandits who dispense it at twenty simoleons per ton, how much coin of the realm, I pray thee, shall the Royal Presence have left with which to purchase New Year's gifts?"

And Scheherezade answered and said unto the King:

"Oh, Mightiness, the answer is not printed in Joe Miller's Joke Book, which proveth that the question is no merry jest. Nevertheless, will I give thee an answer, and the answer is, 'Forget it.'"

And the Sultan was pleased and said, "Verily, that is the answer that I will give unto the coal dealers at the presentation of their bill. Praised be to the Prophet, though coal be scarce there is hot air in exceeding plenty. Tell me, I pray thee, one of thy tales."

And Scheherezade obeyed and spake thus:

"Know, oh King, that in the good old summer time there lived in a far city a couple with one son. And the name of this son was Schemselnihar, and in all the land there was no male child like unto him, if one accepted as fact the testimony of his father and his mother. And upon this, their only son, determined they to bestow all the education which the market afforded, even though the landlord yammered at the gate of their domicile and the proverbial wolf ki-yied in the front hall thereof.

"And it came to pass that by devious ways and much toil did the parents of Schemselnihar amass sufficient store of shekels to send their son to the university. And there joined he the Slippery Club, and the Paresis Club, and the Alpha and Omega Sodality, and the Football Eleven, and the Society for the Wearing of Imported Clothes. And he wore upon his breast numerous pins with mystic letters, and in all the college there was none who could so handily lick a street car conductor, nor who could so successfully avoid study. And each time that he returned home upon the coming of the vacation season did his parents bow before him and exalt him to the skies, saying, 'Verily, oh son of our hearts, thou art a wonder!' And Schemselnihar contradicted them not, for he felt that it was so.

"And upon these vacation sojourns at the home of his youth, did Schemselnihar expand his bosom and wax exceeding chesty. And he sneered at the what-not in the best parlor and scoffed copiously at the hymn tunes which his sister wrested from the melodeon. And he patronized his kinsfolk and they abased themselves before him.

"And it came to pass that Schemselnihar came forth from the university bearing with him the certificate that is bestowed upon the elect. And he commanded that the word be spread abroad in the land that he, Schemselnihar, of the class of Oughty-Ought, was at liberty and that his services might be secured for the positions of Assistant Superintendent of the Universe or Chief Engineer of the Earth. But behold, the number of applications for the said services was as naught with none to carry.

"And Schemselnihar marveled at this, but he said, 'Lo, it is written, "If the mountain will not come to Mohammed, then shall Mohammed perambulate in the direction of the mountain."' And he set forth to secure a position.

"But it came to pass that when he applied unto them that bought and sold in the land, they made answer, saying, 'What canst thou do?' and he answered yet again, 'I can give thee college yells in all the tongues of men, can teach thee how to tackle low, and how to jolly Carrie Nation; incidentally I can tell thee every brand of cigarette that is worth the smoking. Is it not apparent that I can run thy business with one hand tied behind me?'

"And the employer said unto him, 'It is well, but canst thou tell us how to yank the deficit from the ledger and substitute therefor a corpulent dividend?'

"And when he answered them, 'No,' then did they bid the porter remove him to the exterior of the building and call the dog catcher.

"And it came to pass that Schemselnihar returned to his father's house and said, 'Behold, oh Governor, the tradesmen of the land are asses. It behooveth me to remain here at home and write screeds for their enlightenment.'

"And his father frowned upon him and said:

"'True, oh son of mine, but it occurreth to me that there are a few acres of potatoes in the back garden that need hoeing. It behooveth thee to get the hoe and begin, and that without loss of time.'

"And the father of Schemselnihar went into the house and sighed and said unto the wife of his bosom, 'Verily, Mother, it's another gold brick!' And they wept full sore."

And Scheherezade paused and said unto the Sultan:

"Oh, King, live forever! is a college education a good thing?"

And the King answered her, saying,

"Surely an incubator is a good thing, but it cannot hatch a chicken from a doorknob."

And he called for the royal dice box that he might shake with himself for the cigars.

Correspondence

Voucher Check.

From G. J. R., Kansas City, Kan.

I enclose a voucher check which I got up some time since for the Kansas City Live Stock Exchange. The Exchange is well pleased with it and the same form has been adopted by other institutions.

NOTE.—We have pleasure in presenting a reproduction of the voucher check which this correspondent sends us. By examination the reader will perceive that as a fact it is not a check but instead it is a form of receipt, and yet the receipt is somewhat lost by the verbiage used. Finally, when dated and receipted it becomes a draft on the Inter-state National Bank. It is of undoubted interest to our readers and for that reason we have pleasure in presenting it.

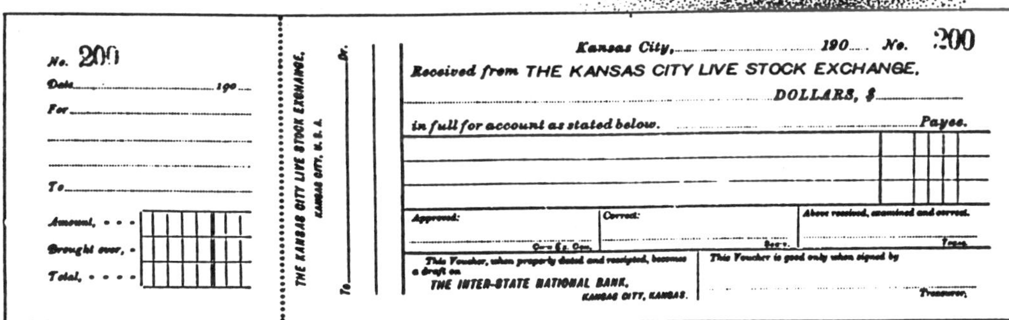

No. 200

Date .... 190..

For ....

To ....

Amount, . . .

Brought over, .

Total, ...

THE KANSAS CITY LIVE STOCK EXCHANGE, KANSAS CITY, U. S. A.

Dr.

To

Kansas City, ... 190.... No. 200

Received from THE KANSAS CITY LIVE STOCK EXCHANGE,

.... DOLLARS, $ ....

in full for account as stated below. .... Payee.

Approved: .... Gen'l Sup. Com.

Correct: .... Secy.

Above received, examined and correct. .... Treas.

This Voucher, when properly dated and receipted, becomes a draft on THE INTER-STATE NATIONAL BANK, KANSAS CITY, KANSAS.

This Voucher is good only when signed by .... Treasurer.

A Kansas City Voucher Check.

When Was the Profit Made?

From E. J. F., Greensboro, N. C.

Hardly a day passes that one does not run across some horrible example of how not to do it. Here is one that came to my notice the present week. Will you please discuss it for me?

A cotton mill bought a supply of cotton at 7 cents a pound and stored it in the warehouse. The market price of this grade of cotton went to 9 cents. The 2 cents per pound increase was equal to a gain of $7,000 on the supply purchased. This $7,000 is incorporated in the monthly report as a gain.

The next month there was a loss on manufacturing of $1,500, yet a gain to the extent of $5,500 was shown. The third month the price of the cotton goes down to 8¼ cents, and this item in the gain report is correspondingly reduced.

ANSWER.—The only satisfactory rule in matters of this kind that we have been able to obtain is based on the question of "When is a profit made?" The answer to this is, not when the market price goes up, but when we take advantage of the market price. The bookkeeper in the cotton mill to which this correspondent refers was consistent in his course, modifying his loss and gain account, as appears above, from time to time, according to the condition of affairs in the market. This, however, is not satisfactory. In fact, it is incorrect.

If we consider manufacturing a manipulation of capital, which it really is, we shall occupy a point of view that will perhaps be better for our purpose than any other. Whereas we had cash we bought with it cotton. This cotton stands in place of the cash we expended for it and must so stand until it is consumed—irrespective of the fluctuations of the market. It was not right, therefore, to take advantage of the advance in market rates as is stated above.

Our correspondent in his letter gives us permission to discuss this question to any length that we see fit, but we believe in the brief reference to it that we have covered every point that is essential. The profit is not made until the goods are sold. Manufacturing is a manipulation of assets. It takes them from one condition and puts them into another. There were no profits made because the market price went up on this cotton. Hence the necessity of making the alteration when the price again went down.

Position of the Practical Bookkeeper.

From J. C. E.

I have read in a recent issue of Commerce, Accounts & Finance your answer, which, by the way, does not answer my letter concerning the position of the practical bookkeepers in the scheme for the creation of a sort of trust for a section of people who may or may not be what they claim to be. I beg to apologize for my ignorance in being altogether unconscious that the proprietors of the paper were championing this combine, or, as your article seems to indicate, you were in fact "it." It seems to me to be a vital and significant indication of your business acumen that you make an uncalled for and personal attack on a subscriber to your journal and hold him up to ridicule through the pen of your "funny man."

NOTE.—Our correspondent's letter, which we have pleasure in submitting to our readers, seems to shoot wide of the mark. We do not recognize what he is talking about and certainly protest against misusing any subscriber to this paper or any other person in its columns. We were not aware that there was any combine being considered, nor do we know of any combine in existence or in contemplation. He would seem to charge us with being "it," but what "it" is we do not know.

KNEW PAPA'S REPERTOIRE.

He was very quiet during the first courses, and every one forgot that he was there. As dessert was being served, however, the host told a story. When he had finished and the laughter had ceased, the little son exclaimed, delightedly, "Now, papa, tell the other one!"—Harper's Magazine.

"HOME-MADE."

"Do you know that if one appreciated such things," observed a Dedham gentleman, as reported by the "Boston Herald," "that one can find much of the humorous in the signs and advertisements he sees in the course of his peregrinations. For that reason I always keep my eyes open for the funny things in this line. The other evening I was in Boston and I came across a peanut vender. He had a rudely lettered shingle, and it conveyed the astonishing information that he had for sale:

"'Fresh baked, home-made peanuts, five cents a bag.'"

COMMERCE ACCOUNTS & FINANCE

A Magazine of Higher Business Education and Practical Administration. Acknowledged Authority in the Profession of Commerce and Consistent Advocate of Methods Up to Date and Above the Table.

JOSEPH CROSBY LINCOLN, - - - Editor.
FRIEND PITTS, JR., - Circulation and Advertising.
E. R. KITTREDGE, - - - Business Manager.

PUBLISHED MONTHLY

SUBSCRIPTION $1 a Year in the United States, Canada and Mexico. Other countries $1.50. Postage prepaid by the Publishers. In the absence of specific orders to stop at the end of the subscription term the paper will be continued and a bill sent. Entered at the New York Postoffice as Second Class mail matter.

COMMERCE, ACCOUNTS & FINANCE COMPANY, Publishers
Twenty-five Pine Street, New York

The publishers of Commerce, Accounts & Finance have undertaken to do something that has never been done before. They have undertaken to prepare a library of practical accounting and business management that shall cover every branch of work and cover it thoroughly and well and in the most up-to-date manner. There have been published innumerable works on bookkeeping, some good, some bad and more indifferent and incomplete. There have been books published dealing with auditing and with business organization and administration; but never, so far as we know, has the entire range of office routine from the materials used by the office boy to the duties and responsibilities of the president of the corporation been brought together, systematized and described as it is intended that they shall be in the business library which is now being made ready by the publishers of this periodical. It is a big proposition, there is no doubt about that, but there is need of such books as these, and the members of the publication committee have undertaken to fill that need.

*

The first bock in the series, "The Tools of Business," is unique. It stands in a class by itself as an encyclopedia of office equipment. Let us suppose that one is about to open an office for the transaction of business. No matter what that business may be, the uses of the present age demand that the office be designed, furnished and equipped in as handsome and complete a manner as the means of the owner or lessee will allow. Antiquated "tools of business' have been supplanted, in this our day, by machines and appliances as far superior to those of our fathers as the Hoe press is superior to that used by Benjamin Franklin. Our man of business, therefore, desires to know what his office must contain in order to be abreast of the times. He turns to the book "The Tools of Business," and there under the several headings he finds information concerning the materials most used in the construction of the floor of his office, the coverings for that floor and for the walls, information concerning the various styles and makes of the desks and chairs, the various standard makes of typewriters, copying presses, duplicating machines, safes, vaults, cash drawers, pens, inks, papers, filing cabinets—in short, every possible fitting and appliance that he may need. By consulting this book he may decide just what he needs to buy in order to make his place of business complete. There remains but to ascertain prices and to buy the goods themselves. It seems to us that this first book of the library is in itself almost invaluable.

*

The "Elements of Bookkeeping" comes next, and though our business man may be informed concerning these "elements," his son or his clerk will find information in the book that is just what he is looking for. To be frank, and judging by experience, the average man of business knows far too little of the principles of bookkeeping, and the lack of knowledge accounts for the ridiculous and slipshod manner in which so many men of affairs permit their books to be kept. Single entry bookkeeping is as obsolete as the hand spinning wheel; in fact, it really is not bookkeeping at all, yet some large concerns depend upon it for their records of business done.

*

Balance Sheet Accounting we believe to be the most up-to-date system of accounting yet devised. Our opinion in this matter is borne out by the testimony of hundreds of prominent business men who are using this system and are delighted with the results attained. A book on the subject, therefore, is something for which there is likely to be a large demand. The volume will tell what Balance Sheet Accounting is, its principles and workings, and how it may be installed to fit any branch of manufacture or trade. "Results always in sight" is the motto of the Balance Sheet system, and as the average merchant is hungering for some scheme of accounting that will tell him at any time exactly how much money he is making or losing, it follows that he will want to buy and read "Balance Sheet Accounting."

*

Auditing is a branch of professional practice that is very important. Many large houses employ one or more auditors; but do these so-called auditors really audit? That is the question. Many of them draw a trial balance and consider the audit complete, but that is not the definition of the term as will be set forth in this book. Its author is an auditor who fills the position for some of the largest banking houses and commercial corporations in the country, and he knows his business. The book on "Auditing" will cover the subject in a way in which it has never before been handled and that will be satisfactory as well as understandable.

The final volume of the forthcoming library is to deal with subjects of vast importance. It will treat of the subjects of the business world, namely, "Business Organization and Administration." The ledger may be well kept, and the salesman may sell large quantities of goods, but if there is a lack of well-organized system and administrative ability the concern will lose money, or, at least, will make but a small percentage of the profit that might come to it were these all-important matters properly adjusted. In the book which concludes the series, business organization and administration will be dealt with in a common-sense, intelligent manner. The experience of successful business managers will be drawn upon for material and their advice will be quoted at length. The various departments of a great business will be dissected, each in turn, and the various cogs, that, fitting one into the other, make up a harmonious and smooth running whole, will be described and their workings explained. It is intended that "Business Organization and Administration" shall be worthy of its title.

*

We have dwelt upon the new library of business at length because we believe its importance justifies the space given it. Commerce, Accounts & Finance feels proud that its name should go forth as sponsor for such an enterprise. If the books when completed are what it is intended they shall be, we think the edition definite of the literature of business for the next twenty years at least will have been issued. Meanwhile, the reader is asked to turn to the advertising pages of this paper and to read what is said there concerning the search for a name for this series of books. The publication committee is in search of a name that will fit the subject, and if the reader can help them out, so much the better for them and, incidentally, for him. The committee have received a number of suggestions. They would like to receive a thousand more, but will be grateful for each one. Get your wits to work, dear reader, and help the committee out.

* * *

In this issue of Commerce, Accounts & Finance is opened a new department that we believe will prove to be both interesting and important. We refer to the department devoted to the School of Business Organization and Administration. In this department will be found this month a general description of the school, its methods and the subjects which are embraced in its courses. As the reader will perceive, these subjects are vital to the profession of business, and to be well grounded in their principles is to be well equipped for what, to the great majority, is the chosen work of life. There are many soldiers in the world, many statesmen, lawyers, doctors, authors, clergymen, and what not, but their number is very small compared to the great army enlisted in the service of commerce and those of its allies, financiering and accounting. It is to the privates in this army, and particularly to the young recruits in its ranks, that the School of Business Organization and Administration should appeal.

*

In the new department, among other matters, will appear each month "Talks With Students" and "Collateral Reading." "Talks With Students" will be what its name implies, a series of helpful dissertations upon the various subjects of the lesson courses.* If a student is perplexed concerning some point in his studies and will write of his trouble to the faculty of the school, his inquiry will, so far as is possible, be answered under the head of "Talks With Students." In this way, all readers of the paper, and in particular all the other students in his course, will be given the information, as well as will he, himself. As an example of this, see the talk concerning the "International Date Line" in this issue. In "Collateral Reading" it is proposed to print much useful matter from current literature and the various authorities bearing upon Grammar, Business Correspondence, Commercial Law, and the other business branches in which the student is interested. The articles in this issue of Commerce, Accounts & Finance are but a foretaste of what is to come. It will be our aim to improve the School department in every possible way and to make it a valuable aid to the student.

NOT THE REAL THING.

Bounder—Charley is a pusher; he always gets there. He's of the true metal, he is.

Stillman—What are you talking about? Brass isn't a metal: it's only a composition.—Boston Transcript.

THE UNKINDEST CUT.

The Philadelphia "Record" chronicled, "Caterpillars are crawling": and an ever-appreciative New York paper not only copied the startling item but gave it the scare-head, "Activity in the Quaker City."

IDENTIFIED.

"Public Opinion" says that a South African constabulary commander wrote to a local troop officer, asking if there were any donkeys in camp. The reply came, in the troop officer's handwriting, "Yes, one—R. H. Smynes, Captain."

A scene in Chicago—As it must seem to strangers who have been reading the papers recently.—Chicago Record-Herald.

The Negotiable Instruments Law*

By THOMAS B. PATON.

Instrument Dishonored by Non-Payment—Notice of Dishonor—Time of Maturity—Computation of Time.

NOTE.—As enacted in New York, the Negotiable Instruments Law is divided into nineteen articles as follows:

1. General Provisions (Sections 1—17)
2. Negotiable Instruments: Form and Interpretation (20—42)
3. Consideration (50—55)
4. Negotiation (60—80)
5. Rights of holder (90—98)
6. Liabilities of parties (110—119)
7. Presentment for payment (130—148)
8. Notice of dishonor (160—189)
9. Discharge (200—206)
10. Bills of exchange (210—215)
11. Acceptance (220—230)
12. Presentment for acceptance (240—248)
13. Protest (260—268)
14. Acceptance for honor (280—290)
15. Payment for honor (300—306)
16. Bills in a set (310—315)
17. Promissory notes and checks (320—325)
18. Notes given for patent rights (330—332)
19. Laws repealed. When takes effect (340—341)

The provisions of the law naturally fall under four general classifications.

a. General Provisions.
b. Negotiable Instruments in General.
c. Bills of Exchange.
d. Promissory Notes and Checks.

The text of the law is the same in all the states (with some slight exceptions which will be noted) but the numbering of the sections, and in some states, of the articles, is not uniform. There is, however, the same continuity of articles and text, except that in some instances "General Provisions" follow, instead of precede the remainder of the act. By following this course of study with reference to the New York act, as above outlined, the reader in each state can apply the same to the law of his own state.

WE come next to the sections which provide and describe when an instrument is dishonored by non-payment and the liability of persons secondarily liable when the instrument is dishonored.

Sec. 143. When Instrument Dishonored by Non-Payment.—The instrument is dishonored by non-payment when:

1. It is duly presented for payment and payment is refused or cannot be obtained; or
2. Presentment is excused and the instrument is overdue and unpaid.

Sec. 144. Liability of Person Secondarily Liable When Instrument is Dishonored.—Subject to the provisions of this act, when the instrument is dishonored by non-payment an immediate right of recourse to all parties secondarily liable theron accrues to the holder.

In section 143 we see it clearly stated that an instrument is dishonored by non-payment when "it is duly presented for payment and payment is refused or cannot be obtained," or when "presentment is excused and the instrument is overdue and unpaid."

The Negotiable Instruments Law abolishes grace on negotiable instruments so that the day of maturity, there being no grace, is the day upon which dishonor happens where the instrument is unpaid. Where an instrument is presented for payment and payment refused before the close of banking or business hours on the day of maturity, the questions arise (1) may notice of dishonor immediately be given before the close of such hours; (2) may suit immediately be instituted to enforce payment of the instrument on the same day, after the fact of dishonor, or must the whole day be allowed to elapse and does the right to bring suit only arise on the day following that of dishonor?

Notice of Dishonor.

So far as the giving of notice of dishonor is concerned, the holder is not bound to present it a second time, and where the instrument is presented during reasonable hours and is dishonored, the authorities have practically agreed that notice of dishonor may be immediately given and that the holder is not obliged to wait until the close of banking or business hours as the case may be, although it is often customary to do so. While the maker or primary debtor upon an instrument has the whole day in which to pay it, the holder may nevertheless, after actual dishonor, immediately give notice, and if the instrument is afterward paid on the same day, the effect of the payment is to render the notice of no avail.

But with regard to the bringing of suit upon a dishonored instrument on the day of maturity, there has been, in different states, considerable conflict of authority, the cases mostly involving instruments which have carried grace, the abolishment of the grace feature being a very recent matter. One line of cases have held to the theory that as the maker has the whole of the last day of grace to make payment, and that as the law knows no fraction of a day, suit cannot be instituted against him until the day of payment has entirely elapsed. And concerning suit against an indorser, it has also been held that suit cannot be instituted immediately after the sending of notice, but sufficient time must elapse for the indorser to be in actual receipt of such notice. To the contrary, many courts have held that while in the case of ordinary contracts the promissor has the whole of the day for their performance and suit cannot be commenced for a breach until that day has passed, yet where the maker of a note or the acceptor of a bill makes it payable on a day certain, his contract is to pay it on demand on any part of that day, if made within reasonable hours; hence, after demand and refusal of payment on the last day of grace, his contract is broken and action may be commenced on the same day against the maker; and after notice has been issued to the indorser, action may be also commenced against him, whether sufficient time has elapsed for him to actually receive it or not.

The Negotiable Instruments Act does not provide a regulation of this disputed question whether suit against the primary debtor, after dishonor, on the day of maturity, is or is not premature; but as to suit against the indorsers of persons secondarily liable, the provision of section 144 that "subject to the provisions of this act" (i. e., subject to the provisions for charging such parties by due notice of dishonor) "when the instrument is dishonored by non-payment, an immediate right of recourse to all parties secondarily liable thereon accrues to the holder," would seem to authorize the conclusion that suit on the same day, after the issuance of notice of dishonor, would not be premature.

Time of Maturity.

We now approach the provision which regulates the time of maturity.

Sec. 145. Time of Maturity.—Every negotiable instrument is payable at the time fixed therein without grace. When the day of maturity falls upon Sunday, or a holiday, the instrument is payable on the next succeeding business day. Instruments falling due on Saturday are to be presented for payment on the next succeeding business day, except that instruments payable on demand may, at the option of the holder, be presented for payment before twelve o'clock noon on Saturday when that entire day is not a holiday.

We have heretofore considered those provisions which regulate the time of maturity with reference to within

---

*Republished from the Banking Law Journal by permission. Copyright, 1899, 1900, 1901 and 1902, by T. B. Paton; all rights reserved. To be revised and published in book form by the author.

what particular hours on the day of maturity the instrument must be presented, both where the instrument is (sec. 135) and is not (sec. 132) payable at a bank. The present section fixes with definiteness the day of maturity itself. In the first place, "every negotiable instrument is payable at the time fixed therein without grace." In these few words the long standing customs and laws attaching three days of grace to the time of payment of certain negotiable instruments are swept away and the instrument becomes payable, according to its terms, without grace.

In Massachusetts a slight deviation has been made in this provision; for by chapter 130 of the laws of 1899 it is enacted that "on all drafts and bills of exchange made payable within this commonwealth at sight, three days of grace shall be allowed, unless there is an express stipulation therein to the contrary;" and so much of the Negotiable Instruments Law as is consistent therewith is repealed.

In North Carolina, also, the grace portion of the above section is not operative by reason of a provision incorporated in a later section in the act that "the laws now in force in this state with regard to days of grace shall remain in force, and shall not be construed to be repealed by this act."

Sundays and Holidays.

Section 145, taking into view the existence of Sundays and of holidays, next provides a uniform rule fixing the day of payment of all instruments which by their terms would otherwise be payable on Sunday or a holiday, namely, the next succeeding business day. The Negotiable Instruments Act does not name the days to be observed as holidays; these are fixed by separate enactment by the legislatures of the various states and, of course, these days are not always the same in different states of the Union.

Finally, by Section 145, the act fixes with definiteness the time of maturity of instruments falling due on Saturday. It provides that instruments falling due on Saturday are to be presented for payment on the next succeeding business day, except that instruments payable on demand may, at the option of the holder, be presented for payment before twelve o'clock noon on Saturday when that entire day is not a holiday. This provision is doubtless made to meet the situation in those states which have enacted Saturday half-holiday laws. The holder of a bill or note, payable on time, which, by its terms, falls due on Saturday, must hold it until the next succeeding business day, generally Monday, to present for payment; but the holder of a demand instrument such as a check, may at his option present it for payment before twelve o'clock noon on any business Saturday. The inquiry comes in right here—What about those states in which the Negotiable Instruments Law has been enacted which have no special Saturday half-holiday legislation?—in other words, where the entire Saturday is a business day, the same as any other day of the week? Why, in such cases, the act virtually makes Saturday a holiday so far as the presentment for payment of time paper is concerned, and precludes its presentment until the next business day; thereby virtually adding two days of grace to all such paper, by extending the time of payment from Saturday to the following Monday.

The details of legislation in this respect in those states in which the Negotiable Instruments Law has been enacted, are as follows:

In the states of New York, Connecticut, Virginia, Pennsylvania, and in the District of Columbia, there is special legislation making Saturday afternoons a half holiday, so that Section 145, enacted in uniform language in such states, is consistent and appropriate in postponing the payment of time paper to the following business day.

In the state of Washington, also, there is special legislation making Saturday afternoon a half holiday so far as the payment of negotiable paper is concerned, so that Section 145, enacted in that state, is also consistent and appropriate.

But in the states of Florida, Massachusetts, Oregon, North Carolina, Tennessee, North Dakota and Utah, unless there has been some very recent change in this last-named state, there is no special half-holiday legislation whatever; Saturday in those states, so far as legislative enactments are concerned, apart from the Negotiable Instruments Act, are business days throughout; so that in those states, the adoption of the Negotiable Instruments Act with this section postponing the payment of time paper from Saturday until Monday, virtually adds two days to the time of payment of such paper, although Saturday afternoons in such states are legally business days. Whether this has been knowingly done, or unintentional, we cannot say; but such at all events is the result.

In Rhode Island the only Saturday half-holiday legislation is special, namely, that permitting certain public offices to close at twelve o'clock on Saturdays. The enactment of the Negotiable Instruments Law in that state likewise postpones payment of time paper from Saturday until Monday.

In Maryland, where the Negotiable Instruments Law has been enacted, there is likewise no general Saturday half-holiday legislation; but in 1900 the legislature made Saturday a half holiday in Cecil County only. The same provisions of the Negotiable Instruments Law postpone the payment of time paper from Saturday until Monday throughout the entire state.

Law in Colorado and Wisconsin.

In only two states in which the Negotiable Instruments Law has been enacted, wherein Saturday afternoon has not been made a half holiday for the entire state, has the language of Section 145 been modified so as to make it consistent with existing conditions. These states are Colorado and Wisconsin. In Colorado, Saturday afternoons have been made half holidays only in cities of 100,000 or more, and only in the months of June, July and August in each year. At other times, and in all other places in the state, Saturday is a business day. Instead of adopting Section 145 entire, the legislature of Colorado wisely modified it so as to read as follows:

"Instruments falling due on any day in any place where any part of such day is a holiday are to be presented for payment on the next succeeding business day, except that instruments payable on demand may, at the option of the holder, be presented for payment during reasonable business hours on the part of such day which is not a holiday.

In the State of Wisconsin there is no Saturday half-holiday legislation, the entire Saturday being a business day. The legislators in that state wisely made Section 145 conform to existing conditions by enacting that portion of the section only which abolishes grace and provides for paper falling due upon Sundays or holidays; omitting entirely the concluding portion of the section that "instruments falling due upon Saturday are to be presented for payment on the next succeeding business day, except that instruments payable on demand may, at the option of the holder, be presented for payment before twelve o'clock noon on Saturday when that entire day is not a holiday." In Wisconsin, therefore, where a man makes a three months note, which by its terms matures on a Saturday, the note is payable and must be presented on Saturday, and is not postponed until the following business day, notwithstanding the general Negotiable Instruments Act, with this feature omitted, prevails in that state.

Computation of Time.

We now come to the section which computes the days which an instrument payable at a fixed period after date, after sight, or after the happening of a specified event, has to run.

Section 146. Time; How Computed.—Where the instrument is payable at a fixed period after date, after sight, or after the happening of a specified event, the time of payment is determined by excluding the day from which the time is to begin to run, and by including the date of payment.

This section follows the rule of the law merchant as universally recognized. The day of payment of a note, payable thirty days after date for example, is arrived at by excluding the day of date, and fixing the day of payment as the thirtieth day thereafter. In case that day falls on Sunday or a holiday, then Section 145, as we have seen, makes the instrument payable on the next succeeding business day. Likewise, if the instrument is payable so many days after sight, or after the happening of a specified event, the day of sight, or of the happening of the event, is excluded.

Payable at Bank.

Sec. 147. Instrument Payable at Bank.—Where the instrument is made payable at a bank it is equivalent to an order to the bank to pay the same for the account of the principal debtor thereon.

This section provides a uniform rule for the payment of instruments made payable at banks, to supplant the conflicting rules which have prevailed in different states.

It was the law of New York State, before the Act, that where a depositor in a bank made his note payable at the bank, the note, in so far as related to its presentment at the bank and the duties of the bank in respect to it, was equivalent to a check drawn by the maker upon the bank where the note was made payable. Hence, not only had the bank the right or authority to pay the note, but it was compelled to do so. The law of Pennsylvania was the same as that of New York in this respect. In some of the other states, the rule was that the bank had authority to pay, but was not obliged to do so in the absence of express instructions from the maker, or the decisions while holding the bank authorized were silent upon the point of obligation; and in still other states, the law was declared that a bank had no right to pay a depositor's note made payable at the bank, in the absence of special instruction so to do, and payment made without such instruction was at its peril. In many states there had been no special decision upon the subject, and bankers were in a quandary as to their authority and duty in the premises.

The Act clears up this matter. An instrument made payable at a bank is equivalent to, or the same thing as, an order to the bank to pay the same for the account of the principal debtor thereon.

The bank, then, at which an instrument—note or acceptance—is made payable by a depositor, must pay the same, if in funds. But suppose a time note is not presented on the precise day of maturity, but a day or two afterward. An interesting question here arises whether the bank's authority and duty to pay is limited to the day of maturity only, or can or must be exercised on a subsequent day? We think in such cases the authority and duty is limited to the day of maturity. Non-presentment on that day discharges indorsers, and leaves to the holder recourse upon the note against the maker alone. Presentment by the holder on a day subsequent to maturity, is presentment of an overdue instrument, to which suspicions attach, and in such case the holder should be left to his recourse upon the maker direct, and the bank, as the latter's paying agent, should not volunteer payment of an instrument which, perchance, the maker might have some good reason for refusing. Of course, where the instrument made payable by a depositor at the bank is in the nature of an acceptance, or demand note, having no precise, fixed day of maturity, the bank's rule of payment would, doubtless, be the same as in case of its depositor's check.

Another interesting question comes up in this connection. A note made payable at a bank, has on it the names of sureties and indorsers, and before maturity is discounted by the bank, which becomes its owner. On the day of maturity the maker has sufficient funds on deposit to pay the note. But the bank, say at the request of the maker, fails to pay or charge up the note against his account and afterward allows him to withdraw his deposit. Does the bank, by such action, release the indorsers and sureties from liability? This is a question upon which the authorities have not been entirely uniform; but the better opinion seems to be that the indorsers and sureties are released. But, taking the same case, except that the bank is not owner of the note, but it is presented by the last holder, and payment refused by the bank at the request of the maker, though in funds, we do not think—although it has been argued to the contrary—that in this case the sureties on the note are released, for here the failure to apply funds of the principal debtor is not by a creditor of the latter, but by his debtor and paying agent, the bank, and its action in not paying is the same as it would take in the case of its depositor's check, payment of which he had stopped.

THE FLY AND THE BELL.

The Fly: "Curfew shall not ring to-night."

The above little artistic creation, which is supposed to be a realistic representation of a bold attempt upon the part of a certain fly to get itself into the pages of history, is amusing on account of the incongruity of the comparative sizes of the fly and the bell. We assume that there is not a man who rests his eye upon this little picture who will not smile at the vanity of the fly in supposing for a minute that his actions could have any restraining effect upon the movement of the bell. And yet these same men are confronted with parallel cases in their daily business life, and the absurdity of the parallel does not appeal to them. Thus the efforts of certain people to stem the tide of modern progress by trying to oppose lawful combinations of capital, despite the fact that every far-seeing and broad-minded economist concedes the fact that such combinations are but one more step in our commercial evolution, are in every way as ridiculous and amusing as is the effort of the fly in the picture to stop the ringing of the curfew.

A WIDE ACQUAINTANCE.

"Yes," said the fat man, "I live in Swamphurst, but I don't know the man you speak of."

"That's funny; he said he had a wide acquaintance in Swamphurst, and I naturally thought he meant you."

Correspondence School of

Business Organization and Administration

"Accounting is the Vital Element of Business"

THE LESSON COURSES.

The lesson courses are arranged in two series: Preparatory and Advanced. The legend on the banner is "Accounting is the Vital Element of Business." Every effort is made, therefore, to get the pupil fully conversant with accounting principles as the foundation of his work and then building thereon to instruct him in Organization and Administration along selected lines.

Each student upon enrollment is subjected to a preliminary examination to put upon our office records the facts of his elementary training. Notation is also made of various personal facts connected with his history, such as age, experience in actual business, references, etc. So far we have found remunerative employment for every one who has been under our charge, and at present the applicants upon our rolls for intelligent help are in excess of our ability to supply. Every one who entrusts himself to our care is assured of a good position on completion of either one of the advanced courses of training.

PREPARATORY COURSES.

A	English Grammar, Composition and Business Rhetoric	$25 00
B	Business Correspondence	15 00
C	Shorthand and Typewriting	25 00
D	Commercial Geography	15 00
E	Financial and Commercial History	15 00
F	Business Arithmetic	15 00
G	Double Entry Bookkeeping	25 00
H	Commercial Law	25 00

ADVANCED COURSES.

1	Accounting, Business Organization and Administration of Machine Shop with Foundry	$100
2	Accounting, Business Organization and Administration of Cotton Mill (Textiles in General)	100
3	Accounting, Business Organization and Administration of Street Car Line	100
4	Accounting, Business Organization and Administration of Department Store	100
5	Accounting, Business Organization and Administration of Country Bank	100
6	Accounting, Business Organization and Administration of Large City Bank	100
7	Accounting, Business Organization and Administration of Book Publishing House	100
8	Accounting, Business Organization and Administration of Periodical Publishing Concern	100
9	Accounting, Business Organization and Administration of Mercantile Business (wholesale)	100
10	Accounting, Business Organization and Administration of Mining	100
11	Accounting, Business Organization and Administration of General Manufacturing	100
12	Accounting, Business Organization and Administration of Installment Merchandising	100

Special courses arranged in the light of particular requirements.

The prices preceding are for single payments with the order. Under proper conditions, and at a slight advance over these rates, we are prepared to concede monthly or quarterly payments.

Time unlimited. Students may enter at any time, and proceed with their work rapidly or slowly as suits their convenience.

The Lesson Courses are all sectionalized. A second section will be forwarded only when proficiency has been shown in the first.

PRELIMINARY EXAMINATION.

(In answering these questions, indicate the questions by numbers. Write on paper 8½ x 11 inches, one side only).

1. Name.
2. Home address.
3. Business address.
4. Married or single.
5. Age.
6. General account of elementary education.
7. General account of business experience.
8. What works on bookkeeping, commerce, finance, etc., have you in your library or that are accessible for reference?
9. Define the principle of debit and credit.
10. Outline the general method of opening a set of books.
11. Describe the general method of closing a set of books.
12. Define "trial balance."
13. Define "balance sheet."
14. About how much time per day can you devote to this course of study?

SAMPLE DESCRIPTIONS.

The following descriptions of courses are samples of all and will serve to give the prospective student an idea of the kind of instruction he will receive.

Preparatory Courses.

One of the greatest difficulties that we have encountered in the instruction that we have been giving in this line the last few years is the lack of thorough grounding in fundamental principles. We have been approached by those desiring instruction as accountants who were deficient in the elements of bookkeeping. We have been approached by those who desire to be drilled as secretaries and amanuenses, who were deficient in ordinary English. For this reason the preparatory courses mentioned in the announcement of this school have been most carefully prepared.

In each of these courses the student is given practical instruction from the outset. All that which is superfluous from the standpoint of every-day, hard-fisted business is relegated to the background, and only that is taught which is applicable to the requirements of business transactions. The illustrations employed are eminently practical and are derived from actual going business.

1.—Machine Shop With Foundry. $100.

In this case the student is supposed to have some machine shop and foundry in mind. If he has the run of the office of such an institution, so much the better. His instruction commences with the charting of the accounts, and is continued, with full explanation of the details which go to make up the accounts. The entering of orders, the analysis of orders, the conveyance of the order to the foreman or superintendent, are each described. Incidentally the methods of handling cash, including petty cash and the bank account, are worked out in all necessary detail. Items in suspense, matters in reserve, and the handling of the different accounts composing the Balance Sheet Ledger are carefully exploited.

After the accounting foundation has been thus broadly laid, the question of the business organization and administration of the shop is undertaken. Various examples are presented, ranging from a very small shop to one of considerable size. The question of business matters as distinct and different from those of shop details is presented, and the relation of one department to another is carefully discussed. The question of a code for managing and operating these several divisions is introduced and illustrated.

2.—Cotton Mill Work. $100.

This subject is intended to cover textiles in general. The accounting foundation is laid broad and deep, covering everything from entering the order and the purchase of material, together with the time keeping and payment of employees, to the final adjustments in the balance sheet. All details are gone over carefully.

On the accounting foundation thus established there is then introduced the question of general organization at the mill, including the business head (president or treasurer as the case may be), the superintendent, the foreman, the overseers. The arrangement of the offices, the duties assigned to each of the occupants thereof, the correspondence, and all other details are carefully gove over.

If the student has the run of a cotton mill or other textile institution, he is encouraged to bring into his work illustrations derived from the actual practice of the establishment under view. His instruction will be so complete as to enable him to take charge of the work and carry it through.

4.—Department Store. $100.

In no line of business is proper organization and efficient administration more necessary than in the department store. In no branch of merchandising does the going balance sheet and profit and loss statement develop to better advantage than in this. There is perhaps no line of business extending more rapidly throughout the country than the department store.

In this course, as in others, the student at the outset is drilled in the accounting and then upon the foundation so laid is given instruction in the matter of arrangement and management.

The accounting taught is made to include every ticket and slip, no matter how insignificant, and the details are so handled that there is no rewriting or copying. The best use of modern devices for economizing labor is carefully pointed out, and the results are displayed in the balance sheet ledger and profit and loss statement, which in this case are made to give their results daily. The margins of profit in the department store are not large. They frequently depend upon the cashing of bills. All these matters are discussed in exhaustive detail.

11.—General Manufacturing. $100.

The student in this course, as well as in others, is drilled first in the principles and practice of the accounts, that which is to be accomplished in this direction being first worked out in chart form.

After the accounting has been thoroughly covered, there is taken up the general question of the purchase of supplies, the care of supplies, the entry of orders in the factory, the relationship of the superintendent to the general office, the relationship of the foreman to the superintendent, with illustrations and provisions for taking care of these several functions.

Where the student has access to a factory, he is encouraged to bring into the work practical illustrations drawn from the methods under view, and at completion he is left in such shape as to be competent to administer the entire responsibilities of the establishment, or to introduce improvements in routine in different divisions as circumstances permit.

TALKS WITH STUDENTS.

The following letter came to us from one of the students in the Course of Commercial Geeography:

In a recent discussion with some friends respecting problems in longitude and time the international date line was mentioned. We discovered, before we got through, that our knowledge of the nature and location of that imaginary division of time was somewhat vague and shadowy, to say the least. Therefore, I appeal to you for enlightenment. How is the date line determined? Is it with reference to the meridian of Greenwich, or to the recognized meridian of any other nation? And between what lines of latitude does it run? If you think the subject of sufficient interest to give it attention, I shall be obliged, and shall thank you for answering my questions and for supplying any other information pertinent to the subject that you may be pleased to furnish.

The meridian at Greenwich, England, is one of the standards of the world for calculating longtitude. When it is midnight on Sunday at Greenwich, it is Sunday at all places from Greenwich to 180 degrees east of Greenwich, and Monday at all places from Greenwich to 180 degrees west of Greenwich. That is, to the same meridian. Ship captains, therefore, who recognize the Greenwich standard, change their time at this 180th meridian. Going eastward, if they should pass this meridian on Sunday, they would change the time on shipboard to Monday. If they should pass the meridian on Sunday while going westward they would make the change to Saturday. This change is made for the purpose of having the correct time of all localities east or west of the 180th meridian.

Similar changes would be made if any other meridian was taken as the standard of reckoning.

The international date line differs slightly from the 180th meridian of any of the world's standards of longitude. The course of this time is far from straight. It does not follow any of the earth's meridians. According to Mr. Olney, the scientist and mathematician, it starts from the Chatham Islands, latitude 44 degrees S., longitude 177 degrees W., runs north and west to the east of New Zealand, New Guinea and Borneo, thence through the Philippines, approaching China near Canton, thence to the northwest of the Japan Islands, thence through the Behring Sea to the North Pole. The date east of this line is generally one day behind that west of it.

For further information on this subject we present to our readers the following article by Mr. Henry Collins, which was published in "The School Bulletin and New York State Educational Journal":

The International Date Line.

If a person should start at midday, that is, when the sun was shining perpendicularly on the meridian passing through the place of starting, and could by any means travel westward, keeping pace with the sun, thus keeping the sun directly over the meridian of the place at which he might be, he would make a complete journey around the globe in twenty-four hours, and arrive at the place of starting at noon the next day. But though twenty-four hours of time have passed, to the traveler the sun has been shining perpendicularly all the time, and the question arises: When or at what point did the traveler change from noon one day to noon the next? For instance, if he should start at Sunday noon and keep the sun in the zenith, he would arrive at the place of starting Monday noon; when did the change take place? It has been noonday to the traveler during the whole journey of twenty-four hours, and to him it is yet Sunday noon; he has apparently lost a day and to obtain the correct date he must drop a day.

The reason for dropping a day can be more fully shown as follows: Remembering that the earth makes one complete revolution on its axis in twenty-four hours, and thus the sun in its apparent diurnal revolution moves over 360 degrees of space in twenty-four hours, it thus moves over 15 degrees of space in one hour; from which it is evident that the difference in longitude which causes the difference in the relative time may be estimated in time, allowing 15 degrees to an hour, or one degree to four minutes. Therefore, suppose, starting from any given point, you travel one degree west, your watch, instead of marking 12 o'clock at noon, according to the correct time at that place, would mark four minutes after twelve. Travel west 15 degrees, and you will find that one o'clock by your watch will be noonday by the sun. Go on to 120 degrees, and when the sun is in the zenith your watch will indicate eight o'clock P. M. Complete your journey around the globe and you will have gained, in this manner, twenty-four hours. From this it will be seen that in order to obtain the correct time twenty-four hours must be subtracted from your time.

On the other hand, if a person could travel eastward at the same speed with which the sun apparently travels westward (the same rate of speed with which the earth revolves on its axis), if he should start at noonday he would meet the sun when exactly on the opposite side of the earth from the place of starting, thus seeing three noondays within twenty-four hours, or apparently gaining a day. This we know to be impossible, since only twenty-four hours of time have passed, while in reality an extra period of light has been gained, and thus to obtain the correct local date a day must be added to your time. By traveling two degrees east you will lose eight minutes of time, as the sun-dial marks noon at fifty-two minutes past eleven by your watch. Going on to 120 degrees, it will be noon at 4 o'clock A. M. by your watch; complete the journey and you will have lost twenty-four hours.

To show further what might happen I quote from an

excellent article on the subject by the late W. D. Henkle, published in the Ohio "Educational Monthly":

Curious Facts.

"If a traveler should leave Columbus, Ohio, at noon on Saturday and go westward, keeping pace with the sun, he would arrive at Columbus at noon on Sunday. His noon would continue for twenty-four hours, and Saturday noon would change to Sunday noon without an intervening night. Where would the change occur? If a man should start from Columbus on Saturday and travel one degree east he would delay the first noon after his arrival four minutes.

"Now if two men should start from Columbus and travel around the earth, one going east and the other going west, and should meet each other at any point, whether half way around or not, it would be found that one would have set the hands of his watch forward four minutes for every degree that he had traveled east, and the other would have set the hands of his watch backward four minutes for every degree he had traveled west. There being 360 degrees of travel, the sum of the minutes of change in the two watches would be exactly twenty-four hours. But the watches at the meeting place would indicate the same hour of the day, and hence the travelers would agree as to the time of the day, but they would differ just one day of the week, the eastward traveler being a day ahead.

"Every 360 degrees traveled jointly by the travelers would make another day's difference in the week, until they should travel jointly seven times 360 degrees, when they would not only agree as to the time of the day, but as to the day of the week. They would, however, disagree seven days as to the days of the month.

"If they should travel jointly twenty-eight times 360 degrees and meet on some day in February in a common year according to the count of the westward traveler, they would agree as to the time of the day, the day of the week, and the day of the month, but not as to the name of the month, the eastward traveler calling it March.

"If they should travel ninety-one times 360 degrees and meet on the same day of April according to the westward traveler, they would agree except as to the month, the eastward traveler calling it July.

"If they should travel jointly 245 times 360 degrees and meet according to the westward traveler in May, they would agree as before, except that the eastward traveler would call it January of the following year.

"Such discrepancies might occur in common years in a dozen other ways. For instance, for ninety-one times 360 degrees, we might also have the months of September and December. In leap years about sixteen such instances might be given, not going beyond 236 times 360 degrees. If they should travel 2,191 times 360 degrees, they would agree as to the time of the day, the day of the week, the day of the month, and the name of the month, but they would differ six years as to the number of the year of the century, provided there should be one intercalary day between their dates.

"To bring about such results, there need be no restriction as to the time of starting or rate of travel. If the two supposed travelers should not live to carry out the plan, there would be the same results if the travel is finally completed by any of their immediate or remote descendants, provided they should retain the same mode of counting."

What is the Date Line?

From this we see that for every time a person travels around the earth in either direction there is a difference in time of one day, and the result is the same, regardless of the rate of speed. In order to avoid the confusion of dates which must necessarily result from this constant gain on one side and loss on the other, it has been proposed to determine upon some line at which eastern-bound travelers shall add a day, and westward travelers shall drop a day from their reckoning, and thus prevent a disagreement in regard to the day of the week. The line at which this addition or subtraction shall be made is what is meant by the date line.

The fact and necessity of such a date line may be shown in a way with which we are all familiar. Take a simple problem in arithmetic on "Longitude and Time." "When it is 9 o'clock A. M., May 1, at Singapore, long. 104 E., what time is it at Manila, long. 121 degrees 30 minutes, E?" The difference of longitude estimated eastward from Singapore is 17 degrees 30 minutes. The application of the ordinary rules of arithmetic gives for an answer ten hours, ten minutes, May 1. But the difference of longitude estimated westward from Singapore is 342 degrees 30 minutes, giving for an answer ten: 10 A. M., April 30. This shows that when the time of day at one place is known, and the longitudes of both places are known, the time of

The "Sandow" of the Situation.—New York World.

day at the other may be obtained in two ways, viz., by using the difference of longitude estimated west, or estimated east. But the dates thus obtained differ by one day; which is correct? Sometimes the one and sometimes the other. In the problem just considered the latter result is correct. In such problems the difference of longitude must be taken in such a direction as not to come across the date line; or if the date line is crossed, the dates must be changed in accordance with the following definition:

The date line is the line at which dates must be made later by one day when crossing it from east to west, and earlier by one day when crossing it from west to east.

The popular idea seems to be that 180 degrees east or west of Greenwich is the point at which this change of date occurs. This is not the fact, although sometimes the case. In general terms it may be defined as a very irregular line, located mostly in the Pacific Ocean, and extending from pole to pole. Let us consider where it is, and why it is placed where it is.

Roman Origin.

The calendars in general use throughout the civilized world originated in Rome. The one most generally adopted is the Gregorian. Russia, and all other countries of the Greek Church, still use the Julian calendar. The two calendars differ as to the day of the month, but agree as to the day of the week.

But whichever calendar is used, all places received their date from Rome. Places receiving dates by westward communication from Rome would naturally be considered earlier in time, at the same instant, and those places receiving dates by eastward communication would be considered later in time at the same instant, and the date lines would naturally occur where these directions of communications met.

Such is the fact. The western part of Europe, the islands of the Atlantic Ocean, the whole of South America and the greater part of North America have received civilization by westward communication from Rome. Therefore there is no date line in the Atlantic, or in America (since the occupation of Alaska by the United States, which will be explained hereafter). The eastern part of Europe and Asia received civilization by eastward communication from Rome. Date lines, therefore, occur in the Pacific Ocean between islands that have received dates by eastward and those that have received them by westward communication. By connecting these two lines we have an irregular line whose general direction is north and south, and which may properly be called the date line, though not always, and perhaps not usually, the line where vessels change dates.

Location.

Beginning therefore, at the north pole, let us trace its course. The northwestern part of British America, formerly known as Russian America, now Alaska, received civilization by eastward communication, therefore its dates would correspond with those of Asia; but the northwestern part of British America received civilization by westward communication, thus the dates there would correspond with those of eastern America and Europe. From this we see that two neighbors, one living in Alaska and one in British America, might differ as to the day of the week. This was often the case before Alaska was purchased by the United States in 1867. On this point we find the following on page 19 of Clark's "Geographical Reader":

"At the town of Sitka, in Alaska, half the population are Russians, who have arrived from Russia across Asia; half of the population are Americans, who have arrived via the United States. Hence, when it is Sunday with the Russians it is Saturday with the Americans; the Russians are busy on Monday while the Americans are in church on Sunday, to the great interruption of business."

Mr. Henkle suspected the inaccuracy of this statement, and wrote to his friend, Marcus Baker, of the coast survey at Washington, to consult Mr. Dall (who has visited Alaska and written much about it) on the subject. He received the following reply, dated April 12, 1879:

"Mr. Dall is not in the office to-day, and I take the liberty therefore to say that the Russians now in Alaska all conform to our calendar. They conform both in respect to the style (not reckoned by the old style as formerly, but by the new style), and they conform also with the time as brought from San Francisco, and not as brought from Siberia. A few Russians remain in Alaska, and church service is held in many small settlements, and always on the same Sunday that we use in the United States. I think that the American time is also used at one station in Siberia, viz., Plover Bay."

By this we see that since the United States has come into possession of Alaska, the dating there has been put back to conform to the rest of the United States. The date line then must pass through Behring Strait; or, according to some authorities, just west of the strait; and if the above remark be true in regard to the station at Plover Bay, then it must pass across the eastern point of Asia.

North of the strait some authorities claim that it passes between Plover and Herald Islands, which holds, as the former was discovered from the eastern continent and the latter from the western.

South of the strait it passes west of Clark's or St. Lawrence Island. This island was discovered by Captain Cook in 1777. Thence it passes west of Goers Island; thence southwesterly between the Aleutian Islands and Asia.

This group is in the Northern Pacific Ocean, extending in a westerly direction from the peninsular promontory of Alaska in North America to the peninsular of Kamschatka, in Asiatic Russia. According to the practice of most recent American geographers, we have comprehended this archipelago under one general name, although Russian geographers usually divide the chain into three several groups, those nearest the eastern coast of Kamschatka, including Behring and Mednoi, or Copper Island, being properly called Aleautian; the central group, the Adreanofskie or Andrenovian; and those nearest the American coast, the Fox Islands. If the inhabitants of all these several groups of islands have changed their dating to correspond with that used on the American continent, then the line should pass west of them all, but if all have not changed, then it should pass between those which have and those which have not changed. Most authorities locate as given above, others placing it east of Behring Island.

It thence passes southwesterly some degrees east of Cape Lopatka and the group of Kurile Islands, thence just east of the Japan Islands, Jesso and Niphon, keeping west of Cuadalupa and Margaret's Islands, but east of Bonin, Loo Choo and Patchoo Islands, and southeast of Formosa.

This island was unknown to the Chinese until about 1403. About 1634 the Dutch established themselves here, and built Fort Zeland on a small island commanding the harbor of the capital Taeman. After retaining possession for twenty-eight years, they were expelled by Coxigina, a famous Chinese rebel, whose successors ruled until 1683, when it was taken by the Chinese. It thus retains the same dating as the Chinese nation proper.

The line then passes through Bashee Channel, just north of the Bashee Islands. It enters the China Sea, east of Hong Kong. It then passes south just west of the Philippine Islands, but keeps east of Palawan Island.

It is here that it reaches its most western point, being about 116 degrees east longitude.

It then takes a southwesterly course, passing through the Sooloo Islands, south of Mindanao and north of Gilolo. Thence it passes east nearly parallel with, but just north of, the equator to a point about 165 degrees just north of Schank Island; thence southwesterly, leaving High Island, Gilbert Archipelago, Taswell Islands, and the De Peyster group on the northeast; thence to a point on Navigator or Samoan Islands to longitude about 268 west; thence it turns south, keeping east of the Navigator, Friendly, Tonga, Vasquez, Kermadec, and Curtis Islands, and west of the Society Islands and Cook's or Harvey Island; thence it continues south, bearing a little to the west, so as to cross, according to some authorities, Chatham Islands; thence to the south pole.

By following this description the line can be traced with a pencil on a map of the world.

Facts of History.

We have now briefly in theory sketched the line, let us study its practical history farther.

As far as Alaska is concerned, that has been settled. The Philippine Islands were discovered by Magellan in 1521, and named in honor of Philip II. of Spain. They had kept the American date, because the Spanish had reached the islands by sailing from the Pacific Coast of America. The result was that Luzon and the Celebes, a Portuguese discovery, although on the same meridian, used different dates: Luzon had the American date; Celebes, the Asiatic. To remedy this, the archbishop of Manila decreed that December 30, 1844, should be immediately followed by January 1, 1845, thus adopting the Asiatic date for the islands under his jurisdiction. Since their occupation by the United States the American dating has been established.

In giving the history of the dating of islands in the South Pacific, I quote again from Mr. Henkle's article:

"The first persons who settled Botany Bay in 1788 were ordered to sail thither by way of Cape Horn, but tempestuous weather compelled them to sail by way of the Cape of Good Hope. This circumstance caused the beginning of Sunday to be twenty-four hours earlier in Australia than it would have been if the original orders had been complied with. A few years later a missionary expedition to Tahiti, one of the Society Islands, in longitude 149 degrees 29 minutes west from Greenwich, was given a like order, but was also compelled by tempestuous weather to sail by way of the Cape of Good Hope, thus giving the earlier dating in the Society Islands, or fourteen hours in advance of that at London or Greenwich. The French took possession of Tahiti in 1846, and the authorities adopted the later dating, observing Sunday and festal days one day later than the resident English missionaries."

It therefore should be, as above described, on the east side of the line.

"If the mutineers of the ship Bounty took, in 1790, to Pitcairn's Island in longitude 130 degrees 8 minutes west, Tahiti dating with the Tahiti men and women whom they took, then Sunday began in Pitcairn Island very nearly as soon in absolute time as it (formerly) did on the eastern boundary of Russian America. In 1856 the descendants of the mutineers, 194 in number, were removed to Norfolk Island, in longitude 168 degrees 68 minutes east. This island had been used as a British penal colony for the most heavily sentenced convicts from 1787 to 1810, and again from 1825 to 1856, it having been abandoned from 1810 to 1825. The penal colony was finally broken up in 1856 to receive the Pitcairn islanders. If the Pitcairn islanders used the earlier dating in Pitcairn Island, then the dating of Norfolk Island suited them, because it was the same as that in Australia. If, however, they used the later dating in Pitcairn Island, on their arrival at Norfolk Island they would be a day behind; but if all the former inhabitants had left, there would have been no need of a change. Indeed, we have a faint recollection that a gen-

And he calls himself a FRIEND of Labor!—New York World.

tleman born on the Island of St. Helena, who had traveled in that part of the world, once told us that the datings in Australia and Norfolk Island were different. If this is so, the above suggestions furnish an explanation."

Some time ago the Rev. S. J. Whitmee, who had been a resident of Samoa, facetiously showed in "Nature" the impracticability of 180 degrees west or east longitude as the date line, because it passed through the northeast point of Vanaw Levu, Taviuni, and another small island of the Fiji group. He also stated that the earliest dating is still used in the Tonga and Samoan (Navigator's) Islands, the chief commercial intercourse of the people being with Australia and New Zealand. He considered these islands as leading the world in matter of time, although the change to later dating had been advocated in Samoa more than once. The eastern part of the Samoan Islands is in longitude 160 degrees west, which is probably about that of the westernmost part of Alaska. Mr. Whitmee may be right as to the Samoans leading the world if the English missionaries have abandoned Tahiti (longitude of flagstaff on Point Venus, 149 degrees 29 minutes W., latitude 17 degrees 29 minutes 15 seconds S.), or have changed their dating to suit the French.

COLLATERAL READING.

GRAMMAR AND RHETORIC.

"Nobody's Else" or "Nobody Else's."

WE have all been taught in school that to say "nobody else's" is incorrect and that one should say "nobody's else" to be strictly within the rules, but in the magazine, "Correct English," which purports to teach the young idea how to speak, the editor says, under the head of "Common Errors of a Careful Speaker":

It is the careful speaker who errs in saying "nobody's else." Nobody else says "nobody's else," for everybody else says "nobody else's.' The careful speaker reads some nice little book on "What to say and what not to say," in which the author warns the reader to beware of the fallacy, "nobody else's." But everybody else who has not read "What to say and what not to say" continues to say "nobody else's," instead of "nobody's else," until the careful speaker feels as if he would like to buy a whole edition of "What to say, etc.," and present a copy to each of his friends.

In the phrase "nobody else," "else," ordinarily an adverb, becomes a quasi-adjective. The writers who object to "nobody else's" say that, inasmuch as an adjective cannot be put in the possessive case, the possession must be indicated by "nobody." This would be true were it not for the fact that the phrase "nobody else" has a unitary meaning, and, in consequence, the possession must be indicated by "else" and not by "nobody." For the benefit of those who may have a lingering desire to cling to "nobody's else" the following rule is given:

"The phrases anybody else, somebody else, nobody else, etc., have a unitary meaning, as if one word, and properly take a possessive case (with the suffix at the end of the phrase): as, "this is somebody else's hat;" "nobody else's children act so."—Century Dictionary.

BUSINESS CORRESPONDENCE.

Rambling Business Letters.

The following letter recently appeared in the "National Advertiser":

With all due respect to the makers of typewriting machines, I think they are largely responsible for a tedious, diffusive style of business correspondence. In the old days when letters were written by hand, they were as concise as politeness allowed. Writing was laborious and time was valuable. But talking to a stenographer is easy, and letters have the rambling careless style of conversation. Ideas are beaten out thin. I have seen a message sprawled over two pages which, in the days of manuscript correspondence, would have been boiled down to less than one page. While I am on the subject, I wonder how much advertising is lost through blunders and omissions in routine correspondence? I believe that in every large establishment there is room for a good letter writer, who will give attention not alone to the substance, but to the form of correspondence. This work calls for qualities not to be found in ordinary clerks.

Commenting on this letter, the "Commercialist" says:

That verbose and sometimes incoherent business letters are altogether too common is apparent to many. Often business men are compelled to give a great deal of time to the study of such letters in the endeavor to understand, from the jumble of words, punctuated erratically or not at all, just what meaning the writer intended to convey, and often this is impossible or at least uncertain. Whether the typewriter is responsible for so much of this as the writer of the above seems to think, we are not prepared to say. It is possible that the men who dictate to stenographers such letters as mentioned, would, if this means were not available, write in about the same strain, since it would be too much trouble and take too much time to acquire a better style. It required time and study, in the days before typewriters were invented, to learn to write clearly and concisely, and it is fair to assume that the man who then took pains with his correspondence would do the same now if he dictated it.

There is a constantly growing need for better business correspondents, and young men who expect to enter commercial life should give the matter their earnest attention. There is an old adage that brevity is the soul of wit. It is also the soul of a business letter, but it must not be so brief as to leave the meaning uncertain. Clearness of statement and simplicity of language are the first requirements, and then the letter must be punctuated so as to bring out fully the meaning. To become a really good letter writer requires study and application, but it will be a long step in the right direction for a young man to take any business letter or even a newspaper, and, after fixing in mind the meaning intended to be conveyed by some sentence or paragraph, try to make the statement in fewer words. A person can soon become more or less proficient at this, and it will almost invariably be found that the statement will be stronger and clearer when the superfluous words that obscured the meaning are eliminated.

The use of punctuation marks should also be studied. Do not allow yourself to fall into the reprehensible habit that many have of using a dash when they are uncertain of the proper mark to use. It is not only confusing to the reader, but it is a sure sign of a lack of information on the part of the writer. Punctuation marks are few in number and the directions for the use of each so simple that one may, without going into the refinements of the subject, be reasonably correct in their use.

Time Wasted in Writing Formalities.

A writer in one of the educational exchanges claims that a vast amount of time is wasted in the formalities of correspondence. We presume that this writer holds that these formalities should be dispensed with, but we confess we do not quite agree with him. Business by its very nature is brisk and quick enough in these days, and whatever small forms of politeness and good fellowship are yet retained in it should, it seems to us, be deemed precious. However, we give the writer's argument:

In typewriting 500 letters you waste one hour in writing "Dear Sir" and "Yours very truly." Now, the total annual number of letters sent through the post all over the world is 8,000,000,000. Of course this is not all commercial correspondence, nor is it all typewritten, but for the purpose of having some statistical starting-point it will be assumed that it is. To write "Dear Sir" and "Yours very truly," for this number of letters would take one typist 16,000,000 hours, allowing 300 working days to the year, about 6,700 years. To translate this into an approximation of its money value, allowing $10 as the salary of the typist and eight hours as the average day's work, the cost would be $3,350,000.

COMMERCIAL GEOGRAPHY.

Geographical Basis of Internal Commerce.

In a recent issue of one of the publications of the Treasury Department, Bureau of Statistics, an article appears under the above head. It is very interesting and the map which accompanies it is still more so. The map was drawn by John Franklin Crowell. We reproduce both the article and the map as important for the students in Commercial Geography:

The internal commerce in the United States may be said to be carried on between six geographical divisions on the basis of the staple industries which are fundamental in the prosperity of the different sections. (1) In New England, dairying, trucking and mixed farming have received their fullest development, and the same may be said of New York and parts of the other Middle States. The entire Northeast, including New England, New York, and the leading Middle States, is also so largely engaged in manufacturing as to comprise what may be called the industrial section of the United States. This group of states is, therefore, closely dependent upon the rest of the country for such raw materials as the other sections supply. (2) The second division is conveniently designated as the Cotton Belt, comprising all that country lying south of the thirty-seventh parallel of latitude and extending west as far as the western boundary of Texas. This whole territory is primarily dependent upon cotton culture for its prosperity. (3) North of this territory, lying between the thirty-fifth and forty-third parallels of latitude and extending to the western boundaries of Kansas and Nebraska, lies the third staple section, which may be called the corn and winter wheat belt of the United States. Within this belt the production of live stock is a basic factor in agriculture. (4) North of the forty-third parallel, extending westward from the Great Lakes to the eastern boundary of Montana and Wyoming, lies the spring wheat belt. (5) The states usually known as the Rocky Mountain States, comprising Montana, Idaho, Wyoming, Colorado, New Mexico, Arizona, Utah and Nevada, is devoted to the production of wool and live stock as fundamental industries of the section. (6) The Pacific Coast States of Washington, Oregon and California are still primarily agricultural. Wheat, barley, live stock, timber and fruits constitute the basis of their prosperity. This geographical grouping of economic activities lies at the basis of the internal commerce of the United States.

The important fact to be noted is that no one of these geographical divisions is economically self-sufficing, and that the characteristic industries of each of these sections determine the nature of its contribution to the internal commerce of the country. New England, New York and the manufacturing portions of Pennsylvania and New Jersey—the industrial section—draw upon each and all of the other sections for subsistence and raw materials. These states, in turn, contribute manufactures and merchandise to the communities which make up other sections. The cotton belt produces approximately 10,000,000 bales of cotton per year, but consumes only about 1,600,000 bales. All of the balance enters into the channels of trade. A quantity exceeding 2,000,000 bales goes to northern mills, the remainder, or 6,400,000 bales, enters into foreign trade after reaching the coast, and is, therefore, not counted further in the volume of internal commerce. In the winter wheat and corn section lie practically all of the great trunk lines reaching from the interior to the Atlantic seaboard. In this section, therefore, the greatest internal movements occur. Within this geographical division also lie the great concentrating centers for grain and live stock, including eight or ten of the largest primary grain markets, and all of the four or five most prominent stock centers. The western half of this division comprises the leading productive areas, and the eastern half includes the country's principal centers of consumption and its greatest iron industries. So that, on the whole, what is known as the central wheat and corn belt contains the main stream of internal commerce of the United States. The spring wheat belt pours its surplus into the channels of trade by way of the head of the lakes, through which its products are carried eastward fully eight hundred miles farther to lower lake ports, and thence distributed by rail and canal to seaboard cities and intermediate centers of consumption.

The Rocky Mountain section contributes primarily to the live stock markets on the Missouri and at Chicago as an eastward movement, and to the demands of the Pacific Coast in a westward movement. Year by year this section has served as a reservoir of supply of raw meterials for those industries dependent upon live stock. The rapidly increasing demands for cattle and hogs in Seattle, Spokane, Portland and other points in the far Northwest have called into existence heavy movements of traffic in this direction from the Mountain States. The inflowing of settlers and the increase of town population within these Mountain States have greatly increased their productive resources. The development of Asiatic, Alaskan and Hawaiin trade has resulted in the establishment of packing houses at nearly all important coast points on the Pacific. Consequently, the Pacific packing industry has begun to compete with similar industries on the Missouri and the lakes. Thus to competing commercial movements have given new prominence to the stock-raising industry in the Mountain States. On the Pacific Coast we have a geographical division within which internal commerce has been growing, but whose foreign trade has advanced possibly still more rapidly. One of the principal movements peculiar to the section is the coast trade from Puget Sound and Columbia River to San Francisco and Southern coast points. Lumber and grain are specially important in this movement. The eastward movement from the Pacific Coast section comprises fruits and vegetables, of which citrus and dried fruits are the leading features. It also includes more recently lumber movements by rail from California and from the Columbia River and Puget Sound regions to states drained by the Missouri River and its tributaries. Still more recently shipments of wheat have been made from Oregon and Washington to the Minnesota Mills, over a distance of nearly 2,000 miles. This latter movement, however, seems to be exceptional, and not likely to become permanent in the distribution of the Pacific Coast surplus grain. Nevertheless, it indicates the far-reaching area covered by the demand of the centralized milling industry of the Northwest for grain. This

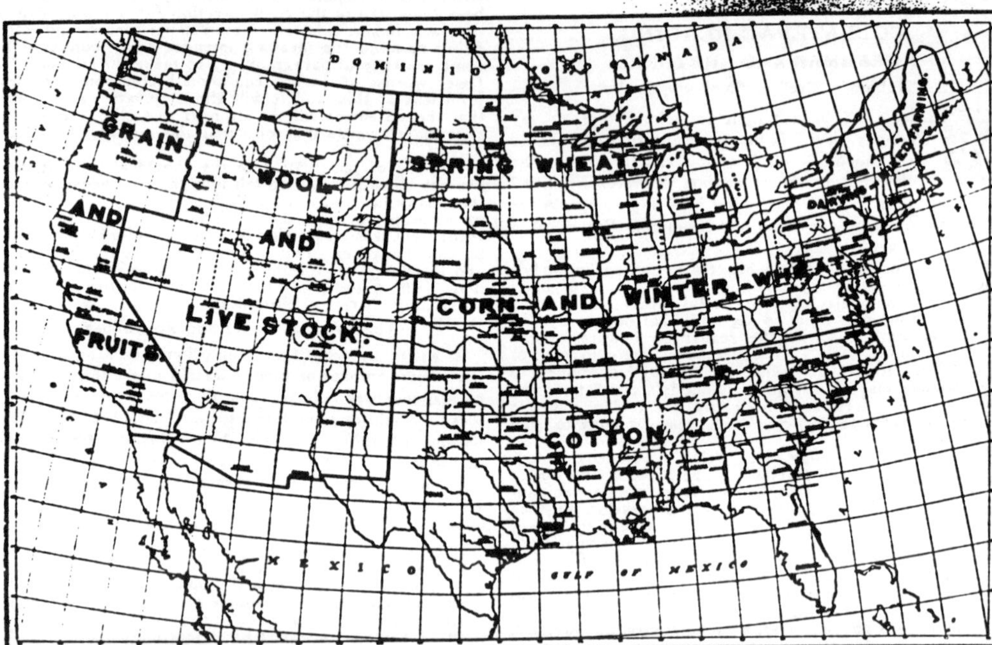

Map showing the Commercial Sections of the United States

demand regularly overreaches national limits. Grain from Canada is continually required for Minnesota milling, just as the cattle industries are growing largely on Mexico to replenish ranges. These few facts indicate characteristic movements in the commerce of the United States between section and section. Under the present economic development no section of the country has reached such a degree of self-sufficiency as to be independent of other sections to both its means of subsistence and its materials in manufacturing. Consequently international commerce is the most necessary of organized agencies for the interchange of the surplus products of industry among the numerous unities which comprise the national life.

The accompanying map shows approximately the division of the United States into these six commercial sections, based on characteristic industries. It also indicates the other supplementary sources of wealth on which internal commerce depends. The statistics of internal trade movement show that both outgoing foreign and the domestic commerce of the country depends principally upon the industries engaged in the production of these staple products. These industries are known as the fundamental or extractive industries, include agriculture, mining, stock-raising, lumbering and fisheries. Manufactures and merchandise contribute a comparatively minor portion of the total tonnage carried in a given year. The dividend-earning tonnage of the western railroads, for example, is found chiefly in the volume of the grain and cattle shipments. Lake transportation is supported primarily by ore, grain and coal freight. The southern railroads rely on cotton, lumber, coal and fruits for their prosperity. Merchandise and manufacturers are rather in a nature of a supplementary contribution to the volume of freight.

Business Subjects in Current Literature

THE approach of the holiday season, while it affected business in a general way, apparently did not change the policy of the magazines so far as the publishing of articles on business subjects was concerned. As has been the case for the past two or three months, a great many articles dealing with the relations of capital and labor were published. Commerce, Accounts & Finance prints below a partial list of the articles on subjects of trade, political economy and banking, that appeared in the periodicals of the world.

Articles on General Subjects.

W. L. Sanders, in Cassier's Magazine, has an article on "Compressed Air in the Machine Shop"; in the same periodical W. H. Booth writes of "The Work-Shop Tool Room"; C. H. Moore, in the Atlantic Monthly, presents an article on "Modern Artistic Handycraft." There is a very interesting paper in The World's Work on "An American Builder in England"; the author's name is not given. J. Barrett, in the North American Review, tells of "America in China," and in Gunton's Magazine "Chinamen as Laborers" are discussed. P. Magnus presents an article on "The Industrial Importance of Technical Education" in the Engineering Magazine; in the Popular Science Monthly "Utilities for Handling Raw Material" are described by W. Fawcett. In Cassier's "The Trend of Machine Tool Design" is discussed by J. Horner; in the Missionary Review Margaret B. Robinson describes her experiences "Among the Coal Miners"; "The Retail Coal Trade" is the title of D. F. Day's paper which appears in the National Geographical Magazine. In Cassier's "Cranes for Machine Shops" are described by G. L. Clark, and in this periodical also appears W. M. McFarland's article on "Electrical Power in the Machine Shop." A. Blauvelt has a paper in Cassier's as well, and he writes of "Fire Prevention for Machine Shops." In The World's Work W. S. Harwood argues for the "Saving of the Fisheries in Our Inland Seas"; in The World's Work also Andrew Carnegie writes of the "Industrial Ascendency of the World"; "A Review of Wireless Telegraphy" is given by A. S. Collins in the Engineering Magazine; among other articles in the same periodical are "Internal Combustion Engines" by W. H. Booth, and "The Cost of Energy in Electrical Supply" by A. D. Adams.

Frank Leslie's Monthly contains a very well-written paper by Agnes C. Laut, whose subject is "Hudson's Bay Company"; "Dangerous Occupations" described by S. E. Moffett in the Cosmopolitan; "The American Ship in 1902" is what W. L. Marven has written about for Scribner; "The Resources and Progress of the South" are described in the Banker's Magazine; "Sugar Industry and Legislation in Europe" by C. S. Griffin, and "The Sugar Question in the United States," by Frank R. Rutter, are the titles of two papers in Quarterly Journal of Economics; in the North American Review O. P. Austin, chief of the bureau of statistics at Washington, has the second in his series of papers on "The Public Debt of the United States"; Bessie Van Vorst writes of "The Woman That Toils" in an article that appears in Everybody's; in McClure's Ida M. Tarbell begins a very interesting series dealing with "The History of the Standard Oil Company"; G. Walsh writes for Gunton's on "The Responsibility of Wealth"; "The Telephone Newspaper is presented by L. Katscher in Pearson's; in the Quarterly Journal of Economics F. A. Fetter discusses "The Round-About Process in the Interest Theory." In the Engineering Magazine is a paper on "The Peat Fuels of Europe" by A. Dal, and in the same publication appears a well-written story dealing with "The Engineer in the Moro Campaign." As an occupation for pleasure and profit Katherine Girling tells us "How to Tool and Emboss Leather."

Beside the articles already mentioned as having appeared in Cassier's Magazine, the following are presented in that periodical: "Limit Gauges in the Workshop," by W. H. Booth; "Modern Foundry Appliances," by B. Moldenke; "Cylindrical Grinding Machines," by J. E. Frantz; "Heating Large Workshops," by H. R. Snell; "Milling Machines in the United States," by C. S. Gingrich; "Factory Depreciation," by E. Mattleson; "Machine Shop Floors," by M. P. Higgins; "Portable Machine Tools," by F. R. Jones, and "The Quality of Product in Piece-Work," by S. E. Thompson.

The foreign magazines contain the following articles: "The Blazing Oil Wells of Baku," by W. G. Fitzgerald, in Cassell's Magazine, of London; "The Inventions of Signor Pino," by C. Iberti, in the Contemporary Review; "The Cunard Agreement," by W. R. Lawson, in the same magazine; "The Reign of Commerce," by G. Trobridge, in the Westminster Review, and "The Commerce and Industry of Japan," in the Quarterly Review. In The Young Man appears an unsigned article on "The Future of British Commerce." "The Making of Diamonds" is described in Chamber's Quarterly, of Edinburgh, and in the Edinburgh Review is a paper on "Government and Trade." In the Revue Artistique, of Paris, a French writer discusses "Insurance for Widows and Orphans."

Banking and Finance.

There were more financial articles than usual. Among them were "A Decade of American Finance," by that veteran financier, J. Cooke; "The Method of Trust Companies," by C. A. Conant, in the American Review of Reviews; "Borrowing Gold to Relieve the Monetary Stringency" in the Banker's Magazine; "Another Revolutionary Increase of Gold," by C. M. Harvey, in The World's Work; "Analysis of a Bank Report," by O. Newfang, in the Banker's Magazine, and "The Practical Work of a Bank" and "Banking in Leading Cities" in the same publication.

In the Banker's Magazine, of London, are these two articles: "New York Banks and the Treasury," by W. R. Lawson, and "The Banking Position in Germany," by W. C. Dreher.

Capital and Labor.

Among the numerous articles on the relations of capital and labor and other economic subjects, we note the following: "The So-Called Beef Trust," by G. B. Fife, in The Century; "Apprentices in the United States," by E. S. Parks, in Cassier's Magazine; "Coal Mines and the Law," by B. Wyman, in The Green Bag; "The Settlement of the Coal Strike," by W. Wellman, in the American Review of Reviews. There are articles on the coal strike in the English Review of Reviews by W. T. Stead, in the Yale Review by P. Roberts, and an unsigned paper in Gunton's. In the Yale Review, also, is an extensive report by the various members of the Industrial Commission. There is another article dealing with the "Triumph of Arbitration in the Coal Strike," in Gunton's. In the North American Review is a paper by J. N. Hobson dealing with "Compulsory Arbitration," and other articles on this subject are "Arbitration—Its Uses and Abuses," by H. Justi, in The Social Service, and "Arbitration In Labor Troubles: Can It be Effective?" by an anonymous writer in The World's Work.

Labor unions and the like are treated of in the following articles: "The Human Side of the Labor Unions," by

M. G. Cunniff, in The World's Work; "Some Phases of the Labor Question," by J. Kelborne, in The Social Service; "A Quarter Century of Strikes," by A. P. Winston, in the Atlantic Monthly: "The Economical Significance of a High Wage Rate," by P. Longmuir, in the Engineering Magazine; "Rewarding Machine Shop Labor," by H. L. Gantt, in Cassier's Magazine, and an article by F. Barter in the same periodical on "Apprentices in Great Britain."

Trusts and corporations, of course, receive their due share of attention, and these are some of the articles dealing with them: "Trusts as Their Makers View Them," by J. H. Bridge, in The World's Work; "The President and the Trusts," by F. Parsons, in The Arena; "An English Substitute for Trusts," by T. L. Baillie, in the Anglo-American; "State Enterprise and Corporations," by G. S. Callender, in the Quarterly Journal of Economics.

Among the articles on the above subjects in the English and Continental periodicals are the following: "Mammoth Trusts and Municipal Trading," by L. Phillips, and "Industrial Troubles in the United States," by B. Taylor, in the Nineteenth Century. T. Good, in the Westminster Review, offers a "Defense of Trade Unionism." In McMillans' Magazine F. W. Bocken writes of "Trusts and Combinations"; in La Revue de Paris L. Tolstoy addresses a letter "To the Laborers," and in the Reforme Sociale H. Valleroux discusses "Workmen's Pensions."

Prominent Men.

Two of the articles dealing with the lives of prominent men in last month's magazines had for their subjects persons closely connected with the great coal strike. One of these articles was by H. T. Newcombe and was entitled "Carroll D. Wright: A Character Sketch." The other was by F. J. Warne, and its title was "John Mitchell, the Labor Leader and the Man." Both of these papers were in the American Review of Reviews. In the London Review of Reviews appeared an unsigned article dealing with "Andrew Carnegie and the Future of the World."

Transportation.

There were very few articles on railways and other methods of transportation, though why this should be is not apparent. Only one of these appeared in an American magazine—that was the article by Mrs. A. S. C. Forbes, on "Mountain Railways," which was printed in the Overland Monthly. In the Pall Mall Magazine, of London, J. S. Montagu presented an article on "The Motor-Car and Its Problems." In the Leisure Hour, of London, Miss Gertrude Bacon writes of "Railway Locomotives," and "The Romance of the Canadian Pacific Railway" is the title of an article by E. A. Reynolds, in Chamber's Journal, of Edinburgh.

THE STORY OF A DICTIONARY.

When the student or the business man, in the course of his day's work, desires to use a word the exact meaning of which may have escaped him, he turns to the revolving bookcase or to the table beside him and takes therefrom the dictionary. The dictionary is a big book, bound, usually, in sheep, with some 2,000 or more pages. The student or the business man by the aid of the thumb index turns to the letter he desires to find, runs his finger down the page until he comes to the word he is seeking, reads the definition, puts the dnctionary back on the table and continues his labor. To him the dictionary has become one of the tools of his trade, and a very handy tool, but, in nine cases out of ten, he is so accustomed to it that he never stops to consider the labor involved in the compilation of such a volume as, for instance, the new Webster's "International." Mark Twain once said in regard to this monumental work: "This is to me the most awe-inspiring of all dictionaries, the most wonderful book that I know of, when I think over the impressive fact that if it had been builded by one man instead of a hundred he would have had to begin it a thousand years ago to have it ready to-day."

But although the great dictionary, in its present form, is the work of at least one hundred men, its conception, away back in the early days of our country's history, was the labor of but one.

Noah Webster, the "schoolmaster of the republic," was a typical scholar—patient, accurate, painstaking. He conceived the idea of a new dictionary of the English language, and year after year, when there was "no money in it" whatever, he patiently worked at the herculean task of preparing, with his own hands, the new lexicon which the rapid development of modern thought and modern life so urgently demanded. Since his day, of course, thousands of new words have been added to the book, and in particular the science of etymology—of the history of words—has made great progress. But Webster laid, in one respect, very enduring foundations. He was a born definer. He discriminated closely and wrote accurately. In this particular his talent was so great it rose to the rank of genius. The most consummate master of the English language in America during this nineteenth century has been Ralph Waldo Emerson; and this "king" among literary men, many years since, paid a particular tribute to this "king" among books, by ascribing to it the highest rank, on account of its exceptional quality, in this matter of precise definition.

But, as time went on, another element of vital force was needed that the development of the book might keep abreast of the higher science and enlarging intellectual life. As time went on, the book needed a "new birth," a recreation, as truly as a man or woman needs a new birth in the course of that development which is the law of human

The Webster "International."

progress. And it was precisely at this point that the activity, push, enterprise of the publisher—the business man—was needed. The men for the work were forthcoming in the persons of George and Charles Merriam (and later Homer Merriam), who bought the copyright of the Webster family, in 1843, published a new edition of the book in 1847; vigorously brought its merits before the American public, and, as fast as they made money by the sale of the book, they poured it back again into the preparation of a new edition, the "Unabridged," which they brought out in the year 1864. In the preparation of this volume literally the best scholarship of the country was employed, in the persons of such men as William D. Whitney, of Yale College; Daniel C. Gilman, now president of Johns Hopkins University; Noah Porter, later president of Yale; and, in the department of etymology, the eminent Dr. C. A. F. Mahn, of Berlin, Prussia. It was a noteworthy enterprise and a noteworthy success. The new book instantly took the highest rank in this country and later in England, judged both by its very large sales and by the enormous volume of spontaneous tributes to its worth from leading lawyers, judges, educators, scientists and men of literary eminence.

But the development of the work, notwithstanding the completeness and temporary adequacy of this edition, went steadily forward. Various tables were added supplementing the main body of the work, and new editions were brought out in the years 1879 and 1884. Then began in good earnest the preparation of the great "International." To describe in detail the immense amount of labor spent in renovating and re-casting the former editions of this last masterpiece would require quite a volume. The best available scholarship of such institutions as Yale and Harvard universities; of such men of science as Professors Edward S. Dana, Herbert A. Newton and William P. Trowbridge; of such lawyers as Francis Wharton; of such musicians as John S. Dwight; of such accomplished men of letters as Professor Henry A. Beers; of such philologists as Professor August Fick, of the University of Gottingen—was employed in bringing this edition to its present perfection.

So, from the comparatively small work of Noah Webster's mind, has grown the mighty compendium of information that lies on our desks to-day. The great dictionary has developed as the nation has developed, and to-day contains the boiled-down wisdom of centuries.

THOUSAND-FOOT STEAMERS.

Vessels of 1,000 feet in length and 40 feet or more draught will have to be reckoned with before very long, and only those sea-ports which have prepared themselves for such visitors will be able to reap the advantages of the commerce which such ships will bring, says a writer in the "Engineering Magazine."

THE REFUTATION OF A SLANDER.

Stubbs—I wonder if it is true that boys who go to college are never fit for work?

Penn—Certainly not. I read about a Yale graduate who is now driving a hack in St. Louis.—Chicago Daily News.

BOOKS OF INTEREST TO BUSINESS MEN.

The A B C of Banks and Banking. —By George M. Coffin. 6¾ x 5 inches; 137 pages. Bound in cloth. Back title gilt. Price, $1.25.

This handy little volume is exactly what its name implies; that is, a presentation of the principles underlying banking in the United States. The author in his preface says that it is designed to appeal to the reader outside as well as inside of a bank. It is by no means the last word or every word about banking. It may be said that it is a primer covering a field that has hitherto been somewhat neglected. The chapter heads are as follows: Banking in General, Various Kinds of Banking, Capital Stock, Shareholders' Rights and Liabilities, Undivided Profits, Dividends and Surplus, Deposits, Checks, Lawful Money Reserve, Issuing Bank Notes, Borrowing Money, Loans and Discounts, Exchanges, Collections, Letters of Credit, Bonds, Mortgages and Stocks, Bank Reports, Examinations, Directors, Executive Officers—Their Powers and Duties, Internal Administration and Bookkeeping, and other suggestions.

Business Law.—By Alonzo R. Weed, L. L. B., of the Boston Bar. 6 x 9¼ inches; 172 pages. Bound in cloth. Cover and back title red. Price, $1.25.

Mr. Weed calls his book "a manual for schools and colleges and for every day use." The titles of the chapters are as follows: Contracts, Principal and Agent, Partnerships, Sales of Personal Property, Bailments and Common Carriers, Negotiable Paper, Deeds, Mortgages and Leases, Collection Laws, Written Rates of Interest, Insurance, Patent Rights, Trade Marks and Copyrights, etc.

The author does not waste words, and yet treats his subjects clearly and comprehensively. In short, he gives the law without the addition of wordy "trimmings."

Introduction to the Study of Economics.—By Charles Jesse Bullock, Ph. D. 7¾ x 5½ inches. 581 pages. Bound in cloth. Cover and back title gilt. Price, $1.25.

This book, the author says, is designed as an introductive text book of economic science. Throughout the volume economics are discussed with special reference to American conditions, and their workings are illustrated by frequent allusions to American experience. There are chapters on the Consumption of Wealth, the Theory of Exchange, the Development of Metallic Money, Money and Credit, and the like.

Political Economy of Humanism.—By Henry Wood. 7¾ x 5¼ inches; 320 pages. Bound in cloth. Cover and back title gilt. Price, $1.25.

Mr. Wood is well known as a writer on various economic subjects, and this book contains a series of able treatises, written in his usual vein, on the relation of the employer to the employed, and the phases of the industrial question and their relation to socialism. Among the questions considered and handled in a conservative spirit and with much common sense, are the following: Supply and Demand, the Law of Competition, Labor and Production, Combinations of Capital, Combinations of Labor, Employers and Profit Sharing, the Obligations and Privileges of Employees, the Unequal Distribution of Wealth, Money and Coinage, Tariffs and Protection, Industrial Education and Gold Production and Values.

The Kite Trust, A Romance of Wealth.—By Lebbeus Harding Rogers. 7¾ x 5½ inches; 475 pages. Illustrated. Price, $1.50.

This is a treatise or series of treatises on economic subjects in the guise of a story. The tale itself concerns three American boys, and is very interesting as well as instructive. The trust idea is explained and an explanation of banking is given. The greenback is dealt with as are also Wall street and stock speculation.

Business Law.—By Thomas Raeburn White, B. L., L. L. B. 5 x 7½ inches; 323 pages. Bound in cloth. Back title gilt. Price, $1.50.

This is a neat, compact and handy book of business for law for the use of students and business men. Among the subjects treated are Contracts, Sales, Partnerships, Corporations, Negotiable Paper and the like. The author's language is plain, and is understandable by any one having no previous knowledge of law. The book's clearness on the essential points of ordinary law should recommend it as a business book for the plain business man who has no time in which to consult a law library.

The Phonographic Dictionary and Phrase Book.—By Benn Pitman and Jerome B. Howard. 5½ x 8 inches; 552 pages. Bound in cloth. Cover title and back title gilt. Price, $3.

This book is the most elaborate shorthand dictionary yet published, with the characters in facsimile. It contains over 120,000 words, and for every one of these words there is a corresponding sign in the Benn Pitman system of shorthand. To the reporter, office or court stenographer, or any one writing the Benn Pitman system of shorthand, the book is invaluable. It is well made, tastefully bound, and is printed on a good quality of paper in clean, plain type.

Grace's Handy Book for Making Rapid Calculations. 8¼ x 5¼ inches. Bound in cloth. 65 pages. Title printed in silver. Price, $1.

The full title of this book is "Merchants', Bankers' and Brokers' Handy Book for Making Rapid Calculations in all Branches of Commercial Requirements, Weights, Measures and Moneys." The volume contains a series of tables for calculating the price of wheat, corn and oat bushels in decimals, for converting cubic meters to cubic feet and cubic feet to meters, meters to lineal yards, superficial feet or square feet to cubic feet, decimal tons to avoirdupois pounds, and the like. To the busy office man who has a great deal of calculating to do, and particularly to the clerk in an export house whose work it is to reckon in United States money the amounts named in foreign invoices, these tables should be very valuable. They are quite complete, and undoubtedly their use will save time.

The Lawrence System of Vocal and Physical Expression.—By Edwin Gordon Lawrence. 4¾ x 6 inches; 128 pages. Bound in cloth. Cover title and back title gilt. Price, $1.

The author says in the preface of this little book that his object has been to place in the hands of lawyers, actors and public speakers in general, a simple system of vocal and physical expression that will enable them to clearly convey thought by word of mouth and emphasize it by the proper action. To the man of affairs who is called upon for a speech on any subject, and who knows what to say but does not know how to say it, this book will be a great help.

The Anatomy of a Railroad Report. —By Thomas F. Woodlock. 7 x 5¼ inches. 121 pages. Bound in cloth. Side and back titles gilt. Price, $1.

This little book is intended for the use of those people who, while interested in railroad investments, are wholly unacquainted with railroad accounts. The book is divided into two sections, the first being the Anatomy of the Railroad Report and the second being Ton-Mile Cost. It treats of phases of the railroad business in concise fashion, but thoroughly and accurately.

Any book in this list will be sent to any address in the United States, Canada or Mexico upon receipt of price. If there is some special book that you require we shall be pleased to hunt it up for you.

Address Commerce, Accounts & Finance, 25 Pine street, New York City.

About a Pay Roll which proves itself, corrects all mistakes in figuring, divides up Pay Roll into several amounts needed to pay each person.

But let us send you a sample leaf, with circular, which tells the whole story.

BARLOW BROS., Grand Rapids, Mich.

Use any pen and your own stationery. If your stationer does not keep it, write for free specimen of work. Beware of infringements. Address Dept.
Pen-Carbon Manifold Co., 145-7-9 Centre St., New York.

HAVE YOU READ

The Kite Trust?

If not, why not? Send $1.50 for a copy to
Commerce, Accounts & Finance,
25 Pine street, New York City.

A New Work on Accounting

A MANUAL OF BOOKKEEPING

By J. THORNTON

THIS attractive volume, comprising over 500 pages, with numerous illustrations, is one of the clearest and most concise surveys of the principles of accounting which has recently appeared. While its illustrations are given in terms of English money the bookkeeping principles discussed are universal.

The work is divided into two leading parts, the first of which is "LAWS AND PRINCIPLES," and the second "APPLICATION."

LAWS AND PRINCIPLES

In the first part there are discussed the Principle of Exchanges, the Principle of Debit and Credit Accounts, the Principle of the Classification of Accounts, the Principle of Ledger Entries, the Principle of Proving, the Principle of Transfer from Preparatory to Final Record, and the Principle of Balancing and Closing the Ledger.

APPLICATION

Under the head of Application the following chapters are presented: Rules and Tools, What Capital Consists of, Capital in Cash, Capital in Bills, Capital in Debts, Capital in Goods, Fixed Capital, Profit and Loss, Capitalist's Accounts, Company Bookkeeping, Errors, and Non-Capitalistic Bookkeeping.

Several chapters are arranged in the form of lessons, following which are questions for class purposes, arranged in such a way, however, as not to detract in the least from the value of the book in the hands of the general reader. A comprehensive index, together with answers to exercises completes the work.

Price, $2.50.—Sent Postpaid to any address in the United States on receipt of price.

Address COMMERCE ACCOUNTS & FINANCE CO.

PUBLISHERS AND BOOKSELLERS - 25 PINE STREET, NEW YORK

PUBLIC ACCOUNTANTS.

Atlanta, Ga.—Ralph H. Brown, 804 Empire Building.

Boston, Mass.—Charles H. Fellows, 174 Summer; New England Audit Company, 45 Milk; J. S. Parsons, 214 Columbus Ave.

Brooklyn, N. Y.—Franklin Allen, Arbuckle Building, 371 Fulton.

Buffalo, N. Y.—W. G. Mowat, 831 Ellicott Square.

Chicago, Ill.—Haskins & Sells, 214 Dearborn.

Davenport, Ia.—J. C. Grabbe, McManus Building.

Detroit, Mich.—H. Naemansson, 496 Putnam Ave.

London, Canada.—Geo. F. Jewell, 361 Dundas.

Montreal, Canada.—George Gontheir, 11-17 Place D'Armes Hill.

New Bedford, Mass.—James L. Hathway, 72 Willis.

New Orleans, La.—P. W. Sherwood, 904 Howard Ave.

New York, N. Y.—Patterson, Teele & Dennis, 30 Broad; Haskins & Sells, 30 Broad; Account, Audit and Assurance Company, 25 Pine; Leon Brummer, 7 Pine; H. F. Searle, 45 Broadway; Hart Bros., Tibbits, Heiron & Co., 11 Broadway; Franklin Allen, Silk Exchange Building, Broadway.

Philadelphia, Pa.—Francis & Sterrett, Penn Mutual Building; Peter Ballingall, German-American Building; Charles W. Thomas, 409 Lippincott Building; Alfred L. Sellers, 1001 Chestnut.

Pittsburgh, Pa.—John Vaughan, 5520 Claybourne; George W. Wood & Co., 341 Fourth Ave.

Providence, R. I.—George R. Allen, 29 Weybosset.

San Francisco, Cal.—Charles L. Lutgen, 218 California; Lester Herrick, 405 Montgomery.

Toronto, Canada.—F. H. Kidd, Bank of Commerce Building.

Windsor, Canada.—F. H. Macpherson, 16 Sandwich, East.

Winnipeg, Canada.—Peter Thornton, 343 Main.

TITLE GUARANTEE AND TRUST COMPANY

Does each year an increasing proportion of the whole business of examining titles and making mortgage loans in New York City. Last year it loaned

Over Thirty-Five Million Dollars

on real estate in New York City. When you buy real estate, or borrow on it, come to this company. Fees moderate and uniform.

Capital and Surplus, $6,000,000

146 Broadway, MANHATTAN. 175 Remsen St., BROOKLYN.

A BUSINESS EDUCATION | **FOR ...ONE... DOLLAR.**

...THE PRACTICAL AGE...

A MONTHLY MAGAZINE full to the brim with helpful suggestions to young men and young women who are struggling successward.

THE BUSINESS HOUSE THAT JACK BUILT, an intensely interesting and highly instructive story of business life, and

APPLIED ENGLISH, an authority on writing and speaking the English language, which no young person can afford to be without, all for ONE DOLLAR.

If you have never seen THE PRACTICAL AGE, send for a free sample copy. Address,

THE PRACTICAL AGE,

Moline, Illinois.

PRENTISS CLOCKS.

SIX TIMES A YEAR

is all that is necessary to wind a Prentiss Clock. Why wind a clock every week when we can sell you one which will require winding but once in sixty days and will keep perfect time? Also Frying-pan, Program and Electrically synchronized clocks. Send for Catalogue No. 282.

THE PRENTISS CLOCK IMPROVEMENT CO.,
Dept. 28, 49 Dey St., New York City

The Theory of Accounts.

JUST PUBLISHED Price, $3.00

Being all questions set in this subject at the New York C. P. A. examinations from December, 1896, to June, 1902, inclusive, with full answers and explanations, by

FREDERICK S. TIPSON, C. P. A.

To follow at short intervals also:

COMMERCIAL LAW, AUDITING,
PRACTICAL ACCOUNTING.

Published by the Author, 150 Nassau Street, NEW YORK

C. P. A. Examinations:

Students thoroughly prepared, either by correspondence or personal instruction, for C. P. A. examinations in all States which grant this diploma. References to students who were successful in January and June, 1900, 1901 and 1902. The only successful candidate at the New York State C. P. A. examination in June, 1900, was coached by

FRED'K S. TIPSON, C. P. A.
150 NASSAU ST., NEW YORK CITY

BUSINESS NEEDS.
Advertisements under this head one cent a word each insertion.

POSITION AS SALESMAN WANTED. An energetic American, thirty-two years old, twelve years' experience as specialty salesman and with first-class record, desires to connect with some enterprising house. Address "Moat," care Commerce, Accounts & Finance.

OLD BOOKS ON ACCOUNTING SUBJECTS.—I want to know about any curious old books on accounting which you may wish to sell. I will pay liberal prices for such books if they are what I desire. Address "Librarian," care Commerce, Accounts & Finance.

WANTED, AN AGENT to take orders. Liberal commission offered the right man. Address "Canvass," care Commerce, Accounts & Finance.

PEN, INK AND PAPER.—I sell all three and I sell them cheaper than most dealers. If I have not what you want in my stock, I will get it for you. Let me make your account books. I make such books well and do not charge de luxe prices. Address, "Stationer," care Commerce, Accounts & Finance.

DO YOU NEED A BOOKKEEPER? I have had experience with good houses. References furnished. Address A. H., care Commerce, Accounts & Finance.

SHIPPING CLERK WANTS WORK. Will begin at a low salary if prospects of advancement warrant. Address J. C., care Commerce, Accounts & Finance.

IF YOU WISH TO LEARN accounting and haven't much time to give to the study, we can tell you how to do it. Address C. S., care Commerce, Accounts & Finance.

LET US SEND YOU PARTICULARS concerning our system of filing invoices. We consider it the best system in use and think we can make you agree with us. If you wish to be convinced, write for circulars, etc., to "Invoice," care Commerce, Accounts & Finance.

Safe Investments
ON
Bond and Mortgage

may be made on desirable property in the

POCONO AND BLUE RIDGE MOUNTAINS OF PENNSYLVANIA

the great natural resort section on the

Lackawanna Railroad

Hotel proprietors are seeking to enlarge their quarters in time for next season's business. They need money for the work. The Lackawanna Railroad has compiled a list of desirable opportunities for placing money in these enterprises, and full particulars may be obtained by addressing

C. W. TEN BROECK, Industrial Agent LACKAWANNA RAILROAD
26 Exchange Place, New York City

WEBSTER'S

THE NEW AND ENLARGED EDITION IS
Standard Authority of the English-Speaking World

All Good Things must win upon their merits. WEBSTER'S INTERNATIONAL DICTIONARY has won a greater distinction and is in more general use than any other work of its kind.

The New Edition has 2364 pages with 5000 illustrations and is printed from new plates throughout. 25,000 new words and phrases have recently been added under the editorship of W. T. Harris, Ph.D., LL.D., United States Commissioner of Education.

LET US SEND YOU FREE
"A Test in Pronunciation" which affords a pleasant and instructive evening's entertainment. Illustrated pamphlet also free.

G. & C. MERRIAM CO., Springfield, Mass.

WEBSTER'S INTERNATIONAL DICTIONARY

INTERNATIONAL DICTIONARY

INVENTORY SHEETS

Stock Taking Made Easy

Simplify Your Methods! *Economize Your Work!*

OUR INVENTORY SHEETS

are now in general use by mercantile houses, as the employment of them provides the **simplest and most economical method of Taking Stock.**

As soon as a sheet (one or more) has been filled, it can be returned to the office for pricing and extensions.

The loose sheets are used temporarily in our **PATENT HOLDERS** with **Special Smooth Insides** for Inventory work. When Inventory is finished, it is bound **Permanently** in our Patent Automatic Binder. As this Binder will hold some 1700 sheets, it can be used to retain the inventories of successive years.

PRICES	
100 Sheets, tableted	$ .75
300 Sheets, tableted	1.75
500 Sheets, tableted	2.75
1000 Sheets, tableted	5.25

PRICES	
Safety Holders, Size No. 2, each	$1.20
Eclipse Holders, Size No. 2, each	1.35
Automatic Binders, Size No 2, each	2.50

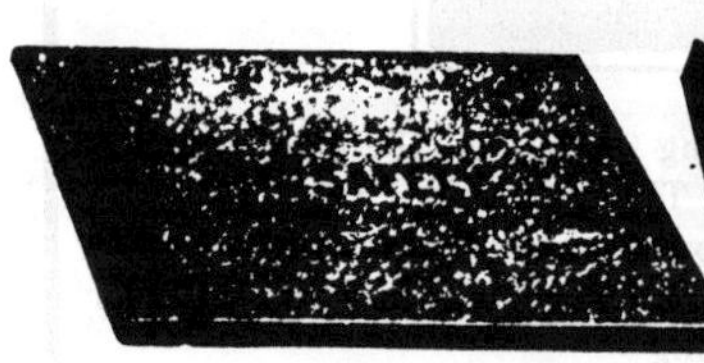

SAFETY HOLDER

HOLDS 1 TO 25 SHEETS

Finely Tempered Steel Spring, Nickel Plated.

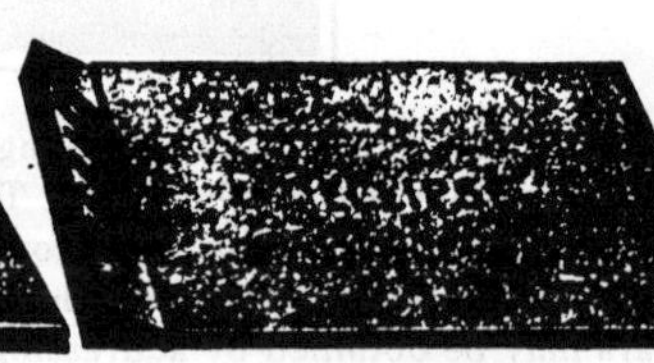

ECLIPSE HOLDER

HOLDS 1 TO 120 SHEETS

Finely Tempered Steel Spring, Nickel Plated.

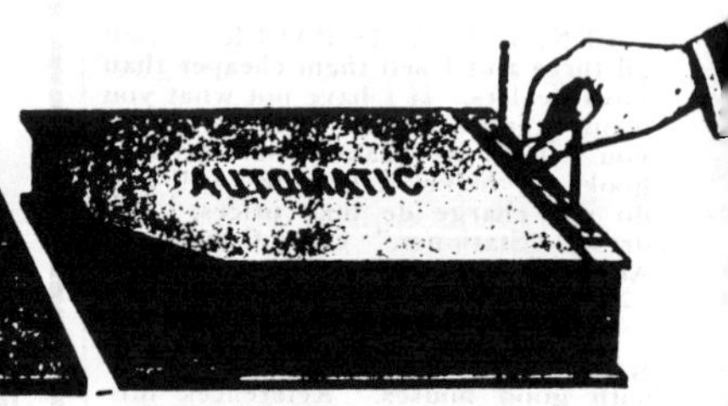

AUTOMATIC BINDER

MADE TO HOLD 100 to 1700 SHEETS

Correspondence solicited regarding, Order Blanks, Holders and Binders.

STATIONERY MANUFACTURING CO.

318 BROADWAY - - NEW YORK

3 06

THE NEW YORK PUBLIC LIBRARY

ASTOR, LENOX AND TILDEN FOUNDATIONS

COMMERCE ACCOUNTS & FINANCE

Volume 5 New York February 1903 Number 2

CONTENTS.

Published Monthly by the Commerce Accounts & Finance Company Twenty-five Pine Street New York

ANNOUNCEMENT EXTRAORDINARY!

A LIBRARY OF PRACTICAL BOOKS FOR THE STUDENT, THE ACCOUNTANT AND THE BUSINESS MAN

What Shall be Its Name?

A COMPETITION WITH THE BOOKS FOR PRIZES

COMMERCE, ACCOUNTS & FINANCE has pleasure in announcing to its readers and to the business public in general that at great expense it has bought the manuscripts, titles and copyrights of the five volumes illustrated in the accompanying cut. It proposes to

Bool s Composing the (?) Library.

use them in furthering the interests of this periodical.

The books will be published one at a time, but our arrangements are so advanced that we feel warranted in promising the complete set in a reasonable length of time.

Each book is to be set from new type, illustrated by original engravings, printed on paper specially made for the purpose, and handsomely bound in cloth with gilt back and side titles. Each book will be upwards of 500 pages in extent, and nothing in the bookmaker's art will be spared to get them up in excellent shape, at once attractive to the eye and convenient for use.

PUBLICATION COMMITTEE.

The set of books will be produced under the direction of the following Publication Committee:

W. H. Grace, chairman, President Commerce, Accounts & Finance Company.

Friend Pitts, Jr., secretary, Treasurer Commerce, Accounts & Finance Company.

A. O. Kittredge, author, President Account, Audit & Assurance Company.

H. M. C. Vedder, Specialist in Accounting and Auditing.

George Young, Textile Accounting and Industrial Operations.

H. W. Courter, General Merchandise and Installment Accounts.

J. A. Cave, Manufacturing Accounts.

J. V. Palmer, Printers' and Publishers' Accounts.

C. H. Sumwalt, of the Correspondence School of Banking.

ADVISORY COUNCILS.

This committee will be supplemented by subcommittees or advisory councils on special topics, the chairman of each of which is a specialist in his own particular branch. These sub-committees will co-operate with the general committee by way of suggestions as to the manner of treating specific topics, the choice of illustration and matters of similar character.

WANTED—A NAME.

The set of books here announced will constitute a library desirable at once for the desk of the business man, the study table of the student and the shelf in reach of the bookkeeper and the clerk while engaged in their daily work. It will also be invaluable to the professional accountant, but **what shall it be called? By what name as a library shall it be introduced to the public?**

We want the most appropriate name as well as the most striking name for this library. It should be something that will give force and character to the several million copies of the announcement which we shall circulate. Who can suggest the right name for the purpose?

There is always wisdom in a multitude of councilors. Therefore, we constitute every one who reads this paragraph a member of our special council on names. Out of the multitude of suggestions thus to be offered we have reason to expect the right idea will come to the top. Just to make it interesting, we propose a friendly contest with prizes.

COMPETITION.

To the person suggesting the name that we finally adopt for this library, we will present a com-

plete set of the books (five volumes). The set so given shall be one of the first off the press and each volume will be properly inscribed over the autograph of the author. To each of ten others who suggest good names, the same being deemed the next best of those we receive, even though we are unable to make use of what they offer, we will give a single volume of the library similarly inscribed over the autograph of the author. Each successful contestant is to have the right of selection.

A subscription for one year to COMMERCE,

The First Volume of the Library to be Issued.

ACCOUNTS & FINANCE goes with each volume sent out as a prize.

This competition will close at 6 o'clock P. M., May 1, 1903.

All entries are to be addressed to LIBRARY NAME COMPETITION, care of COMMERCE, ACCOUNTS & FINANCE, 25 Pine street, New York.

Each competitor is privileged to make as many suggestions of names as he pleases, but only one prize will be awarded to any contestant.

The decision in this competition will be announced in COMMERCE, ACCOUNTS & FINANCE at as early a date as circumstances permit.

EXCLUSIVELY FOR SUBSCRIBERS TO COMMERCE, ACCOUNTS & FINANCE.

The books here announced will not be sold through the trade. The sale will be limited to the cash subscribers to COMMERCE, ACCOUNTS & FINANCE, or to put it otherwise, each volume of the set carries with it a yearly subscription to this periodical.

If you are already a subscriber to COMMERCE, ACCOUNTS & FINANCE, your subscription will be extended for one year for each volume that you purchase.

NO DISCOUNTS TO ANY ONE.

Books will not be sent out on any other terms than those quoted below. The only way to get an advantage in price is to order in advance of publication day.

PRICES.

Either volume, including therewith one yearly subscription to COMMERCE, ACCOUNTS & FINANCE, cash with order, $5.

The set of five volumes, including therewith five yearly subscriptions to COMMERCE, ACCOUNTS & FINANCE, or a single subscription for five years, cash with order, $25.

INSTALLMENT PAYMENTS.

Subscribers, with approved references, may order the set of five volumes at $30, payable $5 with order and the remainder in five monthly installments of $5 each, the title to the books remaining with the publishers until full payment has been made.

Nothing less than a whole set will be furnished on the installment plan.

ADVANCE ORDERS.

Orders in advance of publication will be accepted at the following specially reduced rates:

The set of five volumes, including five yearly subscriptions to COMMERCE, ACCOUNTS & FINANCE, or one subscription for five years, cash with order, $20. Single volumes, including the subscription as above, $4 each.

ORDER OF PUBLICATION.

The arrangement of the volumes in the illustration indicates the order in which they will be produced. "TOOLS OF BUSINESS" will be the first of the set to go to press, following which will be "ELEMENTS OF BOOKKEEPING," "BALANCE SHEET ACCOUNTING," "AUDITING," and "BUSINESS ORGANIZATION AND ADMINISTRATION," in the order named.

The date of publication cannot be named at this time, but the books will be pushed through as rapidly as circumstances make possible. The manuscript for the entire set is in a very forward condition at the present time.

NO ADVERTISING.

There will not be a line of advertising in any of the volumes from cover to cover. Manufacturers' cuts will not be used, but instead new engravings are being made throughout. On the other hand, provision is made, as indicated in the foregoing, for a copy of this periodical to go with each volume. Its advertising pages are open to the business world at reasonable rates, and afford an unequalled opportunity of reaching the very public the advertiser is after.

"TOOLS OF BUSINESS."

The first volume to be brought out as announced above will be "TOOLS OF BUSINESS." This name is to be construed liberally and taken to mean everything from a pen holder to a typewriter, from a chair to a desk and from a method of screening the office window to systems of heating and ventilation.

In this work the author takes up his subject analytically and presents one after another of the several subjects discussed in a most attractive fashion. The scheme of the book is a cyclopedia of office equipment, or a dictionary of those things which

every business man needs to know about in equipping and arranging his business office.

Typewriters, for example, are described analytically and critically. They are divided into classes according to the principles underlying their operation and after those principles have been fully explained, illustrations of different interpretations of those principles are brought forward. The differences between the leading typewriters is clearly defined and the advantages, as well as the disadvantages of some of the cheaper machines are fully set forth.

The office floor is carefully treated, the discussion extending from rugs and mats and carpets to the treatment of the wood of which the floor is composed.

Desks are discussed with respect to the conveniences which they offer, their size, the space occupied and the work to be done. Letter files and cabinets are correspondingly handled. In a similar manner blank books, like ledgers and journals, are discussed with respect to the ends to be accomplished and the materials of which they are composed. Card indexes, loose leaf ledgers, binders and other office appliances are similarly treated.

In future numbers of COMMERCE, ACCOUNTS & FINANCE we shall take pleasure in laying before our readers the personnel of the Sub-Committees or Councils upon whom the Publication Committee depends for advice with respect to details of arrangement, etc. We shall also present in the course of early numbers a complete outline of the contents of this volume.

Address all communications to

COMMERCE, ACCOUNTS & FINANCE COMPANY, 25 PINE STREET, NEW YORK.

BRIEF MENTION.

GENERAL LEW WALLACE, the famous author of "Ben Hur," uses a fountain pen, and in his letter written to the John Holland Gold Pen Company, of 127 East Fourth street, Cincinnati, Ohio, he says that he uses a John Holland Fountain Pen, and finds it "a good, faithful tool, and a happy possession." In their advertising the Holland Company show a facsimile of General Wallace's letter, and a picture of the General himself at the top. For the Holland pen the company claim many advantages, among them being easy, graceful and neat writing from the boldest to the lightest strokes, and an even and steady flow of ink at all times.

OFFICE RULERS are made in all degrees of cheapness, but it is safe to say that a ruler that is very cheap is not a very good ruler. Westcott & Jewell Company, of Seneca Falls, N. Y., make many kinds of rulers, none of which they claim is too cheap and therefore not of good quality. Among the rulers made by this company is the "Autoparel," which is to be used for ruling parallel lines. Serrated soft rubber rollers holds the paper in place while the lines are ruled. The company also makes rubber-back rules, that, it is claimed, stay where they are placed and do not slide.

THE INDELIBA MANUFACTURING COMPANY, of Rochester, N. Y., manufacture the "Indeliba" non-filling typewriter ribbon, for which they claim all sorts of advantages. It does not, so they say, soil the hands or the work, and therefore is the kind that brings business and holds it. The ribbons are put up in little tin boxes and are made in all colors and for all of the leading types or styles of machines. The company also makes the "Dupli-Ka" carbon paper, which is put up in packets containing a dozen sheets each.

A CATALOGUE OF LETTER PRESSES that shows many styles and sizes is that issued by the Rockwell & Rupel Company, of 218 Wabash avenue, Chicago. The company make the Racine Automatic Letter Press, which works with a lever and not with the old-time screw arrangement There are many advantages claimed for the Racine press and the catalogue tells what these advantages are.

AMONG THE NOVELTIES for sale by the New York News Company, of 26 City Hall place, New York, is a paste tube made like the tubes that contain oil paints, and having a brush at the end of the tube. By pressing the tube the paste is forced out through the brush and may be easily spread upon the paper. This paste tube is said to be of special convenience and cleanliness for office use.

A DESK PAD that is flexible and can be rolled up is something of a novelty. The Meyercord-Batterman Company, with offices at Dearborn and Kinsey streets, Chicago, Ill., are manufacturers of a pad of this sort. They call it the "Ever-Clean" desk pad and, so the company states, it is made of a patent composition of pulp and rubber and has a canton-flannel back that will not mar the finest desk. It is made with a finish to match cherry, oak and mahogany desks, and has an interest computing table, postal rates and a rule printed upon it in imitation inlaid wood and pearl. It is claimed for this pad that it can be easily cleaned and is very ornamental.

THE SCALES MANUFACTURED by the Pelouze Scale and Manufacturing Company, with offices at 132 W. Jackson Boulevard, Chicago, Ill., are advertised just now. These scales, judging by the illustrations, are very useful and ornamental little affairs, manufactured in a number of shapes and of several metals. They are said to have a height of three inches and a capacity of one pound by half ounces.

OF LOOSE LEAF LEDGERS there apears to be no end, as these books are made in all sorts of styles and rulings. The Boorum & Pease Company, of 103 Grand street, New York City, manufacture the Shepherds loose leaf ledger which they are advertising extensively. The exclusive advantages claimed for the "Shepherd" are that there are no complex parts to get out of order and that by following the directions any one can operate the book. The illustrations in the catalogue show the "Shepherd" to be carefully made and the makers claim that they are made to carry enough live accounts to satisfy any average demand.

THE SAMUEL C. TATUM COMPANY, of Cincinnati, are advertising the Tatum improved loose sheet transfer binders, which they make in a variety of styles and sizes. The "Tatum" is a post binder for which a number of advantages are claimed. The set screws that hold the cover in place may be released instantly by a half turn, and as they are fast in the cover cannot be removed or lost. The company claims these screws to be a great improvement on the brass knobs which in the ordinary binder screw down from the tops of threaded posts.

THERE HAVE BEEN MANY envelope sealers placed upon the market in recent years, but it appears that there are more to come. The Standard Moistener and Envelope Sealer has just been put on the market by A. A. Weeks, 11 Gold street, New York City. The sealer seems to be a simple arrangement, with a barrel made of steel, finished in nickel and with a cloth tip with which to do the actual moistening. The barrel, of course, contains water, and the company's circulars say that it will contain enough to last a week.

A HANDY COPYHOLDER is that manufactured by the Chicago Writing Machine Company, with offices at 98 Wendell street, in that city. The illustration in the company's advertising matter shows the copyholder to be a convenient little stand for the holding of the stenographer's copybook while she or he is using the typewriter. It, apparently, takes up a small space on the desk and seems to be all right in every respect. The company claim that it will increase results, lessen work and save nerve energy and eyesight.

A Proprietor's Business*

By JOSEPH HARDCASTLE.

THE proprietor must be the central figure in his business. He must possess rights with respect to others, and these others must be under obligation to him.

If a person owes him money, the result of some transaction, he has what is called an equitable right in the money, that is, he cannot go and take the money out of the person's hands, but the person may deliver the money to him, or he may apply to the courts, and in this manner obtain the money, which gives him a legal right in the money, i. e., a right which has been reduced to possession.

We will suppose the money value of the obligations of this character amounts to $10,000 before the act of delivery, consequently his rights over the same property will amount to $10,000. But a person under obligation is a debtor with respect to the persons owning the right, and a person owning a right is a creditor with respect to the person under obligation. And the same fact may be written and spoken of in either one of two ways, or in both ways:

First way:

Persons Under Obligations.	
$10,000	

Second way:

Proprietor Owning Rights.	
	$10,000

Both Ways:

Persons Under Obligations.	
$10,000	

And

Proprietor Owning Rights.	
	$10,000

But persons under obligation we call debtors to the persons owning the rights, and the persons owning the rights we call creditors to the persons under obligation to them.

To use either the first way or the second way, we call single entry of one fact, and to use both ways is double entry of the same fact. This $10,000 in both cases is an asset of the proprietor or a liability of the persons under obligation, but when we write it down in the first way we want to show that it is a liability of the persons under obligation, and writing it down in the second way we want to show that it is an asset of the proprietor.

Custodians of Goods.

Besides, the proprietor may possess goods of various kinds; these for the purpose of bookkeeping may be supposed to be under the custodianship of several persons, each class of goods under its own custodian; thus the keeper of the cash is called a treasurer of goods which can be warehoused, the storekeeper and the proprietor may act in the capacity of custodian to such goods as patent rights. The goods of this class are all constructively in the possession of the proprietor. The custodian's obligation is one of responsibility, and he is called upon to deliver up the goods under his care whenever the proprietor desires him to do so. The law need not be invoked in their case to compel the delivery, the proprietor need only discontinue the custodianship. This custodian under the obligation of responsibility is likewise called a debtor for the goods in his possession to the proprietor, and the proprietor is a creditor for the same goods with respect to the custodian. The custodian will, however, not tolerate the interference of the proprietor with respect to goods in his possession, only for the purpose of delivery. The custodian for certain purposes is the equitable owner, for he can make a complaint to the court against a person who steals any of the goods under his charge. It is not customary, however, in the books of account to have the names of the custodian, and there are advantages in omitting the names of the custodian and instead putting the names of the various goods. For the purpose of understanding the entry of such a kind, it is necessary that we mentally supply a custodian to the goods and make him debtor, although for convenience we shall say the goods are debtor—an absurd statement; so long as we know what it means, there is no harm in using it, and we shall use it. We will suppose the value of the goods under custodianship, real or constructive, belonging to the proprietor is $100,000. This fact may be written in three ways:

First way:

Goods Belonging to Proprietor.	
$100,000	

Second way:

Proprietor Owning Goods.	
	$100,000

Both ways:

Goods.	
$100,000	

And

Proprietor Owning Goods.	
	$100,000

To use either the first way or the second way we have single entry for the same fact, not forgetting that the custodians are the debtors in the first way. To use both ways is double entry of the same fact. But the proprietor's rights against persons and his rights with respect to things constitute the whole of his property. Collecting the accounts by double entry of both the kind of assets and putting into one account the two proprietor accounts we have:

Persons Under Obligations.	
$10,000	

Proprietor Owning Rights and Goods	
	$110,000

Goods.	
$100,000	

Claims of Creditors.

But these assets are subject to a claim of the proprietor's creditors which the proprietor is obligated to meet, which we will suppose to be valued at $5,000. The double entry for these rights and obligations is

Proprietor Under Obligation.	
$5,000	

Creditor's Rights.	
	$5,000

Here these two represent just one fact viewed from opposite points of view. If we now unite these entries with the previous ones we shall express the three facts from two opposite views. The first point of view contains the relation with respect to

*Lecture delivered before the School of Commerce, Accounts and Finance of New York University.

three facts of the proprietor to persons and things external to himself. This is contained in the proprietor's account. The second point of view with respect to the three facts is the point of view of the persons and things external to himself in relation to himself. These persons are of three kinds; two of the kind relating to the proprietor's assets and one kind relating to his obligations. Collecting these we have:

First kind:

Persons and Obligation.

$10,000	

Second kind:

Goods.

$100,000	

Third kind:

Creditor's Rights.

	$5,000

Proprietor's Rights and Goods Less Obligations.

	$105,000

The Proprietor's Account.

The first and second kinds each contain a fact, showing the two kinds of assets of the proprietor; the third kind contains an obligation of the proprietor against the assets in the first and second kind; and these three facts are all repeated in one result in the proprietor's account.

The first kind contains some of proprietor's account.

The second kind contains the remainder of the proprietor's assets.

The third kind contains the assets of the creditors, included in the assets of the first and second kinds, and represents an undivided interest therein for which the proprietor is legally liable, or in other words, the proprietor's liabilities.

The proprietor's account simply gives his net assets or his equity in the business after liquidating his liabilities.

The first and second kinds contain the full scope of proprietor's control as to the property entered in the business, hence often called his activities or active goods.

The third kind contains the orbit of the control exercised over him or under which he suffers, hence called his passivities or passive goods, or his liabilities.

The proprietor's account gives what his activities will be when freed from his passivities, or his net assets.

The above is a sensible view of the accounts at rest when viewed broadly.

Accounts viewed as motion, or in relation to investives, divestive and translative facts:

1. To increase the assets and increase the capital account.
2. To diminish the assets and diminish the capital.
3. To diminish the liabilities and increase the capital.
4. To increase the liabilities and diminish the capital.
5. To increase the assets and diminish the assets.
6. To increase the assets and increase the liabilities.
7. To diminish the assets and diminish the liabilities.
8. To increase the liabilities and diminish the liabilities.
9. A mixture of two or more of these.

It is necessary to have some fixed way in which the accounts are written in the ledger. This is the way we have already used in our diagram. But in writing and speaking about the accounts we often write and speak of them in a different way than that in which they are written. Speaking of the accounts written under Persons, under Obligations, and under Goods, we have:

1. Assets, means property in money value belonging to proprietor, i. e., we disregard the mode of writing.
2. Proprietor's credits means those sums owing by others to him as in the phrase, his goods, chattels and credits.
3. Bills receivable means promissory notes, the property of the proprietor.
4. His capital means his assets, in such phrases as charge his capital with so and so.
5. Bona activa or active goods means the goods he owns so as to control them.
6. His holdings (avoir) means simply his assets.

Creditor's Accounts.

Besides the class just mentioned under the name of Assets, there is another class in which the proprietor, although the legal owner of goods of others which are mingled with his own, the others being the equitable owners who can make the proprietor deliver up the money value for the same. This class is named in the books of accounts, not after the proprietor but after the equitable owner of the same. These equitable owners in the books of accounts are called creditors. But the same class of accounts may be and often is spoken of from the point of view of the proprietor as his liabilites.

Writing the same facts from the outside and from the inside point of view, the total value being expressed in opposite directions, the accounts must always be in balance. The accounts being represented in this double way are presented from both points of view with respect to the persons concerned in the business, and this fact gives a roundness and fullness to them which is advisable, and each of the three kinds has its special functions.

The first gives the specialized assets of the proprietor and are debit accounts.

The second gives his specialized liabilities and are credit accounts.

The third gives the net of the former two, but is not specialized, but collective, giving his financial condition as proprietor of the business and are credit accounts.

Pierpont doesn't seem be such a grasping party after all.—Chicago Record-Herald.

GOOD WILL AN ASSET.

In a recent discussion of reasonable and unreasonable contracts Attorney-General Knox showed that the good will of a man or a firm is a salable asset. In this connection an exchange quotes the Attorney-General as saying:

"Here is a restricted covenant upon the part of the vendor not to engage in competition in a similar business is often the main consideration for the transaction. This covenant is, of course, in restraint of trade, and interferes with competition. But to make a contract such as this illegal is not only restrictive of the liberty of contract, but it is depriving one of his property without due process of law. Good will is property capable of being appraised, bought and sold. In many cases it is the main ingredient of value. It represents all the struggle, industry, tact and judgment that makes success. In estimating the worth of a business it is not infrequently reckoned more valuable than the buildings and machinery that make up the plant. Such a contract has been held reasonable and valid."

OF COURSE.

She—Do they have societies at the Carlisle school?

He—Sure. Haven't you heard of Indian clubs?—Harvard Lampoon.

The National Debts of the World 1*

By O. P. AUSTIN,
Chief of the Bureau of Statistics, Washington, D. C.

THE national debts of the world aggregate, in round terms, thirty-one billions of dollars. In 1790, before the beginning of the Napoleonic wars, they aggregated two and one-half billions. The population of the world to-day is 1,500 millions of people; in 1790 it was 600 millions. The average per capita of the world's national indebtedness to-day, then, is over $20; in 1790 it was $4.

This is the record of a century, a century of activity both in peace and in war, of the introduction of steam, of the construction of a half million miles of railways and a million miles of telegraph, of the building of great fleets and navies, of the maintenance of great armies, of great and costly and destructive wars.

The interest and other annual charges upon this enormous national indebtedness amounts to $1,200,000,000 per annum, a hundred million dollars a month, or as much in a single decade as all the money of the world, while the principal of the debts to-day is nearly three times the total gold, silver and paper money of the entire world combined.

The Growth of National Indebtedness.

How and why has the national indebtedness grown to such vast proportions? Its aggregate to-day is more than twelve times that of 1790, while

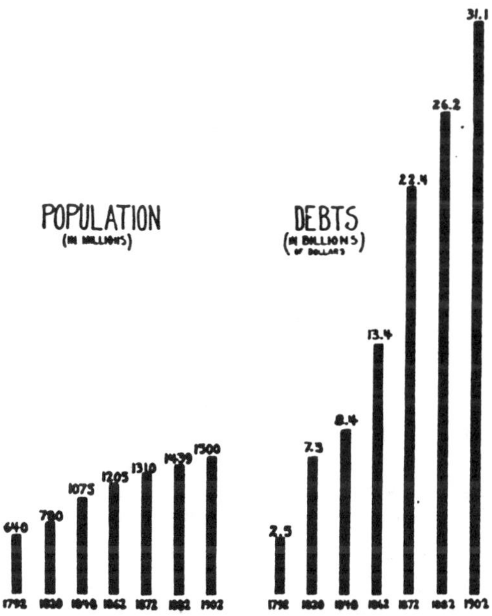

Growth of Population and National Debts of the World—1792-1902.

population is only two and one-half times as much as at that date.

The answer is not a difficult one. The railroads of the world have cost probably thirty billions of dollars, and one-third of them have been built with national funds and are owned by national governments. The other great national works in aid of commerce or for national defense have cost untold sums, aggregating many billions of dollars, and constructed at public expense. The standing armies and navies of the world include four millions of men withdrawn from production and sustained by national governments at a cost of a round billion of dollars per annum in times of peace and of vastly

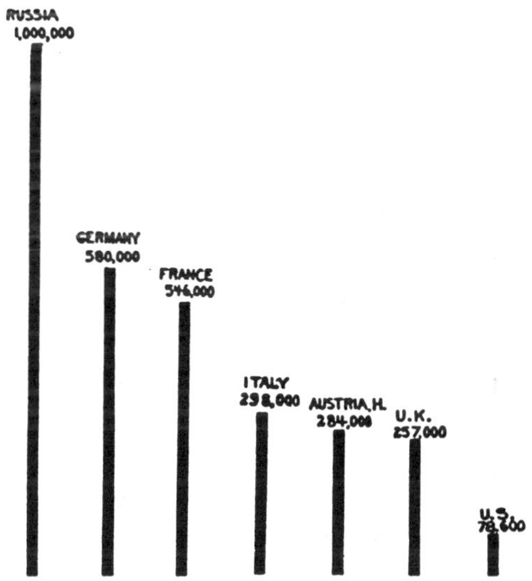

Strength of the Standing Armies of the Principal Countries of the World

more than that sum in times of war. The wars of the period from 1790 to 1902 are estimated to have cost sixteen billions of dollars, or more than one-half the national indebtedness accumulated in that period. Every year adds to the cost of the maintenance of armies, of the construction of navies and of the operations of war. Every year sees new demands upon national governments for the construction of great works in support of commerce and for national defense, for the maintenance of great commercial fleets and for the building of great and costly vessels of war.

The first ninety years of the seventeenth century, a period of comparative peace, added but about two billion dollars to the world's debts. The thirty years from 1790 to 1820, the period which included the Napoleonic wars, added five billions. In the thirty years of comparative peace which followed the national debts increased but about one billion dollars, but in the next thirty years, which included the American Civil, the Balkan and the Franco-Prussian wars, there was an increase of eighteen billions in the national indebtedness bringing the grand total of 1882 up to twenty-six billions of dollars. Following this came large expenditures for standing armies and the construction of great navies, and in the period 1898-1901 the wars between the United States and Spain and between England and South Africa; and now the total national indebtedness stands at thirty-one billions of dollars.

Principal National Debts of the World.

The principal national debts of the world to-day, stated in the order of magnitude and using round millions in the statements, are as follows: France, $5,800,000,000; Russia, $3,167,000,000; United Kingdom, $3,060,000,000; Italy, $2,583,000,000; Germany

*A lecture delivered before Alexander Hamilton Chapter, American Institute of Bank Clerks.

and the German States, $2,573,000,000; Spain, $1,728,000,000; Australia, $1,183,000,000; Austria-Hungary, $1,154,000,000; India, $1,031,000,000; United States, $969,000,000; and all other countries, $8,-375,000,000.

Since the debts of these ten countries aggregate three-fourths of the world's national indebtedness,

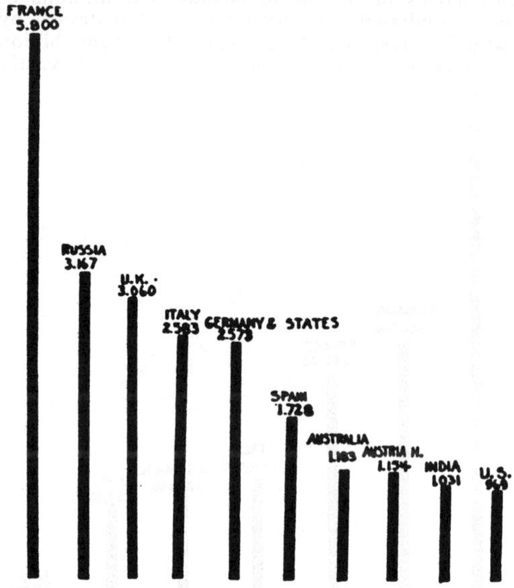

Debt of the Ten Principal Nations of the World in 1902. (In Millions of Dollars.)

they offer a comparatively simple basis for a study of the causes and present conditions of the great and growing indebtedness, and I therefore propose to take up the principal countries in this list and try to analyze briefly their present indebtedness, the principal causes which have led to the creation of these great national obligations, the purposes to which the money thus raised has been devoted, the sources from which it was drawn, the progress which is being made by each in the liquidation of that indebtedness, and the standing which these securities have in the great financial centers of the world. You will note in the statements which I shall present as to the present market value of the principal securities now outstanding and the relation of that price to the original price of issue, that in nearly all cases the issue price was below par. This is a characteristic of the securities issued by most governments other than the United States, that they are in nearly all cases issued at less than par. In a list of forty leading securities of foreign governments named by the Investor's Manual, issued in London, in which the issue and present market prices of the stock are stated, only two classes of securities of consequence are reported as having been issued at or above par, these two being those of the United States and a portion of those issued by British Colonies. An examination of the issue price of the various government securities now outstanding, so far as data are obtainable, justifies the assertion that the outstanding government securities, aggregating thirty-one billions of dollars, call for the payment of fully two billion dollars more than was realized by the governments which issued the securities, and that to this extent the interest payments are in excess of the nominal rates named in the securities. Even the countries whose financial standing cannot be questioned and of the payment of whose securities there can be no reasonable doubt, still follow this custom, the bonds recently issued by the British Government to raise funds for the payment of their war in South Africa having been in all cases sold at less than their face value.

The explanation which is offered is that experience has shown that by this process the rate of interest at which the bonds can be marketed is sufficiently reduced to more than justify the reduction in the sum originally received for the securities. These conditions, however, especially call attention to a fact in which we as citizens of the United States may take an especial pride, and this is that, in spite of the fact that the United States insists upon receiving the par value of all of its securities issued, she has readily sold her securities in recent years at a lower rate of interest than that ever paid by any other nation of the world, and those securities, even at their low interest rate of 2 per cent, are now at a premium in the financial markets of this and other countries.

The Debt of France.

Taking up the principal countries, then, in the order of the magnitude of their national indebtedness, I begin with France. At the beginning of the century her debt amounted to but one hundred and forty million dollars; at the end of the Napoleonic

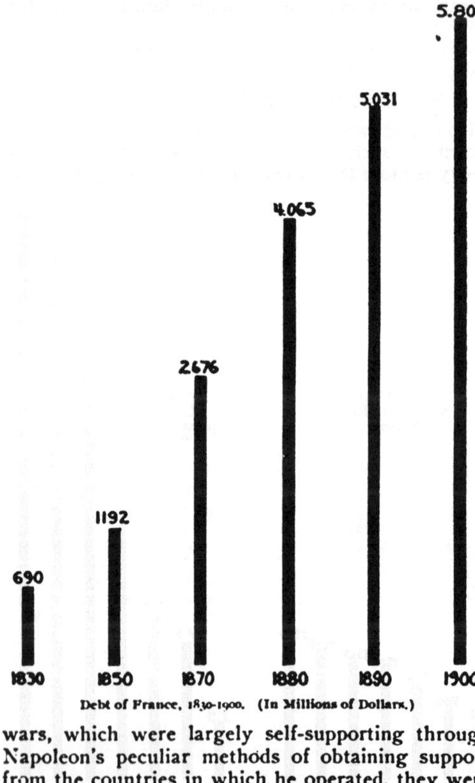

Debt of France, 1830-1900. (In Millions of Dollars.)

wars, which were largely self-supporting through Napoleon's peculiar methods of obtaining support from the countries in which he operated, they were two hundred and fifty million dollars; by 1850 their total had reached a billion dollars; from 1854 to 1870 came the expenses of the wars in the Crimea, Italy, China, Cochin-China, and Mexico, and in 1870 the debt amounted to two thousand four hundred and eighty million dollars, having thus been increased nearly one and one-half billions during that period of wars. The cost of the war with Germany caused an issue of securities in 1871, amounting to five hundred and thirty-six million dollars; another in 1872 of eight hundred millions; and as a result, the national debt stood in 1876 at three thousand eight hundred and fifty-four millions of dollars. These securities issued during the century were sold at prices ranging from 52 per cent. upward, very few reaching as high as 90 per cent. of their face value and only two or three small issues being made in the first half of the century at as high as par. The great loan of 1871 was made at 82½ per cent., and that of 1872 at 84½ per cent. The nominal rate of interest on these securities was 5 per cent., but at the rates at which they were sold, 82½ per cent. and 84½ respectively, were calculated to bring a return of about 6 per cent. on the investment. Since 1872 new issues have been made at lower rates of interest, chiefly for use in refunding the debt and a reduction of interest rates by this process.

About one-half of the debt of France now stands in the form of "perpetual 3 per cent. rentes." These "perpetual" securities, so-called, are a characteristic of a portion of the securities issued by many of the European countries, in which no date for final payment is named, the avowed purpose being to make this portion of the debt permanent, its

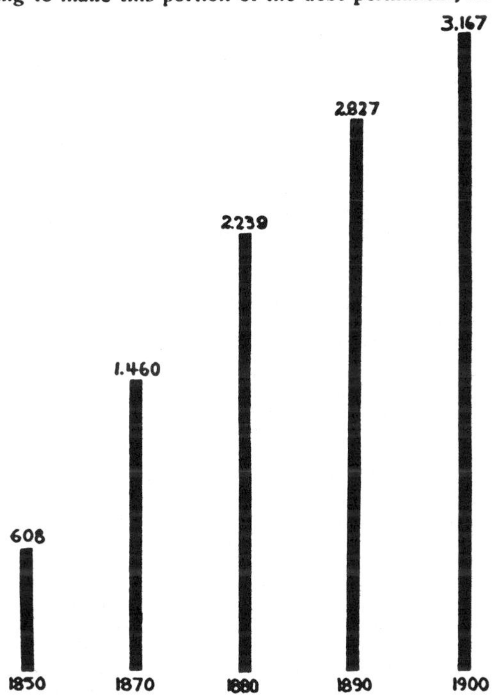

Debt of Russia, 1850-1900. (In Millions of Dollars.)

total being measured in such cases by the annual interest charge rather than by the actual indebtedness. Of these perpetual rentes, the issue of 1886 was made at about eighty per cent.; that of 1891 at 92½ per cent.; and their usual price in the markets is, in most cases, par or slightly above par. It is an interesting fact that the redeemable 3 per cent. rentes, which are an agreement to pay the sum in question in the year 1953, although drawing the same rate of interest and with a fixed date for payment, are, in nearly all cases, quoted in the markets at a lower rate than the "perpetual" rentes bearing the same rate of interest and on which no date is fixed for final payment. Practically all of these securities are held by the people of France, and in this fact, that the interest payments on their enormous national indebtedness are disbursed at home, the French financiers and statesmen justify, in part at least, their enormous national debt, and the neglect of effort to reduce or extinguish that indebtedness.

The Debt of Russia.

The next country to be considered in the order of the magnitude of its debt is Russia, whose national indebtedness amounts to two thousand three hundred million dollars; and this total does not include the guaranteed railroad stock amounting to sixty-four million dollars, nor the bonds of certain

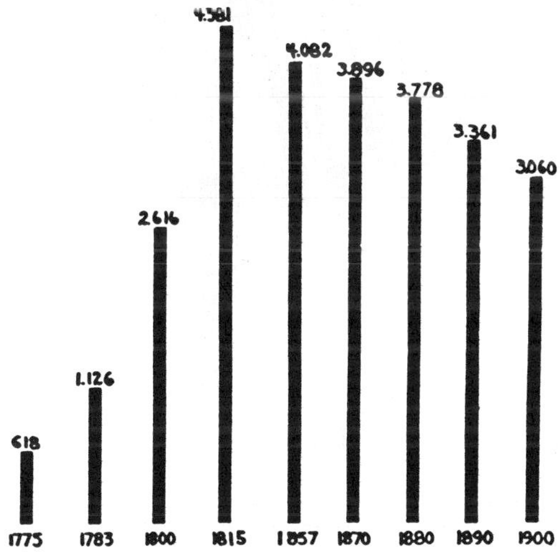

Debt of United Kingdom, 1775-1900. (In Millions of Dollars.)

railway corporations guaranteed by the government, and amounting to over five hundred million dollars. This debt has been practically created in less than a century, the total funded debt in 1817 being less than fifty million dollars, and at the present time over three billions. A very large proportion of this indebtedness was created during the latter part of the century, the liberation of the serfs costing about three hundred million dollars, the Russo-Turkish war over five hundred millions, and the great railway system of the country nearly or quite one and one-half billions; or practically one-half of its present national debt. These securities were issued at rates ranging from 55 to 82 per cent., the issue price of the three per cent. Trans-Caucasian securities having been 55 per cent., but their market prices in the European markets usually range from 85 per cent. to 95 per cent.; while a 4 per cent. issue of 1867, sold originally at 61 per cent., is quoted at par and upward in the markets of London, and a 3 per cent. security issued in 1859 at 66½, usually ranges in price from 80 to 85 per cent. Probably one-half of the Russian securities are held in Russia, chiefly by the great financiers and bankers, differing in this particular from conditions in France, where a large proportion of the national debt is held by the masses. That part of the Russian national debt which is held at home is largely payable in paper currency. The other half of the debt, payable in gold, is chiefly held in foreign countries, especially France and Germany, the larger proportion, however, in France.

What the United Kingdom Owes.

The United Kingdom stands third in the magnitude of its debt, its total national indebtedness at the latest accounts amounting to $3,060,000,000. A very large proportion of this debt has been accumulated since the beginning of the war with the American Colonies in 1776, at which time it stood at about

An Arithmetical Phrase. "One, with two to carry".

six hundred million dollars, being increased during that war over five hundred million dollars and making the total in 1783 a little over one billion dollars. The war period which began in 1793 and was almost continuous until the peace of Paris in 1815, added over three billions of dollars to the national debt, bringing it up to four and one-half billions in 1815. From that date until the year 1855 there was a steady reduction in the indebtedness, but the two years of Russian war added one hundred and fifty millions to the debt, making the total in 1857 a little over four billions. From that date until the beginning of the war in South Africa there was a steady reduction, amounting to over one billion dollars, but the additions made during that war brought the grand total of to-day's indebtedness up to the sum which I have already named, $3,060,000,000.

I have especially mentioned the reductions made in the national indebtedness of the British Government during this period because they are, as I shall show you later, a somewhat unique characteristic in the history of national indebtedness, the instances in which the great nations have materially reduced their indebtedness during the last half century being almost exclusively confined to the United Kingdom and the United States. A very large proportion of the British securities were issued at less than par, ranging from 95 to 98½ per cent., but their prices on the markets of London usually range somewhat above those at which issued, according to the rates of interest and the dates at which they are redeemable. British securities are usually made redeemable at a fixed date, as the custom of considering any considerable part of the national debt permanent or irredeemable does not prevail in that country. Practically all of the national debt of the United Kingdom is held by her own citizens and the interest, therefore, paid at home. One of the methods utilized by the British Government in its debt reduction is that of "terminable annuities," by which persons desiring a fixed income for a long term of years transfer their government securities to the government, which agrees to pay therefor a fixed sum annually for a certain number of years, usually twenty, at which time the obligation terminates.

Origin of the Term "Stocks."

One curious fact in connection with British securities, which may be remarked in passing, is that they are always denominated "stocks." This name seems to have grown out of the fact that persons loaning money to the British Government in early days received, as evidence of their loan, a hazel stick or "stock," with notches cut in it to record the sum so loaned. This stick, when properly notched, was inscribed with the name of the person making the loan and was then cut, lengthwise, into two pieces, and one half given to the person making the loan and the other retained by the government. The stick given to the person making the loan was called his "stock," and that retained by the government the "counter-stock." This custom of designating government securities "stocks" was followed in the United States until 1860, many of the securities bearing the term "stock" in the form printed across their face. Beginning with 1861, however, the securities issued by our government were designated "bonds," and the term "stock" disappeared. In England, however, it has been retained up to the present time. I have been unable to learn, from the most careful inquiry among officers of the government who were in the financial service in 1861, the cause of the change in designation, official or otherwise, but that this change occurred about that date can readily be seen from an examination of the wording printed on the securities issued prior and subsequent to that date.

THE NEW ARITHMETIC.

A correspondent is responsible for the following contribution to Wall street arithmetic, says the New York "Commercial."

10 mills make one trust,
10 trusts make one combine,
10 combines make one merger,
10 mergers make one magnate,
1 magnate makes all the money.

CONCERNING BUTTONS.

In the old days dandies used to adorn themselves with innumerable buttons for purposes of ornament, and the small buttons which still remain on the end of a man's coat sleeve are now about the only relic of this custom. There is an interesting tradition concerning these buttons. It is said that long ago a resourceful king put buttons on the sleeves of his soldiers' coats to prevent them from wiping their noses on them. When handkerchiefs came into vogue the tailor began gradually to reduce the number of buttons on the coat sleeve, until now there are but two, and these for several centuries have had no purpose other than ornamentation

The Coal Speculator Playing with the Public —New York Herald.

THE TALE OF THE DRUMMER WHO KNEW NOT THE COMBINATION

BY JOE LINCOLN

And it was the one thousand and tenth night and the brow of the Sultan was wrinkled and he covered many yards of parchment with figures. And behold when he had finished his figuring he laid aside the scroll and sighed with exceeding weariness, saying:

"Verily, oh Scheherezade, the problem is a hard one If a man hath in his harem four score and ten wives, and if upon the coming of the holiday season doth each wife bestow upon him one hundred bargain-counter cigars, wresting from him the vow that he will smoke each one himself because she gave it to him, and if the man is no longer in the flower of youth, how long, I pray thee, must he continue to burn cabbage after he is dead?"

And Scheherezade knew not how to answer the conundrum of the King, but she said,

"Oh Mightiness, the question is too many for thy servant to handle at her present salary. But comfort thy heart and be glad that thou art not as was King Solomon who had of wives some seven hundred." And, desiring to cheer the heart of the Father of the Faithful, she spake unto him thus:

"Know, oh King, that in the olden time there dwelt in the City of Rhagbagg a certain youth who desired to become a traveling salesman. And he besought the merchants for whom he labored and begged that he might be sent forth into the land and become a drummer. And it came to pass that after a time his employers harkened unto him and he loaded his camels with samples of the goods sold by the merchants, and at the rope factory purchased he many cigars for distribution among his customers and fared forth upon the way rejoicing.

"And behold the name of the youth was Ganem, and upon this, his first trip, sold he but few of the goods of the merchants, for the tradesmen whom he visited questioned him, saying:

"'Wilt this cloth which thou showest us wash without shrinking?'

"And Ganem, being at that time a lover of the truth, answered and said:

"'Not on thy tintype; but verily it will shrink without washing.'

"And the tradesmen scoffed at him and bade him seek the tillers of the soil and among these find a market for his gold-bricks, for they themselves were not in the Rube class.

"And Ganem returned to the City of Rhagbagg and the orders that he had taken were not to be discovered with a microscope, and the merchants were wroth and chided him full sore and found fault with his expense account. And he communed with himself saying:

"'Of a surety the truth is a back number and contains no advertising. Lo! let us test the virtue of prevarication.'

"And upon his second trip the tradesmen questioned him as before, saying: 'Is this ring solid gold which thou offerest us at one dollar a gross?'

"And he laughed scornfully and answered, as one deigning to impart a confidence:

"'Solid? That ring, sayest thou? Why, brother, the gold in that ring is as pure as the advertised analysis of a baking powder, and as solid as a boarding-house doughnut. Know, oh child of darkness, that in our factory none can obtain employment save only those who have taken the gold cure. One thousand gross, sayest thou? Verily, a small order, but the house may be willing to fill it.'

"And when he returned again to Rhagbagg, behold, his order-book was swollen to the extent of the city directory, and the merchants for whom he traveled welcomed him with open arms, and the head of the firm took him to lunch. And although his expense account was infinitely greater than it had been upon the first trip, nevertheless there was no kick coming.

"And it came to pass that he went again upon the road, and his saddle bags were swollen with samples and because of his success was his head swollen to an even greater extent.

"But lo! when on this, his third journey, he did call upon the first tradesman whom he had before visited, that tradesman arose in wrath and blasphemed exceedingly, crying:

"'Dog, thou art he who soaked me with the tin rings, swearing by the Prophet that they were of pure gold! Ho, slaves, bring me my battle-ax and unchain the bloodhounds.'

"And Ganem fled, but in his fleeing did the hounds accompany him for a space and feasted upon certain portions of his raiment.

"And the tradesman called others who had bought of the rings and they harried Ganem about the city and played 'rough house' with him and cast him into the creek that flowed by the walls of the town.

"And that night as he lay in hiding by the wayside, fearing to venture forth, behold there passed a certain drummer that had grown old in the service and had sold much and was still selling.

"And Ganem called unto the aged salesman and bade him pause and hearken unto the tale of one who was up against it, even to the roof. And he laid bare his heart and cried:

"'Lo! I spake the truth and I sold nothing. I lied and I sold but once. Tell me, I pray thee, the secret of the craft, that I may become a winner even as thou art.'

"And the aged drummer smiled sweetly and spake thus:

"'Oh, Ganem, my son, here is my answer: Flour

is not good alone and water is not good alone; but when the skilled cook mingleth flour and water he maketh dough.

"And the aged drummer, having spoken, passed on upon his way and Ganem pondered deeply."

And Scheherezade paused and said unto the Sultan: "Oh King, live forever! What, I pray thee, is the moral of the tale of Ganem?"

And the Father of the Faithful shook his head as one who sorrows, and made answer, saying:

"Verily, I find nothing moral in it."

And, hearing steps approaching from the direction of the harem, he groaned and hurriedly lit another cigar.

BOOKKEEPER VS. AUDITOR.

IT is quite customary of late years for large institutions to employ a man in the capacity of overseer of their accounts whom they call auditor. It is not unusual for the professional auditor to be met by the assertion upon the part of some business man, "Oh! we have a regular auditor in our employ." The question turns upon the meaning of the word auditor. Is a man an auditor because he is called auditor or is he auditor by virtue of what he does? After this question has been answered the next question in order is, "What does the attached auditor do that by any consideration entitles him to the name of auditor?" or "Wherein is he otherwise than chief accountant or head bookkeeper?"

The thoughts underlying this article were precipitated in part by what occurred at New Orleans at the session of the Trust Company Division of the American Bankers' Association. A paper had been read treating upon the audit and examination of trust company accounts. Discussion followed. It was asserted by the manager of one trust company that for some time past they had employed their own special auditor. Someone raised the question concerning his qualifications, and it was pointed out that he was a very trustworthy man, handy with accounts, understood the business and on general principles had been promoted to the position of auditor. Another man took the floor and said that his company also had an auditor, and in answer to questions it developed in this case that his auditor was only the head bookkeeper.

The paper before the house had contained the assertion that it was impossible to audit the accounts of a trust company satisfactorily upon any other basis than laying down first a skeleton balance sheet, which should correctly represent the business of the company, and then to follow out item by item all the details. The fact that the reader of the paper had shown that an intimate knowledge of the business of the trust company was essential to the correct audit led those who were disposed to discuss his remarks to the extreme of saying that no one outside of the company could audit the company's books, and it was along this line that the discussion proceeded.

A step further some one asked if the auditor of one or the other of the two companies, whose managers had just spoken, could not be induced to give to the convention at some future date a complete set of all his blanks. This was equivalent to letting the cat out of the bag. It was evident by the questions which were uppermost in the minds of those taking part in the discussion that it was bookkeeping rather than accounting that they were after; that it was the method of doing things rather than the satisfaction of the correctness in the things done that was uppermost in mind.

Putting aside this instance and allowing the reference which appears above to stand only as an introduction to the subject, the question that we would like to discuss with the reader at this time is, "Can auditing in the best sense of the term be done by a man attached to the company?" By "attached" we mean drawing a regular salary and being a part and parcel of the organization. Can auditing in the proper acceptation of the term be done by such a man satisfactorily? Is such a man in such a capacity entitled to the name auditor? Is he not rather the chief accountant or chief clerk of the establishment? Does not auditing properly considered demand the services of an outside, disinterested person?

It seems to us there can be but one answer to this question. It seems to us that the outside auditor is the one that is being looked for and that the inside or attached man cannot in any way be called auditor. He is instead chief accountant, chief bookkeeper, chief clerk or possibly comptroller, but real auditing comes from the outside. The fact that difficulties beset the steps of the outside auditor, the fact that it is necessary for him to become familiar with all the undertakings of the business is no answer to the general question. Auditing is demanded and it is demanded at the hands of those who are disinterested and who at the same time are experienced in the work and who therefore go at it intelligently.

THE OCCUPATION OF JOSEPH.

In a downtown Sunday-school the first day of this week, one of the teachers read to her small pupils the story of Joseph, of the time when there was a famine in the land, and all of the people flocked into Egypt for grain, says the "New England Grocer." The tale told of how "Joseph opened all of the storehouses and sold unto the Egyptians," and of the coming of Jacob's ten sons with the rest to buy corn. The reading concluded, the teacher indulged in some questions with the idea of testing the Biblical knowledge acquired by the young hopefuls.

"Now, John, tell me who this Joseph was of whom we have been reading. Who was this kindly man who endeavored to relieve the distress of the people?"

John's face was a total blank for a moment, so far as answering the interrogatory was concerned. Then he burst out, triumphant in boyish knowledge, and shouted: "Joseph was a clerk in a grocery store!"

THE ROCK AHEAD.

Jabez—I see by the Bee that Jake Heckman traded horses five times last week, and that he made seven dollars by the transactions.

Ebenezer—That's purty good fer Jake; an' yet, mark my words, this here spirit of commercialism is the very rock on which our American nation is goin' ter be dashed ter splinters!—Puck.

The First Corporation. Noah Floating His Stock.

THE
PUBL...
ASTOR, ... TILDEN ...

Capitalization and Publicity*

By MARTIN A. KNAPP.

THE proposal, as I understand it, is to require all corporations under the control of Congress to make full disclosure of their genesis and operations, to the end, among other things, that it may be clearly seen how the amount of money originally paid in, or the value of the assets at any time owned, compares with the par value of all bonds and stocks which such corporations have issued.

If this will promote the public interest when applied to interstate commerce, it will equally promote that interest when applied to state commerce and private enterprise carried on by corporate methods. The proposed treatment, therefore, includes national and state publicity, comprehensive enough to reach all forms of corporate organization, with the avowed purpose of making all the acts and doings of these artificial persons, including their history and development, as fully known to the general public as they are their respective managers.

Argument of Doubtful Soundness.

With all deference to those who advocate such publicity as a preventative of stock-watering, I venture to doubt the soundness of their argument. Indeed, I hold it unproved that the excessive issue of corporate securities is a source of such danger as to excite public alarm, and I am yet to be convinced that enforced publicity will not be a harmful exercise of public authority.

The capitalization of a company has no relation whatever to the prices at which it sells its products. Of course, the degree to which any concern may approximate the monopoly of a given article does not determine, within limits, the range of obtainable prices: but its power in that case depends wholly upon its control of the market, not at all upon the amount of stocks and bonds which constitute its capital.

When bargaining takes place under conditions of free and active competition, the seller accepts the sum he must take to effect a sale; and this is as true, always and everywhere, of corporations as of individuals. If the seller has to a greater or less extent a monopoly of the article offered, and so escapes the restraint of competition, he names a price which he deems it for his interest to charge; and that price may be influenced by fear of provoking competition, by deference to public sentiment, which would denounce extortion, or even by considerations of a benevolent character; and this is as true, always and everywhere, of corporations as of individuals.

Capitalization is not Monopoly.

When we perceive that capitalization is an entirely distinct and separate thing from monopoly, and cease to confuse things which have no relation to each other, we shall see that the mere factor of stocks and bonds, whether excessive or restricted, has nothing to do with the prices at which the output of corporations is sold.

This being so, it follows that the matter of capitalization in no way concerns the great body of consumers, and that enforced publicity is not required in their interest, since the purchaser buys at the same price, whether the securities outstanding are greater or less than the value of the assets of the corporation in which he deals.

We seek in vain, therefore, for a justification of publicity on the theory that it is needed for the protection of consumers or would contribute to their advantage. This leaves but two classes of persons, few in the aggregate, who have any real interest in corporate publicity, and these are the holders of corporate obligations and those who may desire to buy them for investment or speculation.

In the second place, I maintain that the stockholder as such is not benefited by corporate publicity, and would be harmed rather than helped by its enforcement. The shareholder in a corporation is a quasi partner with the other shareholders, and has a right, corresponding to the right of an actual partner, to know how the business of which he owns a part is managed. This right of the minority stockholder is more or less effectively secured in the charters of corporations or by the statute laws under which they are organized.

Not only is this measure of protection needed, but justice requires that it should be amply afforded. But this is altogether different from general publicity. It is one thing for the stockholder to have knowledge of the concern whose shares he holds; it is quite another thing to furnish the public with the same information.

Publicity is Not Desirable to the Stockholders.

In short, in whatever light the subject is examined, I fail to see that publicity can be desirable or useful to the stockholder. In my judgment it is distinctly against his interest and cannot be defended upon the ground of his advantage.

The justification for this proposal, therefore, must be found, if found at all, in the theory that the state is charged with the duty of safeguarding the investment of capital in corporate securities. To my mind this is a most serious proposition, and I think we should long hesitate before embarking upon such a paternal venture.

Do those who advocate this measure realize the principle involved, the dangers attending its recognition, or the extent to which there may be a demand for its application? I am aware that what is called "over-capitalization" holds a prominent place in the catalogue of corporate offenses, and is emphasized in every count of the indictment against modern combinations.

Nevertheless, I am not convinced that over-capitalization is an evil of such alarming proportions as to require, in the effort to suppress it, a radical change from long accepted views of the functions of government and the inauguration of a legislative policy of such far-reaching import.

In the development of corporate organization we have taken fairly good care to protect the creditors of corporations. I mean by creditors, of course, those who extend them credit, not those who buy or hold their capital obligations. All this is right and requisite, based on sound policy and defensible from every point of view. So, too, the minority stockholder is, or should be, furnished with all needful means for informing himself of the condition and management of the concern in which he is interested, and for redressing any injury which he may have suffered at the hands of those who have excluded him from its administration.

But, so far in the evolution of corporate laws, there has been no attempt to provide assistance or

* Portions of an address by Martin A. Knapp, of the Interstate Commerce Commission, delivered before the American Association for the Advancement of Science, Washington, December 30, 1902.

"The real canal question seems to be "How far will they stretch?"—Minneapolis Journal.

security to the mere investor, except such as may be incidentally afforded by laws designed to safeguard the creditor and the stockholder.

Just why we should undertake to protect those who are seeking investments or engaged in speculation has not been shown to my satisfaction. I do not perceive the necessity or the propriety of such legislation. I regard it at best as a doubtful experiment, not likely to accomplish a useful purpose, and quite certain to have a mischievous outcome.

Stockholders a Small Fraction of the People.

To begin with, the total number of persons who own stocks of any sort is a small fraction of the people. I doubt if there is one in fifty. If the inquiry is confined to those holding stocks in concerns claimed to be over-capitalized, we shall find that they are exceedingly small in number. If from these we deduct the purely speculative purchasers, the stock gamblers, the remainder will be very nearly a negligible quantity.

If we look in another direction, and try to discover how many there are seeking legitimate investments who are liable to be misled or deceived solely on account of a fictitious issue of shares, we shall round up only the most insignificant number. Undoubtedly the avaricious and the unwary are often the victims of outrageous deception. Many a prospectus is filled with fraudulent statements respecting the value of corporate property, and groundless promises of large dividends and rapidly advancing shares.

But the fraud consists in false representations of property and deceitful assurances of gain, not in the mere circumstance that assets of little or no value are capitalized in millions instead of dollars.

Leaving out the speculative and taking into account only those seeking honest investments, ten times more money, to say the least, has been sunk in farm mortgages, suburban lots, patent rights, buying and selling grain, cotton and other commodities, where no corporate shares were dealt in or even existed, than was ever lost on account of the fictitious or excessive issue of corporate securities. If the state is to assume the functions of keeping folly and cupidity from paying twice or ten times what a thing is worth, it surely should assume the guardianship of the largest members and the heaviest losers.

To say that capitalization shall not be greater than the amount of cash actually paid in may, in rare instances, save the feeble-minded from losing their money, but it would also inflict much injury on the general public by hampering the ambitious and placing a handicap upon legitimate enterprise.

To say that shares may be issued only for cash, or for property at its fair value, introduces an alternative which throws the scheme into confusion and leaves it undefended at its weakest point.

If the property to be capitalized is an undeveloped mine, for instance, or an invention like the telephone or wireless telegraphy, by what process will you determine its actual value, or who shall decide on the amount of stock to be issued?

Evil of Watered Stock.

Even if the evil of watered stock is much greater than it appears to me, and however desirable it may be to prevent wrongdoing of this description, I see little good, even to investors, in compelling corporate publicity as a remedy for over-capitalization.

The objections to this plan of corporate publicity do not rest altogether on the negative reasons suggested, for there are independent and affirmative grounds which appear to me important.

Underneath all surface discussion, the real purpose which animates the proposal is, I suppose, the desire by this and other means to check the growth of combination and preserve to the public the benefits of competition.

Our economic philosophy still regards competition, in one form or another, as, after all, the principal reliance to secure fair and reasonable prices for consumable products. We may be obliged in the future to substitute co-operation as the working rule of associated life, but for the present, in common with those who stand for corporate publicity, we must seek to realize as far as possible the advantages of competition.

Assuming this, I ask you to consider the probable effect of publicity upon competitive action. Put in another form the question: Can competition by and between corporations be preserved if they are compelled to make public disclosure of their genesis and operations? Is there not danger that the very thing proposed as an aid to competition will contribute to its downfall, or at least greatly impair its efficiency?

Unless I am quite mistaken the potency of what we call competition results largely as a practical matter, from the ignorance of each contestant as to the strength of his rivals. The actual working of the principle seems to me a series of experiments by which each champion tests the energy and endurance of those who strive against him.

Eager for success each takes the field, fortified with belief in his superior powers, or hopeful that the condition of his adversary may be more desperate than his own. The contest continues because each is in doubt, to a greater or less degree, as to the resources and fortitude of his antagonist.

Out of this very uncertainty springs the disposition of each to measure arms with his fellows; this it is that gives courage for the encounter, whether confidence anticipates conquest or luck is relied upon to escape disaster.

Knowledge Would Reduce Competition.

If each rival knew the other's strength as well as he knows his own, if there were disclosed to him in advance the precise condition of his adversaries in all material respects, and he was conscious that they had equal knowledge respecting himself, would not the contest end before it began?

Where now there is fight there would then be

surrender. Why should either keep up the warfare? Why engage in it at all if he can see from the outset that his rivals are sure to win in the long run? Rather would he lay down his weapons without striking a blow, and join the forces he could not defeat.

On the other hand, if he were provided with full information concerning his rivals, and could see where their weakness exposed them to fatal attack, and they were aware of his knowledge, he would surely expect them to make overtures of peace and not risk an engagement they were certain to lose.

If, then, it is for the public interest to keep up competition; if the general welfare will be conserved by its active operation, I query whether the proposed legislation will not enfeeble the very principle to which it is desired to give new life and vigor.

I cannot but regard corporate publicity of the kind and to the extent advocated by many as a certain and serious hindrance to effective competition. So far from accomplishing the purpose expected in this regard, its practical tendency, in my judgment, would be in the contrary direction. Just as the Sherman Anti-Trust law, which is based upon an economic fallacy, has indirectly aided the very results it was designed to prevent, so the compulsory disclosure of all corporate transactions would, as I believe, undermine the competition it was intended to support. Bearing in mind how rapidly all kinds of business are assuming the corporate form, that the competition of individuals is fast disappearing, and that competition in the future will be mainly between corporations, it seems plain to me that the enforcement of corporate publicity would be an added incentive to industrial combination.

Therefore, as I view the matter, the remedy in question will be worthless to the great mass of people, the consumers, for their troubles are not caused by watered stock and will not be alleviated by publicity. It will not benefit the actual stockholder, for, however much he may need information for himself, his interests would not be promoted by bringing that information to public knowledge.

Against its doubtful and very limited usefulness to the intending purchaser of corporate shares is the danger, not to be lightly estimated, of giving sanction to a principle of extreme paternalism and furnishing a fresh impulse not to compete, but to consolidate.

OPENINGS FOR YOUNG MEN.

While thousands of young men and women throughout the country have taken the civil service examinations and are on the eligible list for appointments in the classified service as clerks, there is a dearth of available applicants for some of the best positions in the Government service. Men and women are needed in almost every department of the Government for a higher class of work than the ordinary applicant for a position under the civil service is capable of performing. So emphatic is this need of the services of specialists that the civil service commission proposes to hold a series of examinations to secure clerks for positions requiring special qualifications.

"We are constantly getting demands from the different departments for skilled men to discharge duties of a more or less technical character," said a member of the Civil Service Commission. "While we have secured an unusually large number of eligibles at our last examinations, the supply does not hold out. They are about to appoint thirty-five additional assistant examiners in the United States Patent Office, and it is our duty to find the men who can fill these places. While the pay is only $100 to start with, there is no branch of the Government service where promotion is so easy and rapid as in the Patent Office. The work of that office is growing with great jumps, Congress having authorized the employment of twenty-five extra assistant examiners only five years ago, and now there are to be thirty-five more. The salary runs all the way from $100 a month to $3,000 a year.

"I don't know of any kind of Government work that is more attractive or desirable to a person having any natural bent for mechanics. The requirements are not severe, but candidates will be expected to be pretty well up in mechanical drawing, and know something about reading plans for technical instruments. The examination will include mathematics, process of manufacture and two or three other subjects, and appointment is practically assured to every person who passes. Mathematicians are wanted in the Navy Department and in the coast and geodetic survey, but there the salaries are not as good as in the Patent Office. New men start at $75 or $90 a month, but splendid opportunities are frequently thrown in the way of these employees to find highly desirable positions outside as a result of the training received in the Government service. I have in mind one of our young men who passed examination and worked for several years as a computer and specialist on the nautical almanac under the chief of the Naval Observatory. He has just resigned his Government position to accept a place in the faculty at Lehigh University. The fact that we can not get enough stenographers and typewriters to satisfy the demands of the department chiefs is an old story. We find plenty of eligibles, but many of them refuse to go into the Government service at the comparatively small salaries that are offered.

RESOLUTIONS ON THE DEATH OF MR. HASKINS.

The accounting fraternity was shocked to learn of the death, on January 9, of Mr. Charles Waldo Haskins, of the firm of Haskins & Sells. Mr. Haskins was prominent not only in accountancy, but in business life generally, and was a member of many societies and social organizations.

At a special meeting of the New York State Society of Certified Public Accountants, held on January 10, the following resolutions were passed:

Whereas, Our beloved president, Charles Waldo Haskins, L. H. M., C. P. A., has been suddenly removed from us by death; therefore be it

Resolved, That we hereby express our deep sense of the loss which this society and the entire accounting profession have sustained; and be it further

Resolved, That the heartfelt sympathy of the members of the society be extended to his bereaved family.

The American Association of Public Accountants also held a special meeting on January 10, and passed the following resolutions:

Whereas, Our member, Charles Waldo Haskins, C. P. A., has been suddenly removed from us by death; therefore be it

Resolved, That we hereby express our deep sense of the loss which this association and the profession generally have sustained. And be it further

Resolved, That the sympathy of the members of this association be extended to his bereaved family. And be it further

Resolved, That these resolutions be engrossed and presented to the family.

The members of these associations attended the funeral in a body.

BOUNDING THE UNITED STATES.

The late Prof. John Fisk liked to tell the story of three patriotic Americans who toasted their native land as follows: The first—"Here's to the United States, bounded on the north by British America, on the south by the Gulf of Mexico, on the east by the Atlantic and on the west by the Pacific." The second—"Here's to the United States, bounded on the north by the North Pole, on the south by the South Pole, on the east by the rising and on the west by the setting sun." The third—"Here's to the United States, bounded on the north by the aurora borealis, on the south by the precession of the equinoxes, on the east by primeval chaos and on the west by the day of judgment."

COMMERCE ACCOUNTS & FINANCE

A Magazine of Higher Business Education and Practical Administration. Acknowledged Authority in the Profession of Commerce and Consistent Advocate of Methods Up to Date and Above the Table.

JOSEPH CROSBY LINCOLN, - - - Editor.
FRIEND PITTS, JR., - Circulation and Advertising.
E. R. KITTREDGE, - - - Business Manager.

PUBLISHED MONTHLY

SUBSCRIPTION $1 a Year in the United States, Canada and Mexico. Other countries $1.50. Postage prepaid by the Publishers. In the absence of specific orders to stop at the end of the subscription term the paper will be continued and a bill sent. Entered at the New York Postoffice as Second Class mail matter.

COMMERCE, ACCOUNTS & FINANCE COMPANY, Publishers
Twenty-five Pine Street, New York

In the untimely death of Charles Waldo Haskins, which occurred January 9, the world loses a broad-minded, enterprising man. As an accountant he was among the leaders of his profession, and was greatly interested in its advancement. In the last decade the profession has taken a great stride forward, and much credit was due to him for his share in this progressive movement. As a business man, he was strong, able and far-seeing. His loss will be greatly felt by all those who had dealings with him The educational world also has received a severe blow, for Mr. Haskins was a leader in the development of the new idea in business education. Although not an old man, he lived to see many of his ideas carried into effect, and to reap a portion, at least, of the reward that was due him.

* * *

The profit-sharing scheme put into operation by the United States Steel Company on January 1 has had such wide publicity through the daily papers that it is scarcely to be supposed that any of our readers have failed to notice it. The scheme essentially is that of allowing the workmen of the corporation, including those engaged with the subsidiary companies, to subscribe to an amount of the preferred stock of the company determined by a percentage on the wages received and giving them the privilege of monthly payments extending over a considerable period. The stock is delivered only when the entire amount of the purchase price has been paid. In the meantime 5 per cent. interest is charged on the amount owing, and the dividends which are 7 per cent. are credited. The subscriber to the stock has the right of selling it at his option whenever it is all paid for, but on the other hand, if he holds it for a period of five years there is a premium of $5 per share in addition to other income. The object in view upon the part of the finance committee who devised this scheme, after much deliberation, is to interest the workmen in the company by which they are engaged in a way to make them feel that they are in a sense working for themselves, and thereby raise the general standard of the force.

*

It was to be expected that this scheme would be attacked. Notwithstanding the very careful explanation by which it was accompanied in presenting it to the public, it was misunderstood in many directions and most mischievously perverted in others. The labor organizations in some instances were emphatic in denouncing the scheme, claiming that it was only another plan of a gigantic corporation to get the better of its laborers. On the other hand a very considerable number of the employees of the United States Steel Company promptly stepped up to the treasurer's office and entered their subscriptions. The success of the scheme has already been demonstrated. This instance is only one of many that might be enumerated at this time, showing the disposition on the part of the managers of large enterprises to divide the profits of the business with those actively engaged in handling the details. There is hardly a paper that has been issued in several weeks past in which some instance of this kind more or less prominent has not been mentioned. Prominent bankers have given their clerks anywhere from 10 to 100 per cent. premium on their salaries for the past year. Railroad companies controlling three-quarters of the mileage of the country have advanced their employees in various amounts. Different industrial corporations have put forth profit-sharing plans more or less elaborate. All these things are of great interest to employees and employers alike.

*

So far as the plan put forth by the United States Steel Company is concerned it will be noticed that it is conceived along new lines. It is a pleasing deviation from various other schemes undertaken in the past, some of which have resulted disastrously to all concerned. That the plan of interesting workmen in the stock of the company is popular is evidenced by the manner in which the general idea has been taken up by other corporations. To the disinterested outsider it would seem that there is no other basis upon which a satisfactory interest can be obtained, and, therefore, that this plan is judicious. The difference between thousands of workmen who might be mentioned and an equal number of employers, who also might be mentioned, is that the first have no understanding of financial affairs while the others have a partial understanding. There is no plan by which the gulf between capital and labor can be so quickly and so satisfactorily bridged as to get the workmen into the habit of investing in the industries with which he is associated. Disaster may possibly follow a plan of this kind. The workman may invest in that which has no secure foundation. On the other hand, there are many secure things available, and therefore little by little he is likely to be educated in the direction of choice in matters of this kind.

* * *

Why should not each one of us tag his signature with two or three letters signifying that he is the possessor of a degree? Degrees are easy to get nowadays, apparently, and are, so to speak, handed out with every pound of tea purchased. Our readers may be interested to learn that a certain Correspondence Institute is now conferring the degree of "Bachelor of Accounts" upon such of its students as pass the final examination in its correspondence course of accounting. "Bachelor of Accounts"—that seems to be a satisfying sort of title. We presume that "B. A." are the mystic letters used to signify this degree, and that therefore they may be annexed to the signature of each proud "Bachelor." These letters, we believe, were formerly supposed to indicate "Bachelor of Arts," a degree which the universities were somewhat chary in bestowing, and which indicated a membership in a rather select body; but now that the same letters stand for "Bachelor of Accounts," and all that is necessary to obtain them is to take a certain correspondence course, why, "B. A.s" should be as thick as flies in the dog days. It behooves each one of us to get in line for a degree; now is the accepted time, and it seems that they are to be had for the asking. We have no doubt that soon there will be "Bachelors of Bricklaying," "Bachelors of Barkeeping," perhaps, even, 'Bachelors of Police." We do not see any limit to the number of bachelors, nor the corresponding number of degrees. Soon a man who may not add two or three letters to his signature will be lonely indeed. Come early and avoid the rush.

TRADE DISCOUNTS.

The subject of trade discounts is one concerning which many pages might be written. There are some trades in which the discounts from list prices are so great as to make the prices themselves look absurd as they appear in the catalogues. This is notably the case in the hardware business where discounts of 70, 10, 5 and 2½ per cent. are sometimes given. In the furniture trade also large discounts from list prices are allowed.

Concerning trade discounts, Mr. Joseph Hardcastle said some time since:

"Often a very suggestive idea may be found by tracing a word to its original source. The English word "monger," signifying a dealer, now used only as a part of a couple of compound words, fish-monger and iron-monger, i. e., a dealer in fish and a dealer in iron, may be traced back to a root used by our Aryan progenitors, signifying one who deceives. In Icelandic we find the same root turning up, signifying a dealer; and again in Anglo-Saxon it appears, conveying the idea of mixing many things.

"We see, then, that there are three ideas hidden in the word; hence, that to be a dealer it is necessary to deceive; and to deceive it is necessary to practice the art of mixing many things, so as to confuse the ideas of the buyer. In our own times, the idea of deception being a necessary part of trade is by no means distinct, in spite of the teachings of political economists that in a good bargain both the buyer and the seller gain by the transaction.

Inherent Deception of Discounts.

"We cannot conceive why the system of compound or trade discounts should be now in vogue, except with the intent to deceive. It is true that price-lists must be published, and that to be compelled to be daily altering them would be a great inconvenience. Granted that a price-list must be published, and that it is necessary that it should serve, say one year, any deviation in the price could be easily made by a single discount. We have, however, to take the world as it is, and not to waste our time in useless efforts to reform it. It is wiser to try to make the most of it as it is, and, in endeavoring to do so, we will try to throw a little light on the subject of trade discounts.

"The order of trade discounts makes no difference in the final cost of goods. Twenty, ten and five; ten, twenty and five; and five, ten and twenty are equivalent sets of trade discounts. Twenty off equals 1-5 off, leaving 4-5 remaining. Ten off equals 1-10 off, leaving 9-10 remaining. Five off equals 1-20 off, leaving 19-20 remaining. And 19-20 of 9-10 of 4-5 equals 19-20 of 4-5 of 9-10 equals 9-10 of 19-20 of 4-5 equals 9-10 of 4-5 of 19-20 equals 4-5 of 9-10 of 19-20 equals 171-250 of the price list as the net cost of the goods. In fact, there has been a real discount of 79-250 or 31 3-5 per cent.

"The sum of the trade discounts we will call the apparent discount, because the sum strikes the judgment as a first impulse. On a careful examination we shall find that the apparent discount should be lessened by a reduction before we arrive at the real discount. In the above case the apparent discount is 35; the reduction, 31 2-5; and the real discount, as we shall see later on, 31 3-5. The question naturally arises, How can we compound several trade discounts so as to form an equivalent single discount? To accomplish this it would be necessary to compound any two, and the resulting discount to compound with a third, and so on until all the trade discounts have been compounded into a single real discount. The order in which the several discounts are taken, as shown, will make no difference.

Rule for Finding Real Discount.

"The following rule will enable the reader to compound any two:

"From the apparent total of two trade discounts subtract 1-100 part of their product, and the remainder will be the real discount equivalent to the two.

"Take 20 and 10. The apparent total discount is 30, from which subtract 1-100 part of 20 x 10 or 2. The result is 28.

"Again take 28 and 5. The apparent total discount is 33, from which take 1-100 part of 28 x 5 or 1 2-5. The result is 31 3-5, the real discount before shown. A little practice will enable the reader to compound either mentally or by pen a series of trade discounts.

"It may be necessary to compare trade discounts at a glance to see which is the more advantageous. In the case where the apparent discounts of two series differ, I believe that the series with the greater apparent discount will have the greater real discount.

"In the case with the apparent discounts of two series, the same as 10, 10 and 10 for one series, and 20, and 5 and 5, the other series, it will be found that the more the discounts of a series approach equality, the less the real discount; and that the more the trade discounts are concentrated into a single discount, the greater the real discount.

"From what we have said it will follow that 10, 10 and 10 are less than 20, 5 and 5.

"There may be cases in which we cannot tell at a glance. In this last case we must calculate the real discounts by the rule given above."

NOT FOR FATHER.

Small Boy—I want to get a bale of hay.

Dealer—What do you want with hay? Is it for your father?

Small Boy—No, sir. It's for our horse.—World's Events.

Commercial Crises. I*

By J. SHIELD NICHOLSON, M.A., D.Sc.

THE title of this paper is "Commercial Crises," but in accordance with common practice the term is used as also covering crises that are in the main monetary or financial. As a matter of history, in most cases, though not in all (crises have been both commercial and financial. For purposes of analysis, however, it is best to consider the two cases separately.

I shall deal first with monetary crises, and for guidance in this part of the subject I shall ask you to accept two principles, the importance of which has been abundantly proved by experience.

Ultimate Solvency.

The first principle is this, namely—

In banking, and more generally in monetary transactions, ultimate solvency is not sufficient. No one doubts for a moment, and even in the most severe crises no one has doubted, the ultimate solvency of the Bank of England. Of this one very striking proof may be offered. In each of the three great crises which followed the passing of the Bank Charter Act of 1844—namely, in 1847, in 1857 and in 1866—this act was suspended by the authority of the government of the day. Now what is the meaning of the suspension of the act? In effect it amounts simply to giving permission to the Bank of England to issue more notes without a corresponding increase of gold. If there had been any doubt of the ultimate solvency of the Bank of England the remedy would have seemed like the joke in "Punch," in which the young lady meets an overdrawn account by sending her banker another of her checks payable to himself by himself. But as a matter of fact the suspension of the act, in two cases indeed the mere announcement of the suspension, was sufficient to restore confidence and allay panic.

Again, to come to our own times, for a long time past the Bank of England has held a reserve of gold —for the notes in the banking department can be immediately converted into gold in the issue department,—the Bank has held a reserve equal to 40 or 50 per cent. of its deposits. In any ordinary bank such a proportion of reserve would seem ridiculously large, even if the term reserve were extended to cover much more than gold. But the Bank of England is the bankers' bank, and although in banking cash and legal tender may be economized to a wonderful degree, in certain cases for certain purposes they are essential. Sometimes nothing but gold itself will suffice, and practically the only reserve of gold is in the Bank of England.

The Second Principle.

The second principle I ask you to apply is really only a special case of the first—namely, that deferred convertibility is not the same thing as immediate convertibility, and suspended convertibility is not the same thing as payment on demand. The case which used to be of most importance was the case of bank notes. For a long period bankers' advances were made for the most part in bank notes, and even fifty years ago it did not seem so preposterous as it would now to suppose that monetary crises would be avoided by the proper regulation of the issues of bank notes. That was the idea by which the Bank Act of 1844, and the corresponding act for Scotland of the next year, were passed. The framers of the Act of 1844 did not mean simply to secure the absolute convertibility of the notes; above all, they wished to prevent excessive issues. Such excessive issues, they supposed, caused an inflation of credit and an inflation of prices, and ultimately led to a crisis. This idea was the subject of a prolonged controversy, which only ceased because bank notes came to be a less and less important part of the credit system, and the Bank of England notes in active circulation positively declined in spite of the growth of trade and population.

But the fundamental idea is by no means dead, though the application must now be different. Those who opposed this "currency principle," as it was termed, or minimised its importance, maintained that if the notes were convertible on demand there could not be an excessive issue. To which the supporters of the stringent limitation of issues by law replied, in effect, that the notes might not as a matter of fact be presented for payment—that as prices rose more might be circulated, and that thus a crisis would eventually be more severe. This view gained the day, and, as I said, the Bank Act of 1844 was passed to prevent crises by limiting the issues of bank notes. Deferred convertibility is usually taken to mean at the option of the debtor; the peccant banker undertakes to cash his notes as if they were letters of exchange payable after so many days or months. Deferred convertibility of this kind was soon shown to be full of danger—witness Scottish banking in the eighteenth century. But there may also be deferred convertibility simply through the inaction of the creditor: the point is, that if the notes are presented for gold, gold will be given, but they are not, as a matter of fact, presented. And indeed the profit of banking for a long time depended mainly on this deferred conversion.

This source of profit may be quite sound in practice, as is proved by experience. At the same time, however, every civilized state has deliberately imposed limits on the issues of bank notes, though the limitation has been achieved in very different ways —as, for example, it is different in England and in Scotland. Time will not allow me to enter into the reasons in detail, but the reference to the universal consensus of opinion ought to be sufficient. Convertibility in itself is not thought to be a sufficient safeguard against the over-issue of bank notes.

But what, it may be asked, is the bearing of the argument on commercial crises under present conditions, when not only issues of bank notes are limited, but the very use of notes is of minor importance? The answer is, that the same principles apply in the case of deposit banking and checks; the notes have been taken for illustration because they are the simplest form of credit instruments.

In deposit banks, just as in banks of issue, in the first place ultimate solvency is not enough; and in the second place, the mere fact that checks are all nominally payable in legal tender on demand is not enough to prevent the unwise extension of credit, and as a consequence excessive speculation and inflation. And yet in this country bankers are practically left to themselves in the management of their deposits, advances and reserves; and while the issues of notes are so strictly regulated, the use

*Address delivered before the Society of Accountants in Edinburgh by the Professor of Political Economy in the University of Edinburgh. Originally published in the Accountants' Magazine.

of checks is from the same point of view altogether unregulated.

In some countries deposit banking has been the subject of legal regulation—notably in the United States—and the want of regulation in this country does not show that there are no dangers in freedom. The system has grown up under various influences instead of being a logical application of principles. The absence of legal regulation may show either that the banks are to be trusted if left to themselves, or that legal control is too difficult to manage or to introduce. Let me again refer to the Bank of England and the account of its functions and position as given in that classic work, Bagehot's "Lombard Street."

The essence of the argument is to show the delicacy and the danger of the present system. No writer has ever made so clear the narrow foundation of our present credit and banking system, and the important part played by the Bank of England, which, strictly speaking, is not a state bank, and the governor and the directors of which are not bankers, but merchants engaged in other businesses. And yet the moral of Bagehot's argument, his general practical conclusion, is not that law and government should at once put an end to such an anomalous state of things, but simply that public opinion should impress on these directors a sense of responsibility, and that some changes should be made in the appointment of the governor and directors so as to admit of greater permanence in the executive, and an admixture of trained bankers. But of legislative control and legal rules for the management of the reserve and deposits there is not a word.

Well, then, the mere fact that deposit banking is left practically free in this country does not show that it is not liable to danger, but simply that under present conditions the danger is not such as can be met in fact by legislative control. The simple truth is that, as in so much of our political and commercial system, so in the most important part of our banking, we rely on the system of national liberty, and we trust more to historical growth than to the logical application of principles.

A financial crisis may arise, broadly speaking, in two ways. In the first place, the ultimate reserve may prove insufficient to meet a sudden strain. Such a strain may arise from events occurring in some foreign country—the outbreak of war, a political revolution, or, it may be, the failure of some foreign banking system. In the past the reserve kept was inadequate, and in times of peril it was mismanaged. This mismanagement of the reserve, if not the cause, was an aggravation of crises. At present the amount is larger, and measures of precaution are taken much sooner; and last, but not least, in times of pressure assistance is afforded more readily when the ultimate security is undoubted. In fact, under present conditions, it seems at first sight hardly conceivable that even a foreign drain could be dangerous to the Bank of England, while any home drain, it may be thought, could be met by the suspension of the Bank Act and the issue of Bank of England notes.

Dangers of the Present System.

But the stability of our present system is by no means perfect. It is now more than a quarter of a century since Bagehot described the dangers of our one-reserve system, and yet at this very time the London bankers are still discussing the best means of diminishing these dangers. There is, fortunately, no question that as regards the management of reserves—especially the reserve of the Bank of England—there has been immense progress since 1866. So great, indeed, has the improvement been, that in spite of the Baring crisis it is seriously maintained by good authorities that crises from this source are no longer to be feared. Seeing, however, that it is little more than ten years since the Bank of England was borrowing gold from the Bank of France and from Russia, this complacency is rather premature. In these days nothing is secure from the attack of combined speculation. So far back as 1866 Overend & Gurney tried to embarrass the Bank of England by the sudden withdrawal of three millions. It is at any rate not beyond the range of possibility that the banking system of this country might be attacked by some great speculative combination in what is generally considered its most vulnerable part.

Senator Hoar as Mrs. Partington.—New York World.

But there is another source of danger. The danger may arise, not in the reserve, but in the credit superstructure. No doubt, here also banks have learned from experience, and they are much more prudent than was formerly the case. Advances are made on better security—in the widest sense of the term—and the funds of the banks are kept more under control. But in a system which rests largely on the good faith and the sound judgment of hundreds and thousands of people, how can we be sure that some gigantic fraud, or at least some disastrous error of judgment, will not be perpetrated? It is on this point that the warning of history is most clear and convincing—and not only ancient history, but history that has been imprinted on the minds of living men.

Even granting that the management of the reserves were perfect, that is only part of the business. There is also danger of excessive competition for business, and the advance of the funds of the banks or of one or more of them beyond the proper range of banking securities—there is the danger of over-confidence, of ignorance and of fraud. Owing to the close interdependence of every part of our credit system, any failure on a large scale may bring down firms that are in no way to blame. No doubt the businesses that are weakest fail the soonest, but the strongest may be unable to bear the strain. And the losses incurred may be such that even the ultimate solvency is not secure. It is true that in banking, conducted on the principles confirmed by experience, there ought to be no danger of ultimate solvency. A bank can apply almost indefinitely the method of dividing the risk, just as an insurance company may itself insure against certain risks by re-insurance. It is true, however, that the principle of insurance is not always so easy of application in banking as it is in life insurance. In times of a great plague the life insurance companies have to meet many claims for deaths, but in times of a great panic banks must meet claims of people who think they are going to die. As we all know, banks have failed in the past, and in all probability will fail in the future, though not to the same extent. The principal danger of banking arises at present, not with reference to ultimate solvency but with reference to immediate demands in times of sudden discredit or alarm. And in this connection it may be observed that although the shock only lasts a short time the recovery may be slow, and during the process of recovery a strain may be imposed on industry generally.

Correspondence School of

Business Organization and Administration

"Accounting is the Vital Element of Business"

TALKS WITH STUDENTS.

Strange as it may seem, many business men do not understand the difference between single entry and double entry bookkeeping, although the difference is as great as that between shadow and substance, between counterfeit and genuine money. Double entry bookkeeping is a system and is founded on scientific principles; single entry is a makeshift, and is founded literally on nothing. Double entry bookkeeping is logical and will lead to accurate conclusions; single entry bookkeeping is without rhyme or reason, and will lead only to confusion and disorder.

Single and Double Entry Discussed.

Bookkeeping by single entry is defined by Webster's dictionary as "the method of keeping books by carrying the record of each transaction to the debit or credit of a single account"; and bookkeeping by double entry is defined as "a mode of bookkeeping in which two entries of every transaction are carried to the ledger, one to the Dr., or left-hand side of one account, and the other to the Cr., or right-hand side of a corresponding account, in order that the one entry may check the other—sometimes called, from the place of its origin, the Italian method."

Let us consider the subject a little in detail.

When a merchant exchanges goods for cash, the cash comes in and the goods go out. This is one of the simplest illustrations we can use. The principle it involves is the same, however, as that involved in every other transaction, whether it be an exchange of goods for goods, goods for debts, goods for service, cash for cash, cash for debts, cash for services, debts for debts, debts for services, or services for services. It is the very nature of an exchange that something must be exchanged for something; there must be an incoming and an outgoing. If the record of an exchange is kept, to be complete it must contain, therefore, entries both of the coming in and of the going out. Two entries, or a double entry, must be made of each transaction, and if this is not done the record will not be complete.

There are many people, however, who do not keep a record of their transactions in this way. The only accounts kept in the ledger are personal accounts. No record is kept of gains and losses, and there is no possibility of determining whether the books are accurate or not. This is single entry bookkeeping. It is sometimes charitably but erroneously called a system. Transactions are recorded to show only one of the two aspects of exchange. Incomings are entered in the ledger without their corresponding outgoings, and outgoings are entered without their corresponding incomings. It is obvious that a ledger kept in this way cannot fail to be an incomplete record, and, therefore, worthless for determining the accuracy of the accounts by proving the books, or for enabling the merchant to know positively whether he is making or losing money, and what special department or departments may be responsible for the conditions that exist.

The object of account keeping is to supply to the business man not only a knowledge of the truth that he is making or losing money, but a careful analysis of the source of his gains and losses. He wants this information not in general terms, but in the form of specific facts. If he is making money, how much he is making, in what special division of his business, and what are the elements that enter actively into the production of that profit? If he is losing money, how much has he lost, where, and from what cause. These are the facts the business man wants to know. But these facts he can never secure by any method of keeping his books that neglects to record one-half of the requisite entries. Such a method is that known as single entry bookkeeping.

This method many of the so-called business colleges and schools formerly taught, greatly to the bewilderment of the pupils, who wondered what they were driving at. Grave examiners would gravely set examination papers thereon, and writers of books on bookkeeping would seriously argue that "single entry is more suited to the operations of retail trade!" But progress in education and knowledge, and the exacting demands of competition in all branches of industry, have made detailed and specific information, full and complete, regarding every division of his business necessary to the merchant who would be successful. For this purpose only double entry bookkeeping is adequate. Every transaction must be recorded in at least two accounts.

On the other hand, says Mr. Thornton in his "Manual of Bookkeeping," there is a method by which the labor of entering each transaction twice may be greatly abridged, by grouping together transactions of a kindred nature, and entering in one total several items, all of which affect one and the same account.

This method is often miscalled single entry. This application of the term is a serious and a mischievous error. The method referred to is really an advanced kind of double entry, and the principle underlying this labor-saving plan is capable of wider application than it often receives.

What Double Entry Does Not Mean.

There is so much confusion on this question of double entry, even in some books on bookkeeping, and still more in the minds of many otherwise well-informed people, that it is necessary here to add a few emphatic cautions as to what double entry does not mean.

1. Double entry does not mean keeping other people's accounts as well as your own.

It is quite true that every transaction affects two persons, but this is not the reason for the double entry that is required. It affects each of these persons in two opposite ways, and for this reason each should make a double entry of it. I do not wish to keep a record in my books of the effect of each one of the multitudinous transactions of my business on A, B, C and all the other people with whom I do business (except in so far as my own rights or obligations are affected thereby), and if I did, it would be often quite impossible. Half of my affairs may be transacted with the unknown individuals, X, Y and Z, whose names and abodes I am alike ignorant of.

2 Double entry does not involve double the clerical labor of single entry.

Many people keep their books in such a manner that, although they have never proved them in their life, comparatively few additional entries would be needed to convert their single entry into double and enable them to do so.

3. Double does not depend upon the keeping of a journal.

4 Double does not need a separate account for each kind of merchandise in which the business deals.

This is entirely a matter for the fancy of the proprietor of the business, who can keep one goods account or twenty or fifty. One is all that is absolutely necessary to double entry.

5. Double entry does not exclude the use of day book and invoice book, nor does the use of these books imply that the system is single entry.

Day book and invoice book are, in reality, portions of a classified journal, and when properly kept they are the means of greatly abridging the bookkeeper's labor.

Let us now take a few examples of ordinary transactions and see how they affect the man of business in two distinct and opposite ways:

Jan. 1, I bought goods for cash, $50.

This increases my stock of goods, and it decreases my stock of cash. It therefore needs a double entry.

Jan. 2, I sell goods to Mr. Jones (on credit), $50.

Here my debts receivable have increased and my goods have decreased. I must therefore make a double entry of the transaction.

Jan. 3, Mr. Jones pays me $50.

Here my cash has increased and my debts receivable have decreased. A single entry of this transaction would therefore be an incomplete one.

Jan. 4, I sold goods to Mr. Barker for cash, $50.

This transaction may be divided into two parts:

(1) I sold goods to Mr. Barker, $50.

(2) Mr. Barker pays me $50.

Whence it is seen to be a combination of the transactions on January 2 and 3, and takes two double entries, or it may be regarded as another instance of the transaction on January 1, "sold goods for cash," and be recorded by one double entry only. That is to say, I need not enter the transaction in Barker's account at all, but if I do I must enter it on both sides of his account; on the Dr. side to show that he became my debtor for the goods sold to him, and also on the Cr. side to show that he became my creditor for the money he paid me. And the effect of these two entries is, of course, to cancel each other, so that the balance of the account remains just as if I had not entered either of them in it.

Enough has been said to indicate that every transaction must be entered in two accounts, and that one of these entries must be a debit and the other a credit. This is the leading principle of double entry bookkeeping and may be briefly stated thus: Every debit has its corresponding credit, and every credit its corresponding debit.

COLLATERAL READING.

GRAMMAR AND RHETORIC.

The Vocabulary of a Child.

In the first section of this course mention is made of the manner in which a child learns to speak. As all of us who are acquainted with children know, the child first learns the names of things, after that he learns to tell us what the things or animals do. For instance, the "fire burns," the "dog barks," etc. This, of course, is the natural method of learning to speak a language. In the "Mount Airy World" was recently printed the following sensible article on the subject of a child's vocabulary. It is interesting not only to teachers, but to all who really desire to use words as they should be used.

A professor at the University of Michigan says that by actual count a child only two years old may use more than two thousand words in a day. If this professor is correct, observers of children hitherto have greatly underestimated the vocabulary of the child. Still all the words a child may use can hardly be classified as belonging to his vocabulary, for children use words of which they do not know the meaning; in fact, the child often follows Lewis Carroll's advice: "Take care of the sound and the sense will take care of itself." As generally understood, one's vocabulary is the list of words one uses intelligently. School children, as any teacher knows, use many words glibly and with grammatical accuracy, yet they have not the slightest idea what the words mean. Frederick Tracy, in a very thoughtful article on the "Language of Childhood," gives the vocabularies of twenty-one children varying in age from nine months to thirty months. The observations were made as accurately as possible, though in no case was there absolute certainty that all the words used intelligently were recorded. The largest vocabulary was that of a Chicago boy in his twenty-eighth month, a vocabulary of six hundred and seventy-seven words. Since a bright Boston boy has a vocabulary of two hundred and eighty-five words when two years old, there is strong reason to doubt that Michigan children of two can use two thousand words unless repeating much that is meaningless to them.

We never have regarded statistics of the above sort as very reliable. That it is difficult, almost impossible, to make an accurate list of the words a child or an adult knows should be apparent to any one giving the matter the least thought. The feat might be placed in the same category with an attempt to count the hair on one's head. If the mind is blank there is no list; if the pate is perfectly bald there is no count, and difficulty of counting increases as you pass on up the cranial exterior from the narrowest possible fringe of hair around the base of the brain. Statistics that are not accurate or at least approximately so are valueless. Now, we admit that it is not difficult to gauge the verbal knowledge of a deaf child for some little time after he begins his education, but he soon reaches a point where the would-be statistician is at sea both as to the number of words the child knows and the number he understands and can use intelligently. The ambition on the part of a few teachers to cram their pupils with verbal husks finds no favor with us. It is more essential that a child can use intelligently the words he knows than that he be possessed of a long list learned by rote.

BUSINESS CORRESPONDENCE.

The Origin of the Postal System.

As all our letters go through the post, and as the postal system plays such an important part in business correspondence, the following article from the "Postman" concerning the origin of the postal system will be interesting to students:

The origin of our postal system, like many of our arts and ancient achievements, is lost in obscurity. Permit me to refer to the Second Chronicles and we read, "The posts went with the letters from the king and his princess throughout all Israel." Job says, "Now my days are swifter than the post; they flee away."

Thus we see, even in those days, the people evidently had a postal system in vogue, however crude it might have been.

The Assyrian and Persian monarchs had established at a day's journey apart, stations where saddle horses were kept in readiness for the messenger to leap into the saddle and carry with great haste the orders of his monarch. The Roman Empire, however, was probably the first to establish what would be termed a postal service. This was not for commerce or for the accommodation of the people in general, but exclusively for military and administrative purposes.

As far as postal communications was concerned, Old Rome, even in her palmiest days, was far inferior to the smallest office in the United States.

While she ruled the whole civilized world, yet her postal system was far from a standard of perfection; but every postal system established afterwards incorporated one word which the Romans used. The word "post" possibly originated from the Roman couriers, who were stationed at posts certain distances apart, to await the dispatches that were to be carried forward.

The writing material of Julius Caesar was not like such as we would buy to-day from our book stores, and it is quite likely that his correspondence was carried on without the aid of a stenographer. He probably wrote upon tablets of wood covered with wax, and formed the letters with a stylus. As these tablets were void of convenient flaps, properly gummed, they were bound together with a cord, and where the cord was tied wax was used to seal it against inspection and was then stamped with his signet ring to insure privacy. Perhaps this is the origin of the franking privileges granted our public officials, especially our congressmen and senators.

How Penny Postage Came to be Established in England.

Newspaper anecdotes are not always trustworthy, but are often very interesting. We give the following anecdote, which was printed in the "New York Tribune," for what it is worth. In connection with our talk on the postal system it is interesting:

Many years ago, when Queen Victoria first began to reign, it cost ninepence to send a letter from one English city to another. In those days the postage was not paid by the sender of the letter, as is now customary, but by the receiver. So, of course, there were many poor people who could not afford to pay ninepence when their mail arrived, and it often happened that they were obliged to forfeit the letters.

One day a man named Rowland Hill was riding on the outskirts of a city, and he saw a postman bring a letter to a young girl and demand ninepence for it. The girl took the letter, scrutinized it carefully and then handed it back to the man, saying she could not afford to pay the postage. Thereupon Rowland Hill, being a kind-hearted man, rode up and insisted upon paying it himself. When the postman had gone, the girl confessed to her benefactor that the letter was from her lover, and to avoid paying ninepence on every letter he made certain marks on the envelope which she alone could decipher.

"But," said Rowland Hill, "don't you know you are doing something very dishonest in thus cheating the government?"

The girl admitted she did, but there was no other way to do.

Hill rode away and meditated over this little incident, and his far-famed idea of "penny postage" was the result. At first he was laughed at by every one, but he fought bravely and finally was rewarded by seeing his idea in practice all over the land.

Postal Checks.

Some time since we printed in this paper a suggestion by Mr. Post, of the New York Postoffice, regarding a system for postal checks. That some such postal check as Mr. Post recommends is necessary most of us feel certain. In the "Baltimore Journal of Commerce" appears an article on the subject of postal checks:

Many of the reforms recommended from year to year by the Postmaster-General are too technical in form or too obscure in effect to catch the popular attention, but this matter of postal checks is an exception. The postal service is at once highly scientific and highly popular, but its scientific advances have to prove their popular value before the public will clamor for them. They have to create their demand, and the experts who think them out have some trouble, without popular support, to get Congress to adopt them.

There should be no such difficulty about postal checks. All of the millions of people who have to send small sums of money through the mails, or who would like to do it instead of using more troublesome ways of payment, see the need of this reform at a glance. The wonder is that they do not reinforce the recommendations of the Postmaster-General by pestering the lives out of their Congressmen till the change in the law shall be made. No betterment in any branch of the public service could be made so easily and cheaply, and at the same time serve the daily convenience of so many people.

Registered letters serve a useful purpose for safe sending of valuables through the mails, and money orders for secure sending of small sums of money. But the latter involve more trouble than most people are willing to take to prevent the loss of such small sums. It is probable that there is more loss now in a year by resort to ordinary letters for sending money than would come with adoption of an easier though less safe way.

What is wanted is a check that can be bought over the counter at any postoffice and cashed at any other. The buyer might be required to write in the name of the paying postoffice as well as that of the payee, though this would make it less convenient. Of course there are practical difficulties about keeping track of the sale and redemption of these wandering checks, but it is exactly the business of the scientific experts of the treasury department to solve such difficulties when created by a strong popular demand. The strongest evidence of imperative demand for postal checks is the fact that the express companies have come into the field to meet it. The government should not confess itself unable to do what private enterprise is doing every day.

COMMERCIAL GEOGRAPHY.

Cost of a Dinner.

We are so accustomed to the use of commonplace articles like pepper, salt, sugar and the other materials that go to make our meals palatable, that we seldom stop to consider how much these articles actually cost in production, transportation and the like, before they are placed upon our table. In the "Outlook" for March 13, 1897, was printed a little article regarding the cost of a dinner, and we reprint it here as being interesting and instructive:

Recently a gentleman who is fond of arithmetic made up his mind that he would find out how much a dinner really costs. This gentleman asked how much a simple dinner that he was eating would cost, and he was told seventy-five cents. He contradicted this, and then made out the following statement about the cost of that dinner. The pepper, he said, came from ten thousand miles away. It grew on a little bush about eight feet high, which must have had a growth of at least five years. The pepper was picked green, it had to be dried in the sun, and this meant employing women. It took one ship and a thousand miles of railroad to bring the pepper to the United States. The tea on the table came from China, and the coffee from South America. The codfish had to be brought from Maine. Men had to be employed to catch the fish; other men and women were employed in drying, packing and boxing it, and it, too, had to make a long railroad journey. The flour of which the bread was made was grown in Dakota; some one owned the land, and that meant the investing of capital; and then he had also to pay wages to workingmen. The flour had to be ground, and the building of the mill and the plant, or machinery, meant more money invested. The millers had to be paid; coopers had to be paid for making the barrels; and, of course, the wood of which the barrels were made had to be cut and sawed and shaped, and this meant the employing of more men. Then the flour had to be shipped over the railroad and handled again by cartment before it came into the house. The salt came from the Indian Reservation in the northwestern part of New York State. The canned peaches came from California, and they too represented the employment of capital and labor. The spices in the cake came from the Spice Islands in the Indian Archipelago. After the gentleman had pointed out what the dinner really cost, he asked what on the table could be raised within the limits of the country where they were living. The answer was: only the corn bread, the butter and buttermilk, and it was decided that the family could not live on those alone. The gentleman estimated that that little dinner represented directly, or indirectly, the employment of five hundred millions of dollars of capital and of five millions of men.

The Romance of Common Things.

As a continuation of the article on the cost of a dinner we print the following little stories of common things

A Bookkeeper's Phrase. "Putting it Down in Round Figures".

connected with the table. The article originally appeared in the "New England Grocer."

The "unspeakable Turk" is said to have been the indirect means of the introduction of coffee to civilization In the seventeenth century, when the Turks in vast numbers laid siege to Vienna, King Sobieski, of Poland, was the intrepid leader who delivered Europe from being overrun by the power of the Osman Empire. Marching out of the city at the head of his 20,000 Poles, he made a detour and gained an eminence at some distance, looking down from which he could see the might of the besieger's forces. Long lines of magnificent tents, looking more like a vast pleasure ground than the abodes of an invading army, stretched on every side. But Sobieski's practised eye soon discerned the lack of order in their arrangement and the loose military discipline displayed by the indolent Turkish ruler, and dashing down with his intrepid followers his very name carried consternation into their ranks and they broke and fled in wild confusion. Their tents, rich with the luxuries of the East, fell into the hands of the victors, who also found in the abandoned camps large quantities of that delightful product of Arabia which has ever since been known as Mocha coffee. Thus when September 12th of this year comes around it will mark the two hundred and nineteenth anniversary of this victory and likewise of the introduction of coffee to civilization.

An old Arab manuscript of the fifteenth century says coffee was used in Abyssinia from time immemorial. Its use had not spread into the neighboring countries, for the Crusaders knew nothing of it. The Egyptians extracted a drink from it called cave, whence the French word cafe.

The Galla, a wandering nation of Africa in ancient times, in their incursions into Abyssinia, being obliged to traverse immense deserts and to travel swiftly, were accustomed to carry nothing with them but coffee roasted till it could be pulverized, and then mixed with butter into balls and put into a leather bag. One of these, the size of a billiard ball, would keep them in strength and spirits during a whole day's march better than bread or meat.

Most writers of the Middle Ages thought cinnamon, ginger, cloves and nutmegs the product all of one and the same tree. An old writer affirms that the distilled water of the flowers of the cinnamon tree excelled far in sweetness all other waters. The fruit yields an oil which was formerly in Ceylon made into candles for the king.

The date tree is the palm of the oases, and supplies food for man and beast. The trees grow from 60 to 80 feet high, and live to a great age. The Arabs say that when Adam was driven out of Eden the date, chief of all fruits, was one of three things he took with him, the other two being the myrtle and an ear of wheat. An ardent spirit, distilled from dates and water, is much used by Mahometans, as it does not come within the prohibition of the Koran against wine.

The fig is supposed to have been the first cultivated fruit tasted by man. In Sicily it is looked upon as ill-omened, as the tree on which Judas Iscariot hanged himself and never to have thrived since. The Germans have a proverb which seems to contradict this opinion, "He who has figs has riches."

The orange is one of those rare trees which produce at the same time fruit, flowers and foliage. The practice of wearing orange blossoms by brides is derived from the Saracens, amongst whom it was regarded as emblematic of happiness and prosperity. This was doubtless the "golden apple" which grew in the fabled gardens of the Hesperides, guarded by the dragon which Hercules slew.

There was much diversity of opinion among ancient writers as to what fruit constituted the Tree of Knowledge which caused mother Eve's undoing, and the fig, the citron, the pomegranite, the orange, the grape and the banana have all been identified as the forbidden fruit, but on what grounds it is difficult to say and the question is likely to remain unsettled.

The blackberry bush is said to have been the burning bush in the midst of which Jehovah appeared to Moses. According to some writers it supplied the crown of thorns for the Crucifixion. The ancients deemed both fruit and flowers efficacious against the bites of serpents, and it was believed that the young shoots, when eaten as a salad, would fasten teeth that were loose. According to an Irish legend, Honor Garrigan, one Sunday during St. Patrick's lifetime, rode up the hill to church, but spying a bunch of ripe blackberries, she dismounted to gather them. Her young servant remonstrated with her on the wickedness of breaking her fast before Holy Communion, but in vain. His mistress ate the blackberries, after which her hunger increased to famine pitch, so that she ate up the boy and then the horse. Then St. Patrick, alarmed by the cries of his congregation, who were afraid she would devour them also, shot her with his bow and arrow, and she was buried in the field outside the churchyard.

England's Pacific Cable.

The sun never sets upon Great Britain's territory; that statement is literally true and has become a proverb. England has now connected her possessions with a telegraph line that reaches around the world and touches at only two points upon other than British territory. An article describing this telegraph was recently published in the "New York Sun," and we quote from it. The "Sun" says:

After long discussion and many delays and difficulties, due in part to the hostility which the great project aroused, the British cable across the Pacific is at last completed and open for business. The length of the cable, allowing 10 per cent. for slack, is 7,986 nautical miles. It extends from Vancouver to Fanning Island, 3,561 miles; Fanning Island to Fiji, 2,093 miles; Fiji to Norfolk Island, 961 miles; Norfolk Island to New Zealand, 537 miles; and Norfolk Island to Queensland, 834 miles.

This great enterprise has been talked about since 1870. At that time Cyrus W. Field evolved a scheme for connecting California with China by way of Alaska and Japan.

The British were much interested in the project and it was widely discussed in England with the idea of laying a British cable across the Pacific. The conclusion finally reached, however, was that Mr. Field's project was impracticable, largely on account of the prevalence of ice in the northern regions and the consequent difficulty of erecting and maintaining the connecting land lines.

For some years nothing more was heard of a British cable across the Atlantic. But at last the scheme of an

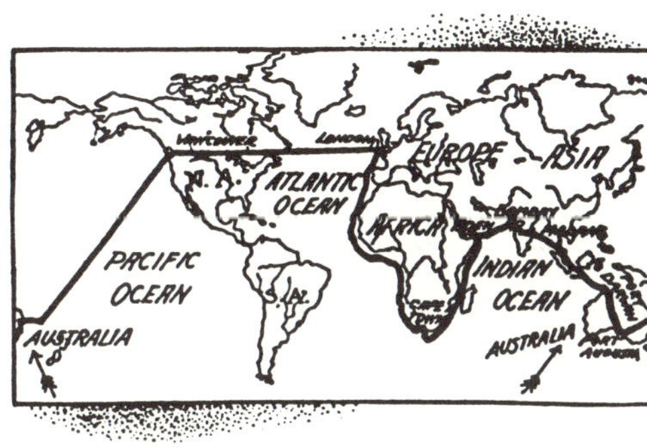

Map of England's "Round-the-World" Telegraph.

all British route linking British Columbia with Australasia came into view and was examined in all its bearings.

As soon as the enterprise began to be very seriously considered opponents of the scheme came forward and urged all sorts of physical and mechanical difficulties in the way of carrying it out It was asserted, for example, that a cable to extend across the Pacific could not possibly be worked; also that it would be impossible to repair the cable because the depths were undoubtedly very much greater than those encountered in the Atlantic.

John Bright, a firm friend of the project, combatted this view. He asserted that from all the facts known with regard to the Pacific the maximum depth to be encountered in laying the cable would probably be found near the Fiji Islands, where it would be necessary to submerge the cable in from 3,300 to 3,400 fathoms.

He pointed out on the other hand that the Atlantic cable of 1869 ran into some 3,200 fathoms and that this was only one example of several of laying cables at a similar depth. His deduction naturally was that a Pacific cable would encounter difficulties, so far as depth was concerned, only slightly greater than in the case of lines then in successful operation.

The difficulty of sending despatches over so long a cable, he declared, might very easily be obviated by landing the cable at various islands on the way across the ocean and relaying the messages. This is the plan that has actually been carried out.

Mr. Bright's prediction as to the depths along the route has been fulfilled in a remarkable manner, though the data on which he founded his statement were very meagre. In surveying the route some 1,900 soundings over 500 fathoms in depth were made. The greatest depth along the entire route is 3,200 fathoms, but the general average is much less.

The financial aspects of the enterprise were then discussed. The British Government finally in 1899 declined to contribute a farthing toward laying the cable.

Mr. Chamberlain definitely announced that the most the government could do was to pay an annual subsidy of $100,000 for a period not exceeding twenty years. He said the government was of the opinion that the cost of the cable should be borne by the colonies interested.

It was only after public opinion in Great Britain had exerted much pressure on the authorities that the government finally decided to become responsible for five-eighteenths of the cost of the cable. The total cost has been nearly $10,000,000, of which Great Britain and Canada have paid five-ninths, New Zealand, one-eighth, and the Australian States have divided the remainder among them.

The fact that Great Britain had no-round-the-world communications except through a number of foreign countries was the great argument that brought about the realization of the project. There were lines of telegraph stretching from England to India and Australasia by way of the Mediterranean and the Red Sea, around Africa and across Europe and Siberia. But every one of these lines of communication would certainly be broken at once in the event of a great European war.

A cable across the Pacific from Canada to Australia would obviate this peril. With the completion of this cable England has telegraphic communications around the world which touch only British soil except at the Cape Verde Islands and Madeira, belonging to her ally, Portugal.

Thus in the event of war the whole machinery of England's vast commerce may be diverted from the European and Asian routes to a route that is practically all British. The English, therefore, believe that the new cable will guarantee to an important extent the security of their trade.

Another advantage of the new line will be the large reduction in the cable rates to Australasia. The rates from South Australia to British Columbia by way of London have been as high as 6s. 3d. a word; and if the message was sent from New Zealand, the rate was increased by the local charge to as high as 7s. 5d. a word, which was almost prohibitory as far as ordinary business is concerned.

It is said that the rate between British Columbia and Australia will now be reduced to two shillings, or 50 cents a word. The importance of this reduction to the business correspondence between these two great members of the British Empire is very evident.

It is estimated that about 2,000,000 words may be transmitted over the new cable in a year.

THE LESSON COURSES.

The lesson courses are arranged in two series: Preparatory and Advanced. The legend on the banner is "Accounting is the Vital Element of Business." Every effort is made, therefore, to get the pupil fully conversant with accounting principles as the foundation of his work and then building thereon to instruct him in Organization and Administration along selected lines.

Each student upon enrollment is subjected to a preliminary examination to put upon our office records the facts of his elementary training. Notation is also made of various personal facts connected with his history, such as age, experience in actual business, references, etc. So far we have found remunerative employment for every one who has been under our charge, and at present the applicants upon our rolls for intelligent help are in excess of our ability to supply. Every one who entrusts himself to our care is assured of a good position on completion of either one of the advanced courses of training.

PREPARATORY COURSES.

A	English Grammar, Composition and Business Rhetoric	$25 00
B	Business Correspondence	15 00
C	Shorthand and Typewriting	25 00
D	Commercial Geography	15 00
E	Financial and Commercial History	15 00
F	Business Arithmetic	15 00
G	Double Entry Bookkeeping	25 00
H	Commercial Law	25 00

ADVANCED COURSES.

1	Accounting, Business Organization and Administration of Machine Shop with Foundry	$100
2	Accounting, Business Organization and Administration of Cotton Mill (Textiles in General)	100
3	Accounting, Business Organization and Administration of Street Car Line	100
4	Accounting, Business Organization and Administration of Department Store	100
5	Accounting, Business Organization and Administration of Country Bank	100
6	Accounting, Business Organization and Administration of Large City Bank	100
7	Accounting, Business Organization and Administration of Book Publishing House	100
8	Accounting, Business Organization and Administration of Periodical Publishing Concern	100
9	Accounting, Business Organization and Administration of Mercantile Business (wholesale)	100
10	Accounting, Business Organization and Administration of Mining	100
11	Accounting, Business Organization and Administration of General Manufacturing	100
12	Accounting, Business Organization and Administration of Installment Merchandising	100

Special courses arranged in the light of particular requirements.

The prices preceding are for single payments with the order. Under proper conditions, and at a slight advance over these rates, we are prepared to concede monthly or quarterly payments.

Time unlimited. Students may enter at any time, and proceed with their work rapidly or slowly as suits their convenience.

The Lesson Courses are all sectionalized. A second section will be forwarded only when proficiency has been shown in the first.

PRELIMINARY EXAMINATION.

(In answering these questions, indicate the questions by numbers. Write on paper 8½ x 11 inches, one side only).

1. Name.
2. Home address.
3. Business address.
4. Married or single.
5. Age.
6. General account of elementary education.
7. General account of business experience.
8. What works on bookkeeping, commerce, finance, etc., have you in your library or that are accessible for reference?
9. Define the principle of debit and credit.
10. Outline the general method of opening a set of books.
11. Describe the general method of closing a set of books.
12. Define "trial balance."
13. Define "balance sheet."
14. About how much time per day can you devote to this course of study?

SAMPLE DESCRIPTIONS.

The following descriptions of courses are samples of all and will serve to give the prospective student an idea of the kind of instruction he will receive.

Preparatory Courses.

One of the greatest difficulties that we have encountered in the instruction that we have been giving in this line the last few years is the lack of thorough grounding in fundamental principles. We have been approached by those desiring instruction as accountants who were deficient in the elements of bookkeeping. We have been approached by those who desire to be drilled as secretaries and amanuenses, who were deficient in ordinary English. For this reason the preparatory courses mentioned in the announcement of this school have been most carefully prepared.

In each of these courses the student is given practical instruction from the outset. All that which is superfluous from the standpoint of every-day, hard-fisted business is relegated to the background, and only that is taught which is applicable to the requirements of business transactions. The illustrations employed are eminently practical and are derived from actual going business.

1.—Machine Shop With Foundry. $100.

In this case the student is supposed to have some machine shop and foundry in mind. If he has the run of the office of such an institution, so much the better. His instruction commences with the charting of the accounts, and is continued, with full explanation of the details which go to make up the accounts. The entering of orders, the analysis of orders, the conveyance of the order to the foreman or superintendent, are each described. Incidentally the methods of handling cash, including petty cash and the bank account, are worked out in all necessary detail. Items in suspense, matters in reserve, and the handling of the different accounts composing the Balance Sheet Ledger are carefully exploited.

After the accounting foundation has been thus broadly

laid, the question of the business organization and administration of the shop is undertaken. Various examples are presented, ranging from a very small shop to one of considerable size. The question of business matters as distinct and different from those of shop details is presented, and the relation of one department to another is carefully discussed. The question of a code for managing and operating these several divisions is introduced and illustrated.

2.—Cotton Mill Work. $100.

This subject is intended to cover textiles in general. The accounting foundation is laid broad and deep, covering everything from entering the order and the purchase of material, together with the time keeping and payment of employees, to the final adjustments in the balance sheet. All details are gone over carefully.

On the accounting foundation thus established there is then introduced the question of general organization at the mill, including the business head (president or treasurer as the case may be), the superintendent, the foreman, the overseers. The arrangement of the offices, the duties assigned to each of the occupants thereof, the correspondence, and all other details are carefully gone over.

If the student has the run of a cotton mill or other textile institution, he is encouraged to bring into his work illustrations derived from the actual practice of the establishment under view. His instruction will be so complete as to enable him to take charge of the work and carry it through.

4.—Department Store. $100.

In no line of business is proper organization and efficient administration more necessary than in the department store. In no branch of merchandising does the going balance sheet and profit and loss statement develop to better advantage than in this. There is perhaps no line of business extending more rapidly throughout the country than the department store.

In this course, as in others, the student at the outset is drilled in the accounting and then upon the foundation so laid is given instruction in the matter of arrangement and management.

The accounting taught is made to include every ticket and slip, no matter how insignificant, and the details are so handled that there is no rewriting or copying. The best use of modern devices for economizing labor is carefully pointed out, and the results are displayed in the balance sheet ledger and profit and loss statement, which in this case are made to give their results daily. The margins of profit in the department store are not large. They frequently depend upon the cashing of bills. All these matters are discussed in exhaustive detail.

11.—General Manufacturing. $100.

The student in this course, as well as in others, is drilled first in the principles and practice of the accounts, that which is to be accomplished in this direction being first worked out in chart form.

After the accounting has been thoroughly covered, there is taken up the general question of the purchase of supplies, the care of supplies, the entry of orders in the factory, the relationship of the superintendent to the general office, the relationship of the foreman to the superintendent, with illustrations and provisions for taking care of these several functions.

Where the student has access to a factory, he is encouraged to bring into the work practical illustrations drawn from the methods under view, and at completion he is left in such shape as to be competent to administer the entire responsibilities of the establishment, or to introduce improvements in routine in different divisions as circumstances permit.

Library Name Contest

We have received a number of communications enclosing lists of names by way of suggestion for the library which Commerce, Accounts & Finance has in preparation at the present time. Merely to help others of our readers who are thinking of this subject, we publish several of the lists below, thereby giving all who are interested an idea of what is in progress. All the names received will, in accordance with the terms of the contest, be turned over to a committee of award, and the decision of this committee will be duly announced in these columns. Notwithstanding the completeness of some of the lists which follow, there is much yet to be said on the subject and the topic is by no means exhausted. We shall be pleased to hear from a large number of our readers on this subject.

From W. W. M., New York.

I enclose a list of fifty names suggested for the Library of Accounts and Business:

1. Practical or Modern Methods Library.
2. Up-to-Date Library.
3. Specialists Library.
4. A. A. A. Library (Accounts, Auditing and Administration).
5. A. A. O. Library (Accounts, Auditing and Organization).
6. "University" Library (Business, Accounts and Finance).
7. Theoretical and Practical Library of Accounting, Business Organization and Finance.
8. "Universal" Library of Accounts, Auditing and Finance.
9. "Complete" Library of Accounts, Auditing and Finance.
10. "Unique" Library of Accounts, Auditing and Finance.
11. Everybody's Library of Accounts, Auditing and Finance.
12. International Library of Accounts, Auditing and Finance.
13. National Library of Accounts, Auditing and Finance.
14. C. P. A. Library of Accounts, Auditing and Finance.
15. "Balance Sheet" Library of Accounts, Auditing and Finance (or any of the other terminations alternatively).
16. The American Encyclopaedia of Accounts, Auditing and Finance.
17. Business and Accounting Library or Encyclopaedia.
18. Encyclopaedia (or Library) of Commerce, Accounts and Finance.
19. Accounting and Commercial Library.
20. Library of Business Organization, Accounts and Finance.
21. Library of Accounting, Business Organization and Auditing.
22. Business and Accounting Economics.
23. Library of Accounting, Business Organization and Administration.
24. Library of Auditing Accounts and Business Management.
25. Library of Industrial Economics.
26. Accountant's and Business Man's Library.
27. "University" Library of Accounts, Auditing and Business Organization.
28. "Industrial Engineering" Library.
29. "Business Engineering" Library.
30. "Commercial Engineering" Library.
31. Library of Advanced Methods in Business Organization, Accounts and Auditing.
32. "Wall Street" Library.
33. Ne Plus Ultra Library.
34. "Financial and Commercial" Library.
35. "Standard" Library.
36. "Educational" Library.
37. "Century" Library.
38. "Progress" Library.
39. Indispensable Library.
40. Institute Library.
41. Premier Library.
42. Royal Library.
43. "Practical" Library of Commerce, Accounts and Finance.
44. School and Counting Room Library of Commerce, Accounts and Finance.
45. Office and Home Library of Commerce, Accounts and Finance.
46. Self-Instructor Library of Commerce, Accounts and Finance.

47. Business Organization and Administration Library.
48. "National Federation" Library. } With any of preceding terminations.
49. "Encyclopaedia" Library. } With any of preceding terminations.
50. Culture or Educational and Reference Library. } With any of preceding terminations.

From C. G. D., Fort Collins, Colo.

I suggest that you call the new publication, "Accountantics, the Office Library."

I am in hopes of being one of the lucky ones, thereby to win one of the valuable volumes.

From D. L., New York.

I submit the following list of names for your library. You will notice that some such phrase as "A Library of" or "Library of" may be prefixed to most of the names given in the list, without injury to the sense:—

1. Advanced Methods for Accountants and Financiers.
2. Business and Common Sense.
3. Systematic Business Methods.
4. Systematic Accounting.
5. Business Principles Applied.
6. Gateway to Success for Accountants and Others.
7. Knowledge and Power—A Guide for Accountants and Financiers.
8. Guide to Success for Business Men.
9. Common Sense Applied to Accounts.
10. Applied Principles in Commerce, Accounts and Finance.
11. Practical Facts in Commerce, Accounts and Finance.
12. Practical Procedure in Commerce, Accounts and Finance.
13. How to Handle Commerce, Accounts and Finance.
14. Conservative Methods for Accountants and Others.
15. Practical Guide for Accountants and Others.
16. Practical Methods for Accountants.
17. Practical Business Methods.
18. Tools of Business, Their Use and Abuse.
19. Business Methods and Procedure.
20. Encyclopaedia of Accounts.
21. Encyclopaedia of Business Knowledge.
22. Accountants' Reference Book.
23. Auditors' Reference Book.
24. Accounting and Finance—A Library of Useful Knowledge.
25. Compendium of Accounts—Commerce and Finance.
26. Technical Knowledge—Accounts, Finance and Business.
27. Complete Technique of Facts and Procedure in Commerce and Finance.
28. Business Man's Reference Book.
29. Commercial Compendium.
30. Useful Hints on Commerce, Accounts and Finance.

From W. N. S., Birmingham, Ala.

I suggest one of the following names for the new library. I hope the list submitted may be of service and that I shall come in for a share of the premiums. I assure you this work is worse than naming the baby.

1. The Commerce, Accounts and Finance Library.
2. The Accountant's Library.
3. The Business Man's Library.
4. The Bookkeeper's Library.
5. The Auditor's Library.
6. The Bookkeeper and Accountant's Library.
7. The Bookkeeper and Auditor's Library.
8. The Bookkeeper's and Business Man's Library.
9. The Auditor's and Business Man's Library.
10. The Auditor's and Accountant's Library.
11. The Accountant's and Business Man's Library.
12. The Bookkeeper's, Accountant's, Auditor's and Business Man's Library.
13. The Grand Library.
14. The Wonderful Library of Business.
15. The Combination Business Library.
16. The Combination Library of Business.
17. The Eureka Library.
18. The Eureka Business Library.
19. The Eureka Library of Business.
20. The Bienvenu (Welcome) Library.
21. The Sovereign Library.
22. The Sovereign Library of Business.
23. The Rex Library.
24. The Rex Library of Business.
25. The Regina Library.
26. The Regina Library of Business.
27. The Multum in Parvo Library.
28. The Relief Library.
29. The Business Man's Helpful Library.
30. The Helpful Library.

John Bull—"A nice mess you've gotten me into!"—New York Herald.

HOW COMPETITION WAS MADE TO PAY.

A merchant relates the following experience: "When I was a young man I set up in trade and took a store where there was not another store within a quarter of a mile, thinking I should do more where there were no others, but at the end of the year I found all that I had made could be put in my eye. I sat down one day thinking my lot was a mighty hard one, and told my clerk that I was going out for awhile, and that he must keep a sharp lookout for customers. I went downtown, and looking around found that two or three stores were doing a very good trade near together, and in passing one of these stores I found the owner quite a talkative man. We put our heads together, and in the course of a week the store directly opposite his received my stock-in-trade and a coat of blue paint on the outside, while his received a coat of green. The first day I did nothing but stand at the door and look pouty at the green store, and my friend stood on his steps looking ditto at me. As people came in I commenced running down the green store, and the latter always run down the blue, so that between us both we built up a trade that was quite lively. People having 'taken sides,' and new comers always purchasing of one or the other, we gradually grew rich, and at the end of some dozen years we settled up, and I found that opposition, or what answered that name, had brought custom and had made my fortune.—Exchange.

ATTRACTIVE RETAIL STORES.

More interest is being manifested by the trade in the question of the adornment of stores. The old idea that there is no need of displaying taste in the arrangement of goods and placing the best foot forward is exploded, says a writer in "The Merchant." Competition has now become too close for a dealer to neglect any art by which he can attract more trade to his place of business. Some, perhaps, are too poor to make the outlay which is requisite for a complete renovation, but every merchant can do something towards putting his place in a better shape. The first thing that ought to be done is to take things out of the way on the floor. Too many grocers strew the whole floor with boxes and baskets, and the customer has to pick his way carefully through them before he can reach a counter or desk. Here is where reform must begin. The doorway should not be crowded, and nothing but attractive goods should be shown on the outside. A lot of poor-looking apples or peaches will frequently drive away customers who would have been drawn in by better ones. The whole place should be kept scrupulously clean, walls white, and floors swept and scoured. On shelves only the attractive-looking packages should be placed, and those which are not neat or pretty should be put in out-of-the-way places. Windows can be made very enticing by placing in them oranges, pretty packages, and things which look well. In these days, when there are so many chromos and pictorial decoration is cheap, every advantage should be taken of them. Heavy goods, which are not attractive to the eye, must be relegated to the end of the store. By adopting these precautions a place of business can be improved very much in appearance, and by this improved appearance trade will be increased.

Correspondence

Accounting and Progressive Bookkeeping.

From F. O. L., Milwaukee.

I am at present a subscriber to four magazines, all of which bid more or less for the patronage of the bookkeeping fraternity. I may mention them: they include Commerce, Accounts & Finance, "Business," "The Bookkeeper," and the London "Accountant." It is my opinion that all of these attempt to cover too much ground and consequently are obliged to "spread it too thin," which materially detracts from the real value of the magazines and practically makes them worthless as a means of education. What I and many other bookkeepers have been looking for many years is a magazine which teaches practical accounting in all its phases and does it thoroughly. For such a magazine I am willing to pay a good price. I am now paying nearly $10 annually for subscriptions to these four magazines, and yet I fail to get what I want.

To make myself clearer. I am at the present time employed as a bookkeeper with a certain mercantile and manufacturing concern, and while I am thoroughly familiar with it and have improved its accounting just as far as it was susceptible of improvement, and know all about the accounting of this particular business, it leaves me no opportunity to familiarize myself with other lines of business, especially manufacturing industries. This is something that cannot be learned from text books, at least not from any that have thus far been published, and I have seen most of them.

A magazine that would during one year take up the thorough treatment and illustration of one subject, say mining and all its accessories, and the next year some other subject, it would seem to me would meet with popular favor with all progressive bookkeepers and certainly ought not to fail to be a remunerative investment for the publishers.

Some years ago Mr. A. O. Kittredge published a magazine called "Business," in connection with which there was published for a period of about two years a supplement called "Practical Accounting." This latter came nearer to my ideal of what a bookkeeper's magazine ought to be than anything I have seen up to the present time.

I have now given you my idea of what I think a magazine that seeks the patronage of the bookkeepers ought to be and you can take it for what it is worth. You no doubt know by experience what takes best with the class of people with which you are dealing. I wish Commerce, Accounts & Finance every success.

NOTE.—We have read and re-read this correspondent's letter to make sure that we correctly apprehend his meaning. Believing that we do understand what he is driving at, we shall venture some general remarks in reply. In the first place it seems to us that our correspondent confuses bookkeeping and accounting. He evidently is seeking after bookkeeping details rather than applications of accounting principles. We fail to read his letter in any other light.

A proper conception of the situation reveals the fact that accounting is accounting, whether applied to a small mercantile business, to a railway system, to a mine, to a bank or to a manufacturing enterprise. Anyone who fails to see the unity of principles underlying all these and many other branches fails to perceive what accounting is. On the other hand, bookkeeping details of each of these branches and many others differ from each other in many essential features. It would be a comparatively easy matter to describe accounting principles for each of these enterprises. It would be a matter which would require a book of the size of an unabridged dictionary to show all of the bookkeeping details.

Again it occurs to us that our correspondent fails to discriminate between business as a going proposition and bookkeeping details. The latter must fit the former, but the latter by no means constitute the former, and between the two, that is, underlying the bookkeeping details, is the application of accounting principles which, as before remarked, he seems to have overlooked or neglected. No man can plan or adapt the accounting of a business that he does not understand. On the other hand, no man can thoroughly understand a business without comprehending the accounts which represent that business.

Our correspondent's course in subscribing to all the periodicals that are issued relating to what he concedes to be his particular corner in the mercantile world, is commendable, but it does not follow that thereby he should have secured absolutely what he requires. The subjects to which the several magazines and periodicals which he enumerates are devoted, should once and for all show wherein he is not to obtain what he asserts he expects. The London "Accountant" is a professional paper published for the edification of members of a great association of public accountants. "The Bookkeeper" is a popular journal with a certain amount of instruction in elementary branches, but running always to the side of large circulation and corresponding general patronage from the advertiser. "Business" is of late leading a nondescript existence, and it is hard to say at the present time just what its scheme is and what it is trying to do. It is apparently largely supported by its reputation of former years. Commerce, Accounts & Finance, as we need not say, is presenting much on higher accounting, something from time to time on adaptations of that accounting to business requirements with a mass of matter of interest both to the general business man and to the accountant, both attached and professional. There are no two of these journals in the same line, and we are not surprised that our correspondent, speaking from the level of a bookkeeper's eyes, fails to find just what he is after.

We are particularly impressed with our correspondent's suggestion that a periodical should during one year take up and thoroughly treat with necessary illustrations a single subject, such as mining and its accessories, and the next year some other, and so on. This, of course, must refer to bookkeeping and bookkeeping details, for as before remarked, accounting in various lines of business is identical, the difference being only in the application of details. We scarcely think it feasible for a journal to undertake work of this kind, for as a fact when it comes down to details there are no two mines running exactly alike, no two railways, no two banks.

We are under many obligations to our correspondent for the frank way in which he has expressed himself, for it gives us the opportunity of discussing the question before our readers.

THE TYPE-PHOUNDER'S PHAULT.

We begin the publication ov the Roccay Mountain Cyclone with some phew diphphiculties in the way. The type-phounders phrom whom we bought our outphit phor this printing ophphice phailed to supply us with any ephs or cays, and it will be phour or phive weex bephore we can get any. The mistaque was not phound out till a day or two ago. We have ordered the missing letters, and will have to get along without them till they come. We don't lique the loox ov this variety ov spelling any better than our readers, but mistax will happen in the best regulated phamilies, and iph the ph's and c's and x's and q's hold out we shall ceep (sound the c hard) the Cyclone whirling aphter a phasion till the sorts arrive. It is no joque to us—it's a serious aphphair.—Exchange.

A QUESTION OF DELICACY.

Rivers was angry. The little water-color painting which he prized highly and had sent out to have properly framed was returned to him cheaply and wretchedly mounted and with finger-marks on the margin of the painting itself.

He strode into the picture framing establishment in a towering rage.

"What do you mean, you blacksmith," he said to the proprietor, "by sending me a job like that? Did you think you were putting a tire on a wagon wheel?"

"Mine friendt," explained the proprietor, "I didn't know dot vos such a delicate chob. I would haf put my delicate man on it."—Chicago Tribune.

BOOKS OF INTEREST TO BUSINESS MEN.

The A B C of Banks and Banking.—By George M. Coffin. 6¾ x 5 inches; 137 pages. Bound in cloth. Back title gilt. Price, $1.25.

This handy little volume is exactly what its name implies; that is, a presentation of the principles underlying banking in the United States. The author in his preface says that it is designed to appeal to the reader outside as well as inside of a bank. It is by no means the last word or every word about banking. It may be said that it is a primer covering a field that has hitherto been somewhat neglected. The chapter heads are as follows: Banking in General, Various Kinds of Banking, Capital Stock, Shareholders' Rights and Liabilities, Undivided Profits, Dividends and Surplus, Deposits, Checks, Lawful Money Reserve, Issuing Bank Notes, Borrowing Money, Loans and Discounts, Exchanges, Collections, Letters of Credit, Bonds, Mortgages and Stocks, Bank Reports, Examinations, Directors, Executive Officers—Their Powers and Duties, Internal Administration and Bookkeeping, and other suggestions.

Business Law.—By Alonzo R. Weed, L. L. B., of the Boston Bar. 6 x 9¼ inches; 172 pages. Bound in cloth. Cover and back title red. Price, $1.25.

Mr. Weed calls his book "a manual for schools and colleges and for every day use." The titles of the chapters are as follows: Contracts, Principal and Agent, Partnerships, Sales of Personal Property, Bailments and Common Carriers, Negotiable Paper, Deeds, Mortgages and Leases, Collection Laws, Written Rates of Interest, Insurance, Patent Rights, Trade Marks and Copyrights, etc.

The author does not waste words, and yet treats his subjects clearly and comprehensively. In short, he gives the law without the addition of wordy "trimmings."

Introduction to the Study of Economics.—By Charles Jesse Bullock, Ph. D. 7¾ x 5½ inches. 581 pages. Bound in cloth. Cover and back title gilt. Price, $1.25.

This book, the author says, is designed as an introductive text book of economic science. Throughout the volume economics are discussed with special reference to American conditions, and their workings are illustrated by frequent allusions to American experience. There are chapters on the Consumption of Wealth, the Theory of Exchange, the Development of Metallic Money, Money and Credit, and the like.

Political Economy of Humanism.—By Henry Wood. 7¾ x 5¼ inches; 320 pages. Bound in cloth. Cover and back title gilt. Price, $1.25.

Mr. Wood is well known as a writer on various economic subjects, and this book contains a series of able treatises, written in his usual vein, on the relation of the employer to the employed, and the phases of the industrial question and their relation to socialism. Among the questions considered and handled in a conservative spirit and with much common sense, are the following: Supply and Demand, the Law of Competition, Labor and Production, Combinations of Capital, Combinations of Labor, Employers and Profit Sharing, the Obligations and Privileges of Employees, the Unequal Distribution of Wealth, Money and Coinage, Tariffs and Protection, Industrial Education and Gold Production and Values.

The Kite Trust, A Romance of Wealth.—By Lebbeus Harding Rogers. 7¾ x 5½ inches; 475 pages. Illustrated. Price, $1.50.

This is a treatise or series of treatises on economic subjects in the guise of a story. The tale itself concerns three American boys, and is very interesting as well as instructive. The trust idea is explained and an explanation of banking is given. The greenback is dealt with as are also Wall street and stock speculation.

Business Law.—By Thomas Raeburn White, B. L., L. L. B. 5 x 7½ inches; 323 pages. Bound in cloth. Back title gilt. Price, $1.50.

This is a neat, compact and handy book of business for law for the use of students and business men. Among the subjects treated are Contracts, Sales, Partnerships, Corporations, Negotiable Paper and the like. The author's language is plain, and is understandable by any one having no previous knowledge of law. The book's clearness on the essential points of ordinary law should recommend it as a business book for the plain business man who has no time in which to consult a law library.

The Phonographic Dictionary and Phrase Book.—By Benn Pitman and Jerome B. Howard. 5½ x 8 inches; 552 pages. Bound in cloth. Cover title and back title gilt. Price, $3.

This book is the most elaborate shorthand dictionary yet published, with the characters in facsimile. It contains over 120,000 words, and for every one of these words there is a corresponding sign in the Benn Pitman system of shorthand. To the reporter, office or court stenographer, or any one writing the Benn Pitman system of shorthand, the book is invaluable. It is well made, tastefully bound, and is printed on a good quality of paper in clean, plain type.

Grace's Handy Book for Making Rapid Calculations. 8¼ x 5¼ inches. Bound in cloth. 65 pages. Title printed in silver. Price, $1.

The full title of this book is "Merchants', Bankers' and Brokers' Handy Book for Making Rapid Calculations in all Branches of Commercial Requirements, Weights, Measures and Moneys." The volume contains a series of tables for calculating the price of wheat, corn and oat bushels in decimals, for converting cubic meters to cubic feet and cubic feet to meters, meters to lineal yards, superficial feet or square feet to cubic feet, decimal tons to avoirdupois pounds, and the like. To the busy office man who has a great deal of calculating to do, and particularly to the clerk in an export house whose work it is to reckon in United States money the amounts named in foreign invoices, these tables should be very valuable. They are quite complete, and undoubtedly their use will save time.

The Lawrence System of Vocal and Physical Expression.—By Edwin Gordon Lawrence. 4¾ x 6 inches; 128 pages. Bound in cloth. Cover title and back title gilt. Price, $1.

The author says in the preface of this little book that his object has been to place in the hands of lawyers, actors and public speakers in general, a simple system of vocal and physical expression that will enable them to clearly convey thought by word of mouth and emphasize it by the proper action. To the man of affairs who is called upon for a speech on any subject, and who knows what to say but does not know how to say it, this book will be a great help.

The Anatomy of a Railroad Report.—By Thomas F. Woodlock. 7 x 5¼ inches. 121 pages. Bound in cloth. Side and back titles gilt. Price, $1.

This little book is intended for the use of those people who, while interested in railroad investments, are wholly unacquainted with railroad accounts. The book is divided into two sections, the first being the Anatomy of the Railroad Report and the second being Ton-Mile Cost. It treats of phases of the railroad business in concise fashion, but thoroughly and accurately.

Any book in this list will be sent to any address in the United States, Canada or Mexico upon receipt of price. If there is some special book that you require we shall be pleased to hunt it up for you.

Address Commerce, Accounts & Finance, 25 Pine street, New York City.

About a Pay Roll which proves itself, corrects all mistakes in figuring, divides up Pay Roll into several amounts needed to pay each person.

But let us send you a sample leaf, with circular, which tells the whole story.

BARLOW BROS., Grand Rapids, Mich.

Use any pen and your own stationery. If your stationer does not keep it, write for free specimen of work. Beware of infringements. Address Dept. Pen-Carbon Manifold Co., 145-7-9 Centre St., New York.

HAVE YOU READ

The Kite Trust?

If not, why not? Send $1.50 for a copy to Commerce, Accounts & Finance, 25 Pine street, New York City.

Account Audit & Assurance Company

25 PINE STREET NEW YORK

WHAT BALANCE SHEET ACCOUNTING DOES.

I.—Initially, it provides an adequate analysis of the accounts of the business, thereby securing a proper representation of the transactions upon the books.

II.—It classifies the daily details of transactions in a way to show "going" results.

III.—The assets of the business are correctly and completely represented at all dates.

IV.—The liabilities of the business are correctly and completely represented at all dates.

V.—The gross profits on goods sold are always shown and there is presented in contrast therewith the total costs of doing business, thereby revealing net profits.

VI.—Among the assets, in the case of a manufacturing business, there are always shown the cost value of the materials and supplies on hand, the cost to date of the work or orders in progress, and the cost of the finished product on hand.

VII.—All this is presented without the preparation of a physical inventory. Inventorying, like counting cash, is resorted to, only for the purpose of verification and proof.

VIII.—The usual fiscal period is abolished. Net profits to date are shown daily (as in department stores), weekly (as in a mercantile business) or once in each four weeks (as in the case of a manufacturing business), according to the time schedule adopted.

IX.—The work of annually or semi-annually closing the books is abolished. The books are always closed and at the same time are always open. Results to date can be easily read from the Balance Sheet Ledger at any and all times.

X.—The labor of maintaining Balance Sheet Accounting, when the system is once in operation, is no greater than that of ordinary double entry. In many cases it has proven to be considerably less.

XI.—The Proof-By-Balance System of Cost Accounts, a constituent element of the Balance Sheet plan, gives the exact cost of goods produced in a factory. There are no estimates. The results are always definite and exact.

XII.—Factories are run at "even keel." The entire cost of the manufacturing department for a given period is balanced by the aggregate of the cost of the individual lots of goods put through.

XIII.—The Balance Sheet System provides that no payments to workmen (pay-roll) shall be made until the amount of their time has been charged to an order in process. Accordingly there is no time paid for that is not accounted for. Charges to orders in process offset the payroll amount. Non-productive labor is handled by prorating its amount over the orders in process.

XIV.—Balance Sheet Accounting is the only system of accounting ever introduced. It is complete. From established premises it reaches definite and exact conclusions.

XV.—Balance Sheet Accounting is eclectic in its elements, and uses as its component parts in the way of ledgers, blanks and forms, various items that are adapted to the purpose in view without reference to their source or origin.

XVI.—Balance Sheet Accounting begins with a balance sheet, ends with a balance sheet and maintains a balance sheet between times.

XVII.—Balance Sheet Accounting facilitates business management. It shows shortages and neglect wherever the same occur. It definitely fixes responsibility. It necessitates order and method in accounting affairs.

XVIII.—Balance Sheet Accounting improves the bookkeeper's position by enabling him to keep all his work up-to-date and by defining a day's duties.

XIX.—In Balance Sheet Accounting there is no back work. Instead, everything is finished as it proceeds.

XX.—The Balance Sheet Ledger upon the business manager's desk in the morning, among other interesting and valuable particulars, gives him the following:

Amount of cash receipts of the preceding day.
Amount of cash disbursements.
Balance on hand and where located.

Amounts charged to customers.
Amounts credited to customers.
Balance owing by customers.

Amounts credited to Purchase Creditors.
Amounts charged to Purchase Creditors.
Balance owing to Purchase Creditors.

Amount of goods (merchandise) taken in.
Amount of goods sent out.
Balance on hand.

Amount of goods sold.
Cost of goods sold.
Gross profit.

Expenses of doing business (viz., clerk hire, rent, advertising, insurance, etc.)

XXI.—Similar facts as to receipts, disbursements and balances are afforded of Notes Receivable and Notes Payable, Sundry Debtors, Sundry Creditors, etc.

XXII.—Balance Sheet Accounting is not "ready made." Instead, it is always "custom made," and made to fit the business after the most careful measurements have been taken. The preceding epitome of Balance Sheet Ledger showings is to be accepted as typical and not as specific.

XXIII.—The Balance Sheet System adapted to your business will give you the exact showings you require, presented in the way you want them and at the time they will be most serviceable to you in planning and managing.

XXIV.—Balance Sheet Accounting is scientific. All its provisions are based upon an accurate and adequate "chart" of the accounts.

XXV.—Balance Sheet Accounting is installed upon the specification plan. A carefully prepared specification, based upon the chart of accounts, is prepared, which stands to the accounting system very much as an architect's specification stands to a building about to be erected.

XXVI.—Each specification is illustrated by drawings of the rulings, blanks and forms required, and by diagrams showing the relationship of the different parts one to the other.

For further particulars, address

Account, Audit and Assurance Company, 25 Pine street, New York.

A New Work on Accounting

A MANUAL OF BOOKKEEPING

By J. THORNTON

THIS attractive volume, comprising over 500 pages, with numerous illustrations, is one of the clearest and most concise surveys of the principles of accounting which has recently appeared. While its illustrations are given in terms of English money the bookkeeping principles discussed are universal.

The work is divided into two leading parts, the first of which is "LAWS AND PRINCIPLES," and the second "APPLICATION."

LAWS AND PRINCIPLES

In the first part there are discussed the Principle of Exchanges, the Principle of Debit and Credit Accounts, the Principle of the Classification of Accounts, the Principle of Ledger Entries, the Principle of Proving, the Principle of Transfer from Preparatory to Final Record, and the Principle of Balancing and Closing the Ledger.

APPLICATION

Under the head of Application the following chapters are presented: Rules and Tools, What Capital Consists of, Capital in Cash, Capital in Bills, Capital in Debts, Capital in Goods, Fixed Capital, Profit and Loss, Capitalist's Accounts, Company Bookkeeping, Errors, and Non-Capitalistic Bookkeeping.

Several chapters are arranged in the form of lessons, following which are questions for class purposes, arranged in such a way, however, as not to detract in the least from the value of the book in the hands of the general reader. A comprehensive index, together with answers to exercises completes the work.

Price, $2.50.—Sent Postpaid to any address in the United States on receipt of price.

Address COMMERCE ACCOUNTS & FINANCE CO.

PUBLISHERS AND BOOKSELLERS - 25 PINE STREET, NEW YORK

PUBLIC ACCOUNTANTS.

Atlanta, Ga.—Ralph H. Brown, 804 Empire Building.

Boston, Mass.—Charles H. Fellows, 174 Summer; New England Audit Company, 45 Milk; J. S. Parsons, 214 Columbus Ave.

Brooklyn, N. Y.—Franklin Allen, Arbuckle Building, 371 Fulton.

Buffalo, N. Y.—W. G. Mowat, 831 Ellicott Square.

Chicago, Ill.—Haskins & Sells, 214 Dearborn.

Davenport, Ia.—J. C. Grabbe, McManus Building.

Detroit, Mich.—H. Naemansson, 496 Putnam Ave.

London, Canada.—Geo. F. Jewell, 361 Dundas.

Montreal, Canada.—George Gontheir, 11-17 Place D'Armes Hill.

New Bedford, Mass.—James L. Hathway, 72 Willis.

New Orleans, La.—P. W. Sherwood, 904 Howard Ave.

New York, N. Y.—Patterson, Teele & Dennis, 30 Broad; Haskins & Sells, 30 Broad; Account, Audit and Assurance Company, 25 Pine; Leon Brummer, 7 Pine; H. F. Searle, 45 Broadway; Hart Bros., Tibbits, Heiron & Co., 11 Broadway; Franklin Allen, Silk Exchange Building, Broadway.

Philadelphia, Pa.—Francis & Sterrett, Penn Mutual Building; Peter Ballingall, German-American Building; Charles W. Thomas, 409 Lippincott Building; Alfred L. Sellers, 1001 Chestnut.

Pittsburgh, Pa.—John Vaughan, 5520 Claybourne; George W. Wood & Co., 341 Fourth Ave.

Providence, R. I.—George R. Allen, 29 Weybosset.

San Francisco, Cal.—Charles L. Lutgen, 218 California; Lester Herrick, 405 Montgomery.

Toronto, Canada.—F. H. Kidd, Bank of Commerce Building.

Windsor, Canada.—F. H. Macpherson, 16 Sandwich, East.

Winnipeg, Canada.—Peter Thornton, 343 Main.

TITLE GUARANTEE AND TRUST COMPANY

Does each year an increasing proportion of the whole business of examining titles and making mortgage loans in New York City. Last year it loaned

Over Thirty-Five Million Dollars

on real estate in New York City. When you buy real estate, or borrow on it, come to this company. Fees moderate and uniform.

Capital and Surplus, $6,000,000

146 Broadway, MANHATTAN. 175 Remsen St., BROOKLYN.

A BUSINESS EDUCATION | **FOR ...ONE... DOLLAR.**

...THE PRACTICAL AGE...

A MONTHLY MAGAZINE full to the brim with helpful suggestions to young men and young women who are struggling successward.

THE BUSINESS HOUSE THAT JACK BUILT, an intensely interesting and highly instructive story of business life, and

APPLIED ENGLISH, an authority on writing and speaking the English language, which no young person can afford to be without, all for ONE DOLLAR.

If you have never seen THE PRACTICAL AGE, send for a free sample copy. Address,

THE PRACTICAL AGE,

Moline, Illinois.

60 DAY CLOCKS

Prentiss 60 day clocks run two months on a single winding, keep perfect time and automatically show the correct date. They are strong, durable, reliable, in fact satisfactory in every way. Right in time; right in price. You ought to have one.

Also Frying-pan, Program, Electric and Synchronized clocks.

Send for Catalogue No. 463.

THE PRENTISS CLOCK IMPROVEMENT CO., DEPT. 46, 49 DEY ST., N. Y. CITY.

Stationery Manufacturing Company

86 FULTON STREET NEW YORK

The Voucher Check.

The voucher check has come to be the check of to-day. A few years ago, in a clumsy and crude form, it was brought forward in the nature of a business experiment. Business men were quick to see and recognize its essential safeguard features, but were also cognizant of its shortcomings in the shape in which it was then presented. Bankers, also, while recognizing the good points of the old-fashioned voucher check, were dissatisfied with its large size and the folding feature, which were its principal drawbacks.

The voucher check, however, even in that crude state, came nearer to being what the business man was looking for in the check line than anything before presented, and many firms adopted it even though it was cumbersome and hard to handle.

Some time ago we began experimenting with the idea of combining the voucher idea with the convenient size of the bank check. After a number of experiments we have succeeded in perfecting several styles of voucher check, that, while embodying all the good features of the old-fashioned folding variety, are yet no larger than the ordinary check furnished to depositors by banks. We have sold a great number of checks of this kind, and in each case they have been hailed as exactly what the business man is looking for—that is, a check that shall show upon its face not only to whom it was drawn and for what amount, but the items for which it is tendered in payment; the correctness of said items and the amount of the check being vouched for by the bookkeeper and the officers of the paying firm or company.

In Fig. 1 is shown a facsimile of one of our styles of voucher check. We ask careful consideration for this design of check, which has not only received the cordial approval of many of the leading firms of this country, but has also been enthusiastically approved by the banks. It overcomes fully all the objections raised against the old-fashioned varieties.

Fig. 1. Face-Voucher Check. Dimensions, 8 1-2 x 3 1-4 inches. Everything on its face, and no folding. (Patent pending.)

Fig. 2 Another form of Face-Voucher Check, with the voucher from differently located. (Patent pending.)

The reader is asked to notice what precedes and follows the voucher form. The voucher itself is drawn in such a way that the endorsement of the check makes it a receipt for the amount, thus avoiding the necessity of stipulating special receipts and the expense later on of filing them. In the process of issuing the check the bookkeeper or ledger clerk first certifies to the correctness of the amount for which the check is drawn; thereafter follows the signature of the firm or the officers of the company as the case may be.

The check drawn in Fig. 2 differs only from that in Fig. 1 in that the voucher form is placed in a different position upon the face of the check. There is no folding, no turning over the check for the filling in of forms upon its back—in short, none of the cumbersome methods that made the old-fashioned voucher check so unhandy.

Many representative firms are using, in connection with these voucher checks, our Multi-Bank Check Register System. Particulars of this system, which does away entirely with the old-style check book, and substitutes therefor something infinitely better and more up-to-date, will be furnished upon application. The checks shown in the illustrations are put up in pads for use with this system.

We are now in a position to furnish at short notice quantities of voucher checks of these general styles, put up in pads or bound and printed to suit the requirements of the firms purchasing them. We are also prepared to submit special designs embodying the general principles of the foregoing. Having at our disposal a competent staff of designers and engravers we are in a position to furnish on order the most handsome and elaborate checks that money can buy.

Prices will be gladly quoted upon request and estimates furnished. We solicit correspondence. Address communications,

Stationery Manufacturing Company, 86 Fulton street, New York City.

R·I·P·A·N·S

There is scarcely any condition of ill-health that is not benefited by the occasional use of a R·I·P·A·N·S Tabule. For sale by Druggists. The Five-Cent packet is enough for an ordinary occasion. The family bottle, 60 cents, contains a supply for a year.

The Theory of Accounts.

JUST PUBLISHED Price, $3.00

Being all questions set in this subject at the New York C. P. A. examinations from December, 1896, to June, 1902, inclusive, with full answers and explanations, by

FREDERICK S. TIPSON, C. P. A.

To follow at short intervals also:

COMMERCIAL LAW, AUDITING, PRACTICAL ACCOUNTING.

Published by the Author, **150 Nassau Street, NEW YORK**

C. P. A. Examinations:

Students thoroughly prepared, either by correspondence or personal instruction, for C. P. A. examinations in all States which grant this diploma. References to students who were successful in January and June, 1900, 1901 and 1902. The only successful candidate at the New York State C. P. A. examination in June, 1900, was coached by

FRED'K S. TIPSON, C. P. A.

150 NASSAU ST., NEW YORK CITY

BUSINESS NEEDS.

Advertisements under this head one cent a word each insertion.

HOW DO YOU FILE YOUR BILLS? If you are filing them in an antiquated fashion and are not satisfied, why not let us tell you about the best system of invoice filing ever devised? Drop a postal to "Bill File," care Commerce, Accounts & Finance.

THERE IS NO REASON why your speech at the banquet should be dull and tiresome. You may have a barrel of ideas but be lacking in the "know how" needed to put them into shape. I have had years of experience in just such work. For a small fee I will take your ideas and embody them in an after-dinner speech that will count for something. Write S. B., care Commerce, Accounts & Finance.

AN ADVERTISING WRITER of experience, now employed by a leading agency, has a little spare time on his hands. He will write ads in this spare time; ads that will bring business. Do you want him to write yours? If so, drop a line to "Adman," care Commerce, Accounts & Finance

BOOKKEEPER WANTED—A good bookkeeper may secure a permanent position by writing "Spice," care Commerce, Accounts & Finance.

A GOOD OFFICE MAN desires a situation where ability and devotion to employers' interests will gain advancement. Good references furnished. Address P. J. K., care Commerce, Accounts & Finance.

IF YOU WISH TO LEARN accounting and haven't much time to give to the study, we can tell you how to do it. Address C. S., care Commerce, Accounts & Finance.

AN INVENTORY OF STOCK to amount to anything should be taken in duplicate and on specially prepared forms. We have such forms in stock and are selling thousands of them. For further information write "Inventory," care Commerce, Accounts & Finance.

Safe Investments

ON

Bond and Mortgage

may be made on desirable property in the

POCONO AND BLUE RIDGE MOUNTAINS OF PENNSYLVANIA

the great natural resort section on the

Lackawanna Railroad

Hotel proprietors are seeking to enlarge their quarters in time for next season's business. They need money for the work. The Lackawanna Railroad has compiled a list of desirable opportunities for placing money in these enterprises, and full particulars may be obtained by addressing

C. W. TEN BROECK, Industrial Agent LACKAWANNA RAILROAD

26 Exchange Place, New York City

WEBSTER'S

THE NEW AND ENLARGED EDITION IS

Standard Authority of the English-Speaking World

All Good Things must win upon their merits. WEBSTER'S INTERNATIONAL DICTIONARY has won a greater distinction and is in more general use than any other work of its kind.

The New Edition has 2364 pages with 5000 illustrations and is printed from new plates throughout. 25,000 new words and phrases have recently been added under the editorship of W. T. Harris, Ph.D., LL.D., United States Commissioner of Education.

LET US SEND YOU FREE

"A Test in Pronunciation" which affords a pleasant and instructive evening's entertainment. Illustrated pamphlet also free.

G. & C. MERRIAM CO., Springfield, Mass.

WEBSTER'S INTERNATIONAL DICTIONARY

INTERNATIONAL DICTIONARY

THE NEW Y[illegible] PUBLIC LIBR[illegible] ASTOR, LENOX AND TILDEN FOUNDAT[illegible]

COMMERCE ACCOUNTS & FINANCE

Volume 5 New York March 1903 Number 3

CONTENTS.

Published Monthly by the Commerce Accounts & Finance Company Twenty-five Pine Street New York

ANNOUNCEMENT EXTRAORDINARY!

A LIBRARY OF PRACTICAL BOOKS FOR THE STUDENT, THE ACCOUNTANT AND THE BUSINESS MAN

What Shall be Its Name?

A COMPETITION WITH THE BOOKS FOR PRIZES

COMMERCE, ACCOUNTS & FINANCE has pleasure in announcing to its readers and to the business public in general that at great expense it has bought the manuscripts, titles and copyrights of the five volumes illustrated in the accompanying cut. It proposes to use them in furthering the interests of this periodical.

Books Composing the (?) Library.

The books will be published one at a time, but our arrangements are so advanced that we feel warranted in promising the complete set in a reasonable length of time.

Each book is to be set from new type, illustrated by original engravings, printed on paper specially made for the purpose, and handsomely bound in cloth with gilt back and side titles. Each book will be upwards of 500 pages in extent, and nothing in the bookmaker's art will be spared to get them up in excellent shape, at once attractive to the eye and convenient for use.

PUBLICATION COMMITTEE.

The set of books will be produced under the direction of the following Publication Committee:

W. H. Grace, chairman, President Commerce, Accounts & Finance Company.

Friend Pitts, Jr., secretary, Treasurer Commerce, Accounts & Finance Company.

A. O. Kittredge, author, President Account, Audit & Assurance Company.

H. M. C. Vedder, Specialist in Accounting and Auditing.

George Young, Textile Accounting and Industrial Operations.

H. W. Courter, General Merchandise and Installment Accounts.

J. A. Cave, Manufacturing Accounts.

J. V. Palmer, Printers' and Publishers' Accounts.

C. H. Sumwalt, of the Correspondence School of Banking.

ADVISORY COUNCILS.

This committee will be supplemented by subcommittees or advisory councils on special topics, the chairman of each of which is a specialist in his own particular branch. These sub-committees will co-operate with the general committee by way of suggestions as to the manner of treating specific topics, the choice of illustration and matters of similar character.

WANTED—A NAME.

The set of books here announced will constitute a library desirable at once for the desk of the business man, the study table of the student and the shelf in reach of the bookkeeper and the clerk while engaged in their daily work. It will also be invaluable to the professional accountant, but **what shall it be called? By what name as a library shall it be introduced to the public?**

We want the most appropriate name as well as the most striking name for this library. It should be something that will give force and character to the several million copies of the announcement which we shall circulate. Who can suggest the right name for the purpose?

There is always wisdom in a multitude of councilors. Therefore, we constitute every one who reads this paragraph a member of our special council on names. Out of the multitude of suggestions thus to be offered we have reason to expect the right idea will come to the top. Just to make it interesting, we propose a friendly contest with prizes.

COMPETITION.

To the person suggesting the name that we finally adopt for this library, we will present a com-

plete set of the books (five volumes). The set so given shall be one of the first off the press and each volume will be properly inscribed over the autograph of the author. To each of ten others who suggest good names, the same being deemed the next best of those we receive, even though we are unable to make use of what they offer, we will give a single volume of the library similarly inscribed over the autograph of the author. Each successful contestant is to have the right of selection.

A subscription for one year to COMMERCE,

The First Volume of the Library to be Issued.

ACCOUNTS & FINANCE goes with each volume sent out as a prize.

This competition will close at 6 o'clock P. M., May 1, 1903.

All entries are to be addressed to LIBRARY NAME COMPETITION, care of COMMERCE, ACCOUNTS & FINANCE, 25 Pine street, New York.

Each competitor is privileged to make as many suggestions of names as he pleases, but only one prize will be awarded to any contestant.

The decision in this competition will be announced in COMMERCE, ACCOUNTS & FINANCE at as early a date as circumstances permit.

EXCLUSIVELY FOR SUBSCRIBERS TO COMMERCE, ACCOUNTS & FINANCE.

The books here announced will not be sold through the trade. The sale will be limited to the cash subscribers to COMMERCE, ACCOUNTS & FINANCE, or to put it otherwise, each volume of the set carries with it a yearly subscription to this periodical.

If you are already a subscriber to COMMERCE, ACCOUNTS & FINANCE, your subscription will be extended for one year for each volume that you purchase.

NO DISCOUNTS TO ANY ONE.

Books will not be sent out on any other terms than those quoted below. The only way to get an advantage in price is to order in advance of publication day.

PRICES.

Either volume, including therewith one yearly subscription to COMMERCE, ACCOUNTS & FINANCE, cash with order, $5.

The set of five volumes, including therewith five yearly subscriptions to COMMERCE, ACCOUNTS & FINANCE, or a single subscription for five years, cash with order, $25.

INSTALLMENT PAYMENTS.

Subscribers, with approved references, may order the set of five volumes at $30, payable $5 with order and the remainder in five monthly installments of $5 each, the title to the books remaining with the publishers until full payment has been made.

Nothing less than a whole set will be furnished on the installment plan.

ADVANCE ORDERS.

Orders in advance of publication will be accepted at the following specially reduced rates:

The set of five volumes, including five yearly subscriptions to COMMERCE, ACCOUNTS & FINANCE, or one subscription for five years, cash with order, $20. Single volumes, including the subscription as above, $4 each.

ORDER OF PUBLICATION.

The arrangement of the volumes in the illustration indicates the order in which they will be produced. "TOOLS OF BUSINESS" will be the first of the set to go to press, following which will be "ELEMENTS OF BOOKKEEPING," "BALANCE SHEET ACCOUNTING," "AUDITING," and "BUSINESS ORGANIZATION AND ADMINISTRATION," in the order named.

The date of publication cannot be named at this time, but the books will be pushed through as rapidly as circumstances make possible. The manuscript for the entire set is in a very forward condition at the present time.

NO ADVERTISING.

There will not be a line of advertising in any of the volumes from cover to cover. Manufacturers' cuts will not be used, but instead new engravings are being made throughout. On the other hand, provision is made, as indicated in the foregoing, for a copy of this periodical to go with each volume. Its advertising pages are open to the business world at reasonable rates, and afford an unequalled opportunity of reaching the very public the advertiser is after.

"TOOLS OF BUSINESS."

The first volume to be brought out as announced above will be "TOOLS OF BUSINESS." This name is to be construed liberally and taken to mean everything from a pen holder to a typewriter, from a chair to a desk and from a method of screening the office window to systems of heating and ventilation.

In this work the author takes up his subject analytically and presents one after another of the several subjects discussed in a most attractive fashion. The scheme of the book is a cyclopedia of office equipment, or a dictionary of those things which

every business man needs to know about in equipping and arranging his business office.

Typewriters, for example, are described analytically and critically. They are divided into classes according to the principles underlying their operation and after those principles have been fully explained, illustrations of different interpretations of those principles are brought forward. The differences between the leading typewriters is clearly defined and the advantages, as well as the disadvantages of some of the cheaper machines are fully set forth.

The office floor is carefully treated, the discussion extending from rugs and mats and carpets to the treatment of the wood of which the floor is composed.

Desks are discussed with respect to the conveniences which they offer, their size, the space occupied and the work to be done. Letter files and cabinets are correspondingly handled. In a similar manner blank books, like ledgers and journals, are discussed with respect to the ends to be accomplished and the materials of which they are composed. Card indexes, loose leaf ledgers, binders and other office appliances are similarly treated.

In future numbers of COMMERCE, ACCOUNTS & FINANCE we shall take pleasure in laying before our readers the personnel of the Sub-Committees or Councils upon whom the Publication Committee depends for advice with respect to details of arrangement, etc. We shall also present in the course of early numbers a complete outline of the contents of this volume.

Address all communications to

COMMERCE, ACCOUNTS & FINANCE COMPANY, 25 PINE STREET, NEW YORK.

BRIEF MENTION

A LARGE ENVELOPE printed in colors and bearing the title "Use Good Envelopes," has reached our desk. It contains the advertising matter of the United States Envelope Company, of Springfield, Mass. The United States Envelope Company are general manufacturers of envelopes, but they are making a specialty of their "Postage Saver" envelopes. The "Postage Saver," as manufactured by this company is one of the "Sealed-yet-open" envelopes of which the Neostyle Envelope Company hold the patents, and the Neostyle Company have granted to the United States Envelope Company a license to manufacture. The "Postage Saver" envelope is in general appearance a sealed envelope, and yet it is not sealed, for one of the flaps at the side is merely folded under; therefore, for circulars and the like these envelopes may be sent through the mail with a one-cent stamp, although to all intents and purposes they seem to be sealed. The "Postage Saver" envelopes are manufactured in a variety of attractive styles and of various qualities of paper. The company says in its circular, "Do not assume because your customers are not all large advertisers that you cannot sell them 'Postage Saver'; the little laundry or the up-to-date grocery around the corner and many small dealers are just as anxious to save five dollars as is the patent medicine man or the large mail-order house to save five thousand dollars."

THE MANHATTAN NOVELTY COMPANY, with offices at 96 Broadway, New York City, are manufacturing the "Dickinson Tabulating Scale for Typewriters." This scale is a simple device, made of metal, which renders it possible to perform billing, tabular and statistical work with the rapidity of ordinary typewriting. In the circular sent out by the company, the principle and operations of this scale are described as being very simple. In addition to the divisions which appear on the typewriter scale commonly used, the Dickinson scale is provided with a groove extending the entire length of the scale. Running in this groove are three slides stamped with O's, spaced regularly, and these slides may be moved to any position on the scale, making it possible to write as many columns as there are slides. It is claimed that the Dickinson scale will fit any machine without alterations or changes of any kind.

"A WONDERFUL TALE" is the title of the folder that Bormay & Co., of 64 Fulton street, New York City, are sending out. The wonderful tale, which the folder says is a true one, is a description of the plant of Bormay & Co., who make engravings of all kinds, and who claim to have the most perfectly equipped and largest plant in the world for the manufacture of engravings by their improved method. The company claims to save for its patrons some twenty per cent. of the cost of engravings, and to manufacture the best engravings that can possibly be made. In the folder are many testimonials from large business houses and from prominent people, all speaking in the highest terms of the engravings made by Bormay & Co.

FOR MANY PURPOSES paste is to be preferred to mucilage. Thaddeus Davids Company, of New York City, are advertising what they claim to be the most perfect paste jar ever made. The name of this jar is "Davids' Perfection Paste Jar," and its main feature is a water well at the side, in which the brush may be kept always clean. The paste is "Davids' White Paste," and is warranted by the company to be of the best quality. The jar is made in two sizes, 5 and 8 oz., and seems to be a very convenient article.

A PAPER PENCIL for some purposes is particularly well adapted. Rosenthal Brothers, of 346 Broadway, New York City, are manufacturing a pencil which they call "No. 622 Paper Pencil," and they claim it to be an ideal and indispensable requisite to the comfort and peace of mind of editors, reporters and business men. The "622 Pencil" is said to have a large lead and one that is soft, smooth and lasting. These are the virtues that many people desire in a pencil, and therefore the "622" ought to be a good one. Rosenthal Brothers say it is, at any rate.

THE CHICAGO SHIPPING AND RECEIPT BOOK COMPANY, with offices at 120 and 122 Fifth avenue, Chicago, are advertising the new style "L Combination Ledger and Binder" that they manufacture. The company claims that for use as a transfer ledger or lock post binder, Style L is absolutely without an equal. It is said to be so made as to fit any size or shape sheet and one that is punched in any manner. It is fitted with an improved rotary wedge lock that works on both posts with a single key. These are only a few of the many advantages which the company claims for this loose leaf ledger, and for further information they are sending to those interested printed matter and circulars describing the ledger in detail.

FROM THE OFFICE of Ames & Rollinson, designers, illuminators and illustrators, with offices at 203 Broadway, New York City, comes a very handsome four-page folder, advertising the firm's business. Ames & Rollinson advertise to prepare finished drawings of any desired style —in line or wash, black-and-white or colors—for reproduction by any process and for any business and social purpose. In this folder are several handsome designs prepared by the office of the company, and the text is well worded and tastily printed. On the fourth page of the folder, in an imitation of ancient English lettering, appears a proclamation bidding "All ye bolde knights and fayre ladys gentlemen and loyale yeomen that do harbor some appreciation of ye fine arts" to appear at the designing chambers of the company, and there inspect "a goodly displaye of rare and curious drawings." The folder altogether is a very artistic piece of work.

MILLER BROTHERS, with offices at 309 Broadway, New York City, are advertising their standard ink erasers, of which they make sixty different numbers in handles of all styles. A good ink eraser is a necessity to the bookkeeper, no matter how careful he may be.

A NEW STYLE POCKET pen and pencil holder is that manufactured by L. D. Van Valkenburg, of Holyoke, Mass. This pocket pencil holder is a small device that clamps over the edge of the vest pocket, and is claimed to be by its maker the neatest, cheapest and most practical holder ever put on the market, and the only one that can be used on a fountain pen.

The History and Development of the Mercantile Agency*

By ARTHUR B. WIGLEY,
Pittsburg Manager of the Mercantile Agency of R. G. Dun & Co.

ACCEPTING your invitation to address you upon the subject of credits and mercantile agency service, I first desire to assure you of the high esteem in which the Credit Men's Association has always been held by our firm. We have a membership in almost all of the local associations, and we are always pleased to receive and give suggestions and ideas as to the best methods of making credits more secure. I believe it is the wish of your committee that I should briefly outline the history of The Mercantile Agency and its growth and development as a factor in the promotion and protection of trade, but first it might be well to glance backward and, if possible, discover the origin of credits.

One would naturally suppose that a credit system would be developed long after cash sales and purchases had been common, yet I am inclined to think that it is a twin brother, born and developed with the cash or rather barter system; for we must remember there was no such thing as money until long after credits became common.

Cain, the son of Adam, was a farmer, raising fruit, vegetables and other products of the soil, whilst Abel was a shepherd and herdsman. It follows that they must have exchanged each other's wares, and it is natural to suppose that Abel's family might need vegetables or fruit many times when the family of Cain had no need of meat and vice versa. It is, therefore, reasonable to suppose that the delivery of the fruits or meats in payment might be postponed to a mutually suitable day.

In the Time of Moses.

That debtor and creditor was a common condition in the time of Moses is plainly shown by his instructions to the Israelites. See Deuteronomy XV, 1 and 6 verses:

(1) "At the end of every seven years thou shalt make a release * * *"

(2) "Every creditor that lendeth anything to his neighbor shall release it; he shall not exact it of his neighbor or his brother * * *"

(3) "Of a foreigner thou mayest exact it again * * *"

(4) "Save when there shall be no poor among you, for the Lord shall greatly bless thee," etc.

Here we have a recognized state of affairs existing in the year of the world possibly 2,500 and after Noah only about 1,000 years, so common as to indicate that even then it had existed from time immemorial. You will also discover in it a very brief, but perfectly effective, bankrupt law, clearing the poor, but not discharging those able to pay their obligations. In it is also a preference in favor of their own people and discrimination against the foreigner, a policy which is still extant.

Demosthenes, the Athenian statesman, said some centuries later: "If you were ignorant of this—that credit is the greatest capital of all toward the acquisition of wealth—you would be utterly ignorant."

Credit is one of the strongest manifestations of the community of interest and the universal brotherhood of man, representing, as it does, some of the noblest sentiments which actuate the human race—trust, confidence and faith. It has played its part in building up the great business marts of the world, and in covering the seas with the commerce of nations. The accumulation of fortunes without number, starting from small beginnings, has been made possible by its beneficent influence. Daniel Webster said: "Credit has done more, a thousand times, to enrich nations than all the mines of the world." But as credit is nothing but postponed payment, and the day of reckoning must come, while it enables the user to do a more extensive business than his real capital would be capable of if he bought for cash only, there must be a proper portion of moneyed capital or other property in his possession for his ventures to rest upon if he is to use his credit with safety to himself and to those who grant it to him. The wrecks upon the sea of credit outnumber the successes so largely that the lesson of experience teaches that constant vigilance is the price of safety. It is not only a question of financial responsibility, which has to be determined by the giver of credit, but the proportion of assets to liabilities, character, habits, experience and capacity of the seeker of it, and his business environment in the shape of local opportunity and competition—all going to make up his chances of success—have to be considered. In fact, the very nature of credit, which is simply turning over to another, in the shape of merchandise, the capital which belongs to one's self, upon his promise to pay for it in the future, renders it imperative that it should be treated as a most serious transaction. The utmost care and the exercise of the keenest intelligence and most prudent judgment is called for in deciding credit risks. A merchant knows about what his margin of profit is, and also that under ordinary conditions he can make sales so as to secure a certain amount of trade, and if his business is conservatively managed as to expenses he can make a success, provided that he does not meet with greater losses by bad debts than he can stand. Should he do so, the result is disaster.

Severe laws to enforce the collection of debts have existed in all ages and all countries, varying in harshness, from taking in bondage and reducing to slavery, down to the laws of imprisonment for debt, which existed in this country and England even to so late a period as fifty years ago, and the pitiful effects of which are so graphically portrayed by Dickens in the "Pickwick Papers" and "Little Dorrit."

I have glanced thus briefly at the history of the subject under discussion, in order that you may realize that the problem before us is no modern invention to be regulated by a few hours' thought and discussion, but it is a subject as old as the human race and its regulation and safeguards have had the closest and most anxious attention of the best lawgivers of all ages. That the question has lost none of its interest is attested by this gathering.

Banks and banking, clearing houses, mortgages, debentures, national, state and personal bonds, notes with endorsements or collateral and a thousand and one other plans and devices have been born and grown to maturity as necessity, that "mother of invention," has required, for the protection and enlargement of credits. Among the rest has come into existence "The Mercantile Agency," whose service you ask me to explain.

The Failure of Arthur Tappan.

In the brief review I have given we came down

* Address delivered before the Pittsburg Credit Men's Association.

to the second quarter of the nineteenth century. About that period, or to be exact, in the year 1837, one of those crushing waves of commercial disaster, which periodically occur, swept over the land, and among the great firms that were wrecked was the greatest of all, that of Arthur Tappan. He was the A. T. Stewart of his day, and his trade and credits extended all over the United States. The firm was never re-established, and Lewis Tappan, his brother, and the manager of his law and credit department, secured deskroom in a small office, and using his knowledge of credits and his acquaintance with lawyers in almost every county in the United States, laid the foundation of our present business, being succeeded by B. Douglass and R. G Dun.

One of the most phenomenal developments in connection with American business history is the growth of the mercantile agency, and it is the best proof which could be offered as to its necessity and usefulness as an auxiliary to the trade of the country, spreading over the immense geographical area of the continent. Commencing, as I have said, in a small way; as a means of systematizing the gathering of credit information, and pooling the expense of obtaining it, for a limited number of New York business houses, it has become an immense organization, having under salary several thousand employees as managers, traveling reporters, or clerks in its one hundred and sixty offices.

Originally each report required was written for and obtained separately, and the functions of the agency were confined to giving the standing of the trader at his own place of residence. These reports were copied in large volumes and subsequent reports added as they were made; then came the system of semi-annual revisions, they being demanded to give at the commencement of each season a tolerably accurate idea of the prosperity or the reverse of the customer. These revisions were made at first entirely by local correspondents, and although necessarily brief, it is surprising with what accuracy the conditions were photographed. Most of our older attorneys took the greatest pride in the correctness of their reports or recommendations, and afterwards when the era of reporting by travelers arrived some of them regarded the innovation as a needless reflection on their abilities, and were quite indignant that any assistance should be offered them in taking care of the districts assigned to their charge. One venerable gentleman in my district (who only recently passed away) had been contemporary with Lewis Tappan, and a number of years ago our traveler had a good deal of difficulty in convincing him that conditions were changed and that old methods had passed away. In the early days of the system of revising by our own traveling reporters, I remember how much we, who had to go out on the road, appreciated a nice old-fashioned conservative district, where "no change to note" and "same as before" covered a large percentage of the reports needed. In those days fifty reports a day were not an unusual average, and these, you must remember, were not single opinions, but confirmed by two or three reliable and respected authorities. Reporters were not expected to search the county or city records, but they were expected to consult (besides our attorneys and correspondents) the best bank and business authorities.

As all reports had to be copied by hand in eight or ten different offices, conciseness and brevity with well-chosen words to express much in little space was one of the requisites of a good reporter. The invention of the typewriter, which enables us to make ten or fifteen copies at once, gave us an opportunity to extend the reports and gave the traveler

Thinking of Handling Him Without Gloves.—Cleveland Plain Dealer.

more freedom in time to obtain, and language to express, his views; so that at the present time ten elaborate reports a day is a good average. In a recent revision, one of my travelers informed me that he had called upon ninety eight per cent. of the persons reported and had secured statements from 70 per cent. These statements had been submitted to the proper local authorities, and also to city references; that is, those from whom he was buying, and the whole digested and incorporated in the reports, thus covering the local opinion and the sellers' or creditors' experience.

As I have several branch offices of the mercantile agency under my charge, I have brought with me, and shall be pleased to leave for your criticism, three reports from each of these offices. They are taken from our records just as they appear there, except that names and places are fictitious. You will find an individual report; a firm report, and corporation report from each place. Some with full statements given, some with partial statements, and some with statements declined. These and similar reports, I believe, have given satisfaction to the local subscribers in the various cities and districts covered, and the local satisfaction or criticism is, in my estimation, the best guide we can have in the construction of a report, because the local subscriber himself has some knowledge of each case and will readily detect flaws and errors which would not be apparent to a credit man at a distance. Whilst on this subject, I wish to inject a deserved compliment to my reporters. The esprit du corps of my men is one of the pleasant features of our business. If my Zanesville people have done well, our Canton men will surpass it, if possible. The Wheeling staff won't be beaten by the other offices, and our Youngstown man comes back and says we will do better than them all.

Speaking to experienced credit men, I would say that nothing is more welcome to us than criticism. We at all times give careful consideration to every question in regard to any report, and reinvestigation is made in all cases when the circumstances require it. I think that no gentleman here will say that the agency is lacking in that courtesy, but occasionally some callow youth, newly inducted into a credit department, will fire at us a request for a report on some brand new mining concern in Colorado, or lumber dealer in Maine, which is ordering machinery or supplies, and the credit man must have the information at once. The members of these firms may have come from the four quarters of the United States, and in order to complete a report we may have to consult Montreal, New York, New Orleans and San Francisco, which takes time: but time and distance are of no account to the youth alluded to, and in about three days we get a lamentation tha

NEW PUBLIC LIB

"the agency service is getting very poor of late, and while deploring the necessity of doing so, we will have to place our patronage elsewhere," etc., etc. These sarcasms, which you will observe are not criticisms, receive the treamtent they merit.

The "Three Cs" of Credit.

In considering the qualifications for credit three "C's" loom up and claim our attention, character, capacity, capital. The intelligent reporter and credit man watches the three "C's" with the most careful vigilance.

Yet after some forty years' experience in mercantile agency work I am almost inclined to substitute character first, character second, character third, because any man may be capable and may have capital, but if he has not the right character you are in danger. Moreover, character is the one peculiar attribute which every man is bound to acquire. A young man starting in business may or may not accumulate money. He may or may not develop capacity, but character, either good or bad, he must acquire, and once acquired he cannot shake it off; it will stick to him until the end. And yet whilst a man is irresistibly compelled to make for himself a character, or reputation of some kind, the uncertainty as to whether his real character is equal to his apparent character is one of the unknown quantities which renders credit insurance a somewhat difficult problem. There are other problems that have to be met, and no doubt will eventually be met and solved, that confront this class of guarantee. I refer to this matter only because it has frequently been asked why a great mercantile agency should not insure its reports. In this connection I may say that it is a recognized duty of a reputable mercantile agency to promote as well as to protect trade, to give to the deserving and striving young man the full value of his merits and reputation, to be an impartial medium between the seeker and dispenser of credits, and it would seem to me that an insurer could hardly occupy that neutral ground. He would naturally lean to the side of conservatism, and, perhaps, at times, be an obstacle in the way of deserving, though new and untried ventures. This, however, is merely theorizing; at present, the mercantile agency occupies an entirely neutral position. It does, however, pay its cordial respects to the credit insurance companies for making the credit dispensers examine more carefully and interpret more correctly than formerly the ratings in the reference book and the detailed reports.

A comparison has been made between the old and new methods, perhaps in favor of the present system, but at this point I am reminded of some of the more careful dispensers of credit in the past whose methods might well be imitated by some of us.

One of the greatest absorbers of mercantile agency information in the past was A. T. Stewart. His method was to send his men to our office and copy from the large old-fashioned records there every report verbatim with all its discrepancies, contradictions, corrections and harmonies, and thus to get in his own credit department an accurate photograph of every customer as he appeared at his own home. The same plan was followed in a modified form by many others of the most shrewd and successful business men all over the country.

The late Charles Arbuthnot, of our own city, made a practice of coming to our office and reading for himself each report on our records in which he was interested, from beginning to end, and many a time some matter, which at home indicated prosperity, such as building a new house or enlarging a store, would be classed by him as injudicious, because the wholesale account was not kept in as good shape as formerly.

Reports Should be Confidential.

One of the great difficulties which confronts the mercantile agency reporter is the carelessness (or worse) with which confidential reports are sometimes handled by subscribers. I regret to say that notwithstanding the contract which exists between us that all reports furnished shall be confidential, it is of almost daily occurrence that people come to our office with a complete copy of their own report, which has been handed to them by some kind friend "in order that they may put themselves right with the agency." I wish to say at this point that the agency never issues a report without having reasonable confidence in its general correctness, and such violations of the contract between us should be and must be frowned upon and stamped out by you if you desire to have the best possible service which the mercantile agency can render.

Personally, I have been in charge of a district reporting some 40,000 names for over a quarter of a century, and I have never had a verdict against us for libel, yet I have been subjected to the annoyance and expense of defending half a dozen suits when we had called a "spade" a "spade" instead of describing it as a "ferruginous implement of agriculture." Similar experience has been had by our managers all over the country, and has made necessary a more cautious wording of reports than would otherwise be desirable, and sometimes the expressions in our reports may be so veiled for our own safety as to require careful interpretation by a competent credit man.

For a number of years past I have made it a rule to invite a statement from business men in Pittsburg and Allegheny at the beginning of each year, thereby giving every one an opportunity to place his condition on our books for his own benefit. A large proportion of the best people avail themselves of this simple and effective means of placing themselves in the proper light in the market. The responses each year grow more numerous as the trader realizes the convenience and advantage to himself of being relieved from entering into elabor-

A Bookkeeping Term—Sun-dry Sales.

ate explanations at the time when purchases are desired. There are still a few who hug the old fetish to their bosom that a "competitor may want to know," etc., but this class has become so rare as now to be almost obsolete.

The doctrine that credit is the business man's most valuable asset has spread over the land, and the intelligent man realizes that credit can only be secured by confidence, and confidence must rest on knowledge. The mercantile agency, therefore, has sought and received an immense mass of information for the benefit alike of the buyer and the seller. Vast numbers of statements are received, investigated and spread on our records, which may never be used or seen, but which are ready to benefit the buyer and protect the seller whenever required.

When called upon by your committee I was asked to touch upon certain special questions, one of which was the matter of fire insurance as a factor in reports. The importance of this subject was enjoined upon me, when as a youth I was first sent out to make reports. I was told to look out for those who did not keep insured, because a "business that did not pay to insure could not pay to follow," and we watched that feature with especial care where the hazard was great and insurance rates high. At the present time it is made one of the most prominent questions which we ask when requesting a statement, or in requiring from our correspondents a report on a new trader. In order to illustrate this point I have brought with me the forms which we use, and which, after making explicit inquiry in regard to the character, abilities, capital, means, etc., contains especial inquiry in heavily lettered type as to insurance. At the present day the carrying of fire insurance is almost universal. The agents of the various companies are constantly pushing their business and urging their patrons to carry a full line, or, at least, eighty per cent. on the value of the properties insured. Our reporters invariably ask those who are making statements for information upon this subject, and yet, though insurance is so uniformly carried, it is almost impossible to obtain explicit information as to the amount and dates of expirations of policies, because those points are known only to the person himself, or to the agent who has placed the insurance. Our travelers tell me that when this question is put, in five cases out of six, the policies have to be hunted up before a correct answer can be given. However, your persistent inquiry as to this feature, and our constant reiteration of the inquiry on the same subject, will have a beneficial effect in directing the attention of the interested party to the necessity of keeping himself amply covered by insurance from loss by fire.

Another point on which I am requested to speak is the possibility of expediting reports where references are given and trade reports desired. This is simply a question of mail and telegraph service, combined with the possibility of interviewing the credit man or the proper person to obtain the desired information. In large cities like Pittsburg and New York several days may elapse before the proper sources of information can be reached.

One of your committee asked me to touch upon the matter of collections. In that department of our business I may say that our circular gives full particulars. We employ the most active and reliable attorneys, and guarantee that all money collected by them will be accounted for. When requested, we make a direct demand or a draft on the debtor at a small charge before sending the claim to our attorney. If the demand meets with no response, or the draft is not honored, the claim is

The Hat's Not Yet Out of Danger.—Minneapolis Journal.

placed in the attorney's hands with such instructions as our clients may order. The agency collects many millions every year. Every cent so collected for sixty years has been paid over to our clients.

The Reference Book.

In using the reference book a careful credit man must bear in mind that a great many changes occur every day. It will surprise many of you to know that the average number of changes each six months is about as follows:

New names added, 150,000; names obliterated, 140,000; changes in ratings, 103,000; changes in styles, 30,000.

I have before me the exact figures for a number of years, and they conform closely to the above, and show an average of nearly 3,000 changes every working day of the year.

The reference book is a ponderous volume, and although we have developed the best possible methods of printing, binding and issuing it rapidly, it follows that some time must elapse between the time it goes to press and its delivery to our subscribers. In the interim the 3,000 changes per diem have been going on, and it is, therefore, manifest that the prudent credit man will make it his business to rely upon the detailed reports which give all these changes as they occur rather than take the chances of selling upon a rating which is based on conditions existing say on the 1st of December, which may have been materially changed on the 1st of January.

WHAT HE WANTED.

Politician—I'll do what I can to get work for you.

Citizen—I don't want work; what I'm after is a city job.—Boston Transcript.

HE HATED TO TELL IT.

At a recent school examination by the school board, an officious member intimated that he would give a certain class a lesson on "wool," relates a writer to the "Scottish American." After lecturing to the children for a considerable time without any appearance of attention from the class, he stopped short and began questioning one dull-looking boy. "Well, my boy," said he, taking hold of the boy's jacket, "what is this jacket made of?" The boy, hanging down his head, remained quite silent. "Come, come, my boy," the member coaxingly said, "don't you know what your jacket is made of?" With eyes still on the floor the boy answered: "It was made oot o' ma faither's auld breeks."

The National Debts of the World. II*

By O. P. AUSTIN,
Chief of the Bureau of Statistics, Washington, D. C.

THE debt of Italy, which ranks next to that of the United Kingdom in size, has grown from four hundred and seventy-five million dollars in 1860 to its present figure, two thousand five hundred and eighty-three millions, and has been chiefly accumulated in the construction of railways, the maintenance of a large standing army, and the construction and maintenance of a large and costly navy. Most of the Italian railways belong to the State, but are now operated by private organizations, to which they are leased, and the telegraph lines, aggregating about twenty-five thousand miles in length, were also constructed by the government. A large proportion of the outstanding obligations still bear interest at 5 per cent., though a small proportion have been funded at 4 and 3 per cent., respectively. A considerable share of the total stands in the form of permanent or perpetual debt, with no fixed date for its final payment. Probably more than one-half of the Italian debt is held in foreign countries, chiefly in France, and more than half the one hundred million dollars of annual interest payments, therefore, goes out of the country every year, thus differing materially from conditions in France, Germany and England, in which the interest payments are made almost wholly to the home population.

The Debt of Germany.

The national debt of Germany is comparatively small, but the debts of the German States are usually included by students of economics in considering the national debts of the world, for the reason that they were largely incurred when the States now composing the German Empire were independent governments and were, therefore, classed among the national debts of Europe; and unless still so included would be misleading in a general survey of the field during a long period of years. Another reason for including the obligations of the German States in a list of national obligations is found in the fact that they were largely created for the construction of railways and other works of national utility now controlled by the German Government. The debt of the German Empire, exclusive of that of the states, which amounted to only thirty million dollars in 1875, is five hundred and sixty millions at the present time; while that of the German States is calculated at a little over two billions, practically all of these obligations being held by the citizens of that country, and the annual interest thus distributed among the home people.

Spain and Her Debt.

The debt of the Spanish Government, which now amounts to one thousand seven hundred and twenty-seven million dollars, has had a somewhat checkered history, having been reduced at various dates, not by the process referred to in the case of the United Kingdom and the United States, but by arbitrary reductions and adjustments with creditors. A very large proportion of this debt is held in foreign countries, chiefly in France, and more than one-half of the eighty million dollars paid in annual interest charges passes out of the country for payment on the securities held abroad.

Australia's Indebtedness.

Next in the list of great national debts is that of Australia, aggregating one thousand one hundred and eighty-three million dollars. This great indebtedness has been accumulated almost wholly in the construction of railways, telegraphs, irrigation works, and other works of national improvement, and has brought the per capita indebtedness of this country of only four millions population to a higher point than that of any other country, the debt of Australia being $263 per capita, against $150 per

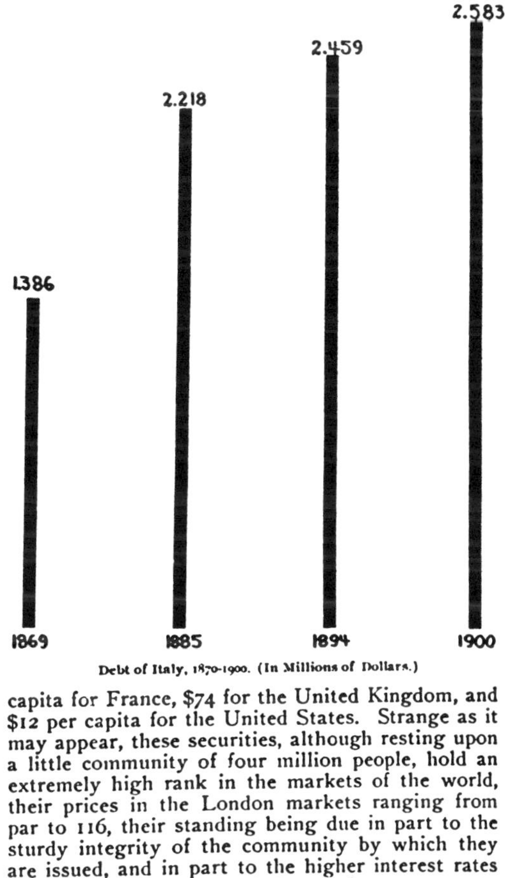

Debt of Italy, 1870-1900. (In Millions of Dollars.)

capita for France, $74 for the United Kingdom, and $12 per capita for the United States. Strange as it may appear, these securities, although resting upon a little community of four million people, hold an extremely high rank in the markets of the world, their prices in the London markets ranging from par to 116, their standing being due in part to the sturdy integrity of the community by which they are issued, and in part to the higher interest rates which they bear, most of them being 4 per cent., although in a few cases the rate is now 3 per cent. It is proper to say, in this connection, that these and other British colonial securities rest solely upon the faith of the community by which they are issued, and are not, as has been supposed by some, guaranteed by the British Government, save in a very few exceptional cases.

The Debt of India.

The debt of India amounts to $1,031,000,000, and of this, about one-half is held in England and denominated "permanent debt in England"; while a large share of that held in India is also considered as a "permanent debt." No part of that debt, whether that held in England or India, is guaranteed by the British Government, the entire debt of India, principal and interest, being chargeable to

* A lecture delivered before Alexander Hamilton Chapter of the American Institute of Bank Clerks.

and paid by the Indian Government. A large share of this debt has been created in the construction of irrigating works and railways, which in many cases return a good profit on the investment, as well as greatly increase the productive powers of the country.

The Debt of the United States.

I come now to a discussion of our own national

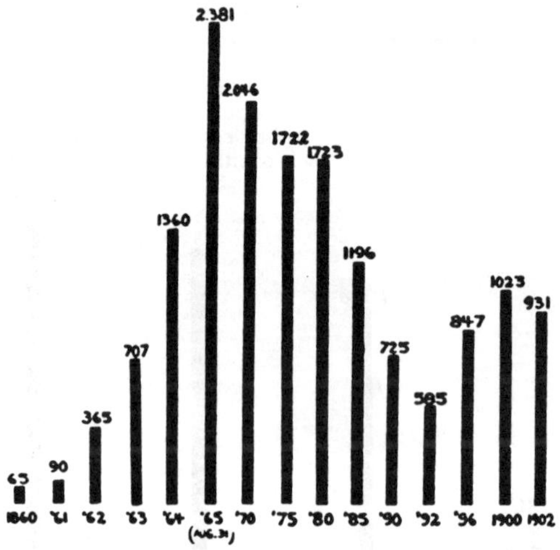

Interest-Bearing Debt of United States, 1860-1902. (In Millions of Dollars.)

debt, the history of which is coincident with the history of the nation. The very act by which the struggling colonies freed themselves from British domination and put themselves in condition to form a nation was in itself productive of an indebtedness large and burdensome to the handful of people, impoverished by a long war and occupying a new and undeveloped country. The history of the obligations incurred during the Revolutionary War would occupy too much time for a discussion of this character, but it is proper to say that the consolidation and adjustment of these obligations, made at the beginning of the present form of government, brought the total national debt at that time, 1790, to the round sum of seventy-five million dollars. In 1803 the Louisiana Territory was purchased for an additional fifteen millions, of which something over three millions was to be paid to citizens of the United States having claims against France and bonds issued for the remainder, bringing the total up to eighty-five millions. This was rapidly reduced until it stood, in 1811, at forty-five millions, but the war of 1812 again increased it, and in 1817 it stood at one hundred and twenty-three millions, which was again rapidly reduced during times of peace until it was practically extinguished in 1835, and the treasury department was actually directed to loan to the various states, in proportion to their population, thirty-seven millions of surplus then in the treasury.

A part of this had been distributed when the financial storm of 1838 burst upon the country and the reduction in revenues caused again an increase of indebtedness followed by heavy expenditures and debt accumulations during the war with Mexico, bringing the total, at the close of that war, up to seventy-five millions. From that time the debt fluctuated, falling and rising with varying conditions of national prosperity until it stood, at the beginning of President Lincoln's administration, at eighty million dollars. The Civil War which followed of course rapidly and enormously increased the national indebtedness, and the history of this growth and of the struggles by which the sums required for carrying on that war were obtained, the interest payments made, and the indebtedness refunded at constantly reducing rates of interest, form one of the most interesting chapters of our national history, the details of which would, however, occupy too much time for their present discussion. The total interest-bearing debt reached high-water mark in August, 1865, amounting to $2,381,000,000, and the annual interest charge one hundred and fifty million dollars. The per capita of indebtedness at that date was $78.25, against $12.27 at the present time, and the annual interest charge $4.29 against 35 cents per capita to-day.

From that time forward began a struggle to meet maturing obligations, to reduce interest rates, and finally for a reduction of the indebtedness. By 1870

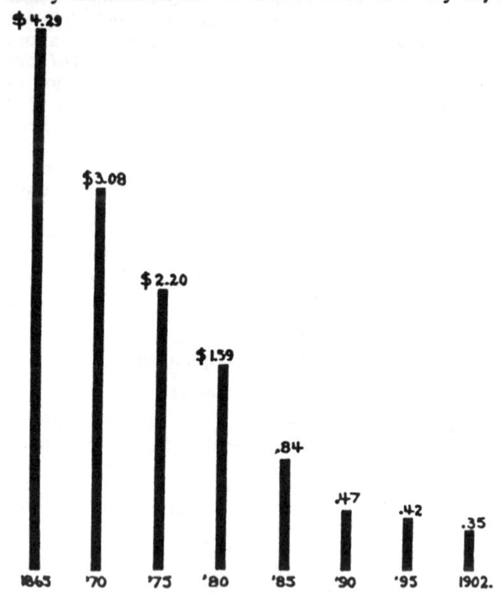

Per Capita Interest Charge of United States Debt, 1865-1902

the interest-bearing debt had fallen from the high-water mark of $2,381,000,000 to two billions of dollars; by 1887 it was one billion, and by 1892 had fallen to five hundred and eighty million dollars, or about one-fourth the figures of 1865, the world having witnessed the unparalleled feat of a debt reduction of $1,800,000,000 in twenty-seven years, an average of sixty-six millions a year, or over five millions a month for the entire period. Between 1893 and 1896 the interest-bearing debt was increased, from causes with which you are familiar, to eight hundred and forty-seven million dollars; and the necessity for available funds at the beginning of the war with Spain brought it again to the billion dollar line, the figure for the year ending June 30, 1899, being $1,046,000,000, but which has now been reduced to $931,000,000 the 1st of July of the present year.

The per capita of debt less cash in the treasury has fallen meantime from practically $77 in 1865 to $12.27, and the per capita interest charge from $4.29 to 35 cents. The rates of interest paid have been steadily reduced from 7.3 per cent. in 1865 to 2 per cent. on about one-half of the national debt, a lower rate of interest than that at which any other government has ever been able to float its securities, and this fact is the more striking because, as I have already said, the securities of most national governments are issued at below par, while those of the United States have never, save in a few exceptional cases many years ago, been sold at less than their face value. Add to this the fact that practically all of our national securities are held by our own people and that in all great emergencies they have come forward with whatever funds might be needed by the government, and frequently with many times the sums thus required, and we may with entire propriety say that the record of our national debt is one for national pride and national congratulation. While other countries of the world have steadily increased their public debts, the two great English-speaking nations, the United Kingdom and the United States, have, at every opportunity in times of peace, reduced their indebtedness, and to-day the United States stand with a per capita indebtedness of 1-6 that of the United Kingdom, and 1-12 that of France, while the per capita interest charge is 1-8 that of the United Kingdom and 1-18 that of France.

The Wealth of the World.

One other question which is suggested by this enormous growth of national indebtedness is, whether or not the wealth and the currency of the world have increased with equal rapidity. I have already shown you that the world's debts have increased about 1,000 per cent. during the century, while its population was increasing but 150 per cent. During that period the gold and silver of the world have, according to the best authorities, increased about 300 per cent., though the proportion of the existing gold and silver which is turned into coin is now much greater than at the beginhing of the nineteenth century; while the utilization of various forms of credit as currency may have increased the world's circulating medium quite in proportion to the increase in its national debts.

Whether national wealth has increased as rapidly as national indebtedness is equally difficult to determine, since official estimates of national wealth were at the beginning of the century made in the case of only a few nations. The wealth of the United Kingdom, France, Spain and the United States in 1800 was estimated at $20,244,640,000, while Mulhall in 1895 estimated their wealth at $195,759,829,000, or practically ten times that at the beginning of the century. The debts of these four nations in 1793 aggregated but $1,630,279,000, and in 1900 were $11,764,000,000, or seven times as much as in 1793. This indicates that in the case of the four nations whose wealth in 1800 can be measured, the wealth figures for 1900 are ten-fold those of 1800, and the debt figures sevenfold those at the beginning of the century. If the rate of growth in wealth which has characterized the four nations whose growth during the century can be measured may be properly applied to the world at large, it may be said that the growth of national wealth has about kept pace with that of national indebtedness, since national wealth in the cases where it can be measured is to-day ten times as great as that at the beginning of the century, and the national debts, where they can be measured, are also to-day about ten times what they were at the beginning of the century.

Divisions of the Great Debts.

The national debts of the world divide themselves into three great groups: (1) those of the English-speaking nations which only increase their debts from the necessities of war or of great public works, and which manfully and persistently reduce them in times of peace; (2) the Germanic and Slavic nations which have increased their debts in wars, by the maintenance of great standing armies and by the construction and ownership of their railroad systems, and, up to the present time, have made little progress in debt reduction; and (3) the Latin nations which have recklessly increased their debts not only by wars and standing armies and public works, but by constant deficits in their national budgets and with no apparent attempt to reduce them until their indebtedness has assumed alarming proportions and is becoming so burdensome as to prove a serious check upon the prosperity and development of these countries themselves.

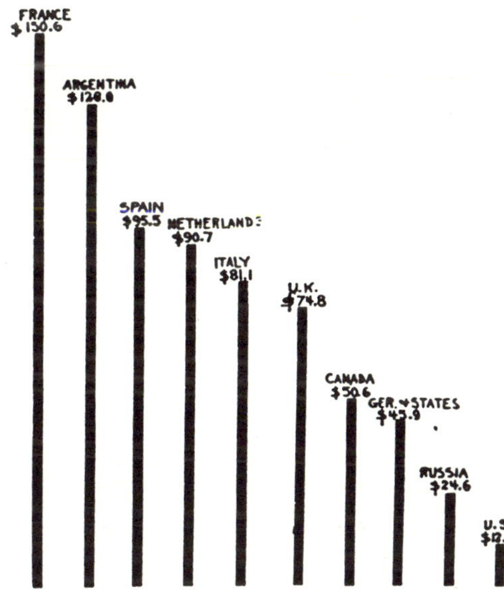

Per Capita Indebtedness of the Ten Principal Nations, 1902.

Conclusions to be Drawn.

What conclusions are we to draw from this rapid and necessarily incomplete survey of the national debt history of the world during the past century and the conditions of to-day? It means that industry and thrift and debt reduction in times of prosperity are as necessary in the nation as in the individual, and that national prosperity as well as individual prosperity must come through a rigorous application of these principles. It means more than that; it means that the nations which exercise caution and self-denial in debt-making and rugged determination in debt-paying, are those which are to become and remain the leading and dominating powers of the world. It means still more than that; that the great English-speaking nations, if they continue in their present course of energy, thrift and conservatism in financial affairs, national and individual, are to not only maintain their present high standing but extend it, until their influence and their example shall make them the leaders of the entire world, and, through that influence and example and leadership, benefit and bless and advance every nation of the world. It means one thing more: that this nation, the greatest of the English-speaking countries, is to be the leader in this great work, and that upon you, gentlemen, the future financiers and statesmen of this nation, rests a grave responsibility, a responsibility which, as I look into your faces, I believe you will assume with fidelity, with dignity and honor to yourselves, your country, and the great people whom you represent.

BALLADS OF BUSINESS · I

THE UNWISDOM OF SOLOMON

BY JOE LINCOLN

Mr. Solomon Stiggles, he kept a small store
In a town by the shore, where his father before
And his grandfather also had kept one of yore,
And the sign lettered o'er the old-fashioned shop door
Read SOLOMON STIGGLES, just that and no more.

Mr. Solomon Stiggles sold sugar and hats
And collars for cats and bedsprings and slats,
And salt, shoes and scissors and bonnets and bats,
And pickles and spats and biscuits and mats,
And calico dresses and poison for rats.

Each morning he came, with a dignified gait
And a manner sedate, to his shop just at eight,
Neither one minute early nor one minute late,
And though callers might prate, he compelled them to wait
The pleasure of Solomon Stiggles the great.

It was Solomon's boast, one he made every day,
That he never would stray from his ancestors' way,
But would carry on business just as did they;
And advertisements gay and show-window display
Were "Undignified—very!" so Stiggles would say.

He sat in his shop all the day like a bump
On a log, or a stump, and his wallet grew plump,
For, with no competition, the folk in a lump,
Though they dubbed him a "chump," came to buy on the jump
Of "the only tin can," so to speak, "on the dump."

But alas for grim Fate, that our peace overthrows!
And though man may propose, 'tis the gods that dispose.
To the town where sat Stiggles in prosperous doze,
Came a chap with a nose and a loud suit of clothes;
His last name was Cohen; his first name was Mose.

And then on a lot that for years had been bare,
In plain sight, I declare, of the Stiggles arm-chair,
Rose a tart little, smart little building in air,
Dressed in signs debonnair, round, oblong and square,
That avowed that MOSE COHEN did business there.

And Mr. Mose Cohen he cared not for pride,
But just pushed it aside and let precedent slide,
While he went after trade with a seven league stride;
And the "booms" that he tried, though most undignified,
Were meant to coax people to buy—and they "buyed."

So Mr. Mose Cohen sold sugar and hats
And collars for cats, and bedsprings and slats,
And salt, shoes and scissors, and bonnets and bats,
And pickles and spats, and biscuits and mats,
While Solomon's patrons were June-bugs and gnats.

And he of the stately conservative mind,
With the methods refined of his grandfather's kind,
Was disgusted at first, and then blustered and whined:
And, as trade fell behind and the profits declined,
He grumbled and grunted and growled—and assigned.

And now when you visit that town by the shore,
If you pause by the door that the signboards galore
Inform us gives entrance to "Cohen's Great Store,"
And a man of three score is seen scrubbing the floor,
That man is S. Stiggles—his salary's "four."

Moral.

The moral is plain—just as plain as the nose
On the face of friend Mose: If you sit down and prose
About grandfather's ways, why, you may as well close!
For, in these days, to doze is to turn up your toes;
And you can't be a "dead one" and win: And that goes.

Interest

By JOSEPH HARDCASTLE.

IF Enterprise is indebted to Thrift $2,000, says this writer in an article published some time since, Thrift is not only entitled to the return of the $2,000, but, in addition, to a compensation for the use of his money, dependent on the time the indebtedness exists. The compensation is called interest, and it is usual to base its amount on the compensation allowed for each $100 for one year. This latter is called the rate per cent. per annum. Suppose Enterprise has been indebted to Thrift $2,000 for four years, and that the compensation he pays for the use of the money is at the rate of $6 for each $100 for one year, then compensation for the use of $100 for one year is $6, and compensation for twenty times $100 or $2,000 for one year is twenty times $6 or $120, and compensation for $2,000 for four years is four times $120, or $480, or 20 x 6 x 4 equals $480, the interest.

But this is not the usual method of calculating interest for years. It is generally preferable to alter the rating, from the rate on $100 to the rate on $1, and in this case the rate on $1 is .06, usually called 6 cents on the dollar. The calculation becomes 2,000 x 6 x 4 equals $480, the interest.

If Enterprise, instead of deferring the payment of the interest to the end of the four years, had paid it annually as it became due, it is evident that Thrift would have had the use of the interest. But Enterprise had the use of the interest without paying for it, and this is called simple interest. If Enterprise has the interest and pays for its use, this is called compound interest. I will return to the original question, considered as simple interest.

Amount loaned		= 2000
Amount due end of first year	= 2000 + 120	= 2120
Amount due end of second year	= 2120 + 120	= 2240
Amount due end of third year	= 2240 + 120	= 2360
Amount due end of fourth year	= 2360 + 120	= 2480

It will be observed that the amounts due increase yearly by $120, a year's interest, forming a series of amounts in arithmetical progression. Except in special cases, which is not necessary here to particularize, the courts of law do not allow interest on interest.

Thrift could not before any interest had accrued have legally bargained that Enterprise should pay him compound interest; but he might have gone to Enterprise after interest had accumulated and, in consideration of having allowed the payment of interest to be deferred, agreed that Enterprise should retain the interest on condition that it should increase the loan to that extent. The debt in this case must be already due, otherwise the interest cannot be thus compounded.

The amounts due by compound interest proceed in geometrical progression, i. e., by multiplication by a constant multiplier. Taking the same question:

Amount loaned	=		2000
Amount due end of 1st year	= 2000	× 1.06	= 2120
Amount due end of 2d year	= 2120	× 1.06	= 2247.20
Amount due end of 3d year	= 2247.20	× 1.06	= 2382.03
Amount due end of 4th year	= 2382.03	× 1.06	= 2524.95

The multiplier is the amount of $1 at the end of one year.

So far we have had no difficulty; but suppose that the time, instead of being in years, is in the fractional part of a year, and that the interest is payable half-yearly, or to speak technically, there are half-yearly rests. The first supposition affects both simple and compound interest; the second, compound interest only.

Fractional Part of a Year.

Most simple interest questions involve the use of the fractional part of a year; hence the necessity of seeing how to represent the fraction. The course of the sun determines the number of days in a year as 365¼ nearly. Practically we get rid of the fraction by considering three out of every four years as consisting of 365 days, and the fourth, which we call leap year, of 366 days. For the purpose of calculating interest we take a step further, and consider the year consisting of 365 days. This we call the true or correct year. The words true and correct are only used relatively as compared with other years used in the calculation of interest. The dilemma which of necessity arises in the case of a leap year being on the above supposition, a year and a day, we get out of it the best way we can.

True simple interest consists in considering each day as a fractional part of 365 days, and is everywhere lawful, even where other methods of establishing the fractional part of a year is made lawful by statute. Calculating true simple interest is simple in principle but irksome in practice, unless we resort to a set of interest tables based on 365 days as the year. There are two other methods in use of calculating simple interest, which are simpler in practice but more artificial, and consequently approximative only.

The first of these, in the State of New York, is legal by statute. The statute decrees that each calendar month shall be considered as 1-12 part of a year, and each day, of days less than a month, as 1-30 part of a calendar month.

The second of these may be called the customary method from its almost universal use by a large class of business men in the country, and considers the year for the purpose of interest calculations as consisting of 360 days, and consequently each day as 1-360th part of a year.

A Calendar Month.

To return to the first of these two methods.

What is a calendar month? Shall the days be counted first and afterwards the months? or vice versa? A calendar month, strictly speaking, is a month as laid down on the calendar. January is a calendar month; February is a calendar month; each of which the law says shall be considered 1-12th part of a year, irrespective of the number of days in each. But with this strict definition of the word calendar the rule laid down by the law would be useless. Custom has extended the meaning of the word. The custom is to call from any day in a month to the same day in the succeeding month a calendar month. For example, from 18th March to 18th April and from 5th of September to 5th October are calendar months. Again, if in the succeeding month there be no day of the month corresponding, then from the day in any month to the last day in a succeeding month is a calendar month. For example, from 30th January to 28th February (or 29th February in a leap year) is a calendar month.

But this loss of one, two or three days at the end of a succeeding month is not to be understood as affecting months following. For example, from 30th January to 30th March is two months.

Counting Months or Days First.

The second question custom has not settled so

definitely. I strongly incline to counting the months first and the days afterwards, as a residue left over. This seems to me the natural way, and I do not know any reason in support of the other course. The two ways may produce different results. For example, from 29th January to 3d October is either eight months, four days, or eight months, five days, thus 29th January to 29th September is eight months, and from 29th September to 3d October is four days. Or from 29th January to 3d February is five days, and from 3d February to 3d October is eight months. Some persons in estimating the days at the end of a month from which they begin to reckon consider that month as consisting of thirty days; but there is no reason or authority for casting out or adding a day, except in the estimation of a whole calendar month as recognized by the statute. This is the method of compound subtraction of the arithmetic. Any of the readers of this paper who wish to study the subject of calendar months will do well to turn their attention to the study of when notes made payable so many months after date become due, and I believe they will come to the conclusion that the above principles are correct. The customary method has likewise its dilemma. As the days approach or exceed 360, the absurdity of the rule becomes apparent. Say we require the interest of 362 days. We may either boldly use this method and thus get the interest for one year, two days, or more timidly adopt some other method.

In concluding this part of my subject I would remark on simple interest—first, that there are no difficulties in calculating simple interest when the time is in years and not fractional. Second, that true simple interest is the most accurate and always legal. Third, New York statute simple interest is sometimes greater than and sometimes less than true simple interest, and in the long run the excesses and deficiencies counterbalance each other. It is the favorite method of lawyers and of the courts of law. It is easier in calculation than the true simple interest, and is the only method which can be used when the interest is for months, quarters and half years. Fourth, the customary method is easy in calculation, but gives a result always too great by 1-72d part of the true simple interest; or otherwise expressed, the true simple interest is 1-73d less than the customary. Calculations made at 6 per cent. by this method are in reality at 6 1-12th per cent. Fifth, each of the many rules given for calculating simple interest may be shown to be founded on one or more of the ideas embraced in the four preceding paragraphs.

In the Receiver of Taxes Office, New York City, interest is calculated on a basis of 365 days to the year In the office of the Clerk of Arrears, New York City, interest is calculated by months and days.

Accrued interest on government and municipal bonds is usually calculated on a basis of 365 days to the year.

Accrued interest on railroad bonds and private bonds and mortgages is calculated by months and days. Interest on loans on collateral by the customary method of 360 days to the year.

On ordinary running accounts for goods sold, or services rendered, where the credit given is indefinite and short, interest is not collectible.

Cash advances made by one person for another ordinarily bear interest; also where a partner draws money out of a firm which belongs to the firm, the partner is liable for interest on the amount; but interest is not chargeable on freight, storage or other charges.

Another American Peril that is Worrying John Bull.—Chicago Inter-Ocean.

Interest is chargeable on a liquidated account, i. e., an account rendered and accepted as correct. The correctness is assumed when the debtor makes no objection within a reasonable time. In an account for merchandise sold on credit, interest is chargeable from and after the maturity of the credit. If it be the custom of a creditor to charge interest, and the custom is known to the debtor, interest is collectible.

I previously stated that simple interest allows the debtor to have the use of interest without paying for it. This is a relic of the prejudice held by our forefathers, that all interest (called usury) is wrong.

Inadequacy of Simple Interest.

The inadequacy of simple interest to solve some questions appears from the following: Suppose twenty years ago I invested $100,000 in unproductive real estate, and that I now wish to ascertain how much the property stands me to (or its effluent cost), allowing interest at 6 per cent. per annum on the investment. It is simply nonsense to add twenty years' interest, or $120,000 to the original cost ($100,000), and to regard the effluent cost as $220,000, for $6,000 a year for interest becomes a burden on the property, and the effluent cost of the property should evidently be the amount of $100,000, at compound interest, for twenty years, or $320,-713.50. A further drawback to calculating by simple interest appears when we wish to capitalize (i e., represent in one sum) many amounts due at different times. The capitalization may be the past, present or future value of many amounts due at different times.

Suppose $1,000 to be due in one year; $1,000 in two years; and $1,000 in three years:

Present value, first amount = $1,000 ÷ 1.06 = $943.40
" second " = 1,000 ÷ 1.12 = 892.86
" third " = 1,000 ÷ 1.12 = 847.46

The capitalization for present time = 943.40 + 892.86 + 847.46 = $2,683.72.

Again, the amount of $1,000, due in one year, in three years is $1,120, two years' interest being added; and the amount of $1,000, due in two years, in three years is $1,060; and the amount of $1,000, due in three years, in three years is $1,000. The capitalization for the end of three years = $1,120 + $1,060 + $1,000 = $3,180.

If both of these capitalizations are true, then they should harmonize; i. e., one be reducible to the other. But the present capitalization, corresponding to the three-year capitalization, $3,180 = $3,180 ÷ $1.18 = $2,694.91, instead of $2,682.72. If the payment had extended over a longer period, and the capitalizations made further apart, the difference would have been greater.

By compound interest this capitalization can be effected; and this is the principal reason that in all cases where capitalization is required, except in ordinary commercial accounts (in which cases simplicity of calculation is preferred to exactness), compound interest is used. This leads us to consider

Compound Interest.

Amounts due, including principal and interest, in compound interest, proceed in geometrical progression. Let $1 be the principal, and .06 the effective rate on $1 for one year, the interest payable yearly.

Amount of $1 at end of five years = 1.06 × 1.06 × 1.06 × 1.06 × 1.06. Here there are five factors, corresponding to the number of year.

Amount loaned on principal		= 1.000000
Amount due end of 1st year	= 1.000000 × 1.06	= 1.060000
" " 2d "	= 1.060000 × 1.06	= 1.123600
" " 3d "	= 1.123600 × 1.06	= 1.191016
" " 4th "	= 1.191016 × 1.06	= 1.262477
" " 5th "	= 1.262477 × 1.06	= 1.338226

Etc., etc.

Similarly, let $1 be the principal, and .03 the effective rate on $1 for one-half year (or .06 the nominal rate on $1 for one year), the interest payable half-yearly.

Amount loaned on principal		= 1.000000
Amount due end of ½ year	= 1.000000 × 1.03	= 1.030000
" " 1 "	= 1.030000 × 1.03	= 1.060900
" " 1½ "	= 1.060900 × 1.03	= 1.092727
" " 2 "	= 1.092727 × 1.03	= 1.125509
" " 2½ "	= 1.125509 × 1.03	= 1.159274

Etc., etc.

This process of calculation is simple in principle, but tedious; and the tediousness can only be got rid of by the use of logarithms, a set of artificial numbers, calculated by means of algebra, corresponding to the natural numbers, and tabulated in books opposite the natural numbers, called Books of Logarithms. By their use multiplication, division, raising of powers and extraction of roots, are very easily and expeditiously performed. Multiplication is performed by addition; division by subtraction; raising of powers by multiplication; and extraction of roots by division. So great is the advantage derived by the use of logarithms that it may be safely said that many questions in compound interest, and some other subjects, cannot be solved without them.

The Uses of Logarithms.

As an illustration of the uses of logarithms let us find the amount of $1 at 6 per cent. per annum for five years, interest payable yearly.

Amount of $1 at end of five years = 1.06 × 1.06 × 1.06 × 1.06. Here there are five factors, corresponding to the number of years.

From a book of logarithms:

The logarithm of 1.06	= .02530587
Consequently the logarithm of 1.06 to the 5th power	= .02530587 × 5
	= .12652935

By referring to the book of logarithms it will be seen that this last number is the logarithm of 1.338226, the correct amount, as may be seen by reference to any one of the tables previously calculated.

If the time contains a fractional part of a year, as in one-half year and four and one-half years, common arithmetic fails us in making the calculation; while by logarithms the calculation is easy. Using logarithms, it will be found that the amounts for one-half year and four and one-half years, respectively, will be as below, one-half and four and one-half being the respective multipliers. We will repeat one of the previous tables, with the amounts for one-half year and four and one-half years inserted in their proper places.

Amount loaned	= 1.000000
Amount due end of ½ year	= 1.029563
" " 1 "	= 1.060000
" " 2 "	= 1.123600
" " 3 "	= 1.191016
" " 4 "	= 1.262477
" " 4½ "	= 1.299800
" " 5 "	= 1.338226

The geometrical progression, which is the law governing compound interest, is in force for the fractional parts of a year, as well as for the year itself The multiplier for the year is 1.06, and for the half year, 1.029363. By using this latter multiplier we can advance the amounts by half years, thus:

Amount due end of ½ year	=1 ×1.029363=1.029363
" " 1 "	=1.029363×1.029363=1.060000
" " 4½ "	=1.262477×1.029363=1.299800
" " 5 "	=1.299800×1.029363=1.338226

In practice, however, it is usual to calculate simple interest for the fractional part of a year. For example, the amount due at the end of five years equals 1.338226, from which subtract the amount due at the end of four years, viz., 1.262477, and we obtain .075749, the interest for the fifth year. For the half year we take the half of this sum, or .037874, which, added to the amount due at end of four years, gives us 1.300351, the amount due at the end of four and one-half years, which is near enough to the true amount, $1.299800.

For those persons requiring to use compound interest, tables have been constructed. If the required rate per cent. is not found in the tables, they either resort to the use of logarithms, or use a calculating machine. If the interest is payable half-yearly, or quarterly, at a nominal rate of, say, 6 per cent. per annum, this gives us 3 per cent. semi-annually, or 1½ quarterly, as the effective rate per cent. for the half year or quarter; and the amount is found for the number of half years, or the number of quarters, fractional parts of a half year or a quarter being found by simple interest, as above.

Compound interest is used in life insurance questions, in annuities certain, in calculating the present value of bonds, for all these require the use of capitalization. Savings banks allow a modified form of compound interest, and commercial accounts frequently at the end of the year add the interest due to form a new principal.

Ensemble—Wonder who Told Him the Trick?—Boston Herald.

COMMERCE ACCOUNTS & FINANCE

A Magazine of Higher Business Education and Practical Administration. Acknowledged Authority in the Profession of Commerce and Consistent Advocate of Methods Up to Date and Above the Table.

JOSEPH CROSBY LINCOLN, - - - Editor.
FRIEND PITTS, JR., - Circulation and Advertising.
E. R. KITTREDGE, - - - Business Manager.

PUBLISHED MONTHLY

SUBSCRIPTION $1 a Year in the United States, Canada and Mexico. Other countries $1.50. Postage prepaid by the Publishers. In the absence of specific orders to stop at the end of the subscription term the paper will be continued and a bill sent. Entered at the New York Postoffice as Second Class mail matter.

COMMERCE, ACCOUNTS & FINANCE COMPANY, Publishers
Twenty-five Pine Street, New York

The office of secretary of the new department of commerce in President Roosevelt's Cabinet is to be filled by George L. Cortelyou. As an example of what American citizenship can do for a real man, Mr. Cortelyou's experience is to be recommended to our readers' attention. George L. Cortelyou is, as the term is nowadays accepted, a young man. He has just passed his fortieth birthday, and has in the ordinary course of events many years of active life before him. He was born in New York City on July 26, 1862, and comes of a distinguished family, his ancestors having been among the leaders in the colonial and revolutionary history of New York State. He graduated from Hempstead Institute in 1879, and later completed his preliminary education at the State Normal School in Westfield, Mass. He had a marked taste for music, and on leaving the normal school entered the New England Conservatory of Music. Later on he determined to enter upon a business career, and began to study stenography as a means toward the end. He soon became known as an expert stenographer.

*

Because of his stenographic ability he obtained a position as private secretary to the postoffice inspector in charge in New York. In July, 1891, he came to Washington as private secretary to the Fourth Assistant Postmaster General. Mr. Cortelyou has always been a stanch Republican, but nevertheless, in 1895, President Cleveland, recognizing his worth, appointed him as his own executive clerk and confidential stenographer. When President McKinley came into office he continued to serve the latter in the same capacity until 1898, when he was appointed assistant secretary to the President. Secretary Porter retiring, Mr. Cortelyou was made secretary to the President. Upon Mr. McKinley's death and the succession of Mr. Roosevelt, Mr. Cortelyou was, at the new President's earnest request, retained in his position. Now he has moved up another round in the ladder, namely to that of secretary of the department of commerce in the President's Cabinet.

*

The moral to be derived from Mr. Cortelyou's rise is so apparent that it needs little comment. Whatever work has been given him to do has been done well. He has worked early and late, and his various employers learned to know that whatever service he was asked to perform would be performed to the best of his ability, and that ability was of a high order. Political positions too often are given to political henchmen without regard to the ability of the applicant. This has not been the case with Secretary Cortelyou. President Cleveland needed a competent executive clerk and confidential stenographer. One may be sure that there were a number of Democratic applicants for the place, but Mr. Cortelyou received the appointment because of his worth and general ability. Appointed under a Democratic President, he continued to serve under a Republican President, and when that President was assassinated served his successor, at the successor's request. We think it safe to assert that in no other country under the sun could this rapid rise have been accomplished in a dozen years, the length of time in which Mr. Cortelyou has risen from stenographer to Cabinet member. His example should be an incentive to other young men, and undoubtedly will be so.

THE WORLD GROWS SMALLER.

It was about thirty years ago that Jules Verne wrote his story "Around the World in Eighty Days." This energetic and resourceful traveler had to hustle and spend money like water for special transportation facilities to accomplish his journey in the wagered time. Jules Verne's story was not merely a romance, says "World's Events." It faithfully set forth the world's transportation conditions as they existed at the time it was written. Eighty days was then the shortest time in which a traveler, try'ng for a record, could hope to complete a tour of the world. Such a tour would have occupied the ordinary traveler, content to accept the ordinary facilities of transportation, considerably longer than eighty days. Before this present year is out, or as soon as the Siberian railway is completed, an ordinary traveler, using the ordinary means of transportation, can journey round the world in forty days. Starting from Paris it will take him eighteen days to reach Vladivostock by rail; from Vladivostock he must make a two days' journey to Yokohama, where he will board a steamer that will land him at Vancouver in twelve days; from Vancouver to New York, via the Canadian Pacific, is a four days' journey; six days on a liner will take him to Cherbourg; and from Cherbourg to his starting point, Paris, is but a step.

IDENTIFIED.

"Are you the defendant?" asked a man in the courtroom, speaking to an old negro. "No, boss," was the reply. "I ain't done nothing to be called names like that. I'se got a lawyer here who does the defensing." "Then who are you?" "I'se the gentleman what stole the chickens."—Green Bag.

UNDERSTOOD THEN.

She—It was fortunate that you were such a fine French scholar. I suppose when you were in Paris you had no difficulty in making yourself understood?

He—Not when I talked English.—Boston Transcript.

Commercial Crises. II*

By J. SHIELD NICHOLSON, M. A., D. Sc.

It is time, however, to observe that crises may arise from causes that are primarily commercial and in which the financial results are secondary. I pass on, then, to consider commercial crises in the more special sense of the term. If we look back on the history of commercial crises we often find that they begin with a bona-fide expansion of trade and industry. Such an expansion may be due to the adoption on a large scale of new methods of production and of transport. Thus, at the end of the eighteenth century so many changes were introduced that the period is often spoken of as the Industrial Revolution. The crisis of 1793 was preceded by a bona-fide expansion of trade, consequent on the increased use of machinery for manufacture and improvement in transport by the greater use of canals. This bona-fide development of industry was accompanied by over-speculation and the undue extension of credit. The crisis was precipitated by political causes, especially the war with France. It was marked by many failures of country banks and a distrust of credit documents. The difficulty was met to some extent by the issue of exchequer bills, but ultimately a continuance of the same unfavorable conditions led to the suspension of cash payments by the Bank of England, and Bank of England notes remained inconvertible till 1819.

The principal cause of the crisis of 1847 was mainly due to the great development of railways. Twenty years before the capital expenditure on railways, then in their infancy, was less than one million a year. Even in 1842-43 the capital expenditure was only about four and one-half millions; then in 1846 the amount authorized by Parliament had risen to one hundred and thiry-two million pounds. This actual authorization of capital for railways was accompanied by a still greater amount of speculation. It has been stated that in 1845—the preceding year—the market value of the various new schemes which were represented by letters of allotment was not less than five hundred million pounds. The speculative rise in shares was enormous. In the Leeds and Thirsk Railway shares with £2 10s. paid rose in a few months to £23 10s.—i. e., nine times the value of the amount paid; in another case shares with £4 paid in January, 1845, were selling at £4 10s., and in September at £42 15s.—again a rise of more than nine times. Here again, though the crisis was commercial in origin, it was in its secondary symptoms financial. The reserve of the Bank of England was reduced to £1,600,000, consols fell to 77¾, and many banks failed. In the end the financial crisis was stayed by the suspension of the Bank Act of 1844.

I have taken these two crises for illustration, because the commercial causes in which they originated were not only perfectly sound, but were destined ultimately to increase enormously the industrial power of the nation. The development of machinery, and the improvement of transport and the means of communication, were unquestionably two of the principal causes of industrial progress in the nineteenth century.

In a case of this kind, which begins with bona-fide causes of prosperity, the prosperity passes into inflation, and the inflation into a crisis, followed by a depression, simply because speculation, aided by credit, anticipates too rapidly the realization of the future.

After the Preliminary Stages.

The process after the preliminary stages is invariably the same. People begin by investing their money in something which they think will yield a good return. This is unquestionably so far legitimate enterprise. There would be no progress if the owners of capital did not take a certain risk in new undertakings. The next step is that the value of the "new thing"—whatever it is—rises. And then people begin to buy the thing not with the idea of getting a good yield from it in the shape of income of some sort, but of getting an extravagant profit by a further rapid rise in value. Very soon the original object is altogether lost sight of, and prices are paid which under no conceivable circumstances could be justified by legitimate business. Then the speculation naturally spreads to other things—many of them hopelessly unsound from the beginning. If a general speculation of this kind is aided by a system of credit that is itself unsound, or at any rate not properly under control, the inflation is pushed to greater extremes than would otherwise be possible. Bad speculation feeds on bad finance. Some speculators, however, are more far-sighted than others, and some credit institutions are more prudent with their advances; speculation for the fall takes the place of speculation for the rise; the fall becomes an avalanche; good and bad are mingled together, and the inevitable crisis is followed by a period of depression of trade and contraction of credit.

Economic history is full of examples of speculation of this kind; sometimes it is purely local and temporary, at other times it seizes a whole nation—it may even affect the whole commercial world; it may be prolonged over a considerable time, and the collapse, when it occurs, is all the more redoubtable. Let me recall one or two famous examples. About the middle of the sixteenth century a German received a present of some tulips from Constantinople, and the flower soon became very popular, especially in Holland. The tulip was discovered to be capable of great variation, and especially amenable to artificial cultivation and experiment. For nearly one hundred years this plant was cultivated with great success in Holland; and the growth of tulips became a very profitable and highly artistic industry. At last the trade became too profitable, and the prices of coveted specimens rose to great heights, and in the year 1634, to quote the pithy description of an old writer, "the whole Dutch nation went mad about tulips." Ordinary trades were neglected for growing tulips; then people began buying the bulbs to sell again at a profit; prices rose every day, and in the course of a year specimens of single bulbs fetched £300, £400 and £550. Then a speculation for the fall began; roots were sold by those who did not possess them, more were sold than were in existence, and perhaps the first specimen of a "corner" was when a number of tulips had been sold of a kind of which there were only two specimens in the market.

This speculation attracted attention in all the exchanges in Holland, the infection spread to other countries, and large sums were remitted to Holland

* Lecture delivered before the Society of Accountants in Edinburgh, by the Professor of Political Economy in the University of Edinburgh. Originally published in the Accountants' Magazine.

for speculation in tulips. At last—but not till 1636—prices reached their climax, and a panic ensued on forced realizations which brought ruin to thousands, and many years passed before the force of the shock was spent. Yet even in this tulip mania there was a basis of reality. The growth of bulbs of all kinds became an important Dutch industry, and is so to this day. The interest of the example lies in its a priori improbability. The subject of the speculation is a new kind of flower, and the country that was afflicted with the mania was the country of the sober-minded, phlegmatic Dutch.

The South Sea Bubble.

The greatest speculative manias on record, with which the nineteenth century has nothing to compare, arose in the first quarter of the eighteenth century—the South Sea Bubble in England, and the Mississippi scheme and the speculation associated with the name of John Law, in France. The greatest and most picturesque of all speculators was John Law: there is little doubt that he was a man of great financial genius, and that his schemes, especially his great bank, only proved unsound when they went beyond his own control. Even the South Sea Bubble saw the promotion of some of the companies which have proved the most prosperous of any on record—as, for example, the New River for supplying London with water.

Facilities for speculation in recent times have no doubt been largely increased by the growth of joint-stock enterprise, especially after the adoption of the principle of limited liability. The possibilities of speculation have been further increased by the enormous expansion of credit, by the great improvements in the means of communication, by the telegraph, and by the extension over a wider and wider area of dealings, not only on the stock exchanges, but on all the markets for important commodities. Nor can we suppose that in the course of two or three centuries there has been a fundamental change in human nature; so far as human nature is concerned, a South Sea Bubble might begin to-morrow; the elementary passions are as strong as ever, including the love of gain and the love of gambling; probably, indeed, so far as the mere desire or the mere greed is concerned, the passion is at present stronger than in many former times when speculation became rampant.

Some of the Causes.

Although, however, both history and theory point to excessive speculation as the principal cause of crises, there are other causes which are too important to be passed over. The whole of modern industry is extremely complex, and the various parts are interdependent, and the whole organization is extremely delicate. Accordingly, any great disturbance in the methods of production, and any dislocation in any of the parts, may indirectly affect the whole system. A great conversion of circulating capital into fixed capital involves a disturbance of this kind. It may happen that more of the fixed capital is created than there is any effective demand for, and also that not enough circulating capital is left for the ordinary business of the country. In such a case as this, even if there is no crisis in the sense of a financial panic, there is a period of inflation, followed by a more or less prolonged depression. And in all probability this creation of fixed capital will be accompanied by excessive speculation in the corresponding companies—e. g., in railways, mines, or it may be even in land itself. The present depression in Germany is said to be largely due to over-speculation in land, associated with a too rapid industrial development.

Again, there is the possibility of general over-production in the sense that markets become overstocked, production becomes unprofitable, and labor finds less employment. Under modern conditions a rise in prices and profits in any one great industry not only stimulates production in that industry, but the movement spreads from trade to trade through the expenditure of the extra profits and wages, and the whole production of the country or of the world is carried on at a higher pressure. Theoretically it may be argued, as by J. S. Mill, that general over-production is impossible, that commodities pay for commodities, that the more there is produced the more there is to exchange. But this theory implies a perfection in the methods of distribution or the possibility of exactly adjusting supply to demand, and of turning capital into new modes of employment, that does not exist in practice.

A general cause, which used to be of the first importance, is found in disturbances affecting the production of raw material, including food. Under old conditions, when each country relied mainly on its own harvests, a series of bad harvests caused universal depression, except to farmers, who were more than compensated by the rise in prices; and a series of good harvests caused general prosperity, except to the farmers, who lost more by the fall in prices. The influence of the harvest in England used to be so great that the price of consols was affected by the weather. Under present conditions the area of supply has been so extended that the deficiency in one part can be met by the abundance of another, and in any case so much is produced, and of such variety, that as regards food, apart from a general war, there is little fear of any real scarcity. With regard to raw material of various kinds there is less room for substitution, and there may be real scarcity, as we have experienced lately as regards coal, and formerly as regards cotton. It was the consideration of the importance of the supplies of food and raw material which led Professor Jevons to formulate what is known as the sun-spot theory of commercial crises—the name is rather startling, but there is nothing unreasonable in the idea.

"It seems probable," argues Jevons, "that commercial crises are connected with a periodic variation of weather affecting all parts of the earth, and probably arising from increased waves of heat received from the sun at average intervals of ten years and a fraction." Cycles of weather of this kind would, of course, greatly affect the production of raw material, including food products, and the oscillation between general abundance and scarcity might very well be associated with inflations and depressions of trade with a crisis at the period of transition.

Periodicity of Crises.

The periodicity of commercial crises at intervals of ten years, or at any rate the regular alternation of inflations and depressions during decennial periods, has been so marked that it is natural to look for some very general cause. The late Mr. Mills, of Manchester, who was an intimate friend of Jevons, and well known as a banker and as an economist, sought for such a general cause, not in external nature in general but in human nature in particular. Mr. Mills was the author of the phrase "credit cycle," and his theory can be best expressed in the biological language that is at present so fashionable. Mr. Mills made a minute examination of the life-history of a credit cycle, and as he conducted his inquiry just after the great crisis of 1866, which had

All Over and King Pin Standing.—Boston Herald.

followed that of 1857, after the allotted time, he had a very fine specimen for illustration. His description of a credit cycle would certainly apply to that period. "During each of these decades," he says, "commercial credit runs through the mutations of a life, having its infancy, growth to maturity, diseased overgrowth, and death by collapse."

Mr. Mills argued that the remedy against the recurrence of crises was the spread of information: and just as some diseases are destroyed by light, so also—this was his main contention—crises may be destroyed by the light of knowledge and of publicity. That most solid of all works on economics, the "Dictionary of Political Economy," edited by Mr Palgrave, seriously asserts that the anticipation of Mr. Mills has been verified in some measure by the course of events.

This theory seems quite reasonable and even plausible in itself. Credit depends to a great extent on confidence, and an inflation of credit involves misplaced confidence. It takes time to recover from the effects of a panic, or even from a narrow escape. After a crisis business is conducted on cautious and sound methods—for a time. Then the saying is verified that John Bull can stand most things, but he cannot stand two per cent. Two per cent. for the bank-rate may be quite satisfactory, but two per cent. for what we have called profit-interest, and nothing in the shape of the wages of speculation, this is the two per cent. against which producers and traders rebel. They prefer their toil enlivened with a little risk, and their gains diversified with a little luck. Thus the period of depression passes into confidence: the panic of the past looks less and less black, and the promise of the future more and more rosy: and a new period of inflation is inaugurated.

Crisis of 1890.

We are too much inclined to think that this ancient history has no lesson for us, and that our methods of business are so sound and so different that all danger of commercial crises is past. We seem to think that steam and electricity have not only revolutionized production and transport, but have also revolutionized human nature. In sober truth, human nature remains much the same, and unless our superior knowledge is used to regulate methods of business these changes in mechanical appliances will only give greater opportunity for mischief. Those who think commercial and financial crises are things of the past have only to recall the Baring crisis of 1890. It is quite true, in this case, that panic was avoided, and that the crisis never became general, and even the offending firm was rehabilitated. But the catastrophe was so near, and for a time the danger looked so serious, that the example loses little of its force by way of warning. It was the practical wisdom, the moral courage, and the keen sense of public duty on the part of a few men that saved the situation. I will conclude this paper by recalling the words used by Mr. Goschen in a speech at Leeds a few weeks after the danger had been surmounted. After telling the audience that we had only escaped disaster by the skin of our teeth, he goes on to describe the serious nature of the crisis. These are the words: "No fertile imagination could exaggerate the gravity of the crisis; and if I attempt to bring home to those who are listening to me now the serious nature of the crisis, I do so in order to accentuate the necessity of their turning their attention to what I may call the necessity for soundness in our banking, and soundness in our currency, transactions. I doubt whether the public has thoroughly realized the extent of the danger to which what is called the banking crisis exposed us all. It was not a question of a narrow circle of financiers or traders. The liabilities were so gigantic, the position of the house was so unique, that interests were at stake far beyond individual fortunes—far beyond the fortunes of any class. We were on the brink of a crisis through which it might have been difficult for the soundest to pass unscathed, for the wealthiest to have escaped. It was a time when none who had liabilities or engagements to pay could say how they could pay them if a condition of things were to continue under which securities could not be realized, under which produce could not be sold, under which bills could not be discounted, under which appeared an absence of cash sufficient to discharge the liabilities of the general public."

There is but one interpretation of these words, and that is—that in the opinion of this eminent authority we were within an ace of a crisis which would have exceeded in intensity the famous crisis of 1866. At the same time, I have no wish to exaggerate the possibility of crises or the dangers that may arise when they do occur. Mr. Goschen spoke when the danger was hardly past; but to us it is already part of ancient history. We can at present afford to be cool spectators and impartial observers. There could, however, be no greater mistake than to suppose that commercial and financial crises are as antiquated as old machinery; they not only may occur, but it is quite possible that for the time being the effects may be still more disastrous than in former times. All we are entitled to say is, that, as in the past, these effects will be obliterated, and commerce will revert to normal conditions.

SLIPPERS MADE OF PAPER.

We are getting on. Now it is said that an American firm means to launch out on the world slippers made of paper! They will suit all the purposes for which slippers are now used, and they will be the greatest boon in the world to weary commercial travelers. What man is there with "soul so dead" that he cannot appreciate the change when, his day's work done, he can sit down in a big easy chair and get rid of his boots. But memories are short, and there are many things to stow away in the portmanteau, and you find yourself sometimes in a far-away hotel minus your slippers. Some day, however, that will be no misfortune. You ring the bell, and a waiter brings you a brand new set of paper slippers at a price which will certainly not ruin you forever.—Echo.

INFORMAL CALL.

The monkey lost his hold and fell into the crocodile's waiting jaws. Even then his wits did not desert him. "I just dropped in for dinner," he said, with an engaging smile.—Yale Record.

The Negotiable Instruments Law*

By THOS. B. PATON.

Payment in Due Course—What Constitutes It?—By Whom Notice of Dishonor is Given—Sufficient Notice.

NOTE.—As enacted in New York, the Negotiable Instruments Law is divided into nineteen articles as follows:

1. General Provisions (Sections 1—17)
2. Negotiable Instruments: Form and Interpretation (20—42)
3. Consideration (50—55)
4. Negotiation (60—80)
5. Rights of holder (90—98)
6. Liabilities of parties (110—119)
7. Presentment for payment (130—148)
8. Notice of dishonor (160—189)
9. Discharge (200—206)
10. Bills of exchange (210—215)
11. Acceptance (220—230)
12. Presentment for acceptance (240—248)
13. Protest (260—268)
14. Acceptance for honor (280—290)
15. Payment for honor (300—306)
16. Bills in a set (310—315)
17. Promissory notes and checks (320—325)
18. Notes given for patent rights (330—332)
19. Laws repealed. When takes effect (340—341)

The provisions of the law naturally fall under four general classifications.

a. General Provisions.
b. Negotiable Instruments in General.
c. Bills of Exchange.
d. Promissory Notes and Checks.

The text of the law is the same in all the states (with some slight exceptions which will be noted) but the numbering of the sections, and in some states, of the articles, is not uniform. There is, however, the same continuity of articles and text, except that in some instances "General Provisions" follow, instead of precede the remainder of the act. By following this course of study with reference to the New York act, as above outlined, the reader in each state can apply the same to the law of his own state.

THE concluding section of Article VI covering "Presentment for Payment," defines when payment is made in due course.

Sec. 148. What Constitutes Payment in Due Course.—Payment is made in due course when it is made at or after the maturity of the instrument to the holder thereof in good faith and without notice that his title is defective.

By Section 200 a negotiable instrument is discharged by payment in due course by or on behalf of the principal debtor, or by payment in due course by the party accommodated, where the instrument is made or accepted for accommodation. Section 148 defines what constitutes payment in due course. Such payment must be made at or after the maturity of the instrument to the holder (i. e., the payee or indorsee of a bill or note, who is in possession of it, or the bearer thereof—Section 2) in good faith and without notice that his title is defective (see Sections 94 and 95, as to good faith and defective title).

Article Eight—Notice of Dishonor.

We now reach the point where a negotiable instrument primarily, to pay it. Section 143 defines when the instrument is dishonored by non-payment, and section 246 when dishonored by non-acceptance. It becomes necessary for the holder, therefore, to look for payment to those parties, drawer, indorser, or both, who are secondarily liable. But in order to preserve their liability, it is necessary that they be promptly notified of the dishonor of the instrument, unless notice is waived or excused, otherwise they will have the right to assume that the instrument has been duly honored, and will be discharged from liability to the holder. Article VIII provides the rules regulating this important subject of notice of dishonor.

Sec. 160. To whom Notice of Dishonor Must be Given.—Except as herein otherwise provided, when a negotiable instrument has been dishonored by non-acceptance or non-payment, notice of dishonor must be given to the drawer and to each indorser, and any drawer or indorser to whom such notice is not given is discharged.

Generally speaking, we see, the parties entitled to notice of dishonor, because of the non-acceptance or non-payment of a negotiable instrument, are the drawer of a bill, and each indorser of a bill or note. The maker of a note, or the acceptor of a bill, is not entitled to notice, because he is the one who, primarily, ought to pay it, and this is so, even though the instrument has been made or accepted for accommodation. The act does not provide for notice of dishonor to one who signs a negotiable instrument as guarantor, and the liability of such an one is left as it exists under the law merchant. The act provides that any drawer or indorser to whom notice of dishonor is not given is discharged from liability on the instrument, and under the law merchant, such discharge also operates to discharge him from any liability on the consideration for the instrument. It is of the utmost importance, therefore, to preserve valuable rights against parties secondarily liable upon, and entitled to notice of dishonor of, negotiable instruments, that the law governing the giving of such notice be carefully observed and followed.

By Whom Notice of Dishonor is Given.

Sec. 161. By Whom Given.—The notice may be given by or on behalf of the holder, or by or on behalf of any party to the instrument who might be compelled to pay it to the holder, and who, upon taking it up would have a right to reimbursement from the party to whom the notice is given.

The notice, it is seen, may be given,

1. By the holder;
2. By some one on his behalf;
3. By any party who might be compelled to pay the holder and who in that event would have the right to reimbursement from the party to whom notice is given;
4. By some one on his behalf.

The object of notice is two-fold; first, to apprise the party to whom it is addressed of the dishonor; and, second, to inform him that the holder, or party giving the notice, looks to him for payment. Hence, it follows that notice can only be given by some party to the instrument, though he need not be the actual holder of the bill at the time. Accordingly, notice is not sufficient if given by

1. A stranger;
2. The maker;
3. The drawee;
4. The acceptor.

While these persons might apprise the notified party of the dishonor, none are in a position to look to him for payment, and cannot inform him to that effect. But a party entitled to give notice might constitute the drawee or acceptor his agent for that purpose.

Agent's Notice.

Sec. 162. Notice Given by Agent.—Notice of dishonor may be given by an agent either in his own name or in the name of any party entitled to give notice, whether that party be his principal or not.

This section relates to cases where the notice is not given personally by the holder or party who might be compelled to pay and look for reimbursement to the notified party, but is given by an agent on behalf of such holder or party. It provides the name in which notice may be given, which may be either

1. Agent's own name; or
2. Principal's name; or
3. Name of any party entitled to give notice, though not agent's own principal.

Cases illustrating the sufficiency of notice given by an

* Republished from the Banking Law Journal by permission. Copyright, 1899, 1900, 1901, 1902 and 1903, by T. B. Paton; all rights reserved. To be revised and published in book form by the author.

agent in the name of a party to the instrument, though not his own principal, are the following:

Chapman v. Keane, 3 Ad. and E. 193. A bill of exchange was indorsed by A to B. B left it with A's clerk, who presented it, and upon dishonor notified the drawer in the name of A. A took up the bill from B, and sued the drawer, who contended that the notice should have been in the name of B, the holder. Held, notice sufficient.

Harrison v. Ruscoe, 15 M. and W. 231. A indorsed a bill to B and B left it with C, who gave notice of dishonor to the drawer, but by mistake and without authority, gave it in A's name instead of B's. In this case, B sued the drawer, and it was held (1) that notice by A would be good, provided he was liable to B and could look to the drawer for reimbursement; in other words, in the event his liability to B was not discharged by laches, or he would have had no right of action against the drawer if he had taken the bill up from B; and (2), that notice by C in A's name, instead of B's; whose agent he was, was sufficient because, though unauthorized, the drawer was not injured.

Effect of Notice on Holder's Behalf.

Sec. 163. Effect of Notice Given on Behalf of Holder.—Where notice is given by or on behalf of the holder, it enures for the benefit of all subsequent holders and all prior parties who have a right of recourse against the party to whom it is given.

Sec. 164. Effect Where Notice is Given by Party Entitled Thereto.—Where notice is given by or on behalf of a party entitled to give notice, it enures for the benefit of the holder and all parties subsequent to the party to whom notice is given.

These two sections provide the rule as to who is benefited by a notice given by or on behalf of the holder, or by or on behalf of a party, other than the holder, entitled to give notice. Notice of dishonor should be given by the holder to all prior parties whom he intends to look to for payment. But while this is best for his own interest, it is, as seen, not absolutely necessary that the notice should come from him, for he is entitled to the benefit of notice given in due time by any party to the instrument who would be liable to him if he, the holder, had himself given him notice of dishonor. If the holder only notifies the last indorser, and he the next preceding, and he the next, and so on to the first, the latter will be liable to all the parties. Again, if the holder notifies all prior indorsers, but one of the intermediate indorsers fails to give notice to prior parties, nevertheless, when compelled to take it up, the notice given the prior parties will enure to his benefit, although not given by him; and so also, if none of the intermediate indorsers between the first indorser and the holder, who have received notice, themselves give notice of dishonor to prior parties, the notice given by the holder will enure to their benefit.

Sec. 165. When Agent May Give Notice.—Where the instrument has been dishonored in the hands of an agent, he may either himself give notice to the parties liable thereon, or he may give notice to his principal. If he give notice to his principal, he must do so within the same time as if he were the holder, and the principal upon receipt of such notice has himself the same time for giving notice as if the agent had been an independent holder.

Many negotiable instruments are transferred by the holder to agents for collection. When dishonored in the hands of the agent, this section, voicing the law merchant, leaves it optional with the agent to himself give notice of dishonor to the parties liable, or to give notice to his principal. In case the agent adopts the latter alternative, the same time is accorded to him to give his principal notice as if he, himself, were the holder, and the principal, upon receipt of such notice, has himself the same time for giving notice, as if the agent had been an independent holder.

It is part of the duty of banks, which as agents receive indorsed negotiable instruments for collection, to give notice of dishonor in the event the instrument is not paid or accepted. Sometimes the bank will send notice, not only to its immediate principal, but also to the drawer and to all prior indorsers. Sometimes it will make out notices for all these parties, and inclose them, in one envelope, with the notice to its principal, that the latter may be conveniently supplied with the means of transmitting notice. The authorities in the past have not been entirely uniform as to the measure of the bank's duty in this regard, but their weight has been to the effect that it is only necessary for a collecting bank to notify its immediate principal. Section 165, as we have seen, makes it optional with the agent either to notify all prior parties or its principal only.

Sufficient Notice.

Sec. 166. When Notice Sufficient.—A written notice need not be signed and an insufficient written notice may be supplemented and validated by verbal communication. A misdescription of the instrument does not vitiate the notice unless the party to whom the notice is given is in fact misled thereby.

The notice of dishonor may be either written or verbal, and this section deals with certain points bearing on the sufficiency of the notice. Where the notice is written, the want of a signature, it is seen, will not affect its validity, providing, of course, it comes from the right party.

Furthermore, where a written notice is, of itself, insufficient, it may be supplemented and validated by a verbal communication, and the sufficiency or insufficiency in such case is a question of fact. Finally, a misdescription of the instrument does not vitiate the notice unless the party to whom the notice is given is in fact misled thereby. Instances of misdescription where the party receiving notice has not been misled, are where the amount of a note has been misstated; the date misdescribed; a bill described as a note; bank at which payable wrongly stated; names of drawer and acceptor transposed; acceptor described by wrong name.

POWER OF THE PRESS.

Managing Editor—Well, what's the trouble?

Assistant—The beauty editor is away, and a woman writes to know what to do with a wrinkle in her forehead.

Managing Editor—Tell her to putty it up and forget it.

Accounting Term. A Running Account.

Inventorying

WHILE the majority of our readers are giving more or less attention to the annual closing of books, the inventorying of stock and the preparation of fiscal statements at the end of an extended period, let us obtrude one or two thoughts about inventorying. We might preface our remarks by referring to the excessive labor of inventorying, the dread which the office man feels all during the year of the inventorying period, and the hard work that is actually done at the time that the inventorying is in operaton. The question arises, why is all this so? Why do you inventory? Why do you go through the stress of closing the books as a preliminary to making out a balance sheet?

We do not want to be presumptuous in our assumption, but nevertheless we venture to say that the thoughtful, logical man who gives attention to this question for a few moments will reach the conclusion that whatever is done in inventorying, or whatever special work is done in connection therewith is nothing more nor less than making up for deficiencies in routine work which existed during the period under review. Inventorying is primarily for the purpose of finding out what goods we have on hand, in order to subtract from the goods we have bought, for the purpose of determining the value of those we have disposed of. Look at the involved reasoning there is in this statement.

Any one who has given attention in the least to business principles from the standpoint of accounts, or any one who has given any thought to the question of exchanges, must have had his attention called to the matter of the value disposed of. When we pay out cash we take account of the disbursement just as much as we take account when we receive cash. Accordingly, the cash account balances and we always have before us by the figures on the cash book a statement of the amount on hand. How is it with merchandise?

We are careful to the last degree to check invoices of goods bought, and there is a merry ha-ha if perchance the dealer from whom we have bought has ventured to charge for goods not sent, or overcharged on any item which the statement contains. But our vigilance stops right here. When it comes to shipping goods we shove them forward regardless, paying no attention to the value of what we are disposing of, but taking great care to charge to the customer the goods so sent out at selling price. We may be selling at a great advance over cost, because the market favors us, or we may be selling out a job lot at less than cost. But the cost value of the goods is never given a thought. We are merely careful to charge the customer what he has agreed to pay.

Conducting business in this way we get mixed up in our accounts, until we throw away our vaunted bookkeeping, and take pencil and paper in hand to inventory in order to find out "where we are at." Contrast with this the thought of inventorying as we go along, of knowing the cost value of goods we dispose of day by day. Contrast with the ordinary merchandise account two accounts, one to be merchandise in fact, namely goods on hand, carried at cost, the other to be the sales account, wherein there is shown the results as between the cost of goods disposed of and the amount received for them.

Debit merchandise account with the cost of goods on hand at the beginning of the period, and thereafter with the cost of the goods received. Credit it day by day with the cost of goods disposed of. In any account conducted on this plan the balance will show the amount of the goods on hand. Debit sales account with the cost of goods disposed of and credit it with the selling price. The balance in this account must be gross profits.

Whenever the question of inventorying comes up, remember that whatever you do in this regard at the end of the year or other fiscal period is only making up for the neglect during the time that the business has been in progress. Contrast with the annual inventory the plan of inventorying as you go along, of knowing the cost value of the goods you dispose of.

Offsets are Dangerous.

In almost every line of business we find managing men prone to employ offsets. We find in some cases that there is no allowance for depreciation of machinery in a factory, for example, because repairs are kept up. We find in other cases that there is no charge for certain classes of cost items because a revenue which is likewise omitted from credits will be an offset to them. The disease is insidious and perhaps infectious. It leads men into paths heretofore untrodden and usually a long way from the truth.

It is better in all cases to make a charge where a charge is due, and make a credit where a credit belongs, rather than to employ the plan of cancellation outside of the books in a way to hide business facts. Two items may offset each other and they may not. If they do, well and good. If they do, the only loss has been the clerical labor. If they do not, the facts of the case are displayed in the balance sheet of the business.

Reserves are to be Used.

The question is frequently addressed us what to do in such and such a case with respect to the reserve which has been accumulated. For example, in the case of a factory a certain amount has been set aside for a number of years against depreciation of machinery. Finally some of the old machinery is thrown out and that of an improved pattern is bought to replace it. To what account shall new machinery be charged? We may lay it down as a rule that does not admit of argument or dispute that reserves are provided for the purpose of being used. But they are to be used intelligently, and that which is reserved against depreciation of machinery, for example, is to be used for keeping the machinery up to the usual degree of efficiency.

In the case of machinery thrown out, the proper asset account should be credited with the cost value of the machinery discarded. We should not part with an asset without taking account of it at cost. Then, in turn, the new machinery bought is to be charged in at its cost.

Suppose, for example, that there has been $100,000 credited to reserves. The offsetting debit having gone into the cost of product; that machinery which cost $25,000 is to be thrown out and new machinery costing $50,000 is to be put in. What are the entries? The cost of the machinery thrown out must be credited to the general account with machinery, and charged against reserves. The machinery brought in should be debited to the general account with machinery. Or, if the machinery brought in, costing $50,000, only takes the place of that which is rejected or thrown out (costing $25,000), then the whole amount should be charged to reserves.

Reserves are made day by day as the business proceeds, by way of an allowance for repairs. The wear of a machine occurs not at the time that the break happens, but during a considerable period preceding the break. As we go along we accumulate a fund with which to pay for repairs when repairs become necessary. We make the repairs to the machine and debit that amount to the reserve for repairs If we are reserving the right amount for repairs, then our annual repair bill will simply consume the reserve for that purpose. If there is a difference, then our reserve allowance should be modified accordingly.

Reserves are made for interest accounts where the amount is payable at the maturity of the loan. We have

The New Secretary of Commerce will be Expected to Act as Jack the Giant Killer.—Minneapolis Journal.

the advantage of the use of the money as we go along, but we pay for it at a future period. That amount should be reserved which is exactly equal to the payment when it comes to be made.

In every business there are bad debts. It is not right to allow the period in which the debt proves itself to be bad to stand the loss. Instead, the loss should be spread over the entire period in which the business is done. Say our loss from bad debts averages $3,120 a year. Manifestly this is in the neighborhood of $60 per week. Sixty dollars per week, then, should be charged into costs of doing business, and a corresponding credit should go to reserves for bad debts. Then as bad debts come along they are charged against this reserve. If our calculations are correct, we shall have reserved just what our bad debts cost us: no more, no less. If the reserve proves too large at the end of a given year, our accounts all having been collected, then it is expedient to reduce the allowance for another year. On the other hand, if the reserve proves too small, it is expedient to increase the rate.

What Is Depreciation?

Where two or three professional accountants are gathered together, some such question as "What is depreciation?" is very likely to be brought up for discussion. It will be found that there are almost as many opinions concerning it as there are persons taking part in the debate.

Some will stoutly maintain that there is no depreciation where repairs are maintained, and yet this argument is easily upset, because when we consider the state of the art we know that new improvements are coming along so rapidly that in certain lines of business it is almost unsafe to buy machinery. Before it can be installed, a new pattern is introduced which would give a competitor undue advantage over one who possessed the old equipment.

As we have elsewhere asserted, reserves are never to be made except they are to be used. A reserve for depreciation is something which is adjusted according to the opinion of the responsible manager of the business in a way to offset that which is being worn out. Having accumulated the credit in the reserve account, it is to be debited with the improvements and betterments which are made in the plant, in the sense of keeping it up to its original degree of efficiency.

Reserves may be defined as profits held back to make good losses. If nothing is held back, then the assets of the company would be depleted in the distribution of profits. Having held back something to make good, whenever the opportunity comes for making good, that which is held back should be freely employed.

There are various concerns throughout the country that believe in writing down their plant from six to twelve per cent per year by reason of depreciation. Not a few will charge against costs of goods manufactured an allowance of five or ten per cent. on the cost of the plant, or will deduct from gross profits this amount before making a showing for dividend purposes. They will credit plant account with the allowance, charging in the one case into the cost of goods produced, and in the other case into loss and gain account the corresponding amount.

Let us see what this leads to. Supposing that the plant is worth $100,000 and the depreciation is $10,000 per year. It must be evident that crediting the plant $10,000 the first year and $10,000 the second year, and so on in succession, that at the end of the tenth year we shall have used up the plant. This, of course, leaves out of the question renewals, betterments and replacements. Now it is hardly to be supposed that if the plant has been in use all this time that at the end of ten years it has no value. Instead, it may have a working value of a considerable amount. In all probability it is insured for anywhere from $40,000 to $60,000. The proprietors, therefore, are placed in the ridiculous position of having an asset, of no value, against which they are carrying an insurance for a considerable amount.

Evidently there is something wrong in the method. If the plant should burn down and the insurance company should resist payment of the policy, and an investigation should follow, and the bookkeeper of the concern should be put upon the stand, we can imagine a shrewd lawyer obtaining from him the confession that notwithstanding the fact that the firm carried insurance to the amount of $60,000, the value of the asset was represented by a row of big ciphers on the books. Then the question would be put to the proprietor, "How is it possible, Sir, that you are carrying insurance on an asset which by your own showing has no value whatsoever?" This certainly would be an awkward predicament.

Contrast with this plan that of allowing the plant or other asset suffering depreciation to remain on the books at its cost value. Credit the depreciation year by year, whatever it may be, to a reserve account. Now, if the plant burns and if the insurance policy is contested, the statement from the bookkeeper is that the account stood on the books at so much—the original cost. What a concern reserves against a contingency has nothing to do with the insurance and is none of the insurance adjuster's business. Instead, it relates solely to a division of profits among stockholders or partners, as the case may be.

OLDEST BIBLICAL MANUSCRIPT.

What is said to be the oldest Biblical manuscript extant was lately discovered in Syria, and is now in safekeeping at Cairo. It comprises the Pentateuch, written in Samaritan characters on gazelle parchment, and its date is the year 116 of the Moslem era, which is equivalent to the year 731, A. D. It is declared to be far older than any of the Hebrew Biblical manuscripts in the libraries of Europe or America. It is stated that the oldest manuscript in the British Museum is of the year 1339, A. D., and this has hitherto been supposed to be the oldest in the world. The newly discovered manuscript contains immediately after the Decalogue a passage of about fifteen lines that do not exist in the authorized version. It is said that this passage is likely to clear up several long-disputed points.

ENGLISH CROWDING OUT FRENCH.

English is more and more taking the place of French as the language of Russian court circles. The Czarina speaks English constantly, and the Czar, too, likes to express himself in the same tongue.

Correspondence School of

Business Organization and Administration

"Accounting is the Vital Element of Business"

TALKS WITH STUDENTS.

In a recent issue we discussed the international date line in response to a request for information on that subject from one of the students in the Institute Course of Commercial Geography. We were pleased at that time to print an article on the subject written by Mr. Henry Collins, and first published in the "School Bulletin and New York State Educational Journal." This we thought would satisfy our correspondent and end the matter, but we reckoned without our host. He wants some more. To appease his hungry longing for knowledge and also to give instruction respecting a question that is of interest to all intelligent people, and a puzzle to many, we reprint from "The School Bulletin" the concluding section of Mr. Collins' article on "The International Date Line."

In an article published in "The School Bulletin" for February, 1876, Professor Haldemann, then vice-president of Cornell University, said:

When New Year's Begins.

"Finally, it may be remarked that, as our date line is identical with no one meridian, there must be a point at its extreme eastern projection which first receives the sun's rays, and where consequently the New Year begins. This point might be called New Year's point. The place which corresponds to this point is Chatham Island."

Chatham Island in longitude about 177 degrees W. was discovered by Broughton in 1791 (named Chatham for his vessel), by westward travel, and this is doubtless the reason that Schedler has placed it on his partly traced international date line. On the other hand, J. P. Maclear, writing May 13, 1878 (see "Nature," May 16, 1878), says that the Fiji Islands, Friendly Islands, Sunday Islands and Chatham Island, have the same dating as Australia, New Zealand and Asia, but that he had forgotten which dating was used in the Navigator's (Samoan) Islands. He asserts also, that the Society Islands had this later dating, the same as the Hawaiian (Sandwich) Islands.

Mr. E. L. Layard, at the British Consulate, Noumea, New Caledona, writes as follows:

"If it is such a deadly sin to work on Sunday, one or the other of Mr. A—— and Mr. B——, coming, one from the east, the other from the west of the 180th meridian, must, if he continues his daily avocations, be in a bad way. Some of our people in Fiji are in this unenviable position, as the line 180 degrees passes through Loma-Loma. I went from Fiji to Tonga in Her Majesty's ship Nymph, and arrived at our destination on Sunday according to our reckoning from Fiji, but on Saturday, according to the proper computation west from Greenwich. We, however, found the natives all keeping Sunday. On my asking the missionaries about it they told me that the missions to that group and the Navigator's, having come from the westward, had determined to observe their Sabbath day as usual, so as not to subject the natives to any puzzle, and agreed to put the dividing line further off, between them and Hawaii, somewhere in the broad ocean, where no metaphysical natives or 'intelligent Zulus' could cross-question them."

The facts in the case as to the dating used in different settlements in and bordering on the Pacific Ocean and the changes therein, have been given.

Different Datings.

The popular idea seems to be that 180 degrees east or west of Greenwich is the point at which the change occurs; but Mr. Henkle has shown that as regards permanent settlements this is not true, and very probably never will be true. National pride is not likely to give to England the right to consider the 180th degree west of Greenwich as having any special advantage over the 180th degree west of Berlin, Paris, Vienna, Rome, Madrid, St. Petersburg, or even Washington, D. C.

"A vessel sailing from San Francisco to Samoa would reach its destination before reaching 180 degrees W. of Greenwich, and would find itself a day behind the Samoans in date. Other illustrations might be given to show that the 180th degree fiction does not remove the difficulty; for instance, as the Philippine Islands use the later dating, a navigator sailing from San Francisco to these islands, who had changed his date at 180 degrees, would find himself a day ahead on his arrival. This would not be the case if he had sailed to Yokohoma or Hong Kong, which have the advance dating. In making a round trip from San Francisco to Yokohoma, a navigator might keep his dating unchanged and thus be right on his return, or he might make two changes, skipping a day on his outward voyage at any time or place on the way, and dropping a day at any time or place on his return.

"Cruising vessels are said not to regard the 180th degree in their dates, as they might in some cases have to change their dating very frequently. In 1855 the English Pacific Squadron was ordered to co-operate with the China fleet. On meeting, their dates differed one day, one having gone by the Cape of Good Hope and the other by Cape Horn. It is said that for a time these fleets, side by side, counted the different days of the week. It has also been asserted that steamers from San Francisco to Japan alter their dates temporarily while in Japan and enter both dates in the log. The truth seems to be that navigators do as they please in this matter."

Scientific Adjustment.

On this I quote from William H. Seward's "Travels Around the World" (see page 34):

"September 16, 1870.—It was a mistake to pronounce our meeting with the steamer America, on the 6th, the event of the voyage. A greater one had just occurred. Our last date is the 14th. This note is written on the 16th. The former entry was certainly made yesterday. The chronometer marked eight o'clock at night at Greenwich, at the very hour when our clock, which keeps the running time, marked eight o'clock in the morning. We are half way around the world from Greenwich, and have lost just half a day. It is quite clear that if we should continue onward making the same discrepancy of time, we should have lost a whole day arriving at Greenwich. We might postpone the readjustment of our ship's time until we reach Greenwich, but the scientific world had wisely decided that this readjustment shall be made in every case by compromise on the 180th meridian, and, therefore, instead of striking out half a day here, we strike out a whole one."

The statement as to what the scientific world has done is hardly yet a fixed fact, and may never be true except approximately or in theory. It, however, shows that the author (Olive Risley Seward) was laboring under what Mr. Henkle is pleased to call the "180th-degree fiction."

Practical Adjustment.

Dr. T. C. Mendenhall, formerly U. S. Consul at Tokio, Japan, says that the rule with Commodore Maury, commander of the Pacific mail steamship "City of Tokio," in which he voyaged from San Francisco, is, in going west, to drop the date of a day providing the 180th degree be passed between midnight and noon, but if between noon and midnight, to drop the succeeding day. He gives the bulletin of two succeeding days posted in the smoking-room as follows:

"Wednesday, September 11, Lat. 34 degrees 40 minutes N., Long. 170 degrees 14 minutes W.

Friday, September 13, Lat. 34 degrees 33 minutes N., Long. 179 degrees 4 minutes E."

Technically, he says, Thursday was dropped, but practically they had half of Thursday, and called the last half of it Friday afternoon. He says that it is so managed that Sunday is neither dropped nor doubled, but that one commander is said to double Sunday whenever it is possible, and to have a cabin service on both days.

From this we see that for settlements the beginning of Sunday or any other day follows a very irregular line, in which changes have been made, growing out of change of allegiance, and that for those afloat changes are made, if at all, when or where the commanders or voyagers please.

Numerous proposals have been made for an initial meridian for all nations, in order to get rid of the many now in use, but no satisfactory proposition has yet been made. M. de Beaumont suggests one running through Behring Strait. Rome has also been suggested for various reasons, among them the fact that it was the home of Old and New style, and need not offend national pride, and because it is nearly on the meridian of Copenhagen, Uraniburg, Leipsig, Munich, Padua, Venice, Christiana, Gotha, Verons and Modena, and not far west of those of Berlin, Prague, Naples and Palermo. This meridian band has been called the great street of the world's observatories. With this suggestion there has been coupled the one that Rome be made 180 degrees and that no degrees be left unmarked, passing somewhere along Behring Strait, and that east and west as applied to longitude be dispensed with.

Another point may be both interesting and instructive. Taking the line as described, its most western point on the Philippine Islands is 117 degrees E., and the most eastern point is 168 degrees W. Using these limits, from the time any given time or day begins to the time it ends is 53 hours. Or taking the eastern part of Alaska, as was formerly done, which is 130 degrees E., and a day remains on the face of the earth for 55 hours and 32 seconds. Taking the former, we can see that for 5 hours each day, by the same calendar, there are three different dates in different parts of the world. These hours in Washington, D. C., and all places on or near that meridian, are from 6:10 A. M. to 11:10 A. M. For instance, during these hours of to-day, January 1, 1881, with us the Navigator's Islands are in the early part of January 2, and the Philippine Islands are finishing December 31, 1880.

These facts are curious and interesting, and possess sufficient practical importance to justify their study. Every intelligent person, with the aid of a globe, may and should become familiar with them. If this essay has enabled anyone better to understand the subject, the object of the author has been attained, in the hope that it will lead to original investigation on the part of the reader.

COLLATERAL READING.

BUSINESS CORRESPONDENCE.

The Postal Law and Delinquent Subscribers.

Students in Business Correspondence should familiarize themselves with the postal laws, in order that they may make no mistakes that will involve them in trouble with the government. The laws dealing with newspaper subscriptions, while having a direct bearing upon almost every citizen of this country—for there are few citizens who do not subscribe to some periodical—seem to be little known. An exchange has compiled seven decisions of the United States Court, bearing upon the subject of newspaper subscriptions. These seven decisions are printed below.

1. Subscribers who do not give express notice to the contrary are considered as wishing to renew their subscriptions.

2. If subscribers order the discontinuance of their periodicals the publisher may continue to send them until all arrearages are paid.

3. If subscribers neglect or refuse to take their periodicals from the postoffice to which they are directed they are responsible until they have settled their bills and ordered them discontinued.

4. If subscribers move to other places without informing the publisher, and the papers are sent to the former address they are held responsible.

5. The courts have decided that refusing to take periodicals from the office or removing and having them called for, is prima facie evidence of intentional fraud.

6. If subscribers pay in advance they are bound to give notice at the end of the time if they do not wish to continue taking it, otherwise the publisher is authorized to send it and the subscriber be responsible until an express notice, with all arrearages, is sent to the publisher.

7. The latest postal laws are such that newspaper publishers can arrest anyone for fraud who takes a paper and refuses to pay for it. Under the law the man who allows his subscription to run along for some time unpaid and then orders it discontinued, or orders the postmaster to mark it "refused," and have a postal card sent notifying the publishers, leaves himself liable to arrest and fine, the same as for theft.

It will be seen that many disputed points are disposed of by these decisions which are certainly only just. If a subscriber doesn't want to renew his subscription let him notify the publisher. The second decision given here will be a surprise to some subscribers. The delinquent must pay up if he desires to discontinue his subscription. Otherwise he is held responsible for as long as the paper is being sent to him, whether he takes it from the postoffice or not.

COMMERCIAL GEOGRAPHY.

The Building of the Pennsylvania Railroad Tunnel.

The gigantic engineering work which the Pennsylvania Railroad has undertaken to complete in a given term of years, namely, the tunnel beneath the Hudson River from Jersey City to New York, will soon be under way. The problem of how to construct this tunnel through the mud and silt that composes the bed of the North River is a matter that has commanded the attention of the best engineers in America since the plan was first outlined. The North River is a stream 50 feet deep with a bed of mud 200 feet thick above the bed-rock. Tunnel builders have found this silt to be the most treacherous material to deal with. The experts have agreed that the tunnel must have support from the bed-rock. It is at the present time an open question whether the support shall be in the form of isolated piers at a distance of 150 feet apart or a continuous pile system on which the tunnel may rest.

The question of driving the tunnel is another matter altogether and that is really the chief problem of construction. In a article published in the New York "Sun" it is stated that two plans are under consideration: one to drive the tunnel by the use of a compressed air chamber, and the other to freeze the mud by a comparatively new process and remove it as sandstone or some other soft rock might be removed.

Charles M. Jacobs, who is the chief engineer of the Pennsylvania's tunnels, submitted a plan to the commission, and as he is the head of the plan builders for the road it has been assumed that the Pennsylvania would adopt it. The Pennsylvania system is manned by scientific engineers. President Cassatt is a graduate of the Troy Polytechnic, and in his command are scores of men who have made a scientific study of the problems of construction. As the choice of the wrong method might mean a tunnel that would sink or shift in the river bed the Pennsylvania experts are going at the problem with great caution.

The Jacobs' plan is to drive each tunnel in the usual manner with a shield, a form that has been employed for many years in tunneling under water levels. The tunnel is to be lined with iron as it is driven. At intervals of 150 feet traps are to be cut in this lining in the bottom of the tunnel, and through them cylinder piers sunk to bed rock. Trusses erected inside the lining and firmly attached to it are to rest on the piers. In this way the trusses will carry all the loads and transit them to the piers, and the lining will be saved that strain.

Since Mr. Jacobs' plan was submitted another has been laid before the commission by Charles Sooysmith, one of

John Bull—We haven't a difference in the world now, Brother Jonathan.
Jonathan—First time in 130 years, John. I'm afeard something 'll happen now so we won't be friends.—Minneapolis Journal.

the consulting engineers of the contractors who are building the rapid transit tunnel. Mr. Sooysmith is known for his achievements in subaqueous construction. When the freezing process for sinking shafts was invented in Germany, Mr. Sooysmith went abroad and got the American rights. He now holds patents on processes and devices for tunnel driving on the same theory. Mr. Sooysmith's scheme differs from that of Mr. Jacobs' in the beginning, because he holds a continuous line of piles to

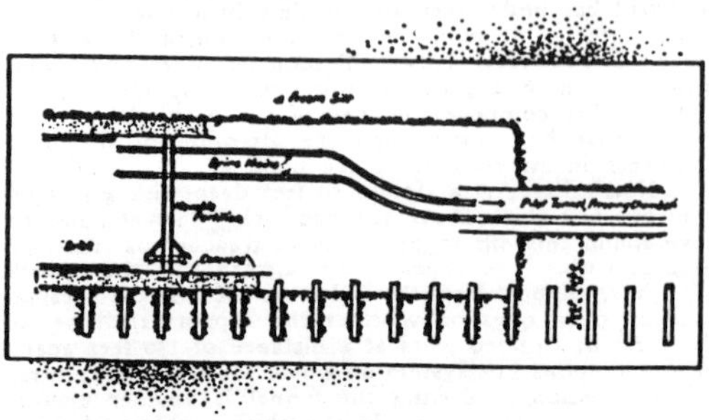

Fig. 1. Arrangement of Freezing Pilot and Method of Constructing the Tunnel Back of it.

be a better rest for the tunnel than the isolated piers. The tunnel structure, unless material is added to give it weight, would be generally lighter than the silt it displaces, and would therefore have a tendency to rise rather than to settle. This would make any provision for a supporting structure unnecessary, were it not that the factor of the varying load and weight and the vibration of traffic is of real importance. The bed of silt which might support a quiescent load indefinitely without settlement might give way at any moment with a lighter load which brought with it a slight pounding. The vibration of the moving trains must be transmitted to a larger mass of the underlying silt so that the shock will be dissipated.

Mr. Sooysmith's plan accepts as true that a continuous pile foundation is the ideal one, and he has called the attention of the commission to the pile piers along the river front, which show how great and permanent the bearing capacity of such a formation may be made.

To sink this line of piles across the river will be comparatively simple. Mr. Sooysmith thinks. A steel tube large enough to receive the pile would be jetted down in the same manner as a pile until its lower end reached the level at which the bottom of the tunnel would be, probably thirty-five feet under the mud. The pile would then be telescoped through the tube and driven through the slit with a Nasmyth hammer, which, with the help of compressed air, may be operated under water.

The piles could easily be driven so that they would be at the exact level desired. With this pile support laid Mr. Sooysmith would then proceed to construct the tunnel by the freezing process.

In Europe this method has been employed in sinking many deep shafts. In this country it has been used but once, for few jobs have called for so much work as to warrant the installation of a refrigerating plant. The system has not been used for horizontal tunnel work, but a number of engineers have given the opinion that it could be operated perfectly for just such a job as the Hudson River tunnels will be.

The difficulty and great cost of constructing subaqueous tunnels by compressed air is due to the difference of hydrostatic head at the top and bottom of the heading and to the size of the shield that is necessary. A small tunnel, not more than six or seven feet in diameter, may be constructed through the most difficult material with comparatively small expense. But the Pennsylvania tunnel tubes are to have an interior diameter of nineteen feet, which will make the excavated tunnel about twenty-three feet in diameter. The driving of so large a tunnel through silt must be slow and highly expensive. The workmen have to cope with the difficulties of working in a compressed air chamber, and accidents costing life and meaning delay and damage to the work done are not infrequent.

The freezing system as it is put to use in shaft sinking consists of sinking vertical pipes around the site of the shaft. These pipes are closed at the bottom, and each contains a smaller pipe open at the bottom. Brine, cooled by an ice machine, is circulated through these pipes until a frozen wall is made, shutting off the water and sand and permitting the excavation and shaft work to be done within the protection of this frozen cofferdam.

For the tunnel work Mr. Sooysmith has planned a small tunnel, to be built in the usual way. This he calls the pilot tunnel. It will be about six feet in diameter in the center line of the main tunnel. This pilot tunnel will be used as a refrigerating chamber. By maintaining a temperature below zero, Fahrenheit, in this chamber the surrounding silt will be frozen into a substance which may be dealt with much like sandstone.

The pilot tunnel will be lined temporarily with metal plates and the refrigerated brine circulated through pipes laid against this lining, leaving the center unobstructed, so that the freezing may follow closely the excavation of the pilot tunnel. The pilot tunnel may be extended while the freezing is going on. As the Pennsylvania tunnels will require a very large excavation, the freezing process would be hastened by pushing out radial tubes from the pilot tunnel and circulating the brine through these. In some work done at Iron Mountain, Mich., the material was frozen to a distance of nine feet in seventy-two days from pipes eight inches in diameter, with brine at zero temperature. Thus the material may be solidified to a sufficient distance to enable the full-sized tunnel to be excavated at one time, still leaving an ample protection of frozen material outside the excavation.

Another plan of procedure which Mr. Sooysmith suggests is not to use the radial pipes, but to do all the freezing from the pilot tunnel, which could be enlarged gradually until it was made of the desired size. This scheme calls for the use of refrigerated air instead of brine.

Experiments in shaft sinking at Iron Mountain and with silt dredged from the Hudson River, have enabled Mr. Sooysmith to estimate very closely the cost of this process. Tests made on the frozen silt show it to be of the strength of good concrete, so that two or three feet of frozen material would suffice to prevent a collapse.

The frozen silt may be blasted and removed in large sections. It is as easy to handle as sandstone, and Mr. Sooysmith believes that the tunnel may be constructed with the greatest speed if this plan be followed.

The pilot tunnel might be built at the rate of ten to fifteen feet a day at a cost of less than $20 a foot. The frozen silt could be mined and brought to the surface, he estimates, at less than $1 a cubic yard.

The silt will remain frozen around the tunnel excavation long enough to permit the construction work, which, however, would follow closely to the finished excavation.

Another question has been raised as to the feasibility of building the tunnel structure of masonry against frozen earth. It is stated that freezing does not seriously, if at all, injure Portland cement, and that it will be possible to keep the temperature of the masonry work above zero long enough to let the cement set, while at the same time the frozen wall outside can be maintained.

Mr. Sooysmith has pointed out to the Pennsylvania engineers' commission that his plan obviates the use of the pneumatic shield, which calls for the construction of a heavy and costly structure of cast iron that would thereafter be subject to the danger of cracking from the vibration of moving trains, a result which would be most serious to an under-water tunnel.

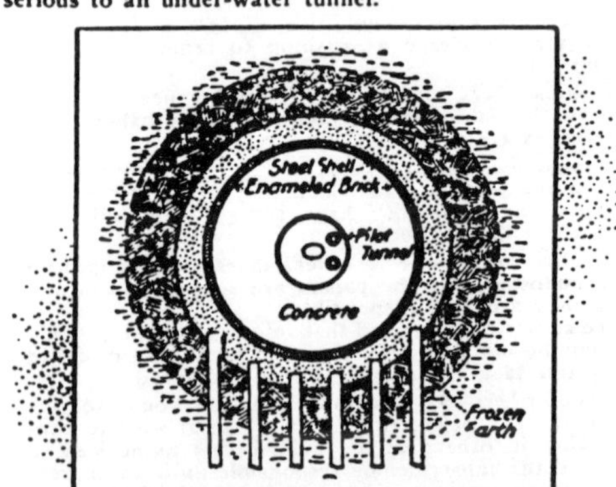

Fig. 2. End View of Tunnel Construction.

The freezing method, he points out, permits the excavation of a chamber, in which, open to inspection at all times, a much better and cheaper tunnel wall may be built, consisting of a steel shell imbedded in concrete. Any desired material or design may be used. Such a tunnel can be built in exact grade and alignment, a matter of much difficulty in driving a tunnel with a shield. By the freezing method the tunnel may be located closer to the bed of the river, thus reducing the grade. Besides these advantages Mr. Sooysmith claims the additional one of a great reduction in expense.

The Management of Scrapbooks

To many men of affairs a scrapbook has become an indispensable appliance. Whether of a size for handy reference at home or in the office, or small and compact for carrying in the pocket, it is of great convenience. The newspapers and magazines are filled with short articles that are worth preserving, and unless these are pasted in a scrapbook they are bound, sooner or later, to be lost. W. L. Brown, in the "Industrial World," gives some hints as to the management of scrapbooks that are worth reading. Mr. Brown says:

The plan for preserving printed extracts which I have devised and herewith describe, although very simple, appears to have been previously unknown to the many to whom I have shown it, and it may therefore be of some interest to those of your readers who desire, as I did, to find a convenient and systematic method for keeping such cuttings. It consists of a set of Mark Twain scrapbooks of a uniform size, 8¼ inches long by 3⅝ inches wide, each book containing twenty-four gummed pages. Such a size is handy for the pocket, whenever it may become necessary to temporarily remove a book. Upon the outside of each book is a gummed label on which is written the title of the subject comprised within, and the entire series is then arranged in alphabetical order in one of my desk drawers, and accessible from my chair. I keep one book for each subject I am interested in; hence, as concerns any one else, the number of books and subjects will depend upon the habits, tastes, profession, or business of the individual. As an illustration of the ground covered, I give my own list of subjects, which would, probably, suit only chemists, and possibly only those doing chemical work for railroads, but the principle applies to any other profession, trade, business or occupation.

1. Adulteration of food. 2. Antiseptics and disinfectants. 3. Apparatus (chemical, etc.). 4. Books (reviews, lists, advertisements, etc.). 5. Butter, cheese. 6. Chemistry—applied to arts and manufactures. 7. Chemistry—tests, reactions. 8. Coal. 9. Colors and dyes. 10. Fats and oils. 11. Health. 12. Indexes. 13. Lacquers, varnishes, etc. 14. Linseed oil. 15. Lubrication. 16. Metallurgy. 17. Metals and alloys. 18. Milk. 19. Mineralogy. 20. Miscellaneous. 21. Paints—miscellaneous. 22. Paints—analysis of. 23. Paints—lectures on. 24. Petroleum and its compounds. 25. Poisons. 26. Preservation of timber. 27. Railroad chemistry. 28. Rails. 29. Receipts. 30. Soaps. 31. Steel and iron. 32. Steel and iron—methods of analysis. 33. Sugar (sorghum, candy, etc.). 34. Tables. 35. Water.

The above set of thirty-five books does not quite fill an ordinary desk drawer. Of course, discretion is to be observed in preserving cuttings, but when such care is used the result will be extremely valuable articles, notes and references. If a subject grows too much for one book add a second, and more if necessary. The above system retains in a convenient form extracts from papers which one does not care to preserve entire. When, for any reason, it is not advisable to cut or paste an article, yet it is wished to have it filed, and when wanted quickly found, use either Breed's scrapbook album, which consists of a number of large envelopes bound together as a book and properly numbered and lettered, or Colton's portfolio file and scrapbook, which is also a number of stout envelopes held together between covers by means of tape. Each envelope of the latter is numbered and ruled for writing on the outside. For letters, papers and printed extracts of larger size there are many more or less extensive, expensive and complicated holders, cases and cabinets well known to business men. A simple one is Pilger's Burlington file, being a large brown paper envelope with twenty-two divisions alphebetically labeled; it pulls out like an accordion. For pamphlets, the Globe case is about the strongest and best. I use a number of them to include many subjects. When one becomes too full the pamphlets should be bound, those of a kind together, and then a book is ready for the library.

Finally the index rerum or commonplace book. Of course, more than one can be prepared; accordingly, as the owner is interested in the sciences, art, literature, etc., but even one made miscellaneous is of value. For this purpose take a large blank book and divide it into twenty-six parts for the letters of the alphabet, giving the greatest number of pages to those letters which begin the greatest number of words in the English language, as B, C, D, P, R, S and T, and from one to four pages to those like J, K, Q, X and Z, etc. For a book of 500 pages the following numbers will divide the pages about as they should be allotted.

A, 37	F, 21	K, 4	P, 40	U, 12
B, 27	G, 15	L, 16	Q, 4	V, 10
C, 52	H, 15	M, 22	R, 25	W, 14
D, 31	I, 16	N, 16	S, 53	X, 1
E, 21	J, 4	O, 14	T, 25	Y, 4
				Z, 1

Now subdivide each group of pages into five parts for the vowels, thus, Aa, Ae, Ai, Ao and Au, and so with the others. References can thus be classified sufficiently closely, the first letter of the principal word of the reference and the first vowel following it determining its place, as bronze under Bo, stell under Se, etc. Where the number of pages given to any letter cannot be evenly divided by five give the preference to "a" and "o" over the others, and to all the other four over "u"; thus for A make them Aa, eight; Ae, eight, and the others seven each or thirty-seven in all. Double or cross references can be indulged in if desired.

The above described systems of keeping track of items, scraps, articles and references if carefully kept up (and really very little time is needed for them when once under full way) will be sufficient to thoroughly post any ordinary person in the particular lines he may be interested in.

AN AWFUL STATE OF THINGS.

In the State of Mass.
There lives a lass
I love to go N. C.;
No other Miss.,
Can e'er, I Wis.,
Be half so dear to Me.

R. I. is blue,
And her cheeks the hue
Of shells where waters swash;
On her pink-white phiz
There Nev. Ariz.
The least complexion Wash.

La! could I win
The heart of Minn.,
I'd ask for nothing more,
But I only dream
Upon the theme
And Conn. it o'er and Ore.

Why is it, pray,
I can't Ala.
This love that makes me Ill.?
N. Y., O., Wy.
Kan. Nev. Ver. I
Propose to her my will?

I shun the task
'Twould be to ask
This gentle maid to wed;
And so, to press
My suit, I guess
Alaska Pa. instead.—Brooklyn Eagle.

INDIGNATION WASTED.

"That coal I bought here a week ago," he said, "is the worst I have had in ten years. There's a great quantity of slate in it, and what isn't slate runs to clinkers."

"Sorry to hear it, Mr. Williams," said the coal dealer's clerk inside the railing, as reported by "Shoe and Leather." "I'll make a memorandum of it. Perhaps the company will give you a rebate of it."

Taking a slip of paper he wrote a few words on it and hung it on a hook.

The customer, happening to glance at the slip of paper, saw this: "G. G. Williams, Bad Egg."

"So I'm a bad egg, am I?" he asked, reddening with indignation.

"Oh, not at all, Mr. Williams," hastily explained the clerk. "That means that the egg coal we sold you turns out to be bad."

And then the customer reddened again, but not from indignation.

Account Audit & Assurance Company

25 PINE STREET NEW YORK

WHAT BALANCE SHEET ACCOUNTING DOES.

I.—Initially, it provides an adequate analysis of the accounts of the business, thereby securing a proper representation of the transactions upon the books.

II.—It classifies the daily details of transactions in a way to show "going" results.

III.—The assets of the business are correctly and completely represented at all dates.

IV.—The liabilities of the business are correctly and completely represented at all dates.

V.—The gross profits on goods sold are always shown and there is presented in contrast therewith the total costs of doing business, thereby revealing net profits.

VI.—Among the assets, in the case of a manufacturing business, there are always shown the cost value of the materials and supplies on hand, the cost to date of the work or orders in progress, and the cost of the finished product on hand.

VII.—All this is presented without the preparation of a physical inventory. Inventorying, like counting cash, is resorted to, only for the purpose of verification and proof.

VIII.—The usual fiscal period is abolished. Net profits to date are shown daily (as in department stores), weekly (as in a mercantile business) or once in each four weeks (as in the case of a manufacturing business), according to the time schedule adopted.

IX.—The work of annually or semi-annually closing the books is abolished. The books are always closed and at the same time are always open. Results to date can be easily read from the Balance Sheet Ledger at any and all times.

X.—The labor of maintaining Balance Sheet Accounting, when the system is once in operation, is no greater than that of ordinary double entry. In many cases it has proven to be considerably less.

XI.—The Proof-By-Balance System of Cost Accounts, a constituent element of the Balance Sheet plan, gives the exact cost of goods produced in a factory. There are no estimates. The results are always definite and exact.

XII.—Factories are run at "even keel." The entire cost of the manufacturing department for a given period is balanced by the aggregate of the cost of the individual lots of goods put through.

XIII.—The Balance Sheet System provides that no payments to workmen (pay-roll) shall be made until the amount of their time has been charged to an order in process. Accordingly there is no time paid for that is not accounted for. Charges to orders in process offset the pay-roll amount. Non-productive labor is handled by prorating its amount over the orders in process.

XIV.—Balance Sheet Accounting is the only system of accounting ever introduced. It is complete. From established premises it reaches definite and exact conclusions.

XV.—Balance Sheet Accounting is eclectic in its elements, and uses as its component parts in the way of ledgers, blanks and forms, various items that are adapted to the purpose in view without reference to their source or origin.

XVI.—Balance Sheet Accounting begins with a balance sheet, ends with a balance sheet and maintains a balance sheet between times.

XVII.—Balance Sheet Accounting facilitates business management. It shows shortages and neglect wherever the same occur. It definitely fixes responsibility. It necessitates order and method in accounting affairs.

XVIII.—Balance Sheet Accounting improves the bookkeeper's position by enabling him to keep all his work up-to-date and by defining a day's duties.

XIX.—In Balance Sheet Accounting there is no back work. Instead, everything is finished as it proceeds.

XX.—The Balance Sheet Ledger upon the business manager's desk in the morning, among other interesting and valuable particulars, gives him the following:

Amount of cash receipts of the preceding day.
Amount of cash disbursements.
Balance on hand and where located.

Amounts charged to customers.
Amounts credited to customers.
Balance owing by customers.

Amounts credited to Purchase Creditors.
Amounts charged to Purchase Creditors.
Balance owing to Purchase Creditors.

Amount of goods (merchandise) taken in.
Amount of goods sent out.
Balance on hand.

Amount of goods sold.
Cost of goods sold.
Gross profit.

Expenses of doing business (viz., clerk hire, rent, advertising, insurance, etc.)

XXI.—Similar facts as to receipts, disbursements and balances are afforded of Notes Receivable and Notes Payable, Sundry Debtors, Sundry Creditors, etc.

XXII.—Balance Sheet Accounting is not "ready made." Instead, it is always "custom made," and made to fit the business after the most careful measurements have been taken. The preceding epitome of Balance Sheet Ledger showings is to be accepted as typical and not as specific.

XXIII.—The Balance Sheet System adapted to your business will give you the exact showings you require, presented in the way you want them and at the time they will be most serviceable to you in planning and managing.

XXIV.—Balance Sheet Accounting is scientific. All its provisions are based upon an accurate and adequate "chart" of the accounts.

XXV.—Balance Sheet Accounting is installed upon the specification plan. A carefully prepared specification, based upon the chart of accounts, is prepared, which stands to the accounting system very much as an architect's specification stands to a building about to be erected.

XXVI.—Each specification is illustrated by drawings of the rulings, blanks and forms required, and by diagrams showing the relationship of the different parts one to the other.

For further particulars, address **Account, Audit and Assurance Company, 25 Pine street, New York.**

BOOKS OF INTEREST TO BUSINESS MEN.

The A B C of Banks and Banking. —By George M. Coffin. 6¼ x 5 inches; 137 pages. Bound in cloth. Back title gilt. Price, $1.25.

This handy little volume is exactly what its name implies; that is, a presentation of the principles underlying banking in the United States. The author in his preface says that it is designed to appeal to the reader outside as well as inside of a bank. It is by no means the last word or every word about banking. It may be said that it is a primer covering a field that has hitherto been somewhat neglected. The chapter heads are as follows: Banking in General, Various Kinds of Banking, Capital Stock, Shareholders' Rights and Liabilities, Undivided Profits, Dividends and Surplus, Deposits, Checks, Lawful Money Reserve, Issuing Bank Notes, Borrowing Money, Loans and Discounts, Exchanges, Collections, Letters of Credit, Bonds, Mortgages and Stocks, Bank Reports, Examinations, Directors, Executive Officers—Their Powers and Duties, Internal Administration and Bookkeeping, and other suggestions.

Business Law.—By Alonzo R. Weed, L. L. B., of the Boston Bar. 6 x 9¼ inches; 172 pages. Bound in cloth. Cover and back title red. Price, $1.25.

Mr. Weed calls his book "a manual for schools and colleges and for every day use." The titles of the chapters are as follows: Contracts, Principal and Agent, Partnerships, Sales of Personal Property, Bailments and Common Carriers, Negotiable Paper, Deeds, Mortgages and Leases, Collection Laws, Written Rates of Interest, Insurance, Patent Rights, Trade Marks and Copyrights, etc.

The author does not waste words, and yet treats his subjects clearly and comprehensively. In short, he gives the law without the addition of wordy "trimmings."

Introduction to the Study of Economics.—By Charles Jesse Bullock, Ph. D. 7¼ x 5½ inches. 581 pages. Bound in cloth. Cover and back title gilt. Price, $1.25.

This book, the author says, is designed as an introductive text book of economic science. Throughout the volume economics are discussed with special reference to American conditions, and their workings are illustrated by frequent allusions to American experience. There are chapters on the Consumption of Wealth, the Theory of Exchange, the Development of Metallic Money, Money and Credit, and the like.

Political Economy of Humanism.—By Henry Wood. 7¼ x 5¼ inches; 320 pages. Bound in cloth. Cover and back title gilt. Price, $1.25.

Mr. Wood is well known as a writer on various economic subjects, and this book contains a series of able treatises, written in his usual vein, on the relation of the employer to the employed, and the phases of the industrial question and their relation to socialism. Among the questions considered and handled in a conservative spirit and with much common sense, are the following: Supply and Demand, the Law of Competition, Labor and Production, Combinations of Capital, Combinations of Labor, Employers and Profit Sharing, the Obligations and Privileges of Employees, the Unequal Distribution of Wealth, Money and Coinage, Tariffs and Protection, Industrial Education and Gold Production and Values.

The Kite Trust, A Romance of Wealth.—By Lebbeus Harding Rogers. 7¼ x 5½ inches; 475 pages. Illustrated. Price, $1.50.

This is a treatise or series of treatises on economic subjects in the guise of a story. The tale itself concerns three American boys, and is very interesting as well as instructive. The trust idea is explained and an explanation of banking is given. The greenback is dealt with as are also Wall street and stock speculation.

Business Law.—By Thomas Raeburn White, B. L., L. L. B. 5 x 7½ inches; 323 pages. Bound in cloth. Back title gilt. Price, $1.50.

This is a neat, compact and handy book of business for law for the use of students and business men. Among the subjects treated are Contracts, Sales, Partnerships, Corporations, Negotiable Paper and the like. The author's language is plain, and is understandable by any one having no previous knowledge of law. The book's clearness on the essential points of ordinary law should recommend it as a business book for the plain business man who has no time in which to consult a law library.

The Phonographic Dictionary and Phrase Book.—By Benn Pitman and Jerome B. Howard. 5½ x 8 inches; 552 pages. Bound in cloth. Cover title and back title gilt. Price, $3.

This book is the most elaborate shorthand dictionary yet published, with the characters in facsimile. It contains over 120,000 words, and for every one of these words there is a corresponding sign in the Benn Pitman system of shorthand. To the reporter, office or court stenographer, or any one writing the Benn Pitman system of shorthand, the book is invaluable. It is well made, tastefully bound, and is printed on a good quality of paper in clean, plain type.

Grace's Handy Book for Making Rapid Calculations. 8¼ x 5¼ inches. Bound in cloth. 65 pages. Title printed in silver. Price, $1.

The full title of this book is "Merchants', Bankers' and Brokers' Handy Book for Making Rapid Calculations in all Branches of Commercial Requirements, Weights, Measures and Moneys." The volume contains a series of tables for calculating the price of wheat, corn and oat bushels in decimals, for converting cubic meters to cubic feet and cubic feet to meters, meters to lineal yards, superficial feet or square feet to cubic feet, decimal tons to avoirdupois pounds, and the like. To the busy office man who has a great deal of calculating to do, and particularly to the clerk in an export house whose work it is to reckon in United States money the amounts named in foreign invoices, these tables should be very valuable. They are quite complete, and undoubtedly their use will save time.

The Lawrence System of Vocal and Physical Expression.—By Edwin Gordon Lawrence. 4¾ x 6 inches; 128 pages. Bound in cloth. Cover title and back title gilt. Price, $1.

The author says in the preface of this little book that his object has been to place in the hands of lawyers, actors and public speakers in general, a simple system of vocal and physical expression that will enable them to clearly convey thought by word of mouth and emphasize it by the proper action. To the man of affairs who is called upon for a speech on any subject, and who knows what to say but does not know how to say it, this book will be a great help.

The Anatomy of a Railroad Report. —By Thomas F. Woodlock. 7 x 5¼ inches. 121 pages. Bound in cloth. Side and back titles gilt. Price, $1.

This little book is intended for the use of those people who, while interested in railroad investments, are wholly unacquainted with railroad accounts. The book is divided into two sections, the first being the Anatomy of the Railroad Report and the second being Ton-Mile Cost. It treats of phases of the railroad business in concise fashion, but thoroughly and accurately.

Any book in this list will be sent to any address in the United States, Canada or Mexico upon receipt of price. If there is some special book that you require we shall be pleased to hunt it up for you.

Address **Commerce, Accounts & Finan.e, 25 Pine street, New York City.**

TITLE GUARANTEE AND TRUST COMPANY

Does each year an increasing proportion of the whole business of examining titles and making mortgage loans in New York City. Last year it loaned

Over Thirty-Five Million Dollars

on real estate in New York City. When you buy real estate, or borrow on it, come to this company. Fees moderate and uniform.

Capital and Surplus, $6,000,000

146 Broadway, MANHATTAN. 175 Remsen St., BROOKLYN.

HAVE YOU READ

The Kite Trust?

If not, why not? Send $1.50 for a copy to

Commerce, Accounts & Finance, 25 Pine street, New York City.

Stationery Manufacturing Company

86 FULTON STREET NEW YORK

The Voucher Check.

The voucher check has come to be the check of to-day. A few years ago, in a clumsy and crude form, it was brought forward in the nature of a business experiment. Business men were quick to see and recognize its essential safeguard features, but were also cognizant of its shortcomings in the shape in which it was then presented. Bankers, also, while recognizing the good points of the old-fashioned voucher check, were dissatisfied with its large size and the folding feature, which were its principal drawbacks.

The voucher check, however, even in that crude state, came nearer to being what the business man was looking for in the check line than anything before presented, and many firms adopted it even though it was cumbersome and hard to handle.

Some time ago we began experimenting with the idea of combining the voucher idea with the convenient size of the bank check. After a number of experiments we have succeeded in perfecting several styles of voucher check, that, while embodying all the good features of the old-fashioned folding variety, are yet no larger than the ordinary check furnished to depositors by banks. We have sold a great number of checks of this kind, and in each case they have been hailed as exactly what the business man is looking for—that is, a check that shall show upon its face not only to whom it was drawn and for what amount, but the items for which it is tendered in payment; the correctness of said items and the amount of the check being vouched for by the bookkeeper and the officers of the paying firm or company.

In Fig. 1 is shown a facsimile of one of our styles of voucher check.

Fig. 1. Face-Voucher Check. Dimensions, 8 1-2 x 3 1-4 inches. Everything on its face, and no folding. (Patent pending.)

We ask careful consideration for this design of check, which has not only received the cordial approval of many of the leading firms of this country, but has also been enthusiastically approved by the banks. It overcomes fully all the objections raised against the old-fashioned varieties.

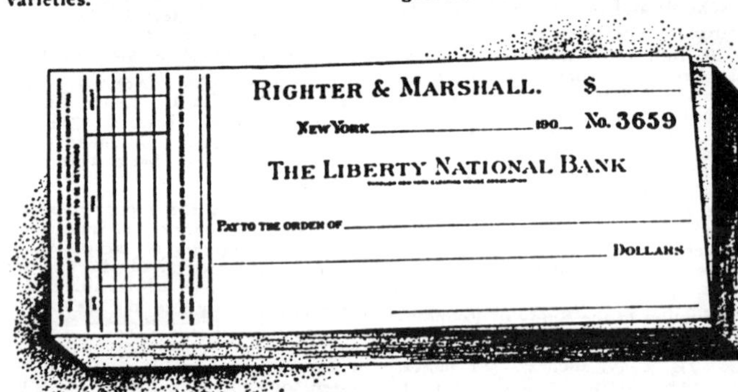

Fig. 2 Another form of Face-Voucher Check, with the voucher form differently located. (Patent pending.)

The reader is asked to notice what precedes and follows the voucher form. The voucher itself is drawn in such a way that the endorsement of the check makes it a receipt for the amount, thus avoiding the necessity of stipulating special receipts and the expense later on of filing them. In the process of issuing the check the bookkeeper or ledger clerk first certifies to the correctness of the amount for which the check is drawn; thereafter follows the signature of the firm or the officers of the company as the case may be.

The check drawn in Fig. 2 differs only from that in Fig. 1 in that the voucher form is placed in a different position upon the face of the check. There is no folding, no turning over the check for the filling in of forms upon its back—in short, none of the cumbersome methods that made the old-fashioned voucher check so unhandy.

Many representative firms are using, in connection with these voucher checks, our Multi-Bank Check Register System. Particulars of this system, which does away entirely with the old-style check book, and substitutes therefor something infinitely better and more up-to-date, will be furnished upon application. The checks shown in the illustrations are put up in pads for use with this system.

We are now in a position to furnish at short notice quantities of voucher checks of these general styles, put up in pads or bound and printed to suit the requirements of the firms purchasing them. We are also prepared to submit special designs embodying the general principles of the foregoing. Having at our disposal a competent staff of designers and engravers we are in a position to furnish on order the most handsome and elaborate checks that money can buy.

Prices will be gladly quoted upon request and estimates furnished. We solicit correspondence. Address communications,

Stationery Manufacturing Company, 86 Fulton street, New York City.

R·I·P·A·N·S

There is scarcely any condition of ill-health that is not benefited by the occasional use of a R·I·P·A·N·S Tabule. For sale by Druggists. The Five-Cent packet is enough for an ordinary occasion. The family bottle, 60 cents, contains a supply for a year.

A New Work on Accounting

A MANUAL OF BOOKKEEPING

By J. THORNTON

THIS attractive volume, comprising over 500 pages, with numerous illustrations, is one of the clearest and most concise surveys of the principles of accounting which has recently appeared. While its illustrations are given in terms of English money the bookkeeping principles discussed are universal.

The work is divided into two leading parts, the first of which is "LAWS AND PRINCIPLES," and the second "APPLICATION."

LAWS AND PRINCIPLES

In the first part there are discussed the Principle of Exchanges, the Principle of Debit and Credit Accounts, the Principle of the Classification of Accounts, the Principle of Ledger Entries, the Principle of Proving, the Principle of Transfer from Preparatory to Final Record, and the Principle of Balancing and Closing the Ledger.

APPLICATION

Under the head of Application the following chapters are presented: Rules and Tools, What Capital Consists of, Capital in Cash, Capital in Bills, Capital in Debts, Capital in Goods, Fixed Capital, Profit and Loss, Capitalist's Accounts, Company Bookkeeping, Errors, and Non-Capitalistic Bookkeeping.

Several chapters are arranged in the form of lessons, following which are questions for class purposes, arranged in such a way, however, as not to detract in the least from the value of the book in the hands of the general reader. A comprehensive index, together with answers to exercises completes the work.

Price, $2.50.—Sent Postpaid to any address in the United States on receipt of price.

Address **COMMERCE ACCOUNTS & FINANCE CO.**

PUBLISHERS AND BOOKSELLERS - 25 PINE STREET, NEW YORK

BUSINESS NEEDS.

Advertisements under this head one cent a word each insertion.

A FEW WORDS ABOUT PRINTING.

Printing is done artistically or it is done inartistically. Some people want cheap printing and some people want the best printing. What kind do you want? I can give you figures on either kind of printing that will give you satisfaction and the goods delivered will insure your future orders. Try an estimate from "The Printing Press," care Commerce, Accounts & Finance.

BOOKS! BOOKS! BOOKS!

Do you need any books? We are glad to furnish you any information about any book that you may want. We will give you prices. We will tell you what book you are looking for, perhaps. At any rate, write "The Old Book Man," care of Commerce, Accounts & Finance.

I AM A THOROUGHLY experienced office man, familiar with the details of office routine and competent to take charge of any force of employees. Am thirty years of age, and can furnish the best of references as to integrity, character and ability. Address "Adaptable," care of Commerce, Accounts & Finance.

WANTED—COMPETENT bookkeeper for railroad machinists and boilermakers in a small town ninety miles from New York City, good wages and fair treatment. Address "G. H. T.," care of Commerce, Accounts & Finance.

IS YOUR SAFE CAPACIOUS enough to hold your books and papers? I act as an intermediary between persons or firms who need safes and those who have them to dispose of. I don't sell new safes for old safes, but I do know people who want your old safe and I can sell you a new safe at the lowest possible price. Second-hand safes at very low figures. In writing to me write to "A Safe Man," care of Commerce, Accounts & Finance.

ROLL TOP DESKS, office furniture and office labor-saving devices can be obtained in every variety of style and price. Write for further information to "T. G. S.," care of Commerce, Accounts & Finance.

MY NAME IS FRED COOK. I have asked you before through these columns if you need any one to write an advertisement for you, prepare a circular or draft out a catalogue. I do these things and do them well enough to earn a good living. Why not drop me a line care of Commerce, Accounts & Finance, and I think that I can show you some things that will interest you.

TYPEWRITERS — SOLD ON weekly payments as low as $1 a week. All styles. Address "Brown," care of Commerce, Accounts & Finance.

BOOKS BOUGHT AND SOLD. Books of every description bought for highest cash prices. Send postal for further information. Address L., 823 B., care Commerce, Accounts & Finance.

A BUSINESS EDUCATION	FOR ..ONE.. DOLLAR.

...THE PRACTICAL AGE...

A MONTHLY MAGAZINE full to the brim with helpful suggestions to young men and young women who are struggling successward.

THE BUSINESS HOUSE THAT JACK BUILT, an intensely interesting and highly instructive story of business life, and

APPLIED ENGLISH, an authority on writing and speaking the English language, which no young person can afford to be without, all for ONE DOLLAR.

If you have never seen THE PRACTICAL AGE, send for a free sample copy. Address,

THE PRACTICAL AGE,

Moline, Illinois.

Use any pen and your own stationery. If your stationer does not keep it, write for free specimen of work. Beware of infringements. Address Dept.

Pen-Carbon Manifold Co., 145-7-9 Centre St., New York.

OUT THIS MONTH

The Science of Loose Leaf Bookkeeping and Accounting

By CHAS. A. SWEETLAND, Public Accountant

UNIQUE AND UP-TO-DATE

THE PIONEER WORK

Covering the practical application in detail of this modern system of accounting. Over 200 pages of valuable information. Of interest to both users and non-users of LOOSE LEAF SYSTEMS.

MR. FRANKLIN, WITH HASKINS & SELLS, NEW YORK, SAYS,
"A magnificent reference."

MR. STONE, HEAD BOOKKEEPER OF MEYER BROS. DRUG CO., ST. LOUIS, SAYS,
"A valuable acquisition."

MR. SYLVANUS, LATE OF HASKINS & SELLS, NEW YORK, SAYS,
"No bookkeeper can afford to be without it."

Price, cloth bound, post paid, $2 00 per copy. Remit by draft or P. O. Order. Published by the author.

CHAS. A. SWEETLAND, Room, 664 Century Building, ST. LOUIS, MO.

The Theory of Accounts.

JUST PUBLISHED Price, $3.00

Being all questions set in this subject at the New York C. P. A. examinations from December, 1896, to June, 1902, inclusive, with full answers and explanations, by

FREDERICK S. TIPSON, C. P. A.

To follow at short intervals also:

COMMERCIAL LAW, AUDITING, PRACTICAL ACCOUNTING.

Published by the Author, 150 Nassau Street, NEW YORK

C. P. A. Examinations:

Students thoroughly prepared, either by correspondence or personal instruction, for C. P. A. examinations in all States which grant this diploma. References to students who were successful in January and June, 1900, 1901 and 1902. The only successful candidate at the New York State C. P. A. examination in June, 1900, was coached by

FRED'K S. TIPSON, C. P. A.

150 NASSAU ST., NEW YORK CITY

PUBLIC ACCOUNTANTS.

Atlanta, Ga.—Ralph H. Brown, 804 Empire Building.

Boston, Mass.—Charles H. Fellows, 174 Summer; New England Audit Company, 45 Milk; J. S. Parsons, 214 Columbus Ave.

Brooklyn, N. Y.—Franklin Allen, Arbuckle Building, 371 Fulton.

Buffalo, N. Y.—W. G. Mowat, 831 Ellicott Square.

Chicago, Ill.—Haskins & Sells, 214 Dearborn.

Davenport, Ia.—J. C. Grabbe, McManus Building.

Detroit, Mich.—H. Naemansson, 496 Putnam Ave.

London, Canada.—Geo. F. Jewell, 361 Dundas.

Montreal, Canada.—George Gontheir, 11-17 Place D'Armes Hill.

New Bedford, Mass.—James L. Hathway, 72 Willis.

New Orleans, La.—P. W. Sherwood, 904 Howard Ave.

New York, N. Y.—Patterson, Teele & Dennis, 30 Broad; Haskins & Sells, 30 Broad; Account, Audit and Assurance Company, 25 Pine; Leon Brummer, 7 Pine; H. F. Searle, 45 Broadway; Hart Bros., Tibbits, Heiron & Co., 11 Broadway; Franklin Allen, Silk Exchange Building, Broadway.

Philadelphia, Pa.—Francis & Sterrett, Penn Mutual Building; Peter Ballingall, German-American Building; Charles W. Thomas, 409 Lippincott Building; Alfred L. Sellers, 1001 Chestnut.

Pittsburgh, Pa.—John Vaughan, 5520 Claybourne; George W. Wood & Co., 341 Fourth Ave.

Providence, R. I.—George R. Allen, 29 Weybosset.

San Francisco, Cal.—Charles L. Lutgen, 218 California; Lester Herrick, 405 Montgomery.

Toronto, Canada.—F. H. Kidd, Bank of Commerce Building.

Windsor, Canada.—F. H. Macpherson, 16 Sandwich, East.

Winnipeg, Canada.—Peter Thornton, 343 Main.

60 DAY CLOCKS

Prentiss 60 day clocks run two months on a single winding, keep perfect time and automatically show the correct date. They are strong, durable, reliable, in fact satisfactory in every way. Right in time; right in price. You ought to have one.

Also Frying pan, Program, Electric and Synchronized clocks. Send for Catalogue No. 463.

THE PRENTISS CLOCK IMPROVEMENT CO. DEPT. 46, 49 DEY ST., N. Y. CITY.

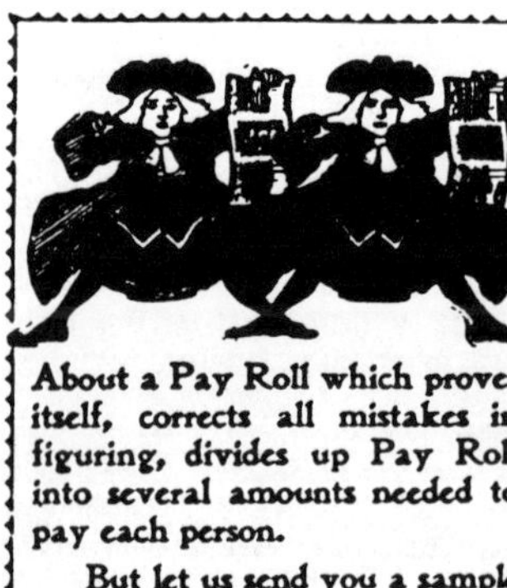

About a Pay Roll which proves itself, corrects all mistakes in figuring, divides up Pay Roll into several amounts needed to pay each person.

But let us send you a sample leaf, with circular, which tells the whole story.

BARLOW BROS., Grand Rapids, Mich.

NEW YORK PUBLIC LIBRARY ASTOR, LENOX AND TILDEN FOUNDATIONS

COMMERCE ACCOUNTS & FINANCE

Volume 5 New York April 1903 Number 4

CONTENTS.

Published Monthly by The Commerce Accounts & Finance Company Twenty-five Pine Street New York

What Do You Do With Your Invoices?

When You Receive a bill for goods bought by you, what do you do with it? Do you hand it to your bookkeeper, who laboriously copies it, figure by figure, in a bulky invoice journal, from which the total amount is posted to the ledger?

When your Bookkeeper has wasted valuable time by the above process, what does he do with the invoice itself? Does he hand it to the office boy or the assistant bookkeeper, who places it in some compartment of a clumsy file along with a dozen other bills from the same house, each of which must be pawed over when this particular one is wanted again?

If You Are Wasting Time and Money by these antiquated methods, aren't you tired of doing so? Would you not welcome a system as far superior to them as the sun is to a kerosene lamp?

THEN USE THE

"Acx" System of Filing Invoices

Simpler, More Convenient and More Serviceable than any other. A time-saving application of elements more or less used in every up-to-date office.

What the "Acx" System Is.

A system of filing invoices by which (1) the copy of the order placed, (2) the record of the receipt of the goods, and (3) the invoices, are brought together on a sheet of the paper of a size and shape to be conveniently handled and preserved in any post binder file.

The "Acx" Invoice Filing Sheet is of manilla, 11 inches long by 8½ inches deep. The directions on it explain its use. Three lines of mucilage are in place on the sheet. The first of these (inside left hand) is entitled "Attach left hand of your order here." All orders should be filled out in duplicate, preferably by the use of carbon sheets, and the retained copy attached to the invoice sheet.

Reduced fac-simile of "Acx" Invoice File Sheet, designed by Account, Audit & Assurance Co., Ltd., 25 Pine Street, New York. Made by Self-Proving Account Book Co., New York. Patented February 8, 1898. May 20, 1902. Other patents pending.

When the goods for which the order is given are received, the count is made and entered upon a "Goods Received Slip," provided for the purpose. This slip is then attached to the Invoice Filing Sheet in the place marked "Attach left hand of Goods Received Here."

When the invoice is checked with the order and the "Goods Received Slip," its upper edge is moistened and laid against the mucilage on the Invoice Filing Sheet in the place marked "Attach top of invoice here." There are then superimposed upon this sheet (1) copy of the order, (2) record of the goods received, and (3) the invoice. The Invoice Filing Sheet is then paged in numerical order in its upper left-hand corner and is ready to be inserted in the binder; the latest invoice always being on top.

No Journalizing, no hunting for lost invoices, orders or goods received records. Order, receipt of goods and invoice all attached to one sheet of stiff paper, numbered and securely bound in a substantial binder, ready for instant reference. Post from this sheet direct to the ledger.

Price $6 a Thousand.

Address orders to

STATIONERY MANUFACTURING COMPANY,

86 Fulton Street, New York City.

A New Work on Accounting

A MANUAL OF BOOKKEEPING

By J. THORNTON

THIS attractive volume, comprising over 500 pages, with numerous illustrations, is one of the clearest and most concise surveys of the principles of accounting which has recently appeared. While its illustrations are given in terms of English money the bookkeeping principles discussed are universal.

The work is divided into two leading parts, the first of which is "LAWS AND PRINCIPLES," and the second "APPLICATION."

LAWS AND PRINCIPLES

In the first part there are discussed the Principle of Exchanges, the Principle of Debit and Credit Accounts, the Principle of the Classification of Accounts, the Principle of Ledger Entries, the Principle of Proving, the Principle of Transfer from Preparatory to Final Record, and the Principle of Balancing and Closing the Ledger.

APPLICATION

Under the head of Application the following chapters are presented: Rules and Tools, What Capital Consists of, Capital in Cash, Capital in Bills, Capital in Debts, Capital in Goods, Fixed Capital, Profit and Loss, Capitalist's Accounts, Company Bookkeeping, Errors, and Non-Capitalistic Bookkeeping.

Several chapters are arranged in the form of lessons, following which are questions for class purposes, arranged in such a way, however, as not to detract in the least from the value of the book in the hands of the general reader. A comprehensive index, together with answers to exercises completes the work.

Price, $2.50.—Sent Postpaid to any address in the United States on receipt of price.

Address COMMERCE ACCOUNTS & FINANCE CO.

PUBLISHERS AND BOOKSELLERS - 25 PINE STREET, NEW YORK

BUSINESS NEEDS.

Advertisements under this head one cent a word each insertion.

A FEW WORDS ABOUT PRINTING.

Printing is done artistically or it is done inartistically. Some people want cheap printing and some people want the best printing. What kind do you want? I can give you figures on either kind of printing that will give you satisfaction and the goods delivered will insure your future orders. Try an estimate from "The Printing Press," care Commerce, Accounts & Finance.

AN EXPERIENCED BOOKKEEPER desires a position. Am at present employed by one of the largest insurance companies in the world, but desire to make a change to some position where prospects for the future are brighter. Best of references. Address "Fidelity," care of Commerce, Accounts & Finance.

A LITERARY WORKER having some spare time on his hands will undertake to prepare booklets, circulars, advertising matter, etc., at reasonable prices. Will also, if requested, supervise the mechanical part of the work, the printing, binding, etc. Has had large experience, is the author of several books and is a regular contributor to the leading periodicals. Address "Writer," care of Commerce, Accounts & Finance.

AN EXPERIENCED OFFICE MANAGER desires to make a change. Salary not the only object. Best of references. Address "Manager," care of Commerce, Accounts & Finance.

IS YOUR SAFE CAPACIOUS enough to hold your books and papers? I act as an intermediary between persons or firms who need safes and those who have them to dispose of. I don't sell new safes for old safes, but I do know people who want your old safe and I can sell you a new safe at the lowest possible price. Second-hand safes at very low figures. In writing to me write to "A Safe Man," care of Commerce, Accounts & Finance.

ROLL TOP DESKS, office furniture and office labor-saving devices can be obtained in every variety of style and price. Write for further information to "T. G. S.," care of Commerce, Accounts & Finance.

ATTRACTIVE ILLUSTRATIONS. I have had twenty years' experience as an illustrator on many of the leading magazines. I also have had a large experience in drawing for advertisers. I work in pen and ink, in wash and in colors. Filling as I do a steady position, I will do outside work in my spare time at prices lower than would otherwise be the case. Address "Sketch," care of Commerce, Accounts & Finance.

TYPEWRITERS — SOLD ON weekly payments as low as $1 a week. All styles. Address "Brown," care of Commerce, Accounts & Finance.

BOOKS BOUGHT AND SOLD. Books of every description bought for highest cash prices. Send postal for further information. Address L., 823 E., care Commerce, Accounts & Finance.

A BUSINESS EDUCATION | FOR ...ONE... DOLLAR.

...THE PRACTICAL AGE...

A MONTHLY MAGAZINE full to the brim with helpful suggestions to young men and young women who are struggling successward.

THE BUSINESS HOUSE THAT JACK BUILT, an intensely interesting and highly instructive story of business life, and

APPLIED ENGLISH, an authority on writing and speaking the English language, which no young person can afford to be without, all for ONE DOLLAR.

If you have never seen THE PRACTICAL AGE, send for a free sample copy. Address,

THE PRACTICAL AGE,

Moline, Illinois.

Use any pen and your own stationery. If your stationer does not keep it, write for free specimen of work. Beware of infringements. Address Dept.

Pen-Carbon Manifold Co., 145-7-9 Centre St., New York.

BRIEF MENTION.

THE COMPTOGRAPH COMPANY have sent out a very handsome panel as the floater for their annual calendar. It is oval in shape, with bronze margin, inside of which is a plaque of blue on which in turn is put the picture of the bust of a woman in fancy dress all done in imitation of water colors. Accompanying this plaque was a handsomely engraved card reading, "With Best Wishes for a Prosperous New Year, The Comptograph Company."

A TASTY BOOKLET is that issued by the National Safe Deposit Company, of New York, with offices on the ground floor of the Mutual Life Building, on Liberty, Nassau and Cedar streets, New York City. The booklet is bound in blue and bears on its cover in gilt letters the words "A Great Mistake." The mistake, so the booklet informs us, is made by those not renting a safe in the vaults of the National Safe Deposit Company. The booklet is illustrated with many handsome halftone cuts, reproductions of photographs, showing the interior of the company's offices and the interior and exterior of their safe deposit boxes. It is a very fine piece of advertising, and apparently the vaults of this company are as secure as anything of the sort can be.

THERE ARE MANY PAPER fasteners in the market but the fastener made by the DeLong Hook and Eye Company, of Philadelphia, Pa., is claimed to be the best fastener made. The company's advertising states that the only vise needed to squeeze this fastener through a dozen sheets of paper is the presence of the thumb and forefinger. The fastener is said to make its own perforations, to clasp and hold, all in one easy second.

THE SCATTERGOOD MUCILAGE bottle is an old favorite, but it holds its friends and makes new ones. The Scattergood Company, of 67 Laurel street, Philadelphia, are advertising this mucilage bottle extensively just at present, and some of their advertising matter is very attractive.

PRINTED IN RED AND BLACK on a fine quality of colored paper is a little folder issued by the Title Guarantee & Trust Company, of Broadway, New York City. It advertises the company's tax registration bureau, and this registration bureau of the Title Guarantee & Trust Company is said to obtain accurate description from the registrar's office records; obtain accurate lot numbers from state tax maps, obtain verified tax bill in September, verified waterrent bill in April, and a good deal more of the same nature. The little folder is well printed and well written, and should be of interest to property holders in Greater New York.

THE L. E. WATERMAN COMPANY, makers of the Waterman Ideal Fountain Pen, are advertising a small book entitled "Waterman Ideal Salesmanship," and the company claims that this book will make its reader a successful pen clerk. The book, we believe, contains lessons in the art of selling the Waterman pen, and will be sent to those selling fountain pens. Further information will be furnished by the L. E. Waterman Company upon request.

A PERPETUAL PENCIL would seem to be a pretty good sort of a thing, and that is what the American Lead Pencil Company, of 491 & 493 Broadway, New York City, are advertising. The pencil is a very neat nickeled and japanned affair, which is made to contain a number of indelible leads, one behind the other. When not in use the lead is pushed up into the pencil, but by pressure at the end of the pencil it drops down into position.

PUBLIC ACCOUNTANTS.

Atlanta, Ga.—Ralph H. Brown, 804 Empire Building.

Boston, Mass.—Charles H. Fellows, 174 Summer; New England Audit Company, 45 Milk; J. S. Parsons, 214 Columbus Ave.

Brooklyn, N. Y.—Franklin Allen, Arbuckle Building, 371 Fulton.

Buffalo, N. Y.—W. G. Mowat, 831 Ellicott Square.

Chicago, Ill.—Haskins & Sells, 214 Dearborn.

Davenport, Ia.—J. C. Grabbe, McManus Building.

Detroit, Mich.—H. Naemansson, 496 Putnam Ave.

London, Canada.—Geo. F. Jewell, 361 Dundas.

Montreal, Canada.—George Gontheir, 11-17 Place D'Armes Hill.

New Bedford, Mass.—James L. Hathway, 72 Willis.

New Orleans, La.—P. W. Sherwood, 904 Howard Ave.

New York, N. Y.—Patterson, Teele & Dennis, 30 Broad; Haskins & Sells, 30 Broad; Account, Audit and Assurance Company, 25 Pine; Leon Brummer, 7 Pine; H. F. Searle, 45 Broadway; Hart Bros., Tibbits, Heiron & Co., 11 Broadway; Franklin Allen, Silk Exchange Building, Broadway.

Philadelphia, Pa.—Francis & Sterrett, Penn Mutual Building; Peter Ballingall, German-American Building; Charles W. Thomas, 409 Lippincott Building; Alfred L. Sellers, 1001 Chestnut.

Pittsburgh, Pa.—John Vaughan, 5520 Claybourne; George W. Wood & Co., 341 Fourth Ave.

Providence, R. I.—George R. Allen, 29 Weybosset.

San Francisco, Cal.—Charles L. Lutgen, 218 California; Lester Herrick, 405 Montgomery.

Toronto, Canada.—F. H. Kidd, Bank of Commerce Building.

Windsor, Canada.—F. H. Macpherson, 16 Sandwich, East.

Winnipeg, Canada.—Peter Thornton, 343 Main.

The Manual of the Self-Proving Accounting System

By A. O. KITTREDGE, C. P. A. *and* J. F. BROWN, *Merchant*

Large Octavo. 328 Pages. 4 Fac-simile Insets and Numerous Other Illustrations. Good Paper, Excellent Typography and Substantial Binding. :: :: ::

A Real Book on Real Accounting

THIS work describes and illustrates a system of accounts adapted to all lines of business, which has for its foundation a Perpetual Balance Sheet. This balance sheet, in place of being made up at intervals, is an integral and going part of the system and keeps the net results of the business constantly before the eye of the manager. It introduces no new elements, but makes various new applications of old principles. A rigid classification of accounts upon balance sheet principles is enforced, and the columnar method of condensation and summarizing is intelligently applied. A given business is represented by the smallest possible number of accounts, and each class of accounts is furnished with books adapted to its special requirements.

No Troublesome Trial Balances

By the SELF-PROVING ACCOUNTING SYSTEM all the terrors of the trial balance—the bookkeeper's bugbear—are entirely overcome. The central feature of the system is the Balance Sheet Ledger, which always shows the exact condition of the business. There is no copying; postings are made from the original entries; there are many new ideas in rulings.

Adapted to Any Line of Business

The SELF-PROVING ACCOUNTING SYSTEM is adapted to any line of business. It is in use in prominent establishments throughout the country covering almost every branch of commerce. The Manual gives complete description of the system so that its application to any required business may readily be made. Especial attention is paid to the requirements of the Installment business, a line hitherto sadly neglected by accountants.

Sent Postpaid on Receipt of $3.00

Stationery Mfg. Co.
86 Fulton Street, New York

Higher Commercial Education

A Symposium on Various Phases of This Subject by the Alumni and Members of the Faculty of the University of Michigan.

[The alumni and members of the faculty of the University of Michigan were asked a short time ago to give their views on the subject of Higher Commercial Education to the "Michigan Alumnus," the graduates' magazine. From the large number of contributions submitted in compliance with this request, Commerce, Accounts & Finance has selected the following as being of interest to all business men.]

WHAT IS HIGHER COMMERCIAL EDUCATION?

By EDWARD D. JONES.

HIGHER commercial education is the effort of universities to respond to the call for a course of study which shall fit young men for responsible positions in industry. It aims to give the theoretical and systematic part of the education of those who are to determine and execute the commercial and financial policy of business enterprises and who will occupy positions as managers of departments of large concerns, as foreign agents and buyers of the same, as officials of banks and of insurance and transportation companies, as merchants, journalists, government employees, including members of the consular and diplomatic services, etc.

This educational departure is of comparatively recent origin and involves some fifteen of the larger universities of this country. It is to be distinguished from training for office and clerical work as given by so-called "commercial colleges," and from trade and technical training such as is given by engineering, agricultural, textile, or other trade schools.

There are two main causes which have led to the introduction of this type of education. The first of these is the increased use of system and science in the conduct of business affairs. This not only makes necessary the selection of men of trained minds, acquainted with science, to superintend the processes of industry, but it has made possible such a formulation of the principles of production that there is now a subject-matter which can be studied, apart from practice, according to the methods of an educational institution, and which is of practical value because it governs practice. As Mr. Arthur Balfour, the First Lord of the Treasury, has recently said: "In the marvelously complicated phenomena of modern trade, commerce, production and manufacture, there is ample scope for the most scientific minds and the most critical intellects; and if commerce is to be treated from that higher and wider viewpoint it must be approached in the broader spirit of impartial scientific investigation."

Such being the condition precedent, the second cause of higher commercial education is found in the response which institutions of higher education have made to it. This involves the birth and growth of a broader conception of the university as an institution to gather in to itself and conserve all knowledge, to represent the interests of all classes of the community in and for which it exists, and to be as broadly useful as is possible, consistent with true learning, in the training of men for the various activities of life. This sentiment which characterizes the modern university man in contrast with the narrower and more exclusive ideas once dominating, was well expressed by President Nicholas Murray Butler in his inaugural address at Columbia University. He said: "In these modern days the university is not apart from the activities of the world, but in them and of them. To fulfil its high calling the university must give, and give freely, to its students; to the world of learning and of scholarship; to the development of trade, commerce and industry; to the community in which it has its home, and to the state and nation whose foster child it is."

The courses of study which have been planned in the various universities differ somewhat in details, but in the main they include the following elements: (1) Studies to give mental discipline or general culture, in which category a prominent place is occupied by history; (2) science, including not only the principles but certain courses in applied science, such as industrial chemistry, the application of physics to industry, and economic geology; (3) economics, under which is included applied economics, economic history, money, banking, finance, and statistics; (4) the technique of industry. This phrase may serve to designate a group of new branches concerned in the study of wealth production and including the extractive and manufacturing industries; commerce, including commercial geography and history and the institutions and methods of internal and foreign commerce; transportation; and business organization, which has to do with the administrative relations existing within an individual business, especially of large size, and with the methods of manipulating the resources of investors to finance great undertakings; (5) commercial law, involving not only the legal liabilities connected with every industrial act, but the principles upon which the state interferes to regulate the competitive struggle; and (6) modern languages.

The successful conduct of such a course of study obviously involves the co-operation of several departments of a university. The humanities are represented in the history, economics, literature and language; the scientific department provides an indispensable element, as does also the law department, while the studies connected with the technique of industry serve as a central topic about which the others can be grouped. In this co-operation is found one of the features of strength in courses of higher commercial education, because the student, while pursuing a unified course of study, has an opportunity to become acquainted with the atmosphere prevailing in the various departments of the university, to know many teachers, to view truth from all sides and in this way develop the habit of independent thought and action, so necessary in industrial pursuits. In this co-operation lies also a valuable means of keeping different departments and colleges of a university in touch and of increasing the common bonds which education of a specialized character usually tends to break asunder.

The possibilities of higher commercial education are only limited by the extent to which science shall revolutionize industry and to which the universities can adapt themselves to the changing needs of the times. There are needed at present teachers who are adequately prepared to teach and also to carry on investigations which shall systematize the knowledge needed for purposes of instruction. Textbooks are also needed in many branches. Some years of experience will be required to show what new subjects are demanded to round out the course of study and what relation these subjects will sustain to one another. One prime necessity in order that a rapid and healthy growth may be made is a permanent means of keeping educational work in constant touch with the business community. As the pursuit of scientific knowledge requires the laboratory; of art, the gallery; of letters, the library; so the study of industry requires access to a field of observation. The various means of accomplishing this at present in use are: the calling of special lecturers from the ranks of men of affairs to the university, the visiting of industrial establishments by students, the copious use of trade and technical literature, the commercial museum connected with a university. Other means have been suggested and can be put into operation with the practical certainty of splendid results as soon as university authorities shall thoroughly appreciate the responsibility which the task of educating the business leaders of the future places in their hands. American universities can in no way more certainly add a numerous and influential element to those who are their friends and backers than by providing adequately for a type of special education which shall meet the approval of intelligent business men. Nor will the good effects of such a policy be confined to any one department of a university, for the patronage of courses in commerce comes largely from persons who would otherwise not enter universities, and an alumnus of a university, no matter what his department or course, is a more intelligent judge and a more ardent friend of the work of all the various departments of his alma mater than is the person who has remained entirely outside the circle of influence of university life and ideals.

HIGHER EDUCATION IN BUSINESS.

By ARCHER BROWN.

A DIFFERENCE of opinion has long existed as to the value of a college education in business. Mr. Carnegie some years ago very forcibly presented the negative side of the controversy, and Mr. Schwab has more recently done the same. There is good reason, however, to think that Mr. Carnegie, in his later years, has reversed his attitude. Otherwise, his gift of ten million dollars to Scottish universities seems contradictory and illogical. It can scarcely be supposed that all the young Scots studying at Edinburgh and Glasgow are destined for the learned professions. If the controversy were to break out afresh to-day, it would doubtless be found that most of our captains of industry who have made their way from humble beginnings would side with those who call for broader education in all large business affairs.

It must be admitted that the business world is steadily coming to recognize that its leaders must be found mainly among those whose minds have been trained in the colleges and technical schools of the country. In a comparatively few years I have noticed a marked change of sentiment in this particular, within the range of my own experience. Ten years ago the great industrial concerns of the country gave preference to the practical man, particularly such as had come up from the ranks in their own organization. Now these same companies are found in close competition for the bright minds in the graduating classes of engineering and technical schools. Modern business is so highly specialized

"Send the Bill to Andy."—New York World.

and in most lines is conducted on so gigantic a scale that the highest premium is put upon mental capacity and trained skill. These qualities are occasionally found among men of narrow education, but in the main they must be looked for among those whose minds have been expanded and disciplined by liberal study.

Within the past few weeks I have learned of more than one large commercial organization which has been compelled to go through its force of men and weed out numbers who, by lack of education, or ambition, have quickly reached the limit of their growth, and fill their places with educated men. The experience is a familiar one in most large manufacturing and commercial companies. The bright boy who has taken to business, perhaps before he has completed his high school course, is generally (though not always) found to have reached his limitation in what might be termed routine work. When it comes to larger lines, which require initiative and originality of thought, the man of trained mental powers comes to the front. He may have got his training by private study or he may have got it at college. At any rate he must have it. And here it might be mentioned that the hard tests of the business world prove that not all of the men who emerge from colleges with degrees are educated, in any real sense. I have known many a man, who, by night work and private study, has made up for the lack of advantages in youth, and whose mind is better trained and stored with useful knowledge than that of the college graduate, whose residence at the university was largely occupied with social and athletic affairs. It is more than ever true to-day that the elements of higher success in the business world are clear thinking and sound judgment. These, of course, must be coupled with unswerving integrity, concentration of purpose, and high executive powers. The old days, when the first Vanderbilt organized steamship and railroad lines in farmer style, or when Daniel Drew carried great speculative accounts in his hat, will not fit present highly organized conditions.

You ask an expression as to what the university should do for the students who come to it for preparation in the business world of to-day. First, I should put the technical training which equips a man for the higher work in the great fields of mining, manufacturing, engineering, etc. There is practically no limit to the demands for men of this class. With their technical training, supported by knowledge of languages, history and sciences, such as our great universities now give them, they have an immense lead in the race over their less favored competitors.

But the general business world calls for a large number of highly trained and competent men in lines where technical education does not apply. The counting house, the factory, the mill, and even the business management of mines, railroads, etc., do not need so much technical and scientific training as a general equipment which contributes to that rare and difficult to define quality known as "executive ability." It is generally called, in the business world, brains. The so-called commercial schools of the day, with their courses in bookkeeping, typewriting, counting house methods, etc., all excellent in their way, do not touch this higher field at all. It is a matter of gratification to the business alumni of Michigan that the regents and faculty have recognized the need of higher commercial education. The special courses, as they are described, touching the organization and administration of industries; the great questions of finance; the application of the principles of chemistry, physics, and mathematics to industrial undertakings, seem to be admirably adapted to the end in view. It is something of a question whether the five years' course in the university which is, apparently, required to secure the degree, is not too long for the average young man, eager to get at the real work of life. The president of Columbia, in his recent address, looking to a shortening of the usual college course for those who are preparing for business or professional life, has touched a point which may well deserve the study of careful educators. It is a pleasure to see the University of Michigan with the leaders in modern and progressive movements, and I trust the new courses in the higher commercial education will be crowded with ambitious students.

FINANCING OF CORPORATIONS.

By ANDREW J. BROCKETT.

"A corporation," says Judge Cooley, "is a body consisting of one or more natural persons, empowered by law to act as an individual, and continued by a succession of members." It is invisible, immortal, has no soul, neither is it subject to the death of the natural body. It is a citizen of the state by whose sovereignty it is created, and its action is determined by the mere majority of its members. All the members may change, but it remains unchanged. They may die, but the corporation remains immortal.

There are many kinds of corporations—those for profit, for charity, for benevolence, for religious purposes, and for pleasure, each requiring its own system of financing.

National banks are managed by a board of directors who are able to command the confidence of a large number of depositors, and the acts of this board are subjected to the constant inspection and surveillance of the United States government, all of their financial operations being carefully regulated by law. If honestly and vigilantly managed, they cannot be otherwise than successful.

The manufacturing corporation should have ample capital, so that its shares of stock should not be worth less than par, and its credit such that it can borrow money at the lowest rate of interest, thereby providing means for the entire output of manufactured goods for one season, or until the sale of goods begins to bring returns, thus keeping resources sufficient to permit buying material required for its products anywhere, and at any time, when it may be obtained for the lowest price, in order to secure for its stockholders the largest percentage of profit in the purchase of raw material, as well as in manufactured goods. It is absolutely necessary in the successful financing of such a corporation to have a broad-minded, competent board of directors, each being familiar with every detail and knowing the value of, and the required quality of each part of the manufactured article, thus determining the price at which it can be sold to make the necessary profit.

Another matter of vital importance is the value of the plant and its annual depreciations. Still another is the expense of selling the finished product, including storage and transportation, together with interest on money invested and temporary

Now for Industrial Peace.—Philadelphia Press.

The Shark—"Don't mind me, old fellow; you're welcome to what's left."—Chicago News.

loans. The sources of profit down to minutest detail should be carefully investigated.

An optimist in business will see everything favorably and make up figures and reports accordingly, while, on the other hand, the conservative man will set forth affairs in a much less favorable light. There is some excuse for the more favorable view in corporation matters, for corporations live on, and it is sometimes absolutely necessary in order to tide over a temporary crisis in business affairs—for the sake of sustaining its credit—to present the best report possible, for corporations often live down losses which would wreck a partnership. A corporation should, however, be more, rather than less, exact than a firm.

Each corporation should select such forms of accounts as suits its particular business. These should embrace such divisions as will enable the management to refer at any time to what is being done in every department, and at what cost, for it is only by accurate accounting that modern business can be successfully carried on.

The main account is that of the general balance sheets in which are regularly stated the other accounts, such as surplus income, or profit and loss, reflecting the changes in general condition during the year. This the investor should carefully study, because on the interpretation of the items included depends one's judgment as to the wisdom of the investment.

The report which every corporation should make to its shareholders and the public—if the public holds the shares—should contain statements of details of every transaction during the year, in order that every one may form his own judgment of the safety of the investment.

A very necessary thing in the financial management of a large corporation is a depreciation account, treating of the expenditures for the care of the plant. The real estate may decline in value, money will be required each year to adjust the buildings more perfectly to the requirements of the business, and yet this may not add anything to the salable value of the property, and should not, therefore, be added in the accounts of the investment in real estate. Machinery, likewise, will wear out, and new inventions may render it practically worthless, so that a partially or entirely new outfit may be required. The conservative course in these cases is the proper one, and a suitable amount to meet such requirements should be set aside to profit and loss.

Unless these matters are carefully attended to the stockholders of a corporation may find, later on, that their securities cover a property of little or no business value. Indeed, unless sufficient sums are thus considered as outside the income of the business, and if dividends are paid larger than should be, just in proportion to the extent to which this is done, the returns received by shareholders are not dividends, but parts of their capital returned to them.

If we say that advancement in material civilization is made possible chiefly through a cheapening of the cost of production for staple articles, and that true progress can be made only as both labor and capital receive their due rewards, we state the conditions of an industrial problem, which point directly toward a more effective organization. Cheaper cost, higher wages, and better profits form a union of blessings which can be realized, if at all, in no other way than through combinations of capital larger in the aggregate, though divided into small ownerships, together with the best mechanical resources, a massing of employees, and an efficient oversight of the whole. Such organizations can be best managed through corporations.

There should be only one kind of stock, and it should all have the same relative value, so that each stockholder should receive the same dividend pro rata. Thus the stockholders will become important factors in sustaining the corporation, because they receive the full benefit of the earning power of the corporation.

CALIFORNIA ACCOUNTANTS ORGANIZE.

The certified public accountants of the State of California have followed the example of their eastern brethren and organized a society. A meeting of the certified public accountants of the state was held at the office of A. G. Platt, No. 503 California street, San Francisco, Cal., on Monday evening, February 23, 1903, for the purpose of completing the organization of the Society of Public Accountants of California. Representatives were present from San Francisco, Oakland, Alameda, Fresno and Stockton, and letters were received from accountants in Los Angeles and Berkeley. A constitution and by-laws for the governments of the society were adopted and the following officers and directors were elected:

Alfred G. Platt, San Francisco, president; J. L. Fields, Alameda, vice-president; Lester Herrick, San Francisco, secretary-treasurer, and Messrs. J. F. Foster, Norman McLaren and A. Wenzelburger, of San Francisco, W. R. Blackman, of Los Angeles, J. B. Harries, of Sausalito, and W. G. Langdon, of Oakland, as directors.

The society intends to begin a campaign of education similar to that carried on by the eastern accounting societies, the idea being, of course, to elevate and maintain a standard of proficiency, integrity and character equal to that required and maintained in other learned professions.

At the meetings, which will be held at stated intervals, professional and business men who are interested in accounting and its kindred subjects, will be asked to attend and address the meetings and to join in discussions. The Society of Certified Public Accountants of California begins its work with enthusiasm. The secretary's office is at 820 Haywood street, San Francisco, Cal.

WAITING ON HER.

"Lady, is anybody waiting on you?" said a floorwalker at a dry goods store to a girl from the country.

"Yes, sir," said the blushing damsel. "That's my young man outside. He wouldn't come in."

Anson O. Kittredge

WHEN Anson O. Kittredge, president of the Account, Audit and Assurance Company, of New York City, and secretary of the American Institute of Bank Clerks, left his office on the 12th of January for a short business trip to Boston, his business associates who took leave of him little thought that he would never again return to his desk. Such, however, was the sad fact, for Mr. Kittredge, while at the Hotel Essex, in Boston, was seized with a sudden and severe illness that terminated in his death in that city on the 23d of March. His loss comes as a great shock to all his friends and acquaintances, for he was in appearance the picture of health and the embodiment of nervous force and energy.

Those who knew Mr. Kittredge well, knew him to be an indefatigable worker, an eminently progressive man and one whose thought was often in advance of his time. Whatever the undertaking with which he was at the time associated, to the furthering of that undertaking he devoted himself body and mind. The term "working hours," as commonly accepted, meant nothing to Mr. Kittredge; all hours were working hours to him when he once became interested in a subject. Although considerate of others, he never spared himself, and it may be that this unselfishness helped to bring about his death at the comparatively early age of fifty-five. He was stricken down while on a business trip. If ever man died in harness, he did.

Anson O. Kittredge

Anson O. Kittredge was born in Dayton, O., on February 19, 1848. His early struggle to obtain an education is typical of many successful Americans. He worked at odd jobs between whiles, cutting wood in the winter and picking berries in the summer, in order to earn money to pay for his schooling. At one time he acted as sexton in a church, and taught school when only seventeen, still keeping up his own studies.

He began his business life as bookkeeper in the stove foundry of Greer & King, in Dayton, O. While there he originated and constructed what was probably the first card ledger ever used. He left the stove foundry to form a partnership with a Mr. Klugle in the sheet metal business at Salem, O. The firm of Klugle & Kittredge was succeeded by Kittredge, Clark & Co., which firm was later incorporated as The Kittredge Cornice and Ornament Works. While with Kittredge, Clark & Co., Mr. Kittredge issued "The Manual of Sheet Metal Architectural Work," a paper-bound book of some seventy-five pages, containing specification of materials, construction of workmanship, tables of sizes and weights and prices of materials, rules and directions for estimates and measurements, tables of various sorts of tin roofing, a glossary of architectural and technical terms in common use, etc.—the first comprehensive publication of the kind issued.

It is characteristic of the man that in the preface of this little book Mr. Kittredge said: "Appreciating the want of such a work felt by the trade and all interested in building, we have undertaken this publication—not, however, with any idea of speculation or direct profit from it. We look for our reward to the accomplishment of another object—the dissemination of accurate information respecting the class of work now in general use throughout the country and the establishment of a standard of prices for all in the trade."

We say that this is characteristic because much of Mr. Kittredge's most valuable work was given to the public at large at a price below the cost of production, with the idea of benefiting the class interested and not with the idea of pecuniary profit. And it it true that more money was made by outsiders through the adaptation of Mr. Kittredge's ideas than was made by the originator of these ideas. In 1874-78 he published "The Sheet Metal Builder," a journal circulating among manufacturers and dealers in sheet metal work, in which he continued the dissemination of accurate information among the trade, commenced in the booklet above referred to.

Mr. Kittredge went to New York in 1878 and sold "The Sheet Metal Builder" to David Williams, publisher of "The Metal Worker" and "The Iron Age." He was always interested in journalism, and for a time after his arrival in New York did space work for "The Metal Worker." His ability being recognized by Mr. Williams, he became editor of that journal and of "Carpentry and Building," which position he held for a number of years. While with "The Metal Worker," he wrote "The Metal Worker Pattern Book," which is yet the standard in use among sheet metal workers.

Mr. Kittredge was always interested in accounting, and in 1886 conceived the idea of publishing a journal which should be the exponent of progressive methods. He therefore began the publication of "The Office," a monthly periodical, which was successful from the start. In 1890 "The Office" was purchased by David Williams and the name changed to "Business—The Office Paper," Mr. Kittredge continuing as editor. During the period from 1878 to 1892 he was editor of "The Metal Worker," "Carpentry and Building" and "Business."

In addition to his editorial work he designed and perfected many sheet-metal working machines, taking out patents on the same for the Vulcan Company, of Philadelphia, an association of sheet metal builders. About 1890 he became interested in water-tube boiler construction, and, assisted by John J. Hogan, developed and patented many improvements in the construction of boilers for domestic and power uses.

In 1892 he severed his connection with "The Metal Worker" and "Carpentry and Building," and incorporated The Kittredge Company, Publishers. "Business" was purchased by the new corporation, and a new paper called "Metal" was started to give better expression of Mr. Kittredge's ideas of what a modern trade paper should be than was possible for him to do in "The Metal Worker." The new paper met with instant appreciation by the members of the trades addressed, so that in the few months of its existence it reached a circulation and advertising patronage rivaling the older publication. The financial support given Mr. Kittredge in the new company was inadequate, however, in view of the hard times of 1893, and "Metal" was discontinued. In 1896, as a further result of the commercial disturbance, "Business" passed out of his control.

Mr. Kittredge, in connection with his other duties, had, as we have said, been much interested in accounting, and at this time, having severed his connection with publishing enterprises, he resolved to devote his entire attention to the accounting profession. Being eminently successful in this, in 1898 he formed the Account, Audit and Assurance Company, of which he remained president until his death. Mr. Kittredge's idea was that the accountant should be something more than is ordinarily understood by the term, and to his practice of the profession he was able to bring to bear his wide experience as a business man and journalist. This faculty assured his success as president of the Account, Audit and Assurance Company, which was marked. This company has installed the Balance Sheet Accounting System in some of the largest business houses of America. Under Mr. Kittredge's personal direction it reorganized among others the accounts of D. Appleton & Co., of New York; John P. Squire & Co., of Boston; The American Cotton Company, of New York; and latterly, completely revised the accounting system at the mines of the Greene Consolidated Copper Company, at La Cananea, Mexico. The finishing touches to this great work were given but a few days before Mr. Kittredge was seized with the illness which caused his death. As an accountant, Mr. Kittredge was one of the prime movers in securing the passage of the law in New York State making the Regents' degree of Certified Public Accountant now considered so valuable by accountants generally.

Always interested in business education for the young man, when the School of Commerce, Accounts and Finance of New York University was founded in 1900, he became professor of the theory and practice of accounts at that school, which position he held until his death.

Probably the crowning work of Mr. Kittredge's career, perhaps the most important of all, was his labor as secretary of the American Institute of Bank Clerks, the educational enterprise begun in 1900 by the American Bankers' Association, at their convention at Richmond, Va. Mr. Kittredge was actively interested in the movement from the start and was made secretary by the board of trustees. He published "The Bulletin," the official organ of the Institute, and organized and carried on the work of the Correspondence School of Banking. Under his direction the American Institute of Bank Clerks grew until it now has some six thousand members, and the organization is in an extremely healthy condition and its growth steadily increases. Subscriptions to "The Bulletin" and enthusiastic commendations of its merit have been received from all parts of the world.

Mr. Kittredge was married in 1869 to Miss Ann E. Peck, of Dayton, O., who survives him. He leaves also one son and two daughters.

It is a matter of regret that the latest photograph taken of Mr. Kittredge, the one here reproduced, was taken about thirteen years ago; he was then forty-two years of age. His hair and mustache had become more gray of later years, but in other respects he had changed little.

AUSTRALIA'S QUEER LAW.

Australia is popularly supposed to be the country which has most nearly solved the puzzling industrial problems of the time, yet some queer laws have been passed under the dictation of the Socialistic-Labor party. One of these is the immigration law. Several years ago a cry was started for "A White Australia," says an English exchange. After a while this law was passed. It says that no person shall be allowed to land in Australia who, when asked by an officer, fails to write out at dictation and sign, in the presence of the officer, a passage of fifty words in a European language.

This means that the customs officers can require any person on any incoming ship to write from dictation fifty words in any European language the officer may choose to select. A very intelligent Frenchman might not be able to write fifty words in Dutch, or a Turk to do the same in Spanish. The law goes further. It says that any person who has entered the country in violation of the law shall be liable to six months' imprisonment or a fine of £50, or both.

The only exceptions are Australians who have been away from the country, ambassadors, soldiers, sailors of the royal navy, and crews of trading vessels in Australian ports. Australian citizens who go abroad are advised to have their photographs taken in no less than four positions so that they may be identified on their return.

Curious as this law is, its mode of enforcement is still more curious. At present it is enforced only against Hindus, who are British subjects, and Japanese, who are not. One party leader said lately: "We don't object to any white people. Germans and Frenchmen make good colonists, and the orders to the customs officers are not to enforce the act against any but Asiatics. But if we choose we could exclude everybody. We could trip a Cambridge B. A. on that act."

The Anglo-Indian Accountant*

By GEORGE CECIL.

WITH the fatal result of "all work and no play" we are acquainted. And though in India the imported accountant is not kept too close to his task, the nature of his relaxations is apt to have a dulling effect upon him. For the amusements of the exiled actuary are not only somewhat limited, but they are—according to circumstances—poor of their kind. Consequently, the social life of the bank or mercantile accountant is often a weariness to the flesh. In a word, it may be his misfortune to be bored to death. And this result is as easily achieved in India's metropolis as in its smallest and most insignificant station.

The few towns in which the expatriated man of figures is likely to find himself are Calcutta, Bombay and Madras; whilst Poonah, Kurachee, Lucknow, Allahabad, Bangalore, Secunderabad and Rawalpindi will also claim him. Occasionally a bank accountant is to be found in Simla, Naini Tal, and other hill sanatoriums. And in the very small mofussil (country) towns—mere villages—of the Bombay Presidency, should a branch of the Bombay Bank exist, a white "assistant"—as clerks are termed in the East—may find himself invested with managerial and accountant duties. Promotion of this nature will naturally enhance his position; but, in the majority of such cases, his means of amusing himself are practically reduced to a minimum. In the first place, there may be but half a dozen other Europeans in the station. Secondly, should several of the English members of the social circle in question (as is sometimes the case) not be on speaking terms, a harmonious interchange of thoughts, ideas and opinions is impossible. And in the third place, in the event of his fellow-exiles being intensely uninteresting, and, consequently, extremely boring, their presence will avail the accountant naught. Thus, should he be unable to take any pleasure in their society, he will be forced to spend his leisure in reading and writing, unless he cares to bicycle; golf or ride by himself. Shooting and pig-sticking is at his diposal—should he be fortunate in being stationed in a district in which sport of this nature is obtainable. Owing to the cheapness of horseflesh, driving is placed within his reach, whilst at auctions a suitable dog-cart may be picked up for as little as the equivalent of two or three pounds. For as (comparatively) infinitesimal a sum as fifty-five rupees (about $16.50) a serviceable pony is to be purchased (provided the accountant is a lightweight). But the exiled actuary who desires to be well mounted will invest in a waler—i. e., a horse of from fifteen to sixteen hands imported from Australia. An animal of this nature will cost from thirty to seventy pounds. The keep of the horse or pony, together with the wages of the sais, will in a small station amount to some fifteen rupees (£1) a month; in the large towns the amount is doubled. It is perhaps interesting in this connection to give a copy of a letter received from a sais by a Poonah accountant, and in which the former besought the latter to take him into his service. Thus:—

Bazaar, Poonah, September 3.

Honourable Sir—I am poor chap of honest sais I knowing work thoroughly I was head sais to general sahib I giving all the satisfaction you take me on I do all the thing you like I keep horse clean and carriages shine I rub harness clean I got very good sartificate (certificates) I wanting ten rupee a month same as all gentlemen giving I train for race master wins cup all saying I good sais so if your Honour giving me this job I doing all the necessary and I will pray ever more for your good health and prosperity. BENI, Sais.

It may be added that such applications are written by baboos (English-speaking native clerks), who perform services of this nature in return for a few pence. More than this, they are sometimes known to furnish their clients with ready-made testimonials (at a price), their leisure being devoted to composing them. Indeed, more than one baboo has grown quite rich by occupying his leisure in this manner. Occasionally the exile who hankers after carriage exercise buys a complete turnout second-hand from a confrere who is returning to England on leave. In this way excellent bargains are frequently made.

"The Club."

"The club" is the great stand-by of the Anglo-Indian accountant. In Calcutta the New Club and the Saturday Club await him, and in Bombay he will be welcomed as a member by the Gymkhana Club, the Yacht Club, and the Bombay Club. Should he be relegated to Bareilly, Cawnpore, Peshawar, or any other small country town, he will be received with open arms by the local club. The inquiring reader may here be reminded that no candidate for membership of any of India's clubs need possess the qualification of gentle birth. In Hindustan the most common and ill-bred white man becomes a member of the station club—provided he is a civil or military official, a partner or a clerk in a business house. Tradesmen and natives alone are exempted from the list of members. The half-caste element, however, are often admitted. But since the semi-European is quite uncivilized, the emigrant who is at all particular in his tastes does not seek his acquaintance. Even at the very small villages a club exists, and it frequently boasts of but three or four patrons—should the place only contain that number of men eligible for membership. It should be borne in mind that ladies are also admitted to Anglo-Indian clubs. But, even with this inducement thrown in, the accountant is apt to find an hour or so at the club a very poor form of amusement.

Every afternoon from about five till eight o'clock the society of the station foregathers at the club. Lawn tennis and Badminton are played in the adjoining grounds—billiards, whist and conversation being indulged in as soon as it becomes dark. In many of the smaller clubs the ladies invade the billiard and card-room, somewhat hampering the players by their artless conversation. During the hot weather cards are usually played in the open air, the card-tables being taken out for that purpose. Over them a punka is rigged up, and a contrivance not unlike a miniature meat-safe is affixed to the lamps, in order that their serenity may not be disturbed by the draught caused by the flapping punka. On first joining an Indian club the newly-arrived accountant will be somewhat astonished at the amount of whiskies-and-sodas and liqueurs disposed of by the members between tea-time and dinner-time; for it appears to be a recognized custom to ask his friends to "have a drink" directly a member accosts them. And the expatriated man of mathematics wonders that he suffers from premature liver complaint.

Dining Out.

Dining out also awaits the exile. In fact, upon the arrival of a married lady in the station the accountant—in common with the other sahibs—is en-

* From the "Accountant's Magazine," of Edinburgh.

titled to call upon her. In return he is invited to dinner, this being the Anglo-Indian method of returning a bachelor's call. He will, in the small towns such as Mhow, Ahmedabad, Ahmednugger and Sialkote, be made an honorary member of the local native infantry messes. He will frequently be asked to dine with the officers. There are also instances of his having been patronized in a similar manner by native cavalry messes. He is not, however, honored in this way by the better class of British regiments serving in the East, most of which are by way of being (so their Anglo-Indian brethren of the sword think) unduly exclusive. In connection with this honorary membership, it is perhaps interesting to note that he sometimes takes all his meals in the mess. By doing so he, usually speaking, succeeds in effecting a saving; for the officers of an Indian Staff Corps regiment being poor, they (very sensibly) put their pride in their pockets and keep a check on the mess expenses. One of them—a Eurasian for choice—keeps an eye to the commissariat, and the wines and whisky are obtained on more or less advantageous terms.

Should the Anglo-Indian accountant live in Calcutta he will be considered, by those who are easily pleased, to be singularly fortunate. For in addition to the usual distractions, he will be able to boat on the river Hooghly and to attend various race and steeple-chase meetings. Picnics to the Botanical Gardens will be placed at his disposal, the aide-de-camp in waiting to the Viceroy will bestow upon him an invitation to the annual state ball, the Lieutenant-Governor (a local dignitary) will invite him to one or two official garden-parties every cold season, and he will be asked to dinner at the houses of innumerable business men. He will be afforded the opportunity of attending a few dances during the winter and rains, and if he is fond of music he will be much pained by the efforts of Calcutta amateurs. For memories of Olitzka's "Amneris," of Plancon's "Landgrave," and of Calve's "Carmen" will have spoilt him for the Anglo-Indian amateur prima donna's conception of what constitutes il bel canto. Nor will the efforts of Bengal baritones compare favorably with those of, say, Kennerley Rumford; whilst those well-meaning ladies who strive to emulate the successes of Florence Schmidt, Fanny Moody, Charles Phillips, and other satisfactory singers, are singularly unsatisfying. From time to time comic operas and plays are put on by amateurs. But since the singing is so bad, pieces of the "Pinafore," "Pirates of Penzance," and "Dorothy" type are not worth listening to when given by Anglo-Indian performers. Plays, however, are often well acted by those adorning Calcutta society. The Australian companies, on the other hand, which from time to time visit India's metropolis, are sadly disappointing; for even if the members of such troupes happen to be competent actors and actresses, their appalling accent ruins their performance. "The Second in Command" or any other "society" piece is, when presented by an antipodean company, a mere burlesque. Yet innumerable exiles are pleased at their efforts.

Listening to the Band.

Amongst the other amusements and recreations awaiting the Anglo-Indian accountant who happens to be domiciled in Calcutta is listening to the band of an evening in the Eden Gardens. Occasionally a British regiment furnishes the orchestra, but more often a particularly dreadful native infantry band is told off for the purpose of entertaining the promenaders. There also exists in Calcutta the "Town Band," the members of which are Eurasians. Their performance is, if anything, rather worse than is that of the musicians alluded to. Sea-trips to Rangoon, Madras and Chittagong are also placed at the disposal of the jaded Calcutta actuary, and Saturday to Monday visits to Darjheeling in the Himalayas are feasible. During the Poojah holidays, which occur in the month of September, and which last for ten days, the accountant will visit Ceylon, deriving considerable benefit from the voyage.

The man of figures who is an inhabitant of Bombay entertains himself in much the same manner as do his Calcutta brethren. He enjoys, in addition, the advantages of sea-bathing. Should he be so inclined, he may yacht and fish. With a view to obtaining a temporary respite from the enervating heat of Hindustan's western capital, the accountant escapes as often as possible to Poonah. In connection with the climate of India it should be borne in mind that, whatever entertainments and pastimes may be placed at the disposal of the bank and commercial accountants, the heat greatly discounts the value of these relaxations. For, though pleasant enough weather prevails for from two to five months in the year—according to the part of India in which the accountant may find himself—the heat is something dreadful. In Bombay a depressing mugginess exists for three-fourths of the year, and in Calcutta, from April till November, the humidity is something awful. In Allahabad and Lucknow, and in other northwestern stations, though the winter is delightful, the hot weather and rains are exceptionally unpleasant. In fact, on the plains of India, wherever one happens to be living during the summer and autumn months, one is certain to be in a disgusting state of perspiration for the greater part of the twenty-four hours. In spite, however, of these drawbacks the exiled accountant takes kindly to cricket and football—however hot it may be.

In conclusion, it may be pointed out that Simla is, on the whole, the least unpleasant of Indian stations in which the European accountant is likely to find himself. With the climate there is nothing the matter, the air being bracing and healthy. For the actuary who can afford it polo exists, satisfactory acting—by the Simla Amateur Dramatic Society—takes place at the Gaiety Theatre, dinner parties and at-homes are given by the dozen, and, to crown all, heat is non-existent. But the Anglo-Indians whose abiding place is Simla are quite as uninteresting as are those who have the misfortune to be relegated to less desirable parts of our exceedingly unpleasant Eastern Empire. It may, therefore, be repeated that the emigrant railway, commercial or bank accountant is frequently bored by the relaxations placed at his disposal.

One Reason for the Child Labor Problem.—New York Herald.

History of a Car of Grain

FROM the great grain fields of the West comes the larger part of the world's cereal foodstuffs. We supply the markets of a goodly share of the globe with our wheat and corn. The farmer sows the seed and reaps the harvest—everyone knows that—but comparatively few know that the modern grain growers of the Western States are speculators as well as farmers. Mr. Charles Taller, an authority on this subject, has said:

The history of a car of grain after it has left its home in the West to contribute to the necessities of man, is usually supposed to be a very uneventful one. The general impression among the uninitiated is that the "honest farmer" hauls the grain to the nearest merchant, who, after honestly weighing his precious commodity, pays the patient toiler in good, hard cash, or its equivalent in a new frock for Sarah Jane, the gude-wife, and various articles of necessary comfort for the dear bairns who constitute his well-stocked quiver; "but the contrary, quite the reverse." The conventional honest farmer seems to have become a relic of the past. He is to-day a full-fledged shark. If you see him standing under a tree among the waving fields of grain, you may think he is figuring up the wages of his harvest hands or the total cost of the six brindle steers that are getting large enough to turn into sirloins and roasts. No; his book says that his "trades" do not suit him exactly in the present condition of the market, for be it known that while his ostensible occupation is a raiser of grain, he is in reality a regular old fox, and irregularly either a bull or a bear as occasion requires or suggests. In short, he is a speculator, and he finds upon examination this morning that he is getting too much "long" grain on his books, and that, too, in the face of a declining market. His bookkeeping for the purposes of his transactions possesses about the same degree of simplicity as the "scalping account" of the "noble red man." The Indian, however, uses only "single entry" when he makes a notch in the handle of his tomahawk; whereas the pale-face records his offenses against humanity by a "double entry" of purchases and sales which, in view of the higher civilization that he is supposed to have reached, may be properly regarded as a double offense.

The Grain-Grower's Accounts.

If the universal mania for speculation had not spread to the rural districts, this degenerate son of a possible noble sire would have no occasion to keep an account of his "deals."

Let us take a look at his "accounts": he has two sides corresponding to debit and credit, and they are for instance:

Bought.	Sold.
5,000 January wheat @ 86⅝	5,000 Jan. wheat @ 86⅞ Made a quarter of a cent which pays his commission merchant for the transaction and leaves him the glory.
10,000 January wheat @ 87	10.000 Jan. wheat @ 87 Which leaves him in debt to his commission merchant ¼c. or $25.
20.000 December wheat @ 87⅞	(Open) Can't sell it.

So he has on his book 20,000 December wheat, or stuff that he must take that month, at the price paid, and his crop of 20,000 bushels on his hands. He is "long of the market," and his face is somewhat in the same condition. But he has an honest pride in knowing that his "books are correct." We are sorry for him; but he does not ask our sympathy, for he is used to it. He has done the same thing every year with varying success. When you hear of "country" trading, it means that the rural accountant is immersed in figures, and the shrewd old speculator on "change" in the city takes careful note of whether the "country" is buying or selling. Well, however, December or January may be running—the reports say that spot wheat is active for milling purposes. So the farmer-speculator rushes his crop to the station in his spring wagons, behind smart trotters, at almost as good a gait as a first-class funeral procession down Broadway. He is reminded, too, by his commission merchant that his deals want to be "margined up," as the market is going against him.

At the nearest station will be found an elevator erected by men who have selected that point of an account of good crops in that section, and have located there for the season. They buy the grain in small and large lots as best they can, usually having to pay the market price for that particular day, and the farmer is pretty apt to know what it is, as it is flashed over the wires like war news during an active campaign. When a carload (20,000 to 40,000 pounds) is secured, they telegraph to the railroad company for a car; the car is loaded and the railroad company issues a bill of lading at a rate of freight that the shipper is assured is a ruinous cut on the tariff rates, and is lower than any one else has gotten or will get. The shipper begins to suspect even the word of a railroad agent, however, when he finds a competitor paying more for the "stuff" though handling it over the same rails. There is always a country banker ready to take, at a paying rate, this bill of lading, with a sight draft on some commission man in the nearest large city.

The commission man pays the draft and "spouts" the bill of lading at his bank till the car arrives, when he sells the grain and deposits proceeds in the bank to cover his overdraft. In this case it is sold by sample, probably within an hour after it reaches the "track"—that is, stops at some spot in the city before being ordered to an elevator. In that case the shippers get the full market value for it, in all likelihood through the simple-minded honesty of the merchant, who has not yet reached that elevated position in the commercial scale that entitles him to the enjoyment of a little joke like the following: Say the car has been consigned to a "large and influential" house, whose transactions are never questioned. Say the car arrives on the 30th of September. The house sends it to an elevator and gets a receipt. Now they have a September delivery to make, which they have sold at say 86; so they take this car, put it into their batch of September deliveries—that month being cornered—and instead of reporting the sale at 86—the price of that day—they wait till next day, October 1, when the market has broken to 80, and take the car "to account" at that price, making report to the shipper as sold regularly that day on arrival. These little tricks help to brace up the profit and loss account in a large house.

The Commission Merchant.

But to return to the car: In the natural course of things proper accounts are to be kept of it upon its arrival. The commission merchant's car clerk, in order to keep track of a good many cars, from a large number of shippers, at different points, has a ledger account for each shipper, giving him credit for the car or cars he may ship, by their car number and initial. As fast as cars are sold the sale number is put opposite the car number in the shape of a charge—so it can be seen what has been accounted for. When the railroad company notifies a commission man that a car has arrived, the notice describes the car by its number, and the clerk turns to a book, upon each page of which are the numbers 1 to 1,000. If the car in question is 75,250 he looks on page 75 and opposite 250 he finds in pencil the page number in the ledger, and from it can at once know who is the shipper and what orders are to be given for the disposal of the car, whether it is to be sampled and sold, sent to elevator and held for a price, or what not. If sold by sample the carload will go into consumption either in that market or be shipped to some other, thus fulfilling its natural and legitimate destiny, thereby escaping its unhappy share in the game of battledore and shuttle-cock, to which it is more likely to be subjected at the hands of the speculator. Let us suppose that it "passes grade"—comes up to the standard of "No. 2 "wheat, for instance—which is the favorite grade for speculative purposes. When we speak of "wheat" we mean "No. 2" wheat. It now goes into elevator, and forever loses its identity as a whole by being dumped into the great "No. 2 Bin," whose contents represent the hopes and fears, the smiles and tears, of the turbulent mass of crazed humanity that surrounds the pit on 'Change. It would be well for the happiness of mankind if this car were allowed to remain just where it is now until it should be called for to be ground into flour, in obedience to the ordinary course of supply and demand. It is not needed yet, for there is always more than enough in these times of peace and plenty. But no; it must go out in the shape of an elevator receipt, which, while representing only one car of grain, becomes eventually the spurious token of countless thousands, in the giddy whirl of speculative manipulation.

To explain in part en passant: The truth is, the custodians of this grain—the elevator people themselves—are speculators, too, and they sometimes find it necessary to quietly issue receipts for grain which they have not got in their bins, in order to "make deliveries" of their own sales. They can avoid detection of the fraud by issuing a receipt for so many thousand bushels without specifying the car numbers, so in this way our car No. 75,250 may be duplicated ad infinitum. But their books are all correct.

Following the Elevator Receipt.

We will follow this elevator receipt that personates our car in its uncertain course. It is likely to stand in place of the grain or a like quantity for many a day. I say a like quantity, for the elevator is not required to deliver this particular grain, but only a like quantity of the same grade. The elevator people do, however, get rid of the poorest and oldest grain first, and keep the freshest and best for the last deliveries. When the grain is sold—by receipt—the seller attaches it to his bill, and the buyer pays on delivery of the receipt the same day. The buyer, under the rules of the Board of Trade of Chicago, undertakes to pay, besides the purchase price of the grain, the storage for the first ten days; but he is entitled to five days in which to take the grain from elevator without paying any more storage. Since the elevator charges 1¼ cent originally, but now ¾ cent per bushel for the first ten days and ½ cent for each ten days following, a receipt can

Shaking them Out.—New York Herald.

be made "regular"—that is five days to take out the grain—by deducting all the storage the buyer would have to pay the elevator except ¾ cent per bushel for the first ten days, which, as I have said, the buyer pays out of his pocket, in addition to the purchase price. For example, if a receipt be dated September 1, and it sold "regular" to-day, we must deduct from the bill:

Storage,	September	1 to 10,	¾ cent.
"	"	11 to 20,	½ cent.
"	"	21 to 30,	½ cent.
"	October	1 to 10,	½ cent.
"	"	11 to 20,	½ cent.
"	"	21 to 30,	½ cent.

2½ cents being all storage beyond that for first ten days, which the buyer pays. In this case, we are obliged to include storage to the 30th, in order to give the buyer the five days, although in doing so we had to give him more than five days. Receipts in such cases are called "fresh," "strictly fresh" and "gilt-edge," according as they have six, eight or more days to take the grain from elevator.

Winter Storage.

Another feature of the storage imbroglio is winter storage. This was an invention to induce, or rather seduce, grain holders to run their stuff into Chicago in the fall and leave it during the winter. It is better to take it a little cheaper than not get it at all—an expedient that has worked well and has kept the elevators full during the winter season. Winter storage then begins November 15 and ends April 15, and the elevator men say: "We will only charge 4 cents for all that long period." That is, on grain received during that time, the storage shall accrue until it has reached 4 cents, and then be free till April 15. The result of this has been to make May the popular speculative month, and on the 1st of May deliveries are made by taking off 4¼ cents, old style, 3¾ cents, new style, on all winter receipts; on May 11, 4¾ cents, old style, 4 cents new style, and so on. One more peculiarity of this ever-perplexing storage deal is that a receipt issued before winter storage began must submit to a further deduction of one-half cent for every ten days, counting back time from November 15. The intricacies of these storage calculations have appalled many a bright accountant, and their successful and ready solution casts into the shade the less exasperating difficulties of the Pons asinorum of our school days. Grain is sold by car lots first, represented by these elevator receipts; but in time they are made up into 5,000 bushel lots, and the latter are used in making deliveries on the "future contracts" as they mature. A 5,000 bushel lot may con-

Uncle Sam: "Don't you worry. There's enough left."—Chicago Inter Ocean.

tain 4,950 to 5,050 bushels to make a proper delivery —1 per cent. variation either way being allowable. This is the Chicago method; other markets allow a variation of 5 per cent.—the larger allowance in keeping with the diminished brain capacity of the un-Chicagoan clerk making up the "5," I suppose; for it is done pretty quickly, sometimes; in fact, amazingly so. When a fellow rushes in upon you a big block of stuff and you have to tear it all to pieces in a jiffy, and make up your "fives" in accordance with your sales with reference to the storages, each receipt differing from the others in bushels and fractional parts, and date of going into elevator.

The Chicago Method.

It is proper to state that in the development of business systems some markets have established a registration of elevator receipts for grain, and in Chicago it is in charge of the state. Receipts cannot be delivered on sales under this system till they have each been registered in a book kept for that purpose, and elevators cannot deliver the grain on those receipts till the registration has been cancelled. The salutary operations of this system are obvious in preventing over-issue of receipts by the elevators for speculative purposes, referred to in another part of this paper. Policy is the best honesty. Another excellent feature in the Chicago Board is the establishment of a clearing house, which works also as a postoffice. Each member of the Board of Trade makes a list of amounts due from and to his fellow members, and brings down the balance, handing in his certified check for the amount of balance against him. These lists must be left at the clearing house before 11 A. M., under a penalty of $5, and at 2:30 P. M. the receivers get a certified check for the amount claimed. A fine of $1 is rigidly enforced for any mistake as in addition or putting down the wrong amount, or any amount not agreed upon between the parties. An expeditious mode of settling trades without passing bills is designated by the euphonious title of "ringing." It is to get rid of trades when a member has the same option bought and sold. For instance: A has November wheat bought of D and sold to B, so he hunts up C, who has November wheat bought of B and sold D; then it stands thus:

A has it sold B.
B " " C.
C " " D.
D " " A.

To settle it out and receive or pay any difference between the bought and sold prices,

A buys it from B and sells D.
B " " C " A.
C " " D " B.
D " " A " C.

All at the settling price fixed by the Board of Trade for the day, and the next morning the differences are settled through the clearing house. I never knew even a lawyer to venture into this field. It appears rather too complicated even to that class of omniscent mortals. When they do go in, it is on the outside, and they place themselves like all the other victims, "in the hands of their friends," the operators on the floor, who understand all these things, oh! so well!

After detailing these peculiar systems it must be pleasant to revert to our car No. 75,250 and tell more about it on its march to the home of the consumer; but no. Its identity is lost. It has plunged into the whirling maelstrom of speculation, along with its fellows, forming these battledore and shuttlecock "fives" that become the toys and playthings of the seething and squirming mass of half-crazed humanity in the "pit" on the floor of the exchange. Our car has become a factor in the causes that consign these men to the incurable cells of insane asylums, or what is less horrible and more frequent, untimely graves, not uncommonly expedited by that baleful balancer of earthly accounts, the five-shooter.

HAD MORE SENSE THAN THE JUDGE.

Chief Justice John Marshall knew that water would tighten a tire on a wheel: and, when he once found a wheel loose, he drove into a little creek. This wet one part of the wheel. Then he drove out and backed his horse. The same part of the wheel went into the water again. Again he tried it, all the time getting the same part of the wheel wet. A negro came along, and, seeing the situation, told the judge to drive into the water again. Then the negro took hold of a spoke, turned it around, and soon had all the wheel wet. Judge Marshall said, "Why, I never thought of doing that." The negro smilingly replied, "Well, some people nat'ly have more sense than some others, anyhow."

WAS AT SEA THEN.

A London clergyman was speaking before sailors once, and used this expression: "Now, friends, you know that, when you are at sea in a storm, the first thing you do is to anchor." A half-concealed laugh went round, and the clergyman knew he had made a mistake. A listener came to him later, and asked him if he had ever been at sea. The minister replied, "Yes, but only when I was delivering that address."

NOT NEW ENGLAND HOSPITALITY.

Senator Hoar, at the New England dinner that was held recently in Philadelphia, talked about New England hospitality.

"It is better now than it used to be," he said, "but it will stand improvement here and there. I remember how I dined not long ago, with a Connecticut farmer, a boyhood friend of mine. For dinner there was turkey. It was an excellent bird and I ate of it heartily. I said:

"'John, this turkey will make a fine hash to-morrow.'

"'Yes, George, it will,' the farmer answered, 'providing that you leave off now.'

"That was not New England hospitality, either. It was just a joke," concluded Senator Hoar.—New York Tribune.

WHAT WAS WANTED.

"Young man," asked the employer, "how can you afford to dress so elaborately and expensively on the salary we pay you?"

"I can't," gloomily answered the young man; "I ought to have more salary."—Chicago Tribune.

COMMERCE ACCOUNTS & FINANCE

A Magazine cf Higher Business Education and Practical Administration. Acknowledged Authority in the Profession of Commerce and Consistent Advocate of Methods Up to Date and Above the Table.

JOSEPH CROSBY LINCOLN, - - - Editor.
FRIEND PITTS, JR., - Circulation and Advertising.
E. R. KITTREDGE, - - - Business Manager.

PUBLISHED MONTHLY

SUBSCRIPTION $1 a Year in the United States, Canada and Mexico. Other countries $1.50. Postage prepaid by the Publishers. In the absence of specific orders to stop at the end of the subscription term the paper will be continued and a bill sent. Entered at the New York Postoffice as Second Class mail matter.

COMMERCE, ACCOUNTS & FINANCE COMPANY, Publishers
Twenty-five Pine Street, New York

The editor of COMMERCE, ACCOUNTS & FINANCE announces to its readers the death in Boston on March 23 of Mr. Anson O. Kittredge, president of the Account, Audit & Assurance Company, of New York. The announcement of Mr. Kittredge's death will come as a great shock to his many friends and admirers throughout the United States. For years he had been among the foremost accountants of the country, a leader in every movement for the betterment and advancement of professional accountancy, and his writings on accounting subjects have been published by most of the leading technical journals. Mr. Kittredge believed that the profession of the public accountant was as dignified as that of any of the so-called "learned professions," and he long believed what is just now coming to be recognized, that is, that the accountant is really a vital force of modern business enterprise.

*

Mr. Kittredge was a man cf strong personality, unsparing in his opposition to what he believed to be wrong and as unswerving in his adherence to what he considered right. No mere questions of policy could influence his fight for truth. He was outspoken in the expression of his views, and although some differed with him, all respected him. As a business educator his work as professor of theoretical and practical accounting in the New York University of the School of Commerce, Accounts and Finance is well known. As a journalist his work as editor of The Metal Worker, Carpentry and Building, Business, and, later in connection with COMMERCE, ACCOUNTS & FINANCE and The Bulletin of the American Institute of Bank Clerks speaks for itself.

Mr. Kittredge had always been a hard worker. No task was too great for him to undertake, and once undertaken it was carried to completion. He was a marvel of industry, working early and late to further the desires of his employers, when he was an employee, and relaxing not at all when he employed others. We do not mean by this that he was inconsiderate to his employees or that he demanded of them more than they could perform; it was merely that, by his untiring energy, he set an example which was inspiring to those beneath him. It was largely owing to Mr. Kittredge's efforts that the law was passed making the Regents' Degree of C. P. A. in New York State, now so greatly sought after by accountants. He was the originator of the Balance Sheet System of Accounting, which is, without doubt, the most up-to-date and comprehensive accounting system yet devised.

*

In addition to his accounting work, Mr. Kittredge was the secretary of the American Institute of Bank Clerks, the educational work undertaken by the American Bankers' Association. He was present at the convention of the Bankers' Association at Richmond in 1900, where the bankers appropriated a large sum of money for the founding of an organization for the education of bank clerks along broad banking lines. The trustees of the Institute are some of the leading bankers of the country. The practical work of the organization was in Mr. Kittredge's hands. He organized the Correspondence School of Banking, which now has students everywhere. Under his direction The Bulletin, the official organ of the Institute, now has probably a larger circulation than any banking magazine published, and has subscribers in all parts of the world. Mr. Kittredge's work as secretary of the Institute will, perhaps, be his greatest monument. If he had done nothing else this work would be sufficient to insure the gratitude of many thousands of his countrymen. His friends were many and his mourners will be numerous.

* * *

The formation of societies of public accountants goes on apace. One was recently formed in New York City and another has just been formed in San Francisco, Cal. These societies of public accountants are bodies which are bound to do great good not only to their members, but to the business world in general. To accountants their meetings should serve as gatherings where much interesting information relating to the profession may be given and obtained. To the business world they should serve as object lessons of what modern accountancy really is and what it is doing for commerce and finance. There should be an accountant's society in every one of the large cities of the country. This undoubtedly will be true some day, but now is the time to set about it. COMMERCE, ACCOUNTS & FINANCE will be glad to receive reports of the meetings of these societies for publication in its columns, and the editor trusts that the secretaries of the societies will be kind enough to send these reports to him.

* * *

POSTPONEMENT.

Owing to the sudden death of Mr. A. O. Kittredge, who had in personal charge the preparation of the manuscript for the five books—"Tools of Business," "Elements of Bookkeeping," "Balance Sheet Accounting," "Auditing" and "Business Organization and Administration"—and the consequent difficulty of continuing the work under the charge of one more or less unfamiliar with Mr. Kittredge's intentions, the publishers are obliged to announce that the production of the books will now be indefinitely postponed. Suitable notice of the date of publication will be given as soon as it is possible to do so.

RAILWAY ACCIDENTS.

Railway accidents in the United States have always been more frequent than in England and on the Continent of Europe. To a great degree the single track system is no doubt responsible for this, but some of the recent accidents in the States and in Canada seem to point to the deplorable fact that the railway employees are not only overworked, but that their number is far too small to insure a sufficient degree of safety to the traveling public. Severe accusations have been laid against the different companies by the press and public, saying that the companies neglect the safety of their passengers in order to be able to pay higher dividends. Some of these accusations are no doubt exaggerated, but the preponderance of railway accidents as compared with England and the Continent of Europe has a very serious aspect. During the fifteen months ending March, 1902, not a single passenger was killed by a train accident in Great Britain, and since that date we remember only one fatal accident occurring in the United Kingdom.

In the United States 282 passengers were killed by railway accidents during the year ending June 30, 1901, while 4,988 passengers were injured. This bad record has been even exceeded by the disasters which have happened between December 26, 1902, and the beginning of the present year. Including Canada, over twenty-six railway accidents have happened during that short period, causing a loss of lives exceeding one hundred, and injuries to more than two hundred passengers. Even the figures quoted tell but a small part of the story of destruction of human life by American railways.

The total number of casualties to persons on account of railway accidents for the year ending June 30, 1901, was 61,794; the killed numbering 8,455, and the injured, 53,339. Out of every 400 employees, one was killed, and out of every 26 employees, one was injured. Of the "train men" proper, the ratio was even greater. One was killed out of every 136, and one injured out of every 13. In Canada, during the year ending June 30, 1901, the total killed were 317; and the injured, 1317; but only 29 were killed through the railway from collisions and derailments.

Another set of figures shows that for the year ending June 30, 1901, one passenger was killed for every 2,153,469 carried, and one injured for every 121,748 carried. Ratios based on the number of miles traveled, however, show that 61,537,548 passenger miles were traveled for each passenger killed; and 3,479,067 for each passenger injured. The corresponding figures for the year ending June 30, 1900, were, however, 64,413,684 for every passenger killed; and 3,885,418 for every passenger injured, showing that the accident ratio grew worse.

If the figures were to hand for 1902 an even worse showing would be made, and Canada's record for that period would be a very black one.

A great part of the accidents in Canada have taken place on the Grand Trunk Railway. The "Railway and Locomotive Engineering," commenting on the cause of the Wanstead accident, says: "The fact, if true, furnishes an example of a certain kind of train dispatch, which should make officials of the Grand Trunk Railway hang their heads with shame." It certainly appears as if, as the "Scientific American" says, "the sanctity of human life is held very much more sacred abroad than here," and its accusations against American railways—that they take enormous risks for the sake of lower costs and larger profits—is such a stern one, that railway officials, if these accusations be true, should try every remedy in their power to make the railways of the United States and Canada as safe as those of Great Britain and the Continent.

THE UNWILLING SUBSCRIBER.

The following extract from a letter sent to me by the First Assistant Postmaster General, R. J. Wynne, will interest all who have periodicals thrust upon them against their will, says "Tip" in the "New York Press":

Up to this time the department has not found a way by which it could interfere in the matter of alleged indebtedness for subscription to a periodical. However, there has been so much questionable work on the part of certain publications which refuse to discontinue when requested by subscribers that I agree with you it is time something should be done. It ought to be possible to put a stop to the mailing of publications to people who are not subscribers and the subsequent placing of the accounts in the hands of bad debt collecting agencies. You understand that it is a somewhat difficult matter to handle, for the reason that a great many newspapers do not require prepayment of subscriptions, and it really is no business of this department whether a responsible subscriber prepays his subscription or not if the publisher is willing to trust him.

The only point the department has to consider is whether, after the subscriber has notified the publisher to discontinue his paper, or after the postmaster has notified the publisher that the subscriber refuses to take the paper from the postoffice, the continuance on the part of the publisher to claim that the addressee still is a subscriber is an attempt upon the publisher's part to obtain money under false or fraudulent representations through the mails, or whether the alleged subscription list is a legitimate subscription list such as would entitle the publisher to the benefits of the pound rate of postage. The question will be considered further.

Washington, March 23.

Mr. Wynne, unfortunately, overlooks the matter of contract or no contract between publisher and subscriber. Even in cases of newspapers which do not demand prepayment of subscription there is always a contract if the publisher is honest. He says to John Brown: "I don't see your name on my list of subscribers, John. If you haven't got the price handy let me send the paper anyhow and you can pay when you're flush." "All right," says Brown. There is the contract, and the publisher may send the paper to Brown as long as he is willing to trust him. And, finally, if Brown refuses to pay, a suit will lie. Country papers take loads of wood, hay, fodder, potatoes, wheat, corn, oats, hams, bacon, mutton—anything they can get for subscriptions and at any time when the articles may be brought to the office. "Bill Jones has been taking our paper for two years and ain't brought that load of lightwood yet," is one of the customary methods of asking a subscriber to settle up.

A SECOND WASHINGTON.

A man was standing in front of a Saranac Lake market the other day. He had a basket and a fishing rod. "Just throw me a dozen perch and bullheads," he said to the owner of the market.

"Certainly," replied the owner, "but why do you ask me to throw them to you?"

"So I can go home and tell my wife I caught them," was the reply. "I may be a poor fisherman, but I am no liar."

Exhibition Accounts and Finance. I*

By JOHN M. MACLEOD, C.A.,

Auditor of the Glasgow International Exhibition, 1901.

THE subject of this paper is "Exhibition Accounts and Finance, and the System of Checking Income and Expenditure." Before entering on the technical portion of the paper, I would say something on the general subject of exhibitions.

To France must be accorded the credit of the conception of the exhibition in somewhat of the form in which we know it at the present day, as the first display of the kind was held at Paris in 1798. Before that date, indeed, there had been a number of exhibitions. They, however, were small and provincial in character, and the Paris Exhibition of 1798 has been generally regarded as the parent of the great industrial exhibitions of modern times. Between 1798 and 1850 about fifteen exhibitions, either of a provincial or municipal description, were organized and inaugurated. Of these, no fewer than eleven were in Paris, and four were British, and were held respectively in London in 1828, in Manchester in 1837, in Leeds in 1839, and Birmingham in 1849. Since 1850 there have been forty-one great exhibitions, of which nineteen were foreign and twenty-two British.

First Great Exhibition in England.

If to France belongs the credit of the idea of exhibitions, to Britain must be awarded the distinction of expanding them into the great international undertakings with which we are now familiar. The era of international exhibitions in this country began with the opening of Sir Joseph Paxton's "Palace of Glass" in Hyde Park, London, by Queen Victoria in May, 1851. The structure, which was of glass and iron, was built at the cost of £193,168, and enclosed twenty acres, and was 1,851 feet in length. It accommodated the works of 13,937 exhibitors, of whom 6,681 were British, 520 colonial, and 6,556 foreign. The exhibition remained open five and a half months, and was visited by 6,039,195 visitors. The greatest number in one day was 109,760, and the admission fees amounted to £423,792, or, including season tickets, £505,107. After all expenses were paid, a surplus of about £150,000 remained, which Her Majesty's Commissioners invested in the purchase of an estate at South Kensington, on which subsequently the South Kensington Museum, the Royal Horticultural Society's Garden, the International Exhibition of 1862, the Albert Memorial Hall, and other institutions have been placed. The exhibition building, now the Crystal Palace, at Sydenham must be familiar to many.

The success, pecuniary and otherwise, of this exhibition gave birth to a numerous train of imitators, among which I shall notice the following:

1855.—In 1855 the "Exposition Universelle," of Paris, was held in the Palace of Industry, a specially erected permanent building. It accommodated 20,839 exhibitors, and, while open from 15th May till 30th November, it was visited by 5,162,330 persons; but the expenses exceeded the income. In this and subsequent exhibitions international collections of pictures formed striking features.

1862.—The next great exhibition in order of time was the London International Exhibition of 1862, for which a guarantee fund of £452,300 was raised. The building was of brick, the main hall being a parallelogram 1,150 feet long by 560 feet wide, which, with annexes, cost £460,000. Remaining open from 1st May till 15th November, it was visited by 6,211,103 persons, and the total receipts were £408,530.

1867.—A second "Exposition Universelle" was opened in Paris on the Champs de Mars in May, 1867. The building was oviform, and the different sections were arranged in concentric bands. By this arrangement visitors could examine the entire collections of any nation by proceeding from the outer band to the center, and special classes of articles from all nations could be visited by making the circuit of the building in any continuous ring. Part of the surrounding park was enclosed for reproductions of national habitations, and the life, clothing, food, and domestic habits of the various peoples were practically illustrated by families brought from all corners of the globe to inhabit the houses of their countries. The "Exposition" was visited by 6,805,969 persons, and the receipts from all sources were £420,735.

1873.—The "Weltausstellung" of Vienna, 1873, a building with a central rotunda 312 feet in diameter, covered by a dome larger than that of St. Peter's at Rome, was constructed by J. Scott Russell, a native of Glasgow. It was visited by 6,740,500 persons during the six months it remained open, and the total receipts amounted to £206,477.

The Centennial Exhibition.

1876.—Across the Atlantic, the Centennial Exhibition of the United States was held in 1876, in Fairmount Park, Philadelphia, and was then described as "the biggest thing that had ever been drawn together." It comprised a main building 1,880 feet long by 464 feet wide, covering twenty-one and one-half acres; a permanent art gallery, a machinery hall, an agricultural hall, and a horticultural hall, extending over forty-six acres. The attendance was 9,910,996.

1878.—It was surpassed in 1878 by a still more gigantic exhibition held in Paris, when on the opening day no fewer than 111,955 persons were admitted, which is claimed to be the largest assemblage ever under the same roof at one time in the history of the world. The total admissions were 16,032,725, or a daily average of 82,000 persons.

Uncle Sam—"Will somebody tell me how the Pup works."—Boston Herald.

*From the "Accountant's Magazine," of Edinburgh.

George Washington Roosevelt:—"Father, I cannot tell a lie, I did it with my little hatchet."—Philadelphia Press.

The gross receipts were 12,653,746 francs, or about £527,239 sterling.

1886.—Passing over various exhibitions held between 1878 and 1886, I briefly notice the great Colonial and Indian Exhibition in London in 1886, where the total attendance was 5,550,745. The highest number on one day was 81,516 and the surplus was £35,235.

During the same year Liverpool held an exhibition, with a total attendance of 2,468,098, and total receipts amounting to £131,032, and an expenditure of £150,167. Not deterred by the loss sustained, they made another effort in the following year, when the attendance was under one million, and the balance was again on the wrong side.

1888.—I must now, before closing these preliminary notices, refer briefly to the Glasgow Exhibition of 1888. It was open 161 days. The total attendance was 5,748,379, and the highest number admitted on one day was 117,901. The gross receipts were £225,928, and the payments £184,858, leaving on hand a surplus, after providing for some contingent claims, of £41,070, which with accrued interest, and the sum realized from buildings, amounting in all to £53,000, was devoted to the promotion of the fine arts in our city, and formed the nucleus of the fund that was raised to erect the palatial building in Kelvingrove for housing the art treasures of past, present and future generations of the citizens.

1901.—Coming now to the Glasgow Exhibition of 1901, I may note that the promoters required to provide (first) funds to meet all preliminary and administrative expenses, and the cost of erecting the buildings, until such time as the revenue from the exhibition began to come in; and (second) funds to meet any deficiency that might arise from the undertaking. The appeal for this guarantee met with a ready response. The corporation guaranteed £5,000, and altogether a sum of £508,916 was subscribed by 1,255 subscribers, in sums varying from £5 to £10,000. The guarantee bonds were lodged with the Clydesdale Bank, and were held by it for behoof of itself and the other banks that might be asked to advance moneys to the exhibition. The total amount borrowed from the banks was £84,500, and the interest paid was £2,892 14s. 4d. These sums were repaid out of rents received for space, payments from contractors in advance, and the first takings of the exhibition, within ten days after the date of opening.

The Method at the Paris Exhibition.

It may be interesting to notice here the difference in the method adopted by the Executive of the Paris Exhibition of 1900. A guarantee was given by the Government of the French Republic, amounting to twenty million francs, say £800,000 sterling, and a similar sum was guaranteed by the municipality of the City of Paris, making together £1,600,000 sterling. The Republic was the promoter, and in its name the invitations were given to foreign nations to participate in the exhibition. An agreement was made with the City of Paris that if there was a surplus—which we know now there was not—it would be equally divided between the state and the city; but if there was a loss, it would be borne by the state alone.

In 1896, under an agreement with the Consortium of Bankers, bonds had been issued to the extent of sixty million francs, equal to £2,400,000 sterling. Each bond had twenty tickets of admission to the exhibition attached, giving the bearer certain privileges as to admission to side shows and return railway fares, together with the chance of drawing prizes valued from £4,000 down to £40, every three months for four years. The whole of these bonds were immediately taken up by the public, and thus the administration of the exhibition received in cash £2,400,000 sterling three years before it was opened. This sum was further increased by the concession granted to theatres, restaurants, panoramas, and other side shows, by about £500,000 sterling. The concessions were sold either by public auction or private bargain, and fetched very high prices, as much as £12,000 being paid for the one for printing and selling the official catalogue.

The originality of the scheme consisted in getting the money not "cash on delivery," but cash three years before delivery, and at the same time insuring the receipts for the admissions at least four years in advance. No money was taken at the gates, only tickets, and these were obliterated as received, and counted and destroyed daily. One curious feature in connection with the scheme was the changing market value of these bonds. As the drawings for the prizes went on, and the remaining chances were reduced, the value of the single admission tickets went steadily down, until a ticket bearing the face value of one franc could be bought for 2d. Thus, towards the end of the exhibition, millions of people enjoyed the privilege of entering at a cost that was 80 per cent. under the regular charge, but without injuring the receipts. Surely a very clever financial arrangement!

The total attendance at the Paris Exhibition, 1900, was 50,860,801. The highest attendance in one day was 652,082. This large number of admissions in one day was exceeded at the Chicago Exhibition of 1893, when 761,000 persons were admitted in one day, the total attendance for the period being 23,000,000.

It is to be earnestly hoped that the financial success attending our two exhibitions in Glasgow will not cause cities to seize upon the idea of imitating them as a means of mere money raising, otherwise we shall have exhibitions becoming as great a nuisance as the modern bazaar. The popularity and attractiveness of our latest exhibition will be readily admitted when we recall the fact that during the 165 days it was open to the public over eleven and one-half million visits were made. As a means of education and mental stimulus to so vast a number of people its value cannot be easily calculated.

Income.

Speaking now in detail of the finances of our last exhibition and the methods of checking income and expenditures, I deal first with income, the chief sources of which were: admissions, royalties and concessions, space rents and miscellaneous receipts. Let us glance at each of these in its order.

Under the head of admissions are embraced season tickets, coupons, railway and steamboat tickets, special tickets, and gate money. The season tickets were of a special design, supplied per contract by one printer only, and numbered consecutively in each class (adult and children) from No. 1 upward. The cashier was responsible for the sale of these. The sale commenced before Christmas, 1900, and altogether 104,357 tickets were sold, made up of 94,391 for adults and 9,966 for children. Three banks, and their city branches, and about thirty shops in various parts of the city, assisted in the sale, and thereby materially lightened the work of the cashier's staff. The auditor was able to check the number of tickets sold by comparing the certificate obtained from the printer of the number issued with the tickets on hand and cash received. Similarly, the coupon tickets were certified and the stock on hand verified. The returns made by the railway and steamboat companies were compared with the books. The largest item of income from admissions was, of course, from the money taken at the gates. The arrangements for admission and the system of checking the cash received were as follows: There were six entrances, at each of which there were turnstiles for admission, arranged as follows: Attendants and exhibitors; payment (adults who paid); payment (children who paid); season ticket holders, and holders of railway, steamboat and coupon tickets. There were thirty-nine turnstiles in all. The records of the registers and the cash were taken from all the gates twice daily, and on certain days three times daily, and the keys of the registers and money boxes were available only on these occasions.

To facilitate the collections, the entrances were divided into three groups, and, exactly at the fixed periods, representatives of the admission department, the cashier's office and the bank were in attendance. Each representative was in possession of a card with the turnstile in his group noted thereon, and with a blank space for the index numbers. The records were taken by each official, and the cash was there and then taken possession of by the Clydesdale Bank. The inspectors from the admission department, when the records of their group were fully taken, returned to the admission office and handed in their cards to two recorders, who entered the figures in a large sheet that already contained the index numbers taken at a previous collection. When all the figures were entered, the differences of the two readings were extended, and when the two recorders agreed on the result, the return was complete and ready for announcement. So perfectly did the system work that Mr. James Laing, the excellent head of the admission department, and his efficient staff were able to announce the total number admitted each day under the separate allocations within fifteen minutes after the entrance gates were closed at 9:30 P. M.

Handling the Cash.

As already stated, the bank officials took possession of the bags containing the cash, and carried them straight to the bank. The bank in due course counted the cash, and sent in a return to the admission department of the money from each cash turnstile. This return was at once compared with the record shown from the register, and the money received entered in the admission sheet. Any difference between the cash and the numbers recorded was noted in a special column in the sheet. The complete daily return from the bank of each day's counting was in the hands of the admission department early the following morning. This often entailed hard work for the bank officials, as after a heavy day the amount of silver was very large. But by working during the early hours of the morning the work was overtaken, and was never at any time an hour in arrear. The arrangement was of immense benefit to the exhibition. It saved an incalculable amount of responsibility and labor to the treasurer's department, and no question could arise as to the counting. The bank's return was final. In addition, it enabled the admission department to check at once the honesty of the men in charge of the turnstile.

At first there were certain differences between the money counted by the bank and the number of admissions by payment shown by the register. In some cases more money was collected than the register recorded, and in other cases less. In the first instance, where more money was collected, this could be accounted for by more than one person in a crowd passing together through a turnstile with only one marking. In the second instance it was possible that the turnstiles might not be working smoothly. In the latter case the men in charge were shifted to turnstiles that had been proved to be in good working order, and if the differences still continued their services were dispensed with. This, however, happened in only a few cases at the commencement of the exhibition, and there is no doubt about the honesty of the men employed at the turnstiles. It is interesting to note that the net result at the close of the exhibition of these daily "shorts" and "overs" was a balance of £75 11s. 1d. in favor of the "overs"—that is to say, £75 11s. 1d. was received in excess of the amount recorded by the registers.

When the charge for admission was reduced to 6d. after five o'clock, a collection was made at that hour, and it was thus easy to calculate the admissions by payment after that time at the reduced rate. The sales of tickets and cash admissions were as follows:

Season tickets, adult, 21s.........	80,624=	£84,655 4 0
Half tickets, adult, 10s. 6d........	13,764=	7,227 13 6
Season tickets, children, 10s. 6d...	7,798=	4,093 19 0
Half tickets, children, 5s..........	2,168=	542 0 0
	104,354	£96,518 16 6
Coupon tickets, adults and children........		£4,060 8 10
Excursion, steamboat, etc., tickets........		2,854 14 0
		£6,915 2 10
Cash drawn at the gates..................		167,957 13 11
Showing a total of...................		£271,391 13 3

The "record" attendance was on 9th November, when the number who passed the turnstiles was 173,266, with gate money amounting to £1,861 11s. 6d., and the lowest on 11th July, when there were but 37,243 visits made. The highest takings at the gates on one day were on 23d September, when £3,589, 7s. was received in cash, and the attendance was 171,960. The lowest takings were £365, 5s. on 7th May, with an attendance of 46,164. The highest attendance at the 1888 exhibition was on the closing day, 10th November, when 117,901 passed the turnstiles; and the highest gate money was on the same day, and amounted to £2,331, 0s. 6d. The lowest gate was on 28th June, when only £181 6s. 9d. was taken. In 1901 the average daily attendance, including the free admissions, was 70,058, and in 1888 it was 35,689. The drawings from the switchback railway, water chute, and Indian theatre were checked by turnstile registers. The numbers were taken at the same time as the collections from the admission gates, and the cash was likewise taken possession of by the bank. The bank also collected the money from the sports ground after each performance, and this was checked with the turnstile registers taken at the same time. Over one hundred foreign and colonial coins were passed at the turnstiles as shillings. As the colonial coins bore the Queen's head it was easy to have them passed in a crush, and the foreign coins were similar in appearance to our shillings. There were two franc pieces dated prior to the battle of Waterloo.

MUST LOVE YOUR WORK.

The following is from the writings of James Russell Lowell:

A merchant, desiring office-help, advertised for a young man. The following morning found some dozen or more applicants for the position. Each in turn was asked to step into the office. One after the other was told that he did not suit. This surprised several of the young men, inasmuch as no cause was given for the curt, but to-the-point, "No, you're not our man."

Another young man entered the office to make his application and the following conversation ensued:

"How old are you?"

"Twenty years."

"What trade have you learned?"

"None."

"What education have you had?"

"Public and high school."

"Do you like to work?"

Those in the other room who overheaerd this question were somewhat surprised when the young man's response came forth unhesitatingly:

"Can't say as I do."

Their surprise was not at its highest point, however, for, hardly had the words left the applicant's mouth, than the proprietor was heard to give vent to the following:

"Good! I wouldn't work unless I had to. I admire honesty and straightforwardness. The job's yours."

Upon telling this story on different occasions, says Mr. Lowell, I have heard remarks like the following: "That's about right," "I'll wager the other fellows didn't like work any better than he did," and "Very few of us would work if we weren't forced to" * * * Young man and young woman, listen to me—if you have no love for your work, if you must drive yourself or be driven to attend to your daily duties in your work, there is something radically wrong with you or the kind of work you have taken up. The man or woman who is doing work which is distasteful to him or which he is not eager to pursue, is not on the highway to success—he will never reach that pinnacle towards which we should all be striving. Your work may be of humble stamp, but if you love it, if you take pleasure in it, if you are constantly striving to advance in it, to become more perfect, you must succeed and will succeed. Progress is made when earnest endeavors are made to reach an ideal, and where determination is backed up by industry the result is positive—success.

The story repeated above has its good points. The merchant's last words were, "I admire honesty and straightforwardness."

We are often surprised when brought face to face with incongruities as exemplified in the proprietor's last reply. How an admirer of honesty and straightforwardness can at the same time stand for such opposite principles is more than is within the comprehension of ordinary mortals.

Honesty in all dealings has been the advice to humanity for years. Dishonest methods have been successful temporarily. Honest methods prevail and rise above dishonest ways of doing business in the long run. It is more desirable to be honest in the pursuit of one's business than to have to meet the sneer, the look of rebuke or contempt which accompanies the gaze of one's friends or employees who realize the means that have been employed to gain certain ends at the cost of honesty and conscience. Be honest because it pays and because it is right.

Straightforwardness and honesty are kinsmen. Let your glance as well as your speech and address be straightforward—unmistakable. The young man who is equipped with health, energy, honesty and straightforwardness will find that many obstacles apparently insurmountable are overcome with ease. Above all,

"Be noble! and the nobleness
That lies in other men,
Sleeping but never dead,
Will rise in majesty to meet thine own."

RECOGNIZABLE.

"Mr. Jones," began old Skinflint, the boss, as he cleared his throat, "you have been in my employ just twenty years to-day, and have proven a good and faithful servant. I propose to make now substantial recognition of your fidelity. Here is a picture of myself as a present."

"Thanks. It's just like you," muttered Jones as he accepted the valuable gift.—Baltimore American.

IN THE SMOKING CAR.

"Here's a good one," said the man from Denver. "What's the difference between a pen and a pencil? Give it up? A pen has to be driven, but a pencil has to be lead. See?"

"The automatic bell buoy beats 'em both," murmured a quiet little chap who had got on at Cleveland. "It rights itself."—Philadelphia Press.

MIGHT HAVE BEEN WORSE.

Governor Odell tells this story of an optimistic parson: A poor Irishman had lost both legs by an accident in a stone quarry, and was in the hospital. "Come, cheer up, my good man," said the parson, brightly. "You've lost a pair of legs, but it's not so bad as it might be." "Shure, I dunno but you're roight," replied the fellow, glumly. "I suppose it would have been a thundering sight worse if I'd ever learned to dance."

OF TWO EVILS.

"He can't afford to let her spend so much money.'

She—Well, perhaps he'd rather have trouble with his creditors than with his wife.

The Tale of the Stranger Who Was Not up to the Times

By JOE LINCOLN.

AND it was the one thousand and eleventh night and the Father of the Faithful, having newly arisen from his couch whereon had he slumbered throughout the day, appeared in his audience chamber, and, behold, his countenance was troubled. And he spake unto Scheherezade, saying:

"Verily, thou chewest gum yesterday, to-day and forever! Lo, with the power of thy jaw could I run a dynamo for the lighting of this abode of happiness. Cease, I pray thee, for a space and answer me this, my question: What thief hath rehypothecated the Royal turban and left this Fedora in its stead?"

And Scheherezade answered and said: "Oh, Concentration of Wisdom, there is thy turban in the bootjack where thou placed it this morning upon thy return from the banquet of the Commercial Travellers' Sodality. That which thou art attempting to fit upon thy massive brow is a slipper."

And the King looked and saw that it was so. And Scheherezade judging it wisest to wait not for an answer, spake yet again with exceeding quickness, saying:

"Know, oh thou whose superlative virtues excelleth even those of the newest breakfast food, hearken unto thy handmaiden. Behold, it came to pass that a certain youth named Ali Cogia lived in the city of Rhagbagg, where he labored in the shop of a merchant. And the ways of the world beyond the gates of the city were unknown to the youth, forasmuch as he had journeyed but little.

"And it came to pass that upon a day the merchant sent for Ali Cogia and bade him journey into a far country, even unto the town of Dingbhatt. And the youth was exceedingly glad, although the importance of his errand bowed him down even as a thousand of brick. And he bade the slaves make ready the camels, while he himself put an edge upon the creases of his trousers and a gloss upon his slippers, that he might cut a dash in the land.

"And behold he journeyed far, until after many days he came unto the city of his seeking, even unto Dingbhat. And there called he upon the merchants with whom it was ordained that he should hold converse. But behold, the merchants were not yet at their shops. And by the timepiece in the pocket of Ali Cogia it was nine of the morning.

"And Ali Cogia spake unto a warder of the city, even unto a copper that slumbered by the wayside. And he communed with the copper thus:

"'Lo, this is a dead town and only waiting for the undertaker. Behold, it is nine of the clock and these merchants are not yet on deck.'

"And the copper drew forth his own timepiece and said:

"'Verily, thy watch is a sprinter and trying for the record. It is now but eight.'

"And Ali Cogia scoffed loudly, forasmuch as his timepiece was a new one and he had set it by the chronometer in the jeweller's window before starting on his journey. And he drew it forth and held it before the copper, saying:

"'To the rear, thou son of rest! to the rear and recline upon a divan. Look thou upon a watch that is a watch.'

"And the copper gazed upon the timepiece of Ali Cogia and grinned and said:

"'From whence comest thou?'

"And Ali Cogia smiled with exceeding loftiness and made answer, saying:

"'From the real thing—even from Rhagbagg.'

"And the copper sighed as one who pities, and spake thus:

"'To the rear thyself, oh unsalted one! Thou carriest the time of Rhagbagg, which is one hour faster than the time of Dingbhatt. It is now but eight of the clock.'

"And Ali Cogia marvelled, but he turned back the hands of his timepiece unto eight, and at nine

by the new time came the merchants and Ali Cogia conversed with them. And behold one of them begged that Ali Cogia would feast with him. And he said:

"'Meet me before the wineshop of Timsul Livan, at twelve thirty.' And Ali Cogia said unto him, 'Sure!'

"But behold, when at twelve thirty Ali Cogia sought the wineshop, the merchant was not therein.

And he waited long but the merchant came not. And at length he spake unto the keeper of the shop, even unto Timsul Livan, and the latter said unto him:

"'Thou art behind the schedule. He that thou waitest for was here at the appointed time, but thou camest not until one of the clock.'

"And Ali Cogia was wroth and said, 'Verily, thou art disconnected with thy battery! It is but one thirty even now and I have sojourned in this poison dispensary several weeks already.'

"And when Timsul Livan saw the watch of Ali Cogia he grinned wearily and said:

"'Art thou not a stranger in the city?'

"And Ali Cogia said 'Praised be to Allah, that's what I am.'

"And Timsul Livan answered him, saying: "Thy watch beareth the time of the city, but most appointments are made by standard time, which is half an hour faster than the time of the city.'

"And Ali Cogia was bewildered and marvelled yet more, but he set his timepiece according to the standard time and fared forth to purchase a sandwich.

"And it came to pass that a merchant with whom he was to deal was to arrive in Dingbhat by the special caravan from the West. And the time of that caravan's arrival was the hour of four that afternoon.

"And behold at the hour of four was he waiting at the door of the inn where the caravan unloaded. But the caravan came not and he marvelled; and he spake unto a porter who was assorting his tips and placing them in barrels—the quarters into the one barrel, the halves into another barrel, and so on. And Ali Cogia said unto the porter:

"'Why, I pray thee, is the four o'clock caravan not here?'

"And the porter answered not but stretched forth his hand. And Ali Cogia, being wise, reached down into his garments and brought forth a coin and made good with the porter. And the porter answered and said:

"'The four o'clock caravan is not here because it is not yet four o'clock.'

"And Ali Cogia was amazed and said:

"'Of a surety, it is four and after four.' And he held forth his timepiece.

"And the porter grinned and said:

"'Yea, verily, boss, but that is standard time and the caravans from the West are run upon Western time, which is one half hour slower than standard time.'

"And Ali Cogia sank upon the floor of the inn and muttered wildly thus:

"'Behold this is the limit. These people come to their labors at the hour set by the city time; and their food they eat by standard time; and their caravans they run by Western time; and they give the glad "Ha! Ha!" to the stranger who carrieth Eastern time. Verily, let me hie hence before they spring another time upon me!'

"And at that instant came unto him the merchant who had invited him to the feast. And the merchant was rejoiced to see him and fell upon his neck, crying:

"'Lo, my heart was sad when I met thee not at noonday; but come, let us seek the playhouse and hear a little ragtime.'

"And Ali Cogia fled howling, and they found him in the square before the temple, rending his garments and casting stones at the town clock. And they wept exceeding sore and led him away to the crazy house.

And Scheherezade paused and said unto the Father of the Faithful, "Oh King, live forever! What thinkest thou of Ali Cogia and the people of Dingbhatt?"

And the Sultan opened his eyes and made answer, saying, "Verily, I think the folk of Dingbhatt gave Ali the time of his life."

And he closed his eyes and slumbered yet again.

GOOD OLD NAMES.

The Indian names that have come down to us are the most euphonious in any language and it is little less than profanation to discard them, and around others that our fathers used there cluster memories, tradition and history that make them almost sacred to those who have heard them from childhood, says the Manchester (N. H.) "Mirror." Think of Penacook as Streeterville, Monadnock as Miller Mountain, Winnipesaukee as Busiel Lake, Kearsarge as Mount Chandler, Chocorua as Sanborn Hill, the Piscataquog River as Goffstown Creek, the Nashua as Hamblett Brook and Massabesic as the Manchester reservoir, and it sends a shudder of disgust through every well-tempered mind. Scarcely less reprehensible is the change from Loon Pond to Highland Lake, from Rattlesnake Hill to Mount Pleasant, from Beaver Dam Meadows to The Intervales and all that class of sentimental revision of our geographies and histories. The old names meant something. The new one are meaningless. Let us stick to the designations of the fathers.

FLOUR OR DOUGH?

He thought it safer to write to the girl's father for her hand. He was an ardent lover, but a poor speller, and his note ran:

"I want your daughter—the flour of your family."

"The flour of my family is good," replied the old man; "are you sure it isn't my dough you're after?"—Yonkers Statesman.

MORE SPIRIT.

A minister opened the Sunday-school class with the well-known hymn, "Little drops of water, little grains of sand." In the middle of the first verse he stopped the singing, and complained strongly of the half-hearted manner in which it was sung. He made a fresh start; "Now, then," he shouted, "little drops of water, and for goodness sake put some spirit into it."

ATTACHMENT.

Teacher—Tommy, can you tell me what animal attaches himself most to man?

Tommy (aged six)—The bulldog, ma'am.—Telegram.

The Negotiable Instruments Law*

By THOS. B. PATON.

Form of Notice of Dishonor—Illustrative Cases—Rules as to Parties to Whom Notice May be Given.

NOTE.—As enacted in New York, the Negotiable Instruments Law is divided into nineteen articles as follows:

1. General Provisions (Sections 1—17)
2. Negotiable Instruments: Form and Interpretation (20—42)
3. Consideration (50—55)
4. Negotiation (60—80)
5. Rights of holder (90—98)
6. Liabilities of parties (110—119)
7. Presentment for payment (130—148)
8. Notice of dishonor (160—189)
9. Discharge (200—206)
10. Bills of exchange (210—215)
11. Acceptance (220—230)
12. Presentment for acceptance (240—248)
13. Protest (260—268)
14. Acceptance for honor (280—290)
15. Payment for honor (300—306)
16. Bills in a set (310—315)
17. Promissory notes and checks (320—325)
18. Notes given for patent rights (330—332)
19. Laws repealed. When takes effect (340—341)

The provisions of the law naturally fall under four general classifications.

a. General Provisions.
b. Negotiable Instruments in General.
c. Bills of Exchange.
d. Promissory Notes and Checks.

The text of the law is the same in all the states (with some slight exceptions which will be noted) but the numbering of the sections, and in some states, of the articles, is not uniform. There is, however, the same continuity of articles and text, except that in some instances "General Provisions" follow, instead of precede the remainder of the act. By following this course of study with reference to the New York act, as above outlined, the reader in each state can apply the same to the law of his own state.

HAVING seen to whom and by whom notice of dishonor may be given, and certain matters bearing on the sufficiency of the notice, we now come to the section which provides the form of notice.

Sec. 167. Form of Notice.—The notice may be in writing or merely oral and may be given in any terms which sufficiently identify the instrument and indicate that it has been dishonored by non-acceptance or non-payment. It may in all cases be given by delivering it personally or through the mails.

In the first place the notice may be in writing or merely oral. This provision embodies the rule of the law merchant that it is not necessary that notice of dishonor of a bill or note should be in writing and that verbal notice is sufficient. The sufficiency of a verbal notice was tested in the Supreme Court of the State of New York as early as the year 1830 in the case of Cuyler v. Stevens, 4 Wend. 566. Payment of a promissory note at maturity had been demanded of the maker at his place of business in Troy, and at his dwelling house in Greenbush, New York, and on the following business day the agent of the holder called at the store of the endorser in the City of Albany, showed him the note, gave him verbal notice of demand and non-payment and informed him that the holder looked to him for payment. When the endorser was sued on the note he contended that the notice of dishonor was insufficient because verbal and not in writing, the parties residing in different counties; but the court held that the verbal notice was sufficient to charge the endorser. The same has been held in other states.

Notice Over the Telephone.

Now that the telephone as a means of communication has come into vogue, an interesting question arises whether verbal notice of dishonor can be given through that medium where the parties giving and receiving notice may be physically separated by many miles. The method of giving notice of dishonor by telephone is probably legal and sufficient, if proved to have been received by the endorser, but a practical objection arises as to the ability of the sender to prove the identity of the recipient, that is, that the party to whom notice has been communicated over the telephone is the identical endorser sought to be charged with notice. That fact proved, we believe the notice would be just as sufficient legally as if verbally communicated face to face. The Court of Appeals of Kansas in the year 1897 had before it a question of the sufficiency of a notice of dishonor by telephone (See Thompson v. Appleby, 14 B. L. J. 391). The court held: While a witness may ordinarily testify to a conversation had by him over the telephone with a person though he is not able to identify the voice of the person responding, yet where it is sought to charge an endorser of a promissory note with liability by a notice of dishonor thus communicated, it must clearly appear that the person responding was the endorser himself; and where the only evidence of giving such notice was the testimony of a witness that he called up the office of the endorser and did not know whether or not it was the endorser or his bookkeeper, or either of them, that responded, it is not error to sustain a demurrer to this testimony, as furnishing no evidence that the notice of dishonor was given.

Having considered the provision that the notice may be in writing or merely oral, we proceed to consider that it "may be given in any terms which sufficiently identify the instrument and indicate that it has been dishonored by non-acceptance or non-payment."

This relates to the terms in which the language of the verbal or written notice may be couched. Any terms are sufficient, provided two main requisites are complied with:

1. That they sufficiently identify the instrument:
2. That they indicate that it has been dishonored by non-acceptance or non-payment.

As to the sufficiency of terms to identify the instrument, we have already seen, in considering section 166, that a misdescription of the instrument does not vitiate the notice unless the party to whom the notice is given is in fact misled thereby, and we gave certain illustrations of misdescription such as of date, amount, character of instrument, names of parties, etc., which the courts held, in particular cases, did not invalidate the notice. It may be gathered from the act that any terms which sufficiently identify the instrument so that the party notified is not misled as to its identity, although it may not be correctly described in one or more particulars, are sufficient. Furthermore, to be sufficient in terms the notice must indicate that it has been dishonored by non-acceptance or non-payment. But it is not necessary, and the act does not require, that the notice should state that the holder looks to the endorser or drawer for payment as this is implied from the fact of giving the notice; nor is it necessary that the fact of demand be stated in the notice.

Cases as Illustrations.

We cite the following cases as illustrative:

In Mills v. Bank of the United States, 11 Wheat. 431, an early case (1826) in the Supreme Court of

* Republished from the Banking Law Journal by permission. Copyright, 1899, 1900, 1901, 1902, and 1903, by T. B. Paton: all rights reserved. To be revised and published in book form by the author.

the United States, the following notice of dishonor was sent to an endorser:

Chillicothe, 22 September, 1819.

Sir—You will hereby take notice that a note drawn by Wood & Ebert dated 20th day of September, 1819, for $3,600, payable to you or order in sixty days at the office of discount and deposit of the Bank of the United States, at Chillicothe, and on which you are endorser, has been protested for non-payment and the holders thereof look to you.

Yours respectfully,
LEVIN BELT,
Mayor of Chillicothe.

Peter Mills, Esq.

The question before the court was whether the notice was sufficient to charge the endorser. The points involved may be seen from the following extract from the opinion of the court, delivered by Mr. Justice Story, which we quote:

"The point is whether the notice sent to the defendant at Chillicothe was sufficient to charge him as endorser. The court (below) was of opinion that it was sufficient, if there was no other note payable in the office at Chillicothe drawn by Wood & Ebert and endorsed by defendant.

"It is contended that this opinion is erroneous because the notice was fatally defective by reason of its not stating who was the holder, by reason of its misdescription of the date of the note, and by reason of its not stating that a demand had been made at the bank when the note was due.

"The first objection proceeds upon a doctrine which is not admitted to be correct; and no authority is produced to support it. No form of notice to an endorser has been prescribed by law. The whole object of it is to inform the party to whom it is sent that payment has been refused by the maker; that he is considered liable; and that payment is expected of him. It is of no consequence to the endorser who is the holder as he is equally bound by the notice, whomsoever he may be; and it is time enough for him to ascertain the true title of the holder when he is called upon for payment.

"The objection of misdescription may be disposed of in a few words. It cannot be for a moment maintained that every variance however immaterial is fatal to the notice. It must be such a variance as conveys no sufficient knowledge to the party of the particular note which has been dishonored. If it does not mislead him, if it conveys to him the real fact without any doubt, the variance cannot be material either to guard his rights or avoid his responsibility. In the present case the misdescription was merely in the date (real date was July 20, 1819). The sum, the parties, the time and place of payment, and the endorsement, were truly and accurately described. The eror too was apparent on the face of the notice. The party was informed that on the 22d of September a note endorsed by him, payable in sixty days, was protested for non-payment, and yet the note itself was stated to be dated on the 20th of the same month and of course only two days before. Under these circumstances the court laid down a rule most favorable to the defendant. It directed the jury to find the notice good if there was no other note payable at the office at Chillicothe drawn by Wood & Ebert and endorsed by defendant. If there was no other note how could the mistake of date possibly mislead the defendant? If he had endorsed but one note for Wood & Ebert how could the notice fail to be full and unexceptional in fact?

"The last objection to the notice is that it does not state that payment was demanded at the bank when the note became due. It is certainly not necessary that the notice should contain such a formal allegation. It is sufficient that it states the

B. J. to J. B.—"We don't play partners in this game. But if that Dutchman raises you I'll try to stay with him."—New York Tribune.

fact of non-payment of the note and that the holder looks to the endorser for indemnity. Whether the demand was duly and regularly made, is matter of evidence to be established at the trial. If it be not legally made, no averment, however accurate, will help the case; and the statement of non-payment and notice is by necessary implication an assertion of right by the holder, founded upon his having complied with the requisites of law against the endorser. In point of fact, in commercial cities, the general, if not universal practice is, not to state in the notice the mode or place of demand, but the mere naked non-payment.

"There was no error in the opinion of the Circuit Court."

A More Recent Case.

The following is a more recent case (1895) from the Court of Errors and Appeals, New Jersey. Saloman v. Pfeister & Vogel Leather Company, 31 Atl. Rep. 602. The notice of protest mailed to the endorser in this case stated that payment of the note had been duly demanded of the maker, that payment was refused, and that the note was protested for non-payment. It was contended that the notice was not sufficient because there was no statement that the holder looked to the endorser for payment. The court said:

"The only question which it is deemed necessary to discuss in this case is whether a notice of protest must contain an express statement that the holder of the protested note will look to the endorser for payment. This question was before our Supreme Court in Burgess v. Vreeland, 24 N. J. Law, 71, in which case there was a failure to state in the notice that the holder looked to the endorser for payment. The chief justice in deciding the case said: 'The object of the notice is to apprise the endorser that the note is dishonored and that he is looked to for payment. It is not necessary to state, in terms, that the holder looks to the endorser for indemnity. It is enough if that fact appears by just and natural implication. The modern cases agree that the fact of giving notice to the endorser that the note is dishonored for non-payment, is in itself a sufficient notice that the endorser is looked to for payment.' Many authorities supporting this rule are cited in the opinion. In the later case of Howard v. Adrian, 30 N. J. Law 41, the rule recognized was that the notice must be sufficient to inform the party, either in express terms or by necessary implication, that the bill or note had been dishonored and that he was looked to for payment.

"In the case in hand the notice mailed to the endorser stated that payment of the note had been duly demanded of the maker, that payment was refused, and that the note was protested for non-payment. The only inference which the endorser could reasonably have drawn from such a notice was that the holder of the note intended to look to him for payment. The liability of the maker to the holder was fixed without presentment and protest, and therefore the only purpose which the holder could have had in sending such notice was to charge the endorser. The notice in this case was sufficient."

Rules as to Parties to Whom Notice May be Given.

We now come to the sections which provide rules as to the parties to whom notice may be given. We saw, by section 160, the general rule that notice of dishonor must be given ti the drawer and to each endorser. But sometimes the drawer or endorser may be represented by an agent; or he may be dead; or the drawer or endorser may be a firm; or two or more parties who are not partners may have signed jointly as drawers or endorsers; or the drawer or endorser may have been adjudged a bankrupt. The following sections, 168-172 inclusive, provide the detailed rules governing such cases:

Sec. 168. To Whom Notice May be Given.—Notice of dishonor may be given either to the party or to his agent in that behalf.

Sec. 169. Notice Where Party is Dead.—When any party is dead, and his death is know to the party giving notice, the notice must be given to the personal representative, if there be one, and if with reasonble diligence he can be found. If there be no personal representative, notice may be sent to the last residence or the last place of business of the deceased.

Sec. 170. Notice to Partners.—Where the parties to be notified are partners, notice to any one partner is notice to the firm, even though there has been a dissolution.

Sec. 171. Notice to Persons Jointly Liable.—Notice to joint parties who are not partners must be given to each of them, unless one of them has authority to receive such notice for the others.

Sec. 172. Notice to Bankrupt.—Where a party has been adjudged a bankrupt or an insolvent, or has made an assignment for the benefit of creditors, notice may be given either to the party himself or to his trustee or assignee.

As above seen, the act provides that the notice may be given either to the party himself or to his agent in that behalf. The following cases will help to an understanding of when notice may be given to an agent.

In Bank of Auburn v. Putnam, 3 Keyes (N. Y.) 343 one B was agent for a joint stock company and had frequently endorsed their business paper and procured it to be discounted by the bank. Notice of dishonor of a note so endorsed was served upon B, and the sufficiency of such a notice to bind the joint stock company was the question involved in the case. The court held that the notice was sufficient. Not only was B the agent to endorse this particular paper for the joint stock company, but he was general agent of the company to endorse and attend to such paper for them. Without going into an examination of the question whether authority to endorse a particular piece of negotiable paper carries with it authority to receive notice of its dishonor, the court held that as B was general agent of the joint stock company in reference to endorsing and taking care of their business paper, notice to him of the dishonor was notice to the company.

The Same Old Game—Chicago News.

In Fassin v. Hubbard, 55 N. Y. 465, the firm of B and H discontinued business, save the adjustment and liquidation of their affairs. A new firm under the same name succeeded it, of which H was a partner. H endorsed a note on account of the old firm "B and H, old firm in liquidation." Notice of dishonor of this note was served upon one B, who acted as the agent of the old firm in the liquidation of its affairs, with knowledge of H. It was contended by H, who was sued as endorser, as a member of the old firm, that notice to B was not sufficient to bind him. But the court upheld its efficiency, saying that B was the general agent for liquidating the affairs of the firm and the notice related to those affairs. Service upon B was, therefore, good service upon H.

Notice Where Party Is Dead.

Concerning the matter of notice where the endorser or drawer is dead, as regulated by section 169, the rule provided is that which has prevailed under the law merchant. The New York case of Stewart v. Eden, 2 Caines 121, decided as early as 1804 is illustrative. A note was dated and endorsed in New York City. Shortly after the endorsement the endorser removed to his country residence and there died. His will was not proved until after the maturity of the note. At its maturity the holder, upon dishonor, sent a messenger with a notice of dishonor directly to the endorser, to the latter's city residence, but as it was closed the notice was rolled up and put into the key-hole of the door. The question before the court, in an action by the holder of the note against the executor of the endorser, was the sufficiency of the notice. The court upheld its sufficiency. We quote the opinion rendered by Livingston J.:

"Ought notice of the maker's default have been sent to the endorser's country house? The note being dated in New York, the maker and endorser are presumed to have resided in and contemplated payment there. It is admitted, indeed, that the endorser did reside in the city at the time of its date, for it is stated that shortly thereafter he went to his country seat, shutting up his house in town. We must take care that while proper diligence be imposed on the holder of negotiable paper, we do not exact from him every possible exertion that might have been made to affect an endorser with knowledge of its being dishonored. If he has done all that a diligent and prudent man could naturally and fairly do under like circumstances; if the law has prescribed no certain way of sending a notice in the given case; if the endorser's own conduct has rendered it difficult to determine in what way the notice ought to be given; and especially if from what has been done it may reasonably be presumed that notice has reached the parties concerned, we should be satisfied and not ask for more. Endorsers, therefore, cannot complain if notices of this nature are permitted to be left at their houses in town notwithstanding their removal into the country during the hot months. It is more reasonable that they leave a person in town to attend to their business than that the holders of their paper be put to the trouble of finding out to what part of the country they have removed and sending after them. It is also probable, especially where the distance between the two houses is only four miles, as it was here, that some communication will be kept up between them, and that a letter left at the dwelling in town will not be long in finding is way to the country. I speak now of a temporary residence in the country; for a permanent removal from the city might render a different course necessary.

"Nor was it fatal to direct the notice to the endorser himself; for as it was not known whether he had made a will, nor who his executors were, until long after, it was fully as probable that it would reach the parties interested by this address as by any other; some one of the deceased's family would either open it or see it safely delivered to an executor. The notice, therefore, was well served and its address proper."

Notice to Partners.

In the case of notice to partners, the rule provided by section 170 is clear and explicit, and perpetuates the common-law rule upon the subject. Notice to any one partner is notice to the firm, even though there has been a dissolution. In the case of Dabney v. Stidger, 12 Miss. 749, a note was endorsed by the partnership of T and D. The partnership was dissolved by the death of D. Thereafter, at maturity, notice of dishonor was served upon T, the surviving partner. In an action against the administrator of the deceased endorser it was contended that the executor or administrator of a deceased partner is entitled to notice of dishonor of a note endorsed by the partners as such, in order to hold the estate liable, but the court held that notice to one partner is notice to all; and the notice of dishonor to T, the surviving partner, after the death of D, was sufficient to bind both T and the estate of D.

In the case of joint endorsement by two or more persons, not partners, the rule provided by section 171, which is the same as the rule of the law merchant, is that notice to joint parties, not partners, must be given to each of them, unless one of them has authority to receive such notice for the others. An illustrative case on this subject is Willis v. Green, 5 Hill (N. Y.) 232. A note payable to J and G was endorsed by both payees, who were not partners. At maturity, notice was mailed to both J and G, directed to Little Falls, where the note had been executed. G. resided in Little Falls, but when the note was given J resided at Salisbury, about eight miles from that place, where he had died, intestate and insolvent, a few days before the note fell due. The question before the court was as to the liability of G. The court held that in order to charge G notice must equally have been served upon J; that the holder had failed to show that the estate of J had been charged by notice of non-payment, for the notice, having been sent to Little Falls, instead of to the place of J's residence at Salisbury, was not sufficient, although it would have been sufficient if it had been sent to the proper place though directed there after the death of J; that, therefore, if there was nothing else in the case, the failure to charge the estate of J by due notice would operate as a discharge of both endorsers. But it further appeared in the case that after the note fell due G, the surviving endorser, had taken from the maker a bond and warrant of attorney to secure the payment of the note and that he had collected nearly the whole amount, and this was held an admission by him that the proper steps had been taken to charge both endorsers, and consequently he was held liable.

Section 172 provides a simple and easily understood rule in case of the bankruptcy, insolvency, or assignment of a drawer or an endorser whom it is sought to charge by notice of dishonor. In such case the holder has the option either to give notice of dishonor to the endorser himself, or to his trustee or assignee.

SENATORIAL JOKES.

John C. Calhoun, when vice-president, did not believe that, as the presiding officer of the Senate, he had any right to call senators to order for words spoken in debate, says a writer in the "Century." John Randolph, of Roanoke, abused this license by opening speech with the words: "Mr. Speaker—I mean Mr. President of the Senate, and would-be President of the United States—which God in His infinite mercy avert!" and then launched into one of his characteristic tirades.

Calhoun's name recalls nullification. When this heresy was at its most rampant stage, the Northern senators depended largely upon John Holmes, of Maine, as champion of their side of the chamber, on account of his ready wit. John Tyler tried to badger him one day by asking what had become of that political firm once mentioned by Randolph as "James Madison, Felix Grundy, John Holmes and the devil."

"The partnership," answered Mr. Holmes, promptly, "has been legally dissolved. The senior member is dead; the second has gone into retirement; the third now addresses you, and the last has gone over to the nullifiers, and is electioneering among the honorable senator's constituents."

Clay and Webster were not habitual humorists, but both had the gift of entertaining as well as of enthralling their audiences. Clay ran most to illustrative anecdote. While he was in the House a prominent politician deserted the Whig party in the hope of starting a general revolt. To his dismay, he found himself quite alone, and then bent all his energies to getting back into good standing. The incident reminded Clay of a story:

"A stage-coach took aboard a passenger who insisted upon riding with the driver, and who diligently drew upon the contents of a bottle carried in his greatcoat pockets. When his potations at last overcame him he fell off. The coach stopped long enough for some charitable travelers to alight and pull the poor fellow out of the mud.

"'Ha!' he exclaimed, as he looked down at his tattered garments, 'we had quite a turnover, didn't we?'

"'Oh, no,' answered one of his rescuers, 'there was no turnover. You only fell off.'

"'I say,' he persisted, 'there was a (hic) turnover, and I leave it to the company.'

"Everyone joined in assuring him that the coach had not upset.

"'Well,' he remarked ruefully, as he tried to climb back to his former perch, 'if I'd known that (hic) I wouldn't have got off.'"

On a certain afternoon the Senate clock got a fit of striking in the midst of one of Webster's most effective speeches. After it had struck fourteen or fifteen, Webster held up one finger. "Mr. President," said he, "the clock is out of order. I have the floor.'"

DIDN'T KNOW WHAT TO MAKE OF IT.

"Well," said the merchant to a young clerk whom he had sent out to collect accounts, "did you have any luck?"

"Some."

"I suppose you got the amount Mr. Fatherington owes. You said he was a personal friend of yours."

"No, I didn't get the money. The fact is, I don't know what to make of my experience there."

"How was it?"

"I went in and said, 'I called to see about a matter—.' I didn't get any further, when he puts in with 'That's all right, my boy; she is yours; take her and be happy.'"

Bookkeeping in a Chinese Laundry

DID you ever have your washing done in a chinese laundry? If so you know all about the ticket system by which you receive back your clothes in proper time with unfailing accuracy. You always find the correct number of pieces in the package, and you never receive your neighbor's linen, nor he yours. The system in a Chinese laundry is simplicity in itself, and yet it is well nigh perfect. The bookkeeping is a prominent feature of it, and John Chinaman is never so busy as to neglect his books, and his books are always so well kept that they never fail to answer any question that may arise. If one's linen is taken to an American laundry or to one conducted by Irish, German or French, no matter how carefully marked the pieces may be, some mark peculiar to the laundry will be affixed. In some of the more careful establishments this will be a colored thread so wrought as to form a designating mark; in others it will be a number applied in indelible ink, and in some it will be a symbol or a combination of letters, or letters and figures. The laundries of some of the large hotels in such cities as Philadelphia, Chicago, Cincinnati, St. Louis, etc., pursue this plan so that a traveler's clothes in the course of time come to have a bewildering array of initials, numbers and symbols. So far as the writer's experience extends, and he has traveled more or less constantly for a long term of years, besides living in several of the cities, the large majority of American laundries in these particulars are far behind Chinese laundries.

A customer enters a Chinese laundry and leaves, say, five shirts, eight collars and five cuffs. John attaches to each of the lot a linen tag marked in tea-chest characters. On each of the shirts is put a tag which reads "Moon"; the eight collars are divided into two bundles of four each and likewise marked "Moon"; the cuffs are similarly labeled. Then in a book John enters the transaction about as follows: November 12, 1886, check "Moon" eighteen pieces—five shirts, eight collars, five cuffs. To the customer he gives a ticket, the duplicate of the entry excepting the items. The next customer is, perhaps, checked "horse." Other favorite check-words are "lion," "devil," "prosperity," "goodness," "man," "angel," etc. These check-words are changed usually once a week, so that the laundryman can tell from his tag the date of any lot of linen. The ticket given a customer has a greater significance under Chinese law than an ordinary receipt and may be justly likened to a pawn-ticket. Its possession is a badge of ownership. In case of loss or destruction the customer should, under Chinese rules, apply to a magistrate and enter into an agreement corresponding to the American indemnity bond. It takes John a long time to realize that a wash-ticket is merely a receipt. Usually three lawsuits and an arrest for larceny are required before he recognizes the difference between Chinese and American law.

The book which the Chinaman uses is of the cheapest possible character. It is home-made, and is very generally composed of manilla paper, loosely stitched together. The writing is done after the Chinese fashion, with a "stick," the ink being similar to the kind draftsmen use, and mixed from time to time as required. What strikes the observer as the most interesting feature is the neatness of the work and the exact system with which it is executed.

John Chinaman's system evidently pays, for proprietors constantly retire, having gained a competence. The average investment in the one thousand or more laundries in New York is said to be less than $200 each. The cost of running depends, of course, upon the amount of business done. In main it is: Rent, $30; gas, $6; fuel, $8; water tax, $1; provisions, $30; one ironer, $60; one washer, $35. In the running cost of the laundry all living expenses are included, the employer and employees eating and living together. Usually in three months, if the neighborhood be good, the profit of the establishment, according to good authority, has arisen to $15 a week. The laundry is then a success and can be maintained or it can be readily sold to the trade for $350. Many Chinamen who speak English and conform to American habits make a living through this fact by opening laundries and selling out as soon as the places pay. Chin Wag Sing, of Mott street, New York, is an example. In four years he is reported as having opened and sold thirty laundries, clearing over $9,000 in the operation. In some instances the good will goes far beyond these figures. That of the laundry at No. 118 Chatham street, New York, a short time since, was valued at $2,500; one on Flatbush avenue, Brooklyn, at $2,200, and one in Chicago at $4,000.

Most laundrymen retire from business after accumulating $1,500 to $2,000. They then return to their native land, buy a small farm, which is put in thorough order, and then come back to the United States to make a second fortune. Wong Sai Ung, of Brooklyn, has, for example, gone to China four times with a large banker's credit on each occasion, and is now busy in his endeavor to make his fifth trip.

SPLITTING UP THE NICKEL.

"You would be surprised to know the vast number of children among the poorer classes in New Orleans who do not clearly understand the value and function of the nickel," said a storekeeper down town, according to the New Orleans "Times-Democrat," and it all results from the popularity of the quartie system, which has always been so much a part of life in this city. They are the small buyers, who run all kinds of errands for the little family to which they belong.

"Purchases, amounting in individual cases to less than five cents, daily amount in the aggregate to thousands of dollars. It is no small part of the retail traffic of the city. The children split a nickel up into very small pieces, buying a penny's worth of this and a penny's worth of that until they leave the store or the market with an armful of little packages which will represent the day's supplies.

"Sometimes they will spend only a part of the nickel, and will get a ticket, or tickets, or maybe pennies in change. Frequently the purchase will amount to 2½ cents, and then they get a paste-board check for the other 2½ cents, which is legal tender at the place issuing it for its face value. Checks or tickets of this kind are extensively used in this city, and they have added greatly to the circulation of a sort of crude subsidiary money.

"One of those checks is as good as gold at the grocery or market stall where it is issued. It is predicated on and gets its value from a redemption fund, just like Uncle Sam's money, except that instead of being redeemable in gold on demand, it is exchangeable at the grocery at its face value for any of the things in stock, or good at the vegetable stall at the market place for 2½ cents' worth of anything on hand when it is presented. It is always good for what it calls for on its face."

BOOKS OF INTEREST TO BUSINESS MEN.

The A B C of Banks and Banking. —By George M. Coffin. 6¼ x 5 inches; 137 pages. Bound in cloth. Back title gilt. Price, $1.25.

This handy little volume is exactly what its name implies; that is, a presentation of the principles underlying banking in the United States. The author in his preface says that it is designed to appeal to the reader outside as well as inside of a bank. It is by no means the last word or every word about banking. It may be said that it is a primer covering a field that has hitherto been somewhat neglected. The chapter heads are as follows: Banking in General, Various Kinds of Banking, Capital Stock, Shareholders' Rights and Liabilities, Undivided Profits, Dividends and Surplus, Deposits, Checks, Lawful Money Reserve, Issuing Bank Notes, Borrowing Money, Loans and Discounts, Exchanges, Collections, Letters of Credit, Bonds, Mortgages and Stocks, Bank Reports, Examinations, Directors, Executive Officers—Their Powers and Duties, Internal Administration and Bookkeeping, and other suggestions.

Business Law.—By Alonzo R. Weed, L. L. B., of the Boston Bar. 6 x 9¼ inches; 172 pages. Bound in cloth. Cover and back title red. Price, $1.25.

Mr. Weed calls his book "a manual for schools and colleges and for every day use." The titles of the chapters are as follows: Contracts, Principal and Agent, Partnerships, Sales of Personal Property, Bailments and Common Carriers, Negotiable Paper, Deeds, Mortgages and Leases, Collection Laws, Written Rates of Interest, Insurance, Patent Rights, Trade Marks and Copyrights, etc.

The author does not waste words, and yet treats his subjects clearly and comprehensively. In short, he gives the law without the addition of wordy "trimmings."

Introduction to the Study of Economics.—By Charles Jesse Bullock, Ph. D. 7¾ x 5½ inches. 581 pages. Bound in cloth. Cover and back title gilt. Price, $1.25.

This book, the author says, is designed as an introductive text book of economic science. Throughout the volume economics are discussed with special reference to American conditions, and their workings are illustrated by frequent allusions to American experience. There are chapters on the Consumption of Wealth, the Theory of Exchange, the Development of Metallic Money, Money and Credit, and the like.

Political Economy of Humanism.—By Henry Wood. 7¾ x 5¼ inches; 320 pages. Bound in cloth. Cover and back title gilt. Price, $1.25.

Mr. Wood is well known as a writer on various economic subjects, and this book contains a series of able treatises, written in his usual vein, on the relation of the employer to the employed, and the phases of the industrial question and their relation to socialism. Among the questions considered and handled in a conservative spirit and with much common sense, are the following: Supply and Demand, the Law of Competition, Labor and Production, Combinations of Capital, Combinations of Labor, Employers and Profit Sharing, the Obligations and Privileges of Employees, the Unequal Distribution of Wealth, Money and Coinage, Tariffs and Protection, Industrial Education and Gold Production and Values.

The Kite Trust, A Romance of Wealth.—By Lebbeus Harding Rogers. 7¾ x 5½ inches; 475 pages. Illustrated. Price, $1.50.

This is a treatise or series of treatises on economic subjects in the guise of a story. The tale itself concerns three American boys, and is very interesting as well as instructive. The trust idea is explained and an explanation of banking is given. The greenback is dealt with as are also Wall street and stock speculation.

Business Law.—By Thomas Raeburn White, B. L., L. L. B. 5 x 7½ inches; 323 pages. Bound in cloth. Back title gilt. Price, $1.50.

This is a neat, compact and handy book of business for law for the use of students and business men. Among the subjects treated are Contracts, Sales, Partnerships, Corporations, Negotiable Paper and the like. The author's language is plain, and is understandable by any one having no previous knowledge of law. The book's clearness on the essential points of ordinary law should recommend it as a business book for the plain business man who has no time in which to consult a law library.

The Phonographic Dictionary and Phrase Book.—By Benn Pitman and Jerome B. Howard. 5½ x 8 inches; 552 pages. Bound in cloth. Cover title and back title gilt. Price, $3.

This book is the most elaborate shorthand dictionary yet published, with the characters in facsimile. It contains over 120,000 words, and for every one of these words there is a corresponding sign in the Benn Pitman system of shorthand. To the reporter, office or court stenographer, or any one writing the Benn Pitman system of shorthand, the book is invaluable. It is well made, tastefully bound, and is printed on a good quality of paper in clean, plain type.

Grace's Handy Book for Making Rapid Calculations. 8¼ x 5¼ inches. Bound in cloth. 65 pages. Title printed in silver. Price, $1.

The full title of this book is "Merchants', Bankers' and Brokers' Handy Book for Making Rapid Calculations in all Branches of Commercial Requirements, Weights, Measures and Moneys." The volume contains a series of tables for calculating the price of wheat, corn and oat bushels in decimals, for converting cubic meters to cubic feet and cubic feet to meters, meters to lineal yards, superficial feet or square feet to cubic feet, decimal tons to avoirdupois pounds, and the like. To the busy office man who has a great deal of calculating to do, and particularly to the clerk in an export house whose work it is to reckon in United States money the amounts named in foreign invoices, these tables should be very valuable. They are quite complete, and undoubtedly their use will save time.

The Lawrence System of Vocal and Physical Expression.—By Edwin Gordon Lawrence. 4¾ x 6 inches; 128 pages. Bound in cloth. Cover title and back title gilt. Price, $1.

The author says in the preface of this little book that his object has been to place in the hands of lawyers, actors and public speakers in general, a simple system of vocal and physical expression that will enable them to clearly convey thought by word of mouth and emphasize it by the proper action. To the man of affairs who is called upon for a speech on any subject, and who knows what to say but does not know how to say it, this book will be a great help.

The Anatomy of a Railroad Report. —By Thomas F. Woodlock. 7 x 5¼ inches. 121 pages. Bound in cloth. Side and back titles gilt. Price, $1.

This little book is intended for the use of those people who, while interested in railroad investments, are wholly unacquainted with railroad accounts. The book is divided into two sections, the first being the Anatomy of the Railroad Report and the second being Ton-Mile Cost. It treats of phases of the railroad business in concise fashion, but thoroughly and accurately.

Any book in this list will be sent to any address in the United States, Canada or Mexico upon receipt of price. If there is some special book that you require we shall be pleased to hunt it up for you.

Address **Commerce, Accounts & Finance, 25 Pine street, New York City.**

The Science of

Loose Leaf Bookkeeping and Accounting

By Chas. A. Sweetland

Public Accountant.

Unique and up-to-date. The Pioneer Work. 250 pages of valuable information. Price, cloth bound, postpaid, $2.00.

Remit by draft or P. O. order.

Published by the author,

Chas. A. Sweetland.

Room 664 Century Bldg. St. Louis Mo.

60 DAY CLOCKS

Prentiss 60 day clocks run two months on a single winding, keep perfect time and automatically show the correct date. They are strong, durable, reliable, in fact satisfactory in every way. Right in time; right in price. You ought to have one.

Also Frying-pan, Program, Electric and Synchronized clocks.

Send for Catalogue No. 463.

THE PRENTISS CLOCK IMPROVEMENT CO.

DEPT. 44, 49 DEY ST., N. Y. CITY.

Stationery Manufacturing Company

86 FULTON STREET NEW YORK

The Voucher Check.

The voucher check has come to be the check of to-day. A few years ago, in a clumsy and crude form, it was brought forward in the nature of a business experiment. Business men were quick to see and recognize its essential safeguard features, but were also cognizant of its shortcomings in the shape in which it was then presented. Bankers, also, while recognizing the good points of the old-fashioned voucher check, were dissatisfied with its large size and the folding feature, which were its principal drawbacks.

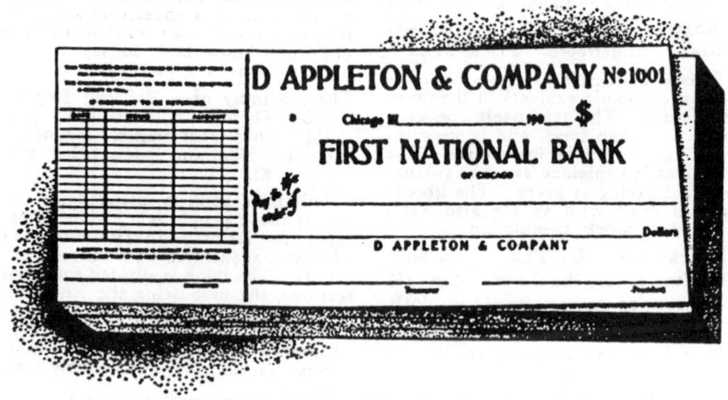

Fig. 1. Face-Voucher Check. Dimensions, 8 1-2 x 3 1-4 inches. Everything on its face, and no folding. (Patent pending.)

The voucher check, however, even in that crude state, came nearer to being what the business man was looking for in the check line than anything before presented, and many firms adopted it even though it was cumbersome and hard to handle.

Some time ago we began experimenting with the idea of combining the voucher idea with the convenient size of the bank check. After a number of experiments we have succeeded in perfecting several styles of voucher check, that, while embodying all the good features of the old-fashioned folding variety, are yet no larger than the ordinary check furnished to depositors by banks. We have sold a great number of checks of this kind, and in each case they have been hailed as exactly what the business man is looking for—that is, a check that shall show upon its face not only to whom it was drawn and for what amount, but the items for which it is tendered in payment; the correctness of said items and the amount of the check being vouched for by the bookkeeper and the officers of the paying firm or company.

In Fig. 1 is shown a facsimile of one of our styles of voucher check. We ask careful consideration for this design of check, which has not only received the cordial approval of many of the leading firms of this country, but has also been enthusiastically approved by the banks. It overcomes fully all the objections raised against the old-fashioned varieties.

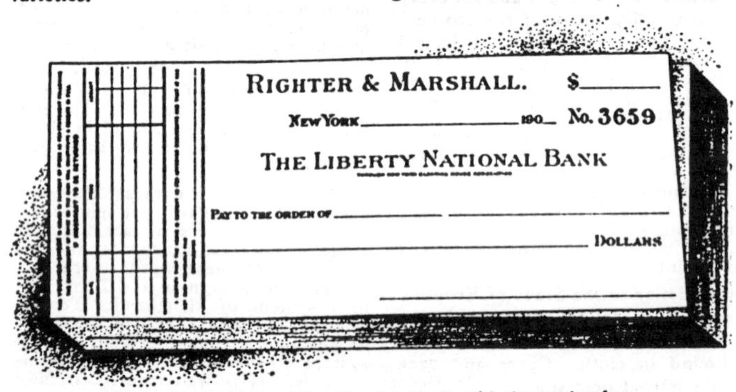

Fig. 2 Another form of Face-Voucher Check, with the voucher form differently located. (Patent pending.)

The reader is asked to notice what precedes and follows the voucher form. The voucher itself is drawn in such a way that the endorsement of the check makes it a receipt for the amount, thus avoiding the necessity of stipulating special receipts and the expense later on of filing them. In the process of issuing the check the bookkeeper or ledger clerk first certifies to the correctness of the amount for which the check is drawn; thereafter follows the signature of the firm or the officers of the company as the case may be.

The check drawn in Fig. 2 differs only from that in Fig. 1 in that the voucher form is placed in a different position upon the face of the check. There is no folding, no turning over the check for the filling in of forms upon its back—in short, none of the cumbersome methods that made the old-fashioned voucher check so unhandy.

Many representative firms are using, in connection with these voucher checks, our Multi-Bank Check Register System. Particulars of this system, which does away entirely with the old-style check book, and substitutes therefor something infinitely better and more up-to-date, will be furnished upon application. The checks shown in the illustrations are put up in pads for use with this system.

We are now in a position to furnish at short notice quantities of voucher checks of these general styles, put up in pads or bound and printed to suit the requirements of the firms purchasing them. We are also prepared to submit special designs embodying the general principles of the foregoing. Having at our disposal a competent staff of designers and engravers we are in a position to furnish on order the most handsome and elaborate checks that money can buy.

Prices will be gladly quoted upon request and estimates furnished. We solicit correspondence. Address communications,

Stationery Manufacturing Company, 86 Fulton street, New York City.

R·I·P·A·N·S

There is scarcely any condition of ill-health that is not benefited by the occasional use of a R·I·P·A·N·S Tabule. For sale by Druggists. The Five-Cent packet is enough for an ordinary occasion. The family bottle, 60 cents, contains a supply for a year.

Account Audit & Assurance Company

25 PINE STREET NEW YORK

WHAT BALANCE SHEET ACCOUNTING DOES.

I.—Initially, it provides an adequate analysis of the accounts of the business, thereby securing a proper representation of the transactions upon the books.

II.—It classifies the daily details of transactions in a way to show "going" results.

III.—The assets of the business are correctly and completely represented at all dates.

IV.—The liabilities of the business are correctly and completely represented at all dates.

V.—The gross profits on goods sold are always shown and there is presented in contrast therewith the total costs of doing business, thereby revealing net profits.

VI.—Among the assets, in the case of a manufacturing business, there are always shown the cost value of the materials and supplies on hand, the cost to date of the work or orders in progress, and the cost of the finished product on hand.

VII.—All this is presented without the preparation of a physical inventory. Inventorying, like counting cash, is resorted to, only for the purpose of verification and proof.

VIII.—The usual fiscal period is abolished. Net profits to date are shown daily (as in department stores), weekly (as in a mercantile business) or once in each four weeks (as in the case of a manufacturing business), according to the time schedule adopted.

IX.—The work of annually or semi-annually closing the books is abolished. The books are always closed and at the same time are always open. Results to date can be easily read from the Balance Sheet Ledger at any and all times.

X.—The labor of maintaining Balance Sheet Accounting, when the system is once in operation, is no greater than that of ordinary double entry. In many cases it has proven to be considerably less.

XI.—The Proof-By-Balance System of Cost Accounts, a constituent element of the Balance Sheet plan, gives the exact cost of goods produced in a factory. There are no estimates. The results are always definite and exact.

XII.—Factories are run at "even keel." The entire cost of the manufacturing department for a given period is balanced by the aggregate of the cost of the individual lots of goods put through.

XIII.—The Balance Sheet System provides that no payments to workmen (pay-roll) shall be made until the amount of their time has been charged to an order in process. Accordingly there is no time paid for that is not accounted for. Charges to orders in process offset the pay-roll amount. Non-productive labor is handled by prorating its amount over the orders in process.

XIV.—Balance Sheet Accounting is the only system of accounting ever introduced. It is complete. From established premises it reaches definite and exact conclusions.

XV.—Balance Sheet Accounting is eclectic in its elements, and uses as its component parts in the way of ledgers, blanks and forms, various items that are adapted to the purpose in view without reference to their source or origin.

XVI.—Balance Sheet Accounting begins with a balance sheet, ends with a balance sheet and maintains a balance sheet between times.

XVII.—Balance Sheet Accounting facilitates business management. It shows shortages and neglect wherever the same occur. It definitely fixes responsibility. It necessitates order and method in accounting affairs.

XVIII.—Balance Sheet Accounting improves the bookkeeper's position by enabling him to keep all his work up-to-date and by defining a day's duties.

XIX.—In Balance Sheet Accounting there is no back work. Instead, everything is finished as it proceeds.

XX.—The Balance Sheet Ledger upon the business manager's desk in the morning, among other interesting and valuable particulars, gives him the following:

Amount of cash receipts of the preceding day.
Amount of cash disbursements.
Balance on hand and where located.

Amounts charged to customers.
Amounts credited to customers.
Balance owing by customers.

Amounts credited to Purchase Creditors.
Amounts charged to Purchase Creditors.
Balance owing to Purchase Creditors.

Amount of goods (merchandise) taken in.
Amount of goods sent out.
Balance on hand.

Amount of goods sold.
Cost of goods sold.
Gross profit.

Expenses of doing business (viz., clerk hire, rent, advertising, insurance, etc.)

XXI.—Similar facts as to receipts, disbursements and balances are afforded of Notes Receivable and Notes Payable, Sundry Debtors, Sundry Creditors, etc.

XXII.—Balance Sheet Accounting is not "ready made." Instead, it is always "custom made," and made to fit the business after the most careful measurements have been taken. The preceding epitome of Balance Sheet Ledger showings is to be accepted as typical and not as specific.

XXIII.—The Balance Sheet System adapted to your business will give you the exact showings you require, presented in the way you want them and at the time they will be most serviceable to you in planning and managing.

XXIV.—Balance Sheet Accounting is scientific. All its provisions are based upon an accurate and adequate "chart" of the accounts.

XXV.—Balance Sheet Accounting is installed upon the specification plan. A carefully prepared specification, based upon the chart of accounts, is prepared, which stands to the accounting system very much as an architect's specification stands to a building about to be erected.

XXVI.—Each specification is illustrated by drawings of the rulings, blanks and forms required, and by diagrams showing the relationship of the different parts one to the other.

For further particulars, address **Account, Audit and Assurance Company, 25 Pine street, New York.**

Charts of Bank

Organization and Administration

ONE of the original and fascinating features of the work of the American Institute of Bank Clerks is a collection of charts showing in a clear and comprehensive manner the arrangement of the working forces of several of the leading banks in different large cities of the country, together with an outline of the duties connected with each department.

What the Charts Show

CHART "A" represents the First National Bank of Chicago, which has a very comprehensive plan of administration. The different departments of the bank are numbered in the chart for ready reference, so that the course of any item may be followed from receipt to final disposition. The main divisions of labor are clearly shown, and the duties of employees set forth in a clear and striking manner.

CHART "B" represents a prominent New York bank doing a large general business. The various departments and the duties of the different clerks therein employed are fully described.

CHART "C" shows the general plan of administration of one of the largest New York banks doing an extensive business with merchants and having a large number of correspondents throughout the country. An examination of the chart shows how this great business is handled.

CHART "D" represents in outline one of the largest and strongest banks in New York. An analysis of the chart shows that loans on collateral security are an important feature of the business transacted, although the bank's customers include numerous corporations of the first magnitude, and a desirable line of out-of-town banks.

CHART "E" represents a New York bank in the wealthy residence district, numbering among its customers many of the "400." The facilities afforded to ladies are a conspicuous and presumably very profitable feature of this institution.

CHART "F" shows the administrative plan of one of the leading banks of Philadelphia, doing a large general business and having numerous correspondents throughout the country.

CHART "G" is not intended to represent any particular institution, but rather to show the distribution of the working force of a typical New York bank of large size and progressive methods.

These charts are a part of the correspondence course of study in Practical Banking, but they have created such general interest that the Institute has arranged to publish them in a handsomely bound booklet, and to use the same as a premium for new subscriptions at $2.00 each.

To each new subscriber to The Bulletin at $2.00, as a premium, one copy Free

Send order and make remittance payable to

American Institute of Bank Clerks

25 Pine Street New York

THE NEW YORK PUBLIC LIBRARY
ASTOR LENOX AND TILDEN FOUNDATIONS

COMMERCE ACCOUNTS & FINANCE

Volume 5 New York May 1903 Number 5

CONTENTS.

Published Monthly by the Commerce Accounts & Finance Company
Twenty-five Pine Street New York

BRIEF MENTION.

THERE ARE ALL SORTS of binders on the market, but the Sisson's binders, made by the J. C. Hall Company, of Providence, R. I., still appear to hold their own. The company makes this binder in a number of sizes, bound with leather backs and cloth sides. In its advertising matter the company states that special sizes of these binders will be made to order. The stock sizes are made for binding letters, invoices, notes and telegrams.

THERE ARE A GREAT many typewriter ribbons on the market, and Messrs. Mittag & Volger, whose principal offices and factories are at Park Ridge, N. J., make the Eureka and the M. M. Yellow box ribbons. The manufacturers have issued their new catalogue, which describes these ribbons and various makes of carbon paper. The catalogue is very attractively printed and will be sent to any one interested upon request.

THE COMPANY THAT advertises the "See that Hump" hook and eye—of course we mean the DeLong Hook and Eye Company, of Philadelphia—are now advertising another specialty, the "Best" fastener. This fastener, which is intended for the binding of sheets of paper and forms, is a small but handy affair. In the company's advertising, which is characteristically bright, the fastener is described as "coming together as easy as a kiss," but it is said to "hang on longer."

PUBLIC ACCOUNTANTS.

Atlanta, Ga.—Ralph H. Brown, 804 Empire Building.

Boston, Mass.—Charles H. Fellows, 174 Summer; New England Audit Company, 45 Milk; J. S. Parsons, 214 Columbus Ave.

Brooklyn, N. Y.—Franklin Allen, Arbuckle Building, 371 Fulton.

Buffalo, N. Y.—W. G. Mowat, 831 Ellicott Square.

Chicago, Ill.—Haskins & Sells, 214 Dearborn.

Davenport, Ia.—J. C. Grabbe, McManus Building.

Detroit, Mich.—H. Naemansson, 496 Putnam Ave.

London, Canada.—Geo. F. Jewell, 361 Dundas.

Montreal, Canada.—George Gonthier, 11-17 Place D'Armes Hill.

New Bedford, Mass.—James L. Hathway, 72 Willis.

New Orleans, La.—P. W. Sherwood, 904 Howard Ave.

New York, N. Y.—Patterson, Teele & Dennis, 30 Broad; Haskins & Sells, 30 Broad; Account, Audit and Assurance Company, 25 Pine; Leon Brummer, 7 Pine; H. F. Searle, 45 Broadway; Hart Bros., Tibbits, Heiron & Co., 11 Broadway; Franklin Allen, Silk Exchange Building, Broadway.

Philadelphia, Pa.—Francis & Sterrett, Penn Mutual Building; Peter Ballingall, German-American Building; Charles W. Thomas, 409 Lippincott Building; Alfred L. Sellers, 1001 Chestnut.

Pittsburgh, Pa.—John Vaughan, 5520 Claybourne; George W. Wood & Co., 341 Fourth Ave.

Providence, R. I.—George R. Allen, 29 Weybosset.

San Francisco, Cal.—Charles L. Lutgen, 218 California; Lester Herrick, 405 Montgomery.

Toronto, Canada.—F. H. Kidd, Bank of Commerce Building.

Windsor, Canada.—F. H. Macpherson, 16 Sandwich, East.

Winnipeg, Canada.—Peter Thornton, 343 Main.

If you are planning a trip to the country this summer be sure to send for "Mountain and Lake Resorts," a little book just issued by the Passenger Department of the Lackawanna Railroad. It will tell you about some of the most delightful summer resorts in the East, the rates of fare, price of board, and other interesting information. The book is profusely illustrated by more than 175 pictures and contains a delightful love story entitled "For Reasons of State." It will be sent free to anyone by addressing T. W. Lee, General Passenger Agent, Lackawanna Railroad, New York City, and enclosing 5 cents in stamps, to cover postage.

The Manual of the Self-Proving Accounting System

By A. O. Kittredge, C. P. A. *and* J. F. Brown, *Merchant*

Large Octavo. 328 Pages. 4 Fac-simile Insets and Numerous Other Illustrations. Good Paper, Excellent Typography and Substantial Binding. :: :: ::

A Real Book on Real Accounting

THIS work describes and illustrates a system of accounts adapted to all lines of business, which has for its foundation a Perpetual Balance Sheet. This balance sheet, in place of being made up at intervals, is an integral and going part of the system and keeps the net results of the business constantly before the eye of the manager. It introduces no new elements, but makes various new applications of old principles. A rigid classification of accounts upon balance sheet principles is enforced, and the columnar method of condensation and summarizing is intelligently applied. A given business is represented by the smallest possible number of accounts, and each class of accounts is furnished with books adapted to its special requirements.

No Troublesome Trial Balances

By the SELF-PROVING ACCOUNTING SYSTEM all the terrors of the trial balance—the bookkeeper's bugbear—are entirely overcome. The central feature of the system is the Balance Sheet Ledger, which always shows the exact condition of the business. There is no copying; postings are made from the original entries; there are many new ideas in rulings.

Adapted to Any Line of Business

The SELF-PROVING ACCOUNTING SYSTEM is adapted to any line of business. It is in use in prominent establishments throughout the country covering almost every branch of commerce. The Manual gives complete description of the system so that its application to any required business may readily be made. Especial attention is paid to the requirements of the Installment business, a line hitherto sadly neglected by accountants.

Sent Postpaid on Receipt of $3.00

Stationery Mfg. Co.
86 Fulton Street, New York

A New Work on Accounting

A MANUAL OF BOOKKEEPING

By J. THORNTON

THIS attractive volume, comprising over 500 pages, with numerous illustrations, is one of the clearest and most concise surveys of the principles of accounting which has recently appeared. While its illustrations are given in terms of English money the bookkeeping principles discussed are universal.

The work is divided into two leading parts, the first of which is "LAWS AND PRINCIPLES," and the second "APPLICATION."

LAWS AND PRINCIPLES

In the first part there are discussed the Principle of Exchanges, the Principle of Debit and Credit Accounts, the Principle of the Classification of Accounts, the Principle of Ledger Entries, the Principle of Proving, the Principle of Transfer from Preparatory to Final Record, and the Principle of Balancing and Closing the Ledger.

APPLICATION

Under the head of Application the following chapters are presented: Rules and Tools, What Capital Consists of, Capital in Cash, Capital in Bills, Capital in Debts, Capital in Goods, Fixed Capital, Profit and Loss, Capitalist's Accounts, Company Bookkeeping, Errors, and Non-Capitalistic Bookkeeping.

Several chapters are arranged in the form of lessons, following which are questions for class purposes, arranged in such a way, however, as not to detract in the least from the value of the book in the hands of the general reader. A comprehensive index, together with answers to exercises completes the work.

Price, $2.50.—Sent Postpaid to any address in the United States on receipt of price.

Address COMMERCE ACCOUNTS & FINANCE CO.

PUBLISHERS AND BOOKSELLERS - 25 PINE STREET, NEW YORK

BUSINESS NEEDS.

Advertisements under this head one cent a word each insertion.

A FEW WORDS ABOUT PRINTING.

Printing is done artistically or it is done inartistically. Some people want cheap printing and some people want the best printing. What kind do you want? I can give you figures on either kind of printing that will give you satisfaction and the goods delivered will insure your future orders. Try an estimate from "The Printing Press," care Commerce, Accounts & Finance.

BOOKS! BOOKS! BOOKS!

Do you need any books? We are glad to furnish you any information about any book that you may want. We will give you prices. We will tell you what book you are looking for, perhaps. At any rate, write "The Old Book Man," care of Commerce, Accounts & Finance.

A LITERARY WORKER having some spare time on his hands will undertake to prepare booklets, circulars, advertising matter, etc., at reasonable prices. Will also, if requested, supervise the mechanical part of the work, the printing, binding, etc. Has had large experience, is the author of several books and is a regular contributor to the leading periodicals. Address "Writer," care of Commerce, Accounts & Finance.

AN EXPERIENCED OFFICE MANAGER desires to make a change. Salary not the only object. Best of references. Address "Manager," care of Commerce, Accounts & Finance.

MY NAME IS FRED COOK. I have asked you before through these columns if you need any one to write an advertisement for you, prepare a circular or draft out a catalogue. I do these things and do them well enough to earn a good living. Why not drop me a line care of Commerce, Accounts & Finance, and I think that I can show you some things that will interest you.

ROLL TOP DESKS, office furniture and office labor-saving devices can be obtained in every variety of style and price. Write for further information to "T. G. S.," care of Commerce, Accounts & Finance.

ATTRACTIVE ILLUSTRATIONS. I have had twenty years' experience as an illustrator on many of the leading magazines. I also have had a large experience in drawing for advertisers. I work in pen and ink, in wash and in colors. Filling as I do a steady position, I will do outside work in my spare time at prices lower than would otherwise be the case. Address "Sketch," care of Commerce, Accounts & Finance.

I AM A THOROUGHLY experienced office man, familiar with the details of office routine and competent to take charge of any force of employees. Am thirty years of age, and can furnish the best of references as to integrity, character and ability. Address "Adaptable," care of Commerce, Accounts & Finance.

A BUSINESS EDUCATION | **FOR ...ONE... DOLLAR.**

...THE PRACTICAL AGE...

A MONTHLY MAGAZINE full to the brim with helpful suggestions to young men and young women who are struggling successward.

THE BUSINESS HOUSE THAT JACK BUILT, an intensely interesting and highly instructive story of business life, and

APPLIED ENGLISH, an authority on writing and speaking the English language, which no young person can afford to be without, all for **ONE DOLLAR.**

If you have never seen THE PRACTICAL AGE, send for a free sample copy. Address,

THE PRACTICAL AGE,

Moline, Illinois.

Use any pen and your own stationery. If your stationer does not keep it, write for free specimen of work. Beware of infringements. Address Dept.

Pen-Carbon Manifold Co., 145-7-9 Centre St., New York.

Stationery Manufacturing Company

86 FULTON STREET NEW YORK

The Voucher Check.

The voucher check has come to be the check of to-day. A few years ago, in a clumsy and crude form, it was brought forward in the nature of a business experiment. Business men were quick to see and recognize its essential safeguard features, but were also cognizant of its shortcomings in the shape in which it was then presented. Bankers, also, while recognizing the good points of the old-fashioned voucher check, were dissatisfied with its large size and the folding feature, which were its principal drawbacks.

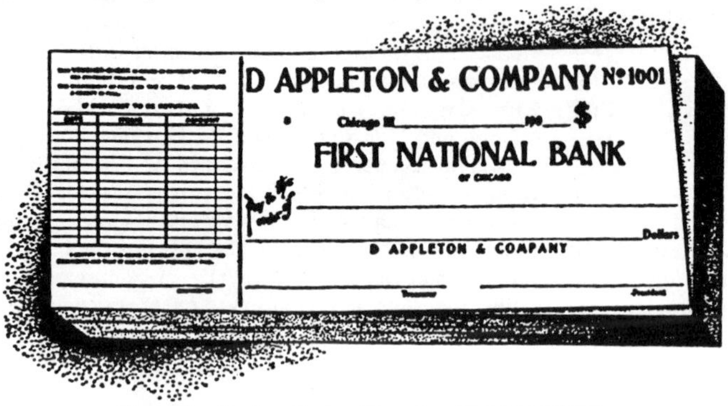

Fig. 1. Face-Voucher Check. Dimensions, 8 1-2 x 3 1-4 inches. Everything on its face, and no folding. (Patent pending.)

The voucher check, however, even in that crude state, came nearer to being what the business man was looking for in the check line than anything before presented, and many firms adopted it even though it was cumbersome and hard to handle.

Some time ago we began experimenting with the idea of combining the voucher idea with the convenient size of the bank check. After a number of experiments we have succeeded in perfecting several styles of voucher check, that, while embodying all the good features of the old-fashioned folding variety, are yet no larger than the ordinary check furnished to depositors by banks. We have sold a great number of checks of this kind, and in each case they have been hailed as exactly what the business man is looking for—that is, a check that shall show upon its face not only to whom it was drawn and for what amount, but the items for which it is tendered in payment; the correctness of said items and the amount of the check being vouched for by the bookkeeper and the officers of the paying firm or company.

In Fig. 1 is shown a facsimile of one of our styles of voucher check. We ask careful consideration for this design of check, which has not only received the cordial approval of many of the leading firms of this country, but has also been enthusiastically approved by the banks. It overcomes fully all the objections raised against the old-fashioned varieties.

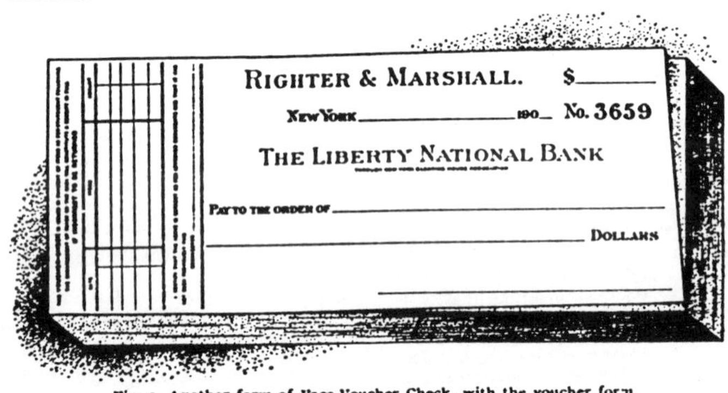

Fig. 2 Another form of Face-Voucher Check, with the voucher form differently located. (Patent pending.)

The reader is asked to notice what precedes and follows the voucher form. The voucher itself is drawn in such a way that the endorsement of the check makes it a receipt for the amount, thus avoiding the necessity of stipulating special receipts and the expense later on of filing them. In the process of issuing the check the bookkeeper or ledger clerk first certifies to the correctness of the amount for which the check is drawn; thereafter follows the signature of the firm or the officers of the company as the case may be.

The check drawn in Fig. 2 differs only from that in Fig. 1 in that the voucher form is placed in a different position upon the face of the check. There is no folding, no turning over the check for the filling in of forms upon its back—in short, none of the cumbersome methods that made the old-fashioned voucher check so unhandy.

Many representative firms are using, in connection with these voucher checks, our Multi-Bank Check Register System. Particulars of this system, which does away entirely with the old-style check book, and substitutes therefor something infinitely better and more up-to-date, will be furnished upon application. The checks shown in the illustrations are put up in pads for use with this system.

We are now in a position to furnish at short notice quantities of voucher checks of these general styles, put up in pads or bound and printed to suit the requirements of the firms purchasing them. We are also prepared to submit special designs embodying the general principles of the foregoing. Having at our disposal a competent staff of designers and engravers we are in a position to furnish on order the most handsome and elaborate checks that money can buy.

Prices will be gladly quoted upon request and estimates furnished. We solicit correspondence. Address communications,

Stationery Manufacturing Company, 86 Fulton street, New York City.

R·I·P·A·N·S

There is scarcely any condition of ill-health that is not benefited by the occasional use of a R·I·P·A·N·S Tabule. For sale by Druggists. The Five-Cent packet is enough for an ordinary occasion. The family bottle, 60 cents, contains a supply for a year.

Balance Sheets and Profit and Loss Accounts*

By WILLIAM STRACHAN, F. S. A. A.

IN every walk of life there is a tendency to be guided by precedent or custom, rather than to think for ourselves and endeavor to arrive at the underlying principles out of which those customs have evolved. I fear that this remark applies to accountants no less than to those engaged in other callings. We are content to be guided largely by what others have done before us, and it is exceedingly difficult to get us to move off the beaten track. It has occurred to me, therefore, that I may afford the Birmingham and Midland Incorporated Accountants' Students some useful topics for discussion if I consider briefly to-night whether certain customs and generally accepted theories about accounts are or are not well founded, and endeavor to present a general view of the aims and objects of a balance sheet and a trading and profit and loss account. You may think that sounds elementary, but sometimes elements are very important.

Balance Sheet.

In the first place, then, what is a balance sheet? I feel sure that if each one in this room were to write down an answer to that question, the result would afford sufficient food for an evening's useful discussion. One would probably say: a statement of assets and liabilities; another, disposed to be more precise: a statement showing on the one side the property and assets of a business, and on the other the capital and liabilities; and a third might say: a statement showing the financial position of the affairs of an individual, firm or company. Now, I submit that not one of these answers is strictly correct. The first two are clearly wrong, and the third could be improved upon. A balance sheet—i. e., an average balance sheet—is not a mere statement of assets and liabilities, neither is it a statement of property and assets on the one hand and capital and liabilities on the other; further than this, it very rarely shows on the face of it the true financial position. I do not say but what the figures are there from which the financial position can be ascertained, but I do say that in nine cases out of ten the surplus which the balance sheet shows is not the real surplus. What, then, is a balance sheet? It is nothing more nor less than a summary of the debit and credit balances in the ledgers, an abstract or epitome of the books. It shows, or ought to show, the state of affairs of the individual or undertaking, but that does not necessarily mean that it unfolds clearly the financial position. It is true the assets are all to be found on one side and the liabilities on the other, but then a number of other items are also there which are neither assets nor liabilities. There are certain things which we are pleased to call nominal or fictitious assets, things which exist only in name, in other words, are non-existent in tangible form. Perhaps the best example of these is "preliminary expenses" carried forward. Goodwill, too, is frequently more or less of a like visionary character, especially when it stands at the exorbitant figure which is often paid for it. I do not say that it is without value, but it is seldom really worth the price paid for it by a company, as the promoter's profit is included.

Then, turning to the other side of the balance sheet, we find such items as reserve fund, debenture redemption fund, forfeited shares account, etc. These are not in any sense liabilities; on the contrary, they are simply nominal accounts representing assets on the other side of the balance sheet. You will frequently see "debenture redemption fund" standing among the liabilities long after the whole of the debentures have been redeemed, that is not only confusing, but also somewhat misleading. I think it would be a good exercise for any student to prepare from a balance sheet, having in it a number of these nominal items, a plain statement of affairs. In other words, let him try on paper to liquidate the company by realizing the assets and paying off the liabilities, and then let him compare the surplus or deficiency with that which appeared on the balance sheet. I am convinced he would agree with me that, although the balance sheet might have exhibited (in the words of the Companies Acts) " a true and correct view of the state of the company's affairs," it did not show the financial position. What does an accountant do when he sets himself to examine or criticise a balance sheet? Why, he simply proceeds to eliminate the nominal item, and thus to see what tangible assets the concern is possessed of, and what actual liabilities those assets will have to meet. He then goes a step further, and divides the assets into two sections—those which are liquid, or really realizable, and those which are not. Then, and not until then, does he know the real financial position. With practice, this capacity for elimination and dissection becomes so familiar to him that he is able, almost unconsciously, to analyze and dissect and accurately weigh the relative values of the debits and credits. This is one of the most important functions that an accountant is called upon to perform, and the ability to perform it efficiently can only be acquired by wide knowledge, careful observation and long practice. But I see no reason why this acquisition, to which I have just referred, should not be applied also to the preparation of balance sheets, with the view of making them disclose more nearly the financial position. Much can be done to render a balance sheet intelligible by stating it in a form that will be readily understood, and I submit that accounts are not generally presented in the most explicit form. For instance, a balance sheet might with advantage be divided up in the following way:—

Balance Sheet.

Liabilities to the Public—	Floating Assets—
Mortgage Debentures.	Cash at Bank and in hand.
Sundry Creditors.	Investment of Sinking Fund.
Liabilities to Shareholders—	Sundry Debtors.
Capital—	Stock-in-Trade.
Ordinary Shares.	Fixed Assets—
Preference Shares.	Plant and Machinery.
Balance, consisting of—	Freeholds and Leaseholds.
Capitalized Profits.	Goodwill.
Reserve Account.	Nominal Accounts—
Sinking Fund.	Preliminary Expenses.
Forfeited Shares Account.	Advertising and Insurance unexpired, and Rents, Rates, etc., paid in advance.
Undivided Profit.	Suspense Account.

The above is not intended to be exhaustive, but simply to indicate the form in which the figures

* A lecture delivered before the Birmingham and Midland Incorporated Accountants' Students' Society of England.

should be stated. Amounts due by the company for advertising, rents, etc., would, of course, appear under "sundry creditors."

I think anyone will admit that if the items were grouped in this way, the real state of affairs would be much more evident to shareholders than if they were set out in the manner we are accustomed to see them. I daresay we might, as auditors, occasionally be met with the objection that a balance sheet in the form I have sketched would be rather too explicit, in other words, would reveal too openly the nakedness of the land; but that does not concern us for the present. What we are endeavoring to arrive at is the best and clearest means of conveying to the public mind the actual state of affairs. The fact is that an ordinary balance sheet is not what it is generally regarded by the public to be, namely, a statement of assets and liabilities, and in the large majority of cases it is quite misleading to use those words as headings.

Shareholders and Balance Sheets.

It may safely be asserted that the usual form of balance sheet is more or less vague and incomprehensible to the average shareholder. This is evidenced by the meaningless remarks, intended for criticism, that are so frequently heard at company meetings. But it may be said that the fault lies with the shareholder; that the figures are there which ought to convey to his mind the true position; and as nobody is excused for ignorance of the law, so we are equally entitled to assume on the part of the public a knowledge of accounts; and, further, it may be pointed out that those who have not acquired that knowledge have at their call a large body of qualified accountants able and willing to enlighten them. That may be so, but it does not relieve us, as accountants, from the obligation of marshalling the figures in the form that is calculated to be most readily understood. I recently heard a press representative, in an after-dinner speech, describing the impression left on his mind by the accounts which were usually submitted at company meetings. He said it was quite evident that the shareholders did not understand them. He had no hesitation in saying that he was in the same happy position himself. As for the directors, all they had to do was to point to the auditor's certificate, and say, "Look, there it is, the accounts are certified." He could not say whether the auditor, who usually sat in the vicinity of the directors, understood them; it could only be assumed from his calm and confident expression that he did. In any case, there was nobody there likely to find out. Now this is, of course, somewhat overdrawn, but it conveys a very realistic idea of what most of us must have witnessed more than once.

Double Account System.

Accounts published in what is known as the "Double Account System" by railway and other companies are even more difficult to follow, and I doubt if five per cent. of the shareholders of those companies have any intelligent conception of what the voluminous array of figures means. Take the balance sheet alone. You will have noticed that it is divided into two parts. First, there is an account of receipts and expenditure on capital account. The balance unexpended on this account is brought into the second section as a liability, and the other debits and credits are then stated in the usual way. The primary object of this, as you are doubtless aware, is to show what has been done with the paid-up capital, and how much remains unapplied. It is, moreover, obligatory in the case of most companies incorporated by special Act of Parliament. But, in addition, there is a principle underlying the practice of treating capital as distinct from revenue. The principle is one that has been adopted by the courts, in the legal decisions of recent years, when deciding what are profits available for dividend. Stated briefly, it is this: The capital expenditure shown in the first section of the balance sheet may not have assets to represent the full value of the original outlay, but, notwithstanding this, the difference between the income and expenditure on revenue account may be treated as profit available for dividend; in other words, there is no obligation on the part of directors to see that the capital expenditure standing in the balance sheet has a full equivalent in assets at any given time. But this statement requires qualification. Part of the capital expenditure is usually in respect of circulating capital, and it has been held that, although depreciation of fixed capital may be ignored, it is incumbent upon a company to maintain the value of its circulating capital.

Fixed and Circulating Capital.

What, then, is the distinction between fixed and circulating capital? It is not easy to satisfactorily define, because a great deal depends upon the nature of the undertaking. What may be fixed capital in one company may be circulating capital in another. The best definition that I can think of is this: Fixed capital is what a company trades with, and circulating capital what it trades in. Or, to put it another way, fixed capital is that which is acquired for permanent retention as an implement or requisite of trade, and not with the view of selling at a profit. Circulating capital is that which is acquired with the specific object of turning it over as quickly as possible, and making a profit by the transaction. Take a simple illustration: A company trades with its plant and machinery; it trades in its goods. The former are acquired as a permanent investment and are fixed capital; the latter are bought for resale and are circulating capital; book debts and bills of exchange, being accessories, are likewise classed under the latter head. We may have our own opinions about the soundness, from a commercial or business point of view, of ignoring depreciation on fixed assets, but the subject is too large to be discussed at length this evening, and I content myself with simply stating the position as we are bound to recognize it in the present state of the law.

Reserves.

Before leaving the balance sheet, I would like to refer in more detail to one or two items that frequently appear therein. First, I will take reserves, which have been the subject of much discussion from time to time. All of you are, doubtless, familiar with the arguments for and against the specific investment of a reserve outside the business. Some go so far as to say that there can be no reserve unless it is so invested, while others contend that the manner of investment is immaterial. My own opinion is that both of these contentions, or theories, are erroneous. There is a want of perception of the distinction, or fundamental difference, between a reserve fund and a reserve account. Personally, I think it is very material whether a reserve is, or is not, separately invested—in fact, it is sometimes absolutely imperative that it should be. Everything depends upon the object for which the reserve is created. The term "reserve fund" is often misapplied. It should only be used where there is a separate investment shown on the other side of the balance sheet to represent it. The term "reserve account," on the other hand, represents an amount of profit set aside and used in the business, instead of being distributed as dividend, or, in the case of a private individual, carried to the credit of capital account and liable to be withdrawn. In either case the reserve is real, but the great difference is that in the one case the hard cash is available to meet a contingency, while in the other, the equivalent of the reserve is in all probability locked up among the fixed assets. Take an example. If a heavy premium is paid for a lease, and a reserve is created for the purpose of renewing that lease on its expiration, an ordinary reserve account would not meet the requirements, because there is no guarantee that when the lease expires there will be cash available to acquire a fresh one, although, of course, there will be a sufficient credit balance on the reserve account. Now take the case of a reserve for depreciation of plant and machinery. In this instance a separate investment is rarely necessary. The renewals are required year by year in comparatively small items, and the sum set aside annually out of profits is at once used for the purpose for which it was intended. I do not say that the precise amount of the reserve will be utilized in any one year, but taking one year with another, over a period, the reserve will be practically absorbed annually by the renewals. It will thus be seen that, in such a case as this, the reserve is equally useful although retained in the business, and, if the concern is a prosperous one, it will probably earn more than double the rate of interest that an outside investment would realize. What I wish chiefly to emphasize is the necessity of distinguishing in the balance sheet between what is really a reserve fund, and what is only a reserve account. Sometimes there will be found a general reserve for no specific purpose, except to enhance the stability of the business. The effect of this, if not separately invested, is simply to make the excess of assets over liabilities so much the greater, and thus afford a better security to creditors. It is simply a reserve account, not a reserve fund.

Sinking Funds.

Sinking funds present some curious features, and are frequently the subject of misconception. A sinking fund is usually created for the purpose of repaying, out of profits, an issue of debentures, or a loan in some form or other. At first sight it might be imagined that when the loan had been repaid the sinking fund would disappear from the balance sheet; but this is not so, and I would like you to understand clearly the reason why such should be the case. It is a good thing to know facts, but it is better still to have a clear conception of the grounds on which those facts are based, and I would advise the younger members present (to whom my remarks are chiefly directed) never to be satisfied with a bare statement of facts, however reliable the authority may be, but always to insist upon logical evidence, for, as a friend of mine used to remark, there is a reason for everything. Well, then, what is the reason for a sinking fund continuing on the balance sheet after its object has been accomplished? It is this: The money which was raised by way of loan has been applied, let us say, in the purchase of additional plant, and if it were expedient and possible to realize that plant at its original cost, when the loan became repayable, there would be no need to create a sinking fund at all; but there is no such intention. The desire is to repay the loan without interfering with the plant, and therefore a certain sum is set aside annually out of profits, and invested so as to accumulate a fund sufficient to repay the loan when it falls due. A liability has thus been discharged without a corresponding reduction of assets. In other words, profits have been capitalized to the amount of the loan, and the excess of assets over liabilities has increased to that extent. There must, therefore, be a credit balance on profit and loss account representing this capitalization (which would be a very awkward thing to explain to shareholders), or else an entry must be made on the debit side of the balance sheet to represent the capitalized profits, and this is the usual course to adopt. After the loan has been discharged, "sinking fund" or "debenture redemption account" is not a proper designation for it. A far better term to use, in my opinion, is "capitalized profits," which exactly explains what has taken place.

Secret Reserves.

In a prosperous company it is not unusual to find what is known as a "secret reserve." It will not be discernible on the balance sheet, and it may not be visible even, in the books. Various methods are adopted for creating such reserves, the most common being to write down certain assets much below their real value. For instance, banks are in the habit of depreciating their freehold premises sometimes to almost vanishing point, while they write down their gilt-edged securities to what are known as "panic prices." In a mercantile concern, plant and machinery is an item which can be readily written down without the knowledge of those outside the management, and sometimes stock-in-trade is subjected to a like treatment. Occasionally, also, the more bold expedient is adopted of creating and building up, from year to year, a distinct fund. The objects of these reserves are various; but that does not concern us for the moment, and the question of their desirability is for the directors and shareholders to decide. But what is the position of the auditor, when he is asked to certify the accounts, where a reserve of this description exists? He is required by statute to state in his report to the shareholders whether, in his opinion, the balance sheet is properly drawn up so as to exhibit a true and correct view of the state of the company's affairs as shown by the books. The true facts can hardly be withheld from the auditor, and he will have to stretch his conscience considerably in order to give an unqualified certificate and report. He is the agent of the shareholders, and it is his duty to acquaint them with anything of moment that the balance sheet does not disclose. The position is, of course, better than it is represented by the accounts, but that is no excuse. The shareholders are entitled to know the true position, otherwise those possessed of the confidential knowledge might use it to their own advantage. It seems to me that it would meet the case if the auditor were to state in his report that such a reserve was in existence, or that certain assets were stated below their true value, without going into the question of figures. The shareholders could then require further information from the board, and it would be for the directors to convince them that it was in the best interests of the company to keep the figures secret.

I recently observed a press report to the effect that a company, carrying on business not very far from Birmingham, when taking steps to alter its articles of association, desired to reserve to the directors express power to create a secret reserve of such an amount as they might deem expedient, without disclosing to the shareholders the extent of same. Whether this alteration in the articles was ultimately sanctioned by the shareholders, I am not in a position to say, but the fact that such a proposal was put forward is sufficient to show that there is a tendency on the part of prosperous companies to withhold from the public view the full measure of their success, and it behooves us, as auditors, to be prepared to deal with such cases when they come before us.

There are many other points in the balance sheet that I might refer to but I must now pass on to the profit and loss account.

Profit and Loss Account.

The profit and loss account, as you are all aware, is usually divided into three sections. The first showing the gross profit, the second the net profit, and the third the appropriation of the profit. With regard to the first of these sections, which is generally termed the trading account, I would like to refer to the method of stating the figures, especially with reference to the stock. The usual practice is to debit the starting stock and purchases, and credit the sales and the finishing stock. This, of course, gives the gross profit quite accurately, and shows the amount of the sales, which is all right so far as it goes, but a trader naturally wants to know something more. The next question that an intelligent man would ask would be—What did those sales cost? In order to arrive at this it is necessary, either mentally or otherwise, to deduct from the total of the debit items the amount of stock on hand at the closing date, which is shown on the opposite side of the account, or to deduct from the total of the credit items the amount of the gross profit. Now, I see no reason why this should be so. It seems much clearer and simpler, to my mind, to deduct the finishing stock from the debit side, instead of adding it to the credit side—that is to say, debit the starting stock and purchases, and deduct the finishing stock and carry out the balance, and on the other side of the account credit the sales. By this means the one side of the account shows the total cost of buying and placing a certain quantity of goods on the market, and the other side shows what they have realized, the difference being the gross profit. When the figures are stated in this form, it greatly facilitates the calculation of the percentage of gross profit, which I think it is always advisable to note on the account in red ink. The percentage, I believe, is usually calculated on the turnover or selling price, but for the purpose of comparing one year with another this is quite misleading. The calculation should be based on the buying price. It is not easy to understand why the former method should ever have been adopted, except, perhaps, as a matter of convenience. It is quite conceivable that a trader might take his day book and see that he has sold so much goods, upon which he reckons to be making, on an average, a certain percentage of gross profit on the selling price, and he might thus come to regard the amount of his sales as the basis of his profit. But it is not a true basis, as can readily be shown. It is not my intention, however, to trouble you with a long dissertation on the subject of percentages to-night, but I would warn you not to be put off with the apology that it is really immaterial as a matter of practice, that it is merely academical. I assure you it is very material. It was only the other day that I had a case before me where the gross profit showed an increase of 12 per cent. when calculated on the cost, and only 4 per cent. when calculated on the turnover.

There is another matter of some importance relating to the stock, and that is with regard to depreciation.

Depreciation of Stock.

In the ordinary course, when stock on hand at the end of the year has depreciated in value, it is brought into the stock sheets at the reduced figure, thus causing a reduction in the normal rate of gross profit on the year's trading. Now, you are all doubtless in the habit of comparing the rates of gross profit, one year with another, when you draw up accounts at the end of the year, and I think you will readily see that if this element of depreciation of stock could be ascertained as a separate item, it would greatly enhance the value of the comparisons. For the moment, I am regarding the matter more from the point of view of the auditor than of the trader, and I submit that by eliminating the depreciation the auditor can form a very fair judgment as to whether the stock-taking is correct, because if it is, the rates of gross profit should be almost uniform year by year, subject to alterations in prices or other arbitrary influences capable of explanation and verification. I suggest, therefore, that it would be very advantageous to have the stock sheets ruled with two-price columns, one being the cost price, or price at last stock taking, and the other the present stock-taking price. The difference between the totals of these two columns would then represent the depreciation written off for the year, and the following method of showing this in the trading account might be adopted:—

To Starting Stock	....		By Sales............	....
" Purchases	....			
		....		
Deduct—				
Finishing Stock	....			
Less Depreciation	....			
		....		
		....		

For the purpose of the trader I would prefer to show on the accounts the percentage of actual profit without eliminating the depreciation. The other course being merely adopted by the auditor for his own satisfaction as a check upon the accuracy of the figures. Stock is almost the only item in a balance sheet that an auditor cannot properly verify, and anything that will be of assistance in that direction should be taken the fullest advantage of.

What are Trading Charges?

A difficulty is sometimes experienced in deciding precisely what the trading and what profit and loss items. But this difficulty will largely disappear if the general relation between the two accounts be clearly understood. What, then, is the trading account intended to show, and what results are we to look for from the profit and loss account? The object of the trading account is to show the total cost of placing the completed goods on the market ready for sale, and the object of the profit and loss account is to show the cost of sale and distribution. The rule to bear in mind, therefore, is that anything which adds to the cost of an article or product, until it is ready for sale, is a trading charge. This will include the purchase-price of the goods, carriage inwards, manufacturing wages, if any, and other factory expenses. The rent of the factory and interest and depreciation on machinery used in manufacture are also, strictly speaking, trading charges, but it is customary to debit them to the profit and loss account. I must confess that I cannot assign any adequate reason for this. They are certainly as much part of the cost of manufacture as the wages, and if the trading account is to be of real value in a manufacturing business, it seems to me that it ought to show, on the one hand, the cost of producing a certain quantity of finished goods, and, on the other hand, the price for which those goods have been sold. Unless this result is achieved, I fail to see that any intelligible purpose is served. The only feasible explanation that occurs to me for stating the figures otherwise, is that rent of factory and depreciation of machinery would not vary directly with the turnover, and would therefore cause the rate of gross profit to fluctuate without any alteration in prices, but simply by reason of a larger or smaller turnover. The fact remains, however, that this fluctuation is real, and not imaginary, and it is the real result that the manufacturer wants to know. The auditor, therefore, requires to work out two rates, one for the use of the manufacturer, showing the actual fluctuation, and the other for his own use, for the purpose of enabling him to form an opinion (a) as to whether the stock is approximately correct, and (b) as to whether the margin of profit, with standing charges eliminated, has been maintained. It is impossible to do more than form an opinion, especially in a manufacturing business (unless proper stock accounts are kept), but no available means of check should be neglected.

All other charges and expenses should be debited to the profit and loss account, and the difference between the gross profit and the net profit will then represent the cost of sale and distribution. For the purpose of comparison, the figures of the previous year should always be shown on the account which is placed before the proprietors or directors. I might here refer to the question of depreciation of plant, furniture, etc. This should always be arrived at on the basis of the life of the article, and should not be written off by way of a percentage on the diminishing balance of the asset standing in the ledger year by year.

The third portion of the account should show, on the credit side, the net profit brought down, to which should be added any undistributed balance brought forward, and any item of income not relating to the business, such as interest on invested money. There would thus be brought into account the whole amount available for distribution. On the debit side should then be set out the manner in which the directors propose that the profits should be appropriated. For example, so much to be carried to reserve account, so much to be set aside to pay a dividend, and the balance to be carried forward to next year.

Higher Commercial Education. II

A Symposium on Various Phases of This Subject by the Alumni and Members of the Faculty of the University of Michigan.

THE COLLEGIATE STUDY OF BANKING.

By FRED M. TAYLOR.

THE question: Will the collegiate study of banking be of advantage to the prospective banker? is best answered by breaking it in two—first, will the systematic study of banking under any conditions pay? second, will such systematic study at the college or university pay? The first question again, is really threefold, according as one has in mind banking practice or banking theory, or banking history. Let us hastily run over these questions in order. Does it pay to study banking practice? Surely there is room for but one answer. No one would deny that a banker, like anyone else, can learn something about his business from the experience of other persons. If proof is wanted we need only to remark on the conduct of bankers themselves. As a class they are exceptionally eager to make and utilize opportunities for studying the best methods of conducting their business. They buy books on banking; subscribe for journals devoted to banking; maintain bankers' associations, both national and local; and finally support a system of correspondence study of banking.

The answer to the second question—Does it pay to study banking theory? is not quite so evident. Yet even in this case not many would be found supporting the negative. Once we have admitted that the study of banking practice pays we can hardly withhold our assent from a similar statement with respect to banking theory. For, speaking generally, banking theory is merely the body of principles which underlies banking practice. In its more elementary stages banking theory asks such questions as these: What amount of reserve is needed to secure the safety of depositors? What sort of assets are safest? What sort of assets are most profitable? What volume of loans can be made on a given basis of reserves in country banks? What volume in city banks? What effect on the profit to be derived from note issues under our national banking system is produced by a high rate of interest in the community? By a high price of government bonds, and so on. Now, of course, it is possible that a banker may act with good judgment in cases where questions like this are involved without having any clear cut opinions on the several points named. In the course of actual practice, men learn to employ a sort of instinctive judgment. But we surely cannot doubt that it would usually be a gain to have clear and definite reasons for a given course of action rather than to trust to a half-blind impression. But perhaps the objector will say that every intelligent banker can and does acquire from reflection upon his own experience a theory of banking—a fairly definite set of principles with respect to the points named. Probably so, yet it surely must be admitted that most men will more easily acquire such principles and can be better assured as to the soundness of those principles through a systematic study of the books devoted to the subject than from their own unaided reflection.

In enumerating above some problems of banking theory, I chose those more immediately related to banking practice. Now, it must be admitted that in studying the theory of banking we take up problems which are more abstract than these—more removed from actual experience. Thus to the ordinary banker the theory of foreign exchange, or of international gold movements, is of little practical value. Yet a thoroughly intelligent banker can scarcely be content to remain in ignorance on matters of this sort. If for no other reason, he wants to be informed in order that as a man of special weight in determining the character of banking legislation, he shall be prepared to form and to help others to form intelligent opinions with respect to any proposed changes in banking laws.

But this protracted argument for the importance of a study of banking theory was hardly necessary. The conduct of bankers themselves, who would not err on the side of giving undue attention to this matter, shows that their authority can be quoted in favor of the proposition here supported. Let me give only one, but that a decisive proof. At the present time the American Bankers' Association maintains an elaborate system of correspondence study for bank clerks which is largely devoted to banking theory. They have a special committee in charge of the matter. They have a paid staff of officers, a secretary and assistants. They organize local chapters, lay out courses of study, conduct examinations, furnish lecturers, and so on. Surely we need no further argument to prove that the study of banking theory pays.

With respect to our third question—Does it pay to study banking history—it is enough to say that the study of history in any field is an almost indispensable accompaniment to the study of theory; for it is almost the only antidote for narrowness or dogmatism of opinion, for the disposition to fancy that there is one way for accomplishing a given result, for the pernicious habit of being governed by a priori ideas rather than by the teachings of experience.

We now come to the final and for our purpose most important question. Does the systematic study of banking in the college or the university pay? Does the study under these conditions offer any material advantages over home study? Assuredly yes. Everyone who has tried to pursue a systematic course of home study knows that it is almost impossible for nine persons out of ten even to persist in such a course of study amid the numberless distractions of actual business life. Further, such a home student is frequently at a loss to understand the statements made by authors, and so frequently feels the need of explanation from some one who has made a special study of the subject. Again, the home student, like every other student, finds coming into his mind new ideas—criticisms, perhaps, on what the books say—and he naturally needs to talk these over with some one to learn how they impress other people, as also to see how they look to himself when set out in language. But under the usual conditions of home study he will have no one to serve him in this way. Now it is hardly necessary to say that most of these and other drawbacks to home study are removed when we undertake the study of any subject at a college or university. At such a place we have an intense spirit of study which makes it easy to keep up one's work, indeed makes it difficult to stop work. We have the specially prepared teacher who can explain and amplify the matter given in books. We have opportunities for exchange of views with those who are studying the same subject. Finally, we have access to a great library containing a much larger variety of authorities than most home-study workers can command. Surely if one is going to study banking he will find it to his advantage to carry on this study at some school.

But perhaps we ought not to leave the subject without giving a word to the other side. For, of course, there is another side. Able and successful bankers could be found who would declare that the collegiate study of banking, instead of being a valuable preparation, is frequently pernicious and at the best useless. In support of this view they would perhaps say that banking as taught in colleges is too theoretical. The time is largely spent on problems which have little or no reference to banking practice. Even if the problems discussed are of importance in practice, at least the treatment is too theoretical—too abstract. Everything is made to turn on conditions which the practical banker never thinks of; while surface facts which he accepts as a guide are quite ignored. At best the point of view is so different that the language of each, even when speaking of the same thing, is unintelligible to the other. The theory of the schools may be very profound and very interesting to the philosophic student; but practical banking has no use for it.

In reply to this indictment two things may be said. First, there is much less truth in these statements than is often believed. College instructors are constantly striving by the study of banking practice to get into touch with the real thing. They are constantly studying and drawing illustrations from the events which are at the time taking place in the business world. They are constantly bringing their theories to the test of practical application. Of course, they are not teaching banking practice—a thing which can far more easily and far more correctly be learned in a banking office—but they do not forget that their students are soon to engage in the actual conduct of banks, and they try to give such an account of banking theory that it will prove of real significance to them in practice.

But, in the second place, even if it be admitted that banking as taught in schools is too theoretical, too abstract for immediate application in the conduct of a bank, it must be remembered that there is no possibility of determining in advance whether any particular phase of theory will in the future be of practical consequence. Those investigations which seem most remote from real life may at any moment come to have an important bearing on banking practice. At the very least, every intelligent banker will certainly find his views of his work broadened by theoretical study, his capacity to reflect intelligently upon it strengthened, his ability to comprehend the issues involved in the controversies of the day increased. Finally, we may console ourselves with the reflection that in any case no particular harm will come. The experience of life will quickly enough bring the student down to the real world. Very soon, far too soon, indeed, the scientific spirit, the interest in the truth for its own sake and without reference to its relation to the profits of his bank, will disappear under the pressure of everyday duties, or at most will survive only as a very mild flavor of the college life which will work no injury to anybody.

THE CAUSES OF BUSINESS FAILURE.

By HARLOW P. DAVOCK.

It has been suggested by some one that the duties of a United States Referee in Bankruptcy, in his relation to a man who has failed in business, are somewhat analogous to those of an undertaker who, in the administering of the last rites to the deceased, sees that the body corporeal is duly buried, covered up and entirely eliminated from the earth's surface.

It is because of familiarity with the final disposition of the wreckage of many unsuccessful business men, that I am called upon to give an opinion as to the cause of the failure of the business man, and to give some deductions from the practical data brought before me.

The present bankruptcy law has been in existence a little over four years, and in the sixteen counties of southeastern Michigan, comprising some eight hundred and fifty thousand inhabitants, there has been an average of one hundred and forty business failures, in bankruptcy, each year. These, with very few exceptions, are made up of persons who, unable to stand the waves of adversity, engulfed in the deep waters of insolvency, have been cast upon the shores of the bankruptcy court, helpless and poverty stricken, seeking again for a new foothold and relief from the waves of indebtedness that have overwhelmed them.

A general cause of the failures of business men is covered by the term "mismanagement," and the lack of that subtle quality of adeptness and success, which is as rare in the man of business as in the lawyer and the doctor. The failure to meet the new way of conducting business, and the standing obstinately by the methods of forty years ago, with the resultant dry rot which inevitably follows, is another reason for the failure of the man in business.

Then there is the question of extravagance in living and business. There seems to be a class of men who, in prosperous times, proceed under the theory that a similar condition will last forever, and when the inevitable cyclone of depression comes, they are utterly unable to diminish their expenses at home, or in their business, and the result which necessarily follows is ruin.

The question of location is a vital one. If one rents or builds in an improper location, business will not come to him, and no matter what the ability of a merchant may be, thus circumstanced he cannot achieve success. There may not be luck in business for the sluggard or incompetent, but environment is a condition which requires the most careful consideration and judgment. About fifty years ago, when railroads were in their infancy, a gentleman of some means, and as results showed, of superior business capacity, decided to carry on his life work as a banker in some city upon the shores of Lake Erie. After using the greatest care and looking over the ground carefully, he decided not to select either Erie, Cleveland, or Toledo, but took another city not far distant, whose future at that time seemed much better than the cities I have named. The result was, that although regarded as a prosperous citizen in the city of his choice, his location enabled him to be worth one hundred thousand dollars, while if he had located in one of the other cities mentioned he would probably have been worth half a million. I once asked an honest and prosperous alumnus of the university how it was that his father, with all his ability, had achieved such little success in the world. The reply, which explained so much, was simply this: "My father bought a poor farm, and it made him a poor man all his life."

I am asked what things, in my judgment, I would most prefer that a young man in whom I was interested, entering the university, should have as a preparation for a business life. I would say first, that as much in business as any walk in life, he should have integrity, character, and industry. This fast-moving world has no time to waste in dealing with unreliable men. The result of the failure of the college man is not his deficiency in the things he has learned, but his lack of those certain other qualities which are absolutely essential to his success, qualities of which but little is known during his college course.

If a man is lazy, if he is unreliable, if he is not in all things honorable and truthful, he may, under the ordinary dispensation of our colleges, go through his university course with a high standing as a student, but this success is evanescent, and without the superior, unknown, last-mentioned qualities, his life will be a failure.

I am asked further what things I would have a young man taught in the university, and what things I would have him avoid? The study of the science of accounts I would deem of great value. A knowledge of bookkeeping does not make the possessor of it simply an accounting machine; false economy, which leads a man to keep his unpaid invoices on the one spindle and his paid invoices on the other; or the ignorance of a man who, putting his money into an untried business, receives a trial balance which he is unable to comprehend, or the assured superiority of the so-called educated man to what he assumes to be the drudgery of business, will in each case lead one to be the prey either of the scoundrel or the optimist, with a strong probability of leading him to ruin and bankruptcy.

The doctrine is as true now as it was one hundred years ago, that one must avoid haste to get rich. Avoid buying on margins, whether it is wheat, copper, iron, or real estate. Avoid extravagance in living, and never forget that when the hard times come, character and credit are a fortune in themselves. With them you may be carried on to success. Without them, when the shadow of adversity comes, and it is likely to come to all who have active business interests, there is no redress and no help; you will be compelled to succumb.

A word as to one class whom I have met in the bankruptcy court—the men who do not endeavor to pay their debts, who obtain credit for the necessities of life, and receiving a fair salary, repudiate their obligations, incurred at the expense, hard labor, and self-denial of their creditors. I take pleasure in saying that there are but few of this class, and of them it can be said that without the respect of their fellowmen, and without the respect of themselves, on every hand they meet with the obloquy which is so justly due them.

To conclude, I should want a young man's life in college to teach him to be exact, thoughtful, and to use good judgment, and above all things to be honest and true. I should want him to abhor everything that savored of chicanery and mere smartness; to avoid extravagance in his business and personal expenditures, and above all, to remember that no success is of value if in gaining the material things of this world he thereby loses the soul of these things which should be of them, as well as of himself.

COMMERCIAL EDUCATION IN SECONDARY AND HIGHER SCHOOLS.

By DURAND W. SPRINGER.

PUBLIC high schools have for many years offered different courses of study, most of which were preparatory to corresponding courses in colleges and universities. The content of these courses has largely been determined by the requirements for admission to college. New subjects and new methods of presentation have usually appeared in college courses prior to their introduction into the high school.

Commercial courses in secondary schools, however, preceded similar courses in higher institutions of learning. The enormous increase in the commercial activities of the United States, coupled with the growth and success of private "business colleges," awakened a demand for this form of education in the public schools.

The earlier commercial courses were intended to provide work similar to that offered in business colleges, and were ordinarily outlined for a single year. In some cases, however, a second year was added in order that some of the more general subjects might be included in the course. The absence of proper equipment was largely due to the fact that competent teachers in this line of work were scarce, and those who were given charge of it did not realize the problem with which they were confronted. Indeed, these earlier courses did not, in most instances, afford a training equal to that obtained at the best business colleges. The short courses were failures. They created wrong impressions in the minds of the students. They belittled business by implying that the preparation required by the successful business man was not as great as that demanded by the successful man in other pursuits. They attracted the inferior class of students. Those who had made a failure in the other courses hoped to find something in the new which they could master. Those whose only ambition was to secure a diploma naturally drifted toward the course which offered the least resistance. They created wrong impressions in the minds of the public as to the disciplinary value of commercial studies. Graduates from a one or two year commercial course were compared with graduates from other four year courses to the disparagement of the former, and in most cases the critics did not take into consideration the fact that the training was from two to four times as long in the one case as in the other.

During the last decade the four year commercial course has been steadily gaining favor, and each fall has witnessed the introduction of many new commercial departments in public high schools. Already six commercial high schools have been established in the largest cities. The courses have been varied and in most cases have been experimental, but in general they have contained two years' work pertaining directly to business, and two years of work taken from other courses but having a bearing upon business in some of its many phases.

The introduction of higher schools of commerce has raised the query: Will a working relation be established between the commercial courses in secondary and higher schools similar to that which has existed between the classical and scientific courses in these schools? In a preliminary report to the department of business education of the National Educational Association, the committee to which was assigned the work of preparing a monograph on commercial education in American public schools made the following statement: "The paramount factor in shaping commercial courses in public schools should be the welfare of the student who goes directly from the high school to his life work. It is expected, however, that such courses will provide a training of such character as will fit the student completing them to enter the schools of commerce and industry now being established by many colleges and universities."

The university of Michigan requires fifteen units of work for admission to its department of literature, science and the arts, in which department the higher commercial courses are given. Of the subjects which may be offered for admission, at least eleven units are found in the commercial courses of the representative high schools. They are English 3, mathematics 3, language (French or German) 2, physics 1, and 2 from either chemistry, history or English literature, usually the first two. Can the high schools reasonably ask the university to accept four units of commercial work in the narrower sense as part of the entrance requirements from those who are to take the course in higher commercial education? The four units would naturally be shorthand and bookkeeping, one each, and economics, commercial law, and history of commerce and industry (each of which is studied for one half year) two units.

The reasonableness of the request would seem to be apparent in view of the following observations. The elements of shorthand and bookkeeping will probably never be taught in colleges, and yet the business man recognizes the value received from a knowledge of these subjects. Shorthand ranks with the languages so far as disciplinary value is concerned. A preliminary knowledge of bookkeeping is expected of those who pursue courses in the science of accounts, and surely it should be considered worthy of being counted as an entrance requirement. Courses in economics, geography, law, and history of commerce and industry are now offered in the higher schools of commerce. The tendency has always been to crowd the study of the elementary principles of the various subjects into the secondary schools in order that more time might be reserved to the higher schools for advanced work. Should the sentiment favoring the three-year college course prevail, this tendency will be more marked than ever. Certainly, the student intending to enter upon a business career would secure a better foundation for his college course from the study of the subjects indicated than he would obtain from the study of physiography, botany, or zoology, which subjects are now accepted for entrance.

With a proper regard for the distinct aims of the commercial courses in high schools and colleges, the problem of adjusting them, so that the former shall be considered preparatory to the latter, ought not to be difficult.

THE MAN WHO DOES THINGS.

Every institution wants him. He is not looking for positions; positions are looking for him, says an exchange. He does not complain, he acts. He accomplishes results, and these accomplished results speak more loudly in his favor than acres of subsidized newspapers. What the world wants, what the world rewards, is the man who does things. Discouragement and failures are meaningless nothings to him; results are the substantial things for which he strives and attains. There is a settled air of assured success in his manners and movements. There is no trouble in selecting him from a crowd. He can be picked out just as unerringly as his opposite, who abides with discouragement and failure, and they leave a more attractive imprint on the countenance. Men who can do things in industrial, commercial and financial life are as scarce as their opposites are plentiful.

The tree of opportunity, heavy with golden fruit, is ever waiting for the man who does things. Opportunities are not scarce, they are plentiful, more plentiful than ever since history was written. They await the poor boy who does things without looking at the clock. People who are always looking at the clock never amount to much in anything. Men who do things never consult the time to see if they can stop; they know time "was made for slaves," not for virile men who enthusiastically do things. Employees who frequently consult the clock will always be employees with no hope of rising.

The man who does things may in his absorption forget his meals or his bed, but this opposite will be ever ready ahead of time for both or either.

Concentration of thought and absorption in inflexible purpose mark the man who does things. Looseness of the thought and scattering of purpose mark the man who never does anything. The public soon knows the one from the other, and accord him the recognition he deserves.

The man who does things is always at a premium, his services never go begging, he is ever welcome, success attends his footsteps, and failure stands aloft from him.

Bucket-Shops, Large and Small

By RICHARD K. JARVIS.

CERTAIN phases there are of our modern life that many people consider to be evil in themselves and to exercise an evil influence, and yet these phases of life are recognized as being like the poor—always with us. The bucket-shop in spite of the many attempts to put it out of existence still remains, and it is a fact that in a great city like New York thousands of people do nothing all day long but sit in these bucket-shops and "speculate," that is, gamble in stocks.

The bucket-shop differs, as almost everyone knows, from the legitimate broker's office, that is, the office of the broker who is a member of one of the stock exchanges, in that no stock is actually bought and none actually sold. The speculators ostensibly buy shares of stock on a margin and, later on, sell them again. If they make a profit on this transaction, from this profit is deducted the bucket-shop's commission for buying and its commission for selling. As a matter of fact, there being no buying and no selling, this commission is the "rake-off" that the bucket-shop gets from the customer, that is to say, it is a part of the rake-off. If the customer loses—if his margin is exhausted and the stock is closed out, the bucket-shop wins the money that the customer has deposited as his margin. If a customer buys and the market goes up and he sells at a higher figure, the bucket-shop loses the difference between the figure at which he bought and that at which he sold minus the commissions before mentioned.

There are all sorts of bucket-shops ranging from luxurious institutions, sometimes bearing names like "The People's Stock Exchange," or "The Public Stock Exchange," and fitted with expensive furniture and patronized by broadcloth-coated speculators, to little dens, dirty and dingy, where messenger boys and newsboys take a "flyer" on the market with a crafty individual who is almost, if not quite, as short of dollars as they are themselves.

For human nature study the customer's room of a big bucket-shop during stock exchange hours is unexcelled. The room itself is usually a large one, perhaps with costly paintings on the walls, certainly with plenty of easy upholstered armchairs and with a long table piled with magazines and papers. In some bucket-shops the magazines on this table are of all kinds, literary and technical. In the majority, however, the publications are all of the financial variety, and the customers scan them eagerly, hoping for "tips" on the market. The tickers, the buzzing machines that make and lose money for those who play with them, are at one side of the room, and directly back of or beside them is a long blackboard, the upper part of which bears the names of the various stocks dealt in upon the stock exchanges of New York, Philadelphia, Boston and Chicago. By stocks we do not necessarily mean railroad shares and the like, for wheat, corn and cotton are mighty factors in bucket-shop gambling.

Scene in a Large Bucket-Shop.—From the N. Y. Sun.

As the tickers record the various sales at the exchanges, boys employed for the purpose mark upon the blackboard the "quotations," the latter being the prices at which these sales were made. On a busy day in Wall street the life of a board boy in a bucket-shop is not to be envied. The customers lounge in the spacious chairs, reading the papers and magazines or talking in low tones with one another, arising from time to time to consult the ticker or to whisper an order in the ears of a clerk.

The blackboard itself, or, as it is in many offices, a wooden rack with grooves in which printed cards bearing the "quotations" are placed, is the most important part of a bucket-shop's machinery, the tickers, of course, excepted. The "quotation" at the upper part of the board and beneath, or in some cases above, the name of each stock, is usually the closing price of the day before, that is, the price at which it sold when the stock exchange closed for that day; there also appear the highest point that it

A Group in a Second-Rate Bucket-Shop

reached in the day's fluctuations and the lowest. The bucket-shop's active day begins when the stock exchange opens at ten o'clock. Then the tickers begin to whirr, the numbered slips begin to appear upon the board, the customers lean forward and grow jubilant or sad as prices rise or fall and the wheel of fortune that will make, or in most cases break, them is spinning furiously.

Even in the most luxurious bucket-shops the customers are not wealthy men. Men of wealth prefer to patronize the legitimate broker's office. These are clerks, men who have had a few thousand dollars left them and want to turn them into millions, gamblers, or Wall street "lame ducks," who, having lost their money in speculation on the exchange are driven perforce to the humbler "flyer" in the bucket-shop. Orders in a bucket-shop are placed on a margin of one per cent. as against ten per cent. in a real broker's office. That is to say, if a customer wishes to buy one hundred shares of any stock selling at a par value of one hundred dollars, he deposits one dollar for each share. This is the case if he merely wishes to protect himself for a one-point drop. If he wishes to be protected further down the scale he puts up more margin, but it is all at the one per cent. rate. There is a great deal of "selling short" in bucket-shops, as in fact there is in the broker's office. In the bucket-shop the customer, having had a "tip" from somewhere or other, believes that N. P., for instance, is going to decline in price, so he gives an order to the clerk to sell one hundred shares "short," depositing his margin the same as before. If the stock goes down he wins. If it goes up he loses.

In the smaller bucket-shops the paraphernalia is similar but much less elaborate, and the customers are also less elaborate in general get-up and appearance. Customers in the smaller bucket-shops are a queer lot of men. They generally appear to have the financial cares of a Morgan upon their shoulders. You meet them everywhere, at the restaurants in particular. They may be eating a piece of pie or a sandwich in some corner lunchroom, but they are discussing the financial movements of the country's securities with apparent ease and asserting that "Sugar" is a "good buy" or "Consolidated Gas" should be sold for a "ten-point drop." Their linen may be soiled and their trousers ragged about their shoe-tops, but they talk stocks just the same.

The "tip" is the great thing in the bucket-shop. Somebody hears from somebody else that Mr. Russell Sage told an uncle of somebody else that it was time to buy a certain stock. Therefore the bucket-shop customers buy, and the bucket-shop usually makes money, because the stock goes the other way. Brokers' clerks, perhaps, come in to gamble on a chance "tip" that they think they have obtained from another clerk in a larger broker's office. In the little bucket-shops the customers are more quickly "cleaned out" than is the case in the big ones. They lose all that they have put up and, perhaps, have not a dollar to buy a night's lodging, but they still cluster around the ticker like moths around a candle. They cannot leave it, apparently.

It is said that in the smaller bucket-shops, where the blackboard is a little affair and the proprietor is board boy, cashier and bookkeeper all in one, bootblacks, newsboys and the like come in to put twenty-five or fifty cents on the market. The proprietors of these bucket-shops are not by any means the prosperous-looking citizens that those of the big establishments are. The big fellows wear diamonds,

A Humble Speculator.

drive fast horses and open wine for their friends. The little chaps are as seedy as their customers and their only safe is their pockets.

Taking it altogether, the bucket-shop is a curious instance of the gambling fever and the anxiety to get rich in a hurry. Everybody that deals with it knows that there is no exchange connection; that no stock is really bought and none sold; that their orders are only "bucketed"—recorded on the sheet that is the holy of holies in the bucket-shop. They know that they are gambling when they go there, and gambling with the chances against them, nevertheless they gamble, being human. There are hundreds of bucket-shops in every city of size, and the chances are that in spite of the measures taken to drive them out of business there will continue to be at least that number until the millenium arrives. Incidentally when one hears his next door neighbor talking of "dealings" in this or that stock, he must not be too ready to believe him a "plunger" on the stock exchange.

The Typewriter and Public Records

ONLY a little while ago nothing but pen-written documents were accepted in the courts and public records were legal only when written with a pen. But although matters of this kind are the last to respond to the drum-beat of improvement, they do respond after a while, and now in many states public records are made on the typewriter.

The gentleman who was at the head of one of the largest concerns engaged in the manufacture of typewriter ribbons, has contributed to one of the New York papers some interesting facts regarding the status of the typewritten record in a number of states and foreign countries, as well as in our own national government.

According to the information furnished by this gentleman from personal experience the question of permanence of typewritten records was raised a number of years ago, when the typewriter came into general use in government offices, and the State of Pennsylvania first passed upon the question by deciding after various tests that some typewriter ribbons made records as lasting as those made with the best record ink, and passing an act making them valid.

Then, some seven or eight years ago, the United States Government, in order to insure permanence of typewriter ribbon records, required manufacturers of such ribbons to send samples for chemical tests, and only such were given contracts to supply ribbons as furnished those which stood the most severe experiments.

Two or three years ago the Canadian Government also made some exhaustive tests with ribbons of various manufacture and found many that made absolutely permanent records, and about the same time the English Government did the same thing, and both are using such ribbons.

In Massachusetts the validity of typewritten records was established by statute in 1899, section 1, chapter 354, Acts of that year, reading as follows:

No person having the care or custody of any public records in any department or office of the commonwealth, or of any county, city or town therein, shall use or permit to be used upon the public record written by him or under his direction, any ink excepting such as is furnished by the commissioner of public records; provided, however, that printing by typewriting machines may be allowed upon such records, subject to the provisions of section 4 herein.

Section 4, chapter 354, provides that:

No person having the care or custody of any public records mentioned in section 1 of this act shall use or permit to be used upon such records any ribbon, pad or other device used for printing by typewriting machines, any ink contained in such ribbon, pad or device, except such as is approved by the commissioner of public records. Such approval shall be withdrawn by the commissioner whenever he finds that an article approved falls below the standard established by him.

In his twelfth annual report, issued in January, 1900, Commissioner of Public Records Robert T. Swan, under the portion of his report entitled "Typewriter Ribbons," says:

"To carry out the provisions of section 4 of chapter 354 of the Acts of 1899, it became necessary to approve ribbons, pads or other devices to be used for printing upon typewriting machines. An investigation, previously made and reported upon, satisfied me that the leading manufacturers could and did make ribbons and pads containing permanent ink, and most of them made them suitable for use on any typewriting machine.

"The establishment of a standard, as of a record ink, was not practicable, for numerous reasons, and there seemed, therefore, no reason why any one ribbon should be designated. Accordingly, manufacturers of good repute who supplied the chief part of the ribbons used in New England, were asked for samples of printing done with ink upon the permanency of which they would stake their reputations. Severe tests of the samples submitted showed the inks to be permanent, and the ribbons and pads of nine manufacturers were approved.

* * *

"The reputation of the manufacturers of the approved ribbons, coupled with the fact that approval is to be withdrawn if a ribbon is found inferior to the sample, would seem to be a sufficient guarantee that the standard will be maintained. Some dissatisfaction has been expressed by persons claiming to be manufacturers, who put ribbons upon the market under certain names, that their ribbons were not approved; but, having satisfied myself that the chief parts of them were made for them, and they had no knowledge of the character of the ink, nor control over it, I declined to approve them.

"A ribbon made by a responsible manufacturer, which had acquired a reputation for permanency under a certain name, might be kept on the market under the same name, but be an entirely different article, made by an irresponsible manufacturer."

It should be stated that these facts and the permanency of typewritten records are only true of two varieties of typewriter ribbons, the "black record" and "indelible," the ink for which is made with a base of pure carbon, like any fine fluid or printer's ink, and hence, from their chemical nature, are as permanent in quality as those inks. This does not apply to any particular brand or manufacture of ribbon, but is true of all black record and indelible ribbons made by the first-class firms.

The colored ribbons, green, blue, purple, etc., are not permanent, and the manufacturers do not claim them to be so, although the better ones make a copy that may last many years.

STONEHENGE.

It has always been a matter of speculation with scientists how old the famous druidical stone monuments at Stonehenge, in southern England, are, says "World's Events." Many have held that they date back to the primitive stone age, while others would not allow them to be older than Roman times.

Excavations round the great Monolite, however, have now brought to light conclusive proof that Stonehenge is a relic of the days before iron or even bronze implements had been introduced into Britain. The excavations have revealed around the foundations a number of stone implements which had evidently been used in dressing the monuments, and which had been thrown away when dulled or broken. Not a sign of a metal tool was found. As it is believed that bronze first put in its appearance in Britain about 1500 B. C., it is evident that the Stonehenge monuments must belong to a very remote age, approximating that which produced the Egyptian pyramid—about 2000 B. C.

EXTINCT ALL RIGHT.

Teacher: "Bessie, name one bird that is now extinct." Little Bessie: "Dick." Teacher: "Dick? What sort of a bird is that?" Little Bessie: "Our canary. The cat extincted him!"—Puck.

COMMERCE ACCOUNTS & FINANCE

A Magazine of Higher Business Education and Practical Administration. Acknowledged Authority in the Profession of Commerce and Consistent Advocate of Methods Up to Date and Above the Table.

JOSEPH CROSBY LINCOLN, - - - Editor.
FRIEND PITTS, JR., - Circulation and Advertising.
E. R. KITTREDGE, - - - Business Manager.

PUBLISHED MONTHLY

SUBSCRIPTION $1 a Year in the United States, Canada and Mexico. Other countries $1.50. Postage prepaid by the Publishers. In the absence of specific orders to stop at the end of the subscription term the paper will be continued and a bill sent. Entered at the New York Postoffice as Second Class mail matter.

COMMERCE, ACCOUNTS & FINANCE COMPANY, Publishers
Twenty-five Pine Street, New York

This issue of Commerce, Accounts & Finance is the last in which the periodical will appear as a monthly magazine. The next number, issued in July, will be in the form of a quarterly, changed as to make-up, improved in quality, enlarged and enriched, and being in every particular what a first-class accounting magazine should be. Subscribers of Commerce, Accounts & Finance will, we feel assured, be more than pleased with the change and with the new magazine in its quarterly form. The subscription list of Commerce, Accounts & Finance contains some of the best known names in accounting and general business in the country, and we have received many gratifying testimonials as to the worth of the publication. We believe that as a quarterly it will retain all its old subscribers and gain many new ones.

* * *

We doubt if the profession of the accountant was ever before so highly considered in this country as it is in this year of our Lord, 1903. In Great Britain the accountant is a person of importance, and his work has long been recognized by the British business man as being almost the mainspring of successful trade. This has not, until recently, been the case over here. The American merchant and manufacturer has been too prone to consider the selling department of his business as the only vital part of the concern. Get good machinery, get good salesmen and make and sell goods; these were his ideas. The accounting department was a sort of necessary evil that was to be tolerated but not encouraged. That the American merchant and manufacturer made money under the system—or lack of system—and pushed his goods to the four corners of the earth is a marvel indeed.

*

But within the last decade there has been an upward movement in the profession of scientific accounting among Americans. Business men of this country no longer confuse the accountant—the man who plans and installs cost systems for mammoth manufactories—with the bookkeeper who merely makes the entries in the books. They know now that a scientific accounting system is to a business man what a carefully arranged plan of battle is to the general of an army. The officers of the army may be gallant and competent, and the private may be daring and willing, but if there is no plan, if every move made is not thought out beforehand and its consequences considered, that army will, in nine cases out of ten, be defeated. You may have the best lot of salesmen in creation, you may have good goods to sell, but if your accounting system is so slovenly that you do not know what your goods cost you, both to make and sell, while you may not meet with an actual defeat, you certainly will not gain the victory that should be yours.

*

To-day there seems to be a grand awakening in the United States to the value of adequate accounting. Hundreds of big business houses are reorganizing their cost systems and their office facilities. The young men who are acting as managers in so many of these large concerns are not content with grandfather's methods, and want something that really does what it claims to do. A sufficient accounting system should show exactly what it costs to manufacture goods, what each department of a factory or warehouse gains or loses in any period of time, what it costs to sell the goods, and exactly how the entire business stands. Nothing less than this will do to-day, and that is why the competent professional accountant is so prominent a figure in the world of commerce.

NO MAN FOR A FUSS.

A Fifeshire farmer gave his herd laddie, Jamie (a half-wit), a ticket to admit him to a sacred recital in a neighboring town, to be given by local talent, and told the lad to be sure and enjoy himself.

The farmer was greatly surprised to find his servant in the kitchen long before the conclusion of the performance, and upon asking him why he had returned from the recital, Jamie replied:

"Weel, maister, ae man yonder began to sing, 'I'm the King of Glory'; then anither said he 'was the King of Glory,' and when I saw three ithers standin' up an' sayin' they were 'the Kings of Glory,' I kent there was to be a fecht, so I cam awa' an' left them to finish it amon' themselves."—Dundee Advertiser.

PROFIT AND LOSS IN COINING.

A strange thing about our coining system is that the government loses money in coining gold, but makes a big profit in coining pennies. For instance, in a $10 gold piece there is exactly $10 worth of gold and 10 per cent. of copper put in to harden the precious metal, besides the cost of minting. A silver piece of money is about half profit, but the penny pays Uncle Sam best of all, as the blanks are purchased at the rate of $7,300 per million. That is, the United States Government obtains for 7 and 3-10 cents the copper blanks, which, by the process of stamping, are transformed into $1 worth of pennies.

Exhibition Accounts and Finance. II*

By JOHN M. MACLEOD, C. A.,
Auditor of the Glasgow International Exhibition, 1901.

BENEATH the second head there are the amounts received from the refreshment and the amusement caterers. As the gross amount of the takings from the refreshments and amusements may be regarded as the cost paid by the visitors for their own entertainment, I give here the figures for the benefit of any who may have a special liking for statistics. There were in all ten separate places of refreshment. Three of these were licensed, and the gross takings from these amounted to £101,546. The temperance restaurants yielded £77,234, of which £23,785, 17s. was received by Miss Cranston, and £26,939, 12s. 9d. by Thomas Jenkins & Co. In addition, the Glasgow Dairy Company drew £5,448, 6s. 4d.; Malcolm Campbell, Ltd., £6,487, 7s. 2d., on account of the fruit and refreshments they sold; and Marcowitch & Company, £2,652, 5s., from cigars, cigarettes, tobacco, etc. The drawings from the ten separate places of refreshment were thus £193,368, 11s. 4d., of which more than one-half—viz., £101,-546, 12s. 1d.—was derived from the licensed premises. Amusements also furnished a very large sum. From the switchback railway £12,706, 19s. 1d. was received. The water chute drew an even larger amount—viz., £16,281, 1s. 10d. Automatic machines gave £5,160, 16s. 3d.; the Indian theatre, £4,884, 1s. 6d.; the shooting jungle, £3,378, 13s. 1d. At the concert hall £3,720, 19s. 6d. was drawn, and the sports ground gave a gross income of £7,829, 5s. 4d. There were other amusements, such as the boats on the Kelvin, the military rifle range, the lifts to the dome, and our little friend, the miniature railway, which together yielded several thousands of pounds. To sum up, the total amount drawn from amusements was £58,869, 15s., and from refreshments and amusements together, £252,238, 6s. 4d.

The Exhibition Executive stipulated that they should receive percentages, varying in amount, from both refreshments and amusements. In the case of the refreshments the percentages ranged from 15 per cent. from the Glasgow Company to 30 per cent. paid by Messrs. McKillop & Mackenzie, 32½ per cent. by Miss Cranston, and 33 1-3 per cent. by T. W. W. Flint. Here again the licensed premises contributed more than one-half of the whole sum received, the Messrs. McKillop paying a percentage of £28,687, 4s. 4d.; Thomas Jenkins, £6,930, 1s. 11d.; The Cabin, Limited, £4,104, 3s. 5d.; T. W. W. Flint, £3,586; Malcolm Campbell, £1,621, 16s. 10d.; the Dairy Company, £817, 5s.; and Marcowitch & Company, £716, 0s. 8d.

Amusements.

In the case of the amusements the percentages were very much higher, ranging from 10 per cent. in respect of the boats on the Kelvin to 60 per cent. for the water chute and Indian theatre, and 80 per cent. for the switchback railway—which latter showed a net profit to the exhibition well on for £10,000, the actual sum being £9,312, 0s. 7d. The water chute also was a lucrative source of revenue to the executive, contributing £5,298, 18s. 5d. The whole takings from the sports ground, £7,829, 5s. 4d., went into the exhibition exchequer, but when the expenses in connection with sports, etc., which came to £6,285, 6s. 7d., and the cost of track, stands and ground, which amounted to £7,550, 1s. 8d., or together to £13,835, 8s. 3d., are taken into account, there is a heavy deficit. It must, however, also be reckoned—although no figure can be put on it—that the attractions on the ground specially drew considerable numbers who paid in addition admission money to the exhibition. A sum of £3,720, 19s. 6d. came from the concert hall. Without giving in detail the percentages got from the other amusements, I may say that the exhibition derived no less a sum than £34,160, 15s. 1d. from amusements. Percentages from refreshments and amusements thus yielded together to the Exhibition Association £88,-202, 10s. 1d. I should explain that in the case of the switchback railway, water chute and Indian theatre, fixed sums were received out of the first takings, in terms of the agreements, towards the cost of the erection of the structures. In the cases of the refreshment caterers the cost of the various buildings was borne by the exhibition, but the internal fittings and decorations were done by the respective caterers at their own expense. In each instance fixed guaranteed minimum payments were provided for, payable by four equal instalments on the first days of May, June, July and August respectively. When the minimum amount was exceeded the percentage became payable weekly. In every case the minimum sums were exceeded. The concessions account was augmented by £5,419, 2s. 5d. for printing, and by other sums for lavatories, photography, bakery and confectionery, which together came to £7,470, 8s. 5d. The total revenue to the exhibition from refreshments, amusements and concessions was £95,672, 18s. 6d. As practically all the refreshment contractors paid to the exhibition a percentage of their drawings, it became necessary to check their takings. A condition in all the agreements with the refreshment contractors was that they should submit to the auditor by a certain date before the opening of the exhibition a statement showing their system of bookkeeping and check on drawings. Another condition provided for the gross drawings being lodged in the bank daily. These conditions were faithfully observed. The method of checking the takings varied according to the nature of the business. The auditor had access to the bank accounts, and to all the contractors' books, and was able to compare the bank accounts with the contractors' cash books. Each contractor handed in to the auditor's office statements showing the daily drawings. These were filed, and after being checked were entered in a book kept for each contractor, and at the end of each week the percentage on the takings was calculated and extended.

Dining Rooms and Bars.

The drawings from each bar and each dining-room were kept separate, and therefore each was run as a separate business. In the bars a full record was kept of all the goods supplied, and the stock was taken each week, which enabled the proprietors to judge what the drawings should have been. In the dining-rooms a cashier was placed at every exit from the kitchen or serving room, and the waiter on passing out had to pay to him the value of the goods he

* From the "Accountant's Magazine," of Edinburgh.

carried. Another person was beside the cashier to see that the proper values were placed in the cash box. These drawings were also checked with the kitchen accounts.

In the rooms where table d'hote was served a separate cashier's box was placed, and the waiter received and paid for tablets that contained a list of all the courses that were marked off as served. The bars connected with the dining-rooms were worked on the same system as the open bars. In the tea-rooms there were cashiers to whom the public paid their bills, at the same time handing in a voucher granted by the waitress for the amount. The counterfoils of the waitresses' books were from time to time summed and compared with the amounts entered in the cash book, and any leakage could be detected. In other cases cash registers were used, and these were checked and compared with the sums lodged in bank.

When the percentage became payable weekly, the auditor made out a certificate of the amount due to the exhibition, and the certificate was passed to the treasurer, who was responsible for the collection of the amount.

Switchback Railway.

Admission to the switchback railway, water chute, boats on the Kelvin, and the Indian theatre was by turnstile, and to the miniature railway and lifts to the dome by tickets numbered consecutively from No. 1 upwards, which were sold by the officials of the exhibition, and collected from the public by the servants of the caterers. The keys of the cash drawers in the automatic machines were kept in the treasurer's office, and the money was collected at stated times by one of his assistants and representatives of the several machine companies, and taken direct to the bank, and counted and lodged in the proper accounts. The drawings from the two shooting ranges were also collected and lodged in bank, and the auditor checked the number of the cartridges issued from the magazine from time to time. The keys of the magazine were kept in the bank.

The contractors' bank accounts were all in the joint names of the finance committee of the exhibition and the respective contractors, and were operated upon, in the case of the restaurants, by the contractors, and in all other cases by the executive. In these latter cases, the shares of the sums lodged belonging to the caterers and the exhibition respectively were, after being certified by the auditor, drawn by checks signed by the finance committee. From what I have just told you it will be seen that the interests of the exhibition were well safeguarded; but it is due to the refreshment contractors to say that at all times they did everything in their power to assist the checking of their drawings.

Space and Rents.

The space for exhibiting purposes was comprised in the various buildings erected at the cost of the exhibition executive, as well as in the buildings of a permanent character belonging to the Corporation of Glasgow, and in other buildings erected by exhibitors. The total area of space available for exhibition purposes was 509,640 square feet, of which no less than 259,580 were in the industrial hall and grand avenue, 155,640 in the machinery hall, 11,400 in the heating and lighting section, 5,000 in the old Kelvingrove Museum, and 78,020 in the Corporation Fine Art Palace. For all space let in the industrial hall and grand avenue, the machinery hall, and the heating and lighting section, a uniform charge of 3s. per square foot was made. The old Museum was let for a lump sum to the Japanese Committee, and the Fine Art Galleries were devoted to the exhibition of pictures, sculpture and other works of art lent to the committee. Ireland, two of our colonies and three foreign countries could not find sufficient space for their purpose within the main buildings, and sites were allotted to them in the grounds, where they erected buildings at their own cost. In the machinery section also similar pressure was felt, and several large exhibitors paid for space in the grounds, whereon they erected suitable housing for their exhibits. The site of this group came to be known as "Machinery Street."

Applications for space were made on forms, which set forth the terms of allotment and the regulations for exhibitors. These forms also provided space for entering a full description of the proposed exhibit and the country to which it belonged. When the date fixed for receiving applications expired (about a year before the opening), it was found that nearly double the amount of the space available had been applied for. The committee had therefore to select the most suitable exhibits and reject the others. The applications were recorded, as they came in, in a book kept for the purpose, and the amount of the deposit accompanying each was entered in its proper column. The allotment letters were made out by the manager's department and handed to the cashier, who, after having them checked and stamped, entered the amount of space allotted and the balance due thereon in their respective columns, and issued them to the applicants. The rejected applications were then extended into a special column and the amounts deposited returned to the owners.

The minimum charge for space was £5, and as it frequently happened that this sum was in excess of the value of the area allotted at 3s. per square foot, in order to be able to check the total amount of cash received as against the total space allotted, a column was kept headed "differences," and all sums in excess were entered in it. It was thus possible to compare the summations of the space book and the amount appearing at the credit of "space account" in the ledger. The several spaces let in the grounds were kept separate in the books, and these were checked separately and compared with the terms stated in the letters of allotment. The total space let was 360,053 square feet 10 square inches (exclusive of the Art Galleries). British exhibitors were allotted 242,308 square feet, for which they paid £27,843, 10s. 9d., and this amount, added to the sums received from the ten foreign and colonial countries which sent exhibits, made a grand total of £34,513, 12s. 11d. To this there falls to be added the sum of £410 for rents of offices received from railway and steamboat companies, amounting together to £34,923, 12s. 11d. In respect of space, therefore, we were not so generous to our exhibitors as our neighbors across the Channel, who gave their exhibitors space free, doubtless thinking that it would be a breach of the laws of hospitality to invite friends to a reception at home and make them pay for their seats.

Sundry Income.

The fourth and remaining source of income to be noticed is of a varied nature and somewhat incidental to the business of the exhibition. The chief items embraced under this head are: storage of empty cases, hire of bath chairs, fees from architects and others, fees for lost season tickets, etc., the receipts from which totalled £753, 7s. 6d. While little remark is needed with regard to this branch, it may be stated that the executive undertook to store the empty cases belonging to the exhibitors at a rate of

1½d. per cubic foot, and after paying rents of stores, taxes, gas, cartage and labor, there was a profit of £346, 1s. 3d. Separate books were kept for storage and bath chairs. The counterfoils of the receipts granted for these items were duly compared with the sums entered in the cash book.

Total Income.

If we now bring together the amount of the several branches of income that we have had under review, they will stand thus:—

1. Admissions	£271,391	13	3
2. Royalties, concessions, sports and concert hall	95,672	18	6
3. Space rents	34,923	12	11
4. Miscellaneous	753	7	6
Making a total income of	£402,741	12	2

It should be stated, however, that although these figures represent the whole of the income proper, they do not include the whole of the money received by the cashier. There were large accounts incurred by the executive for lighting and power, and for hand-railing to enclose the exhibits in the machinery hall and protect the public. Exhibitors who needed special lighting or power required to pay for them, while exhibitors using hand-railing had to pay for it. The electric current meters were surveyed monthly. The survey books were written up in the engineer's office, and the quantity of current consumed extended. The books were then sent to the cashier's office, where the accounts were made out, entered in a "lighting account book," and issued to the consumers. A similar course was followed with the installation and fitting up of lamps, and with the hand-railing.

The auditor compared the entries in the cashier's books with those in the engineer's books and saw that the payments were duly accounted for in the cash book. The sums received for light and power, wiring and lamps, hire of meters, erection and maintenance, and hand-railing, together made £8,008, 10s. 10d. The various sums were posted to the credit of the ledger accounts for lighting and hand-railing respectively, and thereby reduced the amounts debited to these accounts. So far, therefore, as the income side of the accounts are concerned, we have seen that each branch came under the careful scrutiny of the auditor's office, and that the method of checking adopted was effective and complete.

Total Admission.

Before leaving this branch of my subject it may interest you to look at the total number of persons admitted to the exhibition and to the several places of amusement, either by turnstile or ticket. We have already seen that the total admission at the gates was 11,559,649. Add now at—

Switchback railway	1,011,134
Water chute	650,719
Miniature railway	151,731
Boats on the Kelvin	87,117
Indian theatre	195,284
Lifts to dome	195,660
Concert hall (only when by payment)	173,846
Sports grounds	249,001
Swimming gala	2,895

and we have a grand total of no fewer than 14,277,-936 admissions, all of which, as I have shown you, were checked or verified in one way or other.

We turn now to consider the outgoings or expenditure side of the accounts. But before I deal with the figures of the several branches, it may help you to realize the large sums necessarily spent in the organization of such an enterprise if I here merely mention in passing the names of the several committees appointed by the executive council to attain the objects aimed at. These were eighteen in number, and the name of each committee fairly well indicates the nature of the work committed to its care, viz.:—

1. Chairman's Committee.
2. Acting London Committee.
3. Admission, Traffic and Excursion Committee.
4. Building, Lighting and Grounds Committee.
5. Music, Entertainments, Refreshments, Printing and Advertising Committee.
6. Exhibit and Space Committee.
7. Finance Committee.
8. Machinery and Electric Lighting Committee.
9. Agricultural and Horticultural Committee.
10. Chemical Industries Committee.
11. Educational Committee.
12. Mineral Committee.
13. Marine Engineering and Shipbuilding Committee.
14. Textile Committee.
15. Foreign Committee.
16. Indian, Canadian and Colonial Committee.
17. Fine Arts, Scottish History and Archaeology Section Committee.
18. The Women's Section Committee.

Many of these committees appointed sub-committees charged with special duties and responsible to their parent committees, and these were in turn responsible to the executive council, which passed the minutes of the various committees at stated periods.

Checking Accounts.

All liabilities incurred by committees and sub-committees were in the first place submitted to the general manager, who passed them on to the cashier with any comments thereon he deemed necessary. They were then compared by the cashier with contract prices, where such existed, carefully examined as to extensions and additions, and, if correct in these respects, initialed and sent to the committee by which the liability had been incurred. After examination by the proper committee, the accounts, if found in order, were certified correct and returned to the cashier. They were then entered in an "accounts payable" book and submitted to the finance committee, together with checks for payment of the several accounts presented. This committee, having satisfied themselves that the accounts were duly certified, countersigned them, and signed the checks and authorized the payments.

To prevent any account being rendered and passed a second time, as sometimes happens, the cashier kept subsidiary books, in which all accounts for goods received on credit were entered, showing the nature of the goods, date of invoice, and cash book number of the voucher. In the course of the examination of any account, if there was any doubt as to whether it had already been passed or not, a reference to the proper subsidiary account at once revealed the fact, and, in the event of an error, the voucher was easily forthcoming.

Cash Book.

All payments, except for "petty cash," for which a separate cash book was kept, were made by check. As many payments, however, required to be made without the delay involved in waiting for the weekly meeting of the finance committee, when checks were signed in the usual course, a "cashier's bank account" was opened, on which the cashier operated as required for all immediate payments, such as carriage, wages, bandsmen's and artists' fees, and such like. Any payments thus made between the weekly meetings were reported to the next meeting of the committee for homologation, and the vouchers produced to, and signed by, the committee. A rough cash book was kept, which was balanced daily. The general cash book was framed with twelve cash columns on each page, and these columns were headed, on the Dr. side, something like the following:—

1. Bank account.	7. Gate money.
2. Cashier's account.	8. Concert hall account.
3. Space account.	9. Sports account.
4. Storage account.	10. Percentage account.
5. Season tickets account.	11. Sundries account.
6. Coupon tickets, etc., account.	12. Totals.

On the Cr. side the headings were:—

1. Bank account.	7. Insurance account.
2. Cashier's account.	8. Coal and light account.
3. Wages account.	9. Stores account.
4. Carriage account.	10. Buildings account.
5. Printing account.	11. Sundries account.
6. Advertising account.	12. Totals.

These heads were changed from time to time as required by the transactions. When any receipt or payment occurred not classified in any of the headed columns it was entered only in the "totals" column, and posted separately to its proper account. All the headed columns were summed at the end of the month, and the totals only posted to the respective ledger accounts.

Monthly Audit.

The auditor checked the books monthly. The vouchers for the payments were examined to see that they had been duly certified by the proper committees, and were also compared with the entries in the cash book. The pay sheets were made up weekly, certified by the heads of departments, and sent to the cashier. Two of the cashier's assistants made up and checked the wages, and thereafter paid the employees at the office of their respective departments.

Now I come to the final statement of accounts. This has been made up in the form of a short abstract of receipts and payments, with schedules attached, giving all the necessary details and such information as may be of interest. The actual surplus, after allowing for accounts still due to, and for claims due by, the executive, and without crediting any amount yet to be realized from the sale of the buildings, is £30,571, 10s. 1d. The auditor's report precedes the statement of accounts.

From statements of the probable surplus which were publicly made, but which were totally unauthorized and unwarranted, there will no doubt be some disappointment that the surplus is so little. But when one remembers the magnificence of the buildings, the beauty of the grounds, and the costly illuminations of both; that no money was spared in order to bring to the exhibition the finest music that could be obtained in Europe and America; and that the whole was worked not with the object of making money but solely for the enjoyment and edification of the citizens—then you will agree with me in thinking that it is highly creditable to the whole management that there is any surplus at all, and all the more when the surplus is such a substantial one.

There is no doubt that the exhibition was a unique success, which, in my opinion, was due to the following causes: (first), the credit of a large guarantee fund; (second), the work having been begun early, namely, three years before the date of opening; (third), the organization having been divided amongst committees, which included the ablest experts and advisers in the city; (fourth), the management being presided over by one of the most capable and worthy of men in Mr. Hedley, a man of rare organizing power and indefatigable energy; and lastly, a spell of fine and warm weather, somewhat, I regret to say, unusual in our experience.

And now I come to the end of what I am afraid some of you perhaps may consider a wearisome recounting of details. They were necessary, however, in order to give you an idea of the method of conducting the financial work of the "First International Exhibition of the Twentieth Century." In connection with so large an undertaking you can easily understand that without a careful system of bookkeeping and constant checking there might have been serious leakage. The means which were devised to prevent this were effectual. The visitor was counted and tabulated from the time he entered the exhibition until he left it. The turnstile through which he passed clicked out the number which he occupied in the daily throng. His meals were enumerated, and if he sought the exhilaration of a dash down the water chute or a ride on the switchback railway, the act did not pass unrecorded. It was all done, however, so automatically and quickly that the operation never proved irksome.

The exhibition has passed away, it fully realized the end for which it was promoted, and its happy memory will rest for some time to come with those who knew it.

HE DESERVED THE JOB.

The following spicy letter was first printed in "The Catholic Youth." It was written by a young man in answer to an ad. in the "Ledger," of Philadelphia. It is good, no joke, but a fact. It applies to a whole lot of business men who want help at starvation wages.

Dear Sir—I beg to offer myself as an applicant for the position advertised in this morning's "Ledger." I am a young man, thirty-seven years of age, having been connected with the United States Embassy at Madagascar for some time, and feel confident if you will give me a trial I will prove my worth to you. I am not only an experienced bookkeeper, proficient stenographer and typewriter, excellent telegraph operator and erudite college professor, but have several other accomplishments which might make me more desirable than ordinary mortals. I am an experienced snow-shoveller, a first-class corn husker and peanut roaster. I have some knowledge of clipping puppy dogs' ears, and a medal for reciting "Curfew Shall Not Ring To-night." Am a skilled chiropodist and practical, for I can cook, take care of horses, crease trousers, open oysters and repair umbrellas. Being possessed of great physical beauty, I would not only be useful but ornamental, as well lending to the sacred precincts of your office that delightful artistic charm that a Satsuma vase would. I can furnish recommendations from Chauncey M. Depew, Jacob S. Coxey, Kaiser Wilhelm, Captain Clarke, the Prime Minister to Dahomey, and the dog catcher general of Timbuctoo. As to salary, I would feel I was robbing the widowed of bread and taking sponge cake from the orphaned if I were to take advantage of your munificence by accepting the fabulous sum of $3 per week. I would be entirely willing to give my services for less, and by accepting $1.37 it would not only give me a clear conscience, but would also give you an opportuity of increasing your donation to the church, pay your butcher bill, and keep up your life insurance. Really, dear friend, your charity borders on the supernatural, and, to the ordinary mind, appears like reckless extravagance.

I can call to see you any Saturday night after 11 o'clock, or can be seen any Sunday morning in the choir loft of our church (Broad and Dock streets), where I am at present employed as first assistant organ-blower and understudy of the janitor.

Hopefully yours,

SOCRATES M'GOO.

P. S.—Now, honestly, what kind of a man do you expect for $3 per week?

The Negotiable Instruments Law*

By THOS. B. PATON.

Time—Residence—Sufficient Notice Given—Where Notice Must be Sent.

NOTE.—As enacted in New York, the Negotiable Instruments Law is divided into nineteen articles as follows:

1. General Provisions (Sections 1—17)
2. Negotiable Instruments: Form and Interpretation (20—42)
3. Consideration (50—55)
4. Negotiation (60—80)
5. Rights of holder (90—98)
6. Liabilities of parties (110—119)
7. Presentment for payment (130—148)
8. Notice of dishonor (160—189)
9. Discharge (200—206)
10. Bills of exchange (210—215)
11. Acceptance (220—230)
12. Presentment for acceptance (240—248)
13. Protest (260—268)
14. Acceptance for honor (280—290)
15. Payment for honor (300—306)
16. Bills in a set (310—315)
17. Promissory notes and checks (320—325)
18. Notes given for patent rights (330—332)
19. Laws repealed. When takes effect (340—341)

The provisions of the law naturally fall under four general classifications.

a. General Provisions.
b. Negotiable Instruments in General.
c. Bills of Exchange.
d. Promissory Notes and Checks.

The text of the law is the same in all the states (with some slight exceptions which will be noted) but the numbering of the sections, and in some states, of the articles, is not uniform. There is, however, the same continuity of articles and text, except that in some instances "General Provisions" follow, instead of precede the remainder of the act. By following this course of study with reference to the New York act, as above outlined, the reader in each state can apply the same to the law of his own tate.

On the subject of notice of dishonor we have heretofore considered the sections which provide to whom and by whom notice of dishonor may be given and the form and sufficiency of the notice. We now come to the sections which provide as to the time within which notice of dishonor may be given.

Time.

Sec. 173. Time Within Which Notice May Be Given.—Notice may be given as soon as the instrument is dishonored; and unless delay is excused as hereinafter provided, must be given within the times fixed by this act.

Here we see the general range of time fixed, from the earliest moment at which notice may be given, to the latest time. The earliest moment is "as soon as the instrument is dishonored." It is not necessary, after dishonor, for the holder to wait until the close of business hours in anticipation of the possible payment of the instrument later in the day. As soon as the instrument is dishonored, notice may be at once given; and if the instrument is paid later in the day, this nullifies the notice. The extreme limit of time within which notice may be given is provided in the next two sectons, the first regulating the time where the parties reside in the same place; the second, where they reside in different places.

Residence.

Sec. 174. Where Parties Reside in Same Place.—Where the person giving and the person to receive notice reside in the same place, notice must be given within the following times:

1. If given at the place of business of the person to receive notice, it must be given before the close of business hours on the day following;

2. If given at his residence, it must be given before the usual hours of rest on the day following;

3. If sent by mail, it must be deposited in the postoffice in time to reach him in usual course on the day following.

It will be seen that, where the parties reside in the same place, the design of the law is that the notice shall reach the endorser either personally, or his place of business or residence, not later than the close of the day following that of dishonor. It may be either given him personally during that day; or a written notice may be left at his place of business or at his residence, in which event it must be so left before the close of business hours, or the usual hours of rest, respectively; or if it is sent by mail, it must be deposited in the postoffice at such time as will permit of its reaching the endorser in usual course on the day following.

The original rule of the law merchant was that where the parties resided in the same place, notice could not be given by mail, but this rule was subsequently changed in some of the states by statute, and by custom in some of the large cities. Under the above section of the Negotiable Instruments Law, it would seem that notice by mail is authorized where the parties reside in the same place.

Sec. 175. Where Parties Reside in Different Places.—Where the person giving and the person to receive notice reside in different places, the notice must be given within the following times:

1. If sent by mail, it must be deposited in the postoffice in time to go by mail the day following the day of dishonor, or if there be no mail at a convenient hour on that day, by the next mail thereafter.

2. If given otherwise than through the postoffice, then within the time that notice would have been received in due course of mail, if it had been deposited in a postoffice within the time specified in the last subdivision.

Where the parties reside in different places, the usual mode of serving notice is by mail; and there has been some confusion among the authorities as to when notice must be mailed, varying requirements having been that notice must be given by the first mail after dishonor on the same day; that it must be given not later than the first mail of the day following, when there are more than one; and that it may be sent by any mail on the day following. The rule of the Negotiable Instruments Law, it is seen, is that the notice must be deposited in the postoffice in time to go by mail on the day following or, if there be no mail at a conveneient hour on that day, by the next mail thereafter.

Construing this rule in the light of judicial decisions, it means that deposit of the notice in the postoffice, at any time during the day following dishonor, is early enough, providing in time to go by a mail of that day; and if there is only one mail a day, and that closes before business hours, deposit in the postoffice on the first day after dishonor, in time to go by the early morning mail on the second day after dishonor, would be sufficient.

It was held in Lawson v. Farmers' Bank, 1 Ohio St. 206, that a mail which closed at 9.10 A. M., being the only mail of the day after the day of dishonor, was not at an unreasonable or inconvenient hour; while in Chick v. Pillsbury, 24 Me. 458, it was held that 6 A. M. was an inconvenient hour.

*Republished from the Banking Law Journal by permission. Copyright, 1899, 1900, 1901, 1902, and 1903, by T. B. Paton: all rights reserved. To be revised and published in book form by the author.

Where the notice to a party residing in a different place is given by special messenger, express, or otherwise than through the postoffice, the provision is that it must be given him within the time that notice would have reached him in due course, if it had been deposited in the postoffice within the time above specified.

Sufficient Notice Given.

Sec. 176. When Sender Deemed to Have Given Due Notice.—Where notice of dishonor is duly addressed and deposited in the postoffice, the sender is deemed to have given due notice, notwithstanding any miscarriage in the mails.

This perpetuates the common law rule, exempting the sender of notice of dishonor by mail from the consequences of the mistakes or miscarriages which sometimes occur in the United States postal service.

Sec. 177. Deposit in Postoffice; What Constitutes—Notice is deemed to have been deposited in the postoffice when deposited in any branch postoffice or in any letter box under the control of the postoffice department.

This section embraces branch postoffices and letter boxes under the general term "postoffice." Before the passage of the act, cases had come before the courts wherein it was contended that a deposit of notice in a letter-box was not the legal equivalent of depositing in the postoffice, but the courts uniformly held that the deposit of notice in a postoffice box on the street was just the same, in legal effect, as if it had been deposited in a box at the postoffice. The same thing has been held with reference to a notice contained in a letter delivered to a postoffice carrier on the street. In Pearce v. Langfit, 101 Pa. St. 507, the court said: "We think the delivery of a letter to an official letter-carrier is the full equivalent for depositing it in a receiving box or at the postoffice. When left in the former it is for the purpose of being taken therefrom by the carrier, and if left at the postoffice it must be taken from the receptacle there provided for its deposit ,either by the postmaster or by some one of his agents, to be placed in the mail. In either case the letter must come into the personal custody of some one lawfully authorized for the purpose, whose function it is to participate in the transmission of it from the sender to the mail. It certainly can make no difference whether the letter is handed directly to the carrier, or is first deposited in a receiving box, and taken from thence by the same carrier. The postal regulations of the United States require that carriers while on their rounds shall receive all letters prepaid that may be handed to them for mailing. It follows that when such a carrier receives a prepaid letter from a citizen for the purpose of being mailed, he is in the strict performance of his official duty.

Section 177 does not specify that delivery to a carrier is equivalent to deposit in a general or branch postoffice or letter-box, but "in any case not provided for in this act, the rules of the law merchant shall govern."

Time of Notice to Subsequent Party.

Sec. 178. Notice to Subsequent Party; Time of.—Where a party receives notice of dishonor, he has, after the receipt of such notice, the same time for giving notice to antecedent parties that the holder has after the dishonor.

In sections 174 and 175 we have seen the provisions as to the time within which notice must be given to charge an endorser where the parties reside in the same place, and where they reside in a different place. Section 178 provides the rule where there are two or more endorsers to be notified. Each endorser, upon receiving due notice, has the same time to give notice to an antecedent endorser as the holder had, after the dishonor. Where there are, for example, five successive endorsers, and this method of each endorser separately charging each antecedent endorser is adopted, the earliest endorser in point of time would not receive notice until several days after the dishonor, and yet he would be charged with liability. But with reference to the liability of this earliest endorser, if the holder instead of giving notice to his immediate predecessor within the time limited after dishonor, should omit such notice and thereafter serve notice upon the earliest endorser within the time in which he would have received it, had the method of each successive party notifying his immediate antecedent been adopted, yet this would not be sufficient to charge the earliest endorser with liability. This point was raised in Simpson v. Turney, 5 Humphrey (Tenn.) 419. A note, held by a bank, was protested on the 1st of February. One Simpson was the immediate endorser to the bank, and one Turney the next prior endorser. No notice of dishonor whatever was given by the bank on the second day of February, but on the third day of February the bank served notice on Turney. Had the bank notified Simpson on the second and Simpson notified Turney on the third, the latter would have received the notice of dishonor no earlier than he in fact received it from the bank, and would have been held; and in an action by Simpson against Turney to hold him liable as endorser, it was argued by the counsel for the plaintiff that the notice to Turney was in time, just as much as if the bank had first notified Simpson and he in turn had notified Turney, and it was insisted that the notice given by the bank to Turney should inure to Simpson's benefit. But the court said:

"If the notice had been in time and valid, it would by law have inured to his benefit, he being an intermediate party. But a notice of no benefit to the bank, because not fixing the liability of the party notified cannot inure to the benefit of another. So to hold, would be to introduce a new principle into the law merchant. Suppose there were ten endorsers upon a note; if the holder, ten days after the protest, gave notice to the first endorser, this, according to the argument, would fix all the endorsers, for it would be just the time necessary to them to have given notice to each other successively. Upon the direct question raised in this case, Bayley on Bills expressly says: 'Nor is it any excuse that there are several intervening parties between him who gives the notice and the defendant to whom it is given; and if the notice had been communicated through those intervening parties, and each had taken the time the law allows, the defendant would not have had the notice the sooner.'"

Where Notice Must Be Sent.

Sec. 179. Where Notice Must Be Sent.—Where a party has added an address to his signature, notice of dishonor must be sent to that address; but if he has not given such address, then the notice must be sent as follows:

1. Either to the postoffice nearest to his place of residence, or to the postoffice where he is accustomed to receive his letters; or

2. If he live in one place and have his place of business in another, notice may be sent to either place; or

3. If he is sojourning in another place, notice may be sent to the place where he is sojourning.

But where the notice is actually received by the party within the time specified in this act, it will be sufficient, though not sent in accordance with the requirements of this section.

Here we see two broad divisions with respect to where notice must be sent, one where the party has, the other where the party has not, added an address to his signature. In the former case, the notice must be sent to the address given.

In Bartlett v. Robinson, 39 N. Y. 187, a note, dated at New York, was endorsed as follows:

"Charles Robinson, 214 E. 18th street."

The note was protested when due, and the notary mailed notice of dishonor to the endorser addressed as follows:

"Charles Robinson Esq., City of New York."

This notice Robinson never received. It was held the notice was not sufficient to charge him as endorser. Reasonable diligence on the part of the holder in such a case required, the court said, that he mail the notice to the place where the endorser has appointed to receive it.

We will cite the following cases to illustrate the text, where the endorser has not affixed an address to his signature.

Bank of Geneva v. Howlett, 4 Wend. (N. Y.) 328. Notice of dishonor mailed at Geneva, N. Y., to endorser at "Geddesburgh, N. Y." The legal name of the postoffice was "Geddes," not "Geddesburgh," but it was popularly known as "Geddesburgh," and mail addressed to "Geddesburgh" always went to "Geddes," and on this point the court ruled that the notice was sent to Geddes. The endorser resided a mile and a half or two miles nearer to the postoffice at Onondaga Hill than to Geddes, but Geddes was his place of business, and he received letters at both offices. More letters for him individually were received through the office at Onondaga than at Geddes, but all the letters for the company with which he was connected were directed to the latter office. The endorser or his sons were in the habit of calling for letters at the Geddes office, and he kept a postage account there. The court held that under the circumstances notice directed to either office would be good.

Illustrative Cases.

Citizens' Nat. Bank v. Cade, 73 Mich. 449. Notice of dishonor was mailed at Romeo, Mich., to an endorser addressed "Hiram M. Cade. Romeo, Mich." The notary had made diligent inquiry to ascertain Cade's postoffice address and where he received his mail, and was informed that he received it at Romeo. The residence of Cade and his place of business was, at that time, and had been for some years prior thereto, in the township of Ray, Macomb county, Mich., about eight and one-half miles from Romeo and about eighty rods from Ray Center postoffice, at which he was then, and had been for a long time, receiving his mail, and which was his postoffice address. The officers of the bank holding the note knew that Cade resided at Ray at the time the note matured, but did not know that he received his mail at the Ray Center postoffice. The second day after maturity Cade was personally given notice of dishonor at his house in Ray, by one of the bank's officers. Held, Cade did not have any notice at all of the non-payment of the note, such as the law requires.

Northwestern Coal Co. v. Bowman, 69 Iowa, 150. Notice of dishonor to endorser of a check directed to him at Boone, Boone county, Iowa. The evidence showed that endorser's postoffice address was Odebolt, in Sac county. Held, clearly insufficient.

Montgomery County Bank v. Marsh, 7 N. c. 481. An endorser resided in the village of Palatine Bridge, in which there was a postoffice, where he received letters occasionally, and had a place for the transaction of his business in the village of Canajoharie, distant about half a mile from Palatine Bridge, and kept a box in the postoffice at Canajoharie and received most of his letters there. Held, a notice addressed to him at Canajoharie was sufficient to charge him.

Choteau v. Webster, 6 Metc. (Mass.) 1. Daniel Webster, an inhabitant of Boston, endorsed a promissory note that was made payable at a bank in the City of New York, and which the maker failed to pay at maturity. When the note fell due, the endorser was at Washington attending to his duties, at a session of Congress, as a senator from Massachusetts; and he had, at all times, an agent in Boston who had charge of his business in his absence; but the holder of the note had no notice that the endorser had such agent, nor did the endorser request that notice should be sent to him at Boston. Notice of non-payment by the maker was seasonably put into the postoffice at New York, directed to the endorser at Washington, where letters, addressed by mail to members of the Senate, during the session of Congress, were taken from the postoffice by officers of the Senate charged with that duty, and delivered to the members in their places, when the Senate was actually in session, and on other days were delivered, by those officers, at the members' lodgings.

Held, the notice was sufficient to charge the endorser.

Bank of Commerce v. Chambers, 14 Mo. App. 152. Endorser had a general residence or domicile in St. Louis and a general place of business in St. Louis, but his family were sojourning at Selma, Mo., a place without a postoffice, while he was sojourning in Washington, as a member of Congress. Notices were mailed to him addressed to St. Louis, Washington and Selma, respectively. Held (after deciding that the notices mailed to St. Louis were insufficient because holder and endorser both resided in St. Louis). The general notice sent by mail addressed "Hon. R. Graham Frost, Washington, D. C." was a good notice (Citing Choteau v. Webster). This was on December 23, 1880. Congress had, on December 22, taken a recess until January 5th following. The fact that Congress had taken this temporary recess may not have been known to the notary, and if known, it would not necessarily indicate to him that Mr. Frost would be absent from the capital during such recess. If it should indicate this it would not impair the legal sufficiency of the notice: because the controlling rule is that where the endorser has different residences and different places of business, the notice must be sent to the place where, upon diligent inquiry, it seems most likely to reach him with certainty and promptness.

A WAYSIDE SERMON.

Looky how de rich man go—
 Allus in a hurry!
But, thank de Lawd, I des so po'
 I ain't got time ter worry!

Don't keer how de river run—
 How de win' is blowin',
Des de same in rain en sun—
 Reapin' time en sowin'!

Here's de lesson fer de time—
 True enough for all, suh;
Folks what got no hill ter climb
 Ain't got fur ter fall, suh!

What the Accountants are Doing

WASHINGTON C. P. A. LAW.

PUBLIC accountants of Seattle and Tacoma, the two leading Puget Sound cities, recently organized the Washington Association of Public Accountants, and at the very brief session of the Legislature, which closed early in March, succeeded in passing a C. P. A. Law, and the governor has given it his approval.

The new law provides for a state board of accountancy, consisting of five skilled accountants, to be appointed by the governor from a list of fifteen names to be furnished by the Washington Association.

When the bill was on second reading in the house it was amended by some "granger" member so that the age limit reads nineteen years instead of twenty-one. But this will probably not take effect, because applicants for certificates must be United States citizens.

In another respect the law differs from those of other states in that no previous experience is stipulated for in the Waiver clause; it therefore becomes most essential that the law should be administered carefully and at the hands of those who have the best welfare of the profession of the public accountants at heart.

That this bill will be the case we are assured by Mr. George Wilkinson, the secretary of the Federation of Societies of Public Accountants in the United States, who writes from Seattle, under date of March 24, that he has personally seen a large majority of the members of the Washington Association, and finds them to be very much in earnest in the matter and well equipped to maintain the dignity of the profession on the Pacific Coast.

For promptness of action in the face of many discouragements born of ignorance and prejudice, the Washington Accountants deserve great credit in thus having secured the passage of their C. P. A. bill on their first attempt. Several members should receive credit for the work that they have done at Olympia, the capital of the state, but prominently among them should be mentioned Mr. E. G. Shorrock, Mr. C. M. Williams, both of Seattle, and Mr. L. G. Jackson and George Shedden, both of Tacoma.

Pennsylvania Institute of Certified Public Accountants.

The annual meeting of the Pennsylvania Institute of Certified Public Accountants was held at 516 Stephen Girard Building, on Monday, April 20, with a representative gathering of members in attendance.

The report of the treasurer was presented and approved. It showed that the financial affairs of the Institute are in a healthy condition.

The chairman of the committee on education reported that evening classes had been established at the beginning of the winter under the direction of the Institute. The membership was practically limited to assistants in offices of certified public accountants, the total enrollment of the class being nineteen. The interest exhibited in this new movement warrants the belief that a large membership could have been secured if the conditions would have permitted. The instructors for the season were:

Theory of Accounts, Robt. H. Montgomery, C. P. A.; Practical Accounting, Wm. L. Lybrand, C. P. A.; Auditing, James W. Fernley, C. P. A.; Commercial Law, Herbert G. Stockwell, C. P. A.

The chairman of the lecture committee reported that several meetings had been held during the year at the Manufacturers' Club, on each occasion an informal dinner being arranged for by the Institute, followed by addresses or debates. These meetings proved to be of interest and of value to the members, and it is proposed to hold them frequently next year.

The chairman of the committee on library reported that the nucleus of a reference library for the members and students had been begun by the purchase of about thirty volumes of standard accountancy literature, English and American. The volumes have been in active use by the students.

The meeting then proceeded to the election of officers for the ensuing year. All of the officers were re-elected:

William M. Lybrand, president; John Vaughan, vice-president; J. D. Stinger, treasurer; Alfred L. Sellers, secretary.

The following council was elected:

J. E. Sterrett, Herbert G. Stockwell, Charles Lewer, James W. Fernley, Stockton Bates.

Following the election the meeting adjourned to convene again at the annual dinner to be held on May 4, which occasion will mark the close of the season's work.

"SHIN-PLASTER" WOULDN'T DO.

The following happening that is reported by the "New York Sun" as having occurred in that city recently is interesting and amusing:

Considerable fractional currency which was issued by the United States Government in 1864 is being put in circulation in New York City by a retail firm as an advertisement. The result is that street car conductors and many retail dealers have refused to take the money, denouncing it as counterfeit. On the Brighton Beach line of the Brooklyn Rapid Transit Company the other day a passenger who got on the train at Beverley road handed the conductor a 25-cent "shinplaster," which was a familiar piece of money thirty years ago. The conductor, evidently believing the passenger was trying to have fun with him, handed back the 25-cent greenback.

"That's good money," remarked the passenger.

"Oh, pay your fare," replied the conductor. "I've no time for kidding."

The man with the fractional currency insisted that the money was as good as gold, but he produced a nickel when the conductor threatened to throw him off the car.

At the time of the issue of the paper the money shows that John Allison was register of the treasury and F. E. Spinner treasurer. The pieces of paper are only three inches long and two inches wide. On the back of the note is the statement that it is 25 cents in fractional currency of the United States and that it is receivable in payment for all dues except customs.

WANTED TO KNOW.

Usually Miss Sullivan and Miss Keller both use the right hand in speaking and reading, but the left hand is sometimes substituted. Not long ago Miss Sullivan began talking with her left hand, and Mark Twain looked on with deep interest. Finally, he interrupted. "I say," he drawled, "can you tell the truth with your left hand?"

Banks with Branches Vs. Individual Banks*

By B. E. WALKER,
General Manager, Canadian Bank of Commerce, Toronto, Canada.

ALLOW me, before entering upon my subject, to thank you very sincerely for this opportunity of again meeting the bankers of Minneapolis. I have so often been the recipient of warm hospitality in this great city of the Northwest that I do not know whether to be filled with gladness at meeting many of you again, or of deep sorrow for some who are gone and whose places, so far as we who remain are concerned, can never be filled.

I have been asked to speak once more upon the subject of branch banking. It is a rather threadbare subject to me, and I must try, if possible, to present the arguments in a different form as compared with previous addresses.

I do not wish to assert that it is practicable, or that it would be wise if practicable, for the United States to change, by one sweeping movement from individual to branch banking. Banks without branches are a perfectly natural industrial development, which should always have full liberty to exist, and in the United States they are now, by a long and uninterrupted period of growth, so intertwined with the industrial whole that they could only be altered with patience and time.

A Confession of Weakness.

What I do wish to assert is that any attempt by law to prevent branch banking is a direct confession of the weakness inherent in individual banking, because it must be just as clear that branch banking is a perfectly natural industrial development as that individual banking is, and that therefore branch banking should also have as full liberty to exist.

I further wish to assert that the destruction of branch banking by Jackson and others was a misfortune of the gravest character to this country, and that the terrible panics and the heavy and unnatural burden of interest, as compared with other countries, which you have been forced to bear, are due to this barbarous act of destruction. I hope no one will suppose from this statement that I am defending the Bank of the United States as an institution. It lived in a time of paper inflation and of experiment, when some of the simplest principles of finance were not well understood. It had the state for a partner and hence was subject to all sorts of influences which would not have been present if it had merely been a great commercial bank. Branch banking, per se, has nothing to do with these defects, and my contention is that the statesmen of the time should have built up the bank, correcting its errors, instead of destroying it.

I desire also to point out that the fact that branch banking has been impossible in the United States during a period when combinations in all other industries have been the practice rather than the reverse, is an extraordinary anomaly, and that if the economic progress of the United States has been greatly accelerated by combinations which lessen the cost of manufacture and of doing business, then the United States has lost enormously by preventing a species of combinations, and has not the element of possible monopoly which is present in some of the great combinations we have witnessed.

The People Must Have What They Want.

In all democratic countries the people must have what they want, or what they think they want; but the people, as a rule, are ignorant and imagine a vain thing. The people feared a bank monopoly, and therefore idolized Jackson, but the fear was just as groundless then as it would be now. Whatever evils may flow to a nation from the aggregation of too much loanable capital in one institution will, I am sure, be much more evident in individual banks than in banks with many branches. I dare say that a careful study of conditions in New York and London to-day would bear out this conclusion.

It is not, however, that the people were set wrong and have changed but little that disturbs one, but that the individual bankers of the United States are, as a rule, opposed to branch banking, and look upon its re-entrance into the United States as a menace to the existing banks. As an interested person I might wish to see the United States remain unconvinced, but as a sincere well-wisher of this great country I do most heartily wish that every thinking man could be made to see that a great wrong was done seventy years ago, and that gradually, even if only by slow and patient effort, it must be put right.

Reasonableness of Branch Banking.

Allow me therefore to discuss with you the reasonableness of branch banking as opposed to individual banks. I hope to show that in banking on a large scale, where international or interstate commerce is concerned, or where for any reason money needs to be moved about, the natural form of banking, as demonstrated by history, is branch banking. If the concerns of a bank literally do not extend beyond a radius of ten or twenty miles from its door, an individual bank may, under some conditions, be able to perform as good service to the community as a branch, or as the chief office, of a bank with branches. But if the community has affairs at a distance which require the service of a bank, one that has a system of branches and the foreign and other correspondents which such a system develops is pretty sure to be the most capable servant to the public.

There is a general impression that in the new nations, especially in the United States, there is not much respect for precedent, which means practically that there is not much respect for what is to be learned from history. It is indeed clear that much of the progress of this country is due to the willingness to try a new thing because it is new, while in older nations there is a dislike of new things because they are new. But in the United States the result of this indifference to history has often been that old things discarded by more experienced nations turn up as if they were new, and readily get a hearing and perhaps a trial, while other old things which the historical experience of older nations has demonstrated to be good get no hearing, because they have not occurred to the mind of the younger nation as something new.

A Bushel of Money to Buy a Bushel of Wheat.

When, for instance, a Western senator of great wealth and presumably of great ability, not many

*Address delivered at the banquet of Minneapolis Chapter of the American Institute of Bank Clerks.

years ago proposed that the government printing press should provide the money with which to clear off the mortgages on all the farms in the United States, the government being secured by mortgages not exceeding 50 per cent. of the supposed value of the farms, but charging no interest, or a merely nominal rate, it would really have been well if the senator had known that in the eighteenth century the colony of Rhode Island had tried the experiment, and carried it on until it took about a bushel of that kind of money to buy a bushel of wheat, and had then abandoned it.

Now if we admit that the United States can learn from history, what do we find in the experience of other nations in the past and present regarding branch banking? And if we find that the United States is persisting in a system which is opposed to the history and present practice of other nations, is it likely that such a system is wise, even to the exclusion of the mere right to try the other?

Among the very early forms of debt are borrowing money on the security of real estate by rent-charge or mortgage, or on moveable property by a pledge, with a change of possession. For such a purpose an individual banker, provided he were not short of money, would do as well as any other. Another early form of debt is described by the economist as a delayed payment for merchandise. This, in distinction to lending against security, is a real form of credit; but the merchant-banker who gives such credit need not of course have extended affairs and business establishments in more than one place.

When Nations Began to Expand.

But let us consider the mediaeval conditions of Europe when nations began to expand on the industrial side. If a trader on the east coast of England desired to cross the dangerous North Sea in order to buy delft in Holland, or cloths in Flanders, or rarer merchandise in France, how could he accomplish this best, so far as the money side of the trading was concerned? He must have cash when he reached these countries, and to carry the actual gold would put him in peril of his life, besides subjecting him to great loss in the exchange of it for money current in these countries. He goes, however, let us suppose, to some old "Isaac of York" and explains his difficulty. Isaac, belonging to that race which is free from insularity, and has made its livelihood through all the centuries by its superior intelligence, tells him that his brother Jacob lives in Rotterdam, and is known to everybody in trade there, and that he has a cousin in Brussels with whom he has much business, and that in Paris there are two or three of his race who will gladly honor his instructions. He gives the trading Englishman a letter, or perhaps actual bills of exchange, and the trader may now go on his way risking his life perhaps at sea, but not on land, and not risking his precious money, and able to buy his merchandise at the best advantage.

Early Italian Bankers.

A modern banker, acquainted with the complicated development of credit, can readily imagine the evolution from such a simple problem as that of the English trader to those of the twentieth century. But we might have been much more backward to-day in our banking development but for the enormous changes caused by the crusades. When the military leaders of the Christian nations began to move men by tens of thousands from Western Europe to the Far East, it is easy to realize the difficulties they had to encounter. Their soldiers had to be fed and cared for day after day in countries where the language, money and trade conditions were in each case different, and for this the leaders must have money, and in vast quantities as compared with any experience since Roman days. Much of the money they had to borrow, and when borrowed, or possessed in any shape, how could it be made available at the main points of their journey? But behind the armies came the traders, and in such numbers that centuries after the Crusades the trade routes thus established remained as great factors in European commerce. And these traders were not merely those who sought to buy and sell with the people en route, and to largely supply the armies as well, but traders who sought to bring back the finer goods and the art treasure of the East to the newer nations of the West.

Now in the end how was the banking for this great military and trading movement accomplished? By bankers whose names are well known in Italian history. The Medici and Frescobaldi of Florence; the Bardi, Cantoni and Acciajuoli of Geneva; the Conti and Vermigli of Pisa, had offices at Acon, Jaffa, Caesarea, Tripoli, and other places in Cyprus, Syria and Egypt. These bankers with their branches provided the bills of exchange, dealt in the ever changing currencies, lent money to the traders, the military leaders and to the Church, and when the loans were too big for any one house they entered into syndicates to carry them out, as we do now. So important and so profitable was the banking side of the crusades that the Church as such, the Abbots and Knights Hospitallers on their own account, and many other classes, went into the business. But the point I wish to make is that Isaac of York could not have served his trading customer, and the bankers of the Italian cities could not have served the crusaders, without having the elements in their business organization which are to be found in branch-banking and not in individual banking.

In Modern Times.

And here it may be well to remember that this distinction between a bank with branches and one without, would hardly occur in any other country. Elsewhere a bank without branches would be looked upon as a perfectly natural operation in banking, likely to be followed later by the addition of better machinery for doing business at a distance, of such confidential nature as banking, by the establishment of branches, or by close affiliations of a nature akin to branches. If we consider the first house of the Rothschilds and their present position, we have a concrete example. Must it not be clear that the power to impart and to obtain, in absolute confidence with each other alone, information of such moment for trade or financial purposes is a power of almost incalculable value? It may be argued that the Rothschilds are sui generis. Not so, because the Jewish banking houses of international prominence are all similar in the main lines of structure to the great house of the Rothschilds, and many of them much older in their origin.

If you argue that these are forms of banking which have been evolved from earlier conditions, and that those who begin now can, as in many manufacturing businesses, start afresh with a system more suited to modern times, I fear the facts are entirely against such a view. If we study the Bank of France in its relation to the small agriculturist on the one side and to the great problems of state finances on the other, you may argue that it is an exceptional institution; but if you consider the development in so many of the trade centers of the world of the more peculiarly commercial banks of

France, can you doubt that whatever be the public interests to be served, banks with branches are the natural machinery?

Recent Bank Consolidation in London.

Until recently there was a great bank in London without branches. It had developed an enormous city business, and was perhaps as able as any institution in Europe to follow with success its peculiar system of individual banking. There was also in London one of the last of those grand old private banks, and it had under different titles a series of country establishments in which the various members of the family were owners in one form or another. The other day, the bank without branches and the private bank with its series of country establishments were all amalgamated into one joint stock institution.

Was Alexander Hamilton Wrong?

But you may argue that all this is in Europe, and that if the Rothschilds are not sui generis, this country is. But your greatest financial genius, Alexander Hamilton, started you in the course of branch banking when it could hardly be said to be highly developed even in Great Britain. Do the facts of your own financial history prove that he was wrong? Do they not prove, unmistakably, that he was right? But this was in the East, you may say. To this I answer that another financial genius, Hugh McCullock, proved the soundness of branch banking in Indiana fifty years after Hamilton's time. And in the far West out of an express business, the great establishment, with its branches, of Wells, Fargo & Co. arose by the most natural laws of trade.

The world of banking as we find it in Great Britain, France, Germany, Norway and Sweden, Canada, Australia, and indeed almost everywhere except here, has decided in favor of branch banking. You as individuals have a perfect right to conclude that you do not wish to change, but in view of the universal opinion elsewhere in favor of branch banking, do you really think that it is wise to practically forbid it? Can the thing which is good for all the rest of the world, and which was once good for you, be so bad that it has not clear right of existence in your country? As a matter of fact we all know that it is quietly coming. Some branches have been established by state institutions where it is permitted. Large national banks are controlling the management of other banks by some process of affiliation, and the need of such affiliation is being admitted in many quarters.

Difficulties Considered.

It may be thought that I take too little account of the difficulties standing in the way of such a change. In an address at Saratoga in 1895, I tried, at least, to show that I fully appreciate the difficulties, and I have suggested the manner in which, as it appears to me, the first efforts might be made. I certainly do not believe in any violent change from present conditions, but in laws which freely permit both systems. I fear, very much, that the first efforts at branch banking may in some cases result in failure. The business of branch banking must be learned as with any other business, but if once permitted I do not fear for the ultimate results. At Saratoga I ventured to indulge in the following dream:

"I can imagine nothing in banking so attractive s a bank with say $10.000.000 of capital"—this eemed a bold statement at the time. There are already three banks in New York with $10,000,000 of capital, and now there is to be one with a capital of $25,000,000—"a head office in New York, and branches in such cities as Boston, Philadelphia, Buffalo, Pittsburg, Chicago, Minneapolis, Duluth, Cincinnati, St. Louis, Kansas City, Omaha, San Francisco, Galveston, New Orleans, Atlanta and others of similar importance, gathering deposits everywhere, lending only on the choicest mercantile paper, the leading staples of commerce, and the best bond and stock securities, possessing powerful alliances with foreign banks, enabling it to buy and sell foreign exchange and issue letters of credit on all countries—able, indeed, to perform the whole round of functions performed by the great banks of Europe. If the Bank of Montreal can lend $10,000,000 safely in Chicago through an agency, cannot a bank with headquarters in New York do it? If it is safe for hundreds of New England banks to fill their wallets with the paper securities arising from grain, flour and other business in Illinois and Minnesota, purchased through note brokers, or by rediscounting for Western banks, could not branches of Eastern banks do such a business better? And in times of trouble, would not the existence of several such banks, and of many other powerful banks with branches restricted to sections of the United States, be a source of financial strength sufficient to set the pace of courage to the smaller banks, and to the whole mercantile community?"

Since then what mighty changes have been wrought by war, by treaty, and by commerce in the destiny of this nation, and to what an extent do these changes afford arguments for branch banking? Who is to move the sugar crops of the Hawaiian Islands? Who is to care for the trans-Pacific trade with Japan, China, Russia and Australia? Who is to do the banking business arising so rapidly with Cuba and Porto Rico, with Costa Rica and other Central American countries? Who is to care for the banking affairs of the Philippines? If this is to be a nation with dependencies not consisting of people from Anglo-Saxon or other European stocks, then you must through the medium of great institutions, having their head offices in the financial centers of the United States, take charge of such important concerns as the banks and other institutions in these dependencies, confidence and stability in which are absolutely necessary to success.

I trust I have not offended by the manner in which I have presented this very incomplete argument for branch banks. Other arguments I have made elsewhere, touching more closely the smaller aspects of the matter and particularly as to the practical working of the two systems. All that I have said tonight springs solely from a firm friendship for a firm belief in the future of your country, accompanied by sincere regret that in the matter of reforming your currency and your banking so great a nation should spend years in argument when one moment of vigorous, clear-sighted action might set all right.

PROPULSION.

A group of rustics was admiring a stylish motor car in the village street, and the motorist was explaining its principles. "What's the stoof as drives 'er along, mister?" inquired one. "Petroleum, my man; it's petroleum that's the propelling force," was the reply. "Lawks-a-mussy!" said the querist. "Did ye 'eer thot, Garge? It's petroleum as prurpels 'er." "Ho, indeed," said Garge, disdainfully: "that tin't nuthin' oot o' the common. It were petroleum as prurpelled oor Mary Hann right through the kitchen door, and banged 'er opp agen the barn. She troid to light the foire wi' it."—Golden Penny.

Chemistry of an Office Desk

DOUBTLESS those of our readers who are chemists have given some consideration to the chemistry of an office desk. No doubt simple analyses have been made of some of the articles and supplies that are used upon a desk, and much interest has been taken in studying their peculiarities. For the benefit of those who are not experts in this line we append an article which appeared some time ago in the "Popular Science News" bearing this title. It will be found of general interest:

Common Ink.

Common ink, chemically considered, is a substance of much interest. The majority of inks at present used are made from ferrous sulphate (copperas) and infusion of nutgalls. These last contain a peculiar organic acid known as gallotannic acid or tannin; this readily unites with the iron of the copperas, forming ferrous gallotannate, which is nearly colorless and quite soluble in water. On exposure to the air, however, this soon oxidizes to ferric gallotannate, which is an intensely black, insoluble substance. It is this oxidation which causes ink to turn black after exposure to the air, either in the inkstand or on the written page. The solution of the ferrous salt is always used for writing, as it is clear and flows readily from the pen; and a little aniline, or other coloring matter, is added to it to render the writing visible before the true color of the ink is developed by the oxygen of the air.

Solutions of aniline blue or violet are often used for writing purposes, for which their intense coloring power renders them very suitable; their only disadvantage is that they fade quickly, and letters written with such ink, exposed to light and air, soon become illegible.

A fluid of intense black color can be made by adding to an infusion of nutgalls a few grains of vanadate of ammonia dissolved in a little hot water. The coloring matter is not a solid precipitate, but is held in solution, and makes a most excellent ink; but, unfortunately, it is not very permanent. Inks are usually thickened with gum-arabic to give them sufficient "body," while copying-ink only differs from ordinary writing fluid by containing sugar or glycerine, which prevents it from drying too rapidly. When a sheet of paper written over with copying-ink is pressed firmly against a sheet of thin, absorbent paper, previously moistened, a part of the ink is transferred, thus producing a complete copy of the original writing. India ink is simply carbon or lamp-black, mixed with gum, molded into sticks. It is very permanent and does not corrode steel pens, but must be prepared fresh every time it is used. A perfect ink should be a thin, free-flowing liquid of a deep black color when first used, non-corrosive, entirely permanent, not easily removed by chemical agents, and leaving but little residue when evaporated.

Paper.

Writing paper, chemically considered, is nearly pure cellulose. It has the same composition as starch like thousands of other organic bodies which have similar chemical compositions, but widely differing physical properties. The only explanation that can be given of this strange fact is that the atoms are differently arranged in the different substances just as the same figures may be arranged to denote numbers of widely varying values.

Physically considered, paper is a thin sheet of vegetable fibres felted together, and is a striking proof of man's ingenuity. Writing paper is heavily "sized" with a mixture of glue, starch, resin, etc., to give it a hard, smooth surface, suitable for receiving the ink. Blotting paper is a thick, heavy paper entirely unsized, so that it readily absorbs any ink or other fluid brought in contact with it. The ruling of paper is done by a very ingenious machine, so complicated that an apprentice in the paper-ruling business requires several years in which to learn the trade.

Pens and Pencils.

Concerning pens there is little to be said. They are made from the best varieties of steel, which, as our readers know, differs from iron in the amount of carbon, and possibly some other elements, combined with it. Our practical knowledge of the metallurgy of steel is very complete and satisfactory, but there is still much to be learned as to the theoretical part of the science, and the chemical significance and action of the various elements upon iron.

Lead pencils in former times were really made of lead, and pencils with a marking point of metallic silver are occasionally met with; but graphite is now almost exclusively used. This is nearly pure carbon, like charcoal or the diamond, but contains a small amount of iron which some chemists consider to be simply an impurity and not in chemical combination.

Wafers are but little used at present, and are simply small pieces of colored gelatine or gum. They are often colored with the poisonous red-lead, and for this reason should not be moistened in the mouth. They have been superceded by the self-sealing envelopes, on the flap of which is placed a little dextrine or British gum which only needs to be moistened to firmly seal up the envelope. This dextrine is made from starch by the action of heat and acid. It has the same chemical composition as both starch and the cellulose of the paper; that is, chemically speaking, it is isomeric with these substances. This same gum is used upon the backs of postage stamps. It is said that the process of transforming starch into dextrine was discovered accidently by the partial burning of a starch manufactory in England, but we cannot vouch for the truth of the story. Much more might be written regarding the scientific principles involved in the use of sealing-wax, stylographs, hektographs, papyrographs and many other inventions designed to enlighten the labors of the writer, but lack of space forbids a more extended account of them.

FULLY QUALIFIED.

The late Thomas B. Reed liked a good story, even when the point was against him, and liked to tell this one. When he applied for admission to the bar he was examined by the judge of the county court, who asked if the legal tender act just passed was, in his opinion, constitutional. Reed had never considered the matter, but, unwilling to display his ignorance, said confidently that it was. "Well, I will admit you," said the judge. "I examined another young man this morning, and asked him the same question. He replied it was not constitutional. So I admitted him, too. I am always glad to admit young men to the bar who can answer such grave constitutional questions off-hand."
—Green Bag.

Account Audit & Assurance Company

25 PINE STREET NEW YORK

WHAT BALANCE SHEET ACCOUNTING DOES.

I.—Initially, it provides an adequate analysis of the accounts of the business, thereby securing a proper representation of the transactions upon the books.

II.—It classifies the daily details of transactions in a way to show "going" results.

III.—The assets of the business are correctly and completely represented at all dates.

IV.—The liabilities of the business are correctly and completely represented at all dates.

V.—The gross profits on goods sold are always shown and there is presented in contrast therewith the total costs of doing business, thereby revealing net profits.

VI.—Among the assets, in the case of a manufacturing business, there are always shown the cost value of the materials and supplies on hand, the cost to date of the work or orders in progress, and the cost of the finished product on hand.

VII.—All this is presented without the preparation of a physical inventory. Inventorying, like counting cash, is resorted to, only for the purpose of verification and proof.

VIII.—The usual fiscal period is abolished. Net profits to date are shown daily (as in department stores), weekly (as in a mercantile business) or once in each four weeks (as in the case of a manufacturing business), according to the time schedule adopted.

IX.—The work of annually or semi-annually closing the books is abolished. The books are always closed and at the same time are always open. Results to date can be easily read from the Balance Sheet Ledger at any and all times.

X.—The labor of maintaining Balance Sheet Accounting, when the system is once in operation, is no greater than that of ordinary double entry. In many cases it has proven to be considerably less.

XI.—The Proof-By-Balance System of Cost Accounts, a constituent element of the Balance Sheet plan, gives the exact cost of goods produced in a factory. There are no estimates. The results are always definite and exact.

XII.—Factories are run at "even keel." The entire cost of the manufacturing department for a given period is balanced by the aggregate of the cost of the individual lots of goods put through.

XIII.—The Balance Sheet System provides that no payments to workmen (pay-roll) shall be made until the amount of their time has been charged to an order in process. Accordingly there is no time paid for that is not accounted for. Charges to orders in process offset the payroll amount. Non-productive labor is handled by prorating its amount over the orders in process.

XIV.—Balance Sheet Accounting is the only system of accounting ever introduced. It is complete. From established premises it reaches definite and exact conclusions.

XV.—Balance Sheet Accounting is eclectic in its elements, and uses as its component parts in the way of ledgers, blanks and forms, various items that are adapted to the purpose in view without reference to their source or origin.

XVI.—Balance Sheet Accounting begins with a balance sheet, ends with a balance sheet and maintains a balance sheet between times.

XVII.—Balance Sheet Accounting facilitates business management. It shows shortages and neglect wherever the same occur. It definitely fixes responsibility. It necessitates order and method in accounting affairs.

XVIII.—Balance Sheet Accounting improves the bookkeeper's position by enabling him to keep all his work up-to-date and by defining a day's duties.

XIX.—In Balance Sheet Accounting there is no back work. Instead, everything is finished as it proceeds.

XX.—The Balance Sheet Ledger upon the business manager's desk in the morning, among other interesting and valuable particulars, gives him the following:

Amount of cash receipts of the preceding day.
Amount of cash disbursements.
Balance on hand and where located.

Amounts charged to customers.
Amounts credited to customers.
Balance owing by customers.

Amounts credited to Purchase Creditors.
Amounts charged to Purchase Creditors.
Balance owing to Purchase Creditors.

Amount of goods (merchandise) taken in.
Amount of goods sent out.
Balance on hand.

Amount of goods sold.
Cost of goods sold.
Gross profit.

Expenses of doing business (viz., clerk hire, rent, advertising, insurance, etc.)

XXI.—Similar facts as to receipts, disbursements and balances are afforded of Notes Receivable and Notes Payable, Sundry Debtors, Sundry Creditors, etc.

XXII.—Balance Sheet Accounting is not "ready made." Instead, it is always "custom made," and made to fit the business after the most careful measurements have been taken. The preceding epitome of Balance Sheet Ledger showings is to be accepted as typical and not as specific.

XXIII.—The Balance Sheet System adapted to your business will give you the exact showings you require, presented in the way you want them and at the time they will be most serviceable to you in planning and managing.

XXIV.—Balance Sheet Accounting is scientific. All its provisions are based upon an accurate and adequate "chart" of the accounts.

XXV.—Balance Sheet Accounting is installed upon the specification plan. A carefully prepared specification, based upon the chart of accounts, is prepared, which stands to the accounting system very much as an architect's specification stands to a building about to be erected.

XXVI.—Each specification is illustrated by drawings of the rulings, blanks and forms required, and by diagrams showing the relationship of the different parts one to the other.

For further particulars, address **Account, Audit and Assurance Company, 25 Pine street, New York.**

BOOKS OF INTEREST TO BUSINESS MEN.

The A B C of Banks and Banking.—By George M. Coffin. 6¾ x 5 inches; 137 pages. Bound in cloth. Back title gilt. Price, $1.25.

This handy little volume is exactly what its name implies; that is, a presentation of the principles underlying banking in the United States. The author in his preface says that it is designed to appeal to the reader outside as well as inside of a bank. It is by no means the last word or every word about banking. It may be said that it is a primer covering a field that has hitherto been somewhat neglected. The chapter heads are as follows: Banking in General, Various Kinds of Banking, Capital Stock, Shareholders' Rights and Liabilities, Undivided Profits, Dividends and Surplus, Deposits, Checks, Lawful Money Reserve, Issuing Bank Notes, Borrowing Money, Loans and Discounts, Exchanges, Collections, Letters of Credit, Bonds, Mortgages and Stocks, Bank Reports, Examinations, Directors, Executive Officers—Their Powers and Duties, Internal Administration and Bookkeeping, and other suggestions.

Business Law.—By Alonzo R. Weed, L. L. B., of the Boston Bar. 6 x 9¼ inches; 172 pages. Bound in cloth. Cover and back title red. Price, $1.25.

Mr. Weed calls his book "a manual for schools and colleges and for every day use." The titles of the chapters are as follows: Contracts, Principal and Agent, Partnerships, Sales of Personal Property, Bailments and Common Carriers, Negotiable Paper, Deeds, Mortgages and Leases, Collection Laws, Written Rates of Interest, Insurance, Patent Rights, Trade Marks and Copyrights, etc.

The author does not waste words, and yet treats his subjects clearly and comprehensively. In short, he gives the law without the addition of wordy "trimmings."

Introduction to the Study of Economics.—By Charles Jesse Bullock, Ph. D. 7¾ x 5½ inches. 581 pages. Bound in cloth. Cover and back title gilt. Price, $1.25.

This book, the author says, is designed as an introductive text book of economic science. Throughout the volume economics are discussed with special reference to American conditions, and their workings are illustrated by frequent allusions to American experience. There are chapters on the Consumption of Wealth, the Theory of Exchange, the Development of Metallic Money, Money and Credit, and the like.

Political Economy of Humanism.—By Henry Wood. 7¾ x 5¼ inches; 320 pages. Bound in cloth. Cover and back title gilt. Price, $1.25.

Mr. Wood is well known as a writer on various economic subjects, and this book contains a series of able treatises, written in his usual vein, on the relation of the employer to the employed, and the phases of the industrial question and their relation to socialism. Among the questions considered and handled in a conservative spirit and with much common sense, are the following: Supply and Demand, the Law of Competition, Labor and Production, Combinations of Capital, Combinations of Labor, Employers and Profit Sharing, the Obligations and Privileges of Employees, the Unequal Distribution of Wealth, Money and Coinage, Tariffs and Protection, Industrial Education and Gold Production and Values.

The Kite Trust, A Romance of Wealth.—By Lebbeus Harding Rogers. 7¾ x 5½ inches; 475 pages. Illustrated. Price, $1.50.

This is a treatise or series of treatises on economic subjects in the guise of a story. The tale itself concerns three American boys, and is very interesting as well as instructive. The trust idea is explained and an explanation of banking is given. The greenback is dealt with as are also Wall street and stock speculation.

Business Law.—By Thomas Raeburn White, B. L., L. L. B. 5 x 7½ inches; 323 pages. Bound in cloth. Back title gilt. Price, $1.50.

This is a neat, compact and handy book of business for law for the use of students and business men. Among the subjects treated are Contracts, Sales, Partnerships, Corporations, Negotiable Paper and the like. The author's language is plain, and is understandable by any one having no previous knowledge of law. The book's clearness on the essential points of ordinary law should recommend it as a business book for the plain business man who has no time in which to consult a law library.

The Phonographic Dictionary and Phrase Book.—By Benn Pitman and Jerome B. Howard. 5½ x 8 inches; 552 pages. Bound in cloth. Cover title and back title gilt. Price, $3.

This book is the most elaborate shorthand dictionary yet published, with the characters in facsimile. It contains over 120,000 words, and for every one of these words there is a corresponding sign in the Benn Pitman system of shorthand. To the reporter, office or court stenographer, or any one writing the Benn Pitman system of shorthand, the book is invaluable. It is well made, tastefully bound, and is printed on a good quality of paper in clean, plain type.

Grace's Handy Book for Making Rapid Calculations. 8¼ x 5¼ inches. Bound in cloth. 65 pages. Title printed in silver. Price, $1.

The full title of this book is "Merchants', Bankers' and Brokers' Handy Book for Making Rapid Calculations in all Branches of Commercial Requirements, Weights, Measures and Moneys." The volume contains a series of tables for calculating the price of wheat, corn and oat bushels in decimals, for converting cubic meters to cubic feet and cubic feet to meters, meters to lineal yards, superficial feet or square feet to cubic feet, decimal tons to avoirdupois pounds, and the like. To the busy office man who has a great deal of calculating to do, and particularly to the clerk in an export house whose work it is to reckon in United States money the amounts named in foreign invoices, these tables should be very valuable. They are quite complete, and undoubtedly their use will save time.

The Lawrence System of Vocal and Physical Expression.—By Edwin Gordon Lawrence. 4¾ x 6 inches; 128 pages. Bound in cloth. Cover title and back title gilt. Price, $1.

The author says in the preface of this little book that his object has been to place in the hands of lawyers, actors and public speakers in general, a simple system of vocal and physical expression that will enable them to clearly convey thought by word of mouth and emphasize it by the proper action. To the man of affairs who is called upon for a speech on any subject, and who knows what to say but does not know how to say it, this book will be a great help.

The Anatomy of a Railroad Report.—By Thomas F. Woodlock. 7 x 5¼ inches. 121 pages. Bound in cloth. Side and back titles gilt. Price, $1.

This little book is intended for the use of those people who, while interested in railroad investments, are wholly unacquainted with railroad accounts. The book is divided into two sections, the first being the Anatomy of the Railroad Report and the second being Ton-Mile Cost. It treats of phases of the railroad business in concise fashion, but thoroughly and accurately.

Any book in this list will be sent to any address in the United States, Canada or Mexico upon receipt of price. If there is some special book that you require we shall be pleased to hunt it up for you.

Address **Commerce, Accounts & Finance, 25 Pine street, New York City.**

The Science of

Loose Leaf Bookkeeping and Accounting

By Chas. A. Sweetland
Public Accountant.

Unique and up-to-date. The Pioneer Work. 250 pages of valuable information. Price, cloth bound, postpaid, $2.00.

Remit by draft or P. O. order.

Published by the author,

Chas. A. Sweetland.

Room 664 Century Bldg. St. Lou is Mo

60 DAY CLOCKS

Prentiss 60 day clocks run two months on a single winding, keep perfect time and automatically show the correct date. They are strong, durable, reliable, in fact satisfactory in every way. Right in time; right in price. You ought to have one.

Also Frying-pan, Program, Electric and Synchronized clocks.

Send for Catalogue No. 463.

THE PRENTISS CLOCK IMPROVEMENT CO.
DEPT. 46, 46 DEY ST., N. Y. CITY.

What Do You Do With Your Invoices?

When You Receive a bill for goods bought by you, what do you do with it? Do you hand it to your bookkeeper, who laboriously copies it, figure by figure, in a bulky invoice journal, from which the total amount is posted to the ledger?

When your Bookkeeper has wasted valuable time by the above process, what does he do with the invoice itself? Does he hand it to the office boy or the assistant bookkeeper, who places it in some compartment of a clumsy file along with a dozen other bills from the same house, each of which must be pawed over when this particular one is wanted again?

If You Are Wasting Time and Money by these antiquated methods, aren't you tired of doing so? Would you not welcome a system as far superior to them as the sun is to a kerosene lamp?

THEN USE THE

"Acx" System of Filing Invoices

Simpler, More Convenient and More Serviceable than any other. A time-saving application of elements more or less used in every up-to-date office.

What the "Acx" System Is.

A system of filing invoices by which (1) the copy of the order placed, (2) the record of the receipt of the goods, and (3) the invoices, are brought together on a sheet of the paper of a size and shape to be conveniently handled and preserved in any post binder file.

The "Acx" Invoice Filing Sheet is of manilla, 11 inches long by 8½ inches deep. The directions on it explain its use. Three lines of mucilage are in place on the sheet. The first of these (inside left hand) is entitled "Attach left hand of your order here." All orders should be filled out in duplicate, preferably by the use of carbon sheets, and the retained copy attached to the invoice sheet.

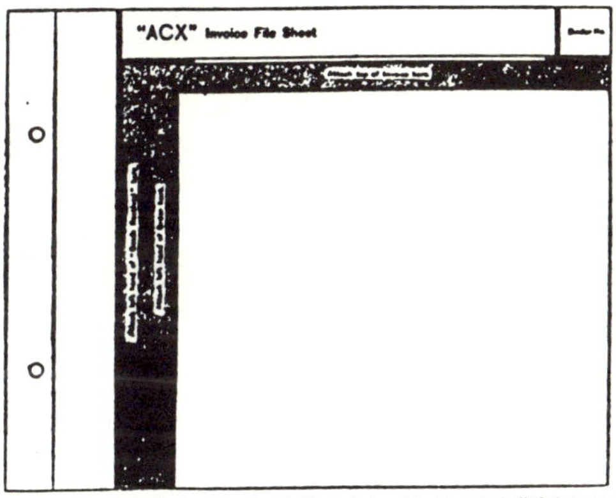

Reduced fac-simile of "Acx" Invoice File Sheet, designed by Account, Audit & Assurance Co., Ltd., 25 Pine Street, New York. Made by Self-Proving Account Book Co., New York. Patented February 8, 1898. May 20, 1902. Other patents pending.

When the goods for which the order is given are received, the count is made and entered upon a "Goods Received Slip," provided for the purpose. This slip is then attached to the Invoice Filing Sheet in the place marked "Attach left hand of Goods Received Here."

When the invoice is checked with the order and the "Goods Received Slip," its upper edge is moistened and laid against the mucilage on the Invoice Filing Sheet in the place marked "Attach top of invoice here." There are then superimposed upon this sheet (1) copy of the order, (2) record of the goods received, and (3) the invoice. The Invoice Filing Sheet is then paged in numerical order in its upper left-hand corner and is ready to be inserted in the binder; the latest invoice always being on top.

No Journalizing, no hunting for lost invoices, orders or goods received records. Order, receipt of goods and invoice all attached to one sheet of stiff paper, numbered and securely bound in a substantial binder, ready for instant reference. Post from this sheet direct to the ledger.

Price $6 a Thousand.

Address orders to

STATIONERY MANUFACTURING COMPANY,

86 Fulton Street, New York City.

Charts of Bank Organization and Administration

ONE of the original and fascinating features of the work of the American Institute of Bank Clerks is a collection of charts showing in a clear and comprehensive manner the arrangement of the working forces of several of the leading banks in different large cities of the country, together with an outline of the duties connected with each department.

What the Charts Show

CHART "A" represents the First National Bank of Chicago, which has a very comprehensive plan of administration. The different departments of the bank are numbered in the chart for ready reference, so that the course of any item may be followed from receipt to final disposition. The main divisions of labor are clearly shown, and the duties of employees set forth in a clear and striking manner.

CHART "B" represents a prominent New York bank doing a large general business. The various departments and the duties of the different clerks therein employed are fully described.

CHART "C" shows the general plan of administration of one of the largest New York banks doing an extensive business with merchants and having a large number of correspondents throughout the country. An examination of the chart shows how this great business is handled.

CHART "D" represents in outline one of the largest and strongest banks in New York. An analysis of the chart shows that loans on collateral security are an important feature of the business transacted, although the bank's customers include numerous corporations of the first magnitude, and a desirable line of out-of-town banks.

CHART "E" represents a New York bank in the wealthy residence district, numbering among its customers many of the "400." The facilities afforded to ladies are a conspicuous and presumably very profitable feature of this institution.

CHART "F" shows the administrative plan of one of the leading banks of Philadelphia, doing a large general business and having numerous correspondents throughout the country.

CHART "G" is not intended to represent any particular institution, but rather to show the distribution of the working force of a typical New York bank of large size and progressive methods.

These charts are a part of the correspondence course of study in Practical Banking, but they have created such general interest that the Institute has arranged to publish them in a handsomely bound booklet, and to use the same as a premium for new subscriptions at $2.00 each.

To each new subscriber to The Bulletin at $2.00, as a premium, one copy Free

Send order and make remittance payable to

American Institute of Bank Clerks

25 Pine Street New York